The New Encyclopedia of Christian Martyrs

The New Encyclopedia of Christian Martyrs

Compiled by
MARK WATER

"The history of Christian martyrdom is, in fact,
the history of Christianity itself."
William Bramley-Moore

BakerBooks
A Division of Baker Book House Co
Grand Rapids, Michigan 49516

Compiled by Mark Water.

Published by Baker Books
a division of Baker Book House Company
P.O. Box 6287, Grand Rapids, MI 49516-6287

Original edition published in English under the title
Encyclopedia of Christian Martyrs by John Hunt Publishing Ltd,
New Alresford, Hants, UK.

Printed in Finland

Book design by Jim Weaver Design, UK

Cover design by Andrew Milne Design, UK
Cover iIllustration: *St Andrew and Philip the Good* by
Guillaume Vrelant © Historial Picture Archive/Corbis.

ISBN 0-8010-1225-2

Library of Congress Cataloging-in-Publication Data is on file at
the Library of Congress, Washington, D.C.

For current information about all releases from Baker Book
House, visit our web site:
http://www.bakerbooks.com

"The noble army of martyrs: praise Thee."

Te Deum Laudamus

Contents

Introduction

"The history of Christian martyrdom is, in fact, the history of Christianity itself; for it is in the arena, at the stake, and in the dungeon that the religion of Christ has won its most glorious triumphs." So wrote William Bramley-Moore in his conclusion to an introduction to an edition of Foxe's *Book of Martyrs.* Today, however, despite our living in a "global village," many, many Christian martyrs, including those of the twenty-first-century, are largely unsung heroes. This history of Christian martyrs gathers together the stories of faithful Christians who gladly gave their lives for the Lord and Master — from Stephen, the first Christian martyr, to those martyred in our day, at the beginning of the new Millennium.

This book testifies to the Christian faith of the martyrs and provides overwhelming evidence of the fulfilment of Jesus Christ's words, "I am sending you prophets and wise men and teachers. Some of them you will kill and crucify; others you will flog in your synagogues and pursue from town to town" (Matthew 23:34).

Martyrdoms were so often unreasonable and totally unjust. Tertullian certainly felt the force of this when he wrote: "The term 'conspiracy' should not be applied to us but rather to those who shout for the blood of the innocent and plead forsooth in justification of their hatred the foolish excuse that the Christians are to blame for every public disaster and every misfortune that befalls the people. If the Tiber rises to the walls, if the Nile fails to rise and flood the fields, if the sky withholds its rain, if there is earthquake or famine or plague, straightaway the cry arises: 'The Christians to the lions!'" (*Defense of Christianity*, 40:1-2).

Why a book on Christian martyrs?

However, the exposure of the corrupt nature of secular and religious authorities is not the main purpose of this book. A.J. Mason provides an excellent answer to the question: "Why a book on Christian martyrs?" in his own introduction to *Historic Martyrs of the Primitive Church*:

> In sending this book to press, it is my hope and prayer that it may not only instruct and interest, but that it may serve to stimulate its readers to a more ardent devotion to the great cause for which the martyrs suffered. They suffered for liberty and conscience, and the service which they thus did for mankind can never be exaggerated. But it was not for liberty of conscience as an abstract principle.
>
> They died for their loyalty to the one holy God amidst the immoralities of a corrupt polytheism. They died because they would not even pretend to put anything else on the same level with the Son of God who was crucified for them. They died because they would not abandon the gospels which tell of his incarnate life, nor absent themselves from the Eucharist [*Thanksgiving* Lord's

Supper] which he instituted to be the bond between himself and us, and between us amongst ourselves. This faith requires to be held today with a force of conviction like theirs; and perhaps there is no better way to brace and strengthen our Christian principles than by dwelling often upon the triumphs which the same faith has won in the past.[1]

The word "martyr"

The word "martyr" derives from the Greek word *martus,* "witness." The word was originally used in the Acts of the Apostles for people who were witnesses of our Lord's life and resurrection: "You will be my witnesses in Jerusalem, and in all Judea and Samaria, and to the ends of the earth" (Acts 1:8). One of the essential qualifications for Judas's replacement was that "one of these must become a witness with us of his [Christ's] resurrection" (Acts 1:22).

In Christian usage the term "martyr" soon acquired the meaning "blood-witness" (see Revelation 2:13), the person who was killed because of his testimony to Jesus. With the spread of persecution the word was used of those who had undergone hardships for the faith, and then "martyr" was restricted in its usage to those who had suffered death on account of their Christian faith. The martyrs were the heroes of the church.

Literature on martyrdoms

A considerable literature on martyrdom was produced in the early church:

1. *Acts of the martyrs*

These were the accounts of the trials (not transcripts of the court proceedings but often based on them), of which the earliest is the *Acts of Justin and his Companions* (AD 165).

2. *Passions*

These were freer accounts of the last days and death of the martyr. The earliest of the authentic passions is *The Martyrdom of Polycarp* (not long after his death in AD 156). "The most poignant of all the martyrs' narratives is called *The Passion of St Perpetua and St Felicity.* It holds a unique place in Christian annals. During the fourth century it was publicly read in the churches of North Africa. It was so popular that St Augustine had to protest that it should not be put on a level with the books of the Bible."[2]

3. *Exhortations*

Important early church leaders, such as Tertullian and Origen, wrote treatises about martyrdom, including accounts of specific martyrdoms.

4. *Panegyrics*

Panegyrics (public speeches in praise of someone) were made on the anniversary of the martyr's death for the edification of the faithful. Many of these are found in the sermons of the church fathers.

5. *Legends*
Later legends were little more than historical romances, based on a few facts but numerous embellishments. Such legends are excluded from this book.

In most cases the descriptions of martyrdoms in this book come from eye-witness accounts or from compilations of written records concerning the martyr's death. These descriptions are usually by people who wrote with white-hot passion, often from a totally committed viewpoint, and sometimes unable to exclude a tirade of abuse being heaped on those responsible for the martyr's death. These descriptions have not been toned down for the purposes of this book, but have been left as they were written, to ensure that today's reader captures the atmosphere of the particular martyrdom. The centrepiece to each entry in this book is the account of the actual martyrdom. This is drawn from an appropriate historical source. Sometimes this will be Foxe's *Book of Martyrs,* at other times the Passions, or Eusebius (who wrote *On the Martyrs of Palestine* as well as entries in his *Ecclesiastical History*), or one of the other reliable accounts of Christian martyrdoms found in Christian writings of recognized credibility, such as Prudentius, Chrysostom, Basil, and Augustine. In the case of martyrdom in the nineteenth and twentieth centuries, details have been drawn from the records of international missionary societies, and such reliable sources as the Keston Institute. This is an appropriate place to acknowledge and thank the many libraries, librarians, archivists, missionaries and missionary organizations who have so freely offered advice and material for inclusion in this book: in particular a deep debt of gratitude is due to The Keston Institute, The London Library, Regent's College Library, Dr Williams's Library, the Catholic Central Library, the Unevangelized Fields Mission (UFM), the Overseas Missionary Fellowship (OMF), the Worldwide Evangelization Crusade (WEC), the Wycliffe Bible Translators and the Africa Evangelical Fellowship.

Foxe's *Book of Martyrs*

More entries in this present compilation are taken from Foxe's *Book of Martyrs* than from any other single source. Many people have wished that Foxe lived today and had brought his book up to date. The Brownists thought this, as is clear from the following dedication, dating back to 1596, from a volume entitled *A True Confession of the Faith of the Brownists*:

> Our God (wee trust) will one day rayse up an other John Foxe, to gather and compile the Actes and Monuments of his later Martyrs, for the vew of posteritie, tho yet they seem to bee buryed in oblivion, and sleep in the dust.[3]

However, Foxe's writings have come under fire from Catholic writers. For example, Edward Norman has written:

> There has been a consistent production of anti-Catholic literature since the Reformation. Some of the works have been classics of English popular culture, like John Foxe's Book of Martyrs (*Acts and Monuments of these latter and*

> *perilous dayes*), first published in 1563. It went through five editions in the reign of Elizabeth I, and, with numerous subsequent republications, became the main source for most people of what Catholicism was like. Foxe represented it as inherently corrupt, authoritarian, foreign, and above all, as implacably opposed to personal freedom.[4]

Catholics have felt so strongly about Foxe's accounts that a book was published in 1870 entitled, *Martyrs Omitted by Foxe, being records of Religious Persecutions in the sixteenth and seventeenth centuries, compiled by a member of the English Church* [not identified]. In this volume, the writer states:

> The object of the compiler of these brief records is a twofold one: To hold up a mirror, that we may see ourselves in our hideous deformity, as breakers of the "law of love," puffed up, as we undoubtedly are, with the grossest, because the most unjustifiable, spiritual pride.
>
> It is also to edify the reader with records of the power of faith in many a last conflict, and with exemplifications of the working of that "law of love," enabling the sufferer to forgive the persecutor, who, like a second Cain, imbrued his hands in his brother's blood.
>
> . . . More than heroes, they [Roman Catholic fellow-Christians who were persecuted and killed] were Christian witnesses to the divine character of the church universal. Their names have been cast out as evil; their good deeds disparaged; their intense faith laughed at; their loftiest motives and last hours misrepresented. But they are not less worthy of our admiration. They were Englishmen. They were English Churchmen. They were sufferers for righteousness' sake. Therefore are they surely blessed. May we all be led to see how craftily the enemies of God's eternal and unalterable truth have put darkness for light, and light for darkness; sweet for bitter, and bitter for sweet; and how successfully souls have been ruined and lost in the process.[5]

The present book includes entries from both Foxe's book and from *Martyrs Omitted by Foxe*.

It is not easy to find an unbiased opinion about Foxe. Certainly his strength was his attention to detail, though it is true that his entries were by no means complete: for example it would appear that he did not have access to translations of documents such as *The Passion of Perpetua*. Perhaps Professor Owen Chadwick can give us the best assessment of Foxe's writings:

> Reformed theologians distrusted the old custom of celebrating a calendar of saints, for they believed the reverence paid to saints to derogate from faith in the one Savior. But at a very early date Protestant writers began to collect historical materials and stories about the deaths at the stake and upon the scaffold. The most famous and influential were the *Book of Martyrs* by Jean Crespin, a French lawyer who fled to Strasbourg and then to Geneva, and who collected the moving and painful agonies of the Huguenot victims; and

the book originally of the same title by the Englishman John Foxe, who fled abroad during the reign of Queen Mary and wrote his *Book of the Martyrs* at Basle between 1556 and 1559. His work, in its later editions known as *Acts and Monuments*, was influenced by that of Crespin, but Foxe's own genius and the different matter make it a great book in its own right. Both Crespin and Foxe were willing to include the death of persons who might doubtfully be claimed for the Reforming cause, and Foxe included at least two persons who had not died at all; but when every allowance is made to modern criticism, they contain much material still indispensable to the historian of the age, and they were sources of power and faith in the Protestant communities to which they were addressed. In England the Convocation of 1571 ordered a copy of Foxe's book to be placed in all cathedrals.[6]

Historical features

Historical features, which are not actual descriptions of martyrdoms, are interspersed throughout this book so that the reader can more fully appreciate the circumstances of particular martyrdoms. While we may know that the early Christians were martyred for not "sacrificing to the gods" we may have little idea about what "sacrificing to the gods" entailed, so the historical feature "Sacrificing to the gods" enlightens us on this. Horrific physical and mental tortures were often the prelude and means of Christian martyrdoms. This book does not dwell on these tortures, but neither does it ignore them. For example, we may read that a Christian martyr was "tortured with a currycomb on the hobby-horse" but without some explanation we shall have little understanding of what actually happened. Eight historical features detail the tortures Christian martyrs were subjected to in the early centuries, which often were used in succeeding centuries as well. For this reason this book is upsetting, as well as challenging and inspiring.

Readers should be prepared for horrific and explicit accounts. The introduction to a book which has graphic illustrations as well as horrific written accounts of the tortures inflicted on Christians states:

> One often hears that certain tortures were inflicted on the first Christians, but, beyond a few vague hints scattered here and there, it is impossible for unlettered folk to imagine the nature of the sufferings they were made to endure. Probably no more awful lesson of man's inhumanity to man, concentrated into so short a space, can be found throughout the annals of literature.
>
> At first sight the descriptions of these tortures may appear to some minds repellent and unreal; but on closer examination we find ourselves wondering – nay, stricken with admiration and astonishment – at the moral grandeur of the men and women who held with such fierce grip and tenacity "the faith once delivered to the saints."[7]

Additional background information is supplied alongside the actual martyrdoms to enable the reader to see what specific challenges faced our Christian brothers and sisters in previous centuries, how they responded, where exactly they drew their spiritual strength from to endure the unspeakable tortures they were put through, and how they remained "faithful unto death."

Choice of entries

The choice of entries for a book of Christian martyrs is controversial. Who should be in and who should be left out? For example, a number of Protestant ministers refused to attend Bonhoeffer's memorial service because, far from viewing him as an authentic Christian martyr, they viewed his acts as misguided and political. Joan of Arc is not officially regarded as a martyr by the Roman Catholic Church, but is put in the category of a "virgin." Then, Bishop Hannington is included as a "martyr" in some Anglican lectionaries, although he was actually killed as an intruder rather than because of his Christian faith. The editorial policy this book takes on this matter is to be inclusive and to include any person who was put to death for their Christian faith. So, for example, all three people just mentioned are included in this compilation. Also included are people who died in the place of others, but usually excluded are people like Gladys Aylward who may have given a life of Christian service in dangerous places and who may have died of disease or because of war or accidents. Butler's *Lives*, commenting on St Vitalis' martyrdom in 62, reminds us that:

> ... we are not all called to the sacrifice of martyrdom; but all are bound to make their whole lives a continued sacrifice of themselves to God, and to perform every action in this perfect spirit of sacrifice. An ardent desire of devoting ourselves totally to God in life and in death, and a cheerful readiness to do and to suffer whatever he requires of us, in order constantly to accomplish his divine will, is a disposition which ought to accompany and to animate all our actions.[8]

Just because a Christian martyr has an entry in a martyrology it does not mean to say that all he or she did or said was exemplary. This point has been underlined in a book referring to Christian saints, which is equally applicable to Christian martyrs:

> It is no part of my purpose to present the saints as perfect, although I would not wish to discourage those who have gained strength from that conviction. The ethical perfection of the saints is not, in my understanding, an article of faith in any Church. St Thomas More is almost certainly the most revered of English saints, but his attitude to heretics is repulsive by our modern standards. St Peter fell and fell again. Augustine's sins before he became a Christian add to the drama of his conversion. But the dismissal of his mistress, the mother of his child, seems harsh to us, though not apparently to him. St Francis of Assisi's treatment of his father makes painful reading. And there are numerous other examples.[9]

The entries are, in the main, in chronological order. However, the first entry is Matthew's account of the crucifixion of Jesus Christ. This is placed at the beginning of the book, not because Jesus Christ's death was a martyrdom, but because so many martyrs referred to Christ's death and because so much writing about Christian martyrs makes reference to his crucifixion. For example, Luke records that as Stephen was being martyred he echoed a prayer Jesus himself prayed: "Then Stephen fell on his knees, and cried out, "Lord, do not hold this sin against them." When he had said this he fell asleep" (Acts 7:60). They start with the Old Testament martyrs and the New Testament martyrs and then the martyrs of the early Christian church under the various emperors.

Under Nero (AD 54-68), Peter and Paul were martyred along with "a huge multitude" who were burned and tortured and put to death in other ways. Under Domitian (AD 81-96) a number of Christians were put to death charged with "atheism" (not publicly recognizing the emperor as a god). Under Trajan (AD 97-117), the most famous martyr was Ignatius of Antioch. Under Antoninus Pius (AD 138-161), the chief martyr was Polycarp of Smyrna. Under Marcus Aurelius (AD 161-180) the best known martyrs were Carpus, Papylus, Agathonica, Justin and his companions, the Scillitan martyrs and the martyrs of Lyons. Under Septimius Severus (AD 193-211) a new era began with Christians being sought out by the state, especially the newly converted and their teachers. During this time Saturus and his pupils Perpetua and Felicitas and their companions were martyred. Under Decius (AD 249-251) many of the martyrs were bishops, such as Fabian of Rome. Under Valerian (AD 253-260) bishops were the main target, along with other ministers as well as Christians of noble birth. Martyrs of the time included Cyprian and Fructuosus. Under Diocletian (AD 292-303), Christians experienced the severest persecutions of the early centuries of the church. This was caused by fear of Christian penetration into the Roman army, including even officers of the high command, and into the higher echelons of the civil service. Scriptures were burned and churches destroyed. Under Constantine, in March 313 complete freedom was restored to Christians by the Edict of Milan and persecution and martyrdom eventually ceased.

The first three centuries of the Christian era are probably the best-known period of martyrdoms. In addition to these, this book relates many of the less well known Christian martyrdoms through the centuries (such as the martyrs of the Coptic church), as well as the better known martyrs of the middle ages, the Reformation and modern times.

Twentieth-century and twenty-first-century martyrs

Christian martyrs of the 17th to 21st are under geographical areas, rather than in a chronological list, although most of these are from the 20th century. There are accounts of the martyrdom of numerous pioneer missionaries throughout the world and the martyrdoms of the first indigenous Christians in a number of countries.

> It appears likely that Dr Paul Carlson was correct when he told Congolese believers, before his martyrdom, that more believers have died for Christ in this century than in all the previous centuries combined. Of course, there is no hard evidence to prove this, since the records of most martyrdoms before the twentieth century are lost, and the name of countless martyrs in this century (those who died in the Soviet Union and China, for example) are not available for scrutiny.[10]

Missionary letters and first-hand accounts of the martyrdoms of Christians are here included of the two places where more Christians have been martyred in the twentieth-century than anywhere else: China and Russia.

A great cloud of witnesses

Hebrews chapter eleven refers to those who through faith "shut the mouths of lions, quenched the fury of the flames, and escaped the edge of the sword," as well as those who "were tortured and refused to be released, so that they might gain a better resurrection. Some faced jeers and flogging, while still others were chained and put in prison. They were stoned; they were sawn in two; they were put to death by the sword. They went about in sheepskins and goatskins, destitute, persecuted and ill-treated – the world was not worthy of them" (Hebrews 11:33-38).

Sadly, just as there were many martyrs in Old Testament days and New Testament days, so there have been countless Christian martyrs through the centuries right up to our own day. The writer to the Hebrews calls these martyrs and other faithful Christians "a cloud of witnesses" by which "we are surrounded" (Hebrews 12:1). Reading the record of this history of Christian martyrs must sober and challenge us, no matter how easy or acutely difficult our personal circumstances may be. This is the way we should act, once we have viewed the roll of honor of the Christian martyrs, according to the writer to the Hebrews: "Since we are surrounded by such a cloud of witnesses . . . let us fix our eyes on Jesus, the author and perfecter of our faith, who for the joy set before him endured the cross, scorning its shame, and sat down at the right hand of the throne of God. Consider him who endured such opposition from sinful men, so that you will not grow weary and lose heart" (Hebrews 12:1-3).

Notes

1 A. J. Mason, *Historic Martyrs of the Primitive Church,* Longmans, 1906, p x.
2 Frank Longford, *Saints*, Hutchinson, 1970, p 23.
3 *A True Confession of the Faith of the Brownists* (1596), reprinted in Albert Peel, *The Noble Army of Congregational Martyrs,* Pilgrim Press, 1948, p 8.
4 Edward Norman, *Roman Catholicism in England,* OUP, 1985, p 4.
5 *Martyrs Omitted by Foxe, being records of Religious Persecutions in the sixteenth and seventeenth centuries, compiled by a member of the English Church,* London: John Hodges, 1870, p xv.
6 Owen Chadwick, *The Reformation,* Penguin, 1972, pp 174-75.

7 *Tortures and Torments of the Christian Martyrs, from the De SS. Martyrum Curciatibus of the Rev Father Gallonia,* translated by A. R. Allinson, London: printed for subscribers, 1903, p. vii.
8 Alban Butler, *The Lives of the Saints,* Dublin: Richard Coyne, 1833, vol I, p 528.
9 Frank Longford, *Saints,* Hutchinson, 1970, pp 197-98.
10 J. and M. Hefley, *By Their Blood: Christian Martyrs of the Twentieth Century,* Milford: Mott Media, 1979 p. 589.

Part One

Bible martyrs

Contents

1. Introduction

The word "martyr" does not occur in the Old Testament. However, the Old Testament records more instances of God's people being put to death on account of their faith than is usually recalled. There are many indications in the Old Testament that God's faithful prophets risked their lives just for being a prophet. "They killed your prophets, who had admonished them in order to turn them back to you" Nehemiah 9:26. In the opening chapters of his prophecy Jeremiah has this graphic description of the martyrdom of some prophets: "Your sword has devoured your prophets like a ravening lion" Jeremiah 2:30.

Jesus' references to the Old Testament martyrs are recorded in the New Testament: "And you say, 'If we had lived in the days of our forefathers, we would not have taken part with them in shedding the blood of the prophets.' So you testify against yourselves that you are the descendants of those who murdered the prophets" Matthew 23:30-31. In the next breath Jesus prophesied that martyrdom awaited some of his followers: "Therefore I am sending you prophets and wise men and teachers. Some of them you will kill and crucify, others you will flog in your synagogues and pursue from town to town. And so upon you will come all the righteous blood that has been shed on earth, from the blood of righteous Abel to the blood of Zechariah son of Berakiah, whom you murdered between the temple and the altar" Matthew 23:34-36.

The scope of this opening chapter of the record of Christian martyrs is limited to martyrdoms recorded in the Old and New Testaments and to some people mentioned in the Bible whose martyrdoms are recorded outside the pages of the Bible.

Perhaps the most famous summary of the martyrs of the Old Testament comes in the book of Hebrews: "Others were tortured and refused to be released, so that they might gain a better resurrection. Some faced jeers and flogging, while still others were chained and put in prison. They were stoned; they were sawn in two; they were put to death by the sword" 11:35-37. Many Bible commentators point out that "sawn in two" could be a reference to the legendary book entitled *Martyrdom of Isaiah* in which Isaiah is sawn in two with a wooden saw on account of prophesying that the future redemption would come through Jesus Christ.

While this opening chapter of this encyclopedia has extracts from the Bible and extracts from books that are outside the canonical books of the Bible this is not meant to imply that any writing is on a par with the uniquely inspired Scriptures. Such writings as The Apocrypha and Pseudepigrapha of the Old Testament and the Acts of Thaddeus should be referred to for the flavor and background they give us, as we might read a novel today, rather than given the status of a wholly accurate and historical account.

2. Christ's crucifixion

While he was still speaking, Judas, one of the Twelve, arrived. With him was a large crowd armed with swords and clubs, sent from the chief priests and the elders of the people. Now the betrayer had arranged a signal with them: "The one I kiss is the man; arrest him." Going at once to Jesus, Judas said, "Greetings, Rabbi!" and kissed him.

Jesus replied, "Friend, do what you came for."

Then the men stepped forward, seized Jesus and arrested him. With that, one of Jesus' companions reached for his sword, drew it out and struck the servant of the high priest, cutting off his ear.

"Put your sword back in its place," Jesus said to him, "for all who draw the sword will die by the sword. Do you think I cannot call on my Father, and he will at once put at my disposal more than twelve legions of angels? But how then would the Scriptures be fulfilled that say it must happen in this way?"

At that time Jesus said to the crowd, "Am I leading a rebellion, that you have come out with swords and clubs to capture me? Every day I sat in the temple courts teaching, and you did not arrest me. But this has all taken place that the writings of the prophets might be fulfilled." Then all the disciples deserted him and fled.

Those who had arrested Jesus took him to Caiaphas, the high priest, where the teachers of the law and the elders had assembled. But Peter followed him at a distance, right up to the courtyard of the high priest. He entered and sat down with the guards to see the outcome.

The chief priests and the whole Sanhedrin were looking for false evidence against Jesus so that they could put him to death. But they did not find any, though many false witnesses came forward.

Finally two came forward and declared, "This fellow said, "I am able to destroy the temple of God and rebuild it in three days."

Then the high priest stood up and said to Jesus, "Are you not going to answer? What is this testimony that these men are bringing against you?" But Jesus remained silent.

The high priest said to him, "I charge you under oath by the living Go: Tell us if you are the Christ, the Son of God."

"Yes, it is as you say," Jesus replied. "But I say to all of you: In the future you will see the Son of Man sitting at the right hand of the Mighty One and coming on the cloud of heaven."

Then the high priest tore his clothes and said, "He has spoken blasphemy! Why do we need any more witnesses? Look, now you have heard the blasphemy. What do you think?"

"He is guilty of death," they answered.

Then they spat in his face and struck him with their fists. Others slapped him and said, "Prophesy to us, Christ. Who hit you?"

Now Peter was sitting out in the courtyard, and a servant girl came to him. "You also were with Jesus of Galilee," she said.

But he denied it before them all. "I don't know what you're talking about," he said.

Then he went out to the gateway, where another girl saw him and said to the people there, "This fellow was with Jesus of Nazareth."

He denied it again, with an oath: "I don't know the man!"

After a little while, those standing there went up to Peter and said, "Surely you are one of them, for your accent gives you away."

Then he began to call down curses on himself and he swore to them, "I don't know the man!"

Immediately a rooster crowed. Then Peter remembered the word Jesus had spoken: "Before the rooster crows, you will disown me three times." And he went outside and wept bitterly.

Early in the morning, all the chief priests and the elders of the people came to the decision to put Jesus to death. They bound him, led him away and handed him over to Pilate, the governor.

When Judas, who had betrayed him, saw that Jesus was condemned, he was seized with remorse and returned the thirty silver coins to the chief priests and the elders. "I have sinned," he said "for I have betrayed innocent blood."

"What is that to us?" they replied. "That's your responsibility."

So Judas threw the money into the temple and left. Then he went away and hanged himself.

The chief priests picked up the coins and said, "It is against the law to put this into the treasury, since it is blood money." So they decided to use the money to buy the potter's field as a burial place for foreigners. That is why it has been called the Field of Blood to this day. Then what was spoken by Jeremiah the prophet was fulfilled: "They took the thirty silver coins, the price set on him by the people of Israel, and they used them to buy the potter's field, as the Lord commanded me."

Meanwhile Jesus stood before the governor, and the governor asked him, "Are you the king of the Jews?"

"Yes, it is as you say," Jesus replied.

When he was accused by the chief priests and the elders, he gave no answer. Then Pilate asked him, "Don't you hear the testimony they are bringing against you?" But Jesus made no reply, not even to a single charge – to the great amazement of the governor.

Now it was the governor's custom at the Feast to release a prisoner chosen by the crowd. At that time they had a notorious prisoner, called Barabbas. So when the crowd had gathered, Pilate asked them, "Which one do you want me to release to you: Barabbas, or Jesus who is called Christ?" For he knew it was out of envy that they had handed Jesus over to him.

While Pilate was sitting on the judge's seat, his wife sent him this message: "Don't have anything to do with that innocent man, for I have suffered a great deal today in a dream because of him."

But the chief priests and the elders persuaded the crowd to ask for Barabbas and to have Jesus executed.

"Which of the two do you want me to release to you?" asked the governor.

"Barabbas," they answered.

"What shall I do, then, with Jesus who is called Christ?" Pilate asked.

They all answered, "Crucify him!"

"Why? What crime has he committed?" asked Pilate.

But they shouted all the louder, "Crucify him!"

When Pilate saw that he was getting nowhere, but that instead an uproar was starting, he took water and washed his hands in front of the crowd. "I am innocent of this man's blood," he said. "It is your responsibility!"

All the people answered, "Let his blood be on us and on our children!"

Then he released Barabbas to them. But he had Jesus flogged, and handed him over to be crucified.

Then the governor's soldiers took Jesus into the Praetorium and gathered the whole company of soldiers round him. They stripped him and put a scarlet robe on him, and then twisted together a crown of thorns and set it on his head. They put a staff in his right hand and knelt in front of him and mocked him. "Hail, king of the Jews!" they said. They spat on him, and took the staff and struck him on the head again and again. After they had mocked him, they took off the robe and put his own clothes on him. Then they led him away to crucify him.

As they were going out, they met a man from Cyrene, named Simon, and they forced him to carry the cross. They came to a place called Golgotha (which means The Place of the Skull). There they offered Jesus wine to drink, mixed with gall; but after tasting it, he refused to drink it. When they had crucified him, they divided up his clothes by casting lots. And sitting down, they kept watch over him there. Above his head they placed the written charge against him: THIS IS JESUS, THE KING OF THE JEWS. Two robbers were crucified with him, one on his right and one on his left. Those who passed by hurled insults at him, shaking their heads and saying, "You who are going to destroy the temple and build it in three days, save yourself! Come down from the cross, if you are the Son of God!"

In the same way the chief priests, the teachers of the law and the elders mocked him. "He saved others," they said, "but he can't save himself! He's the King of Israel! Let him come down now from the cross, and we will believe in him. He trusts in God. Let God rescue him now if he wants him, for he said, "I am the Son of God."" In the same way the robbers who were crucified with him also heaped insults on him.

From the sixth hour until the ninth hour darkness came over all the land. About the ninth hour Jesus cried out in a loud voice, "*Eloi, Eloi, lama sabachthani?*" – which means, "My God, my God, why have you forsaken me?"

When some of those standing there heard this, they said, "He's calling Elijah."

Immediately one of them ran and got a sponge. He filled it with wine vinegar, put it on a stick, and offered it to Jesus to drink. The rest said, "Now leave him alone. Let's see if Elijah comes to save him.'

And when Jesus had cried out again in a loud voice, he gave up his spirit.

At that moment the curtain of the temple was torn in two from top to bottom. The earth shook and the rocks split. The tombs broke upon and the bodies of many holy people who had died were raised to life. They came out of the tombs, and after Jesus" resurrection they went into the holy city and appeared to many people.

When the centurion and those with him who were guarding Jesus saw the earthquake and all that had happened, they were terrified, and exclaimed, "Surely he was the Son of God!"

Many women were there, watching from a distance. They had followed Jesus from Galilee to care for his needs. Among them were Mary Magdalene, Mary the mother of James and Joses, and the mother of Zebedee's sons.

As evening approached, there came a rich man from Arimathea, named Joseph, who had himself become a disciple of Jesus. Going to Pilate, he asked for Jesus" body, and Pilate ordered that it be given to him. Joseph took the body, wrapped it in a clean linen cloth, and placed it in his own new tomb that he had cut out of the rock. He rolled a big stone in front of the entrance to the tomb and went away. Mary Magdalene and the other Mary were sitting there opposite the tomb.

The next day, the one after Preparation Day, the chief priests and the Pharisees went to Pilate. "Sir," they said, "we remember that while he was still alive that deceiver said, "After three days I will rise again." So give the order for the tomb to be made secure until the third day. Otherwise, his disciples may come and steal the body and tell the people that he has been raised from the dead. This last deception will be worse than the first.'

"Take a guard," Pilate answered. "Go, make the tomb as secure as you know how." So they went and made the tomb secure by putting a seal on the stone and posting the guard.

The Bible: Matthew 26:47-27:66

3. Martyrdoms recorded in the Old Testament

ZECHARIAH THE PRIEST

Jesus Christ's summary of the history of martyrdom in the Old Testament:

This generation will be held responsible for the blood of all the prophets that has been shed since the beginning of the world, from the blood of Abel to the blood of Zechariah, who was killed between the altar and the sanctuary.

The Bible: Luke 11:51

After the death of Jehoiada, the officials of Judah came and paid homage to the king, and he listened to them. They abandoned the temple of the Lord, the God of their fathers, and worshiped Asherah poles and idols. Because of their guilt, God's anger came upon Judah and Jerusalem. Although the Lord sent prophets to the people to bring them back to him, and though they testified against them, they would not listen.

Then the Spirit of God came upon Zechariah son of Jehoiada the priest. He stood before the people and said, "This is what God says: "Why do you disobey the Lord's commands? You will not prosper. Because you have forsaken the Lord, he has forsaken you.'

But they plotted against him, and by order of the king they stoned him to death in the courtyard of the Lord's temple. King Joash did not remember the kindness Zechariah's father Jehoiada had shown him but killed his son, who said as he lay dying, "May the Lord see this and call you to account.'

The Bible: 2 Chronicles 24:17-22

URIAH THE PROPHET

Now Uriah son of Shemaiah from Kiriath Jearim was another man who prophesied in the name of the Lord; he prophesied the same things against this city [Jerusalem] and this land as Jeremiah did. When King Jehoiakim and all his officers and officials heard his words, the king sought to put him to death. But Uriah heard of it and fled in fear to Egypt. King Jehoiakim, however, sent Elnathan son of Acbor to Egypt, along with some other men. They brought Uriah out of Egypt and took him to King Jehoiakim, who had him struck down with a sword and his body thrown into the burial place of the common people.

Furthermore, Ahikam son of Shaphan supported Jeremiah, and so he was not handed over to the people to be put to death.
The Bible: Jeremiah 26:20-24

4. Martyrdoms of Old Testament people not recorded in the Old Testament

Isaiah the prophet

Chapter 1

1 And it came to pass in the twenty-sixth year of the reign of Hezekiah king of Judah that he
2 called Manasseh his son. Now he was his only one. And he called him into the presence of Isaiah the son of Amoz the prophet; and into the presence of Josab the son of Isaiah. . . .
6b, 7 And whilst he (Hezekiah) gave commands, Josab the son of Isaiah standing by, Isaiah said to Hezekiah the king, but not in the presence of Manasseh only did he say unto him: "As the Lord liveth, whose name has not been sent into this world, [and as the Beloved of my Lord liveth], and as the Spirit which speaketh in me liveth, all these commands and these words shall be made of none effect by Manasseh thy son, and through the agency of his hands I shall depart mid the torture of
8 my body. And Sammael Malchira shall serve Manasseh, and execute all his desire, and he shall
9 become a follower of Beliar rather than of me. And many in Jerusalem and in Judaea he shall cause to abandon the true faith, and Beliar shall dwell in Manasseh, and by his hands I shall be
10 sawn asunder." And when Hezekiah heard these words he wept very bitterly, and rent his garments,
11 and placed earth upon his head, and fell on his face. And Isaiah said unto him: "The counsel of
12 Sammael against Manasseh is consummated: nought shall avail thee." And on that day Hezekiah
13 resolved in his heart to slay Manasseh his son. And Isaiah said to Hezekiah: ["The Beloved hath made of none effect thy design, and] the purpose of thy heart shall not be accomplished, for with this calling have I been called [and I shall inherit the heritage of the Beloved]."

Chapter 2

1 And it came to pass after that Hezekiah died and Manasseh became king, that he did not remember the commands of Hezekiah his father but forgat them, and Sammael abode in Manasseh
2 and clung fast to him. And Manasseh forsook the service of the God of his father, and he served
3 Satan and his angels and his powers. And he turned aside the house of his father which had been
4 before the face of Hezekiah the words of wisdom and from the service of God. And Manasseh turned aside his heart to serve Beliar; for the angel of lawlessness, who is the ruler of this world, is Beliar, whose name is Matanbuchus. And he delighted in Jerusalem because of Manasseh, and he made him strong in apostatizing (Israel) and in the lawlessness which was spread abroad in Jerusalem
5 And witchcraft and magic increased and divination and augulation, and fornication, [and adultery], and the persecution of the righteous by Manasseh and [Belachira, and] Tobia the Canaanite, and John
6 of Anathoth. And the rest of the acts, behold they are written
7 in the book of the Kings of Judah and Israel. And when Isaiah the son of Amoz saw the lawlessness which was being perpetrated in Jerusalem and the worship of Satan and his wantonness, he
8 withdrew from Jerusalem and settled in Bethlehem of Judah. And there also there was much
9 lawlessness, and withdrawing from Bethlehem he settled on a mountain in a desert place. [And Micaiah the prophet, and

the aged Ananias, and Joel and Habakkuk,
and his son Josab, and many of the faithful
who believed in the ascension into heaven,
withdrew and settled on the mountain.]
10 They were all clothed with garments of
hair, and they were all prophets. And they
had nothing with them but were naked, and
they all lamented with a great lamentation
because of the going
11 astray of Israel. And these eat nothing
save wild herbs which they gathered on the
mountains, and having cooked them, they
lived thereon together with Isaiah the
prophet. And they spent two years of
12 days on the mountains and hills. [And
after this, whilst they were in the desert,
there was a certain man in Samaria named
Belchra, of the family of Zedekiah, the son
of Chenaan, a false prophet whose dwelling
was in Bethlehem. Now Hezekiah the son of
Chanani, who was the brother of his father,
and in the days of Ahab king of Israel had
been the teacher of the 400 prophets of Baal,
13 had himself smitten and reproved
Micaiah the son of Amada the prophet. And
he, Micaiah, had been reproved by Ahab and
cast into prison. (And he was) with
Zedekiah the prophet: they were
14 with Ahaziah the son of Ahab, king in
Samaria. And Elijah the prophet of Tebon of
Gilead was reproving Ahaziah and Samaria,
and prophesied regarding Ahaziah that he
should die on his bed of sickness, and that
Samaria should be delivered into the hand of
Leba Nasa because he had slain
15 the prophets of God. And when the false
prophets, who were with Ahaziah the son of
Ahab and
16 their teacher Gemarias of Mount Joel had
heard – now he was brother of Zedekiah –
when they had heard, they persuaded Ahaziah
the king of Aguaron and slew Micaiah.

Chapter 3

1 And Belchlra recognized and saw the place
of Isaiah and the prophets who were with
him; for he dwelt in the region of
Bethlehem, and was an adherent of
Manasseh. And he prophesied falsely in
Jerusalem, and many belonging to Jerusalem
were confederate with him, and he was a
Samaritan.
2 And it came to pass when Alagar Zagar,
king of Assyria, had come and captured
Samaria and taken the nine (and a half)
tribes captive, and led them away to the
mountains of the Medes and the
3 rivers of Tazon; this (Belchira) while still a
youth, had escaped and come to Jerusalem
in the days of Hezekiah king of Judah, but
he walked not in the ways of his father of
Samaria; for he feared
4 Hezekiah. And he was found in the days
of Hezekiah speaking words of lawlessness in
Jerusalem.
5 And the servants of Hezekiah accused him,
and he made his escape to the region of
Bethlehem.
6 And they persuaded . . . And Belchlra
accused Isaiah and the prophets who were
with him, saying: "Isaiah and those who are
with him prophesy against Jerusalem and
against the cities of Judah that they shall be
laid waste and (against the children of Judah
and) Benjamin also that they shall go into
captivity, and also against thee, O lord the
king, that thou shalt go (bound) with hooks
8 and iron chains": But they prophesy falsely
against Israel and Judah. And Isaiah himself
hath
9 said: "I see more than Moses the prophet."
But Moses said: "No man can see God and
live":
10 and Isaiah hath said: "I have seen God
and behold I live." Know, therefore, O king,
that he is lying. And Jerusalem also he hath
called Sodom, and the princes of Judah and
Jerusalem he hath declared to be the people
of Gomorrah. And he brought many
accusations against Isaiah and the
11 prophets before Manasseh. But Beliar
dwelt in the heart of Manasseh and in the
heart of the
12 princes of Judah and Benjamin and of
the eunuchs and of the councillors of the
king. And the words of Belchira pleased him
[exceedingly], and he sent and seized Isaiah.

Chapter 5

1b, 2 And he sawed him asunder with a
wood-saw. And when Isaiah was being sawn
in sunder Balchra stood up, accusing him,

and all the false prophets stood up, laughing and rejoicing because
3 of Isaiah. And Balchra, with the aid of Mechembechus, stood up before Isaiah,
4 deriding; And Belchlra said to Isaiah: "Say: 'I have lied in all that I have spoken, and likewise
5 the ways of Manasseh are good and right. And the ways also of Balchra and of his associates are
6, 7 good.'" And this he said to him when he began to be sawn in sunder. But Isaiah was (absorbed)
8 in a vision of the Lord, and though his eyes were open, he saw them . And Balchra spake thus to Isaiah: "Say what I say unto thee and I will turn their heart, and I will compel Manasseh
9 and the princes of Judah and the people and all Jerusalem to reverence thee." And Isaiah answered and said: "So far as I have utterance: Damned and accursed be thou and all thy powers and
10, 11 all thy house. For thou canst not take (from me) aught save the skin of my body." And they
12 seized and sawed in sunder Isaiah, the son of Amoz, with a wood-saw. And Manasseh and
13 Balchra and the false prophets and the princes and the people all stood looking on. And to the prophets who were with him he said before he had been sawn in sunder: "Go ye to the region
14 of Tyre and Sidon; for me only hath God mingled the cup." And when Isaiah was being sawn in sunder, he neither cried aloud nor wept, but his lips spake with the Holy Spirit until he was sawn in twain.
The Apocrypha and Pseudepigrapha of the Old Testament

5. Martyrdoms recorded in the New Testament

JOHN THE BAPTIST

Jesus Christ's assessment of John the Baptist

Among those born of women there has not risen anyone greater than John the Baptist.
The Bible: Matthew 11:11, NIV

Martyrdom of John the Baptist (1)

At that time Herod the tetrarch heard the reports about Jesus, and he said to his attendants, "This is John the Baptist; he has risen from the dead! That is why miraculous powers are at work in him."

Now Herod had arrested John and bound him and put him in prison because of Herodias, his brother Philip's wife, for John had been saying to him: "It is not lawful for you to have her." Herod wanted to kill John, but he was afraid of the people, because they considered him a prophet.

On Herod's birthday the daughter of Herodias [although her name is not mentioned in the Bible, Josephus, the Jewish historian, tells us her name: Salome] danced for them and pleased Herod so much that he promised with an oath to give her whatever she asked. Prompted by her mother, she said, "Give me here on a platter the head of John the Baptist." The king was distressed, but because of his oaths and his dinner guests, he ordered that her request be granted and had John beheaded in the prison. His head was brought in on a platter and given to the girl, who carried it to her mother. John's disciples came and took his body and buried it. Then they went and told Jesus.
The Bible: Matthew 14:1-12

Note on John the Baptist

The two New Testament accounts of John the Baptist being beheaded, Matthew 14:1-12 and Mark 6:14-29 do not mention the name of dancer who "pleased" Herod so much. She is just called "the daughter of Herodias". Her name is supplied by Josephus, in a totally different context, when he is discussing the Herodian dynasty. "Herodias . . . had a daughter Salome, after whose birth she undertook to flout the precepts of our fathers by marrying Herod [Antipas], her husband's brother" (*Antiquities* 18:136).

Martyrdom of John the Baptist (2)

1 Not long after this {ie: the appointment of

the seventy) John the Baptist was beheaded by the younger Herod, as is stated in the Gospels. Josephus also records the same fact, making mention of Herodias by name, and stating that, although she was the wife of his brother, Herod made her his own wife after divorcing his former lawful wife, who was the daughter of Aretas, king of Petra, and separating Herodias from her husband while he was still alive.

2 It was on her account also that he slew John, and waged war with Aretas, because of the disgrace inflicted on the daughter of the latter. Josephus relates that in this war, when they came to battle, Herod's entire army was destroyed, and that he suffered this calamity on account of his crime against John.

3 The same Josephus confesses in this account that John the Baptist was an exceedingly righteous man, and thus agrees with the things written of him in the Gospels. He records also that Herod lost his kingdom on account of the same Herodias, and that he was driven into banishment with her, and condemned to live at Vienne in Gaul.

4 He relates these things in the eighteenth book of the Antiquities, where he writes of John in the following words: "It seemed to some of the Jews that the army of Herod was destroyed by God, who most justly avenged John called the Baptist.

5 For Herod slew him, a good man and one who exhorted the Jews to come and receive baptism, practicing virtue and exercising righteousness toward each other and toward God; for baptism would appear acceptable unto Him when they employed it, not for the remission of certain sins, but for the purification of the body, as the soul had been already purified in righteousness.

6 And when others gathered about him (for they found much pleasure in listening to his words), Herod feared that his great influence might lead to some sedition, for they appeared ready to do whatever he might advise. He therefore considered it much better, before any new thing should be done under John's influence, to anticipate it by slaying him, than to repent after revolution had come, and when he found himself in the midst of difficulties. On account of Herod's suspicion John was sent in bonds to the above-mentioned citadel of Mach'ra, and there slain."

Eusebius, Church History, book 1, chapter 11

THE HOLY INNOCENTS

The savage murder of the innocent babies and toddlers by King Herod has been reckoned as an early instance of martyrdom.
Matthew records this horrific slaughter.

Martyrdom of the holy innocents (1)

When Herod realized that he had been outwitted by the Magi, he was furious, and he gave orders to kill all the boys in Bethlehem and its vicinity who were two years old and under, in accordance with the time he had learned from the Magi. Then what was said through the prophet Jeremiah was fulfilled: "A voice is heard in Ramah, weeping and great mourning, Rachel weeping fro her children and refusing to be comforted, because they are no more."

Matthew 2:16-18

Martyrdom of the holy innocents (2)

Say, ye celestial guards, who wait
In Bethlehem, round the Saviour's palace gate,
Say, who are these on golden wings,
That hover o'er the new-born King of kings,
Their palms and garlands telling plain
That they are of the glorious martyr train,
Next to yourselves ordain'd to praise
His name, and brighten as on Him they gaze?

But where their spoils and trophies? where
The glorious dint a martyr's shield should bear?
How chance no cheek among them wears
The deep-worn trace of penitential tears,
But all is bright and smiling love,
As if, fresh-borne from Eden's happy grove,
They had flown here, their King to see,
Nor ever had been heirs of dark mortality?

Ask, and some angel will reply,
"These, like yourselves, were born to sin and die,
"But ere the poison root was grown,

"God set his seal, and mark'd them for his own.
"Baptiz'd in blood for Jesus' sake,
"Now underneath the cross their bed they make,
"Not to be scar'd from that sure rest
"By frighten'd mither's shriek, or warrior's waving crest."

Mindful of these, the first fruits sweet
Borne by the suffering Church her Lord to greet;
Bless'd Jesus ever lov'd to trace
The "innocent brightness" of an infant's face.
He rais'd them from the world and all its harms:
Heirs though they were of sin and shame,
He bless'd them in his own and in his Father's name.

Then, as each fond unconscious child
On th' everlasting Parent sweetly smil'd,
(Like infants sporting on the shore,
That tremble not at Ocean's boundless roar)
Were they not present to thy thought,
All souls, that in their cradles thou hast bought?
But chiefly these, who died for Thee,
That Thou might'st live for them a sadder death to see.

And next to these, thy gracious word
Was as a pledge of benediction, stor'd
For Christian mothers, while they moan
Their treasur'd hopes, just born, baptiz'd, and gone.
Oh joy for Rachel's broken heart!
She and her babes shall meet no more to part;
So dear to Christ her pious haste
To trust them in his arms, for ever safe embrac'd.
She dares not grudge to leave them there,
Where to behold them was her hear's first prayer,

She dares not grieve – but she must weep,
As her pale placid martyr sinks to sleep,
Teaching so well and silently
How, at the shepherd's call, the lamb should die:
How happier far than life the end
Of souls that infant-like beneath their burthen bend.
John Keble, The Christian Year

Stephen: The first Christian martyr

All who were sitting in the Sanhedrin looked intently at Stephen, and they saw that his face was like the face of an angel.
The Bible: Acts 6:15, NIV

At the end of Dr Luke's account of the martyrdom of Stephen he adds a detail about the people involved in killing Stephen: "the witnesses laid their clothes at the feet of a young man named Saul" (Acts 7:58). One consequence of Stephen's martyrdom was the impression it left on the man who was destined to become the greatest teacher and missionary of the early church. A second consequence of Stephen's death, a time of persecution for these first Christians resulting in the spread of Christianity from Jerusalem, is recorded in the opening words of Acts chapter 8: "On that day [Stephen's martyrdom] a great persecution broke out against the church at Jerusalem, and all except the apostles were scattered throughout Judea and Samaria" (Acts 8:1). Like Jesus, Stephen asked God to forgive his murderers.

Martyrdom of Stephen (1)

Now Stephen, a man full of God's grace and power, did great wonders and miraculous signs among the people. Opposition arose, however, from members of the Synagogue of the Freedmen. These men began to argue with Stephen, but they could not stand up against his wisdom or the Spirit by whom he spoke.

Then they secretly persuaded some men to say, "We have heard Stephen speak words of blasphemy against Moses and against God."

So they stirred up the people and the elders and the teachers of the law. They seized Stephen and brought him before the Sanhedrin. They produced false witnesses, who testified, "This fellow never stops speaking against this holy place and against the law. For we have heard him say that this Jesus of Nazareth will destroy this place and change the customs Moses handed down to us."

All who were sitting in the Sanhedrin looked intently at Stephen, and they saw that his face was like the face of an angel. Then the high priest asked him, "Are these charges true?"

To this Stephen replied: "Brothers and fathers, listen to me! The God of glory appeared to our father Abraham while he was still in Mesopotamia . . . You stiff-necked people, with uncircumcised hearts and ears! You are just like your fathers: You always resist the Holy Spirit! Was there ever a prophet your fathers did not persecute? They even killed those who predicted the coming of the Righteous One. And now you have betrayed and murdered him-you who have received the law that was put into effect through angels but have not obeyed it."

When they heard this, they were furious and gnashed their teeth at him. But Stephen, full of the Holy Spirit, looked up to heaven and saw the glory of God, and Jesus standing at the right hand of God. "Look," he said, "I see heaven open and the Son of Man standing at the right hand of God."

At this they covered their ears and yelling at the top of their voices, they all rushed at him, dragged him out of the city and began to stone him. Meanwhile, the witnesses laid their clothes at the feet of a young man named Saul.

While they were stoning him, Stephen prayed, "Lord Jesus, receive my spirit." Then he fell on his knees and cried out, "Lord, do not hold this sin against them." When he had said this, he fell asleep.

And Saul was there, giving approval to his death.

The Bible: Acts 6:8-15; 7:1-2, 51-60 NIV

Martyrdom of Stephen (2)

St. Stephen's death was occasioned by the faithful manner in which he preached the Gospel to the betrayers and murderers of Christ. To such a degree of madness were they excited, that they cast him out of the city and stoned him to death. The time when he suffered is generally supposed to have been at the Passover which succeeded to that of our Lord's crucifixion, and to the era of his ascension, in the following spring.

Upon this a great persecution was raised against all who professed their belief in Christ as the Messiah, or as a prophet. We are immediately told by St. Luke, that "there was a great persecution against the church which was at Jerusalem;" and that "they were all scattered abroad throughout the regions of Judaea and Samaria, except the apostles."

About two thousand Christians, with Nicanor, one of the seven deacons, suffered martyrdom during the "persecution that arose about Stephen."

On the spot where he was martyred, Eudocia, the Empress of Theodosius, erected a superb church.

Foxe's Book of Martyrs, Edited by William Byron Forbush

Martyrdom of Stephen (2) Stephen, deacon and protomartyr

All that we know about Stephen the Protomartyr (that is, the first martyr of the Christian Church) is found in chapters 6 and 7 of the Book of Acts.

The early Christian congregations, like the Jewish synagogues, had a program of assistance for needy widows, and some of the Greek-speaking Jews in the Jerusalem congregation complained that their widows were being neglected. The apostles replied: "We cannot both preach and administer financial matters. Choose seven men from among yourselves, respected, Spirit-filled, and of sound judgement, and let them be in charge of the accounts, and we will devote ourselves to prayer and the ministry of the word." The people accordingly chose seven men, including Stephen, and the apostles laid their hands on them. They are traditionally considered to be the first deacons, although the Scriptures do not use the word to describe them. (The Scriptures do refer to officials called deacons in the local congregations, without being very specific about their duties; and a century or more later, we find the organized charities of each local congregation in the hands of its deacons.)

Stephen was an eloquent and fiery speaker, and a provocative one. (Some readers have speculated that some of his fellow Christians wanted to put him in charge of alms in the hope that he would administer more and talk less.) His blunt declarations that the Temple service was no longer the means by which penitent sinners should seek reconciliation with God enraged the Temple leaders, who caused him to be stoned to death. As he died, he said, "Lord, do not hold this sin against them." One of those who saw the stoning and approved of it was Saul (or Paul) of Tarsus, who took an active part in the general persecution of Christians that followed the death of Stephen, but who was later led to become a Christian himself.

We remember Stephen on December 26, the day after Christmas. Hence the song

Good King Wenceslas looked out
On the feast of Stephen,

describes an action of the king on the day after Christmas Day. The tune used with this song is older than the words and was previously used with a hymn often sung on the feasts of Stephen and other martyrs. It begins:

Christian friends, your voices raise.
Wake the day with gladness.
God himself to joy and praise
turns our human sadness:
Joy that martyrs won their crown,
opened heaven's bright portal,
when they laid the mortal down
for the life immortal.

James Kiefer, Christian Biographies, By kind permission

Martyrdom of Stephen (3)

And still further, Stephen, who was chosen the first deacon by the apostles, and who, of all men, was the first to follow the footsteps of the martyrdom of the Lord, being the first that was slain for confessing Christ, speaking boldly among the people, and teaching them, says: "The God of glory appeared to our father Abraham, ... and said to him, Get thee out of thy country, and from thy kindred, and come into the land which I shall show thee."

But that both the apostles and their disciples thus taught as the Church preaches, and thus teaching were perfected, wherefore also they were called away to that which is perfect – Stephen, teaching these truths, when he was yet on earth, saw the glory of God, and Jesus on His right hand, and exclaimed, "Behold, I see the heavens opened, and the Son of man standing on the right hand of God." These words he said, and was stoned; and thus did he fulfil the perfect doctrine, copying in every respect the Leader of martyrdom, and praying for those who were slaying him, in these words: "Lord, lay not this sin to their charge." Thus were they perfected who knew one and the same God, who from beginning to end was present with mankind in the various dispensations; as the prophet Hosea declares: "I have filled up visions, and used similitudes by the hands of the prophets." Those, therefore, who delivered up their souls to death for Christ's Gospel – how could they have spoken to men in accordance with old-established opinion? If this had been the course adopted by them, they should not have suffered; but inasmuch as they did preach things contrary to those persons who did not assent to the truth, for that reason they suffered. It is evident, therefore, that they did not relinquish the truth, but with all boldness preached to the Jews and Greeks.

Irenaeus, Doctrine of the rest of the Apostles, chapter 10

Irenaeus, Doctrine of the rest of the Apostles, chapter 13

Martyrdom of Stephen (4)
Stephen

As rays around the source of light
Stream upward ere he glow in sight,
And watching by his future flight
Set the clear heavens on fire;

So on the King of Martyrs wait
Three chosen bands, in royal state,
And all earth owns, of good and great,
Is gather'd in that choir.

One presses on, and welcomes death:
One calmly yields his willing breath,
Nor slow, nor hurrying, but in faith

Content to die or live:

And some, the darlings of their Lord,
Play smiling with the flame and sword,
And, ere they speak, to his sure word
Unconscious witness give.

Foremost and nearest to his throne,
By perfect robes of triumph known,
And likest Him in look and tone,
The holy Stephen kneels,

With steadfast gaze, as when the sky
Flew open to his fainting eye,
Which, like a fading lamp, flash'd high,
Seeing what death conceals.

Well might you guess what vision bright
Was present to his raptur'd sight,
Even as reflected streams of light
Their solar source betray –

The glory which our GOD surrounds,
The Son of Man, th'atoning wounds –
He sees them all; and earth's dull bounds
Are melting fast away.

He sees them all – no other view
Could stamp the Saviour's likeness true,
Or with his love so deep embrue
Man's sullen heart and gross –

"Jesu, do Thou my soul receive:
Jesu, do Thou my foes forgive:"
He who would learn that prayer, must live
Under the holy Cross.

He, though he seem on earth to move,
Must glide in air like gentle dove,
From yon unclouded depths above
Must draw his purer breath;

Till men behold his angel face
All radiant with celestial grave,
Martyr all o'er, and meet to trace
The lines of Jesus' death.

John Keble, The Christian Year

Sermon preached on the anniversary of Stephen's martyrdom (1)

Yesterday we celebrated the birth in time of our eternal King. Today we celebrate the triumphant suffering of his soldier. Yesterday our king, clothed in his robe of flesh, left his place int he virgin's womb and graciously visited the world. Today his soldier leaves the tabernacle of his body and goes triumphantly to heaven.

Our king, despite his exalted majesty, came in humility for our sake; yet he did not come empty-handed. He gave of his bounty, yet without any loss to himself. In a marvelous way he changed into wealth the poverty of his faithful followers while remaining in full possession of his own inexhaustible riches. And so the love that brought Christ from heaven to earth raised Stephen from earth to heaven; shown first in the king, it later shone forth in his soldier. His love of God kept him from yielding to the ferocious mob; his love for his neighbor made him pray for those who were stoning him. Love inspired him to reprove those who erred, to make them amend; love led him to pray for those who stoned him, to save them from punishment.

Love, indeed, is the source of all good things; it is an impregnable defense, and the way that leads to heaven. He who walks in love can neither go astray nor be afraid: love guides him, protects him, and brings him to his journey's end.

My brothers, Christ made love the stairway that would enable all Christians to climb to heaven. Hold fast to it, therefore, in all sincerity, give one another practical proof of it, and by your progress in it, make your ascent together.

Fulgentius of Ruspe

Sermon preached on the anniversary of Stephen's martyrdom (2)

How lovely is the inspiration exhibited by those who are good, and how sweet is the joy which they disclose! See, we acquire a feast from a feast and grace from grace. Yesterday the Lord of the universe welcomed us whereas today it is the imitator [Stephen] of the Lord. How are they related to each other? One assumed human nature on our behalf while the other shed it for his Lord. One accepted the cave of this life for us, and the other left it for him. One was wrapped in swaddling clothes for us, and the other was stoned for him. One destroyed death, and the other scorned it.

Brethren, let us hasten to the stadium where the great athlete contends against the wicked adversary of human life by stripping himself in the arena by his confession [of faith] [cf. 1 Cor 4.9]. Indeed, as Paul has said [Heb 12.4], Stephen [Stephanos] has become a spectacle to the world, angels and to men. He was the first to have received the crown [stephanos] of martyrdom, the first to have paved the way for the chorus of martyrs and the first to have resisted sin to the point of shedding blood. It seems to me that the entire host of transcendent powers, angels, and myriads both assist and accompany them [i.e., the martyrs]. If we hear anything honorable in the heavens from among the principalities, powers, thrones, ruling forces and the entire heavenly assembly, their words provide an athletic spectacle by contending with an opponent [cf. Col 1.16 & Eph 1.21].

Let human life resemble a stadium for the contestants where one person contends against another. That antagonist which showed himself hostile to human life from the fall of our first parents until the time of Stephen strove to be victorious over men, yet the great athlete of faith considered his assaults as nothing [cf. Wis 2.24]. Both took up arms against each other: the inventor of death confronted a threat to death, whereas the disciple of life confessed his faith. For who could not help but admire this new type of struggle when truth judged between life and death chronicled the truth? For while the herald of a life hidden [in God] remained unknown, he nevertheless divulged it to men. At once he forsook this life and rightly judged it better to exchange a more honorable life for the present one.

It would be beneficial to accurately record his contest in order to disclose the order of our method by a series of miracles. Recently a powerful wind from heaven scattered every airy, deceptive power of the demons and filled the Apostles' house. Tongues of fire resided in each man corresponding with the number of those who received the grace of the Spirit. All were overcome by shock and confusion with the widely diverse languages immediately which the disciples spoke according to the sound and wonder of tongues and to the astonishment of those from every nation who were dwelling in Jerusalem [cf. Acts 2.2-5]. This was not a result of training and study but was a gift in the form of speaking which suddenly came from the Spirit's inspiration. Those engaged in constructing an earthly tower must speak the same language when building the church's spiritual dwelling. And so, the Holy Spirit's wonderful dispensation introduced grace in order to diffuse it, thereby providing a common benefit for everyone through the medium of the human voice. In this way the preaching of piety might not be limited to one tongue and remain unprofitable for those persons who spoke various tongues.

Even at this early point the Pharisees did not believe with their own ears and concocted to trip up persons astonished by these miraculous events as though new wine had made them [the Apostles] insane [cf. Acts 2.13]. Then Peter's solitary defense captured three thousand souls for Christ [cf. Acts 2.41], after which the church grew in the number of those who had been delivered. Those who were saved opened the temple's Beautiful Gate for the man born lame [cf. Acts 3.2ff] because his miraculous healing both increased and led to the faith persons lame in soul. As a result, many flocked when the faith was preached and sought help from the diverse profusion of grace at which point Stephen, who was wealthy in wisdom and grace by the Spirit, was summoned to assist the Apostles [cf. Acts 6.5]. Let no one think that the name of minister [diakonia] made him inferior to the dignity of the Apostles. Since Paul realized that he was a minister of the mysteries of Christ [cf. 1 Cor 4.1] and the Lord of the universe brought salvation by assuming human, he was not ashamed to be called a minister. As the Apostle says, he was in their midst as one who serves [cf. Lk 22.27] and as one who provides a variety of ministries [cf. 1 Cor 12.5-6].

Just as fire consumes useful material and

bright flames rise on high, so did the Holy Spirit make the rays of grace shine brighter through Stephen's nobility. Similarly, all turned to him because he was gifted with knowledge and training. Those few persons who gathered together seemed to be a dense crowd much like a phalanx which attempted to assail Stephen who was equally serene whether in the company of many or few persons. Then certain persons under the guise of Alexandrians, Libertinians, Cyrenians and men from every place engaged the athlete in a debate regarding the truth. The father of lies assumed a human form and rose against truth which Stephen had spoken [cf. Jn 8.44]. However, the truth brought forth trophies against such lies, and its excellence wonderfully put to flight every assault of deception. The minister of truth sought the truth about the enemy who concealed his substance; rather, he made the truth appear as something which lacks substance. How does this ruse affect the preacher? I believe that it comes from the devil. If any of you shares his strength, the truth destroys it in Stephen. But if that truth is loftier than your machinations, why are you deceitfully planning evil against the vessel of truth in order to destroy what remains of it? Dogs do this when they open their mouths for stones cast to them, yet they cannot touch the person whom threw them. Since true facts repulsed such a lie and could no longer find another champion of deception, all who looked squarely at the manifest truth remembered his own struggle. Stephen directed his energy against his accusers who passed judgment upon him, for they brought false accusations against him while being marked by rage and slander. The Jews brought various accusers against Stephen including judges who were either elected or who were subservient to death and did not know the impact of a ruinous vote levelled against Stephen. For just as experienced athletes bring down their more formidable opponents through vigorous training and thereby make them fall, so did the great Stephen who lay prostrate upon the ground overcome his adversary with difficultly.

From this point began the Apostles' journey throughout the entire world and their preaching. If it were not for [Stephen's] murder and the Jews' rage against the Apostles, perhaps the grace of the Gospel would have been confined to the inhabitants of Jerusalem. Having been driven out by the Jews to another nation, the teaching of the [Christian] mysteries expelled the devil from the world. Thus Samaria received the preaching [cf. Acts 8.14]; salvation reached the eunuch through Philip [Acts 8.26ff]; Paul was a great vessel of election armed against the devil's wrath and his threats against whose arrows he raised a shield [Acts 9.15], thereby abolishing him from the entire earth and making all places accessible to the faith of Christ. As a result, Egyptians, Syrians, Parthians, Mesopotamians, Galatians, Illurians, Macedonians as well as nations from everywhere hastened to hear the preaching. Do you see Stephen's athletic prowess and how the adversary was brought down to ruin although he appeared more excellent than his adversary by making false accusations?

But let us return again to the stadium. How do the calumniators enflame the people? They say, "He does not cease to speak words against this holy place and the Law. For we have heard him say that this Jesus of Nazareth will destroy this place and will change the customs which Moses handed down to us" [Acts 6.13-14]. Such is the allegation presented by the devil's speech, but who pays attention to such rubbish? Against whom do they rage so vehemently and what evil can they detect in his words? They even brought forth another indictment against [Stephen] claiming that he boasted that this place would be destroyed and that the institutes of Moses would be changed. What outrage doe these words contain whether they happen to be true or false? If false, there is no cause for alarm; if true, what unjust ground is there for denunciation? For what had transpired will indeed happen again whether or not we remain silent. Can the murder of him who was denounced earlier relieve persons who are grieving? For example, Jesus the Nazarene was condemned by the same vote of reprisal levelled against Stephen. If he who is unjust vents his wrath, gives place to injustice and alters customs, Stephen is not responsible for these acts but it is Jesus, as the accuser says, and the court is compelled to pass judgement against him who is accused. Oh, what an unfair verdict for those who are listening! Since Jesus, says the judge, changes the laws, Stephen should then be stoned. How did Jesus abrogate the Law when he affirmed its antiquity by saying, "I did not come to abolish the Law but to fulfill it" [Mt 5.17]? Who strengthened his disciples according to the Law? He forbade them to become angry and to commit murder [cf. Mt 5.21-22], rejected adultery out of desire [cf. Mt 5.39], ordered that grief not be repaid since unjust hands cannot lay hold of you [cf. Mt 6.19ff] and wiped out passion, a result of greed, and taught mastery over it. Why were these neither mentioned nor examined when judgement was passed? I do not wish the crowd of those bloodstained judges to be present and do not want to know about places associated with such malevolent persons, the celebrated temple's location, the huge amount of stones, the gold left over which equalled the small amount left in the temple, the sacrifices according to the Law such as the ram, calf, lamb, heifer, dove, turtle-dove and he-goat for averting evil [cf. Lev 16.20ff]. Therefore if they condemn Stephen to death in order to deflect their sadness, they reveal their fruits through that terrible murder. If nothing is left, they claim that the vote counts, not the murder.

But let us see in the succeeding struggles how he who was covered by stones as if they were snow had warded off his murderers and how he returned a variety of thunderbolts against those who cast stones. The Jews knew the Christians' weapons which the great Stephen used to ward off their attacks and who made it the law of life. They were all fierce, standing in a circle, looked at him with a hysterical gaze and brandished a weapon against Stephen in their hands. However, he resembled a priest according to the spiritual law, was a pure sacrifice, submissive, and offered his own body instead of an offering of sprinkled blood. He saw God in the celestial sanctuary, made petition on behalf of those who mistreated him, exchanged their bloodthirstiness for a good deed and cried out in their ears, "Lord, do not hold this sin against them" [Acts 7.60]. By this prayer he expiated their sin which the murderers committed by their transgression and who were exasperated at his prayer. However, this did not prevent them from casting stones until the great Stephen fell into a sweet, blessed sleep as though he were surrounded by tender flowers or by gentle dew.

The athletes have achieved victory before we see those crowned who had engaged in fierce struggles since before seeing the contest, we have attained the goal of their struggles. I believe that we must not neglect them without mentioning the outstanding nature of their witness. This gathering of murderers was so filled with rage that they resorted to bloodshed; their evil was so strong that it restricted their breathing; their glance, appearance and passion was manifested by their teeth as divine Scripture says concerning enraged hearts which gnashed their teeth against him [cf. Acts 7.54]. Being in their midst, he girded himself against their hostile, murderous intent, surmounted their contemptuous intentions, resisted their wrath with patience and their threats with disdain, the fear of death with contempt, hatred with love, ill-will with benevolence and slander with truth.

Not only did the true athlete reveal one type of victory but combatted by countless virtues every form of evil which the Jews devised, thereby resulting in victory. I hear about various contests of strength in gymnasiums when athletes strip themselves naked in the arena and achieve victory against their contenders. Such martyrs are sovereign in the stadium, resisting with their own power every adversary and are as a beacon of triumph for all to see. The false wisdom of the Libertinians, Cyreninas and sages from Alexandria [Acts 6.9] contend against him who is triumphant through true wisdom: courage overcomes fear, disdain conquers threats, charity subdues savagery and truth is victorious over falsehood. They sought to murder him, and their hands were already armed with stones; their glance and breathing through their teeth [M.713] held tightly together revealed their brutality. Nevertheless, he saw them as brothers and greeted them as fathers saying, "Men, brothers and fathers, listen [Acts 7.2]!"

They persuasively devised all sorts of calumny by convening a council of murderers against the truth. [Stephen] neither reproved them out of fear, was unconcerned with impending dangers nor did he consider death; rather, having his soul raised on high and appearing as though her were senseless to everyone gazing upon him, he taught them as though they were foolish children and demonstrated the error of their doctrines with regard to faith. In their presence [Stephen] briefly recounted the story of Abraham as well as the saints who followed him [cf. Acts 7.2-7]. He also added Moses, his birth, upbringing, education, initiation on the mountain, smiting the Egyptians, service to the Israelites and prophesy concerning the mystery of the Lord [cf. Acts 7.20-22, 30, 34, 36-37]. What especially incited this group and fomented their illness was that Moses to whom they were especially devoted was a mentor for their teaching. They rose up against him in order to quiet him, something which Stephen desired in order to end his bitterness. He exited human nature and before he left the body, with pure eyes gazed upon heaven's gates and the temple's interior, the revelation of divine glory and the effulgence of his glory [cf. Acts 7.55-56]. The stamp of the Father's glory [cf. Heb 1.3] could not be described, and the athlete saw his brilliance among men which accommodated itself to human nature. Thus being outside human nature, he shared the angelic nature which seemed like a miracle to these murderers. His face was changed to assume that of the angels and seeing invisible reality, he proclaimed the grace he had beheld [cf. Acts 7.56]. But they blocked their ears and did not wish to see this with their eyes, preferring their own self-righteous since they were not capable of hearing this divine report. However, he shared the grace with those present although he alone was worthy of it: "I see the heavens open and the Son of Man standing at God's right hand" [Acts 7.57]. They exclaimed with a great voice, blocked their ears and unanimously rushed upon him. History recounts a similar uproar in order to show how their actions coincide with the Sodomites, for the judge [God] hears their wicked cry when he says, "The cry of the inhabitants of Sodom and Gomorrah have reached me" [Gen 18.20-21]. Therefore they shouted out in order that the cry against Stephen might be heard.

The athlete fully realized the benefit hidden beneath the murderers' bitterness because they [M.716] who stood in a circle ready to stone him provided him with a crown much like a victor's crown plaited at enemy hands. Therefore [Stephen] warded off their murderous intent by a blessing and being fully aware of their plan to slay him, was prepared to suffer death at their hands. Furthermore, he believed that his enemies had the opportunity of conferring a benefit upon him. For this reason the person who knows Christ wishes to bring his enemies into submission. [Stephen] knew that the Lawgiver was patient, recalled his command to love one's enemies, to do good to those who bear hatred and to pray for one's enemies [cf. Mt 5.44]. But the athlete's goal does not consider human glory; rather, he seeks to overcome the entire world by the magnificence of his triumph and to outstrip human endurance, thereby rejecting every type of praise.

Although [Stephen] acquires victory in accord with every human manner of praise, we should pay attention to the narrative which pertains to the salvation of souls. Just as there are some athletes who have ceased their activity and train youths for athletic competitions through skillful technical maneuvers to vanquish their adversaries, so I think we should be trained by the great Stephen in piety that we might escape the grips of spiritual adversaries [pneumatomachoi]. For those who are mad with rage detract from the Spirit's glory claiming that Stephen is an advocate of their error when he gazed intently at heaven and saw God's glory and Jesus standing at his right hand [Acts 7.55]. They claimed that he perverted the teachings of piety when, if the Spirit should be included along with the Father and Son, why did not Stephen see in his vision the Spirit with the Son? Therefore how did Stephen cause such distress by uttering these words with his hands outstretched? How does his reasonable tactics counteract such distressing words since he countered the incredulity of his adversaries at that very spot? Do you seek, oh pneumatichos, when the Father's glory appears and the Son stands at his right, the location of the Spirit? If the Spirit were present within you, you would not fail to notice what is proposed [of the Spirit] much like those with defective vision who are ignorant of gold lying at their feet. At any rate I have now gotten wind of this and [desire] that you do not subscribe to the rumor devised by the Jews.

How did Stephen see transcendent glory? Who laid bare heaven's gates for him? Was this the work of men? Which of the angels enabled inferior [human] nature soar to that height? Stephen was not alone when he was generously filled with power [M.717] coming from the angels which enabled him to see what he saw. What was recorded? "Stephen was filled with the Holy Spirit and saw the glory of God and his Only-Begotten Son" [Acts 7.55]. As the Prophet says, light cannot be seen unless one is filled with light: "In your light we shall see light" [Ps 35.10] (If observation of the light does not share this same light, how can anyone deprived of the sun's rays see it?). Since the Father's light makes this possible, the Only Begotten [Son's] light emanates through the Holy Spirit which makes it visible. Therefore the Spirit's glory enables us to perceive the glory of both the Father and Son. But can we say that the Gospel is true which says that "No man has ever seen God" [Jn 1.18]? How do the Apostle's words agree with the following, "No man has seen nor can see [God]" [1 Tim 6.16]? If human nature and power can perceive the glory of the Father and Son, their vision must indeed be mistaken. However, history is true and cannot lie. The evil deed of the pneumatomachoi is indeed made clear because Scripture bears witness to similar situations. For Stephen beholds God not in human nature and power but is united by grace to the Holy Spirit who elevates him in order to comprehend God. Therefore, one cannot say that Jesus is Lord apart from the Spirit, as the Apostle says [cf. 1 Tim 6.16, 1 Cor 12.3]. One cannot contemplate the Father's glory because where the Spirit is the Son is seen and is grasped the Father's glory.

But history presents us with another problem, namely, the weapon of impiety coming from the Christomachoi who condemn the Only Begotten [Son], for they consider the One present in the Father's glory to be inferior to his authority. What about Paul? How shall I answer them? What does the prophet David who lived earlier say when he explained the glory of the Only Begotten [Son] by the teaching of the Spirit? David says, "The Lord said to my Lord, 'Sit at my right hand'" [Ps 109.1]. The Apostle says that the Lord is seated at the right hand of God's throne [Col 3.1, Heb 1.3]. If this represents either a place of inferiority or a seat of honor, testimony concerning its magnificence is added in order to signify the loftiness of honor and the reception of true piety. For the Spirit's grace teaches all these things. Stephen, being filled with the Holy Spirit, saw everything and spoke about what he knew. While in the Spirit, David calls "Lord" as the Gospel says [Mt 22.43]; when Paul, speaks of him, he mentions mysteries in the Spirit [1 Cor 14.2]. Therefore if there is one teacher who is in complete harmony, the teaching is the Spirit of truth which was present in divinely inspired persons. Then how can any dissonance be present in teachings? But there is another seat and position which I can easily point out and will now mention it. Instead of showing concern for the body, these words should refer to what is incorporeal. With regard to man, the seat signifies that part of the body's hips which enables it not to continuously bear strain and thereby become weighed down and crooked. On the other hand, an upright position upon one's knees signifies that a person does not rest upon his hips when seated. But when it comes to transcendent nature, sitting and standing have no place with such concepts since each is separate and should be understood respectively. We neither subscribe to a bent position regarding incorporeal nature nor a sitting down with regard to what is formless; rather, we devoutly understand that each represents stability and being unmoved in every good. For standing and sitting apply to God and do not pertain to a difference of words concerning concepts which teach that God is firmly standing and sitting unmoved in the good. The prophet David and the apostle Paul do not comprehend the sitting of the Only Begotten [Son] in the same manner because the Father is standing and the Son is sitting. Indeed, by mentioning only the fact that the Son is sitting, Scripture tells us about the standing of the Son and no longer suggests the sitting of the Father. For just as Paul and David both confessed the Father sitting through the Son's standing at his right, indeed nothing is taught beforehand concerning the Father which is also true regarding Stephen where the Son is standing and revealed in the Father's glory. Thus this image is valid if it appears to be a satisfactory archetype. Goodness is present in what is good, light is present in the light it reflects and primeval beauty is present in everything supported by an appropriate image. Thus we should clearly understand the image of the Son's sitting, the Father's sitting and the standing in the standing which differs from the archetype's properties.

Brothers, you should ponder our words and thoughts and hold them as introductory remarks since Stephen's vision provokes reflection. We are not only spectators of Stephen's contest but since we are full of the Holy Spirit, we share his grace and eradicate adversaries for the glory of our Lord Jesus Christ to whom be glory and power forever and ever. Amen.

Gregory of Nyssa

JAMES, THE APOSTLE

Martyred around AD 30, James the son of Zebedee was one of the twelve apostles of Jesus Christ and brother of the apostle John. This account is the only record preserved in the Bible about the death of any of the first of the twelve apostles.

Jesus said to James and John, "You will drink of the same cup [of suffering] that I drink."

The Bible: Mark 10:39

Martyrdom of James, the apostle (1)

About this time King Herod [Herod Agrippa I] began to persecute some members of the church. He had James, the brother of John, put to death by the sword.

The Bible: Acts 12:1-2

Martyrdom of James, the apostle (2)

The man who informed against James, causing him to be put to death, was so impressed at the way James testified during his court hearing, that he, too, admitted that he was a Christian. So they were both led away to be executed. On the way, the man who had informed on James asked James to forgive him. The apostle did not immediately answer. He considered for a while, and then said to him: "I wish you peace', and kissed him. They were both beheaded at the same time.

And then, as the divine Scripture says,[4] Herod, upon the death of James, seeing that the deed pleased the Jews, attacked Peter also and committed him to prison, and would have slain him if he had not, by the divine appearance of an angel who came to him by night, been wonderfully released from his bonds, and thus liberated for the service of the Gospel. Such was the providence of God in respect to Peter.

Eusebius, The History of the Church, Book 1, chapter 9

ANTIPAS

You did not renounce your faith in me, even in the days of Antipas, my faithful witness, who was put to death in your city . . .

Revelation 2:13

Nobody knows the identity of this Antipas. This passage marks the beginning of the transition of the meaning of Greek *martyrs* from "witness" to "martyr".

6. Martyrdom of New Testament people, not recorded in the New Testament

JAMES, THE LORD'S BROTHER

This James, not to be confused with one of the

twelve apostles, referred to as James the brother of John, was known as "the Lord's Brother", "the Just" and "the Righteous". The risen Jesus appeared to him (see 1 Corinthians 15:7) and this presumably helped him to believe in Jesus, for in John's gospel it is recorded that "For even his own brothers did not believe in him [Jesus]" (John 7:5). James' martyrdom is not recorded in the New Testament.

James himself wrote:
Brothers, as an example of patience in the face of suffering, take the prophets who spoke in the name of the Lord. As you know, we consider blessed those who have persevered. You have heard of Job's perseverance and have seen what the Lord finally brought about. The Lord is full of compassion and mercy.
The Bible: James 5:11, NIV

Martyrdom of James, the Lord's brother (1)

After Paul had successfully appealed to Caesar and was sent off to Rome the disappointed Jews turned their attention to James. They hatched this plot against the Lord's brother, whom the apostles had appointed to the episcopal throne at Jerusalem. They hauled James up in front of a great crowd and demanded that he deny Christ. To their surprise James remained calm and showed unexpected tranquillity before this hostile crowd. James openly declared that our Saviour and Lord, Jesus, was indeed the Son of God. They were unable to stomach this testimony as James was universally acclaimed as a most righteous man.

Clement tells us that they seized James, threw him off a parapet and then clubbed him to death. Hegesippus, in his fifth book, provides the most detailed description of James" martyrdom.

The church was in the control of the apostles, along with James, the Lord's brother, who has always been known as the Righteous. Many people were called James, but only this James was holy from the day he was born. He drank no alcohol and was a vegetarian, and following a Nazirite vow never had his hair cut. Only James was allowed to enter into the Holy Place in the Temple as he wore linen, not woollen, clothes. He was often to be found in the Sanctuary alone, praying on his knees for the people's forgiveness. He worshipped God so much in this way that his knees became as hard as the knees of a camel. Because he was so righteous he became known as James the Righteous.

The Scribes and the Pharisees forced James to stand on the Sanctuary parapet and shouted out to him: "Righteous one, whose testimony we have to accept, you are leading the people astray and encouraging them to follow Jesus, who was crucified. What do you mean by "the door of Jesus"?" [See John 10:9, "I am the gate; whoever enters through me will be saved."] James called back, "Why do you ask me about the Son of Man? He sits in heaven at the right hand of the Great Power, and he will return on heavenly clouds." [James" reply "Why do you ask me about the Son of Man?" shows him using his last moments, like Stephen, to call Jesus by a title which is only used elsewhere by our Lord himself when he spoke about himself.]

Many in the crowd were persuaded by James" words, and cried out: "Hosanna to the Son of David."

The Scribes and Pharisees realised that they had made a big mistake in allowing James to testify about Jesus. "Let us throw him over the parapet so that people will become too afraid to follow him," they plotted. Then they called out: "The Righteous one has gone astray".

So they threw the Righteous one over the parapet, and then stoned him as the fall did not kill him. James knelt down and prayed, "Lord God and Father, I pray thee, forgive them; they do not know what they are doing." They continued to hurl stones at him until the son of Rachabim shouted: "Stop throwing your stones! What do you think you are doing? The Righteous one is praying for you. Then, one of the mob, a fuller, grabbed the club he beat his clothes with and cracked it down on top of the Righteous one's head. So the Righteous one was martyred. He was buried where he fell and his headstone remains there. He was a

genuine witness to both Jews and Gentiles that Jesus is the Christ.
Eusebius, The History of the Church, Book 3

Martyrdom of James, the Lord's brother (2)

The next martyr we meet with, according to St. Luke, in the History of the Acts of the Apostles, was James the son of Zebedee, the elder brother of John, and a relative of our Lord; for his mother Salome was cousin-german to the Virgin Mary. It was not until ten years after the death of Stephen that the second martyrdom took place; for no sooner had Herod Agrippa been appointed governor of Judea, than, with a view to ingratiate himself with them, he raised a sharp persecution against the Christians, and determined to make an effectual blow, by striking at their leaders. The account given us by an eminent primitive writer, Clemens Alexandrinus, ought not to be overlooked; that, as James was led to the place of martyrdom, his accuser was brought to repent of his conduct by the apostle's extraordinary courage and undauntedness, and fell down at his feet to request his pardon, professing himself a Christian, and resolving that James should not receive the crown of martyrdom alone. Hence they were both beheaded at the same time. Thus did the first apostolic martyr cheerfully and resolutely receive that cup, which he had told our Savior he was ready to drink. Timon and Parmenas suffered martyrdom about the same time; the one at Philippi, and the other in Macedonia. These events took place A.D. 44.
James Kiefer, Christian Biographies, By kind permission

St Andrew

Martyrdom of Andrew (1)

This apostle and martyr was the brother of St Peter, and preached the gospel to many Asiatic nations. On arriving at Edessa, the governor of the country, named Egeas, threatened him for preaching against the idols they worshipped. St Andrew, persisting in the propagation of his doctrines, was ordered to be crucified, two ends of the cross being fixed transversely in the ground. [Hence the derivation of the term, St. Andrew's Cross.] He boldly told his accusers that he would not have preached the glory of the cross had he feared to die on it. And again, when they came to crucify him, he said that he coveted the cross, and longed to embrace it. He was fastened to the cross, not with nails, but cords, that his death might be more slow. In this situation he continued two days, preaching the greatest part of the time to the people, and expired on the 30th of November.
John Foxe, The Book of Martyrs, revised with notes and an appendix by W. Bramley-Moore, London, 1869, pp 4-5

Martyrdom of Andrew (2)

What we have all, both presbyters and deacons of the churches of Achaia, beheld with our eyes, we have written to all the churches established in the name of Christ Jesus, both in the east and west, north and south. Peace to you, and to all who believe in one God, perfect Trinity, true Father unbegotten, true Son only-begotten, true Holy Spirit proceeding from the Father, and abiding in the Son, in order that there may be shown one Holy Spirit subsisting in the Father and Son in precious Godhead. This faith we have learned from the blessed Andrew, the apostle of oar Lord Jesus Christ, whose passion also we, having seen it set forth before our eyes, have not hesitated to give an account of, according to the degree of ability we have. Accordingly the proconsul Aegeates, having come into the city of Patras, began to compel those believing in Christ to worship the idols; to whom the blessed Andrew, running up, said: It behoved thee, being a judge of men, to acknowledge thy Judge who is in the heaven, and having acknowledged Him, to worship Him; and worshipping Him who is the true God, to turn away thy thoughts from those which are not true gods.

To whom Aegeates said: Art thou Andrew, who destroyest the temples of the gods, and persuadest men about the religion which, having lately made its appearance, the emperors of the Romans have given orders to suppress?

The blessed Andrew said: The emperors

of the Romans have never recognised the truth. And this the Son of God, who came on account of the salvation of men, manifestly teaches – that these idols are not only not gods, but also most shameful demons, and hostile to the human race, teaching men to offend God, so that, by being offended, He turns away and will not hearken; that therefore, by His turning away and not hearkening, they may be held captive by the devil; and that they might work them to such a degree, that when they go out of the body they may be found deserted and naked, carrying nothing with them but sins.

Aegeates said: These are superfluous and vain words: as for your Jesus, for proclaiming these things to the Jews they nailed him to the tree of the cross. The blessed Andrew answering, said: Oh, if thou wouldst recognize the mystery of the cross, with what reasonable love the Author of the life of the human race for our restoration endured this tree of the cross, not unwillingly, but willingly!

Aegeates said: Seeing that, betrayed by his own disciple, and seized by the Jews, he was brought before the procurator, and according to their request was nailed up by the procurator's soldiers, in what way dost thou say that he willingly endured the tree of the cross?

The holy Andrew said: For this reason I say willingly, since I was with Him when He was betrayed by His disciple. For before He was betrayed, He spoke to us to the effect that He should be betrayed and crucified for the salvation of men, and foretold that He should rise again on the third day. To whom my brother Peter said, Far be it from thee, Lord; let this by no means be. And so, being angry, He said to Peter, Get thee behind me, Satan; for thou art not disposed to the things of God. And in order that He might most fully explain that He willingly underwent the passion, He said to us, I have power to lay down my life, and I have power to take it again. And, last of all, while He was supping with us, He said, One of you will betray me. At these words, therefore, all becoming exceedingly grieved, in order that the surmise might be free from doubt, He made it clear, saying, To whomsoever I shall give the piece of bread out of my hand, he it is who betrays me. When, therefore, He gave it to one of our fellow-disciples, and gave an account of things to come as if they were already present, He showed that He was to be willingly betrayed. For neither did He run away, and leave His betrayer at fault; but remaining in the place in which He knew that he was, He awaited him Aegeates said: I wonder that thou, being a sensible man, shouldst wish to uphold him on any terms whatever; for, whether willingly or unwillingly, all the same, thou admittest that he was fastened to the cross.

The blessed Andrew said: This is what I said, if now thou apprehendest, that great is the mystery of the cross, which, if thou wishest, as is likely, to hear, attend to me. Aegeates said: A mystery it cannot be called, but a punishment.

The blessed Andrew said: This punishment is the mystery of man's restoration. If thou wilt listen with any attention, thou wilt prove it.

Aegeates said: I indeed will hear patiently; but thou, unless thou submissively obey me, shalt receive the mystery of the cross in thyself.

The blessed Andrew answered: If I had been afraid of the tree of the cross, I should not have proclaimed the glory of the cross.

Aegeates said: Thy speech is foolish, because thou proclaimest that the cross is not a punishment, and through thy foolhardiness thou art not afraid of the punishment of death.

The holy Andrew said: It is not through foolhardiness, but through faith, that I am not afraid of the punishment of death; for the death of sins is hard. And on this account I wish thee to hear the mystery of the cross, in order that thou perhaps, acknowledging it, mayst believe, and believing, mayst come somehow or other to the renewing of thy soul. Aegeates said: That which is shown to have perished is for renewing. Do you mean that my soul has perished, that thou makest me come to the renewing of it through the faith, I know not what, of which thou hast spoken?

The blessed Andrew answered: This it is which I desired time to learn, which also I shall teach and make manifest, that though the souls of men are destroyed, they shall be renewed through the mystery of the cross. For the first man through the tree of transgression brought in death; and it was necessary for the human race, that through the suffering of the tree, death, which had come into the world, should be driven out. And since the first man, who brought death into the world through the transgression of the tree, had been produced from the spotless earth, it was necessary that the Son of God should be begotten a perfect man from the spotless virgin, that He should restore eternal life, which men had lost through Adam, and should cut off the tree of carnal appetite through the tree of the cross. Hanging upon the cross, He stretched out His blameless hands for the hands which had been incontinently stretched out; for the most sweet food of the forbidden tree He received gall for food; and taking our mortality upon Himself, He made a gift of His immortality to us.

Aegeates said: With these words thou shalt be able to lead away those who shall believe in thee; but unless thou hast come to grant me this, that thou offer sacrifices to the almighty gods, I shall order thee, after having been scourged, to be fastened to that very cross which thou commendest.

The blessed Andrew said: To God Almighty, who alone is true, I bring sacrifice day by day not the smoke of incense, nor the flesh of bellowing bulls, nor the blood of goats, but sacrificing a spotless lamb day by day on the altar of the cross; and though all the people of the I faithful partake of His body and drink His blood, the Lamb that has been sacrificed remains after this entire and alive. Truly, therefore, is He sacrificed, and truly is His body eaten by the people, and His blood is likewise drunk; nevertheless, as I have said, He remains entire, and spotless, and alive.

Aegeates said: How can this be?

The blessed Andrew said: If thou wouldest know, take the form of a disciple, that thou mayst learn what thou art inquiring after.

Aegeates said: I will exact of thee through tortures the gift of this knowledge.

The blessed Andrew declared: I wonder that thou, being an intelligent man, shouldest fall into the folly of thinking that thou mayst be able to persuade me, through thy tortures, to disclose to thee the sacred things of God. Thou hast heard the mystery of the cross, thou hast heard the mystery of the sacrifice. If thou be lievest in Christ the Son of God, who was crucified, I shall altogether disclose to thee in what manner the Lamb that has been slain may live, after having been sacrificed and eaten, remaining in His kingdom entire and spotless.

Aegeates said: And by what means does the lamb remain in his kingdom after he has been slain and eaten by all the people, as thou hast said?

The blessed Andrew said: If thou believest with all thy heart, thou shalt be able to learn: but if thou believest not, thou shalt not by any means attain to the idea of such truth.

Then Aegeates, enraged, ordered him to be shut up in prison, where, when he was shut up, a multitude of the people came together to him from almost all the province, so that they wished to kill Aegeates, and by breaking down the doors of the prison to set free the blessed Andrew the apostle.

Then the blessed Andrew admonished in these words, saying: Do not stir up the peace of our Lord Jesus Christ into seditious and devilish uproar. For my Lord, when He was betrayed, endured it with all patience; He did not strive, He did not cry out, nor in the streets did any one hear Him crying out. Therefore do ye also keep silence, quietness, and peace; and hinder not my martyrdom, but rather get yourselves also ready beforehand as athletes to the Lord, in order that you may overcome threatenings by a soul that has no fear of man, and that you may get the better of injuries through the endurance of the body. For this temporary fall is not to be feared; but that should be feared which has no end. The fear of men, then, is like smoke which, while it is raised and gathered together, disappears. And those torments ought to be feared which never have an end. For these torments, which happen to be somewhat light, any one can bear; but if they are heavy, they soon destroy life. But those torments are everlasting, where there are daily weepings, and mournings, and lamentations, and never-ending torture, to which the proconsul Aegeates is not afraid to go. Be ye therefore rather prepared for this, that through temporary afflictions ye may attain to everlasting rest, and may flourish for ever, and reign with Christ.

The holy Apostle Andrew having admonished the people with these and such like words through the whole night, when the light of day dawned, Aegeates having sent for him, ordered the blessed Andrew to be brought to him; and having sat down upon the tribunal, he said: I have thought that thou, by thy reflection during the night, hast turned away thy thoughts from folly, and given up thy commendation of Christ that thou mightst be able to be with us, and not throw away the pleasures of life; for it is folly to come for any purpose to the suffering of the cross, and to give oneself up to most shameful punishments and burnings.

The holy Andrew answered: I shall be able to have joy with thee, if thou wilt believe in Christ, and throw away the worship of idols; for Christ has sent me to this province, in which I have acquired for Christ a people not the smallest.

Aegeates said: For this reason I compel thee to make a libation, that these people who have been deceived by thee may forsake the vanity of thy teaching, and may themselves offer grateful libations to the gods; for not even one city has remained in Achaia in which their temples have not been forsaken and deserted. And now, through thee, let them be again restored to the worship of the images, in order that the gods also, who have been enraged against thee, being pleased by this, may bring it about that thou mayst return to their friendship anti ours. But if not, thou awaitest varied tortures, on account of the vengeance of the gods; and after these, fastened to the tree of the cross which thou commendest, thou shall die.

The holy Andrew said: Listen, O son of death and chaff made ready for eternal burnings, to me, the servant of God and apostle of Jesus Christ. Until now I have conversed with thee kindly about the perfection of the faith, in order that thou, receiving the exposition of the truth, being made perfect as its vindicator, mightst despise vain idols, and worship God, who is in the heavens; but since thou remainest in the same shamelessness at last, and thinkest me to be afraid because of thy threats, bring against me whatever may seem to thee greater in the way of tortures. For the more shall I be well pleasing to my King, the more I shall endure in tortures for the confession of His name.

Then the proconsul Aegeates, being enraged, ordered the apostle of Christ to be afflicted by tortures. Being stretched out, therefore, by seven times three soldiers, and beaten with violence, he was lifted up and brought before the impious Aegeates. And he spoke to him thus: Listen to me, Andrew, and withdraw thy thoughts from the outpouring of thy blood; but if thou wilt not hearken to me, I shall cause thee to perish on the tree of the cross.

The holy Andrew said: I am a slave of the cross of Christ, and I ought rather to pray to attain to the trophy of the cross than to be afraid; but for thee is laid up eternal torment, which, however, thou mayst escape after thou hast tested my endurance, if thou wilt believe in my Christ. For I am afflicted about thy destruction, and I am not disturbed about my own suffering. For my suffering takes up a space of one day, or two at most; but thy torment for endless ages shall never come to a close. Wherefore henceforward cease from adding to thy miseries, and lighting up everlasting fire for thyself.

Aegeates then being enraged, ordered the blessed Andrew to be fastened to the cross. And he having left them all, goes up to the cross, and says to it with a clear voice:

Rejoice, O cross, which has been consecrated by the body of Christ, and adorned by His limbs as if with pearls. Assuredly before my Lord went up on thee, thou hadst much earthly fear; but now invested with heavenly longing, thou art fitted up according to my prayer. For I know, from those who believe, how many graces thou hast in Him, how many gifts prepared beforehand. Free from care, then, and with joy, I come to thee, that thou also exulting mayst receive me, the disciple of Him that was hanged upon thee; because thou hast been always faithful to me, and I have desired to embrace thee. O good cross, which hast received comeliness and beauty from the limbs of the Lord; O much longed for, and earnestly desired, and fervently sought after, and already prepared beforehand for my soul longing for thee, take me away from men, and restore me to my Master, in order that through thee He may accept me who through thee has redeemed me.

And having thus spoken, the blessed Andrew, standing on the ground, and looking earnestly upon the cross, stripped himself and gave his clothes to the executioners, having urged the brethren that the executioners should come and do what had been commanded them; for they were standing at some distance. And they having come up, lifted him on the cross; and having stretched his body across with ropes, they only bound his feet, but did not sever his joints, having received this order from the proconsul: for he wished him to be in distress while hanging, and in the night-time, as he was suspended, to be eaten up alive by dogs.

And a great multitude of the brethren stood by, nearly twenty thousand; and having beheld the executioners standing off, and that they had done to the blessed one nothing of what those who were hanged up suffer, they thought that they would again hear something from him; for assuredly, as he was hanging, he moved his head smiling. And Stratocles inquired of him: Why art thou smiling, Andrew, servant of God? Thy laughter makes us mourn and weep, because we are deprived of thee. And the blessed Andrew answered him: Shall I not laugh at all, my son Stratocles, at the empty stratagem of Aegeates, through which he thinks to take vengeance upon us? We have nothing to do with him and his plans. He cannot hear; for if he could, he would be aware, having learned it by experience, that a man of Jesus is unpunished. And having thus spoken, he discoursed to them all in common, for the people ran together enraged at the unjust judgment of Aegeates: Ye men standing by me, and women, and children, and elders, bond and free, and as many as will hear; I beseech you, forsake all this life, ye who have for my sake assembled here; and hasten to take upon you my life, which leads to heavenly things, and once for all despise all temporary things, confirming the purposes of those who believe in Christ. And he exhorted them all, teaching that the sufferings of this transitory life are not worthy to be compared with the future recompense of the eternal life.

And the multitude hearing what was said by him, did not stand off from the place, and the blessed Andrew continued the rather to say to them more than he had spoken. And so much was said by him, that a space of three days and nights was taken up, and no one was tired and went away from him. And when also on the fourth day they beheld his nobleness, and the unweariedness of his intellect, and the multitude of his words, and the serviceableness of his exhortations, and the stedfastness of his soul, and the sobriety of his spirit, and the fixedness of his mind, and the perfection of his reason, they were enraged against Aegeates; and all with one accord hastened to the tribunal, and cried out against Aegeates, who was sitting, saying: What is thy judgment, O proconsul? Thou hast judged wickedly; thy awards are impious. In what has the man done wrong; what evil has he done? The city has been put in an uproar; thou grievest us all; do not betray Caesar's city. Grant willingly to the Achaians a just man; grant willingly to us a God-fearing man; do not put to death a godly man. Four days he has been hanging, and is alive; having eaten nothing, he has filled us all. Take down the man from the cross, and we shall all seek after wisdom; release the man, and to all Achaia will mercy be shown. It is not necessary that he should suffer this, because, though hanging, he does not cease proclaiming the truth.

And when the proconsul refused to listen to them, at first indeed signing with his hand to the crowd to take themselves off, they began to be emboldened against him, being in number about twenty thousand. And the proconsul having beheld that they had somehow become maddened, afraid that something frightful would befall him, rose up from the tribunal and went away with them, having promised to set free the blessed Andrew. And some went on before to tell the apostle the cause for which they came to the place.

While all the crowd, therefore, was exulting that the blessed Andrew was going to be set free, the proconsul having come up, and all the brethren rejoicing along with Maximilla, the blessed Andrew, having heard this, said to the brethren standing by: What is it necessary for me to say to him, when I am departing to the Lord, that will I also say. For what reason hast thou again come to us, Aegeates? On what account dost thou, being a stranger to us, come to us? What wilt thou again dare to do, what to contrive? Tell us. Hast thou come to release us, as having changed thy mind? I would not agree with thee that thou hadst really changed thy mind. Nor would I believe thee, saying that thou art my friend. Dost thou, O proconsul, release him that has been bound? By no means. For I have One with whom I shall be for ever; I have One with whom I shall live to countless ages. To Him I go; to Him I hasten, who also having made thee known to me, has said to me, Let not that fearful man terrify thee; do not think that he will lay hold of thee, who art mine: for he is thine enemy. Therefore, having known thee through him who has turned towards me, I am delivered from thee. But if thou wishest to believe in Christ, there will be opened up for time, as I promised thee, a way of access; but if thou hast come only to release me, I shall not be able after this to be brought down from this cross alive in the body. For I and my kinsmen depart to our own, allowing thee to be what thou art, and what thou dost not know about thyself. For already I see my King, already I worship Him, already I stand before Him, where the fellowship of the angels is, where He reigns the only emperor, where there is light without night, where the flowers never fade, where trouble is never known, nor the name of grief heard, where there are cheerfulness and exultation that have no end. O blessed cross! without the longing for thee, no one enters into that place. But I am distressed, Aegeates, about thine own miseries, because eternal perdition is ready to receive thee. Run then, for thine own sake, O pitiable one, while yet thou canst, lest perchance thou shouldst wish then when thou canst not.

When, therefore, he attempted to come near the tree of the cross, so as to release the blessed Andrew, with all the city applauding him, the holy Andrew said with a loud voice: Do not suffer Andrew, bound upon Thy tree, to be released, O Lord; do not give me who am in Thy mystery to the shameless devil. O Jesus Christ, let not Thine adversary release me, who have been hanged by Thy favour; O Father, let this insignificant man no longer humble him who has known Thy greatness. The executioners, therefore, putting out their hands, were not able at all to touch him. Others, then, and others endeavoured to release him, and no one at all was able to come near him; for their arms were benumbed.

Then the blessed Andrew, having adjured the people, said: I entreat you earnestly, brethren, that I may first make one prayer to my Lord. So then set about releasing me. All the people therefore kept quiet because of the adjuration. Then the blessed Andrew, with a loud cry, said: Do not permit, O Lord, Thy servant at this time to be removed from Thee; for it is time that my body be committed to the earth, and Thou shalt order me to come to Thee. Thou who givest eternal life, my Teacher whom I have loved, whom on this cross I confess, whom I know, whom I possess, receive me, O Lord; and as I have confessed Thee and obeyed Thee, so now in this word hearken to me; and, before my body come down from the cross, receive me to Thyself, that through my departure there may be access to Thee of many of my kindred, finding rest for themselves in Thy majesty.

When, therefore, he had said this, he became in the sight of all glad and exulting; for an exceeding splendour like lightning coming forth out of heaven shone down upon him, and so encircled him, that in consequence of such brightness mortal eyes could not look upon him at all. And the dazzling light remained about the space of half an hour. And when he had thus spoken and glorified the Lord still more, the light withdrew itself, and he gave up the ghost, and along with the brightness itself he departed to the Lord in giving Him thanks.

And after the decease of the most blessed Andrew the apostle, Maximilla being the most powerful of the notable women, and continuing among those who had come, as soon as she learned that the apostle had departed to the Lord, came up and turned her attention to the cross, along with Stratocles, taking no heed at all of those standing by, and with reverence took down the body of the most blessed apostle from the cross. And when it was evening, bestowing upon him the necessary care, she prepared the body for burial with costly spices, and aid it in her own tomb. For she had been parted from Aegeates on account of his brutal disposition and lawless conduct, having chosen for herself a holy and quiet life; and having been united to the love of Christ, she spent her life blessedly along with the brethren.

Aegeates had been very importunate with her, and promised that he would make her mistress of his wealth; but not having been able to persuade her, he was greatly enraged, and was determined to make a public charge against all the people, and to send to Caesar an accusation against both Maximilla and all the people. And while he was arranging these things in the presence of his officers, at the dead of night he rose up, and unseen by all his people, having been tormented by the devil, he fell down from a great height, and rolling into the midst of the market-place of the city, breathed his last.

And this was reported to his brother Stratocles; and he sent his servants, having told them that they should bury him among those who had died a violent death. But he sought nothing of his substance, saying: Let not my Lord Jesus Christ, in whom I have believed, suffer me to touch anything whatever of the goods of my brother, that the condemnation of him who dared to cut off the apostle of the Lord may not disgrace me. These things were done in the province of Achaia, in the city of Patras on the day before the kalends of December, where his good deeds are kept in mind even to this day, to the glory and praise of our Lord Jesus Christ, to whom be glory for ever and ever. Amen.

Author unknown, The Acts of Andrew, Third fragment

The Acts of Andrew are believed to be from the 3rd century, this book details some of the life and ministry of the disciple who was the first to be called to follow Jesus. It includes a brief description of his martyrdom.

Concordia

Peter's wife is never actually mentioned in the New Testament. The closest she comes to being mentioned is when Jesus heals her mother. "When Jesus came into Peter's house, he saw Peter's mother-in-law lying in bed with a fever. He touched her hand and the fever left her, and she got up and began to wait on him" Matthew 8:14-15.

Martyrdom of Concordia (1)

Peter, before his own death, had the pain of witnessing what must have been worse than death to him. The apostle Paul tells us that Peter was accompanied by his wife on his missionary travels. She was probably with him still when Peter went to Rome, and there preceded him to martyrdom. She may have been one of those women of whom Clement speaks as going through a terrible death for the amusement of the Roman crowds. Peter may have seen his wife taken away to be killed, saying, as he looked on that he was happy in his heart, "because she had been called and was going home." "He lifted up his voice," so the ancient story runs, "and addressed her in a very encouraging and comforting manner, speaking to her by name – the name had been forgotten; some late legends give it as Concordia – and saying, "Remember the Lord, Concordia," or whatever her name was. "Such," says the old narrator, "was the marriage of the saints, and their disposition at the last to those whom they loved so dearly.'

Clement of Alexandria quoted by Eusebius, The History of the Church, Book III; in A. J. Mason: The Historic Martyrs of the Primitive Church, Longmans, 1905, pp 9-10

Martyrdom of Concordia (2)

The apostle Peter's wife was martyred before him during the Neronian persecution at Rome. Clement writes: "They relate that the blessed Peter, seeing his own wife led away to execution, was delighted on account of her calling and return to her country, and that he cried to her in a consolatory and encouraging voice, addressing her by name: 'Oh thou, remember ,the Lord!' Such was the marriage of these blessed ones, and such was their perfect affection towards their dearest friends."

Clement, Stromateus

PETER

The evangelist John records Peter talking with the risen Lord Jesus Christ. After telling Peter to "feed my sheep", Jesus predicted how Peter would die: "I tell you the truth, when you were younger you dressed yourself and went where you wanted; but when you are old you will stretch out your hands, and someone else will dress you and lead you where you do not want to go." Commenting on these words, John writes in his Gospel, "Jesus said this to indicate the kind of death by which Peter would glorify God" (John 21:17-19).

Martyrdom of Peter (1)

Outside Rome, on the Appian Way stands a little chapel known as "*Domine, quo vadis?*" – "Lord, whither goes thou?" Bishop Lightfoot, among others, is inclined to believe the story that the Christians at Rome came to Peter at the start of the persecution and begged him to flee from the city. Peter gave in to their pleas. When Peter reached the place where the chapel stands, Jesus Christ met him in the middle of a dark night. The apostle asked his Lord, as he had done before, "What do you want me to do?" The Lord answered him, "I go to Rome, to be crucified again." Peter was quick to understand the meaning behind this rebuke. He returned to Rome and told the Christian brethren what he had seen, and then glorified God by his death, as the Lord had foretold that he would, when he said, "Another shall gird thee and carry thee wither thou wouldest not.'

Ambrose, Epistle 21; in A. J. Mason, The Historic Martyrs of the Primitive Church, Longmans, 1905, p 10

Martyrdom of Peter (2)

When Herod Agrippa caused St James the Great to be put to death, and found that it pleased the Jews, he resolved, in order to ingratiate himself with the people, that Peter should be the next sacrifice. He was accordingly apprehended and thrown into prison; but an angel of the Lord released him, which so enraged Herod, that he ordered the sentinels who guarded the dungeon in which he had been confined to be put to death. St Peter, after various miracles, retired to Rome, where he defeated the artifices and confounded the magic of Simon Magus, a great favourite of the Emperor Nero: he likewise converted to Christianity one of the minions of that monarch, which so exasperated the tyrant, that he ordered both St Peter and St Paul to be apprehended. During the time of their confinement, they converted two of the captains of the guard and forty-seven other people to Christianity. Having been nine months in prison, Peter was brought from thence for execution, when, after being severely scourged, he was crucified with his head downwards; which position, however, was at his own request. His body being taken down, embalmed, and buried in the

Vatican, a church was erected on the spot; but this being destroyed by the Emperor Heliogabalus, the body was concealed till the twentieth bishop of Rome, Cornelius, conveyed it again to the Vatican; afterwards Constantine the Great erected one of the most stately churches over the place.
John Foxe, The Book of Martyrs, revised with notes and an appendix by W. Bramley-Moore, London, 1869, p 6.

Peter and Paul

Martyrdom of Peter and Paul (1)

But not to dwell upon ancient examples, let us come to the most recent spiritual heroes. Let us take the noble examples furnished in our own generation. Through envy and jealousy, the greatest and most righteous pillars [of the Church] have been persecuted and put to death. Let us set before our eyes the illustrious apostles. Peter, through unrighteous envy, endured not one or two, but numerous labours and when he had at length suffered martyrdom, departed to the place of glory due to him. Owing to envy, Paul also obtained the reward of patient endurance, after being seven times thrown into captivity, compelled to flee, and stoned. After preaching both in the east and west, he gained the illustrious reputation due to his faith, having taught righteousness to the whole world, and come to the extreme limit of the west, and suffered martyrdom under the prefects. Thus was he removed from the world, and went into the holy place, having proved himself a striking example of patience.
Eusebius, The History of the Church, chapter 5

Martyrdom of Peter and Paul (2)

Many noble martyrs have sprung from the blood of Ss. Peter and Paul

Thither came also thy blessed brother-Apostle Paul, "the vessel of election," and the special teacher of the Gentiles, and was associated with thee at a time when all innocence, all modesty, all freedom was into jeopardy under Nero's rule. Whose fury, inflamed by excess of all vices, hurled him headlong into such a fiery furnace of madness that he was the first to assail the Christian name with a general persecution, as if God's Grace could be quenched by the death of saints, whose greatest gain it was to win eternal happiness by contempt of this fleeting life. "Precious," therefore, "in the eyes of the Lord is the death of His saints:" nor can any degree of cruelty destroy the religion which is founded on the mystery of Christ's cross. Persecution does not diminish but increase the church, and the Lord's field is clothed with an ever richer crop, while the grains, which fall singly, spring up and are multiplied a hundred-fold. Hence how large a progeny have sprung from these two heaven-sown seeds is shown by the thousands of blessed martyrs, who, rivalling the Apostles' triumphs, have traversed the city far and wide in purple-clad and ruddy-gleaming throngs, and crowned it, as it were with a single diadem of countless gems.
Leo the Great, Sermon 82

Paul

Paul wrote:

Christ will be exalted in my body, whether by life or by death. For to me, to live is Christ and to die is gain.
The Bible: Philippians 1:20-21

Martyrdom of Paul (1)

In the days when Paul was still Saul, he was no stranger to persecution. He instigated imprisonment and executions on numerous early followers of Christ. After Stephen's martyrdom Luke records that "Saul began to destroy the church. Going from house to house, he dragged off men and women and put them in prison" (Acts 8:3). On the road to Damascus, and on the day of his conversion, Dr Luke paints a picture of Saul the persecutor of Christians in these words: "Saul was still breathing out murderous threats against the Lord's disciples. He went to the high priest and asked him for letters to the synagogues in Damascus, so that if he found any there who belonged to the Way, whether men or women, he might take them as prisoners to Jerusalem. As he neared Damascus . . ." (Acts 9:1-3). Most interesting, the words of Jesus that then rang in Saul's ears not only focused on his persecution of Jesus' early followers, but also equated it with persecuting Christ himself: "Saul, Saul, why do you persecute me?" (Acts 9:4).

After Saul became Paul he was on the receiving end of much persecution for the sake of his Lord. Paul writes about some of his hardships in his second letter to the Christians at Corinth and mentions "troubles, hardships and distresses; beatings, imprisonments and riots, and sleepless nights and hunger" (2 Corinthians 6:4-5). Towards the end of this letter Paul gives more details about the persecution he suffered for the sake of Christ: ". . . I have been in prison more frequently, been flogged more severely, and been exposed to death again and again. Five times I received from the Jews the forty lashes minus one. Three times I was beaten with rods, once I was stoned, three times I was shipwrecked, I spent a night and a day in the open sea, I have been constantly on the move. . . . I have known hunger and thirst and have often gone without food; I have been cold and naked. . . . In Damascus the governor under King Aretas had the city of Damascus guarded in order to arrest me. But I was lowered in a basket from a window in the wall and slipped through his hands" (2 Corinthians 11:23-33).

At Iconium, St Paul and St Barnabas were near being stoned to death by the enraged Jews; on which they fled to Lycaonia. At Lystra, St Paul was stoned, dragged out of the city, and left for dead. He, however, happily revived, and escaped to Derbe. At Philippi, Paul and Silas were imprisoned and whipped; and both were again persecuted at Thessalonica. Being afterwards taken at Jerusalem, he was sent to Caesarea, but appealed to Caesar at Rome. Here he continued a prisoner at large for two years; and at length, being released, he visited the churches of Greece and Rome, and preached in France and Spain. Returning to Rome, he was again apprehended, and, by the order of Nero, martyred, by beheading.

About this same time saints James, Philip, Matthew, Mark, Matthias, Jude, Bartholomew, Thomas, and Luke the evangelist also suffered martyrdom for the cause of Christ.

John Foxe, The Book of Martyrs, revised with notes and an appendix by W. Bramley-Moore, London, 1869, pp 6-7

Martyrdom of Paul (2)

Clement, the third bishop of Rome, wrote about some of the sufferings the Christians at Rome went through. Writing to the Corinthian church, Clement, talking about Peter and Paul, calls them "the champions nearest to our own time, noble examples set in our own generation." Of Paul, he writes:

Through jealousy and strife Paul showed us what is the reward of patient endurance. Seven times he was imprisoned; he was driven into exile; he was stoned; he preached both in the east and in the west, and gained a noble renown for his faith, having taught the whole world righteousness and having come to the very bounds of the west; and when he had borne his witness before the rulers, he was set free from the world and passed into the holy place, the greatest pattern of endurance.

Clement of Rome, 5, 6; quoted by A. J. Mason, The Historic Martyrs of the Primitive Church, Longmans, 1905, p 8

JOHN

John the evangelist records Jesus Christ's words: "Greater love has no one than this, that he lay down his life for his friends" (John 15:13)

Martyrdom of John (1)

He was distinguished as a prophet, an apostle, a divine, an evangelist, and a martyr. He is called the beloved disciple, and was brother to James the Great. He was previously a disciple of John the Baptist, and afterwards not only one of the twelve apostles, but one of the three to whom Christ communicated the most secret passages of his life. He founded churches at Smyrna, Pergamos, Sardis, Philadelphia, Laodicea, and Thyatira, to which he directs his Book of Revelation. Being at Ephesus, he was ordered by the Emperor Domitian to be sent bound to Rome, where he was condemned to be cast into a cauldron of boiling oil. [This was a punishment which the philosopher Seneca refers to as being suitable for a slave who had been convicted of a very serious crime.] But here a miracle was wrought in his favour; the oil did him no injury, and Domitian, not being able to put him to death, banished him to Patmos, to labour in the mines, in AD 73. He was, however, recalled by Nerva, who succeeded Domitian, but was deemed a martyr on account of his having undergone an execution, though it did not take effect. He wrote his epistles, gospel and Revelation, each in different style, but they are all equally admired. He was the only apostle who escaped a violent death, and lived the longest of any, he being nearly 100 years of age at the time of his death.

John Foxe, The Book of Martyrs, revised with notes and an appendix by W. Bramley-Moore, London, 1869, p 7

Martyrdom of John (2)

The Apostle John and the Apocalypse

It is said that in this persecution the apostle and evangelist John, who was still alive, was condemned to dwell on the island of Patmos in consequence of his testimony to the divine word. Irenaeus, in the fifth book of his work Against Heresies, where he discusses the number of the name of Antichrist which is given in the so-called Apocalypse of John, speaks as follows concerning him: "If it were necessary for his name to be proclaimed openly at the present time, it would have been declared by him who saw the revelation. For it was seen not long ago, but almost in our own generation, at the end of the reign of Domitian."

To such a degree, indeed, did the teaching of our faith flourish at that time that even those writers who were far from our religion did not hesitate to mention in their histories the persecution and the martyrdoms which took place during it. And they, indeed, accurately indicated the time. For they recorded that in the fifteenth year of Domitian Flavia Domitilla, daughter of a sister of Flavius Clement, who at that time was one of the consuls of Rome, was exiled with many others to the island of Pontia in consequence of testimony borne to Christ.

Eusebius of Caesarea, Church History, Book 3, chapter 18

Philip

Martyrdom of Philip (1)

Was born at Bethsaida, in Galilee and was first called by the name of "disciple." He labored diligently in Upper Asia, and suffered martyrdom at Heliopolis, in Phrygia. He was scourged, thrown into prison, and afterwards crucified, A.D. 54.

Foxe's Book of Martyrs, Edited by William Byron Forbush

Martyrdom of Philip (2)

THE TRAVELS OF PHILIP THE APOSTLE FROM THE FIFTEENTH ACT UNTIL THE END, AND AMONG THEM THE MARTYRDOM

About the time when the Emperor Trajan received the government of the Romans, after Simon the son of Clopas, who was bishop of Jerusalem, had suffered martyrdom in the eighth year of his reign, being the second bishop of the church there after James who bore the name of brother of the Lord, Philip the apostle, going through the cities and regions of Lydia and Asia, preached to all the Gospel of Christ. And having come to the city of Ophioryma, which is called Hierapolis of Asia, he was entertained by a certain believer, Stachys by name. And there was with him also Bartholomew, one of the seventy disciples of the Lord, and his sister Mariamme, and his disciples that followed him. All the men of the city therefore, having left their work, ran to the house of Stachys, hearing about the works which Philip did. And many men and women having assembled in the house of Stachys, Philip along with Bartholomew taught them the things of Jesus.

And Philip's sister Mariamme, sitting in the entry of the house of Stachys, addressed herself to those coming, persuading them to listen to the apostles, saying to them: Our brethren, and sons of my Father in heaven, ye are the excellent riches, and the substance of the city above, the delight of the habitation which God has prepared for those that love Him. Trample under foot the snares of the enemy, the writhing serpent. For his path is crooked, since he is the son of the wicked one, and the poison of wickedness is in him; and his father is the devil, the author of death, and his mother corruption; rage in his eyes and destruction in his mouth, and his path is Hades. Wherefore flee from him that has no substance, the shapeless one that has no shape in all the creation, whether in the heaven or in the earth, whether in the flying creatures or the beasts. For everything is taken away from his shape; for among the beasts of the earth and the fowls of the heaven is the knowledge of him, that the serpent trails his belly and his breast; and Tartarus is his dwelling-place, and he goes in the darkness, since he has confidence in nothing. Flee therefore from him, that his poison may not be poured out into your mouth. But be rather believing. holy, of good works, having no deceit. Take away from yourselves the wicked disposition, that is, the evil desires through which the serpent, the wicked dragon, the prince of evil, has produced the pasture of destruction and death for the soul, since all the desire of the wicked has proceeded from him. And this is the root of iniquity, the maintenance of evils, the death of souls: for the desire of the enemy is armed against the believers, and comes forth from the darkness, and walks in the darkness, taking in hand to war with those who are in the light. For this is the beginning of concupiscence. Wherefore you who wish to come to us, and the rather that God has come through us to you as a father to his own children, wishing to have mercy upon you, and to deliver you from the wicked snare of the enemy, flee from the evil lusts of the enemy, and cast them completely out of your mind, hating openly the father of evils, and loving Jesus, who is light, and life, and truth, and the Saviour of all who desire Him. Having run, therefore, to Him, take hold of Him in love, that He may bring you up out of the pit of the wicked, and having cleansed you, set you blameless, living in truth, in the presence of His Father. And all these things Philip said to the multitudes that had come together to worship as in old times the serpents and the viper, of which also they set up images and worshipped them. Wherefore also they called Hierapolis Ophioryma. And these things having been said by Philip, Bartholomew and Mariamme and his disciples, and Stachys being along with him, all the people gave ear, and a great multitude of them fleeing from the enemy were turned to Jesus, and were added to Philip and those about him. And the faithful were the more confirmed in the love of Christ.

And Nicanora, the wife of the proconsul, lying in bed under various diseases, especially of the eyes, having heard about the Apostle Philip and his teaching, believed in the Lord. For she had even before this heard about Him; and having called upon His name, she was released from the troubles that afflicted her. And rising up, she went forth out of her house through the side door, carried by her own slaves in a silver litter, and went into the house of Stachys, where the apostles were.

And when she came before the gate of the house, Mariamme, the sister of Philip the apostle, seeing her, spoke to her in the Hebrew tongue before Philip and Bartholomew, and all the multitude of those who had believed, saying: Alemakan, Ikasame, Marmare, Nachaman, Mastranan, Achaman; which is, Daughter of the father, thou art my mistress, thou hast been given as a pledge to the serpent; but Jesus our Redeemer has come to deliver thee through us, to break thy bands, and cut them, and to remove them from thee from their root, because thou art my sister, one mother brought us forth twins. Thou hast forsaken thy father, thou hast forsaken the path leading thee to the dwelling-place of thy mother, being in error; thou hast left the temple of that deception, and of the temporary glory, and hast come to us, fleeing from the enemy, because he is the dwelling-place of death. Behold, now thy Redeemer has come to redeem thee; Christ the Sun of righteousness has risen upon thee, to enlighten thee. And when Nicanora, standing before the door, heard these things, she took courage before all, crying out, and saying: I am a Hebrew, and a daughter of the Hebrews; speak with me in the language of my fathers. For, having heard the preaching of my fathers, I was straightway cured of the disease and the troubles that encompassed me. I therefore adore the goodness of God who has caused you to be spoiled even to this city, on account of His true stone held in honour, in order that through you we may receive the knowledge of Him, and may live with you, having believed in Him.

Nicanora having thus spoken, the Apostle Philip, along with Bartholomew and Mariamme and those with them, prayed for her to God, saying: Thou who bringest the dead to life, Christ Jesus the Lord, who hast freed us through baptism from the slavery of death, completely deliver also this woman from the error, the enemy; make her alive in Thy life, and perfect her in Thy perfection, in order that she may be found in the country of her fathers in freedom, having a portion in Thy goodness, O Lord Jesus. And all having sent up the amen along with the Apostle Philip, behold, there came the tyrant, the husband of Nicanora, raging like an unbroken horse; and having laid hold of his wife's garments, he cried out, saying: O Nicanora, did not I leave thee in bed? how hadst thou so much strength as to come to these magicians? And how hast thou been cured of the inflammation of thine eyes? Now, therefore, unless thou tell me who thy physician is, and what is his name, I shall punish thee with various punishments, and shall not have compassion upon thee. And she answering, says to him: O tyrant, cast out from thee this tyranny of thine, forsake this wickedness of thine; abandon this life lasting only for a season; run away from the brutality of thy worthless disposition; flee from the wicked dragon and his lusts; throw from thee the works and the dart of the man- slaying serpent; renounce the abominable and wicked sacrifices of the idols, which are the husbandry of the enemy, the hedge of darkness; make for thyself a life chaste and pure, that being in holiness thou mayst be able to know my Physician, and to get His name. If therefore thou wishest me to be beside thee, prepare thyself to live in chastity and self-restraint, and in fear of the true God, and I shall live with thee all my life; only cleanse thyself from the idols, and from all their filth. And when the gloomy tyrant her husband heard these words of hers, he seized her by the hair of her head, and dragged her along, kicking her, and saying: It will be a fine thing for thee to be cut off by the sword, or to see thee from beside me committing fornication with these foreign magicians; for I see that thou hast fallen into the madness of these deceivers. Thee first of them, therefore, I shall cut off by an evil death; and then, not sparing them, I shall cut their sinews, and put them to a most cruel death. And having turned, he said to those about him: Bring out for me those impostors of magicians. And the public executioners having run into the house of Stachys, and laid hold of the Apostle Philip, and Bartholomew and Mariamme, dragged them along, leading them to where the proconsul was. And the most faithful Stachys followed, and all the faithful. And the proconsul seeing them, gnashed his teeth, saying: Torture these deceivers that have deceived many women, and young men and girls, saying that they are worshippers of God, while they are an abomination. And he ordered thongs of raw hide to be brought, and Philip and Bartholomew and Mariamme to be beaten; and after they had been scourged with the thongs, he ordered their feet to be tied, and them to be dragged through the streets of the city as far as the gate of their temple. And a great crowd was assembled, so that scarcely any one stayed at home; and they all wondered at their patience, as they were being violently and inhumanly dragged along.

And the proconsul, having tortured the Apostle Philip and the saints who were with him, ordered them to be brought, and secured in the temple of the idol of the viper by its priests, until he should decide by what death he should destroy each of them. And many of the crowd believed in the grace of

Christ, and were added to the Apostle Philip, and those with him, having renounced the idol of the viper, and were confirmed in the faith being magnified by the endurance of the saints; and all together with their voice glorified God, saying the amen.

And when they were shut up in the temple of the viper-both Philip the Apostle, and Bartholomew and Mariamme, the priests of the viper assembled in the same place, and a great crowd, about seven thousand men; and having run to the proconsul, they cried out, saying: Avenge us of the foreigners, and magicians, and corrupters and seducers of men. For ever since they came to us, our dry has been filled with every evil deed; and they have also killed the serpents, the sons of our goddess; and they have also shut the temple, and the altar has been desolated; and we have not found the wine which had been brought in order that the viper, having drunk of it, might go to sleep. But if thou wishest to know that they are really, magicians, look and see how they wish to bewitch us, saying, Live in chastity and piety, after believing in God; and how also they have come into the city; and bow also the dragons have not struck them blind, or even killed them; and how also they have not drunk their blood; but even they who keep our city from every foreigner have been cast down by these men. And the proconsul, having heard these things, was the more inflamed with rage, and filled with wrath and threatening; and he was exceedingly enraged, and said to the priests: Why need you speak, when they have bewitched my own wife? And from that time she has spoken to me with strange words; and praying all the night through, she speaks in a strange tongue with a light shining round her; and groaning aloud, she says, Jesus the true light has come to me. And I, having gone forth from my chamber, wished to look down through the window and see Jesus, the light which she spoke of; and like lightning it came upon me, so that I was within a little of being blinded; and from that time forth I am afraid of my wife, on account of her luminous Jesus. Tell me, ye priests, what I am to do. And they said to him: O proconsul, assuredly we are no longer priests; for ever since thou didst shut them up, in consequence of them praying, not only has the temple been shaken from the foundations, but it is also assuredly falling down.

Then the proconsul ordered to bring Philip and those with him forth out of the temple, and to bring them up to the tribunal, saying to the public executioner: Strip Philip and Bartholomew and Mariamme, and search thoroughly to try to find their enchantments. Having therefore first stripped Philip, then Bartholomew, they came also to Mariamme; and dragging her along, they said: Let us strip her naked, that all may see her, how she follows men; for she especially deceives all the women. And the tyrant says to the priests: Proclaim throughout the whole city round about that all should come, men and women, that they may see her indecency, that she travels about with these magicians, and no doubt commits adultery with them. And he ordered Philip to be hanged, and his ankles to be pierced, and to bring also iron hooks, and his heels also to be driven through, and to be hanged head downwards, opposite the temple on a certain tree; and stretch out Bartholomew opposite Philip, having nailed his hands on the wall of the gate of the temple. And both of them smiled, seeing each other, both Philip and Bartholomew; for they were as if they were not tortured: for their punishments were prizes and crowns. And when also they had stripped Mariamme, behold, straightway the semblance of her body was changed in the presence of all, and straightway there was about her a cloud of fire before all; and they could not longer look at all on the place in which the holy Mariamme was, but they all fled from her. And Philip spoke with Bartholomew in the Hebrew tongue saying: Where is our brother John? for, behold, I am being released from the body; and who is he that has prayed for us? Because they have also laid hands on our sister Mariamme, contrary to what is meet; and, behold, they have set fire to the house of Stachys, sayings, Let us burn it, since he entertained them. Dost thou wish then, Bartholomew, fire to come from heaven, and that we should burn them up? And as Philip was thus speaking, behold, also John entered into the city like one of their fellow-citizens; and moving about in the street, he asked: Who are these men, and why are they punished? And they say to him: It cannot be that thou art of our city, and askest about these men, who have wronged many: for they have shut up our gods, and by their magic have cut off both the serpents and the dragons; and they have also raised many of the dead, who have struck us with amazement, detailing many punishments against us, and they wish also, these strangers who are hanging, to pray for fire out of heaven, and to burn up us and our city. Then says John: Let us go, and do you show me them. They led John, therefore, as their fellow-citizen, to where Philip was; and there was there a great crowd, and the proconsul, and the priests. And Philip, seeing John, said to Bartholomew in Hebrew: Brother, John has come, who was in Barek, where the living water is. And John saw Philip hanging head downwards both by the ankles and the heels; and he also saw Bartholomew stretched out on the wall of the temple; and he said to them: The mystery of him that was hanged between the heaven and the earth shall be with you.

And he said also to the men of that city: Ye men who dwell in Ophioryma Hierapolis, great is the ignorance which is among you, for you have erred in the path of error. The dragon breathing has breathed upon you, and blinded you in three ways; that is, he has made you blind in body, and blind in soul, and blind in spirit: and you have been struck by the destroyer. Look upon the whole creation, whether in the earth, or in the heaven, or in the waters, that the serpent has no resemblance to anything above; but he is of the stock of corruption, and has been brought to nothing by God; and on this account he is twisted and crooked, and there is no life in him; and anger, and rage, and darkness, and fire, and smoke are in all his members. And now, therefore, why do you punish these men because they have told you that the serpent is your enemy? And when they heard these words from John, they raised their hands against him, saying: We thought thee to be a fellow-citizen, but now thou hast shown thyself that thou art their companion. Like them, so also thou shalt be put to death; for the priests have intended to squeeze out your blood, and having mixed it with wine, to bring it to the viper to drink it. When, therefore, the priests attempted to lay hold of John, their hands were paralyzed. And John said to Philip: Let us not at all render evil for evil. And Philip said to John: Behold now, where is my Lord Jesus, who told me not to avenge myself? But for my part, I shall not endure it longer; but I will accomplish upon them my threat, and will destroy them all .

And John and Bartholomew and Mariamme restrained him, saying: Our Master was beaten, was scourged, was extended on the cross, was made to drink gall and vinegar, and said, Father, forgive them, for they know not what they do. And this He taught, saying: Learn of me, for I am meek and lowly in heart. Let us also therefore be patient. Philip says: Go away, and do not mollify me; for I will not bear that they have hanged me head down, and pierced my ankles and my heels with irons. And thou, John, beloved of God, how much hast thou reasoned with them, and thou hast not been listened to! Wherefore go away from me, and I will curse them, and they shall be destroyed utterly to a man. And he began to curse them, invoking, and crying out in Hebrew: Abalo, Aremun, Iduthael, Tharseleon, Nachoth, Aidunaph, Teletoloi: that is, O Father of Christ, the only and Almighty God; O God, whom all ages dread, powerful and impartial Judge, whose name is in Thy dynasty Sabaoth. blessed art Thou for everlasting: before Thee tremble dominions and powers of the celestials, and the fire-breathing threats of the cherubic living ones; the King, holy in majesty, whose name came upon the wild beasts of the desert, and they were tamed, and praised Thee with a rational voice; who lookest upon us, and readily grantest our requests; who knewest us before we were fashioned; the Overseer of all: now, I pray, let the great Hades open its mouth; let the great abyss swallow up these the ungodly, who have not been willing to receive the word of truth in this city. So let it be, Sabaoth. And, behold, suddenly the abyss was opened, and the whole of the place in which the proconsul was sitting was swallowed up, and the whole of the temple, and the viper which they worshipped, and great crowds, and the priests of the viper, about seven thousand men, besides women and children, except where the apostles were: they remained unshaken. And the proconsul was swallowed up into the abyss; and their voices came up from beneath, saying, with weeping: Have mercy upon us, O God of Thy glorious apostles, because we now see the judgments of those who have not confessed the crucified One: behold. the cross illumines us. O Jesus Christ, manifest Thyself to us, because we are all coming down alive into Hades, and are being scourged because we have unjustly crucified Thine apostles. And a voice was heard of one, saying: I shall be merciful to you in the cross of light. And there remained both Stachys and all his house, and the wife of the proconsul, and fifty other women who had believed with her upon the Lord, and a multitude besides, both of men and women, and a hundred virgins who had not been swallowed up because of their chastity, having been sealed with the seal of Christ. Then the Lord, having appeared unto Philip, said: O Philip, didst thou not hear: Thou shall not render evil for evil? and why hast thou inflicted such destruction? O Philip, whosoever putteth his hand to the plough, and looketh backwards, is his furrow well set? or who gives up his own lamp to another, and himself sits in darkness? or who forsakes his own dwelling-place, and dwells on a dunghill himself? And who, giving away his own garment in winter, goes naked? or what enemy rejoices in the joy of the man that hates him? and what soldier goes to war without a full suit of armour? and what slave who has fulfilled his master's order will not be commended? and who in the race-coarse, having nobly run, does not receive the prize? and who that has washed his garments willingly defiles them? Behold, my bride chamber is ready; but blessed is he who has been found in it wearing the shining garment: he it is who receives the crown upon his head. Behold, the supper is ready; and blessed is he who is invited, and is ready to go to Him that has invited him. The harvest of the field is much, and blessed is the good labourer. Behold the lilies and all the flowers, and it is the good husbandman who is the first to get a share of them. And how hast thou become, O Philip, unmerciful, having cursed thine enemies in wrath?

Philip says: Why art Thou angry with me, Lord, because I have cursed mine enemies? for why dost Thou not tread them under foot, because they are yet alive in the abyss? And knowest Thou, Lord, that because of Thee I came into this city, and in Thy name I have persecuted all the error of the idols, and all the demons? The dragons have withered away, and the serpents. And since these men have not received Thy light, therefore have I cursed them, and they have gone down to Hades alive. And the Saviour says to Philip: But since thou hast disobeyed me, and hast requited evil for evil, and hast not kept my commandment, on this account thou shalt finish thy course gloriously indeed, and shalt be led by the hand by my holy angels, and shalt come with them even to the paradise of delight; and they indeed shall come beside me into paradise, but thee will I order to be shut outside of paradise for forty days, in terror under the flaming and turning sword, and thou shall groan because thou hast done evil to those who have done evil to thee. And after forty days I shall send my archangel Michael; and he, having taken hold of the sword guarding paradise, shall bring thee into it, and thou shall see all the righteous who have walked in their innocence, and then thou shall worship the glory of my Father in the heavens. Nevertheless the sign of thy departure shall be glorified in my cross. And Bartholomew having gone away into Lycaonia, shall there also be himself crucified; and Mariamme shall lay her body in the river Jordan. But I, O Philip, will not endure thee, because thou hast swallowed up the men into the abyss; but, behold, my Spirit is in them, and I shall bring them up from the dead; and thus they, seeing thee, shall believe in the glory of Him that sent thee. And the Saviour having turned, stretched up His hand, and marked a cross in the air coming down from above even to the abyss, and it was full of light, and had its form after the likeness of a ladder. And all the multitude that had gone down from the city into the abyss came up on the ladder of the luminous cross; but there remained below the proconsul, and the viper which they worshipped. And when the multitude had come up, having looked upon Philip hanging head downwards, they lamented with a great lamentation at the lawless action which they had done. And they also saw Bartholomew, and Mariamme having her former appearance. And. behold, the Lord went up into the heavens in the sight of Philip, and Bartholomew and Mariamme. and Stachys, and all the unbelieving people, and silently they glorified God in fear and trembling. And all the multitudes cried out, saying: He alone is God, whom these men proclaim in truth; He alone is God, who sent these men for our salvation. Let us therefore truly repent for our great error, because we are by no means worthy of everlasting life. Now we believe, because we have seen great wonders, because the Saviour has brought us up from the abyss. And they all fell upon their face, and adored Philip, and entreated him, ready to flee: Do not do another miracle, and again send us away into the abyss. And they prayed that they might become worthy of the appearing of Christ. And Philip, yet hanging, addressed them, and said: Hear and learn how great are the powers of my God, remembering what you have seen below, and how your city has been overturned, with the exception of the house which received me; and now the sweetness of my God has brought you up out of the abyss, and I am obliged to walk round paradise for forty days on your account, because I was enraged against you into requiting you. And this commandment alone I have not kept, in that I did not give you good in return for evil. But I say unto you, From this time forth, in the goodness of God, reject the evil, that you may become worthy of the thanksgiving of the Lord. And some of the faithful ran up to take down Philip, and take off him the iron grapnels, and the hooks out of his ankles. But Philip said: Do not, my children, do not come near me on account of this, for thus shall be my end. Listen to me, ye who have been enlightened in the Lord, that I came to this city, not to make any merchandise, or do any other thing; but I have been destined to go out of my body in this city in the case in which you see me. Grieve not, then, that I am hanging thus; for I bear the stamp of the first man, who was brought to the earth head downwards, and again, through the wood of the cross brought to life out of the death of the transgression. And now I accomplish that which hath been enjoined upon me; for the Lord said to me, Unless you shall make that of you which is down to be up, and that which is on the left to be on the right, you shall not enter into my kingdom. Be ye not therefore likened to the unchanged type, for all the world has been changed, and every soul dwelling in a body is in forgetfulness of heavenly things; but let not us possessing the glory of the heavenly seek that which is without, which is the body and the house of slavery. Be not unbelieving, but believing, and forgive each other's faults. Behold, I hang six days, and I have blame from the true Judge, because I altogether requited you evil, and put a stumbling-block in the way of my rectitude. And now I am going up on high; be not sorrowful, but rather rejoice, because I am leaving this dwelling-place, my body, having escaped from the corruption of the dragon, who punishes every soul that is in sins.

And Philip, having looked round upon the multitudes, said: O ye who have come up out of the dead from Hades, and the swallowing up of the abyss,-and the luminous cross led you up on high, through the goodness of the Father, and the Son, and the Holy Ghost,-He being God became man, having been made flesh out of the Virgin Mary, immortal, abiding in flesh; and having died, He raised the dead, having had pity on mankind, having taken away the sting of sin. He was great, and became small for our sake, until He should enlarge the small, and bring them into His greatness. And He it is who has sweetness; and they spat upon Him, giving Him gall to drink, in order that He might make those who were bitter against Him to taste of His sweetness. Cleave then to Him, and do not forsake Him, for He is our life to everlasting. And when Philip had finished this announcement, he says to them, Loose Bartholomew; and having gone up, they loosed him. And after loosing him, Philip says to him: Bartholomew, my brother in the Lord, thou knowest that the Lord has sent thee with me to this city, and thou hast shared with me in all the dangers with our sister Mariamme; but I know that the going forth from thy body has been appointed in Lycaonia, and it has been decreed to Mariamme to go forth from the body in the river Jordan. Now therefore I command you, that when I have gone forth from my body, you shall build a church in this place; and let the leopard and the kid of the goats come into the church, for a sign to those that believe; and tot Nicanora provide for them until they shall go forth from the body; and when they shall have gone forth, bury them by the gate of the church. And lay your peace upon the house of Stachys, as Christ laid His peace on this city. And let all the virgins who believe stand in that house each day, watching over the sick, walking two and two; but let them have no communication with young men, that Satan may not tempt them: for he is a creeping serpent, and he caused Adam by menus of Eve to slip into death. Let it not be so again in this time as in the case of Eve. But do thou, O Bartholomew, look to them well: and thou shalt give these injunctions to Stachys, and appoint him bishop. Do not entrust the place of the bishopric to a young man, that the Gospel of Christ may not he brought to shame; and let every one that teacheth have his works equal to his words. But I am going to the Lord, and take my body and prepare it for burial with Syriac sheets of paper; and do not put round me flaxen cloth, because the body of my Lord was wrapped in linen. And having prepared my body for burial in the sheets of paper, bind it tight with papyrus reeds, and bury it in the church; and pray for me forty days, in order that the Lord may forgive me the transgression wherein I transgressed, in requiting those who did evil to me. See, O Bartholomew, where my blood shall drop upon the earth, a plant shall spring up from my blood, and shall become a vine, and shall produce fruit of a bunch of grapes; and having taken the cluster, press it into the cup; and having partaken of it on the third day, send up on high the Amen, in order that the offering may be complete. And Philip, having said these things, prayed thus: O Lord Jesus Christ, Father of the ages, King of the light, who hast made us wise in Thy wisdom, and hast given us Thine understanding, and hast bestowed upon us the counsel of Thy goodness, who hast never at any time left us, Thou art He who taketh away the disease of those who flee to Thee for refuge; Thou art the Son of the living God, who hast given us Thy presence of wisdom, who hast given us signs and wonders, and hast turned those who have gone astray; who crownest those who overcome the adversary, Thou excellent Judge. Come now, Jesus, and give me the everlasting crown of victory against every adverse dominion and power, and do not let their dark air hide me when I shall cross the waters of fire and all the abyss. O my Lord Jesus Christ, let not the enemy have ground to accuse me at Thy tribunal: but put on me Thy glorious robe, Thy seal of light that ever shines, until I shall pass by all the powers of the world, and the wicked dragon that lieth in wait for us. Now therefore, my Lord Jesus Christ, make me to meet Thee in the air, having forgiven me the recompense which I recompensed to my enemies; and transform the form of my body into angelic glory, and give me rest in Thy blessedness; and let me receive the promise from Thee which Thou hast promised to Thy saints to everlasting. And having thus spoken, Philip gave up the ghost, while all the multitudes were looking upon him, and weeping, and saying: The life of this spirit has been accomplished in peace.

And they said the Amen. And Bartholomew and Mariamme took down his body, and did as Philip had commanded them, and buried it in that place. And there was straightway a voice out of the heavens: Philip the apostle has been crowned with an incorruptible crown by Jesus Christ, the Judge of the contest. And all shouted out the Amen.

And after the three days the plant of the vine sprouted up where the blood of the holy Philip had dropped. And they did all that had been commanded them by him, offering an offering for forty days, praying without ceasing. And they built the church in that place, having appointed Stachys bishop in the church. And Nicanora and all the faithful assembled, and did not cease, all of them, glorifying God on account of the wonders that had happened among them. And all the city believed in the name of Jesus. And Bartholomew commanded Stachys to baptize those who believed into the name of the Father, and the Son, and the Holy Ghost.

And after the forty days, the Saviour, having appeared in the form of Philip, said to Bartholomew and Mariamme: My beloved brethren, do you wish to rest in the rest of God? Paradise has been opened to me, and I have entered into the glory of Jesus. Go away to the place appointed for you; for the plant that has been set apart and planted in this city shall bear excellent fruit. Having therefore saluted the brethren, and prayed for each of them, they departed from the city of Ophioryma, the Hierapolis of Asia; and Bartholomew departed into Lycaonia, and Mariamme proceeded to the Jordan; and Stachys and those with him remained, maintaining the church in Christ Jesus our Lord, to whom be glory and strength for ever and ever. Amen.

New Testament Apocrypha

Matthew

Whose occupation was that of a toll-gatherer, was born at Nazareth. He wrote his gospel in Hebrew, which was afterwards translated into Greek by James the Less. The scene of his labors was Parthia, and Ethiopia, in which latter country he suffered martyrdom, being slain with a halberd in the city of Nadabah, A.D. 60.

Foxe's Book of Martyrs, Edited by William Byron Forbush

James the Less

Is supposed by some to have been the brother of our Lord, by a former wife of Joseph. This is very doubtful, and accords too much with the Catholic superstition, that Mary never had any other children except our Savior. He was elected to the oversight of the churches of Jerusalem; and was the author of the Epistle ascribed to James in the sacred canon. At the age of ninety-four he was beat and stoned by the Jews; and finally had his brains dashed out with a fuller's club.

Foxe's Book of Martyrs, Edited by William Byron Forbush

Matthias

Of whom less is known than of most of the other disciples, was elected to fill the vacant place of Judas. He was stoned at Jerusalem and then beheaded.

Foxe's Book of Martyrs, Edited by William Byron Forbush

Mark

Was born of Jewish parents of the tribe of Levi. He is supposed to have been converted to Christianity by Peter, whom he served as an amanuensis, and under whose inspection he wrote his Gospel in the Greek language. Mark was dragged to pieces by the people of Alexandria, at the great solemnity of Serapis their idol, ending his life under their merciless hands.

Foxe's Book of Martyrs, Edited by William Byron Forbush

Jude

Martyrdom of Jude (1)

The brother of James, was commonly called Thaddeus. He was crucified at Edessa, A.D. 72.

Foxe's Book of Martyrs, Edited by William Byron Forbush

Martyrdom of Jude (2)

The apostle St. Jude is distinguished from

the Iscariot by the surname of Thaddaus, which signifies in Syriac praising or confession (being of the same import with the Hebrew word Judas), also by that of Lebbaeus, which is given him in the Greek text of St. Matthew. St. Jude was brother to St. James the Less, as he styles himself in his epistle; likewise of St. Simeon of Jerusalem, and of one Joses, who are styled the brethren of our Lord, and were sons of Cleophas and Mary, sister to the Blessed Virgin.

This apostle's kindred and relation to our Saviour exalted him not so much in his Master's eyes as his contempt of the world the ardour of his holy zeal and love, and his sufferings for his sake. It is not known when and by what means he became a disciple of Christ, nothing having been said of him in the gospels before we find him enumerated in the catalogue of the apostles. After the last supper, when Christ promised to manifest himself to every one who should love him, St. Jude asked him why he did not manifest himself to the world? By which question he seems to have expressed his expectation of a secular kingdom of the Messias. Christ by his answer satisfied him that the world is unqualified for divine manifestations, being a stranger and an enemy to what must fit souls for a fellowship with heaven; but that he would honour those who truly love him with his familiar converse, and would admit them to intimate communications of grace and favour.

After our Lord's ascension and the descent of the Holy Ghost, St. Jude set out, with the other great conquerors of the world and hell, to pull down the prince of darkness from his usurped throne; which this little troop undertook to effect armed only with the word of God and his Spirit. Nicephorus, Isidore, and the Martyrologies tell us that St. Jude preached up and down Judea, Samaria, Idumaa, and Syria; especially in Mesopotamia. St. Paulinus says that St. Jude planted the faith in Libya. This apostle returned from his missions to Jerusalem in the year 62, after the martyrdom of his brother, St. James, and assisted at the election of St. Simeon, who was likewise his brother. He wrote a catholic or general epistle to all the churches of the East, particularly addressing himself to the Jewish converts, amongst whom he had principally laboured. St. Peter had written to the same two epistles before this, and in the second had chiefly in view to caution the faithful against the errors of the Simonians, Nicholaits, and Gnostics. The havoc which these heresies continued to make among souls stirred up the zeal of St. Jude, who sometimes copied certain expressions of St. Peter, and seems to refer to the epistles of SS. Peter and Paul as if the authors were then no more. The heretics he describes by many strong epithets and similes, and calls them wandering meteors which seem to blaze for a while but set in eternal darkness. The source of their fall he points out by saying they are murmurers, and walk after their own lusts. The apostle puts us in mind to have always before our eyes the great obligation we lie under of incessantly building up our spiritual edifice of charity, by praying in the Holy Ghost, growing in the love of God, and imploring his mercy through Christ. From Mesopotamia St. Jude travelled into Persia. Fortunatus and the western Martyrologists tell us that the apostle St. Jude suffered martyrdom in Persia; the Menology of the Emperor Basil and some other Greeks say at Arat or Ararat, in Armenia, which at that time was subject to the Parthian empire, and consequently esteemed part of Persia. Many Greeks say he was shot to death with arrows: some add whilst he was tied on across. The Armenians at this day venerate him and St. Bartholomew for the first planters of the faith among them.

Alban Butler, The Lives of the Fathers, Martyrs and Other Principal Saints, volume 3

Simon the Zealot

Surnamed Zelotes, preached the Gospel in Mauritania, Africa, and even in Britain, in which latter country he was crucified, A.D. 74.

Foxe's Book of Martyrs, Edited by William Byron Forbush

Bartholomew

Preached in several countries, and having translated the Gospel of Matthew into the

language of India, he propagated it in that country. He was at length cruelly beaten and then crucified by the impatient idolaters.
Foxe's Book of Martyrs, Edited by William Byron Forbush

THOMAS

Called Didymus, preached the Gospel in Parthia and India, where exciting the rage of the pagan priests, he was martyred by being thrust through with a spear.
Foxe's Book of Martyrs, Edited by William Byron Forbush

LUKE

The evangelist, was the author of the Gospel which goes under his name. He travelled with Paul through various countries, and is supposed to have been hanged on an olive tree, by the idolatrous priests of Greece.
Foxe's Book of Martyrs, Edited by William Byron Forbush

BARNABAS

Was of Cyprus, but of Jewish descent, his death is supposed to have taken place about A.D. 73.

And yet, notwithstanding all these continual persecutions and horrible punishments, the Church daily increased, deeply rooted in the doctrine of the apostles and of men apostolical, and watered plentously with the blood of saints.
Foxe's Book of Martyrs, Edited by William Byron Forbush

TIMOTHY

The ageing apostle Paul's warning to his young protégé: "Everyone who wants to live a godly life in Christ Jesus will be persecuted" (Timothy 3:12).

Under Emperor Domitian's reign there were various tales published in order to injure the Christians. Among other falsehoods, they were accused of indecent nightly meetings, of a rebellious spirit, of murdering their children, and even of being cannibals; and at this time, such was the infatuation of the pagans, that if famine, pestilence, or earthquakes afflicted any of the Roman provinces, it was charged on the Christians. The various kinds of punishments and inflicted cruelties were, during this persecution, imprisonment, racking, searing, broiling, burning, scourging, stoning, hanging, and worrying. Many were lacerated with red-hot pincers, and others were thrown upon the horns of wild bulls. After having suffered these cruelties, the friends of the deceased Christians were refused the privilege of burying their remains.

Among the most distinguished of the martyrs of this period was Timothy, the celebrated disciple of St Paul, and Bishop of Ephesus.

St Paul sent to Timothy to come to him in his last confinement at Rome; and after that great apostle's martyrdom, he returned to Ephesus, where he governed the church till nearly the close of the century. At this period the pagans were about to celebrate a feast, the principal ceremonies of which were, that the people should carry sticks in their hands, go masked, and bear about the streets the images of their gods. When Timothy met the procession, he severely reproved them of their idolatry, which so exasperated them, that they fell upon him with their clubs, and beat him in so dreadful a manner, that he expired two days later.
John Foxe, The Book of Martyrs, revised with notes and an appendix by W. Bramley-Moore, London, 1869, pp 10-11

7. Foxe's Book of Martyrs

THE INFLUENCE OF THE BOOK OF MARTYRS

Title

The full title of John Foxe's famous book, *The Book of Martyrs* is *The Book of Martyrs, Acts and Monuments of these latter and perillous day,* was first published in 1563. It's subtitle reads: A HISTORY OF THE LIVES, SUFFERINGS

AND TRIUMPHANT DEATHS OF THE EARLY CHRISTIAN AND THE PROTESTANT MARTYRS

A source of edification

"After the Bible itself, no book so profoundly influenced early Protestant sentiment as the Book of Martyrs. Even in our time it is still a living force. It is more than a record of persecution. It is an arsenal of controversy, a storehouse of romance, as well as a source of edification."

James Miller Dodds, English Prose

Molded the national character

"When one recollects that until the appearance of the Pilgrim's Progress the common people had almost no other reading matter except the Bible and Foxe's Book of Martyrs, we can understand the deep impression that this book produced; and how it served to mold the national character. Those who could read for themselves learned the full details of all the atrocities performed on the Protestant reformers; the illiterate could see the rude illustrations of the various instruments of torture, the rack, the gridiron, the boiling oil, and then the holy ones breathing out their souls amid the flames. Take a people just awakening to a new intellectual and religious life; let several generations of them, from childhood to old age, pore over such a book, and its stories become traditions as individual and almost as potent as songs and customs on a nation's life."

Douglas Campbell, The Puritan in Holland, England, and America

A monument for the desire for spiritual freedom

"If we divest the book of its accidental character of feud between churches, it yet stands, in the first years of Elizabeth's reign, a monument that marks the growing strength of a desire for spiritual freedom, defiance of those forms that seek to stifle conscience and fetter thought."

Henry Morley, English Writers

A sketch of the author

John Foxe was born at Boston, in Lincolnshire, in 1517, where his parents are stated to have lived in respectable circumstances. He was deprived of his father at an early age; and notwithstanding his mother soon married again, he still remained under the parental roof. From an early display of talents and inclination to learning, his friends were induced to send him to Oxford, in order to cultivate and bring them to maturity.

During his residence at this place, he was distinguished for the excellence and acuteness of his intellect, which was improved by the emulation of his fellow collegians, united to an indefatigable zeal and industry on his part. These qualities soon gained him the admiration of all; and as a reward for his exertions and amiable conduct, he was chosen fellow of Magdalen College; which was accounted a great honor in the university, and seldom bestowed unless in cases of great distinction. It appears that the first display of his genius was in poetry; and that he composed some Latin comedies, which are still extant. But he soon directed his thoughts to a more serious subject, the study of the sacred Scriptures: to divinity, indeed, he applied himself with more fervency than circumspection, and discovered his partiality to the Reformation, which had then commenced, before he was known to its supporters, or to those who protected them; a circumstance which proved to him the source of his first troubles. He is said to have often affirmed that the first matter which occasioned his search into the popish doctrine was that he saw divers things, most repugnant in their nature to one another, forced upon men at the same time; upon this foundation his resolution and intended obedience to that Church were somewhat shaken, and by degrees a dislike to the rest took place.

His first care was to look into both the ancient and modern history of the Church; to ascertain its beginning and progress; to consider the causes of all those controversies which in the meantime had sprung up, and diligently to weigh their effects, solidity, infirmities, etc.

Before he had attained his thirtieth year, he had studied the Greek and Latin fathers, and other learned authors, the transactions of the Councils, and decrees of the consistories, and had acquired a very competent skill in the Hebrew language. In these occupations he frequently spent a considerable part, or even the whole of the night; and in order to unbend his mind after such incessant study, he would resort to a grove near the college, a place much frequented by the students in the evening, on account of its sequestered gloominess. In these solitary walks he was often heard to ejaculate heavy sobs and sighs, and with tears to pour forth his prayers to God. These nightly retirements, in the sequel, gave rise to the first suspicion of his alienation from the Church of Rome. Being pressed for an explanation of this alteration in his conduct, he scorned to call in fiction to his excuse; he stated his opinions; and was, by the sentence of the college convicted, condemned as a heretic, and expelled.

His friends, upon the report of this circumstance, were highly offended, when he was thus forsaken by his own friends, a refuge offered itself in the house of Sir Thomas Lucy, of Warwickshire, by whom he was sent for to instruct his children. The house is within easy walk of Stratford-on-Avon, and it was this estate which, a few years later, was the scene of Shakespeare's traditional boyish poaching expedition. Foxe died when Shakespeare was three years old.

In the Lucy house Foxe afterward married. But the fear of the popish inquisitors hastened his departure thence; as they were not contented to pursue public offences, but began also to dive into the secrets of private families. He now began to consider what was best to be done to free himself from further inconvenience, and resolved either to go to his wife's father or to his father-in-law.

His wife's father was a citizen of Coventry, whose heart was not alienated from him, and he was more likely to be well entreated, or his daughter's sake. He resolved first to go to him; and, in the meanwhile, by letters, to try whether his father-in-law would receive him or not. This he accordingly did, and he received for answer, "that it seemed to him a hard condition to take one into his house whom he knew to be guilty and condemned for a capital offence; neither was he ignorant what hazard he should undergo in so doing; he would, however, show himself a kinsman, and neglect his own danger. If he would alter his mind, he might come, on condition to stay as long as he himself desired; but if he could not be persuaded to that, he must content himself with a shorter stay, and not bring him and his mother into danger."

No condition was to be refused; besides, he was secretly advised by his mother to come, and not to fear his father-in- law's severity; "for that, perchance, it was needful to write as he did, but when occasion should be offered, he would make recompense for his words with his actions." In fact he was better received by both of them than he had hoped for.

By these means he kept himself concealed for some time, and afterwards made a journey to London, in the latter part of the reign of Henry VIII. Here, being unknown, he was in much distress, and was even reduced to the danger of being starved to death, had not Providence interfered in his favor in the following manner:

One day as Mr. Foxe was sitting in St. Paul's Church, exhausted with long fasting, a stranger took a seat by his side, and courteously saluted him, thrust a sum of money into his hand, and bade him cheer up his spirits; at the same time informing him, that in a few days new prospects would present themselves for his future subsistence. Who this stranger was, he could never learn; but at the end of three days he received an invitation from the Duchess of Richmond to undertake the tuition of the children of the Earl of Surry who, together with his father, the Duke of Norfolk, was imprisoned in the Tower, by the jealousy and ingratitude of the king. The children thus confided to his care were, Thomas, who succeeded to the dukedom; Henry, afterwards Earl of Northampton; and Jane who became Countess of Westmoreland. In the performance of his duties, he fully satisfied the expectations of the duchess, their aunt.

These halcyon days continued during the

latter part of the reign of Henry VIII and the five years of the reign of Edward VI until Mary came to the crown, who, soon after her accession, gave all power into the hands of the papists.

At this time Mr. Foxe, who was still under the protection of his noble pupil, the duke, began to excite the envy and hatred of many, particularly Dr. Gardiner, then Bishop of Winchester, who in the sequel became his most violent enemy.

Mr. Foxe, aware of this, and seeing the dreadful persecutions then commencing, began to think of quitting the kingdom. As soon as the duke knew his intention, he endeavored to persuade him to remain; and his arguments were so powerful, and given with so much sincerity, that he gave up the thought of abandoning his asylum for the present.

At that time the Bishop of Winchester was very intimate with the duke (by the patronage of whose family he had risen to the dignity he then enjoyed,) and frequently waited on him to present his service when he several times requested that he might see his old tutor. At first the duke denied his request, at one time alleging his absence, at another, indisposition. At length it happened that Mr. Foxe, not knowing the bishop was in the house, entered the room where the duke and he were in discourse; and seeing the bishop, withdrew. Gardiner asked who that was; the duke answered that he was "his physician, who was somewhat uncourtly, as being new come from the university." "I like his countenance and aspect very well," replied the bishop, "and when occasion offers, I will send for him." The duke understood that speech as the messenger of some approaching danger; and now himself thought it high time for Mr. Foxe to quit the city, and even the country. He accordingly caused everything necessary for his flight to be provided in silence, by sending one of his servants to Ipswich to hire a bark, and prepare all the requisites for his departure. He also fixed on the house of one of his servants, who was a farmer, where he might lodge until the wind became favorable; and everything being in readiness, Mr. Foxe took leave of his noble patron, and with his wife, who was pregnant at the time, secretly departed for the ship.

The vessel was scarcely under sail, when a most violent storm came on, which lasted all day and night, and the next day drove them back to the port from which they had departed. During the time that the vessel had been at sea, an officer, despatched by the bishop of Winchester, had broken open the house of the farmer with a warrant to apprehend Mr. Foxe wherever he might be found, and bring him back to the city. On hearing this news he hired a horse, under the pretence of leaving the town immediately; but secretly returned the same night, and agreed with the captain of the vessel to sail for any place as soon as the wind should shift, only desired him to proceed, and not to doubt that God would prosper his undertaking. The mariner suffered himself to be persuaded, and within two days landed his passengers in safety at Nieuport.

After spending a few days in that place, Mr. Foxe set out for Basle, where he found a number of English refugees, who had quitted their country to avoid the cruelty of the persecutors, with these he associated, and began to write his "History of the Acts and Monuments of the Church," which was first published in Latin at Basle in 1554, and in English in 1563.

In the meantime the reformed religion began again to flourish in England, and the popish faction much to decline, by the death of Queen Mary; which induced the greater number of the Protestant exiles to return to their native country.

Among others, on the accession of Elizabeth to the throne, Mr. Foxe returned to England; where, on his arrival, he found a faithful and active friend in his late pupil, the Duke of Norfolk, until death deprived him of his benefactor: after which event, Mr. Foxe inherited a pension bequeathed to him by the duke, and ratified by his son, the Earl of Suffolk.

Nor did the good man's successes stop here. On being recommended to the queen by her secretary of state, the great Cecil, her majesty granted him the prebendary of Shipton, in the cathedral of Salisbury, which was in a manner forced upon him; for it was with difficulty that he could be persuaded to accept it.

On his resettlement in England, he employed himself in revising and enlarging his admirable Martyrology. With prodigious pains and constant study he completed that celebrated work in eleven years. For the sake of greater correctness, he wrote every line of this vast book with his own hand, and transcribed all the records and papers himself. But, in consequence of such excessive toil, leaving no part of his time free from study, nor affording himself either the repose or recreation which nature required, his health was so reduced, and his person became so emaciated and altered, that such of his friends and relations as only conversed with him occasionally, could scarcely recognize his person. Yet, though he grew daily more exhausted, he proceeded in his studies as briskly as ever, nor would he be persuaded to diminish his accustomed labors. The papists, forseeing how detrimental his history of their errors and cruelties would prove to their cause, had recourse to every artifice to lessen the reputation of his work; but their malice was of signal service, both to Mr. Foxe himself, and to the Church of God at large, as it eventually made his book more intrinsically valuable, by inducing him to weigh, with the most scrupulous attention, the certainty of the facts which he recorded, and the validity of the authorities from which he drew his information.

But while he was thus indefatigably employed in promoting the cause of truth, he did not neglect the other duties of his station; he was charitable, humane, and attentive to the wants, both spiritual and temporal, of his neighbors. With the view of being more extensively useful, although he had no desire to cultivate the acquaintance of the rich and great on his own account, he did not decline the friendship of those in a higher rank who proffered it, and never failed to employ his influence with them in behalf of the poor and needy. In consequence of his well-known probity and charity, he was frequently presented with sums of money by persons possessed of wealth, which he accepted and distributed among those who were distressed. He would also occasionally attend the table of his friends, not so much for the sake of pleasure, as from civility, and to convince them that his absence was not occasioned by a fear of being exposed to the temptations of the appetite. In short his character as a man and as a Christian was without reproach.

Although the recent recollection of the persecutions under Bloody Mary gave bitterness to his pen, it is singular to note that he was personally the most conciliatory of men, and that while he heartily disowned the Roman Church in which he was born, he was one of the first to attempt the concord of the Protestant brethren. In fact, he was a veritable apostle of toleration.

When the plague or pestilence broke out in England, in 1563, and many forsook their duties, Foxe remained at his post, assisting the friendless and acting as the almsgiver of the rich. It was said of him that he could never refuse help to any one who asked it in the name of Christ. Tolerant and large-hearted he exerted his influence with Queen Elizabeth to confirm her intention to no longer keep up the cruel practice of putting to death those of opposing religious convictions. The queen held him in respect and referred to him as "Our Father Foxe."

Mr. Foxe had joy in the fruits of his work while he was yet alive. It passed through four large editions before his decease, and it was ordered by the bishops to be placed in every cathedral church in England, where it was often found chained, as the Bible was in those days, to a lectern for the access of the people.

At length, having long served both the Church and the world by his ministry, by his pen, and by the unsullied luster of a benevolent, useful, and holy life, he meekly resigned his soul to Christ, on the eighteenth of April, 1587, being then in the seventieth year of his age. He was interred in the chancel of St. Giles', Cripplegate; of which parish he had been, in the beginning of Elizabeth's reign, for some time vicar. On the south wall of the chancel is a plain tablet erected to his memory, with this inscription (translated):

TO JOHN FOXE
The most faithful Martyrologist of the Church of England,

The most sagacious Investigator of Historical Antiquity,
The most valiant Defender of Evangelical Truth,
A wondrous worker of miracles,
Who presented the Marian martyrs, like phoenixs, alive from their ashes:
Chiefly to fulfil every duty of filial affection,
Samuel Foxe,
His eldest son,
Erected this monument,
Not without tears.
He died the 18th April, AD 1587
A septuagenarian.
The life of mortal life is the hope of immortal life.

Conclusion to book

And now to conclude, good Christian readers, this present tractation, not for the lack of matter, but to shorten rather the matter for largeness of the volume. In the meantime the grace of the Lord Jesus Christ work with thee, gentle reader, in all thy studious readings. And when thou hast faith, so employ thyself to read, that by reading thou mayest learn daily to know that which may profit thy soul, may teach thee experience, may arm thee with patience, and instruct thee in all spiritual knowledge more and more, to thy perfect comfort and salvation in Christ Jesus, our Lord, to whom be glory in secula seculorum. Amen.

Foxe's Book of Martyrs, Edited by William Byron Forbush, chapter 22

A Catholic perspective

John Foxe was born at Boston in Lincolnshire, England, in 1516, and was educated at Magdalen School and College, Oxford. He joined the more extreme Reformers early in life and under Edward VI acted as tutor to the children of the recently beheaded Earl Of Surrey. In Mary's reign he fled to Germany and joined the exiles at Frankfort. In the controversy which arose there he took sides with Knox and the extremists and after the break up of the Frankfort colony he went to Basle where poverty compelled him to take service with the Protestant printer Oporinus. In 1539 he returned to England and entered the ministry, he was helped by his old pupil the Duke of Norfolk and was mainly occupied with his martyrology. He still belonged to the extremists and objected to the surplice. His opinions interfered with his prospects, but he was not an ambitious man. Though violent and dishonest in controversy, he was personally of a kind and charitable temper. Besides his "Acts and Monuments" he published a number of sermons, translations, and controversial attacks on Catholicism. He died in 1587.

Even before leaving England in 1554 Foxe had begun the story of the persecutions of the Reformers. The result was the publication of a little Latin work dealing mainly with Wyclifism. While at Basle he was supplied by Grindal with reports of the persecution in England and in 1559 he published a large Latin folio of 740 pages which began with Wyclif and ended with Cranmer. After his return to England he began to translate this book and to add to it the results of fresh information. The "Acts and Monuments" were finally published in 1563 but came almost immediately to he known as the "Book of Martyrs". The criticism which the work called forth led to the publication of a "corrected" edition in 1570. Two more (1576 and 1583) came out during his life and five (1596, 1610, 1632, 1641, 1684) within the next hundred years. There have been two modern editions, both unsatisfactory; they are in eight volumes and were published in 1837-41 and 1877. The size may be gathered from the fact that in the edition of 1684 it consists of three folio volumes of 895, 682, and 863 pages respectively. Each page has two columns and over eighty lines. The first volume besides introductory matter contains the story of early Christian persecutions, a sketch of medieval church history and an account of the Wyclifite movement in England and on the continent. The second volume deals with the reigns Henry VII and Edward VI and the third with that of Mary. A large number of official documents such as injunctions, articles of accusation, letters, etc., have been included. The book is illustrated throughout by woodcuts, some of them symbolizing the triumph of the Reformation, most of them depicting the sufferings of the martyrs.

The Convocation of the English Church

ordered in 1571 that copies of the "Book of Martyrs" should be kept for public inspection in all cathedrals and in the houses of church dignitaries. The book was also exposed in many parish churches. The passionate intensity of the style, the vivid and picturesque dialogues made it very popular among Puritan and Low Church families down to the nineteenth century. Even in the fantastically partisan church history of the earlier portion of the book, with its grotesque stories of popes and monks and its motley succession of witnesses to the truth (including the Albigenses, Grosseteste, Dante, and Savonarola) was accepted among simple folk and must have contributed much to anti-Catholic prejudices in England. When Foxe treats of his own times his work is of greater value as it contains many documents and is but largely based on the reports of eyewitnesses; but he sometimes dishonesty mutilates his documents and is quite untrustworthy in his treatment of evidence. He was criticized in his own day by Catholics such as Harpsfield and Father Parsons and by practically all serious ecclesiastical historians.

BIBLIOGRAPHY. The most careful examination of his methods is to be found in Maitland, Essays on the Reformation in England (1849), and in Gairdner, History of the English Church from the ascention of Henry VIII to the Death of Mary (1903); Lee in Dict. of Nat. Biog. Gerard, John Foxe and His Book of Martyrs (Catholic Truth Society, London), includes the opinions of a number of Foxe's critics.

F.F. Urquhart, The Catholic Encyclopedia, Volume 2

8. Bible study on martyrdom

Torrey's New Topic Textbook

Martyrdom

Is death endured for the word of God, and testimony of Christ Re 6:9; 20:4.

Saints

Forewarned of. Mt 10:21; 24:9; Joh 16:2.

Should not fear. Mt 10:28; Re 2:10.

Should be prepared for. Mt 16:24,25; Ac 21:13.

Should resist sin to. Heb 12:4.

Reward of Re 2:10; 6:11.

Inflicted at the instigation of the devil Re 2:10,13.

The Apostasy guilty of inflicting Re 17:6; 18:24.

Of saints, shall be avenged Lu 11:50,51; Re 18:20-24.

Exemplified

Abel. Ge 4:8; 1Jo 3:12.

Ahimelech and his fellow priests. 1Sa 22:18,19.

Prophets and Saints of old. 1Ki 18:4; 19:10; Lu 11:50,51; Heb 11:37.

Uriah. Jer 26:23.

John the Baptist. Mr 6:27.

Peter. Joh 21:18,19.

Stephen. Ac 7:58.

Christians. Ac 9:1; 22:4; 26:10.

James. Ac 12:2.

Antipas. Re 2:13.

Persecution

Christ suffered Ps 69:26; Joh 5:16.

Christ voluntarily submitted to Isa 50:6.

Christ was patient under Isa 53:7.

Saints may expect Mr 10:30; Lu 21:12; Joh 15:20.

Saints suffer, for the sake of God Jer 15:15. Of saints, is a persecution of Christ Zec 2:8; Ac 9:4,5.

All that live godly in Christ, shall suffer 2Ti 3:12.

Originates

Ignorance of God and Christ. Joh 16:3.

Hated to God and Christ. Joh 15:20,24.

Hatred to the gospel. Mt 13:21.

Pride. Ps 10:2.

Mistaken zeal. Ac 13:50; 26:9-11.

Is inconsistent with the spirit of the gospel Mt 26:52.

Men by nature addicted to Ga 4:29.

Preacher of the gospel subject to Ga 5:11.

Is sometimes to death Ac 22:4.

God forsakes not his saints under 2Co 4:9.

God delivers out of Da 3:25,28; 2Co 1:10; 2Ti 3:11.

Cannot separated from Christ Ro 8:35.

Lawful means may be used to escape Mt 2:13; 10:23; 12:14,15.

Saints suffering, should

- Commit themselves to God. 1Pe 4:19.
- Exhibit patience. 1Co 4:12.
- Rejoice. Mt 5:12; 1Pe 4:13.
- Glorify God. 1Pe 4:16.
- Pray for deliverance. Ps 7:1; 119:86.
- Pray for those who inflict. Mt 5:44.
- Return blessing for. Ro 12:14.

The hope of future blessedness supports under 1Co 15:19,32; Heb 10:34,35.

Blessedness of enduring, for Christ's sake Mt 5:10; Lu 6:22.

Pray for those suffering 2Th 3:2.

Hypocrites cannot endure Mt 4:17.

False teachers shrink from Ga 6:12. The wicked

- Addicted to. Ps 10:2; 69:26.
- Active in. Ps 143:3; La 4:19.
- Encourage each other in. Ps 71:11.
- Rejoice in its success. Ps 13:4; Re 11:10.
- Punishment for. Ps 7:13; 2Th 1:6.
- Illustrated. Mt 21:33-39.

Spirit of-Exemplified

- Pharaoh &c. Ex 1:8-14.
- Saul. 1Sa 26:18.
- Jezebel. 1Ki 19:2.
- Zedekiah &c. Jer 38:4-6.
- Chaldeans. Da 3:8-30.
- Pharisees. Mt 12:14.
- Jews. Joh 5:16; 1Th 2:15.
- Herod. Ac 12:1.
- Gentiles. Ac 14:5.
- Paul. Php 3:6; 1Ti 1:13.

Suffering of-Exemplified

- Micaiah. 1Ki 22:27.
- David. Ps 119:161.
- Jeremiah. Jer 32:2.
- Daniel. Da 6:5-17.
- Peter &c. Ac 4:3.
- Apostles. Ac 5:18.
- The Prophets. Ac 7:52.
- The Church. Ac 8:1.
- Paul and Barnabas. Ac 13:50.
- Paul and Silas. Ac 16:23.
- Hebrews. Heb 10:33.
- Saints of old. Heb 11:36.

Easton's Bible Dictionary

Martyr – one who bears witness of the truth, and suffers death in the cause of Christ (Acts 22:20; Rev. 2:13; 17:6). In this sense Stephen was the first martyr. The Greek word so rendered in all other cases is translated "witness." (1.) In a court of justice (Matt. 18:16; 26:65; Acts 6:13; 7:58; Heb. 10:28; 1 Tim. 5:19). (2.) As of one bearing testimony to the truth of what he has seen or known (Luke 24:48; Acts 1:8, 22; Rom. 1:9; 1 Thess. 2:5, 10; 1 John 1:2).

Death of Saints, The.

- A sleep in Christ 1Co 15:18; 1Th 4:14.
- Is blessed Re 14:13.
- Is gain Php 1:21.
- Is full of
- Faith. Heb 11:13.
- Peace. Isa 57:2.
- Hope. Pr 14:32.
- Sometimes desired Lu 2:29.
- Waited for Job 14:14.
- Met with resignation Ge 50:24; Jos 23:14; 1Ki 2:2.
- Met without fear 1Co 15:55.
- Precious in God's sight Ps 116:15.
- God preserves them to Ps 48:14.
- God is with them in Ps 23:4.
- Removes from coming evil 2Ki 22:20; Isa 57:1.
- Leads to
    - Rest. Job 3:17; 2Th 1:7.
    - Comfort. Lu 16:25.
    - Christ's presence. 2Co 5:8; Php 1:23.
    - A crown of life. 2Ti 4:8; Re 2:10.
    - A joyful resurrection. Isa 26:19; Da 12:2.
- Disregarded by the wicked Isa 57:1.
- Survivors consoled for 1Th 4:13-18.
- The wicked wish theirs to resemble Nu 23:10.
- Illustrated Lu 16:22.
- Exemplified
    - Abraham. Ge 25:8.
    - Isaac. Ge 35:29.
    - Jacob. Ge 49:33.
    - Aaron. Nu 20:28.
    - Moses. De 34:5.
    - Joshua. Jos 24:29.
    - Elisha. 2Ki 13:14,20.
    - One thief. Lu 23:43.
    - Dorcas. Ac 9:37.

Scripture Passages about Martyrdom and Persecution

Throughout the history of the Christian church particular Bible verses have been used to encourage Christians in the heat of persecution and the fires of martyrdom. The NIV is used.

1. Hebrews 13:3. Remember those in prison as if you were their fellow prisoners, and those who are mistreated as if you yourselves were suffering.

2. Proverbs 31:8-9. Speak up for those who cannot speak for themselves, for the rights of all who are destitute. Speak up and judge fairly; defend the rights of the poor and needy.

3. Psalms 119:71-72. It was good for me to be afflicted so that I might learn your decrees. The law from your mouth is more precious to me than thousands of pieces of silver and gold.

4. Matthew 25:35-36. For I was hungry and you gave me something to eat, I was thirsty and you gave me something to drink, I was a stranger and you invited me in, I needed clothes and you clothed me, I was sick and you looked after me, I was in prison and you came to visit me.

5. Acts 12:5-10. So Peter was kept in prison, but the church was earnestly praying to God for him. The night before Herod was to bring him to trial, Peter was sleeping between two soldiers, bound with two chains, and sentries stood guard at the entrance. Suddenly an angel of the Lord appeared and a light shone in the cell. He struck Peter on the side and woke him up. "Quick, get up!" he said, and the chains fell off Peter's wrists. Then the angel said to him, "Put on your clothes and sandals." And Peter did so. "Wrap your cloak around you and follow me," the angel told him. Peter followed him out of the prison, but he had no idea that what the angel was doing was really happening; he thought he was seeing a vision. They passed the first and second guards and came to the iron gate leading to the city. It opened for them by itself, and they went through it.

6. 1 Peter 2:19-21. For it is commendable if a man bears up under the pain of unjust suffering because he is conscious of God. But how is it to your credit if you receive a beating for doing wrong and endure it? But if you suffer for doing good and you endure it, this is commendable before God. To this you were called, because Christ suffered for you, leaving you an example, that you should follow in his steps.

7. Hebrews 11:35-38. Others were tortured and refused to be released, so that they might gain a better resurrection. Some faced jeers and flogging, while still others were chained and put in prison. They were stoned; they were sawed in two; they were put to death by the sword. They went about in sheepskins and goatskins, destitute, persecuted and mistreated–the world was not worthy of them. They wandered in deserts and mountains, and in caves and holes in the ground.

8. 1 Peter 1:6-7. In this you greatly rejoice, though now for a little while you may have had to suffer grief in all kinds of trials. These have come so that your faith–of greater worth than gold, which perishes even though refined by fire–may be proved genuine and may result in praise, glory and honor when Jesus Christ is revealed.

9. John 15:19-20. If you belonged to the world, it would love you as its own. As it is, you do not belong to the world, but I have chosen you out of the world. That is why the world hates you. Remember the words I spoke to you: No servant is greater than his master. If they persecuted me, they will persecute you also. If they obeyed my teaching, they will obey yours also.

10. 1 Peter 3:13-14. Who is going to harm you if you are eager to do good? But even if you should suffer for what is right, you are blessed. "Do not fear what they fear; do not be frightened."

11. 1 Peter 4:1-6. Therefore, since Christ suffered in his body, arm yourselves also with

the same attitude, because he who has suffered in his body is done with sin. As a result, he does not live the rest of his earthly life for evil human desires, but rather for the will of God. For you have spent enough time in the past doing what pagans choose to do–living in debauchery, lust, drunkenness, orgies, carousing and detestable idolatry. They think it strange that you do not plunge with them into the same flood of dissipation, and they heap abuse on you. But they will have to give account to him who is ready to judge the living and the dead. For this is the reason the gospel was preached even to those who are now dead, so that they might be judged according to men in regard to the body, but live according to God in regard to the spirit.

12. Isaiah 59:15-16. Truth is nowhere to be found, and whoever shuns evil becomes a prey. The Lord looked and was displeased that there was no justice. He saw that there was no one, he was appalled that there was no one to intervene; so his own arm worked salvation for him, and his own righteousness sustained him.

13. 1 Peter 4:12-19. Dear friends, do not be surprised at the painful trial you are suffering, as though something strange were happening to you. But rejoice that you participate in the sufferings of Christ, so that you may be overjoyed when his glory is revealed. If you are insulted because of the name of Christ, you are blessed, for the Spirit of glory and of God rests on you. If you suffer, it should not be as a murderer or thief or any other kind of criminal, or even as a meddler. However, if you suffer as a Christian, do not be ashamed, but praise God that you bear that name. For it is time for judgment to begin with the family of God; and if it begins with us, what will the outcome be for those who do not obey the gospel of God? And, "If it is hard for the righteous to be saved, what will become of the ungodly and the sinner?" So then, those who suffer according to God's will should commit themselves to their faithful Creator and continue to do good.

14. Romans 5:2-8. And we rejoice in the hope of the glory of God. Not only so, but we also rejoice in our sufferings, because we know that suffering produces perseverance; perseverance, character; and character, hope. And hope does not disappoint us, because God has poured out his love into our hearts by the Holy Spirit, whom he has given us. You see, at just the right time, when we were still powerless, Christ died for the ungodly. Very rarely will anyone die for a righteous man, though for a good man someone might possibly dare to die. But God demonstrates his own love for us in this: While we were still sinners, Christ died for us.

15. 1 Peter 5:8-9. Be self-controlled and alert. Your enemy the devil prowls around like a roaring lion looking for someone to devour. Resist him, standing firm in the faith, because you know that your brothers throughout the world are undergoing the same kind of sufferings.

16. Romans 8:35-39. Who shall separate us from the love of Christ? Shall trouble or hardship or persecution or famine or nakedness or danger or sword? As it is written: "For your sake we face death all day long; we are considered as sheep to be slaughtered." No, in all these things we are more than conquerors through him who loved us. For I am convinced that neither death nor life, neither angels nor demons, Or nor heavenly rulers neither the present nor the future, nor any powers, neither height nor depth, nor anything else in all creation, will be able to separate us from the love of God that is in Christ Jesus our Lord.

17. 1 Thessalonians 3:7-8. Therefore, brothers, in all our distress and persecution we were encouraged about you because of your faith. For now we really live, since you are standing firm in the Lord.

18. Hebrews 10:33-35. Sometimes you were publicly exposed to insult and persecution; at other times you stood side by side with those who were so treated. You sympathized with those in prison and joyfully accepted the confiscation of your property, because you knew that you yourselves had better and

lasting possessions. So do not throw away your confidence; it will be richly rewarded. You need to persevere so that when you have done the will of God, you will receive what he has promised.

19. Revelation 2:10. Do not be afraid of what you are about to suffer. I tell you, the devil will put some of you in prison to test you, and you will suffer persecution for ten days. Be faithful, even to the point of death, and I will give you the crown of life.

20. Hebrews 2:9. But we see Jesus, who was made a little lower than the angels, now crowned with glory and honor because he suffered death, so that by the grace of God he might taste death for everyone.

21. 2 Corinthians 1:2-11. Praise be to the God and Father of our Lord Jesus Christ, the Father of compassion and the God of all comfort, who comforts us in all our troubles, so that we can comfort those in any trouble with the comfort we ourselves have received from God. For just as the sufferings of Christ flow over into our lives, so also through Christ our comfort overflows. If we are distressed, it is for your comfort and salvation; if we are comforted, it is for your comfort, which produces in you patient endurance of the same sufferings we suffer. And our hope for you is firm, because we know that just as you share in our sufferings, so also you share in our comfort. We do not want you to be uninformed, brothers, about the hardships we suffered in the province of Asia. We were under great pressure, far beyond our ability to endure, so that we despaired even of life. Indeed, in our hearts we felt the sentence of death. But this happened that we might not rely on ourselves but on God, who raises the dead. He has delivered us from such a deadly peril, and he will deliver us. On him we have set our hope that he will continue to deliver us, as you help us by your prayers. Then many will give thanks on our behalf for the gracious favor granted us in answer to the prayers of many.

22. 2 Corinthians 6:4-10. Rather, as servants of God we commend ourselves in every way: in great endurance; in troubles, hardships and distresses; in beatings, imprisonments and riots; in hard work, sleepless nights and hunger; in purity, understanding, patience and kindness; in the Holy Spirit and in sincere love; in truthful speech and in the power of God; with weapons of righteousness in the right hand and in the left; through glory and dishonor, bad report and good report; genuine, yet regarded as impostors; known, yet regarded as unknown; dying, and yet we live on; beaten, and yet not killed; sorrowful, yet always rejoicing; poor, yet making many rich; having nothing, and yet possessing everything.

23. Hebrews 2:9. But we see Jesus, who was made a little lower than the angels, now crowned with glory and honor because he suffered death, so that by the grace of God he might taste death for everyone.

24. James 5:10-11,13. Brothers, as an example of patience in the face of suffering, take the prophets who spoke in the name of the Lord. As you know, we consider blessed those who have persevered. You have heard of Job's perseverance and have seen what the Lord finally brought about. The Lord is full of compassion and mercy. Is any one of you in trouble? He should pray. Is anyone happy? Let him sing songs of praise.

25. Revelation 6:9-11. When he opened the fifth seal, I saw under the altar the souls of those who had been slain because of the word of God and the testimony they had maintained. They called out in a loud voice, "How long, Sovereign Lord, holy and true, until you judge the inhabitants of the earth and avenge our blood?" Then each of them was given a white robe, and they were told to wait a little longer, until the number of their fellow servants and brothers who were to be killed as they had been was completed.

26. Hebrews 12:7-9. Endure hardship as discipline; God is treating you as sons. For what son is not disciplined by his father? If you are not disciplined (and everyone undergoes

discipline), then you are illegitimate children and not true sons. Moreover, we have all had human fathers who disciplined us and we respected them for it. How much more should we submit to the Father of our spirits and live! Our fathers disciplined us for a little while as they thought best; but God disciplines us for our good, that we may share in his holiness. No discipline seems pleasant at the time, but painful. Later on, however, it produces a harvest of righteousness and peace for those who have been trained by it.

27. Romans 12:14-21. Be joyful in hope, patient in affliction, faithful in prayer. Share with God's people who are in need. Practice hospitality. Bless those who persecute you; bless and do not curse. Rejoice with those who rejoice; mourn with those who mourn. Live in harmony with one another. Do not be proud, but be willing to associate with people of low position. Do not be conceited. Do not repay anyone evil for evil. Be careful to do what is right in the eyes of everybody. If it is possible, as far as it depends on you, live at peace with everyone. Do not take revenge, my friends, but leave room for God's wrath, for it is written: "It is mine to avenge; I will repay," says the Lord. On the contrary: "If your enemy is hungry, feed him; if he is thirsty, give him something to drink. In doing this, you will heap burning coals on his head." Do not be overcome by evil, but overcome evil with good.

28. Matthew 5:10. Blessed are those who are persecuted because of righteousness, for theirs is the kingdom of heaven.

29. Matthew 5:12. Rejoice and be glad, because great is your reward in heaven, for in the same way they persecuted the prophets who were before you.

30. Matthew 24:9. Then you will be handed over to be persecuted and put to death, and you will be hated by all nations because of me. At that time many will turn away from the faith and will betray and hate each other, and many false prophets will appear and deceive many people. Because of the increase of wickedness, the love of most will grow cold, but he who stands firm to the end will be saved.

31. John 5:16. So, because Jesus was doing these things on the Sabbath, the Jews persecuted him. Jesus said to them, "My Father is always at his work to this very day, and I, too, am working." For this reason the Jews tried all the harder to kill him; not only was he breaking the Sabbath, but he was even calling God his own Father, making himself equal with God.

32. John 15:20-22. Remember the words I spoke to you: "No servant is greater than his master." If they persecuted me, they will persecute you also. If they obeyed my teaching, they will obey yours also. They will treat you this way because of my name, for they do not know the One who sent me. If I had not come and spoken to them, they would be guilty of sin. Now, however, they have no excuse for their sin.

33. Acts 22:4-5. I persecuted the followers of this Way to their death, arresting both men and women and throwing them into prison, as also the high priest and all the Council can testify. I even obtained letters from them to their brothers in Damascus, and went there to bring these people as prisoners to Jerusalem to be punished.

34. 1 Corinthians 4:12-14. We work hard with our own hands. When we are cursed, we bless; when we are persecuted, we endure it; when we are slandered, we answer kindly. Up to this moment we have become the scum of the earth, the refuse of the world. I am not writing this to shame you, but to warn you, as my dear children.

35. 1 Corinthians 15:9-10. For I am the least of the apostles and do not even deserve to be called an apostle, because I persecuted the church of God. But by the grace of God I am what I am, and his grace to me was not without effect. No, I worked harder than all of them–yet not I, but the grace of God that was with me.

36. 2 Corinthians 4:7-18. But we have this treasure in jars of clay to show that this all-surpassing power is from God and not from us. We are hard pressed on every side, but not crushed; perplexed, but not in despair; persecuted, but not abandoned; struck down, but not destroyed. We always carry around in our body the death of Jesus, so that the life of Jesus may also be revealed in our body. For we who are alive are always being given over to death for Jesus' sake, so that his life may be revealed in our mortal body. So then, death is at work in us, but life is at work in you. It is written: "I believed; therefore I have spoken." With that same spirit of faith we also believe and therefore speak, because we know that the one who raised the Lord Jesus from the dead will also raise us with Jesus and present us with you in his presence. All this is for your benefit, so that the grace that is reaching more and more people may cause thanksgiving to overflow to the glory of God. Therefore we do not lose heart. Though outwardly we are wasting away, yet inwardly we are being renewed day by day. For our light and momentary troubles are achieving for us an eternal glory that far outweighs them all. So we fix our eyes not on what is seen, but on what is unseen. For what is seen is temporary, but what is unseen is eternal.

37. 2 Timothy 3:12. In fact, everyone who wants to live a godly life in Christ Jesus will be persecuted, while evil men and impostors will go from bad to worse, deceiving and being deceived.

38. Matthew 16:21-26 From that time on Jesus began to explain to his disciples that he must go to Jerusalem and suffer many things at the hands of the elders, chief priests and teachers of the law, and that he must be killed and on the third day be raised to life. Peter took him aside and began to rebuke him. "Never, Lord!" he said. "This shall never happen to you!" Jesus turned and said to Peter, "Get behind me, Satan! You are a stumbling block to me; you do not have in mind the things of God, but the things of men." Then Jesus said to his disciples, "If anyone would come after me, he must deny himself and take up his cross and follow me. For whoever wants to save his will lose it, but whoever loses his life for me will find it. What good will it be for a man if he gains the whole world, yet forfeits his soul?

39. Luke 22:14-20. When the hour came, Jesus and his apostles reclined at the table. And he said to them, "I have eagerly desired to eat this Passover with you before I suffer. For I tell you, I will not eat it again until it finds fulfillment in the kingdom of God." After taking the cup, he gave thanks and said, "Take this and divide it among you. For I tell you I will not drink again of the fruit of the vine until the kingdom of God comes." And he took bread, gave thanks and broke it, and gave it to them, saying, "This is my body given for you; do this in remembrance of me." In the same way, after the supper he took the cup, saying, "This cup is the new covenant in my blood, which is poured out for you."

40. Acts 3:18-19. But this is how God fulfilled what he had foretold through all the prophets, saying that his Christ would suffer. Repent, then, and turn to God, so that your sins may be wiped out, that times of refreshing may come from the Lord.

41. Acts 26:22-23. But I have had God's help to this very day, and so I stand here and testify to small and great alike. I am saying nothing beyond what the prophets and Moses said would happen–that the Christ would suffer and, as the first to rise from the dead, would proclaim light to his own people and to the Gentiles.

42. 2 Corinthians 1:5-7. For just as the sufferings of Christ flow over into our lives, so also through Christ our comfort overflows. If we are distressed, it is for your comfort and salvation; if we are comforted, it is for your comfort, which produces in you patient endurance of the same sufferings we suffer. And our hope for you is firm, because we know that just as you share in our sufferings, so also you share in our comfort.

43. Philippians 1:29-30. For it has been

granted to you on behalf of Christ not only to believe on him, but also to suffer for him, since you are going through the same struggle you saw I had, and now hear that I still have.

44. 1 Thessalonians 5:9-11. For God did not appoint us to suffer wrath but to receive salvation through our Lord Jesus Christ. He died for us so that, whether we are awake or asleep, we may live together with him. Therefore encourage one another and build each other up, just as in fact you are doing.

45. Hebrews 9:26-28. Then Christ would have had to suffer many times since the creation of the world. But now he has appeared once for all at the end of the ages to do away with sin by the sacrifice of himself. Just as man is destined to die once, and after that to face judgment, so Christ was sacrificed once to take away the sins of many people; and he will appear a second time, not to bear sin, but to bring salvation to those who are waiting for him.

46. Psalm 116:15. Precious in the sight of the Lord is the death of his saints.

47. Romans 8:18. I consider that our present sufferings are not worth comparing with the glory that will be revealed in us.

48. Lamentations 3:12-14. He drew his bow and made me the target for his arrows. He pierced my heart with arrows from his quiver. I became the laughing-stock of all my people; they mock me in song all day long.

49. Psalm 119:51. The arrogant mock me without restraint, but I do not turn from your law.

50. Proverbs 29:10. Bloodthirsty men hate a man of integrity and seek to kill the upright.

The Art of Divine Contentment

Extract from An Exposition of Philippians 4. 11
"I have learned, in whatsoever state I am, therewith to be content."
God hath always propagated religion by sufferings. The foundation of the church hath been laid in blood, and these sanguine showers have ever made it more fruitful. Cain put the knife to Abel's throat, and ever since the church's veins had bled: but she is like the vine, which by bleeding grows, and like the palm-tree, which the more weight is laid upon it, the higher it riseth. The holiness and patience of the saints, under their persecutions, hath much added both to the growth of religion, and the crown. Basil and Tertullian observe of the primitive martyrs, that divers of the heathens seeing their zeal and constancy turned Christians: religion is that Phoenix which hath always revived and flourished in the ashes of holy men. Isaiah sawn asunder, Peter crucified at Rome with his head downwards, Cyprian, bishop of Carthage, and Polycarp of Smyrna, both martyred for religion; yet evermore the truth hath been sealed by blood, and gloriously dispersed; whereupon Julian did forbear to persecute, not out of pity, but envy, because the church grew so fast, and multiplied, as Nazianzen well observes.

Thomas Watson

Stephen's prayer

Lord Jesus, receive my spirit. ... Lord, do not hold this sin against them.

Stephen, as he was being martyred. Acts 7.59-60

Part Two

Martyrs under the Roman Empire (1)

From Nero to Didius Julinaus Pertinax

Time line 54–193

CONTENTS

1. Introduction Martyrs under the Roman Empire

General Survey

The persecutions of Christianity during the first three centuries appear like a long tragedy: first, foreboding signs; then a succession of bloody assaults of heathenism upon the religion of the cross; amidst the dark scenes of fiendish hatred and cruelty the bright exhibitions of suffering virtue; now and then a short pause; at last a fearful and desperate struggle of the old pagan empire for life and death, ending in the abiding victory of the Christian religion. Thus this bloody baptism of the church resulted in the birth of a Christian world. It was a repetition and prolongation of the crucifixion, but followed by a resurrection. Our Lord had predicted this conflict, and prepared His disciples for it. "Behold, I send you forth as sheep in the midst of wolves. They will deliver you up to councils, and in their synagogues they will scourge you; yea and before governors and kings shall ye be brought for My sake, for a testimony to them and to the Gentiles. And brother shall deliver up brother to death, and the father his child: and children shall rise up against parents, and cause them to be put to death. And ye shall be hated of all men for My name's sake: but he that endureth to the end, the same shall be saved." These, and similar words, as well as the recollection of the crucifixion and resurrection, fortified and cheered many a confessor and martyr in the dungeon and at the stake. The persecutions proceeded first from the Jews, afterwards from the Gentiles, and continued, with interruptions, for nearly three hundred years. History reports no mightier, longer and deadlier conflict than this war of extermination waged by heathen Rome against defenseless Christianity. It was a most unequal struggle, a struggle of the sword and of the cross; carnal power all on one side, moral power all on the other. It was a struggle for life and death. One or the other of the combatants must succumb. A compromise was impossible. The future of the world's history depended on the downfall of heathenism and the triumph of Christianity. Behind the scene were the powers of the invisible world, God and the prince of darkness. Justin, Tertullian, and other confessors traced the persecutions to Satan and the demons, though they did not ignore the human and moral aspects; they viewed them also as a punishment for past sins, and a school of Christian virtue. Some denied that martyrdom was an evil, since it only brought Christians the sooner to God and the glory of heaven. As war brings out the heroic qualities of men, so did the persecutions develop the patience, the gentleness, the endurance of the Christians, and prove the world-conquering power of faith.

Number of Persecutions

From the fifth century it has been customary to reckon ten great persecutions: under Nero, Domitian, Trajan, Marcus Aurelius, Septimius Severus, Maximinus, Decius, Valerian, Aurelian, and Diocletian. This number was suggested by the ten plagues of Egypt taken as types (which, however, befell the enemies of Israel, and present a contrast rather than a parallel), and by the ten horns of the Roman beast making war with the Lamb, taken for so many emperors. But the number is too great for the general persecutions, and too small for the provincial and local. Only two imperial persecutions – those, of Decius and Diocletian – extended over the empire; but Christianity was always an illegal religion from Trajan to Constantine, and subject to annoyance and violence everywhere. Some persecuting emperors – Nero, Domitian, Galerius, were monstrous tyrants, but others – Trajan, Marcus Aurelius, Decius, Diocletian – were among the best and most energetic emperors, and were prompted not so much by hatred of Christianity as by zeal for the maintenance of the laws and the power of the government. On the other hand, some of the most worthless emperors – Commodus, Caracalla, and Heliogabalus – were rather favorable to the Christians from sheer caprice. All were equally ignorant of the true character of the new religion.

The Result

The long and bloody war of heathen Rome against the church, which is built upon a rock, utterly failed. It began in Rome under Nero, it ended near Rome at the Milvian bridge, under Constantine. Aiming to exterminate, it purified. It called forth the virtues of Christian heroism, and resulted in the consolidation and triumph of the new religion. The philosophy of persecution is best expressed by the terse word of Tertullian, who lived in the midst of them, but did not see the end: "The blood of the Christians is the seed of the Church."

Religious Freedom

The blood of persecution is also the seed of civil and religious liberty. All sects, schools, and parties, whether religious or political, when persecuted, complain of injustice and plead for toleration; but few practice it when in power. The reason of this inconsistency lies in the selfishness of human nature, and in mistaken zeal for what it believes to be true and right. Liberty is of very slow, but sure growth. The ancient world of Greece and Rome generally was based upon the absolutism of the state, which mercilessly trampled under foot the individual rights of men. It is Christianity which taught and acknowledged them. The Christian apologists first proclaimed, however imperfectly, the principle of freedom of religion, and the sacred rights of conscience. Tertullian, in prophetic anticipation as it were of the modern Protestant theory, boldly tells the heathen that everybody has a natural and inalienable right to worship God according to his conviction, that all compulsion in matters of conscience is contrary to the very nature of religion, and that no form of worship has any value whatever except as far as it is a free voluntary homage of the heart. Similar views in favor of religious liberty were expressed by Justin Martyr, and at the close of our period by Lactantius, who says: "Religion cannot be imposed by force; the matter must be carried on by words rather than by blows, that the will may be affected. Torture and piety are widely different; nor is it possible for truth to be united with violence, or justice with cruelty. Nothing is so much a matter of free will as religion." The Church, after its triumph over paganism, forgot this lesson, and for many centuries treated all Christian heretics, as well as Jews and Gentiles, just as the old Romans had treated the Christians, without distinction of creed or sect. Every state-church from the times of the Christian emperors of Constantinople to the times of the Russian Czars and the South American Republics, has more or less persecuted the dissenters, in direct violation of the principles and practice of Christ and the apostles, and in carnal misunderstanding of the spiritual nature of the kingdom of heaven.

Causes of Roman Persecution.

The policy of the Roman government, the fanaticism of the superstitious people, and the self-interest of the pagan priests conspired for the persecution of a religion which threatened to demolish the tottering fabric of idolatry; and they left no expedients of legislation, of violence, of craft, and of wickedness untried, to blot it from the earth. To glance first at the relation of the Roman state to the Christian religion.

Roman Toleration

The policy of imperial Rome was in a measure tolerant. It was repressive, but not preventive. Freedom of thought was not checked by a censorship, education was left untrammelled to be arranged between the teacher and the learner. The armies were quartered on the frontiers as a protection of the empire, not employed at home as instruments of oppression, and the people were diverted from public affairs and political discontent by public amusements. The ancient religions of the conquered races were tolerated as far as they did not interfere with the interests of the state. The Jews enjoyed special protection since the time of Julius Caesar. Now so long as Christianity was regarded by the Romans as a mere sect of Judaism, it shared the hatred and contempt, indeed, but also the legal protection bestowed on that ancient national religion. Providence had so ordered it that

Christianity had already taken root in the leading cities of the empire before, its true character was understood. Paul had carried it, under the protection of his Roman citizenship, to the ends of the empire, and the Roman proconsul at Corinth refused to interfere with his activity on the ground that it was an internal question of the Jews, which did not belong to his tribunal. The heathen statesmen and authors, even down to the age of Trajan, including the historian Tacitus and the younger Pliny, considered the Christian religion as a vulgar superstition, hardly worthy of their notice. But it was far too important a phenomenon, and made far too rapid progress to be long thus ignored or despised. So soon as it was understood as a new religion, and as, in fact, claiming universal validity and acceptance, it was set down as unlawful and treasonable, a religio illicita; and it was the constant reproach of the Christians: "You have no right to exist."

Roman Intolerance

We need not be surprised at this position. For with all its professed and actual tolerance the Roman state was thoroughly interwoven with heathen idolatry, and made religion a tool of its policy. Ancient history furnishes no example of a state without some religion and form of worship. Rome makes no exception to the general rule. "The Romano-Hellenic state religion" (says Mommsen), "and the Stoic state-philosophy inseparably combined with it were not merely a convenient instrument for every government – oligarchy, democracy, or monarchy – but altogether indispensable, because it was just as impossible to construct the state wholly without religious elements as to discover any new state religion adapted to form a substitute for the old." The piety of Romulus and Numa was believed to have laid the foundation of the power of Rome. To the favor of the deities of the republic, the brilliant success of the Roman arms was attributed. The priests and Vestal virgins were supported out of the public treasury. The emperor was ex-officio the pontifex maximus, and even an object of divine worship. The gods were national; and the eagle of Jupiter Capitolinus moved as a good genius before the world-conquering legions. Cicero lays down as a principle of legislation, that no one should be allowed to worship foreign gods, unless they were recognized by public statute. Maecenas counseled Augustus: "Honor the gods according to the custom of our ancestors, and compel others to worship them. Hate and punish those who bring in strange gods." It is true, indeed, that individuals in Greece and Rome enjoyed an almost unlimited liberty for expressing skeptical and even impious sentiments in conversation, in books and on the stage. We need only refer to the works of Aristophanes, Lucian, Lucretius, Plautus, Terence. But a sharp distinction was made then, as often since by Christian governments, between liberty of private thought and conscience, which is inalienable and beyond the reach of legislation, and between the liberty of public worship, although the latter is only the legitimate consequence of the former. Besides, wherever religion is a matter of state-legislation and compulsion, there is almost invariably a great deal of hypocrisy and infidelity among the educated classes, however often it may conform outwardly, from policy, interest or habit, to the forms and legal acquirements of the established creed. The senate and emperor, by special edicts, usually allowed conquered nations the free practice of their worship even in Rome; not, however, from regard for the sacred rights of conscience, but merely from policy, and with the express prohibition of making proselytes from the state religion; hence severe laws were published from time to time against transition to Judaism.

Obstacles to the Toleration of Christianity

To Christianity, appearing not as a national religion, but claiming to be the only true universal one making its converts among every people and every sect, attracting Greeks and Romans in much larger numbers than Jews, refusing to compromise with any form of idolatry, and threatening in fact the very existence of the Roman state religion, even this limited toleration could not be granted.

The same all-absorbing political interest of Rome dictated here the opposite course, and Tertullian is hardly just in changing the Romans with inconsistency for tolerating the worship of all false gods, from whom they had nothing to fear, and yet prohibiting the worship of the only true God who is Lord over all. Born under Augustus, and crucified under Tiberius at the sentence of the Roman magistrate, Christ stood as the founder of a spiritual universal empire at the head of the most important epoch of the Roman power, a rival not to be endured. The reign of Constantine subsequently showed that the free toleration of Christianity was the death-blow to the Roman state religion. Then, too, the conscientious refusal of the Christians to pay divine honors to the emperor and his statue, and to take part in any idolatrous ceremonies at public festivities, their aversion to the imperial military service, their disregard for politics and depreciation of all civil and temporal affairs as compared with the spiritual and eternal interests of man, their close brotherly union and frequent meetings, drew upon them the suspicion of hostility to the Caesars and the Roman people, and the unpardonable crime of conspiracy against the state. The common people also, with their polytheistic ideas, abhorred the believers in the one God as atheists and enemies of the gods. They readily gave credit to the slanderous rumors of all sorts of abominations, even incest and cannibalism, practiced by the Christians at their religious assemblies and love-feasts, and regarded the frequent public calamities of that age as punishments justly inflicted by the angry gods for the disregard of their worship. In North Africa arose the proverb: "If God does not send rain, lay it to the Christians." At every inundation, or drought, or famine, or pestilence, the fanatical populace cried: "Away with the atheists! To the lions with the Christians!" Finally, persecutions were sometimes started by priests, jugglers, artificers, merchants, and others, who derived their support from the idolatrous worship. These, like Demetrius at Ephesus, and the masters of the sorceress at Philippi, kindled the fanaticism and indignation of the mob against the new religion for its interference with their gains.

Trajan, one of the best and most praiseworthy emperors, honored as the "father of his country," but, like his friends, Tacitus and Pliny, wholly ignorant of the nature of Christianity, was the first to pronounce it in form a proscribed religion, as it had been all along in fact. He revived the rigid laws against all secret societies, and the provincial officers applied them to the Christians, on account of their frequent meetings for worship. His decision regulated the governmental treatment of the Christians for more than a century . It is embodied in his correspondence with the younger Pliny, who was governor of Bithynia in Asia Minor from 109 to 111. Pliny came in official contact with the Christians. He himself saw in that religion only a "depraved and immoderate superstition," and could hardly account for its popularity. He reported to the emperor that this superstition was constantly spreading, not only in the cities, but also in the villages of Asia Minor, and captivated people of every age, rank, and sex, so that the temples were almost forsaken, and the sacrificial victims found no sale. To stop this progress, he condemned many Christians to death, and sent others, who were Roman citizens, to the imperial tribunal. But he requested of the emperor further instructions, whether, in these efforts, he should have respect to age; whether he should treat the mere bearing of the Christian name as a crime, if there were no other offence. To these inquiries Trajan replied: "You have adopted the right course, my friend, with regard to the Christians; for no universal rule, to be applied to all cases, can be laid down in this matter. They should not be searched for; but when accused and convicted, they should be punished; yet if any one denies that be has been a Christian, and proves it by action, namely, by worshiping our gods, he is to be pardoned upon his repentance, even though suspicion may still cleave to him from his antecedents. But anonymous accusations must not be admitted in any criminal process; it sets a bad example, and is contrary to our age" (i.e. to the spirit of Trajan's government). This decision was much milder than might have been expected from a heathen emperor of the old Roman stamp. Tertullian charges it with self- contradiction, as both cruel and lenient, forbidding the search for Christians and yet commanding their punishment, thus declaring them innocent and guilty at the same time. But the emperor evidently proceeded on political principles, and thought that a transient and contagious enthusiasm, as Christianity in his judgment was, could be suppressed sooner by leaving it unnoticed, than by openly assailing it. He wished to ignore it as much as possible. But every day it forced itself more and more upon public attention, as it spread with the irresistible power of truth. This rescript might give occasion, according to the sentiment of governors, for extreme severity towards Christianity as a secret union and a *religio illicita*. Even the humane Pliny tells us that he applied the rack to tender women.

Syria and Palestine suffered heavy persecutions in this reign. Symeon, bishop of Jerusalem, and, like his predecessor James, a kinsman of Jesus, was accused by fanatical Jews, and crucified A.D. 107, at the age of a hundred and twenty years. In the same year (or probably between 110 and 116) the distinguished bishop Ignatius of Antioch was condemned to death, transported to Rome, and thrown before wild beasts in the Colosseum. The story of his martyrdom has no doubt been much embellished, but it must have some foundation in fact, and is characteristic of the legendary martyrology of the ancient church. Our knowledge of Ignatius is derived from his disputed epistles, and a few short notices by Irenaeus and Origen. While his existence, his position in the early Church, and his martyrdom are admitted, everything else about him is called in question. How many epistles he wrote, and when he wrote them, how much truth there is in the account of his martyrdom, and when it took place, when it was written up, and by whom – all are undecided, and the subject of protracted controversy. He was, according to tradition, a pupil of the Apostle John, and by his piety so commended himself to the Christians in Antioch that he was chosen bishop, the second after Peter, Euodius being, the first. But although he was a man of apostolic character and governed the church with great care, he was personally not satisfied, until he should be counted worthy of sealing his testimony with his blood, and thereby attaining to the highest seat of honor. The coveted crown came to him at last and his eager and morbid desire for martyrdom was gratified. The emperor Trajan, in 107, came to Antioch, and there threatened with persecution all who refused to sacrifice to the gods. Ignatius was tried for this offence, and proudly confessed himself a "Theophorus" ("bearer of God") because, as he said, he had Christ within his breast. Trajan condemned him to be thrown to the lions at Rome. The sentence was executed with all haste. Ignatius was immediately bound in chains, and taken over land and sea, accompanied by ten soldiers, whom he denominated his "leopards," from Antioch to Seleucia, to Smyrna, where he met Polycarp, and whence be wrote to the churches, particularly to that in Rome; to Troas, to Neapolis, through Macedonia to Epirus, and so over the Adriatic to Rome. He was received by the Christians there with every manifestation of respect, but would not allow them to avert or even to delay his martyrdom. It was on the 20th day of December, 107, that he was thrown into the amphitheater: immediately the wild beasts fell upon him, and soon naught remained of his body but a few bones, which were carefully conveyed to Antioch as an inestimable treasure. The faithful friends who had accompanied him from home dreamed that night that they saw him; some that he was standing by Christ, dropping with sweat as if he had just come from his great labor. Comforted by these dreams they returned with the relics to Antioch.

Philip Scaff, History of the Christian Church, chapters 13–15

Christians in the Age of the Martyrs: A Defense by the Apologists

The Roman authorities were at first indifferent to Christianity. But they soon showed their hostility to Christians as soon as they refused to worship the ancient pagan deities of Rome, as

Table of persecutions under the Roman Empire: 54-193

EMPEROR	DATES	CONDITIONS	FAMOUS MARTYRS
Nero	54-68	Persecution 64-68	Peter, Paul
Galba, Otho,68-9 Vitellius			
Vespasian	69-79		
Titus	79-81		
Domitian	81-96	Christians charged with atheism	Flavius Clemens, consul and cousin of the Emperor, his wife Domitilla, and Acilius Glabrio, ex-consul
Nerva		96-8	
Trajan	98-117	Pliny the Younger, governor of Bithynia (Letters of Pliny and Trajan, x. 96) instructed in 112 1 Christians were not to be sought out, and anonymous accusations were to be neglected. **2** Those who were regularly accused and who professed to be Christians were to be punished. **3** People who had never been Christians, or who had stopped being Christians, provided they sacrificed, were pardoned These guidelines were followed for the next hundred years, until Septimius Severus.	Ignatius
Hadrian	117-138	Comparative lack of persecution	
Antoninus Pius	138-61	Polycarp	
Marcus Aurelius	161-80	Carpus, Papylus, Agathonica Justin and companions Scillitan martyrs Martyrs of Lyons	
Commodus	180-92	Very little persecution	
Pertinax, Didius Julianus	193	Very little persecution	

well as the emperor. The Christians were accused of disloyalty to their fatherland, of atheism, of hatred towards mankind, of hidden crimes, such as incest, infanticide and ritual cannibalism; likewise they were held responsible for all natural calamities, such as plagues, floods, famines, and even the fire of Rome.

The Christian religion was proclaimed "strana et illicita – strange and unlawful," Senatorial decree AD 35; "exitialis – deadly,"and "detestabilis – hateful," Tacitus; "prava et immodica – wicked and unbridled," Plinius; "nova et malefica – new and harmful" (Svetonius); "tenebrosa et lucifuga – mysterious and opposed to light," Minucius. It was therefore outlawed and persecuted, because it was considered the most dangerous enemy of the power of Rome, which was based upon the ancient national religion and on the emperor's worship.

The first three centuries constitute the age of Martyrs, which ended in 313 with the edict of Milan, by which the emperors Constantine and Licinius gave freedom to the Church. The persecution was not always continuous and universal, nor equally cruel and bloody. Periods of persecution were followed by periods of relative peace.

Christians faced persecution with courage, a very large percentage with heroism, but they did not submit to it without opposition. They defended themselves by refuting the accusations of those crimes as being false and groundless.

In the "Apologies" ("defenses"), prepared by the Christian writers of the time, and often addressed to the emperors, the Christians protested vigorously against their being condemned unjustly, without being known and without being convicted. According to the Apologies, the principle of the senatorial law "Non licet vos esse – you have no right to exist" is unjustifiable and unlawful, because Christians are honest citizens, respectful of laws, loyal to the emperor, hard-working and exemplary both in their private and public life.

1. The Letter to Diognetus

The Letter to Diognetus is apology by an unknown author from the second century. Diognetus appears to have been a high official, and perhaps, like Pliny, was at a loss to know why he was compelled to take action against the Christians. His informant describes him as "seeking earnestly to know what God they believe in, and what that worship of him is which enables them to despise the world, and to brave death."

THEY ARE MEN LIKE OTHERS

Christians are not different because of their country or the language they speak or the way they dress. They do not isolate themselves in their cities nor use a private language; even the life they lead has nothing strange.

Their doctrine does not originate from the elaborate disquisitions of intellectuals, nor do they follow, as many do, philosophical systems which are the fruit of human thinking. They live in Greek or in barbarian (foreign) cities, as the case may be, and adapt themselves to local traditions in dress, food and all usage. Yet they testify to a way which, in the opinion of the many, has something extraordinary about it.

Anonymous Letter to Diognetus

THEY DWELL ON EARTH, BUT ARE CITIZENS OF HEAVEN

They live in their own countries and are strangers. They loyally fulfil their duties as citizens, but are treated as foreigners. Every foreign land is for them a fatherland and every fatherland, foreign.

They marry like everyone, they have children, but they do not abandon their new-born. They have the table in common, but not the bed. They are in the flesh, but do not live according to the flesh (2 Cor 10,3; Rom 8, 12-15). They dwell on earth, but are citizens of heaven.

They obey the laws of the state, but in their lives they go beyond the law. They love everyone, yet are persecuted by everyone. No one really knows them, but all condemn them. They are killed, but go on living. They are poor, but enrich many (2 Cor 6.9-10). They have nothing, but abound in everything. but in that contempt they find glory before God. Their honor is insulted, while their justice is acknowledged.

Anonymous Letter to Diognetus

THEY ANSWER WITH KIND WORDS

When they are cursed, they bless. When they are insulted, they answer with kind words (1 Cor 4,12-13). They do good to others and are punished like evil-doers. When they are punished, they rejoice, as if they were given life. The Jews make war against them as if they were a foreign race. The Greek persecute them, but those who hate them , cannot tell the reason for their hatred.

Anonymous Letter to Diognetus

THEY ARE IN THE WORLD AS THE SOUL IS IN THE BODY

In the way the Christians are in the world, so the soul is in the body. As the soul is diffused in all parts of the body, so Christians are spread in the various cities of the earth. The soul lives in the body, but is not of the body; so Christians live in the world, but are not of the world. As the invisible soul is imprisoned in a visible body, so Christians are a reality quite visible in the world, while the spiritual worship they give to God is invisible.

As the flesh hates the spirit and fights

against it, though not receiving any offence from it, but only because the spirit hinders it in its savoring of harmful joys and pleasures; so the world hates the Christians who have done it no harm, merely because they oppose a way of life based on mere pleasure.

As the soul loves the body and its limbs, which hate it in return, thus Christians love those who hate them. The soul, though it sustains the body, is enclosed in it. So Christians, though they are a support to the world, are confined in the world as a prison. The immortal soul lives in a mortal tent, so Christians live like strangers among corruptible things, awaiting the incorruptibility of heaven.

By mortifying itself in food and drink, the soul is refined and strengthened; so Christians, maltreated and persecuted, grow in number every day. God has assigned them such a high state that they are never to abandon it.

Anonymous Letter to Diognetus

2. Books to Autolicus

The "Books to Autolicus" by Theophilus of Antioch was also written in the second century.

The Christians pay homage to the emperor and pray for him

I shall pay homage to the emperor, but will not adore him; I shall instead pray for him. I adore the true and only God, by whom I know the sovereign was made. Well now, you might ask me: "Why don"t you adore the emperor?". The emperor, given authority by God, must be honored with a proper respect, but he must not be adored.

You see, he is not God; he is only a man whom God has placed in that office not to be adored, but in order that he exercise justice on earth. In a way this authority was entrusted to him by God. As the emperor may not tolerate that his title be taken over by those subject to him, so no one may be adored, save God.

The sovereign must therefore be honored with sentiments of reverence; we must obey him and pray for him: In this way God's will is done.

The life of Christians proves the greatness and beauty of their religion

We find out that Christians have a wise self-control, practice temperance, marry only once, keep chaste, refuse injustice, uproot sin, practice justice, observe the law, have a positive appreciation of piety. God is acknowledged, and truth is regarded as the supreme law.

Grace guards them; peace protects them; the Sacred Word guides them, wisdom teaches them; eternal life directs them. God is their king.

The Book to Auloticus

3. The "Apology" by Aristides

The "Apology" by Aristides also comes from the second century.

Christians observe the divine laws

Christians bear the divine laws impressed on their hearts and observe them in the hope of a future life. For this reason they do not commit adultery, or fornication; don't bear false witness; don't misappropriate the money they have received on deposit; don't crave for what is not due to them; honor father and mother, do good to their neighbor; and when they are appointed judges, judge rightly.

They don't adore idols in human form; whatever they don't want others do to them, they do not do it to anyone. They don't eat meat offered to the gods, because it is contaminated: Their daughters are pure and keep their virginity and shun prostitution; men abstain from every illegitimate union and from all impurity; likewise their women are chaste, in the hope of the great recompense in the next life.

They are kind and charitable

They help those who offend them, making friends of them; do good to their enemies. They don't adore idols; they are kind, good, modest, sincere, they love one another; don't despise widows; protect the orphans; those who have much give without grumbling, to those in need. When they meet strangers, they invite them to their homes with joy, for they recognize them as true brothers, not natural but spiritual.

When a poor man dies, if they become aware, they contribute according to their means for his funeral; if they come to know that some people are persecuted or sent to prison or condemned for the sake of Christ's name, they put their alms together and send them to those in need. If they can do it, they try to obtain their release. When a slave or a beggar is in need of help, they fast two or three days, and give him the food they had prepared for themselves, because they think that he too should be joyful , as he has been called to be joyful like themselves.

THEY LIVE IN JUSTICE AND SANCTITY

They strictly observe the commandments of the Lord, by living in a saintly and right way, as the Lord God has prescribed to them; they give Him thanks each morning and evening for all food and drink and every other thing.

These are, o emperor, their laws; the goods they have to ask God, they ask Him, and so they pass through this world till the end of time; because God has subjected everything to them. Therefore they are grateful to Him, because the whole universe and all creation have been made for them. Surely these people have found truth.

Apology by Aristides

4. "The Apologeticus"

"The Apologeticus" was written by Tertullian, c. 150 – c. 212

CHRISTIANS ARE NOT USELESS AND UNPRODUCTIVE

We are accused of being unproductive in the various fields of activity. But how can you say this of men who live with you, eat with you, wear the same clothes, follow the same way of life and have the same necessities of life?

We remember to give thanks to God, our Lord and Creator, and do not refuse any fruit of his work. There is no doubt that we make use of things with moderation and not in an evil or unrestrained way. We live together with you and often attend the forum, the market-place, the baths, the shops and workshops, the stables, taking part in all activities.

We also are at sea together with you, we serve in the army, we till the land, we carry on trade, we exchange goods and put on sale, for your benefit, the fruits of our work. I really cannot understand how we may appear useless and unproductive for your affairs, when we live with you and for you.

Surely, there are some people who have good grounds for complaining about Christians, as they cannot do any business with them. They are the masters of prostitutes, the procurers and their accomplices; then there come the criminals, the murderers through poison, the sorcerers, the fortune-tellers, the wizards, the astrologers.

What an unbelievable thing is to be unproductive for such people!... And finally, you will never find any Christian in prison, unless he be there for religious reasons.

We have learnt from God to live honest lives.

The Apologeticus, Tertullian

LIST OF THE TEN PERSECUTIONS OF THE EARLY CHRISTIANS BY THE ROMANS

Persecution has been the common lot of Christians ever since the death of Jesus Christ. The persecutions leveled against the Romans against the Christian Church can be divided into ten main ones. Each one is associated with a Roman Emperor.

1. Nero

Nero (Roman emperor AD 54–68), persecution stirred up in AD 64. In this persecution the apostle Peter was crucified in Rome. Paul, the apostle, also suffered in this period under Nero. The first persecution ceased under Vespasian (reigned AD 69–79).

2. Domitian

Domitian (Roman emperor AD 81–96). In this persecution John, the apostle and evangelist, was exiled to Patmos. After the death of Domitian, John was released and came to Ephesus in AD 97, where he wrote his Gospel and where he lived until the time of Trajan.

3. Trajan

Trajan (Roman emperor AD 98–117). Ignatius, the bishop of Antioch suffered in this persecution.

4. Marcus Aurelius

Marcus Aurelius, his other name being Antoninus Verus (Roman emperor AD 161–180). In this persecution suffered Polycarp, the bishop of Smyrna and the Christian martyrs of Lyons and Vienne, two cities in France.

5. Septimius Severus

Septimius Severus (Roman emperor AD 193–211). This persecution had extended to northern Africa, which was a Roman province.

6. Maximinus

Maximinus, Gaius Julius Verus (Roman emperor AD 235–238).

7. Decius

Decius (Roman emperor AD 249–251). In this period Fabian was martyred; Cyprian, bishop of Carthage, was forced into exile; and Origen was imprisoned and tortured.

8. Valerian

Valerian (Roman emperor AD 253–260).

9. Aurelian

Aurelian (Roman emperor AD 270–275).

10. Diocletian

Diocletian (Gaius Aurelius Valerius Diocletianus, reigned AD 284–305) and Maximian (reigned AD 285–305) governed as emperors together. Diocletian began his furious persecution against the Christians in 303. The emperor ordered the doors of the Christian church at Nicomedia, the capital, to be barred, and then burnt the edifice with 600 Christians within. Many edicts were issued by him against Christians. Churches were demolished, Christian books were seized and burnt, Christians were persecuted, imprisoned, tortured and killed. The persecution brought a considerable number of martyrs. The persecution continued until 313, when Emperor Constantine set the Christians at liberty and proclaimed religious freedom.
Eusebius, Church History

The Church History of Eusebius

The best source about these ten persecutions is the *Church History* of Eusebius of Caesarea. Eusebius (c AD 260–340) was an eyewitness of many martyrdoms in Caesarea (an important city in Palestine) during the tenth persecution stirred up by Diocletian. After the persecution ended in 313, Eusebius became the bishop of Caesarea. Eusebius was one of the most voluminous writers of antiquity. His most important work is the Church History, which gives an account of the history of Christianity in ten books from the time of Jesus Christ down to AD 324, the time of Emperor Constantine and the defeat of Licinius. This work refers to many prominent figures of the first three centuries and contains many original sources.

Eusebius as a writer

Eusebius was one of the most voluminous writers of antiquity, and his labors covered almost every field of theological learning. In the words of J.B. Lightfoot he was "historian, apologist, topographer, exegete, critic, preacher, dogmatic writer, in turn. . . . If the permanent utility of an author's labors may be taken as a test of literary excellence, Eusebius will hold a very high place indeed. *The Ecclesiastical History* is unique and indispensable. The Chronicle is the vast storehouse of information relating to the ancient monarchies of the world. The Preparation and Demonstration are the most important contributions to theology in their own province. Even the minor works, such as the *Martyrs of Palestine*, the *Life of Constantine*, the *Questions addressed to*

Stephanus and to Marinus, and others, would leave an irreparable blank, if they were obliterated. And the same permanent value attaches also to his more technical treatises. The Canons and Sections have never yet been superseded for their particular purpose. *The Topography of Palestine* is the most important contribution to our knowledge in its own department. In short, no ancient ecclesiastical writer has laid posterity under heavier obligations."

The Church History

BOOK 1: OUTLINE

1 It is my purpose to write an account of the successions of the holy apostles, as well as of the times which have elapsed from the days of our Savior to our own; and to relate the many important events which are said to have occurred in the history of the Church; and to mention those who have governed and presided over the Church in the most prominent parishes, and those who in each generation have proclaimed the divine word either orally or in writing.

2 It is my purpose also to give the names and number and times of those who through love of innovation have run into the greatest errors, and, proclaiming themselves discoverers of knowledge falsely so-called have like fierce wolves unmercifully devastated the flock of Christ.

3 It is my intention, moreover, to recount the misfortunes which immediately came upon the whole Jewish nation in consequence of their plots against our Savior, and to record the ways and the times in which the divine word has been attacked by the Gentiles, and to describe the character of those who at various periods have contended for it in the face of blood and of tortures, as well as the confessions which have been made in our own days, and finally the gracious and kindly succor which our Savior has afforded them all.

Eusebius, Church History, Book 1, chapter 1

Eusebius the historian

The glorious struggles of the most blessed martyrs, for the honor of Christ the Lord and of our God, are celebrated by perpetual services and an annual solemnity, that while our faithful people know the faith of the martyrs, they may also rejoice in their triumphs, and may rest assured that it is by the protection of these that they themselves are to be protected. For it is held in repute that Eusebius the historian, of sacred memory, bishop of the city of C'sarea, a most blessed priest of excellent life, very learned also in ecclesiastical matters, and to be venerated for his extraordinary carefulness, set forth for every city, in so far as the truth was able to be ascertained, the Holy Spirit announcing the deeds that had been done, – inasmuch as the cities of single provinces and localities or towns have merited being made famous by the heavenly triumphs of martyrs, – set forth, I say, in the time of what rulers the innumerable persecutions were inflicted at the command of officials. Who, although he has not described entire the sufferings of individual martyrs, yet has truly intimated why they ought to be described or celebrated by faithful and devoted Christians. Thus this faithful husbandman has cultivated the grace of God, which has been scattered abroad in all the earth, while, as it were, from a single grain of wheat, plenteous harvests are produced on account of the fertility of the field, and go on in multiplied abundance. So through the narration of the above-mentioned man, diffused from the fountain of a single book, with the ever-spreading writings of the faithful, the celebrating of the sufferings of the martyrs has watered all the earth.

An unknown author in the Passion of the Holy Valerian

2. The martyrdoms

PERSECUTIONS UNDER EMPEROR NERO

The first persecution in the primitive ages of the church was under Nero Domitius, the sixth Emperor of Rome, AD 67. The barbarities inflicted on the Christians, during the first persecution, were such as excited the sympathy of even the Romans themselves. Nero nicely refined upon cruelty, and contrived all manner of punishments for his victims. He had some sewed up in the skins of wild beats, and then worried by dogs till they expired; and others dressed in shirts made stiff with wax, fixed to axle-trees, and set on fire in his garden. This persecution was general throughout the Roman Empire; but it increased rather than diminished the spirit of Christianity. Besides St Paul and St Peter, many others, whose names have not been transmitted to posterity, and who were mostly their converts and followers, suffered.

Among other diabolical outrages, he ordered that the city of Rome should be set on fire, which was done by his officers. While the city was in flames, he went up to the tower of Maecenas, played upon his harp, sung the song of the burning of Troy, and declared that he wished the ruin of all things before his death. Among the noble buildings burnt was the Circus, the place appropriated to civic sports: it was half a mile in length, of an oval form, with rows of seats rising above each other, and capable of receiving with ease upwards of 100,000 spectators. This dreadful conflagration continued nine days.

Nero, finding that a severe odium was cast upon him, determined to charge the whole upon the Christians, at once to excuse himself and have an opportunity of fresh persecutions. But the savagery of this inhuman monster, so far from crushing out the faith which he hated, only tended, in God's good providence, to its extension. The charred ruins of the noble Circus, the bleeding bodies of the slaughtered Christians, the desolated city, when contrasted with the meek, inoffensive lives of those who suffered such tortures, and to whose account the tyrant dared to lay the destruction of that city, exercised an influence among the people in favor of Christianity, the extent of which it is impossible to overrate.

Erastus, the chamberlain of Corinth; Aristarchus, the Macedonian; Trophimus, an Ephesian by birth, and a Gentile by religion, converted by St Paul; Joseph, commonly called Barsabas, and usually deemed one of the seventy; and Ananias, Bishop of Damascus, are among those who perished during this persecution.

John Foxe, The Book of Martyrs, revised with notes and an appendix by W. Bramley-Moore, London, 1869, pp 7-10

Early martyrs of Rome
30 June 64

Ancient Roman historians (non-Christian) relate the first wholesale massacres of Christians by the Roman government as follows: In the year 64, much of the city of Rome burned. It was widely speculated that the Emperor Nero had ordered the fire in order that he might rebuild to his fancy. In order to divert suspicion from himself, Nero accused the Christians of setting the fires, and had many of them put to death in various cruel ways: eaten in the arena by wild beasts, covered with pitch and burned as torches to light the Emperor's nightly revels, and so on. The persecution appears to have been confined to Rome.

James Kiefer, Christian Biographies, By kind permission

The First Persecution

The Persecution under Nero in which Paul and Peter were honored at Rome with Martyrdom on Behalf of Religion

When the government of Nero was now firmly established, he began to plunge into unholy pursuits, and armed himself even against the religion of the God of the universe. To describe the greatness of his depravity does not lie within the plan of the present work. As there are many indeed that have recorded his history in most accurate narratives, every one may at his pleasure learn from them the coarseness of the man's extraordinary madness, under the influence of which, after he had accomplished the destruction of so many myriads without any reason, he ran into such blood-guiltiness that he did not spare even his nearest relatives and dearest friends, but destroyed his mother and his brothers and his wife, with very many others of his own family as he would private and public enemies, with various kinds of deaths. But with all these things this particular in the catalogue of his crimes was still wanting, that he was the first of the emperors who showed himself an enemy of the divine religion. The Roman Tertullian is likewise a witness of this. He writes as follows: "Examine your records. There you will find that Nero was the first that persecuted this doctrine, particularly then when after subduing all the east, he exercised his cruelty against all at Rome. We glory in having such a man the leader in our punishment. For whoever knows him can understand that nothing was condemned by Nero unless it was something of great excellence." Thus publicly announcing himself as the first among God's chief enemies, he was led on to the slaughter of the apostles. It is, therefore, recorded that Paul was beheaded in Rome itself, and that Peter likewise was crucified under Nero. This account of Peter and Paul is substantiated by the fact that their names are preserved in the cemeteries of that place even to the present day. It is confirmed likewise by Caius, a member of the Church, who arose under Zephyrinus, bishop of Rome. He, in a published disputation with Proclus, the leader of the Phrygian heresy, speaks as follows concerning the places where the sacred corpses of the aforesaid apostles are laid: "But I can show the trophies of the apostles. For if you will go to the Vatican or to the Ostian way, you will find the trophies of those who laid the foundations of this church." And that they both suffered martyrdom at the same time is stated by Dionysius, bishop of Corinth, in his epistle to the Romans, in the following words: "You have thus by such an admonition bound together the planting of Peter and of Paul at Rome and Corinth. For both of them planted and likewise taught us in our Corinth. And they taught together in like manner in Italy, and suffered martyrdom at the same time." I have quoted these things in order that the truth of the history might be still more confirmed.

Eusebius of Caesarea, Church History, Book 2, chapter 26

AN HISTORIAN'S VIEWPOINT: TACITUS

The secular historian, Tacitus, relates that when the city of Rome was destroyed by fire (AD 64) the report was widely circulated and believed that the emperor himself had caused the fire, or had at least prevented it from being put out.

To stifle the report, Nero provided others to bear the accusation, in the shape of people who were commonly called "Christians," in detestation of their abominable character. These he visited with every refinement of punishment. First some were arrested who confessed [that they were Christians], and then, on received information, an immense number were convicted, not so much on the charge of arson but on the charge of ill-will towards mankind in general. Their deaths were turned into a form of amusement. They were wrapped in the skins of wild beasts to be torn in pieces by dogs, or were fastened to crosses to be set on fire, and, when the daylight came to an end, were burned for an illumination at night. Nero threw open his own gardens for the spectacle, and made it the occasion of a circus exhibition, mingling with the populace in the costume of a driver, or standing in his chariot. Sympathy was eventually felt for the sufferers, although the objects of it were guilty people who deserved the most extreme punishment: people felt that they were being destroyed not for the benefit of the public but to serve the cruel purpose of one man.

Tacitus, Annals, xv.44; quoted by A. J. Mason, The Historic Martyrs of the Primitive Church, Longmans, 1905, pp. 7-8

VITALIS C. 62

Vitalis was born in Milan and lived in Ravenna where he saw a Christian named Ursicinus, who was condemned to lose his head for his faith, who stood aghast at the sight of death, but seemed happy to yield up his life. Vitalis was extremely moved by this spectacle. The honor of God, which was in danger of being insulted by sin, and the soul of a brother in Christ which appeared to be upon the very brink of apostasy were alarming objects to awake his zeal. He boldly and successfully encouraged Ursicinus to triumph over death, and after his martyrdom, carried off his body, and respectfully interred it.

The judge, whose name was Paulinus, being informed of what he had done, caused him to be apprehended, stretched on the rack, and, after other torments, to be buried alive in a place called Palmtree, in Ravenna. Vitalis' wife, upon returning to Ravenna from Milan, was beaten to death by certain peasants, because she refused to join them in an idolatrous festival and riot.

Alban Butler, The Lives of the Saints, Dublin, 1833, vol I, pp 527-8

Felicitas and her seven sons

A pious widow, Felicitas, who had seven sons, lived in Rome. By the public and edifying example of this lady and her whole family, many idolaters were moved to renounce the worship of their false gods, and to embrace the faith of Christ, which Christians were likewise encouraged by so illustrious a pattern openly to profess. This raised the spleen of the heathenish priests, who complained to the emperor Antoninus that the boldness with which Felicitas publicly practiced the Christian religion, drew many from the worship of the immortal gods who were the guardians and protectors of the empire, and that it was a constant insult on them; who, on that account, were extremely offended and angry with the city and whole state. They added, that in order to appease them, it was necessary to compel this lady and her children to sacrifice to them. Antoninus being himself superstitious was prevailed upon by this remonstrance to send an order to Publius the prefect of Rome, to take care that the priests should be satisfied, and the gods appeased in this matter.

Publius caused the mother and her sons to be apprehended and brought before him. When this was done he took Felicitas aside, and used the strongest inducements to bring her freely to sacrifice to the gods, that he might not be obliged to proceed with severity against her and her sons; but she returned him this answer: "Do not think to frighten me by threats, or to win me by fair speeches. The spirit of God within me will not suffer me to be overcome by Satan, and will make me victorious over all your assaults."

Publius said in a great rage: "Unhappy woman, is it possible you should think death so desirable as not to permit even your children to live, but force me to destroy them by the most cruel torments?"

"My children," replied Felicitas, "will live eternally with Christ if they are faithful to him; but must expect eternal death if they sacrifice to idols."

The next day the prefect, sitting in the square of Mars before his temple, sent for Felicitas and her sons, and said to Felicitas, "Take pity on your children, Felicitas; they are in the bloom of youth, and may aspire to the greatest honors and preferments."

The holy mother answered, "Your pity is really impiety, and the compassion to which you exhort me would make me the most cruel of mothers."

Then turning to her children, Felicitas said, "My son, look up to heaven where Jesus Christ expects you. Be faithful in his love, and fight courageously for your souls."

Publius being exasperated at this behavior, commanded her to be cruelly buffeted, saying, "You are insolent indeed, to give them such advice as this in my presence, in contempt of orders of our princes."

The judge then called the children to him, one after another, and used many artful speeches, mingling promises with threats to induce them to adore the gods.

Januarius, the eldest, experienced his assaults the first, but resolutely answered him, "You advise me to do a thing that is very foolish, and contrary to all reason; but I confide in my Lord Jesus Christ, that he will preserve me from such an impiety." Publius ordered him to be stripped and cruelly scourged, after which he sent him back to prison.

Felix, the second brother, was called next, and commanded to sacrifice. But the generous youth replied, "There is only one God. To him we offer the sacrifice of our hearts. We will never forsake the love which we owe to Jesus Christ. Employ all your artifices; exhaust all inventions of cruelty. You will never be able to overcome our faith."

The other brothers made their answers separately, that they feared not a passing death, but everlasting torments; and that having before their eyes the immortal recompenses of the just, they despised the threats of men. Martialis, who spoke last, said, "All who do not confess Christ to be the true God, shall be cast into eternal flames."

The brothers, after being whipped, were remanded in prison, and the prefect, despairing to be able ever to overcome their resolution, laid the whole process before the emperor. Antoninus having read the interrogatory, gave an order that they should be sent to different judges, and condemned to different deaths. Januarius was scourged to death with whips loaded with plummets of lead. The two next, Felix and Philip, were beaten with clubs till they expired.

Sylvanus, the fourth, was thrown headlong down a steep precipice. The three youngest, Alexander, Vitalis, and Martialis, were beheaded, and the same sentence was executed upon the mother four months later.

Alban Butler, *The Lives of the Saints,* Dublin, 1833, Vol II, pp 43-44

Early Christian teaching about martyrdom

The following extract is taken from *The Didache* or *Teaching of the Twelve Apostles* or, in full, *The Teaching of the Twelve Apostles, to the Gentiles.* Scholars still debate its date and provenance but it is thought to have been written in about AD 80, and to be of Syrian origin.

Concerning the Martyrs.

That It is Reasonable for the Faithful to Supply the Wants of Those Who are Afflicted for the Sake of Christ by the Unbelievers, According to the Constitution of the Lord.

I. If any Christian, on account of the name of Christ, and love and faith towards God, be condemned by the ungodly to the games, to the beasts, or to the mines, do not ye overlook him; but send to him from your labor and your very sweat for his sustenance, and for a reward to the soldiers, that he may be eased and be taken care of; that, as far as lies in your power, your blessed brother may not be afflicted: for he that is condemned for the name of the Lord God is an holy martyr, a brother of the Lord, the son of the Highest, a receptacle of the Holy Spirit, by whom every one of the faithful has received the illumination of the glory of the holy Gospel, by being vouchsafed the incorruptible crown, and the testimony of Christ's sufferings, and the fellowship of His blood, to be made conformable to the death of Christ for the adoption of children. For this cause do you, all ye of the faithful, by your bishop, minister to the saints of your substance and of your labor. But if any one has not, let him fast a day, and set apart that, and order it for the saints. But if any one has superfluities, let him minister more to them according to the proportion of his ability. But if he can possibly sell all his livelihood, and redeem them out of prison, he will be blessed, and a friend of Christ. For if he that gives his goods to the poor be perfect, supposing his knowledge of divine things, much more is he so that does it on account of the martyrs. For such a one is worthy of God, and will fulfil His will by supplying those who have confessed Him before nations and kings, and the children of Israel; concerning whom our Lord declared, saying: "Whosoever shall confess me before men, him will I also confess before my Father." And if these be such as to be attested to by Christ before His Father, you ought not to be ashamed to go to them in the prisons. For if you do this, it will be esteemed to you for a testimony, because the real trial was to them a testimony; and your readiness will be so to you, as being partakers of their combat: for the Lord speaks somewhere to such as these, saying: "Come, ye blessed of my Father, inherit the kingdom prepared for you from the foundation of the world. For I was an hungry, and ye gave me meat; I was thirsty, and ye gave me drink; I was a stranger, and ye took me in; naked, and ye clothed me;

I was sick, and ye visited me; I was in prison, and ye came unto me. Then shall the righteous answer, and say, Lord, when saw we Thee an hungered, and fed Thee? or thirsty, and gave Thee drink? When saw we Thee naked, and clothed Thee? or sick, and visited Thee? When saw we Thee a stranger, and took Thee in? or in prison, and came unto Thee? And He will answer and say unto them, Inasmuch as ye have done it unto one of the least of these my brethren, ye have done it unto me. And these shall go away into life everlasting. Then shall He say unto them on His left hand, Depart from me, ye cursed, into everlasting fire, prepared for the devil and his angels. For I was hungry, and ye gave me no meat; I was thirsty, and ye gave me no drink; I was a stranger, and ye took me not in; naked, and ye clothed me not; sick, and in prison, and ye visited me not. Then shall they also answer and say, Lord when saw we Thee hungry, or thirsty, or a stranger, or naked, or sick, or in prison, and did not minister unto Thee? Then shall He answer and say unto them, Verily I say unto you, Inasmuch as ye have not done it unto one of the least of these, neither have ye done it unto me. And these shall go away unto everlasting punishment."

That We are to Avoid Intercourse with False Brethren When They Continue in Their Wickedness.

II. But if any one who calls himself a brother is seduced by the evil one, and acts wickedness, and is convicted and condemned to death as an adulterer, or a murderer, depart from him, that ye may be secure, and none of you may be suspected as a partner in such an abominable practice; and that no evil report may be spread abroad, as if all Christians took a pleasure in unlawful actions. Wherefore keep far from them. But do you assist with all diligence those that for the sake of Christ are abused by the ungodly and shut up in prison, or who are given over to death, or bonds, or banishment, in order to deliver your fellow-members from wicked hands. And if any one who accompanies with them is caught, and falls into misfortune, he is blessed, because he is partaker with the martyr, and is one that imitates the sufferings of Christ; for we ourselves also, when we oftentimes received stripes from Caiaphas, and Alexander, and Annas, for Christ's sake, "went out rejoicing that we were counted worthy to suffer such things for our Savior." Do you also rejoice when ye suffer such things, for ye shall be blessed in that day.

That We Ought to Afford an Helping Hand to Such as are Spoiled for the Sake of Christ, Although We Should Incur Danger Ourselves.

III. Receive also those that are persecuted on account of the faith, and who "fly from city to city" on account of the Lord's commandment; and assist them as martyrs, rejoicing that ye are made partakers of their persecution, as knowing that they are esteemed blessed by the Lord; for Himself says: "Blessed are ye when men shall reproach you, and persecute you, and say all manner of evil against you falsely, for my sake. Rejoice, and be exceeding glad, because your reward is great in heaven: for so persecuted they the prophets which were before us." And again: "If they have persecuted me, they will also persecute you." And afterwards: "If they persecute you in this city, flee ye to another. For in the world ye have tribulation: for they shall deliver you into the synagogues; and ye shall be brought before rulers and kings for my sake, and for a testimony to them." And, "He that endureth unto the end, the same shall be saved." For he that is persecuted for the sake of the faith, and bears witness in regard to Him, Christ, and endures, is truly a man of God.

That It is an Horrible and Destructive Thing to Deny Christ.

IV. But he that denies himself to be a Christian, that he may not be hated of men, and so loves his own life more than he does the Lord, in whose hand his breath is, is wretched and miserable, as being detestable and abominable, who desires to be the friend of men, but is the enemy of God, having no longer his portion with the saints, but with those that are accursed; choosing instead of the kingdom of the blessed, that eternal fire which is prepared for the devil and his angels: not being any longer hated by men, but rejected by God, and cast out from His presence. For of such a one our Lord declared, saying: "Whosoever shall deny me before men, and shall be ashamed of my name, I also will deny and be ashamed of him before my Father which is in heaven." And again He speaks thus to us ourselves, His disciples: "He that loveth father or mother more than me, is not worthy of me; and he that loveth son or daughter more than me, is not worthy of me; and he that taketh not his cross, and followeth after me, is not worthy of me. He that findeth his life, shall lose it; and he that loseth his life for my sake, shall find it. For what is a man profited, if he shall gain the whole world, and lose his own soul? or what shall a man give in exchange for his soul?" And afterwards: "Fear not them that kill the body, but are not able to kill the soul; but rather fear Him who is able to destroy both soul and body in hell."

That We Ought to Imitate Christ in Suffering, and with Zeal to Follow His Patience.

V. Every one therefore who learns any art, when he sees his master by his diligence and skill perfecting his art, does himself earnestly endeavor to make what he takes in hand like to it. If he is not able, he is not perfected in his work. We therefore who have a Master, our Lord Jesus Christ, why do we not follow His doctrine? – since He renounced repose, pleasure, glory, riches, pride, the power of revenge, His mother and brethren, nay, and moreover His own life, on account of His piety towards His Father, and His love to us the race of mankind; and suffered not only persecution and stripes, reproach and mockery, but also crucifixion, that He might save the penitent, both Jews and Gentiles. If therefore He for our sakes renounced His repose, was not ashamed of the cross, and did not esteem death inglorious, why do not we imitate His sufferings, and renounce on His account even our own life, with that patience which He gives us? For He did all for our sakes, but we do it for our own sakes: for He does not stand in need of us, but we stand in need of His mercy. He only requires the sincerity and readiness of our faith, as the Scripture says: "If thou beest righteous, what doest thou give to Him? or what will He receive at thy hand? Thy wickedness is to a man like thyself, and thy righteousness to a son of man."

That a Believer Ought Neither Rashly to Run into Danger Through Security, Nor to Be Over-Timorous Through Pusillanimity, But to Fly Away for Fear; Yet that If He Does Fall into the Enemy's Hand, to Strive Earnestly, Upon Account of the Crown that is Laid Up for Him.

VI. Let us therefore renounce our parents, and kinsmen, and friends, and wife, and children, and possessions, and all the enjoyments of life, when any of these things become an impediment to piety. For we ought to pray that we may not enter into temptation; but if we be called to martyrdom, with constancy to confess His precious name, and if on this account we be punished, let us rejoice, as hastening to immortality. When we are persecuted, let us not think it strange; let us not love the present world, nor the praises which come from men, nor the glory and honor of rulers, according as some of the Jews wondered at the mighty works of our Lord, yet did not believe on Him, for fear of the high priests and the rest of the rulers: "For they loved the praise of men more than the praise of God." But now, by confessing a good confession, we not only save ourselves, but we confirm those who are newly illuminated, and strengthen the faith of the catechumens. But if we remit any part of our confession, and deny godliness by the faintness of our persuasion, and the fear of a very short punishment, we not only deprive ourselves of everlasting glory, but we shall also become the causes of the perdition of others; and shall suffer double punishment, as affording suspicion, by our denial that that truth which we gloried in so much before is an erroneous doctrine. Wherefore neither let us be rash and hasty to thrust ourselves into dangers, for the Lord says: "Pray that ye fall not into temptation: the spirit indeed is willing, but the flesh is weak." Nor let us, when we do fall into dangers, be fearful or ashamed of our profession. For if a person, by the denial of his own hope, which is Jesus the Son of God, should be delivered from a temporary death, and the next day should fall dangerously sick upon his bed, with a distemper in his bowels, his stomach, or his head, or any of the incurable diseases, as a consumption, or gangrene, or looseness, or iliac passion, or dropsy, or colic, and has a sudden catastrophe, and departs this life; is not he deprived of the things present, and loses those eternal? Or rather, he is within the verge of eternal punishment, "and goes into outer darkness, where is weeping and gnashing of teeth." But let him who is vouchsafed the honor of martyrdom rejoice with joy in the Lord, as obtaining thereby so great a crown, and departing out of this life by his confession. Nay, though he be trot a catechumen, let him depart without trouble; for his suffering for Christ will be to him a more genuine baptism, because he does really die with Christ, but the rest only in a figure. Let him therefore rejoice in the imitation of his Master, since is it thus ordained: "Let every one be perfect, as his Master is." Now his and our Master, Jesus the Lord, was smitten for our sake: He underwent reproaches and revilings with long-suffering. He was spit upon, He was smitten on the face, He was buffeted; and when He had been scourged, He was nailed to the cross. He had vinegar and gall to drink; and when He had fulfilled all things that were written, He said to His God and Father, "Into Thy hands I commend my spirit." Wherefore let him that desires to be His disciple earnestly follow His conflicts: let him imitate His patience, knowing that, although he be burned in the fire by men, he will suffer nothing, like the three children; or if he does suffer anything, he shall receive a reward from the Lord, believing in the one and the only true God and Father, through Jesus Christ, the great High Priest, and Redeemer of our souls, and rewarder of our sufferings. To whom be glory for ever. Amen.

Several Demonstrations Concerning the Resurrection, Concerning the Sibyl, and What the Stoics Say Concerning the Bird Called the Phoenix.

VII. For the Almighty God Himself will raise us up through our Lord Jesus Christ, according to His infallible promise, and grant us a resurrection with all those that have slept from the beginning of the world; and we shall then be such as we now are in our present form, without any defect or corruption. For we shall rise incorruptible: whether we die at sea, or are scattered on the earth, or are torn to pieces by wild beasts and birds, He will raise us by His own power; for the whole world is held together by the hand of God. Now He says: "An hair of your head shall not perish." Wherefore He exhorts us, saying: "In your patience possess ye your souls." But as concerning the resurrection of the dead, and the recompense of reward for the martyrs, Gabriel speaks to Daniel: "And many of them that sleep shall arise out of the dust of the earth, some to everlasting life, and some to shame and everlasting contempt. And they that understand shall shine as the sun, and as the firmament, and as the stars." Therefore the most holy Gabriel foretold that the saints should shine like the stars: for His sacred name did witness to them, that they might understand the truth. Nor is a resurrection only declared for the martyrs, but for all men, righteous and unrighteous, godly and ungodly, that every one may receive according to his desert. For God, says the Scripture, "will bring every work into judgment, with every secret thing, whether it be good or whether it be evil." This resurrection was not believed by the Jews, when of old they said, "Our bones are withered, and we are gone." To whom God answered, and said: "Behold, I open your graves, and will bring you out of them; and I will put my Spirit into you, and ye shall live: and ye shall know that I the Lord have spoken it, and will do it." And He says by Isaiah: "The dead shall rise, and those that are in the graves shall be raised up. And those that rest in the earth shall rejoice, for the dew which is from Thee shall be healing to them." There are indeed many and various things said concerning the resurrection, and concerning the continuance of the righteous in glory, and concerning the punishment of the ungodly, their fall, rejection, condemnation, shame, "eternal fire, and endless worm." Now that, if it had pleased Him that all men should be immortal, it was in His power, He showed in the examples of Enoch and Elijah, while He did not suffer them to have any experience of death. Or if it had pleased Him in every generation to raise those that died, that this also He was able to do He hath made manifest both by Himself and by others; as when He raised the widow's son by Elijah, and the Shunammite's son by Elisha. But we are persuaded that death is not a retribution of punishment, because even the saints have undergone it; nay, even the Lord of the saints, Jesus Christ, the life of them that believe, and the resurrection of the dead. Upon this account, therefore, according to the ancient practice, for those who live in the great city, after the combats He brings a dissolution for a while, that, when He raises up every one, He may either reject him or crown him. For He that made the body of Adam out of the earth will raise up the bodies of the rest, and that of the first man, after their dissolution, (to pay what is owing to the rational nature of man; we mean the continuance in being through all ages. He, therefore, who brings on the dissolution, will Himself procure the resurrection. And He that said, "The Lord took dust from the ground, and formed man, and breathed into his face the breath of life, and man became a living soul," added after the disobedience, "Earth thou art, and unto earth shalt thou return;" the same promised us a resurrection afterwards. For says He: "All that are in the graves shall hear the voice of the Son of God, and they that hear shall live." Besides these arguments, we believe there is to be a resurrection also from the resurrection of our Lord. For it is He that raised Lazarus, when he had been in the grave four days, and Jairus' daughter, and the widow's son. It is He that raised Himself by the command of the Father in the space of three days, who is the pledge of our resurrection. For says He: "I am the resurrection and the life." Now He that brought Jonas in the space of three days, alive and unhurt, out of the belly of the whale, and the three children out of the furnace of Babylon, and Daniel out of the mouth of the lions, does not want power to raise us up also. But if the Gentiles laugh at us, and disbelieve our Scriptures, let at least their own prophetess Sibylla oblige them to believe, who says thus to them in express words:-

"But when all things shall be reduced to dust and ashes,

And the immortal God who kindled the fire shall have quenched it,

God shall form those bones and that ashes into a man again,

And shall place mortal men again as they were before.

And then shall be the judgment, wherein God will do justice,

And judge the world again. But as many mortals as have sinned through impiety

Shall again be covered under the earth;

But so many as have been pious shall live again in the world.

When God puts His Spirit into them, and gives those at once that are godly both life and favor,

Then shall all see themselves."

If, therefore, this prophetess confesses the resurrection, and does not deny the restoration of all things, and distinguishes the godly from the ungodly, it is in vain for them to deny our doctrine. Nay, indeed, they say they can show a resemblance of the resurrection, while they do not themselves believe the things they declare: for they say that there is a bird single in its kind which affords a copious demonstration of the resurrection, which they say is without a mate, and the only one in the creation. They call it a phoenix, and relate that every five hundred years it comes into Egypt, to that which is called the altar of the sun, and brings with it a great quantity of cinnamon, and cassia, and balsam-wood, and standing towards the east, as they say, and praying to the sun, of its own accord is burnt, and becomes dust; but that a worm arises again out of those ashes, and that when the same is warmed it is formed into a new-born phoenix; and when it is able to fly, it goes to Arabia, which is beyond the Egyptian countries.

If, therefore, as even themselves say, a resurrection is exhibited by the means of an irrational bird, wherefore do they vainly disparage our accounts, when we profess that He who by His power brings that into being which was not in being before, is able to restore this body, and raise it up again after its dissolution? For on account of this full assurance of hope we undergo stripes, and persecutions, and deaths. Otherwise we should to no purpose undergo such things if we had not a full assurance of these promises, whereof we profess ourselves to be the preachers. As, therefore, we believe Moses when he says, "In the beginning God made the heaven and the earth; " and we know that He did not want matter, but by His will alone brought those things into being which Christ was commanded to make; we mean the heaven, the earth, the sea, the light, the night, the day, the luminaries, the stars, the fowls, the fishes, and four-footed beasts, the creeping things, the plants, and the herbs; so also will He raise all men up by His will, as not wanting any assistance. For it is the work of the same power to create the world and to raise the dead. And then He made man, who was not a man before, of different parts, giving to him a soul made out of nothing. But now He will restore the bodies, which have been dissolved, to the souls that are still in being: for the rising again belongs to things laid down, not to things which have no being. He therefore that made the original bodies out of nothing, and fashioned various forms of them, will also again revive and raise up those that are dead. For He that formed man in the womb out of a little seed, and created in him a soul which was not in being before,-as He Himself somewhere speaks to Jeremiah, "Before I formed thee in the womb I knew thee; " and elsewhere, "I am the Lord who established the heaven, and laid the foundations of the earth, and formed the spirit of man in him," -will also raise up all men, as being His workmanship; as also the divine Scripture testifies that God said to Christ, His only-begotten, "Let us make man after our image, and after our likeness. And God made man: after the image of God made He him; male and female made He them." And the most divine and patient Job, of whom the Scripture says that it is written, that "he was to rise again with those whom the Lord raises up," speaks to God thus: "Hast not Thou milked me like milk, and curdled me like cheese? Thou hast clothed me with skin and flesh, and hast fenced me with bones and sinews. Thou hast granted me life and favor, and Thy visitation hath preserved my spirit. Having these things within me, I know that Thou canst do all things, and that nothing is impossible with Thee." Wherefore also our Savior and Master Jesus Christ says, that "what is impossible with men is possible with God." And David, the beloved of God, says: "Thine hands have made me, and fashioned me." And again: "Thou knowest my frame." And afterward: "Thou hast fashioned me, and laid Thine hand upon me. The knowledge of Thee is declared to be too wonderful for me; it is very great, I cannot attain unto it." "Thine eyes did see my substance, being yet imperfect; and all men shall be written in Thy book." Nay, and Isaiah says in his prayer to Him: "We are the clay, and Thou art the framer of us." If, therefore, man be His workmanship, made by Christ, by Him most certainly will he after he is dead be raised again, with intention either of being crowned for his good actions or punished for his transgressions. But if He, being the legislator, judges with righteousness; as He punishes the ungodly, so does He do good to and saves the faithful. And those saints who for His sake have been slain by men, "some of them He will make light as the stars, and make others bright as the luminaries," as Gabriel said to Daniel. All we of the faithful, therefore, who are the disciples of Christ, believe His promises. For He that has promised it cannot lie; as says the blessed prophet David: "The Lord is faithful in all His words, and holy in all His works." For He that framed for Himself a body out of a virgin, is also the Former of other men. And He that raised Himself from the dead, will also raise again all that are laid down. He who raises wheat out of the ground with many stalks from one grain, He who makes the tree that is cut down send forth fresh branches, He that made Aaron's dry rod put forth buds, will raise us up in glory; He that raised Him up that had the palsy whole, and healed him that had the withered hand, He that supplied a defective part to him that was born blind from clay and spittle, will raise us up; He that satisfied five thousand men with five loaves and two fishes, and caused a remainder of twelve baskets, and out of water made wine, and sent a piece of money out of a fish's mouth by me Peter to those that demanded tribute, will raise the dead. For we testify all these things concerning Him, and the prophets testify the other. We who have eaten and drunk with Him, and have been spectators of His wonder fill works, and of His life, and of His conduct, and of His words, and of His sufferings, and of His death, and of His resurrection from the dead, and who associated with Him forty days after His resurrection, and who received a command from Him to preach the Gospel to all the world, and to make disciples of all nations, and to baptize them into His death by the authority of the God of the universe, who is His Father, and by the testimony of the Spirit, who is His Comforter, – we teach you all these things which He appointed us by His constitutions, before "He was received up in our sight into heaven," to Him that sent Him. And if you will believe, you shall be happy; but if you will not believe, we shall be found innocent, and clear from your incredulity.

Concerning James the Brother of the Lord, and Stephen the First Martyr

VIII. Now concerning the martyrs, we say to you that they are to be had in all honor with you, as we honor the blessed James the bishop, and the holy Stephen our fellow-servant. For these are reckoned blessed by God, and are honored by holy men, who were pure from all transgressions, immoveable when tempted to sin, or persuaded from good works, without dispute deserving encomiums: of whom also David speaks, "Precious in the sight of the Lord is the death of His holy ones;" and Solomon says, "The memory of the just is with encomiums:" of whom also the prophet speaks, "Righteous men are taken away."

Concerning False Martyrs

IX. These things we have said concerning those that in truth have been martyrs for Christ, but not concerning false martyrs, concerning whom the oracle speaks, "The name of the ungodly is extinguished." For "a faithful witness will not lie, but an unjust witness inflames lies." For he that departs this life in his testimony without lying, for the sake of the truth, is a faithful martyr, worthy to be believed in such things wherein he strove for the word of piety by his own blood.

The Didache (The Teaching of the Twelve Apostles) chapter 5 translated and edited by J. B. Lightfoot

The Second Persecution (1)

The Persecution under Domitian

Domitian, having shown great cruelty toward many, and having unjustly put to death no small number of well-born and notable men at Rome, and having without cause exiled and confiscated the property of a great many other illustrious men, finally became a successor of Nero in his hatred and enmity toward God. He was in fact the second that stirred up a persecution against us, although his father Vespasian had undertaken nothing prejudicial to us.

Eusebius of Caesarea, Church History, Book 3, chapter 17

Domitian commands the Descendants of David to be slain

But when this same Domitian had commanded that the descendants of David should be slain, an ancient tradition says that some of the heretics brought accusation against the descendants of Jude (said to have been a brother of the Savior according to the flesh), on the ground that they were of the lineage of David and were related to Christ himself. Hegesippus relates these facts in the following words. "Of the family of the Lord there were still living the grandchildren of Jude, who is said to have been the Lord's brother according to the flesh. Information was given that they belonged to the family of David, and they were brought to the Emperor Domitian by the Evocatus. For Domitian feared the coming of Christ as Herod also had feared it. And he asked them if they were descendants of David, and they confessed that they were. Then he asked them how much property they had, or how much money they owned. And both of them answered that they had only nine thousand denarii, half of which belonged to each of them; and this property did not consist of silver, but of a piece of land which contained only thirty-nine acres, and from which they raised their taxes and supported themselves by their own labor." Then they showed their hands, exhibiting the hardness of their bodies and the callousness produced upon their hands by continuous toil as evidence of their own labor. And when they were asked concerning Christ and his kingdom, of what sort it was and where and when it was to appear, they, answered that it was not a temporal nor an earthly kingdom, but a heavenly and angelic one, which would appear at the end of the world, when he should come in glory to judge the quick and the dead, and to give unto every one according to his works. Upon hearing this, Domitian did not pass judgment against them, but, despising them as of no account, he let them go, and by a decree put a stop to the persecution of the Church. But when they were released they ruled the churches because they were witnesses and were also relatives of the Lord. And peace being established, they lived until the time of Trajan. These things are related by Hegesippus.

Tertullian also has mentioned Domitian in the following words: "Domitian also, who possessed a share of Nero's cruelty, attempted once to do the same thing that the latter did. But because he had, I suppose, some intelligence, he very soon ceased, and even recalled those whom he had banished." But after Domitian had reigned fifteen years, and Nerva had succeeded to the empire, the Roman Senate, according to the writers that record the history of those days, voted that Domitian's honors should be canceled, and that those who had been unjustly banished should return to their homes and have their property restored to them. It was at this time that the apostle John returned from his banishment in the island and took up his abode at Ephesus, according to an ancient Christian tradition.

Eusebius of Caesarea, Church History, Book 3, chapter 20

The Second Persecution (2)

The Second Persecution under Domitian, A.D. 81

The emperor Domitian, who was naturally inclined to cruelty, first slew his brother, and then raised the second persecution against the Christians. In his rage he put to death some of the Roman senators, some through malice; and others to confiscate their estates. He then commanded all the lineage of David be put to death.

Among the numerous martyrs that suffered during this persecution was Simeon, bishop of Jerusalem, who was crucified; and St. John, who was boiled in oil, and afterward banished to Patmos. Flavia, the daughter of a Roman senator, was likewise banished to Pontus; and a law was made, "That no Christian, once brought before the tribunal, should be exempted from punishment without renouncing his religion."

A variety of fabricated tales were, during this reign, composed in order to injure the Christians. Such was the infatuation of the pagans, that, if famine, pestilence, or earthquakes afflicted any of the Roman provinces, it was laid upon the Christians. These persecutions among the Christians increased the number of informers and many, for the sake of gain, swore away the lives of the innocent.

Another hardship was, that, when any Christians were brought before the magistrates, a test oath was proposed, when, if they refused to take it, death was pronounced against them; and if they confessed themselves Christians, the sentence was the same.

The following were the most remarkable among the numerous martyrs who suffered during this persecution.

Dionysius, the Areopagite, was an Athenian by birth, and educated in all the useful and ornamental literature of Greece. He then traveled to Egypt to study astronomy, and made very particular observations on the great and supernatural eclipse, which happened at the time of our Savior's crucifixion.

The sanctity of his conversation and the purity of his manners recommended him so strongly to the Christians in general, that he was appointed bishop of Athens.

Nicodemus, a benevolent Christian of some distinction, suffered at Rome during the rage of Domitian's persecution.

Protasius and Gervasius were martyred at Milan.

Timothy was the celebrated disciple of St. Paul, and bishop of Ephesus, where he zealously governed the Church until A.D. 97. At this period, as the pagans were about to celebrate a feast called Catagogion, Timothy, meeting the procession, severely reproved them for their ridiculous idolatry, which so exasperated the people that they fell upon him with their clubs, and beat him in so dreadful a manner that he expired of the bruises two days later.

Foxe's Book of Martyrs, Edited by William Byron Forbush

The Third Persecution (1)

Trajan forbids the Christians to be sought after

So great a persecution was at that time opened against us in many places that Plinius Secundus, one of the most noted of governors, being disturbed by the great number of martyrs, communicated with the emperor concerning the multitude of those that were put to death for their faith. At the same time, he informed him in his communication that he had not heard of their doing anything profane or contrary to the laws, except that they arose at dawn and sang hymns to Christ as a God; but that they renounced adultery and murder and like criminal offenses, and did all things in accordance with the laws. In reply to this Trajan made the following decree: that the race of Christians should not be sought after, but when found should be punished. On account of this the persecution which had threatened to be a most terrible one was to a certain degree checked, but there were still left plenty of pretexts for those who wished to do us harm. Sometimes the people, sometimes the rulers in various places, would lay plots against us, so that, although no great persecutions took place, local persecutions were nevertheless going on in particular provinces, and many of the faithful endured martyrdom in various forms. We have taken our account from the Latin Apology of Tertullian which we mentioned above. The translation runs as follows: "And indeed we have found that search for us has been forbidden. For when Plinius Secundus, the governor of a province, had condemned certain Christians and deprived them of their dignity, he was confounded by the multitude, and was uncertain what further course to pursue. He therefore communicated with Trajan the emperor, informing him that, aside from their unwillingness to sacrifice, he had found no impiety in them. And he reported this also, that the Christians arose early in the morning and sang hymns unto Christ as a God, and for the purpose of preserving their discipline forbade murder, adultery, avarice, robbery, and the like. In reply to this Trajan wrote that the race of Christians should not be sought after, but when found should be punished." Such were the events which took place at that time.

Eusebius of Caesarea, Church History, Book 3, chapter 23

The Third Persecution (2)

The third persecution, under Trajan, A.D. 108

In the third persecution Pliny the Second, a man learned and famous, seeing the lamentable slaughter of Christians, and moved therewith to pity, wrote to Trajan, certifying him that there were many thousands of them daily put to death, of which none did any thing contrary to the Roman laws worthy of persecution. "The whole account they gave of their crime or error (whichever it is to be called) amounted only to this – viz. that they were accustomed on a stated day to meet before daylight, and to repeat together a set form of prayer to Christ as a God, and to bind themselves by an obligation – not indeed to commit wickedness; but, on the contrary – never to commit theft, robbery, or adultery, never to falsify their word, never to defraud any man: after which it was their custom to separate, and reassemble to partake in common of a harmless meal."

In this persecution suffered the blessed martyr, Ignatius, who is held in famous reverence among very many. This Ignatius was appointed to the bishopric of Antioch next after Peter in succession. Some do say, that he, being sent from Syria to Rome, because he professed Christ, was given to the wild beasts to be devoured. It is also said of him, that when he passed through Asia, being under the most strict custody of his keepers, he strengthened and confirmed the churches through all the cities as he went, both with his exhortations and preaching of the Word of God. Accordingly, having come to Smyrna, he wrote to the Church at Rome, exhorting them not to use means for his deliverance from martyrdom, lest they should deprive him of that which he most longed and hoped for. "Now I begin to be a disciple. I care for nothing, of visible or invisible things, so that I may but win Christ. Let fire and the cross, let the companies of wild beasts, let breaking of bones and tearing of limbs, let the grinding of the whole body, and all the malice of the devil, come upon me; be it so, only may I win Christ Jesus!" And even when he was sentenced to be thrown to the beasts, such as the burning desire that he had to suffer, that he spake, what time he heard the lions roaring, saying: "I am the wheat of Christ: I am going to be ground with the teeth of wild beasts, that I may be found pure bread."

Trajan being succeeded by Adrian, the latter continued this third persecution with as much severity as his predecessor. About this time Alexander, bishop of Rome, with his two deacons, were martyred; as were Quirinus and Hernes, with their families; Zenon, a Roman nobleman, and about ten thousand other Christians.

In Mount Ararat many were crucified, crowned with thorns, and spears run into their sides, in imitation of Christ's passion. Eustachius, a brave and successful Roman commander, was by the emperor ordered to join in an idolatrous sacrifice to celebrate some of his own victories; but his faith (being a Christian in his heart) was so much greater than his vanity, that he nobly refused it. Enraged at the denial, the ungrateful emperor forgot the service of this skillful commander, and ordered him and his whole family to be martyred.

At the martyrdom of Faustines and Jovita, brothers and citizens of Brescia, their torments were so many, and their patience so great, that Calocerius, a pagan, beholding them, was struck with admiration, and exclaimed in a kind of ecstasy, "Great is the God of the Christians!" for which he was apprehended, and suffered a similar fate.

Many other similar cruelties and rigors were exercised against the Christians, until Quadratus, bishop of Athens, made a learned apology in their favor before the emperor, who happened to be there and Aristides, a philosopher of the same city, wrote an elegant epistle, which caused Adrian to relax in his severities, and relent in their favor.

Adrian dying A.D. 138, was succeeded by Antoninus Pius, one of the most amiable monarchs that ever reigned, and who stayed the persecutions against the Christians.

Foxe's Book of Martyrs, Edited by William Byron Forbush

Clement of Rome

St Clement, Pope, Martyr (A.D. 100)

St Clement, the son of Faustinus, a Roman by birth, was of Jewish extraction; for he tells us himself that he was of the race of Jacob. He was converted to the faith by St. Peter or St. Paul, and was so constant in his attendance on these apostles, and so active in assisting them in their ministry, that St. Jerome and other fathers call him an apostolic man; St. Clement of Alexandria styles him an apostle; and Rufinus, almost an apostle. Some authors attribute his conversion to St. Peter, whom he met at Cesarea with St. Barnabas; but he attended St. Paul at Philippi in 62, and shared in his sufferings there. We are assured by St. Chrysostom that he was a companion of the latter, with SS. Luke and Timothy, in many of his apostolic journeys, labors, and dangers. St. Paul (Phil. iv, 3) calls him his fellow-laborer, and ranks him among those whose names are written in the book of life; a privilege and matter of joy far beyond the power of commanding devils. (Luke x. 17) St. Clement followed St. Paul to Rome, where he also heard St. Peter preach, and was instructed in his school, as St. Irenaeus and Pope Zosimus testify. Tertullian tells us that St. Peter ordained him bishop, by which some understand that he made him a bishop of nations, to preach the gospel in many countries; others, with Epiphanius, that he made him his vicar at Rome, with an episcopal character to govern that church during his absence in his frequent missions. Others suppose he might at first be made bishop of the Jewish church in that city. After the martyrdom of SS. Peter and Paul, St. Linus was appointed Bishop of Rome, and after eleven years, succeeded by St. Cletus. Upon his demise in 89, or rather in 91, St. Clement was placed in the apostolic chair. According to the Liberian Calendar he sat nine years, eleven months, and twenty days.

At Corinth, an impious and detestable division, as our saint called it, happened amongst the faithful, like that which St. Paul had appeased in the same church; and a party rebelled against holy and irreproachable priests and presumed to depose them. It seems to have been soon after the death of Domitian in 96, that St. Clement, in the name of the church of Rome, wrote to them his excellent epistle, a piece highly extolled and esteemed in the primitive church as an admirable work, as Eusebius calls it. It was placed in rank next to the canonical books of the holy scriptures, and with them read in the churches. Whence it was found in the very ancient Alexandrian manuscript copy of the Bible, which Cyril Lucaris sent to our King James I, from which Patrick Young, the learned keeper of that king's library, published it at Oxford in 1633. St. Clement begins his letter by conciliating the benevolence of those who were at variance, tenderly putting them in mind how edifying their behavior was when they were all humble-minded, not boasting of anything, desiring rather to be subject than to govern, to give than to receive, content with the portion God had dispensed to them, listening diligently to his word, having an insatiable desire of doing good, and a plentiful effusion of the Holy Ghost upon all of them. At that time they were sincere, without offence, not mindful of injuries, and all sedition and schism was an abomination to them. The saint laments that they had then forsaken the fear of the Lord, and were fallen into pride, envy, strife, and sedition; and pathetically exhorts them to lay aside all pride and anger, for Christ is theirs who are humble and not theirs who exalt themselves. The scepter of the majesty of God, our Lord Jesus Christ, came not in the show of pride, though he could have done so; but with humility. He bids them look up to the Creator of the world, and think how gentle and patient he is towards his whole creation; also with what peace it all obeys his will, and the heavens, earth, impassable ocean, and worlds beyond it, are governed by the commends of this great master. Considering how near God is to us, and that none of our thoughts are hid from him, how ought we never to do anything contrary to his will, and honor them who are set over us! showing with a sincere affection of meekness, and manifesting the government of our tongues by a love of silence. "Let your children," says the saint, "be bred up in the instruction of the Lord, and learn how great a power humility has with God, how much a pure and holy charity avails with him, and how excellent and great his fear is." It appears by what follows, that some at Corinth boggled at the belief of a resurrection of the flesh, which the saint beautifully shows to be easy to the Almighty power, and illustrates by the vine which sheds its leaves, then buds, spreads its leaves, flowers, and afterwards produces first sour grapes, then ripe fruit; by the morning rising from night; and corn brought forth from seed. The saint adds a strong exhortation to shake off all sluggishness and laziness, for it is only the good workman who receives the bread of his labor. "We must hasten," says he, "with all earnestness and readiness of mind, to perfect every good work, laboring with cheerfulness; for even the Creator and Lord of all things rejoices in his own works." The latter part of this epistle is a pathetic recommendation of humility, peace, and charity. "Let every one," says the saint, "be subject to another, according to the order in which he is placed by the gift of God. Let not the strong man neglect the care of the weak; let the weak see that he reverence the strong. Let the rich man distribute to the necessity of the poor, and let the poor bless God who give :h him one to supply his want. Let the wise man show forth his wisdom, not in words, but in good works. Let him that is humble, never speak of himself, or make show of his actions. Let him that is pure in the flesh, not grow proud of it, knowing that it was another who gave him the gift of continence. They who are great cannot yet subsist without those that are little; nor the little without the great. In our body, the head without the feet is nothing; neither the feet without the head. And the smallest members of our body are yet both necessary and useful to the whole." Thus the saint teaches that the lowest in the church may be the greatest before God, if they are most faithful in the discharge of their respective duties. St. Clement puts pastors and superiors in mind that, with trembling and humility, they should have nothing but the fear of God in view, and take no pleasure in their own power and authority. "Let us," says he, "pray for all such as fall into any trouble or distress; that being endued with humility and moderation, they may submit, not to us, but to the will of God." Fortunatus, who is mentioned by St. Paul, was come from the church of Corinth to Rome, to inform that holy see of their unhappy schism. St. Clement says, he had dispatched four messengers to Corinth with him, and adds, "send them back to us again with all speed in peace and joy, that they may the sooner acquaint us with your peace and concord, so much prayed for and desired by us; and that we may rejoice in your good order." We have a large fragment of a second epistle of St. Clement to the Corinthians, found in the same Alexandrian manuscript of the Bible; from which circumstance it appears to have been also read like the former in many churches, which St. Dionysius of Corinth expressly testifies of that church, though it was not so celebrated among the ancients as the other. In it our saint exhorts the faithful to despise this world and its false enjoyments, and to have those which are promised us always before our eyes; to pursue virtue with all our strength, and its peace will follow us with the inexpressible delights of the promise of what is to come. The necessity of perfectly subduing both the irascible and concupiscible passions of our souls, he lays down as the foundation of a Christian life, in words which St. Clement of Alexandria enforces and illustrates. Besides these letters of St. Clement to the Corinthians, two others have been lately discovered, which are addressed to spiritual eunuchs or virgins. Of these St. Jerome speaks, when he says of certain epistles of St. Clement, "In the epistles which Clement, the successor of the Apostle Peter, wrote to them, that is, to such eunuchs, almost his whole discourse turns upon the excellence of virginity." These two letters were found in a manuscript copy of a Syriac New Testament, by John James Westein, in 1752, and printed by him with a Latin translation at Amsterdam in 1752, and again in 1757. A French translation of them has been published, with short critical notes. These letters are not unworthy this great disciple of St. Peter; and in them the counsels of St. Paul concerning celibacy and virginity are explained, that state is pathetically recommended, without prejudice to the honor due to the holy state of marriage; and the necessity of shunning all familiarity with persons of a different sex, and the like occasions of incontinence is set in a true light. St. Clement with patience and prudence got through the persecution of Domitian. Nerva's peaceable reign being very short, the tempest increased under Trajan, who, even from the beginning of his reign, never allowed the Christian assemblies. It was in the year 100 that the third general persecution was raised by him, which was the more afflicting, as this reign was in other respects generally famed for justice and moderation. Rufin, Pope Zosimus, and the council of Bazas in 452, expressly styles St. Clement a martyr. In the ancient canon of the Roman mass, he is ranked among the martyrs. Eusebius tells us, that St. Clement departed this life in the third year of Trajan, of Christ 100. From this expression some will have it that he died a natural death; but St. Clement says of St. Paul, who certainly died a martyr, that "he departed out of the world." It is also objected, that St. Irenaeus gives the title of martyr only to St. Telesphorus among the popes before St. Eleutherius. But it is certain that some others were martyrs, whatever was the cause of his omission. St. Irenaeus mentions the epistle of

St. Clement yet omits those of St. Ignatius, though in some places he quotes him. Shall we hence argue, that St. Ignatius wrote none? When the Emperor Lewis Debonnair founded the great abbey of Cava, in Abruzzo, four miles from Slaerno, in 872, he enriched it with the relics of St. Clement, pope and martyr, which Pope Adrian sent him, as is related at length in the chronicle of that abbey, with a history of many miracles. These relics remain there to this day. The ancient Church of St. Clement in Rome, in which St. Gregory the Great preached several of his homilies, still retains part of his relics. It was repaired by Clement XI, but still shows entire the old structure of Christian churches, divided into three parts: the narthex, the ambo, and the sanctuary. St. Clement inculcates, that the spirit of Christianity is a spirit of perfect disengagement from the things of this world. "We must," says he, "look upon all the things of this world, as none of ours, and not desire them. This world and that to come are two enemies. We cannot, therefore, be friends to both; but we must resolve which we would forsake, and which we would enjoy. And we think, that it is better to hate the present things, as little, short-lived, and corruptible; and to love those which are to come, which are truly good and incorruptible. Let us contend with all earnestness, knowing that we are now called to the combat. Let us run in the straight road, the race that is incorruptible. This is what Christ saith: keep your bodies pure and your souls without spot, that ye may receive eternal life."

Alban Butler, The Lives of the Fathers, Martyrs and Other Principal Saints

MARTYRDOM OF IGNATIUS (1)
Ignatius of Antioch, Bishop and Martyr: 17 October 107

After the Apostles, Ignatius was the second bishop of Antioch in Syria. His predecessor, of whom little is known, was named Euodius. Whether he knew any of the Apostles directly is uncertain. Little is known of his life except for the very end of it. Early in the second century (perhaps around 107 AD, during the reign of the Emperor Trajan), he was arrested by the Imperial authorities, condemned to death, and transported to Rome to die in the arena. By thus dealing with a leader, the rulers hoped to terrify the rank and file. Instead, Ignatius took the opportunity to encourage them, speaking to groups of Christians at every town along the way. When the prison escort reached the west coast of Asia Minor, it halted before taking ship, and delegations from several Asian churches were able to visit Ignatius, to speak with him at length, to assist him with items for his journey, and to bid him an affectionate farewell and commend him to the grace of God. In response he wrote seven letters that have been preserved: five to congregations that had greeted him, en masse or by delegates (Ephesians, Magnesians, Trallians, Philadelphians, and Smyrnaeans), one to the congregation that would greet him at his destination (Romans), and one to Polycarp, Bishop of Smyrna and disciple of the Apostle John.

The themes of his letters are:

first: the importance of maintaining Christian unity in love and sound doctrine (with warnings against factionalism and against the heresy of Docetism – the belief that Christ was not fully human and did not have a material body or really suffer and die):

second: the role of the clergy as a focus of Christian unity:

third: Christian martyrdom as a glorious privilege, eagerly to be grasped.

He writes: "I am God's wheat, ground fine by the lion's teeth to be made purest bread for Christ.

No early pleasures, no kingdoms of this world can benefit me in any way. I prefer death in Christ Jesus to power over the farthest limits of the earth. He who died in place of us is the one object of my quest. He who rose for our sakes is my one desire. The time for my birth is close at hand. Forgive me, my brothers. Do not stand in the way of my birth to real life; do not wish me stillborn. My desire is to belong to God. Do not, then, hand me back to the world. do not try to tempt me with material things.

Let me attain pure light. Only on my arrival there can I be fully a human being. Give me the privilege of imitating the passion of my God."

James Kiefer, Christian Biographies, By kind permission

St. Ignatius of Antioch

Also called Theophorus (ho Theophoros); born in Syria, around the year 50; died at Rome between 98 and 117.

More than one of the earliest ecclesiastical writers have given credence, though apparently without good reason, to the legend that Ignatius was the child whom the Savior took up in His arms, as described in Mark 9:35. It is also believed, and with great probability, that, with his friend Polycarp, he was among the auditors of the Apostle St. John. If we include St. Peter, Ignatius was the third Bishop of Antioch and the immediate successor of Evodius (Eusebius, "Hist. Eccl.", II, iii, 22). Theodoret ("Dial. Immutab.", I, iv, 33a, Paris, 1642) is the authority for the statement that St. Peter appointed Ignatius to the See of Antioch. St. John Chrysostom lays special emphasis on the honor conferred upon the martyr in receiving his episcopal consecration at the hands of the Apostles themselves ("Hom. in St. Ig.", IV. 587). Natalis Alexander quotes Theodoret to the same effect (III, xii, art. xvi, p. 53).

All the sterling qualities of ideal pastor and a true soldier of Christ were possessed by the Bishop of Antioch in a preeminent degree. Accordingly, when the storm of the persecution of Domitian broke in its full fury upon the Christians of Syria, it found their faithful leader prepared and watchful. He was unremitting in his vigilance and tireless in his efforts to inspire hope and to strengthen the weaklings of his flock against the terrors of the persecution. The restoration of peace, though it was short-lived, greatly comforted him. But it was not for himself that he rejoiced, as the one great and ever-present wish of his chivalrous soul was that he might receive the fullness of Christian discipleship through the medium of martyrdom. His desire was not to remain long unsatisfied. Associated with the writings of St. Ignatius is a work called "Martyrium Ignatii", which purports to be an account by eyewitnesses of the martyrdom of St. Ignatius and the acts leading up to it. In this work, which such competent Protestant critics as Pearson and Ussher regard as genuine, the full history of that eventful journey from Syria to Rome is faithfully recorded for the edification of the Church of Antioch. It is certainly very ancient and is reputed to have been written by Philo, deacon of Tarsus, and Rheus Agathopus, a Syrian, who accompanied Ignatius to Rome. It is generally admitted, even by those who regarded it as authentic, that this work has been greatly interpolated.

According to these Acts, in the ninth year of his reign, Trajan, flushed with victory over the Scythians and Dacians, sought to perfect the universality of his dominion by a species of religious conquest. He decreed, therefore, that the Christians should unite with their pagan neighbors in the worship of the gods. A general persecution was threatened, and death was named as the penalty for all who refused to offer the prescribed sacrifice. Instantly alert to the danger that threatened, Ignatius availed himself of all the means within his reach to thwart the purpose of the emperor. The success of his zealous efforts did not long remain hidden from the Church's persecutors. He was soon arrested and led before Trajan, who was then sojourning in Antioch. Accused by the emperor himself of violating the imperial edict, and of inciting others to like transgressions, Ignatius valiantly bore witness to the faith of Christ. If we may believe the account given in the "Martyrium", his bearing before Trajan was characterized by inspired eloquence, sublime courage, and even a spirit of exultation. Incapable of appreciating the motives that animated him, the emperor ordered him to be put in chains and taken to Rome, there to become the food of wild beasts and a spectacle for the people.

That the trials of this journey to Rome were great we gather from his letter to the Romans (par. 5): "From Syria even to Rome

I fight with wild beasts, by land and sea, by night and by day, being bound amidst ten leopards, even a company of soldiers, who only grow worse when they are kindly treated." Despite all this, his journey was a kind of triumph. News of his fate, his destination, and his probable itinerary had gone swiftly before. At several places along the road his fellow-Christians greeted him with words of comfort and reverential homage. It is probable that he embarked on his way to Rome at Seleucia, in Syria, the nearest port to Antioch, for either Tarsus in Cilicia, or Attalia in Pamphylia, and thence, as we gather from his letters, he journeyed overland through Asia Minor. At Laodicea, on the River Lycus, where a choice of routes presented itself, his guards selected the more northerly, which brought the prospective martyr through Philadelphia and Sardis, and finally to Smyrna, where Polycarp, his fellow-disciple in the school of St. John, was bishop. The stay at Smyrna, which was a protracted one, gave the representatives of the various Christian communities in Asia Minor an opportunity of greeting the illustrious prisoner, and offering him the homage of the Churches they represented. From the congregations of Ephesus, Magnesia, and Tralles, deputations came to comfort him. To each of these Christian communities he addressed letters from Smyrna, exhorting them to obedience to their respective bishops, and warning them to avoid the contamination of heresy. These, letters are redolent with the spirit of Christian charity, apostolic zeal, and pastoral solicitude. While still there he wrote also to the Christians of Rome, begging them to do nothing to deprive him of the opportunity of martyrdom.

From Smyrna his captors took him to Troas, from which place he dispatched letters to the Christians of Philadelphia and Smyrna, and to Polycarp. Besides these letters, Ignatius had intended to address others to the Christian communities of Asia Minor, inviting them to give public expression to their sympathy with the brethren in Antioch, but the altered plans of his guards, necessitating a hurried departure, from Troas, defeated his purpose, and he was obliged to content himself with delegating this office to his friend Polycarp. At Troas they took ship for Neapolis. From this place their journey led them overland through Macedonia and Illyria. The next port of embarkation was probably Dyrrhachium (Durazzo). Whether having arrived at the shores of the Adriatic, he completed his journey by land or sea, it !s impossible to determine. Not long after his arrival in Rome he won his long-coveted crown of martyrdom in the Flavian amphitheater. The relics of the holy martyr were borne back to Antioch by the deacon Philo of Cilicia, and Rheus Agathopus, a Syrian, and were interred outside the gates not far from the beautiful suburb of Daphne. They were afterwards removed by the Emperor Theodosius II to the Tychaeum, or Temple of Fortune which was then converted into a Christian church under the patronage of the martyr whose relics it sheltered. In 637 they were translated to St. Clement's at Rome, where they now rest. The Church celebrates the feast of St. Ignatius on 1 February.

The character of St. Ignatius, as deduced from his own and the extant writings of his contemporaries, is that of a true athlete of Christ. The triple honor of apostle, bishop, and martyr was well merited by this energetic soldier of the Faith. An enthusiastic devotion to duty, a passionate love of sacrifice, and an utter fearlessness in the defense of Christian truth, were his chief characteristics. Zeal for the spiritual well-being of those under his charge breathes from every line of his writings. Ever vigilant lest they be infected by the rampant heresies of those early days; praying for them, that their faith and courage may not be wanting in the hour of persecution; constantly exhorting them to unfailing obedience to their bishops; teaching them all Catholic truth ; eagerly sighing for the crown of martyrdom, that his own blood may fructify in added graces in the souls of his flock, he proves himself in every sense a true, pastor of souls, the good shepherd that lays down his life for his sheep.

COLLECTIONS

The oldest collection of the writings of St. Ignatius known to have existed was that made use of by the historian Eusebius in the first half of the fourth century, but which unfortunately is no longer extant. It was made up of the seven letters written by Ignatius whilst on his way to Rome; These letters were addressed to the Christians of Ephesus (Pros Ephesious); of Magnesia (Magnesieusin); of Tralles (Trallianois); of Rome (Pros Romaious); of Philadelphia (Philadelpheusin); of Smyrna (Smyrnaiois); and to Polycarp (Pros Polykarpon).

John B. O'Connor, The Catholic Encyclopedia, Volume 7

EXTRACTS FROM IGNATIUS WRITINGS

Some Christians could hardly wait for martyrdom. The best known example of this is Ignatius of Antioch.

Ignatius of Antioch was the third bishop of Antioch and considered an apostolic Father because he heard the Apostle John preach. About 110 A.D. he was sentenced to a martyr's death in the arena by the Emperor Trajan. On the journey to Rome he wrote seven letters, which are his only surviving letters. They are addressed to Christian communities at Ephesus, Magnesia, Tralles, Rome, Philadelphia and Smyrna, including a personal one to Bishop Polycarp of Smyrna. The authenticity of the letters is universally accepted by Catholic and Protestant scholars.

Stand firm like an anvil

The times require thee, as pilots require winds, and as one tossed at sea requires a haven. Be vigilant as God's athlete. Stand firm like an anvil under the blows of the hammer. It is the part of a great athlete to receive blows and to conquer. Be yet more diligent than you are, learn to know the times.

Ignatius, Letter to bishop Polycarp of Smyrna

Suffering brings us near to God

Make me suffer to become food for the wild beasts, through whose instrumentality it will be granted me to attain God... Then shall I truly be a disciple of Christ... I know what is for my benefit... Let fire and the cross; let the crowds of wild beasts; let tearings, breakings, and dislocations of bones; letting cutting off of members; let shatterings of the whole body; and let all the dreadful torments of the devil come upon me: only let me attain to Jesus Christ.

St Ignatius of Antioch, Letter to the Romans

He who is near the sword is near God

He who is near the sword is near God; he that is among the wild beasts is in company with God; provided only he be so in the name of Jesus Christ. I undergo all these things that I may suffer together with Him, He inwardly strengthening me.

St Ignatius of Antioch, Letter to the Smyrnaeans

IGNATIUS' LETTER TO THE EPHESIANS

Ignatius of Antioch, Letters of Ignatius (before 117 A.D.).

On the journey to his martyrdom in Rome, the Bishop of Antioch (a disciple of the Apostle John) writes to the Ephesian, Magnesian, Trallian, Roman, Philadelphian, and Smyrnaean churches, as well as to his fellow Bishop, Polycarp.

Introduction

Ignatius, who is also called Theopharus, to the Church which is at Ephesus, in Asia, deservedly most happy, being blessed in the greatness and fulness of God the Father, and predestinated before the beginning of time, that it should be always for an enduring and unchangeable glory, being united and elected through the true passion by the will of the Father, and Jesus Christ, our God: Abundant happiness through Jesus Christ, and His undefiled grace. Ignatius, who is also called Theophorus, to the Church which is at Ephesus, in Asia, deservedly most happy, being blessed in the greatness and fulness of God the Father, and predestinated before the beginning of time, that it should be always for an enduring and unchangeable glory, being united and elected through the true passion by the will of God the Father, and of our Lord Jesus Christ our Savior : Abundant happiness through Jesus Christ, and His undefiled joy.

Chapter 1: Praise of the Ephesians

I have become acquainted with your name, much-beloved in God, which ye have acquired by the habit of righteousness, according to the faith and love in Jesus Christ our Savior. Being the followers of God, and stirring up yourselves by the blood of God, ye have perfectly accomplished the work which was beseeming to you. For, on hearing that I came bound from Syria for the common name and hope, trusting through your prayers to be permitted to fight with beasts at Rome, that so by martyrdom I may indeed become the disciple of Him "who gave Himself for us, an offering and sacrifice to God,"[ye hastened to see me]. I received, therefore, your whole multitude in the name of God, through Onesimus, a man of inexpressible love, and your bishop in the flesh, whom I pray you by Jesus Christ to love, and that you would all seek to be like him. And blessed be He who has granted unto you, being worthy, to obtain such an excellent bishop.

Ignatius' letter to the Romans

Ignatius, who is also called Theophorus, to the Church which has obtained mercy, through the majesty of the Mast High Father, and Jesus Christ, His only-begotten Son; the Church which is beloved and enlightened by the will of Him that willeth all things which are according to the love of Jesus Christ our God, which also presides in the place of the report of the Romans, worthy of God, worthy of honor, worthy of the highest happiness, worthy of praise, worthy of obtaining her every desire, worthy of being deemed holy, and which presides over love, is named from Christ, and from the Father, and is possessed of the Spirit, which I also salute in the name of Almighty God, and of Jesus Christ His Son: to those who are united, both according to the flesh and spirit, to every one of His commandments, who are filled inseparably with all the grace of God, and are purified from every strange taint, [I wish] abundance of happiness unblameably, in God, even the Father, and our Lord Jesus Christ.

Chapter 1: As a prisoner, I hope to see you

Through prayer to God I have obtained the privilege of seeing your most worthy faces, even as I earnestly begged might be granted me; for as a prisoner in Christ Jesus I hope to salute you, if indeed it be the will [of God] that I be thought worthy of attaining unto the end. For the beginning has been well ordered, if I may obtain grace to cling to my lot without hindrance unto the end. For I am afraid of your love, lest it should do me an injury. For it is easy for you to accomplish what you please; but it is difficult for me to attain to God, if ye spare me. But it is difficult for me to attain to God, if ye do not spare me, under the pretense of carnal affection.

Chapter 2: Do not save me from martyrdom

For it is not my desire to act towards you as a man-pleaser, but as pleasing God, even as also ye please Him. For neither shall I ever have such [another] opportunity of attaining to God; nor will ye, if ye shall now be silent, ever be entitled to the honor of a better work. For if ye are silent concerning me, I shall become God's; but if you show your love to my flesh, I shall again have to run my race. Pray, then, do not seek to confer any greater favor upon me than that I be sacrificed to God while the altar is still prepared; that, being gathered together in love, ye may sing praise to the Father, through Christ Jesus, that God has deemed me, the bishop of Syria, worthy to be sent for from the east unto the west. It is good to set from the world unto God, that I may rise again to Him. For it is not my desire that ye should please men, Out God, even as also ye do please Him. For neither shall I ever hereafter have such an opportunity of attaining to God; nor will ye, if ye shall now be silent, ever be entitled to s the honor of a better work. For if ye are silent concerning me, I shall become

God's; but if ye show your love to my flesh, I shall again have to run my race. Pray, then, do not seek to confer any greater favor upon me than that I be sacrificed to God, while the altar is still prepared; that, being gathered together in love, ye may sing praise to the Father, through Christ Jesus, that God has deemed me, the bishop of Syria, worthy to be sent for from the east unto the west, and to become a martyr in behalf of His own precious sufferings, so as to pass from the world to God, that I may rise again unto Him.

Chapter 3: Pray rather that I may obtain martyrdom

Ye have never envied any one; ye have taught others. Now I desire that those things may be confirmed [by your conduct], which in your instructions ye enjoin [on others]. Only request in my behalf both inward and outward strength, that I may not only speak, but [truly] will; and that I may not merely be called a Christian, but really be found to be one. For if I be truly found [a Christian], I may also be called one, and be then deemed faithful, when I shall no longer appear to the world. Nothing visible is eternal. "For the things which are seen are temporal, but the things which are not seen are eternal."

Chapter 4: Allow me to fall a prey to the wild beasts

I write to the Churches, and impress on them all, that I shall willingly die for God, unless ye hinder me. I beseech of you not to show an unseasonable good-will towards me. Suffer me to become food for the wild beasts, through whose instrumentality it will be granted me to attain to God. I am the wheat of God, and let me be ground by the teeth of the wild beasts, that I may be found the pure bread of Christ. Rather entice the wild beasts, that they may become my tomb, and may leave nothing of my body; so that when I have fallen asleep [in death], I may be no trouble to any one. Then shall I truly be a disciple of Christ, when the world shall not see so much as my body. Entreat Christ for me, that by these instruments I may be found a sacrifice [to God]. I do not, as Peter and Paul, issue commandments unto you. They were apostles; I am but a condemned man: they were free, while I am, even until now, a servant. But when I suffer, I shall be the freedman of Jesus, and shall rise again emancipated in Him. And now, being a prisoner, I learn not to desire anything worldly or vain.

Chapter 5: I desire to die

From Syria even unto Rome I fight with beasts, both by land and sea, both by night and day, being bound to ten leopards, I mean a band of soldiers, who, even when they receive benefits, show themselves all the worse. But I am the more instructed by their injuries [to act as a disciple of Christ]; "yet am I not thereby justified." May I enjoy the wild beasts that are prepared for me; and I pray they may be found eager to rush upon me, which also I will entice to devour me speedily, and not deal with me as with some, whom, out of fear, they have not touched. But if they be unwilling to assail me, I will compel them to do so. Pardon me

Chapter 6: By death I shall attain true life

All the pleasures of the world, and all the kingdoms of this earth, shall profit me nothing. It is better for me to die in behalf of Jesus Christ, than to reign over all the ends of the earth. "For what shall a man be profited, if he gain the whole world, but lose his own soul?"" Him I seek, who died for us: Him I desire, who rose again for our sake. This is the gain which is laid up for me. Pardon me, brethren: do not hinder me from living, do not wish to keep me in a state of death; and while I desire to belong to God, do not ye give me over to the world. Suffer me to obtain pure light: when I have gone thither, I shall indeed be a man of God. Permit me to be an imitator of the passion of my God. If any one has Him within himself, let him consider what I desire, and let him have sympathy with me, as knowing how I am straitened.

Chapter 7: Why I desire to die

The prince of this world would fain carry me

away, and corrupt my disposition towards God. Let none of you, therefore, who are [in Rome] help him; rather be ye on my side, that is, on the side of God. Do not speak of Jesus Christ, and yet set your desires on the world. Let not envy find a dwelling-place among you; nor even should I, when present with you, exhort you to it, be ye persuaded to listen to me, but rather give credit to those things which I now write to you. For though I am alive while I write to you, yet I am eager to die. My love has been crucified, and there is no fire in me desiring to be fed; but there is within me a water that liveth and speaketh, saying to me inwardly, Come to the Father. I have no delight in corruptible food, nor in the pleasures of this life. I desire the bread of God, the heavenly bread, the bread of life, which is the flesh of Jesus Christ, the Son of God, who became afterwards of the seed of David and Abraham; and I desire the drink of God, namely His blood, which is incorruptible love and eternal life.

Chapter 8: Look on me with your favor

I no longer wish to live after the manner of men, and my desire shall be fulfilled if ye consent. "I am crucified with Christ: nevertheless I live; yet no longer I, since Christ liveth in me." I entreat you in this brief letter: do not refuse me; believe me that I love Jesus, who was delivered [to death] for my sake. "What shall I render to the Lord for all His benefits towards me ?" Now God, even the Father, and the Lord Jesus Christ, shall reveal these things to you, [so that ye shall know] that I speak truly. And do ye pray along with me, that I may attain my aim in the Holy Spirit. I have not written to you according to the flesh, but according to the will of God. If I shall suffer, ye have loved me; but if I am rejected, ye have hated me.

Chapter 9: Pray for the church in Syria

Remember in your prayers the Church which is in Syria, which, instead of me, has now for its shepherd the Lord, who says, "I am the good Shepherd." And He alone will oversee it, as well as your love towards Him. But as for me, I am ashamed to be counted one of them; for I am not worthy, as being the very last of them, and one born out of due time. But I have obtained mercy to be somebody, if I shall attain to God. My spirit salutes you, and the love of the Churches which have received me in the name of Jesus Christ, and not as a mere passerby. For even those Churches which were not near to me in the way, have brought me forward, city by city.

Chapter 10: Conclusion

Now I write these things to you from Smyrna by the Ephesians, who are deservedly most happy. There is also with me, along with many others, Crocus, one dearly beloved by me. As to those who have gone before me from Syria to Rome for the glory of God, I believe that you are acquainted with them; to whom, [then,] do ye make known that I am at hand. For they are all worthy, both of God and of you; and it is becoming that you should refresh them in all things. I have written these things unto you, on the day before the ninth of the Kalends of September (that is, on the twenty-third day of August). Fare ye well to the end, in the patience of Jesus Christ. Amen.

The Epistle of Ignatius' letter to the Tarsians

Introduction

Ignatius, who is also called Theophorus, to the Church which is at Tarsus, saved in Christ, worthy of praise, worthy of remembrance, and worthy of love: Mercy and peace from God the Father, and the Lord Jesus Christ, be ever multiplied.

Chapter 1: His own sufferings; exhortation to steadfastness

From Syria even unto Rome I fight with beasts not that I am devoured by brute beasts, for these, as ye know, by the will of God, spared Daniel, but by beasts in the shape of men, in whom the merciless wild beast himself lies hid, and pricks and wounds me day by day. But none of these hardships "move me, neither count I my life dear unto myself," in such a way as to love it better than the Lord.

Wherefore I am prepared for [encountering] fire, wild beasts, the sword or the cross, so that only I may see Christ my Savior and God, who died for me. I therefore, the prisoner of Christ, who am driven along by land and sea, exhort you: "stand fast in the faith," and be ye steadfast, "for the just shall live by faith;" be ye unwavering, for "the Lord causes those to dwell in a house who are of one and the same character."

The Martyrdom of Ignatius (2)

Chapter 1: Ignatius' desire for martyrdom

When Trajan, not long since, succeeded to the empire of the Romans, Ignatius, the disciple of John the apostle, a man in all respects of an apostolic character, governed the Church of the Antiochians with great care, having with difficulty escaped the former storms of the many persecutions under Domitian, inasmuch as, like a good pilot, by the helm of prayer and fasting, by the earnestness of his teaching, and by his [constant spiritual labor, he resisted the flood that rolled against him, fearing [only] lest he should lose: any of those who were deficient in courage, or apt to suffer from their simplicity. Wherefore he rejoiced over the tranquil state of the Church, when the persecution ceased for a little time, but was grieved as to himself, that he had not yet attained to a true love to Christ, nor reached the perfect rank of a disciple. For he inwardly reflected, that the confession which is made by martyrdom, would bring him into a yet more intimate relation to the Lord. Wherefore, continuing a few years longer with the Church, and, like a divine lamp, enlightening every one's understanding by his expositions of the [Holy] Scriptures, he [at length] attained the object of his desire.

Chapter 2: Ignatius is condemned by Trajan

For Trajan, in the ninth year of his reign, being lifted up [with pride], after the victory he had gained over the Scythians and Dacians, and many other nations, and thinking that the religious body of the Christians were yet wanting to complete the subjugation of all things to himself, and [thereupon] threatening them with persecution unless they should agree to worship daemons, as did all other nations, thus compelled all who were living godly lives either to sacrifice [to idols] or die. Wherefore the noble soldier of Christ [Ignatius], being in fear for the Church of the Antiochians, was, in accordance with his own desire, brought before Trajan, who was at that time staying at Antioch, but was in haste [to set forth] against Armenia and the Parthians. And when he was set before the emperor Trajan, [that prince] said unto him, "Who art thou, eked wretch, who settest thyself to transgress our commands, and persuadest others to do the same, so that they should miserably perish?" Ignatius replied, "No one ought to call Theophorus wicked; for all evil spirits have departed from the servants of God. But if, because I am an enemy to these [spirits], you call me wicked in respect to them, I quite agree with you; for inasmuch as I have Christ the King of heaven [within me], I destroy all the devices of these [evil spirits]." Trajan answered, "And who is Theophorus?" Ignatius replied, "He who has Christ within his breast." Trajan said, "Do we not then seem to you to have the gods in our mind, whose assistance we enjoy in fighting against our enemies?" Ignatius answered, "Thou art in error when thou callest the daemons of the nations gods. For there is but one God, who made heaven, and earth, and the sea, and all that are in them; and one Jesus Christ, the only-begotten Son of God, whose kingdom may I enjoy." Trajan said, "Do you mean Him who was crucified under Pontius Pilate?" Ignatius replied, "I mean Him who crucified my sin, with him who was the inventor of it, and who has condemned [and cast down] all the deceit and malice of the devil under the feet of those who carry Him in their heart." Trajan said, "Dost thou then carry within thee Him that was crucified?" Ignatius replied, "Truly so; for it is written, "I will dwell in them, and walk in them."" Then Trajan pronounced sentence as follows: "We command that Ignatius, who affirms that he carries about within him Him that was crucified, be bound by soldiers, and carried to the great [city] Rome, there to be devoured by the beasts, for the gratification of the people." When the holy martyr heard this sentence, he cried out with joy, "I thank thee, O Lord, that Thou hast vouchsafed to honor me with a perfect love towards Thee, and hast made me to be bound with iron chains, like Thy Apostle Paul." Having spoken thus, he then, with delight, clasped the chains about him; and when he had first prayed for the Church, and commended it with tears to the Lord, he was hurried away by the savage cruelty of the soldiers, like a distinguished ram the leader of a goodly flock, that he might be carried to Rome, there to furnish food to the bloodthirsty beasts.

Chapter 3: Ignatius sails to Smyrna

Wherefore, with great alacrity and joy, through his desire to suffer, he came down from Antioch to Seleucia, from which place he set sail. And after a great deal of suffering he came to Smyrna, where he disembarked with great joy, and hastened to see the holy Polycarp, [formerly] his fellow-disciple, and [now] bishop of Smyrna. For they had both, in old times, been disciples of St. John the Apostle. Being then brought to him, and having communicated to him some spiritual gifts, and glorying in his bonds, he entreated of him to labor along with him for the fulfilment of his desire; earnestly indeed asking this of the whole Church (for the cities and Churches of Asia had welcomed the holy man through their bishops, and presbyters, and deacons, all hastening to meet him, if by any means they might receive from him some spiritual gift), but above all, the holy Polycarp, that, by means of the wild beasts, he soon disappearing from this world, might be manifested before the face of Christ.

Chapter 4: Ignatius writes to the churches

And these things he thus spake, and thus testified, extending his love to Christ so far as one who was about to secure heaven through his good confession, and the earnestness of those who joined their prayers to his in regard to his [approaching] conflict; and to give a recompense to the Churches, who came to meet him through their rulers, sending(9) letters of thanksgiving to them, which dropped spiritual grace, along with prayer and exhortation. Wherefore, seeing all men so kindly affected towards him, and fearing lest the love of the brotherhood should hinder his zeal towards the Lord, while a fair door of suffering martyrdom was opened to him, he wrote to the Church of the Romans the Epistle.

Chapter 5: Ignatius is brought to Rome

Having therefore, by means of this Epistle, settled, as he wished, those of the brethren at Rome who were unwilling [for his martyrdom]; and setting sail from Smyrna (for Christophorus was pressed by the soldiers to hasten to the public spectacles in the mighty [city] Rome, that, being given up to the wild beasts in the sight of the Roman people, he might attain to the crown for which he strove), he [next] landed at Troas. Then, going on from that place to Neapolis, he went [on foot] by Philippi through Macedonia, and on to that part of Epirus which is near Epidamnus; and finding a ship in one of the seaports, he sailed over the Adriatic Sea, and entering from it on the Tyrrhene, he passed by the various islands and cities, until, when Puteoli came in sight, he was eager there to disembark, having a desire to tread in the footsteps of the Apostle Paul. But a violent wind arising did not suffer him to do so, the ship being driven rapidly forwards; and, simply expressing his delight over the love of the brethren in that place, he sailed by. Wherefore, continuing to enjoy fair winds, we were reluctantly hurried on in one day and a night, mourning [as we did] over the coming departure from us of this righteous man. But to him this happened just as he wished, since he was in haste as soon as possible to leave this world, that he might attain to the Lord whom he loved. Sailing then into the Roman harbor, and the unhallowed sports being just about to close, the soldiers began to be annoyed at our slowness, but the bishop rejoicingly yielded to their urgency.

Chapter 6: Ignatius is devoured by the beasts at Rome

They pushed forth therefore from the place which is called Portus; and (the fame of all relating to the holy martyr being already spread abroad) we met the brethren full of fear and joy; rejoicing indeed because they were thought worthy to meet with Theophorus, but struck with fear because so eminent a man was being led to death. Now he enjoined some to keep silence who, in their fervent zeal, were saying that they would appease the people, so that they should not demand the destruction of this just one. He being immediately aware of this through the Spirit, and having saluted them all, and begged of them to show a true affection towards him, and having dwelt [on this point] at greater length than in his Epistle, and having persuaded them not to envy him hastening to the Lord, he then, after he had, with all the brethren kneeling [beside him], entreated the Son of God in behalf of the Churches, that a stop might be put to the persecution, and that mutual love might continue among the brethren, was led with all haste into the amphitheater. Then, being immediately thrown in, according to the command of Caesar given some time ago, the public spectacles being just about to close (for it was then a solemn day, as they deemed it, being that which is called the thirteenth in the Roman tongue, on which the people were wont to assemble in more than ordinary numbers), he was thus cast to the wild beasts close, beside the temple, that so by them the desire of the holy martyr Ignatius should be fulfilled, according to that which is written, "The desire of the righteous is acceptable [to God]," to the effect that he might not be troublesome to any of the brethren by the gathering of his remains, even as he had in his Epistle expressed a wish beforehand that so his end might be. For only the harder portions of his holy remains were left, which were conveyed to Antioch and wrapped in linen, as an inestimable treasure left to the holy Church by the grace which was in the martyr.

Chapter 7: Ignatius appears in a vision after his death

Now these things took place on the thirteenth day before the Kalends of January, that is, on the twentieth of December, Sun and Senecio being then the consuls of the Romans for the second time. Having ourselves been eye-witnesses of these things, and having spent the whole night in tears within the house, and having entreated the Lord, with bended knees and much prayer, that He would give us weak men full assurance respecting the things which were done, it came to pass, on our filling into a brief slumber, that some of us saw the blessed Ignatius suddenly standing by us and embracing us, while others beheld him again praying for us, and others still saw him dropping with sweat, as if he had just come from his great labor, and standing by the Lord. When, therefore, we had with great joy witnessed these things, and had compared our several visions together, we sang praise to God, the giver of all good things, and expressed our sense of the happiness of the holy [martyr]; and now we have made known to you both the day and the time [when these things happened], that, assembling ourselves together according to the time of his martyrdom, we may have fellowship with the champion and noble martyr of Christ, who trode under foot the devil, and perfected the course which, out of love to Christ, he had desired, in Christ Jesus our Lord; by whom, and with whom, be glory and power to the Father, with the Holy Spirit, for evermore! Amen.

Martyrdom Ignatii

Martyrdom of Ignatius (3)

"I battle with beasts . . . and would to God I were once come to the beasts which are prepared for me." (Ignatius, writing to Polycarp at Smyrna)

The most illustrious victim of the persecution under Emperor Trajan was the great Ignatius, bishop of Antioch, in Syria.

Emperor Trajan commanded the martyrdom of Ignatius, Bishop of Antioch. This holy man, when an infant, Christ took in his arms, and showed to his disciples, as one that would be a pattern of humility and innocence: he received the gospel afterwards from St John the Evangelist, and was exceedingly zealous in his mission and ministry. He boldly vindicated the faith of Christ before the emperor, for which he was cast into prison, and was cruelly tormented; for, after being dreadfully scourged, he was compelled to hold fire in his hands, and at the same time, papers dipped in oil were put to his sides and lighted. His flesh was then torn with hot pincers, and at last he was dispatched by the fury of wild beasts.

Ignatius had either presentiment or information of his fate; for writing to Polycarp, at Smyrna, he thus described his adventures:

"From Syria, even till I came to Rome, had I battle with beasts, as well by sea as land, both day and night, being bound in the midst of a cruel legion of soldiers who, the more benefits they received at my hands, behaved so much the worse unto me. And would to God I were once come to the beasts which are prepared for me; which also I wish with gaping mouths were ready to come upon me, whom also I will provoke that they, without delay, may devour me. And if they will not, unless they be provoked, I will then enforce them against myself. Now begin I to be a scholar; I esteem no visible things, nor yet invisible things, so that I may get or obtain Christ Jesus. Let the fire, the gallows, the wild beasts, the breaking bones, the pulling asunder of members, the bruising of my whole body, and the torments of the devil and hell itself come upon me, so that I may win Christ Jesus."

John Foxe, The Book of Martyrs, revised with notes and an appendix by W. Bramley-Moore, London, 1869, pp 11-13

PLINY'S WRITINGS

Pliny the Younger, 62?–c.113, was a notable orator and statesman. He is remembered for his letters, which are an excellent mirror of Roman life.

Pliny the Younger was governor of Pontus/Bithynia from 111-113 AD. We have a whole set of exchanges of his letters with the emperor Trajan on a variety of administrative political matters. The following letters are his most famous, in which Pliny encounters Christianity for the first time.

A letter from Pliny the younger, while he was governor of Bithynia, to the Emperor Trajan requested instructions about how to deal with Christians who were brought before him.

I have taken part in the trial of a Christian, and therefore I do not know what it is that they are commonly punished for, and with what degree of allowance, nor what direction the investigation should take. I have been much perplexed to know whether any distinction should be made between one age and another, or whether the weak and tender should be treated in exactly the same way as the strong; whether those who repent should be pardoned, or whether if a person has once been a Christian he should gain nothing by ceasing to be so; whether the very name Christianity is liable to punishment, apart from disgraceful conduct, or the disgraceful conduct which is attached to the name.

[Clearly Pliny thought that there might be nothing to punish in Christianity itself.]

Meanwhile, this is the method which I have followed with those who were brought before me as Christians. I have asked them directly whether they were Christians. If they confessed, I have asked them a second and a third time, with threats of punishment; if they persisted I have ordered them to be executed. I had no doubt that whatever the thing which they confessed amounted to, their obstinacy at any rate, and their inflexible stubbornness, deserved to be punished.

There then follows the earliest description of Christian ways given by a non-Christian.

Yet they affirmed that their fault or their error came to no more than this – that it was their custom to assemble on a fixed day before daylight, and to repeat alternately among themselves a song to Christ as to a god, and to bind themselves by an oath – not to any crime, but that they would not commit theft or robbery or adultery, that they would not break their word, and that when called upon to produce a thing entrusted to them they would not repudiate the trust. When this was done, they said that it had been their habit to depart and then come together again later to take a meal, but an ordinary harmless meal, and this they had ceased to do after the issue of my edict forbidding the existence of organized associations, as you commanded.

This made me think it more necessary to find out from two female slaves, who were called *ministrae* (deaconesses), how far the account was true. So I tortured them, but discovered nothing beyond a degraded and extravagant superstition. So I adjourned the hearing and had recourse to you. The matter seemed to me worth troubling you with, particularly because so many people were imperilled. Many of every age and every rank, and of both sexes too, are and will be in danger. It is not only the cities, but even the villages and the country, that are penetrated by this catching superstition.

Pliny, Letter 10

Trajan to Pliny

You observed proper procedure, my dear Pliny, in sifting the cases of those who had been denounced to you as Christians. For it is not possible to lay down any general rule to serve as a kind of fixed standard. They are not to be sought out; if they are denounced and proved guilty, they are to be punished, with this reservation, that whoever denies that he is a Christian and really proves it – that is, by worshiping our gods – even though he was under suspicion in the past, shall obtain pardon through repentance. But anonymously posted accusations ought to have no place in any prosecution. For this is both a dangerous kind of precedent and out of keeping with the spirit of our age.

Acts of Sharbil

In the fifteenth year of the Sovereign Ruler Trajan Caesar, and in the third year of King Abgar the Seventh, which is the year 416 of the kingdom of Alexander king of the Greeks, and in the priesthood of Sharbil and Barsamya, Trajan Caesar commanded the governors of the countries under his dominion that sacrifices and libations should be increased in all the cities of their administration, and that those who did not sacrifice should be seized and delivered over to stripes, and to the tearing of combs, and to bitter inflictions of all kinds of tortures, and should afterwards receive the punishment of the sword.

Now, when the command arrived at the town of Edessa of the Parthians, there was a great festival, on the eighth of Nisan, on the third day of the week: the whole city was gathered together by the great altar which was in the middle of the town, opposite the Record office, all the gods having been brought together, and decorated, and sitting in honor, both Nebu and Bel together with their fellows. And all the priests were offering incense of spices and libations, and an odor of sweetness was diffusing itself around, and sheep and oxen were being slaughtered, and the sound of the harp and the drum was heard in the whole town. And Sharbil was chief and ruler of all the priests; and he was honored above all his fellows, and was clad in splendid and magnificent vestments; and a headband embossed with figures of gold was set upon his head; and at the bidding of his word everything that he ordered was done. And Abgar the king, son of the gods, was standing at the head of the people. And they obeyed Sharbil, because he drew nearer to all the gods than any of his fellows, and as being the one who according to that which he had heard from the gods returned an answer to every man.

And, while these things were being done by the command of the king, Barsamya, the bishop of the Christians, went up to Sharbil, he and Tiridath the elder and Shalula the deacon; and he said to Sharbil, the high priest: The King Christ, to whom belong heaven and earth, will demand an account at thy hands of all these souls against whom thou art sinning, and whom thou art misleading, and turning away from the God of verity and of truth to idols that are made and deceitful, which are not able to do anything with their hands – moreover also thou hast no pity on thine own soul, which is destitute of the true life of God; and thou declarest to this people that the dumb idols talk with thee; and, as if thou wert listening to something from them, thou puttest thine ear near to one and another of them, and sayest to this people: The god Nebu bade me say to you," On account of your sacrifices and oblations I cause peace in this your country;" and: Bel saith, "I cause great plenty in your land;" and those who hear this from thee do not discern that thou art greatly deceiving them – because "they have a mouth and speak not, and they have eyes and see not with them;" it is ye who bear up them, and not they who bear up you, as ye suppose; and it is ye who set tables before them, and not they who feed you. And now be persuaded by me touching that which I say to thee and advise thee. If thou be willing to hearken to me, abandon idols made, and worship God the Maker of all things, and His Son Jesus Christ. Do not, because He put on a body and became man and was stretched out on the cross of death, be ashamed of Him and refuse to worship Him: for, all these things which He endured – it was for the salvation of men and for their deliverance. For this One who put on a body is God, the Son of God, Son of the essence of His Father, and Son of the nature of Him who begat Him: for He is the adorable brightness of His Godhead, and is the glorious manifestation of His majesty, and together with His Father He existed from eternity and from everlasting, His arm, and His right hand, and His power, and His wisdom, and His strength, and the living Spirit which is from Him, the Expiator and Sanctifier of all His worshiper. These are the things which Palut taught us, with whom thy venerable self was acquainted; and thou knowest that Palut was the disciple of Addaeus the apostle. Abgar the king also, who was older than this Abgar, who himself worshiped idols as well as thou, he too believed in the King Christ, the Son of Him whom thou callest Lord of all the gods. For it is forbidden to Christians to worship anything that is made, and is a creature, and in its nature is not God: even as ye worship idols made by men, who themselves also are made and created. Be persuaded, therefore, by these things which I have said to thee, which things are the belief of the Church: for I know that all this population are looking to thee, and I am well assured that, if thou be persuaded, many also will persuaded with thee. Sharbil said to him: Very acceptable to me are these thy words which thou hast spoken before me; yea, exceedingly acceptable are they to me. But, as for me, I know that I am outcast from all these things, and there is no longer any remedy for me. And, now that hope is cut off from me, why weariest thou thyself about a man dead and buried, for whose death there is no hope of resuscitation? For I am slain by paganism, and am become a dead man, the property of the Evil One: in sacrifices and libations of imposture have I consumed all the days of my life.

And, when Barsamya the bishop heard these things, he fell down before his feet, and said to him: There is hope for those who turn, and healing for those that are wounded. I myself will be surety to thee for the abundant mercies of the Son Christ: that He will pardon thee all the sins which thou hast committed against Him, in that thou hast worshiped and honored His creatures instead of Himself. For that Gracious One, who extended Himself on the cross of death, will not withhold His grace from the souls that comply with His precepts and take refuge in His kindness which has been displayed towards us. Like as He did towards the robber, so is He able to do to thee, and also to those who are like thee. Sharbil said to him: Thou, like a skillful physician, who suffers pain from the pain of the afflicted, hast done well in that thou hast been concerned about me. But at present, because it is the festival to-day of this people, of every one of them, I cannot go down with thee to-day to the church. Depart thou, and go down with honor; and to-morrow at night I will come down to thee: I too have henceforth renounced for myself the gods made with hands, confess the Lord Christ, the Maker of all men. And the next day Sharbil arose and went down to Barsamya by night, he and Babai his sister; and he was received by the whole church. And he said to them: Offer for me prayer and supplication, that Christ may forgive me all the sins that I have committed against Him in all this long course of years. And, because they were in dread of the persecutors, they arose and gave him the seal of salvation, whilst he confessed the Father, and the Son, and the Holy Spirit. And, when all the city had heard that he was gone down to the church, there began to be a consternation among the multitude; and they arose and went down to him, and saw him clad in the fashion of the Christians. And he said to them: May the Son Christ forgive me all the sins that I have committed against you, and all in which I made you think that the gods talked with me, whereas they did not talk; and, forasmuch as I have been to you a cause of abomination, may I now be to you a cause of good: instead of worshiping, as formerly, idols made with hands, may ye henceforth worship God the Maker. And, when they had heard these things, there remained with him a great congregation 678 of men and of women; and Labu also, and Hafsai, and Barcalba, and Avida, chief persons of the city. They all said to Sharbil: Henceforth we also renounce that which thou hast renounced, and we confess the King Christ, whom thou hast confessed.

But Lysanias, the judge of the country, when he heard that Sharbil had done this, sent by night and carded him off from the church. And there went up with him many Christians. And he sat down, to hear him and to judge him, before the altar which is in the middle of the town, where he used to sacrifice to the gods. And he said to him: Wherefore hast thou renounced the gods, whom thou didst worship, and to whom thou didst sacrifice, and to whom thou wast made chief of the priests, and lo! dost today confess Christ, whom thou didst formerly deny? For see how those Christians, to whom thou art gone, renounce not that which they have held, like as thou hast renounced that in which thou wast born. If thou art assured of the gods, how is it that thou hast renounced them this day? But, if on the contrary thou art not assured, as thou declarest concerning them, how is it that thou didst once sacrifice to them and worship them?

Sharbil said: When I was blinded in my mind, I worshiped that which I knew not; but to-day, inasmuch as I have obtained the clear eyes of the mind, it is henceforth impossible that I should stumble at carved stones, or that I should any longer be the cause of stumbling to others. For it is a great disgrace to him whose eyes are open, if he goes and falls into the pit of destruction.

The judge said: Because thou hast been priest of the venerable gods, and hast been partaker of the mystery of those whom the mighty emperors worship, I will have patience with thee, in order that thou mayest be persuaded by me, and not turn away from the service of the gods; but, if on the contrary thou shall not be persuaded by me, by those same gods whom thou hast renounced I swear that, even as on a man that is a murderer, so will I inflict tortures on thee, and will avenge on thee the wrong done to the gods, whom thou hast rebelled against and renounced, and also the insult which thou hast poured upon them; nor will I leave untried any kind of tortures which I will not inflict on thee; and, like as thine honor formerly was great, so will I make thine ignominy great this day.

Sharbil said: I too, on my part, am not content that thou shouldest look upon me as formerly, wheel I worshiped gods made with hands; but look thou upon me to-day and question me as a Christian man renouncing idols and confessing the King Christ.

The judge said: How is it that thou art not afraid of the emperors, nor moved to shame by those who are listening to thy trial, that thou sayest, "I am a Christian"? But promise that thou wilt sacrifice to the gods, according to thy former custom, so that thy honor may be great, as formerly – lest I make to tremble at thee all those who have believed like thyself.

Sharbil said: Of the King of kings I am afraid, but at any king of earth I tremble not, nor yet at thy threats towards me, which lo! thou utterest against the worshiper of Christ: whom I confessed yesterday, and lo! I am brought to trial for His sake to-day, like as He Himself was brought to trial for the sake of sinners like me.

The judge said: Although thou have no pity on thyself, still I will have pity on thee, and refrain from cutting off those hands of thine with which thou hast placed incense before the gods, and from stopping with thy blood those ears of thine which have heard their mysteries, and thy tongue which has interpreted and explained to us their secret things. Of those gods lo! I am afraid, and I have pity on thee. But, if thou continue thus, those gods be my witnesses that I will have no pity on thee!

Sharbil said: As a man who art afraid of the emperors and tremblest at idols, have thou no pity on me. For, as for me, I know not what thou sayest: therefore also is my mind not shaken or terrified by those things which thou sayest. For by thy judgments shall all they escape from the judgment to come who do not worship that which is not God in its own nature.

The judge said: Let him be scourged with thongs, because he has dared to answer me thus, and has resisted the command of the emperors, and has not appreciated the honor which the gods conferred on him: inasmuch as, lo! he has renounced them.

And he was scourged by ten men, who laid hold on him, according to the command of the judge.

Sharbil said: Thou art not aware of the scourging of justice in that world which is to come. For thou wilt cease, and thy judgments also will pass away; but justice will not pass away, nor will its retributions come to an end.

The judge said: Thou art so intoxicated with this same Christianity, that thou dost not even know before whom thou art judged, and by whom it is that thou art scourged – even by those who formerly held thee in honor, and paid adoration to thy priesthood in the gods. Why dost thou hate honor, and love this ignominy? For, although thou speakest contrary to the law, yet I myself cannot turn aside from the laws of the emperors.

Sharbil said: As thou takest heed not to depart from the laws of the emperors, and if moreover thou depart from them thou knowest what command they will give concerning thee, so do I also take heed not to decline from the law of Him who said, "Thou shalt not worship any image, nor any likeness;" and therefore will I not sacrifice to idols made with hands: for long enough was the time in which I sacrificed to them, when I was in ignorance.

The judge said: Bring not upon thee punishment in addition to the punishment which thou hast already brought upon thee. Enough is it for thee to have said, "I will not sacrifice:" do not dare to insult the gods, by calling them manufactured idols whom even the emperors honor.

Sharbil said: But, if on behalf of the emperors, who are far away and not near at hand and not conscious of those who treat their commands with contempt, thou biddest me sacrifice, how is it that on behalf of idols, who lo! are present and are seen, but see not, thou biddest me sacrifice? Why, hereby thou hast declared before all thy attendants that, because they have a mouth and speak not, lo! thou art become a pleader for them: dumb idols "to whom their makers shall be like," and "every one that trusteth upon them" shall be like thee.

The judge said: It was not for this that thou wast called before me – that, instead of paying the honor which is due, thou shouldst despise the emperors. But draw near to the gods and sacrifice, and have pity on thyself, thou self-despiser!

Sharbil said: Why should it be requisite for thee to ask me many questions, after that which I have said to thee: "I will not sacrifice"? Thou hast called me a self-despiser? But would that from my childhood I had had this mind and had thus despised myself, which was perishing!

The judge said: Hang him up, and tear him with combs on his sides. – And while he was thus torn he cried aloud and said: It is for the sake of Christ, who has secretly caused His light to arise upon the darkness of my mind. And, when he had thus spoken, the judge commanded again that he should be torn with combs on his face.

Sharbil said: It is better that thou shouldest inflict tortures upon me for not sacrificing, than that I should be judged there for having sacrificed to the work of men's hands.

The judge said: Let his body be bent backwards, and let straps be tied to his hands and his feet; and, when he has been bent backwards, let him be scourged on his belly.

And they scourged him in this manner, according to the command of the judge.

Then he commanded that he should go up to the prison, and that he should be east into a dark dungeon. And the executioners, and the Christians who had come up with him from the church, carried him, because he was not able to walk upon his feet in consequence of his having been bent backwards. And he was in the gaol many days.

But on the second of Ilul, on the third day of the week, the judge arose and went down to his judgment-hall by night; and the whole body of his attendants was with him; and he commanded the keeper of the prison, and they brought him before him. And the judge said to him: This long while hast thou been in prison: what has been thy determination concerning those things on which thou wast questioned before me? Dost thou consent to minister to the gods according to thy former custom, agreeably to the command of the emperors?

Sharbil said: This has been my determination in the prison, that that with which I began before thee, I will finish even to the last; nor will I play false with my word. For I will not again confess idols, which I have renounced; nor will I renounce the King Christ, whom I have confessed.

The judge said: Hang him up by his right hand, because he has withdrawn it from the gods that he may not again offer incense with it, until his hand with which he ministered to the gods be dislocated, because he persists in this saying of his. And, while he was suspended by his hand, they asked him and said to him: Dost thou consent to sacrifice to the gods? But he was not able to return them an answer, on account of the dislocation of his arm. And the judge commanded, and they loosed him and took him down. But he was not able to bring his arm up to his side, until the executioners pressed it and brought it up to his side.

The judge said: Put on incense, and go whithersoever thou wilt, and no one shall compel thee to be a priest again. But, if thou wilt not, I will show thee tortures bitterer than these.

Sharbil said: As for gods that made not the heavens and the earth, may they perish from under these heavens! But thou, menace me not with words of threatening; but, instead of words, show upon me the deeds of threatening, that I hear thee not again making mention of the detestable name of gods!

The judge said: Let him be branded with the brand of bitter fire between his eyes and upon his cheeks. And the executioners did so, until the smell of the branding reeked forth in the midst of the judgment-hall: but he refused to sacrifice.

Sharbil said: Thou hast heard for thyself from me, when I said to thee "Thou art not aware of the smoke of the roasting of the fire which is prepared for those who, like thee, confess idols made by hands, and deny the living God, after thy fashion."

The judge said: Who taught thee all these things, that thou shouldest speak before me thus – a man who was a friend of the gods and an enemy of Christ, whereas, lo! thou art become his advocate.

Sharbil said: Christ whom I have confessed, He it is that hath taught me to speak thus. But there needeth not that I should be His advocate, for His own mercies are eloquent advocates for guilty ones like me, and these will avail to plead on my behalf in the day when the sentences shall be eternal.

The judge said: Let him be hanged up, and let him be torn with combs upon his former wounds; also let salt and vinegar be rubbed into the wounds upon his sides. Then he said to him: Renounce not the gods whom thou didst formerly confess.

Sharbil said: Have pity on me and spare me again from saying that there be gods, and powers, and fates, and nativities. On the contrary, I confess one God, who made the heavens, and the earth, and the seas, and all that is therein; and the Son who is from Him, the King Christ.

The judge said: It is not about this that thou art questioned before me – viz.: what is the belief of the Christians which thou hast confessed; but this is what I said to thee, "Renounce not those gods to whom thou wast made priest."

Sharbil said: Where is that wisdom of thine and of the emperors of whom thou makest thy boast, that ye worship the work of the hands of the artificers and confess them, whilst the artificers themselves, who made the idols, ye insult by the burdens and imposts which ye lay upon them? The artificer standeth up at thy presence, to do honor to thee; and thou standest up in the presence of the work of the artificer, and dost honor it and worship it.

The judge said: Thou art not the man to call others to account for these things; but from thyself a strict account is demanded, as to the cause for which thou hast renounced the gods, and refusest to offer them incense like thy fellow-priests.

Sharbil said: Death on account of this is true life: those who confess the King Christ, He also will confess before His glorious Father.

The judge said: Let lighted candles be brought, and let them be passed round about his face and about the sides of his wounds. And they did so a long while.

Sharbil said: It is well that thou burnest me with this fire, that so I may be delivered from "that fire which is not quenched, and the worm that dieth not," which is threatened to those who worship things made instead of the Maker: for it is forbidden to the Christians to honor or worship anything except the nature of Him who is God Most High. For that which is made and is created is designed to be a worshiped of its Maker, and is not to be worshiped along with its Creator, as thou supposest.

The governor said: It is not this for which the emperors have ordered me to demand an account at thy hands, whether there be judgment and the rendering of an account after the death of men; nor yet about this do I care, whether that which is made is to be honored or not to be honored. What the emperors have commanded me is this: that, whosoever will not sacrifice to the gods and offer incense to them, I should employ against him stripes, and combs, and sharp swords.

Sharbil said: The kings of this world are conscious of this world only; but the King of all kings, He hath revealed and shown to us that there is another world, and a judgment in reserve, in which a recompense will be made, on the one hand to those who have served God, and on the other to those who have not served Him nor confessed Him. Therefore do I cry aloud, that I will not again sacrifice to idols, nor will I offer oblations to devils, nor will I do honor to demons!

The judge said: Let nails of iron be driven in between the eyes of the insolent fellow, and let him go to that world which he is looking forward to, like a fanatic.

And the executioners did so, the sound of the driving in of the nails being heard as they were being driven in sharply.

Sharbil said: Thou hast driven in nails between my eyes, even as nails were driven into the hands of the glorious Architect of the creation, and by reason of this did all orders of the creation tremble and quake at that season. For these tortures which lo! thou art inflicting on me are nothing in view of that judgment which is to come. For those "whose ways are always firm," because "they have not the judgment of God before their eyes," and who on this account do not even confess that God exists – neither will He confess them.

The judge said: Thou sayest in words that there is a judgment; but I will show thee in deeds: so that, instead of that judgment which is to come, thou mayest tremble and be afraid of this one which is before thine eyes, in which lo! thou art involved, and not multiply thy speech before me.

Sharbil said: Whosoever is resolved to set God before his eyes in secret, God will also be at his right hand; and I too am not afraid of thy threats of tortures, with which thou dost menace me and seek to make me afraid.

The judge said: Let Christ, whom thou hast confessed, deliver thee from all the tortures which I have inflicted on thee, and am about further to inflict on thee; and let Him show His deliverance towards thee openly, and save thee out of my hands.

Sharbil said: This is the true deliverance of Christ imparted to me – this secret power which He has given me to endure all the tortures thou art inflicting on me, and whatsoever it is settled in thy mind still further to inflict upon me; and, although thou hast plainly seen it to be so, thou hast refused to credit my word.

The judge said: Take him away from before me, and let him be hanged upon a beam the contrary way, head downwards; and let him be beaten with whips while he is hanging.

And the executioners did so to him, at the door of the judgment-hall.

Then the governor commanded, and they brought him in before him. And he said to him: Sacrifice to the gods, and do the will of the emperors, thou priest that hatest honor and lovest ignominy instead!

Sharbil said: Why dost thou again repeat thy words, and command me to sacrifice, after the many times that thou hast heard from me that I will not sacrifice again? For it is not any compulsion on the part of the Christians that has kept me back from sacrifices, but the truth they hold: this it is that has delivered me from the error of paganism.

The judge said: Let him be put into a chest of iron like a murderer, and let him be scourged with thongs like a malefactor. And the executioners did so, until there remained not a sound place on him.

Sharbil said: As for these tortures, which thou supposest to be bitter, out of the midst of their bitterness will spring up for me fountains of deliverance and mercy in the day of the eternal sentences.

The governor said: Let small round pieces of wood be placed between the fingers of his hands, and let these be squeezed upon them vehemently.

And they did so to him, until the blood came out from under the nails of his fingers.

Sharbil said: If thine eye be not satisfied with the tortures of the body, add still further to its tortures whatsoever thou wilt.

The judge said: Let the fingers of his hands be loosed, and make him sit upon the ground; and bind his hands upon his knees, and thrust a piece of wood under his knees, and let it pass over the bands of his hands, and hang him up by his feet, thus bent, head downwards; and let him be scourged with thongs. And they did so to him.

Sharbil said: They cannot conquer who fight against God, nor may they be overcome whose confidence is God; and therefore do I say, that "neither fire nor sword, nor death nor life, nor height nor depth, can separate my heart from the love of God, which is in our Lord Jesus Christ."

The judge said: Make hot a ball of lead and of brass, and place it under his armpits.

And they did so, until his ribs began to be seen.

Sharbil said: The tortures thou dost inflict upon me are too little for thy rage against me – unless thy rage were little and thy tortures were great.

The judge said: Thou wilt not hurry me on by these things which thou sayest; for I have room in my mind to bear long with thee, and to behold every evil and shocking and bitter thing which I shall exhibit in the torment of thy body, because thou wilt not consent to sacrifice to the gods whom thou didst formerly worship.

Sharbil said: Those things which I have said and repeated before thee, thou in thine unbelief knowest not how to hear: now, supposest thou that thou knowest those things which are in my mind?

The judge said: The answers which thou givest will not help thee, but will multiply upon thee inflictions manifold.

Sharbil said: If the several stories of thy several gods are by thee accepted as true, yet is it matter of shame to us to tell of what sort they are. For one had intercourse with boys, which is not right; and another fell in love with a maiden, who fled for refuge into a tree, as your shameful stories tell.

The judge said: This fellow, who was formerly a respecter of the gods, but has now turned to insult them and has not been afraid, and has also despised the command of the emperors and has not trembled – set him to stand upon a gridiron heated with fire.

And the executioners did so, until the under part of his feet was burnt off.

Sharbil said: If thy rage is excited at my mention of the abominable and obscene tales of thy gods, how much more does it become thee to be ashamed of their acts! For lo! if a person were to do what one of thy gods did, and they were to bring him before thee, thou wouldest pass sentence of death upon him.

The judge said: This day will I bring thee to account for thy blasphemy against the gods, and thine audacity in insulting also the emperors; nor will I leave thee alone until thou offer incense to them, according to thy former custom.

Sharbil said: Stand by thy threats, then, and speak not falsely; and show towards me in deeds the authority of the emperors which they have given thee; and do not thyself bring reproach on the emperors with thy falsehood, and be thyself also despised in the eyes of thine attendants!

The judge said: Thy blasphemy against the gods and thine audacity towards the emperors have brought upon thee these tortures which thou art undergoing; and, if thou add further to thine audacity, there shall be further added to thee inflictions bitterer than these.

Sharbil said: Thou hast authority, as judge: do whatsoever thou wilt, and show no pity.

The judge said: How can he that hath had no pity on his own body, so as to avoid suffering in it these tortures, be afraid or ashamed of not obeying the command of the emperors?

Sharbil said: Thou hast well said that I am not ashamed: because near at hand is He that justifieth me, and my soul is caught up in rapture towards him. For, whereas I once provoked Him to anger by the sacrifices of idols, I am this day pacifying Him by the inflictions I endure in my person: for my soul is a captive to God who became man.

The judge said: It is a captive, then, that I am questioning, and a madman without sense; and with a dead man who is burnt, lo! am I talking.

Sharbil said: If thou art assured that I am mad, question me no further: for it is a madman that is being questioned; nay, rather, I am a dead man who is burnt, as thou hast said.

The judge said: How shall I count thee a dead man, When lo! thou hast cried aloud, "I will not sacrifice?"

Sharbil said: I myself, too, know not how to return thee an answer, since thou hast called me a dead man and yet turnest to question me again as if alive.

The judge said: Well have I called thee a dead man, because thy feet are burnt and thou carest not, and thy face is scorched and thou holdest thy peace, and nails are driven in between thine eyes and thou takest no account of it, and thy ribs are seen between the furrows of the combs and thou insultest the emperors, and thy whole body is mangled and maimed with stripes and thou blasphemest against the gods; and, because thou hatest thy body, lo! thou sayest whatsoever pleaseth thee.

Sharbil said: If thou callest me audacious because I have endured these things, it is fit that thou, who hast inflicted them upon me, shouldest be called a murderer in thy acts and a blasphemer in thy words.

The judge said: Lo! thou hast insulted the emperors, and likewise the gods; and lo! thou insultest me also, in order that I may pronounce sentence of death upon thee quickly. But instead of this, which thou lookest for, I am prepared yet further to inflict upon thee bitter and severe tortures.

Sharbil said: Thou knowest what I have said to thee many times: instead of denunciations of threatening, proceed to show upon me the performance of the threat, that thou mayest be known to do the will of the emperors.

The judge said: Let him be torn with combs upon his legs and upon the sides of his thighs. And the executioners did so, until his blood flowed and ran down upon the ground.

Sharbil said: Thou hast well done in treating me thus: because I have heard that one of the teachers of the Church hath said, "Scars are on my body, that I may come to the resurrection from the place of the dead." Me too, who was a dead man out of sight, lo! thine inflictions bring to life again.

The judge said: Let him be torn with combs on his face, since he is not ashamed of the nails which are driven in between his eyes.

And they tore him with combs upon his cheeks, and between the nails which were driven into them.

Sharbil said: I will not obey the emperors, who command that to be worshiped and honored which is not of the nature of God, and is not God in its nature, but is the work of him that made it.

The judge said: Like as the emperors worship, so also worship thou; and that honor which the judges render, do thou render also.

Sharbil said: Even though I insult that which is the work of men and has no perception and no feeling of anything, yet do not thou insult God, the Maker of all, nor worship along with Him that which is not of Him, and is foreign to His nature.

The judge said: Does this your doctrine so teach you, that you should insult the very luminaries which give light to all the regions of the earth?

Sharbil said: Although it is not enjoined upon us to insult them, yet it is enjoined upon us not to worship them nor honor them, seeing that they are things made: for this were an insufferable wrong, that a thing made should be worshiped along with its Maker; and it is an insult to the Maker that His creatures should be honored along with Himself.

The judge said: Christ whom thou confessest was hanged on a tree; and on a tree will I hang thee, like thy Master.

And they hanged him on a tree a long while.

Sharbil said: As for Christ, whom lo! thou mockest – see how thy many gods were unable to stand before Him: for lo! they are despised and rejected, and are made a laughing-stock and a jest by those who used formerly to worship them.

The judge said: How is it that thou renouncest the gods, and confessest Christ, who was hanged on a tree?

Sharbil said: This cross of Christ is the great boast of the Christians, since it is by this that the deliverance of salvation has come to all His worshiper, and by this that they have had their eyes enlightened, so as not to worship creatures along with the Creator.

The governor said: Let thy boasting of the cross be kept within thy own mind, and let incense be offered by thy hands to the gods.

Sharbil said: Those who have been delivered by the cross cannot any longer worship and serve the idols of error made with hands: for creature cannot worship creature, because it is itself also designed to be a worshiped of Him who made it; and that it should be worshiped along with its Maker is an insult to its Maker, as I have said before.

The governor said: Leave alone thy books which have taught thee to speak thus, and perform the command of the emperors, that thou idle not by the emperors' law.

But Sharbil said: Is this, then, the justice of the emperors, in whom thou takest such pride, that we should leave alone the law of God and keep their laws?

The governor said: The citation of the books in which thou believest, and from which thou hast quoted – it is this which has brought upon thee these afflictions: for, if thou hadst offered incense to the gods, great would have been thine honor, like as it was formerly, as priest of the gods.

Sharbil said: To thine unbelieving heart these things seem as if they were afflictions; but to the true heart "affliction imparts patience, and from it comes also experience, and from experience likewise the hope" of the confessor.

The governor said: Hang him up and tear him with combs upon his former wounds.

And, from the fury with which the judge urged On the executioners, his very bowels were almost seen. And, lest he should die under the combs and escape from still further tortures, he gave orders and they took him down.

And, when the judge saw that he was become silent and was not able to return him any further answer, he refrained from him a little while, until he began to revive.

Sharbil said: Why hast thou had pity upon me for even this little time, and kept me back from the gain of a confessor's death?

The governor said: I have not had pity on thee at all in refraining for a little while: thy silence it was that made me pause a little; and, if I had power beyond the law of the emperors, I should like to lay other tortures upon thee, so as to be more fully avenged on thee for thine insult toward the gods: for in despising me thou hast despised the gods; and I, on my part, have borne with thee and tortured thee thus, as a man who so deserves.

And the judge gave orders, and suddenly the curtain fell before him for a short time; and he settled and drew up the sentence which he should pronounce against him publicly.

And suddenly the curtain was drawn back again; and the judge cried aloud and said: As regards this Sharbil, who was formerly priest of the gods, but has turned this day and renounced the gods, and has cried aloud "I am a Christian," and has not trembled at the gods, but has insulted them; and, further, has not been afraid of the emperors and their command; and, though I have bidden him sacrifice to the gods according to his former custom, has not sacrificed, but has treated them with the greatest insult: I have looked into the matter, and decided, that towards a man who doeth these things, even though he were now to sacrifice, it is not fit that any mercy should be shown; and that it is not fit that he should any longer behold the sun of his lords, because he has scorned their laws. I give sentence that, according to the law of the emperors, a strap be thrust into the mouth of the insulter, as into the mouth of a murderer, and that he depart outside of the city of the emperors with haste, as one who has insulted the lords of the city and the gods who hold authority over it. I give sentence that he be sawn with a saw of wood, and that, when he is near to die, then his head be taken off with the sword of the headsmen.

And forthwith a strap was thrust into his mouth with all speed, and the executioners hurried him off, and made him run quickly upon his burnt feet, and took him away outside of the city, a crowd of people running after him. For they had been standing looking on at his trial all day, and wondering that he did not suffer under his afflictions: for his countenance, which was cheerful, testified to the joy of his heart. And, when the executioners arrived at the place where he was to receive the punishment of death, the people of the city were with them, that they might see whether they did according as the judge had commanded, and hear what Sharbil might say at that season, so that they might inform the judge of the country.

And they offered him some wine to drink, according to the custom of murderers to drink. But he said to them: I will not drink, because I wish to feel the saw with which ye saw me, and the sword which ye pass over my neck; but instead of this wine, which will not be of any use to me, give me a little time to pray, while ye stand. And he stood up, and looked toward the east, and lifted up his voice and said: Forgive me, Christ, all the sins I have committed against Thee, and all the times in which I have provoked Thee to anger by the polluted sacrifices of dead idols; and have pity on me and save me, and deliver me from the judgment to come; and be merciful to me, as Thou wast merciful to the robber; and receive me like the penitents who have been converted and have turned to Thee, as Thou also hast turned to them; and, whereas I have entered into Thy vineyard, at the eleventh hour, instead of judgment, deliver me from justice: let Thy death, which was for the sake of sinners, restore to life again my slain body in the day of Thy coming.

And, when the Sharirs of the city heard these things, they were very angry with the executioners for having given him leave to pray.

And, while the nails were remaining which had been driven in between his eyes, and his ribs were seen between the wounds of the combs, and while from the burning on his sides and the soles of his feet, which were scorched and burnt, and from the gashes of the combs on his face, and on his sides, and on his thighs, and on his legs, the blood was flowing and running down, they brought carpenters' instruments, and thrust him into a wooden vice, and tightened it upon him until the bones of his joints creaked with the pressure; then they put upon him a saw of iron, and began sawing him asunder; and, when he was just about to die, because the saw had reached to his mouth, they smote him with the sword and took off his head, while he was still squeezed down in the vice.

And Babai his sister drew near and spread out her skirt and caught his blood; and she said to him: May my spirit be united with thy spirit in the presence of Christ, whom thou hast known and believed.

And the Sharirs of the city ran and came and informed the judge of the things which Sharbil had uttered in his prayer, and how his sister had caught his blood. And the judge commanded them to return and give orders to the executioners that, on the spot where she had caught the blood of her brother, she also should receive the punishment of death. And the executioners laid hold on her, and each one of them severally put her to torture; and, with her brother's blood upon her, her soul took its flight from her, and they mingled her blood with his. And, when the executioners were entered into the city, the brethren and young men s ran and stole away their two corpses; and they laid them in the burial-place of the father of Abshelama the bishop, on the fifth of Ilul, the eve of the Sabbath.

I wrote these Acts on paper – I, Marinus, and Anatolus, the notaries; and we placed them in the archives of the city, where the papers of the kings are placed.

This Barsamya, the bishop, made a disciple of Sharbil the priest. And he lived in the days of Binus, bishop of Rome; in whose days the whole population of Rome assembled together, and cried out to the praetor of their city, and said to him: There are too many strangers in this our city, and these cause famine and clearness of everything: but we beseech thee to command them to depart out of the city. And, when he had commanded them to depart out of the city, these strangers assembled themselves together, and said to the praetor: We beseech thee, my lord, command also that the bones of our dead may depart with us. And he commanded them to take the bones of their dead, and to depart. And all the strangers assembled themselves together to take the bones of Simon Cephas and of Paul, the apostles; but the people of Rome said to them: We will not give you the bones of the apostles. And the strangers said to them: Learn ye and understand that Simon, who is called Cephas, is of Bethsaida of Galilee, and Paul the apostle is of Tarsus, a city of Cilicia. And, when the people of Rome knew that this matter was so, then they let them alone. And, when they had taken them up and were removing them from their places, immediately there was a great earthquake; and the buildings of the city were on the point of falling down, and the city was near being overthrown. And, when the people of Rome saw it, their turned and besought the strangers to remain in their city, and that the bones might be laid in their places again. And, when the bones of the apostles were returned to their places, there was quietness, and the earthquakes ceased, and the winds became still, and the air became bright, and the whole city became cheerful. And when the Jews and pagans saw it, they also ran and fell at the feet of Fabianus, the bishop of their city, the Jews crying out: We confess Christ, whom we crucified: He is the Son of the living-God, of whom the prophets spoke in their mysteries. And the pagans also cried out and said to him: We renounce idols and carved images, which are of no use, and we believe in Jesus the King, the Son of God, who has come and is to come again. And, what ever other doctrines there were in Rome and in all Italy, the followers of these also renounced their doctrines, like as the pagans had renounced theirs, and confessed the Gospel of the apostles, which was preached in the church.

Here end the Acts of Sharbil the confessor.

Marinus, and Anatolus

Martyrdom of Barsamya, bishop of Edessa

Many Christians who have undergone great privations, trials or tortures, but who have not been put to death, are nonetheless acclaimed as martyrs.

In the year four hundred and sixteen of the kingdom of the Greeks [A.D. 105], that is the fifteenth year of the reign of the sovereign ruler, our lord, Trajan Caesar, in the consulship of Commodus and Cyrillus [Cerealis], the day after Lysinus, the judge of the country, had heard the case of Sharbil the priest; as the judge was sitting in his judgment-hall, the Sharirs of the city came before him and said to him:

"We give information before thine Excellency concerning Barsamya, the leader of the Christians, that he went up to Sharbil, the priest, as he was standing and ministering before the venerable gods, and sent and called him to him secretly, and spoke to him, quoting from the books in which he reads in the church where their congregation meets, and recited to him the belief of the Christians, and said to him, "It is not right for thee to worship many gods, but only one God, and His Son Jesus Christ" – until he made him a disciple, and induced him to renounce the gods whom he had formerly worshiped; and by means of Sharbil himself also many have become disciples, and are gone down to the church, and lo! this day they confess Christ; and even Avida, and Nebo, and Barcalba, and Hafsai, honorable and chief persons of the city, have yielded to Sharbil in this. We, accordingly, as Sharirs of the city, make this known before thine Excellency, in order that we may not receive punishment as offenders for not having declared before thine Excellency the things which were spoken in secret to Sharbil by Barsamya the guide of the church. Thine Excellency now knoweth what it is right to command in respect of this said matter."

And, immediately that the judge heard these things, he sent the Sharirs of the city, and some of his attendants with them, to go down to the church and bring up Barsamya from the church. And they led him and brought him up to the judgment-hall of the judge; and there went up many Christians with him, saying: We also will die with Barsamya, because we too are of one mind with him in respect to the doctrine of which he made Sharbil a disciple, and in all that he spoke to him, and in all that Sharbil received from him, so that he was persuaded by him, and died for the sake of that which he heard from him.

And the Sharirs of the city came, and said to the judge: Barsamya, as thine Excellency commanded, lo! is standing at the door of the judgement-hall of thy Lordship; and honorable chief-persons of the city, who became disciples along with Sharbil, lo! are standing by Barsamya, and crying out, "We will all die with Barsamya, who is our teacher and guide."

And, when the judge heard those things which the Sharirs of the city had told him, he commanded them to go out and write down the names of the persons who were crying out, "We will all die with Barsamya." And, when they went out to write down the names of these persons, those who so cried out were too many for them, and they were not able to write down their names, because they were so many: for the cry kept coming to them from all sides, that they "would die for Christ's sake along with Barsamya." And, when the tumult of the crowd became great, the Sharirs of the city turned back, and came in to the judge, and said to him: We are not able to write down the names of the persons who are crying aloud outside, because they are too many to be numbered. And the judge commanded that Barsamya should be taken up to the prison, so that the crowd might be dispersed which was collected together about him, lest through the tumult of the multitude there should be some mischief in the city. And, when he went up to the gaol, those who had become disciples along with Sharbil continued with him.

And after many days were passed the judge rose up in the morning and went down to his judgement-hall, in order that he might hear the case of Barsamya. And the judge commanded, and they brought him from the prison; and he came in and stood before him. The officers said: Lo, he standeth before thine Excellency.

The judge said: Art thou Barsamya, who hast been made ruler and guide of the people of the Christians, and didst make a disciple of Sharbil, who was chief-priest of the gods, and used to worship them?

Barsamya said: It is I who have done this, and I do not deny it; and I am prepared to die for the truth of this.

The judge said: How is it that thou wast not afraid of the command of the emperors, so that, when the emperors commanded that every one should sacrifice, thou didst induce Sharbil, when he was standing and sacrificing to the gods and offering incense to them, to deny that which he had confessed, and confess Christ whom he had denied?

Barsamya said: I was assuredly made a shepherd of men, not for the sake of those only who are found, but also for the sake of those who have strayed from the fold of truth, and become food for the wolves of paganism; and, had I not sought to make Sharbil a disciple, at my hands would his blood have been required; and, if he had not listened to me, I should have been innocent of his blood.

The judge said: Now, therefore, since thou hast confessed that it was thou that madest Sharbil a disciple, at thy hands will I require his death; and on this account it is right that thou rather than he shouldest be condemned before me, because by thy hands he has died the horrible deaths of grievous tortures for having abandoned the command of the emperors and obeyed thy words.

Barsamya said: Not to my words did Sharbil become a disciple, but to the word of God which He spoke: "Thou shalt not worship images and likenesses of men." And it is not I alone that am content to die the death of Sharbil for his confession of Christ, but also all the Christians, members of the church, are likewise eager for this, because they know that they will secure their salvation before God thereby.

The judge said: Answer me not in this manner, like Sharbil thy disciple, lest thine own torments be worse than his; but promise that thou wilt sacrifice before the gods on his behalf.

Barsamya said: Sharbil, who knew not God, I taught to know [Him]: and dost thou bid -me-, who have known God from my youth, to renounce God? God forbid that I should do this thing!

The judge said: Ye have made the whole creation disciples of the teaching of Christ ; and lo ! they renounce the many gods whom the many worshiped. Give up this way of thinking, [Lit. "this mind"] lest I make those who are near tremble at thee as they behold thee to- day, and those also that are afar off as they hear of the torments to which thou art condemned.

Barsamya said: If God is the help of those who pray to Him, who is he that can resist them? Or what is the power that can prevail against them? Or thine own threats — what can they do to them : to men who, before thou give commandment concerning them that they shall die, have their death [already] set before their eyes, and are expecting it every day?

The judge said : Bring not the subject of Christ before my judgment- seat ; but, instead of this, obey the command of the emperors, who command to sacrifice to the gods.

Barsamya said: Even though we should not lay the subject of Christ before thee, [yet] the sufferings of Christ are portrayed and fixed in the worshiper of Christ ; and, even more than thou hearkenest to the commands of the emperors, do we Christians hearken to the commands of Christ the King of kings.

The judge said: Lo ! thou hast obeyed Christ and worshiped him up to this day : henceforth obey the emperors, and worship the gods whom the emperors worship.

Barsamya said: How canst thou bid me renounce that in which I was born ? when lo ! thou didst exact [punishment] for this at the hand of Sharbil, and saidst to him : Why has thou renounced the paganism in which thou wast born, and confessed Christianity to which thou wast a stranger ? Lo ! even before I came into thy presence thou didst thyself give testimony [on the matter] beforehand, and saidst to Sharbil : the Christians, to whom thou art gone [over], do not renounce that in which they were born, but continue in it. Abide, therefore, by the word, which thou hast spoken.

The judge said: Let Barsamya be scourged, because he has rebelled against the command of the emperors, and has caused those also who were obedient to the emperors to rebel with him.

And, when he had been scourged by five men he said to him: Reject not the command of the emperors, nor insult the emperor's gods.

Barsamya said: Thy mind is greatly blinded, O judge, and so also is that of the emperors who gave thee authority; nor are the things that are manifest seen by you; nor do ye perceive that lo! the whole creation worships Christ; and thou sayest to me, Do not worship Him, as if I alone worshiped Him – Him who the watchers above worship on high.

The judge said: But if ye have taught men to worship Christ, who is that has persuaded those above to worship Christ?

Barsamya said: Those above have themselves preached, and have taught those below concerning the living worship of the King Christ, seeing that they worship Him, and His Father, together with His divine Spirit.

The judge said: Give up these things which your writings teach you, and which ye teach also to others, and obey those things which the emperors have commanded, and spurn not their laws – lest ye be spurned by means of the sword from the light of this venerable sun.

Barsamya said: The light which passeth away and abideth not is not the true light, but is only the similitude of that true light, to whose beams darkness cometh not near, which is reserved and standeth fast for the true worshiper of Christ.

The judge said: Speak not before me of anything else instead of that about which I have asked thee, lest I dismiss thee from life to death, for denying this light which is seen and confessing that which is not seen.

Barsamya said: I cannot leave alone that about which thou askest me, and speak of that about which thou dost not ask me. It was thou that spakest to me about the light of the sun, and I said before thee that there is a light on high which surpasses in its brightness that of the sun which thou dost worship and honor. For an account will be required of thee for worshiping thy fellow creature instead of God thy Creator.

The judge said: Do not insult the very sun, the light of creatures, nor set thou at nought the command of the emperors, nor contentiously resist the lords of the country, who have authority in it.

Barsamya said: Of what avail is the light of the sun to a blind man that cannot see it? For without the eyes of the body, [we know], it is not possible for its beams to be seen. So that by this thou mayest know that it is the work of God, forasmuch as it has no power of its own to show its light to the sightless.

The judge said: When I have tortured thee as thou deservest, then will I write word about thee to the Imperial government, reporting what insult thou hast offered to the gods, in that thou madest a disciple of Sharbil the priest, one who honored the gods, and that ye despise the laws of the emperors, and that ye make no account of the judges of the countries, and live like barbarians, though under the authority of the Romans.

Barsamya said: Thou dost not terrify me by these things which thou sayest. It is true, I am not in the presence of the emperors to-day; yet lo! before the authority which the emperors have given thee I am now standing, and I am brought to trial, because I said, I will not renounce God, to whom the heavens and the earth belong, nor His Son Jesus Christ, the King of all the earth.

The judge said: If thou art indeed assured of this, that thou art standing and being tried before the authority of the emperors, obey their commands, and rebel not against their laws, lest like a rebel thou receive the punishment of death.

Barsamya said: But if those who rebel against the emperors, even when they justly rebel, are deserving of death, as thou sayest; for those who rebel against God, the King of kings, even the punishment of death by the sword is too little.

The judge said: It was not that thou shouldest expound in my judgement-hall that thou wast brought in before me, because the trial on which thou standest has but little concern with expounding, but much concern with the punishment of death, for those who insult the emperors and comply not with their laws.

Barsamya said: Because God is not before your eyes, and ye refuse to hear the word of God; and graven images that are of no use, "which have a mouth and speak not," are accounted by you as though they spake, because your understanding is blinded by the darkness of paganism in which ye stand–

The judge [interrupting] said: Leave off those things thou art saying, for they will not help thee at all, and worship the gods, before the bitter [tearing of] combs and harsh tortures come upon thee.

Barsamya said: Do thou too leave off the many questions which lo! thou askest me, and at once give command for the stripes and the combs with which thou dost menace me: for thy words will not help thee so much as thy inflictions will help me.

The judge said: Let Barsamya be hanged up and torn with combs.

And at that very moment there came to him letters from Alusis the chief proconsul, father of emperors [probably Lusius Quietus, Trajan's general in the East]. And he commanded, and they took down Barsamya, and he was not torn with combs; and they took him outside of the hall of judgement.

And the judge commanded that the nobles, and the chief persons, and the princes, and the honorable persons of the city, should come before him, that they might hear what was the order that was issued by the emperors, by the hand of the proconsuls, the rulers of the countries under the authority of the Romans. And it was found that the emperors had written by the hand of the proconsuls to the judges of the countries: "since our Majesty commanded that there should be a persecution against the people of the Christians, we have heard and learned, from the Sharirs whom we have in the countries under the dominion of our Majesty, that the people of the Christians are persons who eschew murder, and sorcery, and adultery, and theft, and bribery and fraud, and those things for which the laws of our Majesty also exact punishment from those who commit them. We, therefore, in our impartial justice, have commanded that on account of these things the persecution of the sword shall cease from them, and that there shall be rest and quietness in all our dominions, they continuing to minister according to their custom and no man hindering them. It is not, however, towards them that we show clemency, but towards their laws, agreeing as they do with the laws of our Majesty. And, if any man hinder them after this our command, that sword which is ordered by us to descend upon those who despise our command, the same do we command to descend upon those who despise this decree of our clemency."

And, when this command of the emperor's clemency was read, the whole city rejoiced that there was quietness and rest for every man. And the judge commanded, and they released Barsamya, that he might go down to his church. And the Christians went up in great numbers to the judgement-hall, together with a great multitude of the population of the city, and they received Barsamya with great and exceeding honor, repeating psalms before him, according to their custom; there went also the wives of the chief of the wise men. And they thronged about him, and saluted him, and called him "the persecuted confessor," "the companion of Sharbil the martyr." And he said to them: Persecuted I am, like yourselves; but from the tortures and combs of Sharbil and his companions I am clean escaped. And they said to him: We have heard from thee that a teacher of the church has said, "The will, according to what it is, so is it accepted." [2 Cor. 8:12] And, when he was entered into the church, he and all the people that were with him, he stood up and prayed, and blessed them and sent them away to their homes rejoicing and praising God for the deliverance which He had wrought for them and for the church.

And the day after Lysinas the judge of the country had set his hand to these Acts, he was dismissed from his authority.

I, Zenophilus, and Patrophilus are the notaries who wrote these Acts, Diodorus and Euterpes, Sharirs of the city, bearing witness with us by setting-to their hand, as the ancient laws of the ancient kings commanded.

This Barsamya, bishop of Edessa, who made a disciple of Sharbil, the priest of the same city, lived in the days of Fabianus, bishop of the city of Rome. And ordination to the priesthood was received by Barsamya from Abshelama, who was bishop in Edessa; and by Abshelama ordination was received from Palut the First; and by Palut ordination was received from Serapion, bishop of Antioch; and by Serapion ordination was received from Zephyrinus, bishop of Rome; and Zephyrinus of Rome received ordination from Victor of the same place, Rome; and Victor received ordination from Eleutherius; and Eleutherius received it from Soter; and Soter received it from Anicetus; and Anicetus received it from Pius; and Pius received it from Telesphorus; and Telesphorus received it from Xystus; and Xystus received it from Alexander; and Alexander received it from Evartis; and Evartis received it from Cletus; and Cletus received it from Linus; and Linus received it from Simon Cephas; and Simon Cephas received it from our Lord, together with his fellow-apostles, on the first day of the week, the day of the ascension of our Lord to His glorious Father, which was the fourth day of Heziran, which was in the nineteenth year of the reign of Tiberius Caesar, in the consulship of Rufus and Rubelinus, which year was the year 341 of the kingdom of the Greeks; for in the year 309 occured the advent of our Savior in the world, according to the testimony which we ourselves have found in a correct register among the archives, which errs not at all in whatever it sets forth.

Here endeth the martyrdom of Barsamya, bishop of Edessa.

Marinus, and Anatolus

Tortures of the First Christian Martyrs

1: The cross and stakes

Of the cross, of stakes, and other means whereby the bodies of Christians remaining steadfast in their confession of Christ were suspended.

a. Martyrs suspended by one foot.

b. Martyrs suspended by both feet.

c. Martyrs raised on the cross, head uppermost.

d. Martyrs nailed to the cross, head downwards.

e. Martyrs hung up by both arms with heavy weights attached to the feet.

f. Christian women martyrs suspended by their hair.

g. Martyrs hung up by one arm only, with ponderous stones attached to their feet.

h. Martyrs suspended by both feet with a great stone fastened to the neck.

i. Sometimes the blessed martyrs, after being smeared with honey, were bound to stakes fixed to the ground, and so exposed to the rays of the sun, to be tortured by the bites and stings of flies and bees.

j. Martyrs suspended by one foot; one leg is bent at the knee, which is constricted by means of an iron ring, the other being weighed with a heavy mass of iron.

k. Martyrs suspended by their thumbs, with heavy stones attached to their feet.

l. Christians hung up, and a slow fire kindled underneath to suffocate them with the smoke.

m. Martyrs were suspended by their feet and at the same time pounded with hammers.

n. Martyrs were suspended by the hands, which were tied behind their backs, and heavy weights fastened to their feet and round their neck.

o. Martyrs were suspended by the hands, which were tied behind his back, and had the shoulders weighed down with lumps of salt. Wooden gags were forced into their mouths.

Source: Tortures and Torments of the Christian Martyrs, from the "De SS. Martyrum Cruciatibus of Gallonio, translated by A.R. Allinson (London and Paris, printed for the subscribers, 1903), pp. 34-37

EUSTATHIUS

We say we are Christians, we proclaim it to the whole world, even under the hands of the executioner, and in the midst of all the torments you inflict upon us to compel us to unsay it. Torn and mangled, and weltering in our blood, we cry out as loud as we are able to cry, That we are worshipers of God through Christ.

Tertullian, Apologeticus, c. 21

General Eustathius, under Emperor Trajan, was returning victorious from a successful campaign against the Barbarians. And it came to pass that as he did this Emperor Trajan died and he was replaced by Adrian (Hadrian), who was an exceedingly irreligious man, and was more wicked than all the other kings who had reigned before him. And when Eustathius was returning from the war the Emperor went out to meet him, according to the custom of the Roman Emperors, and he brought with him all his nobles, because of the long list of all the places which Eustathius had captured. And Eustathius, because of his valor, whereof he was conscious, and because of his meeting with his wife and sons, was filled to the uttermost with his joy. And when he had come into the city the Emperor went and entered into the temple of Apollo, but Eustathius did not go in with him, and remained outside. And the Emperor called him, and asked him why he did not come into the temple of Apollo, saying, "Thou must pour out a libation to the gods in return for thy victory, and because thou has returned from the war, and thou must offer up sacrifices of thanksgiving to them."

Then the Emperor was wroth when he heard these things from Eustathius, and he made him withdraw from him as if he had been a pagan, he and his wife and his sons, and he spake unto them words of terror and threats of destruction. And the saints neither regarded them nor were they frightened at all. And when the Emperor saw their lack of concern and their faith in the Christ, he commanded them to be taken too the stadium, and for a mighty lion to be let loose in the stadium. And when the lion advanced to attack them he stood still before the saints, and bent his legs and worshiped them, and he laid his head also down to the ground. And afterwards he came out of the stadium and departed. And when the Emperor saw this great sight, and that the wild beast would not attack them, he fell into doubt. And he commanded them to make a brazen bull, so that they might cast the saints into it and burn them. And the multitude gathered together to see the strife and the spectacle of the saints. The Emperor's servants seized them with mechanical devices to lift them up in the brazen bull.

Then the blessed Eustathius entreated the honorable people to allow them to pray, and he spread out his hands, he and his wife and his sons, and they prayed, saying: "O Lord God of the Powers, whom no man hath ever seen, but whom now we see according to his wish, hearken thou now unto us who cry unto thee. Make thou our prayer to be perfect with one thought, namely the confession of thy name and thy holy faith. Make thou us worthy to be counted among the holy martyrs, and let the threat of this fire which is round about us become to us the dew of refreshing, so that our bodies, O Lord, may gain strength thereby."

Then the saints delivered themselves over to the soldiers, who cast them into the brazen instrument. And having been thrown in the flame of fire it enveloped them, and they ascribed glory to the Holy Trinity, unto whom victory belongeth, and after a short time they delivered up their souls into the hands of God. And the fire did not scorch their bodies in the least degree, nor the hair of their heads.

And after three days the wicked Emperor Hadrian came to the place wherein the saints had finished their fight, an he commanded that the brazen bull should be opened, so that he might be able to see what had happened to the saints. And when it had been opened they found the bodies of the saints in a perfect state of preservation, and there were no marks of destruction whatever in them, and they seemed to be still alive. And when they had brought them out and laid them on the ground, great awe and wonder came upon every one who stood near them, and the bodies of the saints were brilliantly white like snow. The evil Hadrian looked on them, was filled with wonder and fear, and went away. The multitude who were standing there cried out, "Great art thou, O God of the Christians! Thou art indeed the only Great God, Jesus the Christ, and there is no other god besides thee. for thou didst not permit any harm to reach the bodies of these saints, nay, they have become brilliantly white and shining, and they send forth great light with glory and gladness."

And when the evening had come the Christians came and carried away the bodies of the martyred saints, and they laid them in an honorable place secretly in the city of Rome.

E. A. Wallis Budge (ed.), Coptic Martyrdom in the Dialect of Upper Egypt, British Museum, 1914, pp 376-80 (extract from BM oriental manuscript 6783)

SYMPHOROSA AND HER SEVEN SONS

Symphorosa and her seven sons: Crescens, Julian, Nemesius, Primativus, Justin, Stacteus, Eugeniusc: 120

According to Paulinus, after the destruction of Jerusalem, Emperor Adrian (Hadrian) erected Jupiter where Christ rose from the dead, a marble Venus on the place of Christ's crucifixion; and at Bethlehem, a grotto consecrated in honor of Adonis, to whom he also dedicated the cave where Christ was born. This prince, towards the end of his reign abandoned himself more than ever to acts of cruelty, and being awaked by a fit of superstition he again drew his sword against the innocent flock of Christ. He built a magnificent country palace at Tibur, now Tivoli, sixteen miles from Rome, on the banks of the river Teverone. Here he placed whatever could be procured most curious out of all the provinces. Having finished the building he intended to dedicate it by heathenish ceremonies which he began by offering sacrifices, in order to induce the idols to deliver their oracles. The demons answered: "The widow Symphorosa and her seven sons daily torment us by invoking their God; if they sacrifice, we promise to be favorable to your vows."

Symphorosa was well known for relieving Christians who suffered for their faith. Adrian, whose superstition was alarmed at the answer of his gods or their priests, ordered that Symphorosa and her sons should be seized, and brought before him. She came with joy in her countenance, praying all the way for herself and her children, that God would grant them the grace to confess his holy name with constancy. The emperor exhorted them at first in mild terms to sacrifice.

Symphorosa answered: "My husband Getusius and his brother Amantius, being your tribunes, have suffered various torments for the name of Jesus Christ rather than sacrifice to idols; and they have vanquished your demons by their death, choosing to be beheaded rather than to overcome. The death they suffered drew upon them ignominy among men, but glory among the angels; and they now enjoy eternal life in heaven."

The emperor, changing his voice, said to her in an angry tone, "Either sacrifice to the most powerful gods, with thy sons, or thou thyself shalt be offered up as a sacrifice together with them."

Symphorosa answered: "Your gods cannot receive me as a sacrifice; but if I am burnt for the name of Jesus Christ my death will increase the torment which your devils endure in their flames. But can I hope for so great a happiness as to be offered with my children a sacrifice to the true and living God?"

Adrian said, "Either sacrifice to my gods, or you shall all miserably perish."

Symphorosa said: "Do not imagine that

fear will make me change; I desire to be at rest with my husband whom you put to death for the name of Jesus Christ."

The emperor then ordered her to be carried to the temple of Hercules, where she was first buffeted on the cheeks, and afterward hung up by the hair of her head. When no torments were able to shake her invincible soul, the emperor gave orders that she should be thrown into the river with a great stone fastened about her neck.

The next day the emperor sent for her seven sons all together, and exhorted them to sacrifice and not imitate the obstinacy of their mother. He added the severest threats, but finding all to be in vain, he ordered seven stakes with engines and pulleys to be planted round the temple of Hercules, and the pious youths to be bound upon them; their limbs were in this posture tortured and stretched in such a manner that the bones were disjointed in all parts of their bodies. The young noblemen, far from yielding under the violence of their tortures, were encouraged by each other's example, and seemed more eager to suffer than the executioners were to torment.

At length the emperor commanded them to be put to death, in the same place where they were, but in different ways. The eldest, called Crescens, had his throat cut; the second, called Julian, was stabbed in the chest; Nemesius, the third, was pierced with a lance in his heart; Primativus received his wound in the belly, Justin in the back, Stacteus on his sides, and Eugenius the youngest died by his body being cleft asunder into two parts across his chest from the head down.

Alban Butler, The Lives of the Saints, Dublin, 1833, volume II, pp 90-91

The Fourth Persecution, under Marcus Aurelius

Soter, bishop of the church of Rome, died after an episcopate of eight years, and was succeeded by Eleutherus, the twelfth from the apostles. In the seventeenth year of the Emperor Antoninus Verus, the persecution of our people was rekindled more fiercely in certain districts on account of an insurrection of the masses in the cities; and judging by the number in a single nation, myriads suffered martyrdom throughout the world. A record of this was written for posterity, and in truth it is worthy of perpetual remembrance. A full account, containing the most reliable information on the subject, is given in our Collection of Martyrdoms, which constitutes a narrative instructive as well as historical. I will repeat here such portions of this account as may be needful for the present purpose. Other writers of history record the victories of war and trophies won from enemies, the skill of generals, and the manly bravery of soldiers, defiled with blood and with innumerable slaughters for the sake of children and country and other possessions. But our narrative of the government of God will record in ineffaceable letters the most peaceful wars waged in behalf of the peace of the soul, and will tell of men doing brave deeds for truth rather than country, and for piety rather than dearest friends. It will hand down to imperishable remembrance the discipline and the much-tried fortitude of the athletes of religion, the trophies won from demons, the victories over invisible enemies, and the crowns placed upon all their heads.

Eusebius of Caesarea, Church History, Book 5, Introduction

The Martyrs, beloved of God, kindly ministered to the persecuted

Such things happened to the churches of Christ under the above-mentioned emperor, from which we may reasonably conjecture the occurrences in the other provinces. It is proper to add other selections from the same letter, in which the moderation and compassion of these witnesses is recorded in the following words: "They were also so zealous in their imitation of Christ, who, being in the form of God, counted it not a prize to be on an equality with God," that, though they had attained such honor, and had borne witness, not once or twice, but many times, having been brought back to prison from the wild beasts, covered "with burns and scars and wounds, yet they did not proclaim themselves witnesses, nor did they suffer us to address them by this name. If any one of us, in letter or conversation, spoke of them as witnesses, they rebuked him sharply. For they conceded cheerfully the appellation of Witness to Christ the faithful and true Witness," and "firstborn of the dead," and prince of the life of God; and they reminded us of the witnesses who had already departed, and said, "They are already witnesses whom Christ has deemed worthy to be taken up in their confession, having sealed their testimony by their departure; but we are lowly and humble confessors."

And they besought the brethren with tears that earnest prayers should be offered that they might be made perfect. They showed in their deeds the power of "testimony," manifesting great boldness toward all the brethren, and they made plain their nobility through patience and fearlessness and courage, but they refused the title of Witnesses as distinguishing them from their brethren, being filled with the fear of God." A little further on they say: "They humbled themselves under the mighty hand, by which they are now greatly exalted. They defended all, but accused none. They absolved all, but bound none. And they prayed for those who had inflicted cruelties upon them, even as Stephen, the perfect witness, "Lord, lay not this sin to their charge." But if he prayed for those who stoned him, how much more for the brethren !" And again after mentioning other matters, they say: "For, through the genuineness of their love, their greatest contest with him was that the Beast, being choked, might cast out alive those whom he supposed he had swallowed. For they did not boast over the fallen, but helped them in their need with those things in which they themselves abounded, having the compassion of a mother, and shedding many tears on their account before the Father. They asked for life, and he gave it to them, and they shared it with their neighbors. Victorious; over everything, they departed to God. Having always loved peace, and having commended peace to us they went in peace to God, leaving no sorrow to their mother, nor division or strife to the brethren, but joy and peace and concord and love."

This record of the affection of those blessed ones toward the brethren that had fallen may be profitably added on account of the inhuman and unmerciful disposition of those who, after these events, acted unsparingly toward the members of Christ.
Eusebius of Caesarea, Church History, Book 5, chapter 2

The Fourth Persecution, Under Marcus Aurelius Antoninus, A.D. 162

Marcus Aurelius, followed about the year of our Lord 161, a man of nature more stern and severe; and, although in study of philosophy and in civil government no less commendable, yet, toward the Christians sharp and fierce; by whom was moved the fourth persecution.

The cruelties used in this persecution were such that many of the spectators shuddered with horror at the sight, and were astonished at the intrepidity of the sufferers. Some of the martyrs were obliged to pass, with their already wounded feet, over thorns, nails, sharp shells, etc. upon their points, others were scourged until their sinews and veins lay bare, and after suffering the most excruciating tortures that could be devised, they were destroyed by the most terrible deaths.

Germanicus, a young man, but a true Christian, being delivered to the wild beasts on account of his faith, behaved with such astonishing courage that several pagans became converts to a faith which inspired such fortitude.

Polycarp, the venerable bishop of Smyrna, hearing that persons were seeking for him, escaped, but was discovered by a child. After feasting the guards who apprehended him, he desired an hour in prayer, which being allowed, he prayed with such fervency, that his guards repented that they had been instrumental in taking him. He was, however, carried before the proconsul, condemned, and burnt in the market place.

The proconsul then urged him, saying, "swear, and I will release thee; – reproach Christ."

Polycarp answered, "Eighty and six years

have I served him, and he never once wronged me; how then shall I blaspheme my King, Who hath saved me?" At the stake to which he was only tied, but not nailed as usual, as he assured them he should stand immovable, the flames, on their kindling the fagots, encircled his body, like an arch, without touching him; and the executioner, on seeing this, was ordered to pierce him with a sword, when so great a quantity of blood flowed out as extinguished the fire. But his body, at the instigation of the enemies of the Gospel, especially Jews, was ordered to be consumed in the pile, and the request of his friends, who wished to give it Christian burial, rejected. They nevertheless collected his bones and as much of his remains as possible, and caused them to be decently interred.

Metrodorus, a minister, who preached boldly, and Pionius, who made some excellent apologies for the Christian faith, were likewise burnt. Carpus and Papilus, two worthy Christians, and Agatonica, a pious woman, suffered martyrdom at Pergamopolis, in Asia.

Felicitatis, an illustrious Roman lady, of a considerable family, and the most shining virtues, was a devout Christian. She had seven sons, whom she had educated with the most exemplary piety.

Januarius, the eldest, was scourged, and pressed to death with weights; Felix and Philip, the two next had their brains dashed out with clubs; Silvanus, the fourth, was murdered by being thrown from a precipice; and the three younger sons, Alexander, Vitalis, and Martial, were beheaded. The mother was beheaded with the same sword as the three latter.

Justin, the celebrated philosopher, fell a martyr in this persecution. He was a native of Neapolis, in Samaria, and was born A.D. 103. Justin was a great lover of truth, and a universal scholar; he investigated the Stoic and Peripatetic philosophy, and attempted the Pythagorean; but the behavior of our of its professors disgusting him, he applied himself to the Platonic, in which he took great delight. About the year 133, when he was thirty years of age, he became a convert to Christianity, and then, for the first time, perceived the real nature of truth.

He wrote an elegant epistle to the Gentiles, and employed his talents in convincing the Jews of the truth of the Christian rites; spending a great deal of time in traveling, until he took up his abode in Rome, and fixed his habitation upon the Viminal mount.

He kept a public school, taught many who afterward became great men, and wrote a treatise to confuse heresies of all kinds. As the pagans began to treat the Christians with great severity, Justin wrote his first apology in their favor. This piece displays great learning and genius, and occasioned the emperor to publish an edict in favor of the Christians.

Soon after, he entered into frequent contests with Crescens, a person of a vicious life and conversation, but a celebrated cynic philosopher; and his arguments appeared so powerful, yet disgusting to the cynic, that he resolved on, and in the sequel accomplished, his destruction.

The second apology of Justin, upon certain severities, gave Crescens the cynic an opportunity of prejudicing the emperor against the writer of it; upon which Justin, and six of his companions, were apprehended. Being commanded to sacrifice to the pagan idols, they refused, and were condemned to be scourged, and then beheaded; which sentence was executed with all imaginable severity.

Several were beheaded for refusing to sacrifice to the image of Jupiter; in particular Concordus, a deacon of the city of Spolito.

Some of the restless northern nations having risen in arms against Rome, the emperor marched to encounter them. He was, however, drawn into an ambuscade, and dreaded the loss of his whole army. Enveloped with mountains, surrounded by enemies, and perishing with thirst, the pagan deities were invoked in vain; when the men belonging to the militine, or thundering legion, who were all Christians, were commanded to call upon their God for succor. A miraculous deliverance immediately ensued; a prodigious quantity of rain fell, which, being caught by the men, and filling their dykes, afforded a sudden and astonishing relief. It appears that the storm which miraculously flashed in the face of the enemy so intimidated them, that part deserted to the Roman army; the rest were defeated, and the revolted provinces entirely recovered.

This affair occasioned the persecution to subside for some time, at least in those parts immediately under the inspection of the emperor; but we find that it soon after raged in France, particularly at Lyons, where the tortures to which many of the Christians were put, almost exceed the powers of description.

The principal of these martyrs were Vetius Agathus, a young man; Blandina, a Christian lady, of a weak constitution; Sanctus, a deacon of Vienna; red hot plates of brass were placed upon the tenderest parts of his body: Biblias, a weak woman, once an apostate; Attalus, of Pergamus; and Pothinus, the venerable bishop of Lyons, who was ninety years of age. Blandina, on the day when she and the three other champions were first brought into the amphitheater, she was suspended on a piece of wood fixed in the ground, and exposed as food for the wild beasts; at which time, by her earnest prayers, she encouraged others. But none of the wild beasts would touch her, so that she was remanded to prison. When she was again produced for the third and last time, she was accompanied by Ponticus, a youth of fifteen, and the constancy of their faith so enraged the multitude that neither the sex of the one nor the youth of the other were respected, being exposed to all manner of punishments and tortures. Being strengthened by Blandina, he persevered unto death; and she, after enduring all the torments heretofore mentioned, was at length slain with the sword.

When the Christians, upon these occasions, received martyrdom, they were ornamented, and crowned with garlands of flowers; for which they, in heaven, received eternal crowns of glory.

It has been said that the lives of the early Christians consisted of "persecution above ground and prayer below ground." Their lives are expressed by the Coliseum and the catacombs. Beneath Rome are the excavations which we call the catacombs, which were at once temples and tombs. The early Church of Rome might well be called the Church of the Catacombs. There are some sixty catacombs near Rome, in which some six hundred miles of galleries have been traced, and these are not all. These galleries are about eight feet high and from three to five feet wide, containing on either side several rows of long, low, horizontal recesses, one above another like berths in a ship. In these the dead bodies were placed and the front closed, either by a single marble slab or several great tiles laid in mortar. On these slabs or tiles, epitaphs or symbols are engraved or painted. Both pagans and Christians buried their dead in these catacombs. When the Christian graves have been opened the skeletons tell their own terrible tale. Heads are found severed from the body, ribs and shoulder blades are broken, bones are often calcined from fire. But despite the awful story of persecution that we may read here, the inscriptions breathe forth peace and joy and triumph. Here are a few:

"Here lies Marcia, put to rest in a dream of peace."

"Lawrence to his sweetest son, borne away of angels."

"Victorious in peace and in Christ."

"Being called away, he went in peace."

Remember when reading these inscriptions the story the skeletons tell of persecution, of torture, and of fire.

But the full force of these epitaphs is seen when we contrast them with the pagan epitaphs, such as:

"Live for the present hour, since we are sure of nothing else."

"I lift my hands against the gods who took me away at the age of twenty though I had done no harm."

"Once I was not. Now I am not. I know nothing about it, and it is no concern of mine."

"Traveler, curse me not as you pass, for I am in darkness and cannot answer."

The most frequent Christian symbols on the walls of the catacombs, are, the good shepherd with the lamb on his shoulder, a ship under full sail, harps, anchors, crowns, vines, and above all the fish.

Foxe's Book of Martyrs, Edited by William Byron Forbush

Persecutions under Marcus Aurelius. A.D. 161-180

Marcus Aurelius Antoninus: (b. 121, d. 180)

Marcus Aurelius, the philosopher on the throne, was a well-educated, just, kind, and amiable emperor, and reached the old Roman ideal of self-reliant Stoic virtue, but for this very reason he had no sympathy with Christianity, and probably regarded it as an absurd and fanatical superstition. He had no room in his cosmopolitan philanthropy for the purest and most innocent of his subjects, many of whom served in his own army. He was flooded with apologies of Melito, Miltiades, Athenagoras in behalf of the persecuted Christians, but turned a deaf ear to them. Only once, in his Meditations, does he allude to them, and then with scorn, tracing their noble enthusiasm for martyrdom to "sheer obstinacy" and love for theatrical display. His excuse is ignorance. He probably never read a line of the New Testament, nor of the apologies addressed to him. Belonging to the later Stoical school, which believed in an immediate absorption after death into the Divine essence, he considered the Christian doctrine of the immortality of the soul, with its moral consequences, as vicious and dangerous to the welfare of the state. A law was passed under his reign, punishing every one with exile who should endeavor to influence people's mind by fear of the Divinity, and this law was, no doubt, aimed at the Christians. At all events his reign was a stormy time for the church, although the persecutions cannot be directly traced to him. The law of Trajan was sufficient to justify the severest measures against the followers of the "forbidden" religion. About the year 170 the apologist Melito wrote: "The race of the worshiper of God in Asia is now persecuted by new edicts as it never has been heretofore; shameless, greedy sycophants, finding occasion in the edicts, now plunder the innocent day and night." The empire was visited at that time by a number of conflagrations, a destructive flood of the Tiber, an earthquake, insurrections, and particularly a pestilence, which spread from Ethiopia to Gaul. This gave rise to bloody persecutions, in which government and people united against the enemies of the gods and the supposed authors of these misfortunes. Celsus expressed his joy that "the demon" [of the Christians] was "not only reviled, but banished from every land and sea," and saw in this judgment the fulfilment of the oracle: "the mills of the gods grind late." But at the same time these persecutions, and the simultaneous literary assaults on Christianity by Celsus and Lucian, show that the new religion was constantly gaining importance in the empire.

In 177, the churches of Lyons and Vienne, in the South of France, underwent a severe trial. Heathen slaves were forced by the rack to declare, that their Christian masters practiced all the unnatural vices which rumor charged them with; and this was made to justify the exquisite tortures to which the Christians were subjected. But the sufferers, "strengthened by the fountain of living water from the heart of Christ," displayed extraordinary faith and steadfastness, and felt, that "nothing can be fearful, where the love of the Father is, nothing painful, where shines the glory of Christ." The most distinguished victims of this Gallic persecution were the bishop Pothinus, who, at the age of ninety years, and just recovered from a sickness, was subjected to all sorts of abuse, and then thrown into a dismal dungeon, where he died in two days; the virgin Blandina, a slave, who showed almost superhuman strength and constancy under the most cruel tortures, and was at last thrown to a wild beast in a net; Ponticus, a boy of fifteen years, who could be deterred by no sort of cruelty from confessing his Savior. The corpses of the martyrs, which covered the streets, were shamefully mutilated, then burned, and the ashes cast into the Rhone, lest any remnants of the enemies of the gods might desecrate the soil. At last the people grew weary of slaughter, and a considerable number of Christians survived. The martyrs of Lyons distinguished themselves by true humility, disclaiming in their prison that title of honor, as due only, they said, to the faithful and true witness, the Firstborn from the dead, the Prince of life (Rev. 1:5), and to those of his followers who had already sealed their fidelity to Christ with their blood. About the same time a persecution of less extent appears to have visited Autun (Augustodunum) near Lyons. Symphorinus, a young man of good family, having refused to fall down before the image of Cybele, was condemned to be beheaded. On his way to the place of execution his own mother called to him: "My son, be firm and fear not that death, which so surely leads to life. Look to Him who reigns in heaven. Today is thy earthly life not taken from thee, but transferred by a blessed exchange into the life of heaven."

The story of the "thundering legion" rests on the fact of a remarkable deliverance of the Roman army in Hungary by a sudden shower, which quenched their burning thirst and frightened their barbarian enemies, A.D. 174. The heathens, however, attributed this not to the prayers of the Christian soldiers, but to their own gods. The emperor himself prayed to Jupiter: "This hand, which has never yet shed human blood, I raise to thee." That this event did not alter his views respecting the Christians, is proved by the persecution in South Gaul, which broke out three years later. Of isolated cases of martyrdom in this reign, we notice that of Justin Martyr, at Rome, in the year 166. His death is traced to the machinations of Crescens, a Cynic philosopher. Marcus Aurelius was succeeded by his cruel and contemptible son, Commodus (180-192), who wallowed in the mire of every sensual debauchery, and displayed at the same time like Nero the most ridiculous vanity as dancer and singer, and in the character of buffoon; but he was accidentally made to favor the Christians by the influence of a concubine, Marcia, and accordingly did not disturb them. Yet under his reign a Roman senator, Apollonius, was put to death for his faith.
Philip Scaff, History of the Christian Church, chapter 20

Symeon

Symeon, Bishop of Jerusalem, suffers Martyrdom

It is reported that after the age of Nero and Domitian, under the emperor whose times we are now recording, a persecution was stirred up against us in certain cities in consequence of a popular uprising. In this persecution we have understood that Symeon, the son of Clopas, who, as we have shown, was the second bishop of the church of Jerusalem, suffered martyrdom. Hegesippus, whose words we have already quoted in various places, is a witness to this fact also. Speaking of certain heretics he adds that Symeon was accused by them at this time; and since it was clear that he was a Christian, he was tortured in various ways for many days, and astonished even the judge himself and his attendants in the highest degree, and finally he suffered a death similar to that of our Lord. But there is nothing like hearing the historian himself, who writes as follows: "Certain of these heretics brought accusation against Symeon, the son of Clopas, on the ground that he was a descendant of David and a Christian; and thus he suffered martyrdom, at the age of one hundred and twenty years, while Trajan was emperor and Atticus governor." And the same writer says that his accusers also, when search was made for the descendants of David, were arrested as belonging to that family. And it might be reasonably assumed that Symeon was one of those that saw and heard the Lord, judging from the length of his life, and from the fact that the Gospel makes mention of Mary, the wife of Clopas, who was the father of Symeon, as has been already shown. The same historian says that there were also others, descended from one of the so-called brothers of the Savior, whose name was Judas, who, after they had borne testimony before Domitian, as has been already recorded, on behalf of faith in Christ, lived until the same reign. He writes as follows: "They came, therefore, and took the lead of every church as witness and as relatives of the Lord. And profound peace being established in every church, they remained until the reign of the Emperor Trajan, and until the above-mentioned Symeon, son of Clopas, an uncle of the Lord, was informed against by the heretics, and was himself in like manner accused for the same cause before the governor Atticus. And after being tortured for many days he suffered martyrdom, and all, including even the proconsul, marveled that, at the age of one hundred and twenty years, he could endure so much. And orders were given that he should be crucified." In addition to these things the same man, while recounting the events of that period, records that the Church up to that time had remained a pure and uncorrupted virgin, since, if there were any that attempted to corrupt the sound norm of the preaching of salvation, they lay until then concealed in obscure darkness. But when the sacred college of apostles had suffered death in various forms, and the generation of those that had been deemed worthy to hear the inspired wisdom with their own ears had passed away, then the league of godless error took its rise as a result of the folly of heretical teachers, who, because none of the apostles was still living, attempted henceforth, with a bold face, to proclaim, in opposition to the preaching of the truth, the "knowledge which is falsely so-called."

Eusebius, Church History, book 1, chapter 32

Martyrdom of Polycarp (1)
23 February 156

Polycarp was Bishop of Smyrna (today known as Izmir), a city on the west coast of Turkey. The letters to the "seven churches in Asia" at the beginning of the book of Revelation include a letter to the church in Smyrna, identifying it as a church undergoing persecution.

Polycarp is said to have known the Apostle John, and to have been instructed by him in the Christian faith. Polycarp, in his turn, was known to Irenaeus, who later became Bishop of Lyons in what is now France. We have Irenaeus's brief memoir of Polycarp; a letter to Polycarp from Ignatius of Antioch, written around 115 AD when Ignatius was passing through Turkey, being sent in chains to Rome to be put to death; a letter from Polycarp to the church at Philippi, written at the same time; and an account of the arrest, trial, conviction, and martyrdom of Polycarp, written after his death by one or more members of his congregation.

Polycarp was denounced to the government, arrested, and tried on the charge of being a Christian. When the proconsul urged him to save his life by cursing Christ, he replied: "Eighty-six years I have served him, and he never did me any wrong. How can I blaspheme my King who saved me?" The magistrate was reluctant to kill a gentle old man, but he had no choice.

Polycarp was sentenced to be burned. As he waited for the fire to be lighted, he prayed:

Lord God Almighty, Father of your blessed and beloved child Jesus Christ, through whom we have received knowledge of you, God of angels and hosts and all creation, and of the whole race of the upright who live in your presence: I bless you that you have thought me worthy of this day and hour, to be numbered among the martyrs and share in the cup of Christ, for resurrection to eternal life, for soul and body in the incorruptibility of the Holy Spirit. Among them may I be accepted before you today, as a rich and acceptable sacrifice, just as you, the faithful and true God, have prepared and foreshown and brought about. For this reason and for all things I praise you, I bless you, I glorify you, through the eternal heavenly high priest Jesus Christ, your beloved child, through whom be glory to you, with him and the Holy Spirit, now and for the ages to come. Amen.

The fire was then lit and shortly thereafter a soldier stabbed Polycarp to death by order of the magistrate. His friends gave his remains honorable burial, and wrote an account of his death to other churches.

James Kiefer, Christian Biographies, By kind permission

Martyrdom of Polycarp (2)

In the book of Revelation, one of the seven letters is addressed to the church at Smyrna, and includes these words:

> *"Be faithful, even to the point of death,*
> *and I will give you the crown of life."*
> *(Revelation 2:10)*

Polycarp was bishop of Smyrna and the leading Christian figure in Roman Asia in the reign of the emperor Antoninus Pius. According to Irenaeus, Polycarp "had fellowship with John [the apostle] and with the others who had seen the Lord". Polycarp's long life made him a very important link between the early church and the apostles.

The church of God at Smyrna to the church of God at Philomelium and to all communities of the holy, catholic church everywhere. . . . We are writing to you, brethren, to tell you how many people suffered martyrdom, especially blessed Polycarp.

Late in the day Polycarp's pursuers came up together and found him hiding in a cottage, lying in an upper room. It was within Polycarp's power to flee from there to another place, but he refused to do so, saying, "God's will be done."

So when Polycarp heard them arrive he came down and talked with them. The soldiers were amazed at his age and his courage and that so much trouble had been taken to arrest such an elderly man.

The soldiers brought Polycarp back into the city, riding on a donkey. The head of the police, Herod, met him. Herod's father, Nicetes, transferred Polycarp into a carriage, sat next to him, and tried to make him change his mind. Nicetes urged Polycarp, "Tell me, what harm is done if one says that Caesar is Lord? Go on, make a sacrifice to Caesar, and then you will save your skin."

To start with Polycarp made no reply, but as they pressed him, he said, "I do not intend to do what you advise me."

Once they had failed to persuade Polycarp they dragged him from the carriage into the stadium where there was such a tremendous noise that it was impossible for anyone to be heard.

Polycarp was brought before the Proconsul who also tried to persuade him to change his mind: "Think of your old age. Just do as everybody else does and swear by the genius of Caesar; repent; say, "Away with the Atheists."" ["Atheists here does not refer to people who do not believe in God, but to people, like Polycarp, who refused to acknowledge that Caesar was a divine god who should be worshiped and receive sacrifices.]

Polycarp then studied the crowd of lawless heathen in the stadium, waved his hand in their direction, looked up to heaven with a groan, and said, "Away with the Atheists."

The Proconsul was insistent and repeated, "swear, and we will release you; deny Christ."

Polycarp replied:

> "Eighty and six years have I served him,
> and he has done me no wrong;
> how then can I blaspheme my King
> who saved me?"

Still the Proconsul urged Polycarp: "swear by the genius of Caesar."

"If you really think that I would swear by the genius of Caesar then you forget who I am. Take note, I am a Christian. If you want to learn the Christian faith, appoint a day, and grant me a hearing."

The Proconsul replied, "I have wild beasts and if you do not change your mind I will throw you to them."

Polycarp said, "Order them to be brought. We are not allowed to change our minds from what is good to what is evil, only to change from what is evil to what is good."

The Proconsul said, "As you despise the wild beasts, you will be destroyed by fire, if you do not change your mind."

So Polycarp said, "The fire you threaten me with only burns for a short time and then it goes out. You are ignorant of the future fire of judgment which is never put out and which is reserved for the ungodly. So what are you waiting for? Do what you want to do. I have to be burnt alive."

Saying these things, and other things as well, Polycarp was inspired with courage and joy, and his appearance was filled with grace, so that not only did it not faint at the many things that were said to him, but on the contrary the proconsul was amazed and sent his own herald to proclaim three times in the middle of the stadium, "Polycarp has confessed himself to be a Christian." When this was proclaimed by the herald, the whole multitude, both the Gentiles and the Jews who lived in Smyrna, cried out with uncontrollable anger in loud shouts, "This is the teacher of Asia, the father of the Christians, the puller down of our gods, who teaches numbers not to sacrifice nor worship." After they had said this they called out to Asiarch Philip requesting that a lion be set loose on Polycarp. But he replied that this would be unlawful, as the games had already ended. Then the crowd decided to shout out in unison that Polycarp should be burnt alive. For it was necessary that Polycarp's vision be fulfilled, which he had about his pillow which he saw on fire while he was praying. Polycarp then turned and said prophetically to those who were with him, "I must be burnt alive."

This was no sooner said than done. In a moment the mob collected logs and faggots from the workshops and the baths and the Jews proved to be especially zealous about this, as usual. When the pyre had been completed they were about to nail Polycarp to the stake, but he said,

> "Let me be as I am: He that gave me power to abide the fire will grant me too, without your making me fast with nails, to abide untroubled on the pyre."

So they did not nail him to the stake but just bound him to it. Polycarp put his hands behind him and was bound, like a godly ram out of a great flock for an offering, a whole burnt offering made ready and acceptable to God. Then he looked up to heaven and prayed:

> "O Lord God Almighty, you are the Father of your much loved and blessed Son Jesus Christ, through whom we have received our knowledge of you. You are the God of the angels and the powers and the God of the whole creation and of everyone who worships you. I praise you that you have counted me worthy of this day and hour so that I can be counted as one of the martyrs in the suffering of Christ and then to the resurrection to eternal life of both the body and the soul with the Holy Spirit. May I be welcomed with them today into your presence as an acceptable sacrifice. As you planned that this should happen, may it now be fulfilled since you are the faithful and true God. On account of this and for every other reason I praise you, bless you, and glorify you through the everlasting and heavenly high priest Jesus Christ, your much loved Son. It is through him we come to you in the company of the Holy Spirit, to whom we give glory now and for ever. Amen."

As soon as Polycarp had completed his prayer and offered up his Amen the fire was kindled. A great flame blazed out, and we who saw it, and who have been preserved to tell the story, saw something marvelous. The fire took the shape of an arch, like a ship's sail blown by the wind, and this made a wall around the martyr's body. His body was at the center of this, not at all like burning flesh, but like baked bread, or like gold and silver in a furnace. We smelled a sweet perfume in the air, like frankincense or some other precious spice.

Eventually when the unholy people saw that Polycarp's body was not being consumed by the fire, they ordered that he should be killed and they stabbed him with as dagger. As they did this a spurt of blood gushed out and put the fire out, to the amazement of all the spectators.

Such is the story of the blessed Polycarp, who with the eleven from Philadelphia was martyred in Smyrna. The blessed Polycarp was martyred on the second day of the first part of the month Xanthicus, on the seventh day before the Kalends of March, on a high Sabbath, at the eighth hour. He was taken by Herodes, when Philip of Tralles was chief priest, in the proconsulship of Statius Quadratus, in the everlasting reign of Jesus Christ; to whom be glory, honor, majesty, and a throne eternal, from generation to generation. Amen.

We pray that you may be of good cheer, brethren, while you walk by the word of Jesus Christ according to the gospel, with whom be glory to God for the salvation of the elect saints; even as blessed Polycarp suffered martyrdom, in whose footsteps God grant that we may be found in the kingdom of Jesus Christ.

This account was copied by Gaius from the papers of Irenaeus, a disciple of Polycarp, Gaius having been himself a companion of Irenaeus. And I, Socrates, wrote it down in Corinth from the copy of Gaius. Grace be with you all.

E. C. E. Owen, Some Authentic Acts of the Early Martyrs, Oxford, 1927. (Church at Smyrna for the Church at Philomelium.)

Encyclical letter from the Church at Smyrna for the Church at Philomelium

The encyclical epistle of the church at Smyrna concerning the martyrdom of the holy Polycarp

The Church of God which sojourns at Smyrna, to the Church of God sojourning in Philomelium, and to all the congregations of the Holy and Catholic Church in every place: Mercy, peace, and love from God the Father, and our Lord Jesus Christ, be multiplied.

Chapter 1: Subject of Which We Write.

We have written to you, brethren, as to what relates to the martyrs, and especially to the blessed Polycarp, who put an end to the persecution, having, as it were, set a seal upon it by his martyrdom. For almost all the events that happened previously [to this one], took place that the Lord might show us from above a martyrdom becoming the Gospel. For he waited to be delivered up, even as the Lord had done, that we also might become his followers, while we look not merely at what concerns ourselves but have regard also to our neighbors. For it is the part of a true and well-founded love, not only to wish one's self to be saved, but also all the brethren.

Chapter 2: The Wonderful Constancy of the Martyrs.

All the martyrdoms, then, were blessed and noble which took place according to the will of God. For it becomes us who profess greater piety than others, to ascribe the authority over all things to God. And truly, who can fail to admire their nobleness of mind, and their patience, with that love towards their Lord which they displayed?-who, when they were so torn with scourges, that the frame of their bodies, even to the very inward veins and arteries, was laid open, still patiently endured, while even those that stood by pitied and bewailed them. But they reached such a pitch of magnanimity, that not one of them let a sigh or a groan escape them; thus proving to us all that those holy martyrs of Christ, at the very time when they suffered such torments, were absent from the body, or rather, that the Lord then stood by them, and communed with them. And, looking to the grace of Christ, they despised all the torments of this world, redeeming themselves from eternal punishment by [the suffering of] a single hour. For this reason the fire of their savage executioners appeared cool to them. For they kept before their view escape from that fire which is eternal and never shall be quenched, and looked forward with the eyes of their heart to those good things which are laid up for such as endure; things "which ear hath not heard, nor eye seen, neither have entered into the heart of man," but were revealed by the Lord to them, inasmuch as they were no longer men, but had already become angels. And, in like manner, those who were condemned to the wild beasts endured dreadful tortures, being stretched out upon beds full of spikes, and subjected to various other kinds of torments, in order that, if it were possible, the tyrant might, by their lingering tortures, lead them to a denial [of Christ].

Chapter 3: The Constancy of Germanicus. The Death of Polycarp is Demanded.

For the devil did indeed invent many things against them; but thanks be to God, he could not prevail over all. For the most noble Germanicus strengthened the timidity of others by his own patience, and fought heroically with the wild beasts. For, when the proconsul sought to persuade him, and urged him to take pity upon his age, he attracted the wild beast towards himself, and provoked it, being desirous to escape all the more quickly from an unrighteous and impious world. But upon this the whole multitude, marveling at the nobility of mind displayed by the devout and godly race of Christians, cried out, "Away with the Atheists; let Polycarp be sought out!"

Chapter 4: Quintus the Apostate.

Now one named Quintus, a Phrygian, who was but lately come from Phrygia, when he saw the wild beasts, became afraid. This was the man who forced himself and some others to come forward voluntarily [for trial]. Him the proconsul, after many entreaties, persuaded to swear and to offer sacrifice. Wherefore, brethren, we do not commend those who give themselves up [to suffering], seeing the Gospel does not teach so to do.

Chapter 5: The Departure and Vision of Polycarp.

But the most admirable Polycarp, when he first heard [that he was sought for], was in no measure disturbed, but resolved to continue in the city. However, in deference to the wish of many, he was persuaded to leave it. He departed, therefore, to a country house not far distant from the city. There he stayed with a few [friends], engaged in nothing else night and day than praying for all men, and for the Churches throughout the world, according to his usual custom. And while he was praying, a vision presented itself to him three days before he was taken; and, behold, the pillow under his head seemed to him on fire. Upon this, turning to those that were with him, he said to them prophetically," I must be burnt alive."

Chapter 6: Polycarp is Betrayed by a Servant.

And when those who sought for him were at hand, he departed to another dwelling, whither his pursuers immediately came after him. And when they found him not, they seized upon two youths [that were there], one of whom, being subjected to torture, confessed. It was thus impossible that he should continue hid, since those that betrayed him were of his own household. The Irenarch then (whose office is the same as that of the Cleronomus), by name Herod, hastened to bring him into the stadium. [This all happened] that he might fulfil his special lot, being made a partaker of Christ, and that they who betrayed him might undergo the punishment of Judas himself.

Chapter 7: Polycarp is Found by His Pursuers.

His pursuers then, along with horsemen, and taking the youth with them, went forth at supper-time on the day of the preparation with their usual weapons, as if going out against a robber. And being come about evening [to the place where he was], they found him lying down in the upper room of a certain little house, from which he might have escaped into another place; but he refused, saying, "The will of God be done." So when he heard that they were come, he went down and spake with them. And as those that were present marveled at his age and constancy, some of them said. "Was so much effort made to capture such a venerable man? Immediately then, in that very hour, he ordered that something to eat and drink should be set before them, as much indeed as they cared for, while he besought them to allow him an hour to pray without disturbance. And on their giving him leave, he stood and prayed, being full of the grace of God, so that he could not cease for two full hours, to the astonishment of them that heard him, insomuch that many began to repent that they had come forth against so godly and venerable an old man.

Chapter 8: Polycarp is Brought into the City.

Now, as soon as he had ceased praying, having made mention of all that had at any time come in contact with him, both small and great, illustrious and obscure, as well as the whole Catholic Church throughout the world, the time of his departure having arrived, they set him upon an ass, and conducted him into the city, the day being that of the great Sabbath. And the Irenarch Herod, accompanied by his father Nicetes (both riding in a chariot), met him, and taking him up into the chariot, they seated themselves beside him, and endeavored to persuade him, saying, "What harm is there in saying, Lord Caesar, and in sacrificing, with the other ceremonies observed on such occasions, and so make sure of safety? "But he at first gave them no answer; and when they continued to urge him, he said, "I shall not do as you advise me." So they, having no hope of persuading him, began to speak bitter words unto him, and cast him with violence out of the chariot, insomuch that, in getting down from the carriage, he dislocated his leg [by the fall]. But without being disturbed, and as if suffering nothing, he went eagerly forward with all haste, and was conducted to the stadium, where the tumult was so great, that there was no possibility of being heard.

Chapter 9: Polycarp Refuses to Revile Christ.

Now, as Polycarp was entering into the stadium, there came to him a voice from heaven, saying, "Be strong, and show thyself a man, O Polycarp!" No one saw who it was that spoke to him; but those of our brethren who were present heard the voice. And as he was brought forward, the tumult became great when they heard that Polycarp was taken. And when he came near, the proconsul asked him whether he was Polycarp. On his confessing that he was, [the proconsul] sought to persuade him to deny [Christ], saying, "Have respect to thy old age," and other similar things, according to their custom, [such as], "swear by the fortune of Caesar; repent, and say, Away with the Atheists." But Polycarp, gazing with a stern countenance on all the multitude of the wicked heathen then in the stadium, and waving his hand towards them, while with groans he looked up to heaven, said, "Away with the Atheists." Then, the proconsul urging him, and saying, "swear, and I will set thee at liberty, reproach Christ;" Polycarp declared, "Eighty and six years have I served Him, and He never did me any injury: how then can I blaspheme my King and my Savior?"

Chapter 10: Polycarp Confesses Himself a Christian.

And when the proconsul yet again pressed

him, and said, "swear by the fortune of Caesar," he answered, "since thou art vainly urgent that, as thou sayest, I should swear by the fortune of Caesar, and pretendest not to know who and what I am, hear me declare with boldness, I am a Christian. And if you wish to learn what the doctrines of Christianity are, appoint me a day, and thou shalt hear them." The proconsul replied, "Persuade the people." But Polycarp said, "To thee I have thought it right to offer an account [of my faith]; for we are taught to give all due honor (which entails no injury upon ourselves) to the powers and authorities which are ordained of God.28 But as for these, I do not deem them worthy of receiving any account from me."

Chapter 11: No Threats Have Any Effect on Polycarp.

The proconsul then said to him, "I have wild beasts at hand ; to these will I cast thee, except thou repent." But he answered, "Call them then, for we are not accustomed to repent of what is good in order to adopt that which is evil; and it is well for me to be changed from what is evil to what is righteous." But again the proconsul said to him, "I will cause thee to be consumed by fire, seeing thou despisest the wild beasts, if thou wilt not repent." But Polycarp said, "Thou threatenest me with fire which burneth for an hour, and after a little is extinguished, but art ignorant of the fire of the coming judgment and of eternal punishment, reserved for the ungodly. But why tarriest thou? Bring forth what thou wilt."

Chapter 12: Polycarp is Sentenced to Be Burned.

While he spoke these and many other like things, he was filled with confidence and joy, and his countenance was full of grace, so that not merely did it not fall as if troubled by the things said to him, but, on the contrary, the proconsul was astonished, and sent his herald to proclaim in the midst of the stadium thrice, "Polycarp has confessed that he is a Christian." This proclamation having been made by the herald, the whole multitude both of the heathen and Jews, who dwelt at Smyrna, cried out with uncontrollable fury, and in a loud voice, "This is the teacher of Asia, the father of the Christians, and the overthrower of our gods, he who has been teaching many not to sacrifice, or to worship the gods." Speaking thus, they cried out, and besought Philip the Asiarch to let loose a lion upon Polycarp. But Philip answered that it was not lawful for him to do so, seeing the shows of wild beasts were already finished. Then it seemed good to them to cry out with one consent, that Polycarp should be burnt alive. For thus it behooved the vision which was revealed to him in regard to his pillow to be fulfilled, when, seeing it on fire as he was praying, he turned about and said prophetically to the faithful that were with him, "I must be burnt alive."

Chapter 13: The Funeral Pile is Erected

This, then, was carried into effect with greater speed than it was spoken, the multitudes immediately gathering together wood and fagots out of the shops and baths; the Jews especially, according to custom, eagerly assisting them in it. And when the funeral pile was ready, Polycarp, laying aside all his garments, and loosing his girdle, sought also to take off his sandals,-a thing he was not accustomed to do, inasmuch as every one of the faithful was always eager who should first touch his skin. For, on account of his holy life, he was, even before his martyrdom, adorned with every kind of good. Immediately then they surrounded him with those substances which had been prepared for the funeral pile. But when they were about also to fix him with nails, he said, "Leave me as I am; for He that giveth me strength to endure the fire, will also enable me, without your securing me by nails, to remain without moving in the pile."

Chapter 14: The Prayer of Polycarp

They did not nail him then, but simply bound him. And he, placing his hands behind him, and being bound like a distinguished ram [taken] out of a great flock for sacrifice, and prepared to be an acceptable burnt-offering unto God, looked up to heaven, and said, "O Lord God Almighty, the Father of thy beloved and blessed Son Jesus Christ, by whom we have received the knowledge of Thee, the God of angels and powers, and of every creature, and of the whole race of the righteous who live before thee, I give Thee thanks that Thou hast counted me, worthy of this day and this hour, that I should have a part in the number of Thy martyrs, in the cup of thy Christ, to the resurrection of eternal life, both of soul and body, through the incorruption [imparted] by the Holy Ghost. Among whom may I be accepted this day before Thee as a fat and acceptable sacrifice, according as Thou, the ever-truthful God, hast fore-ordained, hast revealed beforehand to me, and now hast fulfilled. Wherefore also I praise Thee for all things, I bless Thee, I glorify Thee, along with the everlasting and heavenly Jesus Christ, Thy beloved Son, with whom, to Thee, and the Holy Ghost, be glory both now and to all coming ages. Amen."

Chapter 15: Polycarp is Not Injured by the Fire

When he had pronounced this amen, and so finished his prayer, those who were appointed for the purpose kindled the fire. And as the flame blazed forth in great fury, we, to whom it was given to witness it, beheld a great miracle, and have been preserved that we might report to others what then took place. For the fire, shaping itself into the form of an arch, like the sail of a ship when filled with the wind, encompassed as by a circle the body of the martyr. And he appeared within not like flesh which is burnt, but as bread that is baked, or as gold and silver glowing in a furnace. Moreover, we perceived such a sweet odor [coming from the pile], as if frankincense or some such precious spices had been smoking there.

Chapter 16: Polycarp is Pierced by a Dagger

At length, when those wicked men perceived that his body could not be consumed by the fire, they commanded an executioner to go near and pierce him through with a dagger. And on his doing this, there came forth a dove, and a great quantity of blood, so that the fire was extinguished; and all the people wondered that there should be such a difference between the unbelievers and the elect, of whom this most admirable Polycarp was one, having in our own times been an apostolic and prophetic teacher, and bishop of the Catholic Church which is in Smyrna. For every word that went out of his mouth either has been or shall yet be accomplished.

Chapter 17: The Christians are Refused Polycarp's Body

But when the adversary of the race of the righteous, the envious, malicious, and wicked one, perceived the impressive nature of his martyrdom, and [considered] the blameless life he had led from the beginning, and how he was now crowned with the wreath of immortality, having beyond dispute received his reward, he did his utmost that not the least memorial of him should be taken away by us, although many desired to do this, and to become possessors of his holy flesh. For this end he suggested it to Nicetes, the father of Herod and brother of Alce, to go and entreat the governor not to give up his body to be buried, "lest," said he, "forsaking Him that was crucified, they begin to worship this one." This he said at the suggestion and urgent persuasion of the Jews, who also watched us, as we sought to take him out of the fire, being ignorant of this, that it is neither possible for us ever to forsake Christ, who suffered for the salvation of such as shall be saved throughout the whole world (the blameless one for sinners), nor to worship any other. For Him indeed, as being the Son of God, we adore; but the martyrs, as disciples and followers of the Lord, we worthily love on account of their extraordinary affection towards their own King and Master, of whom may we also be made companions and fellow-disciples!

Chapter 18: The Body of Polycarp is Burned

The centurion then, seeing the strife excited

by the Jews, placed the body in the midst of the fire, and consumed it. Accordingly, we afterwards took up his bones, as being more precious than the most exquisite jewels, and more purified than gold, and deposited them in a fitting place, whither, being gathered together, as opportunity is allowed us, with joy and rejoicing, the Lord shall grant us to celebrate the anniversary of his martyrdom, both in memory of those who have already finished their course, and for the exercising and preparation of those yet to walk in their steps.

Chapter 19: Praise of the Martyr Polycarp

This, then, is the account of the blessed Polycarp, who, being the twelfth that was martyred in Smyrna (reckoning those also of Philadelphia), yet occupies a place of his own in the memory of all men, insomuch that he is everywhere spoken of by the heathen themselves. He was not merely an illustrious teacher, but also a pre-eminent martyr, whose martyrdom all desire to imitate, as having been altogether consistent with the Gospel of Christ. For, having through patience overcome the unjust governor, and thus acquired the crown of immortality, he now, with the apostles and all the righteous [in heaven], rejoicingly glorifies God, even the Father, and blesses our Lord Jesus Christ, the Savior of our souls, the Governor of our bodies, and the Shepherd of the Catholic Church throughout the world.

Chapter 20: This Epistle is to Be Transmitted to the Brethren

Since, then, ye requested that we would at large make you acquainted with what really took place, we have for the present sent you this summary account through our brother Marcus. When, therefore, ye have yourselves read this Epistle, be pleased to send it to the brethren at a greater distance, that they also may glorify the Lord, who makes such choice of His own servants. To Him who is able to bring us all by His grace and goodness into his everlasting kingdom, through His only-begotten Son Jesus Christ, to Him be glory, and honor, and power, and majesty, for ever. Amen. Salute all the saints. They that are with us salute you, and Evarestus, who wrote this Epistle, with all his house.

Chapter 21: The Date of the Martyrdom

Now, the blessed Polycarp suffered martyrdom on the second day of the month Xanthicus just begun, the seventh day before the Kalends of May, on the great Sabbath, at the eighth hour. He was taken by Herod, Philip the Trallian being high priest, Statius Quadratus being proconsul, but Jesus Christ being King for ever, to whom be glory, honor, majesty, and an everlasting throne, from generation to generation. Amen.

Chapter 22: Salutation

We wish you, brethren, all happiness, while you walk according to the doctrine of the Gospel of Jesus Christ; with whom be glory to God the Father and the Holy Spirit, for the salvation of His holy elect, after whose example the blessed Polycarp suffered, following in whose steins may we too be found in the kingdom of Jesus Christ!

These things Caius transcribed from the copy of Irenaeus (who was a disciple of Polycarp), having himself been intimate with Irenaeus. And I Socrates transcribed them at Corinth from the copy of Caius. Grace be with you all.

And I again, Pionius, wrote them from the previously written copy, having carefully searched into them, and the blessed Polycarp having manifested them to me through a revelation, even as I shall show in what follows. I have collected these things, when they had almost faded away through the lapse of time, that the Lord Jesus Christ may also gather me along with His elect into His heavenly kingdom, to whom, with the Father and the Holy Spirit, be glory for ever and ever. Amen.

Pionius

Martyrdom of Polycarp (3)

St Polycarp was one of the most illustrious of the apostolic fathers, who, being the immediate disciples of the apostles, received instructions from their mouths, and inherited of them the spirit of Christ in a degree so much the more eminent as they lived nearer the fountain head. He embraced Christianity very young, about the year 80, was a disciple of the apostles, in particular of St. John the Evangelist, and was constituted by him Bishop of Symrna, probably before his banishment to Patmos in 96, so that he governed that important see seventy years. He seems to have been the angel or bishop of Smyrna who was commended above all the bishops of Asia by Christ himself in the Apocalypse, and the only one without a reproach. Our Savior encouraged him under his poverty, tribulation, and persecutions, especially the calumnies of the Jews, called him rich in grace, and promised him the crown of life by martyrdom. This saint was respected by the faithful to a degree of veneration. He formed many holy disciples, among whom were St. Irenaeus and Papias. When Florinus, who had often visited St. Polycarp, had broached certain heresies, St. Irenaeus wrote to him as follows: "These things were not taught you by the bishops who preceded us. I could tell you the place where the blessed Polycarp sat to preach the word of God. It is yet present to my mind with what gravity he everywhere came in and went out; what was the sanctity of his deportment, the majesty of his countenance and of his whole exterior, and what were his holy exhortations to the people. I seem to hear him now relate how he conversed with John and many others who had seen Jesus Christ; the words he had heard from their mouths. I can protest before God that if this holy bishop had heard of any error like yours, he would have immediately stopped his ears, and cried out, according to his custom, Good God! that I should be reserved to these times to hear such things! That very instant he would have fled out of the place in which he had heard such doctrine." St. Jerome mentions that St. Polycarp met at Rome the heretic Marcion in the streets, who resenting that the holy bishop did not take that notice of him which he expected, said to him, "Do you not know me, Polycarp?" "Yes," answered the saint, "I know you to be the firstborn of Satan." He had learned this abhorrence of the authors of heresy, who knowingly and willingly adulterate the divine truths, from his master, St. John, who fled out of the bath in which he saw Cerinthus. St. Polycarp kissed with respect the chains of St. Ignatius, who passed by Smyrna on the road to his martyrdom, and who recommended to our saint the care and comfort of his distant church of Antioch, which he repeated to him in a letter from Troas, desiring him to write in his name to those churches of Asia to which he had not leisure to write himself. St. Polycarp wrote a letter to the Philippians shortly after, which is highly commended by St. Irenaeus, St. Jerome, Eusebius, Photius, and others, and is still extant. It is justly admired both for the excellent instructions it contains and for the simplicity and perspicuity of the style, and was publicly read in the church in Asia in St. Jerome's time. In it he calls a heretic, as above, the eldest son of Satan. About the year 158 he undertook a journey of charity to Rome, to confer with Pope Anicetus about certain points of discipline, especially about the time of keeping Easter, for the Asiatic churches kept it on the fourteenth day of the vernal equinoctial moon, as the Jews did, on whatever day of the week it fell; whereas Rome, Egypt, and all the West observed it on the Sunday following. It was agreed that both might follow their custom without breaking the bands of charity. St. Anicetus, to testify his respect, yielded to him the honor of celebrating the Eucharist in his own church. We find no further particulars concerning our saint recorded before the acts of his martyrdom.

In the sixth year of Marcus Aurelius and Lucius Verus, Statius Quadratus being proconsul of Asia, a violent persecution broke out in that country, in which the faithful gave heroic proofs of their courage and love of God, to the astonishment of the infidels. When they were torn to pieces with scourges till their very bowels were laid bare, amidst the moans and tears of the spectators, who were moved with pity at the sight of their torments, not one of them gave so much as a single groan, so little regard had they for their own flesh in the cause of God. No kinds of torture, no inventions of cruelty, were forborne to force them to a conformity to the pagan worship of the times. Germanicus, who had been brought to Smyrna with eleven or twelve other Christians, signalized himself above the rest, and animated the most timorous to suffer. The proconsul in the amphitheater called upon him with tenderness, entreated him to have some regard for his youth, and to value at least his life, but he, with a holy impatience, provoked the beasts to devour him, to leave this wicked world. One Quintus, a Phrygian, who had presented himself to the judge, yielded at the sight of the beast let out upon him, and sacrificed. The authors of these acts justly condemn the presumption of those who offered themselves to suffer, and say that the martyrdom of St. Polycarp was conformable to the gospel, because he exposed not himself to the temptation, but waited till the persecutors laid hands on him, as Christ our Lord taught us by his own example. The spectators, seeing the courage of Germanicus and his companions, and being fond of their impious bloody diversions, cried out, "Away with the impious! let Polycarp be sought for!" The holy man, though fearless, had been prevailed upon by his friends to withdraw and conceal himself in a neighboring village during the storm, spending most of his time in prayer. Three days before his martyrdom, he in a vision saw his pillow on fire, from which he understood by revelation, and foretold his companions, that he should be burnt alive.

When the persecutors were in quest of him he changed his retreat, but was betrayed by a boy, who was threatened with the rack unless he discovered him. Herod, the Irenarch, or keeper of the peace, whose office it was to prevent misdemeanors and apprehend malefactors, sent horsemen by night to beset his lodgings. The saint was above stairs in bed, but refused to make his escape, saying, "God's will be done." He went down, met them at the door, ordered them a handsome supper, and sired only some time for prayer before he went with them. This granted, he began his prayer standing, which he continued in that posture for two hours, recommending to God his own flock and the whole church with so much earnestness and devotion that several of those that were come to seize him repented they had undertaken the commission. They set him on an ass, and were conducting him towards the city when he was met on the road by Herod and his father Nicetes, who took him into their chariot, and endeavored to persuade him to a little compliance, saying, "What harm is there in saying Lord Caesar, or even in sacrificing, to escape death?" By the word Lord was meant nothing less than a kind of deity or godhead. The bishop at first was silent, in imitation of our Savior, but being pressed, he gave them this resolute answer, "I shall never do what you desire of me." At these words, taking off the mask of friendship and compassion, they treated him with scorn and reproaches, and thrust him out of the chariot with such violence that his leg was bruised by the fall. The holy man went forward cheerfully to the place where the people were assembled. Upon his entering it a voice from heaven was heard by many, "Polycarp, be courageous, and act manfully." He was led directly to the tribunal of the proconsul, who exhorted him to respect his own age, to swear by the genius of Caesar, and to say, "Take away the impious," meaning the Christians. The saint, turning towards the people in the pit, said, with a stern countenance, "Exterminate the wicked," meaning by this expression either a wish that they might cease to be wicked by their conversion to the faith of Christ, or this was a prediction of the calamity which befell their city in 177, when Smyrna was overturned by an earthquake, as we read in Dion and Aristides.[8] The proconsul repeated, "swear by the genius of Caesar, and I discharge you; blaspheme Christ." Polycarp replied, "I have served him these fourscore and six years, and he never did me any harm, but much good, and how can I blaspheme my King and my Savior? If you require of me to swear by the genius of Caesar, as you call it, hear my free confession- I am a Christian; but if you desire to learn the Christian religion, appoint a time, and hear me." The proconsul said, "Persuade the people." The martyr replied, "I addressed my discourse to you, for we are taught to give due honor to princes as far as is consistent with religion. But the populace is an incompetent judge to justify myself before." Indeed rage rendered them incapable of hearing him.

The proconsul then assuming a tone of severity, said: "I have wild beasts." "Call for them," replied the saint: "for we are unalterably resolved not to change from good to evil. It is only good to pass from evil to good." The proconsul said: "If you contemn the beasts, I will cause you to be burnt to ashes." Polycarp answered: "You threaten me with a fire which burns for a short time and then goes out, but are yourself ignorant of the judgment to come, and of the fire of everlasting torments which is prepared for the wicked. Why do you delay? Bring against me what you please." Whilst he said this and many other things, he appeared in a transport of joy and confidence, and his countenance shone with a certain heavenly grace and pleasant cheerfulness, insomuch that the proconsul himself was struck with admiration. However, he ordered a crier to make public proclamation three times in the middle of the Stadium (as was the Roman custom in capital cases): "Polycarp hath confessed himself a Christian." At this proclamation the whole multitude of Jews and Gentiles gave a great shout, the latter crying out, "This is the great teacher of Asia; the father of the Christians; the destroyer of our gods, who preaches to men not to sacrifice to or adore them." They applied to Philip the Asiarch to let loose a lion upon Polycarp. He told them that it was not in his power, because those shows had been closed. Then they unanimously demanded that he should be burnt alive. Their request was no sooner granted but every one ran with all speed to fetch wood from the baths and shops. The pile being prepared, Polycarp put off his garments, untied his girdle, and began to take off his shoes, an office he had not been accustomed to, the Christians having always striven who should do these things for him, regarding it as a happiness to be admitted to touch him. The wood and other combustibles were heaped all round him. The executioners would have nailed him to the stake; but he said to them: "suffer me to be as I am. He who gives me grace to undergo this fire will enable me to stand still without that precaution." They therefore contented themselves with tying his hands behind his back, and in this posture looking up towards heaven, he prayed as follows: "O Almighty Lord God, Father of thy beloved and blessed Son Jesus Christ, by whom we have received the knowledge of thee, God of angels, powers, and every creature, and of all the race of the just that live in thy presence! I bless thee for having been pleased in thy goodness to bring me to this hour, that I may receive a portion in the number of thy martyrs, and partake of the chalice of thy Christ, for the resurrection to eternal life, in the incorruptibleness of the holy Spirit. Amongst whom grant me to be received this day as a pleasing sacrifice, such an one as thou thyself hast prepared, that so thou mayest accomplish what thou, O true and faithful God! hast foreshown. Wherefore, for all things I praise, bless, and glorify thee, through the eternal high priest Jesus Christ, thy beloved Son, with whom, to Thee and the Holy Ghost be glory now and for ever. Amen." He had scarce said Amen when fire was set to the pile, which increased to a mighty flame. But behold a wonder, say the authors of these acts, seen by us reserved to attest it to others; the flames forming themselves into an arch, like the sails of a ship swelled with the wind, gently encircled the body of the martyr, which stood in the middle, resembling not roasted flesh, but purified gold or silver, appearing bright through the flames; and his body sending forth such a fragrancy that we seemed to smell precious spices. The blind infidels were only exasperated to see his body could not be consumed, and ordered a spearman to pierce him through, which he did, and such a quantity of blood issued out of his left side as to quench the fire. The malice of the devil ended not here: he endeavored to obstruct the relics of the martyr being carried off by the Christians; for many desired to do it, to show their respect to his body. Therefore, by the suggestion of Satan, Nicetes advised the proconsul not to bestow it on the Christians, lest, said he, abandoning the crucified man, they should adore Polycarp: the Jews suggested this, "Not knowing," say the authors of the acts, "that we can never forsake Christ, nor adore any other, though we love the martyrs, as his disciples and imitators, for the great love they bore their king and master." The centurion, seeing a contest raised by the Jews, placed the body in the middle, and burnt it to ashes. "We afterwards took up the bones," say they, "more precious than the richest jewels or gold, and deposited them decently in a place at which may God grant us to assemble with joy, to celebrate the birthday of the martyr." Thus these disciples and eye-witnesses. It was at two o"clock in the afternoon, which the authors of the acts call the eighth hour, in the year 166, that St. Polycarp received his crown, according to Tillemont; but in 169, according to Basnage. His tomb is still shown with great veneration at Smyrna, in a small chapel. St. Irenaeus speaks of St. Polycarp as being of an uncommon age.

The epistle of St. Polycarp to the Philippians, which is the only one among those which he wrote that has been preserved, is, even in the dead letter, a standing proof of the apostolic spirit with which he was animated, and of that profound humility, perfect meekness, burning charity, and holy zeal, of which his life was so admirable an example. The beginning is an effusion of spiritual joy and charity with which he was transported at the happiness of their conversion to God, and their fervor in divine love. His extreme abhorrence of heresy makes him immediately fall upon that of the Docaetae against which he arms the faithful, by clearly demonstrating that Christ was truly made man, died, and rose again: in which his terms admirably express his most humble and affectionate devotion to our divine Redeemer, under these great mysteries of love. Besides walking in truth, he takes notice, that to be raised with Christ in glory, we must also do his will, keep all his commandments, and love whatever he loved; refraining from all fraud, avarice, detraction, and rash judgment; repaying evil with good forgiving and showing mercy to others that we ourselves may find mercy. "These things," says he, "I write to you on justice, because you incited me; for neither I, nor any other like me, can attain to the wisdom of the blessed and glorious Paul, into whose epistles if you look, you may raise your spiritual fabric by strengthening faith, which is our mother, hope following, and charity towards God, Christ, and our neighbor preceding us. He who has charity is far from all sin." The saint gives short instructions to every particular state, then adds, "Every one who hath not confessed that Jesus Christ is come in the flesh, is antichrist; and who hath not confessed the suffering of the cross, is of the devil; and who hath drawn the oracles of the Lord to his passions, and hath said that there is no resurrection nor judgment, he is the oldest son of Satan." He exhorts to watching always in prayer, lest we be led into temptation; to be constant in fasting, persevering, joyful in hope, and in the pledge of our justice, which is Christ Jesus, imitating his patience; for, by suffering for his name, we glorify him. To encourage them to suffer, he reminds them of those who had suffered before their eyes: Ignatius, Zozimus, and Rufus, and some of their own congregation, "who are now," says our saint, "in the place which is due to them with the Lord, with whom they also suffered."

Alban Butler

Ptolemy and Lucius

About the same date as Polycarp's martyrdom, a group of martyrdoms took place in Rome which illustrate how Christians were put to death just for professing to be Christians, and with no other charges being laid against them.

After a woman had been converted to Christ she refused to join her heathen husband in practices which were against her conscience. Eventually she tried to obtain a "divorce" – a legal release from her husband. The profligate husband denounced her as a Christian. The woman appealed to the emperor to delay her case coming to trial until she had settled her own private affairs, and the request was granted. The divorced husband turned his anger on Ptolemy, the person who had taught his wife the Christian faith. The husband had a friend who was a centurion. He persuaded the centurion to arrest Ptolemy, and throw him into prison, and "to interrogate him on this one point, whether he were a Christian."

Ptolemy, who was a guileless and truthful man, confessed that he was, and after a lengthy imprisonment was brought before Urbicus, a prefect in Rome. Like the centurion, Urbicus only asked Ptolemy if he was a Christian. Ptolemy owed everything good in his life to Christianity. He stated that he was a Christian, and he was condemned to death. As he was led away from the tribunal, a Christian called Lucius cried out, "This man has not been convicted of adultery, or murder, or robbery, or any other crime; you punish him just because he acknowledged Christ's name. Urbicus, that is not a judgement that suits an emperor called Pius, nor Caesar's son, the philosopher, or the Senate – the sacred Senate."

Urbicus replied, "I suppose that you are the same as Ptolemy."

"Certainly, replied Lucius.

The prefect then ordered Lucius to share the same fate as Ptolemy. Lucius thanked him, and a third Christian who behaved in the same way was included with the former two.

Justin, Apol ii.2; quoted by A. J. Mason, The Historic Martyrs of the Primitive Church, Longmans, 1905, pp 30-1

THE MARTYRS OF LYONS (1)

2 June 177

At Lyons and Vienne, in Gaul, there were missionary centers which had drawn many Christians from Asia and Greece. Persecution began in 177.

At first, Christians were excluded from the public baths, the market place, and from social and public life. They were subject to attack when they appeared in public, and many Christian homes were vandalized. At this point the government became involved, and began to take Christians into custody for questioning. Some slaves from Christian households were tortured to obtain confessions, and were induced to say that Christians practiced cannibalism and incest. These charges were used to arouse the whole city against the Christians, particularly against Pothinus, the aged bishop of Lyons; Sanctus, a deacon; Attalus; Maturus, a recent convert; and Blandina, a slave. Pothinus was beaten and then released, to die of his wounds a few days later. Sanctus was tormented with red-hot irons. Blandina, tortured all day long, would say nothing except, "I am a Christian, and nothing vile is done among us." Finally, the survivors were put to death in the public arena.

James Kiefer, Christian Biographies, By kind permission

THE MARTYRS OF LYONS (2)

Under Marcus Aurelius Antoninus Verus many Christians were martyred, especially in parts of Asia and France. Such were the cruelties used in this persecution that many of the spectators shuddered with horror at the sight, and were astonished at the intrepidity of the sufferers. Some of the martyrs were obliged to pass, with their already wounded feet, over thorns, nails, and sharp shells; others were scourged till their sinews and veins lay bare; and after suffering most excruciating tortures, they were destroyed by the most terrible deaths.

At Lyons the martyrs were compelled to sit in hot iron chairs till their flesh was broiled. Some were sewn up in nets, and thrown on the horns of wild bulls; and the carcasses of those who died in prison, previous to the appointed time of execution, were thrown to dogs. Indeed, so far did the malice of the pagans proceed, that they set guards over the bodies while the beasts were devouring them, lest the friends of the deceased should get them by stealth; and the offal left by the dogs was ordered to be burnt.

To start with they endured like heroes whatever the crowds did to them: shouts of abuse, being dragged along the ground, attacked, stoned, imprisoned, and everything else that wild crowds inflict on their enemies. They were herded into the forum and tried by the tribune and city authorities in front of the whole town. As soon as they confessed Christ they were locked up in prison and had to wait for the governor. When they were later brought before him they had to suffer all the cruelties that were reserved for Christians.

Vettius

Vettius Epagathus was one of our group. He was full of love for God and for his neighbor. Even though he was young you could say of him the same as was said of the elderly Zacharias, that he kept all of God's commandments most diligently (see Luke 1:6). He was zealous for God (see Romans 10:2) and was continually full of spiritual fervor (see Romans 12:10). He found the unjust sentence against the Christians unbearable and applied for permission to speak on behalf the Christians. Amid the jeers of the crowd the governor dismissed his request by asking, "Are you a Christian? As Vettius replied clearly, "I am," he joined the ranks of the martyrs.

Blandina

The full force of the crowd, the soldiers and the governor fell on Sanctus, the deacon from Vienne; on Maturus, who had been only recently baptized, who nevertheless faced his ordeal like a hero, and Attalus, a pillar of the church at Pergamum, where he was born. Blandina was also attacked. Through Blandina Christ demonstrated that the things that are despised in the eyes of men are held in high esteem by God (see 1 Corinthians 1:28). This was exemplified in Blandina's love for Christ. Everyone, including Blandina's mistress, who was facing the prospect of martyrdom, was living in fear of persecution. Blandina was full of such courage that her torturers fell exhausted from their exertions and did not know what else they could do to her. They could not believe that she still breathed, even though she was full of gaping wounds and her body was a mangled mess. They thought that one of their tortures would have been enough to kill her and could not understand how she had survived. Ignoring her great sufferings Blandina still uttered the words, at the end of the day, "I am a Christian. I have done nothing to be ashamed of."

Sanctus

Sanctus also endured the ravages of inhuman cruelty with superhuman strength. His torturers expected the severity of his tortures to force him to recant. But his resistance was so powerful that when questioned he refused to reveal his name, race, place of birth or nationality. He replied, in Latin, to each question: "I am a Christian." The governor and his torturers became so angry with Sanctus that they applied red-hot copper plates to his private parts. Sanctus did not yield as he was strengthened by the divine water of life that flows from the heart of Christ [see John 7:38; 19:34]. However his body bore all the marks of his sufferings and looked like one great wounded mass of flesh, without any human shape left to it. But Christ achieved through this suffering body wonderful things as the opponent of Christianity was completely defeated. Sanctus suffering also demonstrated to everyone that there is no need to be afraid where the Father's love is present, and that nothing can harm Christ's followers where Christ's glory is present [see 1 John 4:18; 2 Corinthians 8:23].

A few days after this wicked people put Sanctus back on the rack thinking that his tortured body would now be unable to resist any further pain, as he experienced excruciating pain at the slightest touch on his body. His torturers also hoped to frighten other Christians by making this example of Sanctus. However, to their amazement, Sanctus body regained its former shape and he could move his limbs once again. So, through Christ's grace, Sanctus second time on the rack resulted in his cure and not in further punishment.

Biblis

Biblis, who had previously denied Christ, was not tortured. Her torturers thought that they would quickly break her resistance. But on the rack she regained her strength. She replied to her accusers, "How could we possibly eat children when we refuse to eat food sacrifice to idols?" (Acts 15:29). From that moment on she rejoined the ranks of the other Christians.

The devil used other methods of persecution when individual tortures failed. The saints were incarcerated in dark, filthy prisons, with their legs stretched apart to the fifth hole in the stocks. Many young Christians died under these tortures inside prisons.

Ponthinus

Blessed Pothinus, more than ninety years old, and extremely frail, was dragged in front of the tribunal. When he was asked by the governor, "Who is the Christian's god?" Pothinus replied, "If you had any understanding you would know." At that Pothinus was viciously struck to the ground and no allowance was made for his old age. He was then dragged off to prison, barely able to breathe, where he died two days later.

Maturus, Sanctus, Blandina, and Attalus were taken to the amphitheater so that they could be thrown to the wild beasts. But, before that happened, Maturus and Sanctus were tortured for a second time. they had to endure being whipped, a local custom, being mauled by wild beasts, and every other torture that the mad mob demanded. They were then placed in iron chairs which roasted their bodies and nearly suffocated them in the process. However, Sanctus continued to mumble the words, "I am a Christian," as he declared his Christian faith. Maturus and Sanctus appalling suffering replaced the contests between the gladiators that day. After being made a spectacle to the whole universe they were sacrificed (1 Corinthians 4:9).

Blandina, hanging from a post, was given as food to the wild beasts in the arena. She hung there in the shape of a cross and gave great encouragement to other Christians who were martyred. As they looked at her hanging there, they were reminded of the privilege in sharing in Christ's sufferings. None of the wild beasts attacked Blandina that day, so she was cut down and returned to prison.

Attalus

The crowd demanded that Attalus, a man of considerable note, should be brought into the arena. He arrived in the arena, with a clear conscience and fully prepared to face the ordeal, as he had trained so hard in Christ's school. He was paraded around the amphitheater with a placard on him which read: "This is Attalus – the Christian", as the crowds hurled all kinds of abuse at him. When the governor realized that he was a Roman he ordered that he should be returned to prison.

Caesar had given orders that they should be put to death by torture, unless they decided to deny Christ, in which case they should be released. The governor ordered them to be put on trial in front of him at the start of a local festival which attracted huge numbers of people. After they were examined again those who were Roman citizens were beheaded and the others put into the arena with the wild beasts. To appease the crowd, the governor put Attalus in with the wild beasts. He was then put in the iron chair and burnt from where he cried out: "Look what you are doing! You are eating men. But we do not eat people or indulge in any such evil practices." Just before he died he was asked, "What name does God have?" Attalus replied: "God does not have a name like any human person."

Blandina was brought out, as the crowning glory of these sports. She came with a fifteen-year-old called Ponticus. Blandina and Ponticus had been forced to watch the fate of their fellow Christians and had infuriated the crowd because they had stood firm in their faith. Blandina encouraged her younger Christian brother through all his tortures until he eventually gave up his spirit to God. Blandina then had to endure all the sufferings she had witnessed. She was whipped, thrown to the wild beasts and roasted on the griddle. Last of all she was put in a basket which tossed by a bull. Blandina's martyrdom resulted in the onlookers admitting that they had never seen a woman suffer such tortures so well for such a long time.

Even the dead and mangled bodies were abused during the following six days. Then they were finally burnt to ashes and their ashes thrown into the Rhone, so that no earthly trace of them might be left. Their torturers believed that his would ensure that "they would have no hope of resurrection, in which they trust and through which they introduce among us a strand, new religion, and by which they endure tortures and are prepared to meet death with joy. Let us see now if they will rise again, and if their God can help them and deliver them from our hands".

Eusebius, The History of the Church, Book 5, chapter 1

Epipodius and Alexander

The persecution at Lyons continued for some years, and Epipodius and Alexander were martyred the year after Blandina.

Epipodius and Alexander, friends from their school days, were unable to escape from Lyons and so lived in hiding in an area in the city known as Pierre Encise. Thorough search for any remaining Christians was made in Lyons. They were discovered and taken off quickly, so quickly that Epipodius only had time to put on one shoe, leaving the other one to be treasured as a relic by the widow who had cared for them. After three days in prison they were examined and they confessed that they were Christians. To deprive them of their mutual support they were tried separately.

Epipodius bore his tortures bravely. When the crowds shouted for worse tortures the magistrate, in order to maintain the dignity of his office, ordered Epipodius to be executed with the sword at once. Two days later Alexander was brought to the bar. On refusing to offer incense, he was beaten by three executioners in succession. After they had finished he still confessed, "The gods of the heathen are devils. I commit my will to God Almighty." The magistrate said that as the Christians liked to prolong their torments and boast about them, he would not allow them to do this. He ordered that Alexander should be crucified without delay. He died quickly as his body was exhausted through the scourging which it had received. With his last breath he called on Christ.

Ruinart's Acta Primorum Martyrum Sincera; quoted by A. J. Mason, The Historic Martyrs of the Primitive Church, Longmans, 1905, pp 57-8

Symphorian

At about the same time as the martyrs of Lyons suffered, Symphorian lived in Autun, a town renowned for being the center for orgies linked to the Phrygian worship of Cymbele, or Berecynthia. During a great celebration of the festival of this goddess, Symphorian was seen not to give the customary marks of reverence to Berecynthia. Since Christians were being rounded up Symphorian was brought before the governor, Heraclius.

Heraclius asked the usual questions about his name and position. Symphorian replied, "I am a Christian, my name is Symphorian."

"Are you a Christian?" answered the governor in surprise. "You must have escaped our attention. There are few of you in these parts. Why do you despise the figure of the mother of the gods, and refuse to worship it?"

"I have already told you," replied Symphorian, "that I am a Christian. I worship the true God, who reigns in heaven. I do not worship the image of a devil. If you would allow me to I would break it up with a hammer."

The magistrate declared that he was not only guilty of sacrilege, but of treason. Heraclius ordered the lictors to beat him and put him in prison. After a few days Symphorian was brought to the court again and asked if he would worship the gods, but he refused. "I fear the Almighty God who made me," he replied, "and I serve him only. You have my body in your power for a while, but not my soul."

The judge condemned him to be beheaded. As we was led out of the gate of the city, his mother called out to him from the city wall, "My son! Symphorian, my son! Think of the living God. Be steadfast. It is no loss of life for you today, but a change for the better."

A. J. Mason, The Historic Martyrs of the Primitive Church, Longmans, 1905, pp 58-9

THE ACTS OF CARPUS, PAPYLUS AND AGATHONICA 161-9

Carpus, Papylus and Agathonica were martyred at Pergamos at about the same time as the churches at Lyons and Vienne were being persecuted.

While the proconsul was in residence at Pergamus blessed Carpus and Papylus, Christ's martyrs, were brought before him. Having taken his seat on the tribunal the proconsul asked, "What is your name?"

The blessed one replied, "My first name and chosen name is Christian, but, if you want to know my earthly name, it is Carpus."

The proconsul said: "You are aware of Augusti's commands, that you must both worship the gods who govern the world, so I now order you both to come forward and sacrifice."

Carpus replied, "I am a Christian, I worship Christ, the son of God, who came in the latter times for our salvation and delivered us from the deceit of the devil, and to such idols I do not sacrifice. No matter what you may do to me, it is impossible for me to sacrifice to fake representations of demons. People of sacrifice to them are similar to them. For just as "true worshiper – those who, according to the divine teaching of our Lord, "worship God in spirit and in truth" – are made like God's glory and are immortal with him, taking part in eternal life through the Word, so also those who worship these idols are like the demons and will perish with them in hell. So, be assured, Proconsul, I will not sacrifice to these."

The proconsul angrily replied, "sacrifice, both of you, and don't behave like fools."

Carpus replied, smiling, "Perish the gods that have not made the heaven and earth!"

The proconsul said: "You must sacrifice: for so the Emperor commanded."

Carpus answered: "The living do not sacrifice to the dead."

The proconsul said: "Do the gods seem to you to be dead?"

Carpus said: "Would you hear the answer? These were never even men, nor ever lived, that they should die. Do you wish to learn that this is true? Take away from them your homage which you suppose they receive at your hands, and you shall know they are nothing, things of the earth earthy and destroyed by time. For our God who is timeless and made the ages himself remains indestructible and everlasting, being ever the same and admitting neither of increase nor of decrease, but these are made by men and destroyed, as I said, by time. And do not marvel that they give oracles and deceive. For the Devil, having fallen in the beginning from his place of glory, would fain by his own villainy make of none effect the fatherly love of God for man, and being hard pressed by the saints contends with them and prepares wars beforehand and forecast announces them to his own. Likewise also from the things that happen to us daily he, being more ancient than the years, by his experience foretells the future evil which he himself intends to do. For by the decree of God knowledge as well as wickedness are his, and by God's permission he tempts man, seeking to turn him from holiness. Be convinced therefore, O consul, that you are living in no small folly."

The proconsul said: "By enduring much idle talk from you I have led you to blaspheme the gods and the Augusti. So that it goes no further with you, will you sacrifice? Or what have you to say?"

Carpus answered: "It is impossible for me to sacrifice, for I have never sacrificed to idols."

So the proconsul ordered him to be hung up and scraped. Carpus cried out: "I am a Christian." And after this torture had continued for a long time, he was exhausted and unable to speak.

So the proconsul left Carpus, and turned to Papylus, and said to him, "Are you a councillor?""

And he answered: "I am a citizen."

The proconsul said: "A citizen of which city?"

Papylus answered, "Of Thyatira."

The proconsul said: "Have you any children?"

Papylus answered, "Yes, and many of them, thanks be to God!"

Then someone in the crowd shouted out, "He means that some of the Christians are his children in the faith."

The proconsul said: "Why do you lie, saying that you have children?"

Papylus answered: "Would you learn that I do not lie, but speak the truth? In every district and city I have children in God."

The proconsul said: "Will you sacrifice? Or what will you say?"

Papylus answered: "I have served God since I was a youth, and I have never sacrificed to idols, since I am a Christian, and you cannot learn anything more than this from me; for there is nothing greater or nobler than this for me to say."

So he was also hung up and scraped three times with two instruments of torture at the same time, but he uttered no sound, but as a noble athlete withstood the wrath of the Enemy.

When the proconsul saw their great endurance he gave orders that they should be burnt alive. They were both taken at once to the amphitheater, so that they might leave this world quickly. Papylus was nailed to the stake, lifted up, and as the fire approached him, he prayed and gave up his soul peacefully. Carpus was then nailed and he smiled on them, so that the spectators asked, "What are you laughing about?" The blessed Carpus said, ""I saw the glory of the Lord, and I was glad, and at the same time I was leaving you and have no part in your evil actions." When the soldier piled up the wood and lit it the saintly Carpus said, as he hung, "We too were born of the same mother Eve and have the same flesh as you, but looking to the judgement seat of truth let us endure everything." After he said this, as the fire approached him, he said, "Blessed art thou, Lord Jesus Christ, Son of God, because thou didst count me also the sinner worthy of this part in thee!" Then Carpus gave up his soul.

A certain Agathonica standing and beholding the glory of the Lord, which Carpus said that he had seen, and perceiving the invitation to be from heaven, immediately raised her voice, "This dinner has been prepared for me; of this glorious dinner therefore I must take part and eat."

But the people cried out, saying, "Take pity on your son."

The blessed Agathonica said, "He has God who can have pity on him, for his is the Protector of everyone; but I must leave." Then she took off her outer clothes and threw herself on the stake, rejoicing. But the spectators lamented and said, "Terrible sentence, unjust orders!" When Agathonica was lift up on the stake and felt the burning flames, she cried out three times, "Lord, Lord, Lord help me, for I flee to Thee."

And so she gave up her spirit, and was perfected with the saints, whose remains the Christians secretly took up and carefully guarded to the glory of Christ and the praise of his martyrs, because to him belong glory and power, to the Father and to the Son and to the Holy Spirit, now and always and for ever and ever. Amen.

E. C. E. Owen (trans.), Some Authentic Acts of the Early Martyrs, Oxford, 1927, pp 42-46

Martyrdom of Justin (1)

"You can kill, but you cannot harm us." (Justin, Apology)

The Christian church fared worse under the emperor Marcus Aurelius than it had done under any emperor since the times of Nero and Domitian. The most famous martyr under Marcus Aurelius was the philosopher Justin.

Justin, the celebrated philosopher, fell martyr under Emperor Marcus Aurelius Antoninus Verus persecution. He was born in Neapolis, in Samaria, in 103. He traveled into Egypt, the country where the polite tour of that age made for improvement. At Alexandria he was informed of everything relative to the seventy interpreters of the Septuagint version of the Scriptures, and shown the rooms, or, rather, cells, in which their work was performed: the story being that each of the seventy translators was confined during his work in a separate apartment, and that subsequently, on their comparing their independent translations of the Old Testament into Greek, they were found to be practically identical. About 133, when he was thirty years old, he became a convert to Christianity. Justine wrote an elegant letter to the Gentiles, to convert them to the faith he had newly acquired. As the pagans began to treat the Christians with great severity, Justin wrote his first apology in their favor, and addressed it to the Emperor Antoninus, and to the senate and to the people of Rome in general. This piece, which occasioned the emperor to publish an edict in favor of the Christians, displays great learning and genius.

A short time later, he entered into debates with Crescens, a celebrated cynic philosopher; and his arguments appeared so powerful, yet disgusting, to the cynic, that he resolved on his destruction. Justin's second apology upon fresh severities gave Crescens an opportunity of prejudicing the emperor against the writer of it; upon which Justin and six of his companions were apprehended.

John Foxe, The Book of Martyrs, revised with notes and an appendix by W. Bramley-Moore, London, 1869, pp 14-15

Justin Martyr, Philosopher, Apologist, and Martyr

Justin was born around 100 (both his birth and death dates are approximate) at Flavia Neapolis (ancient Shechem, modern Nablus) in Samaria (the middle portion of Israel, between Galilee and Judea) of pagan Greek parents. He was brought up with a good education in rhetoric, poetry, and history. He studied various schools of philosophy in Alexandria and Ephesus , joining himself first to Stoicism, then Pythagoreanism, then Platonism, looking for answers to his questions. While at Ephesus, he was impressed by the steadfastness of the Christian martyrs, and by the personality of an aged Christian man whom he met by chance while walking on the seashore. This man spoke to him about Jesus as the fulfilment of the promises made through the Jewish prophets. Justin was overwhelmed. "straightway a flame was kindled in my soul," he writes, "and a love of the prophets and those who are friends of Christ possessed me." Justin became a Christian, but he continued to wear the cloak that was the characteristic uniform of the professional teacher of philosophy. His position was that pagan philosophy, especially Platonism, is not simply wrong, but is a partial grasp of the truth, and serves as "a schoolmaster to bring us to Christ." He engaged in debates and disputations with non-Christians of all varieties, pagans, Jews, and heretics. He opened a school of Christian philosophy and accepted students, first at Ephesus and then later at Rome. There he engaged the Cynic philosopher Crescens in debate, and soon after was arrested on the charge of practicing an unauthorized religion. (It is suggested that Crescens lost the debate and denounced Justin to the authorities out of spite.) He was tried before the Roman prefect Rusticus, refused to renounce Christianity, and was put to death by beheading along with six of his students, one of them a woman. A record of the trial, probably authentic, is preserved, known as The Acts of Justin the Martyr.

Three works of Justin have been preserved.

His First Apology (in the sense of "defense" or "vindication") was addressed (around 155) to the Emperor Antoninus Pius and his adopted sons. (It is perhaps worth noting that some of the fiercest persecutors of the Christians were precisely the emperors who had a strong sense of duty, who were fighting to maintain the traditional Roman values, including respect for the gods, which they felt had made Rome great and were her only hope of survival.) He defends Christianity as the only rational creed, and he includes an account of current Christian ceremonies of Baptism and the Eucharist (probably to counteract distorted accounts from anti-Christian sources).

The Second Apology is addressed to the Roman Senate. It is chiefly concerned to rebut specific charges of immorality and the like that had been made against the Christians. He argues that good Christians make good citizens, and that the notion that Christianity undermines the foundations of a good society is based on slander or misunderstanding.

The Dialog With Trypho The Jew is an account of a dialog between Justin and a Jewish rabbi named Trypho(n) (probably a real conversation with a real rabbi, although it may be suspected that Justin in editing it later gave himself a few good lines that he wished he had thought of at the time), whom he met while promenading at Ephesus shortly after the sack of Jerusalem in 135. Trypho had fled from Israel, and the two men talked about the Jewish people and their place in history, and then about Jesus and whether he was the promised Messiah. A principal question is whether the Christian belief in the deity of Christ can be reconciled with the uncompromising monotheism of the Scriptures. The dialogue is a valuable source of information about early Christian thought concerning Judaism and the relation between Israel and the Church as communities having a covenant relation with God. Toward the end of the dialog, Trypho asks, "suppose that I were to become a Christian. Would I be required to give up keeping kosher and other parts of the Jewish law?" Justin replies: "Christians are not agreed on this. Some would say that you must give them up. Others, such as myself, would say that it would be quite all right for you, as a Jewish convert to Christianity, to keep kosher and otherwise observe the Law of Moses, provided that you did not try to compel other converts to do likewise, and provided that you clearly understand that keeping kosher will not save you. It is only Christ who saves you." They finally part friends, with Trypho saying, "You have given me food for thought. I must consider this further."

An interesting feature is the dispute about texts. Justin would quote a passage from the Septuagint (LXX), the standard Greek translation of the Jewish Scriptures, and Trypho would reply, "That is not an accurate translation of the Hebrew. You Christians have been tampering with the text!" He never (at least as reported by Justin) denies that Justin is correctly quoting the Greek manuscripts as they existed at the time, never brings forward an uncorrupted translation that has been preserved by Greek-speaking Jews.

The subsequent history of this dispute about translations is that the Jews, who had produced the LXX translation between 285 and 132 BC, repudiated it as unreliable and produced several subsequent translations, chiefly that of Aquila (around 140), which were close literal translations of the received Hebrew text – what we may by an anachronism call the Masoretic Text (MT). Many Christians, on the other hand, noted that the LXX is the version usually quoted in the New Testament, even when it differs from the Hebrew. They recalled a Jewish story to the effect that the translation had been produced by 70 (or 72) scholars (hence the name), each working separately, and that their results when compared agreed perfectly; and they took this story as an indication that the LXX was an inspired translation, and that when it disagreed with the Hebrew, so much the worse for the Hebrew! The earliest Latin versions of the Bible (known collectively as the Old Latin (OL)) are translated from the LXX. However, when Jerome was called to produce a new version of the Latin Bible, he translated directly from the Hebrew (except for the Psalms, where he produced two versions), and this reduced the prestige of the LXX in the West. For many years scholars, noting the differences between the LXX and the MT, supposed that the LXX was simply a sloppy translation. However, the Dead Sea Scrolls included many Hebrew manuscripts of portions of Old Testament books (Samuel is the outstanding example) that had readings that agreed with the LXX against the MT. Accordingly, it is now widely held that the LXX is an accurate translation of Hebrew manuscripts representing one of several versions, but not always the version that ultimately prevailed in Hebrew circles and came to be what we call the MT. As for why it happened that the LXX was so often better suited to Christian purposes in proof-texting than the MT, several explanations come to mind:

The early Christians, who were for the most part Greek-speakers, started their search for good proof texts by reading the LXX, and they accordingly found all the places where the LXX gives them what they want and the MT doesn't, while they completely missed all the places where the MT gives them what they want and the LXX doesn't.

The Jews, in their subsequent sorting out of their various manuscript traditions, wherever the rival claims of two readings were otherwise roughly balanced, tended to be more hospitable to a reading that did not furnish aid and comfort to their opponents.

The early Christians, being Greek-speakers steeped in the LXX, tended to remember the details of life of Christ in a way that was colored by the LXX. For example (not a very good example), Matthew (27:34) tells us that before Our Lord was crucified, he was offered wine with gall added. It is unlikely that gall was actually used (it has no relevant pharmacological properties), and I assume that Matthew was using the term simply to refer generically to a bitter-tasting substance. However, his use of this particular term is undoubtedly influenced by Psalm 69:21, considered as a prophecy of the crucifixion. As noted, this is not a very good example, because it does not involve the wording of the LXX. But my point is that a Christian writer, describing an event in the life of Christ while thinking of an Old Testament passage that he believes foreshadows that event, will, without sacrificing factual accuracy, naturally allow that passage to affect his choice of details to mention and words in which to describe them, and if he has been reading the LXX, then the LXX will be a more impressive version to cite than the MT if you are trying to match the event as recorded with the alleged prediction of it.

From the First Apology:

On finishing the prayers we greet each other with a kiss. Then bread and a cup of water mixed with wine are brought to the leader and he, taking them, sends up praise and glory to the Father of the Universe through the name of the Son and of the Holy Spirit, and offers thanksgiving at some length that we have been deemed worthy to receive these things. When the leader has finished the prayers and thanksgivings, the whole congregation assents, saying, "Amen." ("Amen" is Hebrew for "so be it.") Then those whom we call deacons give to each of those present a portion of the consecrated bread and wine and water, and they take it to the absent.

Justin's works are found in the multi-volumed set called: The Ante-Nicene Fathers
James Kiefer, Christian Biographies, By kind permission

Martyrdom of Justin (2)
Examination of Justin by the prefect

In the time of the lawless adherents of idolatry, evil decrees were passed against the godly Christians, both in the towns and in the countryside, to force them to offer libations to vain idols. After the holy men had been arrested they were brought in front of the Roman prefect called Rusticus.

When they were brought before the judgement seat, Rusticus the prefect said to Justin: "First of all obey the gods, and make submission to the princes."

Justin said, "To obey the commands of our Savior Jesus Christ is not worthy of blame or condemnation."

The prefect Rusticus said, "What doctrines do you hold?"

Justin said, "I have endeavored to make myself acquainted with all doctrines, but I have given my assent to the true doctrines of the Christians, whether they please the holders of false beliefs or not."

The prefect Rusticus said, "Do those doctrines please you, miserable man?"

Justin said, "Yes, for the belief in accordance with which I follow them is right."

The prefect Rusticus said, "What belief do you mean?"

Justin said, "That which we religiously profess concerning the God of the Christians, in whom we believe, one God, existing from the beginning, Maker and Artificer of the whole creation, seen and unseen; and concerning our Lord Jesus Christ, the Son of God, who hath also been proclaimed afore time by the prophets as about to come to the race of men for herald of salvation and for master of true disciples. And I, being but a man, regard what I say to be of little worth in comparison with his infinite Godhead, but there is a power in prophecy, and that I acknowledge; therein has proclamation been made beforehand about him of whom I just spoke as the Son of God. For I know that from the beginning the prophets foretold his coming among men."

Examination of Justin continued

The prefect Rusticus said, "Where do you meet together?"

Justin said, "Where each wills and can. Do you really think that we all meet in the same place? Not so: for the God of the Christians is not confined by place, but being unseen fills heaven and earth, and is worshiped and glorified by the faithful everywhere."

The prefect Rusticus said, "Tell me, where do you meet, or in what place do you gather your disciples?"

Justin said, "I lodge above the house Martin, near the baths of Timothy, and during all this time (this is my second visit to Rome) I have known no other place of meeting but his house. And if any wished to come to me, I imparted to him the word of truth."

Rusticus said, "To come to the point then, are you a Christian?"

Justin said, "Yes, I am a Christian."

Examination of Chariton and others

The prefect Rusticus said to Chariton, "What do you say, Chariton?"

Chariton said, "I am a Christian by God's gift."

Rusticus the prefect asked the woman Charito, "What do you say, Charito?"

Charito said, "I am a Christian by the grace of God."

Rusticus said to Euelpistus: "And what are you?"

Euelpistus, a slave of Caesar, answered, "I also am a Christian, freed by Christ, and share by the grace of Christ in the same hope."

The prefect Rusticus said to Hierax, "Are you also a Christian?"

Hierax said: "Yes, I am a Christian, for I worship and adore the same God."

The prefect Rusticus said, "Did Justin make you Christians?"

Hierax said, "I was, and shall ever be, a Christian."

A man called Paeon stood up and said: "I also am a Christian."

The prefect Rusticus said, "Who taught you?"

Paeon said: "I received from my parents this good confession."

Euelpistus said, "I listened indeed gladly to the words of Justin, but I too received Christianity from my parents."

The prefect Rusticus said, "Where are your parents?"

Euelpistus said: "In Cappadocia."

Rusticus said to Hierax, "Where are your parents?"

He answered, saying, "Our true father is Christ, and our mother our faith in him. My earthly parents are dead, and I was dragged away from Iconium in Phrygia before coming here."

The prefect Rusticus said to Liberian, "And what do you say? Are you a Christian? Are you an unbeliever like the rest?"

Liberian said: "I also am a Christian; for I am a believer and adore the only true God."

Rusticus threatens the Christians with death

The prefect Rusticus said to Justin, "Listen, you that are said to be a learned man, and think that you are acquainted with true doctrine, if you shall be scourged and beheaded, are you persuaded that you will ascend to heaven?"

Justin said, "I hope if I endure these things to have his gifts. For I know that for all who so live there abides until the consummation of the whole world the free gift of God."

The prefect Rusticus said, "Do you then think that you will ascend to heaven, to receive certain rewards?"

Justin said, "I do not think, I know and am fully persuaded."

The prefect Rusticus said, "Let us now come to the pressing matter in hand. Agree together and sacrifice with one accord to the gods."

Justin said, "No one who is rightly minded turns from true belief to false."

The prefect Rusticus said, "If you do not obey, you will be punished without mercy."

Justin said, "If we are punished for the sake of our Lord Jesus Christ we hope to be saved, for this shall be our salvation and confidence before the more terrible judgement seat of our Lord and Savior who shall judge the whole world."

So also said the other martyrs, "Do what you will. For we are Christians and offer no sacrifice to idols."

Sentence pronounced and executed

Rusticus the prefect gave sentence, "Let those who will not sacrifice to the gods and yield to the command of the Emperor be scourged and led away to be beheaded in accordance with the laws."

The holy martyrs went out glorifying God to the customary place and were beheaded, and fulfilled their testimony by the confession of their Savior. And some of the faithful took their bodies by stealth and laid them in a convenient place, the grace of our Lord Jesus Christ working with them, to whom be glory for ever and ever. Amen.
Eusebius, The History of the Church, Book 6

MARTYRDOM OF JUSTIN (3)

Christian apologist, born at Flavia Neapolis, about A.D. 100, converted to Christianity about A.D. 130, taught and defended the Christian religion in Asia Minor and at Rome, where he suffered martyrdom about the year 165. Two "Apologies" bearing his name and his "Dialogue with the Jew Tryphon" have come down to us.

Justin's life

Among the Fathers of the second century his life is the best known, and from the most authentic documents. In both "Apologies and in his "Dialogue" he gives many personal details, e.g. about his studies in philosophy and his conversion; they are not, however, an autobiography, but are partly idealized, and it is necessary to distinguish in them between poetry and truth; they furnish us however with several precious and reliable clues. For his martyrdom we have documents of undisputed authority. In the first line of his "Apology" he calls himself "Justin, the son of Priscos, son of Baccheios, of Flavia Neapolis, in Palestinian Syria". The date of his birth is uncertain, but would seem to fall in the first years of the second century. He received a good education in philosophy, an account of which he gives us at the beginning of his "Dialogue with the Jew Tryphon"; he placed himself first under a Stoic, but after some time found that he had learned nothing about God and that in fact his master had nothing to teach him on the subject. A Peripatetic whom he then found welcomed him at first but afterwards demanded a fee from him; this proved that he was not a philosopher. A Pythagorean refused to teach him anything until he should have learned music, astronomy, and geometry. Finally a Platonist arrived on the scene and for some time delighted Justin. This account cannot be taken too literally; the facts seem to be arranged with a view to showing the weakness of the pagan philosophies and of contrasting them with the teachings of the Prophets and of Christ. The main facts, however, may be accepted; the works of Justin seem to show just such a philosophic development as is here described, Eclectic, but owing much to Stoicism and more to Platonism. He was still under the charm of the Platonistic philosophy when, as he walked one day along the seashore, he met a mysterious old man; the conclusion of their long discussion was that he soul could not arrive through human knowledge at the idea of God, but that it needed to be instructed by the Prophets who, inspired by the Holy Ghost, had known God and could make Him known.

. . . St. Justin lived certainly some time at Ephesus; the Acts of his martyrdom tell us that he went to Rome twice and lived "near the baths of Timothy with a man named Martin". He taught school there, and in the aforesaid Acts of his martyrdom we read of several of his disciples who were condemned with him. In his second "Apology" (iii) Justin says: "I, too, expect to be persecuted and to be crucified by some of those whom I have named, or by Crescens, that friend of noise and of ostentation." Indeed Tatian relates (Discourse, xix) that the Cynic philosopher Crescens did pursue him and Justin; he does not tell us the result and, moreover, it is not certain that the "Discourse" of Tatian was written after the death of Justin. Eusebius (Hist. eccl., IV, xvi, 7, 8) says that it was the intrigues of Crescens which brought about the death of Justin; this is credible, but not certain; Eusebius has apparently no other reason for affirming it than the two passages cited above from Justin and Tatian. St. Justin was condemned to death by the prefect, Rusticus, towards A.D. 165, with six companions, Chariton, Charito, Evelpostos, Pæon, Hierax, and Liberianos. We still have the authentic account of their martyrdom.

The examination ends as follows:

"The Prefect Rusticus says: Approach and sacrifice, all of you, to the gods. Justin says: No one in his right mind gives up piety for impiety. The Prefect Rusticus says: If you do not obey, you will be tortured without mercy. Justin replies: That is our desire, to be tortured for Our Lord, Jesus Christ, and so to be saved, for that will give us salvation and firm confidence at the more terrible universal tribunal of Our Lord and Savior. And all the martyrs said: Do as you wish; for we are Christians, and we do not sacrifice to idols. The Prefect Rusticus read the sentence: Those who do not wish to sacrifice to the gods and to obey the emperor will be scourged and beheaded according to the laws. The holy martyrs glorifying God betook themselves to the customary place, where they were beheaded and consummated their martyrdom confessing their Savior."

. . . The role of St. Justin may be summed up in one word: it is that of a witness. We behold in him one of the highest and purest pagan souls of his time in contact with Christianity, compelled to accept its irrefragable truth, its pure moral teaching, and to admire its superhuman constancy. He is also a witness of the second-century Church which he describes for us in its faith, its life, its worship, at a time when Christianity yet lacked the firm organization that it was soon to develop but the larger outlines of whose constitution and doctrine are already luminously drawn by Justin. Finally, Justin was a witness for Christ unto death.

Jules Lebreton, The Catholic Encyclopedia, Volume 8

The Scillitan saints

Introduction to the Passion of the Scillitan Martyrs

The Scillitan Martyrs were condemned and executed at Carthage on the 17th July, A.D. 180. The martyrs belonged to Scili, a place in that part of Numidia which belonged to proconsular Africa. The proconsul at the time, who is said by Tertullian to have been the first to draw the sword against the Christians there, was P. Vigellius Saturninus. The consuls for the year were Praesens II. and Condianus. Marcus Aurelius had died only a few months before.

Records about martyrdoms inflicted by the sword in Scillium, part of the African diocese of Carthage, are contained in Acts of Martyrdom. These are the oldest Acts in existence in Africa, and are excellent examples of Acts as they are based on official reports, and have very little added by any editors. Seven men and five women, who became known as the Scillium martyrs, appeared before Saturninus at Carthage.

In the consulship of Praesens, then consul for the second time, and Claudian, on the 17th of July, Speratus, Nartzalus and Cittinus, Donata, Secunda, Vestia were brought to trial at Carthage in the council chamber. The proconsul Saturninus said to them, "You may merit the indulgence of our Lord and Emperor, if you return to a right mind."

Speratus said, "We have never done harm to any, we have never lent ourselves to wickedness; we have never spoken ill of anyone, but have given thanks when ill-treated, because we hold our own Emperor in honor."

The proconsul Saturninus said, "We also are religious people, and our religion is simple, and we swear by the genius of our

Lord the Emperor, and pray for his safety, as you also ought to do."

Speratus said, "If you will give me a quiet hearing, I will tell you the mystery of simplicity."

Saturninus said, "If you begin to speak evil of our sacred rites, I will give you no hearing; but swear rather by the genius of our Lord the Emperor."

Speratus said, "I do not recognize the empire of this world; but rather I serve that God, whom no man has seen nor can see. I have not stolen, but if I buy anything, I pay the tax, because I recognize my Lord, the King of kings and Emperor of all peoples."

The proconsul Saturninus said to the rest, "Cease to be of this persuasion."

Speratus said, "The persuasion that we should do murder, or bear false witness, that is evil."

The proconsul Saturninus said, "Have no part in this madness."

Cittinus said, "We have nobody else to fear except the Lord our God who is in heaven."

Donata said, "Give honor to Caesar as unto Caesar, but fear to God."

Vestia said, "I am a Christian."

Secunda said, "I wish to be none other than what I am."

The proconsul Saturninus said to Speratus, "Do you persist in being a Christian?"

Speratus said, "I am a Christian." And all agreed with this statement.

The proconsul Saturninus said, "Do you want any time to consider your position?"

Speratus said, "When the right is so clear, there is nothing to consider."

The proconsul Saturninus said, "What have you in your case?"

Speratus said, "The books, and letters of a just man, one Paul."

The proconsul Saturninus said, "Take a reprieve of thirty days and think it over."

Speratus repeated, "I am a Christian." And all were of the same mind.

The proconsul Saturninus read out the sentence from his note book: "Whereas Speratus, Nartzalus, Cittinus, Donata, Vestia, Secunda, and the rest have confessed that they live in accordance with the religious rites of the Christians, and, when an opportunity was given them to return to the ways of the Romans, they persisted in their obstinacy, it is our pleasure that they should suffer by the sword."

Speratus said, "Thanks be to God!"

Nartzalus said, "Today we are martyrs in heaven, thanks be to God!"

The proconsul Saturninus commanded that proclamation be made by the herald, "I have commanded Speratus, Nartzalus, Cittinus, Donata, Vestia, Secunda, Veturius, Felix, Aquilinus, Laetantius, Januaria, Generosa, to be led out for execution.

They all said, "Thanks be to God!

And so all were crowned with martyrdom together, and reign with the Father and Son and Holy Spirit for ever and ever. Amen.

Eusebius, The History of the Church, Book 6

Caecilia, Valerian, Tiburtius and Maximus

Towards the end of Marcus Aurelius' reign a famous saint was killed in Rome – St Caecilia. She was a daughter of the illustrious Roman family of the Caecilii, and had been brought up a Christian from childhood. She persuaded both her husband Valerian and his younger brother Tiburtius to receive Christian instruction from the elder Urban. He lived on the family property on the Appian Way and baptized them. At this time some Christians were martyred in the city of Rome. Local laws prevented their bodies from being buried. But the two brothers tried to bury the bodies, thus bringing themselves to the notice of the authorities, and they were arrested.

In reply to an accusation that he was mad, Tiburtius said, "No, the Lord Jesus Christ, whom I have received into my inmost parts, has possession of them, and speaks through me." When Valerian came into court, the prefect told him that his brother was mad. Valerian replied that he only knew one doctor for the mind, who was Christ, the Son of God. He added that eternal sorrow awaited those who lived the life of the world.

"What?" cried the prefect, "shall we and the invincible emperors have eternal sorrow, while you have perfect joy?"

Valerian answered, "What are you and what are your emperors but frail men, who are born and must die when your time comes, and are responsible to God for the power which you have received from him?"

The prefect said, "We are wasting our time in irrelevant conversation. Offer to the gods, and you may leave."

The brothers answered, "We do not sacrifice to the gods, we sacrifice every day to God."

The prefect asked them the name of their god. Valerian replied, "You will not find the name of God, not if you were to soar with wings."

"Is not Jupiter the name of a god?" said the prefect.

"No," said Valerian, "it is the name of a corrupt and wicked man. Your own writers show him to be a murderer and a criminal."

The prefect ordered them to be beaten with sticks. Valerian called out to the Christians who looked on, who also coveted their Roman citizenship, "Roman Citizens, do not let my sufferings frighten you away from the truth, but stand firm in the faith of our holy Lord, knowing that those who worship the gods of wood and stone will suffer everlasting tribulation." Later they were led out to a place called Pagus Triopius, four miles outside the city, and given one last opportunity to offer incense in the temple of Jupiter. They refused to offer incense, knelt down and were beheaded by a sword. It is said that the head official of the court, Maximus, was so moved by the brothers' behavior that he linked himself to their religion, and was also put to death for this. Caecilia buried the three bodies in the neighboring cemetery, called Praetextatus.

Perhaps for her part in these burials Caecilia was arrested. She told the prefect that she was freeborn and from a noble family. The prefect accused her of being proud and trying to use her position to her advantage. Caecilia replied, "Pride is one thing, and firmness is another. I spoke firmly, but not proudly."

The prefect replied, "You know that the emperors have ordered that those who do not deny that they are Christians will be punished, and those who deny that they are Christians will be released." Caecilia refused to offer incense and so was ordered back to her own house where she was to be suffocated in a hot bath. As this proved unsuccessful an executioner beheaded her in her home.
Editor

The Acts of Apollonius

The philosopher Apollonius was beheaded in Rome in 185.

In the persecution Emperor Commodus inflicted on the Christians Perennis was proconsul of Asia. After the apostle Apollonius, who came from Alexandria, was arrested Perennis put him on trial.

PROCONSUL PERENNIS: Are you a Christian, Apollonius?

APOLLONIUS: Yes, I am a Christian. I fear and worship the God who made heaven, earth, the sea and all that is in them.

PROCONSUL PERENNIS: Be advised, Apollonius, and swear by the emperor Commodus, our lord.

APOLLONIUS: Listen to my defense, Perennis. If you disobey God's commandments you become a criminal because you are denying God. God's commands are full of justice and truth. We believe them to be the word of God and they teach us never take oaths.

PROCONSUL PERENNIS: Sacrifice to the gods and to emperor Commodus' statue.

APOLLONIUS: The sacrifice we Christians offer is one of prayer. In fact we daily pray for the emperor Commodus. Be we believe that he rules not by the will of humans, but through God's decree.

PROCONSUL PERENNIS: I will give you one day to think about your fate.

Three days later Apollonius was asked if he had changed his mind. He replied in this way:

APOLLONIUS: I am aware of the Senate's decree, but my God whom I serve is not made with human hands. I can never worship gold, or iron or bronze or silver, or any deaf and dumb idols. You are wrong on many counts to indulge in such worship.

Firstly, you are wrong in God's sight because your idols are unable to respond to you.

Secondly, you are wrong in God's sight because you worship the fruit of nature, such things as onions and garlic which once they have passed through the stomach go into sewers.

Thirdly, you are wrong in God's sight because you worship animals.

Fourthly, you are wrong in God's sight because you worship man-made gods such as Dionysus, Heracles and Zeus."

PROCONSUL PERENNIS: Senate's decree forbids anyone to be a Christian.

APOLLONIUS: Man's decrees have no power over God's decrees. The more you kill these poor, innocent people, the more God will raise up more of them. Everyone is in God's hands, kings and senators, to free men and slaves. After we die we come to the time of judgment. We do not think that it is difficult to die for the God of truth.

PROCONSUL PERENNIS: So does death give you pleasure?

APOLLONIUS: Perennis, I love life, but that does not make me fear death. But the life which I prefer above everything is eternal life. This is the life that is in store for those who live faithfully on this earth. We believe in the immortal soul, judgment following death, the resurrection of the dead and that God will be our judge. Even if you believe that all this is foolishness we gladly take these illusions with us which have helped us to live.

PROCONSUL PERENNIS: I hoped that you would say goodbye to your beliefs and join us in worshiping the gods.

APOLLONIUS: I hoped that my words would have opened the eyes of your soul so that you would worship the God who created the world.

PROCONSUL PERENNIS: Even though I would like to set you free, Apollonius, emperor Commodus's decree prevents me. However, I will ensure that your death will not be painful.

Perennis then ordered Apollonius to be beheaded. Perennis responded by saying that Perennis' sentence would bring him eternal life.

3. Christian writings

A collection of the writings, prayers and the spoken words of the martyrs and about the martyrs and martyrdom and persecution of Christians from the period 54-193.

A. It is the Part of the Wicked to Vex the Righteous: Clement of Rome

Saint Clement I, or Clement of Rome (c AD 30-100), bishop of Rome, mentioned by Paul the apostle as a fellow worker (Philippians 4:3), was the first of the ecclesiastical writers called Apostolic Fathers. His Epistle to the Corinthians was considered a canonical book of the Bible until the 4th century and was held in high esteem. Here we present an excerpt of this letter dealing with the persecutors and the purpose of the martyrdom of Christians.

Clement's first letter to the Corinthians Chapter 45: It is part of the wicked to vex the righteous

Ye are fond of contention, brethren, and full of zeal about things which do not pertain to salvation. Look carefully into the Scriptures, which are the true utterances of the Holy Spirit. Observe that nothing of an unjust or counterfeit character is written in them. There you will not find that the righteous were cast off by men who themselves were holy. The righteous were indeed persecuted, but only by the wicked. They were cast into prison, but only by the unholy; they were stoned, but only by transgressors; they were slain, but only by the accursed, and such as had conceived an unrighteous envy against them. Exposed to such sufferings, they endured them gloriously. For what shall we say, brethren? Was Daniel cast into the den of lions by such as feared God? Were Ananias, and Azarias, and Mishael shut up in a furnace of fire by those who observed the great and glorious worship of the Most High? Far from us be such a thought! Who, then, were they that did such things? The hateful, and those full of all wickedness, were roused to such a pitch of fury, that they inflicted torture on those who served God with a holy and blameless purpose [of heart], not knowing that the Most High is the Defender and Protector of all such as with a pure conscience venerate His all-excellent name; to whom be glory for ever and ever. Amen. But they who with confidence endured [these things] are now heirs of glory and honor, and have been exalted and made illustrious by God in their memorial for ever and ever. Amen.

Clement

B. Manners of the Christians and the Reason of Their Persecution

The Epistle of Mathetes to Diognetus

The author (Mathetes) of this Epistle from around AD 130 calls himself "a disciple of the Apostles". He might have been a catechumen of Paul or of one of the apostle's associates. Here we present two chapters from this letter dealing with the life and manners of the Christians and the reason they are persecuted.

Chapter 5: The Manners of the Christians

For the Christians are distinguished from other men neither by country, nor language, nor the customs which they observe. For they neither inhabit cities of their own, nor employ a peculiar form of speech, nor lead a life which is marked out by any singularity. The course of conduct which they follow has not been devised by any speculation or deliberation of inquisitive men; nor do they, like some, proclaim themselves the advocates of any merely human doctrines. But, inhabiting Greek as well as barbarian cities, according as the lot of each of them has determined, and following the customs of the natives in respect to clothing, food, and the rest of their ordinary conduct, they display to us their wonderful and confessedly striking method of life. They dwell in their own countries, but simply as sojourners. As citizens, they share in all things with others, and yet endure all things as if foreigners. Every foreign land is to them as their native country, and every land of their birth as a land of strangers. They marry, as do all [others]; they beget children; but they do not destroy their offspring. They have a common table, but not a common bed. They are in the flesh, but they do not live after the flesh. They pass their days on earth, but they are citizens of heaven. They obey the prescribed laws, and at the same time surpass the laws by their lives. They love all men, and are persecuted by all. They are unknown and condemned; they are put to death, and restored to life. They are poor, yet make many rich; they are in lack of all things, and yet abound in all; they are dishonored, and yet in their very dishonor are glorified. They are evil spoken of, and yet are justified; they are reviled, and bless; they are insulted, and repay the insult with honor; they do good, yet are punished as evil-doers. When punished, they rejoice as if quickened into life; they are assailed by the Jews as foreigners, and are persecuted by the Greeks; yet those who hate them are unable to assign any reason for their hatred.

Chapter 6: The Relation of Christians to the World

To sum up all in one word what the soul is in the body, that are Christians in the world. The soul is dispersed through all the members of the body, and Christians are scattered through all the cities of the world. The soul dwells in the body, yet is not of the body; and Christians dwell in the world, yet are not of the world. The invisible soul is guarded by the visible body, and Christians are known indeed to be in the world, but their godliness remains invisible. The flesh hates the soul, and wars against it, though itself suffering no injury, because it is prevented from enjoying pleasures; the world also hates the Christians, though in nowise injured, because they abjure pleasures. The soul loves the flesh that hates it, and [loves also] the members; Christians likewise love those that hate them. The soul is imprisoned in the body, yet preserves that very body; and Christians are confined in the world as in a prison, and yet they are the preservers of the world. The immortal soul dwells in a mortal tabernacle; and Christians dwell as sojourners in corruptible [bodies], looking for an incorruptible dwelling in the heavens. The soul, when but ill-provided with food and drink, becomes better; in like manner, the Christians, though subjected day by day to punishment, increase the more in number. God has assigned them this illustrious position, which it were unlawful for them to forsake.

The Epistle of Mathetes to Diognetus

C. Quotations about martyrdom

Let me be given to the wild beasts, for by their means I can attain to God. I am God's wheat, and I am being ground by the teeth of the beasts so that I may be like pure bread.

Ignatius of Antioch

Now do I begin to be a disciple of my Master, Christ.

Ignatius of Antioch, traveling cheerfully to the place where he was to be thrown to the lions.

[Nero] laid the guilt, and inflicted the most cruel punishments, upon a set of people who were held in abhorrence for their crimes, and popularly called Christians. ... Their sufferings at their execution were aggravated by insult and mockery, for some were disguised in the skins of wild beasts and worried to death by dogs, some were crucified, and others were wrapped in pitched shirts and set on fire when the day closed, that they might serve as lights to illuminate the night. Nero lent his own gardens for these executions.

Tacitus

You can kill us, but you can't hurt us.

Justin Martyr

When I was delighting in the doctrines of Plato, and heard the Christians slandered, and saw them fearless of death ... I perceived that it was impossible that they could be living in wickedness and pleasure.

Justin Martyr

No one makes us afraid or leads us into captivity as we have set our faith on Jesus. For though we are beheaded, and crucified, and exposed to beasts and chains and fire and all other forms of torture, it is plain that we do not forsake the confession of our faith, but the more things of this kind which happen to us the more are there others who become believers and truly religious through the name of Jesus.

Justin Martyr

In our case [as Christians] we are hated for our name.

Athenagoras

Let us therefore become imitators of His endurance; and if we should suffer for His name's sake, let us glorify Him. For He gave this example to us in His own person, and we believed this.

Polycarp

Eighty and six years have I now served Christ, and he has never done me the least wrong; how, then, can I blaspheme my King and my Savior?

Polycarp, in reply to the Roman Proconsul commanding him to swear allegiance to Caesar, saying, "Swear, and I will set thee at liberty; reproach Christ."

Justin Martyr on trial

The saints were seized and brought before the prefect of Rome, whose name was Rusticus. As they stood before the judgment seat, Rusticus the prefect said to Justin, "Above all, have faith in the gods and obey the emperors."

Justin replied, "We cannot be accused or condemned for obeying the commands of our Savior, Jesus Christ."

Rusticus said, "What system of teaching do you profess?"

Justin said, "I have tried to learn about every system, but I have accepted the true doctrines of the Christians, though these are not approved by those who are held fast by error."

The prefect Rusticus said, "Are those

doctrines approved by you, wretch that you are?"

Justin said, "Yes, for I follow them with their correct teaching."

The prefect Rusticus said, "What sort of teaching is that?"

Justin said, "Worship the God of the Christians. We hold him to be from the beginning the one creator and maker of the whole creation, of things seen and things unseen. We worship also the Lord Jesus Christ, the Son of God."

Rusticus said, "You are a Christian, then?"

Justin said, "Yes, I am a Christian."

The prefect said to Justin, "You are called a learned man and think you know what is true teaching. Listen: if you were scourged and beheaded, are you convinced that you would go up to heaven?"

Justin said, "I hope that I shall enter God's house if I suffer in that way. For I know that God's favor is stored up until the end of the whole world for all who have lived good lives."

The prefect Rusticus said, "Do you have an idea that you will go up to heaven to receive some suitable rewards?"

Justin said, "It is not an idea that I have; it is something I know well and hold to be most certain."

The prefect Rusticus said, "Now let us come to the point at issue, which is necessary and urgent. Gather round then and with one accord offer sacrifice to the gods."

Justin said, "No one who is right-thinking stoops from true worship to false worship."

The prefect Rusticus said, "If you do not do as you are commanded you will be tortured without mercy."

Justin said, "We hope to suffer torment for the sake of our Lord Jesus Christ, and so be saved."

In the same way the other martyrs also said, "Do what you will. We are Christians; we do not offer sacrifice to idols."

The prefect Rusticus pronounced sentence, saying, "Let those who have refused to sacrifice to the gods and to obey the command of the emperor be scourged and led away to suffer capital punishment according to the ruling of the laws." Glorifying God, the holy martyrs were beheaded, and so fulfilled their witness of martyrdom in confessing their faith in their Savior. The Acts of the Martyrdom of Saint Justin and his Companions

The joy of martyrdom

It is said concerning many of the martyrs, that when they foreknew, either by revelation or by information received from one of their friends, the day on which they were to receive the crown of martyrdom, they did not taste anything the preceding night, but from evening till morning they stood keeping vigil in prayer, glorifying God in psalms, hymns, and spiritual odes, and they looked forward to that hour with joy and exaltation, waiting to meet the sword in their fast as ones prepared for the nuptials. Therefore let us also be vigilant, we who are called to an unseen martyrdom so as to receive the crowns of sanctification, so that we may never give our enemies a sign of denial with any member or part of our body.
St Isaac The Syrian (Ascetical Homilies, Hom. 37).

Martyrdom is fullness

Martyrdom is fullness, not because it finishes a human life but because it brings love to the fullest point.
Clement of Alexandria

D. Prayers of the Martyrs

Father, make us more like Jesus. Help us to bear difficulty, pain, disappointment and sorrow, knowing that in your perfect working and design you can use such bitter experiences to mold our characters and make us more like our Lord. We look with hope to the day when we will be completely like Christ, because we will see him as he is. ...

I am God's wheat. May I be grounded by the teeth of the wild beasts until I become the fine wheat bread that is Christ's. My passions are crucified, there is no heat in my flesh, a stream flows murmuring inside me; deep down in me it says: Come to the Father.
Ignatius of Antioch, prior to his martyrdom

Lord, almighty God, Father of your beloved and blessed Son Jesus Christ, through whom we have come to the knowledge of yourself, God of angels, of powers, of all creation, of all the saints who live in your sight, I bless you for judging me worthy of this day, this hour, so that in the company of the martyrs I may share the cup of Christ, your anointed one, and so rise again to eternal life in soul and body, immortal through the power of the Holy Spirit. May I be received among the martyrs in your presence today as a rich and pleasing sacrifice. God of truth, stranger to falsehood, you have prepared this and revealed it to me and now you have fulfilled your promise.

Polycarp. This is the prayer he prayed as he was burned at the stake, c. 155

4. Acts of the Martyrs

In a strict sense the Acts of the Martyrs are the official records of the trials of early Christian martyrs made by the notaries of the court. In a wider sense, however, the title is applied to all the narratives of the martyrs' trial and death. In the latter sense, they may be classified as follows:

Official reports of the interrogatories (acta, gesta). Those extant, like the "Acta Proconsulis (Cyprian, "Ep. lxxvii ") are few in number and have only come down to us in editions prepared with a view to the edification of the faithful. The "Passio Cypriani" and "Acta Martyrum Scillitanorum" are typical of this class. Of these the former is a composite work of three separate documents showing the minimum of editorial additions in a few connecting phrases. The first document gives an account of the trial of Cyprian in 257, the second, his arrest and trial in 258, the third, of his martyrdom.

Non-official records made by eye-witnesses or at least by contemporaries recording the testimony of eye-witnesses. Such are the "Martyrium S. Polycarpi", admitting though it does much that may be due to the pious fancy of the eye-witnesses. The "Acta SS. Perpetuµ et Felicitatis is perhaps of all extant Acta the most beautiful and famous, for it includes the autograph notes of Perpetua and Saturus and an eye-witness's account of the martyrdom. And to these must be added the "Epistola Ecclesiarum Viennensis et Lugdunensis", telling the story of the martyrs of Lyons, and other Acta not so famous.

Documents of a later date than the martyrdom based on Acta of the first or second class, and therefore subjected to editorial manipulation of various kinds. It is this class which affords the critic the greatest scope for his discernment. What distinguishes these Acta from the subsequent classes is their literary basis. The editor was not constructing a story to suit oral tradition or to explain a monument. He was editing a literary document according to his own taste and purpose. The class is numerous and its contents highly debatable, for though additional study may raise any particular Acta to a higher class, it is far more likely as a rule to reduce it.

Besides these three classes of more or less reliable documents, many others pass under the name of Acta Martyrum, though their historicity is of little or no value. They are romances, either written around a few real facts which have been preserved in popular or literary tradition, or else pure works of the imagination, containing no real facts whatever. Among the historical romances we may instance the story of Felicitas and her seven sons, which in its present form seems to be a variation of IV Maccabees, viii, 1, though there can be no doubt of the underlying facts, one of which has actually been confirmed by De Rossi's discovery of the tomb of Januarius, the eldest son in the narrative. The Roman "Legendarium" can claim no higher class than this; so that, apart from monumental, liturgical, and topographical traditions, much of the literary evidence for the great martyrs of Rome is embedded in historical romances. It may be a matter for surprise that there should be such a class of Acta as the imaginative romances, which have no facts at all for their foundation. But they were the novels of those days which unfortunately came to be taken as history. Perhaps such is the case with the story of Genesius the Comedian who was suddenly converted while mimicking the Christian mysteries, and the Acts of Didymus and Theodora, the latter of whom was saved by the former, a Christian soldier, from a punishment worse than death. And even less reputable than these so-called Acta are the story of Barlaam and Josaphat which is the Christian adaptation of the Buddha legend, the Faust-legend of Cyprian of Antioch, and the romance of the heroine who, under the various names of Pelagia, Marina, Eugenia, Margaret, or Apollinaria is admitted in man's dress to a monastery, convicted of misconduct, and posthumously rehabilitated. St. Liberata also, the bearded lady who was nailed to a cross, is a saint of fiction only, though the romance was probably invented with the definite purpose of explaining the draped figure of a crucifix.

Still these two classes of romantic Acta can hardly be regarded as forgeries in the strict sense of that term. They are literary figments, but as they were written with the intention of edifying and not deceiving the reader, a special class must be reserved for hagiographical forgeries. To this must be relegated all those Acts, Passions, Lives, Legends, and Translations which have been written with the express purpose of perverting history, such, for instance, as the legends and translations falsely attaching a saint's name to some special church or city. Their authors disgraced the name of hagiographer, and they would not merit mention were it not that conscious deceit has in consequence been attributed to those hagiographers, who, having for their object to edify and not to instruct, have written Acta which were meant to be read as romances and not as history.

Besides these detached Acta Martyrum, there are other literary documents concerning the life and death of the martyrs which may be mentioned here. The Calendaria were lists of martyrs celebrated by the different Churches according to their different dates. The Martyrologies represent collections of different Calendaria and sometimes add details of the martyrdom. The Itineraries are guide-books drawn up for the use of pilgrims to the sanctuaries of Rome; they are not without their utility in so far as they reveal, not only the resting places of the great dead, but also the traditions which were current in the seventh century. The writings of the Fathers of the Church also embody many references to the martyrs, as, for instance, the sermons of St. Basil, Chrysostom, Augustine, Peter Chrysologus, and John Damascene.

Finally there are to be considered the collections of Lives, intended for public and private reading. Most important of all are the "Historia Ecclesiastica" of Eusebius (265-340), and his "De Martyribus Palestinus"; but unfortunately his martyron synagoge or Collection of Acts of the Martyrs, to which he refers in the preface of the fifth book of his "Historia Ecclesiastica", is no longer extant. The fourteen poems of Aurelius Prudentius Clemens, published in 404 as the "Persitephanon liber", celebrated the praises of the martyrs of Spain and Italy; but as the author allowed himself the license of the poet with his material, he is not always reliable. The writers of the Middle Ages are responsible for a very large element of the fictitious in the stories of the martyrs; they did not even make a proper use of the material they had at their disposal. Gregory of Tours was the first of these medieval hagiographers with his "De virtutibus S. Martini", "De gloria Confessorum", and "De vitis Sanctorum". Simeon Metaphrastes is even less reliable; it has even been questioned whether he was not consciously deceitful. But the most famous collection of the Middle Ages was the "Golden Legend" of Jacopo de Soragine, first printed in 1476. All these medieval writers include saints as well as martyrs in their collections. So do Mombritius (Milan, 1476), Lipomanus (Venice, 1551), and Surius (Cologne, 1570). J. Faber Stapulensis included only Martyrs in his "Martyrum agones antiquis ex monumentis genuine descriptos", and they are only the martyrs whose feasts are celebrated in the month of January. But an epoch was marked in the history of the martyrs by the "Acta primorum martyrum sincera et selecta" of the Benedictine Theodore Ruinart (Paris, 1689) and frequently reprinted (Ratisbon, 1858). Other collections of Acta, subsequent to Ruinart's are Ilbachius, "Acta Martyrum Vindicata" (Rome, 1723). S. Assemai, "Acta SS. Martyrum orient. et occ." (Rome, 1748). T. Mamachii "Origines et Antiquitates Christianae" (Rome, 1749). The critical study of the Acta Martyrum has been vigorously prosecuted within the last few years, and the standpoint of the critics considerably changed since the attempt of Ruinart to make his selection of Acta. Many of his Acta Sincera will no longer rank as sincera; and if they be arranged in different classes according to their historicity very few can claim a place in our first or second class. But on the other hand the discovery of texts and the archaeological researches of De Rossi and others have confirmed individual stories of martyrdom. And a general result of criticism has been to substantiate such main facts as the causes of persecution, the number and heroism of the martyrs, the popularity of their cults, and the historicity of the popular heroes.

The chief problem, therefore, for modern critics is to discover the literary history of the Acta which have come down to us. It cannot be denied that some attempt was made at the very first to keep the history of the Church's martyrs inviolate. The public reading of the Acta in the churches would naturally afford a guarantee of their authenticity; and this custom certainly obtained in Africa, for the Third Council of Carthage (c. 47) permitted the reading of the "Passiones Martyrum cum anniversarii dies eorum celebrentur". There was also an interchange of Acta between different Churches as we see from the "Martyrium S. Polycarpi" and the "Epistola Ecclesiae Viennensis et Lugdunensis". But it is not known to what extent those customs were practiced. And during the persecutions of Diocletian there must have been a wholesale destruction of documents, with the result that the Church would lose the accounts of its Martyr's history. This seems to be especially true of Rome, which possesses so few authentic Acta in spite of the number and fame of its martyrs; for the Romans had apparently lost the thread of these traditions as early as the second half of the fourth century. The poems of Prudentius, the Calendaria, and even the writings of Pope Damasus show that the story of the persecutions had fallen into obscurity. Christian Rome had her martyrs beneath her feet, and celebrated their memory with intense devotion, and yet she knew but little of their history.

Under these circumstances it is not improbable that the desire of the faithful for fuller information would easily be satisfied by raconteurs who, having only scanty material at their disposal, would amplify and multiply the few facts preserved in tradition and attach what they considered suitable stories to historical names and localities. And in the course of time it is argued these legends were committed to writing, and have come down to us as the Roman legendarium. In support of this severe criticism it is urged that the Roman Acta are for the most part not earlier than the sixth century (Dufourcq), and that spurious Acta were certainly not unknown during the period. The Roman Council of 494 actually condemned the public reading of the Acta (P. L., LIX, 171-2). And this Roman protest had been already anticipated by the Sixth Council of Carthage (401) which protested against the cult of martyrs whose martyrdom was not certain (canon 17). St. Augustine (354-340) also had written: "Though for other martyrs we can hardly find accounts which we can read on their festivals, the Passion of St. Stephen is in a canonical book" (Sermo, 315, P. L., XXXVIII, 1426). Subsequently in 692 the Trullan Council at Constantinople excommunicated those who were responsible for the reading of spurious Acta. The supposition, therefore, of such an origin for the Roman legends is not improbable. And unfortunately the Roman martyrs are not the only ones whose Acta are unreliable. Of the seventy-four separate Passions included by Ruinart in his Acta Sincera, the Bollandist Delehaye places only thirteen in the first or second class, as original documents. Further study of particular Acta may, of course, raise this number; and other original Acta may be discovered. The labors of such critics as Gebhardt, Franchi de Cavalieri, Le Blant, Conybeare, Harnack, the Bollandists, and many others, have in fact, not infrequently issued in this direction, while at the same time they have gathered an extensive bibliography around the several Acta. These must therefore be valued on their respective merits. It may, however, be noticed here that the higher criticism is as dangerous when applied to the Acts of the Martyrs as it is for the Holy Scriptures. Arguments may of course, be drawn from the formal setting of the document, its accuracy in dates, names, and topography, and still stronger arguments from what may be called the informal setting given to it unconsciously by its author. But in the first case the formal setting can surely be imitated, and it is unsafe therefore to seek to establish historicity by such an argument. It is equally unsafe to presume that the probability of a narrative, or its simplicity is a proof that it is genuine. Even the improbable may contain more facts of history than many a narrative which bears the appearance of sobriety and restraint. Nor is conciseness a sure proof that a document is of an early date; St. Mark's Gospel is not thus proved to be the earliest of the Synoptics. The informal setting is more reliable; philology and psychology are better tests than dates and geography, for it needs a clever romancer indeed to identify himself so fully with his heroes as to share their thoughts and emotions. And yet even with this concession to higher criticism, it still remains true that the critic is on safer ground when he has succeeded in establishing the pedigree of his document by external evidence.

James Bridge, The Catholic Encyclopedia, Volume 9

5. The catacombs

Origin and History of the Catacomb

The Catacombs of Rome and other cities open a new chapter of Church history, which has recently been dug up from the bowels of the earth. Their discovery was a revelation to the world as instructive and important as the discovery of the long lost cities of Pompeii and Herculaneum, and of Nineveh and Babylon. Eusebius says nothing about them; the ancient Fathers scarcely allude to them, except Jerome and Prudentius, and even they give us no idea of their extent and importance. Hence the historians till quite recently have passed them by in silence. But since the great discoveries of Commendatore De Rossi and other archaeologists they can no longer be ignored. They confirm, illustrate, and supplement our previous knowledge derived from the more important literary remains.

The name of the Catacombs is of uncertain origin, but is equivalent to subterranean cemeteries or resting-places for the dead. First used of the Christian cemeteries in the neighborhood of Rome, it was afterwards applied to those of Naples, Malta, Sicily, Alexandria, Paris, and other cities.

It was formerly supposed that the Roman Catacombs were originally sand-pits (*arenariae*) or stone-quarries (*lapidicinae*), excavated by the heathen for building material, and occasionally used as receptacles for the vilest corpses of slaves and criminals. But this view is now abandoned on account of the difference of construction and of the soil. A few of the catacombs, however, about five out of thirty, are more or less closely connected with abandoned sand-pits.

The catacombs, therefore, with a few exceptions, are of Christian origin, and were excavated for the express purpose of Christian burial. Their enormous extent, and the mixture of heathen with Christian symbols and inscriptions, might suggest that they were used by heathen also; but this is excluded by the fact of the mutual aversion of Christians and idolaters to associate in life and in death. The mythological features are few, and adapted to Christian ideas.

Another erroneous opinion, once generally entertained, regarded the catacombs as places of refuge from heathen persecution. But the immense labor required could not have escaped the attention of the police. They were, on the contrary, the result of toleration. The Roman government, although (like all despotic governments) jealous of secret societies, was quite liberal towards the burial clubs, mostly of the poorer classes, or associations for securing, by regular contributions, decent interment with religious ceremonies. Only the worst criminals, traitors, suicides, and those struck down by lightning (touched by the gods) were left unburied. The pious care of the dead is an instinct of human nature, and is found among all nations. Death is a mighty leveler of distinctions and preacher of toleration and charity; even despots bow before it, and are reminded of their own vanity; even hard hearts are moved by it to pity and to tears. "*De mortuis nihil nisi bonum.*"

The Christians enjoyed probably from the

beginning the privilege of common cemeteries, like the Jews, even without an express enactment. Galienus restored them after their temporary confiscation during the persecution of Valerian (260).

Being mostly of Jewish and Oriental descent, the Roman Christians naturally followed the Oriental custom of cutting their tombs in rocks, and constructing galleries. Hence the close resemblance of the Jewish and Christian cemeteries in Rome. The ancient Greeks and Romans under the empire were in the habit of burning the corpses (*crematio*) for sanitary reasons, but burial in the earth (*humatio*), outside of the city near the public roads, or on hills, or in natural grottos, was the older custom; the rich had their own sepulchers (*sepulcra*).

In their catacombs the Christians could assemble for worship and take refuge in times of persecution. Very rarely they were pursued in these silent retreats. Once only it is reported that the Christians were shut up by the heathen in a cemetery and smothered to death.

Most of the catacombs were constructed during the first three centuries, a few may be traced almost to the apostolic age. After Constantine, when the temporal condition of the Christians improved, and they could bury their dead without any disturbance in the open air, the cemeteries were located above ground, especially above the catacombs, and around the basilicas; or on other land purchased or donated for the purpose. Some catacombs owe their origin to individuals or private families, who granted the use of their own grounds for the burial of their brethren; others belonged to churches. The Christians wrote on the graves appropriate epitaphs and consoling thoughts, and painted on the walls their favorite symbols. At funerals they turned these dark and cheerless abodes into chapels; under the dim light of the terra-cotta lamps they committed dust to dust, ashes to ashes, and amidst the shadows of death they inhaled the breath of the resurrection and life everlasting. But it is an error to suppose that the catacombs served as the usual places of worship in times of persecution; for such a purpose they were entirely unfitted; even the largest could accommodate, at most, only twenty or thirty persons within convenient distance.

The devotional use of the catacombs began in the Nicene age, and greatly stimulated the worship of martyrs and saints. When they ceased to be used for burial they became resorts of pious pilgrims. Little chapels were built for the celebration of the memory of the martyrs. St. Jerome relates, how, while a school-boy, about A.D. 350, he used to go with his companions every Sunday to the graves of the apostles and martyrs in the crypts at Rome, "where in subterranean depths the visitor passes to and fro between the bodies of the entombed on both walls, and where all is so dark, that the prophecy here finds its fulfillment: The living go down into Hades. Here and there a ray from above, not falling in through a window, but only pressing in through a crevice, softens the gloom; as you go onward, it fades away, and in the darkness of night which surrounds you, that verse of Virgil comes to your mind:

"Horror ubique animos, simul ipsa silentia terrent."

The poet Prudentius also, in the beginning of the fifth century, several times speaks of these burial places, and the devotions held within them.

Pope Damasus (366–384) showed his zeal in repairing and decorating the catacombs, and erecting new stair-cases for the convenience of pilgrims. His successors kept up the interest, but by repeated repairs introduced great confusion into the chronology of the works of art.

The barbarian invasions of Alaric (410), Genseric (455), Ricimer (472), Vitiges (537), Totila (546), and the Lombards (754), turned Rome into a heap of ruins and destroyed many valuable treasures of classical and Christian antiquity. But the pious barbarism of relic hunters did much greater damage. The tombs of real and imaginary saints were rifled, and cartloads of dead men's bones were translated to the Pantheon and churches and chapels for more convenient worship. In this way the catacombs gradually lost all interest, and passed into decay and complete oblivion for more than six centuries.

In the sixteenth century the catacombs were rediscovered, and opened an interesting field for antiquarian research. The first discovery was made May 31, 1578, by some laborers in a vineyard on the Via Salaria, who were digging *pozzolana*, and came on an old subterranean cemetery, ornamented with Christian paintings, Greek and Latin inscriptions and sculptured sarcophagi. "In that day," says De Rossi, "was born the name and the knowledge of Roma Sotterranea." One of the first and principal explorers was Antonio Bosio, "the Columbus of this subterranean world." His researches were published after his death (Roma, 1632). Filippo Neri, Carlo Borromeo, and other restorers of Romanism spent, like St. Jerome of old, whole nights in prayer amid these ruins of the age of martyrs. But Protestant divines discredited these discoveries as inventions of Romish divines seeking in heathen sand-pits for Christian saints who never lived, and Christian martyrs who never died.

In the present century the discovery and investigation of the catacombs has taken a new start, and is now an important department of Christian archaeology. The dogmatic and sectarian treatment has given way to a scientific method with the sole aim to ascertain the truth. The acknowledged pioneer in this subterranean region of ancient church history is the Cavalier John Baptist de Rossi, a devout, yet liberal Roman Catholic. His monumental Italian work (*Roma Sotterranea,* 1864–1877) has been made accessible in judicious condensations to French, German, and English readers by Allard (1871), Kraus (1873 and 1879), Northcote & Brownlow (1869 and 1879). Other writers, Protestant as well as Roman Catholic, are constantly adding to our stores of information. Great progress has been made in the chronology and the interpretation of the pictures in the catacombs.

And yet the work is only begun. More than one half of ancient Christian cemeteries are waiting for future exploration. De Rossi treats chiefly of one group of Roman catacombs, that of Callistus. The catacombs in Naples, Syracuse, Girgenti, Melos, Alexandria, Cyrene, are very imperfectly known; still others in the ancient apostolic churches may yet be discovered, and furnish results as important for church history as the discoveries of Ilium, Mycenae, and Olympia for that of classical Greece.

Description of the catacombs

The Roman catacombs are long and narrow passages or galleries and cross-galleries excavated in the bowels of the earth in the hills outside and around the city, for the burial of the dead. They are dark and gloomy, with only an occasional ray of light from above. The galleries have two or more stories, all filled with tombs, and form an intricate net-work or subterranean labyrinth. Small compartments (*loculi*) were cut out like shelves in the perpendicular walls for the reception of the dead, and rectangular chambers (*cubicula*) for families, or distinguished martyrs. They were closed with a slab of marble or tile. The more wealthy were laid in sarcophagi. The ceiling is flat, sometimes slightly arched. Space was economized so as to leave room usually only for a single person; the average width of the passages being 2 to 3 feet. This economy may be traced to the poverty of the early Christians, and also to their strong sense of community in life and in death. The little oratories with altars and episcopal chairs cut in the tufa are probably of later construction, and could accommodate only a few persons at a time. They were suited for funeral services and private devotion, but not for public worship.

The galleries were originally small, but gradually extended to enormous length. Their combined extent is counted by hundreds of miles, and the number of graves by millions.

The oldest and best known of the Roman cemeteries is that of St. Sebastian, originally called *Ad Catacumbas*, on the Appian road, a little over two miles south of the city walls. It was once, it is said, the temporary resting-place of the bodies of St. Peter and St. Paul, before their removal to the basilicas named after them; also of forty-six bishops of Rome, and of a large number of martyrs.

The immense cemetery of Pope Callistus (218–223) on the Via Appia consisted originally of several small and independent burial grounds (called Lucinae, Zephyrini, Callisti, Hippoliti). It has been thoroughly investigated by De Rossi. The most ancient part is called after Lucina, and measures 100 Roman feet in breadth by 180 feet in length. The whole group bears the name of Callistus, probably because his predecessor, Zephyrinus "set him over the cemetery" (of the church of Rome). He was then a deacon. He stands high in the estimation of the Roman church, but the account given of him by Hippolytus is quite unfavorable. He was certainly a remarkable man, who rose from slavery to the highest dignity of the church.

The cemetery of Domitilla (named in the fourth century St. Petronillae, Nerei et Achillei) is on the Via Ardeatina, and its origin is traced back to Flavia Domitilla, grand-daughter or great-grand-daughter of Vespasian. She was banished by Domitian (about A.D. 95) to the island of Pontia "for professing Christ." Her chamberlains (*eunuchi cubicularii*), Nerus and Achilleus, according to an uncertain tradition, were baptized by St. Peter, suffered martyrdom, and were buried in a farm belonging to their mistress. In another part of this cemetery De Rossi discovered the broken columns of a subterranean chapel and a small chamber with a fresco on the wall, which represents an elderly matron named "Veneranda," and a young lady, called in the inscription "Petronilla martyr," and pointing to the Holy Scriptures in a chest by her side, as the proofs of her faith. The former apparently introduces the latter into Paradise. The name naturally suggests the legendary daughter of St. Peter. But Roman divines, reluctant to admit that the first pope had any children (though his marriage is beyond a doubt from the record of the Gospels), understand Petronilla to be a spiritual daughter, as Mark was a spiritual son, of the apostle (1 Pet. 5:13), and make her the daughter of some Roman Petronius or Petro connected with the family of Domitilla.

Other ancient catacombs are those of Pruetextatus, Priscilla (St. Silvestri and St. Marcelli), Basilla (S. Hermetis, Basillae, Proti, et Hyacinthi), Maximus, St. Hippolytus, St. Laurentius, St. Peter and Marcellinus, St. Agnes, and the Ostrianum (Ad Nymphas Petri, or Fons Petri, where Peter is said to have baptized from a natural well). De Rossi gives a list of forty-two greater or lesser cemeteries, including isolated tombs of martyrs, in and near Rome, which date from the first four centuries, and are mentioned in ancient records.

The furniture of the catacombs is instructive and interesting, but most of it has been removed to churches and museums, and must be studied outside. Articles of ornament, rings, seals, bracelets, neck-laces, mirrors, tooth-picks, ear-picks, buckles, brooches, rare coins, innumerable lamps of clay (terra-cotta), or of bronze, even of silver and amber, all sorts of tools, and in the case of children a variety of playthings were inclosed with the dead. Many of these articles are carved with the monogram of Christ, or other Christian symbols. (The lamps in Jewish cemeteries bear generally a picture of the golden candlestick).

A great number of flasks and cups also, with or without ornamentation, are found, mostly outside of the graves, and fastened to the grave-lids. These were formerly supposed to have been receptacles for tears, or, from the red, dried sediment in them, for the blood of martyrs. But later archaeologists consider them drinking vessels used in the agapae and oblations. A superstitious habit prevailed in the fourth century, although condemned by a council of Carthage (397), to give to the dead the eucharistic wine, or to put a cup with the consecrated wine in the grave.

The instruments of torture which the fertile imagination of credulous people had discovered, and which were made to prove that almost every Christian buried in the catacombs was a martyr, are simply implements of handicraft. The instinct of nature prompts the bereaved to deposit in the graves of their kindred and friends those things which were constantly used by them. The idea prevailed also to a large extent that the future life was a continuation of the occupations and amusements of the present, but free from sin and imperfection.

On opening the graves the skeleton appears frequently even now very well preserved, sometimes in dazzling whiteness, as covered with a glistening glory; but falls into dust at the touch.

Pictures and Sculptures

The most important remains of the catacombs are the pictures, sculptures, and epitaphs.

1. Pictures.
These have already been described in the preceding chapter. They are painted *al fresco* on the wall and ceiling, and represent Christian symbols, scenes of Bible history, and allegorical conceptions of the Savior. A few are in pure classic style, and betray an early origin when Greek art still flourished in Rome; but most of them belong to the period of decay. Prominence is given to pictures of the Good Shepherd, and those biblical stories which exhibit the conquest of faith and the hope of the resurrection. The mixed character of some of the Christian frescos may be explained partly from the employment of heathen artists by Christian patrons, partly from old reminiscences. The Etrurians and Greeks were in the habit of painting their tombs, and Christian Greeks early saw the value of pictorial language as a means of instruction. In technical skill the Christian art is inferior to the heathen, but its subjects are higher, and its meaning is deeper.

2. Sculpture
The works of sculpture are mostly found on sarcophagi. Many of them are collected in the Lateran Museum. Few of them date from the ante-Nicene age. They represent in relief the same subjects as the wall-pictures, as far as they could be worked in stone or marble, especially the resurrection of Lazarus, Daniel among the lions, Moses smiting the rock, the sacrifice of Isaac.

Among the oldest Christian sarcophagi are those of St. Helena, the mother of Constantine (d. 328), and of Constantia, his daughter (d. 354), both of red porphyry, and preserved in the Vatican Museum. The sculpture on the former probably represents the triumphal entry of Constantine into Rome after his victory over Maxentius; the sculpture on the latter, the cultivation of the vine, probably with a symbolical meaning.

The richest and finest of all the Christian sarcophagi is that of Junius Bassus, Prefect of Rome, A.D. 359, and five times Consul, in the crypt of St. Peter's in the Vatican. It was found in the Vatican cemetery (1595). It is made of Parian marble in Corinthian style. The subjects represented in the upper part are the sacrifice of Abraham, the capture of St. Peter, Christ seated between Peter and Paul, the capture of Christ, and Pilate washing his hands; in the lower part are the temptation of Adam and Eve, suffering Job, Christ's entrance into Jerusalem, Daniel among the lions, and the capture of St. Paul.

Epitaphs

"Rudely written, but each letter
Full of hope, and yet of heart-break,
Full of all the tender pathos of the Here
and the Hereafter."

To perpetuate, by means of sepulchral inscriptions, the memory of relatives and friends, and to record the sentiments of love and esteem, of grief and hope, in the face of death and eternity, is a custom common to all civilized ages and nations. These epitaphs are limited by space, and often provoke rather than satisfy curiosity, but contain nevertheless in poetry or prose a vast amount of biographical and historical information. Many a grave-yard is a broken record of the church to which it belongs.

The Catacombs abound in such monumental inscriptions, Greek and Latin, or strangely mixed (Latin words in Greek characters), often rudely written, badly spelt, mutilated, and almost illegible, with and without symbolical figures. The classical languages were then in a process of decay, like classical eloquence and art, and the great majority of Christians were poor and illiterate people. One name only is given in the earlier epitaphs, sometimes the age, and the day of burial, but not the date of birth.

More than fifteen thousand epitaphs have been collected, classified, and explained by De Rossi from the first six centuries in Rome alone, and their number is constantly increasing. Benedict XIV. founded, in 1750, a Christian Museum, and devoted a hill in the Vatican to the collection of ancient sarcophagi. Gregory XVI. and Pius IX.

patronized it. In this Lapidarian Gallery the costly pagan and the simple Christian inscriptions and sarcophagi confront each other on opposite walls, and present a striking contrast. Another important collection is in the Kircherian Museum, in the Roman College, another in the Christian Museum of the University of Berlin. The entire field of ancient epigraphy, heathen and Christian in Italy and other countries, has been made accessible by the industry and learning of Gruter, Muratori, Marchi, De Rossi, Le Blant, Böckh, Kirchhoff, Orelli, Mommsen, Henzen, Hübner, Waddington, McCaul.

The most difficult part of this branch of archaeology is the chronology (the oldest inscriptions being mostly undated). Their chief interest for the church historian is their religion, as far as it may be inferred from a few words.

The key-note of the Christian epitaphs, as compared with the heathen, is struck by Paul in his words of comfort to the Thessalonians, that they should not sorrow like the heathen who have no hope, but remember that, as Jesus rose from the dead, so God will raise them also that are fallen asleep in Jesus.

Hence, while the heathen epitaphs rarely express a belief in immortality, but often describe death as an eternal sleep, the grave as a final home, and are pervaded by a tone of sadness, the Christian epitaphs are hopeful and cheerful. The farewell on earth is followed by a welcome from heaven. Death is but a short sleep; the soul is with Christ and lives in God, the body waits for a joyful resurrection: this is the sum and substance of the theology of Christian epitaphs. The symbol of Christ (*Ichthys*) is often placed at the beginning or end to show the ground of this hope. Again and again we find the brief, but significant words: "in peace;" "he" or "she sleeps in peace;" "live in God," or "in Christ;" "live forever." "He rests well." "God quicken thy spirit." "Weep not, my child; death is not eternal." "Alexander is not dead, but lives above the stars, and his body rests in this tomb." "Here Gordian, the courier from Gaul, strangled for the faith, with his whole family, rests in peace. The maid servant, Theophila, erected this."

At the same time stereotyped heathen epitaphs continued to be used but of course not in a polytheistic sense), as "sacred to the funeral gods," or "to the departed spirits." The laudatory epithets of heathen epitaphs are rare, but simple terms of natural affection very frequent, as "My sweetest child;" "Innocent little lamb;" "My dearest husband;" "My dearest wife;" "My innocent dove;" "My well-deserving father," or "mother." A. and B. "lived together" (for 15, 20, 30, 50, or even 60 years) "without any complaint or quarrel, without taking or giving offence." Such commemoration of conjugal happiness and commendations of female virtues, as modesty, chastity, prudence, diligence, frequently occur also on pagan monuments, and prove that there were many exceptions to the corruption of Roman society, as painted by Juvenal and the satirists.

Some epitaphs contain a request to the dead in heaven to pray for the living on earth. At a later period we find requests for intercession in behalf of the departed when once, chiefly through the influence of Pope Gregory I., purgatory became an article of general belief in the Western church. But the overwhelming testimony of the oldest Christian epitaphs is that the pious dead are already in the enjoyment of peace, and this accords with the Savior's promise to the penitent thief, and with St. Paul's desire to depart and be with Christ, which is far better. Take but this example: "Prima, thou livest in the glory of God, and in the peace of our Lord Jesus Christ."

Selection of Roman Epitaphs

The following selection of brief epitaphs in the Roman catacombs is taken from De Rossi, and Northcote, who give *facsimiles* of the original Latin and Greek. Comp. also the photographic plates in Roller, vol. I. Nos. X, XXXI, XXXII, and XXXIII; and vol. II. Nos. LXI, LXII, LXV, and LXVI.

1. To dear Cyriacus, sweetest son. Mayest thou live in the Holy Spirit.

2. Jesus Christ, Son of God, Savior. To Pastor, a good and innocent son, who lived 4 years, 5 months and 26 days. Vitalis and Marcellina, his parents.

3. In eternal sleep (*somno aeternali*). Aurelius

Gemellus, who lived ... years and 8 months and 18 days. His mother made this for her dearest well-deserving son. In peace. I commend [to thee], Bassilla, the innocence of Gemellus.

4. Lady Bassilla [= Saint Bassilla], we, Crescentius and Micina, commend to thee our daughter Crescen [tina], who lived 10 months and ... days.

5. Matronata Matrona, who lived a year and 52 days. Pray for thy parents.

6. Anatolius made this for his well-deserving son, who lived 7 years, 7 months and 20 days. May thy spirit rest well in God. Pray for thy sister.

7. Regina, mayest thou live in the Lord Jesus (*vivas in Domino Jesu*).

8. To my good and sweetest husband Castorinus, who lived 61 years, 5 months and 10 days; well-deserving. His wife made this. Live in God!

9. Amerimnus to his dearest, well-deserving wife, Rufina. May God refresh thy spirit.

10. Sweet Faustina, mayest thou live in God.

11. Refresh, O God, the soul of ....

12. Bolosa, may God refresh thee, who lived 31 years; died on the 19th of September. In Christ.

13. Peace to thy soul, Oxycholis.

14. Agape, thou shalt live forever.

15. In Christ. To Paulinus, a neophyte. In peace. Who lived 8 years.

16. Thy spirit in peace, Filmena.

17. In Christ. Aestonia, a virgin; a foreigner, who lived 41 years and 8 days. She departed from the body on the 26th of February.

18. Victorina in peace and in Christ.

19. Dafnen, a widow, who whilst she lived burdened the church in nothing.

20. To Leopardus, a neophyte, who lived 3 years, 11 months. Buried on the 24th of March. In peace.

21. To Felix, their well-deserving son, who lived 23 years and 10 days; who went out of the world a virgin and a neophyte. In peace. His parents made this. Buried on the 2d of August.

22. Lucilianus to Bacius Valerius, who lived 9 years, 8 [months], 22 days. A catechumen.

23. Septimius Praetextatus Caecilianus, servant of God, who has led a worthy life. If I have served Thee [O Lord], I have not repented, and I will give thanks to Thy name. He gave up his soul to God (at the age of) thirty-three years and six months. [In the crypt of St. Cecilia in St. Callisto. Probably a member of some noble family, the third name is mutilated. De Rossi assigns this epitaph to the beginning of the third century.]

24. Cornelius. Martyr. Ep. [iscopus].

The Autun Inscription

This Greek inscription was discovered A.D. 1839 in the cemetery Saint Pierre l'Estrier near Autun (Augustodunum, the ancient capital of Gallia Aeduensis), first made known by Cardinal Pitra, and thoroughly discussed by learned archaeologists of different countries. See the *Spicilegium Solesmense* (ed. by Pitra), vols. I.-III., Raf. Garrucci, *Monuments d' epigraphie ancienne,* Paris 1856, 1857; P. Lenormant, *Mémoire sur l' inscription d' Autun*, Paris 1855; H. B. Marriott, *The Testimony of the Catacombs,* Lond. 1870, pp. 113–188. The Jesuit fathers Secchi and Garrucci find in it conclusive evidence of transubstantiation and purgatory, but Marriott takes pains to refute them. Comp. also Schultze, *Katak.* p. 118. The Ichthys-symbol figures prominently in the inscription, and betrays an early origin, but archaeologists differ: Pitra, Garrucci and others assign it to A.D. 160–202; Kirchhoff, Marriott, and Schultze, with greater probability, to the end of the fourth or the beginning of the fifth century, Lenormant and Le Blant to the fifth or sixth. De Rossi observes that the characters are not so old as the ideas which they express. The inscription has some gaps which must be filled out by conjecture. It is a memorial of Pectorius to his parents and friends, in two parts; the first six lines are an acrostic (*Ichthys*), and contain words of the dead (probably the mother); in the second part the son speaks. The following is the translation (partly conjectural) of Marriott (*l.c.* 118):

"Offspring of the heavenly Ichthys, see that a heart of holy reverence be thine, now that from Divine waters thou hast received, while yet among mortals, a fount of life that is to immortality. Quicken thy soul, beloved one, with ever-flowing waters of wealth-giving wisdom, and receive the honey-sweet food of the Savior of the saints. Eat with a longing hunger, holding Ichthys in thine hands."

"To Ichthys ... Come nigh unto me, my Lord [and] Savior [be thou my Guide] I entreat Thee, Thou Light of them for whom the hour of death is past."

"Aschandius, my Father, dear unto mine heart, and thou [sweet Mother, and all] that are mine ... remember Pectorius."

Lessons of the Catacombs

The catacombs represent the subterranean Christianity of the ante-Nicene age. They reveal the Christian life in the face of death and eternity. Their vast extent, their solemn darkness, their labyrinthine mystery, their rude epitaphs, pictures, and sculptures, their relics of handicrafts worship, and martyrdom give us a lively and impressive idea of the social and domestic condition, the poverty and humility, the devotional spirit, the trials and sufferings, the faith and hope of the Christians from the death of the apostles to the conversion of Constantine. A modern visitor descending alive into this region of the dead, receives the same impression as St. Jerome more than fifteen centuries ago: he is overcome by the solemn darkness, the terrible silence, and the sacred associations; only the darkness is deeper, and the tombs are emptied of their treasures. "He who is thoroughly steeped in the imagery of the catacombs," says Dean Stanley, not without rhetorical exaggeration, "will be nearer to the thoughts of the early church than he who has learned by heart the most elaborate treatise even of Tertullian or of Origen."

The discovery of this subterranean necropolis has been made unduly subservient to polemical and apologetic purposes both by Roman Catholic and Protestant writers. The former seek and find in it monumental arguments for the worship of saints, images, and relics, for the cults of the Virgin Mary, the primacy of Peter, the seven sacraments, the real presence, even for transubstantiation, and purgatory; while the latter see there the evidence of apostolic simplicity of life and worship, and an illustration of Paul's saying that God chose the foolish, the weak, and the despised things of the world to put to shame them that are wise and strong and mighty.

A full solution of the controversial questions would depend upon the chronology of the monuments and inscriptions, but this is exceedingly uncertain. The most eminent archaeologists hold widely differing opinions. John Baptist de Rossi of Rome, the greatest authority on the Roman Catholic side, traces some paintings and epitaphs in the crypts of St. Lucina and St. Domitilia back even to the close of the first century or the beginning of the second. On the other hand, J. H. Parker, of Oxford, an equally eminent archaeologist, maintains that fully three-fourths of the fresco-paintings belong to the latest restorations of the eighth and ninth centuries, and that "of the remaining fourth a considerable number are of the sixth century." He also asserts that in the catacomb pictures "there are no religious subjects before the time of Constantine," that "during the fourth and fifth centuries they are entirely confined to Scriptural subjects," and that there is "not a figure of a saint or martyr before the sixth century, and very few before the eighth, when they became abundant." Renan assigns the earliest pictures of the catacombs to the fourth century, very few (in Domitilla) to the third. Theodore Mommsen deems De Rossi's argument for the early date of the *Coemeterium Domitillae* before A.D. 95 inconclusive, and traces it rather to the times of Hadrian and Pius than to those of the Flavian emperors.

But in any case it is unreasonable to seek in the catacombs for a complete creed any more than in a modern grave-yard. All we can expect there is the popular elements of eschatology, or the sentiments concerning death and eternity, with incidental traces of the private and social life of those times. Heathen, Jewish, Mohammedan, and Christian cemeteries have their characteristic peculiarities, yet all have many things in common which are inseparable from human nature. Roman Catholic cemeteries are easily recognized by crosses, crucifixes, and reference to purgatory and prayers for the dead; Protestant cemeteries by the frequency of Scripture passages in the epitaphs, and the expressions of hope and joy in prospect of the immediate transition of the pious dead to the presence of Christ. The catacombs have a character of their own, which distinguishes them from Roman Catholic as well as Protestant cemeteries.

Their most characteristic symbols and pictures are the Good Shepherd, the Fish, and the Vine. These symbols almost wholly disappeared after the fourth century, but to the mind of the early Christians they vividly expressed, in childlike simplicity, what is essential to Christians of all creeds, the idea of Christ and his salvation, as the only comfort in life and in death. The Shepherd, whether from the Sabine or the Galilean hills, suggested the recovery of the lost sheep, the tender care and protection, the green pasture and fresh fountain, the sacrifice of life: in a word, the whole picture of a Savior. The popularity of this picture enables us to understand the immense popularity of the Pastor of Hermas, a religious allegory which was written in Rome about the middle of the second century, and read in many churches till the fourth as a part of the New Testament (as in the Sinaitic Codex). The Fish expressed the same idea of salvation, under a different form, but only to those who were familiar with the Greek (the anagrammatic meaning of *Ichthys*) and associated the fish with daily food and the baptismal water of regeneration. The Vine again sets forth the vital union of the believer with Christ and the vital communion of all believers among themselves.

Another prominent feature of the catacombs is their hopeful and joyful eschatology. They proclaim in symbols and words a certain conviction of the immortality of the soul and the resurrection of the body, rooted and grounded in a living union with Christ in this world. These glorious hopes comforted and strengthened the early Christians in a time of poverty, trial, and persecution. This character stands in striking contrast with the preceding and contemporary gloom of paganism, for which the future world was a blank, and with the succeeding gloom of the mediaeval eschatology which presented the future world to the most serious Christians as a continuation of penal sufferings. This is the chief, we may say, the only *doctrinal*, lesson of the catacombs.

On some other points they incidentally shed new light, especially on the spread of Christianity and the origin of Christian art. Their immense extent implies that Christianity was numerically much stronger in heathen Rome than was generally supposed. Their numerous decorations prove conclusively, either that the primitive Christian aversion to pictures and sculptures, inherited from the Jews, was not so general nor so long continued as might be inferred from some passages of ante-Nicene writers, or, what is more likely, that the popular love for art inherited from the Greeks and Romans was little affected by the theologians, and ultimately prevailed over the scruples of theorizers.

The first discovery of the catacombs was a surprise to the Christian world, and gave birth to wild fancies about the incalculable number of martyrs, the terrors of persecution, the subterranean assemblies of the early Christians, as if they lived and died, by necessity or preference, in darkness beneath the earth. A closer investigation has dispelled the romance, and deepened the reality.

There is no contradiction between the religion of the ante-Nicene monuments and the religion of the ante-Nicene literature. They supplement and illustrate each other. Both exhibit to us neither the mediaeval Catholic nor the modern Protestant, but the post-apostolic Christianity of confessors and martyrs, simple, humble, unpretending, unlearned, unworldly, strong in death and in the hope of a blissful resurrection; free from the distinctive dogmas and usages of later times; yet with that strong love for symbolism, mysticism, asceticism, and popular superstitions which we find in the writings of Justin Martyr, Tertullian, Clement of Alexandria, and Origen.

Philip Scaff

Part Three

Martyrs under the Roman Empire (2)

From Septimius Severus to Numerian

Time line 193–284

Contents

Laurentius (St Laurence): James Kiefer
John Foxe
Sermon by Leo the Great, on the Feast of Laurence
Sermon by Augustine on the feast of Laurence
The pupils of Origen who became martyrs: Eusebius
The eighth persecution, under Valerian: Eusebius
The peace under Gallienus: Eusebius
The eighth persecution: John Foxe
Temporary repose, 260-303: Philip Scaff
Arcadius: Alban Butler
Acts of Fructuosus and his deacons: E.C.E. Owen
Tortures of the first Christian martyrs: 5. Iron claws, hooks and currycombs
Cyprian: James Kiefer
John Foxe
Eusebius
John Chapman
The Life and Passion of Cyprian, bishop and martyr by Pontius the deacon
Cyprian's letter to the martyrs and confessors: Letter 8
Cyprian's letter to Moyses and Maximus
Reply from Moyses, Maximus, Nicostratus
Cyprian's letter to Nemesianus and other martyrs in the mines: Letter 76
Reply from Nemesianus, Dativus, Felix, and Victor, to Cyprian: Letter 77
Reply from Lucius: Letter 78
Reply from Felix, Jader, Polianus: Letter 79
Cyprian's letter to Sergius, Rogatianus, and other confessors in prison: Letter 80
Cyprian announces the death of pope Sixtus II: Letter 81
Cyprian's letter to the clergy and people about his withdrawal, a little before his martyrdom: Letter 82
Desiring martyrdom: Treatise 6
Cyprian's exhortation to martyrdom: Treatise 11
The benefits of martyrdom: To Quirinius
The glory of martyrdom
James and Marian: E.C.E. Owen
300 martyrs John Foxe
Cyril A.J. Mason
Marinus and Asterius: John Foxe
The ninth persecution (1): Eusebius
The ninth persecution (2): John Foxe

1. Introduction

Table of persecutions under the Roman Empire (2) 193–284

EMPEROR	DATES	CONDITIONS	FAMOUS MARTYRS
Septimius Severus	193-211	Persecution was now regulated by new edicts. Christians were not accused by a private prosecutor, but sought out by the state. Newly converted Christians, not old Christians persecuted.	Saturus Perpetua & Felicitas
Geta and Caracalla	211-217	Same as Septimius Severus	
Macrinus	217-8	No persecution	
Heliogabalus	218-22	No persecution	
Alexander Severus	222-35	No persecution	
Maximus the Thracian	237-8	Persecution mainly against leaders	
The two Gordians	237-8	No persecution	
Gordianus III	238-44	No persecution	
Philip the Arabian	244-9	No persecution	
Decius	249-51	All Christians had to produce certificates of sacrifice according to the edict of 250 Exile, confiscation of goods, torture, imprisonment on a worldwide scale	Many of the martyrs were bishops: Fabian of Rome
Gallus	251-2	New edict issued to compel Christians to sacrifice	
Volusian	252		
Aemilian	253		
Valerian	253-60	Peace until 257 First edict imposed death penalty of Christians who went to their own worship services; bishops and priests were ordered to sacrifice to gods. Second edict: Bishops, priests and deacons were to be killed at once if they refused to sacrifice.	Cyprian, Fructuosus & his deacons James and Marian, Aemilian
Gallienus	260-8	Cemeteries and other places of worship were allowed Only little persecution	Marinus
Claudius II	270-5		
Tacitus	275-6		
Probus	276-82		
Carus	282-3		
Carinus & Numerian	283-4		

Condition of the Church from Septimius Severus to Philip the Arabian. A.D. 193-249

With Septimius Severus (193-211), who was of Punic descent and had a Syrian wife, a line of emperors (Caracalla, Heliogabalus, Alexander Severus) came to the throne, who were rather Oriental than Roman in their spirit, and were therefore far less concerned than the Antonines to maintain the old state religion. Yet towards the close of the second century there was no lack of local persecutions; and Clement of Alexandria wrote of those times: "Many martyrs are daily burned, confined, or beheaded, before our eyes." In the beginning of the third century (202) Septimius Severus, turned perhaps by Montanistic excesses, enacted a rigid law against the further spread both of Christianity and of Judaism. This occasioned violent persecutions in Egypt and in North Africa, and produced some of the fairest flowers of martyrdom. In Alexandria, in consequence of this law, Leonides, father of the renowned Origen, was beheaded. Potamiaena, a virgin of rare beauty of body and spirit, was threatened by beastly passion with treatment worse than death, and, after cruel tortures, slowly burned with her mother in boiling pitch. One of the executioners, Basilides, smitten with sympathy, shielded them somewhat from abuse, and soon after their death embraced Christianity, and was beheaded. He declared that Potamiaena had appeared to him in the night, interceded with Christ for him, and set upon his head the martyr's crown. In Carthage some catechumens, three young men and two young women, probably of the sect of the Montanists, showed remarkable steadfastness and fidelity in the dungeon and at the place of execution. Perpetua, a young woman of noble birth, resisting, not without a violent struggle, both the entreaties of her aged heathen father and the appeal of her helpless babe upon her breast, sacrificed the deep and tender feelings of a daughter and a mother to the Lord who died for her. Felicitas, a slave, when delivered of a child in the same dungeon, answered the jailor, who reminded her of the still keener pains of martyrdom: "Now I suffer, what I suffer; but then another will suffer for me, because I shall suffer for him." All remaining firm, they were cast to wild beasts at the next public festival, having first interchanged the parting kiss in hope of a speedy reunion in heaven. The same state of things continued through the first years of Caracalla (211-217), though this gloomy misanthrope passed no laws against the Christians. The abandoned youth, El-Gabal, or Heliogabalus (218-222), who polluted the throne by the blackest vices and follies, tolerated all the religions in the hope of at last merging them in his favorite Syrian worship of the sun with its abominable excesses. He himself was a priest of the god of the sun, and thence took his name. His far more worthy cousin and successor, Alexander Severus (222-235), was addicted to a higher kind of religious eclecticism and syncretism, a pantheistic hero-worship. He placed the busts of Abraham and Christ in his domestic chapel with those of Orpheus, Apollonius of Tyana, and the better Roman emperors, and had the gospel rule, "As ye would that men should do to you, do ye even so to them," engraven on the walls of his palace, and on public monuments. His mother, Julia Mammaea, was a patroness of Origen. His assassin, Maximinus the Thracian (235-238), first a herdsman, afterwards a soldier, resorted again to persecution out of mere opposition to his predecessor, and gave free course to the popular fury against the enemies of the gods, which was at that time excited anew by an earthquake. It is uncertain whether he ordered the entire clergy or only the bishops to be killed. He was a rude barbarian who plundered also heathen temples. The legendary poesy of the tenth century assigns to his reign the fabulous martyrdom of St. Ursula, a British princess, and her company of eleven thousand (according to others, ten thousand) virgins, who, on their return from a pilgrimage to Rome, were murdered by heathens in the neighborhood of Cologne. This incredible number has probably arisen from the misinterpretation of an inscription.

Philip Scaff, History of the Christian Church, chapter 21

The Fifth Persecution under Severus

When Severus began to persecute the churches, glorious testimonies were given everywhere by the athletes of religion. This was especially the case in Alexandria, to which city, as to a most prominent theater, athletes of God were brought from Egypt and all Thebais according to their merit, and won crowns from God through their great patience under many tortures and every mode of death. Among these was Leonides, who was called the father of Origen, and who was beheaded while his son was still young. How remarkable the predilection of this son was for the Divine Word, in consequence of his father's instruction, it will not be amiss to state briefly, as his fame has been very greatly celebrated by many.

Eusebius of Caesarea, Church History, Book 6, chapter 1

The Fifth Persecution, Commencing with Severus, A.D. 192

Severus, having been recovered from a severe fit of sickness by a Christian, became a great favorer of the Christians in general; but the prejudice and fury of the ignorant multitude prevailing, obsolete laws were put in execution against the Christians. The progress of Christianity alarmed the pagans, and they revived the stale calumny of placing accidental misfortunes to the account of its professors, A.D. 192.

But, though persecuting malice raged, yet the Gospel shone with resplendent brightness; and, firm as an impregnable rock, withstood the attacks of its boisterous enemies with success. Tertullian, who lived in this age, informs us that if the Christians had collectively withdrawn themselves from the Roman territories, the empire would have been greatly depopulated.

Victor, bishop of Rome, suffered martyrdom in the first year of the third century, A.D. 201. Leonidus, the father of the celebrated Origen, was beheaded for being a Christian. Many of Origen's hearers likewise suffered martyrdom; particularly two brothers, named Plutarchus and Serenus; another Serenus, Heron, and Heraclides, were beheaded. Rhais had boiled pitch poured upon her head, and was then burnt, as was Marcella her mother. Potainiena, the sister of Rhais, was executed in the same manner as Rhais had been; but Basilides, an officer belonging to the army, and ordered to attend her execution, became her convert.

Basilides being, as an officer, required to take a certain oath, refused, saying, that he could not swear by the Roman idols, as he was a Christian. Struck with surprise, the people could not, at first, believe what they heard; but he had no sooner confirmed the same, than he was dragged before the judge, committed to prison, and speedily afterward beheaded.

Irenaeus, bishop of Lyons, was born in Greece, and received both a polite and a Christian education. It is generally supposed that the account of the persecutions at Lyons was written by himself. He succeeded the martyr Pothinus as bishop of Lyons, and ruled his diocese with great propriety; he was a zealous opposer of heresies in general, and, about A.D. 187, he wrote a celebrated tract against heresy. Victor, the bishop of Rome, wanting to impose the keeping of Easter there, in preference to other places, it occasioned some disorders among the Christians. In particular, Irenaeus wrote him a synodical epistle, in the name of the Gallic churches. This zeal, in favor of Christianity, pointed him out as an object of resentment to the emperor; and in A.D. 202, he was beheaded.

The persecutions now extending to Africa, many were martyred in that quarter of the globe; the most particular of whom we shall mention.

Perpetua, a married lady, of about twenty-two years. Those who suffered with her were, Felicitas, a married lady, big with child at the time of her being apprehended, and Revocatus, catechumen of Carthage, and a slave. The names of the other prisoners, destined to suffer upon this occasion, were Saturninus, Secundulus, and Satur. On the day appointed for their execution, they were led to the amphitheater. Satur, Saturninus, and Revocatus were ordered to run the gauntlet between the hunters, or such as had the care of the wild beasts. The hunters being drawn up in two ranks, they ran between, and were severely lashed as they passed. Felicitas and Perpetua were stripped, in order to be thrown to a mad bull, which made his first attack upon Perpetua, and stunned her; he then darted at Felicitas, and gored her dreadfully; but not killing them, the executioner did that office with a sword. Revocatus and Satur were destroyed by wild beasts; Saturninus was beheaded; and Secundulus died in prison. These executions were in the 205, on the eighth day of March.

Speratus and twelve others were likewise beheaded; as was Andocles in France. Asclepiades, bishop of Antioch, suffered many tortures, but his life was spared.

Cecilia, a young lady of good family in Rome, was married to a gentleman named Valerian. She converted her husband and brother, who were beheaded; and the maximus, or officer, who led them to execution, becoming their convert, suffered the same fate. The lady was placed naked in a scalding bath, and having continued there a considerable time, her head was struck off with a sword, A.D. 222.

Calistus, bishop of Rome, was martyred, A.D. 224; but the manner of his death is not recorded; and Urban, bishop of Rome, met the same fate A.D. 232.

Foxe's Book of Martyrs, Edited by William Byron Forbush

2. The martyrdoms

Perpetua and Her Companions, Martyrs at Carthage 7 March 202

During a persecution of Christians under the emperor Septimius Severus, a group of Christians died together in the arena at Carthage. Their final days have been recorded for us in a document that is partly in their own words, and partly in those of an anonymous narrator (sometimes thought to be Tertullian). What follow are extracts, sometimes condensed, from that document.

Vivia Perpetua was a catchumen (i.e. a convert not yet baptized), well educated and from a prosperous family, about 22 years old, married and apparently recently widowed, with a child at her breast, and with two brothers and both parents still living. (Her father was not a Christian.) Felicity (Latin: Felicitas) was a slave woman in advanced pregnancy. With them were Revocatus (also a slave), Saturninus, and Secundus.

They were arrested and placed in a dungeon, but after a few days two deacons visited the prison and by a gift of money to the jailers arranged (1) that they should have an interval in the better part of the prison to refresh themselves, and (2) that Perpetua should be allowed to keep her child with her.

Perpetua had a vision in which she saw a golden ladder, guarded by a fierce dragon, but she climbed it, stepping on the dragon's head to do so. At the top, she found herself in a green meadow, with many white-robed figures, and in their midst a shepherd, who welcomed her and gave her a morsel of cheese from the sheep-milk. She awakened and understood that their martyrdom was certain.

Perpetua writes:

> After a few days there was a report that we were to have a hearing in court. And my father came to me from the city, worn out with anxiety. He came up to me, that he might cast me down, saying: "Have pity, my daughter, on my grey hairs. Have pity on your father, if I am worthy to be called a father by you. If with these hands I have brought you up to this flower of your age, if I have preferred you to all your brothers, do not deliver me up to the scorn of men. Have regard to your brothers, have regard to your mother and your aunt, have regard to your son, who will not be able to live after you. Lay aside your courage, and do not bring us all to destruction; for none of us will speak in freedom if you should suffer anything."

> These things said my father in his affection, kissing my hands, and throwing himself at my feet, and with tears he called me not Daughter, but Lady. And I grieved over the grey hairs of my father, that he alone of all my kindred would have no joy in my death. And I comforted him, saying, "On that scaffold, whatever God wills shall happen. For know that we are not placed in our own power but in that of God." And he departed from me in sorrow.

Perpetua had had a brother who died of cancer when he was eight years old. She prayed for him, and received assurance in a vision that all was well with him.

Her narrative continues:

> After a few days, Pudens, an assistant overseer of the prison, began to hold us in high esteem, seeing that God was with us, and he admitted many of the brethren to see us, that we and they might be mutually refreshed.

Perpetua had another vision, in which she saw herself fighting against a gladiator in the arena, and winning. She understood this to signify victory over the devil.

Saturus also had a vision, which he records in his own words, in which he and the others, having died in the arena, are borne by angels into a beautiful garden, where they greet other martyrs who have gone before them, and are brought before the throne of God, surrounded by twenty-four elders (see Revelation 4), who greet them and say, "Enter into joy." Perpetua says to Saturus: "I was joyful in the flesh, and here I am more joyful still."

The narrator writes:

> Now Felicitas was eight months pregnant, and the law did not allow a pregnant woman to be executed. She was accordingly fearful that her death would be postponed, and instead of dying with her fellow Christians she would be put to death later in the company of some group of criminals. She and her companions accordingly prayed, and Felicity went into labor, with the pains normal to an eight-month delivery. And a servant of the jailers said to her, "If you cry out like that now, what will you do when you are thrown to the beasts, which you despised when you refused to sacrifice?" And she replied: "Now it is I that suffer what I suffer; but then Another will be in me, who will suffer for me, because I also am about to suffer for Him." Thus she brought forth a little girl, whom a certain sister brought up as her own.

The day of their victory shone forth, and they proceeded from the prison to the amphitheater, as if to an assembly, joyous and of brilliant countenance. At the gate, the guards were going to dress them in the robes of those dedicated to Saturn and to Ceres. But that noble-minded woman [Perpetua?] said: "We are here precisely for refusing to honor your gods. By our deaths we earn the right not to wear such garments." The guards recognized the justice of her words, and let them wear their own clothing.

The men of their company were scheduled to be killed by beasts, but the wild boar turned on its keeper instead, and the bear refused to leave its cage. The leopard, however, attacked Saturus and mortally wounded him. He bade farewell to his guard, Pudens, encouraging him to obey God rather than man, and then fell unconscious.

For the young women there was prepared a fierce cow. Perpetua was first led in. She was tossed, and when she saw her tunic torn from her side, she drew it as a veil over her middle, rather mindful of her modesty than of her sufferings. Then the was called up again, and bound up her disheveled hair, for it is not becoming for a martyr to die with disheveled hair, which is a sign of mourning. She saw Felicity wounded, and took her hand and raised her up, and at the demand of the populace they were given a respite.

Now all the prisoners were to be slain with the sword, and they went to the center of the arena, first exchanging a farewell kiss of peace. The others died unmoving and silent, but when the awkward hand of the young executioner bungled her death-stroke, Perpetua cried out in pain, and herself guided his hand to her throat. Possibly such a woman could not have been slain unless she herself willed it, because she was feared by the impure spirit.

James Kiefer, Christian Biographies, By kind permission

Perpetua and Felicitas

Perpetua was martyred 7th March, 203, in the amphitheater at Carthage. She was about twenty-two years of age.

The persecutions about this time extended to Africa, and many were martyred in that part of the globe; the principal of whom was Perpetua, a married lady with an infant child at her breast.

Certain young catechumens were arrested, Revocatus and his servant Felicitas, Saturninus, and Secundulus. Among these also Vibia Perpetua, well- born, liberally educated, honorably married, and having an infant son at her breast. She was about twenty-two years of age.

Pages from Perpetua's diary, written from prison

When I was still with my companions, and my father in his affection for me was endeavoring to upset my by arguments and overthrow my resolution, I said, "Father, do you see this waterpot lying here?"

"I see it," he said.

And I said to him, "Can it be called by any other name than what it is?"

And he answered, "No,"

"So also I cannot call myself anything else than what I am, a Christian."

Then my father, furious at the word "Christian", threw himself upon me as though to pluck out my eyes; but he was satisfied with annoying me; he was in fact vanquished, he and his devil's arguments. Then I thanked the Lord for being parted for a few days from my father, and was refreshed by his absence. During those few days we were baptized, and the Holy Spirit bade me make no other petition after the holy water save for bodily endurance. A few days later we were put in prison; and I was in great fear, because I had never known such darkness. What a day of horror! Terrible heat, thanks to the crowds! Rough handling by the soldiers! To crown all I was tormented there by anxiety for my baby. Then my baby was brought to be and I suckled him, for he was already faint for lack of food. I obtained leave for my baby to remain in prison with me and my prison suddenly became a palace to me, and I would rather have been there than anywhere else.

The procurator Hilarian said to me: "Spare your father's white hairs; spare the tender years of your child. Offer a sacrifice for the safety of the Emperors."

And I answered, "No."

"Are you a Christian!" said Hilarian.

And I answered: "I am."

Then he passed sentence on all of us, and condemned us to the beasts. I sent at once the deacon Pomponius to my father to ask for my baby. But my father refused to give him. And as God willed, neither had he any further wish for my breasts, nor did they become inflamed; that I might not be tortured by anxiety for the baby and pain in my breasts.

As for Felicitas, she was also visited by God's grace. Being eight months pregnant, and as the day for the spectacle grew near she was in great sorrow in case her pregnancy prevented or delayed her martyrdom, since it is against the law for pregnant women to be exposed for punishment. Her fellow martyrs were also deeply grieved at the thought of leaving so good a comrade and fellow-traveler behind alone on the way to the same hope. So in one flood of common lamentation they poured their prayers to the Lord two days before the games. Immediately after the prayer her pains came upon her. And since from the natural difficulty of an eight-months' labor she suffered much in child-birth, one of the warders said to her: "You who so suffer now, what will you do when you are flung to the beasts which, when you refused to sacrifice, you despised?" And she answered: "Now I suffer what I suffer: but Another will be in me who will suffer for me, because I too am to suffer for him." So she gave birth to a girl, whom one of the sisters brought up as her own daughter.

The day of their victory dawned, and they

proceeded from the prison to the amphitheater, as if they were on their way to heaven, with happy and gracious looks; trembling, if at all, not with fear but joy. Perpetua followed with shining steps, as the true wife of Christ, as the darling of God, abashing with the high spirit in her eyes the gaze of all. Felicitas also rejoicing that she had safely given birth so that she might fight the beasts, from blood to blood, from midwife to gladiator, to find in her second baptism her child- birth washing.

For the young women the Devil made ready a mad heifer, an unusual animal selected for this reason, that he wished to match their sex with that of the beast. And so after being stripped and enclosed in nets they [Felicitas and Perpetua] were brought into the arena. The people were horrified, beholding in the one a tender girl, in the other a woman fresh from childbirth, with milk dripping from her breasts.

They were brought into the open, that, when the sword pierced their bodies, these might lend their eyes for partners in the murder. When Perpetua's turn came to receive the sword, she was struck on the bone and cried out, and herself guided to her throat the wavering hand of the young untried gladiator. Perhaps so great a woman, who was feared by the unclean spirit, could not otherwise be slain except she willed.

O valiant and blessed martyrs! O truly called and chosen to the glory of Jesus Christ our Lord! He who magnifies, honors, and adores that glory should recite to the edification of the church these examples also, not less precious at least than those of old; that some new instances of virtue may testify that one and the self-same Spirit is working to this day with the Father, God Almighty, and with his Son Jesus Christ our Lord, to whom belong splendor and power immeasurable for ever and ever. Amen.

E. C. E. Owen (trans.), Some Authentic Acts of the Early Martyrs, Oxford, 1927, pp 78-92

Tortures of the first Christian martyrs (2) Wheels, pulleys and presses

a. Martyrs had their limbs interwoven in the spokes of a wheel, on which they were left exposed for days until they died.

b. Martyrs were bound on a narrow wheel, which was revolved, so that their bodies were horribly mangled on iron spikes fixed underneath.

c. Martyrs were bound to the circumference of a wheel which was then revolved over a fire kindled underneath.

d. Martyrs were crushed in the press, just as grapes and olives are pressed in making wine and oil.

e. Martyrs were bound, sometimes by their hands, and sometimes by their feet, to the ropes of the pulleys one way and to the stakes the other; then the ropes were pulled tight, according to the judges' instructions, and their bodies were miserably stretched and racked.

f. Martyrs, with hands bound behind their backs, were hoisted in the air by a rope and pulley above spikes or sharp flints below them, on to which they were let fall.

Source: Tortures and Torments of the Christian Martyrs, from the "De SS. Martyrum Cruciatibus" of Gallonio, translated by A.R. Allinson (London and Paris, printed for the subscribers, 1903), pp. 34-37

Cecilia

Cecilia cultivated young patrician whose ancestors loomed large in Rome's history. She vowed her virginity to God, but her parents married her to Valerian of Trastevere. She told her new husband that she was accompanied by an angel, but in order to see it, he must be purified. He agreed to be purified, and was baptized. Returning from the ceremony, he found her in prayer accompanied by a praying angel. The angel placed a crown on each of their heads, and offered Valerian a favor; he asked that his brother be baptized.

During the persecutions, the two brothers gave proper burial to martyrs. In their turn they were arrested and martyred for their faith. Cecilia buried them at her villa on the Apprian Way, and was arrested. In about 117 Cecilia was ordered to sacrifice to false gods; when she refused, she was suffocated for a while, and when that didn't kill her, she was beheaded.

The Acts of Cecilia states that: "While the profane music of her wedding was heard, Cecilia was singing in her heart a hymn of love for Jesus, her true spouse." It was this phrase that led to her association with music, singers, and musicians.

The Life of Saint Cecilia

Saint Cecilia the holy virgin was come of the noble lineage of the Romans, and from the time that she lay in her cradle she was fostered and nourished in the faith of Christ, and always bare in her breast the gospel hid, and never ceased day ne night from holy prayers but recommended to God always her virginity.

And when this blessed virgin should be spoused to a young man named Valerian, and the day of wedding was come, and was clad in royal clothes of gold, but under she wore the hair[-shirt], and she hearing the organs making melody, she sang in her heart only to God saying, "O lord I beseech thee that myn heart and body may be undefouled so that I be not confounded."

And every second and third day she fasted commending herself unto our Lord whom she dreaded. The night came that she should go to bed with her husband as the custom is, and when they were both in their chamber alone, she said to him in this manner: "O my best beloved and sweet husband, I have a counsel to tell thee, if so be that thou wilt keep it secrete and swear that ye shall bewreye [reveal] it to no man." To whom Valerian said that he would gladly promise and swear never to bewreye it.

And then she said to him, "I have an angel that loveth me which ever keepeth my body whether I sleep or wake and if he may find that ye touch my body by vilainy or foul and polluted love, certainly he shall anon slay you, and so should ye lose the flower of your youth and if so be that thou love me in holy love and cleanness, he shall love thee as he loveth me and shall show to thee his grace."

Then Valerian, corrected by the will of God, having dread, said to her, "If thou wilt that I believe that thou sayest to me, show to me that angel that thou speakest of, and if I find veritable that he be the angel of God, I shall do that thou sayest. And if so be that thou love another man than me, I shall slay both him and thee with my sword."

Cecilia answered to him, "If thou wilt believe and baptize thee thou shalt well now see him. Go then forth to Via Appia which is three mile out of this town and there thou shalt find Pope Urban with poor folks. And tell him these words that I have said. And when he hath purged you from sin by baptism, then when ye come again ye shall see the angel."

And forth went Valerian and found this holy man Urban louting [lurking] among the burials [catacombs], to whom he reported the words that Cecilia had said. And Saint Urban for joy gan [did] hold up his hand and the tears fell out of his eyes, and said, "O mighty God Jesus Christ sower of chaste counsel and keeper of us all, receive the fruit of the seed that thou hast sown in Cecilia. For like a busy bee she serveth thee. For the spouse whom she hath taken, which was like a wode [crazed] lion, she hath sent him hither like as a meek lamb." And with that word appeared suddenly an old man y-clad in white clothes, holding a book written with letters of gold, whom Valerian seeing, for fear fell down to the ground, as he had been dead.

Whom the old man raised and took up and read in this wise: "One God, one faith, one baptism. One God and father of all, above all, and in us all everywhere." And when this old man had read this, he said, "Believest thou this or doubtest thou it? Say yea or nay."

Then Valerian cried, saying "There is no thing truer under heaven." Then vanished this old man away. Then Valerian received baptism of Saint Urban and returned home to Saint Cecilia whom he found within her chamber speaking with an angel. And this angel had two crowns of roses and lilies which he held in his hand, of which he gave one to Cecilia and that other to Valerian saying "Keep ye these crowns with an undefouled and a clean body, for I have brought them to you from paradise, and they shall never fade nor wither nor lose their savor; nor they may not be seen but of them to whom chastity pleaseth. And thou Valerian because thou hast used profitable counsel, demand what thou wilt."

To whom Valerian said, "There is no thing in this world to me lever [dearer] than my brother whom I would fain that he might know this very truth with me."

To whom the angel said, "Thy petition pleaseth our lord, and ye both shall come to him by the palm of martyrdom." And anon Tiburce his brother and came and entered in to this chamber. And anon he felt the sweet odor of the roses and lilies, and marveled from whence it came.

Then Valerian said, "We have crowns which thine eyes may not see and like as by my prayers thou hast felt the odor of them. So if thou wilt believe, thou shalt see the crowns of roses and lilies that we have. Then Cecilia and Valerian began to preach to Tiburce of the joy of heaven. And also they preached to him of the Incarnation of our Lord and of his passion, and did so much that Tiburce was converted, baptized by St Urban, and from than forth he had so much grace of God that every day he saw angels and all that ever he required of our Lord he obtained.

After Almachius, provost of Rome, which put to death many Christian men, heard say that Tiburce and Valerian buried Christian men that were martyred and gave all their good to poor people. He called them to him, and after long disputation he commanded that they should go to the statue or image of Jupiter for to do sacrifice or else they should be beheaded. And as they were led they preached the faith of our lord to one called Maximus that they converted him to the Christian faith, and they promised to him that if he had very repentance and firm creadance that he should see the glory of heaven, which their souls should receive at the hour of their passions. And that he himself should have the same if he would believe.

Then Maximus got leave of the tormentors for to have them home to his house. And the said Maximus with al his household and all the tormentors were turned to the faith. Then came Saint Cecilia thider with priests and baptized them. And afterward when the morning came Saint Cecilia said to them, "Now ye knights of Christ cast away from you the works of darkness and clothe you with the arms of light." And then they were led four mile out of the town and brought tofore the image of Jupiter. But in no wise they would do sacrifice nor incense to the idol, but humbly with great devotion kneeled down and there were beheaded. And Saint Cecilia took their bodies and buried them.

Then Maximus that saw this thing said that he saw in the hours of their passion angels clear shining, and their souls ascend into heaven which bare up. Wherefore many were converted to the Christian faith.

And when Almache heard that Maximus was Christianed he did do beat him with plomettes of lead so long til he gave up his spirit and died, whose body Saint Cecilia buried by Valerian, and after Almache commanded that Cecilia should be brought unto his presence for to do sacrifice to Jupiter, and she so preached to them that came for her that she converted them to the faith which wept sore that so fair a maid and so noble should be put to death.

Then she said to them, "O ye good young men, it is nothing to lose the youth but to change it — that is to give clay and take therefor gold, to give a foul habitacle [habitation] and take a precious, to give a little corner and to take a right great place; God rewardeth for one simple an hundred fold. Believe ye this that I have said." And they said, "We believe Christ to be very God which hath such a servant."

Then Saint Urban was called and four hundred and more were baptized.

Then Almache calling tofore him Saint Cecilia said to her, "Of what condition art thou?" And she said that she was of a noble kynrede. To whom Almachius said, "I demand thee of what religion art thou?"

Then Cecilia said, "Then begannest thou thy demand folyly that wouldest have two answers in one demand."

To whom Almache said, "From whence cometh thy rude answer?"

And she sayd, "Of good conscience and faith not feigned."

To whom Almachius said, "Knowest thou not of what power I am?"

And she said, "Thy power is little to dread, for it is like a bladder full of wind, which with the pricking of a needle is anon gone away and come to nought."

To whom Almache said, "In wronge beganest thou and in wrong thou perseverest. Knowest thou not how our princes have given me power to give life and to slay?"

And she said, "Now shal I prove thee a liar against the very truth. Thou mayst wel take the life from them that live, but to them that be dead thou mayst give no life. Therfore thou art a minister not of life but of death."

To whom Almachius said, "Now lay apart thy madness and do sacrifice to the gods."

To whom Cecilia said, "I wot never where thou hast loste thy sight, for them that thou sayest be goddes, we see them stones. Put thine hand and by touching thou shalt learn that which thou mayst not see with thine eyes."

Then Almachius was wroth and commanded her to be led into her house and there to be burned in a burning baine [bath] which her seemed was a place cool and wel attempered. Then Almachius, hearing that, commanded that she should be beheaded in the same bath. Then the tormentor smote at her three strokes and could not smite off her heed. And the fourth stroke he might not by the law smite and so left her there lying half alive and half dead.

And she lived three dayes after in that mannere, and gave all that she had to poor people and continually preached the faith all that while and all them that she converted she sente to Urban, for to be baptized and said "I have asked respite three days that I might commend to you these soules. And that ye should hallow of mine house a church."

And then, at the end of three days she slept in our Lord, and Saint Urban wyth his deacons buried her body among the bishops and hallowed her house into a church, in which unto this day is the service unto our Lord.

She suffered her passion about the year of our Lord two hundred and xxiij in the time of Alexaunder the emperor. And it is read in another place that she suffered in the time of Marcius Aurelius, which reigned about the year of our Lord two hundred and twenty.

Then let us devoutly pray unto our Lord that by the merits of this holy virgin and martyr Saint Cecilia we may come to his everlasting bliss in heaven. Amen.

Thus endeth the Life of Saint Cecilia Virgin and Martyr.

Edited from Golden Legend, 1483

The Persecution under Maximinus

The Roman emperor, Alexander, having finished his reign in thirteen years, was succeeded by Maximinus Caesar. On account of his hatred toward the household of Alexander, which contained many believers, he began a persecution, commanding that only the rulers of the churches should be put to death, as responsible for the Gospel teaching. Thereupon Origen composed his work On Martyrdom, and dedicated it to Ambrose and Protoctetus, a presbyter of the parish of Caesarea, because in the persecution there had come upon them both unusual hardships, in which it is reported that they were eminent in confession during the reign of Maximinus, which lasted but three years. Origen has noted this as the time of the persecution in the twenty-second book of his Commentaries on John, and in several epistles.

Eusebius of Caesarea, Church History, Book 6, chapter 28

The Sixth Persecution, under Maximus, A.D. 235

A.D. 235, was in the time of Maximinus. In Cappadocia, the president, Seremianus, did all he could to exterminate the Christians from that province.

The principal persons who perished under this reign were Pontianus, bishop of Rome; Anteros, a Grecian, his successor, who gave offence to the government by collecting the acts of the martyrs, Pammachius and Quiritus, Roman senators, with all their families, and many other Christians; Simplicius, senator; Calepodius, a Christian minister, thrown into the Tyber; Martina, a noble and beautiful virgin; and Hippolitus, a Christian prelate, tied to a wild horse, and dragged until he expired.

During this persecution, raised by Maximinus, numberless Christians were slain without trial, and buried indiscriminately in heaps, sometimes fifty or sixty being cast into a pit together, without the least decency.

The tyrant Maximinus dying, A.D. 238, was succeeded by Gordian, during whose reign, and that of his successor Philip, the Church was free from persecution for the space of more than ten years; but in A.D. 249, a violent persecution broke out in Alexandria, at the instigation of a pagan priest, without the knowledge of the emperor.

Foxe's Book of Martyrs, Edited by William Byron Forbush

Hippolytus

Hippolytus was apprehended, and interrogated on the rack in Rome; but the prefect of the city, having filled it with Christian blood, went to Ostia to extend the persecution in those parts of the country, and ordered our saint and several other Christians who were then in prison at Rome, to be conducted thither after him. Hippolytus was taken out of prison and the prefect, who had gone ahead of the prisoners, ascended his tribunal, surrounded with his executioners, and various instruments of torture. The confessors were ranged in several companies before him, and by their emaciated faces, the length of their hair, and the filth with which they were covered, showed how much they had suffered by their long imprisonment.

The judge, finding that he was not able to prevail with any of them by torments, at length condemned them all to be put to death. Some he caused to be beheaded, others to be crucified, others burnt, and some to be put out to sea in rotten vessels, which immediately foundered. When the venerable old man, Hippolytus, was in his turn brought to him loaded with chains, a crowd of young people cried out to the judge that he was a chief among the Christians, and ought to be put to death by some new and remarkable kind of punishment.

"What is his name?" said the prefect.

They answered, "Hippolytus."

The prefect said, "Then let him be treated like Hippolytus, and dragged by wild horses." By this sentence he alluded to Hippolytus, the son of Theseus, who, flying from the indignation of his father, met a monster, the sight of which frightened his horses, so that he fell from his chariot, and, being entangled in the harness, was dragged along, and torn in pieces. No sooner was the order given but the people set themselves to work in assisting the executioners. Out of the country, where untamed horses were kept, they took a pair of the most furious and unruly they could meet with, and tied a long rope between them instead of a pole, to which they fastened the martyr's feet. Then they provoked the horses to run away by loud cries, whipping and pricking them.

The last words which the martyr was heard to say as they started, were, "Lord, they tear my body, receive thou my soul." The horses dragged him away furiously into the woods, through brooks, and over ditches, briars, and rocks, leaving the mangled parts of his body scattered all about.

Alban Butler, The Lives of the Saints, Dublin, 1833, volume 2, pp 228-29

Julian of Cilicia

In the year 249, Decius being Emperor of Rome, a dreadful persecution was begun against the Christians. This was occasioned partly by the hatred he bore to his predecessor Philip, who was deemed a Christian, and partly by his jealousy concerning the amazing progress of Christianity; for the heathen temples were almost forsaken, and the Christian churches crowded with proselytes. Decius, provoked at this, attempted, as he said, to extirpate the name of Christian. The pagans in general were ambitious to enforce the imperial decrees upon the occasion, and looked upon the murder of a Christian as a merit to be coveted. The martyrs were, therefore, innumerable.

Julian, born in Cilicia, as we are informed by St Chrysostom, was seized for being a Christian. He was tortured, but remained inflexible; and though often brought from prison for execution, was remanded, to suffer greater cruelties. He at length was obliged to travel for twelve months together, from town to town, that he might be exposed to the insults of the people.

When all attempts to make him recant his religion were ineffective, he was brought before a judge, stripped, and whipped in a dreadful manner. He was then put into a leather bag, with a number of serpents and scorpions, and in that condition thrown into the sea.

John Foxe, The Book of Martyrs, revised with notes and an appendix by W. Bramley-Moore, London, 1869, pp 23-4

The Acts of Pionius

The martyrdom of St Pionius and his companions in Smyrna took place in 250.

The priest Pionius, Asclepias , a woman confessor of the faith, Sabina, and a few others were celebrating the vigil of an anniversary of the martyrdom of Polycarp together. Pionius had a premonition that they were to be arrested the next day. To dramatically illustrate this he took three cords and put them round the necks of Sabina, Asclepias and himself.

The temple guard Polemon arrived as their service was ending. He demanded that they should sacrifice meet that had been offered to idols. Polemon reminded them about the emperor's decrees that stipulated that they must sacrifice to the gods. Pionius replied, "We know God's orders which state that we must only worship him." Polemon ordered them into the square to obey the emperor's commands. Asclepias and Sabina confirmed Pionius' reply and said, "We will only obey the living God." As they were taken to the square passers-by noticed the strange cords they were wearing and a fascinated crowd gathered. By the time they arrived in the square the place was packed with people.

Pionius began his defense: "People of Smyrna, the beauty of your city has inspired great pride and produced Homer, the son of Meles, now listen to my words. You sneer at apostates and you despise weak people who put up no resistance when they sacrifice. The Greeks among you should remember the words of your Homer, who said that it was sacrilege to laugh at a dying person. You Jews should remember Moses' words, "If you see the donkey of someone who hates you fallen down under its load, do not leave it there; be sure to help him with it" [Exodus 23:5, NIV]. You should also recall Solomon's words, "Do not gloat when your enemy falls; when he stumbles, do not let your heart rejoice" [Proverbs 24:17, NIV]. As far as I am concerned, I am only being faithful to my master. I choose to die rather than to break his word. So I refuse to worship and bow down before your golden gods."

Some of the crowd tried to dissuade them. They warned Sabina that she would be sent to a public brothel if she did not offer sacrifice to the gods. Polemon then ordered each of them to sacrifice. They refused and so were taken off to prison. In the morning the prisoners were taken off to be executed by Theophilus, a cavalry officer, and Polemon, the temple guard. They told than that their bishop, Euctemon had recently sacrificed and that they should follow his example. As they were being led into the temple the prisoners struggled and kicked hoping to stop the soldiers from taking them into the temple. But they were overpowered. The apostate bishop, Euctemon, stood by the altar and Lepidus then interrogated the prisoners.

LEPIDUS: Ponius, why do you refuse to sacrifice?

PIONIUS: We refuse to sacrifice because we are Christians.

LEPIDUS: Who is the god you worship?

PIONIUS: The God who made heaven, earth, the sea, and all that is in them.

LEPIDUS: Is this the God who was killed on a cross?

PIONIUS: This is the God who was sent into the world to save the world.

Pionius had pointed out that they could not execute them as their proconsul was not present. The prisoners were returned to their prison cell. When the proconsul had arrived in Smyrna Pionius was brought before him and then sentenced to die: "Since Pionius confesses that he is a Christian we condemn him to be burnt alive." Pionius was taken to the stadium where he took off his clothes and stretched himself out on a cross asking the soldier to hammer in the nails. After this was completed Pionius was told that it was still not too late to change his mind. If he did change his mind the nails would be removed. Pionius replied that he had felt the point of the nails and that he was now impatient to die so that he could wake up again speedily, referring to the resurrection.

Pionius' cross was then erected next to Metrodorus, a Marcionite priest who was also being executed. Faggots were placed round them and set on fire. As the flames rose Pionius opened his eyes and said, "Amen. Lord, receive my spirit." He then let out a short groan and died, crossing over the narrow divide into eternal life. This took place at 10.00 on Saturday 11 March, in the reign of our Lord Jesus Christ, to whom be glory for ever and ever. Amen.

Edited from several sources

St. Pionius

Martyred at Smyrna, 12 March, 250.

Pionius, with Sabina and Asclepiades, was arrested on 23 February, the anniversary of St. Polycarp's martyrdom. They had passed the previous night in prayer and fasting. Knowing of his impending arrest, Pionius had fastened fetters round the necks of himself and his companions to signify that they were already condemned. People seeing them led off unbound might suppose that they were prepared, like so many other Christians in Smyrna, the bishop included, to sacrifice. Early in the morning, after they had partaken of the Holy Bread and of water, they were conducted to the forum. The place was thronged with Greeks and Jews, for it was a great Sabbath and therefore a general holiday in the city – an indication of the importance of the Jews in Smyrna. Pionius harangued the multitude. He begged the Greeks to remember what Homer had said about not mocking the corpse of an enemy. Let them refrain therefore from mocking those Christians who had apostatized. He then turned to the Jews and quoted Moses and Solomon to the same effect. He ended with a vehement refusal to offer sacrifice. Then followed the usual interrogatories and threats, after which Pionius and his companions were relegated to prison, to await the arrival of the proconsul. Here they found other confessors, among them a Montanist. Many pagans visited them, and Christians who had sacrificed, lamenting their fall. The latter Pionius exhorted to repentance. A further attempt before the arrival of the proconsul was made to force Pionius and his companions into an act of apostasy. They were carried off to a temple where every effort was made to compel them to participate in a sacrifice. On 12 March, Pionius was brought before the proconsul who first tried persuasion and then torture. Both having failed, Pionius was condemned to be burnt alive. He suffered in company with Metrodorus, a Marcionite priest. His feast is kept by the Latins ion 1 Feb.; by the Greeks on 11 March. The true day of his martyrdom, according to the Acts, was 12 March. Eusebius ("H.E.", IV, xv; "Chron.", p. 17, ed. Schoene) places the martyrdom in the reign of Antoninus. His mistake was probably due to the fact that he found the martyrdom of Pionius in a volume containing the Acts of Martyrs of an earlier date. Possibly his MS. lacked the chronological note in our present ones. For the life of Polycarp by Pionius, see Polycarp, Saint. Did Pionius before his martyrdom celebrate with bread and water? We know from St. Cyprian (Ep. 63) that this abuse existed in his time. But note (1) the bread is spoken of as Holy, but not the water; (2) it is unlikely that Pionius would celebrate with only two persons present. It is more likely therefore that we have an account, not of a celebration, but of a private Communion (see Funk, "Abhandlungen", I, 287).

J.F. Bacchus, The Catholic Encyclopedia, Volume 12

Tortures of the first Christian martyrs (3) The wooden horse and other instruments which stretched the limbs

a. The wooden horse, or hobby horse

* The horse among the Ancients was an engine of wood fashioned to resemble a real horse, and having two small, channeled wheels, or pulleys, in the two ends, which were hollowed out to receive them. Over these axles ropes were led and the wheels revolved, by which means the person tied to them was racked and stretched in different directions.
* The tormentors took ropes and tied one to the martyr's feet and one to the martyr's hands, which had been twisted behind him.
* The other ends of these ropes were attached to a winch or windlass which was fixed to the horse's legs. As the windlass was turned, so the body of the martyr was stretched, until every limb was strained and every joint dislocated.

b. Stocks

Stocks were wooden contrivances, where prisoner's legs were constrained, constricted and confined. Blessed martyrs had their legs stretched and forcibly drawn apart even to the fourth and fifth hole of the instrument.

c. Shackles

Shackles were wooden instruments with round holes, into which feet and necks of prisoners were inserted, and fixed there in such a way that they could not withdraw them again.

d. Thongs

A thong was a kind of bond used for securing the feet or neck. Martyrs, firmly bound with thongs around their feet and hands, were violently tugged by four men in all directions until limb was torn from limb.

e. Fetters

Fetters were snares or nooses in which feet were secured.

f. Manacles

Manacles were bands for the hands.

"The English heretics at this present moment (1591) are busied unceasingly in malignantly and cruelly afflicting them of the orthodox faith by means of iron manacles, or handcuffs as they call them. These are a sort of instrument whereby a man is hung up and tortured, his two hands being put through an iron ring toothed inside, and violently squeezed. Indeed, so fierce and intense is the pain that unless the back is allowed to lean somewhat against the wall and the tips of the toes to touch the floor, the man will fall incontinently into a dead faint."

g. Neck collar

Neck collars were a sort of necklace or neckband for condemned criminals, made of wood or iron, which imprisoned their necks firmly, as the yoke doth with oxen.

h. Chains

A chain is an iron bond in which slaves or prisoners are made fast to hinder their escaping.

Tortures and Torments of the Christian Martyrs, from the "De SS. Martyrum Cruciatibus" of Gallonio, translated by A.R. Allinson (London and Paris, printed for the subscribers, 1903), pp. 68-70

Maximus

A few months after Pionius' martyrdom Maximus voluntarily told the proconsul of Ephesus, Optimus, that he was a Christian. The following dialogue took place.

OPTIMUS: What is your name?

MAXIMUS: I am called Maximus.

OPTIMUS: What is your position?
MAXIMUS: I was free born, but I am now a servant of Christ.
OPTIMUS: What is your profession?
MAXIMUS: I am an ordinary tradesman.
OPTIMUS: Are you a Christian?
MAXIMUS: Yes. Even though I am a sinner, I am a Christian.
OPTIMUS: Are you not aware of the imperial decrees which have recently arrived?
MAXIMUS: Which ones?
OPTIMUS: That Christians are to leave their unprofitable superstition and acknowledge the true sovereign, who is supreme over all, and to worship his gods.
MAXIMUS: I know about the iniquitous ordinance of the king of this world, and that is why I came forward to you.
OPTIMUS: Then sacrifice to the gods.
MAXIMUS: I sacrifice to no one except to the only God, to whom I am thankful to say that I have sacrificed from my childhood.
OPTIMUS: Sacrifice, if you want your life to be spared. If you do not, I will have you tortured.
MAXIMUS: This is what I have always wanted. This is why I presented myself to you, so I could exchange this miserable temporal existence for eternal life.

The proconsul ordered Maximus to be beaten with rods. As this was being carried out, Optimus said, "Sacrifice, Maximus, so that you can be released from these sufferings."

"These are no sufferings," Maximus answered, "which are borne in the name of our Lord Jesus Christ, they are soothing ointment. It would be real suffering for me – everlasting suffering – if I departed from my Lord's commands, which I have learned in his Gospel."

The proconsul than had Maximus strung up on the hobby-horse. As the torture proceeded, Optimus said again, "Unhappy man, even now give up your folly, and sacrifice, that you may gain your life."

"I shall gain my life," Maximus replied, "if I do not sacrifice. If I sacrifice, I lose it." The thought of the communion of saints comforted the sufferer in his pains. "I do not feel the rods," he cried, "nor the hooks, nor the fire. The grace of Christ abides in me, and by the prayers of all the saints it will save me for ever. The saints passed through this conflict, and left us the example of their virtues."

The proconsul then gave his final sentence. For his refusal to obey the sacred laws and to sacrifice to the great goddess Diana, "the divine clemency," which the proconsul had in his power, ordered Maximus to be stoned to death, as an example to the Christians.

A. J. Mason, The Historic Martyrs of the Primitive Church, Longmans, 1905, pp 135-6

Nichomachus, Dionysia, Andrew and Paul

At Troas, three more Christians were presented to proconsul Optimus, Nichomachus, Andrew and Paul.

Nichomachus said "I am a Christian," when asked about his religion. The other two said the same.

The magistrate said, "Sacrifice to the gods, as you are commanded."

Nichomachus answered, "As you are aware, a Christian may not sacrifice to devils."

He was hung up and tortured for a long time. He bore the torture until he was completely exhausted and could hardly breathe. The unhappy man cried out, "It is a mistake. I never was a Christian; I sacrifice to the gods." He was instantly taken down. The sacrificial flesh was put to his dying hands and lips as he last spasm seized him. He fell forwards, and, gnawing his tongue, died an apostate.

There was a young girl, sixteen years old, called Dionysia, among the spectators. She was a Christian. This sight so horrified her, that she could not help crying out, "Poor, miserable wretch! For the sake of one short moment you have indescribable pains that will last for ever."

Dionysia was dragged forward.

Optimus asked, "Are you a Christian?"

"Yes," she replied, "I am a Christian. That is why I am sorry for that poor man, because he could not endure a little to find eternal rest."

"He is at rest," replied the proconsul, "the great Diana and Venus have taken him. Now follow his example and sacrifice, or you will be roughly handled and then burned alive."

The girl replied, "My God is greater than you, so I am not afraid of your threats. He will enable me to endure whatever you inflict on me."

The next day, Andrew and Paul, Nichomachus' two companions were brought before the judge again. The priests of Diana were set on them being punished. The two men refused to sacrifice to Diana or to any other god. They said that they could not recognize any of the devils whom the heathen worshipped, and that they had never worshipped any other than the only true God. The crowd were incensed and the proconsul thought it best to hand them over to them to be stoned to death, rather than the more usual form of execution. Their feet were lashed together, and they were dragged outside the town to die.

Meanwhile, the young Dionysia had spent a night in dreadful pain at the hands of ruffians. In the morning, as she was being led to be sentenced, she met the crowd who were dragging Andrew and Paul to their death. With a quick movement, she managed to free herself from her guard, and flung herself on the other Christians, crying, "Let me die with you on earth, that I may live with you in heaven." But the proconsul would not allow her to share their kind of martyrdom. He gave orders to Dionysia to be separated from them and to be beheaded.

A. J. Mason, The Historic Martyrs of the Primitive Church, Longmans, 1905, pp 137-9

Persecutions under Decius, and Valerian. A.D. 249-260. Martyrdom of Cyprian

Decius Trajan (249-251), an earnest and energetic emperor, in whom the old Roman spirit once more awoke, resolved to root out the church as an atheistic and seditious sect, and in the year 250 published an edict to all the governors of the provinces, enjoining return to the pagan state religion under the heaviest penalties. This was the signal for a persecution which, in extent, consistency, and cruelty, exceeded all before it. In truth it was properly the first which covered the whole empire, and accordingly produced a far greater number of martyrs than any former persecution. In the execution of the imperial decree confiscation, exile, torture, promises and threats of all kinds, were employed to move the Christians to apostasy. Multitudes of nominal Christians, especially at the beginning, sacrificed to the gods (*sacrificati, thurificati*), or procured from the, magistrate a false certificate that they had done so (*libellatici*), and were then excommunicated as apostates (*lapsi*); while hundreds rushed with impetuous zeal to the prisons and the tribunals, to obtain the confessor's or martyr's crown. The confessors of Rome wrote from prison to their brethren of Africa: "What more glorious and blessed lot can fall to man by the grace of God, than to confess God the Lord amidst tortures and in the face of death itself; to confess Christ the Son of God with lacerated body and with a spirit departing, yet free; and to become fellow-sufferers with Christ in the name of Christ? Though we have not yet shed our blood, we are ready to do so. Pray for us, then, dear Cyprian, that the Lord, the best captain, would daily strengthen each one of us more and more, and at last lead us to the field as faithful soldiers, armed with those divine weapons (Eph. 6:2) which can never be conquered." The authorities were specially severe with the bishops and officers of the churches. Fabianus of Rome, Babylas of Antioch, and Alexander of Jerusalem, perished in this persecution. Others withdrew to places of concealment; some from cowardice; some from Christian prudence, in hope of allaying by their absence the fury of the pagans against their flocks, and of saving their own lives for the good of the church in better times. Among the latter was Cyprian, bishop of Carthage, who incurred much censure by his course, but fully vindicated himself by his pastoral industry during his absence, and by his subsequent martyrdom. He says concerning the matter: "Our Lord commanded us in times of persecution to yield and to fly. He taught this, and he practiced it himself. For since the martyr's crown comes by the grace of God, and cannot be gained before the appointed hour, he who retires for a time, and remains true to Christ, does not deny his faith, but only abides his time." The poetical legend of the seven brothers at Ephesus, who fell asleep in a cave, whither they had fled, and awoke two hundred years afterwards, under Theodosius II. (447), astonished to see the once despised and hated cross now ruling over city and country, dates itself internally from the time of Decius, but is not mentioned before Gregory of Tours in the sixth century. Under Gallus (251-253) the persecution received a fresh impulse thorough the incursions of the Goths, and the prevalence of a pestilence, drought, and famine. Under this reign the Roman bishops Cornelius and Lucius were banished, and then condemned to death. Valerian (253-260) was at first mild towards the Christians; but in 257 he changed his course, and made an effort to check the progress of their religion without bloodshed, by the banishment of ministers and prominent laymen, the confiscation of their property, and the prohibition of religious assemblies.

Martyrdom of Cyprian

These measures, however, proving fruitless, he brought the death penalty again into play.

The most distinguished martyrs of this persecution under Valerian are the bishops Sixtus II. of Rome, and Cyprian of Carthage. When Cyprian received his sentence of death, representing him as an enemy of the Roman gods and laws, he calmly answered: "Deo gratias!" Then, attended by a vast multitude to the scaffold, he proved once more, undressed himself, covered his eyes, requested a presbyter to bind his hands, and to pay the executioner, who tremblingly drew the sword, twenty-five pieces of gold, and won the incorruptible crown (Sept. 14, 258). His faithful friends caught the blood in handkerchiefs, and buried the body of their sainted pastor with great solemnity. Gibbon describes the martyrdom of Cyprian with circumstantial minuteness, and dwells with evident satisfaction on the small decorum which attended his execution. But this is no fair average specimen of the style in which Christians were executed throughout the empire. For Cyprian was a man of the highest social standing and connection from his former eminence, as a rhetorician and statesman. His deacon, Pontius relates that "numbers of eminent and illustrious persons, men of mark family and secular distinction, often urged him, for the sake of their old friendship with him, to retire." We shall return to Cyprian again in the history of church government, where he figures as a typical, ante-Nicene high-churchman, advocating both the visible unity of the church and episcopal independence of Rome. The much lauded martyrdom of the deacon St. Laurentius of Rome, who pointed the avaricious magistrates to the poor and sick of the congregation as the richest treasure of the church, and is said to have been slowly roasted to death (Aug. 10, 258) is scarcely reliable in its details, being first mentioned by Ambrose a century later, and then glorified by the poet Prudentius. A Basilica on the Via Tiburtina celebrates the memory of this saint, who occupies the same position among the martyrs of the church of Rome as Stephen among those of Jerusalem.
Philip Scaff, History of the Christian Church, chapter 22

The Seventh Persecution

The Persecution under Decius, and the Sufferings of Origen

After a reign of seven years Philip was succeeded by Decius. On account of his hatred of Philip, he commenced a persecution of the churches, in which Fabianus suffered martyrdom at Rome, and Cornelius succeeded him in the episcopate. In Palestine, Alexander, bishop of the church of Jerusalem, was brought again on Christ's account before the governor's judgment seat in Caesarea, and having acquitted himself nobly in a second confession was cast into prison, crowned with the hoary locks of venerable age. And after his honorable and illustrious confession at the tribunal of the governor, he fell asleep in prison, and Mazabanes became his successor in the bishopric of Jerusalem. Babylas in Antioch, having like Alexander passed away in prison after his confession, was succeeded by Fabius in the episcopate of that church.

But how many and how great things came upon Origen in the persecution, and what was their final result, as the demon of evil marshaled all his forces, and fought against the man with his utmost craft and power, assaulting him beyond all others against whom he contended at that time, and what and how many things he endured for the word of Christ, bonds and bodily tortures and torments under the iron collar and in the dungeon; and how for many days with his feet stretched four spaces in the stocks he bore patiently the threats of fire and whatever other things were inflicted by his enemies; and how his sufferings terminated, as his judge strove eagerly with all his might not to end his life; and what words he left after these things, full of comfort to those needing aid, a great many of his epistles show with truth and accuracy.

Eusebius of Caesarea, Church History, Book 6, chapter 39

Dionysius

The Events which happened to Dionysius

I shall quote from the epistle of Dionysius to Germanus an account of what befell the former. Speaking of himself, he writes as follows:

"I speak before God, and he knows that I do not lie. I did not flee on my own impulse nor without divine direction. But even before this, at the very hour when the Decian persecution was commanded, Sabinus sent a frumentarius to search for me, and I remained at home four days awaiting his arrival. But he went about examining all places, roads, rivers, and fields, where he thought I might be concealed or on the way. But he was smitten with blindness, and did not find the house, for he did not suppose, that being pursued, I would remain at home. And after the fourth day God commanded me to depart, and made a way for me in a wonderful manner; and I and my attendants and many of the brethren went away together. And that this occurred through the providence of God was made manifest by what followed, in which perhaps we were useful to some." Farther on he relates in this manner what happened to him after his flight:

"For about sunset, having been seized with those that were with me, I was taken by the soldiers to Taposiris, but in the providence of God, Timothy was not present and was not captured. But coming later, he found the house deserted and guarded by soldiers, and ourselves reduced to slavery."

After a little he says:

"And what was the manner of his admirable management? for the truth shall be told. One of the country people met Timothy fleeing and disturbed, and inquired the cause of his haste. And he told him the truth. And when the man heard it (he was on his way to a marriage feast, for it was customary to spend the entire night in such gatherings), he entered and announced it to those at the table. And they, as if on a preconcerted signal, arose with one impulse, and rushed out quickly and came and burst in upon us with a shout. Immediately the soldiers who were guarding us fled, and they came to us lying as we were upon the bare couches. But I, God knows, thought at first that they were robbers who had come for spoil and plunder. So I remained upon the bed on which I was, clothed only in a linen garment, and offered them the rest of my clothing which was lying beside me. But they directed me to rise and come away quickly.

Then I understood why they were come, and I cried out, beseeching and entreating them to depart and leave us alone. And I requested them, if they desired to benefit me in any way, to anticipate those who were carrying me off, and cut off my head themselves. And when I had cried out in this manner, as my companions and partners in everything know, they raised me by force. But I threw myself on my back on the ground; and they seized me by the hands and feet and dragged me away. And the witnesses of all these occurrences followed: Gaius, Faustus, Peter, and Paul.

But they who had seized me carried me out of the village hastily, and placing me on an ass without a saddle, bore me away."

Dionysius relates these things respecting himself.

Eusebius of Caesarea, Church History, Book 6, chapter 40

The Seventh Persecution, Under Decius, A.D. 249

This was occasioned partly by the hatred he bore to his predecessor Philip, who was deemed a Christian and was partly by his jealousy concerning the amazing increase of Christianity; for the heathen temples began to be forsaken, and the Christian churches thronged.

These reasons stimulated Decius to attempt the very extirpation of the name of Christian; and it was unfortunate for the Gospel, that many errors had, about this time, crept into the Church: the Christians were at variance with each other; self-interest divided those whom social love ought to have united; and the virulence of pride occasioned a variety of factions.

The heathens in general were ambitious to enforce the imperial decrees upon this occasion, and looked upon the murder of a Christian as a merit to themselves. The martyrs, upon this occasion, were innumerable; but the principal we shall give some account of.

Fabian, the bishop of Rome, was the first person of eminence who felt the severity of this persecution. The deceased emperor, Philip, had, on account of his integrity, committed his treasure to the care of this good man. But Decius, not finding as much as his avarice made him expect, determined to wreak his vengeance on the good prelate. He was accordingly seized; and on January 20, A.D. 250, he suffered decapitation.

Julian, a native of Cilicia, as we are informed by St. Chrysostom, was seized upon for being a Christian. He was put into a leather bag, together with a number of serpents and scorpions, and in that condition thrown into the sea.

Peter, a young man, amiable for the superior qualities of his body and mind, was beheaded for refusing to sacrifice to Venus. He said, "I am astonished you should sacrifice to an infamous woman, whose debaucheries even your own historians record, and whose life consisted of such actions as your laws would punish. No, I shall offer the true God the acceptable sacrifice of praises and prayers." Optimus, the proconsul of Asia, on hearing this, ordered the prisoner to be stretched upon a wheel, by which all his bones were broken, and then he was sent to be beheaded.

Nichomachus, being brought before the proconsul as a Christian, was ordered to sacrifice to the pagan idols. Nichomachus replied, "I cannot pay that respect to devils, which is only due to the Almighty." This speech so much enraged the proconsul that Nichomachus was put to the rack. After enduring the torments for a time, he recanted; but scarcely had he given this proof of his frailty, than he fell into the greatest agonies, dropped down on the ground, and expired immediately.

Denisa, a young woman of only sixteen years of age, who beheld this terrible judgment, suddenly exclaimed, "O unhappy wretch, why would you buy a moment's ease at the expense of a miserable eternity!" Optimus, hearing this, called to her, and Denisa avowing herself to be a Christian, she was beheaded, by his order, soon after.

Andrew and Paul, two companions of Nichomachus, the martyr, A.D. 251, suffered martyrdom by stoning, and expired, calling on their blessed Redeemer.

Alexander and Epimachus, of Alexandria, were apprehended for being Christians: and, confessing the accusation, were beat with staves, torn with hooks, and at length burnt in the fire; and we are informed, in a fragment preserved by Eusebius, that four female martyrs suffered on the same day, and at the same place, but not in the same manner; for these were beheaded.

Lucian and Marcian, two wicked pagans, though skillful magicians, becoming converts to Christianity, to make amends for their former errors, lived the lives of hermits, and subsisted upon bread and water only. After some time spent in this manner, they became zealous preachers, and made many converts. The persecution, however, raging at this time, they were seized upon, and carried before Sabinus, the governor of Bithynia. On being asked by what authority they took upon themselves to preach, Lucian answered, "That the laws of charity and humanity obliged all men to endeavor the conversion of their neighbors, and to do everything in their power to rescue them from the snares of the devil."

Lucian having answered in this manner, Marcian said, "Their conversion was by the same grace which was given to St. Paul, who, from a zealous persecutor of the Church, became a preacher of the Gospel."

The proconsul, finding that he could not prevail with them to renounce their faith, condemned them to be burnt alive, which sentence was soon after executed.

Trypho and Respicius, two eminent men, were seized as Christians, and imprisoned at Nice. Their feet were pierced with nails; they were dragged through the streets, scourged, torn with iron hooks, scorched with lighted torches, and at length beheaded, February 1, A.D. 251.

Agatha, a Sicilian lady, was not more remarkable for her personal and acquired endowments, than her piety; her beauty was such, that Quintian, governor of Sicily, became enamored of her, and made many attempts upon her chastity without success. In order to gratify his passions with the greater conveniency, he put the virtuous lady into the hands of Aphrodica, a very infamous and licentious woman. This wretch tried every artifice to win her to the desired prostitution; but found all her efforts were vain; for her chastity was impregnable, and she well knew that virtue alone could procure true happiness. Aphrodica acquainted Quintian with the inefficacy of her endeavors changed his lust into resentment. On her confessing that she was a Christian, he determined to gratify his revenge, as he could not his passion. Pursuant to his orders, she was scourged, burnt with red-hot irons, and torn with sharp hooks. Having borne these torments with admirable fortitude, she was next laid naked upon live coals, intermingled with glass, and then being carried back to prison, she there expired on February 5, 251.

Cyril, bishop of Gortyna, was seized by order of Lucius, the governor of that place, who, nevertheless, exhorted him to obey the imperial mandate, perform the sacrifices, and save his venerable person from destruction; for he was now eighty-four years of age. The good prelate replied that as he had long taught others to save their souls, he should only think now of his own salvation. The worthy prelate heard his fiery sentence without emotion, walked cheerfully to the place of execution, and underwent his martyrdom with great fortitude.

The persecution raged in no place more than the Island of Crete; for the governor, being exceedingly active in executing the imperial decrees, that place streamed with pious blood.

Babylas, a Christian of a liberal education, became bishop of Antioch, A.D. 237, on the demise of Zebinus. He acted with inimitable zeal, and governed the Church with admirable prudence during the most tempestuous times.

The first misfortune that happened to Antioch during his mission, was the siege of it by Sapor, king of Persia; who, having overrun all Syria, took and plundered this city among others, and used the Christian inhabitants with greater severity than the rest, but was soon totally defeated by Gordian.

After Gordian's death, in the reign of Decius, that emperor came to Antioch, where, having a desire to visit an assembly of Christians, Babylas opposed him, and absolutely refused to let him come in. The emperor dissembled his anger at that time; but soon sending for the bishop, he sharply reproved him for his insolence, and then ordered him to sacrifice to the pagan deities as an expiation for his offence. This being refused, he was committed to prison, loaded with chains, treated with great severities, and then beheaded, together with three young men who had been his pupils. A.D. 251.

Alexander, bishop of Jerusalem, about this time was cast into prison on account of his religion, where he died through the severity of his confinement.

Julianus, an old man, lame with the gout, and Cronion, another Christian, were bound on the backs of camels, severely scourged, and then thrown into a fire and consumed. Also forty virgins, at Antioch, after being imprisoned, and scourged, were burnt.

In the year of our Lord 251, the emperor Decius having erected a pagan temple at Ephesus, he commanded all who were in that city to sacrifice to the idols. This order was nobly refused by seven of his own soldiers, viz. Maximianus, Martianus, Joannes, Malchus, Dionysius, Seraion, and Constantinus. The emperor wishing to win these soldiers to renounce their faith by his entreaties and lenity, gave them a considerable respite until he returned from an expedition. During the emperor's absence, they escaped, and hid themselves in a cavern; which the emperor being informed of at his return, the mouth of the cave was closed up, and they all perished with hunger.

Theodora, a beautiful young lady of Antioch, on refusing to sacrifice to the Roman idols, was condemned to the stews, that her virtue might be sacrificed to the brutality of lust. Didymus, a Christian, disguised himself in the habit of a Roman soldier, went to the house, informed Theodora who he was, and advised her to make her escape in his clothes. This being effected, and a man found in the brothel instead of a beautiful lady, Didymus was taken before the president, to whom confessing the truth, and owning that he was a Christian the sentence of death was immediately pronounced against him. Theodora, hearing that her deliverer was likely to suffer, came to the judge, threw herself at his feet, and begged that the sentence might fall on her as the guilty person; but, deaf to the cries of the innocent, and insensible to the calls of justice, the inflexible judge condemned both; when they were executed accordingly, being first beheaded, and their bodies afterward burnt.

Secundianus, having been accused as a Christian, was conveyed to prison by some soldiers. On the way, Verianus and Marcellinus said, "Where are you carrying the innocent?" This interrogatory occasioned them to be seized, and all three, after having been tortured, were hanged and decapitated.

Origen, the celebrated presbyter and catechist of Alexandria, at the age of sixty-four, was seized, thrown into a loathsome prison, laden with fetters, his feet placed in the stocks, and his legs extended to the utmost for several successive days. He was threatened with fire, and tormented by every lingering means the most infernal imaginations could suggest. During this cruel temporizing, the emperor Decius died, and Gallus, who succeeded him, engaging in a war with the Goths, the Christians met with a respite. In this interim, Origen obtained his enlargement, and, retiring to Tyre, he there remained until his death, which happened when he was in the sixty-ninth year of his age.

Gallus, the emperor, having concluded his wars, a plague broke out in the empire: sacrifices to the pagan deities were ordered by the emperor, and persecutions spread from the interior to the extreme parts of the empire, and many fell martyrs to the impetuosity of the rabble, as well as the prejudice of the magistrates. Among these were Cornelius, the Christian bishop of Rome, and Lucius, his successor, in 253.

Most of the errors which crept into the Church at this time arose from placing human reason in competition with revelation; but the fallacy of such arguments being proved by the most able divines, the opinions they had created vanished away like the stars before the sun.

Foxe's Book of Martyrs, Edited by William Byron Forbush

Martyrdom of Fabian (1)

Fabian, bishop and martyr

20 January 250

Fabian was Bishop of Rome for 14 years. He organized the city of Rome into parishes and appointed scribes to record the lives of the martyrs for posterity. When the Emperor Decius began a persecution of Christians, probably the first one to be waged simultaneously in all parts of the Empire, Fabian was one of the first to be put to

death, setting a courageous example for others. His tombstone, with the inscription dimly visible, can still be seen at Rome.
James Kiefer, Christian Biographies, By kind permission

Martyrdom of Fabian (2)

Pope St. Fabian (FABIANUS)
Pope (236-250), the extraordinary circumstances of whose election is related by Eusebius (Hist. Eccl., VI, 29). After the death of Anterus he had come to Rome, with some others, from his farm and was in the city when the new election began. While the names of several illustrious and noble persons were being considered, a dove suddenly descended upon the head of Fabian, of whom no one had even thought. To the assembled brethren the sight recalled the Gospel scene of the descent of the Holy Spirit upon the Savior of mankind, and so, divinely inspired, as it were, they chose Fabian with joyous unanimity and placed him in the Chair of Peter. During his reign of fourteen years there was a lull in the storm of persecution. Little is known of his pontificate. The "Liber Pontificalis" says that he divided Rome into seven districts, each supervised by a deacon, and appointed seven subdeacons, to collect, in conjunction with other notaries, the "acta" of the martyrs, i.e. the reports of the court-proceedings on the occasion of their trials (cf. Eus., VI, 43). There is a tradition that he instituted the four minor orders. Under him considerable work was done in the catacombs. He caused the body of Pope St. Pontianus to be exhumed, in Sardinia, and transferred to the catacomb of St. Callistus at Rome. Later accounts, more or less trustworthy, attribute to him the consecration (245) of seven bishops as missionaries to Gaul, among them St. Denys of Paris (Greg. of Tours, Hist. Francor., I, 28, 31). St. Cyprian mentions (Ep., 59) the condemnation by Fabian for heresy of a certain Privatus (Bishop of Lambaesa) in Africa. The famous Origen did not hesitate to defend, before Fabian, the orthodoxy of his teaching (Eus. Hist. Eccl., VI, 34). Fabian died a martyr (20 Jan., 250) at the beginning of the Decian persecution, and was buried in the Crypt of the Popes in the catacomb of St. Callistus, where in recent times (1850) De Rossi discovered his Greek epitaph (Roma Sotterranea II, 59): "Fabian, bishop and martyr." The decretals ascribed to him in Pseudo-Isidore are apocryphal.
P. Gabriel Meier The Catholic Encyclopedia, Volume 5

Letters between the Churches of Rome and of Carthage

The church of Rome and the church of Carthage were often in contact.

The Church of Rome to the Church of Carthage

The Church of Rome, during the persecution of emperor Decius, wrote to the Church of Carthage about how it had been enabled to remain faithful to Christ.

Rome, early 250.
" ... The Church resists strong in the faith. It is true that some have yielded, being alarmed at the possibility that their high social position might attract attention, or from simple human frailty. Nevertheless, though they are now separated from us, we have not abandoned them in their defection, but have helped them and keep still close to them, so that by penance they may be rehabilitated and pardoned by Him who can forgive. Indeed if we were to leave them to their own resources, their fall would become irreparable.
Try and do the same, dearest brothers, extending your hand to those who have fallen, that they may rise again. Thus, if they should be arrested, they may this time feel strong enough to confess the faith and redress their former error.
Allow me also to remind you of what course to take on another problem. Those who surrendered in the time of trial, and are now ill and have repented and want communion with the Church, should be helped. Widows and other persons unable to present themselves spontaneously, as also those in prison or far from home, ought to have people ready to look after them. Nor should catechumens who

have fallen ill remain disappointed in their expectation of help.

The brethren who are in prison, the clergy and the entire Church, that watches so carefully over those who call on the Lord's name, salute you. In return we also ask you to remember us."

Letter 8, 2-3

The Bishop of Carthage to the Church of Rome

When Cyprian was informed of pope Fabian's death, he wrote this letter to the priests and deacons in Rome.

Carthage, early 250.

My dear brothers,

News of the death of my saintly fellow-bishop was still uncertain and information doubtful, when I received your letter brought by subdeacon Crementius, telling me fully of his glorious death. Then I rejoiced, as his admirable governing of the Church had been followed by a noble end.

For this I share your gladness, as you honor the memory of so solemn and splendid a witness, communicating to us also the glorious recollection you have of your bishop, and offering us such an example of faith and fortitude.

Indeed, harmful as the fall of a leader is to his subjects, no less valuable and salutary for his brethren is the example of a bishop firm in his faith... My wish, dearest brothers, is for your continued welfare.

Cyprian, Letter 1

Cyprian, bishop of Carthage to pope Cornelius

Cyprian pays homage to the testimony and fidelity shown by the Pope Cornelius and by the Church of Rome: "a magnificent testimony of a Church entirely united in one spirit and one voice". Foreseeing an imminent time of trial also for the Church of Carthage, Cyprian asks for the brotherly help of prayer and charity.

CARTHAGE, AUTUMN 153

Cyprian to Cornelius, his brother bishop.

We know, dearest brother, of your faith, your fortitude and your open witness. All this does you great honor and it gives me so much joy that I feel myself part of and companion in your merits and undertakings.

Since indeed the Church is one, and one and inseparable is love, and one and unbreakable is the harmony of hearts, what priest singing the praises of another does not rejoice as though they were his own glory? And what brother would not feel happy at the joy of his brethren? Certainly none can imagine the exultation and great joy there has been among us here when we have learnt such fine things, like the proofs of strength you have given.

You have led your brethren to testify their faith, and that very confession of yours has been strengthened further by that of the brethren. Thus, while you have gone before the others in the path of glory, and have shown yourself ready to be the first in testifying for all, you have persuaded the people too to confess the same faith.

So we cannot decide what to praise more in you, your prompt and unshakeable faith or your community's indivisible fraternal charity. In all its splendor, the courage of the bishop leading his people has been manifested, and the fidelity of the people in full solidarity with their bishop has been a great and shining example. Through all of you, the Church of Rome has given a magnificent testimony, entirely united in one spirit and one voice.

In this way, dear brother, the faith which the Apostle recognized and praised in your community, has shown forth. We may say that he, then, already foresaw prophetically and celebrated your courage and your indomitable fortitude. Already then he recognized your merits which were to make you glorious. He exalted the deeds of the fathers, foreseeing those of their sons.

With your complete harmony and strength of spirit, you have given all Christians a shining example of constancy and unity.

Dear brother, the Lord in his Providence forewarns us that the hour of trial is at hand. God in his goodness and eagerness for our salvation gives us helpful promptings for the coming struggle. So, in the name of charity which binds us together, let us help one another, persevering with the entire community, with fasts, vigils and prayer. These are for us the heavenly arms which keep us firm and strongly united, and make us persevere. These are the spiritual weapons and the divine arrows which protect us.

Let us remember one another in harmony and spiritual brotherhood. Let us pray for each other at all times and in all places, and let us try to lessen our sufferings with mutual charity.

Cyprian, Letter 60, 1-2

Cassian

Cassian was a Christian schoolmaster, and taught children to read and write at Imola, a city twenty-seven miles from Ravenna in Italy. A violent persecution was raised against the church, probably that of Decius or Valerian, and Cassian was taken up, and interrogated by the governor of the province. As he constantly refused to sacrifice to the gods, the barbarous judge having informed himself of what profession he was, commanded that his own scholars should stab him to death with their iron writing pencils, called styles; for at that time it was the custom for scholars to write upon wax laid on a board of boxed wood, in which they formed the letters with an iron style or pencil, sharp at one end, but blunt and smooth at the other, to erase what was to be effaced or corrected.

Cassian was exposed naked in the middle of two hundred boys; among whom some threw their tablets, pencils, and penknives at his face and head, and often broke them upon his body; others cut his flesh, or stabbed him with their penknives, and others pierced him with their pencils, sometimes only tearing the skin and flesh, and sometimes raking in his very bowels. Some made it their barbarous sport to cut part of their writing-task in his tender skin. Thus, covered with his own blood, and wounded in every part of his body, he cheerfully bade his little executioners not to be afraid; and to strike him with greater force; not meaning to encourage them in this sin, but to express the ardent desire he had to die for Christ.

Alban Butler, The Lives of the Saints, Dublin, 1833, volume 2, pp 230-31

Trypho and Respicius

Trypho and Respicius were Christians from Apamea, in Bithynia. The irenarch, head of police, had arrested the Christians in response to Decius' edict and had brought them to Nicaea for trial. They were told that they must choose between sacrificing to the gods and being burned alive. They said that to be burned alive for Christ would be a great privilege, and encouraged the magistrate to carry out the edict's instructions.

"Sacrifice," said the magistrate. "I see that you are mature, intelligent people."

"Ah," cried Trypho, "in our Lord Jesus Christ we have indeed a good understanding."

As the command was given that they should be tortured they threw off their clothes and freely offered themselves to their executors. This went on for three hours. The judge, who did not want them to be killed if it could be helped, sent them back to prison. It was a common practice for Roman governors, when they wanted prisoners to comply with their demands, to take them with them from place to place, loaded down with chains and fetters. The governor of Bithynia was going on a hunting expedition, and he forced Trypho and Respicius to go with him. It was bitter winter weather, and the ground was frozen hard, so Trypho's and Respicius' feet were covered with chilblains.

When the expedition was over, they were examined. "Will you be corrected in the future?" the magistrate asked.

"We correct ourselves every day, before the Lord," Trypho answered, "whom we serve without ceasing." They were returned to prison and when they were next brought out before the magistrate, he said to them, "Have compassion on yourselves, and sacrifice to the gods. I think that you are beginning to become wise." But these kind words could not make them change their minds.

"The best compassion we can show ourselves is to unwaveringly confess our Lord Jesus Christ, the true Judge, who shall come to judge everyone's deeds."

The magistrate ordered nails to be hammered through their feet and then for them to walk through the wintry streets of the town. The men said that the nails had only pierced their shoes, and not their flesh. The magistrate, astonished at their perseverance, had their hands tied behind their backs and had them thrashed until their persecutors were exhausted. The claw and the torches followed, but without effect. At last the judge said, "Stop being stupid. Think how men of your age should act."

Respicius answered that they would never bow down to stocks and stones, because they served the true God, and him only, "As we have such a Lord," he said, "no pains can ever separate us from his love."

The following day the judge ordered them to be beaten with loaded thongs. Then he read out this judgement: "These Phrygian youths, who are Christians, and refuse to obey the imperial commands, are sentenced to be beheaded." The martyrs were led out to be executed. They lifted up their hands, crying to the Lord Jesus Christ to receive their souls, and so submitted to the penalty that had been pronounced on them.

A. J. Mason, The Historic Martyrs of the Primitive Church, Longmans, 1905, pp 140-1

NESTOR

Nestor was bishop of Perga, Pamphylia's leading city, during Decius' reign, where St Paul landed after coming from Cyprus on his first missionary journey. Bishop Nestor was brought before governor Epolius of Lycia and Pamphylia, in chains.

GOVERNOR EPOLIUS: Are you the teacher of the Christian religion?

BISHOP NESTOR: If you have already information about me you need ask no more questions, as I am glad to tell you that I am the teacher and guide of the Christians at Perga.

GOVERNOR EPOLIUS: Leave your vain religion and turn to the immortal gods.

BISHOP NESTOR: You may inflict every kind of torture on my body, and throw me to the fire or for food to the wild beasts, but I will never deny the name of Christ, which is above every name. Who would be so stupid to turn from the Creator God and offer sacrifices to wicked devils and unconscious images?

GOVERNOR EPOLIUS: Do you teach, then, that the world was made by the Crucified One?

BISHOP NESTOR: The co-eternal Son and Word of God, who sits on his Father's throne, beheld the infatuation you Greeks have for the creatures around you, and your misguided devotion to images which cannot help you, and had divine compassion for the work of his own hands. He would have all men to be saved and come to the knowledge of the truth. Since it was impossible for men to look on his godhead without an intermediary, it pleased him to live among men under a veil, and teach them the way of salvation through suffering. But for his voluntary act of surrendering his flesh to the infuriated Jews to be crucified, we Christians would not be able to despise the torments which you think fit to inflict on us.

GOVERNOR EPOLIUS: You have presumed on my self-restraint to prolong your meaningless talk. Now leave this vain hope, and come and sacrifice, that your life may not end abruptly and in sorrow.

BISHOP NESTOR: I have already told you that you have my consent to do with me as you think fit. Bodily pains will not move me away from the faith of the true God, my Savior.

GOVERNOR EPOLIUS: Hang this piece of adamant on the wood and let him be well scraped and currycombed. [The order was executed, but Nestor did not utter a word.] Tell me in one word, will you be with us, or with your Christ?

BISHOP NESTOR: With my Christ I am, and always was, and always will be.

Epolius ordered him to be taken to the field outside the town, and there fastened with nails through all his joints, and left there, guarded by soldiers to die a lingering death. As he hung there Nestor encouraged the Christians who came close to him to persevere in their Christian profession of the one who suffered for them. After many hours death released him.

A. J. Mason, The Historic Martyrs of the Primitive Church, Longmans, 1905, pp 141-4

How should Christians conduct themselves when persecuted?

Chapter 37

Unjust persecutions endured for Christ's name are sights worthy of God. Brave pagans and holy martyrs are compared with each other. Christians do not attend public shows and processions are they are sacrilegious and cruel.

How beautiful is the spectacle to God when a Christian does battle with pain; when he is drawn up against threats, and punishments, and tortures; when, mocking the noise of death, he treads under foot the horror of the executioner; when he raises up his liberty against kings and princes, and yields to God alone, whose he is; when, triumphant and victorious, he tramples upon the very man who has pronounced sentence against him! For he has conquered who has obtained that for which he contends. What soldier would not provoke peril with greater boldness under the eyes of his general? For no one receives a reward before his trial, and yet the general does not give what he has not: he cannot preserve life, but he can make the warfare glorious. But God's soldier is neither forsaken in suffering, nor is brought to an end by death. Thus the Christian may seem to be miserable; he cannot be really found to be so. You yourselves extol unfortunate men to the skies; Mucius Scaevola, for instance, who, when he had failed in his attempt against the king, would have perished among the enemies unless he had sacrificed his right hand. And how many of our people have borne that not their right hand only, but their whole body, should be burned–burned up without any cries of pain, especially when they had it in their power to be sent away! Do I compare men with Mucius or Aquilius, or with Regulus? Yet boys and young women among us treat with contempt crosses and tortures, wild beasts, and all the bugbears of punishments, with the inspired patience of suffering. And do you not perceive, O wretched men, that there is nobody who either is willing without reason to undergo punishment, or is able without God to bear tortures? Unless, perhaps, the fact has deceived you, that those who know not God abound in riches, flourish in honors, and excel in power. Miserable men! in this respect they are lifted up the higher, that they may fall down lower. For these are fattened as victims for punishment, as sacrifices they are crowned for the slaughter. Thus in this respect some are lifted up to empires and dominations, that the unrestrained exercise of power might make a market of their spirit to the unbridled licence that is Characteristic of a ruined soul. For, apart from the knowledge of God, what solid happiness can there be, since death must come? Like a dream, happiness slips away before it is grasped. Are you a king? Yet you fear as much as you are feared; and however you may be surrounded with abundant followers, yet you are alone in the presence of danger. Are you rich? But fortune is ill trusted; and with a large traveling equipage the brief journey of life is not furnished, but burdened. Do you boast of the fasces and the magisterial robes? It is a vain mistake of man, and an empty worship of dignity, to glitter in purple and to be sordid in hind. Are you elevated by nobility of birth? do you praise your parents? Yet we are all born with one lot; it is only by virtue that we are distinguished. We therefore, who are estimated by our character and our modesty, reasonably abstain from evil pleasures, and from your pomps and exhibitions, the origin of which in connection with sacred things we know, and condemn their mischievous enticements. For in the chariot games who does not shudder at the madness of the people brawling among themselves? or at the teaching of murder in the gladiatorial games? In the scenic games also the madness is not less, but the debauchery is more prolonged: for now a mimic either expounds or shows forth adulteries; now nerveless player, while he feigns lust, suggests it; the same actor disgraces your gods by attributing to them adulteries, sighs, hatreds; the same provokes your tears with pretended sufferings, with vain gestures and expressions. Thus you demand murder, in fact, while you weep at it in fiction.

The Octavius of Minucius Felix

TORTURES OF THE FIRST CHRISTIAN MARTYRS (4) SCOURGING

The heathen, after they had bound Christians to the horse, frequently beat them pitifully with rods, cudgels, and whips.

a. Lashes

The lashes as used by the ancients were thongs made of leather, employed usually for the correction of slaves.

b. Cudgels

* Martyrs were tied to a post set upright in the ground, or to a stake or pillar, and persistently beaten with cudgels, strong wooden staffs, until they died.
* Martyrs were also bound to four stakes, by their wrists and ankles and beaten with cudgels.
* Martyrs were laid naked on iron spikes and violently beaten with a cudgel.
* Martyrs were bound hand and foot, laid on the ground, and beaten with a cudgel.

c. Rods

* Rods for beating offenders were generally made of thin twigs of trees, but sometimes they were made from iron or lead.
* The custom of the Ancients was, when prisoners were scourged, first to strip the same, and then to whip them over the back, or belly, or other portion of the body, with rods or other instruments of flagellation.

d. Scorpions

Scorpions were knotty or prickly rods.

e. Loaded scourges

Loaded scourges were a sort of whipping instrument made of cords or thongs, with little lead balls attached to the ends, which were inflicted on the loins, back and neck of a condemned person.

f. Martyrs were buffeted, kicked and pounded with fists.

g. Martyrs were stoned to death.

h. Martyrs had their faces bruised and jaws broken with stones.

i. Martyrs were crushed under huge stones.

In the Acts of the Blessed Martyr St Theopompus it is written: "Hereon the holy man was led forth from his prison and stretched face upward on the ground and bound fast to stakes. Then, a huge boulder, which eight men could hardly lift, was laid on his belly."

Tortures and Torments of the Christian Martyrs, from the De SS. Martyrum Cruciatibus of the Rev Father Gallonio, translated by A. R. Allinson, London and Paris: printed for the subscribers, 1903 pp 91-4

THE MARTYRS IN ALEXANDRIA

Martyrs who suffered at Alexandria during Decius' reign 249-51

Eusebius, in a letter to Fabius, bishop of Antioch, relates as follows the sufferings of the martyrs in Alexandria under Decius.

The persecution among us did not begin with the royal decree, but preceded it an entire year. The prophet and author of evils to this city, whoever he was, previously moved and aroused against us the masses of the heathen, rekindling among them the superstition of their country. And being thus excited by him and finding full opportunity for any wickedness, they considered this the only pious service of their demons, that they should slay.

They seized first an old man named Metras, and commanded him to utter impious words. But as he would not obey, they beat him with clubs, and tore his face and eyes with sharp sticks, and dragged him out of the city and stoned him. Then they carried to their idol temple a faithful woman, named Quinta, that they might force her to worship. And as she turned away in detestation, they bound her feet and dragged her through the entire city over the stone-paved streets, and dashed her against the millstones, and at the same time scourged her; then, taking her to the same place, they stoned her to death. Then all with one impulse rushed to the homes of the pious, and they dragged forth whomsoever any one knew as a neighbor, and despoiled and plundered them. They took for themselves the more valuable property; but the poorer articles and those made of wood they scattered about and burned in the streets, so that the city appeared as if taken by an enemy. But the brethren withdrew and went away, and "took joyfully the spoiling of their goods," like those to whom Paul bore witness. I know of no one unless possibly some one who fell into their hands, who, up to this time, denied the Lord. Then they seized also that most admirable virgin, Apollonia, an old woman, and, smiting her on the jaws, broke out all her teeth. And they made a fire outside the city and threatened to burn her alive if she would not join with them in their impious cries. And she, supplicating a little, was released, when she leaped eagerly into the fire and was consumed. Then they seized Serapion in his own house, and tortured him with harsh cruelties, and having broken all his limbs, they threw him headlong from an upper story. And there was no street, nor public road, nor lane open to us, by night or day; for always and everywhere, all of them cried out that if any one would not repeat their impious words, he should immediately be dragged away and burned. And matters continued thus for a considerable time.

But a sedition and civil war came upon the wretched people and turned their cruelty toward us against one another. So we breathed for a little while as they ceased from their rage against us. But presently the change from that milder reign was announced to us, and great fear of what was threatened seized us. For the decree arrived, almost like unto that most terrible time foretold by our Lord, which if it were possible would offend even the elect.

All truly were affrighted. And many of the more eminent in their fear came forward immediately; others who were in the public service were drawn on by their official duties; others were urged on by their acquaintances. And as their names were called they approached the impure and impious sacrifices. Some of them were pale and trembled as if they were not about to sacrifice, but to be themselves sacrifices and offerings to the idols; so that they were jeered at by the multitude who stood around, as it was plain to every one that they were afraid either to die or to sacrifice. But some advanced to the altars more readily, declaring boldly that they had never been Christians. Of these the prediction of our Lord is most true that they shall "hardly" be saved. Of the rest some followed the one, others the other of these classes, some fled and some were seized. And of the latter some continued faithful until bonds and imprisonment, and some who had even been imprisoned for many days yet abjured the faith before they were brought to trial. Others having for a time endured great tortures finally retracted. But the firm and blessed pillars of the Lord being strengthened by him, and having received vigor and might suitable and appropriate to the strong faith which they possessed, became admirable witnesses of his kingdom. The first of these was Julian, a man who suffered so much with the gout that he was unable to stand or walk. They brought him forward with two others who carried him.

One of these immediately denied. But the other, whose name was Cronion, and whose surname was Eunus, and the old man Julian himself, both of them having confessed the Lord, were carried on camels through the entire city, which, as you know, is a very large one, and in this elevated position were beaten and finally burned in a fierce fire, surrounded by all the populace.

But a soldier, named Besas, who stood by them as they were led away rebuked those who insulted them. And they cried out against him, and this most manly warrior of God was arraigned, and having done nobly in the great contest for piety, was beheaded. A certain other one, a Libyan by birth, but in name and blessedness a true Macar, was strongly urged by the judge to recant; but as he would not yield he was burned alive. After them Epimachus and Alexander, having remained in bonds for a long time, and endured countless agonies from scrapers and scourges, were also consumed in a fierce fire. And with them there were four women. Ammonarium, a holy virgin, the judge tortured relentlessly and excessively, because she declared from the first that she would utter none of those things which he commanded; and having kept her promise truly, she was dragged away. The others were Mercuria, a very remarkable old woman, and Dionysia, the mother of many children, who did not love her own children above the Lord. As the governor was ashamed of torturing thus ineffectually, and being always defeated by women, they were put to death by the sword, without the trial of tortures. For the champion, Ammonarium, endured these in behalf of all.

The Egyptians, Heron and Ater and Isidorus, and with them Dioscorus, a boy about fifteen years old, were delivered up. At first the judge attempted to deceive the lad by fair words, as if he could be brought over easily, and then to force him by tortures, as one who would readily yield. But Dioscorus was neither persuaded nor constrained. As the others remained firm, he scourged them cruelly and then delivered them to the fire. But admiring the manner in which Dioscorus had distinguished himself publicly, and his wise answers to his persuasions, he dismissed him, saying that on account of his youth he would give him time for repentance. And this most godly Dioscorus is among us now, awaiting a longer conflict and more severe contest.

But a certain Nemesion, who also was an Egyptian, was accused as an associate of robbers; but when he had cleared himself before the centurion of this charge most foreign to the truth, he was informed against as a Christian, and taken in bonds before the governor. And the most unrighteous magistrate inflicted on him tortures and scourgings double those which he executed on the robbers, and then burned him between the robbers, thus honoring the blessed man by the likeness to Christ.

A band of soldiers, Ammon and Zeno and Ptolemy and Ingenes, and with them an old man, Theophilus, were standing close together before the tribunal. And as a certain person who was being tried as a Christian, seemed inclined to deny, they standing by gnashed their teeth, and made signs with their faces and stretched out their hands, and gestured with their bodies. And when the attention of all was turned to them, before any one else could seize them, they rushed up to the tribunal saying that they were Christians, so that the governor and his council were affrighted. And those who were on trial appeared most courageous in prospect of their sufferings, while their judges trembled. And they went exultingly from the tribunal rejoicing in their testimony; God himself having caused them to triumph gloriously."

Others of whom Dionysius gives an Account

Many others, in cities and villages, were torn asunder by the heathen, of whom I will mention one as an illustration. Ischyrion was employed as a steward by one of the rulers. His employer commanded him to sacrifice, and on his refusal insulted him, and as he remained firm, abused him. And as he still held out he seized a long staff and thrust it through his bowels and slew him.

Why need I speak of the multitude that wandered in the deserts and mountains, and perished by hunger, and thirst, and cold, and sickness, and robbers, and wild beasts? Those of them who survived are witnesses of their election and victory. But I will relate one occurrence as an example. Chaeremon, who was very old, was bishop of the city called Nilus. He fled with his wife to the Arabian mountain and did not return. And though the brethren searched diligently they could not find either them or their bodies. And many who fled to the same Arabian mountain were carried into slavery by the barbarian Saracens. Some of them were ransomed with difficulty and at a large price others have not been to the present time. I have related these things, my brother, not without an object, but that you may understand how many and great distresses came upon us. Those indeed will understand them the best who have had the largest experience of them.

A little further on he adds: These divine martyrs among us, who now are seated with Christ, and are sharers in his kingdom, partakers of his judgment and judges with him, received some of the brethren who had fallen away and become chargeable with the guilt of sacrificing. When they perceived that their conversion and repentance were sufficient to be acceptable with him who by no means desires the death of the sinner, but his repentance, having proved them they received them back and brought them together, and met with them and had fellowship with them in prayers and feasts. What counsel then, brethren, do you give us concerning such persons? What should we do? Shall we have the same judgment and rule as theirs, and observe their decision and charity, and show mercy to those whom they pitied? Or, shall we declare their decision unrighteous, and set ourselves as judges of their opinion, and grieve mercy and overturn order?

These words Dionysius very properly added when making mention of those who had been weak in the time of persecution.
Eusebius of Caesarea, Church History, Book 6, chapter 41

POLYEUCTUS

At the same time that the martyrs of Alexandria were killed in the district of Melitene, near to the border of Armenia, Polyeuctus was martyred.

Polyeuctus, and his inseparable friend, Nearchus, were soldiers in the same legion. Nearchus was a Christian, but Polyeuctus was not. When Decius' edict was published, Nearchus was greatly upset and stopped befriending Polyeuctus. Polyeuctus asked Nearchus why he did this, and so discovered the danger that now threatened his friend. Polyeuctus decided to throw in his lot with Nearchus. Polyeuctus had a dream which seemed to confirm this decision. In his dream he saw a figure, whom he took to be Christ, approach him and strip him of his dirty military cloak and replace it with a much more glorious one, as bright as light. At the same time his visitor placed him on a winged horse. Polyeuctus reminded Nearchus that he had always listened with respect when he had told him about Christ and read the scriptures to him. He now said that he would expose the stupidity of idolatry, and all the deception that went with it.

Nearchus was delighted with this news, but he doubted that Polyeuctus would be able to resist sacrificing. Polyeuctus was confident about this matter, but just troubled that he might be put to death before he was able to be baptized, and so not be accepted by Christ. Nearchus reassured him about this, telling him that the penitent thief who confessed Christ on the cross was accepted, even though he died unbaptized. Polyeuctus's soul was on fire. He went with Nearchus to the place where Decius' edict was pinned up, read it through scornfully, and then pulled it down and tore it up. A few moments after this a procession carrying idols back to the temple from a tour around the streets passed them. The zeal of the new convert overcame all thought of caution, and Polyeuctus went up to the idols, threw them on the ground and trampled on them.

Felix, the local magistrate who had to enforce the edict, was Polyeuctus's father-in-law. He was deeply upset about what had happened. He pleaded with Polyeuctus to do nothing more until he had spoken with his wife. Polyeuctus replied that his wife and child meant nothing to him if they did not follow the same path that he had taken. The attendants beat Polyeuctus's face with rods for saying this, but Polyeuctus remained unmoved. Polyeuctus then rebuked his father-in-law for giving himself over to the ungodly will of perishing people, and for trying to deflect his love for his Savior by mentioning his wife and child. Polyeuctus's wife, crying her heart out, came to him and told him off for breaking "the twelve god". Polyeuctus told her that there were plenty more gods like that and pleaded with her to follow his religious conversion and take hold of eternal life.

Felix conferred with his advisors and then sentenced Polyeuctus to death by being beheaded. The martyr waited calmly for the death sentence to be carried out, talking all the time with his fellow Christians. He saw, he said, a young man leading him on – doubtless he meant Christ – and felt sure that, unbaptized as he was, the seal of Christ was on him. His last words, words of encouragement and affection, were spoken to his friend Nearchus.

A. J. Mason, The Historic Martyrs of the Primitive Church, Longmans, 1905, pp 121-2

AGATHA, MARTYRED 251

Feast: February 5

We have her panegyrics, by St. Aldhelm, in the seventh, and St. Methodius, Patriarch of Constantinople, in the ninth centuries; also a hymn in her honor among the poems of Pope Damasus, and another by St. Isidore of Seville, in Bollandus, p. 596. The Greeks have interpolated her acts; but those in Latin are very ancient. They are abridged by Tillemont, t. 3, p. 409. See also Rocci Pyrrho, in Sicilia Sacra, on Palermo, Catana, and Malta.

The cities of Palermo and Catana, in Sicily, dispute the honor of her birth; but they do much better who, by copying her virtues, and claiming her patronage, strive to become her fellow-citizens in heaven. It is agreed that she received the crown of martyrdom at Catana, in the persecution of Decius, in the third consulship of that prince, in the year of our Lord 251. She was of a rich and illustrious family, and having been consecrated to God from her tender years, triumphed over many assaults upon her chastity. Quintianus, a man of consular dignity, bent on gratifying both his lust and avarice, imagined he should easily compass his wicked designs on Agatha's person and estate by means of the emperor's edict against the Christians. He therefore caused her to be apprehended and brought before him at Catana. Seeing herself in the hands of the persecutors, she made this prayer: "Jesus Christ, Lord of all things, you see my heart, you know my desire-possess alone all that I am. I am your sheep, make me worthy to overcome the devil." She wept, and prayed for courage and strength all the way she went. On her appearance, Quintianus gave orders for her being put into the hands of Aphrodisia, a most wicked woman, who, with six daughters, all prostitutes, kept a common stew. The saint suffered in this infamous place assaults and stratagems against her virtue infinitely more terrible to her than any tortures or death itself. But placing her confidence in God, she never ceased with sighs and most earnest tears to implore his protection, and by it was an overmatch for all their hellish attempts the whole month she was there. Quintianus, being informed of her constancy after thirty days, ordered her to be brought before him. The virgin, in her first interrogatory, told him that to be a servant of Jesus Christ was the most illustrious nobility and true liberty. The judge, offended at her resolute answers, commanded her to be buffeted and led to prison. She entered it with great joy, recommending her future conflict to God. The next day she was arraigned a second time at the tribunal, and answered with equal constancy that Jesus Christ was her life and her salvation. Quintianus then ordered her to be stretched on the rack, which torment was usually accompanied with stripes, the tearing of the sides with iron hooks, and burning them with torches or matches. The governor, enraged to see her suffer all this with cheerfulness, commanded her breast to be tortured, and afterwards to be cut off. At which she made him this reproach: "Cruel tyrant, do you not blush to torture this part of my body, you that sucked the breasts of a woman yourself? "He remanded her to prison, with a severe order that neither salves nor food should be allowed her. But God would be himself her physician, and the apostle St. Peter in a vision comforted her, healed all her wounds,. and filled her dungeon with a heavenly light.

Quintianus, four days after, not the least moved at the miraculous cure of her wounds, caused her to be rolled naked over live coals mixed with broken potsherds. Being carried back to prison, she made this prayer: "Lord, my Creator, you have ever protected me from the cradle; you have taken me from the love of the world, and given me patience to suffer: receive now my soul." After which words she sweetly gave up the ghost. Her name is inserted in the canon of the mass in the calendar of Carthage, as ancient as the year 530, and in all martyrologies of the Latins and Greeks. Pope Symmachus built a church in Rome on the Aurelian Way under her name, about the year 500, which is fallen to decay. St. Gregory the Great enriched a church which he purged from the Arian impiety with her relics, which it still possesses. This church had been rebuilt in her honor by Ricimer, general of the Western Empire, in 460. Gregory II built another famous church at Rome, under her invocation, in 726, which Clement VIII gave to the congregation of the Christian doctrine. St. Gregory the Great ordered some of her relics to be placed in the church of the monastery of St. Stephen, in the Isle of Capreae, now Capri. The chief part, which remained at Catana, was carried to Constantinople by the Greek general, who drove the Saracens out of Sicily about the year 1040; these were brought back to Catana in 1127, a relation of which translation, written by Mauritius, who was then bishop, is recorded by Rocci Pyrrho and Bollandus. The same authors relate in what manner the torrent of burning sulphur and stones which issue from mount Aetna, in great eruptions, was several times averted from the walls of Catana by the veil of St. Agatha, (taken out of her tomb,) which was carried in procession. Also that through her inter. cession, Malta (where she is honored as patroness of the island) was pre served from the Turks who invaded it in 1551. Small portions of relics cf. St. Agatha are said to be distributed in many places.

The perfect purity of intention by which St. Agatha was entirely dead to the world and herself, and sought only to please God, is the circumstance which sanctified her sufferings, and rendered her sacrifice complete. The least cross which we bear, the least action which we perform in this disposition, will be a great holocaust, and a most acceptable offering. We have frequently something to offer – sometimes an aching pain in the body, at other times some trouble of mind, often some disappointment, some humbling rebuke, or reproach, or the like. If we only bear these trials with patience when others are witnesses, or if we often speak of them, or are fretful under them, or if we bear patiently public affronts or great trials, yet sink under those which are trifling, and are sensible to small or secret injuries, it is evident that we have not attained to true purity of intention in our patience; that we are not dead to ourselves. We profess ourselves ready to die for Christ, yet cannot bear the least cross or humiliation. How agreeable to our divine spouse is the sacrifice of a soul which suffers in silence, desiring to have no other witness of her patience than God alone, who sends her trials; which shuns superiority and honors, but takes all care possible that no one knows the humility or modesty of such a refusal; which suffers humiliations and seeks no comfort or reward but from God. This simplicity and purity of heart; this love of being hid in God, through Jesus Christ, is the perfection of all our sacrifices, and the complete victory over self-love, which it attacks and forces out of its strongest entrenchments: this says to Christ, with St. Agatha, "Possess alone all that I am."

Alban Butler, The Lives of the Saints, Dublin, 1833, volume 1

Homily on Agatha

My fellow Christians, our annual celebration of a martyr's feast has brought us together. Agatha achieved renown in the early Church for her noble victory. For her, Christ's death was recent, his blood was still moist. Her robe is the mark of her faithful witness to Christ.

Agatha, the name of our saint, means "good." She was truly good, for she lived as a child of God. Agatha, her goodness coincides with her name and her way of life. She won a good name by her noble deeds, and by her name she points to the nobility of those deeds. Agatha, her mere name wins all men over to her company. She teaches them by her example to hasten with her to the true Good, God alone.

Extract from a homily on Agatha by Methodius of Sicily

Martyrdom of Lawrence (1)

Laurence, Deacon and Martyr
10 August 258

Laurence (or Lawrence) was chief of the seven deacons of the congregation at Rome, the seven men who, like Stephen and his companions (Acts 6:1-6), were in charge of administering the church budget, particularly with regard to the care of the poor. In 257, the emperor Valerian began a persecution aimed chiefly at the clergy and the laity of the upper classes. All Church property was confiscated and meetings of Christians were forbidden. The bishop of Rome, Sixtus II, and most of his clergy were executed on 7 August 258, and Laurence on the 10th. This much from the near-contemporary records of the Church.

The accounts recorded about a century later by Ambrose (see 7 Dec) and the poet Prudentius say that, as Sixtus was being led to his death, Laurence followed him, saying, "Will you go to heaven and leave me behind?" and that the bishop replied, "Be comforted, you will follow me in three days." They go on to say that the Roman prefect, knowing that Laurence was the principal financial officer, promised to set him free if he would surrender the wealth of the Church. Laurence agreed, but said that it would take him three days to gather it. During those three days, he placed all the money at his disposal in the hands of trustworthy stewards, and then assembled the sick, the aged, and the poor, the widows and orphans of the congregation, presented them to the prefect, and said, "These are the treasures of the Church." The enraged prefect ordered him to be roasted alive on a gridiron. Laurence bore the torture with great calmness, saying to his executioners at one time, "You may turn me over; I am done on this side." The spectacle of his courage made a great impression on the people of Rome, and made many converts, while greatly reducing among pagans the belief that Christianity was a socially undesirable movement that should be stamped out.

The details of these later accounts have been disputed, on the grounds that a Roman citizen would have been beheaded. However, it is not certain that Laurence was a citizen, or that the prefect could be counted on to observe the law if he were. More serious objections are these:

The detailed accounts of the martyrdom of Laurence confuse the persecution under Decius with the persecution under Valerian, describing the latter, not as an emperor, but as the prefect of Rome under the emperor Decius.

We have early testimony that Bishop Sixtus and his deacons were not led away to execution, but were summarily beheaded on the scene of their arrest.

For these reasons, the Bollandist Pere Delahaye and others believe that Laurence was simply beheaded in 258 with his bishop and fellow deacons. On this theory, it remains unexplained how he became so prominent and acquired so elaborate an account of his martyrdom.

Lawrence's emblem in art is (naturally) a gridiron.

James Kiefer, Christian Biographies, By kind permission

Martyrdom of Lawrence (2)

Laurentius (St Laurence)

"These are the true treasures of the church." (Laurentius)

Emperor Valerian governed with moderation, and treated the Christians with special leniency and respect; but in the year 257, an Egyptian magician, named Macriamus, gained a great ascendancy over him, and persuaded him to persecute the Christians. Edicts were accordingly published, and the persecution lasted for three and a half years.

Laurentius, generally called Laurence, the principal of the deacons, was taught and preached under Sextus, Bishop of Rome, and followed him to the place of execution; when Sextus predicted that he should met him in heaven three days after. Laurentius considering this as a certain indication of his own approaching martyrdom, on his return collected all the Christian poor, and distributed among them the treasures of the church which had been committed to his care, thinking the money could not be better disposed of, or less liable to fall into the hands of pagans. His conduct alarmed the persecutors, who seized him, and commanded him to give an immediate account to the emperor of the church treasures.

Laurentius promised to satisfy them, but begged a short respite to put things in proper order: three days being granted him, he was suffered to depart. Then with great diligence he collected together a great number of aged, and helpless poor, and went to the magistrate, presenting them to him, saying: "These are the true treasures of the church."

Provoked at this disappointment, and thinking that he was being ridiculed, the governor ordered Laurentius to be immediately scourged. He was beaten with iron rods, set upon a wooden horse, and had his limbs dislocated. He endured these tortures with such fortitude and perseverance, that he was ordered to be fastened to a large gridiron, with a slow fire under it, that his death might be more tedious. But his astonishing constancy during these trials, and his serenity of countenance under such excruciating torments, gave the spectators so exalted an idea of the dignity and truth of the Christian religion, that many immediately became converts.

Having lain for some time upon the gridiron, the martyr called out to the emperor, who was present, in a kind of jocose Latin couplet, which may be thus translated:

This side is broil'd sufficient to be food
For all who wish it to be done and good."

On this the executioner turned him, and after having lain a considerable time longer, he had still strength and spirit enough to triumph over the tyrant, by telling him, with great serenity, that he was roasted enough, and only wanted serving up. He then cheerfully lifted up his eyes to heaven, and with calmness yielded his spirit to the Almighty. This happened on the 10th August 258.

John Foxe, The Book of Martyrs, revised with notes and an appendix by W. Bramley-Moore, London, 1869, pp 23-4

Sermon preached on the Feast of S. Laurence the Martyr (1)

The example of the martyrs is most valuable

Whilst the height of all virtues, dearly-beloved, and the fulness of all righteousness is born of that love, wherewith God and one's neighbor is loved, surely in none is this love found more conspicuous and brighter than in the blessed martyrs; who are as near to our Lord Jesus, Who died for all men, in the imitation of His love, as in the likeness of their suffering. For, although that Love, wherewith the Lord has redeemed us, cannot be equaled by any man's kindness, because it is one thing that a man who is doomed to die one day should die for a righteous man, and another that One Who is free from the debt of sin should lay down His life for the wicked: yet the martyrs also have done great service to all men, in that the Lord Who gave them boldness, has used it to show that the penalty of death and the pain of the cross need not be terrible to any of His followers, but might be imitated by many of them. If therefore no good man is good for himself alone, and no wise man's wisdom befriends himself only, and the nature of true virtue is such that it leads many away from the dark error on which its light is shed, no model is more useful in teaching God's people than that of the martyrs. Eloquence may make intercession easy, reasoning may effectually persuade; but yet examples are stronger than words, and there is more teaching in practice than in precept.

The saint's martyrdom described

And how gloriously strong in this most excellent manner of doctrine the blessed martyr Laurentius is, by whose sufferings to-day is marked, even his persecutors were able to feel, when they found that his wondrous courage, born principally of love for Christ, not only did not yield itself, but also strengthened others by the example of his endurance. For when the fury of the gentile potentates was raging against Christ's most chosen members, and attacked those especially who were of priestly rank, the wicked persecutor's wrath was vented on Laurentius the deacon, who was pre-eminent not only in the performance of the sacred rites, but also in the management of the church's property , promising himself double spoil from one man's capture: for if he forced him to surrender the sacred treasures, he would also drive him out of the pale of true religion. And so this man, so greedy of money and such a foe to the truth, arms himself with double weapon: with avarice to plunder the gold; with impiety to carry off Christ. He demands of the guileless guardian of the sanctuary that the church wealth on which his greedy mind was set should be brought to him. But the holy deacon showed him where he had them stored, by pointing to the many troops of poor saints, in the feeding and clothing of whom he had a store of riches which he could hot lose, and which were the more entirely safe that the money had been spent on so holy a cause.

The description of his sufferings continued

The baffled plunderer, therefore, frets, and blazing out into hatred of a religion, which had put riches to such a use, determines to pillage a still greater treasure by carrying off that sacred deposit , wherewith he was enriched, as he could find no solid hoard of money in his possession. He orders Laurentius to renounce Christ, and prepares to ply the deacon's stout courage with frightful tortures: and, when the first elicit nothing, fiercer follow. His limbs, torn and mangled by many cutting blows, are commanded to be broiled upon the fire in an iron framework , which was of itself already hot enough to burn him, and on which his limbs were turned from time to time, to make the torment fiercer, and the death more lingering.

Laurentius has conquered his persecutor

Thou gainest nothing, thou prevailest nothing, O savage cruelty. His mortal frame is released from thy devices, and, when Laurentius departs to heaven, thou art vanquished. The flame of Christ's love could not be overcome by thy flames, and the fire which burnt outside was less keen than that which blazed within. Thou didst but serve the martyr in thy rage, O persecutor: thou didst but swell the reward in adding to the pain. For what did thy cunning devise, which did not redound to the conqueror's glory, when even the instruments of torture were counted as part of the triumph? Let us rejoice, then, dearly- beloved, with spiritual joy, and make our boast over the happy end of this illustrious man in the Lord, Who is "wonderful in His saints," in whom He has given us a support and an example, and has so spread abroad his glory throughout the world, that, from the rising of the sun to its going down, the brightness of his deacon's light doth shine, and Rome is become as famous in Laurentius as Jerusalem was ennobled by Stephen. By his prayer and intercession we trust at all times to be assisted; that, because all, as the Apostle says, "who wish to live holily in Christ, suffer persecution," we may be strengthened with the spirit of love, and be fortified to overcome all temptations by the perseverance of steadfast faith. Through our Lord Jesus Christ, etc.

Leo, Sermon 85

Sermon preached on the Feast of S. Laurence the Martyr (2)

The Roman Church commends to us today the anniversary of the triumph of Saint Lawrence. For on this day he trod the furious pagan world underfoot and flung aside its allurements, and so gained victory over Satan's attack on his faith.

As you have often heard, Lawrence was a deacon of the Church at Rome. There he ministered the sacred blood of Christ; there for the sake of Christ's name he poured out his own blood. Saint John the apostle was evidently teaching us about the mystery of the Lord's supper when he wrote: "Just as Christ laid down his life for us, so we ought to lay down our lives for the brethren." My brethren, Lawrence understood this and, understanding, he acted on it. In his life he loved Christ; in his death he followed in his footsteps.

Brethren, we too must imitate Christ if we truly love him. We shall not be able to render better return on that love than by modeling our lives on his. "Christ suffered for us, leaving us an example, that we should follow in his steps." The holy martyrs followed Christ even to shedding their life's blood, even to reproducing the very likeness of his passion. They followed him, but not they alone. It is not true that the bridge was broken after the martyrs crossed; nor is it true that after they had drunk from it, the fountain of eternal life dried up.

On no account may any class of people despair, thinking that God has not called them. Christ suffered for all. What the Scriptures say of him is true: "He desires all men to be saved and to come to knowledge of the truth."

I tell you again and again, my brethren, that on no account may any class of people despair, thinking that God has not called them. Christ suffered for all. What the Scriptures say of him is true: "He desires all men to be saved and to come to knowledge of the truth."

Extract from a sermon by Saint Augustine

THE PUPILS OF ORIGEN WHO BECAME MARTYRS

The first of these was Plutarch, who was mentioned just above. As he was led to death the man of whom we are speaking being with him at the end of his life, came near being slain by his fellow-citizens, as if he were the cause of his death. But the providence of God preserved him at this time also.

After Plutarch, the second martyr among the pupils of Origen was Serenus, who gave through fire a proof of the faith which he had received.

The third martyr from the same school was Heraclides, and after him the fourth was Hero. The former of these was as yet a catechumen, and the latter had but recently been baptized. Both of them were beheaded. After them, the fifth from the same school proclaimed as an athlete of piety was another Serenus, who, it is reported, was beheaded, after a long endurance of tortures. And of women, Herais died while yet a catechumen, receiving baptism by fire, as Origen himself somewhere says.

Basilides may be counted the seventh of these. He led to martyrdom the celebrated Potamiaena, who is still famous among the people of the country for the many things which she endured for the preservation of her chastity and virginity. For she was blooming in the perfection of her mind and her physical graces. Having suffered much for the faith of Christ, finally after tortures dreadful and terrible to speak of, she with her mother, Marcella, was put to death by fire.

They say that the judge, Aquila by name, having inflicted severe tortures upon her entire body, at last threatened to hand her over to the gladiators for bodily abuse. After a little consideration, being asked for her decision, she made a reply which was regarded as impious.

Thereupon she received sentence immediately. and Basilides, one of the officers of the army, led her to death. But as the people attempted to annoy and insult her with abusive words, he drove back her insulters, showing her much pity and kindness. And perceiving the man's sympathy for her, she exhorted him to be of good courage, for she would supplicate her Lord for him after her departure, and he would soon receive a reward for the kindness he had shown her.

Having said this, she nobly sustained the issue, burning pitch being poured little by little, over various parts of her body, from the sole of her feet to the crown of her head. Such was the conflict endured by this famous maiden.

Not long after this Basilides, being asked by his fellow-soldiers to swear for a certain reason, declared that it was not lawful for him to swear at all, for he was a Christian, and he confessed this openly. At first they thought that he was jesting, but when he continued to affirm it, he was led to the judge, and, acknowledging his conviction before him, he was imprisoned. But the brethren in God coming to him and inquiring the reason of this sudden and remarkable resolution, he is reported to have said that Potamiaena, for three days after her martyrdom, stood beside him by night and place a crown on his head and said that she had besought the Lord for him and had obtained what she asked, and that soon she would take him with her.

Thereupon the brethren gave him the seal of the Lord; and on the next day, after giving glorious testimony for the Lord, he was beheaded. And many others in Alexandria are recorded to have accepted speedily the word of Christ in those times.

Eusebius, Church History, book 6, chapters 4-5

The Eighth Persecution under Valerian

Gallus and the other rulers, having held the government less than two years, were overthrown, and Valerian, with his son Gallienus, received the empire. The circumstances which Dionysius relates of him we may learn from his epistle to Hermammon, in which he gives the following account:

"And in like manner it is revealed to John; "For there was given to him," he says, "a mouth speaking great things and blasphemy; and there was given unto him authority and forty and two months." It is wonderful that both of these things occurred under Valerian; and it is the more remarkable in this case when we consider his previous conduct, for he had been mild and friendly toward the men of God, for none of the emperors before him had treated them so kindly and favorably; and not even those who were said openly to be Christians received them with such manifest hospitality and friendliness as he did at the beginning of his reign. For his entire house was filled with pious persons and was a church of God.

But the teacher and ruler of the synagogue of the Magi from Egypt persuaded him to change his course, urging him to slay and persecute pure and holy men because they opposed and hindered the corrupt and abominable incantations. For there are and there were men who, being present and being seen, though they only breathed and spoke, were able to scatter the counsels of the sinful demons. And he induced him to practice initiations and abominable sorceries and to offer unacceptable sacrifices; to slay innumerable children and to sacrifice the offspring of unhappy fathers; to divide the bowels of new-born babes and to mutilate and cut to pieces the creatures of God, as if by such practices they could attain happiness."

He adds to this the following: "Splendid indeed were the thank-offerings which Macrianus brought them for the empire which was the object of his hopes. He is said to have been formerly the emperor's general finance minister; yet he did nothing praiseworthy or of general benefit, but fell under the prophetic saying, "Woe unto those who prophesy from their own heart and do not consider the general good." For he did not perceive the general Providence, nor did he look for the judgment of Him who is before all, and through all, and over all. Wherefore he became an enemy of his Catholic Church, and alienated and estranged himself from the compassion of God, and fled as far as possible from his salvation. In this he showed the truth of his own name."

And again, farther on he says: "For Valerian, being instigated to such acts by this man, was given over to insults and reproaches, according to what was said by Isaiah: "They have chosen their own ways and their abominations in which their soul delighted; I also will choose their delusions and will render unto them their sins." But this man madly desired the kingdom though unworthy of it, and being unable to put the royal garment on his crippled body, set forward his two sons to bear their father's sins. For concerning them the declaration which God spoke was plain, "Visiting the iniquities of the fathers upon the children unto the third and fourth generation of them that hate me." For heaping on the heads of his sons his own evil desires, in which he had met with success, he wiped off upon them his own wickedness and hatred toward God."

Dionysius relates these things concerning Valerian.

Eusebius of Caesarea, Church History, Book 7, chapter 10

The Peace under Gallienus

Shortly after this Valerian was reduced to slavery by the barbarians, and his son having become sole ruler, conducted the government more prudently. He immediately restrained the persecution against us by public proclamations, and directed the bishops to perform in freedom their customary duties, in a rescript which ran as follows:

"The Emperor Caesar Publius Licinius Gallienus, Pius, Felix, Augustus, to Dionysius, Pinnas, Demetrius, and the other bishops. I have ordered the bounty of my gift to be declared through all the world, that they may depart from the places of religious worship. And for this purpose you may use this copy of my rescript, that no one may molest you. And this which you are now enabled lawfully to do, has already for a long time been conceded by me. Therefore Aurelius Cyrenius, who is the chief administrator of affairs, will observe this ordinance which I have given."

I have given this in a translation from the Latin, that it may be more readily understood. Another decree of his is extant addressed to other bishops, permitting them to take possession again of the so-called cemeteries.

Eusebius of Caesarea, Church History, Book 7, chapter 13

The Eighth Persecution, Under Valerian, A.D. 257

Began under Valerian, in the month of April, 257, and continued for three years and six months. The martyrs that fell in this persecution were innumerable, and their tortures and deaths as various and painful. The most eminent martyrs were the following, though neither rank, sex, nor age were regarded.

Rufina and Secunda were two beautiful and accomplished ladies, daughters of Asterius, a gentleman of eminence in Rome. Rufina, the elder, was designed in marriage for Armentarius, a young nobleman; Secunda, the younger, for Verinus, a person of rank and opulence. The suitors, at the time of the persecution's commencing, were both Christians; but when danger appeared, to save their fortunes, they renounced their faith. They took great pains to persuade the ladies to do the same, but, disappointed in their purpose, the lovers were base enough to inform against the ladies, who, being apprehended as Christians, were brought before Junius Donatus, governor of Rome, where, A.D. 257, they sealed their martyrdom with their blood.

Stephen, bishop of Rome, was beheaded in the same year, and about that time Saturninus, the pious orthodox bishop of Toulouse, refusing to sacrifice to idols, was treated with all the barbarous indignities imaginable, and fastened by the feet to the tail of a bull. Upon a signal given, the enraged animal was driven down the steps of the temple, by which the worthy martyr's brains were dashed out.

Sextus succeeded Stephen as bishop of Rome. He is supposed to have been a Greek by birth or by extraction, and had for some time served in the capacity of a deacon under Stephen. His great fidelity, singular wisdom, and uncommon courage distinguished him upon many occasions; and the happy conclusion of a controversy with some heretics is generally ascribed to his piety and prudence. In the year 258, Marcianus, who had the management of the Roman government, procured an order from the emperor Valerian, to put to death all the Christian clergy in Rome, and hence the bishop with six of his deacons, suffered martyrdom in 258.

Let us draw near to the fire of martyred Lawrence, that our cold hearts may be warmed thereby. The merciless tyrant, understanding him to be not only a minister of the sacraments, but a distributor also of the Church riches, promised to himself a double prey, by the apprehension of one soul. First, with the rake of avarice to scrape to himself the treasure of poor Christians; then with the fiery fork of tyranny, so to toss and turmoil them, that they should wax weary of their profession. With furious face and cruel countenance, the greedy wolf demanded where this Lawrence had bestowed the substance of the Church: who, craving three days' respite, promised to declare where the treasure might be had. In the meantime, he caused a good number of poor Christians to be congregated. So, when the day of his answer was come, the persecutor strictly charged him to stand to his promise. Then valiant Lawrence, stretching out his arms over the poor, said: "These are the precious treasure of the Church; these are the treasure indeed, in whom the faith of Christ reigneth, in whom Jesus Christ hath His mansion-place. What more precious jewels can Christ have, than those in whom He hath promised to dwell? For so it is written, "I was an hungered, and ye gave me meat: I was thirsty, and ye gave me drink: I was a stranger, and ye took me in." And again, "Inasmuch as ye have done it unto one of the least of these my brethren, ye have done it unto me." What greater riches can Christ our Master possess, than the poor people in whom He loveth to be seen?"

O, what tongue is able to express the fury and madness of the tyrant's heart! Now he stamped, he stared, he ramped, he fared as one out of his wits: his eyes like fire glowed, his mouth like a boar formed, his teeth like a hellhound grinned. Now, not a reasonable man, but a roaring lion, he might be called.

"Kindle the fire (he cried) – of wood make no spare. Hath this villain deluded the emperor? Away with him, away with him: whip him with scourges, jerk him with rods, buffet him with fists, brain him with clubs. Jesteth the traitor with the emperor? Pinch him with fiery tongs, gird him with burning plates, bring out the strongest chains, and the fire-forks, and the grated bed of iron: on the fire with it; bind the rebel hand and foot; and when the bed is fire-hot, on with him: roast him, broil him, toss him, turn him: on pain of our high displeasure do every man his office, O ye tormentors."

The word was no sooner spoken, but all was done. After many cruel handlings, this meek lamb was laid, I will not say on his fiery bed of iron, but on his soft bed of down. So mightily God wrought with his martyr Lawrence, so miraculously God tempered His element the fire; that it became not a bed of consuming pain, but a pallet of nourishing rest.

In Africa the persecution raged with peculiar violence; many thousands received the crown of martyrdom, among whom the following were the most distinguished characters:

Cyprian, bishop of Carthage, an eminent prelate, and a pious ornament of the Church. The brightness of his genius was tempered by the solidity of his judgment; and with all the accomplishments of the gentleman, he blended the virtues of a Christian. His doctrines were orthodox and pure; his language easy and elegant; and his manners graceful and winning: in fine, he was both the pious and polite preacher. In his youth he was educated in the principles of Gentilism, and having a considerable fortune, he lived in the very extravagance of splendor, and all the dignity of pomp.

About the year 246, Coecilius, a Christian minister of Carthage, became the happy instrument of Cyprian's conversion: on which account, and for the great love that he always afterward bore for the author of his conversion, he was termed Coecilius Cyprian. Previous to his baptism, he studied the Scriptures with care and being struck with the beauties of the truths they contained, he determined to practice the virtues therein recommended. Subsequent to his baptism, he sold his estate, distributed the money among the poor, dressed himself in plain attire, and commenced a life of austerity. He was soon after made a presbyter; and, being greatly admired for his virtues and works, on the death of Donatus, in A.D. 248, he was almost unanimously elected bishop of Carthage.

Cyprian's care not only extended over Carthage, but to Numidia and Mauritania. In all his transactions he took great care to ask the advice of his clergy, knowing that unanimity alone could be of service to the Church, this being one of his maxims, "That the bishop was in the church, and the church in the bishop; so that unity can only be preserved by a close connexion between the pastor and his flock."

In A.D. 250, Cyprian was publicly proscribed by the emperor Decius, under the appellation of Coecilius Cyprian, bishop of the Christians; and the universal cry of the pagans was, "Cyprian to the lions, Cyprian to the beasts." The bishop, however, withdrew from the rage of the populace, and his effects were immediately confiscated. During his retirement, he wrote thirty pious and elegant letters to his flock; but several schisms that then crept into the Church, gave him great uneasiness. The rigor of the persecution abating, he returned to Carthage, and did everything in his power to expunge erroneous opinions. A terrible plague breaking out in Carthage, it was as usual, laid to the charge of the Christians; and the magistrates began to persecute accordingly, which occasioned an epistle from them to Cyprian, in answer to which he vindicates the cause of Christianity. A.D. 257, Cyprian was brought before the proconsul Aspasius Paturnus, who exiled him to a little city on the Lybian sea. On the death of this proconsul, he returned to Carthage, but was soon after seized, and carried before the new governor, who condemned him to be beheaded; which sentence was executed on the fourteenth of September, A.D. 258.

The disciples of Cyprian, martyred in this persecution, were Lucius, Flavian, Victoricus, Remus, Montanus, Julian, Primelus, and Donatian.

At Utica, a most terrible tragedy was exhibited: three hundred Christians were, by the orders of the proconsul, placed round a burning limekiln. A pan of coals and incense being prepared, they were commanded either to sacrifice to Jupiter, or to be thrown into the kiln. Unanimously refusing, they bravely jumped into the pit, and were immediately suffocated.

Fructuosus, bishop of Tarragon, in Spain, and his two deacons, Augurius and Eulogius, were burnt for being Christians.

Alexander, Malchus, and Priscus, three Christians of Palestine, with a woman of the same place, voluntarily accused themselves of being Christians; on which account they were sentenced to be devoured by tigers, which sentence was executed accordingly.

Maxima, Donatilla, and Secunda, three virgins of Tuburga, had gall and vinegar given them to drink, were then severely scourged, tormented on a gibbet, rubbed with lime, scorched on a gridiron, worried by wild beasts, and at length beheaded.

It is here proper to take notice of the singular but miserable fate of the emperor Valerian, who had so long and so terribly persecuted the Christians. This tyrant, by a stretagem, was taken prisoner by Sapor, emperor of Persia, who carried him into his own country, and there treated him with the most unexampled indignity, making him kneel down as the meanest slave, and treading upon him as a footstool when he mounted his horse. After having kept him for the space of seven years in this abject state of slavery, he caused his eyes to be put out, though he was then eighty-three years of age. This not satiating his desire of revenge, he soon after ordered his body to be flayed alive, and rubbed with salt, under which torments he expired; and thus fell one of the most tyrannical emperors of Rome, and one of the greatest persecutors of the Christians.

A.D. 260, Gallienus, the son of Valerian, succeeded him, and during his reign (a few martyrs excepted) the Church enjoyed peace for some years.

Foxe's Book of Martyrs, Edited by William Byron Forbush

Temporary Repose, 260-303

Gallienus (260-268) gave peace to the church once more, and even acknowledged Christianity as a religio licita. And this calm continued forty years; for the edict of persecution, issued by the energetic and warlike Aurelian (270-275), was rendered void by his assassination; and the six emperors who rapidly followed, from 275 to 284, let the Christians alone. The persecutions under Carus, Numerianus and Carinus from 284 to 285 are not historical, but legendary. During this long season of peace the church rose rapidly in numbers and outward prosperity. Large and even splendid houses of worship were erected in the chief cities, and provided with collections of sacred books and vessels of gold and silver for the administration of the sacraments. But in the same proportion discipline relaxed, quarrels, intrigues, and factions increased, and worldliness poured in like a flood. Hence a new trial was a necessary and wholesome process of purification.

Philip Scaff, History of the Christian Church, chapter 23

Arcadius

Arcadius probably lived in Caesarea, the capital city of Mauritania, during the last years of Emperor Valerian's reign. Every day new sacrileges were committed; the faithful were compelled to assist at superstitious sacrifices, to lead victims crowned with flowers through the streets, to burn incense before idols, and to celebrate the enthusiastic feasts of Bacchus. Arcadius, seeing his city in great confusion, left his estate, and withdrew to a solitary place in the neighboring country, serving Jesus Christ in watching, prayer, and other exercises of a penitential life.

His flight could not be long a secret; for his not appearing at the public sacrifices made the governor send soldiers to his house, who surrounded it, forced open the doors, and finding one of his relations in it, who said all he could to justify his kinsman's absence, they seized him, and the governor ordered him to be kept in close custody till Arcadius should be taken. The martyr, informed of his friend's danger, and burning with a desire to suffer for Christ, went into the city, and presenting himself to the judge, said: "If on my account you detain my innocent relation in chains, release him; I, Arcadius, am come in person to give an account of myself, and to declare to you, that he knew not where I was."

"I am willing," answered the judge, "to pardon not only him, but you also, on condition that you will sacrifice to the gods."

Arcadius replied, "How can you propose to me such a thing? Do you not know the Christians, or do you believe that the fear of death will ever make me swerve from my duty? Jesus Christ is my life, and death is my gain. Invent what torments you please; but know that nothing shall make me a traitor to my God."

The governor, in a rage, paused to devise some unheard-of torment for him. Iron hooks seemed too easy; neither plummets of lead, nor cudgels could satisfy his fury; the very rack he thought by much too gentle. At last, imagining he had found a manner of death suitable to his purpose, he said to the ministers of his cruelty, "Take him, and let him see and desire death, without being able to obtain it. Cut off his limbs joint by joint, and execute this so slowly, that the wretch may know what it is to abandon the gods of his ancestors for the unknown deity."

The executioners dragged Arcadius to the place, where many other victims of Christ had already suffered: a place dear and sweet to all who sigh after eternal life. Here the martyr lifts up his eyes to heaven, and implores strength from above; then stretches out his neck, expecting to have his head cut off; but the executioner bid him hold out his hand, and joint after joint chopped off his fingers, arms, and shoulders. Laying the saint afterward on his back, he in the same barbarous manner cut off his toes, feet, legs, and thighs, one after another, with invincible patience and courage, repeating these words, "Lord, teach me thy wisdom." For the tyrants had forgotten to cut out his tongue. Arcadius, surveying his scattered limbs all around him said, "Happy members, now dear to me, as you at last truly belong to God, being all made a sacrifice to him." Then, turning to the people, he said, "You who have been present at this bloody tragedy, learn that all torments seem as nothing to one, who has an everlasting crown before his eyes. Your gods are not gods; renounce your worship. He alone for whom I suffer and die, is the true God. He comforts and upholds me in the condition you see me. To die for him is to live; to suffer for him is to enjoy the greatest delights."

Arcadius then expired and the pagans were astonished at such a miracle of patience.

Alban Butler, The Lives of the Saints, Dublin, 1833, volume I, pp 48-49

ACTS OF FRUCTUOSUS AND HIS DEACONS

Fructuosus was bishop of Tarragona in Spain, martyred on January 21, 259, during the reign of Emperors Gallienus and Valerian.

During the reigns of Valerian and Gallienus, in the consulship of Aemilian and Bassus, on Sunday the 16th of January, Fructuosus the bishop and the deacons Augurius and Eulogius ere arrested. In prison Fructuosus was resolute, rejoicing in the Lord's crown, to which he had been called, never stopped praying. With him were the brethren, cheering him and asking him to keep them in mind.

The next day, still in prison, he baptized our brother, Rogatian. On Friday 21st of January Aemilian the governor ordered, "Admit Fructuosus the bishop, and Augurius and Eulogius."

The officials replied, "They are in court."

Aemilian the governor said to Fructuosus the bishop: "Have you heard what the Emperors have ordered?"

Fructuosus the bishop answered, "I do not know what they have ordered. I am, however, a Christian."

Aemilian the governor said, "They have ordered that the gods are to be worshiped."

Fructuosus the bishop said, "I worship one God, who "made heaven and earth, the sea and all that in them is."

Aemilian said, "Do you know that there are gods?"

Fructuosus the bishop answered, "I know no such thing."

Aemilian said: "You shall know later."

Fructuosus the bishop looked to the Lord and began to pray silently.

Aemilian the governor said, "Who is to be obeyed, who is to be feared, who is to be adored if the gods are not worshiped and the images of the Emperor are not adored?"

Aemilian the governor said to Augurius the deacon: "Pay no heed to the words of Fructuosus."

Augurius the deacon answered: "I worship God the Almighty."

Aemilian the governor said to Eulogius the deacon, "Do you worship Fructuosus also?"

Eulogius the deacon answered, "I do not worship Fructuosus, but I worship him whom Fructuosus also worships."

Aemilian the governor said to Fructuosus the bishop, "Are you a bishop?"

Fructuosus the bishop answered, "I am."

Aemilian said, "You were." And he gave sentence that they should be burnt alive.

When Fructuosus the bishop was being led out with his deacons to the amphitheater, the people began to express their grieve, as he was greatly loved, not only by the brethren, but by the pagans as well. For he was just as a bishop should be, as the blessed apostle Paul had said through Holy Spirit, a teacher of the Gentiles. So the brethren who knew that he was on his way to so great a glory, rejoiced rather than grieved. When many, out of brotherly love, offered them a cup of drugged wine to drink, he said, "The hour for breaking our fast has not arrived yet."

When he came to the amphitheater, our brother and fellow-soldier, Felix, clasped his right hand, and begged him to remember him. Fructuosus replied out aloud, "I must have in mind the Catholic church, which is dispersed from the East even to the West."

Then Fructuosus was heard to say, under the guidance, and indeed, in the words of the Holy Spirit: "You will not lack a shepherd for long, nor will the love or the promise of the Lord fail you either here or hereafter. For what you see in front of you seems the illness of but one hour." They were like Ananias, Azarias, and Misael, for with them the Divine Trinity was visible. For each of them at his place in the fire the Father was present, the Son gave help, and the Holy Spirit walked in the middle of the fire. When their ropes which bound them were burned they knelt down, rejoicing and assured of resurrection, and, holding out their arms as a symbol of the Lord's victory, prayed to the Lord until they gave up their souls.

E. C. E. Owen, Some Authentic Acts of the Early Martyrs, Oxford, 1927, pp 100-103

TORTURES OF THE FIRST CHRISTIAN MARTYRS (5) IRON CLAWS, HOOKS AND CURRYCOMBS

a. Iron claws

First, two longish pieces of iron were fastened together, just in the same way as those forming a smith's iron pincers are used to be joined and paired together. Their ends were rounded and towards the ends slightly hollowed, so that little spears or spikes could be fixed there, for the greater convenience of the tormentors mangling those set on the wooden horse or tied to stakes or hung up aloft, whether ordinary criminals or the blessed martyrs. Iron pincers were also used to torture the martyrs.

b. Iron hooks

Iron hooks were longish sticks, or miniature spears, which had an iron at one end, curved and bent back on itself. These hooks were used to tear the skin off martyrs.

c. Iron currycombs

For tearing the flesh from faithful Christians iron combs were used. These combs resembled those used to comb wool.

d. Shards, (fragments of broken pottery)

Sometimes the sides, bellies, thighs and legs of Christians were lacerated in a very cruel way with fragments of pottery. Eusebius, in his History, wrote: "In the Thebaid all hitherto described cruelties were exceeded. For here the tormentors would take shards of pottery instead of claws and tear and lacerate the whole body till they did scrape the skin from off the flesh."

Tortures and Torments of the Christian Martyrs, from the "De SS. Martyrum Cruciatibus' of the Rev Father Gallonio, translated by A. R. Allinson, London and Paris: printed for the subscribers, 1903, pp 106-108

MARTYRDOM OF CYPRIAN (1)
Cyprian of Carthage, Bishop and Martyr
13 September 258

Cyprian was born around 200 AD in North Africa, of pagan parents. He was a prominent trial lawyer and teacher of rhetoric. Around 246 he became a Christian, and in 248 was chosen Bishop of Carthage. A year later the persecution under the Emperor Decius began, and Cyprian went into hiding. He was severely censured for this (unjustly on my view – see Mt 2:13; 10:23; 24:16). After the persecution had died down, it remained to consider how to deal with the lapsed, meaning with those Christians who had denied the faith under duress. Cyprian held that they ought to be received back into full communion after suitable intervals of probation and penance, adjusted to the gravity of the denial. In this he took a middle course between Novatus, who received apostates with no probation at all, and Novatian, who would not receive them back at all, and who broke communion with the rest of the Church over this issue, forming a dissident group particularly strong in Rome and Antioch. (Novatus, somewhat surprisingly, ended up joining the party of Novatian.) Cyprian, who held the same position as the Bishop of Rome on the treatment of the lapsed, wrote urging the Christians of Rome to stand with their bishop.

Later, the question arose whether baptisms performed by heretical groups ought to be recognized as valid by the Church, or whether converts from such groups ought to be rebaptized. Cyprian favored re-baptism, and Bishop Stephen of Rome did not. The resulting controversy was not resolved during Cyprian's lifetime.

During the reign of the Emperor Valerian, Carthage suffered a severe plague epidemic. Cyprian organized a program of medical relief and nursing of the sick, available to all residents, but this did not prevent the masses from being convinced that the epidemic resulted from the wrath of the gods at the spread of Christianity. Another persecution arose, and this time Cyprian did not flee. He was arrested, tried, and finally beheaded on 14 September 258. (Because 14 is Holy Cross Day, he is usually commemorated on a nearby open day.) We have an account of his trial and martyrdom.

Many of his writings have been preserved. His essay On The Unity of The Catholic Church stresses the importance of visible, concrete unity among Christians, and the role of the bishops in guaranteeing that unity. It has greatly influenced Christian thought, as have his essays and letters on Baptism and the Lord's Supper. He has been quoted both for and against the Roman Catholic claims for Papal authority.

James Kiefer, Christian Biographies, By kind permission

Martyrdom of Cyprian (2)

The Acts of Cyprian record the martyrdom of one of Africa's most well-known martyrs, Cyprian, in 258. After Tertullian, Cyprian was the second most important Latin-speaking leader of the church. As he became the first martyr-bishop of North Africa his views gained added weight.

Persecution raged in Africa, and thousands received the crown of martyrdom, among whom was Cyprian, Bishop of Carthage. He was educated in his youth in the maxims of the heathen, and having considerable fortune, he lived in great splendor. Around 246, Coecilius, a Christian minister of Carthage, became the instrument of Cyprian's conversion; on which account he was termed Coecilius Cyprian.

Before his baptism he studied the Scriptures with care, and being struck with the excellence of the truths they contained, he determined to practise the virtues they recommended. After his baptism he sold his estate, distributed the money among the poor, dressed himself in plain attire, and commenced a life of austerity and solitude. Soon he was made a presbyter and being greatly admired for his virtues and his works, on the death of Donatus, in 248 he was elected Bishop of Carthage. In all his transactions he took great care to ask the advice of his clergy, knowing that unanimity alone could be of service to the church: this being one of his maxims, "That the bishop was in the church, and the church in the bishop; so that unity can only be preserved by a close connection between the pastor and his flock."

In 250 Cyprian was proscribed by the Emperor Decius, and the cry of the pagans was, "Cyprian to the lions! Cyprian to the beasts!" The bishop, however, withdrew from the rage of the people, and his effects were confiscated. When the persecution died down he returned to Carthage and did everything in his power to expel false doctrines. A plague now breaking out in Carthage, it was laid to the charge of the Christians: and the magistrates began to persecute them accordingly; this occasioned the letter from them to Cyprian, in reply to which he vindicates the cause of Christianity.

Cyprian was brought before the pro-consul Aspasius Paternus, in 257, and after being commanded to conform to the religion of the empire, he boldly made a confession of his faith. This did not occasion his death, but an order was made for his banishment to a little city on the Libyan Sea. On the death of the pro-consul who banished him, he returned to Carthage, but was soon seized, and taken to the new governor.

John Foxe, The Book of Martyrs, revised with notes and an appendix by W. Bramley-Moore, London, 1869, pp 24-26

Martyrdom of Cyprian (3)

On August 30th at Carthage in his private room Paternus the proconsul said to Cyprian the bishop, "The most sacred Emperors Valerian and Gallienus have thought fit to send me a letter, in which they have commanded that those who do not observe the Roman religion must recognize the

Roman rites. I have therefore made inquiries concerning yourself. What answer have you to give me?"

Cyprian the bishop said, "I am a Christian and a bishop. I know no other God but the One True God, who "made heaven and earth, the sea, and all that in them is". This God we Christians serve, and him we pray day and night for ourselves, and for all men, and for the safety of the Emperors themselves."

The proconsul Paternus said, "Is your will constant in this?"

Cyprian the bishop answered, "A good will, which knows God, cannot be altered."

The proconsul Paternus said, "Can you then in accordance with the order of Valerius and Gallienus go into exile to the city of Curubis?"

Cyprian the bishop said, "I will go."

The proconsul Paternus said, "They have thought fit to write to me not about bishops only, but also about priests. I want to know therefore from you who the priests are, who live in this city."

Cyprian the bishop replied, "It is an excellent and beneficial provision of your laws that informers are forbidden. They cannot therefore be revealed and reported by me."

The proconsul Paternus said, "They shall be found by me." And added, "The emperors have also given instructions that in no place shall meetings be held, nor shall any enter the cemeteries. If therefore any fail to observe these beneficial instructions, he shall suffer death."

Cyprian the bishop answered, "Do as you are instructed."

Then the proconsul Paternus ordered the blessed Cyprian to be banished. And as he stayed a long time in exile, the proconsul Aspasius Paternus was succeeded as proconsul by Galerius Maximus, who ordered the holy bishop Cyprian to be recalled from his banishment and brought before him.

Cyprian was under house arrest in Saturn Street, between the temple of Venus and the temple of Public Welfare. There the whole congregation of the brethren gathered. When holy Cyprian was informed about this he ordered that the young women should be protected as they had all stayed in the street outside the official's door.

On the next day, the 14th of September, Cyprian was brought before Galerius Maximus as he sat in judgement in Sauciolum Hall.

Galerius Maximus asked Cyprian, "Are you Thascius Cyprianus?"

Cyprian the bishop answered, "I am."

Galerius Maximus the proconsul said, "Have you taken on yourself to be Pope of people holding sacrilegious opinions?"

Cyprian the bishop answered, "Yes."

Galerius Maximus the proconsul said, "The most sacred Emperors have commanded you to perform the rite."

Cyprian the bishop answered, "I refuse."

Galerius Maximus the proconsul said, "Consider your own interest."

Cyprian the bishop answered, "Do as you are ordered. In so clear a case there is no need for debate."

Galerius Maximus having conferred with the council gave sentence reluctantly: "You have lived for a long time holding sacrilegious opinions, and have formed an abominable conspiracy, and have set yourself up as an enemy of the gods of Rome and religious ordinances, nor have the pious and most sacred Emperors Valerian and Gallienus, the Augusti, and Valerian, the most noble Caesar, been able to recall you to the observance of their rites. So you will be an example to all those who have joined you. Discipline will be vindicated in your blood.

With these words he read from his tablets the sentence: "It is our pleasure that Thascius Cyprianus should be executed by the sword!"

Cyprian the bishop said, "Thanks be to God!"

After this sentence the crowd of brethren cried: "Let us also be beheaded with him." So there arose an uproar among the brethren, and a great crowd accompanied him. So the same Cyprian was let out to the land of Sextus, and there he took off his mantle, and knelt on the ground, and bowed in prayer to the Lord. And when he took off his dalmatic and handed it to the deacons, he stood in his linen clothes and waited for the executioner. When the executioner arrived Cyprian told his friends to give him twenty-five golden coins. Napkins and handkerchiefs were laid on the ground in front of Cyprian by the brethren. Then blessed Cyprian bound his eyes with his own hand, but, as he could not tie the ends of the handkerchief for himself, the priest Julianus and Julianus the sub-deacon tied them for him.

So the blessed Cyprian suffered, and his body was laid out near by to satisfy the curiosity of the pagans. Then it was taken away at night, accompanied by tapers and torches, and triumphant prayers to the burial ground of Macrobius Candidianus the procurator, which is on the Mappalian way next to the fishponds. A few days later Galerius Maximus the proconsul died.

The most blessed martyr Cyprian suffered on the 14th day of September under Emperors Valerian and Gallienus, in the reign of our Lord Jesus Christ, to whom belong honor and glory for ever and ever. Amen.
Eusebius, The History of the Church, Book 6

St. Cyprian of Carthage

Bishop and martyr

Of the date of the saint's birth and of his early life nothing is known. At the time of his conversion to Christianity he had, perhaps, passed middle life. He was famous as an orator and pleader, had considerable wealth, and held, no doubt, a great position in the metropolis of Africa. We learn from his deacon, St. Pontius, whose life of the saint is preserved, that his mien was dignified without severity, and cheerful without effusiveness. His gift of eloquence is evident in his writings. He was not a thinker, a philosopher, a theologian, but eminently a man of the world and an administrator, of vast energies, and of forcible and striking character. His conversion was due to an aged priest named Caecilianus, with whom he seems to have gone to live. Caecilianus in dying commended to Cyprian the care of his wife and family. While yet a catechumen the saint decided to observe chastity, and he gave most of his revenues to the poor. He sold his property, including his gardens at Carthage. These were restored to him (Dei indulgentiâ restituti, says Pontius), being apparently bought back for him by his friends; but he would have sold them again, had the persecution made this imprudent. His baptism probably took place c. 246, presumably on Easter eve, 18 April.

The Decian persecution

The prosperity of the Church during a peace of thirty-eight years had produced great disorders. Many even of the bishops were given up to worldliness and gain, and we hear of worse scandals. In October, 249, Decius became emperor with the ambition of restoring the ancient virtue of Rome. In January, 250, he published an edict against Christians. Bishops were to be put to death, other persons to be punished and tortured till they recanted. On 20 January Pope Fabian was martyred, and about the same time St. Cyprian retired to a safe place of hiding. His enemies continually reproached him with this. But to remain at Carthage was to court death, to cause greater danger to others, and to leave the Church without government; for to elect a new bishop would have been as impossible as it was at Rome. He made over much property to a confessor priest, Rogatian, for the needy. Some of the clergy lapsed, others fled; Cyprian suspended their pay, for their ministrations were needed and they were in less danger than the bishop. Form his retreat he encouraged the confessors and wrote eloquent panegyrics on the martyrs. Fifteen soon died in prison and one in the mines. On the arrival of the proconsul in April the severity of the persecution increased. St. Mappalicus died gloriously on the 17th. Children were tortured, women dishonored. Numidicus, who had encouraged many, saw his wife burnt to alive, and was himself half burnt, then stoned and left for dead; his daughter found him yet living; he recovered and Cyprian made him a priest. Some, after being twice tortured, were dismissed or banished, often beggared.

But there was another side to the picture.

At Rome terrified Christians rushed to the temples to sacrifice. At Carthage the majority apostatized. Some would not sacrifice, but purchased libelli, or certificates, that they had done so Some bought the exemption of their family at the price of their own sin. Of these libellatici there were several thousands in Carthage. Of the fallen some did not repent, others joined the heretics, but most of them clamored for forgiveness and restoration. Some, who had sacrificed under torture, returned to be tortured afresh. Castus and Aemilius were burnt for recanting, others were exiled; but such cases were necessarily rare. A few began to perform canonical penance. The first to suffer at Rome had been a young Carthaginian, Celerinus. He recovered, and Cyprian made him a lector. His grandmother and two uncles had been martyrs, but his two sisters apostatized under fear of torture, and in their repentance gave themselves to the service of those in prison. Their brother was very urgent for their restoration. His letter from Rome to Lucian, a confessor at Carthage, is extant, with the reply of the latter. Lucian obtained from a martyr named Paul before his passion a commission to grant peace to any who asked for it, and he distributed these "indulgences" with a vague formula: "Let such a one with his family communicate". Tertullian speaks in 197 of the "custom" for those who were not at peace with the Church to beg this peace from the martyrs. Much later, in his Montanist days (c. 220) he urges that the adulterers whom Pope Callistus was ready to forgive after due penance, would now get restored by merely imploring the confessors and those in the mines. Correspondingly we find Lucian issuing pardons in the name of confessors who were still alive, a manifest abuse. The heroic Mappalicus had only interceded for his own sister and mother. It seemed now as if no penance was to be enforced upon the lapsed, and Cyprian wrote to remonstrate. Meanwhile official news had arrived from Rome of the death of Pope Fabian, together with an unsigned and ungrammatical letter to the clergy of Carthage from some of the Roman clergy, implying blame to Cyprian for the desertion of his flock, and giving advice as to the treatment of the lapsed. Cyprian explained his conduct (Ep. xx), and sent to Rome copies of thirteen of the letter he had written from his hiding-place to Carthage. The five priests who opposed him were now admitting at once to communion all who had recommendations from the confessors, and the confessors themselves issued a general indulgence, in accordance with which the bishops were to restore to communion all whom they had examined. This was an outrage on discipline, yet Cyprian was ready to give some value to the indulgences thus improperly granted, but all must be done in submission to the bishop. He proposed that *libellatici* should be restored, when in danger of death, by a priest or even by a deacon, but that the rest should await the cessation of persecution, when councils could be held at Rome and at Carthage, and a common decision be agreed upon. Some regard must be had for the prerogative of the confessors, yet the lapsed must surely not be placed in a better position than those who had stood fast, and had been tortured, or beggared, or exiled. The guilty were terrified by marvels that occurred. A man was struck dumb on the very Capitol where he had denied Christ. Another went mad in the public baths, and gnawed the tongue which had tasted the pagan victim. In Cyprian's own presence an infant who had been taken by its nurse to partake at the heathen altar, and then to the Holy Sacrifice offered by the bishop, was though in torture, and vomited the Sacred Species it had received in the holy chalice. A lapsed woman of advanced age had fallen in a fit, on venturing to communicate unworthily. Another, on opening the receptacle in which, according to custom, she had taken home the Blessed Sacrament for private Communion, was deterred from sacrilegiously touching it by fire which came forth. Yet another found nought within her pyx save cinders. About September, Cyprian received promise of support from the Roman priests in two letters written by the famous Novatian in the name of his colleagues. In the beginning of 251 the persecution waned, owing to the successive appearance of two rival emperors. The confessors were released, and a council was convened at Carthage. By the perfidy of some priests Cyprian was unable to leave his retreat till after Easter (23 March). But he wrote a letter to his flock denouncing the most infamous of the five priests, Novatus, and his deacon Felicissimus (Ep. xliii). To the bishop's order to delay the reconciliation of the lapsed until the council, Felicissimus had replied by a manifesto, declaring that none should communicate with himself who accepted the large alms distributed by Cyprian's order. The subject of the letter is more fully developed in the treatise "De Ecclesiae Catholicae Unitate" which Cyprian wrote about this time (Benson wrongly thought it was written against Novatian some weeks later). This celebrated pamphlet was read by its author to the council which met in April, that he might get the support of the bishops against the schism started by Felicissimus and Novatus, who had a large following. The unity with which St. Cyprian deals is not so much the unity of the whole Church, the necessity of which he rather postulates, as the unity to be kept in each diocese by union with the bishop; the unity of the whole Church is maintained by the close union of the bishops who are "glued to one another", hence whosoever is not with his bishop is cut off from the unity of the Church and cannot be united to Christ; the type of the bishop is St. Peter, the first bishop. Protestant controversialists have attributed to St. Cyprian the absurd argument that Christ said to Peter what He really meant for all, in order to give a type or picture of unity. What St. Cyprian really says is simply this, that Christ, using the metaphor of an edifice, founds His Church on a single foundation which shall manifest and ensure its unity. And as Peter is the foundation, binding the whole Church together, so in each diocese is the bishop. With this one argument Cyprian claims to cut at the root of all heresies and schisms. It has been a mistake to find any reference to Rome in this passage (De Unit., 4).

The lapsed

With regard to the lapsed the council had decided that each case must be judged on its merits, and that libellatici should be restored after varying, but lengthy, terms of penance, whereas those who had actually sacrificed might after life-long penance receive Communion in the hour of death. But any one who put off sorrow and penance until the hour of sickness must be refused all Communion. The decision was a severe one. A recrudescence of persecution, announced, Cyprian tells us, by numerous visions, caused the assembling of another council in the summer of 252 (so Benson and Nelke, but Ritsch and Harnack prefer 253), in which it was decided to restore at once all those who were doing penance, in order that they might be fortified by the Holy Eucharist against trial. In this persecution of Gallus and Volusianus, the Church of Rome was again tried, but this time Cyprian was able to congratulate the pope on the firmness shown; the whole Church of Rome, he says, had confessed unanimously, and once again its faith, praised by the Apostle, was celebrated throughout the whole world (Ep. lx). About June 253, Cornelius was exiled to Centumcellae (Civitavecchia), and died there, being counted as a martyr by Cyprian and the rest of the Church. His successor Lucius was at once sent to the same place on his election, but soon was allowed to return, and Cyprian wrote to congratulate him. He died 5 March, 254, and was succeeded by Stephen, 12 May, 254.

Martrydom

The empire was surrounded by barbarian hordes who poured in on all sides. The danger was the signal for a renewal of persecution on the part of the Emperor Valerian. At Alexandria St. Dionysius was exiled. On 30 August, 257, Cyprian was brought before the Proconsul Paternus in his secretarium. His interrogatory is extant and forms the first part of the "Acta proconsularia" of his martyrdom. Cyprian declares himself a Christian and a bishop. He serves one God to Whom he prays day and night for all men and for the safety of the emperor. "Do you persevere in this?" asks Paternus. "A good will which knows God cannot be altered." "Can you, then, go into exile at Curubis?" "I go." He is asked for the names of the priests also, but replies that delation is forbidden by the laws; they will be found easily enough in their respective cities. On September he went to Curubis, accompanied by Pontius. The town was lonely, but Pontius tells us it was sunny and pleasant, and that there were plenty of visitors, while the citizens were full of kindness. He relates at length Cyprian's dream on his first night there, that he was in the proconsul's court and condemned to death, but was reprieved at his own request until the morrow. He awoke in terror, but once awake he awaited that morrow with calmness. It came to him on the very anniversary of the dream. In Numidia the measurers were more severe. Cyprian writes to nine bishops who were working in the mines, with half their hair shorn, and with insufficient food and clothing. He was still rich and able to help them. Their replies are preserved, and we have also the authentic Acts of several African martyrs who suffered soon after Cyprian. In August, 258, Cyprian learned that Pope Sixtus had been put to death in the catacombs on the 6th of that month, together with four of his deacons, in consequence of a new edict that bishops, priests, and deacons should be at once put to death; senators, knights, and others of rank are to lose their goods, and if they still persist, to die; matrons to be exiled; Caesarians (officers of the fiscus) to become slaves. Galerius Maximus, the successor of Paternus, sent for Cyprian back to Carthage, and in his own gardens the bishop awaited the final sentence. Many great personages urged him to fly, but he had now no vision to recommend this course, and he desired above all to remain to exhort others. Yet he hid himself rather than obey the proconsul's summons to Utica, for he declared it was right for a bishop to die in his own city. On the return of Galerius to Carthage, Cyprian was brought from his gardens by two principes in a chariot, but the proconsul was ill, and Cyprian passed the night in the house of the first princeps in the company of his friends. Of the rest we have a vague description by Pontius and a detailed report in the proconsular Acts. On the morning of the 14th a crowd gathered "at the villa of Sextus", by order of the authorities. Cyprian was tried there. He refused to sacrifice, and added that in such a matter there was no room for thought of the consequences to himself. The proconsul read his condemnation and the multitude cried, "Let us be beheaded with him!" He was taken into the grounds, to a hollow surrounded by trees, into which many of the people climbed. Cyprian took off his cloak, and knelt down and prayed. Then he took off his dalmatic and gave it to his deacons, and stood in his linen tunic in silence awaiting the executioner, to whom he ordered twenty-five gold pieces to be given. The brethren cast cloths and handkerchiefs before him to catch his blood. He bandaged his own eyes with the help of a priest and a deacon, both called Julius. So he suffered. For the rest of the day his body was exposed to satisfy the curiosity of the pagans. But at night the brethren bore him with candles and torches, with prayer and great triumph, to the cemetery of Macrobius Candidianus in the suburb of Mapalia. He was the first Bishop of Carthage to obtain the crown of martyrdom.

Writings

The correspondence of Cyprian consists of eighty-one letters. Sixty-two of them are his own, three more are in the name of councils. From this large collection we get a vivid picture of his time. The first collection of his writings must have been made just before or just after his death, as it was known to Pontius. It consisted of ten treatises and seven letters on martyrdom. To these were added in Africa a set of letters on the baptismal question, and at Rome, it seems, the correspondence with Cornelius, except Ep. xlvii. Other letters were successively aggregated to these groups, including letters to Cyprian or connected with him, his collections of Testimonies, and many spurious works. To the treatises already mentioned we have to add a well-known exposition of the Lord's Prayer; a work on the simplicity of dress proper to consecrated virgins (these are both founded on Tertullian); "On the Mortality", a beautiful pamphlet, composed on the occasion of the plague which reached Carthage in 252, when Cyprian, with wonderful energy, raised a staff of workers and a great fund of money for the nursing of the sick and the burial of the dead. Another work, "On Almsgiving", its Christian character, necessity, and satisfactory value, was perhaps written, as Watson has pointed out, in reply to the calumny that Cyprian's own lavish gifts were bribes to attach men to his side. Only one of his writings is couched in a pungent strain, the "ad Demetrianum", in which he replies in a spirited manner to the accusation of a heathen that Christianity had brought the plague upon the world. Two short works, "On Patience" and "On Rivalry and Envy", apparently written during the baptismal controversy, were much read in ancient times. St. Cyprian was the first great Latin writer among the Christians, for Tertullian fell into heresy, and his style was harsh and unintelligible. Until the days of Jerome and Augustine, Cyprian's writings had no rivals in the West. Their praise is sung by Prudentius, who joins with Pacian, Jerome, Augustine, and many others in attesting their extraordinary popularity.

John Chapman, The Catholic Encyclopedia, Volume 4

The Life and Passion of Cyprian, Bishop and Martyr

1. Although Cyprian, the devout priest and glorious witness of God, composed many writings whereby the memory of his worthy name survives; and although the profuse fertility of his eloquence and of God's grace so expands itself in the exuberance and richness of his discourse, that he will probably never cease to speak even to the end of the world; yet, since to his works and deserts it is justly due that his example should be recorded in writing, I have thought it wall to prepare this brief and compendious narrative. Not that the life of so great a man can be unknown to any even of the heathen nations, but that to our posterity also this incomparable and lofty pattern may be prolonged into immortal remembrance. It would assuredly be hard that, when our fathers have given such honor even to lay-people and catechumens who have obtained martyrdom, for reverence of their very martyrdom, as to record many, or I had nearly said, well nigh all, of the circumstances of their sufferings, so that they might be brought to our knowledge also who as yet were not born, the passion of such a priest and such a martyr as Cyprian should be passed over, who, independently of his martyrdom, had much to teach, and that what he did while he lived should be hidden from the world. And, indeed, these doings of his were such, and so great, and so admirable, that I am deterred by the contemplation of their greatness, and confess myself incompetent to discourse in a way that shall be worthy of the honor of his deserts, and unable to relate such noble deeds in such a way that they may appear as great as in fact they are, except that the multitude of his glories is itself sufficient for itself, and needs no other heraldry. It enhances my difficulty, that you also are anxious to hear very much, or if it be possible every thing, about him, longing with eager warmth at least to become acquainted with his deeds, although now his living words are silent. And in this behalf, if I should say that the powers of eloquence fail me, I should say too little. For eloquence itself fails of suitable powers fully to satisfy your desire. And thus I am sorely pressed on both sides, since he burdens me with his virtues, and you press me hard with your entreaties.

2. At what point, then, shall I begin, – from what direction shall I approach the description of his goodness, except from the beginning of his faith and from his heavenly birth? inasmuch as the doings of a man of God should not be reckoned from any point except from the time that he was born of God. He may have had pursuits previously, and liberal arts may have imbued his mind

while engaged therein; but these things I pass over; for as yet they had nothing to do with anything but his secular advantage. But when he had learned sacred knowledge, and breaking through the clouds of this world had emerged into the light of spiritual wisdom, if I was with him in any of his doings, if I have discerned any of his more illustrious labors, I will speak of them; only asking meanwhile for this indulgence, that whatever I shall say too little (for too little I must needs say) may rather be attributed to my ignorance than subtracted from his glory. While his faith was in its first rudiments, he believed that before God nothing was worthy in comparison of the observance of continency. For he thought that the heart might then become what it ought to be, and the mind attain to the full capacity of truth, if he trod under foot the lust of the flesh with the robust and healthy vigor of holiness. Who has ever recorded such a marvel? His second birth had not yet enlightened the new man with the entire splendor of the divine light, yet he was already overcoming the ancient and pristine darkness by the mere dawning of the light. Then – what is even greater – when he had learned from the reading of Scripture certain things not according to the condition of his novitiate, but in proportion to the earliness of his faith, he immediately laid hold of what he had discovered, for his own advantage in deserving well of God. By distributing his means for the relief of the indigence of the poor, by dispensing the purchase-money of entire estates, he at once realized two benefits, – the contempt of this world's ambition, than which nothing is more pernicious, and the observance of that mercy which God has preferred even to His sacrifices, and which even he did not maintain who said that he had kept all the commandments of the law; whereby with premature swiftness of piety he almost began to be perfect before he had learnt the way to be perfect. Who of the ancients, I pray, has done this? Who of the most celebrated veterans in the faith, whose hearts and ears have throbbed to the divine words for many years, has attempted any such thing, as this man – of faith yet unskilled, and whom, perhaps, as yet nobody trusted – surpassing the age of antiquity, accomplished by his glorious and admirable labors? No one reaps immediately upon his sowing; no one presses out the vintage harvest from the trenches just formed; no one ever yet sought for ripened fruit from newly planted slips. But in him all incredible things concurred. In him the threshing preceded (if it may be said, for the thing is beyond belief) – preceded the sowing, the vintage the shoots, the fruit the root.

3. The apostle's epistle says that novices should be passed over, lest by the stupor of heathenism that yet clings to their unconfirmed minds, their untaught inexperience should in any respect sin against God. He first, and I think he alone, furnished an illustration that greater progress is made by faith than by time. For although in the Acts of the Apostles the eunuch is described as at once baptized by Philip, because he believed with his whole heart, this is not a fair parallel. For he was a Jew, and as he came from the temple of the Lord he was reading the prophet Isaiah, and he hoped in Christ, although as yet he did not believe that He had come; while the other, coming from the ignorant heathens, began with a faith as mature as that with which few perhaps have finished their course. In short, in respect of God's grace, there was no delay, no postponement, – I have said but little, – he immediately received the presbyterate and the priesthood. For who is there that would not entrust every grade of honor to one who believed with such a disposition? There are many things which he did while still a layman, and many things which now as a presbyter he did – many things which, after the examples of righteous men of old, and following them with a close imitation, he accomplished with the obedience of entire consecration – that deserved well of the Lord. For his discourse concerning this was usually, that if he had read of any one being set forth with the praise of God, he would persuade us to inquire on account of what doings he had pleased God. If Job, glorious by God's

testimony, was called a true worshiped of God, and one to whom there was none upon earth to be compared, he taught that we should do whatever Job had previously done, so that while we are doing like things we may call forth a similar testimony of God for ourselves. He, contemning the loss of his estate, gained such advantage by his virtue thus tried, that he had no perception of the temporal losses even of his affection. Neither poverty nor pain broke him down; the persuasion of his wife did not influence him; the dreadful suffering of his own body did not shake his firmness. His virtue remained established in its own home, and his devotion, rounded upon deep roots, gave way under no onset of the devil tempting him to abstain from blessing his God with a grateful faith even in his adversity. His house was open to every comer. No widow returned from him with an empty lap; no blind man was unguided by him as a companion; none faltering in step was unsupported by him for a staff; none stripped of help by the hand of the mighty was not protected by him as a defender. Such things ought they to do, he was accustomed to say, who desire to please God. And thus running through the examples of all good men, by always imitating those who were better than others he made himself also worthy of imitation.

4. He had a close association among us with a just man, and of praiseworthy memory, by name Caecilius, and in age as well as in honor a presbyter, who had converted him from his worldly errors to the acknowledgment of the true divinity. This man he loved with entire honor and all observance, regarding him with an obedient veneration, not only as the friend and comrade of his soul, but as the parent of his new life. And at length he, influenced by his attentions, was, as well he might be, stimulated to such a pitch of excessive love, that when he was departing from this world, and his summons was at hand, he commended to him his wife and children; so that him whom he had made a partner in the fellowship of his way of life, he afterwards made the heir of his affection.

5. It would be tedious to go through individual circumstances, it would be laborious to enumerate all his doings. For the proof of his good works I think that this one thing is enough, that by the judgment of God and the favor of the people, he was chosen to the office of the priesthood and the degree of the episcopate while still a neophyte, and, as it was considered, a novice. Although still in the early days of his faith, and in the untaught season of his spiritual life, a generous disposition so shone forth in him, that although not yet resplendent with the glitter of office, but only of hope, he gave promise of entire trustworthiness for the priesthood that was coming upon him. Moreover, I will not pass over that remarkable fact, of the way in which, when the entire people by God's inspiration leapt forward in his love and honor, he humbly withdrew, giving place to men of older standing, and thinking himself unworthy of a claim to so great honor, so that he thus became more worthy. For he is made more worthy who dispenses with what he deserves. And with this excitement were the eager people at that time inflamed, desiring with a spiritual longing, as the event proved, not only a bishop, – for in him whom then with a latent foreboding of divinity they were in such wise demanding, they were seeking not only a priest, – but moreover a future martyr. A crowded fraternity was besieging the doors of the house, and throughout all the avenues of access an anxious love was circulating. Possibly that apostolic experience might then have happened to him, as he desired, of being let down through a window, had he also been equal to the apostle in the honor of ordination. It was plain to be seen that all the rest were expecting his coming with an anxious spirit of suspense, and received him when he came with excessive joy. I speak unwillingly, but I must needs speak. Some resisted him, even that he might overcome them; yet with what gentleness, how patiently, how benevolently he gave them indulgence! how mercifully he forgave them, reckoning them afterwards, to the astonishment of many, among his closest

and, most intimate friends! For who would not be amazed at the forgetfulness of a mind so retentive?

6. Henceforth who is sufficient to relate the manner in which he bore himself? – what pity was his? what vigor? how great his mercy? how great his strictness? So much sanctity and grace beamed from his face that it confounded the minds of the beholders. His countenance was grave and joyous. Neither was his severity gloomy, nor his affability excessive, but a mingled tempering of both; so that it might be doubted whether he most deserved to be revered or to be loved, except that he deserved both to be revered and to be loved. And his dress was not out of harmony with his countenance, being itself also subdued to a fitting mean. The pride of the world did not inflame him, nor yet did an excessively affected penury make him sordid, because this latter kind of attire arises no less from boastfulness, than does such an ambitious frugality from ostentation. But what did he as bishop in respect of the poor, whom as a catechumen he had loved? Let the priests of piety consider, or those whom the teaching of their very rank has trained to the duty of good works, or those whom the common obligation of the Sacrament has bound to the duty of manifesting love. Cyprian the bishop's cathedra received such as he had been before, – it did not make him so.

7. And therefore for such merits he at once obtained the glory of proscription also. For nothing else was proper than that he who in the secret recesses of his conscience was rich in the full honor of religion and faith, should moreover be renowned in the publicly diffused report of the Gentiles. He might, indeed, at that time, in accordance with the rapidity wherewith he always attained everything, have hastened to the crown of martyrdom appointed for him, especially when with repeated calls he was frequently demanded for the lions, had it not been needful for him to pass through all the grades of glory, and thus to arrive at the highest, and had not the impending desolation needed the aid of so fertile a mind. For conceive of him as being at that time taken away by the dignity of martyrdom. Who was there to show the advantage of grace, advancing by faith? Who was there to restrain virgins to the fitting discipline of modesty and a dress worthy of holiness, as if with a kind of bridle of the lessons of the Lord? Who was there to teach penitence to the lapsed, truth to heretics, unity to schismatics, peacefulness and the law of evangelical prayer to the sons of God? By whom were the blaspheming Gentiles to be overcome by retorting upon themselves the accusations which they heap upon us? By whom were Christians of too tender an affection, or, what is of more importance, of a too feeble faith in respect of the loss of their friends, to be consoled with the hope of futurity? Whence should we so learn mercy? whence patience? Who was there to restrain the ill blood arising from the envenomed malignity of envy, with the sweetness of a wholesome remedy? Who was there to raise up such great martyrs by the exhortation of his divine discourse? Who was there, in short, to animate so many confessors sealed with a second inscription on their distinguished brows, and reserved alive for an example of martyrdom, kindling their ardor with a heavenly trumpet? Fortunately, fortunately it occurred then, and truly by the Spirit's direction, that the man who was needed for so many and so excellent purposes was withheld from the consummation of martyrdom. Do you wish to be assured that the cause of his withdrawal was not fear? to allege nothing else, he did suffer subsequently, and this suffering he assuredly would have evaded as usual, if he had evaded it before. It was indeed that fear – and rightly so – that fear which would dread to offend the Lord – that fear which prefers to obey God's commands rather than to be crowned in disobedience. For a mind dedicated in all things to God, and thus enslaved to the divine admonitions, believed that even in suffering itself it would sin, unless it had obeyed the Lord, who then bade him seek the place of concealment.

8. Moreover, I think that something may here be said about the benefit of the delay, although I have already touched slightly on

the matter. By what appears subsequently to have occurred, it follows that we may prove that that withdrawal was not conceived by human pusillanimity, but, I as indeed is the case, was truly divine. The unusual and violent rage of a cruel persecution had laid waste God's people; and since the artful enemy could not deceive all by one fraud, wherever the incautious soldier laid bare his side, there in various manifestations of rage he had destroyed individuals with different kinds of overthrow. There needed some one who could, when men were wounded and hurt by the various arts of the attacking enemy, use the remedy of the celestial medicine according to the nature of the wound, either for cutting or for cherishing them. Thus was preserved a man of an intelligence, besides other excellences, also spiritually trained, who between the resounding waves of the opposing schisms could steer the middle course of the Church in a steady path. Are not such plans, I ask, divine? Could this have been done without God? Let them consider who think that such things as these can happen by chance. To them the Church replies with clear voice, saying, "I do not allow and do not believe that such needful then are reserved without the decree of God."

9. Still, if it seem well, let me glance at the rest. Afterwards there broke out a dreadful plague, and excessive destruction of a hateful disease invaded every house in succession of the trembling populace, carrying off day by day with abrupt attack numberless people, every one from his own house. All were shuddering, fleeing, shunning the contagion, impiously exposing their own friends, as if with the exclusion of the person who was sure to die of the plague, one could exclude death itself also. There lay about the meanwhile, over the whole city, no longer bodies, but the carcases of many, and, by the contemplation of a lot which in their turn would be theirs, demanded the pity of the passers-by for themselves. No one regarded anything besides his cruel gains. No one trembled at the remembrance of a similar event. No one did to another what he himself wished to experience. In these circumstances, it would be a wrong to pass over what the pontiff of Christ did, who excelled the pontiffs of the world as much in kindly affection as he did in truth of religion. On the people assembled together in one place he first of all urged the benefits of mercy, teaching by examples from divine lessons, how greatly the duties of benevolence avail to deserve well of God. Then afterwards he subjoined, that there was nothing wonderful in our cherishing our own people only with the needed attentions of love, but that he might become perfect who would do something more than the publican or the heathen, who, overcoming evil with good, and practicing a clemency which was like the divine clemency, loved even his enemies, who would pray for the salvation of those that persecute him, as the Lord admonishes and exhorts. God continually makes His sun to rise, and from time to time gives showers to nourish the seed, exhibiting all these kindnesses not only to His people, but to aliens also. And if a man professes to be a son of God, why does not he imitate the example of his Father? "It becomes us," said he, "to answer to our birth; and it is not fitting that those who are evidently born of God should be degenerate, but rather that the propagation of a good Father should be proved in His offspring by the emulation of His goodness."

10. I omit many other matters, and, indeed, many important ones, which the necessity of a limited space does not permit to be detailed in more lengthened discourse, and concerning which this much is sufficient to have been said. But if the Gentiles could have heard these things as they stood before the rostrum, they would probably at once have believed. What, then, should a Christian people do, whose very name proceeds from faith? Thus the ministrations are constantly distributed according to the quality of the men and their degrees. Many who, by the straitness of poverty, were unable to manifest the kindness of wealth, manifested more than wealth, making up by their own labor a service dearer than all riches. And under such a teacher, who would not press forward to be

found in some part of such a warfare, whereby he might please both God the Father, and Christ the Judge, and for the present so excellent a priest? Thus what is good was done in the liberality of overflowing works to all men, not to those only who are of the household of faith. Something more was done than is recorded of the incomparable benevolence of Tobias. He must forgive, and forgive again, and frequently forgive; or, to speak more truly, he must of right concede that, although very much might be done before Christ, yet that something more might be done after Christ, since to His times all fulness is attributed. Tobias collected together those who were slain by the king and cast out, of his own race only.

11. Banishment followed these actions, so good and so benevolent. For impiety always makes this return, that it repays the better with the worse. And what God's priest replied to the interrogation of the proconsul, there are Acts which relate. In the meantime, he is excluded from the city who had done some good for the city's safety; he who had striven that the eyes of the living should not suffer the horrors of the infernal abode; he, I say, who, vigilant in the watches of benevolence, had provided – oh wickedness! with unacknowledged goodness – that when all were forsaking the desolate appearance of the city, a destitute state and a deserted country should not perceive its many exiles. But let the world look to this, which accounts banishment a penalty. To them, their country is too dear, and they have the same name as their parents; but we abhor even our parents themselves if they would persuade us against God. To them, it is a severe punishment to live outside their own city; to the Christian, the whole of this world is one home. Wherefore, though he were banished into a hidden and secret place, yet, associated with the affairs of his God, he cannot regard it as an exile. In addition, while honestly serving God, he is a stranger even in his own city. For while the continency of the Holy Spirit restrains him from carnal desires, he lays aside the conversation of the former man, and even among his fellow-citizens, or, I might almost say, among the parents themselves of his earthly life, he is a stranger. Besides, although this might otherwise appear to be a punishment, yet in causes and sentences of this kind, which we suffer for the trial of the proof of our virtue, it is not a punishment, because it is a glory. But, indeed, suppose banishment not to be a punishment to us, yet the witness of their own conscience may still attribute the last and worst wickedness to those who can lay upon the innocent what they think to be a punishment. I will not now describe a charming place; and, for the present, I pass over the addition of all possible delights. Let us conceive of the place, filthy in situation, squalid in appearance, having no wholesome water, no pleasantness of verdure, no neighboring shore, but vast wooded rocks between the inhospitable jaws of a totally deserted solitude, far removed in the pathless regions of the world. Such a place might have borne the name of exile, if Cyprian, the priest of God, had come thither; although to him, if the ministrations of men had been wanting, either birds, as in the case of Elias, or angels, as in that of Daniel, would have ministered. Away, away with the belief that anything would be wanting to the least of us, so long as he stands for the confession of the name. So far was God's pontiff, who had always been urgent in merciful works, from needing the assistance of all these things.

12. And now let us return with thankfulness to what I had suggested in the second place, that for the soul of such a man there was divinely provided a sunny and suitable spot, a dwelling, secret as he wished, and all that has before been promised to be added to those who seek the kingdom and righteousness of God. And, not to mention the number of the brethren who I visited him, and then the kindness of the citizens themselves, which supplied to him everything whereof he appeared to be deprived, I will not pass over God's wonderful visitation, whereby He wished His priest in exile to be so certain of his passion that was to follow, that in his full confidence of the threatening martyrdom, Curubis possessed not only an exile, but a

martyr too. For on that day whereon we first abode in the place of banishment (for the condescension of his love had chosen me among his household companions to a voluntary exile: would that he could also have chosen me to share his passion!), "there appeared to me," said he, "ere yet I was sunk in the repose of slumber, a young man of unusual stature, who, as it were, led me to the praetorium, where I seemed to myself to be led before the tribunal of the proconsul, then sitting. When he looked upon me, he began at once to note down a sentence on his tablet, which I knew not, for he had asked nothing of me with the accustomed interrogation. But the youth, who was standing at his back, very anxiously read what had been noted down. And because he could not then declare it in words, he showed me by an intelligible sign what was contained in the writing of that tablet. For, with hand expanded and flattened like a blade, he imitated the stroke of the accustomed punishment, and expressed what he wished to be understood as clearly as by speech, – I understood the future sentence of my passion. I began to ask and to beg immediately that a delay of at least one day should be accorded me, until I should have arranged my property in some reasonable order. And when I had urgently repeated my entreaty, he began again to note down, I know not what, on his tablet. But I perceived from the calmness of his countenance that the judge's mind was moved by my petition, as being a just one. Moreover, that youth, who already had disclosed to me the intelligence of my passion by gesture rather than by words, hastened to signify repeatedly by secret signal that the delay was granted which had been asked for until the morrow, twisting his fingers one behind the other. And I, although the sentence had not been read, although I rejoiced with very glad heart with joy at the delay accorded, yet trembled so with fear of the uncertainty of the interpretation, that the remains of fear still set my exulting heart beating with excessive agitation."

13. What could be more plain than this revelation? What could be more blessed than this condescension? Everything was foretold to him beforehand which subsequently followed. Nothing was diminished of the words of God, nothing was mutilated of so sacred a promise. Carefully consider each particular in accordance with its announcement. He asks for delay till the morrow, when the sentence of his passion was under deliberation, begging that he might arrange his affairs on the day which he had thus obtained. This one day signified a year, which he was about to pass in the world after his vision. For, to speak more plainly, after the year was expired, he was crowned, on that day on which, at the commencement of the year, the fact had been announced to him. For although we do not read of the day of the Lord as a year in sacred Scripture, yet we regard that space of time as due in making promise of future things. Whence is it of no consequence if, in this case, under the ordinary expression of a day, it is only a year that in this place is implied, because that which is the greater ought to be fuller in meaning. Moreover, that it was explained rather by signs than by speech, was because the utterance of speech was reserved for the manifestation of the time itself. For anything is usually set forth in words, whenever what is set forth is accomplished. For, indeed, no one knew why this had been shown to him, until afterwards, when, on the very day on which he had seen it, he was crowned. Nevertheless, in the meantime, his impending suffering was certainly known by all, but the exact day of his passion was not spoken of by any of the same, just as if they were ignorant of it. And, indeed, I find something similar in the Scriptures. For Zacharias the priest, because he did not believe the promise of a son, made to him by the angel, became dumb; so that he asked for tablets by a sign, being about to write his son's name rather than utter it. With reason, also in this case, where God's messenger declared the impending passion of His priest rather by signs, he both admonished his faith and fortified His priest. Moreover, the ground of asking for delay arose out of his

wish to arrange his affairs and settle his will. Yet what affairs or what will had he to arrange, except ecclesiastical concerns? And thus that last delay was received, in order that whatever had to be disposed of by his final decision concerning the care of cherishing the poor might be arranged. And I think that for no other reason, and indeed for this reason only, indulgence was granted to him even by those very persons who had ejected and were about to slay him, that, being at hand, he might relieve the poor also who were before him with the final or, to speak more accurately, with the entire outlay of his last stewardship. And therefore, having so benevolently ordered matters, and so arranged them according to his will, the morrow drew near.

14. Now also a messenger came to him from the city from Xistus, the good and peace-making priest, and on that account most blessed martyr. The coming executioner was instantly looked for who should strike through that devoted neck of the most sacred victim; and thus, in the daily expectation of dying, every day was to him as if the crown might be attributed to each. In the meantime, there assembled to him many eminent people, and people of most illustrious rank and family, and noble with the world's distinctions, who, on account of ancient friendship with him, repeatedly urged his withdrawal; and, that their urgency might not be in some sort hollow, they also offered places to which he might retire. But he had now set the world aside, having his mind suspended upon heaven, and did not consent to their tempting persuasions. He would perhaps even then have done what was asked for by so many and faithful friends, if it had been bidden him by divine command. But that lofty glory of so great a man must not be passed over without announcement, that now, when the world was swelling, and of its trust in its princes breathing out hatred of the name, he was instructing God's servants, as opportunity was given, in the exhortations of the Lord, and was animating them to tread trader foot the sufferings of this present time by the contemplation of a glory to come hereafter. Indeed, such was his love of sacred discourse, that he wished that his prayers in regard to his suffering might be so answered, that he would be put to death in the very act of speaking about God.

15. And these were the daily acts of a priest destined for a pleasing sacrifice to God, when, behold, at the bidding of the proconsul, the officer with his soldiers on a sudden came unexpectedly on him, – or rather, to speak more truly, thought that he had come unexpectedly on him, at his gardens, – at his gardens, I say, which at the beginning of his faith he had sold, and which, being restored by God's mercy, he would assuredly have sold again for the use of the poor, if he had not wished to avoid ill-will from the persecutors. But when could a mind ever prepared be taken unawares, as if by an unforeseen attack? Therefore now he went forward, certain that what had been long delayed would be settled. He went forward with a lofty and elevated mien, manifesting cheerfulness in his look and courage in his heart. But being delayed to the morrow, he returned from the praetorium to the officer's house, when on a sudden a scattered rumor prevailed throughout all Carthage, that now Thascius was brought forward, whom there was nobody who did not know as well for his illustrious fame in the honorable opinion of all, as on account of the recollection of his most renowned work. On all sides all men were flocking together to a spectacle, to us glorious from the devotion of faith, and to be mourned over even by the Gentiles. A gentle custody, however, had him in charge when taken and placed for one night in the officer's house; so that we, his associates and friends, were as usual in his company. The whole people in the meantime, in anxiety that nothing should be done throughout the night without their knowledge, kept watch before the officer's door. The goodness of God granted him at that time, so truly worthy of it, that even God's people should watch on the passion of the priest. Yet, perhaps, some one may ask what was the reason of his returning from the praetorium to the officer. And some think that this arose

from the fact, that for his own part the proconsul was then unwilling. Far be it from me to complain, in matters divinely ordered, of slothfulness or aversion in the proconsul. Far be it from me to admit such an evil into the consciousness of a religious mind, as that the fancy of man should decide the fate of so blessed a martyr. But the morrow, which a year before the divine condescension had foretold, required to be literally the morrow.

16. At last that other day dawned – that destined, that promised, that divine day – which, if even the tyrant himself had wished to put off, he would not have had any power to do so; the day rejoicing at the consciousness of the future martyr; and, the clouds being scattered throughout the circuit of the world, the day shone upon them with a brilliant sun. He went out from the house of the officer, though he was the officer of Christ and God, and was walled in on all sides by the ranks of a mingled multitude. And such a numberless army hung upon his company, as if they had come with an assembled troop to assault death itself. Now, as he went, he had to pass by the race-course. And rightly, and as if it had been contrived on purpose, he had to pass by the place of a corresponding struggle, who, having finished his contest, was running to the crown of righteousness. But when he had come to the praetorium, as the proconsul had not yet come forth, a place of retirement was accorded him. There, as he sat moistened after his long journey with excessive perspiration (the seat was by chance covered with linen, so that even in the very moment of his passion he might enjoy the honor of the episcopate), one of the officers ("Tesserarius "), who had formerly been a Christian, offered him his clothes, as if he might wish to change his moistened garments for drier ones; and he doubtless coveted nothing further in respect of his proffered kindness than to possess the now blood-stained sweat of the martyr going to God. He made reply to him, and said, "We apply medicines to annoyances which probably to-day will no longer exist." Is it any wonder that he despised suffering in body who had despised death in soul? Why should we say more? He was suddenly announced to the proconsul; he is brought forward; he is placed before him; he is interrogated as to his name. He answers who he is, and nothing more.

17. And thus, therefore, the judge reads from his tablet the sentence which lately in the vision he had not read, – a spiritual sentence, not rashly to be spoken, – a sentence worthy of such a bishop and such a witness; a glorious sentence, wherein he was called a standard-bearer of the sect, and an enemy of the gods, and one who was to be an example to his people; and that with his blood discipline would begin to be established. Nothing could be more complete, nothing more true, than this sentence. For all the things which were said, although said by a heathen, are divine. Nor is it indeed to be wondered at, since priests are accustomed to prophesy of the passion. He had been a standard-bearer, who was accustomed to teach concerning the bearing of Christ's standard; he had been an enemy of the gods, who commanded the idols to be destroyed. Moreover, he gave example to his friends, since, when many were about to follow in a similar manner, he was the first in the province to consecrate the first-fruits of martyrdom. And by his blood discipline began to be established; but it was the discipline of martyrs, who, emulating their teacher, in the imitation of a glory like his own, themselves also gave a confirmation to discipline by the very blood of their own example.

18. And when he left the doors of the praetorium, a crowd of soldiery accompanied him; and that nothing might be wanting in his passion, centurions and tribunes guarded his side. Now the place itself where he was about to suffer is level, so that it affords a noble spectacle, with its trees thickly planted on all sides. But as, by the extent of the space beyond, the view was not attainable to the confused crowd, persons who favored him had climbed up into the branches of the trees, that there might not even be wanting to him (what happened in the case of Zacchaeus), that he was gazed upon from the trees. And now, having with his own hands bound his eyes, he tried to hasten the slowness of the executioner,

whose office was to wield the sword, and who with difficulty clasped the blade in his failing right hand with trembling fingers, until the mature hour of glorification strengthened the hand of the centurion with power granted from above to accomplish the death of the excellent man, and at length supplied him with the permitted strength. O blessed people of the Church, who as well in sight as in feeling, and, what is more, in outspoken words, suffered with such a bishop as theirs; and, as they had ever heard him in his own discourses, were crowned by God the Judge! For although that which the general wish desired could not occur, viz. that the entire congregation should suffer at once in the fellowship of a like glory, yet whoever under the eyes of Christ beholding, and in the hearing of the priest, eagerly desired to suffer, by the sufficient testimony of that desire did in some sort send a missive to God, as his ambassador.

19. His passion being thus accomplished, it resulted that Cyprian, who had been an example to all good men, was also the first who in Africa imbued his priestly crown with blood of martyrdom, because he was the first who began to be such after the apostles. For from the time at which the episcopal order is enumerated at Carthage, not one is ever recorded, even of good men and priests, to have come to suffering. Although devotion surrendered to God is always in consecrated men reckoned instead of martyrdom; yet Cyprian attained even to the perfect crown by the consummation of the Lord; so that in that very city in which he had in such wise lived, and in which he had been the first to do many noble deeds, he also was the first to decorate the insignia of his heavenly priesthood with glorious gore. What shall I do now? Between joy at his passion, and grief at still remaining, my mind is divided in different directions, and twofold affections are burdening a heart too limited for them. Shall I grieve that I was not his associate? But yet I must triumph in his victory. Shall I triumph at his victory? Still I grieve that I am not his companion. Yet still to you I must in simplicity confess, what you also are aware of, that it was my intention to be his companion. Much and excessively I exult at his glory; but still more do I grieve that I remained behind.

Pontius the deacon

To the Martyrs and Confessors

Cyprian commends the African martyrs for the perseverance and urges them to continue to be faithful as they remember their colleague Mappalicus.

Cyprian to the martyrs and confessors in Christ our Lord and in God the Father, everlasting salvation. I gladly rejoice and am thankful, most brave and blessed brethren, at hearing of your faith and virtue, wherein the Church, our Mother, glories. Lately, indeed, she gloried, when, in consequence of an enduring confession, that punishment was undergone which drove the confessors of Christ into exile; yet the present confession is so much the more illustrious and greater in honor as it is braver in suffering. The combat has increased, and the glory of the combatants has increased also. Nor were you kept back from the struggle by fear of tortures, but by the very tortures themselves you were more and more stimulated to the conflict; bravely and firmly you have returned with ready devotion, to contend in the extremest contest. Of you I find that some are already crowned, while some are even now within reach of the crown of victory; but all whom the danger has shut up in a glorious company are animated to carry on the struggle with an equal and common warmth of virtue, as it behoves the soldiers of Christ in the divine camp: that no allurements may deceive the incorruptible steadfastness of your faith, no threats terrify you, no sufferings or tortures overcome you, because "greater is He that is in us, than he that is in the world; " nor is the earthly punishment able to do more towards casting down, than is the divine protection towards lifting up. This truth is proved by the glorious struggle of the brethren, who, having become leaders to the rest in overcoming their tortures, afforded an example of virtue and faith, contending in the strife, until the strife yielded, being overcome. With what praises can I commend you, most courageous brethren? With what vocal proclamation can I extol the strength of your heart and the perseverance of your faith? You have borne the sharpest examination by torture, even unto the glorious consummation, and have not yielded to sufferings, but rather the sufferings have given way to you. The end of torments, which the tortures themselves did not give, the crown has given. The examination by torture waxing severer, continued for a long time to this result, not to overthrow the steadfast faith, but to send the men of God more quickly to the Lord. The multitude of those who were present saw with admiration the heavenly contest, – the contest of God, the spiritual contest, the battle of Christ,-saw that His servants stood with free voice, with unyielding mind, with divine virtue-bare, indeed, of weapons of this world, but believing and armed with the weapons of faith. The tortured stood more brave than the torturers; and the limbs, beaten and torn as they were, overcame the hooks that bent and tore them. The scourge, often repeated with all its rage, could not conquer invincible faith, even although the membrane which enclosed the entrails were broken, and it was no longer the limbs but the wounds of the servants of God that were tortured. Blood was flowing which might quench the blaze of persecution, which might subdue the flames of Gehenna with its glorious gore. Oh, what a spectacle was that to the Lord,-how sublime, how great, how acceptable to the eyes of God in the allegiance and devotion of His soldiers! As it is written in the Psalms, when the Holy Spirit at once speaks to us and warns us: "Precious in the sight of the Lord is the death of His saints." Precious is the death which has bought immortality at the cost of its blood, which has received the crown from the consummation of its virtues. How did Christ rejoice therein! How willingly did He both fight and conquer in such servants of His, as the protector of their faith, and giving to believers as much as he who taketh believes that he receives! He was present at His own contest; He lifted up, strengthened, animated the champions and assertors of His name. And He who once conquered death on our behalf, always conquers it in us. "When they," says He, "deliver you up, take no thought what ye shall speak: for it shall be given you in that hour what ye shall speak. For it is not ye that speak, but the Spirit of your Father which speaketh in you." The present struggle has afforded a proof of this saying. A voice filled with the Holy Spirit broke forth from the martyr's mouth when the most blessed Mappalicus said to the proconsul in the midst of his torments, "You shall see a contest to-morrow." And that which he said with the testimony of virtue and faith, the Lord fulfilled. A heavenly contest was exhibited, and the servant of God was crowned ill the struggle of the promised fight. This is the contest which the prophet Isaiah of old predicted, saying, "It shall be no light contest for you with men, since God appoints the struggle." And in order to show what this struggle would be, he added the words, "Behold, a virgin shall conceive and bear a son, and ye shall call His name Emmanuel." This is the struggle of our faith in which we engage, in which we conquer, in which we are crowned. This is the struggle which the blessed Apostle Paul has shown to us, in which it behoves us to run and to attain the crown of glory. "Do ye not know," says he, "that they which run in a race, run all indeed, but one receiveth the prize? So run that ye may obtain." "Now they do it that they may receive a corruptible crown, but we an incorruptible." Moreover, setting forth his own struggle, and declaring that he himself should soon be a sacrifice for the Lord's sake, he says, "I am now ready to be offered, and the time of my assumption is at hand. I have fought a good fight, I have finished my course, I have kept the faith: henceforth there is laid up for me a crown of righteousness, which the Lord, the righteous judge, shall give me at that day; and not to me only, but unto all them also that love His appearing."

This fight, therefore, predicted of old by the prophets, begun by the Lord, waged by the apostles, Mappalicus promised again to the proconsul in his own name and that of his colleagues. Nor did the faithful voice deceive in his promise; he exhibited the fight to which he had pledged himself, and he received the reward which he deserved. I not only beseech but exhort the rest of you, that you all should follow that martyr now most blessed, and the other partners of that engagement,-soldiers and comrades, steadfast in faith, patient in suffering, victors in tortures,-that those who are united at once by the bond of confession, and the entertainment of a dungeon, may also be united in the consummation of their virtue and a celestial crown; that you by your joy may dry the tears of our Mother, the Church, who mourns over the wreck and death of very many; and that you may confirm, by the provocation of your example, the steadfastness of others who stand also. If the battle shall call you out, if the day of your contest shall come engage bravely, fight with constancy, as knowing that you are fighting under the eyes of a present Lord, that you are attaining by the confession of His name to His own glory; who is not such a one as that He only looks on His servants, but He Himself also wrestles in us, Himself is engaged,-Himself also in the struggles of our conflict not only crowns, but is crowned. But if before the day of your contest, of the mercy of God, peace shall supervene, let there still remain to you the sound will and the glorious conscience. Nor let any one of you be saddened as if he were inferior to those who before you have suffered tortures, have overcome the world and trodden it under foot, and so have come to the Lord by a glorious road. For the Lord is the "searcher out of the reins and the hearts." He looks through secret things, and beholds that which is concealed. In order to merit the crown from Him, His own testimony alone is sufficient, who will judge us. Therefore, beloved brethren, either case is equally lofty and illustrious,-the former more secure, to wit, to hasten to the Lord with the consummation of our victory,-the latter more joyous; a leave of absence, after glory, being received to flourish in the praises of the Church. O blessed Church of ours, which the honor of the divine condescension illuminates, Which in our own times the glorious blood of martyrs renders illustrious! She was white before in the works of the brethren; now she has become purple in the blood of the martyrs. Among her flowers are wanting neither roses nor lilies. Now let each one strive for the largest dignity of either honor. Let them receive crowns, either white, as of labors, or of purple, as of suffering. In the heavenly camp both peace and strife have their own flowers, with which the soldier of Christ may be crowned for glory. I bid you, most brave and beloved brethren, always heartily farewell in the Lord; and have me in remembrance.

Fare ye well.

Cyprian, Letter 8

Cyprian's letter to Moyses and Maximus and the other Roman confessors

Beloved brethren, greeting. I had already known from rumor, most brave and blessed brethren, the glory of your faith and virtue, rejoicing greatly and abundantly congratulating you, that the highest condescension of our Lord Jesus Christ should have prepared you for the crown by confession of His name. For you, who have become chiefs and leaders in the battle of our day, have set forward the standard of the celestial warfare; you have made a beginning of the spiritual contest which God has purposed to be now waged by your valor; you, with unshaken strength and unyielding firmness, have broken the first onset of the rising war. Thence have arisen happy openings of the fight; thence have begun good auspices of victory. It happened that here martyrdoms were consummated by tortures. But he who, preceding in the struggle, has been made an example of virtue to the brethren, is on common ground with the martyrs in honor. Hence you have delivered to us garlands woven by your hand, and have pledged your brethren from the cup of salvation.

2. To these glorious beginnings of confession and the omens of a victorious warfare, has been added the maintenance of discipline, which I observed from the vigor of your letter that you lately sent to your colleagues joined with you to the Lord in confession, with anxious admonition, that the sacred precepts of the Gospel and the commandments of life once delivered to us should be kept with firm and rigid observance. Behold another lofty degree of your glory; behold, with confession, a double title to deserving well of God,–to stand with a firm step, and to drive away in this struggle, by the strength of your faith, those who endeavor to make a breach in the Gospel, and bring impious hands to the work of undermining the Lord's precepts: to have before afforded the

indications of courage, and now to afford lessons of life. The Lord, when, after His resurrection, He sent forth His apostles, charges them, saying, "All power is given unto me in heaven and in earth. Go ye therefore, and teach all nations, baptizing them in the name of the Father, and of the Son, and of the Holy Ghost: teaching them to observe all things whatsoever I have commanded you." And the Apostle John, remembering this charge, subsequently lays it down in his epistle: "Hereby," says he, "we do know that we know Him, if we keep His commandments. He that saith he knoweth Him, and keepeth not His commandments, is a liar, and the truth is not in him." You prompt the keeping of these precepts; you observe the divine and heavenly commands. This is to be a confessor of the Lord; this is to be a martyr of Christ, – to keep the firmness of one's profession inviolate among all evils, and secure. For to wish to become a martyr for the Lord, and to try to overthrow the Lord's precepts; to use against Him the condescension that He has granted you: to become, as it were, a rebel with arms that you have received from Him: this is to wish to confess Christ, and to deny Christ's Gospel. I rejoice, therefore, on your behalf, most brave and faithful brethren; and as much as I congratulate the martyrs there honored for the glory of their strength, so much do I also equally congratulate you for the crown of the Lord's discipline. The Lord has shed forth His condescension in manifold kinds of liberality. He has distributed the praises of good soldiers and their spiritual glories in plentiful variety. We also are sharers in your honor; we count your glory our glory, whose times have been brightened by such a felicity, that it should be the fortune of our day to see the proved servants of God and Christ's soldiers crowned. I bid you, most brave and blessed brethren, ever heartily farewell; and remember me.

Cyprian

Reply from Moyses, Maximus, Nicostratus, and the Other Confessors to Cyprian's Letter

In this letter the writers gratefully acknowledge the consolation which the roman confessors had received from Cyprian's letter. To them, martyrdom is not a punishment, but a happiness. The words of the gospel stimulate their faith. As far as the lapsed are concerned they are content to abide by Cyprian's judgment.

1. To Caecilius Cyprian, bishop of the church of the Carthaginians, Moyses and Maximus, presbyters, and Nicostratus and Rufinus, deacons, and the other confessors persevering in the faith of the truth, in God the Father, and in His Son Jesus Christ our Lord, and in the Holy Spirit, greeting. Placed, brother, as we are among various and manifold sorrows, on account of the present desolations of many brethren throughout almost the whole world, this chief consolation has reached us, that we have been lifted up by the receipt of your letter, and have gathered some alleviation for the griefs of our saddened spirit. From which we can already perceive that the grace of divine providence wished to keep us so long shut up in the prison chains, perhaps for no other reason than that, instructed and more vigorously animated by your letter, we might with a more earnest will attain to the destined crown. For your letter has shone upon us as a calm in the midst of a tempest, and as the longed-for tranquillity in the midst of a troubled sea, and as repose in labors, as health in dangers and pains, as in the densest darkness, the bright and glowing light. Thus we drank it up with a thirsty spirit, and received it with a hungry desire; so that we rejoice to find ourselves by it sufficiently fed and strengthened for encounter with the foe. The Lord will reward you for that love of yours, and will restore you the fruit due to this so good work; for he who exhorts is not less worthy of the reward of the crown than he who suffers; not less worthy of praise is he who has taught, than he who has acted also; he is not less to be honored who has warned, than he who has fought; except that sometimes the weight of glory more redounds to him who trains, than to him who has shown himself a teachable learner; for the latter, perchance, would not have bad what he has practiced, unless the former had taught him.

2. Therefore, again, we say, brother Cyprian, we have received great joy, great comfort, great refreshment, especially in that you have described, with glorious and deserved praises, the glorious, I will not say, deaths, but immortalities of martyrs. For such departures should have been proclaimed with such words, that the things which were related might be told in such manner as they were done. Thus, from your letter, we saw those glorious triumphs of the martyrs; and with our eyes in some sort have followed them as they went to heaven, and have contemplated them seated among angels, and the powers and dominions of heaven. Moreover, we have in some manner perceived with our ears the Lord giving them the promised testimony in the presence of the Father. It is this, then, which also raises our spirit day by day, and inflames us to the following of the track of such dignity.

3. For what more glorious, or what more blessed, can happen to any man from the divine condescension, than to confess the Lord God, in death itself, before his very executioners? Than among the raging and varied and exquisite tortures of worldly power, even when the body is racked and torn and cut to pieces, to confess Christ the Son of God with a spirit still free, although departing? Than to have mounted to heaven with the world left behind? Than, having forsaken men, to stand among the angels? Than, all worldly impediments being broken through, already to stand free in the sight of God? Than to enjoy the heavenly kingdom without any delay? Than to have become an associate of Christ's passion in Christ's name? Than to have become by the divine condescension the judge of one's own judge? Than to have brought off an unstained conscience from the confession of His name? Than to have refused to obey human and sacrilegious laws against the faith? Than to have borne witness to the truth with a public testimony? Than, by dying, to have subdued death itself, which is dreaded by all? Than, by death itself, to have attained immortality? Than when torn to pieces, and tortured by all the instruments of cruelty, to have overcome the torture by the tortures themselves? Than by strength of mind to have wrestled with all the agonies of a mangled body? Than not to have shuddered at the flow of one's own blood? Than to have begun to love one's punishments, after having faith to bear them? Than to think it an injury to one's life not to have left it?

4. For to this battle our Lord, as with the trumpet of His Gospel, stimulates us when He says, "He that loveth father or mother more than me is not worthy of me: and he that loveth his own soul more than me is not worthy of me. And he that taketh not his cross, and followeth after me, is not worthy of me." And again, "Blessed are they which are persecuted for righteousness" sake: for theirs is the kingdom of heaven. Blessed shall ye be, when men shall persecute you, and hate you. Rejoice, and be exceeding glad: for so did their fathers persecute the prophets which were before you." And again," Because ye shall stand before kings and powers, and the brother shall deliver up the brother to death, and the father the son, and he that endureth to the end shall be saved;" and "To him that overcometh will I give to sit on my throne, even as I also overcame and am set down on the throne of my Father." Moreover the apostle: "Who shall separate us from the love of Christ? shall tribulation, or distress, or persecution, or famine, or nakedness, or peril, or sword? (As it is written, For thy sake are we killed all the day long; we are accounted as sheep for the slaughter.) Nay, in all these things we are more than conquerors for Him who hath loved us."

5. When we read these things, and things of the like kind, brought together in the Gospel, and feel, as it were, torches placed under us, with the Lord's words to inflame our faith, we not only do not dread, but we even provoke the enemies of the truth; and we have already conquered the opponents of God, by the very fact of our not yielding to them, and have subdued their nefarious laws against the truth. And although we have not yet shed our blood, we are prepared to shed it. Let no one think that this delay of our departure is any clemency; for it obstructs us, it makes a hindrance to our glory, it puts off heaven, it withholds the glorious sight of God. For in a contest of this kind, and in the kind of

contest when faith is struggling in the encounter, it is not true clemency to put off martyrs by delay. Entreat therefore, beloved Cyprian, that of His mercy the Lord will every day more and more arm and adorn every one of us with greater abundance and readiness, and will confirm and strengthen us by the strength of His power; and, as a good captain, will at length bring forth His soldiers, whom He has hitherto trained and proved in the camp of our prison, to the field of the battle set before them. May He hold forth to us the divine arms, those weapons that know not how to be conquered, – the breastplate of righteousness, which is never accustomed to be broken, – the shield of faith, which cannot be pierced through, – the helmet of salvation, which cannot be shattered, – and the sword of the Spirit, which has never been wont to be injured. For to whom should we rather commit these things for him to ask for us, than to our so reverend bishop, as destined victims asking help of the priest?

6. Behold another joy of ours, that, in the duty of your episcopate, although in the meantime you have been, owing to the condition of the times, divided from your brethren, you have frequently confirmed the confessors by your letters; that you have ever afforded necessary supplies from your own just acquisitions; that in all things you have always shown yourself in some sense present; that in no part of your duty have you hung behind as a deserter. But what more strongly stimulated us to a greater joy we cannot be silent upon, but must describe with all the testimony of our voice. For we observe that you have both rebuked with fitting censure, and worthily, those who, unmindful of their sins, had, with hasty and eager desire, extorted peace from the presbyters in your absence, and those who, without respect for the Gospel, had with profane facility granted the holiness of the Lord unto dogs, and pearls to swine; although a great crime, and one which has extended with incredible destructiveness almost over the whole earth, ought only, as you yourself write, to be treated cautiously and with moderation, with the advice of all the bishops, presbyters, deacons, confessors, and even the laymen who abide fast, as in your letters you yourself also testify; so that, while wishing unseasonably to bring repairs to the ruins, we may not appear to be bringing about other and greater destruction, for where is the divine word left, if pardon be so easily granted to sinners? Certainly their spirits are to be cheered and to be nourished up to the season of their maturity, and they are to be instructed from the Holy Scriptures how great and surpassing a sin they have committed. Nor let them be animated by the fact that they are many, but rather let them be checked by the fact that they are not few. An unblushing number has never been accustomed to have weight in extenuation of a crime; but shame, modesty, patience, discipline, humility, and subjection, waiting for the judgment of others upon itself, and bearing the sentence of others upon its own judgment, – this it is which proves penitence; this it is which skins over a deep wound; this it is which raises up the ruins of the fallen spirit and restores them, which quells and restrains the burning vapor of their raging sins. For the physician will not give to the sick the food of healthy bodies, lest the unseasonable nourishment, instead of repressing, should stimulate the power of the raging disease, – that is to say, lest what might have been sooner diminished by abstinence, should, through impatience, be prolonged by growing indigestion.

7. Hands, therefore, polluted with impious sacrifices must be purified with good works, and wretched mouths defiled with accursed food must be purged with words of true penitence, and the spirit must be renewed and consecrated in the recesses of the faithful heart. Let the frequent groanings of the penitents be heard; let faithful tears be shed from the eyes not once only, but again and again, so that those very eyes which wickedly looked upon idols may wash away, with tears that satisfy God, the unlawful things that they had done. Nothing is necessary for diseases but patience: they who are weary and weak wrestle with their pain; and so at length hope for health, if, by tolerating it, they can overcome their suffering; for unfaithful is the scar which the physician has too quickly produced; and the healing is undone by any

little casualty, if the remedies be not used faithfully from their very slowness. The flame is quickly recalled again to a conflagration, unless the material of the whole fire be extinguished even to the extremest spark; so that men of this kind should justly know that even they themselves are more advantaged by the very delay, and that more trusty remedies are applied by the necessary postponement. Besides, where shall it be said that they who confess Christ are shut up in the keeping of a squalid prison, if they who have denied Him are in no peril of their faith? Where, that they are bound in the cincture of chains in God's name, if they who have not kept the confession of God are not deprived of communion? Where, that the imprisoned martyrs lay down their glorious lives, if those who have forsaken the faith do not feel the magnitude of their dangers and their sins? But if they betray too much impatience, and demand communion with intolerable eagerness, they vainly utter with petulant and unbridled tongues those querulous and invidious reproaches which avail nothing against the truth, since they might have retained by their own right what now by a necessity, which they of their own free will have sought, they are compelled to sue for. For the faith which could confess Christ, could also have been kept by Christ in communion. We bid you, blessed and most glorious father, ever heartily farewell in the Lord; and have us in remembrance.

Letter 26

Cyprian to Nemesianus and other martyrs in the mines

Cyprian extols and commends the martyrs in the mines. He contrasts, in a beautiful antithesis the tortures of each, with the consolations of each.

1. Cyprian to Nemesianus, Felix, Lucius, another Felix, Litteus, Polianus, Victor, Jader, and Dativus, his fellow-bishops, also to his fellow-presbyters and deacons, and the rest of the brethren in the mines, martyrs of God the Father Almighty, and of Jesus Christ our Lord, and of God our preserver, everlasting greeting. Your glory, indeed, would demand, most blessed and beloved brethren, that I myself should come to see and to embrace you, if the limits of the place appointed me did not restrain me, banished as I am for the sake of the confession of the Name. But in what way I can, I bring myself into your presence; and even though it is not permitted me to come to you in body and in movement, yet in love and in spirit I come expressing my mind in my letter, in which mind I joyfully exult in those virtues and praises of yours, counting myself a partaker with you, although not in bodily suffering, yet in community of love. Could I be silent and restrain my voice in stillness, when I am made aware of so many and such glorious things concerning my dearest friends, things with which the divine condescension has honored you, so that part of you have already gone before by the consummation of their martyrdom to receive from their Lord the crown of their deserts? Part still abide in the dungeons of the prison, or in the mines and in chains, exhibiting by the very delays of their punishments, greater examples for the strengthening and arming of the brethren, advancing by the tediousness of their tortures to more ample titles of merit, to receive as many payments in heavenly rewards, as days are now counted in their punishments. I do not marvel, most brave and blessed brethren, that these things have happened to you in consideration of the desert of your religion and your faith; that the Lord should thus have lifted you to the lofty height of glory by the honor of His glorification, seeing that you have always flourished in His Church, guarding the tenor of the faith, keeping firmly the Lord's commands; in simplicity, innocence; in charity, concord; modesty in humility, diligence in administration, watchfulness in helping those that suffer, mercy in cherishing the poor, constancy in defending the truth, judgment in severity of discipline. And that nothing should be wanting to the example of good deeds in you, even now, in the confession of your voice and the suffering of your body, you provoke the minds of your brethren to divine martyrdom, by exhibiting yourselves as leaders of virtue, that while the flock follows its pastors, and imitates what it sees to be done by those set over it, it may be crowned with the like merits of obedience by the Lord.

2. But that, being first severely beaten with clubs, and ill-used, you have begun by sufferings of that kind, the glorious firstlings of your confession, is not a matter to be execrated by us. For a Christian body is not very greatly terrified at clubs, seeing all its hope is in the Wood. The servant of Christ acknowledges the sacrament of his salvation: redeemed by wood to life eternal, he is advanced by wood to the crown. But what wonder if, as golden and silver vessels, you have been committed to the mine that is the home of gold and silver, except that now the nature of the mines is changed, and the places which previously had been accustomed to yield gold and silver have begun to receive them? Moreover, they have put fetters on your feet, and have bound your blessed limbs, and the temples of God with disgraceful chains, as if the spirit also could be bound with the body, or your gold could be stained by the contact of iron. To men who are dedicated to God, and attesting their faith with religious courage, such things are ornaments, not chains; nor do they bind the feet of the Christians for infamy, but glorify them for a crown. Oh feet blessedly bound, which are loosed, not by the smith but by the Lord! Oh feet blessedly bound, which are guided to paradise in the way of salvation! Oh feet bound for the present time in the world, that they may be always free with the Lord! Oh feet, lingering for a while among the fetters and cross-bars, but to run quickly to Christ on a glorious road! Let cruelty, either envious or malignant, hold you here in its bonds and chains as long as it will, from this earth and from these sufferings you shall speedily come to the kingdom of heaven. The body is not cherished in the mines with couch and cushions, but it is cherished with the refreshment and solace of Christ. The frame wearied with labors lies prostrate on the ground, but it is no penalty to lie down with Christ. Your limbs unbathed, are foul and disfigured with filth and dirt; but within they are spiritually cleansed, although without the flesh is defiled. There the bread is scarce; but man liveth not by bread alone, but by the word of God. Shivering, you want clothing; but he who puts on Christ is both abundantly clothed and adorned. The hair of your half-shorn bead seems repulsive; but since Christ is the head of the man, anything whatever must needs become that head which is illustrious on account of Christ's name. All that deformity, detestable and foul to Gentiles, with what splendor shall it be recompensed! This temporal and brief suffering, how shall it be exchanged for the re ward of a bright and eternal honor, when, according to the word of the blessed apostle, "the Lord shall change the body of our humiliation, that it may be fashioned like to the body of His brightness!"

3. But there cannot be felt any loss of either religion or faith, most beloved brethren, in the fact that now there is given no opportunity there to God's priests for offering and celebrating the divine sacrifices; yea, you celebrate and offer a sacrifice to God equal precious and glorious, and that will greatly profit you for the retribution of heavenly rewards, since the sacred Scripture speaks, saying, "The sacrifice of God is a broken spirit; a contrite and humbled heart God doth not despise." You offer this sacrifice to God; you celebrate this sacrifice without intermission day and night, being made victims to God, and exhibiting yourselves as holy and unspotted offerings, as the apostle exhorts and says, "I beseech you therefore, brethren, by the mercies of God, that ye present your bodies a living sacrifice, holy, acceptable unto God. And be not conformed to this world; but be ye transformed by the renewing of your mind, that ye may prove what is that good, and acceptable, and perfect will of God."

4. For this it is which especially pleases God; it is this wherein our works with greater deserts are successful in earning God's good-will; this it is which alone the obedience of our faith and devotion can render to the Lord for His great and saving benefits, as the Holy Spirit declares and witnesses in the Psalms: "What shall I render," says He, "to the Lord for all His benefits towards me? I will take the cup of salvation, and I will call upon the name of the Lord. Precious in the sight of the Lord is the death of His saints." Who would not gladly and readily receive the cup of salvation? Who would not with joy and gladness desire that in which he himself also may render somewhat unto His Lord? Who would not bravely and

unfalteringly receive a death precious in the sight of the Lord, to please His eyes, who, looking down from above upon us who are placed in the conflict for His name, approves the willing, assists the struggling, crowns the conquering with the recompense of patience, goodness, and affection, rewarding in us whatever He Himself has bestowed, and honoring what He has accomplished?

5. For that it is His doing that we conquer, and that we attain by the subduing of the adversary to the palm of the greatest contest, the Lord declares and teaches in His Gospel, saying, "But when they deliver you up, take no thought how or what ye shall speak; for it shall be given you in that same hour what ye shall speak. For it is not ye that speak, but the Spirit of your Father which speaketh in you." And again: "settle it therefore in your hearts, not to meditate before what ye shall answer; for I will give you a month and wisdom, which your adversaries shall not be able to resist." In which, indeed, is both the great confidence of believers, and the gravest fault of the faithless, that they do not trust Him who promises to give His help to those who confess Him, and do not on the other hand fear Him who threatens eternal punishment to those who deny Him.

6. All which things, most brave and faithful soldiers of Christ, you have suggested to your brethren, fulfilling in deeds what ye have previously taught in words, hereafter to be greatest in the kingdom of heaven, as the Lord promises and says, "Whosoever shall do and teach so, shall be called the greatest in the kingdom of heaven." Moreover, a manifold portion of the people, following your example, have confessed alike with you, and alike have been crowned, associated with you in the bond of the strongest charity, and separated from their prelates neither by the prison nor by the mines; in the number of whom neither are there wanting virgins in whom the hundred-fold are added to the fruit of sixty-fold, and whom a double glory has advanced to the heavenly crown. In boys also a I courage greater than their age has surpassed their years in the praise of their confession, so that every sex and every age should adorn the blessed flock of your martyrdom.

7. What now must be the vigor, beloved brethren, of your victorious consciousness, what the loftiness of your mind, what exultation in feeling, what triumph in your breast, that every one of you stands near to the promised reward of God, are secure from the judgment of God, walk in the mines with a body captive indeed, but with a heart reigning, that you know Christ is present with you, rejoicing in the endurance of His servants, who are ascending by His footsteps and in His paths to the eternal kingdoms! You daily expect with joy the saving day of your departure; and already about to withdraw from the world, you are hastening to the rewards of martyrdom, and to the divine homes, to behold after this darkness of the world the purest light, and to receive a glory greater than all sufferings and conflicts, as the apostle witnesses, and says, "The sufferings of this present time are not worthy to be compared with the glory that shall be revealed in us." And because now your word is more effectual in prayers, and supplication is more quick to obtain what is sought for in afflictions, seek more eagerly, and ask that the divine condescension would consummate the confession of all of us; that from this darkness and these snares of the world God would set us also free with you, sound and glorious; that we who here are united in the bond of charity and peace, and have stood together against the wrongs of heretics and the oppressions of the heathens, may rejoice together in the heavenly kingdom. I bid you, most blessed and most beloved brethren, ever farewell in the Lord, and always and everywhere remember me.

Cyprian, Letter 76

Reply from Nemesianus, Dativus, Felix, and Victor, to Cyprian

This letter, and the next two letters, have similar themes. They thank Cyprian for his assistance and comfort. As there are three separate letters replying to just one letter from Cyprian it has been deduced that the bishops who wrote them were in different sections of the mines.

Nemesianus, Dativus, Felix, and Victor,

1. Nemesianus, Dativus, Felix, and Victor, to their brother Cyprian, in the Lord eternal salvation. You speak, dearly beloved Cyprian, in your letters always with deep meaning, as suits the condition of the time, by the assiduous reading of which letters both the wicked are corrected and men of good faith are confirmed. For while you do not cease in your writings to lay bare the hidden mysteries, you thus make us to grow in faith, and men from the world to draw near to belief. For by whatever good things you have introduced in your many books, unconsciously you have described yourself to us. For you are greater than all men in discourse, in speech more eloquent, in counsel wiser, in patience more simple, in works more abundant, in abstinence more holy, in obedience more humble, and in good deeds more innocent. And you yourself know, beloved, that our eager wish was, that we might see you, our teacher and our lover, attain to the crown of a great confession.

2. For, in the proceedings before the proconsul; as a good and true teacher you first have pronounced that which we your disciples, following you, ought to say before the president. And, as a sounding trumpet, you have stirred up God's soldiers, furnished with heavenly arms, to the close encounter; and fighting in the first rank, you have slain the devil with a spiritual sword: you have also ordered the troops of the brethren, on the one hand and on the other, with your words, so that snares were on all sides laid for the enemy, and the severed sinews of the very carcase of the public foe were trodden under foot. Believe us, dearest, that your innocent spirit is not far from the hundred-fold reward, seeing that it has feared neither the first onsets of the world, nor shrunk from going into exile, nor hesitated to leave the city, nor dreaded to dwell in a desert place; and since it furnished many with an example of confession, itself first spoke the martyr-witness. For it provoked others to acts of martyrdom by its own example; and not only began to be a companion of the martyrs already departing from the world, but also linked a heavenly friendship with those who should be so.

3. Therefore they who were condemned with us give you before God the greatest thanks, beloved Cyprian, that in your letter you have refreshed their suffering breasts; have healed their limbs wounded with clubs; have loosened their feet bound with fetters; have smoothed the hair of their half-shorn head; have illuminated the darkness of the dungeon; have brought down the mountains of the mine to a smooth surface; have even placed fragrant flowers to their nostrils, and have shut out the foul odor of the smoke. Moreover, your continued gifts, and those of our beloved Quirinus, which you sent to be distributed by Herennianus the sub-deacon, and Lucian, and Maximus, and Amantius the acolytes, provided a supply of whatever had been wanting for the necessities of their bodies. Let us, then, be in our prayers helpers of one another: and let us ask, as you have bidden us, that we may have God and Christ and the angels as supporters in all our actions. We bid you, lord and brother, ever heartily farewell, and have us in mind. Greet all who are with you. All ours who are with us love you, and greet you, and desire to see you.
Letter 77

Lucius, the African bishop and martyr, replies to Cyprian

1. To Cyprian our brother and colleague, Lucius, and all the brethren who are with me in the Lord, greeting. Your letter came to us, dearest brother, while we were exulting and rejoicing in God that He had armed us for the struggle, and had made us by His condescension conquerors in the battle; the letter, namely, which you sent to us by Herennianus the sub-deacon, and Lucian, and Maximus, and Amantius the acolytes, which when we read we received a relaxation in our bonds, a solace in our affliction, and a support in our necessity; and we were aroused and more strenuously animated to bear whatever more of punishment might be awaiting us. For before our suffering we were called forth by you to glory, who first afforded us guidance to confession of the name of Christ. We indeed, who follow the footsteps of your confession, hope for an equal grace with you. For he who

is first in the race is first also for the reward; and you who first occupied the course thence have communicated this to us from what you began, showing doubtless the undivided love wherewith you have always loved us, so that we who had one Spirit in the bond of peace might have the grace of your prayers, and one crown of confession.

2. But in your case, dearest brother, to the crown of confession is added the reward of your labors – an abundant measure which you shall receive from the Lord in the day of retribution, who have by your letter presented yourself to us, as you manifested to us that candid and blessed breast of yours which we have ever known, and in accordance with its largeness have uttered praises to God with us, not as much as we deserve to hear, but as much as you are able to utter. For with your words you have both adorned those things which had been less in-strutted in us, and have strengthened us to the sustaining of those sufferings which we bear, as being certain of the heavenly rewards, and of the crown of martyrdom, and of the kingdom of God, from the prophecy which, being filled with the Holy Spirit, you have pledged to us in your letter. All this will happen, beloved, if you will have us in mind in your prayers, which I trust you do even as we certainly do.

3. And thus, O brother most longed-for, we have received what you sent to us from Quirinus and from yourself, a sacrifice from every clean thing. Even as Noah offered to God, and God was pleased with the sweet savor, and had respect unto his offering, so also may He have respect unto yours, and may He be pleased to return to you the reward of this so good work. But I beg that you will command the letter which we have written to Quirinus to be sent forward. I bid you, dearest brother and earnestly desired, ever heartily farewell, and remember us. Greet all who are with you. Farewell.

Letter 78

Felix, Jader, Polianus, and the rest of the martyrs, reply to Cyprian

To our dearest and best beloved Cyprian, Felix, Jader, Polianus, together with the presbyters and all who are abiding with us at the mine of Sigua, eternal health in the Lord. We reply to your salutation, dearest brother, by Herennianus the sub-deacon, Lucian and Maximus our brethren, strong and safe by the aid of your prayers, from whom we have received a sum under the name of an offering, together with your letter which you wrote, and in which you have condescended to comfort us as if we were sons, out of the heavenly words. And we have given and do give thanks to God the Father Almighty through His Christ, that we have been thus comforted and strengthened by your address, asking from the candor of your mind that you would deign to have us in mind in your constant prayers, that the Lord would supply what is wanting in your confession and ours, which He has condescended to confer on us. Greet all who abide with you. We bid you, dearest brother, ever heartily farewell in God. I Felix wrote this; I Jader subscribed it; I Polianus read it. I greet my lord Eutychianus.

Letter 79

Cyprian to Sergius, Rogatianus, and the Other Confessors in Prison

Cyprian consoles Rogatianus and his colleagues, the confessors in prison, and gives them the example of the martyrs Rogatianus the elder and Felicissimus. This letter was written while Cyprian himself was in exile.

1. Cyprian to Sergius and Rogatianus, and the rest of the confessors in the Lord, everlasting health. I salute you, dearest and most blessed brethren, myself also desiring to enjoy the sight of you, if the state in which I am placed would permit me to come to you. For what could happen to me more desirable and more joyful than to be now close to you, that you might embrace me with those hands, which, pure and innocent, and maintaining the faith of the Lord, have rejected the profane obedience? What more pleasant and sublime than now to kiss your lips, which with a glorious voice have confessed the Lord, to be looked upon even in presence by your eyes, which, despising the world, have become worthy of looking upon God? But since opportunity is not afforded me to share in this

joy, I send this letter in my stead to your ears and to your eyes, by which I congratulate and exhort you that you persevere strongly and steadily in the confession of the heavenly glory; and having entered on the way of the Lord's condescension, that you go on in the strength of the Spirit, to receive the crown, having the Lord as your protector and guide, who said, "Lo, I am with you alway, even unto the end of the world." O blessed prison, which your presence has enlightened! O blessed prison, which sends the men of God to heaven! O darkness, more bright than the sun itself, and clearer than the light of this world, where now are placed temples of God, and your members are to be sanctified by divine confessions!

2. Nor let anything now be revolved in your hearts and minds besides the divine precepts and heavenly commands, with which the Holy Spirit has ever animated you to the endurance of suffering. Let no one think of death, but of immortality; nor of temporary punishment, but of eternal glory; since it is written, "Precious in the sight of the Lord is the death of His saints;" and again, "A broken spirit is a sacrifice to God: a contrite and humble heart God doth not despise." And again, where the sacred Scripture speaks of the tortures which consecrate God's martyrs, and sanctify them in the very trial of suffering: "And if they have suffered torments in the sight of men, yet is their hope full of immortality; and having been a little chastised, they shall be greatly rewarded: for God proved them, and found them worthy of Himself. As gold in the furnace hath He tried them, and received them as a sacrifice of a burnt-offering, and in due time regard shall be had unto them. The righteous shall shine, and shall run to and fro like sparks among the stubble. They shall judge the nations, and have dominion over the people; and their Lord shall reign for ever." When, therefore, you reflect that you shall judge and reign with Christ the Lord, you must needs exult and tread under foot present sufferings, in the joy of what is to come; knowing that from the beginning of the world it has been so appointed that righteousness should suffer there in the conflict of the world, since in the beginning, even at the first, the righteous Abel was slain, and thereafter all righteous men, and prophets, and apostles who were sent. To all of whom the Lord also in Himself has appointed an example, teaching that none shall attain to His kingdom but those who have followed Him in His own way, saying, "He that loveth his life in this world shall lose it; and he that hateth his life in this world shall keep it unto life eternal." And again: "Fear not them which kill the body, but are not able to kill the soul: but rather fear Him who is able to destroy both soul and body in hell." Paul also exhorts us that we who desire to attain to the Lord's promises ought to imitate the Lord in all things. "We are," says he, "the sons of God: but if sons, then heirs; heirs of God, and joint-heirs with Christ; if so be that we suffer with Him, that we may also be glorified together." Moreover, he added the comparison of the present time and of the future glory, saying, "The sufferings of this present time are not worthy to be compared with the coming glory which shall be revealed in us." Of which brightness, when we consider the glory, it behoves us to bear all afflictions and persecutions; because, although many are the afflictions of the righteous, yet those are delivered from them all who trust in God.

3. Blessed women also, who are established with you in the same glory of confession, who, maintaining the Lord's faith, and braver than their sex, not only themselves are near to the crown of glory, but have afforded an example to other women by their constancy! And lest anything should be wanting to the glory of your number, that each sex and every age also might be with you in honor, the divine condescension has also associated with you boys in a glorious confession; representing to us something of the same kind as once did Ananias, Azarias, and Misael, the illustrious youths to whom, when shut up in the furnace, the fires gave way, and the flames gave refreshment, the Lord being present with them, and proving that against His confessors and martyrs the heat of hell could have no power, but that they who trusted in God should always continue unhurt and safe in all dangers. And I beg you to consider more carefully, in accordance with your religion, what must have been the faith in these youths which could deserve such full

acknowledgment from the Lord. For, prepared for every fate, as we ought all to be, they say to the king, "O king Nebuchadnezzar, we are not careful to answer thee in this matter; for our God whom we serve is able to deliver us from the burning fiery furnace; and He will deliver us out of thine hand, O king! But if not, be it known unto thee, O king, that we will not serve thy gods, nor worship the golden image which thou hast set up." Although they believed, and, in accordance with their faith, knew that they might even be delivered from their present punishment, they still would not boast of this, nor claim it for themselves, saying, "But if not." Lest the virtue of their confession should be less without the testimony of their suffering, they added that God could do all things; but yet they would not trust in this, so as to wish to be delivered at the moment; but they thought on that glory. of eternal liberty and security.

4. And you also, retaining this faith, and meditating day and night, with your whole heart prepared for God, think of the future only, with contempt for the present, that you may be able to come to the fruit of the eternal kingdom, and to the embrace and kiss, and the sight of the Lord, that you may follow in all things Rogatianus the presbyter, the glorious old man who, to the glory of our time, makes a way for you by his religious courage and divine condescension, who, with Felicissimus our brother, ever quiet and temperate, receiving the attack of a ferocious people, first prepared for you a dwelling in the prison, and, marking out the way for you in some measure, now also goes before you. That this may be consummated in you, we beseech the Lord in constant prayers, that from beginnings going on to the highest results, He may cause those whom He has made to confess, also to be crowned. I bid you, dearest and most beloved brethren, ever heartily farewell in the Lord; and may you attain to the crown of heavenly glory. Victor the deacon, and those who are with me, greet you.

Cyprian, Letter 80

Cyprian announces the death of pope Sixtus II

Severe persecution had been decreed by Emperor Valerian. Bishop Xistus had suffered martyrdom at Rome. Cyprian encourages Successus to strengthen his colleagues, so that they may each be a good example to their flocks, even if this means martyrdom. In this way Cyprian passes on the news about the church at Rome to the Churches of Africa.

Carthage, August 258.
To Successus, on hearing news from Rome about the persecution

My dearest brother, I was unable to send you a letter earlier because none of the clergy of this Church could move, being all under persecution, which however, thank God, found them inwardly most ready to pass at once to heaven. I now send you what news I have.

The envoys I sent to Rome have returned. I sent them to verify and report the decision taken by the authorities concerning myself, whatever it may be, and so put an end to all the speculations and uncontrolled hypotheses which circulated. And now here is the truth, duly ascertained.

Emperor Valerian has sent the Senate his rescript by which he has decided that bishops, priests and deacons shall immediately be put to death. Senators, notables and those who have the title of Roman knighthood shall be deprived of all dignities, as well as of their possessions. If they are obstinate in profess Christianity, even after the confiscation, they will be condemned to capital punishment.

Christians matrons will have all their goods confiscated and then be sent into exile. All imperial functionaries who have professed faith or should do so now, will suffer the same confiscation. They will then be arrested and registered for forced labor on the imperial estates.

Valerian also adds to the rescript a copy of a letter he has sent to the provincial governors concerning myself. I expect this letter any day and hope to receive it quickly, keeping myself firm and strong in faith. My decision in the face of martyrdom is quite clear. I am waiting for it, full of confidence that I shall receive the crown of eternal life from the goodness and generosity of God.

I have to report that Sixtus suffered martyrdom with four deacons on 6th of August, while he was in the "Cemetery" area (the catacombs of St. Callixtus).

The Roman authorities have a rule that all who are denounced as Christians must be executed and their goods forfeited to the imperial treasury.

I ask that what I have reported be made known to our colleagues in the episcopate, so that by their exhortations our communities may be encouraged and ever more prepared for the spiritual combat. This will stimulate them to consider not so much death as the blessings of immortality, and to consecrate themselves to the Lord with ardent faith and heroic fortitude, to delight and not to fear at the thought of testifying their faith. The soldiers of God and of Christ know very well that their immolation is not so much a death but a crown of glory.

To you, dear brother, my greetings in the Lord.

Cyprian, Letter 81

Cyprian's letter to the clergy and people about his withdrawal, a little before his martyrdom

When Cyprian, an elderly man, was told that messengers had been sent to arrest him so he could be punished in Utica, he withdrew. In case it was thought that he had done so for fear of death, he explains his reasons for doing this. He says that he is determined to be martyred in Carthage, in front of his own people, and nowhere else. This letter was written in AD 258.

1. Cyprian to the presbyters and deacons, and all the people, greeting. When it had been told to us, dearest brethren, that the gaolers had been sent to bring me to Utica, and I had been persuaded by the counsel of those dearest to me to withdraw for a time from my gardens, as a just reason was afforded I consented. For the reason that it is fit for a bishop, in that city in which he presides over the Church of the Lord, there to confess the Lord, and that the whole people should be glorified by the confession of their prelate in their presence. For whatever, in that moment of confession, the confessor-bishop speaks, he speaks in the mouth of all, by inspiration of God. But the honor of our Church, glorious as it is, will be mutilated if I, a bishop placed over another church, receiving my sentence or my confession at Utica, should go thence as a martyr to the Lord, when indeed, both for my own sake and yours, I pray with continual supplications, and with all my desires entreat, that I may confess among you, and there suffer, and thence depart to the Lord even as I ought. Therefore here in a hidden retreat I await the arrival of the proconsul returning to Carthage, that I may hear from him what the emperors have commanded upon the subject of Christian laymen and bishops, and may say what the Lord will wish to be said at that hour.

2. But do you, dearest brethren, according to the discipline which you have ever received from me out of the Lord's commands, and according to what you have so very often learnt from my discourse, keep peace and tranquillity; nor let any of you stir up any tumult for the brethren, or voluntarily offer himself to the Gentiles. For when apprehended and delivered up, he ought to speak, inasmuch as the Lord abiding in us speaks in that hour, who willed that we should rather confess than profess. But for the rest, what it is fitting that we should observe before the proconsul passes sentence on me for the confession of the name of God, we will with the instruction of the Lord arrange in common May our Lord make you, dearest brethren, to remain safe in His Church, and condescend to keep you. So be it through His mercy.

Letter 82

Desiring martyrdom

We begin gladly to desire martyrdom as we learn not to fear death. But perchance some one may object, and say, "It is this, then, that saddens me in the present mortality, that I, who had been prepared for confession, and had devoted myself to the endurance of suffering with my whole heart and with abundant courage, am deprived of martyrdom, in that I am anticipated by death." In the first place, martyrdom is not in your power, but in the condescension of God; neither can you say that you have lost what you do not know whether you would deserve to receive. Then, besides, God the searcher of the reins and heart, and the investigator and knower of secret things, sees you, and praises and approves you; and He who sees that your virtue was ready in you, will give you a reward for your virtue. Had Cain, when he offered his gift to God, already slain his brother? And yet God, foreseeing the fratricide conceived in his mind, anticipated its condemnation. As in that case the evil thought and mischievous intention were foreseen by a foreseeing God, so also in God's servants, among whom confession is purposed and martyrdom conceived in the mind, the intention dedicated to good is crowned by God the judge. It is one thing for the spirit to be wanting for martyrdom, and another for martyrdom to have been wanting for the spirit. Such as the Lord finds you when He calls you, such also He judges you; since He Himself bears witness, and says, "And all the churches shall know that I am the searcher of the reins and heart." For God does not ask for our blood, but for our faith. For neither Abraham, nor Isaac, nor Jacob were slain; and yet, being honored by the deserts of faith and righteousness, they deserved to be first among the patriarchs, to whose feast is collected every one that is found faithful, and righteous, and praiseworthy.

Cyprian, Treatise 6

Cyprian's exhortation to martyrdom

This is addressed to Fortunatus

Preface

1. You have desired, beloved Fortunatus that, I since the burden of persecutions and afflictions is lying heavy upon us, and in the ending and completion of the world the hateful time of Antichrist is already beginning to draw near, I would collect from the sacred Scriptures some exhortations for preparing and strengthening the minds of the brethren, whereby I might animate the soldiers of Christ for the heavenly and spiritual contest. I have been constrained to obey your so needful wish, so that as much as my limited powers, instructed by the aid of divine inspiration, are sufficient, some arms, as it were, and defenses might be brought forth from the Lord's precepts for the brethren who are about to fight. For it is little to arouse God's people by the trumpet call of our voice, unless we confirm the faith of believers, and their valor dedicated and devoted to God, by the divine readings.

2. But what more fitly or more fully agrees with my own care and solicitude, than to prepare the people divinely entrusted to me, and an army established in the heavenly camp, by assiduous exhortations against the darts and weapons of the devil? For he cannot be a soldier fitted for the war who has not first been exercised in the field; nor will he who seeks to gain the crown of contest be rewarded on the racecourse, unless he first considers the use and skilfulness of his powers. It is an ancient adversary and an old enemy with whom we wage our battle: six thousand years are now nearly completed since the devil first attacked man. All kinds of temptation, and arts, and snares for his overthrow, he has learned by the very practice of long years. If he finds Christ's soldier unprepared, if unskilled, if not careful and watching with his whole heart; he circumvents him if ignorant, he deceives him incautious, he cheats him inexperienced. But if a man, keeping the Lord's precepts, and bravely adhering to Christ, stands against him, he must needs be conquered, because Christ, whom that man confesses, is un-conquered.

3. And that I might not extend my discourse, beloved brother, to too great a length, and fatigue my hearer or reader by the abundance of a too diffuse style, I have made a compendium; so that the titles being placed first, which every one ought both to know and to have in mind, I might subjoin sections of the Lord s word, and establish what I had proposed by the authority of the divine teaching, in such wise as that I might not appear to have sent you my own treatise so much, as to have suggested material for others to discourse on; a proceeding which will be of advantage to individuals with increased benefit. For if I were to give a man a garment finished and ready, it would be my garment that another was making use of, and probably the thing made for another would be found little fitting for his figure of stature and

body. But now I have sent you the very wool and the purple from the Lamb, by whom we were redeemed and quickened; which, when you have received, you will make into a coat for yourself according to your own will, and the rather that you will rejoice in it as your own private and special garment. And you will exhibit to others also what we have sent, that they themselves may be able to finish it according to their will; so that that old nakedness being covered, they may all bear the garments of Christ robed in the sanctification of heavenly grace.

4. Moreover also, beloved brethren, I have considered it a useful and wholesome plan in an exhortation so needful as that which may make martyrs, to cut off all delays and tardiness in our words, and to put away the windings of human discourse, and set down only those things which God speaks, wherewith Christ exhorts His servants to martyrdom. Those divine precepts themselves must be supplied, as it were, for arms for the combatants. Let them be the incitements of the warlike trumpet; let them he the clarion-blast for the warriors. Let the ears be roused by them; let the minds be prepared by them; let the powers both of soul and body be strengthened to all endurance of suffering. Let us only who, by the Lord's permission, have given the first baptism to believers, also prepare each one for the second; urging and teaching that this is a baptism greater in grace, more lofty in power, more precious in honor – a baptism wherein angels baptize – a baptism in which God and His Christ exult – a baptism after which no one sins any more – a baptism which completes the increase of our faith – a baptism which, as we withdraw from the world, immediately associates us with God. In the baptism of water is received the remission of sins, in the baptism of blood the crown of virtues. This thing is to be embraced and desired, and to be asked for in all the entreaties of our petitions, that we who are God's servants should be also His friends.

Summary

1. Therefore, in exhorting and preparing our brethren, and in arming them with firmness of virtue and faith for the heralding forth of the confession of the Lord, and for the battle of persecution and suffering, we must declare, in the first place, that the idols which man makes for himself are not gods. For things which are made are not greater than their maker and fashioner; nor can these things protect and preserve anybody, which themselves perish out of their temples, unless they are preserved by man. But neither are those elements to be worshiped which serve man according to the disposition and ordinance of God.

2. The idols being destroyed, and the truth concerning the elements being manifested, we must show that God only is to be worshiped.

3. Then we must add, what is God's threatening against those who sacrifice to idols.

4. Besides, we must teach that God does not easily pardon idolaters.

5. And that God is so angry with idolatry, that He has even commanded those to be slain who persuade others to sacrifice and serve idols.

6. After this we must subjoin, that being redeemed and quickened by the blood of Christ, we ought to prefer nothing to Christ, because He preferred nothing to us, and on our account preferred evil things to good, poverty to riches, servitude to rule, death to immortality; that we, on the contrary, in our sufferings are preferring the riches and delights of paradise to the poverty of the world, eternal dominion and kingdom to the slavery of time, immortality to death, God and Christ to the devil and Antichrist.

7. We must urge also, that when snatched from the jaws of the devil, and freed from the snares of this world, if they begin to be in difficulty and trouble, they must not desire to return again to the world, and so lose the advantage of their withdrawal therefrom.

8. That we must rather urge on and persevere in faith and virtue, and in completion of heavenly and spiritual grace, that we may attain to the palm and to the crown.

9. For that afflictions and persecutions are brought about for this purpose, that we may be proved.

10. Neither must we fear the injuries and penalties of persecutions, because greater is the Lord to protect than the devil to assault.

11. And lest any one should be frightened and troubled at the afflictions and persecutions which we suffer in this world, we must prove that it was before foretold that the world would hold us in hatred, and that it would arouse persecutions against us; that from this very thing, that these things come to pass, is manifest the truth of the divine promise, in recompenses and rewards which shall afterwards follow; that it is no new thing which happens to Christians, since from the beginning of the world the good have suffered, and have been oppressed and slain by the unrighteous.

12. In the last place, it must be laid down what hope and what reward await the righteous and martyrs after the struggles and the sufferings of this time, and that we shall receive more in the reward of our suffering than what we suffer here in the passion itself.

Exhortation to martyrdom

1. THAT IDOLS ARE NOT GODS, AND THAT THE ELEMENTS ARE NOT TO BE WORSHIPED IN THE PLACE OF GODS.

In the cxiiith Psalm it is shown that "the idols of the heathen are silver and gold, the work of men's hands. They have a mouth, and speak not; eyes have they, and see not. They have ears, and hear not; neither is there any breath in their mouth. Let those that make them be made like unto them." Also in the Wisdom of Solomon: "They counted all the idols of the nations to be gods, which neither have the use of eyes to see, nor noses to draw breath, nor ears to hear, nor fingers on their hands to handle; and as for their feet, they are slow to go. For man made them, and he that borrowed his own spirit fashioned them; but no man can make a god like unto himself. For, since he is mortal, he worketh a dead thing with wicked hands; for he himself is better than the things which he worshipeth, since he indeed lived once, but they never." In Exodus also: "Thou shalt not make to thee an idol, nor the likeness of anything." Moreover, in Solomon, concerning the elements: "Neither by considering the works did they acknowledge who was the workmaster; but deemed either fire, or wind, or the swift air, or the circle of the stars, or the violent water, or the sun, or the moon, to be gods. On account of whose beauty, if they thought this, let them know how much more beautiful is the Lord than they. Or if they admired their powers and operations, let them understand by them, that He that made these mighty things is mightier than they."

2. THAT GOD ALONE MUST BE WORSHIPED.

"As it is written, Thou shall worship the Lord thy God, and Him only shalt thou serve." Also in Exodus: "Thou shalt have none other gods beside me." Also in Deuteronomy: "see ye, see ye that I am He, and that there is no God beside me. I will kill, and will make alive; I will smite, and I will heal; and there is none who can deliver out of mine hands." In the Apocalypse, moreover: "And I saw another angel fly in the midst of heaven, having the everlasting Gospel to preach over the earth, and over all nations, and tribes, and tongues, and peoples, saying with a loud voice, Fear God rather, and give glory to Him: for the hour of His judgment is come; and worship Him that made heaven and earth, and the sea, and all that therein is." So also the Lord, in His Gospel, makes mention of the first and second commandment, saying, "Hear, O Israel, The Lord thy God is one God;" and, "Thou shalt love thy Lord with all thy heart, and with all thy soul, and with all thy strength. This is the first; and the second is like unto it, Thou shall love thy neighbor as thyself. On these two commandments hang all the law and the prophets." And once more: "And this is life eternal, that they may know Thee, the only and true God, and Jesus Christ, whom Thou hast sent."

3. WHAT IS GOD'S THREATENING AGAINST THOSE WHO SACRIFICE TO IDOLS?

In Exodus: "He that sacrificeth unto any gods but the Lord only, shall be rooted out." Also in Deuteronomy: "They sacrificed unto demons, and not to God." In Isaiah also: "They worshiped those which their fingers have made; and the mean man was bowed down, and the great man was humbled: and I will not forgive them." And again: "To them hast thou poured out drink-offerings, and to them thou hast offered sacrifices. For these, therefore, shall I not be angry, saith the Lord?" In Jeremiah also: "Walk ye not after other gods, to serve them; and worship them not, and provoke me not in the works of your hands, to destroy you." In the Apocalypse too: "If any man worship the beast and his image, and receive his mark in his forehead or in his hand, he shall also drink of the wine of the wrath of God, which is mixed in the cup of His wrath, and shall be punished with fire and brimstone before the eyes of the holy angels, and before the eyes of the Lamb: and the smoke of their torments shall ascend for ever and ever: and they shall have no rest day or night, whosoever worship the beast and his image."

4. That God does not easily pardon idolaters.

Moses in Exodus prays for the people, and does not obtain his prayer, saying: "I pray, O Lord, this people hath sinned a great sin. They have made them gods of gold. And now, if Thou forgivest them their sin, forgive it; but if not, blot me out of the book which Thou hast written. And the Lord said unto Moses, If any one hath sinned against me, him will I blot out of my book." Moreover, when Jeremiah besought for the people, the Lord speaks to him, saying: "And pray not thou for this people, and entreat not for them in prayer and supplication; because I will not hear in the time wherein they shall call upon me in the time of their affliction." Ezekiel also denounces this same anger of God upon those who sin against God, and says: "And the word of the Lord came unto me, saying, Son of man, whatsoever land sinneth against me, by committing an offence, I will stretch forth mine hand upon it, and will crush the support of the bread thereof; and I wills send into it famine, and I will take away from it man and beast. And though these three men were in the midst of it, Noah, Daniel, and Job, they shall not deliver sons nor daughters; they themselves only shall be delivered." Likewise in the first book of Kings: "If a man sin by offending against another, they shall beseech the Lord for him; but if a man sin against God, who shall entreat for him?"

5. That God is so angry against idolatry, that He has even enjoined those to be slain who persuade others to sacrifice and serve idols.

In Deuteronomy: "But if thy brother, or thy son, or thy daughter, or thy wife which is in thy bosom, or thy friend which is the fellow of thine own soul, should ask thee secretly, saying, Let us go anti serve other gods, the gods of the nations, thou shalt not consent unto him, and thou shalt not hearken unto him, neither shall thine eye spare him, neither shalt thou conceal him, declaring thou shalt declare concerning him. Thine hand shall be upon him first of all to put him to death, and afterwards the hand of all the people; and they shall stone him, and he shall die, because he hath sought to turn thee away from the Lord thy God." And again the Lord speaks, and says, that neither must a city be spared, even though the whole city should consent to idolatry: "Or if thou shalt hear in one of the cities which the Lord thy God shall give thee, to dwell there, saying, Let us go and serve other gods, which thou hast not known, slaying thou shalt kill all who are in the city with the slaughter of the sword, and bum the city with fire, and it shall be without habitation for ever. Moreover, it shall no more be rebuilt, that the Lord may be turned from the indignation of His anger. And He will show thee mercy, and He will pity thee, and will multiply thee, if thou wilt hear the voice of the Lord thy God, and wilt observe His precepts." Remembering which precept and its force, Mattathias slew him who had approached the altar to sacrifice. But if before the coming of Christ these precepts concerning the worship of God and the despising of idols were observed, how much more should they be regarded since Christ's advent; since He, when He came, not only exhorted us with words, but with deeds also, but after all wrongs and contumelies, suffered also, and was crucified, that He might teach us to suffer and to die by His example, that there might be no excuse for a man not to suffer for Him, since He suffered for us; and that since He suffered for the sins of others, much rather ought each to suffer for his own sins. And therefore in the Gospel He threatens, and says: "Whosoever shall confess me before men, him will I also confess before my Father which is in heaven; but whosoever shall deny me before men, him will I also deny before my Father which is in heaven." The Apostle Paul also says: "For if we die with Him, we shall also live with Him; if we suffer, we shall also reign with Him; if we deny Him, He also will deny us." John too: "Whosoever denieth the Son, the same hath not the Father; he that acknowledgeth the Son, hath both the Son and the Father." Whence the Lord exhorts and strengthens us to contempt of death, saying: "Fear not them which kill the body, but are not able to kill the soul; but rather fear Him which is able to kill soul and body in Gehenna." And again: "He that loveth his life shall lose it; and he who hateth his life in this world, shall keep it unto life eternal."

6. THAT, BEING REDEEMED AND QUICKENED BY THE BLOOD OF CHRIST, WE OUGHT TO PREFER NOTHING TO CHRIST.

In the Gospel the Lord speaks, and says: "He that loveth father or mother more than me, is not worthy of me; and he that loveth son or daughter more than me, is not worthy of me; and he that taketh not his cross and followeth me, is not worthy of me." So also it is written in Deuteronomy: "They who say to their father and their mother, I have not known thee, and have not acknowledged their own children, these have kept Thy precepts, and have observed Thy covenant." Moreover, the Apostle Paul says: "Who shall separate us from the love of Christ? shall tribulation, or distress, or persecution, or hunger, or nakedness, or peril, or sword? As it is written, Because for Thy sake we are killed all the day long, we are counted as sheep for the slaughter. Nay, in all these things we overcome on account of Him who hath loved us." And again: "Ye are not your own, for ye are bought with a great price. Glorify and bear God in your body." And again: "Christ died for all, that both they which live may not henceforth live unto themselves, but unto Him which died for them, and rose again."

7. THAT THOSE WHO ARE SNATCHED FROM THE JAWS OF THE DEVIL, AND DELIVERED FROM THE SNARES OF THIS WORLD, OUGHT NOT AGAIN TO RETURN TO THE WORLD, LEST THEY SHOULD LOSE THE ADVANTAGE OF THEIR WITHDRAWAL THEREFROM.

In Exodus the Jewish people, prefigured as a shadow and image of us, when, with God for their guardian and avenger, they had escaped the most severe slavery of Pharaoh and of Egypt – that is, of the devil and the world – faithless and ungrateful in respect of God, murmur against Moses, looking back to the discomforts of the desert and of their labor; and, not understanding the divine benefits of liberty and salvation, they seek to return to the slavery of Egypt – that is, of the world whence they had been drawn forth – when they ought rather to have trusted and believed on God, since He who delivers His people from the devil and the world, protects them also when delivered. "Wherefore hast thou thus done with us," say they, "in casting us forth out of Egypt? It is better for us to serve the Egyptians than to die in this wilderness. And Moses said unto the people, Trust, and stand fast, and see the salvation which is from the Lord, which He shall do to you to-day. The Lord Himself shall fight for you, and ye shall hold your peace." The Lord, admonishing us of this in His Gospel, and teaching that we should not return again to the devil and to the world, which we have renounced, and whence we have escaped, says: "No man looking back, land putting his hand to the plough, is fit for the kingdom of God." And again: "And let him that is in the field not return back. Remember Lot's wife." And lest any one should be retarded by any covetousness of wealth or attraction of his own people from following Christ, He adds, and says: "He that forsaketh not all that he hath, cannot be my disciple."

8. THAT WE MUST PRESS ON AND PERSEVERE IN FAITH AND VIRTUE, AND IN COMPLETION OF HEAVENLY AND SPIRITUAL GRACE, THAT WE MAY ATTAIN TO THE PALM AND THE CROWN.

In the book of Chronicles: "The Lord is with you so long as ye also are with Him; but if ye forsake Him, He will forsake you." In Ezekiel also: "The righteousness of the righteous shall not deliver him in what day soever he may transgress." Moreover, in the Gospel the Lord speaks, and says: "He that shall endure to the end, the same shall be saved." And again: "If ye shall abide in my word, ye shall be my disciples indeed; and ye shall know the truth, and the truth shall make you free." Moreover, forewarning us that we ought always to be ready, and to stand firmly equipped and armed, He adds, and says: "Let your loins be girded about, and your lamps burning, and ye yourselves like unto men that wait for their lord when he shall return from the wedding, that when he cometh and knocketh they may open unto him. Blessed are those servants whom their lord, when he cometh, shall find watching." Also the blessed Apostle Paul, that our faith may advance and grow, and attain to the highest point, exhorts us, saying: "Know ye not, that they which run in a race run all indeed, yet one receiveth the prize? So run, that ye may obtain. And they, indeed, that they may receive a corruptible crown; but ye an incorruptible." And again: "No man that warreth for God binds himself to anxieties of this world, that he may be able to please Him to whom he hath approved himself. Moreover, also, if a man should contend, he will not be crowned unless he have fought lawfully." And again: "Now I beseech you, brethren, by the mercy of God, that ye constitute your bodies a living sacrifice, holy, acceptable unto God; and be not conformed to this world, but be ye transformed in the renewing of your spirit, that ye may prove what is the will of God, good, and acceptable, and perfect." And again: "We are children of God: but if children, then heirs; heirs indeed of God, but joint-heirs with Christ, if we suffer together, that we may also be glorified together." And in the Apocalypse the same exhortation of divine preaching speaks, saying, "Hold fast that which thou hast, lest another take thy crown;" which example of perseverance and persistence is pointed out in Exodus, when Moses, for the overthrow of Amalek, who bore the type of the devil, raised up his open hands in the sign and sacrament of the cross, and could not conquer his adversary unless when he had steadfastly persevered in the sign with hands continually lifted up. "And it came to pass," says he, "when Moses raised up his hands, Israel prevailed; but when he let down h s hands, Amalek grew mighty. And they took a stone and placed it under him, and he sate thereon. And Aaron and Hur held up his hands on the one side and on the other side, and Moses' hands were made steady even to the going down of the sun. Anti Jesus routed Amalek and all his people. And the Lord said unto Moses, Write this, and let it be a memorial in a book, and tell it in the ears of Jesus; because in destroying I will destroy the remembrance of Amalek from under heaven."

9. That afflictions and persecutions arise for the sake of our being proved.

In Deuteronomy, "The Lord your God proveth you, that He may know if ye love the Lord. your God with all your heart, and with all your soul, and with all your strength."(9) And again, Solomon: "The furnace proveth the potter's vessel, and righteous men the trial of tribulation." Paul also testifies similar things, and speaks, saying: "We glory in the hope of the glory of God. And not only so, but we glory in tribulations also; knowing that tribulation worketh patience, and patience experience, and experience hope; and hope maketh not ashamed, because the love of God is shed abroad in our hearts by the Holy Spirit who is given unto us." And Peter, in his epistle, lays it down, and says: "Beloved, be not surprised at the fiery heat which falleth upon you, which happens for your trial; and fail not, as if some new thing were happening unto you. But as often as ye communicate with the sufferings of Christ, rejoice in all things, that also in the revelation made of His glory you may rejoice with gladness. If ye be reproached in the name of Christ, happy are ye; because the name of the majesty and power of the Lord resteth upon you; which indeed according to them is blasphemed, but according to us is honored."

10. That injuries and penalties of persecutions are not to be feared by us, because greater is the Lord to protect than the devil to assault.

John, in his epistle, proves this, saying: "Greater is He who is in you than he that is in the world." Also in the cxviith Psalm: "I will not fear what man can do unto me; the Lord is my helper." And again: "These in chariots, and those in horses; bat we will glory in the name of the Lord our God. They themselves are bound, and they have fallen; but we have risen up, and stand upright." And even more strongly the Holy Spirit, teaching and showing that the army of the devil is not to be feared, and that, if the foe should declare war against us, our hope consists rather in that war itself; and that by that conflict the righteous attain to the reward of the divine abode and eternal salvation, – lays down in the twenty-sixth Psalm, and says: "Though an host should be arrayed against me, my heart shall not fear; though war should rise up against me, in that will I put my hope. One hope have I sought of the Lord, this will I require; that I may dwell in the house of the Lord all the days of my life." Also in Exodus, the Holy Scripture declares that we are rather multiplied and increased by afflictions, saying: "And the more they afflicted them, so much the more they became greater, and waxed stronger." And in the Apocalypse, divine protection is promised to our sufferings. "Fear nothing of these things," it says, "which thou shalt suffer." Nor does any one else promise to us security and protection, than He who also speaks by Isaiah the prophet, saying: "Fear not; for I have redeemed thee, and called thee by thy name: thou art mine. And if thou passest through the water, I am with thee, and the rivers shall not overflow thee. And if thou passest through the fire, thou shalt not be burned, and the flame shall not burn thee; for I, the Lord thy God, the Holy One of Israel, am He who maketh thee safe." Who also promises in the Gospel that divine help shall not be wanting to God's servants in persecutions, saying: "But when they shall deliver you up, take no thought how or what ye shall speak. For it shall be given you in that hour what ye shall speak. For it is not ye who speak, but the Spirit of your Father who speaketh in you." And again: "settle it in your hearts not to meditate before how to answer. For I will give you a mouth and wisdom, which your adversaries shall not be able to resist." As in Exodus God speaks to Moses when he delayed and trembled to go to the people, saying: "Who hath given a mouth to man? and who hath made the stammerer? and who the deaf man? and who the seeing, and the blind man? Have not I, the Lord God? And now go, and I will open thy mouth, and will instruct thee what thou shall say." Nor is it difficult for God to open the mouth of a man devoted to Himself, and to inspire constancy and confidence in speech to His confessor; since in the book of Numbers He made even a she-ass to speak against the prophet Balaam. Wherefore in persecutions let no one think what danger the devil is bringing in, but let him indeed consider what help God affords; nor let human mischief overpower the mind, but let divine protection strengthen the faith; since every one, according to the Lord's promises and the deservings of his faith, receives so much from God's help as he thinks that he receives. Nor is there anything which the Almighty is not able to grant, unless the failing faith. of the receiver be deficient and give way.

11. THAT IT WAS BEFORE PREDICTED THAT THE WORLD WOULD HOLD US IN ABHORRENCE, AND THAT IT WOULD STIR UP PERSECUTIONS AGAINST US, AND THAT NO NEW THING IS HAPPENING TO THE CHRISTIANS, SINCE FROM THE BEGINNING OF THE WORLD THE GOOD HAVE SUFFERED, AND THE RIGHTEOUS HAVE BEEN OPPRESSED AND SLAIN BY THE UNRIGHTEOUS.

The Lord in the Gospel forewarns and foretells, saying: "If the world hates you, know that it first hated me. If ye were of the world, the world would love what is its own: but because ye are not of the world, and I have chosen you out of the world, therefore the world hateth you. Remember the word that I spoke unto you, The servant is not greater than his master. If they have persecuted me, they will persecute you also." And again: "The hour will come, that every one that killeth you will think that he doeth, God service; but they will do this because they have not known the Father nor me. But these things have I told you, that when the hour shall come ye may remember them, because I told you." And again: "Verily, verily, I say unto yon, That ye shall weep and lament, but the world shall rejoice; ye shall be sorrowful, but your sorrow shall be turned into joy." And again: "These things have I spoken unto you, that in me ye may have peace; but in the world ye shall have tribulation: but be of good confidence, for I have overcome the world." And when He was interrogated by His disciples concerning the sign of His coming, and of the consummation of the world, He answered and said: "Take care lest any deceive you: for many shall come in my name, saying, I am Christ; and shall deceive many. And ye shall begin to hear of wars, and rumors of wars; see that ye be not troubled: for these things must needs come to pass, but the end is not yet. For nation shall rise against nation, and kingdom against kingdom: and there shall be famines, and earthquakes, and pestilences, in every place. But all these things are the beginnings of travailings. Then they shall deliver you up into affliction, and shall kill you: and ye shall be hateful to all nations for my name's sake. And then shall many be offended, and shall betray one another, and shall hate one another. And many false prophets shall arise, and shall seduce many; and because wickedness shall abound, the love of many shall wax cold. But he who shall endure to the end, the same shall be saved. And this Gospel of the kingdom shall be preached through all the world, for a testimony to all nations; and then shall come the end. When, therefore, ye shall see the abomination of desolation which is spoken of by Daniel the prophet, standing in the holy place (let him who readeth understand), then let them which are in Judea flee to the mountains; and let him which is on the house-roof not go down to take anything from the house; and let him who is in the field not return back to carry away his clothes. But woe to them that are pregnant, and to those that are giving suck in those days! But pray ye that your flight be not in the winter, nor on the Sabbath-day: for there shall be great tribulation, such as has not arisen from the beginning of the world until now, neither shall arise. And unless those days should be shortened, no flesh should be saved; but for the elect's sake those days shall be shortened. Then if any one shall say unto you, Lo, here is Christ, or, Lo, there; believe him not. For there shall arise false Christs, and false prophets, and shall show great signs and wonders, to cause error, if it be possible, even to the elect. But take ye heed: behold, I have foretold you all things. If, therefore, they shall say to you, Lo, he is in the desert; go not forth: lo, he is in the sleeping chambers; believe it not. For as the flashing of lightning goeth forth from the east, and appeareth even to the west, so also shall the coming of the Son of man be. Wheresoever the carcase shall be, there shall the eagles be gathered together. But immediately after the affliction of those days the sun shall be darkened, and the moon shall not give her light, and the stars shall fall from heaven, and the powers of heaven shall be moved: and then shall appear the sign of the Son of man in heaven: and all the tribes of the earth shall lament, and shall see the Son of man coming in the clouds of heaven with great power and glory. And He shall send His angels with a great trumpet, and they shall gather together His elect from the four winds, from the heights of heaven, even into the farthest bounds thereof."

And these are not new or sudden things which are now happening to Christians; since the good and righteous, and those who are devoted to God in the law of innocence and the fear of true religion, advance always through afflictions, and wrongs, and the severe and manifold penalties of troubles, in the hardship of a narrow path. Thus, at the very beginning of the world, the righteous Abel was the first to be shin by his brother; and Jacob was driven into exile, and Joseph was sold, and king Saul persecuted the merciful David; and king Ahab endeavored to oppress Elias, who firmly and bravely asserted the majesty of God. Zacharias the priest was slain between the temple and the altar, that himself might there become a sacrifice where he was accustomed to offer sacrifices to God. So many martyrdoms of the righteous have, in fact, often been celebrated; so many examples of faith and virtue have been set forth to future generations. The three youths, Ananias, Azarias, and Misael, equal in age, agreeing in love, steadfast in faith, constant in virtue, stronger than the flames and penalties that urged them, proclaim that they only obey God, that they know Him alone, that they worship Him alone, saying: "O king Nebuchodonosor, there is no need for us to answer thee in this matter. For the God whom we serve is able to deliver us out of the furnace of burning fire; and He will deliver us from thy hands, O king. And if not, be it known unto thee, that we do not serve thy gods, and we do not adore the golden image which thou hast set up." And Daniel, devoted to God, and filled with the Holy Spirit, exclaims and says: "I worship nothing but the Lord my God, who founded the heaven and the earth."

Tobias also, although under a royal and tyrannical slavery, yet in feeling and spirit free, maintains his confession to God, and sublimely announces both the divine power and majesty, saying: "In the land of my captivity I confess to Him, and I show forth His power in a sinful nation." What, indeed, do we find in the Maccabees of seven brethren, equals alike in their lot of birth and virtues, filling up the number seven in the sacrament of a perfected completion? Seven brethren were thus associating in martyrdom. As the first seven days in the divine arrangement containing seven thousand of years, as the seven spirits and seven angels which stand and go in and out before the face of God, and the seven-branched lamp in the tabernacle of witness, and the seven golden candlesticks in the Apocalypse, and the seven columns in Solomon upon which Wisdom built her house I so here also the number seven of the brethren, embracing, in the quantity of their number, the seven churches, as likewise in the first book of Kings we read that the barren hath borne seven. And in Isaiah seven women lay hold on one man, whose name they ask to be called upon them. And the Apostle Paul, who refers to this lawful and certain number, writes to the seven churches. And in the Apocalypse the Lord directs His divine and heavenly precepts to the seven churches and their angels, which number is now found in this case, in the seven brethren, that a lawful consummation may be completed. With the seven children is manifestly associated also the mother, their origin and root, who subsequently begat seven churches, she herself having been first, and alone founded upon a rock by the voice of the Lord. Nor is it of no account that in their sufferings the mother alone is with her children. For martyrs who witness themselves as the sons of God in suffering are now no more counted as of any father but God, as in the Gospel the Lord teaches, saying, "Call no man your father upon earth; for one is your Father, which is in heaven." But what utterances of confessions did they herald forth! how illustrious, how great proofs of faith did they afford! The king Antiochus, their enemy – yea, in Antiochus Antichrist was set forth – sought to pollute the mouths of martyrs, glorious and unconquered in the spirit of confession, with the contagion of swine's flesh; and when he had severely beaten them with whips, and could prevail nothing, commanded iron plates to be heated, which being heated and made to glow, he commanded him who had first spoken, and had more provoked the king with the constancy of his virtue and faith, to be brought up and roasted, his tongue having first been pulled out and cut off, which had confessed God; and this happened the more gloriously to the martyr. For the tongue which had confessed the name of God, ought itself first to go to God.

Then in the second, sharper pains having been devised, before he tortured the other limbs, he tore off the skin of his head with the hair, doubtless with a purpose in his hatred. For since Christ is the head of the man, and God is the head of Christ, he who tore the head in the martyr was persecuting God and Christ in that head. But he, trusting in his martyrdom, and promising to himself from the retribution of God the reward of resurrection, exclaimed and said, "Thou indeed impotently destroyest us out of this present life; but the King of the world will raise us up, who die for His laws, unto the eternal resurrection of life."

The third being challenged, quickly put forth his tongue; for he had learned from his brother to despise the punishment of cutting off the tongue. Moreover, he firmly held forth his hands to be cut off, greatly happy in such a mode of punishment, since it was his lot to imitate, by stretching forth his hands, the form of his Lord's passion. And also the fourth, with like virtue, despising the tortures, and answering, to restrain the king, with a heavenly voice exclaimed, and said, "It is better that those who are given to death by men should wait for hope from God, to be raised up by Him again to eternal life. For to thee there shall be no resurrection to life."

The fifth, besides treading under foot the torments of the king, and his severe and various tortures, by the strength of faith, animated to prescience also and knowledge of future events by the Spirit of divinity, foretold to the king the wrath of God, and the vengeance that should swiftly follow. "Having power," said he, "among men, though thou art corruptible, thou doest what thou wilt. But think not that our race is forsaken of God. Abide, and see His great power, how He will torment thee and thy seed." What alleviation was that to the martyr! how substantial a comfort in his sufferings, not to consider his own torments, but to predict the penalties of his tormentor! But in the sixth, not his bravery only, but also his humility, is to be set forth; that the martyr claimed nothing to himself, nor even made an account of the honor of his own confession with proud words, but rather ascribed it to his sins that he was suffering persecution from the king, while he attributed to God that afterwards he should be avenged. He taught that martyrs are modest, that they were confident of vengeance, and boasted nothing in their suffering. "Do not," said he, "needlessly err; for we on our own account suffer these things, as sinning against our God. But think not thou that thou shall be unpunished, who darest to fight against God." Also the admirable mother, who, neither broken down by the weakness of her sex, nor moved by her manifold bereavement, looked upon her dying children with cheerfulness, and did not reckon those things punishments of her darlings, but glories, giving as great a witness to God by the virtue of her eyes, as her children had given by the tortures and suffering of their limbs; when, after the punishment and slaying of six, there remained one of the brethren, to whom the king promised riches, and power, and many things, that his cruelty and ferocity might be soothed by the satisfaction of even one being subdued, and asked that the mother would entreat that her son might be cast down with herself; she entreated, but it was as became a mother of martyrs – as became one who was mindful of the law and of God – as became one who loved her sons not delicately, but bravely. For she entreated, but it was that he would confess God. She entreated that the brother would not be separated from his brothers in the alliance of praise and glory; then only considering herself the mother of seven sons, if it should happen to her to have brought forth seven sons, not to the world, but to God.

Therefore arming him, and strengthening him, and so bearing her son by a more blessed birth, she said, "O son, pity me that bare thee ten months in the womb, and gave thee milk for three years, and nourished thee and brought thee up to this age; I pray thee, O son, look upon the heaven and the earth; and having considered all the things which are in them, understand that out of nothing God made these things and the human race. Therefore, O son, do not fear that executioner; but being made worthy of thy brethren, receive death, that in the same mercy I may receive thee with thy brethren." The mother's praise was great in her exhortation to virtue, but greater in the fear of God and in the truth of faith, that she promised nothing to herself or her son from the honor of the six martyrs, nor believed that the prayer of the brothers would avail for the salvation of one who should deny, but rather persuaded him to become a sharer in their suffering, that in the day of judgment he might be found with his brethren. After this the another also dies with her children; for neither was anything else becoming, than that she who had borne and made martyrs, should be joined in the fellowship of glory with them, and that she herself should follow those whom she had sent before to God. And lest any, when the opportunity either of a certificate or of any such matter is offered to him whereby he may deceive, should embrace the wicked part of deceivers, let us not be silent, moreover, about Eleazar, who, when an opportunity was offered him by the ministers of the king, that having received the flesh which it was allowable for him to partake of, he might pretend, for the misguiding of the king, that he ate those things which were forced upon him from the sacrifices and unlawful meats, would not consent to this deception, saying that it was fitting neither for his age nor nobility to feign that, whereby others would be scandalized and led into error; if they should think that Eleazar, being ninety years old, had left and betrayed the law of God, and had gone over to the manner of aliens; and that it was not of so much consequence to gain the short moments of life, and so incur eternal punishment from an offended God. And he having been long tortured, and now at length reduced to extremity, while he was dying in the midst of stripes and tortures, groaned and said, "O Lord, that hast the holy knowledge, it is manifest that although I might be delivered from death, I suffer the severest pains of body, being beaten with scourges; but with my mind, on account of Thy fear, I willingly suffer these things." Assuredly his faith was sincere and his virtue sound, and abundantly pure, not to have regarded king Antiochus, but God the Judge, and to have known that it could not avail him for salvation if he should mock and deceive man, when God, who is the judge of our conscience, and who only is to be feared, cannot at all be mocked nor deceived. If, therefore, we also live as dedicated and devoted to God – if we make our way over the ancient and sacred footsteps of the righteous, let us go through the same proofs of sufferings, the same testimonies of passions, considering the glory of our time the greater on this account, that while ancient examples may be numbered, yet that subsequently, when the abundance of virtue and faith was in excess, the Christian martyrs cannot be numbered, as the Apocalypse testifies and says: "After these things I beheld a great multitude, which no man could number, of every nation, and of every tribe, and people, and language, standing in the sight of the throne and of the Lamb; and they were clothed in white robes, and palms were in their hands; and they said with a loud voice, Salvation to our God, who sitteth upon the throne, and unto the Lamb! And one of the elders answered and said unto me, Who are those which are arrayed in white robes, and whence come they? And I said unto him, My lord, thou knowest. And he said unto me, These are they who have come out of great tribulation, and have washed their robes, and made them white in the blood of the Lamb. Therefore are they before the throne of God, and serve Him day and night in His temple." But if the assembly of the Christian martyrs is shown and proved to be so great, let no one think it a hard or a difficult thing to become a martyr, when he sees that the crowd of martyrs cannot be numbered.

12. What hope and reward remains for the righteous and for martyrs after the conflicts and sufferings of this present time.

The Holy Spirit shows and predicts by Solomon, saying: "And although in the sight of men they suffered torments, yet their hope is full of immortality. And having been troubled in a few things, they shall be in many happily ordered, because God has tried them, and has found them worthy of Himself. As gold in the furnace, He hath tried them; and as whole burnt-offerings of sacrifice, He hath received them, and in its season there will be respect of them. They will shine and run about as sparks in a place set with reeds. They shall judge the nations, and have dominion over the peoples; and their Lord shall reign for ever." In the same also our vengeance is described, and the repentance of those who persecute and molest us is announced. "Then," saith he," shall the righteous stand in great constancy before such as have afflicted them, and who have taken away their labors; when they see it, they shall be troubled with a horrible fear: and they shall marvel at the suddenness of their unexpected salvation, saying among themselves, repenting and groaning for anguish of spirit, These are they whom we had sometime in derision and as a proverb of reproach. We fools counted their life madness, and their end to be without honor. How are they numbered among the children of God, and their lot is among the saints! Therefore have we erred from the way of truth, and the light of righteousness hath not shined unto us, and the sun hath not risen upon us. We have been wearied in the way of unrighteousness and perdition, and have walked through hard deserts, but have not known the way of the Lord. What hath pride profited us, or what hath the boasting of riches brought to us? All these things have passed away like a shadow." Likewise in the cxvth Psalm is shown the price and the reward of suffering: "Precious," it says, "in the sight of the Lord is the death of His saints. In the cxxvth Psalm also is expressed the sadness of the struggle, and the joy of the retribution: "They who sow," it says. "in tears, shall reap in joy. As they walked, they walked and wept, casting their seeds; but as they come again, they shall come in exultation, bearing their sheaves." And again, in the cxviiith Psalm: "Blessed are those that are undefiled in the way, who walk in the law of the Lord. Blessed are they who search His testimonies, and seek Him out with their whole heart." Moreover, the Lord in the Gospel, Himself the avenger of our persecution and the rewarder of our suffering, says: "Blessed are they who suffer persecution for righteousness' sake, for theirs is the kingdom of heaven." And again: "Blessed shall ye be when men shall hate you, and shall separate you, and shall expel you, and shall revile your name as evil, for the Son of man's sake. Rejoice ye in that day, and leap for joy; for, behold, your reward is great in heaven." And once more: "Whosoever shall lose his life for my sake, the same shall save it." Nor do the rewards of the divine promise attend those alone who are reproached and slain; but if the passion itself, be wanting to the faithful, while their faith has remained sound and unconquered, and having forsaken and contemned all his possessions, the Christian has shown that he is following Christ, even be also is honored by Christ among the martyrs, as He Himself promises and says: "There is no man that leaveth house, or land, or parents, or brethren, or wife, or children, for the kingdom of God's sake, but shall receive seven times as much in this present time, and in the world to come eternal life." In the Apocalypse also He says the same thing: "And I saw," saith he, "the souls of them that were slain for the name of Jesus and the word of God." And when he had placed those who were slain in the first place, he added, saying: "And whosoever had not worshiped the image of the beast, neither had received his mark upon their forehead or in their hand;" all these he joins together, as seen by him at one time in the same place, and says, "And they lived and reigned with Christ." He says that all live and reign with Christ, not only who have been slain; but even whosoever, standing in firmness of the faith and in the fear of God, have not worshiped the image of the beast, and have not consented to his deadly and sacrilegious edicts.

13. That we receive more as the reward of our suffering than what we endure here in the suffering itself.

The blessed Apostle Paul proves; who by the divine condescension, being caught up into the third heaven and into paradise, testifies that he heard unspeakable words, who boasts that he saw Jesus Christ by the faith of sight, who professes that which he both learnt and saw with the greater truth of consciousness, and says: "The sufferings of this present time are not worthy to be compared with the coming glory which shall be revealed in us." Who, then, does not with all his powers labor to attain to such a glory that he may become the friend of God, that he may at once rejoice with Christ, that after earthly tortures and punishments he may receive divine rewards? If to soldiers of this world it is glorious to return in triumph to their country when the foe is vanquished, how much more excellent and greater is the glory, when the devil is overcome, to return in triumph to paradise, and to bring back victorious trophies to that place whence Adam was ejected as a sinner, after casting down him who formerly had cast him down; to offer to God the most acceptable gift – an uncorrupted faith, and an unyielding virtue of mind, an illustrious praise of devotion; to accompany Him when He shall come to receive vengeance from His enemies, to stand at His side when He shall sit to judge, to become co-heir of Christ, to be made equal to the angels; with the patriarchs, with the apostles. with the prophets, to rejoice in the possession of the heavenly kingdom! Such thoughts as these, what persecution can conquer, what tortures can overcome? The brave and steadfast mind, founded in religious meditations, endures; and the spirit abides unmoved against all the terrors of the devil and the threats of the world, when it is strengthened by the sure and solid faith of things to come. In persecutions, earth is shut up, but heaven is opened; Antichrist is threatening, but Christ is protecting; death is brought in, but immortality follows; the world is taken away from him that is slain, but paradise is set forth to him restored; the life of time is extinguished, but the life of eternity is realized. What a dignity it is, and what a security, to go gladly from hence, to depart gloriously in the midst of afflictions and tribulations; in a moment to close the eyes with which men and the world are looked upon, and at once to open them to look upon God and Christ! Of such a blessed departure how great is the swiftness! You shall be suddenly taken away from earth, to be placed in the heavenly kingdoms. It behoves us to embrace these things in our mind and consideration, to meditate on these things day and night. If persecution should fall upon such a soldier of God, his virtue, prompt for battle, will not be able to be overcome. Or if his call should come to him before, his faith shall not be without reward, seeing it was prepared for martyrdom; without loss of time, the reward is rendered by the judgment of God. In persecution, the warfare, – in peace, the purity of conscience, is crowned.

Cyprian, Treatise 11

THE BENEFITS OF MARTYRDOM.

In the Proverbs of Solomon: "The faithful martyr delivers his soul from evils." Also in the same place: "Then shall the righteous stand in great boldness against them who have afflicted them, and who took away their labors. When they see them, they shall be disturbed with a horrible fear; and they shall wonder at the suddenness of their unhoped-for salvation, saying among themselves, repenting and groaning with distress of spirit, These are they whom some time we had in derision, and in the likeness of a proverb; we fools counted their life madness, and their end without honor. How are they reckoned among the children of God, and their lot among the saints! Therefore we have wandered from the way of truth, and the light of righteousness has not shined upon us, and the sun has not risen upon us. We have been wearied in the way of iniquity and of perdition, and we have walked through difficult solitudes; but we have not known the way of the Lord. What hath pride profited us? or what hath the boasting of riches brought to us? All these things have passed away as a shadow." Of this same thing in the cxvth Psalm: "Precious in the sight of the Lord is the death of His saints." Also in the cxxvth Psalm: "They who sow in tears shall reap in joy. Walking they walked, and wept as they cast their seeds; but coming they shall come in joy, raising up their laps." Of this same thing in the Gospel according to John: "He who loveth his life shall lose it; and he that hateth his life in this world shall find it to life eternal." Also in the same place: "But when they shall deliver you up, take no thought what ye shall speak; for it is not ye who speak, but the Spirit of your Father which speaketh in you." Also in the same place: "The hour shall come, that every one that killeth you shall think he doeth service to God I but they shall do this also because they have not known the Father nor me." Of this same matter, according to Matthew: "Blessed are they which shall suffer persecution for righteousness' sake; for theirs is the kingdom of heaven." Also in the same place: "Fear not them which kill the body, but are not able to kill the soul; but rather fear Him which is able to kill the soul and body in Gehenna." Also in the same place: "Whosoever shall confess me before men, him also will I confess before my Father which is in heaven; but he who shall deny me before men, him also will I deny before my Father which is in heaven. And he that shall endure to the end, the same shall be saved."

Of this same thing, according to Luke: "Blessed shall ye be when men shall hate you, and shall separate you (from their company), and shall drive you out, and shall speak evil of your name, as wicked, for the Son of man's sake. Rejoice in that day, and exult; for, lo, your reward is great in heaven." Also in the same place: "Verily I say unto you, There is no man that leaveth house, or parents, or brethren, or wife, or children, for the sake of the kingdom of God, and does not receive seven times as much in this present time, but in the world to come life everlasting." Of this same thing in the Apocalypse: "And when he had opened the fifth seal, I saw under the altar of God the souls of them that were slain on account of the word of God and His testimony. And they cried with a loud voice, saying, How long, O Lord, holy and true, dost Thou not judge and avenge our blood on them that dwell on the earth? And unto every one of them were given white robes; and it was said to them, that they should rest still for a short time, until the number of their fellow-servants, and of their brethren, should be fulfilled, and they who shall afterwards be slain, after their example." Also in the same place: "After these things I saw a great crowd, which no one among them could number, from every nation, and from every tribe, and from every people and tongue, standing before the throne and before the Lamb; and they were clothed with white robes, and palms were in their hands. And they said with a loud voice, Salvation to our God, that sitteth upon the throne, and to the Lamb. And one of the elders answered and said to me, What are these which are clothed with white robes? who are they, and whence have they come? And I said unto him, My lord, thou knowest. And he said unto me, These are they who have come out of great tribulation, and have washed their robes, and made them white in the blood of the Lamb. Therefore they are before the throne of God, and serve Him day and night in His temple; and He who sitteth upon the throne shall dwell among them. They shall neither hunger nor thirst ever; and neither shall the sun fall upon them, nor shall they suffer any heat: for the Lamb who is in the midst of the throne shall protect them, and shall lead them to the fountains of the waters of life; and God shall wipe away every tear from their eyes." Also in the same place: "He who shall overcome I will give him to eat of the tree of life, which as in the paradise of my God." Also in the same place: "Be thou faithful even unto death, and I will give thee a crown of life." Also in the same place: "Blessed shall they be who shall watch, and shall keep their garments, lest they walk naked, and they see their shame."

Of this same thing, Paul in the second Epistle to Timothy: "I am now offered up, and the time of my assumption is at hand. I have fought a good fight, I have finished my course, I have kept the faith. There now remains for me a crown of righteousness, which the Lord, the righteous Judge, will give me in that day; and not only to me, but to all also who love His appearing." Of this same thing to the Romans: "We are the sons of God: but if sons and heirs of God, we are also joint-heirs with Christ; if we suffer together, that we may also be magnified together." Of this same thing in the cxviiith Psalm: "Blessed are they who are undefiled in the way, and walk in the law of the Lord. Blessed are they who search into His testimonies."

Cyprian, letter to his son Quirinius

The Glory of Martyrdom

1. Although, beloved brethren, it is unfitting, while my speaking to you receives this indulgence, to profess any trepidation, and it very little becomes me to diminish the glory of so great a devotion by the confession of an incipient doubt; yet at the same time I say that my mind is divided by that very deliberation, being influenced by the desire of describing the glory, and restrained from speaking by the magnitude of the virtue (to be described); since it is either not becoming to be silent, or it is perilous to say too little, save that to one who is tossing in doubt this consideration alone is helpful, that it would appear easy for him to be pardoned who has not feared to dare. Wherefore, beloved brethren, although my mental capacity is burdened by the importance of the subject in such a way, that in proportion as it puts itself forth in declaring the dignity of martyrdom, in that degree it is overwhelmed by the very weight of the glory, and by its estimation of all those things concerning which, when it speaks most, it fails, by its address being weakened, and broken, and self-entangled, and does not with free and loosened reins display the might of

such glory in the liberal eloquence of discourse; yet, if I am not mistaken, some power there will be in my utterance, which, when fortified by the appeal of the work itself, may here and there pour forth what the unequal consciousness of my ability withheld from my words. Since, therefore, beloved brethren, involved as we are in affairs so many and important, we are endeavoring with all eagerness and labor to confirm the excellent and most beautiful issues of salvation, I do not fear being so deterred by any slothful dread as to be withheld or rendered powerless; since, if any one should desire to look into that of which we are considering, the hope of devotion being taken into account, and the very magnitude of the thing being weighed, he would rather wonder that I could have dared at all, in a matter wherein both the vastness of the subject oppressed me, and the earnestness of its own desire drove my mind, confused with its joy, into mental difficulties. For who is there whom such a subject would not alarm? who is there whom it would not overthrow with the fear of its own wonder!

2. For there is indeed, unless I am mistaken, even in the very power of conscience, a marvelous fear which at once disturbs and inflames us; whose power, the more closely you look into, the more the dreadful sense of its obligation is gathered from its very aspect of venerable majesty. For assuredly you ought to consider what glory there is in expiating any kind of defilement of life, and the foulness of a polluted body, and the contagions gathered from the long putrefaction of vices, and the worldly guilt incurred by so great a lapse of time, by the remedial agency of one stroke, whereby both reward may be increased, and guilt may be excluded. Whence every perfection and condition of life is included in martyrdom. This is the foundation of life and faith, this is the safeguard of salvation, this is the bond of liberty and honor; and although there are also other means whereby the light may be attained, yet we more easily arrive at nearness to the promised reward, by help of these punishments, which sustain us.

3. For consider what glory it is to set aside the lusts of this life, and to oppose a mind withdrawn from all commerce with nature and the world, to all the opposition of the adversary, and to have no dread of the cruelty of the torturer; that a man should be animated by the suffering whereby he might be believed to be destroyed, and should take to himself, as an enhancement of his strength, that which the punisher thinks will aggravate his torments. For although the hook, springing forth from the stiffening ribs, is put back again into the wound, and with the repeated strokes of the whip the returning lash is drawn away with the rent portions of the flesh; still he stands immoveable, the stronger for his sufferings, revolving only this in his mind, that in that brutality of the executioners Christ Himself is suffering more in proportion to what he suffers. For since, if he should deny the Lord, he would incur guilt on His behalf for whom he ought to have overcome, it is essential that He should be seen to bear all things to whom the victory is due, even in the suffering.

4. Therefore, since martyrdom is the chief thing, there are three points arising out of it on which we have proposed to ourselves to speak: What it is, how great it is, and of what advantage it is. What, then, is martyrdom? It is the end of sins, the limit of dangers, the guide of salvation, the teacher of patience, the home of life, on the journey to which those things moreover befall which in the coming crisis might be considered torments. By this also testimony is borne to the Name, and the majesty of the Name is greatly enhanced: not that in itself that majesty can be diminished, or its magnitude detracted from, by the guilt of one who denies it; but that it redounds to the increase of its glory, when the terror of the populace that howls around is giving to suffering, fearless minds, and by the threats of snarling hatred is adding to the title whereby Christ has desired to crown the man, that in proportion as he has thought that he conquered, in that proportion his courage has grown in the struggle. It is then, therefore, that all the vigor of faith is brought to bear, then facility of belief is approved, when you encounter the speeches and the reproaches of the rabble, and when you strengthen yourself by a religious mind against those madnesses of the people, – overcoming, that is, and

repelling whatever their blasphemous speech may have uttered to wrong Christ in your person; as when the resisting breakwater repels the adverse sea, although the waves dash and the rolling water again and again beats upon it, yet its immoveable strength abides firm, and does not yield even when covered over by the waves that foam around, until its force is scattered over the rocks and loses itself, and the conquered billow lying upon the rocks retires forth into the open spaces of the shore.

5. For what is there in these speeches other than empty discourse, and senseless talk, and a depraved pleasure in meaningless words? As it is written: "They have eyes, and they see not; ears have they, and they hear not." "Their foolish heart is made sluggish, lest at any time they should be converted, and I should heal them." For there is no doubt but that He said this of all whose hardened mind and obstinate brutality of heart is always driven away and repugnates from a vital devotion, folly leading them, madness dragging them, in fine, every kind of ferocity enraging them, whereby they are instigated as well as carried away, so that in their case their own deeds would be sufficient for their punishment, their guilt would burden the very penalty of the persecution inflicted.

6. The whole of this tends to the praise of martyrdom, the whole illuminates the glory of suffering wherein the hope of time future is beheld, wherein Christ Himself is engaged, of whom are given the examples that we seek, and whose is the strength by which we resist. And that in this behalf something is supplied to us to present, is surely a lofty and marvelous condescension, and such as we are able neither mentally to conceive nor fully to express in words. For what could He with His liberal affection bestow upon us more, than that He should be the first to show forth in Himself what He would reward with a crown in others? He became mortal that we might be immortal, and He underwent the issue of human destiny, by whom things human are governed; and that He might appear to have given to us the benefit of His having suffered, He gave us confession. He suggested martyrdoms; finally, He, by the merits of His nativity, imputed all those things whereby the light (of life) may be quenched, to a saving remedy, by His excellent humility, by His divine strength. Whoever have deserved to be worthy of this have been without death, have overcome all the foulest stains of the world, having subdued the condition of death.

7. For there is no doubt how much they obtain from the Lord, who have preferred God's name to their own safety, so that in that judgment-day their blood-shedding would make them better, and the blood spill would show them to be spotless. Because death makes life more complete, death rather leads to glory. Thus, whenever on the rejoicing wheat-stalks the ears of corn distended by rains grow full, the abundant harvests are forced by the summer; thus, as often as the vine is pruned by the knife from the tendrils that break forth upon it, the bunch of grapes is more liberally clothed. For whatever is of advantage by its injury turns out for the increase of the time to come; just as it has often been of avail to the fields to let loose the flames, that by the heat of the wandering conflagration the blind breathing-holes of the earth might be relaxed. It has been useful to parch the light stalks with the crackling fire, that the pregnant corn-field might raise itself higher, and a more abundant grain might flourish on the breeding stems. Therefore such also is first of all the calamity, and by and by the fruit of martyrdom, that it so contemns death, that it may preserve life in death.

8. For what is so illustrious and sublime, as by a robust devotion to preserve all the vigor of faith in the midst of so many weapons of executioners? What so Meat and honorable, as in the midst of so many swords of the surrounding guards, again and again to profess in repeated words the Lord of one's liberty and the author of one's salvation? – and especially if you set before your eyes that there is nothing more detestable than dishonor, nothing baser than slavery, that now you ought to seek nothing else, to ask for nothing else, than that you should be snatched from the slaughters of the world, be delivered from the ills of the world, and be engaged only as an alien from the contagion of earth, among the ruins of a globe that is

speedily to perish? For what have you to do with this light, if you have the promise of an eternal light? What interest have you in this commerce of life and nature, if the amplitude of heaven is awaiting you? Doubtless let that lust of life keep hold, but let it be of those whom for unatoned sin the raging fire will torture with eternal vengeance for their crimes. Let that lust of life keep hold, but let it be of those to whom it is both a punishment to die, and a torment to endure (after death). But to you both the world itself is subjected, and the earth yields, if, when all are dying, yon are reserved for this fate of being a martyr. Do we not behold daily dyings? We behold new kinds of death of the body long worn out with raging diseases, the miserable re-suits of some plague hitherto inexperienced; and we behold the destruction of wasted cities, and hence we may acknowledge how great is to be considered the dignity of martyrdom, to the attainment of the glory of which even the pestilence is beginning to compel us.

9. Moreover, beloved brethren, regard, I beseech you, this consideration more fully; for in it both salvation is involved, and sublimity accounted of, although I am not unaware that you abundantly know that we are supported by the judgments of all who stand fast, and that you are not ignorant that this is the teaching handed down to us, that we should maintain the power of so great a Name without any dread of the warfare; because we whom once the desire of an everlasting remembrance has withheld from the longing for this light, and whom the anticipations of the future have wrenched away, and whom the society of Christ so longed for has kept aloof from all wickedness, shrink from offering our soul to death except it be in the way of yielding to a mischief, and that those benefits of God must no longer be retained and clung to by us, since beyond the burning up of these things the reward is so great as that human infirmity can hardly attain sufficiently to speak of it. Heaven lies open to our blood; the dwelling-place of Gehenna gives way to our blood; and among all the attainments of glory, the title of blood is sealed as the fairest, and its crown is designated as most complete.

10. Thus, whenever the soldier returns from the enemy laden with triumphant spoils, he rejoices in his wounds. Thus, whenever the sailor, long harassed with tempests, arrives at safe shores, he reckons his happiness by the dangers that he has suffered. For, unless I am mistaken, that is assuredly a joyous labor whereby safety is found. Therefore all things must be suffered, all things must be endured; nor should we desire the means of rejoicing for a brief period, and being punished with a perpetual burning. For you ought to remember that you are bound, as it were, by a certain federal paction, out of which arises the just condition either of obtaining salvation, or the merited fearfulness of punishment. You stand equally among adverse things and prosperous, in the midst of arms and darts; and on the one hand, worldly ambition, on the other heavenly greatness, incites you.

11. If you fear to lose salvation, know that you can die; and, moreover, death should be contemned by you, for whom Christ was slain. Let the examples of the Lords passion, I beseech you, pass before your eyes; let the offerings, and the rewards, and the distinctions prepared come together before you, and look carefully at both events, how great a difficulty they have between them. For you will not be able to confess unless you know what a great mischief you do if you deny. Martyrs rejoice in heaven; the fire will consume those who are enemies of the truth. The paradise of God blooms for the witnesses; Gehenna will enfold the deniers, and eternal fire will burn them up. And, to say nothing of other matters, this assuredly ought rather to urge us, that the confession of one word is maintained by the everlasting confession of Christ; as it is written, "Whosoever shall confess me on earth before men, him also will I confess before my Father, and before His angels." To this are added, by way of an enhancement of glory, the adornments of virtue; for He says, "The righteous shall shine as sparks that run to and fro among the stubble; they shall judge the nations, and shall have dominion over the peoples."

12. For it is a great glory, beloved brethren, to adorn the life of eternal salvation with the dignity of suffering: it is a great sublimity before the face of the Lord, and under the

gaze of Christ, to contemn without a shudder the torments inflicted by human power. Thus Daniel, by the constancy of his faith, overcame the threats of the king and the fury of raging lions, in that he believed that none else than God was to be adored. Thus, when the young men were thrown into the furnace, the fire raged against itself. because, being righteous, they endured the flames, and guarded against those of Gehenna, by believing in God, whence also they received things worthy of them: they were not delayed to a future time: they were not reserved for the reward of eternal salvation. God saw their faith; that what they had promised to themselves to see after their death, they merited to see in their body. For how great a reward was given them in the present tribulation could not be estimated. If there was cruelty, it gave way; if there was flame, it stood still. For there was one mind to all of them, which neither violence could break down nor wrath could subvert; nor could the fear of death restrain them from the obedience of devotion. Whence by the Lord's grace it happened, that in this manner the king himself appeared rather to be punished in those men (who were slain), whilst they escape whom he had thought to slay.

13. And now, beloved brethren, I shall come to that point whence I shall very easily be able to show you how highly the virtue of martyrdom is esteemed, which, although it is well known to all, and is to be desired on account of the insignia of its inborn glory, yet in the desire of its enjoyment has received more enhancement from the necessity of the times. Because if any one be crowned at that season in which he supposes himself to be crowned, if perchance he should die, he is greatly rewarded. Therefore, sublime and illustrious as martyrdom is, it is the more needful now, when the world itself is turned upside down, and, while the globe is partially shattered, failing nature is giving evidence of the tokens of its final destruction. For the rain-cloud hangs over us in the sky, and the very air stretches forth the mournful rain(curtain); and as often as the black tempest threatens the raging sea, the glittering lightning-flashes glow terribly in the midst of the opening darkness of the clouds. Moreover, when the deep is lashed into immense billows, by degrees the wave is lifted up, and by degrees the foam whitens, until at length you behold it rush in such a manner, that on those rocks on which it is hurled, it throws its foam higher than the wave that was vomited forth by the swelling sea. You read that it is written, that we must pay even the uttermost farthing. But the martyrs alone are relieved of this obligation; because they who trust to their desires for eternal salvation, and have overcome their longings for this life, have been made by the Lord's precepts free from the universal suffering. Therefore from this especially, beloved brethren, we shall be able to set forth what great things the virtue of martyrdom is able to fulfil.

14. And, to pass over everything else, we ought to remember what a glory it is to come immaculate to Christ – to be a sharer in His suffering, and to reign in a perpetual eternity with the Lord – to be free from the threatening destruction of the world, and not to be mixed up with the bloody carnage of wasting diseases in a common lot with others; and, not to speak of the crown itself, if, being situated in the midst of these critical evils of nature, you had the promise of an escape from this life, would you not rejoice with all your heart? If, I say, while tossing amid the tempests of this world, a near repose should invite you, would you not consider death in the light of a remedy? Thus, surrounded as you are with the knives of the executioners, and the instruments of testing tortures, stand sublime and strong, considering how great is the penalty of denying, in a time when you are unable to enjoy, the world for the sake of which you would deny, because indeed the Lord knew that cruel torments and mischievous acts of punishment would be armed against us for our destruction, in order that He might make us strong to endure the all. son, says He, "if thou come to serve God, stand fast in righteousness, and fear, and prepare thy soul for temptation." Moreover, also, the blessed Apostle Paul exclaimed, and said, "To me to live is Christ, and to die is gain."

15. Wherefore, beloved brethren, with a

firm faith, with a robust devotion, with a virtue opposed to the fierce threatenings of the world, and the savage murmurs of the attending crowds, we must resist and not fear, seeing that ours is the hope of eternity and heavenly life, and that our ardor is inflamed with the longing for the light, and our salvation rejoices in the promise of immortality. But the fact that our hands are bound with tightened bonds, and that heavy links fastened round our necks oppress us with their solid weight, or that our body strained on the rack hisses on the red-hot plates, is not for the sake of seeking our blood, but for the sake of trying us. For in what manner should we be able to recognize even the dignity of martyrdom, if we were not constrained to desire it, even at the price of the sacrifice of our body? I indeed have known it, and I am not deceived in the truth of what I say, when the cruel hands of the persecutors were wrenching asunder the martyr's limbs, and the furious torturer was ploughing up his lacerated muscles, and still could not overcome him. I have known it by the words of those who stood around. "This is a great matter. Assuredly I know not what it is – that he is not subdued by suffering, that he is not broken down by wearing torments." Moreover, there were other words of those who spoke: "And yet I believe he has children: for he has a wife associated with him in his house; and yet he does not give way to the bond of his offspring, nor is he withdrawn by the claim of his family affection from his steadfast purpose. This matter must be known, and this strength must be investigated, even to the very heart; for that is no trifling confession, whatever it may be, for which a man suffers, even so as to be able to die."

16. Moreover, beloved brethren, so great is the virtue of martyrdom, that by its means even he who has wished to slay you is constrained to believe. It is written, and we read: "Endure in suffering, and in thy humiliation have patience, because gold and silver are tried by the fire." Since, therefore, the Lord proves us by earthly temptations, and Christ the Judge weighs us by these worldly ills, we must congratulate ourselves, and rejoice that He does not reserve us for those eternal destructions, but rejoices over us as purged from all contagion. But from those whom He adopts as partners of His inheritance, and is willing to receive into the kingdom of heaven, what else indeed does He ask than a walk in integrity? He Himself has said that all things are His, both those things which are displayed upon the level plains, and which lift themselves up into sloping hills; and moreover, whatever the greatness of heaven surrounds, and what the gliding water embraces in the circum-fluent ocean. But if all things are within His ken, and He does not require of us anything but sincere actions, we ought, as He Himself has said, to be like to gold. Because, when you behold in the glistening ore the gold glittering under the tremulous light, and melting into a liquid form by the roaring flames (for this also is generally the care of the workmen), whenever from the panting furnaces is vomited forth the glowing fire, the rich flame is drawn away from the access of the earth in a narrow channel, and is kept back by sand from the refluent masses of earth. Whence it is necessary to suffer all things, that we may be free from all wickedness, as He has said by His prophet: "And though in the sight of men they have suffered torments, yet is their hope full of immortality; and being vexed in a few things, they shall be well rewarded in many things, because God has tried them, and has found them worthy of Himself, and has received them as a sacrifice of burnt-offering."

17. But if ambitious dignity deter you, and the amount of your money heaped up in your stores influence you – a cause which ever distracts the intentions of a virtuous heart, and assails the soul devoted to its Lord with a fearful trembling – I beg that you would again refer to the heavenly words. For it is the very voice of Christ who speaks, and says, "Whosoever shall lose his life for my name's sake, shall receive in this world a hundred fold, and in the world to come shall possess eternal life." And we ought assuredly to reckon nothing greater, nothing more advantageous, than this. For although in the nature of your costly garments the purple dye flows into figures, and in the slackening threads the gold

strays into a pattern, and the weighty metals to which you devote yourselves are not wanting in your excavated treasures; still, unless I am mistaken, those things will be esteemed vain and purposeless, if, while all things else are added to you, salvation alone is found to be wanting; even as the Holy Spirit declares that we can give nothing in exchange for our soul. For He says, "If you should gain the whole world, and lose your own soul, what shall it profit you, or what exchange shall a man give for his soul?" For all those things which we behold are worthless, and such as resting on weak foundations, are unable to sustain the weight of their own mass. For whatever is received from the world is made of no account by the antiquity of time. Whence, that nothing should be sweet or dear that might be preferred to the desires of eternal life, things which are of personal right and individual law are cut off by the Lord's precepts; so that in the undergoing of tortures, for instance, the son should not soften the suffering father, and private affection should not change the heart that was previously pledged to enduring strength, into another disposition. Christ of His own right ordained that truth and salvation alone must be embraced in the midst of great sufferings, under which wife, and children, and grandchildren, under which all the offspring of one's bowels, must be forsaken, and the victory be claimed.

18. For Abraham also thus pleased God, in that he, when tried by God, spared not even his own son, in behalf of whom perhaps he might have been pardoned had he hesitated to slay him. A religious devotion armed his hands; and his paternal love, at the command of the Lord who bade it, set aside all the feelings of affection. Neither did it shock him that he was to shed the blood of his son, nor did he tremble at the word; nevertheless for him Christ had not yet been slain. For what is dearer than He who, that you might not sustain anything unwillingly in the present day, first of all Himself suffered that which He taught others to suffer? What is sweeter than He who, although He is our God and Lord, nevertheless makes the man who suffers for His sake His fellow-heir in the kingdom of heaven? Oh grand – I know not what! – whether that reason scarcely bears to receive that consciousness, although it always marvels at the greatness of the rewards; or that the majesty of God is so abundant, that to all who trust in it, it even offers those things which, while we were considering what we have done, it had been sin to desire. Moreover, if only eternal salvation should be given, for that very perpetuity of living we should be thankful. But now, when heaven and the power of judging concerning others is bestowed in the eternal world, what is there wherein man's mediocrity may not find itself equal to all these trials? If you are assailed with injuries, He was first so assailed. If yon are oppressed with reproaches, you are imitating the experience of God. Whence also it is but a little matter whatever you undergo for Him, seeing that you can do nothing more, unless that in this consists the whole of salvation, that He has promised the whole to martyrdom. Finally, the apostle, to whom all things were always dear, while he deeply marveled at the greatness of the promised benefits, said, "I reckon that the sufferings of this present time are not worthy to be compared to the glory that is to follow, which shall be revealed in us." Because he was musing in his own mind how great would be the reward, that to him to whom it would be enough to be free from death, should be given not only the prerogative of salvation, but also to ascend to heaven: to heaven which is not constrained into darkness, even when light is expelled from it, and the day does not unfold into light by alternate changes; but the serene temperature of the liquid air unfolds a pure brightness through a clearness that reddens with a fiery glow.

19. It now remains, beloved brethren, that we are bound to show what is the advantage of martyrdom, and that we should teach that especially, so that the fear of the future may stimulate us to this glorious title. Because those to whom great things are promised, seem to have greater things which they are bound to fear. For the soldier does not arouse himself to arms before the enemy have brandished their hostile weapons; nor does a man withdraw his ship in an anchorage, unless

the fear of the deep have checked his courage. Moreover also, while eager for his wealth, the considerate husbandman does not stir up the earth with a fortunate ploughshare, before the crumbling glebe is loosened into dust by the rain that it has received. Thus this is the natural practice of every man, to be ignorant of what is of advantage, unless you recognize what has been mischievous. Whence also a reward is given to all the saints, in that the punishment of their deeds is inflicted on the unrighteous. Therefore what the Lord has promised to His people is doubtful to none, however ignorant he is; but neither is there any doubt what punitive fires He threatens. And since my discourse has led me thus to argue about both these classes of things in a few words, as I have already spoken of both, I will briefly explain them.

20. A horrible place, of which the name is Gehenna, with an awful murmuring and groaning of souls bewailing, and with flames belching forth through the horrid darkness of thick night, is always breathing out the raging fires of a smoking furnace, while the confined mass of flames is restrained or relaxed for the various purposes of punishment. Then there are very many degrees of its violence, as it gathers into itself whatever tortures the consuming fire of the heat emitted can supply. Those by whom the voice of the Lord has been rejected, and His control contemned, it punishes with different dooms; and in proportion to the different degree of deserving of the forfeited salvation it applies its power, while a portion assigns its due distinction to crime. And some, for example, are bowed down by an intolerable load, some are hurried by a merciless force over the abrupt descent of a precipitous path, and the heavy weight of clanking chains bends over them its bondage. Some there are, also, whom a wheel is closely turning, and an unwearied dizziness tormenting; and others whom, bound to one another with tenacious closeness, body clinging to body compresses: so that both fire is devouring, and the load of iron is weighing down, and the uproar of many is torturing.

21. But those by whom God has always been sought or known, have never lost the position which Christ has given them, where grace is found, where in the verdant fields the luxuriant earth clothes itself with tender grass, and is pastured with the scent of flowers; where the groves are carried up to the lofty hill-top, and where the tree clothes with a thicker foliage whatever spot the canopy, expanded by its curving branches, may have shaded. There is no excess of cold or of heat, nor is it needed that in autumn the fields should rest, or, again in the young spring, that the fruitful earth should bring forth. All things are of one season: fruits are borne of a continued summer, since there neither does the moon serve the purpose of her months, nor does the sun run his course along the moments of the hours, nor does the banishment of the light make way for night. A joyous repose possesses the people, a calm home shelters them, where a gushing fountain in the midst issues from the bosom of a broken hollow, and flows in sinuous mazes by a course deep-sounding, at intervals to be divided among the sources of rivers springing from it. Here there is the great praise of martyrs, here is the noble crown of the victors, who have the promise of greater things than those whose rewards are more abundant. And that either their body is thrown to wild beasts, or the threatening sword is not feared, is shown as the reason of their dignity, is manifested as the ground of their election. Because it would have been inconsistent, that he who had been judged equal to such a duty, should be kept among earthly vices and corruptions.

22. For you deserve, O excellent martyrs, that nothing should be denied to you who are nourished with the hope of eternity and of light; whose absolute devotion, and whose mind dedicated to the service of heaven, is evidently seen. Deservedly, I say deservedly, nothing to you is forbidden to wish for, since by your soul this world is looked down upon, and the alienated appearance of the time has made you to shudder, as if it were a confused blindness of darkness; to whom this world is always regarded in the light of a dungeon, its dwellings for restraints, in a life which has always been esteemed by you as a period of delay on a journey. Thus, indeed, in the

triumph of victory he is snatched from these evils, whom no vain ambition with pompous step has subdued, nor popular greatness has elated, but whom, burning with heavenly desire, Christ has added to His kingdom.

23. There is nothing, then, so great and venerable as the deliverance from death, and the causing to live, and the giving to reign for ever. This is fitting for the saints, needful for the wretched, pleasing to all, in which the good rejoice, the abject are lifted up, the elect are crowned. Assuredly God, who cares for all, gave to life a certain medicine as it were in martyrdom, when to some He assigned it on account of their deserving, to others He gave it on account of His mercy. We have assuredly seen very many distinguished by their faith, come to claim this illustrious name, that death might ennoble the obedience of their devotion. Moreover, also, we have frequently beheld others stand undismayed, that they might redeem their sins committed, and be regarded as washed in their gore by His blood; and so being slain they might live again, who when alive were counted slain. Death assuredly makes life more complete, death finds the glory that was lost. For in this the hope once lost is regained, in this all salvation is restored. Thus, when the seed-times shall fail on the withering plains, and the earth shall be parched with its dying grass, the river has delighted to spring forth from the sloping hills, and to soothe the thirsty fields with its gushing streams, so that the vanquished poverty of the land might be dissolved into fruitful wheat-stems, and the corn-field might bristle up the thicker for the counterfeited showers of rain.

24. What then, beloved brethren, shall I chiefly relate, or what shall I say? When all dignified titles thus combine in one, the mind is confused, the perception is misled; and in the very attempt to speak with brilliancy, my unworthy discourse vanishes away. For what is there to be said which can be sufficient, when, if you should express the power of eternal salvation, its attending glories come in your way; if you would speak of its surroundings, its greatness prevents you? The things at the same time are both in agreement and in opposition, and there is nothing which appears worthy to be uttered. Thus the instances of martyrdom have held in check the impulses of daring speech, as if entangled and ensnared by an opponent. What voice, what lungs, what strength, can undertake to sustain the form of such a dignity? At the confession of one voice, adverse things give way, joyous things appear, kingdoms are opened, empires are prepared, suffering is overcome, death is subdued, life is preferred, and the resisting weapons of a mischievous enemy are broken up. If there is sin, it perishes; if there is crime, it is left behind. Wherefore I beseech you, weigh this in your minds, and from my address receive so much as you know that you can feel.

25. Let it present itself to your eyes, what a day that is, when, with the people looking on, and all men watching, an undismayed devotion is struggling against earthly crosses and the threats of the world; how the minds in suspense, and hearts anxious about the tremblings of doubt, are agitated by the dread of the timid fearfulness of those who are congratulating them! What an anxiety is there, what a prayerful entreaty, what desires are recorded, when, with the victory still wavering, and the crown of conquest hanging in doubt over the head while the results are still uncertain, and when that pestilent and raving confession is inflamed by passion, is kindled by madness, and finally, is heated by the fury of the heart, and by gnashing threats! For who is ignorant how great a matter this is, that our, as it were, despised frailty, and the unexpected boldness of human strength, should not yield to the pangs of wounds, nor to the blows of tortures, – that a man should stand fast and not be moved, should be tortured and still not be overcome, but should rather be armed by the very suffering whereby he is tormented?

26. Consider what it is, beloved brethren: set before your perceptions and your minds all the endurance of martyrdom. Behold, indeed, in the passion of any one you will, they who are called martyrs rejoice as being already summoned out of the world; they rejoice as being messengers of all good men; they rejoice in like manner as elected. Thus the Lord rejoices in His soldier, Christ rejoices in the

witness to His name. It is a small matter that I am speaking of, beloved brethren; it is a small matter, so great a subject in this kind of address, and so marvelous a difficulty has been undertaken by me; but let the gravity of the issue, I beseech you, not be wanting for my own purpose, knowing that as much can be said of martyrdom as could be appreciated. Whence also this alone has been the reason of my describing its glory, not that I judged myself equal and fitted for its praise, but that I saw that there was such a virtue in it, that however little I might say about it, I should profess that I had said as much as I possible. For although the custody of faith may be preferred to the benefit of righteousness, and an immaculate virginity may recognize itself as better than the praises of all; yet it is necessary that even it should give place to the claim of blood, and be made second to a gory death. The former have chosen what is good, the latter have imitated Christ.

27. But now, beloved brethren, lest any one should think that I have placed all salvation in no other condition than in martyrdom, let him first of all look especially at this, that it is not I who seem to speak, that am of so great importance, nor is the order of things so arranged that the promised hope of immortality should depend on the strength of a partial advocacy. But since the Lord has testified with His own mouth, that in the Father's possession are many dwellings, I have believed that there is nothing greater than that glory whereby those men are proved who are unworthy of this worldly life. Therefore, beloved brethren, striving with a religious rivalry, as if stirred up with some incentive of reward, let us submit to all the abundance and the endurance of strength. For things passing away ought not to move us, seeing that they are always being pressed forward to their own overthrow, not only by the law proposed to them, but even by the very end of time. John exclaims, and says, "Now is the axe laid to the root of the tree; " showing, to wit, and pointing out that it is the last old age of all things. Moreover, also, the Lord Himself says, "Walk while ye have the light, lest the darkness lay hold upon you." But if He has foretold that we must walk in that time, certainly He shows that we must at any rate walk.

28. And to return to the praise of martyrdom, there is a word of the blessed Paul, who says; "Know ye not that they who run in a race strive many, but one receiveth the prize? But do ye so run, that all of you may obtain." Moreover also elsewhere, that be may exhort us to martyrdom, he has called us fellow-heirs with Christ; nay, that he might omit nothing, he says, "If ye are dead with Christ, why, as if living in the world, do ye make distinctions?" Because, dearest brethren, we who bear the rewards of resurrection, who seek for the day of judgment, who, in fine, are trusting that we shall reign with Christ, ought to be dead to the world. For you can neither desire martyrdom till you have first hated the world, nor attain to God's reward unless you have loved Christ. And he who loves Christ does not love the world. For Christ was given up by the world, even as the world also was given up by Christ; as it is written, "The world is crucified unto me, and I unto the world." The world has been an object of affection to none whom the Lord has not previously condemned; nor could he enjoy eternal salvation who has gloried in the life of the world. That is the very voice of Christ, who says: "He that loveth his life in this world, shall lose it in the world to come; but he that hateth his life in this world, shall find it in the world to come." Moreover, also, the Apostle Paul says: "Be ye imitators of me, as I also am of Christ." And the same elsewhere says: "I wish that all of you, if it were possible, should be imitators of me."

29. He said this who suffered, and who suffered for this cause, that he might imitate the Lord; and assuredly he wished us also to suffer for this cause, that through him we might imitate Christ. If thou art righteous, and believest in God, why fearest thou to shed thy blood for Him whom thou knowest to have so often suffered for thee? In Isaiah He was sawn asunder, in Abel He was slain, in Isaac He was offered up, in Joseph He was sold into slavery, in man He was crucified. And I say nothing of other matters, such as neither my discourse is able to tell nor my mind to bear. My

consciousness is overcome by the example of His humility; and when it considers what things befell when He suffered, it marvels that He should suffer on whose behalf all things quaked. The day fled into the night; the light gave up all things into darkness; and, its mass being inclined backwards and forwards, the whole earth was jarred, and burst open; the dead were disturbed, the graves were laid bare, and as the tombs gaped open into the rent of the earth, bodies returning to the light were restored; the world trembled at the flowing of His blood; and the veil which hung from the opening of the temple was rent, and all the temple uttered a groan. For which cause it is a great matter to imitate Him who, in dying, convicted the world. Therefore when, after the example of the Lord's passion, and after all the testimony of Christ, you lay down your life, and fear not to shed your blood, everything must absolutely give way to martyrdom. Inestimable is the glory of martyrdom, infinite its measure, immaculate its victory, invaluable its title, immense its triumph; because he who is presented to Him with the special glory of a confessor, is adorned with the kindred blood of Christ.

30. Therefore, beloved brethren, although this is altogether of the Lord's promise and gift, and although it is given from on high, and is not received except by His will, and moreover, can neither be expressed in words nor described by speech, nor can be satisfied by any kind of powers of eloquence, still such will be your benevolence, such will be your charity and love, as to be mindful of me when the Lord shall begin to glorify martyrdom in your experience. That holy altar encloses you within itself, that great dwelling-place of the venerable Name encloses you within itself, as if in the folds of a heart's embrace: the powers of the everlasting age sustain you, and that by which you shall ever reign and shall ever conquer. O blessed ones! and such as truly have your sins remitted, if, however, you who are Christ's peers ever have sinned! O blessed ones ! whom the blood of the Lord has dyed from the beginning of the world, and whom such a brightness of snowy clothing has deservedly invested, and the whiteness of the enfolding robe has adorned! Finally, I myself seem to myself to behold already, and, as far as is possible to the mind of man, that divine and illustrious thing occurs to my eyes and view. I seem, I say to myself, already to behold, that that truly noble army accompanies the glory and the path of their Christ. The blessed band of victors will go before His face; and as the crowds become denser, the whole army, illuminated as it were by the rising of the sun, will ascribe to Him the power. And would that it might be the lot of such a poor creature as myself to see that sight! But the Lord can do what He is believed not to deny to your petitions.

Cyprian, On the glory of martyrdom

Passion of James and Marian

James and Marian were martyred during Valerian's reign on May 6th, 259.

"Do not desire death on a sick-bed, in childbirth, or by a mild fever, but by martyrdom to the honor of him who suffered for you." (Tertullian: fuga, 9; De Anima, 55)

James and Marian were arrested because they persisted in confessing the Name. They were tortured severely by the police, who also had a centurion and the magistrates of Cirta, the Devil's priests, to assist them, as if faith, which sets no store about the body, could be broken through the mangling of limbs.

Marian was hung up to be torn by his thumbs, and not by his hands, in order to inflict greater pain. In addition to this different weights were fixed to his feet so that his whole body would be torn in two. You were unsuccessful, you wicked pagans, against God's temple and against the joint hear with Christ. Even though you hung up his limbs, racked his sides, tore his bowels, my Marian, trusting in God, grew in spirit as much as he grew in body. Eventually the cruelty of his torturers was defeated, and he was locked up in prison to the sound of great rejoicing. There, with James and the other brethren, he celebrated the joy of the Lord's victory in repeated prayer.

James and Marian were later brought out to be executed by being beheaded. After Marian as blindfolded, filled with the spirit of prophecy she spoke about the avenging of the blood of the righteous, and as if from the height of heaven threatened various earthly plagues, famines, and earthquakes. Through this prophetic utterance the faith of the martyr not only triumphed over the heathen but sounded a triumphant note in the ears of God's saints.

When everything was over Marian's mother, with a joy like that of the mother in the days of the Maccabees, certain that her son's passion had ended, began to congratulate not only him, but herself as well, who had borne such a son.

E. C. E. Owen (trans.), Some Authentic Acts of the Early Martyrs, Oxford, 1927, pp 13-17

300 MARTYRS

Perhaps one of the most dreadful events in the history of martyrdom was that which took place at Utica, where 300 Christians were, by the orders of the pro-consul, placed around a burning lime-kiln. A pan of coals and incense being prepared, they were commanded either to sacrifice to Jupiter or to be thrown into the kiln. Unanimously refusing, they bravely jumped into the pit, and were suffocated immediately.

John Foxe, The Book of Martyrs, revised with notes and an appendix by W. Bramley-Moore, London, 1869, p 26

CYRIL

At Caesarea in Cappadocia, a young martyr, named Cyril, won great renown.

The boy Cyril was wholly unconcerned that the police brought him before the magistrate for openly professing to be a follower of Christ.

MAGISTRATE: I forgive you, boy, and so does your father. He will take you home again. You can have all your comforts of home back if you will be a good boy and think about what you are doing.

CYRIL: I do not mind being punished for what I have done. I am very happy with God, in spite of being turned out. I shall have a better home later on. I am glad to become poor, that I may be rich. I am not afraid of a good death. I see a better life before me.

The magistrate did not want the boy to be put to death. He thought that the sight of an execution would bring him to his senses. He ordered Cyril's hands to be tied, and led to the fire. The officials reported that the boy was unmoved and showed no sign of fear.

MAGISTRATE: You have seen the fire, boy, and the sword. Be good, and you shall enjoy yourself at home again with your father.

CYRIL: It was a great shame that you brought me back from the fire and the sword, which I was prepared to endure.

Some of the bystanders were moved to tears. But Cyril told them that they would have rejoiced if they had known where he was going. He asked for no better way of spending his life. And so he went to his death.

A. J. Mason, The Historic Martyrs of the Primitive Church, Longmans, 1905, pp 199-200

MARINUS AND ASTERIUS

Marinus was noted for his wealth and family at Caesarea in Palestine, and around 272 was about to be appointed a centurion, as he was due promotion to this vacant position. But another soldier complained that Marinus should not be appointed centurion as he was a Christian, and that he should be appointed in Marinus' place. Achaeus, the governor of Palestine, asked Marinus if was a Christian. When Marinus affirmed this the governor gave him three hours to change his mind.

The bishop of Caesarea, Theotecnus, was told about the matter. He went to Marinus and took him away from the tribunal and led him by the hand to the church. There, pointing to the sword which Marinus wore, and then to a book of the gospels, the bishop asked the soldier which he was going to choose. Marinus, without hesitation, stretched out his right hand and took hold of the sacred book.

"Adhere steadfastly then to God," said the bishop, "and he will strengthen you, and you shall obtain what you have chosen. Depart in peace."

Being summoned again before the judge, Marinus professed his faith with greater resolution and alacrity than before, and was immediately led away just as he was, and beheaded.

Asterius, a Roman senator, in great favor with the emperors, and well known to all on account of his birth and great estate, was present at Marinus' martyrdom. Even though he was richly dressed, he took away the dead body on his shoulders, and having sumptuously adorned it, gave it a decent burial. Rufinus adds that Asterius was beheaded for this action.

John Foxe, The Book of Martyrs, revised with notes and an appendix by W. Bramley-Moore, London, 1869, pp 292-3

The Ninth Persecution (1)

Such was Aurelian's treatment of us at that time; but in the course of his reign he changed his mind in regard to us, and was moved by certain advisers to institute a persecution against us. And there was great talk about this on every side. But as he was about to do it, and was, so to speak, in the very act of signing the decrees against us, the divine judgment came upon him and restrained him at the very verge of his undertaking, showing in a manner that all could see clearly, that the rulers of this world can never find an opportunity against the churches of Christ, except the hand, that defends them permits it, in divine and heavenly judgment, for the sake of discipline and correction, at such times as it sees best.

After a reign of six years, Aurelian was succeeded by Probus.

Eusebius of Caesarea, Church History, Book 7, chapter 30

The Ninth Persecution Under Aurelian, A.D. 274

The principal sufferers were: Felix, bishop of Rome. This prelate was advanced to the Roman see in 274. He was the first martyr to Aurelian's petulance, being beheaded on the twenty- second of December, in the same year.

Agapetus, a young gentleman, who sold his estate, and gave the money to the poor, was seized as a Christian, tortured, and then beheaded at Praeneste, a city within a day's journey of Rome.

These are the only martyrs left upon record during this reign, as it was soon put to a stop by the emperor's being murdered by his own domestics, at Byzantium.

Aurelian was succeeded by Tacitus, who was followed by Probus, as the latter was by Carus: this emperor being killed by a thunder storm, his sons, Carnious and Numerian, succeeded him, and during all these reigns the Church had peace.

Diocletian mounted the imperial throne, A.D. 284; at first he showed great favor to the Christians. In the year 286, he associated Maximian with him in the empire; and some Christians were put to death before any general persecution broke out. Among these were Felician and Primus, two brothers.

Marcus and Marcellianus were twins, natives of Rome, and of noble descent. Their parents were heathens, but the tutors, to whom the education of the children was intrusted, brought them up as Christians. Their constancy at length subdued those who wished them to become pagans, and their parents and whole family became converts to a faith they had before reprobated. They were martyred by being tied to posts, and having their feet pierced with nails. After remaining in this situation for a day and a night, their sufferings were put an end to by thrusting lances through their bodies.

Zoe, the wife of the jailer, who had the care of the before-mentioned martyrs, was also converted by them, and hung upon a tree, with a fire of straw lighted under her. When her body was taken down, it was thrown into a river, with a large stone tied to it, in order to sink it.

In the year of Christ 286, a most remarkable affair occurred; a legion of soldiers, consisting of six thousand six hundred and sixty-six men, contained none but Christians. This legion was called the Theban Legion, because the men had been raised in Thebias: they were quartered in the east until the emperor Maximian ordered them to march to Gaul, to assist him against the rebels of Burgundy. They passed the Alps into Gaul, under the command of Mauritius, Candidus, and Exupernis, their worthy commanders, and at length joined the emperor. Maximian, about this time, ordered a general sacrifice, at which the whole army was to assist; and likewise he commanded that they should take the oath of allegiance and swear, at the same time, to assist in the extirpation of Christianity in Gaul. Alarmed at these orders, each individual of the Theban Legion absolutely refused either to sacrifice or take the oaths prescribed. This so greatly enraged Maximian, that he ordered the legion to be decimated, that is, every tenth man to be selected from the rest, and put to the sword. This bloody order having been put in execution, those who remained alive were still inflexible, when a second decimation took place, and every tenth man of those living was put to death. This second severity made no more impression than the first had done; the soldiers preserved their fortitude and their principles, but by the advice of their officers they drew up a loyal remonstrance to the emperor. This, it might have been presumed, would have softened the emperor, but it had a contrary effect: for, enraged at their perseverance and unanimity, he commanded that the whole legion should be put to death, which was accordingly executed by the other troops, who cut them to pieces with their swords, September 22, 286.

Alban, from whom St. Alban's, in Hertfordshire, received its name, was the first British martyr. Great Britain had received the Gospel of Christ from Lucius, the first Christian king, but did not suffer from the rage of persecution for many years after. He was originally a pagan, but converted by a Christian ecclesiastic, named Amphibalus, whom he sheltered on account of his religion. The enemies of Amphibalus, having intelligence of the place where he was secreted, came to the house of Alban; in order to facilitate his escape, when the soldiers came, he offered himself up as the person they were seeking for. The deceit being detected, the governor ordered him to be scourged, and then he was sentenced to be beheaded, June 22, A.D. 287.

The venerable Bede assures us, that, upon this occasion, the executioner suddenly became a convert to Christianity, and entreated permission to die for Alban, or with him. Obtaining the latter request, they were beheaded by a soldier, who voluntarily undertook the task of executioner. This happened on the twenty-second of June, A.D. 287, at Verulam, now St. Alban's, in Hertfordshire, where a magnificent church was erected to his memory about the time of Constantine the Great. The edifice, being destroyed in the Saxon wars, was rebuilt by Offa, king of Mercia, and a monastery erected adjoining to it, some remains of which are still visible, and the church is a noble Gothic structure.

Faith, a Christian female, of Acquitain, in France, was ordered to be broiled upon a gridiron, and then beheaded; A.D. 287.

Quintin was a Christian, and a native of Rome, but determined to attempt the propagation of the Gospel in Gaul, with one Lucian, they preached together in Amiens; after which Lucian went to Beaumaris, where he was martyred. Quintin remained in Picardy, and was very zealous in his ministry. Being seized upon as a Christian, he was stretched with pulleys until his joints were dislocated; his body was then torn with wire scourges, and boiling oil and pitch poured on his naked flesh; lighted torches were applied to his sides and armpits; and after he had been thus tortured, he was remanded back to prison, and died of the barbarities he had suffered, October 31, A.D. 287. His body was sunk in the Somme.

Foxe's Book of Martyrs, Edited by William Byron Forbush

3. Christian writings

A collection of the writings, prayers and the spoken words of the martyrs and about the martyrs and martyrdom and persecution of Christians from the period 284 – 313.

A. Cyprian: The lapsed

Christians at this time were divided about what should happen to fellow-Christians who had not managed to withstand persecution. As soon as there was a lull in persecution

Christians had to decide whether they would welcome back into the ranks of their fellowship those who had not been faithful in the face of persecution.

Chapter 1

Behold beloved brethren, peace has been restored to the Church, and, what recently seemed difficult to the incredulous and impossible to the perfidious, our security has by divine aid and retribution been re-established. Our minds are returning to gladness, and with the passing of the cloud and storm of oppression tranquillity and serenity have shone forth again. Praises must be given to God, and His blessings and gifts must be celebrated by the giving of thanks, although not even in the persecution did our voice cease to give thanks. For it is not possible even for an enemy to prevent us, who love God with our whole heart and soul and power, from proclaiming His blessings and praises always and everywhere with glory. The day longed for by the prayers of all of us has come, and after the horrible and loathsome darkness of a long night the world has shone forth illuminated by the light of the Lord.

Chapter 2

With happy countenances we look upon the confessors illustrious by the proclaiming of a good name and glorious in the praise of virtue and the faith; clinging to them with holy kisses we embrace them whom we have desired with a divine and insatiable eagerness. The white-robed cohort of Christ's soldiers is at hand, who by a steadfast formation have broken the turbulent ferocity of an attacking persecution, prepared to suffer imprisonment, armed to endure death. Bravely have you opposed the world, a glorious spectacle have you furnished God, you have been an example to your brethren who will follow you. Your religious voice uttered the name of Christ, in whom it has once confessed that it believed; your illustrious hands, which had been accustomed only to divine works, have resisted the sacrilegious sacrifices; your mouths sanctified by heavenly food after (receiving) the body and blood of the Lord have rejected the profane contagion of the leavings of the idols; your head has remained free from the impious and wretched veil with which the captive heads of those performing the sacrifices were there veiled; your brow pure with the sign of God could not endure the crown of the devil, it reserved itself for the crown of the Lord. With what a joyful bosom does the Mother Church receive you as you return from heaven! How happily, with what rejoicing does she open her gates that with united forces, you may enter bringing back trophies from a prostrate enemy! With the man in triumph women too come, who in their struggle with the world have also overcome their sex. Virgins come with the double glory of their warfare and boys surpassing their years in virtue. Furthermore, the rest of the multitude of those who stand follow your glory, accompany your footsteps with marks of praise very close and almost joined with your own. The same sincerity of heart is in these, the same integrity of a tenacious faith. Relying on the unshaken foundation of heavenly precepts, and strengthened by the evangelical traditions, no prescribed exiles, no destined torments, no penalties as to property or body terrified them. The day for examining their faith was set, but he who is mindful that he has renounced the world knows no day in the world, nor does he now compute the earthly seasons who hopes for eternity from God.

Chapter 3

Let no one, brethren, let no one cut short this glory, let no one by malicious detraction weaken the uncorrupted firmness of those who stand. When the time appointed for the recanters had passed, whoever had not professed in that time to be a Christian confessed that he was. The first title to victory is for him who has fallen in the hands of the Gentiles to confess the Lord; the second step to glory is to make a cautious withdrawal and then to keep himself for God. The one is a public confession; the other private. The former conquers the judge of the world; the latter satisfied with God as his judge guards a conscience pure by integrity of heart. In the former case fortitude is quicker; in the latter solicitude is more secure. The one, as his hour approached, was then found ready; the other perhaps was delayed because he had left his estate and had withdrawn, for he would not deny; surely he would have confessed, had he also been seized.

Chapter 4

One grief saddens these heavenly crowns of the martyrs, these spiritual glories of the confessors, these very great and illustrious virtues of the brethren who stand – the violent enemy has torn away a part of our vitals and has thrown it away in the ruin of his destruction. What shall I do in this situation, dearest brethren? As I waver in the varying tide of emotion, what or how shall I speak? There is need of tears rather than words to express the grief with which the blow to our body is to be mourned, with which the manifold loss of our once numerous people is to be lamented. For who is so hard and without feeling, who so forgetful of brotherly love that as he stands ;n the midst of the manifold destruction of his people and their sad remains deformed by great squalor he can keep his eyes dry and with a sudden burst of weeping not express his lamentations with tears rather than with words? I grieve, brethren, I grieve with you nor does my own integrity and sanity beguile me to soothe my own grief, since the shepherd is wounded more by the wound of his flock. I join my heart with each one; I share in the grievous burden of sorrow and death. I wail with those who wail; I weep with those who weep; I believe myself to be cast down with those who are cast down. At the same time my limbs were pierced by the darts of the raging enemy; their cruel swords have passed through my vitals. My mind was not able to remain immune and free from the attacks of persecution; among my prostrate brethren, my compassion has also prostrated me.

Chapter 5

Nevertheless, most beloved brethren, the cause of truth must be kept, and the gloomy darkness of the cruel persecution ought not have so blinded our senses that nothing of light and clarity has remained whereby the divine precepts can be perceived. If the cause of the disaster is known, the remedy for the wound also is found. The Lord wished his family to be proved, and, because a long peace had corrupted the discipline divinely handed down to us, a heavenly rebuke has aroused a prostrate and, I might say, sleeping faith, and, although we deserved more on account of our sins, the most merciful Lord has so moderated all things, that all that has happened seemed an examination rather than a persecution.

Chapter 6

Everyone was eager to increase his estate, and, forgetful of what the believers in apostolic times either had done before or always should have done, with the insatiable ardor of covetousness they applied themselves to increasing their possessions. Among the priests there was no devout religion; in their ministries no sound faith, in their works no mercy, in their morals no discipline. Among men the beard was defaced; faces were painted among women, eyes were falsified after God's hands had completed them, hair was colored in deception. There were crafty frauds to deceive the hearts of the simple, subtle schemes for circumventing the brethren. They joined with infidels in the bond of matrimony; they prostituted the members of Christ to the Gentiles. They not only swore rashly, but committed perjury also; they looked down with haughty arrogance upon those placed over them; they maligned one another with an envenomed tongue; they quarreled with one another with stubborn hatred. Many bishops, who ought to be a source of encouragement and an example to the rest, contemning their divine charge came under the charge of secular kings; after abandoning their thrones and deserting the people, they wandered through foreign provinces and sought the market places for gainful business; while their brethren in the Church were starving, they wished to possess money in abundance; they seized estates by crafty deceits; they increased their capital by multiplying usuries. What do not such as we deserve to suffer for such sins, when already long ago divine censure warned us and said: "If they forsake my law and walk not in my precepts, if they violate my statutes, and keep not my commandments, I will punish their crimes with a rod, and their sins with stripes."

Chapter 7

These things were foreshadowed to us and predicted before. But we, unmindful of the law handed down and of its observation, have brought it about by our sins that while we contemn the mandates of the Lord we have come by severer remedies to the correction of our sins and a probation of our faith, and not indeed have we at last turned to the fear of the Lord so as to undergo this reproof and divine probation of ours patiently and bravely. Immediately at the first words of the threatening enemy a very large number of the brethren betrayed their faith, and were laid low not by the attack of persecution, rather they laid themselves low by their own voluntary lapse. What so unheard of, I ask, what so new had come, that, as if with the rise of unknown and unexpected circumstances, the pledged to Christ should be dissolved with headlong rashness? Did not both the prophets first and the apostles afterwards announce these events? Have not they, filled with Holy Spirit, predicted the oppressions of the just, and the injuries of the Gentiles always? Does not holy Scripture ever arming our faith and strengthening the servants of God with its heavenly voice say: "The Lord thy God shalt thou worship and him only shalt thou serve"? Does it not say again, pointing out the wrath of the divine indignation and forewarning of the fear of punishment: "They have adored those whom their fingers have made, and man hath bowed himself down, and man hath been debased, and I shall not forgive them." And again God speaks, saying: "He that sacrificeth to gods shall be put to death, save only to the Lord." Later in the gospel also did not the Lord, a teacher in words and a consummator in deeds, teaching what would be done and doing whatever He had taught, forewarn us first of what is now taking place and will take place? Did He not before establish eternal punishments for those who deny Him and salutary rewards for those who confess Him?

Chapter 8

For some, ah misery! all these things have fallen away and have receded from memory. They did not wait at least to ascend when apprehended, to deny when questioned. Many were conquered before the battle, were prostrated without a conflict, and they did not leave this for themselves – to seem to sacrifice to idols unwillingly. Moreover they ran to the market place, of their own accord they hastened to death, as if they formerly desired it, as if they were embracing an occasion granted to them, which they had cheerfully desired. How many on that occasion were put off by the magistrates as evening came on, how many also begged that their destruction be not put off! What violence can such a one plead as an excuse, with which to purge his crime, when he himself rather performed the violence that brought about his ruin? When of their own accord they came to the capitol, when they freely approached yielding to the dire crime, did not their footsteps falter, their sight darken, their vitals tremble, their limbs fail, their senses become dull, their tongues cleave, their speech fail? Could the servant of God, who had already renounced the devil and the world, stand there and speak and renounce Christ? Was that altar, which he had approached to die, not a funeral pyre for him? And as for the altar of the devil, which he had seen smoke and smell with a foul fetor, ought he not to have shuddered at it as if the funeral and sepulcher of his own life and to have fled from it? Why, oh wretch, do you bring a sacrificial offering with you, why a victim for supplication? You yourself have come to the altars as a sacrificial offering, you yourself as a victim; you have immolated your salvation there, your hope; there you have cremated your faith in those fires.

Chapter 9

But for many their own destruction was not

enough. By mutual exhortations people were driven to their destruction. Death was proposed for one and another in the lethal cup. And that nothing might be lacking to cap the crime, infants also, placed in the arms of parents or led by them, lost as little ones what they had gained at the very first beginning of their nativity." When the day of judgment comes, will they not say: "We have done nothing; we have not abandoned the Lord's bread and cup and of our own accord hastened to profane contaminations. The perfidy of others has ruined us; we have found our parents parricides. They have denied us the Church as Mother, God as Father, so that, while we still small and improvident and unaware of so great a crime were joined through others into a sharing in the crimes, we were caught in the deceit of others"?

Chapter 10

There is not, alas, any just and serious reason which excuses so great a crime. The fatherland should have been abandoned, the loss of personal property suffered. For what man, who is born and dies, does not at some time have to abandon his fatherland and suffer the loss of personal property? Let not Christ be abandoned; let not the loss of one's salvation and one's eternal home be the object of fear. Behold, the Holy Spirit through the prophet cries out: "Depart, depart, go ye out from thence, touch no unclean thing, go out of the midst of her, be ye apart, you that carry the vessels of the Lord." And do not those who are the vessels of the Lord and the temple of God, lest they be forced to touch the unclean thing and be polluted and corrupted by deadly foods, go out from the midst and withdraw? In another place also a voice from heaven is heard admonishing what the servants of God should do and saying: "Go out from her, my people, that you may not share in her sins, and that you may not receive of her plagues." He who goes out and withdraws does not become a sharer in the sin but he indeed who is discovered as a companion in the crime is himself also seized by the plagues. And so the Lord commanded to withdraw and flee in time of persecution, and He both taught that it should be done and did it. For since the crown descends upon us according to the good pleasure of God, and cannot be received unless the hour for assuming it has come, whoever abiding in Christ withdraws for a time does not deny the faith, but awaits the time; but he who, when he did not withdraw, fell, remained to deny it.

Chapter 11

The truth, brethren, must not be concealed, nor must the matter and cause of our wound be kept silent. Blind love of one's personal property has deceived many; nor could they have been prepared or ready for departing, when their possessions bound them like fetters. Those fetters were for those who remained, those chains by which virtue was retarded, and faith hard pressed, and mind bound, and the soul imprisoned, so that they who clung to earthly things became as booty and food for the serpent who, according to the words of God, devours the earth. Therefore, the Lord, the teacher of good things, warning for the future, says: "If thou wilt be perfect, sell all thy possessions and give to the poor and thou shalt have treasure in heaven; and come, follow me." If the rich did this, they would not perish by their riches; laying up a treasure in heaven they would not now have an enemy and a domestic conqueror; their heart and mind and feeling would be in heaven, if their treasure were in heaven; nor could he be conquered by the world, who had nothing in the world with which to be conquered. He would follow the Lord, loosed and free, as the Apostles and many in apostolic times, and some others often did, who, abandoning their possessions and their parents, clung to the undivided ties of Christ.

Chapter 12

But how can they follow Christ who are held back by the chain of their personal property? Or, how can they seek heaven, and ascend to the sublime and lofty, who are weighed down by earthly desires? They think that they possess, who rather are possessed, slaves of their own property, not lords as regards their money but rather the bond-slaves of their money. The Apostle refers to this time, to these men, when he says: "But those who seek to become rich fall into temptation and a snare and into many harmful desires which plunge men into destruction and damnation. For covetousness is the root of all evils, and some seeking riches have strayed from the faith and have involved themselves in many troubles." But with what rewards does the Lord invite us to contempt of personal wealth? With what wages does He compensate for these small and trifling losses of this present time? "There is no one," He says, "who has left house, or land, or parents, or brothers, or wife, or sons for the kingdom of God's sake who does not receive a seven-fold in this present time, and in the world to come life everlasting." Since these things are known and have been ascertained from the truth of God who makes the promise, not only is a loss of this kind not to be feared but even to be desired, for the Lord Himself again proclaims and gives warning: "Blessed shall you be when men persecute you, and separate you and shut you out and reject your name as evil because of the Son of man. Rejoice on that day and exult, for behold your reward is great in heaven."

Chapter 13

But later torments had come, and severe sufferings threatened those who resisted. He can complain about torments who was overcome by torments; he can offer the excuse of pain who has been overcome by pain. Such a one can ask and say: "surely I wished to contend bravely, and mindful of my oath I took up the arms of devotion and faith; but as I found in the contest the various tortures and extended punishments overcome me. My mind stood firm and faith strong, and my soul struggled long and unshaken with the excruciating pains. But when, as the cruelty of a most severe judge broke forth afresh, fatigued as I was, the scourges now for the first time slashed me, the cudgels now bruised me, the rack now stretched me, the claw now dug into me, the flame now scorched me, my flesh deserted me in the struggle, the weakness of my vitals gave way, not my soul but my body yielded in the suffering." Such a plea can quickly advance to forgiveness; an excuse of this kind can be worthy of pity. Thus in these circumstances the Lord once forgave Cestus and Aemilius; thus, although conquered in the first encounter, he made them victorious in the second battle, so that they became stronger than the fires who previously had yielded to the fires, and in what they had been overcome, in this they overcame. They made their entreaties by pity not of tears but of wounds, not with a wailing voice alone, but with laceration and pain of body. Blood instead of lamentations came forth, and instead of tears gore poured out from their half burnt vitals.

Chapter 14

But now, what wounds can the conquered show, what injuries to gaping vitals, what tortures of the limbs, when faith did not fail in combat, but perfidy arrived before the combat? Nor does the necessity of the crime excuse him who was caught, where the crime is of the will. I do not say this to burden the cases of the brethren, but rather to stimulate the brethren to prayers of satisfaction. For since it is written: "They that call you blessed, send you into error, and destroy the way of your steps," he who consoles the sinner with flattering blandishments furnishes the means for sinning, and does not check transgressions but nourishes them. But he who rebukes at the same time that he instructs with firmer counsels urges a brother on to salvation. "Whom I love," says the Lord, "I rebuke and chastise." Thus also ought the priest of the Lord not to deceive by deceptive submissions but to provide with salutary remedies. A physician is unskilled who handles the swelling folds of wounds with a sparing hand, and increases the poison inclosed within the deep recesses of the vital organs as he cares for it. The wound must be opened and cut and treated by a sterner remedy, by cutting out the corrupting parts. Although the sick man, impatient by reason of his pain, cries out, shrieks, and complains, he will give thanks afterwards, when he has experienced good health.

Chapter 15

For, very beloved brethren, a new kind of devastation has emerged and, as if the storm of persecution had raged too little, there has been added to the heap, under the title of mercy, a deceiving evil and an alluring destruction. Contrary to the rigor of the Gospel, contrary to the law of the Lord and God because of the temerity of certain persons communion with the rash is related, an empty and false peace, dangerous to those who grant it and of no benefit to those who receive it. They do not seek the patience important for health, nor the true medicine derived from satisfaction. Penance is excluded from their hearts; the memory of a most serious and extreme sin is removed. The wounds of the dying are concealed, and the deadly blow fixed in the deep and secret vitals is concealed by dissimulated pain. Returning from the altars of the devil they approach the holy place of the Lord with hands befouled and reeking with smell; still almost belching forth the death-bearing food of idols, even now with jaws breathing forth their crime and redolent with the fatal contagion they invade the body of the Lord, when the divine Scripture stands in their way, and cries out, saying: "Everyone that is clean shall eat of the flesh, and whatever soul shall eat of the flesh of the saving sacrifice which is the Lord, and his uncleanness is upon him, that soul shall perish from his people." Let the Apostle likewise bear witness, saying: "You cannot drink of the cup of the Lord and the cup of devils; you cannot be partakers of the table of the Lord and of the table of devils." He likewise threatens the stubborn and the perverse, and denounces them, saying: "Whoever eats the bread and drinks the cup of the Lord unworthily will be guilty of the body and blood of the Lord."

Chapter 16

Spurning and despising all these warnings, before their sins have been expiated, before confession of their crime has been made, before their conscience has been purged by the sacrifice and hand of the priest, before the offense of an angry and threatening Lord has been appeased, violence is done to His body and blood, and they sin more against the Lord with their hands and mouth than when they denied the Lord. They think that to be peace which some truck with deceiving words. That is not peace but war, nor is he joined with the Church who is separated from the Gospel. Why do they call an injury a kindness? Why do they refer to impiety by the term "piety"? Why do they interrupt the lamentation of penance and pretend to communicate with those who ought to weep continually and to entreat their Lord? This is of the same nature to the lapsed as hail to the harvests, a violent storm to the trees, a destructive pestilence to cattle, a raging tempest to ships. They destroy the solace of hope, they pull up the roots, with their unwholesome words they creep on to deadly contagion, they dash the ship upon rocks lest it arrive within the harbor. That kind of facility does not grant peace but takes it away, nor does it bestow communion but stands in the way of salvation. This is another persecution and another temptation, by which a subtle enemy attacking the lapsed still further approaches with a concealed devastation, so that lamentation is hushed, grief is made silent, the memory of sin vanishes, the groaning of the heart is repressed, the weeping of the eyes is halted, nor is the Lord implored with a long and full penitence, although it is written: "Remember whence thou hast fallen and do penance."

Chapter 17

Let no man betray himself; let no man deceive himself. The Lord alone can have mercy. He alone can grant pardon for sins which were committed against Him, who bore our sins, who grieved for us, whom God delivered up for our sins. Man cannot be greater than God, nor can the servant by his own indulgence remit or forego what has been committed against the Lord by a more serious sin, lest to him still lapsed this too be added to his crime, if he does not know that it has been proclaimed: "Cursed be the man that hath hope in man." The Lord must be implored; the Lord must be placated by our own satisfaction, who said that He denied him who denied (Him), who alone received every judgment from the Father. We believe indeed that the merits of the martyrs and the works of the righteous have very great power with the Judge, but (this will be) when the day of judgment shall come, when after the end of this age and of the world His people shall stand before the tribunal of Christ.

Chapter 18

But if anyone with precipitate haste rashly thinks that he can grant remission of sins to all or dares to rescind the precepts of the Lord, not only is this of no advantage to the lapsed but it is even a hindrance. Not to have observed the judgment of the Lord, and to think that His mercy is not first to be implored, but after contemning the Lord to presume on one's own power, is to have provoked His wrath. Under the altar of God the souls of the slain martyrs cry out with a loud voice saying: "How long, O Lord holy and true, does Thou refrain from judging and from avenging our blood on those who dwell on earth." And they are ordered to be quiet and to continue to have patience. Does someone think that anyone can wish to become good by remitting and pardoning sins at random or that he can defend others before he himself is vindicated? The martyrs order something to be done; if just, if lawful, if not contrary to the Lord Himself, they are to be done by the priest of God; let the agreement be ready and easy on the part of the one obeying, if there has been religious moderation on the part of him asking. The martyrs order something to be done. If what they order is not written in the law of the Lord, we must first know, that they have obtained from the Lord what they ask, then do what they order. For what has been assured by man's promise cannot be seen at once to have been granted by the divine majesty.

Chapter 19

For Moses also sought pardon for the sins of the people and yet did not receive it when he sought it for those sinning. "I beseech Thee, O Lord," he said, "this people hath sinned a heinous sin, and now, if you forgive their sin, forgive; but if not, strike me out of the book that thou hast written. And the Lord said to Moses: If anyone hath sinned against me, him will I strike out of my book." That friend of God, that one who had often spoken face to face with the Lord was unable to obtain what he sought, nor did he placate the displeasure of an indignant God by his intercession. God praises Jeremias, and proclaims, saying: "Before I formed thee in the womb, I knew thee; and before thou comest forth out of the womb, I sanctified thee, and made thee a prophet unto the nations," and He said to him as he frequently interceded and prayed for the sins of the people: "Do not pray for this people and do not take up praise and prayer for them, for I will not hear them in the time of their cry to me, in the time of their affliction." Who was more righteous than Noah, who, when the earth was replete with sins was alone found righteous upon the earth? Who more glorious than Daniel? Who stronger in firmness of faith for enduring martyrdom, happier in God's favors, who when he fought so often conquered and when he conquered survived? Who was more diligent in good works than Job, stronger in temptations, more patient in suffering, more submissive in fear, more true in faith? And yet God said that, if they should ask, He would not grant. When the prophet Ezekiel interceded for the sins of the people, God said: "Whatever land shall sin against me, so as to transgress grievously, I will stretch forth my hand upon it, and will break the staff of bread thereof, and will send famine upon it, and will destroy man and beast out of it. And if these three men, Noah, Daniel, and Job, shall be in it, they shall deliver neither sons nor daughters, but they only shall be delivered." Therefore, not all that is sought is in the prejudgment of the seeker, but in the decision of the giver, and human opinion takes or assumes nothing to itself unless the divine pleasure also assents.

Chapter 20

In the Gospel the Lord speaks saying:

"Everyone who acknowledges me before men, him will I also acknowledge before my Father who is in heaven; but whoever denies me, even I shall deny him." If he does not deny him who denies, neither does he acknowledge him who acknowledges. The Gospel cannot be firm in part and waver in part. Either both must be strong or both must lose the force of truth. If those who deny will not be guilty of a crime, neither do those who acknowledge receive the reward of virtue. Furthermore, if the faith which has conquered is crowned, the perfidy also which has been conquered must be punished. Thus the martyrs either can be of no avail, if the Gospel can be broken, or if the Gospel cannot be broken, they who become martyrs according to the Gospel cannot act contrary to the Gospel. Let no one, most beloved brethren, no one defame the dignity of the martyrs; let no one destroy their glories and crowns. The strength of an uncorrupted faith remains sound, and no one can say or do anything against Christ whose hope and faith and virtue and glory is entirely in Christ, so that they who have performed the mandates of God Himself cannot be the authors of anything being done by the bishops contrary to the mandate of God. Is anyone greater than God or more merciful than divine goodness, who either wishes that undone which God suffered to be done, or, as if He had too little power to protect His Church, thinks that we can be saved by his own help?

Chapter 21

But if these things have been accomplished with God's knowledge or all these have come to pass without His permission, let divine Scripture teach the unteachable and admonish the forgetful as it speaks in these words: "Who hath given Jacob for a spoil and Israel to those who plundered him? Hath not God against whom they have sinned and were unwilling to walk in His ways and to hear His law? And He hath poured out upon them the indignation of fury." And elsewhere it testifies saying: "Indeed does not the hand of God prevail to save, or, has He burdened His ear that He does not hear? But your sins make a division between you and your God, and because of your sins he hath turned away His face from you lest He have pity." Let us consider our sins, and reviewing the secrets of our action and mind let us weigh the merits of our conscience. Let it return to our hearts that we have not walked in the ways of the Lord, have rejected the law of God, have never been willing to keep His precepts and saving counsels.

Chapter 22

What good do you feel with respect to him, what fear, what faith do you believe there was in him whom fear was unable to correct, whom persecution itself has not reformed. His high and erect neck has not been bent because he has fallen; his puffed up and proud mind has not been broken because he has been conquered. On his back and wounded he threatens those who stand and are sound, and because he does not immediately receive the Lord's body in his sullied hands or drink of the Lord's blood with a polluted mouth, he rages sacrilegiously against the priests. And, oh that excessive madness of yours, frenzied one, you rage at him who struggles to avert God's anger from you; you threaten him who beseeches the Lord's mercy for you, who feels your wound which you yourself do not feel, who pours forth tears for you which you yourself perhaps do not pour forth. You pile up and increase your crime still more, and, when you yourself are implacable towards the bishops and priests of God, do you think that the Lord can be placated about you?

Chapter 23

Accept and admit what we say. Why do your deaf ears not hear the salutary precepts which we advise? Why do your blind eyes not see the way of penitence which we place before you? Why does your closed and insane mind not perceive the vital remedies which we both learn and teach from the heavenly Scriptures? If certain incredulous ones have less faith in the future events, let them at least have fear for the present. Behold, what punishments we perceive of those who have denied, what sad deaths of those do we mourn! Not even here can they be without punishment, although the day of punishment has not yet come. Meanwhile certain ones are punished, that the rest may be guided aright. The torments of a few are examples for all.

Chapter 24

One of these who of his own accord went up to the capital to deny became mute after he had denied Christ. The punishment began there where the crime also began, so that he could no longer ask who did not have words for prayers of mercy. Another was stationed in the baths – for this was lacking to her crime and evils, so that she proceeded at once even to the baths, who had lost the grace of the life-giving laver – but there she who was unclean being seized by an unclean spirit lacerated with her teeth the tongue which had either fed or spoken impiously. After the polluted food had been consumed, the madness of the mouth worked its own destruction. She herself was her own executioner and was not able to survive long thereafter; being tortured by the pain of her belly and vitals she died.

Chapter 25

Hear what took place in my very presence and with me as a witness. Some parents in hasty flight, with little consideration because of their fear, left their little daughter in the care of a nurse. The nurse handed the abandoned girl over to the magistrates. There before the idol where the people were gathering, because she was unable as yet to eat meat because of her age, they gave her bread mixed with wine, which itself had been left over from the immolation of those who were being destroyed. Afterwards the mother recovered her daughter. But the girl was unable to mention and point out the crime that had been committed as she was unable previously to understand and prevent it. Through ignorance, therefore, it came about that the mother brought the child with her to us as we were offering the Sacrifice. Moreover, the girl having mingled with the holy people, being impatient of our supplication and prayer, was now shaken with weeping and was now tossed about by the vacillating motion of her mind; as if under the compulsion of a torturer the soul of the girl still of tender years was trying to confess with such signs as she was able a consciousness of the deed. But when the solemnities were completed and the deacon began to offer the cup to those present, and when, as the rest were receiving, her turn came, the little girl with an instinct of divine majesty turned her face away, compressed her mouth with tightening lips, and refused the cup. The deacon, however, persisted and poured into the mouth of the child, although resisting, of the sacrament of the cup. Then there followed sobbing and vomiting. In the body and mouth which had been violated the Eucharist could not remain; the draught consecrated in the blood of the Lord burst forth from the polluted vitals. So great is the power of the Lord, so great His majesty. The secrets of the shades are detected under His light, nor did hidden crimes deceive the priest of God.

Chapter 26

So much about the infant who as yet did not have the years of speaking of a crime committed by others against herself. But that lady of advanced age and settled in more advanced years, who crept stealthily upon us as we sacrificed, taking food and a sword for herself, and admitting, as it were, a kind of deadly poison, within her jaws and body, began presently to be tormented by frenzy of soul, and suffering the misery no longer of persecution but of her sin, fell quivering and trembling. The crime of her hidden conscience was not long unpunished and concealed. She who had deceived man felt God as an avenger. And when a certain women tried with unclean hands to open her box, in which was the holy (body) of the Lord, thereupon she was deterred by rising fire from daring to touch it. And another man who, himself defiled, after the celebration of the sacrifice dared secretly to take a part with the rest, was unable to eat or handle the holy of the Lord, and found when he opened his hands that he was carrying a cinder. By the evidence of one it was shone that the Lord withdraws when He is denied, and that what is received is of no benefit to the undeserving, when the grace of salvation is changed as the holy escapes into a cinder. How many are daily filled with unclean spirits; how many are shaken out of their minds by the fury of madness even to insanity! It is not necessary to go over the death of each one, when over the varied ruins of the world the punishment of sins is as varied as the multitude of sinners is numerous. Let everyone consider not what another has suffered but what he himself deserves to suffer, and let him not believe that he has escaped, if in the meantime punishment has put him off, since he should fear the more whom the wrath of God the Judge has reserved for Himself.

Chapter 27

Let them not persuade themselves that they should not do penance, who, although they have not contaminated their hands by impious sacrifices, yet have defiled their consciences with certificates. That profession is of one who denies; the testimony is of a Christian who rejects what he had been. He said that he had done what another actually did, and, although it is written: "You cannot serve two masters," he served a secular master, he submitted to his edict, he obeyed human authority rather than God. He should have seen whether he published what he committed with less scandal or less guilt among men; however, he will not be able to escape and avoid God as his judge, for the Holy Spirit says in the Psalms: "Thine eyes have seen my imperfection and all will be written in thy book," and again: "Man looks upon the face, but God upon the heart." Let the Lord Himself also forewarn and instruct you with these words: "And all the churches shall know that I am He who searches the desires and hearts." He perceives the concealed and the secret, and considers the hidden, nor can anyone evade the eyes of God who says: "Am I a God at hand, and not a God afar off? Shall a man be hid in secret places and I not see him? He sees the hearts and breasts of each one, and, when about to pass judgment not only on our deeds but also on our words and thoughts, He looks into the minds and the wills conceived in the very recess of a still closed heart.

Chapter 28

Finally, of how much greater faith and better fear are they who, although bound by no crime of sacrifice or of certificate, since however they have even thought of this, confessing this very thing with grief and simply before the priests of God, make a conscientious avowal, remove the weight of their souls, seek the saving remedy for their wounds however small and slight knowing that it is written: "God is not mocked." God cannot be mocked and deceived, nor can He be deluded by any treacherous cunning. Rather does he sin more who, thinking of God as if human, believes that he is escaping the punishment of his crime, if he has not admitted the crime openly. Christ in His precepts says: "Whoever is ashamed of me, of him shall the Son of man be ashamed." Does he think himself a Christian who is either ashamed or fears to be a Christian? How can he be with Christ, who either blushes or fears to belong to Christ? Clearly he might have sinned less by not looking upon idols, and by not profaning the sanctity of the faith under the eyes of a populace that stood about and cast insults, by not polluting his hands with the deadly sacrifices, and by not defiling his mouth with the wretched food. This is of benefit to this extent, that the fault is less, not that the conscience is without guilt. He can more easily arrive at a forgiveness of his crime, but he is not free from crime. Let him not cease doing penance and beseeching the mercy of the Lord, lest what seems less in the quality of his sin be increased by his failure to give satisfaction to it.

Chapter 29

Let each one confess his sin, I beseech you, brethren, while he who has sinned is still in this world, while his confession can be admitted, while the satisfaction and remission effected through the priest is pleasing with the Lord. Let us turn to the Lord with our whole mind, and, expressing repentance for our sin with true grief, let us implore God's mercy. Let the soul prostrate itself before Him; let sorrow give satisfaction to Him; let our every hope rest upon Him. He Himself tells how we ought to ask. He says: "Be converted to me with all your hearts, in fasting and in weeping, and in mourning, and rend your hearts and not your garments." Let us return to the Lord with a whole heart; let us placate His wrath and displeasure by fastings, weepings, and mournings, as He Himself admonishes.

Chapter 30

Do we think that he laments with a whole heart, implores the Lord with fastings, weepings, and mournings, who from the first day of his crime daily frequents the baths, who, feeding on rich banquets and distended by fuller dainties, belches forth the undigested food on the next day, and does not share his food and drink with the needy poor? How does he, who goes forth joyous and happy, weep over his death, and, although it is written: "You shall not change the form of your beard," plucks his beard and adorns his face? And is he eager to please anyone who displeases his God? Or does she groan and moan who has time to put on the elegance of pricey garments but not to think of the robe of Christ which she has lost; to receive precious ornaments and costly necklaces, but not to weep over the loss of the divine and heavenly ornament? Although you put on foreign robes and silken dresses, you are naked. Although you decorate yourself with gold and pearls and gems, without the adornment of Christ you are unsightly. And you who dye your hair, now at least cease in the midst of your sorrows, and you who paint the edges of your eyes by lines of black powder, now at least wash your eyes with tears. If you had lost any dear one of yours by his passing away in death, you would grieve and mourn sorrowfully; with a disordered countenance, changed dress, unkempt hair, gloomy countenance, dejected face you would show the signs of sorrow. Wretched woman, you have lost your soul; spiritually dead you have begun to live on here, and although yourself walking about you have begun to carry your own death. And do you not groan bitterly; do you not mourn continually; do you not go in hiding either because of the shame of your crime or for the continuing of your lamentation? Behold still worse are the wounds of sinning, behold, greater the transgressions – to have sinned and not to give satisfaction, to have transgressed and not to bemoan transgressions.

Chapter 31

Ananias, Azarias, and Misahel, illustrious and noble youths, did not refrain from making confession to God not even midst the flames and fires of a raging furnace. Although possessed of a good conscience and often well deserving of the Lord by obedience of faith and fear, they did not cease to retain their humility and to give satisfaction to God not even midst the glorious martyrdoms themselves of their virtues. Divine Scripture speaks in these words: "Azarias standing prayed and opened his mouth and made confession to God together with his companions in the midst of fire." Daniel also after the manifold grace of his faith and innocence, after the esteem of the Lord often repeated with regard to his virtues and praises, strives still further by fastings to merit God; wraps himself in sackcloth and ashes as he sorrowfully makes confession, saying: "Lord God, great and strong and terrible who keepest the covenant and mercy to them that love thee and keep thy commandments, we have sinned, we have committed iniquity, we have been ungodly, we have transgressed and gone aside from thy precepts and thy judgments, we have not hearkened to thy servants in what they have spoken in thy name to our kings and to all the nations and to the whole world. To thee, O Lord, to thee is justice, but to us confusion."

Chapter 32

These things the meek, these the simple, this the innocent have done in meriting well of the majesty of God; and those who have denied the Lord refuse to satisfy the Lord and to entreat Him! I beseech you, brethren, acquiesce in the remedies of salvation, obey the better counsels, join your tears with our tears, write your groans with ours. We implore you that we may be able to implore the Lord for you; we turn our very prayers to you first, with which we pray to God for you, that He may be merciful. Do full penance, prove the sorrow of a soul that sorrows and laments.

Chapter 33

Let neither the imprudent error nor the vain stupidity of some move you, who, although they were involved in so grave a crime were struck by such blindness of soul that they neither realized their sins nor lamented them. This is the greater plague of an angry God, as it is written: "And God gave them a spirit of rebellion," and again: "For they have not received the love of truth that they might be saved. Therefore, God sends them a misleading influence that they may believe falsehood, that all may be judged who have not believed truth, but have taken pleasure in injustice." Taking pleasure unjustly and mad by the alienation of a damaged mind, they contemn the precepts of the Lord, neglect the medicine of their wound, are unwilling to do penance. Improvident before their sin was committed, obstinate after their sin, neither steadfast before nor suppliant afterwards, when they ought to have stood fast, they fell, when they ought to fall down and prostrate themselves before God, they think that they stand. Of their own accord they assumed peace for themselves, although no one granted it, seduced by false promises and linked with apostates and infidels they accept error for truth; they regard communion with those who are not communicants as valid; they believe men against God, who have not believed God against men.

Chapter 34

Flee from such men with all your power; and with wholesome caution those who cling to pernicious contacts. Their speech spreads like a cancer; their speech leaps over barriers like a pestilence; their harmful and poisoned persuasion kills worse than persecution itself. Repentance remains there for giving satisfaction. Those who do away with repentance for crime, close the way to satisfaction. So it happens that, when by the rashness of some a false salvation is either promised or believed, the hope of true salvation is taken away.

Chapter 35

But do you, brethren, who are inclined toward fear of the Lord and whose minds, although set in destruction, are mindful of their evils, repenting and grieving view your sins, recognize the very serious crime of your conscience, open the eyes of your hearts to an understanding of your shortcomings, neither despairing of the mercy of the Lord nor yet already laying claim to pardon. As God by reason of His affection as father is always indulgent and good, so by reason of His majesty as judge He is to be feared. Let us weep as greatly as the extent of our sinning. For a deep wound let there not be lacking a careful and long cure; let the repentance be no less than the crime. Do you think that God can be easily placated, whom you denied with perfidious words, above whom you set your property, whose temple you violated with sacrilegious contamination? Do you think that He easily has mercy on you, whom you have said was not yours? You ought to pray and beseech more intently, to pass the day grieving, to spend your nights in wakefulness and weeping, to spend all your time in mournful lamentation, to cling to ashes prone on the ground, to wallow in sackcloth and squalor, to wish for no garment now after losing the cloak of Christ, to prefer fasting after the food of the devil, to devote yourself to just works by which sins are purged, to enter frequently upon alms-giving, by which souls are liberated from death. What the adversary tried to take away, let Christ receive; your property ought not to be retained now or to be cherished, by which one has been both deceived and conquered. Wealth is to be avoided as an enemy, as a thief to be fled, as a sword to be feared by those who possess it, and as a poison. To this extent only might that which has remained be of benefit, that by means of it crime and sin may be redeemed. Let your works be done without delay and in abundance; let every means be evoked for the healing of the wound; let the Lord, who is to be our judge, be put in our debt by our resources and faculties. Thus did faith flourish under the Apostles; thus did the first people of the believers keep the mandates of Christ – they were ready; they were generous. They gave all to be distributed by the Apostles and they were not redeeming such sins.

Chapter 36

If anyone performs prayer with his whole heart, if he groans with genuine lamentations and tears of repentance, if by continuous just works he turns the Lord to the forgiveness of his sin, such can receive His mercy, who has offered His mercy with these words: "When you turn and lament, then you shall be saved and shall know where you have been"; and again: I desire not the death of the dying, says the Lord in the Lord's own words: "Turn," he says, "to the Lord your God, for He is gracious and merciful, patient and rich in mercy and who turns his thought toward the evil that has been done." He can grant mercy; He can turn aside His judgment. He can with indulgence pardon him who is repentant, who performs good works, who beseeches; He can regard as acceptable whatever the martyrs have sought and the priests have done for such. Or, if anyone has moved Him more by his own atonements, has placated His wrath, His rightful indignation by just supplication. He gives arms again with which the vanquished may be armed. He repairs and invigorates his strength so that his restored faith may flourish. The soldier will seek his contest again; he will repeat its fight; he will provoke the enemy; he has become indeed stronger for the battle through suffering. He who has thus satisfied God, who by repentance for his deed, who by shame for his sin has conceived more of both virtue and faith from the very sorrow for his lapsing, after being heard and aided by the Lord, will cause the Church to rejoice, which he recently had saddened, and will merit not alone the pardon of God but a crown.

Treatise 3

B. Clement of Alexandria's Writing on Persecution

The praises of martyrdom

Whence, as is reasonable, the gnostic, when Galled, obeys easily, and gives up his body to him who asks; and, previously divesting himself of the affections of this carcase, not insulting the tempter, but rather, in my opinion, training him and convincing him, "From what honor and what extent of wealth fallen," as says Empedocles, here for the future he walks with mortals. He, in truth, bears witness to himself that he is faithful and loyal towards God; and to the tempter, that he in vain envied him who is faithful through love; and to the Lord, of the inspired persuasion in reference to His doctrine, from which he will not depart through fear of death; further, he confirms also the truth of preaching by his deed, showing that God to whom he hastes is powerful. You will wonder at his love, which he conspicuously shows with thankfulness, in being united to what is allied to him, and besides by his precious blood, shaming the unbelievers. He then avoids denying Christ through fear by reason of the command; nor does he sell his faith in the hope of the gifts prepared, but in love to the Lord he will most gladly depart from this life; perhaps giving thanks both to him who afforded the cause of his departure hence, and to him who laid the plot against him, for receiving an honorable reason which he himself furnished not, for showing what he is, to him by his patience, and to the Lord in love, by which even before his birth he was manifested to the Lord, who knew the martyr's choice. With good courage, then, he goes to the Lord, his friend, for whom he voluntarily gave his body, and, as his judges hoped, his soul, hearing from our Savior the words of poetry, "Dear brother," by reason of the similarity of his life. We call martyrdom perfection, not because the man comes to the end of his life as others, but because he has exhibited the perfect work of love. And the ancients laud the death of those among the Greeks who died in war, not that they advised people to die a violent death, but because he who ends his life in war is released without the dread of dying, severed from the body without experiencing previous suffering or being enfeebled in his soul, as the people that suffer in diseases. For they depart in a state of effeminacy and desiring to live; and therefore they do not yield up the soul pure, but bearing with it their lusts like weights of lead; all but those who have been conspicuous in virtue. Some die in battle with their lusts, these being in no respect different from what they would have been if they had wasted away by disease.

If the confession to God is martyrdom, each soul which has lived purely in the knowledge of God, which has obeyed the commandments, is a witness both by life and word, in whatever way it may be released from the body,-shedding faith as blood along its whole life till its departure. For instance, the Lord says in the Gospel, "Whosoever shall leave father, or mother, or brethren," and so forth, "for the sake of the Gospel and my name," he is blessed; not indicating simple martyrdom, but the gnostic martyrdom, as of the man who has conducted himself according to the rule of the Gospel, in love to the Lord (for the knowledge of the Name and the understanding of the Gospel point out the gnosis, but not the bare appellation), so as to leave his worldly kindred, and wealth, and every possession, in order to lead a life free from passion. "Mother" figuratively means Country and sustenance; "fathers" are the laws of civil polity: which must be contemned thankfully by the high-souled just man; for the sake of being the friend of God, and of obtaining the right hand in the holy place, as the Apostles have done.

Then Heraclitus says, "Gods and men honor those slain in battle; "and Plato in the fifth book of the Republic writes, "Of those who die in military service, whoever dies after winning renown, shall we not say that he is chief of the golden race? Most assuredly." But the golden race is with the gods, who are in heaven, in the fixed sphere, who chiefly hold command in the providence exercised towards men. Now some of the heretics who have misunderstood the Lord, have at once an impious and cowardly love of life; saying that the true martyrdom is the knowledge of the only true God (which we also admit), and that the man is a self-murderer and a suicide who makes confession by death; and adducing other similar sophisms of cowardice. To these we shall reply at the proper time; for they differ with us in regard to first principles. Now we, too, say that those who have rushed on death (for there are some, not belonging to us, but sharing the name merely, who are in haste to give themselves up, the poor wretches dying through hatred to the Creator-these, we say, banish themselves without being martyrs, even though they are punished publicly. For they do not preserve the characteristic mark of believing martyrdom, in as much as they have not known the only true God, but give themselves up to a vain death, as the Gymnosophists of the Indians to useless fire.

But since these falsely named calumniate the body, let them learn that the harmonious mechanism of the body contributes to the understanding which leads to goodness of nature. Wherefore in the third book of the Republic, Plato, whom they appeal to loudly as an authority that disparages generation, says, "that for the sake of harmony of soul, care must be taken for the body," by which, he who announces the proclamation of the truth, finds it possible to live, and to live well. For it is by the path of life and health that we learn gnosis. But is he who cannot advance to the height without being occupied with necessary things, and through them doing what tends to knowledge, not to choose to live well? In living, then, living well is secured. And he who in the body has devoted himself to a good life, is being sent on to the state of immortality.

The blessedness of the martyr

Then he who has lied and shown himself unfaithful, and revolted to the devil's army, in what evil do we think him to be? He belies, therefore, the Lord, or rather he is cheated of his own hope who believes not God; and he believes not who does not what He has commanded.

And what? Does not he, who denies the Lord, deny himself? For does he not rob his Master of His authority, who deprives himself of his relation to Him? He, then, who denies the Savior, denies life; for "the light was life." He does not term those men of little faith, but faithless and hypocrites, who have the name inscribed on them, but deny that they are really believers. But the faithful is called both servant and friend. So that if one loves himself, he loves the Lord, and confesses to salvation that he may save his soul. Though you die for your neighbor out of love, and regard the Savior as our neighbor (for God who saves is said to be nigh in respect to what is saved); you do so, choosing death on account of life, and suffering for your own sake rather than his. And is it not for this that he is called brother? he who, suffering out of love to God, suffered for his own salvation; while he, on the other hand, who dies for his own salvation, endures for love to the Lord. For he being life, in what he suffered wished to suffer that we might live by his suffering.

"Why call ye me Lord, Lord," He says, "and do not the things which I say? " For "the people that loveth with their lips, but have their heart far away from the Lord," is another people, and trust in another, and have willingly sold themselves to another; but those who perform the commandments of the Lord, in every action "testify," by doing what He wishes, and consistently naming the Lord's name; and "testifying" by deed to Him in whom they trust, that they are those "who have crucified the flesh, with the affections and lusts." "If we live in the Spirit, let us also walk in the Spirit." "He that soweth to his flesh, shall of the flesh reap corruption; but he that soweth to the Spirit, shall of the Spirit reap life everlasting."

But to those miserable men, witness to the Lord by blood seems a most violent death, not knowing that such a gate of death is the beginning of the true life; and they will understand neither the honors after death, which belong to those who have lived holily, nor the punishments of those who have lived unrighteously and impurely. I do not say only from our Scriptures (for almost all the commandments indicate them); but they will not even hear their own discourses. For the Pythagorean Theano writes, "Life were indeed a feast to the wicked, who, having done evil, then die; were not the soul immortal, death would be a godsend." And Plato in the Phaedo, "For if death were release from everything," and so forth. We are not then to think according to the Telephus of Aeschylus, "that a single path leads to Hades." The ways are many, and the sins that lead thither. Such deeply erring ones as the unfaithful are, Aristophanes properly makes the subjects of comedy. "Come," he says, "ye men of obscure life, ye that are like the race of leaves, feeble, wax figures, shadowy tribes, evanescent, fleeting, ephemeral." And Epicharmus, "This nature of men is inflated skins." And the Savior has said to us, "The spirit is willing, but the flesh is weak." "Because the carnal mind is enmity against God," explains the apostle: "for it is not subject to the law of God, neither indeed, can be. And they that are in the flesh cannot please God." And in further explanation continues, that no one may, like Marcion regard the creature as evil. "But if Christ be in you, the body is dead because of sin; but the Spirit is life because of righteousness." And again: "For if ye live after the flesh, ye shall die. For I reckon that the sufferings of this present time are not worthy to be compared to the glory which shall be revealed in us. If we suffer with Him, that we also may be glorified together as joint-heirs of Christ. And we know that all things work together for good to them that love God, to them that are called according to the purpose. For whom He did foreknow, He also did predestinate to be conformed to the image of His Son, that He might be the first-born among many brethren. And whom He did predestinate, them He also called; and whom He called, them He also justified; and whom He justified, them He also glorified."

You see that martyrdom for love's sake is taught. And should you wish to be a martyr for the recompense of advantages, you shall hear again. "For we are saved by hope: but hope that is seen is not hope: for what a man seeth, why doth he yet hope for? But if we hope for that we see not, then do we with patience wait for it." "But if we also suffer for righteousness" sake," says Peter, "blessed are we. Be not afraid of their fear, neither be troubled. But sanctify the Lord God in your hearts: and be ready always to give an answer to him that asks a reason of the hope that is in you, but with meekness and fear, having a good conscience; so that in reference to that for which you are spoken against, they may be ashamed who calumniate your good conversation in Christ. For it is better to suffer for well-doing. if the will of God, than for evil-doing." But if one should captiously say, And how is it possible for feeble flesh to resist the energies and spirits of the Powers? well, let him know this, that, confiding in the Almighty and the Lord, we war against the principalities of darkness, and against death. "Whilst thou art yet speaking," He says, "Lo, here am I." See the invincible Helper who shields us. "Think it not strange, therefore, concerning the burning sent for your trial, as though some strange thing happened to you; But, as you are partaken in the sufferings of Christ, rejoice; that at the revelation of His glory ye may rejoice exultant. If ye be reproached in the name of Christ, happy are ye; for the Spirit of glory and of God resteth on you." As it is written, "Because for Thy sake we are killed all the day long; we are accounted as sheep for the slaughter. Nay, in all these things we are more than conquerors, through Him that loved us."

"What you wish to ascertain from my mind,
You shall not ascertain, not were you to apply
Horrid saws from the crown of my head to the soles of my feet,
Not were you to load me with chains,"

says a woman acting manfully in the tragedy. And Antigone, contemning the proclamation of Creon, says boldly: "It was not Zeus who uttered this proclamation."

But it is God that makes proclamation to us, and He must be believed. "For with the heart man believeth unto righteousness; and with the mouth confession is made unto salvation. Wherefore the Scripture saith, "Whosoever believeth on Him shah not be put to shame." Accordingly Simonides justly writes, "It is said that virtue dwells among all but inaccessible rocks, but that she speedily traverses a pure place. Nor is she visible to the eyes of all mortals. He who is not penetrated by heart-vexing sweat will not scale the summit of manliness." And Pindar says:

"But the anxious thoughts of youths, revolving with toils,
Will find glory: and in time their deeds
Will in resplendent ether splendid shine."

Aeschylus, too, having grasped this thought, says:

"To him who toils is due,
As product of his toil, glory from the gods."

"For great Fates attain great destinies," according to Heraclitus:

"And what slave is there, who is careless of death?"

"For God hath not given us the spirit of bondage again to fear; but of power, and love, and of a sound mind. Be not therefore ashamed of the testimony of our Lord, or of me his prisoner," he writes to Timothy. Such shall he be "who cleaves to that which is good," according to the apostle, "who hates evil, having love unfeigned; for he that loveth another fulfilleth the law." If, then, this God, to whom we bear witness, be as He is, the God of hope, we acknowledge our hope, speeding on to hope, "saturated with goodness, filled with all knowledge."

The Indian sages say to Alexander of Macedon: "You transport men's bodies from place to place. But you shall not force our souls to do what we do not wish. Fire is to men the greatest torture, this we despise." Hence Heraclitus preferred one thing, glory, to all else; and professes "that he allows the crowd to stuff themselves to satiety like cattle."

"For on account of the body are many toils,
For it we have invented a roofed house,
And discovered how to dig up silver, and sow the land,
And all the rest which we know by names."

To the multitude, then, this vain labor is desirable. But to us the apostle says, "Now we know this, that our old man is crucified with Him, that the body of sin might be destroyed, that henceforth we should not serve sin." Does not the apostle then plainly add the following, to show the contempt for faith in the case of the multitude? "For I think that God hath set forth us the apostles last, as appointed to death: we are made a spectacle to the world, and to angels, and to men. Up to this present hour we both hunger, and thirst, and are naked, and are beaten, and are feeble, and labor, working with our hands. Being reviled, we bless; being persecuted, we endure; being defamed, we entreat; we are become as it were the offscourings of the world." Such also are the words of Plato in the Republic: "The just man, though stretched on the rack, though his eyes are dug out, will be happy." The Gnostic will never then have the chief end placed in life, but in being always happy and blessed, and a kingly friend of God. Although visited with ignominy and exile, and confiscation, and above all, death, he will never be wrenched from his freedom, and signal love to God. "The charity which bears all things, endures all things," is assured that Divine Providence orders all things well. "I exhort you," therefore it is said, "Be followers of me." The first step to salvation is the instruction accompanied with fear, in consequence of which we abstain from what is wrong; and the second is hope, by reason of which we desire the best things; but love, as is fitting, perfects, by training now according to knowledge. For the Greeks, I know not how, attributing events to unreasoning necessity, own that they yield to them unwillingly. Accordingly Euripides says:

"What I declare, receive from me, madam:
No mortal exists who has not toil;
He buries children, and begets others,
And he himself dies, And thus mortals are afflicted."

Then he adds:

"We must bear those things which are inevitable
according to nature, and go through them:
Not one of the things which are necessary is formidable for mortals."

And for those who are aiming at perfection there is proposed the rational gnosis, the foundation of which is "the sacred Triad." "Faith, hope, love; but the greatest of these is love." Truly, "all things are lawful, but all things are not expedient," says the apostle: "all things are lawful for me, but all things edify not." And, "Let no one seek his own advantage, but also that of his neighbor," so as to be able at once to do and to teach, building and building up. For that "the earth is the Lord's, and the fulness thereof," is admitted; but the conscience of the weak is supported. "Conscience, I say, not his own, but that of the other; for why is my liberty judged of by another conscience? For if I by grace am partaker, why am I evil spoken of I for that for which I give thanks? Whether therefore ye eat, or drink, or whatsoever ye do, do all to the glory of God." "For though we walk in the flesh, we do not war after the flesh; for the weapons of our warfare are not carnal, but mighty through God to the demolition of fortifications, demolishing thoughts, and every high thing which exalteth itself against the knowledge of Christ." Equipped with these weapons, the Gnostic says: O Lord, give opportunity, and receive demonstration; let this dread event pass; I contemn dangers for the love I bear to Thee.

"Because alone of human things
Virtue receives not a recompense from without,
But has itself as the reward of its toils."

"Put on therefore, as the elect of God, holy and beloved, bowels of mercies, kindness, humbleness, meekness, long-suffering. And above all these, love, which is the bond of perfection. And let the peace of God reign in your hearts, to which also ye are called in one body; and be thankful," ye who, while still in the body, like the just men of old, enjoy impassibility and tranquillity of soul.

Christ's sayings about martyrdom.

On martyrdom the Lord hath spoken explicitly, and what is written in different places we bring together. "But I say unto you, Whosoever shall confess in Me before men, the Son of man also shall confess before the angels of God; but whosoever shall deny Me before men, him will I deny before the angels." "Whosoever shall be ashamed of Me or of My words in this adulterous and sinful generation, of him shall the Son of man also be ashamed when He cometh in the glory of His Father with His angels. Whosoever therefore shall confess in Me before men, him will I also confess before my Father in heaven. "And when they bring you before synagogues, and rulers, and powers, think not: beforehand how ye shall make your defense, or what ye shall say. For the Holy Spirit shall teach you in the same hour what ye must say."

In explanation of this passage, Heracleon, the most distinguished of the school of Valentinians, says expressly, "that there is a confession by faith and conduct, and one with the voice. The confession that is made with the voice, and before the authorities, is what the most reckon the only confession. Not soundly: and hypocrites also can confess with this confession. But neither will this utterance be found to be spoken universally; for all the saved have confessed with the confession made by the voice, and departed. Of whom are Matthew, Philip, Thomas, Levi, and many others. And confession by the lip is not universal, but partial. But that which He specifies now is universal, that which is by deeds and actions corresponding to faith in Him. This confession is followed by that which is partial, that before the authorities, if necessary, and reason dictate. For he will confess rightly with his voice who has first confessed by his disposition. And he has well used, with regard to those who confess, the expression "in Me, "and applied to those who deny the expression"Me."For those, though they confess Him with the voice, yet deny Him, not confessing Him in their conduct. But those alone confess "in Him, "who live in the confession and conduct according to Him, in which He also confesses, who is contained in them and held by them. Wherefore "He never can deny Himself."And those deny Him who are not in Him. For He said not, "Whosoever shall deny"in Me, but "Me."For no one who is in Him will ever deny Him. And the expression "before men" applies both to the saved and the heathen similarly by conduct before the one, and by voice before the other. Wherefore they never can deny Him. But those deny Him who are not in Him." So far Heracleon. And in other things he seems to be of the same sentiments with us in this section; but he has not adverted to this, that if some have not by conduct and in their life "confessed Christ before men," they are manifested to have believed with the heart; by confessing Him with the mouth at the tribunals, and not denying Him when tortured to the death. And the disposition being confessed, and especially not being changed by death at any time, cuts away all passions which were engendered by corporeal desire. For there is, so to speak, at the close of life a sudden repentance in action, and a true confession toward Christ, in the testimony of the voice. But if the Spirit of the Father testifies in us, how can we be any more hypocrites, who are said to bear testimony with the voice alone? But it will be given to some, if expedient, to make a defense, that by their witness and confession all may be benefitted-those in the Church being confirmed, and those of the heathen who have devoted themselves to the search after salvation wondering and being led to the faith; and the rest seized with amazement. So that confession is by all means necessary. For it is in our power. But to make a defense for our faith is not universally necessary. For that does not depend on us. "But he that endureth to the end shall be saved." For who of those who are wise would not choose to reign in God, and even to serve? So some "confess that they know God," according to the apostle; "but in works they deny Him, being abominable and disobedient, and to every good work reprobate." And these, though they confess nothing but this, will have done at the end one good work. Their witness, then, appears to be the cleansing away of sins with glory. For instance, the Shepherd says: "You will escape the energy of the wild beast, if your heart become pure and blameless." Also the Lord Himself says: "Satan hath desired to sift you; but I have prayed." Alone, therefore, the Lord, for the purification of the men who plotted against Him and disbelieved Him, "drank the cup; "in imitation of whom the apostles, that they might be in reality Gnostics, and perfect, suffered for the Churches which they founded. So, then, also the Gnostics who tread in the footsteps of the apostles ought to be sinless, and, out of love to the Lord, to love also their brother; so that, if occasion call, enduring without stumbling, afflictions for the Church, "they may drink the cup." Those who witness in their life by deed, and at the tribunal by word, whether entertaining hope or surmising fear, are better than those who confess salvation by their mouth alone. But if one ascend also to love, he is a really blessed and true martyr, having confessed perfectly both to the commandments and to God, by the Lord; whom having loved, he acknowledged a brother, giving himself up wholly for God, resigning pleasantly and lovingly the man when asked, like a deposit.

Those who offered themselves for martyrdom reproved

When, again, He says, "When they persecute you in this city, flee ye to the other," He does not advise flight, as if persecution were an evil thing; nor does He enjoin them by flight to avoid death, as if in dread of it, but wishes us neither to be the authors nor abettors of any evil to any one, either to ourselves or the persecutor and murderer. For He, in a way, bids us take care of ourselves. But he who disobeys is rash and foolhardy. If he who kills a man of God sins against God, he also who presents himself before the judgment-seat becomes guilty of his death. And such is also the case with him who does not avoid persecution, but out of daring presents himself for capture. Such a one, as far as in him lies, becomes an accomplice in the crime of the persecutor. And if he also uses provocation, he is wholly guilty, challenging the wild beast. And similarly, if he afford any cause for conflict or punishment, or retribution or enmity, he gives occasion for persecution. Wherefore, then, we are enjoined not to cling to anything that belongs to this life; but "to him that takes our cloak to give our coat," not only that we may continue destitute of inordinate affection, but that we may not by retaliating make our persecutors savage against ourselves, and stir them up to blaspheme the name.

Exhortation to the heathen, book 4, chapter 4

C. SCORPIACE

Antidote for the Scorpion's Sting. Chapter 1

The earth brings forth, as if by suppuration, great evil from the diminutive scorpion. The poisons are as many as are the kinds of it, the disasters as many as are also the species of it, the pains as many as are also the colors of it. Nicander writes on the subject of scorpions, and depicts them. And yet to smite with the tail – which tail will be whatever is prolonged from the hindmost part of the body, and scourges – is the one movement which they all use when making an assault. Wherefore that succession of knots in the scorpion, which in the inside is a thin poisoned vein, rising up with a bow – like bound, draws tight a barbed sting at the end, after the manner of an engine for shooting missiles. From which circumstance they also call after the scorpion, the warlike implement which, by its being drawn back, gives an impetus to the arrows. The point in their case is also a duct of extreme minuteness, to inflict the wound; and where it penetrates, it pours out poison. The usual time of danger is the summer season: fierceness hoists the sail when the wind is from the south and the south-west. Among cures, certain substances supplied by nature have very great efficacy; magic also puts on some bandage; the art of healing counteracts with lancet and cup. For some, making haste, take also beforehand a protecting draught; but sexual intercourse drains it off, and they are dry again. We have faith for a defense, if we are not smitten with distrust itself also, in immediately making the sign and adjuring, and besmearing the heel with the beast. Finally, we often aid in this way even the heathen, seeing we have been endowed by God with that power which the apostle first used when he despised the viper's bite. What, then, does this pen of yours offer, if faith is safe by what it has of its own? That it may be safe by what it has of its own also at other times, when it is subjected to scorpions of its own. These, too, have a troublesome littleness, and are of different sorts, and are armed in one manner, and are stirred up at a definite time, and that not another than one of burning heat. This among Christians is a season of persecution. When, therefore, faith is greatly agitated, and the Church burning, as represented by the bush, then the Gnostics break out, then the Valentinians creep forth, then all the opponents of martyrdom bubble up, being themselves also hot to strike, penetrate, kill. For, because they know that many are artless and also inexperienced, and weak moreover, that a very great number in truth are Christians who veer about with the wind and conform to its moods, they perceive that they are never to be approached more than when fear has opened the entrances to the soul, especially when some display of ferocity has already arrayed with a crown the faith of martyrs. Therefore, drawing along the tail hitherto, they first of all apply it to the feelings, or whip with it as if on empty space. Innocent persons undergo such suffering. So that you may suppose the speaker to be a brother or a heathen of the better sort. A sect troublesome to nobody so dealt with! Then they pierce. Men are perishing without a reason. For that they are perishing, and without a reason, is the first insertion. Then they now strike mortally. But the unsophisticated souls know not what is written, and what meaning it bears, where and when and before whom we must confess, or ought, save that this, to die for God, is, since He preserves me, not even artlessness, but folly, nay madness. If He kills me, how will it be His duty to preserve me? Once for all Christ died for us, once for all He was slain that we might not be slain. If He demands the like from me in return, does He also look for salvation from my death by violence? Or does God importune for the blood of men, especially if He refuses that of bulls and he-goats? Assuredly He had rather have the repentance than the death of the sinner. And how is He eager for the death of those who are not sinners? Whom will not these, and perhaps other subtle devices containing heretical poisons, pierce either for doubt if not for destruction, or for irritation if not for death? As for you, therefore, do you, if faith is on the alert, smite on the spot the scorpion with a curse, so far as you can, with your sandal, and leave it dying in its own stupefaction? But if it gluts the wound, it drives the poison inwards, and makes it hasten into the bowels; forthwith all the former senses become dull, the blood of the mind freezes, the flesh of the spirit pines away, loathing for the Christian name is accompanied by a sense of sourness. Already the understanding also seeks for itself a place where it may throw up; and thus, once for all, the weakness with which it has been smitten breathes out wounded faith either in heresy or in heathenism. And now the present state of matters is such, that we are in the midst of an intense heat, the very dog-star of persecution, – a state originating doubtless with the dog-headed one himself. Of some Christians the fire, of others the sword, of others the beasts, have made trial; others are hungering in prison for the martyrdoms of which they have had a taste in the meantime by being subjected to clubs and claws besides. We ourselves, having been appointed for pursuit, are like hares being hemmed in from a distance; and heretics go about according to their wont. Therefore the state of the times has prompted me to prepare by my pen, in opposition to the little beasts which trouble our sect, our antidote against poison, that I may thereby effect cures. You who read will at the same time drink. Nor is the draught bitter. If the utterances of the Lord are sweeter than honey and the honeycombs, the juices are from that source. If the promise of God flows with milk and honey, the ingredients which go to make that draught have the smack of this. "But woe to them who turn sweet into bitter, and light into darkness." For, in like manner, they also who oppose martyrdoms, representing salvation to be destruction, transmute sweet into bitter, as well as light into darkness; and thus, by preferring this very wretched life to that most blessed one, they put bitter for sweet, as well as darkness for light.

Chapter 2

But not yet about the good to be got from martyrdom must we learn, without our having first heard about the duty of suffering it; nor must we learn the usefulness of it, before we have heard about the necessity for it. The (question of the) divine warrant goes first – whether God has willed and also commanded ought of the kind, so that they who assert that it is not good are not plied with arguments for thinking it profitable save when they have been subdued. It is proper that heretics be driven to duty, not enticed. Obstinacy must be conquered, not coaxed. And, certainly, that will be pronounced beforehand quite good enough, which will be shown to have been instituted and also enjoined by God. Let the Gospels wait a little, while I set forth their root the Law, while I ascertain the will of God from those writings from which I recall to mind Himself also: "I am," says He, "God, thy God, who have brought thee out of the land of Egypt. Thou shalt have no other gods besides me. Thou shalt not make unto thee a likeness of those things which are in heaven, and which are in the earth beneath, and which are in the sea under the earth. Thou shalt not worship them, nor serve them. For I am the Lord thy God." Likewise in the same book of Exodus: "Ye yourselves have seen that I have talked with you from heaven. Ye shall not make unto you gods of silver, neither shall ye make unto you gods of gold." To the following effect also, in Deuteronomy: "Hear, O Israel; The Lord thy God is one: and thou shalt love the Lord thy God with all thy heart and all thy might, and with all thy soul." And again: "Neither do thou forget the Lord thy God, who brought thee forth from the land of Egypt, out of the house of bondage. Thou shalt fear the Lord thy God, and serve Him only, and cleave to Him, and swear by His name. Ye shall not go after strange gods, and the gods of the nations which are round about you, because the Lord thy God is also a jealous God among you, and lest His anger should be kindled against thee, and destroy thee from off the face of the earth." But setting before them blessings and curses, He also says: "Blessings shall be yours, if ye obey the commandments of the Lord your God, whatsoever I command you this day, and do not wander from the way which I have commanded you, to go and serve other gods whom ye know not." And as to rooting them out in every way: "Ye shall utterly destroy all the places wherein the nations, which ye shall possess by inheritance, served their gods, upon mountains and hills, and under shady trees. Ye shall overthrow all their altars, ye shall overturn and break in pieces their pillars, and cut down their groves, and burn with fire the graven images of the gods themselves, and destroy the names of them out of that place." He further urges, when they (the Israelites) had entered the land of promise, and driven out its nations: "Take heed to thy self, that thou do not follow them after they be driven out from before thee, that thou do not inquire after their gods, saying, As the nations serve their gods, so let me do likewise." But also says He: "If there arise among you a prophet himself, or a dreamer of dreams, and giveth thee a sign or a wonder, and it come to pass, and he say, Let us go and serve other gods, whom ye know not, do not hearken to the words of that prophet or dreamer, for the Lord your God proveth you, to know whether ye fear God with all your heart and with all your soul. After the Lord your God ye shall go, and fear Him, and keep His commandments, and obey His voice, and serve Him, and cleave unto Him. But that prophet or dreamer shall die; for he has spoken to turn thee away from the Lord thy God." But also in another section. "If, however, thy brother, the son of thy father or of thy mother, or thy son, or thy daughter, or the wife of thy bosom, or thy friend who is as thine own soul, solicit thee, saying secretly, Let us go and serve other gods, which thou knowest not, nor did thy fathers, of the gods of the nations which are round about thee, very nigh unto thee or far off from thee, do not consent to go with him, and do not hearken to him. Thine eye shall not spare him, neither shalt thou pity, neither shalt thou preserve him; thou shall certainly inform upon him. Thine hand shall be first upon him to kill him, and afterwards the hand of thy people; and ye shall stone him, and he shall die, seeing he has sought to turn thee away from the Lord thy God." He adds likewise concerning cities, that if it appeared that one of these had, through the advice of unrighteous men, passed over to other gods, all its inhabitants should be slain, and everything belonging to it become accursed, and all the spoil of it be gathered together into all its places of egress, and be, even with all the people, burned with fire in all its streets in the sight of the Lord God; and, says He, "it shall not be for dwelling in for ever: it shall not be built again any more, and there shall cleave to thy hands nought of its accursed plunder, that the Lord may turn from the fierceness of His anger." He has, from His abhorrence of idols, framed a series of curses too: "Cursed be the man who maketh a graven or a molten image, an abomination, the work of the hands of the craftsman, and putteth it in a secret place." But in Leviticus He says: "Go not ye after idols, nor make to yourselves molten gods: I am the Lord your God." And in other passages: "The children of Israel are my household servants; these are they whom I led forth from the land of Egypt: I am the Lord your God. Ye shall not make you idols fashioned by the hand, neither rear you up a graven image. Nor shall ye set up a remarkable stone in your land (to worship it): I am the Lord your God." These words indeed were first spoken by the Lord by the lips of Moses, being applicable certainly to whomsoever the Lord God of Israel may lead forth in like manner from the Egypt of a most superstitious world, and from the abode of human slavery. But from the mouth of every prophet in succession, sound forth also utterances of the same God, augmenting the same law of His by a renewal of the same commands, and in the first place announcing no other duty in so special a manner as the being on guard against all making and worshiping of idols; as when by the mouth of David He says: "The gods of the nations are silver and gold: they have eyes, and see not; they have ears, and hear not; they have a nose, and smell not; a mouth, and they speak not; hands, and they handle not; feet and they walk not. Like to them shall be they who make them, and trust in them."

Chapter 3

Nor should I think it needful to discuss whether God pursues a worthy course in forbidding His own name and honor to be given over to a lie, or does so in not consenting that such as He has plucked from the maze of false religion should return again to Egypt, or does so in not suffering to depart from Him them whom He has chosen for Himself. Thus that, too, will not require to be treated by us, whether He has wished to be kept the rule which He has chosen to appoint, and whether He justly avenges the abandonment of the rule which He has wished to be kept; since He would have appointed it to no purpose if He had not wished it kept, and would have to no purpose wished it kept if He had been unwilling to uphold it. My next step, indeed, is to put to the test these appointments of God in opposition to false religions, the completely vanquished as well as also the punished, since on these will depend the entire argument for martyrdoms. Moses was apart with God on the mountain, when the people, not brooking his absence, which was so needful, seek to make gods for themselves, which, for his own part, he will prefer to destroy. Aaron is importuned, and commands that the earrings of their women be brought together, that they may be thrown into the fire. For the people were about to lose, as a judgment upon themselves, the true ornaments for the ears, the words of God. The wise fire makes for them the molten likeness of a calf, reproaching them with having the heart where they have their treasure also, – in Egypt, to wit, which clothed with sacredness, among the other animals, a certain ox likewise. Therefore the slaughter of three thousand by their nearest relatives, because they had displeased their so very near relative God, solemnly marked both the commencement and the deserts of the trespass. Israel having, as we are I told in Numbers, turned aside at Sethim, the people go to the daughters of Moab to gratify their lust: they are allured to the idols, so that they committed whoredom with the spirit also: finally, they eat of their defiled sacrifices; then they both worship the gods of the nation, and are admired to the rites of Beelphegor. For this lapse, too, into idolatry, sister to adultery, it took the slaughter of twenty-three thousand by the swords of their countrymen to appease the divine anger. After the death of Joshua the son of Nave they forsake the God of their fathers, and serve idols, Baalim and Ashtaroth; and the Lord in anger delivered them up to the hands of spoilers, and they continued to be spoiled by them, and to be sold to their adversaries, and could not at all stand before their enemies. Whithersoever they went forth, His hand was upon them for evil, and they were greatly distressed. And after this God sets judges (critas), the same as our censors, over them. But not even these did they continue steadfastly to obey. So soon as one of the judges died, they proceeded to transgress more than their fathers had done by going after the gods of others, and serving and worshiping them. Therefore the Lord was angry. "Since, indeed," He says, "this nation have transgressed my covenant which I established with their fathers, and have not hearkened to my voice, I also will give no heed to remove from before them a man of the nations which Joshua left at his death." And thus, throughout almost all the annals of the judges and of the kings who succeeded them, while the strength of the surrounding nations was preserved, He meted wrath out to Israel by war and captivity and a foreign yoke, as often as they turned aside from Him, especially to idolatry.

Chapter 4

If, therefore, it is evident that from the beginning this kind of worship has both been forbidden – witness the commands so numerous and weighty – and that it has never been engaged in without punishment following, as examples so numerous and impressive show, and that no offence is counted by God so presumptuous as a trespass of this sort, we ought further to perceive the purport of both the divine threatenings and their fulfillments, which was even then commended not only by the not calling in question, but also by the enduring of martyrdoms, for which certainly He had given occasion by forbidding idolatry. For otherwise martyrdoms would not take place. And certainly He had supplied, as a warrant for these, His own authority, willing those events to come to pass for the occurrence of which He had given occasion. At present (it is important), for we are getting severely stung concerning the will of God, and the scorpion repeats the prick, denying the existence of this will, finding fault with it, so that he either insinuates that there is another god, such that this is not his will, or none the less overthrows ours, seeing such is his will, or altogether denies this will of God, if he cannot deny Himself. But, for our part, contending elsewhere about God, and about all the rest of the body of heretical teaching, we now draw before us definite lines for one form of encounter, maintaining that this will, such as to have given occasion for martyrdoms, is that of not another god than the God of Israel, on the ground of the commandments relating to an always forbidden, as well as of the judgments upon a punished, idolatry. For if the keeping of a command involves the suffering of violence, this will be, so to speak, a command about keeping the command, requiring me to suffer that through which I shall be able to keep the command, violence namely, whatever of it threatens me when on my guard against idolatry. And certainly (in the case supposed) the Author of the command extorts compliance with it. He could not, therefore, have been unwilling that those events should come to pass by means of which the compliance will be manifest. The injunction is given me not to make mention of any other god, not even by speaking, – as little by the tongue as by the hand, – to fashion a god, and not to worship or in any way show reverence to another than Him only who thus commands me, whom I am both bid fear that I may not be forsaken by Him, and love with my whole being, that I may die for Him. Serving as a soldier under this oath, I am challenged by the enemy. If I surrender to them, I am as they are. In maintaining this oath, I fight furiously in battle, am wounded, hewn in pieces, slain. Who wished this fatal issue to his soldier, but he who sealed him by such an oath?

Chapter 5

You have therefore the will of my God. We have cured this prick. Let us give good heed to another thrust touching the character of His will. It would be tedious to show that my God is good, – a truth with which the Marcionites have now been made acquainted by us. Meanwhile it is enough that He is called God for its being necessary that He should be believed to be good. For if any one make the supposition that God is evil, he will not be able to take his stand on both the constituents thereof: he will be bound either to affirm that he whom he has thought to be evil is not God, or that he whom he has proclaimed to be God is good. Good, therefore, will be the will also of him who, unless he is good, will not be God. The goodness of the thing itself also which God has willed – of martyrdom, I mean – will show this, because only one who is good has willed what is good. I stoutly maintain that martyrdom is good, as required by the God by whom likewise idolatry is forbidden and punished. For martyrdom strives against and opposes idolatry. But to strive against and oppose evil cannot be ought but good. Not as if I denied that there is a rivalry in evil things with one another, as well as in good also; but this ground for it requires a different state of matters. For martyrdom contends with idolatry, not from some malice which they share, but from its own kindness; for it delivers from idolatry. Who will not proclaim that to be good which delivers from idolatry? What else is the opposition between idolatry and martyrdom, than that between life and death? Life will be counted to be martyrdom as much as idolatry to be death. He who will call life an evil, has death to speak of as a good. This frowardness also appertains to men, – to discard what is wholesome, to accept what is baleful, to avoid all dangerous cures, or, in short, to be eager to die rather than to be healed. For they are many who flee from the aid of physic also, many in folly, many from fear and false modesty. And the healing art has manifestly an apparent cruelty, by reason of the lancet, and of the burning iron, and of the great heat of the mustard; yet to be cut and burned, and pulled and bitten, is not on that account an evil, for it occasions helpful pains; nor will it be refused merely because it afflicts, but because it afflicts inevitably will it be applied. The good accruing is the apology for the frightfulness of the work. In short, that man who is howling and groaning and bellowing in the hands of a physician will presently load the same hands with a fee, and proclaim that they are the best operators, and no longer affirm that they are cruel. Thus martyrdoms also rage furiously, but for salvation. God also will be at liberty to heal for everlasting life by means of fires and swords, and all that is painful. But you will admire the physician at least even in that respect, that for the most part he employs like properties in the cures to counteract the properties of the diseases, when he aids, as it were, the wrong way, succoring by means of those things to which the affliction is owing. For he both checks heat by heat, by laying on a greater load; and subdues inflammation by leaving thirst unappeased, by tormenting rather; and contracts the superabundance of bile by every bitter little draught, and stops hemorrhage by opening a vein in addition. But you will think that God must be found fault with, and that for being jealous, if He has chosen to contend with a disease and to do good by imitating the malady, to destroy death by death, to dissipate killing by killing, to dispel tortures by tortures, to disperse punishments by punishments, to bestow life by withdrawing it, to aid the flesh by injuring it, to preserve the soul by snatching it away. The wrongheadedness, as you deem it to be, is reasonableness; what you count cruelty is kindness. Thus, seeing God by brief (sufferings) effects cures for eternity, extol your God for your prosperity; you have fallen into His hands, but have happily fallen. He also fell into your sicknesses. Man always first provides employment for the physician; in short, he has brought upon himself the danger of death. He had received from his own Lord, as from a physician, the salutary enough rule to live according to the law, that he should eat of all indeed (that the garden produced) and should refrain from only one little tree which in the meantime the Physician Himself knew as a perilous one. He gave ear to him whom he preferred, and broke through self-restraint. He ate what was forbidden, and, surfeited by the trespass, suffered indigestion tending to death; he certainly richly deserving to lose his life altogether who wished to do so. But the inflamed tumor due to the trespass having been endured until in due time the medicine might be mixed, the Lord gradually prepared the means of healing – all the rules of faith, they also bearing a resemblance to (the causes of) the ailment, seeing they annul the word of death by the word of life, and diminish the trespass – listening by a listening of allegiance.

Thus, even when that Physician commands one to die, He drives out the lethargy of death. Why does man show reluctance to suffer now from a cure, what he was not reluctant then to suffer from a disorder? Does he dislike being killed for salvation, who did not dislike being killed for destruction? – Will he feel squeamish with reference to the counter poison, who gaped for the poison?

Chapter 6

But if, for the contest's sake, God had appointed martyrdoms for us, that thereby we might make trial with our opponent, in order that He may now keep bruising him by whom man chose to be bruised, here too generosity rather than harshness in God holds sway. For He wished to make man, now plucked from the devil's throat by faith, trample upon him likewise by courage, that he might not merely have escaped from, but also completely vanquished, his enemy. He who had called to salvation has been pleased to summon to glory also, that they who were rejoicing in consequence of their deliverance may be in transports when they are crowned likewise. With what good-will the world celebrates those games, the combative festivals and superstitious contests of the Greeks, involving forms both of worship and of pleasure, has now become clear in Africa also. As yet cities, by sending their congratulations severally, annoy Carthage, which was presented with the Pythian game after the racecourse had attained to an old age. Thus, by the world it has been believed to be a most proper mode of testing proficiency in studies, to put in competition the forms of skill, to elicit the existing condition of bodies and of voices, the reward being the informer, the public exhibition the judge, and pleasure the decision. Where there are mere contests, there are some wounds: fists make reel, heels kick like butting rams, boxing-gloves mangle, whips leave gashes. Yet there will be no one reproaching the superintendent of the contest for exposing men to outrage. Suits for injuries lie outside the racecourse. But to the extent that those persons deal in discoloration, and gore, and swellings, he will design for them crowns, doubtless, and glory, and a present, political privileges, contributions by the citizens, images, statues, and – of such sort as the world can give – an eternity of fame, a resurrection by being kept in remembrance. The pugilist himself does not complain of feeling pain, for he wishes it; the crown closes the wounds, the palm hides the blood: he is excited more by victory than by injury. Will you count this man hurt whom you see happy? But not even the vanquished himself will reproach the superintendent of the contest for his misfortune. Shall it be unbecoming in God to bring forth kinds of skill and rules of His own into public view, into this open ground of the world, to be seen by men, and angels, and all powers? – to test flesh and spirit as to steadfastness and endurance? – to give to this one the palm, to this one distinction, to that one the privilege of citizenship, to that one pay? – to reject some also, and after punishing to remove them with disgrace? You dictate to God, forsooth, the times, or the ways, or the places in which to institute a trial concerning His own troop (of competitors) as if it were not proper for the Judge to pronounce the preliminary decision also. Well now, if He had put forth faith to suffer martyrdoms not for the contest's sake, but for its own benefit, ought it not to have had some store of hope, for the increase of which it might restrain desire of its own, and check its wish in order that it might strive to mount up, seeing they also who discharge earthly functions are eager for promotion? Or how will there be many mansions in our Father's house, if not to accord with a diversity of deserts? How will one star also differ from another star in glory, unless in virtue of disparity in their rays? But further, if, on that account, some increase of brightness also was appropriate to loftiness of faith, that gain ought to have been of some such sort as would cost great effort, poignant suffering, torture, death. But consider the requital, when flesh and life are paid away – than which in man there is nought more precious, the one from the hand of God, the other from His breath – that the very things are paid away in obtaining the benefit of which the benefit consists; that the very things are expended which may be acquired; that the same things are the price which are also the commodities. God had foreseen also other weaknesses incident to the condition of man, – the stratagems of the enemy, the deceptive aspects of the creatures, the snares of the world; that faith, even after baptism, would be endangered; that the most, after attaining unto salvation, would be lost again, through soiling the wedding-dress, through failing to provide oil for their torchlets – would be such as would have to be sought for over mountains and woodlands, and carried back upon the shoulders. He therefore appointed as second supplies of comfort, and the last means of succor, the fight of martyrdom and the baptism – thereafter free from danger – of blood. And concerning the happiness of the man who has partaken of these, David says: "Blessed are they whose iniquities are forgiven, and whose sins are covered. Blessed is the man to whom the Lord will not impute sin." For, strictly speaking, there cannot any longer be reckoned ought against the martyrs, by whom in the baptism (of blood) life itself is laid down. Thus, "love covers the multitude of sins; " and loving God, to wit, with all its strength (by which in the endurance of martyrdom it maintains the fight), with all its life (which it lays down for God), it makes of man a martyr. Shall you call these cures, counsels, methods of judging, spectacles, (illustrations of) even the barbarity of God? Does God covet man's blood? And yet I might venture to affirm that He does, if man also covets the kingdom of heaven, if man covets a sure salvation, if man also covets a second new birth. The exchange is displeasing to no one, which can plead, in justification of itself, that either benefit or injury is shared by the parties making it.

Chapter 7

If the scorpion, swinging his tail in the air, still reproach us with having a murderer for our God, I shall shudder at the altogether foul breath of blasphemy which comes stinking from his heretical mouth; but I will embrace even such a God, with assurance derived from reason, by which reason even He Himself has, in the person of His own Wisdom, by the lips of Solomon, proclaimed Himself to be more than a murderer: Wisdom (Sophia), says He has slain her own children. Sophia is Wisdom. She has certainly slain them wisely if only into life, and reasonably if only into glory. Of murder by a parent, oh the clever form! Oh the dexterity of crime! Oh the proof of cruelty, which has slain for this reason, that he whom it may have slain may not die! And therefore what follows? Wisdom is praised in hymns, in the places of egress; for the death of martyrs also is praised in song. Wisdom behaves with firmness in the streets, for with good results does she murder her own sons. Nay, on the top of the walls she speaks with assurance, when indeed, according to Esaias, this one calls out, "I am God's; "and this one shouts, "In the name of Jacob; "and another writes, "In the name of Israel." O good mother! I myself also wish to be put among the number of her sons, that I may be slain by her; I wish to be slain, that I may become a son. But does she merely murder her sons, or also torture them? For I hear God also, in another passage, say, "I will burn them as gold is burned, and will try them as silver is tried." Certainly by the means of torture which fires and punishments supply, by the testing martyrdoms of faith. The apostle also knows what kind of God he has ascribed to us, when he writes: "If God spared not His own Son, but gave Him up for us, how did He not with Him also give us all things? " You see how divine Wisdom has murdered even her own proper, first-born and only Son, who is certainly about to live, nay, to bring back the others also into life. I can say with the Wisdom of God; It is Christ who gave Himself up for our offences. Already has Wisdom butchered herself also. The character of words depends not on the sound only, but on the meaning also, and they must be heard not merely by ears, but also by minds. He who does not understand, believes God to be cruel; although for him also who does not understand, an announcement has been made to restrain his harshness in understanding otherwise than aright. "For who," says the apostle," has known the mind of the Lord? or who has been His counselor, to teach Him? or who has pointed out to Him the way of understanding? " But, indeed, the world has held it lawful for Diana of the Scythians, or Mercury of the Gauls, or Saturn of the Africans, to be appeased by human sacrifices; and in Latium to this day Jupiter has human blood given him to taste in the midst of the city; and no one makes it a matter of discussion, or imagines that it does not occur for some reason, or that it occurs by the will of his God, without having value. If our God, too, to have a sacrifice of His own, had required martyrdoms for Himself, who would have reproached Him for the deadly religion, and the mournful ceremonies, and the altar-pyre, and the undertaker-priest, and not rather have counted happy the man whom God should have devoured?

Chapter 8

We keep therefore the one position, and, in respect of this question only, summon to an encounter, whether martyrdoms have been commanded by God, that you may believe that they have been commanded by reason, if you know that they have been commanded by Him, because God will not command ought without reason. Since the death of His own saints is precious is His sight, as David sings, it is not, I think, that one which falls to the lot of men generally, and is a debt due by all (rather is that one even disgraceful on account of the trespass, and the desert of condemnation to which it is to be traced), but that other which is met in this very work – in bearing witness for religion, and maintaining the fight of confession in behalf of righteousness and the sacrament. As saith Esaias, "See how the righteous man perisheth, and no one layeth it to heart; and righteous men are taken away, and no one considereth it: for from before the face of unrighteousness the righteous man perisheth, and he shall have honor at his burial." Here, too, you have both an announcement of martyrdoms, and of the recompense they bring. From the beginning, indeed, righteousness suffers violence. Forthwith, as soon as God has begun to be worshiped, religion has got ill-will for her portion. He who had pleased God is slain, and that by his brother. Beginning with kindred blood, in order that it might the more easily go in quest of that of strangers, ungodliness made the object of its pursuit, finally, that not only of righteous persons, but even of prophets also. David is persecuted; Elias put to flight; Jeremias stoned; Esaias cut asunder; Zacharias butchered between the altar and the temple, imparting to the hard stones lasting marks of his blood. That person himself, at the close of the law and the prophets, and called not a prophet, but a messenger, is, suffering an ignominious death, beheaded to reward a dancing-girl. And certainly they who were wont to be led by the Spirit of God used to be guided by Himself to martyrdoms; so that they had even already to endure what they had also proclaimed as requiring to be borne. Wherefore the brotherhood of the three also, when the dedication of the royal image was the occasion of the citizens being pressed to offer worship, knew well what faith, which alone in them had not been taken captive, required, – namely, that they must resist idolatry to the death. For they remembered also the words of Jeremias writing to those over whom that captivity was impending: "And now ye shall see borne upon (men's) shoulders the gods of the Babylonians, of gold and silver and wood, causing fear to the Gentiles. Beware, therefore, that ye also do not be altogether like the foreigners, and be seized with fear while ye behold crowds worshiping those gods before and behind, but say in your mind, Our duty is to worship Thee, O Lord." Therefore, having got confidence from God, they said, when with strength of mind they set at defiance the king's threats against the disobedient: "There is no necessity for our making answer to this command of yours. For our God whom we worship is able to deliver us from the furnace of fire and from your hands; and then it will be made plain to you that we shall neither serve your idol, nor worship your golden image which you have set up." O martyrdom even without suffering perfect! Enough did they suffer! enough were they burned, whom on this account God shielded, that it might not seem that they had given a false representation of His power. For forthwith, certainly, would the lions, with their pent-up and wonted savageness, have devoured Daniel also, a worshiped of none but

God, and therefore accused and demanded by the Chaldeans, if it had been right that the worthy anticipation of Darius concerning God should have proved delusive. For the rest, every preacher of God, and every worshiped also, such as, having been summoned to the service of idolatry, had refused compliance, ought to have suffered, agreeably to the tenor of that argument too, by which the truth ought to have been recommended both to those who were then living and to those following in succession, – (namely), that the suffering of its defenders themselves bespeak trust for it, because nobody would have been willing to be slain but one possessing the truth. Such commands as well as instances, remounting to earliest times, show that believers are under obligation to suffer martyrdom.

Chapter 9

It remains for us, lest ancient times may perhaps have had the sacrament (exclusively) their own, to review the modern Christian system, as though, being also from God, it might be different from what preceded, and besides, therefore, opposed thereto in its code of rules likewise, so that its Wisdom knows not to murder her own sons! Evidently, in the case of Christ both the divine nature and the will and the sect are different from any previously known! He will have commanded either no martyrdoms at all, or those which must be understood in a sense different from the ordinary, being such a person as to urge no one to a risk of this kind as to promise no reward to them who suffer for Him, because He does not wish them to suffer; and therefore does He say, when setting forth His chief commands, "Blessed are they who are persecuted for righteousness' sake, for theirs is the kingdom of heaven." The following statement, indeed, applies first to all without restriction, then specially to the apostles themselves: "Blessed shall ye be when men shall revile you, and persecute you, and shall say all manner of evil against you, for my sake. Rejoice and be exceeding glad, since very great is your reward in heaven; for so used their fathers to do even to the prophets." So that He likewise foretold their having to be themselves also slain, after the example of the prophets. Though, even if He had appointed all this persecution in case He were obeyed for those only who were then apostles, assuredly through them along with the entire sacrament, with the shoot of the name, with the layer of the Holy Spirit, the rule about enduring persecution also would have had respect to us too, as to disciples by inheritance, and, (as it were,)bushes from the apostolic seed. For even thus again does He address words of guidance to the apostles: "Behold, I send you forth as sheep in the midst of wolves; "and, "Beware of men, for they will deliver you up to the councils, and they will scourge you in their synagogues; and ye shall be brought before governors and kings for my sake, for a testimony against them and the Gentiles," etc. Now when He adds, "But the brother will deliver up the brother to death, and the father the child; and the children shall rise up against their parents, and cause them to be put to death," He has dearly announced with reference to the others, (that they would be subjected to) this form of unrighteous conduct, which we do not find exemplified in the case of the apostles. For none of them had experience of a father or a brother as a betrayer, which very many of us have. Then He returns to the apostles: "And ye shall be hated of all men for my name's sake." How much more shall we, for whom there exists the necessity of being delivered up by parents too! Thus, by allotting this very betrayal, now to the apostles, now to all, He pours out the same destruction upon all the possessors of the name, on whom the name. along with the condition that it be an object of hatred, will rest. But he who will endure on to the end – this man will be saved. By enduring what but persecution, – betrayal, – death? For to endure to the end is nought else than to suffer the end. And therefore there immediately follow, "The disciple is not above his master, nor the servant above his own lord; "because, seeing the Master and Lord Himself was steadfast in suffering persecution, betrayal and death, much more will it be the duty of His servants and disciples to bear the same, that they may not seem as if superior to Him, or to have got an immunity from the assaults of unrighteousness, since this itself should be glory enough for them, to be conformed to the sufferings of their Lord and Master; and, preparing them for the endurance of these, He reminds them that they must not fear such persons as kill the body only, but are not able to destroy the soul, but that they must dedicate fear to Him rather who has such power that He can kill both body and soul, and destroy them in hell. Who, pray, are these slayers of the body only, but the governors and kings aforesaid – men, I ween? Who is the ruler of the soul also, but God only? Who is this but the threatener of fires hereafter, He without whose will not even one of two sparrows falls to the ground; that is, not even one of the two substances of man, flesh or spirit, because the number of our hairs also has been recorded before Him? Fear ye not, therefore. When He adds, "Ye are of more value than many sparrows," He makes promise that we shall not in vain – that is, not without profit – fall to the ground if we choose to be killed by men rather than by God. "Whosoever therefore will confess in me before men, in him will I confess also before my Father who is in heaven; and whosoever shall deny me before men, him will I deny also before my Father who is in heaven." Clear, as I think, are the terms used in announcing, and the way to explain, the confession as well as the denial, although the mode of putting them is different. He who confesses himself a Christian, beareth witness that he is Christ's; he who is Christ's must be in Christ. If he is in Christ, he certainly confesses in Christ, when he confesses himself a Christian. For he cannot be this without being in Christ. Besides, by confessing in Christ he confesses Christ too: since, by virtue of being a Christian, he is in Christ, while Christ Himself also is in him. For if you have made mention of day, you have also held out to view the element of light which gives us day, although you may not have made mention of light. Thus, albeit He has not expressly said, "He who will confess me," (yet) the conduct involved in daily confession Is not different from what is meant in our Lord's declaration. For he who confesses himself to be what he is, that is, a Christian, confesses that likewise by which he is it, that is, Christ. Therefore he who has denied that he is a Christian, has denied in Christ, by denying that he is in Christ while he denies that he is a Christian; and, on the other hand, by denying that Christ is in him, while He denies that he is in Christ, he will deny Christ too. Thus both he who will deny in Christ, will deny Christ, and he who will confess in Christ will confess Christ. It would have been enough, therefore, though our Lord had made an announcement about confessing merely. For, from His mode of presenting confession, it might be decided beforehand with reference to its opposite too – denial, that is – that denial is repaid by the Lord with denial, just as confession is with confession. And therefore, since in the mold in which the confession has been cast the state of (the case with reference to) denial also may be perceived, it is evident that to another manner of denial belongs what the Lord has announced concerning it, in terms different from those in which He speaks of confession, when He says, "Who will deny me," not "Who will deny in me." For He had foreseen that this form of violence also would, for the most part, immediately follow when any one had been forced to renounce the Christian name, – that he who had denied that he was a Christian would be compelled to deny Christ Himself too by blaspheming Him. As not long ago, alas, we shuddered at the struggle waged in this way by some with their entire faith, which had had favorable omens. Therefore it will be to no purpose to say, "Though I shall deny that I am a Christian, I shall not be denied by Christ, for I have not denied Himself." For even so much will be inferred from that denial, by which, seeing he denies Christ in him by denying that he is a Christian, he has denied Christ Himself also. But there is more, because He threatens likewise shame with shame (in return): "Whosoever shall be ashamed of me before men, of him will I also be ashamed before my Father who is in heaven." For He was aware that denial is produced even most of all by shame, that the state of the mind appears in the forehead, and that the wound of shame precedes that in the body.

Chapter 10

But as to those who think that not here, that is, not within this environment of earth, nor during this period of existence, nor before men possessing this nature shared by us all, has confession been appointed to be made, what a supposition is theirs, being at variance with the whole order of things of which we have experience in these lands, and in this life, and under human authorities! Doubtless, when the souls have departed from their bodies, and begun to be put upon trial in the several stories of the heavens, with reference to the engagement (under which they have come to Jesus), and to be questioned about those hidden mysteries of the heretics, they must then confess before the real powers and the real men, – the Teleti, to wit, and the Abascanti, and the Acineti of Valentinus! For, say they, even the Demiurge himself did not uniformly approve of the men of our world, whom he counted as a drop of a bucket, and the dust of the threshing-floor, and spittle and locusts, and put on a level even with brute beasts. Clearly, it is so written. Yet not therefore must we understand that there is, besides us, another kind of man, which – for it is evidently thus (in the case proposed) – has been able to assume without invalidating a comparison between the two kinds, both the characteristics of the race and a unique property. For even if the life was tainted, so that condemned to contempt it might be likened to objects held in contempt, the nature was not forthwith taken away, so that there might be supposed to be another under its name. Rather is the nature preserved, though the life blushes; nor does Christ know other men than those with reference to whom He says, "Whom do men say that I am? " And, "As ye would that men should do to you, do ye likewise so to, them." Consider whether He may not have I preserved a race such that He is looking for a testimony to Himself from them, as well as I consisting of those on whom He enjoins the interchange of righteous dealing. But if I should urgently demand that those heavenly men be described to me, Aratus will sketch more easily Perseus and Cepheus, and Erigone, and Ariadne, among the constellations. But who prevented the Lord from clearly prescribing that confession by men likewise has to be made where He plainly announced that His own would be; so that the statement might have run thus: "Whosoever shall confess in me before men in heaven, I also will confess in him before my Father who is in heaven? "He ought to have saved me from this mistake about confession on earth, which He would not have wished me to take part in, if He had commanded one in heaven; for I knew no other men but the inhabitants of the earth, man himself even not having up to that time been observed in heaven. Besides, what is the credibility of the things (alleged), that, being after death raised to heavenly places, I should be put to the test there, whither I would not be translated without being already tested, that I should there be tried in reference to a command where I could not come, but to find admittance? Heaven lies open to the Christian before the way to it does; because there is no way to heaven, but to him to whom heaven lies open; and he who reaches it will enter. What powers, keeping guard at the gate, do I hear you affirm to exist in accordance with Roman superstition, with a certain Carnus, Forculus, and Limentinus? What powers do you set in order at the railings? If you have ever read in David, "Lift up your gates, ye princes, and let the everlasting gates be lifted up; and the King of glory shall enter in; " if you have also heard from Amos, "Who buildeth up to the heavens his way of ascent, and is such as to pour forth his abundance (of waters) over the earth; " know that both that way of ascent was thereafter leveled with the ground, by the footsteps of the Lord, and an entrance thereafter opened up by the might of Christ, and that no delay or inquest will meet Christians on the threshold, since they have there to be not discriminated from one another, but owned, and not put to the question, but received in. For though you think heaven still shut, remember that the Lord left here to Peter and through him to the Church, the keys of it, which every one who has been here put to the question, and also made confession, will carry with him. But the devil stoutly affirms that we must confess there, to persuade us that we must deny here. I shall send before me fine documents, to be sure, I shall carry with me excellent keys, the fear of them who kill the body only, but do nought against the soul: I shall be graced by the neglect of this command: I shall stand with credit in heavenly places, who could not stand in earthly: I shall hold out against the greater powers, who yielded to the lesser: I shall deserve to be at length let in, though now shut out. It readily occurs to one to remark further, "If it is in heaven that men must confess, it is here too that they must deny." For where the one is, there both are. For contraries always go together. There will need to be carried on in heaven persecution even, which is the occasion of confession or denial. Why, then, do you refrain, O most presumptuous heretic, from transporting to the world above the whole series of means proper to the intimidation of Christians, and especially to put there the very hatred for the name, where Christ rules at the right hand of the Father? Will you plant there both synagogues of the Jews – fountains of persecution – before which the apostles endured the scourge, and heathen assemblages with their own circus, forsooth, where they readily join in the cry, Death to the third race? But ye are bound to produce in the same place both our brothers, fathers, children, mothers-in-law, daughters-in-law and those of our household, through whose agency the betrayal has been appointed; likewise kings, governors, and armed authorities, before whom the matter at issue must be contested. Assuredly there will be in heaven a prison also, destitute of the sun's rays or full of light unthankfully, and fetters of the zones perhaps, and, for a rack-horse, the axis itself which whirls the heavens round. Then, if a Christian is to be stoned, hail-storms will be near; if burned, thunderbolts are at hand; if butchered, the armed Orion will exercise his function; if put an end to by beasts, the north will send forth the bears, the Zodiac the bulls and the lions. He who will endure these assaults to the end, the same shall be saved. Will there be then, in heaven, both an end, and suffering, a killing, and the first confession? And where will be the flesh requisite for all this? Where the body which alone has to be killed by men? Unerring reason has commanded us to set forth these things in even a playful manner; nor will any one thrust out the bar consisting in this objection (we have offered), so as not to be compelled to transfer the whole array of means proper to persecution, all the powerful instrumentality which has been provided for dealing with this matter, to the place where he has put the court before which confession should be made. Since confession is elicited by persecution, and persecution ended in confession, there cannot but be at the same time, in attendance upon these, the instrumentality which determines both the entrance and the exit, that is, the beginning and the end. But both hatred for the name will be here, persecution breaks out here, betrayal brings men forth here, examination uses force here, torture rages here, and confession or denial completes this whole course of procedure on the earth. Therefore, if the other things are here, confession also is not elsewhere; if confession is elsewhere, the other things also are not here. Certainly the other things are not elsewhere; therefore neither is confession in heaven. Or, if they will have it that the manner in which the heavenly examination and confession take place is different, it will certainly be also incumbent on them to devise a mode of procedure of their own of a very different kind, and opposed to that method which is indicated in the Scriptures. And we may be able to say, Let them consider (whether what they imagine to exist does so), if so be that this course of procedure, proper to examination and confession on earth – a course which has persecution as the source in which it originates, and which pleads dissension in the state – is preserved to its own faith, if so be that we must believe just as is also written, and understand just as is spoken. Here I endure the entire course (in question), the Lord Himself not appointing a different quarter of the world for my doing so. For what does He add after finishing with confession and denial? "Think not that I am come to send peace on earth, but a sword," – undoubtedly on the earth. "For I am come to set a man at variance against his father, and the daughter against her mother, and the mother-in-law against her daughter-in-law. And a man's foes shall be they of his own household." For so is it brought to pass, that the brother delivers up the brother to death, and the father the son: and the children rise up against the parents, and cause them to die. And he who endureth to the end let that man be saved. So that this whole course of procedure characteristic of the Lord's sword, which has been sent not to heaven, but to earth, makes confession also to be there, which by enduring to the end is to issue in the suffering of death.

Chapter 11

In the same manner, therefore, we maintain that the other announcements too refer to the condition of martyrdom. "He," says Jesus, "who will value his own life also more than me, is not worthy of me," – that is, he who will rather live by denying, than die by confessing, me; and "he who findeth his life shall lose it; but he who loseth it for my sake shall find it." Therefore indeed he finds it, who, in winning life, denies; but he who thinks that he wins it by denying, will lose it in hell. On the other hand, he who, through confessing, is killed, will lose it for the present, but is also about to find it unto everlasting life. In fine, governors themselves, when they urge men to deny, say, "Save your life; "and, "Do not lose your life." How would Christ speak, but in accordance with the treatment to which the Christian would be subjected? But when He forbids thinking about what answer to make at a judgment-seat, He is preparing His own servants for what awaited them, He gives the assurance that the Holy Spirit will answer by them; and when He wishes a brother to be visited in prison, He is commanding that those about to confess be the object of solicitude; and He is soothing their sufferings when He asserts that God will avenge His own elect. In the parable also of the withering of the word after the green blade had sprung up, He is drawing a picture with reference to the burning heat of persecutions. If these announcements are not understood as they are made, without doubt they signify something else than the sound indicates; and there will be one thing in the words, another in their meanings, as is the case with allegories, with parables, with riddles. Whatever wind of reasoning, therefore, these scorpions may catch (in their sails), with whatever subtlety they may attack, there is now one line of defense: an appeal will be made to the facts themselves, whether they occur as the Scriptures represent that they would; since another thing will then be meant in the Scriptures if that very one (which seems to be so) is not found in actual facts. For what is written, must needs come to pass. Besides, what is written will then come to pass, if something different does not. But, lo! we are both regarded as persons to be hated by all men for the, sake of the name, as it is written; and are delivered up by our nearest of kin also, as it is written; and are brought before magistrates, and examined, and tortured, and make confession, and are ruthlessly killed, as it is written. So the Lord ordained. If He ordained these events otherwise, why do they not come to pass otherwise than He ordained them, that is, as He ordained them? And yet they do not come to pass otherwise than He ordained. Therefore, as they come to pass, so He ordained; and as He ordained, so they come to pass. For neither would they have been permitted to occur otherwise than He ordained, nor for His part would He have ordained otherwise than He would wish them to occur. Thus these passages of Scripture will not mean ought else than we recognize in actual facts; or if those events are not yet taking place which are announced, how are those taking place which have not been announced? For these events which are taking place have not been announced, if those which are announced are different, and not these which are taking place. Well now, seeing the very occurrences are met with in actual life which are believed to have been expressed with a different meaning in words, what would happen if they were found to have come to pass in a different manner than had been revealed? But this will be the waywardness of faith, not to believe what has been demonstrated, to assume the truth of what has not been demonstrated. And to this waywardness I will offer the following objection also, that if these events, which occur as is written, will not be the very ones which are announced, those too (which are meant) ought not to occur as is written, that they themselves also may not, after the example of these others, be in danger of exclusion, since there is one thing in the words and another in the facts; and there remains that even the events which have been announced are not seen when they occur, if they are announced otherwise than they have to occur. And how will those be believed (to have come to pass), which will not have been announced as they come to pass? Thus heretics, by not believing what is announced as it has been shown to have taken place, believe what has not been even announced.

Chapter 12

Who, now, should know better the marrow of the Scriptures than the school of Christ itself? – the persons whom the Lord both chose for Himself as scholars, certainly to be fully instructed in all points, and appointed to us for masters to instruct us in all points. To whom would He have rather made known the veiled import of His own language, than to him to whom He disclosed the likeness of His own glory – to Peter, John, and James, and afterwards to Paul, to whom He granted participation in (the joys of) paradise too, prior to his martyrdom? Or do they also write differently from what they think – teachers using deceit, not truth? Addressing the Christians of Pontus, Peter, at all events, says, "How great indeed is the glory, if ye suffer patiently, without being punished as evildoers! For this is a lovely feature, and even hereunto were ye called, since Christ also suffered for us, leaving you Himself as an example, that ye should follow His own steps." And again: "Beloved, be not alarmed by the fiery trial which is taking place among you, as though some strange thing happened unto you. For, inasmuch as ye are partakers of Christ's sufferings, do ye rejoice; that, when His glory shall be revealed, ye may be glad also with exceeding joy. If ye are reproached for the name of Christ, happy are ye; because glory and the Spirit of God rest upon you: if only none of you suffer as a murderer, or as a thief, or as an evil-doer, or as a busybody in other men's matters; yet (if any man suffer) as a Christian, let him not be ashamed, but let him glorify God on this behalf." John, in fact, exhorts us to lay down our lives even for our brethren, affirming that there is no fear in love: "For perfect love casteth out fear, since fear has punishment; and he who fears is not perfect in love." What fear would it be better to understand (as here meant), than that which gives rise to denial? What love does he assert to be perfect, but that which puts fear to flight, and gives courage to confess? What penalty will he appoint as the punishment of fear, but that which he who denies is about to pay, who has to be slain, body and soul, in hell? And if he teaches that we must die for the brethren, how much more for the Lord, – he being sufficiently prepared, by his own Revelation too, forgiving such advice! For indeed the Spirit had sent the injunction to the angel of the church in Smyrna: "Behold, the devil shall cast some of you into prison, that ye may be tried ten days. Be thou faithful unto death, and I will give thee a crown of life." Also to the angel of the church in Pergamus (mention was made) of Antipas, the very faithful martyr, who was slain where Satan dwelleth. Also to the angel of the church in Philadelphia (it was signified) that he who had not denied the name of the Lord was delivered from the last trial. Then to every conqueror the Spirit promises now the tree of life, and exemption from the second death; now the hidden manna with the stone of glistening whiteness, and the name unknown (to every man save him that receiveth it); now power to rule with a rod of iron, and the brightness of the morning star; now the being clothed in white raiment, and not having the name blotted out of the book of life, and being made in the temple of God a pillar with the inscription on it of the name of God and of the Lord, and of the heavenly Jerusalem; now a sitting with the Lord on His throne, – which once was persistently refused to the sons of Zebedee. Who, pray, are these so blessed conquerors, but martyrs in the strict sense of the word? For indeed theirs are the victories whose also are the fights; theirs, however, are the fights whose also is the blood. But the souls of the martyrs both peacefully rest in the meantime under the altar, and support their patience by the assured hope of revenge; and, clothed in their robes, wear the dazzling halo of brightness, until others also may fully share in their glory. For yet again a countless throng are revealed, clothed in white and distinguished by palms of victory, celebrating their triumph doubtless over Antichrist, since one of the elders says, "These are they who come out of that great tribulation, and have washed their robes, and made them white in the blood of the Lamb." For the flesh is the clothing of the soul. The uncleanness, indeed, is washed away by baptism, but the stains are changed into dazzling whiteness by martyrdom. For Esaias also promises, that out of red and scarlet there will come forth the whiteness of snow and wool. When great Babylon likewise is represented as drunk with the blood of the saints, doubtless the supplies needful for her drunkenness are furnished by the cups of martyrdoms; and what suffering the fear of martyrdoms will entail, is in like manner shown. For among all the castaways, nay, taking precedence of them all, are the fearful. "But the fearful," says John – and then come the others – " will have their part in the lake of fire and brimstone." Thus fear, which, as stated in his epistle, love drives out, has punishment.

Chapter 13

But how Paul, an apostle, from being a persecutor, who first of all shed the blood of the church, though afterwards he exchanged the sword for the pen, and turned the dagger into a plough, being first a ravening wolf of Benjamin, then himself supplying food as did Jacob, – how he, (I say,) speaks in favor of martyrdoms, now to be chosen by himself also, when, rejoicing over the Thessalonians, he says, "So that we glory in you in the churches of God, for your patience and faith in all your persecutions and tribulations, in which ye endure a manifestation of the righteous judgment of God, that ye may be accounted worthy of His kingdom, for which ye also suffer! As also in his Epistle to the Romans: "And not only so, but we glory in tribulations also, being sure that tribulation worketh patience, and patience experience, and experience hope; and hope maketh not ashamed." And again: "And if children, then heirs, heirs indeed of God, and joint-heirs with Christ: if so be that we suffer with Him, that we may be also glorified together. For I reckon that the sufferings of this time are not worthy to be compared with the glory which shall be revealed in us." And therefore he afterward says: "Who shall separate us from the love of God? Shall tribulation, or distress, or famine, or nakedness, or peril, or sword? (As it is written: For Thy sake we are killed all the day long; we have been counted as sheep for the slaughter,) Nay, in all these things we are more than conquerors, through Him who loved us. For we are persuaded, that neither death, nor life, nor power, nor height, nor depth, nor any other creature, shall be able to separate us from the love of God, which is in Christ Jesus our Lord." But further, in recounting his own sufferings to the Corinthians, he certainly decided that suffering must be borne: "In labors, (he says,) more abundant, in prisons very frequent, in deaths oft. Of the Jews five times received I forty stripes, save one; thrice was I beaten with rods; once was I stoned," and the rest. And if these severities will seem to be more grievous than martyrdoms, yet once more he says: "Therefore I take pleasure in infirmities, in reproaches, in necessities, in persecutions, in distresses for Christ's sake." He also says, in verses occurring in a previous part of the epistle: "Our condition is such, that we are troubled on every side, yet not distressed; and are in need, but not in utter want; since we are harassed by persecutions, but not forsaken; it is such that we are east down, but not destroyed; always bearing about in our body the dying of Christ." "But though," says he, "our outward man perisheth" – the flesh doubtless, by the violence of persecutions – "yet the inward man is renewed day by day" – the soul, doubtless, by hope in the promises. "For our light affliction, which is but for a moment, worketh for us a far more exceeding and eternal weight of glory; while we look not at the things which are seen, but at the things which are not seen. For the things which are seen are temporal" – he is speaking of troubles; "but the things which are not seen are eternal" – he is promising rewards. But writing in bonds to the Thessalonians, he certainly affirmed that they were blessed, since to them it had been given not only to believe on Christ, but also to suffer for His sake. "Having," says he, "the same conflict which ye both saw in me, and now hear to be in me." "For though I are offered upon the sacrifice, I joy and rejoice with you all; in like manner do ye also joy and rejoice with me." You see what he decides the bliss of martyrdom to be, in honor of which he is providing a festival of mutual joy. When at length he had come to be very near the attainment of his desire, greatly rejoicing in what he saw before him, he writes in these terms to Timothy: "For I am already being offered, and the time of my departure is at hand. I have fought the good fight, I have finished my course, I have kept the faith; there is laid up for me the crown which the Lord will give me on that day" – doubtless of his suffering

love, and of a sound mind." For we suffer with power from love toward God, and with a sound mind, when we suffer for our blamelessness. But further, if He anywhere enjoins endurance, for what more than for sufferings is He providing it? If anywhere He tears men away from idolatry, what more than martyrdoms takes the lead, in tearing them away to its injury?

Chapter 14

No doubt the apostle admonishes the Romans to be subject to all power, because there is no power but God, and because (the ruler) does not carry the sword without reason, and is the servant of God, nay also,says he, a revenger to execute wrath upon him that doeth evil. For he had also previously spoken thus: "For rulers are not a terror to a good work, but to an evil. Wilt thou then not be afraid of the power? Do that which is good, and thou shall have praise of it. Therefore he is a minister of God to thee for good. But if thou do that which is evil, be afraid." Thus he bids you be subject to the powers, not an opportunity occurring for his avoiding martyrdom, but when he is making an appeal in behalf of a good life, under the view also of their being as it were assistants bestowed upon righteousness, as it were handmaids of the divine court of justice, which even here pronounces sentence beforehand upon the guilty. Then he goes on also to show how he wishes you to be subject to the powers, bidding you pay "tribute to whom tribute is due, custom to whom custom," that is, the things which are Caesar's to Caesar, and the things which are God's to God; but man is the property of God alone. Peter, no doubt, had likewise said that the king indeed must be honored, yet so that the king be honored only when he keeps to his own sphere, when he is far from assuming divine honors; because both father and mother will be loved along with God, not put on an equality with Him. Besides, one will not be permitted to love even life more than God.

Chapter 15

Now, then, the epistles of the apostles also are well known. And do we, (you say), in all respects guileless souls and doves merely, love to go astray? I should think from eagerness to live. But let it be so, that meaning departs from their epistles. And yet, that the apostles endured such sufferings, we know: the teaching is clear. This only I perceive in running through the Acts. I am not at all on the search. The prisons there, and the bonds, and the scourges, and the big stones, and the swords, and the onsets by the Jews, and the assemblies of the heathen, and the indictments by tribunes, and the hearing of causes by kings, and the judgment-seats of proconsuls and the name of Caesar, do not need an interpreter. That Peter is struck, that Stephen is overwhelmed by stones, that James is slain as is a victim at the altar, that Paul is beheaded has been written in their own blood. And if a heretic wishes his confidence to rest upon a public record, the archives of the empire will speak, as would the stones of Jerusalem. We read the lives of the Caesars: At

Rome Nero was the first who stained with blood the rising faith. Then is Peter girt by another, when he is made fast to the cross. Then does Paul obtain a birth suited to Roman citizenship, when in Rome he springs to life again ennobled by martyrdom. Wherever I read of these occurrences so soon as I do so, I learn to suffer; nor does it signify to me which I follow as teachers of martyrdom, whether the declarations or the deaths of the apostles, save that in their deaths I recall their declarations also. For they would not have suffered ought of a kind they had not previously known they had to suffer. When Agabus, making use of corresponding action too, had foretold that bonds awaited Paul, the disciples, weeping and entreating that he would not venture upon going to Jerusalem, entreated in vain. As for him, having a mind to illustrate what he had always taught, he says, "Why weep ye, and grieve my heart? But for my part, I could wish not only to suffer bonds, but also to die at Jerusalem, for the name of my Lord Jesus Christ." And so they yielded by saying, "Let the will of the Lord be done; "feeling sure, doubtless, that sufferings are included in the will of God. For they had tried to keep him back with the intention not of dissuading, but to show love for him; as yearning for (the preservation of) the apostle, not as counseling against martyrdom. And if even then a Prodicus or Valentinus stood by, suggesting that one must not confess on the earth before men, and must do so the less in truth, that God may not (seem to) thirst for blood, and Christ for a repayment of suffering, as though He besought it with the view of obtaining salvation by it for Himself also, he would have immediately heard from the servant of God what the devil had from the Lord: "Get thee behind me, Satan; thou art an offence unto me. It is written, Thou shalt worship the Lord thy God, and Him only shalt thou serve." But even now it will be right that he hear it, seeing that, long after, he has poured forth these poisons, which not even thus are to injure readily any of the weak ones, if any one in faith will drink, before being hurt, or even immediately after, this draught of ours.

Tertullian, translated by S. Thelwall

De Fuga in Persecutione: Fleeing persecution

Should Christians flee from persecution? Chapter one

My brother Fabius, you very lately asked, because some news or other were communicated, whether or not we ought to flee in persecution For my part, having on the spot made some observations in the negative suited to the place and time, I also, owing to the rudeness of some persons, took away with me the subject but half treated, meaning to set it forth now more fully by my pen; for your inquiry had interested me in it, and the state of the times had already on its own account pressed it upon me. As persecutions in increasing number threaten us, so the more are we called on to give earnest thought to the question of how faith ought to receive them, and the duty of carefully considering it concerns you no less, who no doubt, by not accepting the Comforter, the guide to all truth, have, as was natural, opposed us hitherto in regard to other questions also. We have therefore applied a methodical treatment, too, to your inquiry, as we see that we must first come to a decision as to how the matter stands in regard to persecution itself, whether it comes on us from God or from the devil, that with the less difficulty we may get on firm ground as to our duty to meet it; for of everything one's knowledge is clearer when it is known from whom it has its origin. It is enough indeed to lay it down, (in bar of all besides,) that nothing happens without the will of God. But lest we be diverted from the point before us, we shall not by this deliverance at once give occasion to the other discussions if one make answer. Therefore evil and sin are both from God; the devil henceforth, and even we ourselves, are entirely free. The question in hand is persecution. With respect to this, let me in the meantime say, that nothing happens without God's will; on the ground that persecution is especially worthy of God, and, so to speak, requisite, for the approving, to wit, or if you will, the rejection of His professing servants. For what is the issue of persecution, what other result comes of it, but the approving and rejecting of faith, in regard to which the Lord will certainly sift His people? Persecution, by means of which one is declared either approved or rejected, is just the judgment of the Lord. But the judging properly belongs to God alone. This is that fan which even now cleanses the Lord's threshing-floor – the Church, I mean – winnowing the mixed heap of believers, and separating the grain of the martyrs from the chaff of the deniers; and this is also the ladder of which Jacob dreams, on which are seen, some mounting up to higher places, and others going down to lower. So, too, persecution may be viewed as a contest. By whom is the conflict proclaimed, but by Him by whom the crown and the rewards are offered? You find in the Revelation its edict, setting forth the rewards by which He incites to victory – those, above all, whose is the distinction of conquering in persecution, in very deed contending in their victorious struggle not against flesh and blood, but against spirits of wickedness. So, too, you will see that the adjudging of the contest belongs to the same glorious One, as umpire, who calls us to the prize. The one great thing in persecution is the promotion of the glory of God, as He tries and casts away, lays on and takes off. But what concerns the glory of God will surely come to pass by His will. And when is trust in God more strong, than when there is a greater fear of Him, and when persecution breaks out? The Church is awe-struck. Then is faith both more zealous in preparation, and better disciplined in fasts, and meetings, and prayers, and lowliness, in brotherly-kindness and love, in holiness and temperance. There is no room, in fact, for ought but fear and hope. So even by this very thing we have it clearly proved that persecution, improving as it does the servants of God, cannot be imputed to the devil.

Chapter two

If, because injustice is not from God, but from the devil, and persecution consists of injustice (for what more unjust than that the bishops of the true God, that all the followers of the truth, should be dealt with after the manner o the vilest criminals?), persecution therefore seems to proceed from the devil, by whom the injustice which constitutes persecution is perpetrated, we ought to know, as you have neither persecution without the injustice of the devil, nor the trial of faith without persecution, that the injustice necessary for the trial of faith does not give a warrant for persecution, but supplies an agency; that in reality, in reference to the trial of faith, which is the reason of persecution, the will of God goes first, but that as the instrument of persecution, which is the way of trial, the injustice of the devil follows. For in other respects, too, injustice in proportion to the enmity it displays against righteousness affords occasion for attestations of that to which it is opposed as an enemy, that so righteousness may be perfected in injustice, as strength is perfected in weakness. For the weak things of the world have been chosen by God to confound the strong, and the foolish things of the world to confound its wisdom. Thus even injustice is employed, that righteousness may be approved in putting unrighteousness to shame. Therefore, since the service is not of free-will, but of subjection (for persecution is the appointment of the Lord for the trial of faith, but its ministry is the injustice of the devil, supplied that persecution may be got up), we believe that persecution comes to pass, no question, by the devil's agency, but not by the devil's origination. Satan will not be at liberty to do anything against the servants of the living God unless the Lord grant leave, either that He may overthrow Satan himself by the faith of the elect which proves victorious in the trial, or in the face of the world show that apostatizers to the devil's cause have been in reality His servants. You have the case of Job, whom the devil, unless he had received authority from God, could not have visited with trial, not even, in fact, in his property, unless the Lord had said, "Behold, all that he has I put at your disposal; but do not stretch out your hand against himself." In short, he would not even have stretched it out, unless afterwards, at his request, the Lord had granted him this permission also, saying, "Behold, I deliver him to you; only preserve his life." So he asked in the case of the apostles likewise an opportunity to tempt them, having it only by special allowance, since the Lord in the Gospel says to Peter, "Behold, Satan asked that he might sift you as grain; but I have prayed for you that your faith fail not; " that is, that the devil should not have power granted him sufficient to endanger his faith. Whence it is manifest that both things belong to God shaking of faith as well as the shielding of it, when both are sought from Him – the shaking by the devil, the shielding by the Son. And certainly, when the Son of God has faith's protection absolutely committed to Him, beseeching it of the Father, from whom He receives all power in heaven and on earth, how entirely out of the question is it that the devil should have the assailing of it in his own power! But in the prayer prescribed to us, when we say to our Father, "Lead us not into temptation " (now what greater temptation is there than persecution?), we acknowledge that that comes to pass by His will whom we beseech to exempt us from it. For this is what follows, "But deliver us from the wicked one," that is, do not lead us into temptation by giving us up to the wicked one, for then are we delivered from the power of the devil, when we are not handed over to him to be tempted. Nor would the devil's legion have had power over the herd of swine unless they had got it from God; so far are they from having power over the sheep of God. I may say that the bristles of the swine, too, were then counted by God, not to speak of the hairs of holy men. The devil, it must be owned, seems indeed to have power – in this case really his own – over those who do not belong to God, the nations being once for all counted by God as a drop of the bucket, and as the dust of the threshing-floor, and as the spittle of the mouth, and so thrown open to the devil as, in a sense, a free possession. But against those who belong to the household of God he may not do ought as by any right of his own, because the cases marked out in Scripture show when – that is, for what reasons – he may touch them. For either, with a view to their being approved, the power of trial is granted to him, challenged or challenging, as in the instances already referred to, or, to secure an opposite result, the sinner is handed over to him, as though he were an executioner to whom belonged the inflicting of punishment, as in the case of Saul. "And the Spirit of the Lord," says Scripture, "departed from Saul, and an evil spirit from the Lord troubled and stifled him; " or the design is to humble, as the apostle tells us, that there was given him a stake, the messenger of Satan, to buffet him; and even this son of thing is not permitted in the case of holy men, unless it be that at the same time strength of endurance may be perfected in weakness. For the apostle likewise delivered Phygellus and Hermogenes over to Satan that by chastening they might be taught not to blaspheme. You see, then, that the devil receives more suitably power even from the servants of God; so far is he from having it by any fight of his own.

Chapter three

Seeing therefore, too, these cases occur in persecutions more than at other times, as there is then among us more of proving or rejecting, more of abusing or punishing, it must be that their general occurrence is permitted or commanded by Him at whose will they happen even partially; by Him, I mean, who says, "I am He who make peace and create evil," that is, war, for that is the antithesis of peace. But what other war has our peace than persecution? If in its issues persecution emphatically brings either life or death, either wounds or healing, you have the author, too, of this. "I will smite and heal I will make alive and put to death." "I will burn them," He says, "as gold is burned; and I will try them," He says, "as silver is tried," for when the flame of persecution is consuming as, then the steadfastness of our faith is proved. These will be the fiery darts of the devil, by which faith gets a ministry of burning and kindling; yet by the will of God. As to this I know not who can doubt, unless it be persons with frivolous and frigid faith, which seizes upon those who with trembling assemble together in the church. For you say, seeing we assemble without order, and assemble at the same time, and flock in large numbers to the church, the heathen are led to make inquiry about us, and we are alarmed lest we awaken their anxieties. Do ye not know that God is Lord of all? And if it is God's will, then you shall suffer persecution; but if it is not, the heathen will be still. Believe it most surely, if indeed you believe in that God without whose will not even the sparrow, a penny can buy, falls to the ground. But we, I think, are better than many sparrows.

Chapter four

Well, then, if it is evident from whom persecution proceeds, we are able at once to satisfy your doubts, and to decide from these introductory remarks alone, that men should not flee in it. For if persecution proceeds from God, in no way will it be our duty to flee from what has God as its author; a twofold reason opposing; for what proceeds from God ought not on the one hand to be avoided, and it cannot be evaded on the other. It ought not to be avoided, because it is good; for everything must be good on which God has cast His eye. And with this idea has perhaps this statement been made in Genesis, "And God saw because it is good; "not that He would have been ignorant of its goodness unless He had seen it, but to indicate by this expression that it was good because it was viewed by God. There are many events indeed happening by the will of God, and happening to somebody's harm. Yet for all that, a thing is therefore good because it is of God, as divine, as reasonable; for what is divine, and not reasonable and good? What is good, yet not divine? But if to the universal apprehension of mankind this seems to be the case, in judging, man's faculty of apprehension does not predetermine the nature of things, but the nature of things his power of apprehension. For every several nature is a certain definite reality, and it lays it on the perceptive power to perceive it just as it exists. Now, if that which comes from God is good indeed in its natural state (for there is nothing from God which is not good, because it is divine, and reasonable), but seems evil only to the human faculty, all will be right in regard to the former; with the latter the fault will lie. In its real nature a very good thing is chastity, and so is truth, and righteousness; and yet they are distasteful to many. Is perhaps the real nature on this account sacrificed to the sense of perception? Thus persecution in its own nature too is good, because it is a divine and reasonable appointment; but those to whom it comes as a punishment do not feel it to be pleasant. You see that as proceeding from Him, even that evil has a reasonable ground, when one in persecution is cast out of a state of salvation, just as you see that you have a reasonable ground for the good also, when one by persecution has his salvation made more secure. Unless, as it depends on the Lord, one either perishes irrationally, or is irrationally saved, he will not be able to speak of persecution as an evil, which, while it is under the direction of reason, is, even in respect of its evil, good. So, if persecution is in every way a good, because it has a natural basis, we on valid grounds lay it down, that what is good ought not to be shunned by us, because it is a sin to refuse what is good; besides that, what has been looked upon by God can no longer indeed be avoided, proceeding as it does from God, from whose will escape will not be possible. Therefore those who think that they should flee, either reproach God with doing what is evil, if they flee from persecution as an evil (for no one avoids what is good); or they count themselves stronger than God: so they think, who imagine it possible to escape when it is God's pleasure that such events should occur.

Chapter five

But, says some one, I flee, the thing it belongs to me to do, that I may not perish, if I deny; it is for Him on His part, if He chooses, to bring me, when I flee, back before the tribunal. First answer me this: Are you sure you will deny if you do not flee, or are you not sure? For if you are sure, you have denied already, because by presupposing that you will deny, you have given yourself up to that about which you have made such a presupposition; and now it is vain for you to think of flight, that you may avoid denying, when in intention you have denied already. But if you are doubtful on that point, why do you not, in the incertitude of your fear wavering between the two different issues, presume that you are able rather to act a confessor's part, and so add to your safety, that you may not flee, just as you presuppose denial to send you off a fugitive? The matter stands thus – we have either both things in our own power, or they wholly lie with God. If it is ours to confess or to deny, why do we not anticipate the nobler thing, that is, that we shall confess? If you are not willing to confess, you are not willing to suffer; and to be unwilling to confess is to deny. But if the matter is wholly in God's hand, why do we not leave it to His will, recognizing His might and power in that, just as He can bring us back to trial when we flee, so is He able to screen us when we do not flee; yes, and even living in the very heart of the people? Strange conduct, is it not, to honor God in the matter of flight from persecution, because He can bring you back from your flight to stand before the judgment-seat; but in regard of witness-bearing, to do Him high dishonor by despairing of power at His hands to shield you from danger? Why do you not rather on this, the side of constancy and trust in God, say, I do my part; I depart not; God, if He choose, will Himself be my protector? It beseems us better to retain our position in submission to the will of God, than to flee at our own will. Rutilius, a saintly martyr, after having ofttimes fled from persecution from place to place, nay, having bought security from danger, as he thought, by money, was, notwithstanding the complete security he had, as he thought, provided for himself, at last unexpectedly seized, and being brought before the magistrate, was put to the torture and cruelly mangled, – a punishment, I believe, for his fleeing, – and thereafter he was consigned to the flames, and thus paid to the mercy of God the suffering which he had shunned. What else did the Lord mean to show us by this example, but that we ought not to flee from persecution because it avails us nothing if God disapproves?

Chapter six

Nay, says some one, he fulfilled the command, when he fled from city to city. For so a certain individual, but a fugitive likewise has chosen to maintain, and others have done the same who are unwilling to understand the meaning of that declaration of the Lord, that they may use it as a cloak for their cowardice, although it has had its persons as well as its times and reasons to which it specially applies. "When they begin," He says, "to persecute you, flee from city to city," We maintain that this belongs specially to the persons of the apostles, and to their times and circumstances, as the following sentences will show, which are suitable only to the apostles: "Do not go into the way of the Gentiles, and into a city of the Samaritans do not enter: but go rather to the lost sheep of the house of Israel." But to us the way of the Gentiles is also open, as in it we in fact were found, and to the very last we walk; and no city has been excepted. So we preach throughout all the world; nay, no special care even for Israel has been laid upon us, save as also we are bound to preach to all nations, Yes, and if we are apprehended, we shall not be brought into Jewish councils, nor scourged in Jewish synagogues, but we shall certainly be cited before Roman magistrates and judgment-seats. So, then, the circumstances of the apostles even required the injunction to flee, their mission being to preach first to the lost sheep of the house of Israel. That, therefore, this preaching might be fully accomplished in the case of those among whom this behoved first of all to be carried out – that the sons might receive bread before the dogs, for that reason He commanded them to flee then for a time – not with the object of eluding danger, under the plea strictly speaking which persecution urges (rather He was in the habit of proclaiming that they would suffer persecutions, and of teaching that these must be endured); but in order to further the proclamation of the Gospel message, lest by their being at once put down, the diffusion of the Gospel too might be prevented. Neither were they to flee to any city as if by stealth, but as if everywhere about to proclaim their message; and for this, everywhere about to undergo persecutions, until they should fulfil their teaching. Accordingly the Savior says, "Ye will not go over all the cities of Israel." So the command to flee was restricted to the limits of Judea. But no command that shows Judea to be specially the sphere for preaching applies to us, now that the Holy Spirit has been poured out upon all flesh. Therefore Paul and the apostles themselves, mindful of the precept of the Lord, bear this solemn testimony before Israel, which they had now filled with their doctrine – saying, "It was necessary that the word of God should have been first delivered to you; but seeing ye have rejected it, and have not thought yourselves worthy of eternal life, lo, we turn to the Gentiles." And from that time they turned their steps away, as those who went before them had laid it down, and departed into the way of the Gentiles, and entered into the cities of the Samaritans; so that, in very deed, their sound went forth into all the earth, and their words to the end of the world. If, therefore, the prohibition against setting foot in the way of the Gentiles, and entering into the cities of the Samaritans, has come to an end, why should not the command to flee, which was issued at the same time, have come also to an end? Accordingly, from the time when, Israel having had its full measure, the apostles went over to the Gentiles, they neither fled from city to city, nor hesitated to suffer. Nay, Paul too, who had submitted to deliverance from persecution by being let down from the wall, as to do so was at this time a matter of command, refused in like manner now at the close of his ministry, and after the injunction had come to an end, to give in to the anxieties of the disciples, eagerly entreating him that he would not risk himself at Jerusalem, because of the sufferings in store for him which Agabus had foretold; but doing the very opposite, it is thus he speaks, "What do ye, weeping and disquieting my heart? For I could wish not only to suffer bonds, but also to die at Jerusalem, for the name of my Lord Jesus Christ." And so they all said, "Let the will of the Lord be done." What was the will of the Lord? Certainly no longer to flee from persecution. Otherwise they who had wished him rather to avoid persecution, might also have adduced that prior will of the Lord, in which He had commanded flight. Therefore, seeing even in the days of the apostles themselves, the command to flee was temporary, as were those also relating to the other things at the same time enjoined, that [command] cannot continue with us which ceased with our teachers, even although it had not been issued specially for them; or if the Lord wished it to continue, the apostles did wrong who were not careful to keep fleeing to the last.

Chapter seven

Let us now see whether also the rest of our Lord's ordinances accord with a lasting command of flight. In the first place, indeed, if persecution is from God, what are we to think of our being ordered to take ourselves out of its way, by the very party who brings it on us? For if He wanted it to be evaded, He had better not have sent it, that there might not be the appearance of His will being thwarted by another will. For He wished us either to suffer persecution or to flee from it. If to flee, how to suffer? If to suffer, how to flee? In fact, what utter inconsistency in the decrees of One who commands to flee, and yet urges to suffer, which is the very opposite! "Him who will confess Me, I also will confess before My Father." How will he confess, fleeing? How flee, confessing? "Of him who shall be ashamed of Me, will I also be ashamed before My Father." If I avoid suffering, I am ashamed to confess. "Happy they who suffer persecution for My name's sake." Unhappy, therefore, they who, by running away, will not suffer according to the divine command. "He who shall endure to the end shall be saved." How then, when you bid me flee, do you wish me to endure to the end? If views so opposed to each other do not comport with the divine dignity, they clearly prove that the command to flee had, at the time it was given, a reason of its own, which we have pointed out. But it is said, the Lord, providing for the weakness of some of His people, nevertheless, in His kindness, suggested also the haven of flight to them. For He was not able even without flight – a protection so base, and unworthy, and servile – to preserve in persecution such as He knew to be weak! Whereas in fact He does not cherish, but ever rejects the weak, teaching first, not that we are to fly from our persecutors, but rather that we are not to fear them. "Fear not them who are able to kill the body, but are unable to do ought against the soul; but fear Him who can destroy both body and soul in hell." And then what does He allot to the fearful? "He who will value his life more than Me, is not worthy of Me; and he who takes not up his cross and follows Me, cannot be My disciple." Last of all, in the Revelation, He does not propose flight to the "fearful," but a miserable portion among the rest of the outcast, in the lake of brimstone and fire, which is the second death.

Chapter eight

He sometimes also fled from violence Himself, but for the same reason as had led Him to command the apostles to do so: that is, He wanted to fulfil His ministry of teaching; and when it was finished, I do not say He stood firm, but He had no desire even to get from His Father the aid of hosts of angels: finding fault, too, with Peter's sword. He likewise acknowledged, it is true, that His "soul was troubled, even unto death," and the flesh weak; with the design, (however,) first of all, that by having, as His own, trouble of soul and weakness of the flesh, He might show you that both the substances in Him were truly human; lest, as certain persons have now brought it in, you might be led to think either the flesh or the soul of Christ different from ours; and then, that, by an exhibition of their states, you might be convinced that they have no power at all of themselves without the spirit. And for this reason He puts first "the willing spirit," that, looking to the natures respectively of both the substances, you may see that you have in you the spirit's strength as well as the flesh's weakness; and even from this may learn what to do, and by what means to do it, and what to bring under what, – the weak, namely, under the strong, that you may not, as is now your fashion, make excuses on the ground of the weakness of the flesh, forsooth, but put out of sight the strength of the spirit. He also asked of His Father, that if it might be, the cup of suffering should pass from Him. So ask you the like favor; but as He did, holding your position, – merely offering supplication, and adding, too, the other words: "but not what I will, but what Thou wilt." But when you run away, how will you make this request? taking, in that case, into your own hands the removal of the cup from you, and instead of doing what your Father wishes, doing what you wish yourself.

Chapter nine

The teaching of the apostles was surely in everything according to the mind of God: they forgot and omitted nothing of the Gospel. Where, then, do you show that they renewed the command to flee from city to city? In fact, it was utterly impossible that they should have laid down anything so utterly opposed to their own examples as a command to flee, while it was just from bonds, or the islands in which, for confessing, not fleeing from the Christian name, they were confined, they wrote their letters to the Churches. Paul bids us support the weak, but most certainly it is not when they flee. For how can the absent be supported by you? By bearing with them? Well, he says that people must be supported, if anywhere they have committed a fault through the weakness of their faith, just as (he enjoins) that we should comfort the faint-hearted; he does not say, however, that they should be sent into exile. But when he urges us not to give place to evil, he does not offer the suggestion that we should take to our heels, he only teaches that passion should be kept under restraint; and if he says that the time must be redeemed, because the days are evil, he wishes us to gain a lengthening of life, not by flight, but by wisdom. Besides, he who bids us shine as sons of light, does not bid us hide away out of sight as sons of darkness. He commands us to stand steadfast, certainly not to act an opposite. part by fleeing; and to be girt, not to play the fugitive or oppose the Gospel. He points out weapons, too, which persons who intend to run away would not require. And among these he notes the shield too, that ye may be able to quench the darts of the devil, when doubtless ye resist him, and sustain his assaults in their utmost force. Accordingly John also teaches that we must lay down our lives for the brethren; much more, then, we must do it for the Lord. This cannot be fulfilled by those who flee. Finally, mindful of his own Revelation, in which he had heard the doom of the fearful, (and so) speaking from personal knowledge, he warns us that fear must be put away. "There is no fear," says he, "in love; but perfect love casteth out fear; because fear has torment" – the fire of the lake, no doubt. "He that feareth is not perfect in love" – to wit, the love of God. And yet who will flee from persecution, but he who fears? Who will fear, but he who has not loved? Yes; and if you ask counsel of the Spirit, what does He approve more than that utterance of the Spirit? For, indeed, it incites all almost to go and offer themselves in martyrdom, not to flee from it; so that we also make mention of it. If you are exposed to public infamy, says he, it is for your good; for he who is not exposed to dishonor among men is sure to be so before the Lord. Do not be ashamed; righteousness brings you forth into the public gaze. Why should you be ashamed of gaining glory? The opportunity is given you when you are before the eyes of men. So also elsewhere: seek not to die on bridal beds, nor in miscarriages, nor in soft fevers, but to die the martyr's death, that He may be glorified who has suffered for you.

Chapter ten

But some, paying no attention to the exhortations of God, are readier to apply to themselves that Greek versicle of worldly wisdom, "He who fled will fight again; "perhaps also in the battle to flee again. And when will he who, as a fugitive, is a defeated man, be conqueror? A worthy soldier he furnishes to his commander Christ, who, so amply armed by the apostle, as soon as he hears persecution's trumpet, runs off from the day of persecution. I also will produce in answer a quotation taken from the world: "Is it a thing so very sad to die? " He must die, in whatever way of it, either as conquered or as conqueror. But although he has succumbed in denying, he has yet faced and battled with the torture. I had rather be one to be pitied than to be blushed for. More glorious is the soldier pierced with a javelin in battle, than he who has a safe skin as a fugitive. Do you fear man, O Christian? – you who ought to be feared by the angels, since you are to judge angels; who ought to be feared by evil spirits, since you have received power also over evil spirits; who ought to be feared by the whole world, since by you, too, the world is judged. You are Christ-clothed, you who flee before the devil, since into Christ you have been baptized. Christ, who is in you, is treated as of small account when you give yourself back to the devil, by becoming a fugitive before him. But, seeing it is from the Lord you flee, you taunt all runaways with the futility of their purpose. A certain bold prophet also had fled from the Lord, he had crossed over from Joppa in the direction of Tarsus, as if he could as easily transport himself away from God; but I find him, I do not say in the sea and on the land, but, in fact, in the belly even of a beast, in which he was confined for the space of three days, unable either to find death or even thus escape from God. How much better the conduct of the man who, though he fears the enemy of God, does not flee from, but rather despises him, relying on the protection of the Lord; or, if you will, having an awe of God all the greater, the more that he has stood in His presence, says, "It is the Lord, He is mighty. All things belong to Him; wherever I am, I am in His hand: let Him do as He wills, I go not away; and if it be His pleasure that I die, let Him destroy me Himself, while I save myself for Him. I had rather bring odium upon Him by dying by His will, than by escaping through my own anger."

Chapter eleven

Thus ought every servant of God to feel and act, even one in an inferior place, that he may come to have a more important one, if he has made some upward step by his endurance of persecution. But when persons in authority themselves – I mean the very deacons, and presbyters, and bishops – take to flight, how will a layman be able to see with what view it was said, Flee from city to city? Thus, too, with the leaders turning their backs, who of the common rank will hope to persuade men to stand firm in the battle? Most assuredly a good shepherd lays down his life for the sheep, according to the word of Moses, when the Lord Christ had not as yet been revealed, but was already shadowed forth in himself: "If you destroy this people," he says, "destroy me also along with it." But Christ, confirming these foreshadowings Himself, adds: "The bad shepherd is he who, on seeing the wolf, flees, and leaves the sheep to be torn in pieces." Why, a shepherd like this will be tuned off from the farm; the wages to have been given him at the time of his discharge will be kept from him as compensation; nay, even from his former savings a restoration of the master's loss will be required; for "to him who hath shall be given, but from him who hath not shall be taken away even that which he seemeth to have. Thus Zechariah threatens: "Arise, O sword, against the shepherds, and pluck ye out the sheep; and I will turn my hand against the shepherds." And against them both Ezekiel and Jeremiah declaim with kindred threatenings, for their not only wickedly eating of the Sheep, – they feeding themselves rather than those committed to their charge, – but also scattering the flock, and giving it over, shepherdless, a prey to all the beasts of the field. And this never happens more than when in persecution the Church is abandoned by the clergy. If any one recognizes the Spirit also, he will hear him branding the runaways. But if it does not become the keepers of the flock to flee when the wolves invade it – nay, if that is absolutely unlawful (for He who has declared a shepherd of this sort a bad one has certainly condemned him; and whatever is condemned has, without doubt, become unlawful) – on this ground it will not be the duty of those who have been set over the Church to flee in the time of persecution. But otherwise, if the flock should flee, the overseer of the flock would have no call to hold his ground, as his doing so in that case would be, without good reason, to give to the flock protection, which it would not require in consequence of its liberty, forsooth, to flee.

Chapter twelve

So far, my brother, as the question proposed by you is concerned, you have our opinion in answer and encouragement. But he who inquires whether persecution ought to be shunned by us must now be prepared to consider the following question also: Whether, if we should not flee from it, we should at least buy ourselves off from it. Going further than you expected, therefore, I will also on this point give you my advice, distinctly affirming that persecution, from which it is evident we must not flee, must in like manner not even be bought off. The difference lies in the payment; but as flight is a buying off without money, so buying off is money-flight. Assuredly you have here too the counseling of fear. Because you fear, you buy yourself off; and so you flee. As regards your feet, you have stood; in respect of the money you have paid, you have run away. Why, in this very standing of yours there was a fleeing from persecution, in the release from persecution which you bought; but that you should ransom with money a man whom Christ has ransomed with His blood, how unworthy is it of God and His ways of acting, who spared not His own Son for you, that He might be made a curse for us, because cursed is he that hangeth on a tree, – Him who was led as a sheep to be a sacrifice, and just as a lamb before its shearer, so opened He not His mouth; but gave His back to the scourges, nay, His cheeks to the hands of the smiter, and turned not away His face from spitting, and, being numbered with the transgressors, was delivered up to death, nay, the death of the cross. All this took place that He might redeem us from our sins. The sun ceded to us the day of our redemption; hell re-transferred the right it had in us, and our covenant is in heaven; the everlasting gates were lifted up, that the King of Glory, the Lord of might, might enter in, after having redeemed man from earth, nay, from hell, that he might attain to heaven. What, now, are we to think of the man who strives against that glorious One, nay, slights and defiles His goods, obtained at so great a ransom – no less, in truth, than His most precious blood? It appears, then, that it is better to flee than to fall in value, if a man will not lay out for himself as much as he cost Christ. And the Lord indeed ransomed him from the angelic powers which rule the world – from the spirits of wickedness, from the darkness of this life, from eternal judgment, from everlasting death. But you bargain for him with an informer, or a soldier or some paltry thief of a ruler – under, as they say, the folds of the tunic – as if he were stolen goods whom Christ purchased in the face of the whole world, yes, and set at liberty. Will you value, then, this free man at any price, and possess him at any price, but the one, as we have said, it cost the Lord, – namely, His own blood? (And if not,) why then do you purchase Christ in the man in whom He dwells, as though He were some human property? No otherwise did Simon even try to do, when he offered the apostles money for the Spirit of Christ. Therefore this man also, who in buying himself has bought the Spirit of Christ, will hear that word, "Your money perish with you, since you have thought that the grace of God is to be had at a price!" Yet who will despise him for being (what he is), a denier? For what says that extorter? Give me money: assuredly that he may not deliver him up, since he tries to sell you nothing else than that which he is going to give you for money. When you put that into his hands, it is certainly your wish not to be delivered up. But not delivered up, had you to be held up to public ridicule? While, then, in being unwilling to be delivered up, you are not willing to be thus exposed; by this unwillingness of yours you have denied that you are what you have been unwilling to have it made public that you are. Nay, you say, While I am unwilling to be held up to the public as being what I am, I have acknowledged that I am what I am unwilling to be so held up as being, that is, a Christian. Can Christ, therefore, claim that you, as a witness for Him, have steadfastly shown Him forth? He who buys himself off does nothing in that way. Before one it might, I doubt not, be said, You have confessed Him; so also, on the account of your unwillingness to confess Him before many you have denied Him. A man's very safety will pronounce that he has fallen while getting out of persecution's way. He has fallen, therefore, whose desire has been to escape. The refusal of martyrdom is denial. A Christian is preserved by his wealth, and for this end has his treasures, that he may not suffer, while he will be rich toward God. But it is the case that Christ was rich in blood for him. Blessed therefore are the poor, because, He says, the kingdom of heaven is theirs who have the soul only treasured up. If we cannot serve God and mammon, can we be redeemed both by God and by mammon? For who will serve mammon more than the man whom mammon has ransomed? Finally, of what example do you avail yourself to warrant your averting by money the giving of you up? When did the apostles, dealing with the matter, in any time of persecution trouble, extricate themselves by money? And money they certainly had from the prices of lands which were laid down at their feet, there being, without a doubt, many of the rich among those who believed – men, and also women, who were wont, too, to minister to their comfort. When did Onesimus, or Aquila, or Stephen, give them aid of this kind when they were persecuted? Paul indeed, when Felix the governor hoped that he should receive money for him from the disciples, about which matter he also dealt with the apostle in private, certainly neither paid it himself, nor did the disciples for him. Those disciples, at any rate. who wept because he was equally persistent in his determination to go to Jerusalem, and neglectful of all means to secure himself from the persecutions which had been foretold as about to occur there, at last say, "Let the will of the Lord be done." What was that will? No doubt that he should suffer for the name of the Lord, not that he should be bought off. For as Christ laid down His life for us, so, too, we should do for Him; and not only for the Lord Himself, nay, but likewise for our brethren on His account. This, too, is the teaching of John when he declares, not that we should pay for our brethren, but rather that we should die for them. It makes no difference whether the thing not to be done by you is to buy off a Christian, or to buy one. And so the will of God accords with this. Look at the condition – certainly of God's ordaining, in whose hand the king's heart is – of kingdoms and empires. For increasing the treasury there are daily provided so many appliances – registerings of property, taxes in kind benevolences, taxes in money; but never up to this time has ought of the kind been provided by bringing Christians under some purchase-money for the person and the sect, although enormous gains could be reaped from numbers too great for any to be ignorant of them. Bought with blood, paid for with blood, we owe no money for our head, because Christ is our Head. It is not fit that Christ should cost us money. How could martyrdoms, too, take place to the glory of the Lord, if by tribute we should pay for the liberty of our sect? And so he who stipulates to have it at a price, opposes the divine appointment. Since, therefore, Caesar has imposed nothing on us after this fashion of a tributary sect – in fact, such an imposition never can be made, – with Antichrist now close at hand, and gaping for the blood, not for the money of Christians how can it be pointed out to me that there is the command, "Render to Caesar the things which are Caesar's? " A soldier, be he an informer or an enemy, extorts money from me by threats, exacting nothing on Caesar's behalf; nay, doing the very opposite, when for a bribe he lets me go Christian as I am, and by the laws of man a criminal. Of another sort is the denarius which I owe to Caesar, a thing belonging to him, about which the question then was started, it being a tribute coin due indeed by those subject to tribute, not by children. Or how shall I render to God the things which are God's, certainly, therefore, His own likeness and money inscribed with His name, that is, a Christian man? But what do I owe God, as I do Caesar the denarius, but the blood which His own Son shed for me? Now if I owe God, indeed, a human being and my own blood; but I am now in this juncture, that a demand is made upon me for the payment of that debt, I am undoubtedly guilty of cheating God if I do my best to withhold payment. I have well kept the commandment, if, rendering to Caesar the things which are Caesar's, I refuse to God the things which are God's!

Chapter thirteen

But also to every one who asks me I will give on the plea of charity, not under any intimidation. Who asks? He says. But he who uses intimidation does not ask. One who threatens if he does not receive, does not crave, but compels. It is not alms he looks for, who comes not to be pitied, but to be feared. I will give, therefore, because I pity, not because I fear, when the recipient honors God and returns me his blessing; not when rather he both believes that he has conferred a favor on me, and, beholding his plunder, says, "Guilt money." Shall I be angry even with an enemy? But enmities have also other grounds. Yet withal he did not say a, betrayer, or persecutor, or one seeking to terrify you by his threats. For how much more shall I heap coals upon the head of a man of this sort, if I do not redeem myself by money? "In like manner," says Jesus, "to him who has taken away your coat, grant even your cloak also." But that refers to him who has sought to take away my property, not my faith. The cloak, too, I will grant, if I am not threatened with betrayal. If he threatens, I will demand even my coat back again. Even now, the declarations of the Lord have reasons and laws of their own. They are not of unlimited or universal application. And so He commands us to give to every one who asks, yet He Himself does not give to those who ask a sign. Otherwise, if you think that we should give indiscriminately to all who ask, that seems to me to mean that you would give, I say not wine to him who has a fever, but even poison or a sword to him who longs for death. But how we are to understand," Make to yourselves friends of mammon," let the previous parable teach you. The saying was addressed to the Jewish people; inasmuch as, having managed ill the business of the Lord which had been entrusted to them, they ought to have provided for themselves out of the men of mammon, which we then were, friends rather than enemies, and to have delivered us from the dues of sins which kept us from God, if they bestowed the blessing upon us, for the reason given by the Lord, that when grace began to depart from them, they, betaking themselves to our faith, might be admitted into everlasting habitations. Hold now any other explanation of this parable and saying you like, if only you clearly see that there is no likelihood of our opposers, should we make them friends with mammon, then receiving us into everlasting abodes. But of what will not cowardice convince men? As if Scripture both allowed them to flee, and commanded them to buy off! Finally, it is not enough if one or another is so rescued. Whole Churches have imposed tribute en masse on themselves. I know not whether it is matter for grief or shame when among hucksters, and pickpockets, and bath-thieves, and gamesters, and pimps, Christians too are included as taxpayers in the lists of free soldiers and spies. Did the apostles, with so much foresight, make the office of overseer of this type, that the occupants might be able to enjoy their rule free from anxiety, under color of providing (a like freedom for their flocks)? For such a peace, forsooth, Christ, returning to His Father, commanded to be bought from the soldiers by gifts like those you have in the Saturnalia!

Chapter fourteen

But how shall we assemble together? say you; how shall we observe the ordinances of the Lord? To be sure, just as the apostles also did, who were protected by faith, not by money; which faith, if it can remove a mountain, can much more remove a soldier. Be your safeguard wisdom, not a bribe. For you will not have at once complete security from the people also, should you buy off the interference of the soldiers. Therefore all you need for your protection is to have both faith and wisdom: if you do not make use of these, you may lose even the deliverance which you have purchased for yourself; while, if you do employ them, you can have no need of any ransoming. Lastly, if you cannot assemble by day, you have the night, the light of Christ luminous against its darkness. You cannot run about among them one after another. Be content with a church of threes. It is better that you sometimes should not see your crowds, than subject yourselves (to a tribute bondage). Keep pure for Christ His betrothed virgin; let no one make gain of her. These things, my brother, seem to you perhaps harsh and not to be endured; but recall that God has said, "He who receives it, let him receive it," that is, let him who does not receive it go his way. He who fears to suffer, cannot belong to Him who suffered. But the man who does not fear to suffer, he will be perfect in love-in the love, it is meant, of God; "for perfect love casteth out fear." "And therefore many are called, but few chosen." It is not asked who is ready to follow the broad way, but who the narrow. And therefore the Comforter is requisite, who guides into all truth, and animates to all endurance. And they who have received Him will neither stoop to flee from persecution nor to buy it off, for they have the Lord Himself, One who will stand by us to aid us in suffering, as well as to be our mouth when we are put to the question.

Tertullian, Fleeing persecution, translated by S. Thelwall

C. QUOTATIONS ABOUT MARTYRDOM

Through zeal and envy, the most faithful and righteous pillars of the church have been persecuted even to the most grievous deaths.

Clement of Rome

A Church without martyrs is a Church which is dying.

Origen

Part Four

From Diocletian to Constantine

Time line 284–313

CONTENTS

Basilides and Potamiaena:	Eusebius
Crispina:	Editor
Martyrs at Nicomedia:	A.J. Mason
Theodotus:	A.J. Mason
Eustratius, Eugenius, Auxentius, Mardarius and Orestes:	A.J. Mason
Claudius, Asterius, Neon, Domnina and Theonilla:	A.J. Mason
Januarius:	The Coptic Church
Christian Martyrdom:	Philip Scaff
Peter, Bishop of Alexandria:	Anastasius the Librarian
Procopius:	A.J. Mason
Alphaeus and Zacchaeus:	A.J. Mason
Habib:	The Coptic Church
Shamuna, Guria, and Habib:	Simeon Mataphrastes
Guria and Shamuna::	A homily by Mar Jacob
George, Soldier and Martyr:	James Kiefer
Pancras:	Alban Butler
Agnes of Rome:	James Kiefer
	Alban Butler
Vincent of Saragossa:	James Kiefer
Catherine of Alexandria:	James Kiefer
The Forty Martyrs of Sebaste:	James Kiefer
Agapius and Thecla:	A.J. Mason
Apphian:	A.J. Mason
Ennatha and Valentina:	A.J. Mason
Agape, Chione and Irene:	A.J. Mason
Irenaeus:	A.J. Mason
Quirinus:	A.J. Mason
Maxima and Donatilla:	A.J. Mason
Theodota:	Alban Butler
Felix:	A.J. Mason
Bademus:	Alban Butler
Sabas:	Alban Butler
Alban:	Editor
	Bede
	J.C. Robertson
The Edict of Milan:	Lactantius
Rise of the Worship of Martyrs and Relics:	Philip Scaff
Persecution under Julian the Apostate:	Philip Scaff
Martyrs at Merum in Phrygia, under Julian:	Socrates Scholasticus
Usthazanes:	Sozomen's Memoir
Symeon:	Sozomen's Memoir

1. Introduction

Table of persecutions under the Roman Empire (3)

EMPEROR	DATES	CONDITIONS	FAMOUS MARTYRS
Diocletian alone	284-6		
Diocletian and Maximian	286-92		
Diocletian and Maximian Augusti	292-304	Diocletian's first edict (303):	
Constantius and Galerius Caesars		churches destroyed, scriptures burnt, Christians to be stripped of honours. Many Christians killed. Second edict: Christian leaders imprisoned. Third edict: Imprisoned clergy cruelly tortured if they refused to sacrifice. Fourth edict: 304. War of extermination: all Christians to be killed if they refused to sacrifice.	
Constantius and Gelerius Augusti	305	Persecution in Europe, Asia and Egypt under Galerius and Máximinus	
Severus and Maximinus Daia Caesars			
Galerius, Maximinus Daia	307-313		Marcellus
Constantine (already Caesar, 306)			Cassian
Licinius		Toleration granted to Christians	Christian soldiers
Maximian			Procopius
Maxentius			
In 313 Constantine, through the edict of Milan, gave complete freedom to Christians.		Persecution soon stopped.	

The Diocletian Persecution, A.D. 303-311

The forty years' repose was followed by the last and most violent persecution, a struggle for life and death. "The accession of the Emperor Diocletian is the era from which the Coptic Churches of Egypt and Abyssinia still date, under the name of the 'Era of Martyrs.' All former persecutions of the faith were forgotten in the horror with which men looked back upon the last and greatest: the tenth wave (as men delighted to count it) of that great storm obliterated all the traces that had been left by others. The fiendish cruelty of Nero, the jealous fears of Domitian, the unimpassioned dislike of Marcus, the sweeping purpose of Decius, the clever devices of Valerian, fell into obscurity when compared with the concentrated terrors of that final grapple, which resulted in the destruction of the old Roman Empire and the establishment of the Cross as the symbol of the world's hope." Diocletian (284-305) was one of the most judicious and able emperors who, in a trying period, preserved the sinking state from dissolution. He was the son of a slave or of obscure parentage, and worked himself up to supreme power. He converted the Roman republican empire into an Oriental despotism, and prepared the way for Constantine and Constantinople. He associated with himself three subordinate co-regents, Maximian (who committed suicide, 310), Galerius (d. 311), and Constantius Chlorus (d. 306, the father of Constantine the Great), and divided with them the government of the immense empire; thereby quadrupling the personality of the sovereign, and imparting vigor to provincial administration, but also sowing the seed of discord and civil war. Gibbon calls him a second Augustus, the founder of a new empire, rather than the restorer of the old. He also compares him to Charles V, whom he somewhat resembled in his talents, temporary success and ultimate failure, and voluntary retirement from the cares of government. In the first twenty years of his reign Diocletian respected the toleration edict of Gallienus. His own wife Prisca his daughter Valeria, and most of his eunuchs and court officers, besides many of the most prominent public functionaries, were Christians, or at least favorable to the Christian religion. He himself was a superstitious heathen and an oriental despot. Like Aurelian and Domitian before him, he claimed divine honors, as the vicar of Jupiter Capitolinus. He was called, as the Lord and Master of the world, *Sacratissimus Dominus Noster*; he guarded his Sacred Majesty with many circles of soldiers and eunuchs, and allowed no one to approach him except on bended knees, and with the forehead touching the ground, while he was seated on the throne in rich vestments from the far East. "Ostentation," says Gibbon, "was the first principle of the new system instituted by Diocletian."

As a practical statesman, he must have seen that his work of the political restoration and consolidation of the empire would lack a firm and permanent basis without the restoration of the old religion of the state. Although he long postponed the religious question, he had to meet it at last. It could not be expected, in the nature of the case, that paganism should surrender to its dangerous rival without a last desperate effort to save itself. But the chief instigator of the renewal of hostility, according to the account of Lactantius, was Diocletian's co-regent and son-in-law, Galerius, a cruel and fanatical heathen. He prevailed at last on Diocletian in his old age to authorize the persecution which gave to his glorious reign a disgraceful end. In 303 Diocletian issued in rapid succession three edicts, each more severe than its predecessor. Maximian issued the fourth, the worst of all, April 30, 304. Christian churches were to be destroyed; all copies of the Bible were to be burned; all Christians were to be deprived of public office and civil rights; and at last all, without exception, were to sacrifice to the gods upon pain of death. Pretext for this severity was afforded by the occurrence of fire twice in the palace of Nicomedia in Bithynia, where Diocletian resided . It was strengthened by the tearing down of the first edict by an imprudent Christian (celebrated in the Greek church under the name of John), who vented in that way his abhorrence of such "godless and tyrannical rulers," and was gradually roasted to death with every species of cruelty. But the conjecture that the edicts were occasioned by a conspiracy of the Christians who, feeling their rising power, were for putting the government at once into Christian hands, by a stroke of state, is without any foundation in history. It is inconsistent with the political passivity of the church during the first three centuries, which furnish no example of rebellion and revolution. At best such a conspiracy could only have been the work of a few fanatics; and they, like the one who tore down the first edict, would have gloried in the deed and sought the crown of martyrdom.

The persecution began on the twenty-third day of February, 303, the feast of the

Terminalia (as if to make an end of the Christian sect), with the destruction of the magnificent church in Nicomedia, and soon spread over the whole Roman empire, except Gaul, Britain, and Spain, where the co-regent Constantius Chlorus, and especially his son, Constantine the Great (from 306), were disposed, as far as possible, to spare the Christians. But even here the churches were destroyed, and many martyrs of Spain (St. Vincentius, Eulalia, and others celebrated by Prudentins), and of Britain (St. Alban) are assigned by later tradition to this age.

The persecution raged longest and most fiercely in the East under the rule of Galerius and his barbarous nephew Maximin Daza, who was intrusted by Diocletian before his retirement with the dignity of Caesar and the extreme command of Egypt and Syria. He issued in autumn, 308, a fifth edict of persecution, which commanded that all males with their wives and servants, and even their children, should sacrifice and actually taste the accursed offerings, and that all provisions in the markets should be sprinkled with sacrificial wine. This monstrous law introduced a reign of terror for two years, and left the Christians no alternative but apostasy or starvation. All the pains, which iron and steel, fire and sword, rack and cross, wild beasts and beastly men could inflict, were employed to gain the useless end. Eusebius was a witness of this persecution in Caesura, Tyre, and Egypt, and saw, with his own eyes, as he tells us, the houses of prayer razed to the ground, the Holy Scriptures committed to the flames on the market places, the pastors hunted, tortured, and torn to pieces in the amphitheatre. Even the wild beasts, he says, not without rhetorical exaggeration, at last refused to attack the Christians, as if they had assumed the part of men in place of the heathen Romans; the bloody swords became dull and shattered; the executioners grew weary, and had to relieve each other; but the Christians sang hymns of praise and thanksgiving in honor of Almighty God, even to their latest breath. He describes the heroic sufferings and death of several martyrs, including his friend, "the holy and blessed Pamphilus," who after two years of imprisonment won the crown of life (309), with eleven others—a typical company that seemed to him to be "a perfect representation of the church." Eusebius himself was imprisoned, but released. The charge of having escaped martyrdom by offering sacrifice is without foundation. In this, as in former persecutions, the number of apostates who preferred the earthly life to the heavenly, was very great.

To these was now added also the new class of the traditores, who delivered the holy Scriptures to the heathen authorities, to be burned. But as the persecution raged, the zeal and fidelity of the Christians increased, and martyrdom spread as by contagion. Even boys and girls showed amazing firmness. In many the heroism of faith degenerated to a fanatical courting of death; confessors were almost worshipped, while yet alive; and the hatred towards apostates distracted many congregations, and produced the Meletian and Donatist schisms. The number of martyrs cannot be estimated with any degree of certainty. The seven episcopal and the ninety-two Palestinian martyrs of Eusebius are only a select list bearing a similar relation to the whole number of victims as the military lists its of distinguished fallen officers to the large mass of common soldiers, and form therefore no fair basis for the calculation of Gibbon, who would reduce the whole number to less than two thousand. During the eight years of this persecution the number of victims, without including the many confessors who were barbarously mutilated and condemned to a lingering death in the prisons and mines, must have been much larger. But there is no truth in the tradition (which figures in older church histories) that the tyrants erected trophies in Spain and elsewhere with such inscriptions as announce the suppression of the Christian sect. The martyrologies date from this period several legends, the germs of which, however, cannot now be clearly sifted from the additions of later poesy. The story of the destruction of the legio Thebaica is probably an exaggeration of the martyrdom of St.

Mauritius, who was executed in Syria, as tribunus militum, with seventy soldiers, at the order of Maximin.

The martyrdom of Barlaam, a plain, rustic Christian of remarkable constancy, and of Gordius, a centurion (who, however, was tortured and executed a few years later under Licinius, 314) has been eulogized by St. Basil. A maiden of thirteen years, St. Agnes, whose memory the Latin church has celebrated ever since the fourth century, was, according to tradition, brought in chains before the judgment- seat in Rome; was publicly exposed, and upon her steadfast confession put to the sword; but afterwards appeared to her grieving parents at her grave with a white lamb and a host of shining virgins from heaven, and said: "Mourn me no longer as dead, for ye see that I live. Rejoice with me, that I am forever united in heaven with the Saviour, whom on earth I loved with all my heart." Hence the lamb in the paintings of this saint; and hence the consecration of lambs in her church at Rome at her festival (Jan. 21), from whose wool the pallium of the archbishop is made. Agricola and Vitalis at Bologna, Gervasius and Protasius at Milan, whose bones were discovered in the time of Ambrose Janurius, bishop of Benevent, who became the patron saint of Naples, and astonishes the faithful by the annual miracle of the liquefaction of his blood, and the British St. Alban, who delivered himself to the authorities in the place of the priest he had concealed in his house, and converted his executioner, are said to have attained martyrdom under Diocletian.

Philip Scaff, History of the Christian Church, chapter 24

The Tenth Persecution, Under Diocletian, A.D. 303

Under the Roman emperors, commonly called the Era of the Martyrs, was occasioned partly by the increasing number and luxury of the Christians, and the hatred of Galerius, the adopted son of Diocletian, who, being stimulated by his mother, a bigoted pagan, never ceased persuading the emperor to enter upon the persecution, until he had accomplished his purpose.

The fatal day fixed upon to commence the bloody work, was the twenty-third of February, A.D. 303, that being the day in which the Terminalia were celebrated, and on which, as the cruel pagans boasted, they hoped to put a termination to Christianity. On the appointed day, the persecution began in Nicomedia, on the morning of which the prefect of that city repaired, with a great number of officers and assistants, to the church of the Christians, where, having forced open the doors, they seized upon all the sacred books, and committed them to the flames.

The whole of this transaction was in the presence of Diocletian and Galerius, who, not contented with burning the books, had the church levelled with the ground. This was followed by a severe edict, commanding the destruction of all other Christian churches and books; and an order soon succeeded, to render Christians of all denomination outlaws.

The publication of this edict occasioned an immediate martyrdom, for a bold Christian not only tore it down from the place to which it was affixed, but execrated the name of the emperor for his injustice. A provocation like this was sufficient to call down pagan vengeance upon his head; he was accordingly seized, severely tortured, and then burned alive.

All the Christians were apprehended and imprisoned; and Galerius privately ordered the imperial palace to be set on fire, that the Christians might be charged as the incendiaries, and a plausible pretence given for carrying on the persecution with the greater severities. A general sacrifice was commenced, which occasioned various martyrdoms. No distinction was made of age or sex; the name of Christian was so obnoxious to the pagans that all indiscriminately fell sacrifices to their opinions. Many houses were set on fire, and whole Christian families perished in the flames; and others had stones fastened about their necks, and being tied together were driven into the sea. The persecution became general in all the Roman provinces, but more particularly in the east; and as it lasted ten years, it is impossible to ascertain the numbers martyred, or to enumerate the various modes of martyrdom.

Racks, scourges, swords, daggers, crosses, poison, and famine, were made use of in various parts to dispatch the Christians; and invention was exhausted to devise tortures against such as had no crime, but thinking differently from the votaries of superstition.

A city of Phrygia, consisting entirely of Christians, was burnt, and all the inhabitants perished in the flames.

Tired with slaughter, at length, several governors of provinces represented to the imperial court, the impropriety of such conduct. Hence many were respited from execution, but, though they were not put to death, as much as possible was done to render their lives miserable, many of them having their ears cut off, their noses slit, their right eyes put out, their limbs rendered useless by dreadful dislocations, and their flesh seared in conspicuous places with red-hot irons.

It is necessary now to particularize the most conspicuous persons who laid down their lives in martyrdom in this bloody persecution.

Sebastian, a celebrated martyr, was born at Narbonne, in Gaul, instructed in the principles of Christianity at Milan, and afterward became an officer of the emperor's guard at Rome. He remained a true Christian in the midst of idolatry; unallured by the splendors of a court, untouched by evil examples, and uncontaminated by the hopes of preferment. Refusing to be a pagan, the emperor ordered him to be taken to a field near the city, termed the Campus Martius, and there to be shot to death with arrows; which sentence was executed accordingly. Some pious Christians coming to the place of execution, in order to give his body burial, perceived signs of life in him, and immediately moving him to a place of security, they, in a short time effected his recovery, and prepared him for a second martyrdom; for, as soon as he was able to go out, he placed himself intentionally in the emperor's way as he was going to the temple, and reprehended him for his various cruelties and unreasonable prejudices against Christianity. As soon as Diocletian had overcome his surprise, he ordered Sebastian to be seized, and carried to a place near the palace, and beaten to death; and, that the Christians should not either use means again to recover or bury his body, he ordered that it should be thrown into the common sewer. Nevertheless, a Christian lady named Lucina, found means to remove it from the sewer, and bury it in the catacombs, or repositories of the dead.

The Christians, about this time, upon mature consideration, thought it unlawful to bear arms under a heathen emperor. Maximilian, the son of Fabius Victor, was the first beheaded under this regulation.

Vitus, a Sicilian of considerable family, was brought up a Christian; when his virtues increased with his years, his constancy supported him under all afflictions, and his faith was superior to the most dangerous perils. His father, Hylas, who was a pagan, finding that he had been instructed in the principles of Christianity by the nurse who brought him up, used all his endeavors to bring him back to paganism, and at length sacrificed his son to the idols, June 14, A.D. 303.

Victor was a Christian of a good family at Marseilles, in France; he spent a great part of the night in visiting the afflicted, and confirming the weak; which pious work he could not, consistently with his own safety, perform in the daytime; and his fortune he spent in relieving the distresses of poor Christians. He was at length, however, seized by the emperor Maximian's decree, who ordered him to be bound, and dragged through the streets. During the execution of this order, he was treated with all manner of cruelties and indignities by the enraged populace. Remaining still inflexible, his courage was deemed obstinacy. Being by order stretched upon the rack, he turned his eyes toward heaven, and prayed to God to endue him with patience, after which he underwent the tortures with most admirable fortitude. After the executioners were tired with inflicting torments on him, he was conveyed to a dungeon. In his confinement, he converted his jailers, named Alexander, Felician, and Longinus. This affair coming to the ears of the emperor, he ordered them immediately to be put to death, and the jailers were accordingly beheaded. Victor was then again put to the rack, unmercifully beaten with batons, and again sent to prison. Being a third time examined concerning his religion, he persevered in his principles; a small altar was then brought, and he was commanded to offer incense upon it immediately. Fired with indignation at the request, he boldly stepped forward, and with his foot overthrew both altar and idol. This so enraged the emperor Maximian, who was present, that he ordered the foot with which he had kicked the altar to be immediately cut off; and Victor was thrown into a mill, and crushed to pieces with the stones, A.D. 303.

Maximus, governor of Cilicia, being at Tarsus, three Christians were brought before him; their names were Tarachus, an aged man, Probus, and Andronicus. After repeated tortures and exhortations to recant, they, at length, were ordered for execution.

Being brought to the amphitheater, several beasts were let loose upon them; but none of the animals, though hungry, would touch them. The keeper then brought out a large bear, that had that very day destroyed three men; but this voracious creature and a fierce lioness both refused to touch the prisoners. Finding the design of destroying them by the means of wild beasts ineffectual, Maximus ordered them to be slain by the sword, on October 11, A.D. 303.

Romanus, a native of Palestine, was deacon of the church of Caesarea at the time of the commencement of Diocletian's persecution. Being condemned for his faith at Antioch, he was scourged, put to the rack, his body torn with hooks, his flesh cut with knives, his face scarified, his teeth beaten from their sockets, and his hair plucked up by the roots. Soon after he was ordered to be strangled, November 17, A.D. 303.

Susanna, the niece of Caius, bishop of Rome, was pressed by the emperor Diocletian to marry a noble pagan, who was nearly related to him. Refusing the honor intended her, she was beheaded by the emperor's order.

Dorotheus, the high chamberlain of the household to Diocletian, was a Christian, and took great pains to make converts. In his religious labors, he was joined by Gorgonius, another Christian, and one belonging to the palace. They were first tortured and then strangled.

Peter, a eunuch belonging to the emperor, was a Christian of singular modesty and humility. He was laid on a gridiron, and broiled over a slow fire until he expired.

Cyprian, known by the title of the magician, to distinguish him from Cyprian, bishop of Carthage, was a native of Natioch. He received a liberal education in his youth, and particularly applied himself to astrology; after which he traveled for improvement through Greece, Egypt, India, etc. In the course of time he became acquainted with Justina, a young lady of Antioch, whose birth, beauty, and accomplishments, rendered her the admiration of all who knew her. A pagan gentleman applied to Cyprian, to promote his suit with the beautiful Justina; this he undertook, but soon himself became converted, burnt his books of astrology and magic, received baptism, and felt animated with a powerful spirit of grace. The conversion of Cyprian had a great effect on the pagan gentleman who paid his addresses to Justina, and he in a short time embraced Christianity. During the persecutions of Diocletian, Cyprian and Justina were seized upon as Christians, the former was torn with pincers, and the latter chastised; and, after suffering other torments, both were beheaded.

Eulalia, a Spanish lady of a Christian family, was remarkable in her youth for sweetness of temper, and solidity of understanding seldom found in the capriciousness of juvenile years. Being apprehended as a Christian, the magistrate attempted by the mildest means, to bring her over to paganism, but she ridiculed the pagan deities with such asperity, that the judge, incensed at her behavior, ordered her to be tortured. Her sides were accordingly torn by hooks, and her breasts burnt in the most shocking manner, until she expired by the violence of the flames, December, A.D. 303.

In the year 304, when the persecution reached Spain, Dacian, the governor of Terragona, ordered Valerius the bishop, and Vincent the deacon, to be seized, loaded with irons, and imprisoned. The prisoners being firm in their resolution, Valerius was banished, and Vincent was racked, his limbs dislocated, his flesh torn with hooks, and he was laid on a gridiron, which had not only a fire placed under it, but spikes at the top, which ran into his flesh. These torments neither destroying him, nor changing his resolutions, he was remanded to prison, and confined in a small, loathsome, dark dungeon, strewed with sharp flints, and pieces of broken glass, where he died, January 22, 304. His body was thrown into the river.

The persecution of Diocletian began particularly to rage in A.D. 304, when many Christians were put to cruel tortures and the most painful and ignominious deaths; the most eminent and particular of whom we shall enumerate.

Saturninus, a priest of Albitina, a town of Africa, after being tortured, was remanded to prison, and there starved to death. His four children, after being variously tormented, shared the same fate with their father.

Dativas, a noble Roman senator; Thelico, a pious Christian; Victoria, a young lady of considerable family and fortune, with some others of less consideration, all auditors of Saturninus, were tortured in a similar manner, and perished by the same means.

Agrape, Chionia, and Irene, three sisters, were seized upon at Thessalonica, when Diocletian's persecution reached Greece. They were burnt, and received the crown of martyrdom in the flames, March 25, A.D. 304. The governor, finding that he could make no impression on Irene, ordered her to be exposed naked in the streets, which shameful order having been executed, a fire was kindled near the city wall, amidst whose flames her spirit ascended beyond the reach of man's cruelty.

Agatho, a man of a pious turn of mind, with Cassice, Philippa, and Eutychia, were martyred about the same time; but the particulars have not been transmitted to us.

Marcellinus, bishop of Rome, who succeeded Caius in that see, having strongly opposed paying divine honors to Diocletian, suffered martyrdom, by a variety of tortures, in the year 324, comforting his soul until he expired with the prospect of these glorious rewards it would receive by the tortures suffered in the body.

Victorius, Carpophorus, Severus, and Severianus, were brothers, and all four employed in places of great trust and honor in the city of Rome. Having exclaimed against the worship of idols, they were apprehended, and scourged, with the plumbetae, or scourges, to the ends of which were fastened leaden balls. This punishment was exercised with such excess of cruelty that the pious brothers fell martyrs to its severity.

Timothy, a deacon of Mauritania, and Maura his wife, had not been united together by the bands of wedlock above three weeks, when they were separated from each other by the persecution. Timothy, being apprehended, as a Christian, was carried before Arrianus, the governor of Thebais, who, knowing that he had the keeping of the Holy Scriptures, commanded him to deliver them up to be burnt; to which he answered, "Had I children, I would sooner deliver them up to be sacrificed, than part with the Word of God." The governor being much incensed at this reply, ordered his eyes to be put out, with red-hot irons, saying, "The books shall at least be useless to you, for you shall not see to read them." His patience under the operation was so great that the governor grew more exasperated; he, therefore, in order, if possible, to overcome his fortitude, ordered him to be hung up by the feet, with a weight tied about his neck, and a gag in his mouth. In this state, Maura his wife, tenderly urged him for her sake to recant; but, when the gag was taken out of his mouth, instead of consenting to his wife's entreaties, he greatly blamed her mistaken love, and declared his resolution of dying for the faith. The consequence was, that Maura resolved to imitate his courage and fidelity and either to accompany or follow him to glory. The governor, after trying in vain to alter her resolution, ordered her to be tortured, which was executed with great severity. After this, Timothy and Maura were crucified near each other, A.D. 304.

Sabinus, bishop of Assisium, refusing to sacrifice to Jupiter, and pushing the idol from him, had his hand cut off by the order of the governor of Tuscany. While in prison, he converted the governor and his family, all of whom suffered martyrdom for the faith. Soon after their execution, Sabinus himself was scourged to death, December, A.D. 304.

Tired with the farce of state and public business, the emperor Diocletian resigned the imperial diadem, and was succeeded by Constantius and Galerius; the former a prince of the most mild and humane disposition and the latter equally remarkable for his cruelty and tyranny. These divided the empire into two equal governments, Galerius ruling in the east, and Constantius in the west; and the people in the two governments felt the effects of the dispositions of the two emperors; for those in the west were governed in the mildest manner, but such as resided in the east felt all the miseries of oppression and lengthened tortures.

Among the many martyred by the order of Galerius, we shall enumerate the most eminent.

Amphianus was a gentleman of eminence in Lucia, and a scholar of Eusebius; Julitta, a Lycaonian of royal descent, but more celebrated for her virtues than noble blood. While on the rack, her child was killed before her face. Julitta, of Cappadocia, was a lady of distinguished capacity, great virtue, and uncommon courage. To complete the execution, Julitta had boiling pitch poured on her feet, her sides torn with hooks, and received the conclusion of her martyrdom, by being beheaded, April 16, A.D. 305.

Hermolaus, a venerable and pious Christian, or a great age, and an intimate acquaintance of Panteleon's, suffered martyrdom for the faith on the same day, and in the same manner as Panteleon.

Eustratius, secretary to the governor of Armina, was thrown into a fiery furnace for exhorting some Christians who had been apprehended, to persevere in their faith.

Nicander and Marcian, two eminent Roman military officers, were apprehended on account of their faith. As they were both men of great abilities in their profession, the utmost means were used to induce them to renounce Christianity; but these endeavors being found ineffectual, they were beheaded.

In the kingdom of Naples, several martyrdoms took place, in particular, Januaries, bishop of Beneventum; Sosius, deacon of Misene; Proculus, another deacon; Eutyches and Acutius, two laymen; Festus, a deacon; and Desiderius, a reader; all, on account of being Christians, were condemned by the governor of Campania to be devoured by the wild beasts. The savage animals, however, would not touch them, and so they were beheaded.

Quirinus, bishop of Siscia, being carried before Matenius, the governor, was ordered to sacrifice to the pagan deities, agreeably to the edicts of various Roman emperors. The governor, perceiving his constancy, sent him to jail, and ordered him to be heavily ironed; flattering himself, that the hardships of a jail, some occasional tortures and the weight of chains, might overcome his resolution. Being decided in his principles, he was sent to Amantius, the principal governor of Pannonia, now Hungary, who loaded him with chains, and carried him through the principal towns of the Danube, exposing him to ridicule wherever he went. Arriving at length at Sabaria, and finding that Quirinus would not renounce his faith, he ordered him to be cast into a river, with a stone fastened about his neck. This sentence being put into execution, Quirinus floated about for some time, and, exhorting the people in the most pious terms, concluded his admonitions with this prayer: "It is no new thing, O all-powerful Jesus, for Thee to stop the course of rivers, or to cause a man to walk upon the water, as Thou didst Thy servant Peter; the people have already seen the proof of Thy power in me; grant me now to lay down my life for Thy sake, O my

God." On pronouncing the last words he immediately sank, and died, June 4, A.D. 308. His body was afterwards taken up, and buried by some pious Christians.

Pamphilus, a native of Phoenicia, of a considerable family, was a man of such extensive learning that he was called a second Origen. He was received into the body of the clergy at Caesarea, where he established a public library and spent his time in the practice of every Christian virtue. He copied the greatest part of the works of Origen with his own hand, and, assisted by Eusebius, gave a correct copy of the Old Testament, which had suffered greatly by the ignorance or negligence of former transcribers. In the year 307, he was apprehended, and suffered torture and martyrdom.

Marcellus, bishop of Rome, being banished on account of his faith, fell a martyr to the miseries he suffered in exile, January 16, A.D. 310.

Peter, the sixteenth bishop of Alexandria, was martyred November 25, A.D. 311, by order of Maximus Caesar, who reigned in the east.

Agnes, a virgin of only thirteen years of age, was beheaded for being a Christian; as was Serene, the empress of Diocletian. Valentine, a priest, suffered the same fate at Rome; and Erasmus, a bishop, was martyred in Campania.

Soon after this the persecution abated in the middle parts of the empire, as well as in the west; and Providence at length began to manifest vengeance on the persecutors. Maximian endeavored to corrupt his daughter Fausta to murder Constantine her husband; which she discovered, and Constantine forced him to choose his own death, when he preferred the ignominious death of hanging after being an emperor near twenty years.

Constantine was the good and virtuous child of a good and virtuous father, born in Britain. His mother was named Helena, daughter of King Coilus. He was a most bountiful and gracious prince, having a desire to nourish learning and good arts, and did oftentimes use to read, write, and study himself. He had marvellous good success and prosperous achieving of all things he took in hand, which then was (and truly) supposed to proceed of this, for that he was so great a favorer of the Christian faith. Which faith when he had once embraced, he did ever after most devoutly and religiously reverence.

Thus Constantine, sufficiently appointed with strength of men but especially with strength of God, entered his journey coming towards Italy, which was about the last year of the persecution, A.D. 313. Maxentius, understanding of the coming of Constantine, and trusting more to his devilish art of magic than to the good will of his subjects, which he little deserved, durst not show himself out of the city, nor encounter him in the open field, but with privy garrisons laid wait for him by the way in sundry straits, as he should come; with whom Constantine had divers skirmishes, and by the power of the Lord did ever vanquish them and put them to flight.

Notwithstanding, Constantine yet was in no great comfort, but in great care and dread in his mind (approaching now near unto Rome) for the magical charms and sorceries of Maxentius, wherewith he had vanquished before Severus, sent by Galerius against him. Wherefore, being in great doubt and perplexity in himself, and revolving many things in his mind, what help he might have against the operations of his charming, Constantine, in his journey drawing toward the city, and casting up his eyes many times to heaven, in the south part, about the going down of the sun, saw a great brightness in heaven, appearing in the similitude of a cross, giving this inscription, In hoc vince, that is, "In this overcome."

Eusebius Pamphilus doth witness that he had heard the said Constantine himself oftentimes report, and also to swear this to be true and certain, which he did see with his own eyes in heaven, and also his soldiers about him. At the sight whereof when he was greatly astonished, and consulting with his men upon the meaning thereof, behold, in the night season in his sleep, Christ appeared to him with the sign of the same cross which he had seen before, bidding him to make the figuration thereof, and to carry it in his wars before him, and so should we have the victory.

Constantine so established the peace of the Church that for the space of a thousand years we read of no set persecution against the Christians, unto the time of John Wickliffe.

So happy, so glorious was this victory of Constantine, surnamed the Great! For the joy and gladness whereof, the citizens who had sent for him before, with exceeding triumph brought him into the city of Rome, where he was most honorably received, and celebrated the space of seven days together; having, moreover, in the market place, his image set up, holding in his right hand the sign of the cross, with this inscription: "With this wholesome sign, the true token of fortitude, I have rescued and delivered our city from the yoke of the tyrant."

We shall conclude our account of the tenth and last general persecution with the death of St. George, the titular saint and patron of England. St. George was born in Cappadocia, of Christian parents; and giving proofs of his courage, was promoted in the army of the emperor Diocletian. During the persecution, St. George threw up his command, went boldly to the senate house, and avowed his being a Christian, taking occasion at the same time to remonstrate against paganism, and point out the absurdity of worshipping idols. This freedom so greatly provoked the senate that St. George was ordered to be tortured, and by the emperor's orders was dragged through the streets, and beheaded the next day.

The legend of the dragon, which is associated with this martyr, is usually illustrated by representing St. George seated upon a charging horse and transfixing the monster with his spear. This fiery dragon symbolizes the devil, who was vanquished by St. George's steadfast faith in Christ, which remained unshaken in spite of torture and death.

Foxe's Book of Martyrs, Edited by William Byron Forbush

SACRIFICING TO THE GODS

The Emperor Diocletian took counsel and decided to do the things that were unseemly before God, Jesus the Christ; and this is what he did. He made seventy images of gold, and gave unto them the name of "gods", which they certainly were not. To thirty-five of these he gave names of gods, and to thirty-five the name of goddesses; now the number of his other gods and goddesses amount to one hundred and forty.

And the Emperor Diocletian affixed a decree on the outside of the door of the Palace, wherein it was written thus: "I, the Emperor Diocletian command that from Romania, in the north, to Pelak, in the south, every man, whether he be eparch, or general, or count, or bishop, or elder, or deacon, or reader, or servant, of free man, or soldier, or countryman, shall worship my gods. And any one among these who shall say, "I am a Christian," shall be remembered, and he shall died by the sword. And as for you, O all ye noblemen of high senatorial rank, and officers at court, ye shall give effect to this decree in such a way that every man shall worship my gods; for these are the gods who give us victory in battle, and it is they who are the protectors of you yourselves, and they give strength unto you and unto the whole army. Therefore, he that doth not rise up early in the morning, and come at dawn to me so that we may go into the temple together and offer up sacrifices to the gods, he, I say, that doth not come here shall be cast into the sea, so that all men may know that I am king, and that there is no other king besides me."

And it came to pass at dawn, on the first day of the month Parmoute, that the Emperor Diocletian, and all his army, and the eparchs, and the generals went into the temple. And the Emperor took his seat upon the throne, and he caused the herald to make a proclamation, saying, " all ye Roman people, come ye and offer up sacrifice." And the Emperor made an altar of silver and a vessel wherein to burn incense of gold; and he made a great pedestal of gold, and he placed it before the altar so that the statue of Apollo might be set upon it. And the Emperor commanded them to bring frankincense, and the finest flour of wheat, and the purest oil, and rare old wine, and pour them out upon the altar whereon was blazing fire. And afterwards they lighted two hundred candles on golden candlesticks, and four hundred candles on silver candlesticks, and two hundred white horses drew his gods into the temple.

And when they had brought his gods into the temple the Emperor Diocletian stood up on his throne, and he lifted his crown off his head, and set it upon the head of the statue of Apollo, and he bowed down and worshiped it three times, saying, "Thou art the god who livest, O Apollo, the greatest of the gods, who dost give unto us victory in war." And after the Emperor had worshipped Apollo, his three fellow Caesars Romanus, Basileides, and Euaios, came and worshipped Apollo also.

E. A. Wallis Budge (ed.), Coptic Martyrdom etc. in the Dialect of Upper Egypt, British Museum, 1914, pp 121-23

2. The martyrdoms

Leo

Leo, an aged ascetic, lived about this time, at Patara, on the southern coast of Asia Minor.

A friend of Leo's, Paregorius, had been martyred under Decius, and Leo felt deeply grieved that his life had been spared. The proconsul Lollianus visited Patara while the festival to the god Serapis was being held, and the officials used this opportunity to enforce the edict which compelled all the inhabitants to join in the sacrificial acts. Leo saw the people streaming to the festival, and withdrew to pray where Paregorius' relics had been buried, as he often did. He returned home with his mind full of the thoughts of his martyred friend. That night he dreamed that he and Paregorius stood in the middle of a river in full flood. In spite of the current Leo saw that he could easily reach the point Paregorius had reached in front of him.

The next day he set out for his friend's grave, travelling on a road that went past the temple of Fortune. Leo cast caution aside. He went into the temple and broke the lamps and tapers, shouting aloud, "If you think that the gods have any power, let them defend themselves."

Leo was arrested and brought before the governor. He defended his actions by saying that lights and tapers were vain and senseless things, and that what the true God cared about was a contrite heart and humble soul. He exhorted the magistrate to honor God and his only Son, the Savior of the world and creator of souls.

The magistrate replied that this was irrelevant to the charge. He was told that he would be set free, so long as he obeyed the edict, but Leo refused to worship gods that were no gods. Leo was lashed, but Leo's heart was caught up with the Lord, and he seemed to feel nothing. The patient magistrate was willing to forgo an act of sacrifice if Leo would only repeat after him the formula, Great are the gods.

"Great they are," answered the martyr, "to destroy the souls that believe in them." At last the patience of the official ran out. Giving in to the demands of the crowd he ordered the old man to be dragged away by the feet and thrown into the fast flowing stream that passed through the town. Leo burst out with thanksgiving to God who allowed him so soon to be reunited to his friend Paregorius, and prayed for the conversion of his killers. He was dead before they reached the rock from which they hurled him.

A. J. Mason, The Historic Martyrs of the Primitive Church, Longmans, 1905, pp 200-1

Victor the General

Emperor Diocletian went throughout the city, saying, "When ye shall have finished offering up your sacrifices you shall eat and ye shall drink at the door of the temple of Apollo and Artemis, and ye shall glorify them, for it is they who have made the heavens, and the earth, and the sea, and mankind." And the Emperor went back to the Palace at the time of the morning meal, and he called Romanus the general and said to him, "Take this edict, and make the rest of the multitude offer up sacrifice before you leave them." Then Romanus the general took the edict from the hand of the Emperor, and he gave orders to the people, saying, "O Romans, offer ye up sacrifice."

And it came to pass that when all the people had offered up sacrifice, it came to the turn of his son to offer up sacrifice. Now he was a young man of nineteen years of age, and he worshipped God, and held his commandments in fear. Romanus the general said to Apa Victor, his son, "O my son Victor, it is now thy turn to worship the gods of the Emperor, in whose honour the whole city is keeping this feast day, especially Apollo, the greatest of the gods."

And Apa Victor looked into his father's face, saying, "O my father, hath this foolishness obtained such a hold upon thee this day as too make thee forsake the God of heaven for the sake of the glory that is vanity? Remember, therefore that which our Lord Jesus saith in the Gospel, "Whosoever denieth me before men, him will I myself deny before my Father, who is in the heavens, and before his holy angels' [Matthew 10:33]."

While Apa Victor was saying these words all the soldiers of the army were looking at him and at his father. Then Romanus said, "O my son Victor, listen to me, and offer up sacrifice, and let us bring to an end our trouble in this place."

Apa Victor replied, "Get thee away from this sin which leads to death."

And his father was filled with indignation, and he swore an oath, saying, "By Apollo, the greatest of the gods, I will deliver thee over to the Emperor so that he may destroy thee."

Apa Victor said to his father, "Yesterday thou didst worship God and I was thy son; but today I am not thy son, because thou hast made thyself disobedient to God, and thou dost worship idols."

The Devil filled the heart of the father of Apa Victor, and he made him to deliver Apa Victor over into the hands of Diocletian the Emperor. And Emperor Diocletian made the soldiers fasten Apa Victor's hands behind him, and he tied him to the tail of a horse, and shaved the crown of his head, and se suspended a bell from his neck, and four soldiers with palm branches in their hands, beat him, and they dragged him naked round about through all the city, and a herald went before him crying out, "These things are done unto this man because he will not offer up sacrifice to the gods of the Emperor"; and they went through every part of the city with him.

Apa Victor was then exiled and tortured by Duke Sebastianus. Then the Duke made his servants strip Apa Victor naked, and cut his sinews, and fastened his hands behind him, and drove skewers through him. Then the Duke said to him, "Offer up sacrifice."

And Apa Victor said to him, "I will not offer up sacrifice."

Later, the Duke ordered his servants to break the joints in his legs and arms until his bones stuck out through his skin. And Apa Victor said to him, "I give thanks unto Thee, O my Lord Jesus the Christ, because all the joy of the Christ has drawn high unto me."

Then the Duke passed the sentence of death on Apa Victor and ordered his soldiers to cut off his head.

E. A. Wallis Budge (ed.), Coptic Martyrdom etc. in the Dialect of Upper Egypt, British Museum, 1914, pp 256-98

[The above extracts are taken from a translation of British Museum Manuscript Oriental, No 7022. This manuscript comes from a group of Coptic texts of an important series of ten martyrdoms, lives of great ascetics, discourses on asceticism and the history of the angel of death. All of them are dated and written in the dialect of Upper Egypt and were only first published by the British Museum in 1914.]

Pope Petros and the Seal of the Martyrs

The year 284 was the year Diocletian became emperor, and ordered the longest and fiercest persecution the Christians ever experienced. He remained in office until 305. The Copts who lost their lives under Diocletian, were over eight hundred thousands. Then in the wake of his atrocities Diocletian became blind and mentally deranged. Ironically, when his own people deserted him, an old Christian woman nursed him. By so doing, she obeyed our Lord who commands us to love our enemies and bless those who persecute us.

To keep alive the memory of the martyrs who laid down their lives for their faith, the Coptic calendar commenced with the year 284 AD. as its starting point. The Copts follow the same calendar system of the ancient Egyptians. The Coptic year begins on September 11th and has twelve months of thirty days each, and a short month of five days (or six days on leap years.)

During the celebration of the martyrdom of the apostles Peter and Paul, Sophia entered the church. Deeply in her heart, she asked the Lord, before his holy altar, to give her a child. That night she saw in a vision two old men dressed in white telling her that her prayers were answered, and she would be given a son, and he would be called Peter, after the apostle, for he would be a Father of a whole nation.

In due time Peter was born and when he was seven years old, his parents offered him to the patriarch Abba Theonas, just like the Prophet Samuel had been offered. He became like the patriarch's own son, and was consecrated by him first as a reader, then a deacon, then a priest. He grew up to be learned, chaste and upright, and in due time his knowledge, wisdom and understanding earned for him the surname of "Excellent Doctor of the Christian religion".

When the patriarch Abba Theonas was dying, he counseled the church leaders to choose Peter as his successor. Thus Peter, the son of promise, became the father of a nation and the seventeenth successor of St. Mark in the year 285 A.D.

The years in which Abba Petros guided the church were years of excessive stress. Storms raged from outside, in the form of the most terrible persecutions the Christians were subjected too, and storms from inside in the form of the Arian heresy that was equally dangerous to the Christian faith. Like the able captain of a ship, Peter did his utmost to cope with both storms.

The persecutions that were unleashed against the Christians when Abba Petros became patriarch were those ordered by Emperor Diocletian. They lasted over ten years and did not end until the Patriarch himself was martyred. Since he was the last one to lose his life for the faith under Diocletian, he is called to this day in church history "The seal of the Martyrs".

The tortures and executions were carried on day in and day out, year in and year out, without respite. The Copts who lost their lives in this seventh persecution, and suffered under Diocletian, were over hundred thousands. During the fourth year of the persecutions, Abba Petros felt it necessary to pass special regulations concerning the acceptance of repentant apostates back into the communion of the church. So, he drew up fourteen canons which came to be considered as veritable monument of church disciplines. One of the principals set in the canons was that a Christian could be baptized only once. The truth of this principle was confirmed by an incident which took place at the time.

A Christian woman who lived in Antioch had two sons whom she had been unable to baptize because their father had obeyed the Emperor and gave up his faith. Quietly, she boarded a ship to Alexandria and took them with her. While yet off shore, the ship ran into a storm, and she was afraid that her sons might die without having been baptized. So, she wounded herself, and with her blood made the sign of the cross upon the foreheads of her two sons, and baptized them in the name of the Holy Trinity. However, the ship arrived to Alexandria, and she took them to church to have them baptized with other children. When their turn came, and Abba Petros attempted to immerse them in the Holy Water, the water froze. He tried three times, and the same thing happened. The Patriarch in surprise asked the mother, and she told him what she had done on the way. He was astonished and glorified God, "Thus, says the church that there is only one baptism ".

When Diocletian realized that after so many years of persecutions, the Christians of Egypt were not exterminated, but were increasing in number because of the heroism of the martyrs, he became very angry. He ordered that the religious leaders be arrested and tortured, thinking that by doing so, he would break the spirit of the people. Six of the Bishops were arrested but as no amount of torture would induce them to renounce their faith, they were martyred. When Abba Petros heard of their martyrdom, he fell on his knees and offered thanks to God for having kept them steadfast until the end.

Finally, it was decided that it was Abba Petros' turn. The Emperors soldiers laid hands on him and led him to prison. When news of his arrest went around, a large crowd of his devoted people gathered together and went to the prison in one big mass and there clamored for his freedom. Hearing their loud shouting and fearing that their behavior might bring calamity on them, Abba Petros decided to interfere. He told the officers if they granted him the opportunity to speak to them and pacify them, he would immediately give himself up so that there would be no more trouble on his account. The officers complied and led him to where he could address the crowd. In words of compassion and assurance, he spoke to the multitudes and pleaded with them to depart in peace. They obeyed him. After they dispersed, Abba Petros signaled to the officers that they could now take him as he was ready.

On the way to be executed, he was asked if he had any special request to make. He replied that he would like to be allowed to visit the church of St. Mark. His request was granted, and he was permitted a few minutes there. He went in, knelt in prayer and fervently asked God to accept his life as a ransom for his people. Soon after he ended his petition a voice was heard saying "Amen".

The soldiers then led him to be executed. For a while no one dared raise a hand against him, for they beheld his face like that of an angle. Then one of the officers took out twenty five pieces of gold and said, "this I will give to the one who dares behead this sage". The sight of gold made one of the soldiers take courage and strike the Saint's head off.

Having beheaded him, the soldiers went away, leaving him where he fell. Soon after that, the faithful heard the news and came rushing in tears, and carried away the remains of their pleased Patriarch and buried him in St. Mark Church. The martyrdom of Abba Petros inaugurated a period of peace, that is why he is called "The Seal of Martyrs".

St George Coptic Orthodox Church, by kind permission

Victorinus and his six companions: 284

These seven martyrs were citizens of Corinth, and confessed their faith before Tertius the proconsul, in their own country, in 249, in the beginning of Decius' reign. After their torments they went to Egypt, either voluntarily or by compulsion, where at Diospolis, the capital of Thebais, they completed their martyrdom, in 284, in the reign of Numerian, under the governor of Sabinus.

After the governor had tried the constancy of the martyrs by racks, scourges, and various inventions of cruelty, he had Victorinus thrown into a great mortar. The executioners began to pound his feet and legs, saying to him at every stroke, "spare yourself, wretch. It depends on you to escape this death, if you will only renounce your new God."

The prefect became furious at his constancy, so commanded that his head should be beaten to pieces. The sight of this mortar, far from intimidating Victorinus' companions, seemed to inspire them with greater ardour to be treated in the same way. So when the tyrant threatened Victor with the same death, he said to the executioner, "In that is salvation and true felicity prepared for me!" He was immediately cast into it and beaten to death.

Nicephorus, the third martyr, was impatient of delay, and leaped of his own accord into the bloody mortar. The judge was enraged at his boldness, and commanded not one, but many executioners at once to pound him in the same way.

The judge caused Claudian, the fourth

martyr, to be chopped in pieces, and his bleeding joints to be thrown at the feet of those who still lived. He expired, after his feet, hands, arms, legs, and thighs were cut off.

The tyrant, pointing to his mangled limbs and scattered bones, said to the remaining three companions, "You can avoid this punishment. I do not compel you to suffer."

The martyrs answered with one voice: "On the contrary, we rather pray that if you have any other more exquisite torment you would inflict it on us. We are determined never to violate the fidelity which we owe to God, or to deny Jesus Christ our Saviour, for he is our God, from whom we have our being, and to whom alone we aspire."

The tyrant became almost distracted with fury, and commanded Diodorus to be burnt alive, Serapion to be beheaded, and Papias to be drowned.

Alban Butler, The Lives of the Saints, Dublin, 1833, volume 1, p 272

BARLAAM

An obscure country life, which this saint had led from his childhood, in a village near Antioch, in manual labour, which he sanctified by a heroic spirit and practice of Christian piety, prepared him for the crown of martyrdom. He was imprisoned for his zealous confession of the name of Christ and when he was called to the bar, the judge laughed at his rustic speech. In spite of his anger the judge could not but admire exceedingly Barlaam's greatness of soul, his virtue, and his meek constancy, which even gathered strength by his long imprisonment. He was cruelly scourged; but no sigh, no word of complaint was extorted from him. He was then hoisted on the rack, and his bones in many parts dislocated. Amidst these torments, such was the joy which was painted by his countenance, that one would have judged he had been seated at some delicious banquet, or on a throne. The prefect threatened him with death, and caused swords and axes fresh stained with the blood of martyrs to be displayed before him. But Barlaam viewed them without being daunted, and, without words, his meek and composed countenance spoke a language which confounded and disconcerted the persecutors.

He was therefore remanded in prison, and the judge, who was ashamed to see himself vanquished by an illiterate peasant, studied to invent some new artifice or torment, resolving to revenge his gods, whom he thought injured by the saint's constancy. At length he flattered himself that he had found out a method by which the martyr should be compelled, in spite of all his resolution, to offer sacrifice. Barlaam was brought out of prison, and an altar with burning coals upon it being made ready for sacrifice, the martyr's hand was forcibly held over the flames, and the incense with live coals was laid upon it, that, if he shook the coals off his hand, he might be said to offer sacrifice by throwing the incense into the fire upon the altar. The saint, fearing the scandal and very shadow of the crime, though by throwing off the fire to save his hand, he could not be reasonably be esteemed to have meant to sacrifice, kept his hand steady whilst the coals burnt quite through it, and so, with the incense, dropped upon the altar. At such an instance of fortitude the taunts and scoffs of the heathens were converted into admiration. God, soon after this victory, called his soldier to himself, to crown him with glory.

Alban Butler, The Lives of the Saints, Dublin, 1833, volume 2, pp 903-4

COPTIC PERSECUTIONS

During the first two centuries the Church of Alexandria seems to have been freer from official persecution at the hands of the Roman Government than its sister churches of Rome and Antioch. Two causes may have contributed to this: (1) the privileged political and religious status in Egypt of Jews from whom the Government found it difficult to distinguish the Christians; (2) Roman citizenship having never been extended to the Egyptians, except in a few individual cases, the inhabitants of Egypt were free from the obligations of the Roman state religion and consequently there was no reason for persecution. For it is well known that the only cause of the persecutions in the first and second centuries was the incompatibility of the Christian faith with the state religion, which every Roman citizen, the Jews excepted, was obliged to practice, though free otherwise to follow any other form of religion he chose.

Persecution of Severus (200-11)

But when Septimius Severus by a special edict (about A. D. 200) forbade under severe punishment "to make Jews and Christians," the law applied to all subjects of the Roman Empire whether citizens or not; the Egyptian Church with its famous catechetical school of Alexandria, and the fresh impulse given by Demetrius to the diffusion of Christianity throughout the country, seem to have attracted the attention of the emperor, who had just visited Egypt. The school broke up just at that time; and its director, Clement of Alexandria, being obliged to leave Egypt, the youthful Origen attempted to reorganize it. He was soon arrested by the newly-appointed prefect Aquila. Shortly before, under Lætus, his father Leonidas had been the first victim of the persecution. Origen had earnestly encouraged him to stand firm in his confession, and was himself now longing for a martyr's death. His desire was frustrated through the efforts of his mother and friends. But he had the consolation of assisting and encouraging a number of his pupils who died for the faith. Plutarch, who had been his first disciple, Serenus (burnt), Heraclides, a catechumen, and Hero, a neophyte (both beheaded), a woman, Herais, a catechumen (burnt), another, Serenus (beheaded), and Basilides, a soldier attached to the office of Aquila. Potamiæna, a young Christian woman, had been condemned to be sunk by degrees in a cauldron of boiling pitch and was being led to death by Basilides, who on the way protected her against the insults of the mob. In return for his kindness the martyr promised him not to forget him with her Lord when she reached her destination. Soon after Potamiæna's death Basilides was asked by his fellow-soldiers to take a certain oath; on answering that he could not do it, as he was a Christian, at first they thought he was jesting, but seeing he was in earnest they denounced him and he was condemned to be beheaded. While waiting in jail for his sentence to be carried out some Christians (Origen being possibly one of them) visited him and asked him how he happened to be converted; he answered that three days after her death, Potamiæna had appeared to him by night and placed a crown on his head as a pledge that the Lord would soon receive him into his glory. Potamiæna appeared to many other persons at that time, calling them to faith and martyrdom (Euseb., "Hist. Eccl.", VI, iii-v). To these conversions, Origen, an eyewitness, testifies in his "Contra Celsum" (I, 46; P. G., XI, 746). Marcella, mother of Potamiæna, who likewise perished by fire, is the only other martyr whose name is recorded in authentic sources, but we are told of legions of Christians that were sent to Alexandria from all points of Egypt and Thebaid as picked athletes directed to the greatest and most famous arena of the world (Euseb., "Hist. Eccl.", VI, i).

Persecution of Decius (249-51)

Severus died in 211. Authentic sources mention no further official persecution of the Christians of Egypt until the edict of Decius, A. D. 249. This enactment, the exact tenor of which is not known, was intended to test the loyalty of all Roman subjects to the national religion, but it contained also a special clause against the Christians, denouncing the profession of Christianity as incompatible with the demands of the State, proscribing the bishops and other church officials, and probably also forbidding religious meetings. Disobedience to the imperial orders was threatened with severe punishments, the nature of which in each individual case was left to the discretion or zeal of the magistrates (see Gregg, "Decian Persecution", 75 sqq.). During the long period of peace the Egyptian Church had enjoyed since Severus' death it had rapidly increased in numbers and wealth, much, it seems, to the detriment of its power of endurance. And the fierce onslaught of Decius found it quite unprepared for the struggle. Defections were numerous, especially among the rich, in whom, says St.

Dionysus, was verified the saying of Our Lord (Matt., xix, 23) that it is difficult for them to be saved (Euseb., "Hist. Eccl.", VI, xli, 8). Dionysius was then the occupant of the chair of St. Mark. The particulars of the persecution, and of the popular outbreak against the Christians in Alexandria (A. D. 249) are known to us almost exclusively from his letters as preserved by Eusebius. Decius' death in A. D. 251 put an end to the persecution.

Persecution of Valerian (257-61)

The persecution of Valerian was even more severe than that of Decius. Dionysius who is again our chief authority lays the responsibility for it to the emperor's chief counselor, Macrianus "teacher and ruler of the Magi from Egypt" (Euseb., "Hist. eccl.", VII, x, 4). A first edict published in 257 ordered all bishops, priests, and deacons to conform with the state religion under penalty of exile and prohibited the Christians from holding religious assemblies under penalty of death (Healy, "Valerian Persecution", 136). In 258 a second edict was issued sentencing to death bishops, priests, and deacons, and condemning laymen of high rank to degradation, exile, and slavery, or even death in case of obstinacy, according to an established scale of punishments (Healy, ibid., 169 sq.), confiscation of property resulting ipso facto in every case. Dionysius was still in the chair of St. Mark. On receipt of the first edict Æmilianus, then Prefect of Egypt, immediately seized the venerable bishop with several priests and deacons and on his refusal to worship the gods of the empire exiled him to Kephro in Libya. There he was followed by some brethren from Alexandria and others soon joined him from the provinces of Egypt, and Dionysius managed not only to hold the prohibited assemblies but also to convert not a few of the heathens of that region where the word of God had never been preached. Æmilianus was probably ignorant of these facts which even under the provisions of the first edict made the bishop and his companions liable to capital punishment, Desiring however to have all the exiles in one district nearer at hand where he could seize them all without difficulty whenever he wished, he ordered their transfer to Mareotis, a marshy district south-west of Alexandria, "a country", Dionysius says, "destitute of brethren and exposed to the annoyances of the travelers and incursions of robbers', and assigned them to different villages throughout that desolate region. Dionysius and his companions were stationed at Colluthion, near the highway, so they could be seized first. This new arrangement, which had caused no small apprehension to Dionysius, turned out much better than the former one. If intercourse with Egypt was more difficult, it was easier with Alexandria; Dionysius had the consolation of seeing his friends more frequently, those who were nearer to his heart, and he could hold partial meetings with them as was customary in the most remote suburbs of the capital (Euseb., "Hist. eccl.", VII, xi, 1-7). This is unfortunately all we know of Valerian persecution in Egypt. The portion of Dionysius' letter to Domitius and Didymus in which Eusebius refers to the persecution of Valerian (loc. cit., VII, xx) belongs rather to the Decian times. It is to be regretted that Eusebius did not preserve for us in its entirety Dionysius' letter "to Hermammon and the brethren in Egypt, describing at length the wickedness of Decius and his successors and mentioning the peace under Gallienus".

Immediately after Valerian's capture by the Persians (260?) his son Gallienus (who had been associated with him in the empire for several years) published edicts of toleration if not of recognition in favor of the Christians (see McGiffert's note 2 to Eusebius, "Hist. eccl.", VII, xiii). But Egypt having fallen to the lot of Macrianus it is probable that he withheld the edicts or that the terrible civil war which then broke out in Alexandria between the partisans of Gallienus and those of Macrianus delayed their promulgation.

Persecutions of Diocletian (303-5) and Maximinus (305-13)

For reasons on which sources either disagree or are silent (see Duchesne, "Hist. anc. de l"église", II, 10 sq.; McGiffert in "select Lib. of Nicene and Post-Nicene Fathers, N. S.", I, 400), Diocletianus, whose household was full of Christians, suddenly changed his attitude towards Christianity and initiated the longest and bloodiest persecutions against the Church. Lactantius informs us (De mort. persec., IX) that Diocletian acted on the advice of a council of dignitaries in which Galerius played the principal part. It was in A. D. 303, the nineteenth year of his reign, and the third of Peter Alexandrinus as Bishop of Alexandria. Egypt and Syria (as part of the Diocese of Orient) were directly under the rule of Diocletian. This general outbreak had been preceded for three years at least by a more or less disguised persecution in the army. Eusebius says that a certain magister militum Veturius, in the sixteenth year of Diocletian, forced a number of high rank officers to prove their loyalty by the usual test of sacrificing to the gods of the empire, on penalty of losing their honours and privileges. Many "soldiers of Christ's kingdom" cheerfully gave up the seeming glory of this world and a few received death "in exchange for their pious constancy" (Euseb., "Hist. eccl.", VIII, iv; "Chron.", ed. Schöne, II, 186 sq.). On 23 February, 303, the Church of Nicomedia was torn down by order of the emperors. The next day (thus Lact., op. cit., xiii. Euseb. says "in March, on the approach of the Passion"), a first edict was published everywhere ordering the churches to be destroyed, the Holy Scriptures to be burned, and inflicting degradation on those in high rank and slavery on their households. Two other edicts soon followed, one ordering the imprisonment of all church officials, the other commanding them to sacrifice to the gods (Euseb., op. cit., VIII, ii, 4, 5; vi, 8, 10). In 304, while Diocletian was seriously ill, a fourth edict was issued commanding all the people to sacrifice at once in the different cities and offer libations to the idols (Euseb., "Mart. Pal.", III, i). On 1 May, 305, both Diocletian and Maximian Herculius retired officially from the public life and a tetrarchy was organized with Galerius and Constantius as Augusti and Severus and Maximinus Daia as Cæsars; and a new apportionment of the empire was made, Egypt and Syria with the rest of the Diocese of Orient going to Maximinus. Superstitious in the extreme, surrounded by magicians without whom he did not venture to move even a finger, ferocious and dissolute, Maximinus was far more bitter against the Christians than Galenius himself.

To give a fresh impetus to the persecution, he published again (305) in his provinces, in his own name, the fourth edict which had been issued the year before by all the members of the tetrarchy, thus making it clear that no mercy was to be expected from him (Euseb., "Mart. Pal.", IV, viii). In 307, after the death of Constantius, his son Constantine was made second Cæsar and Severus promoted to the rank of Augustus. The following year Severus, defeated by Maxentius, was obliged to take his own life and his place and rank was given by Galerius to Licinius. Maximinus then assumed the title of Augustus against the wish of Galerius who nevertheless had to recognize him and bestowed the same title on Constantine. It was probably on the occasion of this quarrel with Galerius that Maximinus for a short while in the summer of 308 relaxed somewhat his measures against the Christians. "Relief and liberty were granted to those who for Christ's sake were labouring in the mines of the Thebaid" (Mart. Pal., IX, i). But suddenly in the autumn of the same year he issued another edict (so-called fifth edict) ordering the shrines of the idols to be speedily rebuilt and all the people, even infants at the breast, to be compelled to sacrifice and taste of the offerings. At the same time he commanded the things for sale in the markets to be sprinkled with the libations from the sacrifices, the entrance to the public baths to be contaminated similarly (Mart. Pal., IX, ii). And when three years later (April, 311) Galerius, devoured by a terrible disease and already on the point of death, finally softened toward the Christians and asked them to pray to their God for his recovery, Maximinus significantly kept aloof (Hist. eccl., VIII, xvii). His name does not appear with those of Galerius, Constantinus, and Licinius, in the heading of the edict of toleration, which, moreover, was never promulgated in his provinces. However, probably to placate his two colleagues on the occasion of a new apportionment of the power as a result of Galerius' death, he told his chief official, Sabinus, to instruct the governors and other magistrates to relax the persecution. His orders received wider interpretation than he expected, and while his attention was directed by the division of the Eastern empire between himself and Licinius, the confessors who were awaiting trial in the prisons were released and those who had been condemned to the mines returned home in joy and exultation.

This lull had lasted about six months when Maximinus resumed the persecution, supposedly at the request of the various cities and towns who petitioned him not to allow the Christians to dwell within their walls. But Eusebius declares that in the case of Antioch the petition was Maximinus' own work, and that the other cities had sent their memorials at the solicitation of his officials who had been instructed by himself to that effect. On that occasion he created in each city a high-priest whose office it was to make daily sacrifices to all the (local) gods, and with the aid of the priests of the former order of things, to restrain the Christians from building churches and holding religious meetings, publicly or privately (Eusebius, op. cit., IX, ii, 4; Lactant., op. cit., XXXVI). At the same time everything was done to excite the heathens against the Christians. Forged Acts of Pilate and of Our Lord, full of every kind of blasphemy against Christ, were sent with the emperor's approval to all the provinces under him, with written commands that they should be posted publicly in every place and that the schoolmasters should give them to their scholars instead of their customary lessons to be studied and learned by heart (Euseb., op. cit., IX, v). Members of the hierarchy and others were seized on the most trifling pretext and put to death without mercy. In the case of Peter of Alexandria no cause at all was given. He was arrested quite unexpectedly and beheaded without explanation as if by command of Maximinus (ibid., IX, vi). This was in April, 312, if not somewhat earlier. In the autumn of the same year Constantine defeated Maximinus and soon after conjointly with Licinius published the edict of Milan, a copy of which was sent to Maximinus with an invitation to publish it in his own provinces. He met their wishes half way, publishing instead of the document received an edict of tolerance, but so full of false, contradictory statements and so reticent on the points at issue, that the Christians did not venture to hold meetings or even appear in public (Euseb., "Hist. eccl.", IX, ix, 14-24). It was not, however, until the following year, after his defeat at Adrianople (30 April, 313) at the hands of Licinius, with whom he was contending for the sole supremacy over the Eastern empire, that he finally made up his mind to enact a counterpart of the edict of Milan, and grant full and unconditional liberty to the Christians. He died soon after, consumed by "an invisible and God-sent fire" (Hist. eccl., IX, x, 14). Lactantius says he took poison at Tarsus, where he had fled (op. cit., 49).

Effects of the persecutions

On the effects of the persecutions in Egypt, Alexandria, and the Thebaid in a general way we are well informed by ocular witnesses, such as Phileas, Bishop of Thmuis, in a letter to his flock which has been preserved by Eusebius (Hist. eccl., VIII, x), who visited Egypt towards the end of the persecution, and seems to have been imprisoned there for the faith. Eusebius speaks of large numbers of men in groups from ten to one hundred, with young children and women put to death in one day, and this not for a few days or a short time, but for a long series of years. He describes the wonderful ardour of the faithful, rushing one after another to the judgment seat and confessing themselves Christians, the joy with which they received their sentence, the truly Divine energy with which they endured for hours and days the most excruciating tortures; scraping, racking, scourging, quartering, crucifixion head downwards, not only without complaining, but singing and offering up hymns and thanksgiving to God till their very last breath. Those who did not die in the midst of their tortures were killed by the sword, fire, or drowning (Euseb., "Hist. eccl.", VIII, viii, 9). Frequently they were thrown again into prison to die of exhaustion or hunger. If perchance they recovered under the care of friends and were offered their freedom on condition of sacrificing, they cheerfully chose again to face the judge and his executioners (Letter of Phileas, ibid., 10). Not all, however, received their crowns at the end of a few hours or days. Many were condemned to hard labour in the quarries of Porphyry in Assuan, or, especially after A. D. 307, in the still more dreaded copper mines of Phûnon (near Petra, see Revue Biblique, 1898, p. 112), or in those of Cilicia. Lest they should escape, they were previously deprived of the use of their left legs by having the sinews cut or burnt at the knee or at the ankle, and again their right eyes were blinded with the sword and then destroyed to the very roots by fire. In one year (308) we read of 97, and again of as many as 130, Egyptian confessors thus doomed to a fate far more cruel than death, because of the remoteness of the crown they were impatient to obtain and the privation of the encouraging presence and exhortations of sympathetic bystanders (Mart. Pal., VIII, i, 13).

God in at least two instances related by Eusebius inspired the tyrant to shorten the conflict of those valiant athletes. At his command forty of them, among whom were many Egyptians, were beheaded in one day at Zoara near Phûnon. With them was Silvanus of Gaza, a bishop who had been ministering to their souls. On the same occasion, Bishops Peleus and Nilus, a presbyter, and a layman, Patermuthius, all from Egypt, were condemned to death by fire probably at Phûnon, A. D. 309 (Euseb., "Mart. Pal.", XIII, Cureton, pp. 46-8). Besides Peter of Alexandria, but a few of the many who suffered death illustriously at Alexandria and throughout Egypt and the Thebaid are recorded by Eusebius, viz., Faustus, Dius, and Ammonius, his companions, all three presbyters of the Church of Alexandria, also Phileas, Bishop of Thmuis and three other Egyptian bishops; Hesychius (perhaps the author of the so-called Hesychian recension, see Hastings, "Dict. of the Bible", IV, 445), Pachymius, and Theodorus (Hist. eccl., VIII, xiii, 7); finally Phioromus, "who held a high office under the imperial government at Alexandria and who administered justice every day attended by a military guard corresponding to his rank and Roman dignity" (ibid., ix, 7). The dates of their confessions, with the exception of that of St. Peter (see above) are not certain.

Egyptian martyrs in Syria and Palestine

Among these, Eusebius mentions Pæsis and Alexander, beheaded at Cæsarea in 304, with six other young confessors. Hearing that on the occasion of a festival the public combat of the Christians who had lately been condemned to the wild beasts would take place, they presented themselves, hands bound, to the governor and declared themselves Christians in the hope of being sent to the arena. But they were thrown in prison, tortured, and finally were beheaded (Mart. Pal., IV, iii). Elsewhere we read of five young Egyptians who were cast before different kinds of ferocious beasts, including bulls goaded to madness with red-hot irons, but none of which would attack the athletes of Christ who, though unbound, stood motionless in the arena, their arms stretched out in the form of a cross, earnestly engaged in prayer. Finally they were also beheaded and cast into the sea (Hist. eccl., VIII, vii). We must also mention with Eusebius a party of Egyptians who had been sent to minister to the confessors in Cilicia. They were seized as they were entering Ascalon. Most of them received the same sentence as those whom they had gone to help, being mutilated in their eyes and feet, and sent to the mines. One, Ares, was condemned to be burnt, and two, Probus (or Primus) and Elias, were beheaded, A. D. 308 (Mart. Pal., X, i). The following year five others who had accompanied the confessors to the mines in Cilicia were returning to their homes when they were arrested as they were passing the gates of Cæsarea, and were put to death after being tortured, A. D. 309 (ibid., vi-xiii).

We close this section with the name of Ædesius, a young Lycian and brother of Apphianus (Mart. Pal., IV). He had been condemned to the mines of Palestine. Having somehow been released, he came to Alexandria and fell in with Hierocles, the governor, while he was trying some Christians. Unable to contain his indignation at the sight of the outrages inflicted by this magistrate on the modesty of some pure women, he went forward and with words and deeds overwhelmed him with shame and disgrace. Forthwith he was committed to the executioners, tortured and cast into the sea (Mart. Pal., V, ii-iii). This glorious page of the history of the Church of Egypt is not of course quite free from some dark spots. Many were overcome by the tortures at various stages of their confessions and apostatized more or less explicitly.

Persecution of Diocletian in the acts of martyrs of the Coptic church

The Acts of Martyrs of Egypt in their present form have been, with few exceptions, written in Coptic, and were currently read in the churches and monasteries of Egypt at least from the ninth to the eleventh century. Later they were, like the rest of the Coptic literature, translated into Arabic and then into Ethiopic for the use of the Abyssinian Church.

Bringing together the data furnished by the "Acts of Claudius' (P., 175, and A., 3), and Theodore Stratelates (B-H, 157), we can easily reconstruct the primitive Coptic version of the beginning of the persecution as follows: In the nineteenth year of Diocletian, as the Christians were preparing to celebrate the Passion, an edict was issued everywhere, ordering their churches to be destroyed, their Holy Scriptures burnt, and their slaves liberated, while other edicts were promulgated demanding the imprisonment and punishment of the ministers of the Christian Church unless they sacrificed to the gods. This is unmistakably a translation of Eusebius, "Hist. eccl.", VIII, ii, 4-5, and although it shows three omissions, viz., the indication of the month; the mention that this was the first edict, and the third provision of the edict, together with the wrong translation of the fourth clause, however, two of the omissions are supplied by the "Acts of Epime" (B-H, 122; comp. Didymus H., 285), in which we find as heading of the general edict (fourth edict, see p. 707c) these curious words: This was the first edict [apographê] that was against all the saints. He [the king] got up early on the first day of the month of Pharmuthi [27 March-25 April], as he was to pass into a new year and wrote an edict [diatagma] etc. It needs but a superficial comparison between Eusebius, "Hist. eccl.", VIII, ii, 4-5, and "Mart. Pal.", III, i, to see that the italics in the Coptic version above belong to the former passage, while the rest represent a distorted rendering of the latter. The Coptic has even retained to some extent the difference of style in the two places, having apographê for graphê in the first case and diatagma for prostagma in the latter. The other omission, viz., the third clause of the edict, may be lurking in some other text already extant or yet to be discovered. As for having misunderstood the fourth clause of the edict, the Coptic compiler may well be forgiven his error in view of the divergence of opinion still obtaining among scholars as to the right interpretation of this somewhat obscure passage. (See McGiffert on the passage, note 6. In this case, as the reader may have observed, we have departed from McGiffert's translation in supplying "their" before "household", thus making this fourth clause in reality a continuation of the third one.) Here is now another passage in which the text of Eusebius is gradually transformed so as to lose practically everything of its primitive aspect. In the "Acts of Theodore the Eastern" (one of the most legendary compositions in the Coptic Martyrology), we read that Diocletian, having written the edict, handed it to one of the magistrates, Stephen by name, who was standing by him. Stephen took it and tore it up in the presence of the king. Whereupon the latter grasped his sword and cut Stephen in twain, and wrote the edict over again which he sends all over the world (P., 120 sq.). The legend process has begun, to say the least. Yet everybody will recognize in this story a translation, distorted as it may be, of Eusebius, VIII, v (those in Nicomedia). As in Eusebius it is a man in high rank who tears the edict. Only in Eusebius the edict was posted up instead of being handed by the emperor, and the act took place "while two of the emperors were in the same city" not "in the presence of the emperor"; finally, Eusebius does not say with what death the perpetrator of the act met (Lactantius, "De mort. persec.", XIII, says he was burnt). In the "Acts of Epime", the legend takes another step forward. A young soldier of high rank, seeing the edict (posted up) takes off his sword-belt and presents himself to the king. The king asks him who he is. The soldier answers that he is Christodorus, son of Basilides the Stratelates, but that henceforth he shall not serve an impious king, but confess Christ. Then the king takes the sword of one of the soldiers and runs it through the young man (B-H, 122 sq.). There is almost nothing left of Eusebius' account of this story. In fact it looks as if the writer of the "Acts of Epime" had taken it from those of Theodore the Eastern, or some other already distorted version of the Eusebian account, and spoiled it still more in his effort to conceal his act of plagiarism.

We could cite many more passages of the Acts of martyrs of Egypt, thus reproducing more or less exactly, yet unmistakably, the account of the persecution of Diocletian as given by Eusebius. In fact almost every chapter of the eighth book of his "History" is represented there by one or more passages, also some chapters of the seventh and ninth books, and of the book on the Martyrs of Palestine, so that there can be no serious doubt as to the existence of a Coptic history of the persecution of Diocletian based on Eusebius, This may have been a distinct work, or it may have been part of the Coptic church history, in twelve books, of which considerable fragments are known to be extant. From that same Coptic church history were taken, possibly, the several excerpts from Eusebius to be found in the "History of the Patriarchs' of Severus of Ashmunein, and it might be one of the Coptic and Greek works to which this author refers as having been used by him . However, it seems more likely that the Coptic and Greek works spoken of by Severus were lives of the individual patriarchs, the compilers of which may have used either Eusebius' original text or more probably the Coptic work in question.

H.Hyvernat, The Catholic Encyclopedia, Volume 11

The Theban Legion

Diocletian became emperor in 284. His persecution was so terrible that all former persecutions seemed to the Christians as nothing in comparison with it. They called the date of Diocletian's accession "the Era of Martyrs".

A remarkable affair occurred in 286. A legion of soldiers, consisting of 6,666 men, contained none but Christians. This was called the Theban Legion, because the men had been raised in Thebais. They were quartered in the East till the Emperor Maximian ordered them to march to Gaul, to assist him against the rebels of Burgundy. About this time Maximian ordered a general sacrifice, at which the whole army were to assist; and he commanded that they should take oaths of allegiance, and swear, at the same time, to assist him in the extermination of Christianity from Gaul. Terrified at these orders, each individual of the Theban Legion absolutely refused either to sacrifice or take the oaths prescribed. This so enraged Maximian, that he ordered the legion to be decimated-that is, every tenth man to be selected from the rest, and put to the sword. This cruel order having been put into execution, those who remained alive were still inflexible, when a second decimation took place, and every tenth man of those living were again put to the sword.

The second severity made no more impression than the first; the soldiers preserved their fortitude and their principles; but, on the advice of their officers, drew up a remonstrance to the emperor, in which they told him that they were his subjects and his soldiers, but could not, at the same time, forget the Almighty; that they received their pay from him, and their existence from God.

"While your commands," they said, "are not contradictory to those of our common Master, we shall always be ready to obey, as we have been hitherto; but when the orders of our prince and those of the Almighty differ, we must always obey the latter. Our arms are devoted to the emperor's use, and shall be directed against his enemies; but we cannot submit to stain our hands with Christian blood; and how, indeed, could you, O Emperor, be sure of our allegiance and fidelity, should we violate our obligation to our God, in whose service we were solemnly engaged before we entered the army? You command us to search out and to destroy the Christians: it is not necessary to look any farther for people of that denomination; we ourselves are such, and we glory in the name. We saw our companions fall without the least opposition or murmuring, and thought them happy in dying for the sake of Christ. Nothing shall make us lift up our hands against our sovereign; we had rather die wrongfully, and by that means preserve our innocence, than live under a load of guilt: whatever you command we are ready to suffer; we confess ourselves to be Christians, and therefore cannot persecute Christians, nor sacrifice to idols."

Such a declaration, it might be presumed, would have prevailed with the emperor, but it had the opposite effect; for, enraged at their perseverance and unanimity, he commanded that the whole legion should be put to death, which was then executed by the other troops, who cut them to pieces with their swords. This barbarous transaction occurred on the 22nd of September 286.

John Foxe, The Book of Martyrs, revised with notes and an appendix by W. Bramley-Moore, London, 1869, pp 27-28

Saint Maurice and the Theban Legion

A traveler on the highway that leads from Geneva to Rome, will notice a small and a very old Swiss town called "saint Maurice". This town was known in the Roman times as "Aguanum", an important communication center. It was there that a Coptic officer named Maurice and 6600 of his fellow soldiers died for the sake of Christ at the hands of the impious Emperor Maximian (285-305 AD). The story of these martyrs, commonly known as the Theban Legion has been preserved for us by Saint Eucher, the bishop of Lyons, who died in 494 AD. The bishop starts the account of the martyrdom of these valiant soldiers by the following introduction: "Here is the story of the passion of the holly Martyrs who have made Aguanum illustrious with their blood. It is in honour of this heroic martyrdom that we narrate with our pen the order of events as it came to our ears. We often hear, do we not, a particular locality or city is held in high honor because of one single martyr who died there, and quite rightly, because in each case the saint gave his precious soul to the most high God. How much more should this sacred place, Aguanum, be reverenced, where so many thousands of martyrs have been slain, with the sword, for the sake of Christ." Under "Maximian", who was an Emperor of the Roman Commonwealth (Empire) with Diocletian as his colleague, an uprising of the Gauls known as "Bagaude" forced Maximian to march against them with an army of which one unit was the Thebian Legion composed of 6600 men. This unit had been recruited from upper Egypt and consisted entirely of Christians. They were good men and soldiers who, even under arms, did not forget to render to God the things of God, and to Caesar the things of Caesar. After the revolt was quelled, the Emperor Maximian issued an order that the whole army should join offering sacrifices for the Roman gods for the success of their mission. The order included killing Christians (probably as a sacrifice to the Roman gods). Only the Thebian Legion dared to refuse to comply with the orders. The legion withdrew itself, encamped near Aguanum and refused to take part in these rites. Maximian was then resting in a near-by place called Octudurum. When these news came to him , he repeatedly commanded them to obey his rules and orders, and upon their constant and unanimous refusal, he ordered that the legion should be "decimated". Accordingly, every tenth man was put to death. A second "decimation" was ordered unless the men obeyed the order given but their was a great shout through the legion camp: they all declared that they would never allow themselves to carry out such a sacrilegious order. They had always the horror of idolatry, they had been brought up as Christians and were instructed in the One Eternal God and were ready to suffer extreme penalties rather than do any thing contrary to their religion. When Maximian heard these news, he got angrier than ever. Like a savage beast, he ordered the second decimation to be carried out, intending that the remainder should be compelled to do what they hitherto refused. Yet they still maintained their resolve. After the second decimation, Maximian warned the remainder of the Theban legion that it was of no use for them to trust in their number, for if they persisted in their disobedience, not a man among them would be able to escape death. The greatest mainstay of their faith in this crisis was undoubtedly their captain Maurice, with his lieutenants Candid, the first commanding officer, and "Exuperius' the "Compidoctor". He fired the hearts of the soldiers with the fervor by his encouragement. Maurice, calling attention to the example of their faithful fellow soldiers, already martyrs, persuaded them all be ready to die in their turn for the sake of their baptismal vow (The promise one makes at his baptismal to renounce Satan and his abominable service and to worship only God). He reminded them of their comrades who had gone to heaven before them. At his words, a glorious eagerness for martyrdom burned in the hearts of those most blessed men. Fired thus by the lead of their officers, the Theban legion sent to Maximian (who was still enraged) a reply as loyal as it is brave: "Emperor, we are your soldiers but also the soldiers of the true God. We owe you military service and obedience, but we cannot renounce Him who is our Creator and Master, and also yours even though you reject Him. In all things which are not against His law, we most willingly obey you, as we have done hitherto. We readily oppose your enemies whoever they are, but we cannot stain our hands with the blood of innocent people (Christians). We have taken an oath to God before we took one to you, you cannot place any confidence in our second oath if we violate the other (the first). You commanded us to execute Christians, behold we are such. We confess God the Father the creator of all things and His Son Jesus Christ, God. We have seen our comrades slain with the sword, we do not weep for them but rather rejoice at their honor. Neither this, nor any other provocation have tempted us to revolt. Behold, we have arms in our hands, but we do not resist, because we would rather die innocent than live by any sin." When Maximian heard this, he realized that these men were obstinately determined to remain in their Christian faith, and he despaired of being able to turn them from their constancy. He therefore decreed, in a final sentence, that they should be rounded up, and the slaughter completed. The troops sent to execute this order came to the blessed legion and drew their swords upon those holy men who, for love of life, did not refuse to die. They were all slain with the sword. They never resisted in any way. Putting aside their weapons, they offered their necks to the executioners. Neither their numbers nor the strength of arms tempted them to uphold the justice of their cause by force. They kept just one thing in their minds, that they were bearing witness to him who was lead to death without protest, and who, like a lamb, opened not his mouth; but that now, they them selves, sheep in the Lord's flock, were to be massacred as it by ravaging wolves. Thus, by the savage cruelty of this tyrant, that fellowship of the saints was perfected. For they despised things present in hope of things to come. So was slain that truly angelic legion of men who, we trust, now praise the Lord God of Hosts, together with the legions of Angels, in heaven forever.

Not all the members of the legion were at Aguanum at the time of the massacre. Others were posted along the military highway linking Switzerland with Germany and Italy. These were progressively and methodically martyred wherever they were found.

Some of the most celebrated saints who were martyred are:

In Switzerland

The following five Saints were martyred at Aguanum place (also this city is known now as Saint Maurice en Valais), along with the rest of their cohort.. – Saint Maurice – Saint Exuperius – Saint Candid – Saint Innocent – Saint Vitalis

The following two Saints were found at Solothurn along with 66 others: – Saint Ursus – Saint Victor.

In Zurich, the following Saints were martyred: – Saint Felix – Saint Regula – Saint Exuperantius In Zurzach: – Saint Verena of Zurzach.

In Italy

The following saint was martyred in Bergamo: – Saint Alexander

The following saints were martyred in Turino: – Saint Octavious – Saint Adventor – Saint Sotutor

The following saint was martyred in Piacenza: – Saint Antonius of Piancenza

The following saints were martyred in the Cottian Alps: – Saint Constantius – Saint Alverius – Saint Sabastianus – Saint Magius.

The following saints were martyred in Pinerolo: – Saint Maurelius – Saint Georgius – Saint Tiberius

The following saints were martyred in Milano: – Saint Maximius – Saint Cassius – Saint Secundus – Saint Severinus – Saint Licinius

The following saint was martyred in Ventimilia among many others: – Saint Secundus of Ventimilia

In Germany

The following saints were martyred in Terier along with many others of their comrades: – Saint Tyrsus – Saint Palmatius – Saint Bonifatius

The following two saints were martyred in Bonn among many others in their cohort: – Saint Cassius – Saint Florentius

The following saint was martyred along with 318 others in Cologne: – Saint Gereon

The following two saints were martyred along with 330 others in Xanten: – Saint Victor – Saint Mallosius During their martyrdom, numerous miracles happened, which undoubtedly largely contributed to the massive conversion of the inhabitants of these regions to Christianity.

Saint Maurice and the Theban Legion in the Coptic Tradition: The Coptic Church

Tortures of the First Christian Martyrs (6) Burning

For all the heathen bade Christians of either sex, to the scorn of Christ, to be racked on the horse and mangled with scourges, and iron claws, and to be stretched in the stocks to the fourth and fifth hole, yet was not their savage rage thereby exhausted. So they would often pour quicklime or molten lead or boiling oil over their fresh wounds, or else order the same to be torn open with shards of pottery or violently rubbed and scrubbed with hair cloths, and lastly, command the unhappy beings in this evil case to be horribly burned with red-hot plates, torches, and blazing brands.

a. Red-hot plates (fiery plates)

Plates of iron were heated in the fire and applied to the bare flesh of the blessed martyrs and held there until it had miserably burned the same.

b. Torches

Torches were made from pinewood or twisted and waxed or pitched rope. Martyrs were torched as they hung from the horse or suspended by their feet by a pulley.

c. Brazen bull

The brazen bull was the most exceedingly cruel sort of punishment in use among the ancients, into which anyone who was to be tortured was thrown through an opening or door in its side. Then the door was shut, and a fire was lighted about the bull causing the imprisoned person to suffer unexampled agonies, and by their lamentations and cries to imitate the bellowing of a bull. And this brazen contrivance was so cunningly wrought to the likeness of a real bull that movement and voice alone were lacking to persuade folk that it was a living animal.

d. Brazen pot

A brazen pot was a very capacious vessel made of brass, into which condemned people were stripped and thrown, to be boiled or seethed therein.

e. Brazen cauldron

Very large cauldrons, made of bronze, were filled with boiling oil or pitch, molten lead or wax and the victims thrown in, sometimes head first.

f. Burning coals

Martyrs were forced to walk over burning coals and have boiling pitch poured over their head. Also martyrs were roasted on burning coals as they were made to lie down on the burning coals with their hands and feet bound.

g. Martyrs were sent to sea in a ship filled with combustibles and set on fire.

h. Frying pan

The frying pan was a wide open dish or plate, made of metal, which was filled with oil, pitch, resin or sulphur and then placed over a fire. When it began to bubble and boil, then were Christians of either sex thrown into it. Such as had persisted steadfastly and boldly in their profession of Christ's faith, to the end they might be roasted and fried like fishes cast into boiling oil.

i. Gridiron, or, iron bed

The gridiron was framed of three iron bars set lengthwise and a span distant one from the other, one finger thick, two broad, and of a length suitable for its purpose, with seven or more shorter pieces of iron placed crosswise, and likewise separated a span from each other. There were fixed at each corner and in the middle supports, also of iron, raising the framework a little off the ground and serving as legs. The victim was laid on the gridiron, with his legs and arms bound to the four corners, that his tender limbs might be stretched and racked. This done, fire was set underneath.

j. Iron chair

Martyrs were tied hand and foot to iron chairs which were then placed over a burning fire. Sometimes a red-hot helmet, or morion, was also placed on the martyr's head.

k. Iron tunic and iron shoes

Martyrs were dressed in heated iron tunics and forced to put on red-hot shoes, which consumed the flesh from their bones.

l. Martyrs had their eyes burned out with a lighted brand.

m. Martyrs had their hands filled with incense mingled with live coals, which became so painful to hold that they let them go, and so were said to have made sacrifice to an idol.

n. Red-hot helmet, or, morion

Sometimes a red-hot helmet, or morion, was also placed on the martyr's head.

This is illustrated by the history of the martyrdom of St Clement of Ancyra and that of St Justus, a soldier, where it is written: "The day of trial of the holy martyr St Justus, who was of the city of Rome, a soldier under the Tribune Claudius. Returning once from a victory over the Barbarians, he saw a cross appearing before him like a crystal, and heard a voice coming from it. Instructed by it in the mystery of godly piety, he distributed on his arrival in Rome all his goods to the poor, exulting in the faith of Christ.

But when this came to the ears of the Tribune, and Christ's martyr would in no way deny the profession he had made, he sent him to the Governor Magnentius. Questioned by him and found constant in his steadfastness to the Christian faith, he was ordered to be scourged with whips of rawhide, and afterwards to have his head capped with a fiery helmet, and iron balls heated red-hot to be put under his armpits. All these torments the blessed martyr bore unflinchingly, blessing God all the time, until he was finally thrown into a furnace, where he gave up the ghost."

Tortures and Torments of the Christian Martyrs, from the "De SS. Martyrum Cruciatibus" of the Rev Father Gallonio, translated by A. R. Allinson, London and Paris: printed for the subscribers, 1903, pp 115-117

QUINTIN

Quintin was a Roman full of zeal for the kingdom of Jesus Christ, and burning with a holy desire to make his powerful name and the mysteries of his love and mercy known among the infidels. He left his own country, renounced all prospects of preferment, and, attended by Lucian of Beauvais, made his way to Gaul. They preached the faith together in that country till they reached Amiens in Picardy, where they parted. Lucian went to Beauvais where he was later martyred. Quintin stayed at Amiens, endeavouring by his prayers and labours to make that country a portion of the Lord's inheritance. The reward of his charitable labours was the crown of martyrdom, which he received at the beginning of the reign of Maximian Herculeus, who was associated in the empire by Diocletian, in 286.

Maximian made Rictus Varus prefect of the praetorium. Rictus Varus hated the Christian religion. When he heard that it was making progress at Amiens, he resolved to cut him off who was the author of this. When he arrived at Amiens he ordered Quintin to be seized, thrown into prison, and loaded with chains. The next day the holy preacher was brought before the prefect, who assailed his constancy with promises and threats; and, finding him proof against both, ordered him to be whipped unmercifully, and then confined to a close dungeon without the liberty of receiving either comfort or assistance from the faithful. In two other examinations before the same magistrate, his limbs were stretched with pulleys on the rack till his joints were dislocated: his body was torn with rods of iron wife: boiled pitch and oil were poured on his back, and lighted torches applied to his sides. The holy martyr, strengthened by him whose cause he defended, remained superior to all the cruel arts of his barbarous persecutor, and preserved a perfect tranquillity of mind in the midst of such torments as filled the spectators with horror.

When Rictus Varus left Amiens for Augusta Veromandum, he ordered Quintin to be brought along. There he made fresh attacks on Christ's champion. He had Quintin's body pierced with two iron wires from the neck to the thighs, and iron nails to be struck under his nails, and in his flesh in many places, particularly into his skull; and, lastly, his head to be cut off.

Alban Butler, The Lives of the Saints, Dublin, 1833, volume 2, pp 765-66

MAXIMILIAN

In 295, while Dion, the proconsul of Africa, was engaged in levying new troops, a young man, Maximilian, was brought before him to be measured, as he sat in the forum at Theveste. The proconsul asked him his name, but he answered, "Why should you want to know my name? I cannot serve in the army, I am a Christian.

There were many Christians in the army and Dion would not listen to the excuse. "Measure him," he said.

While they were doing this, Maximilian repeated, "I cannot serve. I cannot do what is wrong."

"Measure his height," said the proconsul. He was five feet ten. "Let him be marked," said the proconsul.

Maximilian resisted. "I cannot do it," he said. "I cannot serve."

"You had better serve," said Dion, "or it will be the worse for you."

"I cannot," repeated the young man; "cut off my head if you like, but I cannot be a soldier of the world; I am a soldier of my God."

Maximilian's father was standing by. It was his business to collect the money paid by conscripts who wished to commute their service for a fine. The proconsul suspected that there was some collusion between the father and the son.

"Who has induced you to behave like this?" he asked the young man.

"My own mind," replied Maximilian, "and He who called me."

Dion turned to Victor, the father. "Give your son good advice," he said.

"He knows his own business," replied Victor. "He has his own ideas of what is good for him."

"Serve," repeated Dion to Maximilian, "and take the badge."

"I will not take the badge," he answered, "I already have the sign of Christ my God."

"I will soon despatch you to your Christ," said Dion.

"I wish you would do it at once," the young man retorted, "that is my glory."

Dion said no more, but ordered the officials to hang the lead badge round his neck. But Maximilian resisted having the distasteful emblem put on him.

"I will not take the badge of worldly warfare," he cried, "if you put it on me, I shall tear it off. It is of no use. I am a Christian. It is unlawful for me to wear this bit of lead round my neck after receiving the sign of my Lord Jesus Christ, the Son of the living God, whom you do not know, but who suffered for our salvation, whom God delivered up for our sins. All we Christians are his servants. We follow him as the Prince of life and the Author of salvation."

"Take the badge, I say, and serve," persisted Dion, "or you will come to a bad end."

"I shall not come to an end," replied the enthusiastic man. "My service is for my own Lord. I cannot engage in worldly warfare. I have already told you that I am a Christian."

Dion the proconsul answered, "There are Christian soldiers in the sacred bodyguard of our lords Diocletian and Maximian, Constantius and Maximus: they serve."

But no argument would convince Maximilian. "I suppose," he said, "that they know what is good for them; but I am a Christian, and cannot do what is wrong."

"What wrong do men do who serve in the army?" the proconsul asked.

"I need not tell you," said Maximilian, "you know well enough what they do."

Once more the proconsul urged him to comply: "Come," he said, "serve, or else if you flout service, you are on the way to perish."

"I shall not perish," answered Maximilian, "and if I pass out of the world, my soul lives with Christ my Lord."

The proconsul's patience was exhausted, and he had the following sentence read out, from his tablet: "Maximilian has disloyally refused the oath of service, and is therefore adjudged to be beheaded."

The young man, twenty-one years old, answered, "Thanks be to God."

As they led him to the place of execution, he said to the Christians near him, "Beloved brethren, hasten with all your might and with eager desire that you may be permitted to see the Lord, and that he may bestow on you a crown like mine." His death was instantaneous.

Maximilian's mother, Pompeiana, received the body from the magistrate, and laid it in her own bedroom. Then she carried it to Carthage and buried it close to the grave of the martyr Cyprian. A fortnight later, the mother herself died, and was buried in the same spot. "His father, Victor," adds the simple and touching record, "returned to his home with great joy, giving thanks to God that he had sent such a gift before him to the Lord, and determined to follow after."

A. J. Mason, The Historic Martyrs of the Primitive Church, Longmans, 1905, pp 207-9

Aneyra and the seven martyrs

Of, female victims of Diocletian's persecution, 304. They were unmarried, about 70 years old, and notable for piety and good works. When the persecution was determined upon, Theotecnus, a magician, a philosopher and pervert from Christianity, was dispatched as governor to Galatia to root out Christianity. Among the earliest victims were the seven virgins, Tecusa, Alexandra, Faina, Claudia, Euphrasia, Matrona, Julitta. Theotecnus called upon them to offer incense, and upon their refusal condemned them to the public brothel, from which they escaped scatheless on account of their age, and by the ingenuity of Tecusa their leader. He then ordered them to officiate as priestesses of Diana and Minerva in washing. their statues according to the annual custom of Ancyra. They were accordingly carried naked through the streets to a neighboring lake, where garlands and white garments were offered them in which to fulfil his commands. Upon their refusal Theotecnus ordered them to be drowned in the lake, with heavy stones tied round their necks lest their bodies should be recovered and buried by their fellow Christians. Many legends have gathered round the story.

Wace, Dictionary of Christian Biography

History of the Arians
Chapter 7

47. Persecution at Alexandria

After he had accomplished all that he desired against the Churches in Italy, and the other parts; after he had banished some, and violently oppressed others, and filled every place with fear, he at last turned his fury, as it had been some pestilential disorder, against Alexandria. This was artfully contrived by the enemies of Christ; for in order that they might have a show of the signatures of many Bishops, and that Athanasius might not have a single Bishop in his persecution to whom he could even complain, they therefore anticipated his proceedings, and filled every place with terror, which they kept up to second them in the prosecution of their designs. But herein they perceived not through their folly that they were not exhibiting the deliberate choice of the Bishops, but rather the violence which themselves had employed; and that, although his brethren should desert him, and his friends and acquaintance stand afar off, and no one be found to sympathize with him and console him, yet far above all these, a refuge with his God was sufficient for him. For Elijah also was alone in his persecution, and God was all in all to the holy man. And the Savior has given us an example herein, who also was left alone, and exposed to the designs of His enemies, to teach us, that when we are persecuted and deserted by men, we must not faint, but place our hope in Him, and not betray the Truth. For although at first truth may seem to be afflicted, yet even they who persecute shall afterwards acknowledge it.

48. Attacks Upon the Alexandrian Church

Accordingly they urge on the Emperor, who first writes a menacing letter, which he sends to the Duke and the soldiers. The Notaries Diogenius and Hilarius , and certain Palatines with them, were the bearers of it; upon whose arrival those terrible and cruel outrages were committed against the Church, which I have briefly related a little above , and which are known to all men from the protests put forth by the people, which are inserted at the end of this history, so that any one may read them. Then after these proceedings on the part of Syrianus, after these enormities had been perpetrated, and violence offered to the Virgins, as approving of such conduct and the infliction of these evils upon us, he writes again to the senate and people of Alexandria, instigating the younger men, and requiring them to assemble together, and either to persecute Athanasius, or consider themselves as his enemies. He however had withdrawn before these instructions reached them, and from the time when Syrianus broke into the Church; for he remembered that which was written, "Hide thyself as it were for a little moment, until the indignation be overpast ." One Heraclius, by rank a Count, was the hearer of this letter, and the precursor of a certain George that was despatched by the Emperor as a spy, for one that was sent from him cannot be a Bishop; God forbid. And so indeed his conduct and the circumstances which preceded his entrance sufficiently prove.

55. Irruption into the Great Church.
The Gentiles accordingly, as purchasing by their compliance the safety of their idols, and certain of the trades , subscribed, though unwillingly, from fear of the threats which he had held out to them; just as if the matter had been the appointment of a general, or other magistrate. Indeed what as heathen, were they likely to do, except whatever was pleasing to the Emperor? But the people having assembled in the great Church (for it was the fourth day of the week), Count Heraclius on the following day takes with him Cataphronius the Prefect of Egypt, and Faustinus the Receiver-General , and Bithynus a heretic; and together they stir up the younger men of the common multitude who worshiped idols, to attack the Church, and stone the people, saying that such was the Emperor's command. As the time of dismissal however had arrived, the greater part had already left the Church, but there being a few women still remaining, they did as the men had charged them, whereupon a piteous spectacle ensued. The few women had just risen from prayer and had sat down when the youths suddenly came upon them naked with stones and clubs. Some of them the godless wretches stoned to death; they scourged with stripes the holy persons of the Virgins, tore off their veils and exposed their heads, and when they resisted the insult, the cowards kicked them with their feet. This was dreadful, exceedingly dreadful; but what ensued was worse, and more intolerable than any outrage. Knowing the holy character of the virgins, and that their ears were unaccustomed to pollution, and that they were better able to bear stones and swords than expressions of obscenity, they assailed them with such language. This the Arians suggested to the young men, and laughed at all they said and did; while the holy Virgins and other godly women fled from such words as they would from the bite of asps, but the enemies of Christ assisted them in the work, nay even, it may be, gave utterance to the same; for they were well-pleased with the obscenities which the youths vented upon them.

56. The Great Church Pillaged
After this, that they might fully execute the orders they had received (for this was what they earnestly desired, and what the Count and the Receiver- General instructed them to do), they seized upon the seats, the throne, and the table which was of wood , and the curtains of the Church, and whatever else they were able, and carrying them out burnt them before the doors in the great street, and cast frankincense upon the flame. Alas! who will not weep to hear of these things, and, it may be, close his ears, that he may not have to endure the recital, esteeming it hurtful merely to listen to the account of such enormities? Moreover they sang the praises of their idols, and said, "Constantius hath become a heathen, and the Arians have acknowledged our customs;" for indeed they scruple not even to pretend heathenism, if only their heresy may be established. They even were ready to sacrifice a heifer which drew the water for the gardens in the Caesareum ; and would have sacrificed it, had it not been a female ; for they said that it was unlawful for such to be offered among them.

58. General Persecution at Alexandria
The Gentiles, when they beheld these things, were seized with fear, and ventured on no further outrage; but the Arians were not even yet touched with shame, but, like the Jews when they saw the miracles, were faithless and would not believe, nay, like Pharaoh, they were hardened; they too having placed their hopes below, on the Emperor and his eunuchs. They permitted the Gentiles, or rather the more abandoned of the Gentiles, to act in the manner before described; for they found that Faustinus, who is the Receiver-General by style, but is a vulgar person in habits, and profligate in heart, was ready to play his part with them in these proceedings, and to stir up the heathen. Nay, they undertook to do the like

themselves, that as they had modeled their heresy upon all other heresies together, so they might share their wickedness with the more depraved of mankind. What they did through the instrumentality of others I described above; the enormities they committed themselves surpass the bounds of all wickedness; and they exceed the malice of any hangman. Where is there a house which they did not ravage? where is there a family they did not plunder on pretense of searching for their opponents? where is there a garden they did not trample under foot? what tomb did they not open, pretending they were seeking for Athanasius, though their sole object was to plunder and spoil all that came in their way? How many men's houses were sealed up! The contents of how many persons' lodgings did they give away to the soldiers who assisted them! Who had not experience of their wickedness? Who that met them but was obliged to hide himself in the market-place? Did not many an one leave his house from fear of them, and pass the night in the desert? Did not many an one, while anxious to preserve his property from them, lose the greater part of it? And who, however inexperienced of the sea, did not choose rather to commit himself to it, and to risk all its dangers, than to witness their threatenings? Many also changed their residences, and removed from street to street, and from the city to the suburbs. And many submitted to severe fines, and when they were unable to pay, borrowed of others, merely that they might escape their machinations.

60. Martyrdom of Eutychius

Moreover, imitating the savage practices of Scythians, they seized upon Eutychius a Subdeacon, a man who had served the Church honourably, and causing him to be scourged on the back with a leather whip, till he was at the point of death, they demanded that her should be sent away to the mines; and not simply to any mine, but to that of Phaeno, where even a condemned murderer is hardly able to live a few days. And what was most unreasonable in their conduct, they would not permit him even a few hours to have his wounds dressed, but caused him to be sent off immediately, saying, "If this is done, all men will be afraid, and henceforward will be on our side." After a short interval, however, being unable to accomplish his journey to the mine on account of the pain of his stripes, he died on the way. He perished rejoicing, having obtained the glory of martyrdom. But the miscreants were not even yet ashamed, but in the words of Scripture, "having bowels without mercy," they acted accordingly, and now again perpetrated a satanic deed. When the people prayed them to spare Eutychius and besought them for him, they caused four honourable and free citizens to be seized, one of whom was Hermias who washed the beggars' feet; and after scourging them very severely, the Duke cast them into the prison. But the Arians, who are more cruel even than Scythians, when they had seen that they did not die from the stripes they had received, complained of the Duke and threatened, saying, "We will write and tell the eunuchs, that he does not flog as we wish." Hearing this he was afraid, and was obliged to beat the men a second time; and they being beaten, and knowing for what cause they suffered and by whom they had been accused, said only, "We are beaten for the sake of the Truth, but we will not hold communion with the heretics: beat us now as thou wilt; God will judge thee for this." The impious men wished to expose them to danger in the prison, that they might die there; but the people of God observing their time, besought him for them, and after seven days or more they were set at liberty.

Chapter 8

64. Persecution in Egypt

Who would call them even by the name of Gentiles; much less by that of Christians? Would any one regard their habits and feelings as human, and not rather those of wild beasts, seeing their cruel and savage conduct? They are more worthless than public hangmen; more audacious than all other heretics. To the Gentiles they are much inferior, and stand far apart and separate from them. I have heard from our fathers, and I believe their report to be a faithful one, that long ago, when a persecution arose in the time of Maximian, the grandfather of Constantius, the Gentiles concealed our brethren the Christians, who were sought after, and frequently suffered the loss of their own substance, and had trial of imprisonment, solely that they might not betray the fugitives. They protected those who fled to them for refuge, as they would have done their own persons, and were determined to run all risks on their behalf. But now these admirable persons, the inventors of a new heresy, act altogether the contrary part; and are distinguished for nothing but their treachery. They have appointed themselves as executioners, and seek to betray all alike, and make those who conceal others the objects of their plots, esteeming equally as their enemy both him that conceals and him that is concealed. So murderous are they; so emulous in their evil-doings of the wickedness of Judas.

65. Martyrdom of Secundus of Barka

The crimes these men have committed cannot adequately be described. I would only say, that as I write and wish to enumerate all their deeds of iniquity, the thought enters my mind, whether this heresy be not the fourth daughter of the horse-leach in the Proverbs, since after so many acts of injustice, so many murders, it hath not yet said, "It is enough." No; it still rages, and goes about seeking after those whom it has not yet discovered, while those whom it has already injured, it is eager to injure anew. After the night attack, after the evils committed in consequence of it, after the persecution brought about by Heraclius, they cease not yet to accuse us falsely before the Emperor (and they are confident that as impious persons they will obtain a hearing), desiring that something more than banishment may be inflicted upon us, and that hereafter those who do not consent to their impieties may be destroyed. Accordingly, being now emboldened in an extreme degree, that most abandoned Secundus of Pentapolis, and Stephanus his accomplice, conscious that their heresy was a defence of any injustice they might commit, on discovering a Presbyter at Barka who would not comply with their desires (he was called Secundus, being of the same name, but not of the same faith with the heretic), they kicked him till he died. While he was thus suffering he imitated the Saint, and said, "Let no one avenge my cause before human judges; I have the Lord for my avenger, for whose sake I suffer these things at their hands." They however were not moved with pity at these words, nor did they feel any awe of the sacred season; for it was during the time of Lent that they thus kicked the man to death.

79. Behavior of the Meletians Contrasted with That of the Alexandrian Christians

Such is the effect of that iniquitous order which was issued by Constantius. On the part of the people there was displayed a ready alacrity to submit to martyrdom, and an increased hatred of this most impious heresy; and yet lamentations for their Churches, and groans burst from all, while they cried unto the Lord, "spare Thy people, O Lord, and give not Thine heritage unto Thine enemies to reproach ;" but make haste to deliver us out of the hand of the lawless. For behold, "they have not spared Thy servants, but are preparing the way for Antichrist." For the Meletians will never resist him, nor will they care for the truth, nor will they esteem it an evil thing to deny Christ. They are men who have not approached the word with sincerity; like the chameleon they assume every various appear ante; they are hirelings of any who will make use of them. They make not the truth their aim, but prefer before it their present pleasure; they say only, "Let us eat and drink, for tomorrow we die." Such a profession and faithless temper is more worthy of Epicritian players than of Meletians. But the faithful servants of our Saviour, and the true Bishops who believe with sincerity, and live not for themselves, but for the Lord; these faithfully believing in our Lord Jesus Christ, and knowing, as I said before, that the charges which were alleged against the truth were false, and plainly fabricated for the sake of the Arian heresy, perceiving all this, as defenders and preachers of the truth, chose rather, and endured to be insulted and driven into banishment, than to subscribe against him, and to hold communion with the Arian madmen. They forgot not the lessons they had taught to others; yea, they know well that great dishonour remains for the traitors, but for them which confess the truth, the kingdom of heaven; and that to the careless and such as fear Constantius will happen no good thing; but for them that endure tribulations here, as sailors reach a quiet haven after a storm, as wrestlers receive a crown after the combat, so these shall obtain great and eternal joy and delight in heaven;- such as Joseph obtained after those tribulations; such as the great Daniel had after his temptations and the manifold conspiracies of the courtiers against him; such as Paul now enjoys, being crowned by the Saviour; such as the people of God everywhere expect. They, seeing these things, were not infirm of purpose, but waxed strong in faith, and increased in their zeal more and more. Being fully persuaded of the calumnies and impieties of the heretics, they condemn the persecutor, and in heart and mind run together the same course with them that are persecuted, that they also may obtain the crown of Confession.

81. The People of the Catholic Church in Alexandria, Which is Under the Government of the Most Reverend Bishop Athanasius, Make This Public Protest by Those Whose Names are Under-Written.

We have already protested against the nocturnal assault which was committed upon ourselves and the Lord's house; although in truth there needed no protest in respect to proceedings with which the whole city has been already made acquainted. For the bodies of the slain which were discovered were exposed in public, and the bows and arrows and other arms found in the Lord's house loudly proclaim the iniquity. But whereas after our Protest already made, the most illustrious Duke Syrianus endeavors to force all men to agree with him, as though no tumult had been made, nor any had perished (wherein is no small proof that these things were not done according to the wishes of the most gracious Emperor Augustus Constantius; for he would not have been so much afraid of the consequences of this transaction, had he acted therein by command); and whereas also, when we went to him, and requested him not to do violence to any, nor to deny what had taken place, he ordered us, being Christians, to be beaten with clubs; thereby again giving proof of the nocturnal assault which has been directed against the Church:- We therefore make also this present Protest, certain of us being now about to travel to the most religious Emperor Augustus: and we adjure Maximus the Prefect of Egypt, and the Controllers , in the name of Almighty God, and for the sake of the salvation of the most religious Augustus Constantius, to relate all these things to the piety of Augustus, and to the authority of the most illustrious Prefects . We adjure also the masters of vessels, to publish these things everywhere, and to carry them to the ears of the most religious Augustus, and to the Prefects and the Magistrates in every place, in order that it may be known that a war has been waged against the Church, and that, in the times of Augustus Constantius, Syrianus has caused virgins and many others to become martyrs. As it dawned upon the fifth before the Ides of February , that is to say, the fourteenth of the month Mechir, while we were keeping vigil in the Lord's house, and engaged in our prayers (for there was to be a communion on the Preparation); suddenly about midnight, the most illustrious Duke Syrianus attacked us and the Church with many legions of soldiers armed with naked swords and javelins and other warlike instruments, and wearing helmets on their heads; and actually while we were praying, and while the lessons were being read, they broke down the doors. And when the doors were burst open by the violence of the multitude, he gave command, and some of them were shooting; others shouting, their arms rattling, and their swords flashing in the light of the lamps; and forthwith virgins were being slain, many men trampled down, and falling over one another as the soldiers came upon them, and several were pierced with arrows and perished. Some of the soldiers also were betaking themselves to plunder, and were stripping the virgins, who were more afraid of being even touched by them than they were of death. The Bishop continued sitting upon his throne, and exhorted all to pray. The Duke led on the attack, having with him Hilarius the notary, whose part in the proceedings was shown in the sequel. The Bishop was seized, and barely escaped being torn to pieces; and having fallen into a state of insensibility, and appearing as one dead, he disappeared from among them, and has gone we know not whither. They were eager to kill him. And when they saw that many had perished, they gave orders to the soldiers to remove out of sight the bodies of the dead. But the most holy virgins who were left behind were buried in the tombs, having attained the glory of martyrdom in the times of the most religious Constantius. Deacons also were beaten with stripes even in the Lord's house, and were shut up there. Nor did matters stop even here: for after all this had happened, whosoever pleased broke open any door that he could, and searched, and plundered what was within. They entered even into those places which not even all Christians are allowed to enter. Gorgonius, the commander of the city force, knows this, for he was present. And no unimportant evidence of the nature of this hostile assault is afforded by the circumstance, that the armor and javelins and swords borne by those who entered were left in the Lord's house. They have been hung up in the Church until this time, that they might not be able to deny it: and although they sent several times Dynamius the soldier, as well as the Commander of the city police, desiring to take them away, we would not allow it, until the circumstance was known to all. Now if an order has been given that we should be persecuted we are all ready to suffer martyrdom. But if it be not by order of Augustus, we desire Maximus the Prefect of Egypt and all the city magistrates to request of him that they may not again be suffered thus to assail us. And we desire also that this our petition may be presented to him, that they may not attempt to bring in hither any other Bishop: for we have resisted unto death, desiring to have the most Reverend Athanasius, whom God gave us at the beginning, according to the succession of our fathers; whom also the most religious Augustus Constantius himself sent to us with letters and oaths. And we believe that when his Piety is informed of what has taken place, he will be greatly displeased, and will do nothing contrary to his oaths, but will again give orders that our Bishop Athanasius shall remain with us. To the Consuls to be elected after the Consulship of the most illustrious Arbaethion and Collianus, on the seventeenth Mechir, which is the day before the Ides of February.

Athanasius, bishop of Alexandria, History of the Arians

Eusebius

"about the end of the third century"

In the reign of Diocletian and Maximian, before they had published any new edicts against the Christians, Eusebius, a holy priest, a man eminently endowed with the spirit of prayer, and all apostolical virtues, suffered death for the faith, probably in Palestine. The emperor Maximian happening to be in that country, an information was lodged with Maxentius, president of the province, against Eusebius, that he distinguished himself by his zeal in invoking and preaching Christ, and the holy man was apprehended, and brought before him. The people stirred up Maxentius, by their furious clamours against the servant of Christ.

MAXENTIUS: Sacrifice to the gods freely, or you shall be made to do it against your will.

EUSEBIUS: There is a greater law which says, "Thou shalt adore the Lord thy God, and him alone shalt thou serve."

MAXENTIUS: Choose either to offer

sacrifice, or to suffer the most rigorous torments.

EUSEBIUS: It is not consistent with reason for a person to adore stones, that which nothing is viler or more brittle.

MAXENTIUS: These Christians are a hardened race of men, to whom it seems desirable rather to die than to live.

EUSEBIUS: It is impious to despise the light for the sake of darkness.

MAXENTIUS: You grow more obstinate by lenity and entreaties. I therefore lay them aside, and frankly tell you, that, unless you sacrifice, you shall be burnt alive.

EUSEBIUS: As to that, I am in no pain. The more severe or cruel the torments are, the greater will the crown be.

Upon this, Maxentius ordered that he should be stretched on the rack, and his sides rent with iron hooks. Eusebius repeated, whilst he was tormenting, "Lord Jesus preserve me. Whether we live or die, we are yours."

The president was amazed at his constancy and fortitude, and after some time, commanded that he should be taken off the rack. Then he said to him, "Do you know the decree of the senate, which commands all to sacrifice to the gods?"

Eusebius answered, "The command of God is to take place before that of man."

Maxentius ordered Eusebius' guards to confine him until the next day. Maxentius went to the prince, and said, "Great emperor, I have found a seditious man who is disobedient to the laws, and even denies to my face that the gods have any power, and refuses to sacrifice, or to adore your name."

The emperor answered, "Let him be brought before me."

A person present, who had seen Eusebius at the prefect's tribunal, said, "If you see him, you will be moved by his speech."

The emperor replied, "Is he such a man that he can even change me?"

The prefect then spoke, "He will change not only you, but the minds of all the people. If you once behold his looks, you will feel yourself strangely moved to follow his inclinations."

The emperor, however, ordered him to be brought in. As Eusebius entered, everyone was struck in beholding the dazzling brightness which appeared in his countenance, the joy and the affecting composure, sweetness, and undaunted courage which shone in his looks and eye, and the gracefulness of his air, and whole mien, which in his venerable old age seemed to breathe an air of virtue above what is human. The emperor fixed his eyes steadfastly upon him, as if he beheld in him something divine, and spoke thus, "Old man, why are you come before me? Speak, and do not be afraid." Seeing him silent, he said, "speak freely; answer my questions. I desire that you be saved."

Eusebius answered, "If I hope to be saved by man, I can no longer expect salvation from God. If you excel in dignity and power, we are, nevertheless, all mortal alike. Neither will I be afraid to repeat before you what I have already declared. I am a Christian: nor can I adore wood and stones; but I most readily obey the true God whom I know, and whose goodness I have experienced."

The emperor said to the president, "What harm is it if this man adores the God of whom he speaks, as above all others?"

Maximian replied, "Be not deceived, most invincible emperor; he does not call what you imagine God, but I know not what Jesus, whom our nation or ancestors never knew." The emperor said, "Go you forth, and judge him according to justice and the laws. I will not be judge in such an affair."

Maxentius went out and ascended his tribunal, saying to Eusebius, "sacrifice, or torments and flames must be your portion."

Eusebius replied, "My soul, which is God's, cannot be hurt by your torments. I persevere firm in the holy law to which I have adhered from my cradle."

The president then condemned him to be beheaded.

Alban Butler, The Lives of the Saints, Dublin, 1833, volume 2, pp 234-35

Second Arian Persecution Under Constantius

But the inheritors of the opinions and impiety of Eusebius and his fellows, the eunuch Leontius, who ought not to remain in communion even as a layman, because he mutilated himself that he might henceforward be at liberty to sleep with one Eustolium, who is a wife as far as he is concerned, but is called a virgin; and George and Acacius, and Theodorus, and Narcissus, who are deposed by the Council; when they heard and saw these things, were greatly ashamed. And when they perceived the unanimity and peace that existed between Athanasius and the Bishops (they were more than four hundred, from great Rome, and all Italy, from Calabria, Apulia, Campania, Bruttia, Sicily, Sardinia, Corsica, and the whole of Africa; and those from Gaul, Britain, and Spain, with the great Confessor Hosius; and also those from Pannonia, Noricum, Siscia, Dalmatia, Dardania, Dacia, Moesia, Macedonia, Thessaly, and all Achaia, and from Crete, Cyprus, and Lycia, with most of those from Palestine, Isauria, Egypt, the Thebais, the whole of Libya, and Pentapolis); when I say they perceived these things, they were possessed with envy and fear; with envy, on account of the communion of so many together; and with fear, lest those who had been entrapped by them should be brought over by the unanimity of so great a number, and henceforth their heresy should be triumphantly exposed, and everywhere proscribed.

Relapse of Ursacius and Valens

First of all they persuade Ursacius, Valens and their fellows to change sides again, and like dogs to return to their own vomit, and like swine to wallow again in the former mire of their impiety; and they make this excuse for their retractation, that they did it through fear of the most religious Constans. And yet even had there been cause for fear, yet if they had confidence in what they had done, they ought not to have become traitors to their friends. But when there was no cause for fear, and yet they were guilty of a lie, are they not deserving of utter condemnation? For no soldier was present, no Palatine or Notary had been sent, as they now send them, nor yet was the Emperor there, nor had they been invited by any one, when they wrote their recantation. But they voluntarily went up to Rome, and of their own accord recanted and wrote it down in the Church, where there was no fear from without, where the only fear is the fear of God, and where every one has liberty of conscience. And yet although they have a second time become Arians, and then have devised this unseemly excuse for their conduct, they are still without shame.

Constantius Changes Sides Again

In the next place they went in a body to the Emperor Constantius, and besought him, saying, "When we first made our request to you, we were not believed; for we told you, when you sent for Athanasius, that by inviting him to come forward, you are expelling our heresy. For he has been opposed to it from the very first, and never ceases to anathematize it. He has already written letters against us into all parts of the world, and the majority of men have embraced communion with him; and even of those who seemed to be on our side, some have been gained over by him, and others are likely to be. And we are left alone, so that the fear is, lest the character of our heresy become known, and henceforth both we and you gain the name of heretics. And if this come to pass, you must take care that we be not classed with the Manichaeans. Therefore begin again to persecute, and support the heresy, for it accounts you its king." Such was the language of their iniquity. And the Emperors when in his passage through the country on his hasty march against Magnentius, he saw the communion of the Bishops with Athanasius, like one set on fire, suddenly changed his mind, and no longer remembered his oaths, but was alike forgetful of what he had written and regardless of the duty he owed his brother. For in his letters to him, as well as in his interview with Athanasius, he took oaths that he would not act otherwise than as the people should wish, and as should be agreeable to the Bishops. But his zeal for impiety caused him at once to forget all these things. And yet one ought not to wonder that after so many letters and so many oaths Constantius had altered his mind, when we remember that Pharaoh of old, the tyrant of Egypt, after frequently promising and by that means obtaining a remission of his punishments, likewise changed, until he at last perished together with his associates.

Constantius Begins to Persecute

He compelled then the people in every city to change their party; and on arriving at Aries and Milan, he proceeded to act entirely in accordance with the designs and suggestions of the heretics; or rather they acted themselves, and receiving authority from him, furiously attacked every one. Letters and orders were immediately sent hither to the Prefect, that for the future the corn should be taken from Athanasius and given to those who favoured the Arian doctrines, and that whoever pleased might freely insult them that held communion with him; and the magistrates were threatened if they did not hold communion with the Arians. These things were but the prelude to what afterwards took place under the direction of the Duke Syrianus. Orders were sent also to the more distant parts, and Notaries despatched to every city, and Palatines, with threats to the Bishops and Magistrates, directing the Magistrates to urge on the Bishops, and informing the Bishops that either they must subscribe against Athanasius, and hold communion with the Arians, or themselves undergo the punishment of exile, while the people who took part with them were to understand that chains, and insults, and scourgings, and the loss of their possessions, would be their portion. These orders were not neglected, for the commissioners had in their company the Clergy of Ursacius and Valens, to inspire them with zeal, and to inform the Emperor if the Magistrates neglected their duty. The other heresies, as younger sisters of their own, they permitted to blaspheme the Lord, and only conspired against the Christians, not enduring to hear orthodox language concerning Christ. How many Bishops in consequence, according to the words of Scripture, were brought before rulers and kings, and received this sentence from magistrates, "subscribe, or withdraw from your churches, for the Emperor has commanded you to be deposed!" How many in every city were roughly handled, lest they should accuse them as friends of the Bishops! Moreover letters were sent to the city authorities, and a threat of a fine was held out to them, if they did not compel the Bishops of their respective cities to subscribe. In short, every place and every city was full of fear and confusion, while the Bishops were dragged along to trial, and the magistrates witnessed the lamentations and groans of the people.

Persecution by Constantius

Such were the proceedings of the Palatine commissioners; on the other hand, those admirable persons, confident in the patronage which they had obtained, display great zeal, and cause some of the Bishops to be summoned before the Emperor, while they persecute others by letters, inventing charges against them; to the intent that the one might be overawed by the presence of Constantius, and the other, through fear of the commissioners and the threats held out to them in these pretended accusations, might be brought to renounce their orthodox and pious opinions. In this manner it was that the Emperor forced so great a multitude of Bishops, partly by threats, and partly by promises, to declare, "We will no longer hold communion with Athanasius." For those who came for an interview, were not admitted to his presence, nor allowed any relaxation, not so much as to go out of their dwellings, until they had either subscribed, or refused and incurred banishment thereupon. And this he did because he saw that the heresy was hateful to all men. For this reason especially he compelled so many to add their names to the small number of the Arians, his earnest desire being to collect together a crowd of names, both from envy of the Bishop, and for the sake of making a shew in favour of the Arian impiety, of which he is the patron; supposing that he will be able to alter the truth, as easily as he can influence the minds of men. He knows not, nor has ever read, how that the Sadducees and the Herodians, taking unto them the Pharisees, were not able to obscure the truth; rather it shines out thereby more brightly every day, while they crying out, "We have no king but Caesar," and obtaining the judgment of Pilate in their favour, are nevertheless left destitute, and wait in utter shame, expecting shortly to become bereft, like the partridge, when they shall see their patron near his death.

Persecution is from the Devil

Now if it was altogether unseemly in any of the Bishops to change their opinions merely from fear of these things, yet it was much more so, and not the part of men who have confidence in what they believe, to force and compel the unwilling. In this manner it is that the Devil, when he has no truth on his side, attacks and breaks down the doors of them that admit him with axes and hammers. But our Saviour is so gentle that He teaches thus, "If any man wills to come after Me," and, "Whoever wills to be My disciple;" and coming to each He does not force them, but knocks at the door and says, "Open unto Me, My sister, My spouse;" and if they open to Him, He enters in, but if they delay and will not, He departs from them. For the truth is not preached with swords or with darts, nor by means of soldiers; but by persuasion and counsel. But what persuasion is there where fear of the Emperor prevails? or what counsel is there, when he who withstands them receives at last banishment and death? Even David, although he was a king, and had his enemy in his power, prevented not the soldiers by an exercise of authority when they wished to kill his enemy, but, as the Scripture says, David persuaded his men by arguments, and suffered them not to rise up and put Saul to death. But he, being without arguments of reason, forces all men by his power, that it may be shown to all, that their wisdom is not according to God, but merely human, and that they who favor the Arian doctrines have indeed no king but Caesar; for by his means it is that these enemies of Christ accomplish whatsoever they wish to do. But while they thought that they were carrying on their designs against many by his means, they knew not that they were making many to be confessors, of whom are those who have lately made so glorious a confession, religious men, and excellent Bishops, Paulinus Bishop of Treveri, the metropolis of the Gauls, Lucifer, Bishop of the metropolis of Sardinia, Eusebius of Vercelli in Italy, and Dionysius of Milan, which is the metropolis of Italy. These the Emperor summoned before him, and commanded them to subscribe against Athanasius, and to hold communion with the heretics; and when they were astonished at this novel procedure, and said that there was no Ecclesiastical Canon to this effect, he immediately said, "Whatever I will, be that esteemed a Canon; the "Bishops' of Syria let me thus speak. Either then obey, or go into banishment."

Banishment of the Western Bishops Spread the Knowledge of the Truth

When the Bishops heard this they were utterly amazed, and stretching forth their hands to God, they used great boldness of speech against him teaching him that the kingdom was not his, but God's, who had given it to him, Whom also they bid him fear, lest He should suddenly take it away from him. And they threatened him with the day of judgment, and warned him against infringing Ecclesiastical order, and mingling Roman sovereignty with the constitution of the Church, and against introducing the Arian heresy into the Church of God. But he would not listen to them, nor permit them to speak further, but threatened them so much the more, and drew his sword against them, and gave orders for some of them to be led to execution; although afterwards, like Pharaoh, he repented. The holy men therefore shaking off the dust, and looking up to God, neither feared the threats of the Emperor, nor betrayed their cause before his drawn sword; but received their banishment, as a service pertaining to their ministry. And as they passed along, they preached the Gospel in every place and city , although they were in bonds, proclaiming the orthodox faith, anathematizing the Arian heresy, and stigmatizing the recantation of Ursacius and Valens. But this was contrary to the intention of their enemies; for the greater was the distance of their place of banishment, so much the more was the hatred against them increased, while the wanderings of these men were but the heralding of their impiety. For who that saw them as they passed along, did not greatly admire them as Confessors, and renounce and abominate the others, calling them not only impious men, but executioners and murderers, and everything rather than Christians?

Athanasius, bishop of Alexandria, History of the Arian, part 4

Egyptian martyrs

Egyptian martyrs at Tyre We know about the Egyptian martyrs, (martyred from 305 onwards), who became shining lights in Palestine and at Tyre in Phoenicia. Nobody could have been but amazed at the harsh floggings, the man-eating beasts which followed when they were attacked by panthers, various bears, bulls enraged by red-hot irons, and wild boars. I saw the courage of these martyrs myself and the divine power of the presence of the One to whom they testified, our Saviour Jesus Christ himself, who was clearly seen in these martyrs. For a long time the man-eating beasts would not go near the bodies of God's beloved people, but rather attacked their handlers. The holy champions stood naked, waving their arms to attack the attention of the wild beasts which left them unmolested. To the astonishment of the spectators this went of for a long time, until a second and then a third group of wild beasts were introduced which then all ravaged the same martyr.

Nothing can outstrip the amazing, fearless courage of these saints and the endurance of their young bodies. A man, not yet twenty years old, would stand up without chains, spread out his arms in the shape of a cross, and concentrate his mind totally on unhurried prayers to the Almighty. A supernatural power stopped the mouths of these wild beasts. Then a wild bull was introduced. The bull attacked and mangled everyone in sight with his horns, except for the group of five holy martyrs, whom he refused to even approach. Even when the bull was provoked with red-hot irons he did not attack the martyrs. Different wild beasts were then sent in but even these did not attack their intended victims. In the end the martyrs were each butchered with a sword. They were not buried in the ground but thrown into the waves of the sea. Egyptian martyrs in Egypt Great numbers of men and women and children, who despised this passing life, faced death in a variety of ways for the sake of our Savior's teaching. Some were flogged without mercy, some put on the rack, some scraped, and some endured countless other tortures. Some were burnt alive, others drowned in the sea, while others gladly bared their necks to the executioner's axe. Some died as they were being tortured, some starved to death, some were crucified like common criminals but some were nailed in an upside down position, head down, to inflict even more pain, and others were starved to death as they slowly died on the cross.

Egyptian martyrs at Thebais

These martyrs were torn to shreds from head to toe with claw-like potsherds until they expired. Women, stripped naked without a stitch of clothing, were lifted up a single foot by rope and so exposed in this shameful way to the crowds. Some were tied to tree stumps and then killed in terrible agony as follows. With the help of machinery the strongest branches of these trees were drawn close to each other and one leg of the martyr was then tied to each of the tree branches. Then the branches were allowed to released and they flew back to their normal positions and the martyr's limbs were torn apart in a second. They did this, not just for a few days or a few weeks, but year after year. Sometimes ten people were killed in this way and on other days thirty or sixty people were killed. On some days over one hundred people were killed by a succession of different punishments.

As I was in these places, I witnessed these

executions personally. Some martyrs were beheaded, others were burnt alive. On some days, so many were killed that the axehead became blunt. I saw a great enthusiasm on the part of those who placed their trust in God's Christ. As soon as one group had been sentenced to death, another group would jump up on the platform and tell the judge that they were Christians. They ignored the terrifying ordeal of the tortures inflicted on them. They were completely devoted to God and welcomed the sentence of death with joy. They sang hymns of thanksgiving to the God of the universe until they could breath no more.

Some of these martyrs were noted for their wealth, and learning, but they put everything in second place to their faith in our Saviour and Lord Jesus Christ. One such person was Philoromus , a leading Roman official in Alexandria. Another was the Bishop of Thumus, Phileas , a man noted for his public work and his writings about philosophy. Many prominent officials, including the judge himself, implored these two people to recant and so save their wives and children from suffering. But nothing made them swerve from their love of our Saviour, who warned his followers to confess him and not deny him. They stood rocklike against all the judge's insults and threats and were both beheaded."

Eusebius, The History of the Church, Book 8

TORTURES OF THE FIRST CHRISTIAN MARTYRS (7) OTHER INSTRUMENTS OF TORTURE

Eusebius says in his *Ecclesiastical History*: "The hands of the executioners failed, and albeit succeeding one another in relays, the men were wearied out, and the edge of the sword blunted. Myself saw the tormentors sit back exhausted, recover strength, regain breath, take fresh swords – and yet the day not be long enough for all the torments to be inflicted! Nevertheless, not one of all the band, not so much as one child of tender years, could be frightened back from affronting death; the one and only thing each dreaded was, that when the hurrying sun ended the short day, he should be left behind, divided from the society of his martyred comrades. Thus did they, one and all, steadfastly and boldly trusting to the faith, welcome with joy and exultation a present death as the beginning of eternal life. In a word, while the first batches were being slaughtered, the rest would stand singing psalms and hymns to God, each waiting his own turn of martyrdom, that so they might breathe forth their last breath in praises to the Almighty."

Mighty the failure of these servants of Satan, and great their foolishness! Verily did they tumble into the pit they had dug for the saints to fall into. Again and again did they condemn – but all in vain – their Christian adversaries to be:

a. Stabbed to death with countless blows of iron writing styles, (schoolboys' pens);
b. Struck over with nails, either their whole body or some special part of it;
c. Cut in half with saws;
d. Transfixed with spears;
e. Pierced with swords;
f. Shot with arrows;
g. Their bellies to be gashed open and the inwards torn out;
h. Their throats to be cut;
i. To be beheaded
j. To be disfigured with brands and markings;
k. Their heads to be pounded with axes or clubs, and dashed to pieces;
l. Women's bosoms to be amputated;
m. Women's tongues, hands and feet, as well as men's, to be cut away;
n. Their legs to be broken;
o. Stripped naked and led through the public streets
p. Buried alive in the earth, either up to their necks, or half buried with arms tied behind them, and left to perish.
q. Shut up in a leaden box and drowned in a river.
r. Sewn up in a bag, together with a cock, a viper, an ape, or a dog, and thrown into the nearest stream or river.
s. Where two trees could be found growing near together, a branch of each being bent down so as to meet, to either of these one of the martyr's feet was tied in such a way that the boughs which had been forcibly drawn

together, when let go, returned with a bound to their natural position and, tearing the man's body in two which was fastened to them, rent his limbs asunder and bare them back with them.

Tortures and Torments of the Christian Martyrs, from the "De SS. Martyrum Cruciatibus" of the Rev Father Gallonio, translated by A.R. Allinson, London and Paris, 1903, Limited Edition, printed for the subscribers, pp. 139-141

GENESIUS

Genesius , a comedian Christ who, to show the power of his grace, and the extent of his mercy, called a publican to the apostleship, honoured with the glory of martyrdom this saint, drawn from the stage.

The emperor Diocletian, coming to Rome, was entertained by people on the stage. In a comedy which was acted in his presence, one of the players took it into his head to represent, in a ludicrous manner, the ceremonies of the Christian baptism, which could not fail to divert the assembly, who held this religion, and its mysteries, in the utmost contempt and derision.

This player, Genesius, who had learned some things concerning the Christian rites from friends who zealously professed that religion, laid himself down on the stage, pretending to be sick, and said, "Ah! My friends, I find a great weight upon me; and would gladly be eased."

The others answered, "What shall we do to give thee ease?"

"You senseless creatures," said Genesius, "I am resolved to die a Christian, that God may receive me on this day of my death, as one who seeks his salvation by fleeing from idolatry and superstition."

Then a priest and exorcist were called, that is to say, two actors. They sat next to his bed-side, and said, "Well, my child, why did you send for us?"

Here Genesius, being suddenly converted by a divine inspiration, replied, not in jest, but seriously, "Because I desire to receive the grace of Jesus Christ and to be born again, that I may be delivered from my sins."

The other actors mimicked the whole ceremony of baptism with him, but Genesius in earnest answered the usual interrogations, and on being baptised was clothed with a white garment. After this, other actors, dressed like soldiers, to carry on the jest, seized Genesius, and presented him to the emperor, to be examined, as the martyrs were wont to be. Then Genesius declared himself openly, and said aloud, standing on the stage, "Hear, O emperor, and all you that are here present, officers of the army, philosophers, senators, and people, what I am going to say. I never yet so much as heard the name of a Christian but I was struck with horror, and detested my very relations because they professed that religion. I informed myself concerning its rites and mysteries only that I might the more heartily despise it, and inspire you with the utmost contempt for the same; but whilst I was washed with the water, and examined, I had no sooner answered sincerely that I believed, than I saw a company of bright angels over my head, who recited out of a book all the sins I had committed from my childhood; and having afterward plunged the book into the water which had been poured upon me in your presence, they showed me the book whiter than snow. Wherefore, I advise you, O great and mighty emperor, and all ye people here present, who have ridiculed these mysteries, to believe, with me, that Jesus Christ is the true Lord; that he is the light and the truth; and that it is through him you may obtain the forgiveness of your sins."

Diocletian, highly enraged at these words, ordered him to be most inhumanly beaten with clubs, and afterward to be put into the hands of Plautian, the prefect of the praetorium, that he might compel him to sacrifice. Palutian commanded him to be put on the rack, where he was torn with iron hooks for a considerable time, and then burnt with torches. The martyr endured these torments with constancy, and persisted crying out, ".There is no other Lord of the universe besides him whom I have seen. Him I adore and serve, and to him I will adhere, though I should suffer a thousand deaths for his sake. No torments shall remove Jesus Christ from my heart or mouth. I regret exceedingly my former errors, and that I once detested his holy name, and came so late to his service. At length his head was struck off.

Alban Butler, The Lives of the Saints, Dublin, 1833, volume 2, pp 319-30

Acts of Marcellus

Marcellus was martyred in Diocletian's reign, October 30, 298

In the city of Tingis, while Fortunatus was governor, the date for celebrating the Emperor's birthday came round. While everyone was feasting at banquets and sacrificing, a certain Marcellus, a centurion from the Trajan legion, deeming those banquets to be pagan, threw down his soldier's belt in front of the legion's standards in the camp. Then he called out in a loud voice, "I serve Jesus Christ the eternal king." He also threw his vine-switch and weapons away, adding, "From now on I stop serving your Emperors, and I refuse to worship your wooden and stone gods, which are deaf and dumb idols. If these are the terms of service, making men offer sacrifice to gods and Emperors, I know throw away my vine-switch and belt, I renounce the standards, and refuse to serve." The soldiers were dumbfounded to hear about this. They seized him and reported him to Anastasius Fortunatus, the legion's commander, who ordered him to be thrown into prison. After the feasting was over Fortunatus, sitting in judgement, ordered the centurion, Marcellus, to be brought before him. When Marcellus, one of the centurions of Asta, was brought in, Anastasius Fortunatus the governor said, "What did you mean by taking of your weapons, contrary to military regulations, and throwing your belt and vine-switch away?"

Marcellus answered, "On the 21st of July, in the presence of the standards of your legion, as you were celebrating the Emperor's birthday, I declared publicly that I was a Christian and that I could not serve under Roman allegiance, but only under the allegiance of Jesus Christ the son of God the Father Almighty."

Anastasius Fortunatus the governor said, "I cannot ignore your rash behaviour, so I will report this matter to the Emperors and to Caesar. You will be referred, unhurt, to my lord, Aurelius Agricolan, Deputy for the Prefects of the Guard. (The writer of these official proceedings was Caecilius.)

On the 30th October at Tigris, Marcellus, one of the centurions of Asta, having been brought into court, was officially summoned. "Fortunatus the governor has referred Marcellus, a centurion, to your authority. There is in court a letter dealing with his case, which at your command I will read."

Agricolan said, "Let it be read."

The official report was as follows: "From Fortunatus to you, my lord, and so forth. This soldier, having thrown away his soldier's belt, and having testified that he was a Christian, publicly said many blasphemous things against the gods and against Caesar. So we have sent him to you that you may take whatever action your eminence sees appropriate."

After the letter had been read, Agricolan said, "Did you say these things as appear in the governor's official report?"

Marcellus answered, "I did."

Agricolan said, "Did you hold the rank of first class centurion?"

Marcellus answered, "I did."

Agricolan said, "What possessed you to throw away the emblems of your allegiance and to speak as you did?"

Marcellus answered, "There is no madness in those who fear the Lord."

Agricolan said, "Did you say everything that the governor's report states?"

Marcellus answered, "I did."

Agricolan said, "Did you throw away your weapons?"

Marcellus answered, "I did. For it is wrong for a Christian, who serves the Lord Christ, to serve the cares of the world."

Agricolan said, "The actions of Marcellus must be punished." And he announced the following sentence: "Marcellus, who held the rank of first class centurion, having admitted that he has disgraced himself by publicly throwing off his allegiance, and having put this on record, as it stated in the governor's official report, along with other mad utterances, it is our pleasure that he is put to death by the sword."

When Marcellus was being led out to be executed he said to Agricolan, "May God bless you! For a martyr should leave this world in this way."

And after he had said these words he was beheaded, dying for the name of our Lord Jesus Christ, who is glorious for ever and ever. Amen.

E. C. E. Owen (trans.), Some Authentic Acts of the Early Martyrs, Oxford, 1927, pp 122-24

Nicander and Marcian

Two soldiers, Nicander and Marcian were martyred, probably at the same time as Marcellus, probably at Dorostorum, in the Moesian province, which later became known as Bulgaria.

Governor of the province of Moesia, Maximus, said to Nicander and Marcian, "If you are acquainted with the orders of the emperors, which require you to sacrifice to the gods, step up and obey the orders."

"It is only required," Nicander answered, "of those who are willing to sacrifice. We are Christians, and cannot be bound by such a requirement."

Maximus pointed out that by refusing they would forfeit their pay rise and promotion, and asked why they should incur the loss.

"Because," answered Nicander, "the riches of the ungodly are a pollution to men who desire to serve God."

"You need only honour the gods with a grain of incense," the governor pleaded.

Nicander replied, "How can a Christian man worship stocks and stones, and forsake the everlasting God whom we worship, who made all things of nothing, and who is able to save both me and all who trust in him?"

Nicander's wife, Daria, was present. Even though Nicander had been away at war for a long time Daria, with the intensity of a Christian woman's love, set herself to encourage her husband in his resolution, and said, "My lord, take good heed that you do it not. Take good heed, my lord, that you deny not our Lord Jesus Christ. Look up to heaven, and you will there see him to whom you are bound in loyalty and conscience. He is your helper."

Maximus, the governor, heard some of these remarks. "You bad woman," he exclaimed, "why do you want your husband to die?"

"That he may live with God," she replied, "and never die."

"No, no," said the governor, "it is nothing of the sort. You want to be married to a better husband, and so are in a hurry to rid yourself of your present husband."

"If you imagine that I think such a thing, and that I plan to do as you say," replied the brave woman, "kill me first for Christ's sake."

"I shall certainly not do as you wish," replied Maximus, "but you shall be put in prison."

All this time Marcian had been silent and unquestioned. The governor now addressed him: "What do you say, Marcian?" he inquired.

"I say the same as my fellow-soldier," he replied.

Maximus answered, "You shall be thrust into prison together, then, and shall assuredly suffer the penalty."

Later, Maximus pronounced the death penalty on them both. On their way to their execution, they were accompanied by their friends. Nicander's wife was there, and with her a man called Papian, whose brother Pasicrates had suffered martyrdom recently. Papian carried in his arms Nicander and Daria's young child. Marcian's wife and their child were also there, but Marcian's wife was either a heathen or a nominal Christian. She tore her clothes and shouted aloud, "I told you in the prison that it would come to this. I was afraid that this would happen, and shed many tears about this. Woe is me! Will you not reply to me? Take pity on my, my lord. Look at your darling little son. Turn your face towards us, and do not disown us. Why are you in such a hurry? Where are you going? Why do you hate us? You have been carried off like a sheep to the slaughter."

Marcian did eventually turn to the poor woman, and said, "How long has Satan blinded your mind and soul? Go your way and let me go mine. Allow me to perfect my martyrdom for God."

A Christian called Zoticus clasped Marcian's hand, and encouraged him, saying, "Be of good courage, the Lord be with you, you have fought the good fight. How can we weak ones have such faith? Remember the promises which the Lord has made, and which he will so soon pay. Perfect Christians are you indeed: blessed are you."

The unhappy wife was still following with her cries, attempting to hold Marcian back. "Hold my wife," said Marcian to Zoticus, and Zoticus did so.

When they came to the place for the execution, the spirit of the martyr relented a little. Looking around, Marcian called his wife to him. He kissed her, and said, "Depart in the Lord. You cannot bear to see me celebrate my martyrdom, with your mind beguiled by the evil one." Marcian kissed his child, and looking up to heaven said, "Lord God Almighty, take Thou care of him." Then the two martyrs embraced one another, and stepped a few paces apart to be put to death.

At that moment, however, Marcian saw Nicander's wife vainly attempting to push through the crowd to her husband. Stretching out his hand to her, while the people made way for him, he brought her to Nicander.

"God be with you," said the husband.

"Be of good cheer, good my lord," said his wife. "show them how you can strive. I spent ten years at home without you, and there was not a moment when I was not wishing to God that I might see you. Now I have seen you, and I am glad that you are setting out for the land of life. I shall sing louder now. How proud I shall be, to be a martyr's wife! Be of good courage, my lord. Bear your witness to God, that you may deliver me also from everlasting death."

The Christians then had such great confidence in the power of a martyr's prayer. Handkerchiefs were bound round the eyes of Nicander and Marcian, and in a moment the skilled stroke of the sword sent them where they desired to be.

Ruinart 484

Passion of Cassian

This is linked to the Acts of Marcellus, December 3, 298.

When Aurelius Agricolan was acting as deputy for the Prefects of the Praetorian Guard, as he was preparing to hear the case of the holy martyr Marcellus , the blessed Cassian was the secretary. When Marcellus, one of the centurions of Asta, was brought into court at Tingis on the 30th of October, Aurelius Agricolan, acting as judge, threatened Marcellus as he attempted to deflect him from standing for Christ. But the blessed Marcellus was so unswerving that everyone thought of him as the judge's judge, as he testified that he was Christ's soldier and that he could not serve the cares of the world. This made Aurelius Agricolan speak in great anger.

Cassian was recording the proceedings, but when he saw that Aurelius Agricolan, defeated by the martyr's great devotion, pronounced the death sentence, he vowed that he would write nothing more down. He threw the pen and note book onto the ground. To the astonishment of the staff, and as Marcellus laughed, Aurelius Agricolan, trembling, leapt up from the bench and demanded to know why Cassian had thrown his notebooks down with an oath. Blessed Cassian replied that Agricolan had handed down an unjust sentence. To avoid being contradicted any more, Agricolan ordered Cassian to be taken away at once and to be thrown into prison.

The blessed martyr Marcellus had laughed because, through the Holy Spirit, he knew what was going to happen, and he rejoiced that Cassian would be his companion in martyrdom. On the 3rd of December, Cassian was brought before the same court that Marcellus had been tried before. He made a similar statement as Marcellus had made and the same replies as Marcellus and received the same sentence as Marcellus. In this way he achieved the victory of martyrdom, through the help of our Lord Jesus Christ, to whom belong honour and glory, excellency and power for ever and ever. Amen.

E. C. E. Owen (trans.), Some Authentic Acts of the Early Martyrs, Oxford, 1927, pp 125-6

Afra

Early on in her life Afra was a prostitute. During the Diocletian persecutions, she and her mother Hilaria hid their bishop. He converted them, and Afra devoted herself to working with the poor until her martyrdom. Afra suffocated from smoke inhalation while being burned alive in about 304.
Editor

Euplius

Sicily, 304

In Sicily, in 304, under the ninth consulate of Diocletian, and the eighth of Maximian, on the 12th August, in the city of Catana, Euplius, a deacon, was brought to the governor's audience-chamber, and attending on the outside of the curtain, cried out, "I am a Christian, and shall rejoice to die for the name of Jesus Christ." The governor, Calvisianus, who was of consular dignity, heard him, and ordered that he who had made that outcry should be brought in, and presented before him.

Euplius went in with the book of the gospels in his hand. One of Calvisianus' friends, Maximus, said, "You ought not to keep such writings, countrary to the edicts of the emperors."

Calvisianus said to Euplius: "Where had you those writings? Did you bring them from your own house?"

Euplius replied that he had no house but that he was seized with the book about him. The judge bid him read something from it. The martyr opened it, and read the following verses: "Blessed are they who suffer persecution for justice sake, for theirs is the kingdom of heaven" (Matthew 5:10); and in another place: "He that will come after me, let him take up his cross, and follow me" (Matthew 16:24).

The judge asked what that meant.

The martyr answered, "It is the law of my Lord, which has been given to me."

Euplius answered, "By Jesus Christ, the Son of the living God."

Calvisianus then pronounced this order: "since his confession is evident, let him be delivered up to the executioners, and examined on the rack." This was immediately done, and the martyr was interrogated accordingly.

While they were tormenting him the same day, Calvisianus asked him if he persisted in his former sentiments. Euplius, making the sign of the cross on his forehead with the hand that he had at liberty, said, "What I formerly said I now declare again, that I am a Christian, and read the holy scriptures." He added that he dared not deliver up the sacred writings as that would offend God, and that he preferred to die as this would bring him eternal life.

Calvisianus ordered him to be hoisted on the rack, and more cruelly tormented. The martyr said, while he was tormented, "I thank thee, O Lord Jesus Christ, that I suffer for thy sake: save me, I beseech thee."

Calvisianus said, "Lay aside thy folly; adore our gods, and thou shalt be set at liberty."

Euplius answered, "I adore Jesus Christ: I detest the devils. Do what you please; add new torments; for I am a Christian. I have long desired to be in the condition in which I now am."

After the executioners had tormented him a long time, Calvisianus bade them desist, and said: "Wretch, adore the gods; worship Mars, Apollo, and Aesculapius."

Euplius replied, "I adore the Father, Son, and Holy Spirit. I worship the holy Trinity, besides whom there is no God."

Calvisianus said, "sacrifice, if you would be delivered."

Euplius answered, "I sacrifice myself now to Jesus Christ my God. All your efforts to move me are to no purpose. I am a Christian." Then Calvisianus gave orders for increasing his torments.

While the executioners were exerting their utmost in tormenting him, Euplius prayed thus, "I thank thee, my God; Jesus Christ, succour me. It is for thy name's sake that I endure these torments." This he repeated several times. When his strength failed him, his lips were seen still to move, the martyr continuing the same or like prayer with his lips when he could no longer do it with his voice.

At length Calvisianus went behind the

curtain, and dictated his sentence, which a secretary wrote. Afterward he came out with a tablet in his hand, and read the following sentence, "I command that Euplius, a Christian, be put to death by the sword, for condemning the prince's edicts, blaspheming the gods, and not repenting. Take him away.

The executioners hung the book of the gospels, which the martyr had with him when he was seized, about his neck, and the public crier proclaimed before him, "This is Euplius the Christian, an enemy of the gods and the emperors."

Euplius continued very cheerful, and repeated as he went, "I give thanks to Jesus Christ my God. Confirm, O Lord, what thou hast wrought in me." When he was come to the place of execution, he prayed a long time on his knees, and once more returning thanks, presented his neck to the executioner, who cut off his head. The Christians carried off his body, embalmed and buried it

Alban Butler, The Lives of the Saints, Dublin, 1833, volume 2, pp 280-82

St. Theodore of Amasea

Surnamed Tyro (Tiro), not because he was a young recruit, but because for a time he belonged to the Cohors Tyronum (Nilles, Kal. man., I, 105), called of Amasea from the place where he suffered martyrdom, and Euchaita from the place, Euchais, to which his body had been carried, and where he was held in such veneration that the city was frequently spoken of as Theodoropolis. His martyrdom seems to have taken place 17 Feb., 306, under the Emperors Galerius Maximian and Maximin, for on this day the Menologies give his feast. The Greeks and Armenians honour him also on the first Saturday of Lent, while the Roman Martyrology records him on 9 Nov. In the twelfth century his body was transferred to Brindisi, and he is there honoured as patron; his head is enshrined at Gaeta. There are churches bearing his name at Constantinople, Jerusalem, Damascus, and other places of the East. An ancient church of Venice, of which he is titular, is said to have been built by Narses. At the foot of the Palatine in Rome is a very old church, circular in shape and dedicated to S. Teodoro, whom the Roman people call S. Toto, which was made a collegiate church by Felix IV. The people showed their confidence in the saint by bringing their sick children to his temple. His martyrdom is represented in the choir of the cathedral of Chartres by thirty-eight glass paintings of the thirteenth century (Migne, "Dict. iconogr.", 599). He is invoked against storms. Emblems: temple, torch, crocodile, pyre, crown of thorns.

St. Gregory of Nyssa delivered a panegyric on his feast and gave several data concerning his life and martyrdom (P.G., XLVI, 741, and Ruinart, 505). The oldest text of the "Martyrium S. Theodori Tironis' was published by Delehaye in "Les legendes grecques des saints militaires', p. 227, but it is considered largely interpolated (Anal. Boll., XXX, 323). St. Theodore is said to have been born in the East (Syria or Armenia are mentioned by some writers). He enlisted in the army and was sent with his cohort to winter quarters in Pontus. When the edict against the Christians was issued by the emperors, he was brought before the Court at Amasea and asked to offer sacrifice to the gods. Theodore, however, denied their existence and made a noble profession of his belief in the Divinity of Jesus Christ. The judges, pretending pity for his youth, gave him time for reflection. This he employed in burning the Temple of Cybele. He was again taken prisoner, and after many cruel torments was burned at the stake.

Francis Mershman, The Catholic Encyclopedia, Volume 14

Panegyric: Praise of Blessed Theodore the Great Martyr

You, the people who belong to Christ, a holy flock, a royal priesthood which had come from every place, city and the countryside, what is the source of that sign which brought you to this sacred place? Who are you who hasten here and planned this [journey] beforehand? Is it not the season of winter which is untroubled by war, when armed soldiers are not present, sailors set sail over the foamy [waves] and the farmer puts to rest the ox used for plowing in the stall? It is not clear that the holy martyr sounded the trumpet from among the roster of warriors, rouses people from diverse regions to a place of rest, proclaims a home, not in preparation for war but to a sweet and attractive peace for Christians? We believe that in the year when the barbarian invasion stopped and the horrible war against the savage Sythians came to an end we witnessed no frightening, terrible war, no triple crested helmet nor a brandished sword glittering in the sun, but the all-powerful cross of Christ which wards them off, the means by which he obtained glory through his suffering. Furthermore, I ask you to consider closely those who keep blameless religious observance such as the martyrs who compose an outstanding assembly of the just as well as those deemed worthy of recompense while still in the world. Let me affirm that they are still with us. Their great honor is open for all to see: by recognizing the fruit of piety, you must strive to share in their reverence. Desire the honors which Christ dispenses according to the worthiness of his athletes. But if it pleases him that we may enjoy future benefits which a pure hope offers to the just when the judge of our lives comes to us, we may see the company of the saints which is so magnificent and glorious. For the soul which is ascending is fond of residing in its own inheritance and converses in an incorporeal manner with its own brethren; the body a deserving and immaculate vehicle for that purpose which never allows the harm originating from its own passions to reside with incorruptibility. Enwrapped with much honor and solicitude, it dwells in this holy place as an inestimable treasure reserved for the time of regeneration and shares the uniqueness with regard to other bodies. For this common death which is similar in nature has no comparison. There are other abominable matters, for example, no one should lightly disregard the tomb but is this person opens himself to persuasion, he is liable to have no share in the repugnance of this present age, thereby avoiding the burden of the human condition. Should a person come to a place similar to our assemble today where the memory of the just and the rest of the saints is present, first consider this house's great dignity to which souls are lead. God's temple is brightly adorned with magnificence and is embellished with decorations, pictures of animals which masons have fashioned with delicate silver figures. It exhibits images of flowers made in the likeness of the martyr's virtues, his struggles, sufferings, the various savage actions of tyrants, assaults, that fiery furnace, the athlete's blessed consummation and the human form of Christ presiding over all these events. They are like a book skillfully interpreting by means of colors which express the martyr's struggles and glorify the temple with resplendent beauty. The pictures located on the walls are eloquent by their silence and offer significant testimony; the pavement on which people tread is combined with small stones and is significant to mention in itself. These spectacles strike the senses and delight the eye by drawing us near to [the martyr's] tomb which we believe to be both a sanctification and blessing. If anyone takes dust from the martyr's resting place, it is a gift and a deserving treasure. Should a person have both the good fortune and permission to touch the relics, this experience is a highly valued prize and seems like a dream both to those who were cured and whose wish was fulfilled. The body appears as if it were alive and healthy: the eyes, mouth, ears as well as the other senses are a cause for pouring out tears of reverence and emotion. In this way one implores the martyr who intercedes on our behalf and is an attendant of God for imparting those favors and blessings which people seek. From all this, oh devout people, learn that "the death of his holy ones is admirable before the Lord" [Ps 115.6], for all men comprise one and the same body; they share the same substance as one dough and are carried off to death. However, the martyr's suffering bestows grace which is lovable, joyful and undeniable as the text above teaches. Therefore we believe that appearances hold out the promise of future blessings procured from trials endured in the world. Many are those who pursue [pleasures of] the stomach, vainglory and the rubbish of all this world's charms while neglecting that which is to come; rather, such persons believe that death puts an end to all these things [Phil 3.19]. But a thoughtful person will learn about great matters from that which is small and about archetypes from shadows. To whom will the honor of kings go? Who will be remembered among men with regard to that arrogance resulting from visible reality? Which general who has captured fortified cities and has enslaved many peoples is celebrated as this soldier, poor man and conscript whom Paul has armed [Eph 6.11] and whom the angels have anointed for combat and whom Christ has crowned with victory [2Tim 4.8]? Since these words unite you to the martyr's trials, follow the saint's uncommon example and forsake any useless pursuit because everyone loves such things. The fatherland is majestic by reason of beholding the sun. Job is noble because he came from the [land of the] sun's rising and continued to observe those customs with which he was acquainted [Job 1.3].

On the other hand, the martyr possesses the entire earth and every citizen who dwells under the sun. However, a list of armed men is taken from that vicinity when their regiment is transferred to our region where its leaders post them to rest during the winter. But when war suddenly arises not by an incursion of barbarians but by Satan's ordinance and decree which God opposes (for every Christian is put under the ban of a severe prescription and is condemned to death), the thrice blessed [Theodore] reveals his piety and gives witness everywhere to his faith in Christ in addition to being inscribed upon the forehead with a confession. He is no longer a novice nor untried by battle and combat but has fortified his soul to resist dangers; he is neither afraid nor a coward reluctant to speak. The evil spirits have convened a court along with their leaders and taxiarchs which is reminiscent of Herod and Pilate who condemned the Lord to be crucified by a similar judgment. They said, "What is the source of your courage, you who dare to mock the king's decree? Do you not submit in trembling to those royal decrees? Do you not worship the authorities who are in power?" Maximianus was then king whom these leaders served. With stern countenance and resolute mind [Theodore] responded to their charges by saying, "I do not know the gods because they are false, whereas you err by honoring and addressing them, having been influenced by demons who have deceived you from [the worship of] God [cf. Jn 3.18]. But as for me, Christ is God, the Only Begotten Son of God. Therefore on behalf of the true religion and by confessing him, let him who inflicts wounds go ahead and cut; let him who strikes thrash; let him who burns lead to the flame, and let him who is grieved by my words cut out my tongue. Each member of the body needs patience bestowed by the Creator." The tyrants were at a loss by these words and could not sustain the first refutation of his integrity because this youth was bursting with passion and sought death as if it were a sweet drink. For a brief period the [persecutors] were at a loss and took counsel with regard to future action. One of the military leaders with a refined demeanor scorned the martyr by the following response: "Theodore, are you the Son of God? Was he born to suffer as a man? My god was not born for this purpose, but I believe that he is a son and that his birth befits his divinity. But you and your childish, pathetic reasoning should make you blush and hide due to your profession in an effeminate god whom, like a mother, you worship her twelve sons who gave birth to a multitude of demons just like a hare or a sow which effortlessly conceive and give birth!" The tyrants mocked the saint by this two pronged attack of idolatry and under the guise of clemency said, "Give us a short time to consider such madness. Perhaps by giving him a brief rest he might change his mind for the better." These [despots] called wisdom insanity, reckoned madness and label derangement eloquence just like drunks who vehemently berate sober persons. However, this pious man and soldier of Christ made full use of manly behavior in the respite allotted to him. What did he do? You certainly have enough time to ponder over his tale with joy. The gods' temple erected to their mythical mother was located in the capitol city of Amasea by a river bank where such mislead persons devised their folly. But the noble man remained fearless while his detractors watched for an opportune moment and a occasion because they yearned to accuse him of setting a fire and impatiently expected him to admit it. Once everyone learned of this incident (for a blazing fire started in the midst of the city), [Theodore] did not disclose the deed nor hasten to speak about it. However, it was certainly clear to [his accuser's] arrogance and to the confusion of their great joy that this incident was a source of distress for the temple and its graven image. It was reported to the magistrates that he was responsible for burning the temple and a judgment more fearful than the first resulted due to his provocation.

Once the [judges] took their seats in court, the magistrate eloquently questioned Theodore who stood in their midst and who quickly turned the interrogation into a confession [of faith]. Since they could not accuse him and their fearful threats had no effect, they changed their tactics and benignly attempted to withdraw the accusation by offering him promises. "If you wish to submit to our counsel," they said, "we will at once reinstate your renown from such disgrace, change your ignominy into honor and will swear that you share in the glory which belongs to the office of chief priest." When he heard of this honor, the thrice-blessed [Theodore] said, "I judge the priests of idols as wretched men and pity the attendants of such vain practices. I both greatly feel for and loath the chief priest. He is among the worst and most miserable of men, a fact which is more unimaginable than any unjust circumstance; he is the cruelest of murderers and is more wanton than any dissolute person. Therefore let your devastating actions run their course. Tell me, you who make such depraved promises, by choosing a life of piety and righteousness with respect to God, it is better to be a outcast in God's house than to dwell in the tents of the wicked [Ps 83.11]? I pity the kingdom's subjects to whom you continuously read the iniquitous law because its authority is considerable. They can keep the title of chief priest for themselves, cloth themselves with dark purple in imitation of evil chief priests and wrap their melancholy with bright dignity. When approaching the impure altar, they sacrifice butchered birds before kings, examine the entails of wretched cattle, sell meat stained with blood and defile their clothing." After the just man had uttered these words, the leaders no longer feigned goodwill but accused him as being most disrespectful of the gods, contemptuous of kings and a blasphemer. First they tortured him by tearing his body which they had suspended upon a tree. While the executioners were vigorously at work, he remained steadfast, constant and sang about his torments from the Psalm, "I will bless the Lord at all times, his praise ever in my mouth" [Ps 33.2]. Those torments of the flesh diminished while he sang and were as though another man were being mistreated. In this fashion the prison sanctioned his punishment. Another phenomenon occurred with regard to the saint: at night he heard a multitude singing, and those outside saw their radiant splendor in the dead of night. This marvelous visitation troubled the prison guard and a sound emanated from inside the cell; no one was present except the martyr who remained at peace with the other sleeping prisoners. After many such events, [Theodore] was strengthened by his confession and piety, and they brought a vote of condemnation upon him. He was ordered to be burned and in the way finished his wonderful, blessed journey to God. However, [Theodore] left behind a lesson from his agony: he summoned the people, taught the church, put demons to flight, brought angelic peace, implored benefits from God, healed various illnesses in that place, provided a safe haven for those tossed by afflictions, was a rich treasury for the poor, a quiet inn of rest for travelers and a continuous festal celebration. If we keep the yearly festival, an enthusiastic multitude will always be in attendance; the highway leading there bore them along like ants with some going and other departing.

Therefore, oh blessed anniversary graciously provided by the Creator, we flock to your festival with the martyrs' holy band which worships a common God. By recalling the victory of our many struggles, you return to us, and when you arrive, you provide us with a day of celebration. We beseech you, whether you dwell in the air above or in some celestial circle or angelic chorus, that you assist the Lord or worship him as a faithful servant with the powers and virtues. Come from that place to those who beseech you, invisible friend! You have learned of his death, a means by which you might give double thanks to God who conferred this favor through one passion and one pious confession that you may rejoice in the blood he shed and in the grievous fire he endured. As a result you will have as worthy ministers those who witnessed the spectacle. We lack many benefactors. Intercede on behalf of the people that they may share one kingdom because the martyr's country is one of affliction whose citizens and brethren and kinsmen have died and have been honored. We fear afflictions and expect danger because we are close to the ungodly Sythians who grieve us with war. As a soldier, fight for us; as a martyr, grant courage to your fellow servants. Since you have prevailed over this life yet are familiar with humanity's sufferings and needs, grant peace that the festivals may continue, that the furious, insolent, mad barbarians might not triumph over the temples or altars and that they might not tread the holy place. We who have been kept safe and unharmed ponder your beneficence and implore protection for the future. Should we experience stress and dishonor, let your people beseech the chorus of your fellow martyrs; the prayers of many just people will exonerate sin. Remember Peter, awaken Paul along with John the theologian and beloved disciple, who are solicitous on behalf of the churches which they have founded and on whose behalf they endured dangers and death. They did not engage in idol worship which was inimical to our head [Christ] in order that heresy may resemble thorns to pluck out vines, that weeds might not suffocate wheat, that no rock hinder the true, rich dew and that anything without root may show the power of the fertile word [cf. Mt 13.25, 7, 20]. But by the power of your intercession and those with you, oh marvelous and most bright among the martyrs, the young shoot will return to you, the flourishing citizenship of Christians will endure to the end in the splendid, fruitful field of faith in Christ which always bears the fruit of eternal life in Christ Jesus Lord. To him with the Father and Holy Spirit be glory, power and honor now and forever. Amen.

Gregory of Nyssa

The Passion of Serge and Bacchus

Under the rule of the emperor Maximian gross superstition held sway over the human race, for people worshiped and made sacrifices to stones and wood, the devices of human beings, and they consumed obscene offerings. Those unwilling to sacrifice were subjected to torture and harsh punishment and compelled to serve the demons. A decree [to this effect] with severe threats was posted in the markets of every city. The purity of the air was defiled with the diabolical smell from the altars and the darkness of idolatrous error was reckoned a matter of state. It was then that Serge and Bacchus, like stars shining joyously over the earth, radiating the light of confession of and faith in our Savior and Lord Jesus Christ, began to grace the palace, honored by the emperor Maximian. The blessed Serge was the primicerius of the school of the Gentiles, a friend of the emperor and who had great familiarity with him, so that Maximian promptly acceded to his requests. Thus the blessed Serge, having a certain friend Antiochus, was able to arrange for him to become the governor of the province of Augusto-Euphrates.

The blessed Bacchus himself happened to be the secundarius of the school of the Gentiles. Being as one in their love for Christ, they were also undivided from each other in the army of the world, united not by the way of nature, but in the manner of faith, always singing and saying, "Behold, how good and how pleasant it is for brethren to dwell together in unity!" They were adept and excellent soldiers of Christ, cultivating assiduously the inspired writings to combat diabolical error, and fighting vigorously in battle to defeat the enemy.

But the malicious and evil spirit afflicted with envy some of those who had been brought to the school of the Gentiles, and they, seeing [the saints] so honorably received in the imperial chambers, so advanced in military rank, and on such familiar terms with the emperor, and being unable to bring any other instrument of malice against them, accused them to the emperor of being Christians.

Waiting for a moment when the saints would not be standing near the emperor, and finding him alone, they said to him, "such zeal for the cult of the holiest and greatest gods has your immortal majesty that in those holy rescripts of yours which are everywhere disseminated you have commanded that all unwilling to honor and worship them, and in submission to your righteous doctrine, should perish in great torment. How is it then that Serge and Bacchus, the directors of our school, enjoy such familiarity with your eternal power, when they worship Christ, whom those called Jews executed, crucifying him as a criminal; and by persuading many others they draw them away from the worship of the gods?"

When he heard this the emperor refused to believe it and said, "I do not think you speak the truth that Serge and Bacchus are not devoted to the veneration and worship of the gods, since I have such a pure affection for them, and they would hardly be worthy of it they were not truly faithful in their piety toward the gods. But if, as you say, they belong to that unholy religion, they shall now be exposed. Once I have summoned them without their knowing of the charges that have been brought against them, I will go with them into the temple of mighty Zeus, and if they sacrifice and eat of the holy offerings, you yourselves shall bear the risk of the slander of which you are guilty. If they refuse to sacrifice, they shall incur the penalty appropriate for their impiety. For the gods would not have the shield-bearers of my empire be impious and ungrateful."

"We, O Emperor," replied the accusers, "moved by zeal and affection for the gods, have brought before your undying majesty what we have heard regarding them. It is for your unfailing wisdom to discover their impiety."

Straightaway the emperor sent for them. They entered with the customary retinue of guards and imperial pomp. The emperor received them and went in their company to the temple of Zeus. Once he had entered, Maximian offered libations with the whole army, partook of the sacrificial offerings, and looked around. He did not see the blessed Serge and Bacchus. They had not gone into the temple, because they thought it impious and unholy to see them offering and consuming unclean sacrifices. They stood outside and prayed as with one mouth, saying, "King of Kings and Lord of lords, who alone possess immortality and inhabit unapproachable light, shed light on the eyes of their minds, because they walk in the darkness of their unknowing; they have exchanged your glory, incorruptible God, for the likeness of corruptible men and birds and beasts and snakes; and they worship the created rather than you, the creator. Turn them to knowledge of you, that they may know you, the one true God, and your only-begotten Son, our Lord Jesus Christ, who for us and for our salvation suffered and rose from the dead, that he might free us from the bonds of the law and rescue us from the folly of vain idols. Preserve us, God, pure and spotless in the path of your martyrs, walking in your commandments."

While this prayer was yet in their mouths, the emperor sent some of the guard standing near him and commanded them to be brought into the temple. When they had entered, the emperor said to them, "It appears that, counting on my great friendship and kindness – for which the gods have been your defenders and advocates – you have seen fit to disdain imperial law and to become deserters and enemies of the gods. But I will not spare you if indeed those things spoken of you prove to be true. Go, then, to the altar of mighty Zeus, make sacrifice and consume, like everyone else, the mystical offerings."

In reply the noble soldiers of Christ, the martyrs Serge and Bacchus, answered: "We, O Emperor, are obliged to render to you earthly service of this corporal body; but we have a true and eternal king in heaven, Jesus the Son of God, who is the commander of our souls, our hope and our refuge of salvation. To him every day we offer a holy, living sacrifice, our thoughtful worship. We do not sacrifice to stones or wood, nor do we bow to them. Your gods have ears, but they do not hear the prayers of humans; just as they have noses but do not smell the sacrifice brought them, have mouths but do not speak, hands but do not feel, feet but do not walk. "They that make them," as the Scripture says, "are like unto them: so is every one that trusteth in them because Thou are with us."

The emperor's countenance was transformed with anger; immediately he ordered their belts cut off, their tunics and all other military garb removed, the gold torcs taken from around their necks, and women's clothing placed on them; thus they were to be paraded through the middle of the city to the palace, bearing heavy chains around their necks. But when they were led into the middle of the marketplace the saints sang and chanted together, "Yea, though we walk through the valley of the shadow of death, we will fear no evil, Lord"; and this apostolic saying: "Denying ungodliness and worldly lusts, and putting off the form of the old man, naked in faith we rejoice in you, Lord, because you have clothed us with the garment of salvation, and have covered us with the robe of righteousness; as brides you have decked us with women's gowns and joined us together for you [or: "joined us to you"] through our confession. You, Lord, commanded us, saying, "Ye shall be brought before governors and kings for my sake.... But when they deliver you up, take no thought how or what ye shall speak: for it shall be given you in that same hour what ye shall speak. For it is not ye that speak, but the Spirit of your Father which speaketh in you." Rise, Lord, help us and rescue us for your name's sake; strengthen our souls that we may not be separated from you and the impious may not say, "Where is their God?"

When they reached the palace Maximian summoned them and said, "Most wicked of all men, so much for the friendship which I had bestowed on you, thinking you to have proper respect for the gods, and which you, confident of my openness and affection, have despised, brazenly offering me in return that which is against the law of obedience and subjection. But why should you blaspheme the gods as well, through whom the human race enjoys such abundant peace? Do you not realize that the Christ whom you worship was the son of a carpenter, born out of wedlock of an adulterous mother, whom those called Jews executed by crucifixion, because he had become the cause of dissensions and numerous troubles among them, leading them into error with magic and claiming to be a god? The very great race of our gods were all born of legal marriage, of the most high Zeus, who is thought to be the most holy, giving birth through his marriage and union with the blessed Hera. I imagine that you will have also heard that the heroic and twelve greatest labors were worthy of a god, those of heavenly Hercules, born of Zeus."

The noble soldiers of Christ answered, "Your majesty is mistaken. These are myths that ring in the ears of the simpler men and lead them to destruction. He whom you say to have been born of adultery as the son of a carpenter, he is God, the son of the True God, with and through whom was all made. He established the heavens, he made the earth, the abyss and the great sea he bounded with sand, he adorned the heavens with the multitude of stars, the sun he invented for the illumination of the day and as a torch in the night he devised the moon. He divided the darkness from the light, he imposed measure on the day and limits on the night, in wisdom he brought forth all things from nonbeing to being. In these last days he was born upon the earth for the salvation of humankind, not from the desire of a man, nor the desire of the flesh, but from the Holy Spirit and an ever-virgin girl, and living among humans he taught us to turn from the error of vain idols and to know him and his father. He is true God of true God, and in accord with an unknowable plan he died for the salvation of the human race, but he plundered hell and rose on the third day in the power of his divinity, and he established incorruptibility and the resurrection of the dead to eternal life."

Beside himself with rage on hearing these things, the emperor ordered that their accusers be enrolled in their positions in the army and said to them, "I am sending you to Duke Antiochus, thrice-cursed ones – the very man you were able to promote to such rank because of the friendship and familiarity you had with me – so that you will realize how great is the honor you have lost by speaking against the gods and how trivial a court you merit for the worst punishments, since the greatness of the gods has apprehended and brought your blasphemy to the judgment seat for justice."

Immediately he sent them to Duke Antiochus, ordering that their entire bodies be bound with heavy chains, and that they be sent thus to Eastern parts through a succession of officials. He also wrote a letter along these lines: "From Maximian, eternal emperor and triumphant ruler of all, greetings to Duke Antiochus. The wisdom of the greatest gods is unwilling that any men should be impious and hostile to their worship, especially shield and spear-bearers of our empire. Wherefore I commend to your severity the vile Serge and Bacchus, convicted with apposite proof of belonging to the unholy sect of the Christians and plainly deserving of the worst punishment, whom I consider unworthy of the administration of imperial justice. If they should be persuaded by you to change their minds and sacrifice to the gods, then treat them with their own innate humanity, free them from the prescribed torments and punishments, assure them of our forgiving kindness and that they will receive back immediately their appropriate military rank and be better off now than they were before. But if they will not be persuaded and persist in their unholy religion, subject them to the severest penalties of the law and remove from them hope of long life with the penalty of the sword. Farewell."

The same day the officials took them out of the city as far as the twelfth mark, and when evening overtook them they stopped at an inn. About midnight an angel of the Lord appeared and said to [the saints], "Take courage and fight against the devil and his evil spirits, as noble soldiers and athletes of Christ, and once you have thrown the enemy put him under your feet so that when you appear before the king of glory we, the host of the army of angels, may come to greet you singing the hymn of victory, conferring on you the trophies of triumph and the crowns of perfect faith and unity.

When morning came they rose and took the road with great joy and alacrity. There were also some of their household servants with them, united with them in longing for the love of Christ, and in true love for their corporal masters, on account of which they would not leave them when they were in such straits. They heard them discussing with each other the appearance of the angel in the night.

Taking the road, the two chanted psalms together and prayed as if with one mouth, thus, "We have rejoiced in the way of martyrdom, as much as in all riches. We will meditate in thy precepts and search out thy ways. We will delight ourselves in thy statutes: we will not forget thy word. Deal bountifully with thy servants, that we may live and keep thy word."

As the emperor had commanded, the soldiers of Christ were sent from city to city through a succession of changing officials with great security along the road of martyrdom laid down for them, until they were brought to the eparchy of Augusto-Euphrates, which was on the borders next to the people of the Saracens, to a certain fortress called Barbalisus where Duke Antiochus had his seat.

Appearing promptly before him around the ninth hour, their custodians handed over the emperor's letter and also the holy martyrs Serge and Bacchus. Antiochus rose from his dais and accepted the emperor's rescript in his purple general's cloak; when he had read it he summoned privately the official in charge and told him, "Take the prisoners and secure them in the military prison, seeing that apart from the usual constraints they do not suffer anything, and do not place their feet in full manacles of wood. Bring them to the bench of my justice tomorrow, so that I can hear them at the prescribed time, according to the law." The official took them and bound them as the duke had commanded him. When it was evening, they sang together and prayed, as with one mouth, speaking thus: "Thou, Lord, brakest the heads of the dragons in the waters; thou didst cleave the fountain and the flood; thou hast set all the borders of the earth. Cast thine eye upon us, O Lord, for the enemy hath reproached us, and the foolish people have blasphemed thy holy name. Deliver not the souls of those confessing thee to men more savage than beasts, forget not the congregation of thy poor forever. Have respect unto thy covenant: for the dark places of the earth are full of the habitations of cruelty. Let us not be returned humbled, ashamed: so that we, thy humble servants, may praise thy name. Forget not the voice of thine enemies: the pride of them that hate thee ascendeth continually against us, thy servants, and in vain have the people hated us. But do thou, O Lord, rescue us and free us for thy name's sake."

Then, while they slept for a while, an angel of the Lord appeared to them and said, "Take heart, stand fast and unmovable in your faith and love. It is God who aids and watches over you."

Rising from their sleep and reporting to their household the apparition of the angel, they were encouraged and began to chant again: "In my distress I cried unto the Lord, and he heard me from his holy mountain. I laid me down and slept; for the Lord sustained me. We will not be afraid of thousands of people, that have set themselves against us round about. Arise, Lord, and save us, O our God: for salvation belongeth unto the Lord: thy blessing is upon thy people."

On the following day, when the duke was seated on the bench of justice in the praetorium, he summoned the commentarius and said, "Bring in the prisoners." The latter responded, "They are at hand before the righteous bench of your authority." When the saints appeared, he commanded the emperor's letter to be read. Once this was done, Duke Antiochus, prompted by his associate, announced, "It is incumbent on you to obey the orders of the glorious emperor, our lord, and to sacrifice to the gods and become worthy of their benevolence. Since you were unwilling to do this, you have forfeited great glory, and having made yourselves unworthy, were discharged from the military and deprived of all your former wealth. Nonetheless, if you will now obey me and sacrifice to the gods to earn their goodwill, you could earn even greater honor and glory than before, and receive back your military rank and more besides.

"This was prescribed in the letter sent to me, as you yourselves have heard. Being humane, the most holy emperor has disposed that if you repent of those things you have rashly done, and now sacrifice to the gods, you may yet enjoy his favor. Wherefore I, feeling compassion for you, and mindful of your friendship and kindness – especially yours, my Lord Serge, for I myself have benefited from your generosity – advise you that if you will not do this, you force me to obey our lord the emperor and to see that his orders concerning you are strictly observed."

In reply the saints declared, "We have left all and followed Christ, so that heedless of earthly and temporal honor, we may become rivals of the angels in heaven, and ignoring terrestrial and corruptible wealth, we may heap up treasure in heaven. What profit would it be if we gained the whole world, but lost our souls? Do not, therefore, so advise us, Antiochus. For your tongue is forked, and the poison of adders is under your lips. You will hardly be able to change our minds while God himself encourages us. Do, therefore, what you will; we will not sacrifice to wood, nor worship stones. We serve Christ, the son of God, the eternal ruler, before whom "every knee should bow, of things in heaven, and things on earth, and things under the earth," and whom every tongue should confess. Your gods are man-made idols: if they were divine, they themselves would command humans, and would not [need to] be avenged through human design on those who decline to serve and worship them."

The duke rejoined, "We do not avenge the gods. It is through their disposition that all the powers of our enemies have been subjected to us. But we call you to justice because of your accursed and unholy superstition."

To which the saints responded, "It is you who are accursed and unholy, and all those persuaded by you to sacrifice to demons and worship insensate stones and wood. All of them will soon be cast eternally into flames, and you also will be punished with them."

In a great rage the duke commanded that the blessed Serge be taken from the praetorium and returned to prison; the blessed Bacchus he ordered held for flogging. The henchmen went at this until they collapsed exhausted and near dead on the floor. When they could go on no longer, he directed that [Bacchus] be turned over on his stomach to be beaten with four whips of rawhide, saying to him, "Let's see if your Christ will free you from my hands." From the first hour until evening they wore away his flesh; blood flowed everywhere; both his stomach and liver were ruptured.

The blessed Bacchus said to Antiochus: "The devil's servants, your torturers have failed; your impudence is overthrown; the tyrant Maximian is conquered; your father the devil has been put to shame. The more the man without is ravaged by your blows, the more the man within is renewed in preparation for the eternal life to come."

After he said this, there was a great voice from heaven: "Come, rest henceforth in the kingdom prepared for you, my noble athlete and soldier, Bacchus." Those standing by hearing the voice were stupefied and struck dumb. He himself, having borne the blows so long, gave up his spirit to the angels.

The duke, frustrated by his defeat, ordered that his remains not be buried, but thrown out and exposed as meat to the dogs, beasts, and birds outside the camp. Then he rose and left. When the body was tossed some distance from the camp, a crowd of animals gathered around it. The birds flying above would not allow the bloodthirsty beasts to touch it, and kept guard through out the night.

In the morning, some of the monks who lived nearby in caves came and collected the body the animals – as if they were rational human beings – had been mourning. They buried him in one of their caves.

Meanwhile the blessed Serge, deeply depressed and heartsick over the loss of Bacchus, wept and cried out, "No longer, brother and fellow soldier, will we chant together, 'Behold, how good and how pleasant it is for brethren to dwell together in unity!' You have been unyoked from me and gone up to heaven, leaving me alone on earth, bereft [literally, "made single"], without comfort." After he uttered these things, the same night the blessed Bacchus suddenly appeared to him with a face as radiant as an angel's, wearing an officer's uniform, and spoke to him. "Why do you grieve and mourn, brother? If I have been taken from you in body, I am still with you in the bond of union, chanting and reciting, 'I will run the way of thy commandments, when thou hast enlarged my heart.' Hurry then, yourself, brother, through beautiful and perfect confession to pursue and obtain me, when finishing the course. For the crown of justice for me is with you." At daybreak when he rose he related to those who were with him how he had seen the blessed Bacchus in the night and in what sort of garb.

The next day the duke planned to go out of the fortress of Barbalisus to that of Souros, and commanded that the blessed Serge follow. He enjoined him to sacrifice, but the latter, with noble judgment, refused his blandishments. When they reached the castle of Souros, Antiochus took his seat in the praetorium, summoned the blessed Serge, and told him, "The most sacrilegious Bacchus refused to sacrifice to the gods and chose to die violently; he got the death he deserved. But you, my lord Serge, why give yourself over to such misery by following that deceptive and impious cult. Mindful of your kindness to me I am disposed to mercy; and it embarrasses me that you were the cause of my having obtained this authority, since now you stand in the dock as the accused, and I sit on the bench as the prosecutor."

To this Christ's witness answered, "Antiochus, this very suffering and present disgrace will stand as a patron for me of great eloquence and eternal glory with the king of heaven and of earth and of every living thing, Jesus Christ, the Son of God. If only you would now heed me and recognize my God and king, Christ, and be as circumspect in regard to the heavenly ruler, Christ, as you are in dealing with earthly kings, you would provide yourself with power unending and perpetual glory. For earthly rulers pass quickly, as the psalm says: 'Ye shall die like men, and fall like one of the princes.' And again, 'I have seen the wicked highly exalted, and lifted up like the cedars of Libanus. And I passed by, and lo, he was not: and I sought him and his place was not found.'"

The duke replied, "spare us this idiocy and ignorant foolishness; sacrifice to the gods in obedience to the holy command of our ruler, the emperor Maximian. If you will not, know that you force me to forget all that has come to me through you and to subject you to the most rigorous punishment decreed by law."

Serge answered, "Do as you will. I have Christ to preserve me, who said, 'Fear not them which kill the body, but are not able to kill the soul; but rather fear him which is able to destroy both soul and body in hell.' The body is subject to you: torture and punish it if you wish. But bear in mind that even if you kill my body, you can not dominate my soul – neither you nor your father, Satan."

The duke responded angrily: "It appears that my patience has served only to prod you along the path of willfulness." He summoned the official in charge and told him, "Fasten long nails in his boots, sticking straight up, and then put them on him." Once the boots were on, Antiochus sat in his carriage, directed that the animals be driven fiercely all the way to Tetrapyrgium, and ordered the blessed one to run in front of him. Tetrapyrgium is nine miles from Syrum. While he ran, the blessed one sang, "I waited patiently for the Lord, and he inclined unto me. He brought me up also out of a horrible pagan pit, out of the miry clay of idolatry, and set my feet upon a rock, and establishes my goings."

When they reached the castle of Tetrapyrgium the duke said, "It amazes me, Serge, that having first been kept in such confinement you can now sustain these bitter torments." The most holy martyr answered, "These tortures are not bitter to me, but sweeter than honey." The duke got out of the chariot and went in to breakfast, indicating that [Serge] should be retained in the soldiers' custody.

In the evening [Serge] sang psalms. "Those who did eat of my bread hath lifted up their heels against me, and with the cords of hideous torture they have laid a net for my feet, hoping to trip me up. But rise, Lord, outrun them and cause them to stumble, and rescue my soul from the wicked." About midnight an angel of the Lord came to him and healed him, restoring his feet completely. In the morning, mounting the bench, the duke ordered him brought in, thinking he would be unable to walk and would have to be carried, on account of his feet. When he saw him coming, walking a considerable distance and not limping at all, he was astounded, and exclaimed, "The man is a sorcerer. This must be how he managed to enjoy such familiarity with the emperor: he accomplished it through sorcery. What I am seeing is the proof of what they said about him. I would have thought it wholly impossible for him to walk on his feet after having been disabled by the torture inflicted on him yesterday. By the gods I am confounded at seeing him now walk as if nothing had happened!"

When the blessed Serge stood before the bench Antiochus addressed him. "Come to your senses even now, sacrifice to the gods, and you will avoid further torture. I will spare you out of respect for your kindness. If you will not, know that the witchcraft with which you devised to heal yourself will not avail you."

To which the blessed Serge replied, "If only you could escape the intoxication of diabolical error. I am in my senses in the Lord who has trampled the weapons of your father the devil under the feet of his humble servant, and has given me victory over you, and sent his angel to heal me. It is you who are the magician, and those who worship demons. It is the cult of your nameless idols that invented every sorcery, that is the beginning and cause and conclusion of all evil."

Antiochus sat down on his carriage even angrier, and commanded [Serge] to run before him wearing the same boots as far as the castle of Rosafae, another nine miles from Tetrapyrgium. When they came to the castle of Rosafae, the duke said to the blessed Serge, "Has the agony of the nails untied the knot of your idiocy? Are you prepared now to sacrifice to the gods, or will you persist in this insane obsession?"

The noblest martyr rejoined, "Know this, Antiochus: with this foolishness I will dissolve and undo your malicious and wicked strength. Do what you will: I will not worship demons, nor sacrifice to idols. Blameless in this, I strive to offer sacrifice only to my Lord."

Seeing that he remained steadfast and immovable in his faith and confession of Christ, the duke pronounced sentence against him: "You have rendered yourself unworthy of the favor of the gods, Serge, and become a member of the unholy sect called Christians, injuring the great good of our ruler, the emperor Maximian, by refusing to comply with his holy decree and sacrifice to the gods. For this the law requires that you suffer the penalty of the sword." A number of those present shouted out that the sentence issued against him was just. The guards came immediately and gagged his holy lips, took him out of the courtroom, and led him away to be executed.

A great crowd of men, women, and children followed, to see the blessed one meet his end. Seeing the beauty blooming in his face, and the grandeur and nobility of his youth, they wept bitterly over him and bemoaned him. The beasts of the region left their lairs and gathered together with the people, doing no injury to the humans, and bewailed with inarticulate sounds the passing of the holy martyr.

When they reached the place where the holy martyr of Christ was to meet his end, he called on the guards to allow him a little time to pray. Extending his hands to heaven, he said, "The beasts of the field and the birds of the sky, recognizing your dominion and rule, Lord, have gathered together for the glory of your holy name, so that you will incline and wish of your goodness to turn through their unreason the reason of humans to knowledge of you. For you wish all to be saved and to come to knowledge of the truth. When you lay death upon them, accept their repentance, Lord, and do not remember the sin of ignorance which they have perpetrated against us for your sake. Enlighten the eyes of their minds and lead them to the knowledge of you. Receive, Lord, my spirit, and give it rest in the heavenly tents with all the others whom you have found acceptable. To you do I commend my soul, which you have rescued from the snares of the devil."

Saying this and signing himself, he knelt and was beheaded, giving up his spirit to the angels. A voice from heaven said, "Come, also, Serge, soldier and victor, to the kingdom prepared for you. The hosts of angels, the ranks of patriarchs, the choirs of apostles and prophets, the souls of the just all await your coming to share with them the wonderful things in store for you there."

Translated by John Boswell from the Greek "Passio antiquior SS. Sergii et Bacchi Graece nunc primum edita," AB 14 (Brussels, 1895)

Julius

The elderly Julius was tried and condemned by Maximus.

Maximus was capable of recognising excellence, and, at the start of Julius' trial he was anxious to befriend Julius.

MAXIMUS: Julius, I see that you are a sensible and serious man. Take my advice therefore, and sacrifice to the gods.

JULIUS: I will not do as you desire, nor run into sin and eternal punishment.

MAXIMUS: If you think that sin, let it be laid to my charge. I will apply force to you, that it may not look as if you had complied willingly. Then you can go home with no further anxiety.

The offer was all the more seductive because it was so kindly intended; but Julius saw behind the indulgent governor the evil power which spoke through him.

JULIUS: You cannot draw me away from my eternal Lord. I cannot deny God. Give sentence against me, therefore, as a Christian.

MAXIMUS: Unless you will be obedient to the imperial orders and sacrifice I will cut your head off.

JULIUS: That is a good thought. I beseech you, religious governor, by the health of the emperors, to put it in execution, and give sentence upon me, that my desires may be fulfilled.

MAXIMUS: You are in such a hurry to die. You think that you will suffer for some praiseworthy object.

JULIUS: If I am permitted to suffer in this way everlasting glory will await me.

MAXIMUS: If you were suffering for your country and for the laws you would have everlasting praise.

JULIUS: It is indeed for the laws that I shall suffer, but the laws are God's laws.

MAXIMUS: Laws which are bequeathed to you by a dead man who was crucified. See what a fool you are, to make more of a dead man than of the live emperors.

JULIUS: He died for our sins that he might bestow on us eternal life, but he is God who endures for ever, and whoever confesses him shall have eternal life, and whoever denies him eternal punishment.

MAXIMUS: I am sorry for you and I advise you to sacrifice and live with us.

JULIUS: If I live with you it is death to me, but if I die, I live.

MAXIMUS: You have chosen death rather than life.

JULIUS: I have chosen death for the moment and then life everlasting.

The following sentence was then pronounced: "Julius, who refuses to obey the orders of the emperors, is to receive capital punishment."

Julius was taken out to be executed. His last words were, "O Lord Jesus Christ, for whose name's sake I suffer thus, vouchsafe to set my spirit among thy saints." He was then beheaded.

A. J. Mason, The Historic Martyrs of the Primitive Church, Longmans, 1905, pp 218-9

Sebastian

"He was prepared for his second martyrdom."

Sebastian was born at Narbonee, in Gaul, instructed in Christianity at Milan, and was later an officer in the Imperial Guard at Rome. He remained a Christian in the middle of idolatry, untainted by evil examples around him. He was informed against and betrayed; but being of rank too considerable to be put to death without the emperor's orders, Emperor Diocletian was acquainted with the persecution.

On hearing the accusation, he sent for Sebastian, and charged him with being an enemy of the gods of the empire. Sebastian replied that proof of his faithfulness was in praying to the only true God for the well being and prosperity of the emperor and the government. Incensed at this reply, the emperor ordered him to be taken to the Campus Martius, and there to be shot to death the arrows, which sentence was carried out. A few Christians attended the execution, in order to bury his body, and they perceived signs of life in him. They took him away and shortly he recovered and was prepared for his second martyrdom.

As soon as he was able to walk, he placed himself in the emperor's way as he was going to the temple. The appearance of a person supposed to be dead astonished the emperor, nor did the words of the martyr less surprise him, for he began to reprehend him for his cruelties, and for his prejudices against Christianity. Having overcome his surprise, he ordered Sebastian to be seized and beaten to death, and his body thrown into a common sewer.

John Foxe, The Book of Martyrs, revised with notes and an appendix by W. Bramley-Moore, London, 1869, p 30

Tarachus, Probus and Andronicus

While Maximus, Governor of Cilicia, was at Tarsus, three Christians were brought before him. Tarachus, the eldest, was asked by Maximus what he was. The prisoner replied, "A Christian." This reply offending the governor, he again made the demand, and was answered in a similar manner. The governor then told him that he ought to sacrifice to the gods, as the only way to promotion, riches, and honours; and that the emperors themselves did what he recommended him to perform. Tarachus answered that avarice was a sin, and gold itself an idol as abominable as any other. As for promotion, he desired it not, as he could not in conscience accept any place which would subject him to worship idols; and with regard to honours, he desired none greater than the honourable title of Christian. As to the emperors themselves, he added, that they were deceived in worshipping idols, and misled by the devil himself. For this speech his jaws were broken. He was then scourged, loaded with chains, and thrown into a dungeon, to remain there till the trials of the other two prisoners.

Probus was then brought before Maximus, who asked his name. The prisoner answered, the most valuable name that he could boast of was that of a Christian. To this Maximus replied: "Your name of Christian will be of little service to you; be therefore guided by me; sacrifice to the gods, engage my friendship, and the favor of the emperor." Probus answered that as he had relinquished a considerable fortune to become a soldier of Christ, it might appear evident that he neither cared for his friendship nor the favour of the emperor. Probus was then scourged; and Demetrius, the officer, observing how his blood flowed, advised him to comply; but his only answer was, that those severities were agreeable to him.

"What!" cried Maximus. "Does he still persist in his madness?"

To which Probus rejoined, "That character is wrongly bestowed on one who refuses to worship idols." After being scourged, suffering with as much intrepidity as before, and still repeating, "The more my body suffers and loses blood, the more my soul will grow vigorous, and be a gainer," he was committed to prison, and his feet and hands were stretched on the stocks.

Andronicus was next brought up, when being asked the usual questions, he said, "I am a Christian, a native of Ephesus, and descended from one of the first families in that city." He was ordered to undergo punishments similar to those of Tarachus and Probus, and then was remanded to prison. Having been confined some days, the three prisoners were brought before Maximus, who began to reason with Tarachus, expressed the hope that he would change his mind. Finding himself mistaken, Maximus ordered him to be tortured in a variety of ways: fire was placed in the palms of his hands; he was hung up by his feet; a mixture of salt and vinegar was poured into his nostrils: and in this state he was remanded to his dungeon.

Probus being called, and asked if he would sacrifice, replied: "I come better prepared to die than before; for what I have already suffered has only confirmed me in my resolution. Employ your whole power on me, and you will find that neither you, nor your masters the emperors, nor the gods whom you serve, nor the devil, who is your father, shall oblige me to adore idols whom I know not." The governor, however, pressed him to sacrifice to Jupiter; but Probus turned his casuistry into ridicule, and said, "shall I pay divine honours to Jupiter, to one who married his own sister to a debauchee, as he is even acknowledged to have done by your priests and poets?" Provoked at this speech, the governor ordered him to be struck on the mouth for uttering blasphemy. His body was then seared with hot irons; he was put on the rack, and scourged; his head was shaved, and red-hot coals placed on the crown of his head; and after all these tortures, he was remanded in prison.

When Andronicus was again brought before Maximus, the latter attempted to deceive him, by pretending that Tarachus and Probus had repented of their obstinacy, and owned the gods of the empire. To this the prison answered, "I cannot believe that they have renounced their hopes in our God, nor will I fall short of them in faith in our common Saviour. Thus armed, I neither now your gods nor your authority; fulfil your threats, employ every cruel art in your power; I am prepared to bear it for the sake of Christ." For this answer he was scourged, and his wounds rubbed with salt.

These intrepid Christians were brought to a third examination, when they retained their constancy, were again tortured, and at length ordered to be executed. They were brought to the amphitheater where several beasts were let loose on them; but none of the animals, though hungry, would touch them. Maximus was so incensed at this circumstance, that he rebuked the keeper, and ordered him to produce a beast that would execute the business for which he was wanted. The keeper then brought out a large bear that had that day destroyed three men; but this creature, and a fierce lioness, also refused to touch the Christians. Finding the design of destroying them by the means of wild beasts ineffectual, Maximus ordered them to be slain by a sword, which was done on the 11th of October, 303.

John Foxe, The Book of Martyrs, revised with notes and an appendix by W. Bramley-Moore, London, pp 31-34

Tortures of the First Christian Martyrs (8) Martyrs Condemned to the Wild Beasts

It was customary with the Ancients in former days to condemn criminals, or Christians if it so happened, to the wild beasts.

a. Savage dogs. In the Acts of the holy martyr St Benignus, we read, "The most wicked Emperor commanded him to be shut up in prison, and a great stone with a hole through it to be brought, and his feet to be fixed therein with molten lead, and red-hot bradawls to be stuck lengthwise into his fingers under the nails, and for six days neither food nor drink to be given him; moreover that twelve savage dogs should be imprisoned along with him, maddened with hunger and thirst, to the end these might tear him in pieces, and the goal to be watched by soldiers."

b. Martyrs were imprisoned in a net, and so exposed to be tossed by a savage bull.

c. Martyrs were wrapped in a wild beasts's hide, and so left to be torn by animals.

Tortures and Torments of the Christian Martyrs, from the "De SS. Martyrum Cruciatibus" of the Rev Father GAllonio, translated by A.R.Allinson, London and Paris, 1903, Limited Edition, printed for the subscribers, pp. 159-161

Basilides and Potamiaena

Basilides, virgin, martyred at the beginning of the third century, under Emperor Maximian, and the soldier Potamiaena, who took Basilides to her execution.

The praises of Potamiaena are still widely sung today. She had guarded her chastity against all lovers even though her body and mind were in full flower. She ended her indescribably horrible tortures by being burnt to death. It is reported that her judge, Aquila, after subjecting her body to dreadful tortures, threatened to hand her body over to the gladiators so they could abuse her. She was led away to her execution by a member of the armed forces, Basilides. He showed kindness to Potamiaena as he kept the abusive crowd away from her. After Potamiaena had been led away she prayed for Basilides, and her prayer was answered quickly. Potamiaena showed unbelievable courage in her martyrdom, as, slowly, drop by drop, boiling pitch was poured all over her body, from the tip of her toes to the crown of her head.

Soon after this Basilides was asked to take an oath but refused to do so, stating that he was unable to do this because he was a Christian (see Matthew 5:34). To start with everybody thought he was joking, but, eventually, he was brought before a magistrate and then imprisoned. When his Christian brothers visited him and asked what made his so determined, it is reported that he said that three days after Potamiaena's martyrdom she appeared to him and placed a wreath on his head. In this vision he saw that Potamiaena had her prayer answered and that he would soon stand at her side. The brothers then bestowed the seal of the Lord on him [baptised him], and the following day Basilides, as a noble witness for his Lord, was beheaded.

Eusebius, The History of the Church, Book 6

Crispina

The Acts of Crispina *record the martyrdom of a mother called Crispina in Theveste, Numidia, in 304, and took place during the Galerian's persecution, the last persecution of the Roman Empire.*

"A martyrdom never falls within human plans, for the true martyr is the one who has become the instrument of God." T.S. Eliot

On December 5th, in Diocletian's ninth consulate and Maximian's eighth, Anulinus, the proconsul, sat on his judgement seat, in the colony of Theveste. The court's clerk said, "Crispina of Thagore has defied the edict of our masters and lords. If you order it, she will be heard."

ANULINUS: Bring her to us.

Crispina came in.

ANULINUS: Crispina, are you aware of the indictment?

CRISPINA: No. What does it say?

ANULINUS: Make sacrifices to all our gods so that our emperors will be protected. The law is promulgated by Diocletian, Maximian, pious Augusti, and Constantius and Maximus, our most noble Caesars.

CRISPINA: I have never sacrificed before. I will not sacrifice now – except to the one true God, our Saviour Jesus Christ, his Son, who was born and suffered.

ANULINUS: You must renounce your superstition and bow down before the statues of the Roman gods.

CRISPINA: Every day I call upon almighty God, and know no other gods other than him.

ANULINUS: You are insolent and stupid. You will pay for keeping to your beliefs.

CRISPINA: Whatever may happen to me, I am prepared to suffer in the name of the faith which I have embraced.

ANULINUS: I repeat: you must submit to the imperial orders.

CRISPINA: I do submit, but only to the commands of my Lord Jesus Christ.

ANULINUS: You will be beheaded if you continue to ignore the emperor's orders. You must obey them. You should know that everyone in Africa has sacrificed.

CRISPINA: Nobody will ever make me sacrifice to demons. I sacrifice to the Lord who made heaven and earth, the sea and all that is in them.

ANULINUS: If you want to stay alive and practise your religion you must serve these gods.

CRISPINA: A religion that tortures those who will not join them is no religion.

ANULINUS: You will have to obey if you are not to escape the punishment laid down by the law.

CRISPINA: I am prepared to endure torture, but I will never defile my soul by coming into contact with man-made idols of stone.

Anulinus told the clerk of the court,

Degrade her. Shave her head with the razor!

CRISPINA: I will believe your gods if they speak. I would not have appeared before your tribunal if I was not seeking my salvation.

ANULINUS: Do you want to live for a long time, or to die in agony, like so many of your friends?

CRISPINA: If I wished to die and hand over

my soul to the flames of eternal fire I would have faith in your demons.

ANULINUS: You will be beheaded unless you worship our venerable gods.

CRISPINA: I thank God for dying in such a way. I totally accept being beheaded for my God's sake. I will not sacrifice to your imaginary gods who are both dumb and deaf. ANULINUS: Do you persist in your mad resolve?

CRISPINA: My eternal God caused me to be born, saved me through the living water of baptism, is with me now, and strengthens me in my trials. Thanks to my God I shall escape sacrilege.

ANULINUS: We can no longer endure this insolence. Read the charge against her again.

The proconsul Anulinus then read this sentence from his tablets: "Crispina persists in her infamous superstition and will not sacrifice to our gods. In the name of Augustus' sacred law I pronounce that you are chastised by the sword."

CRISPINA: I bless my God and thank him for giving me grace to be free in this way from you. Thanks be to God.

Crispina then made the sign of the cross on her forehead, laid bare her neck, and was beheaded for the name of our Saviour Jesus Christ, to whom be honour for ever and ever. Amen.

Editor

MARTYRS AT NICOMEDIA

Peter

In Nicomedia the rulers ordered a certain man to offer sacrifice. Because he refused, he was stripped, and tied up naked, and whipped with loaded whips which tore into his flesh. This was to continue until he agreed to sacrifice. As he did not give in to this his wounds were then bathed in salt and vinegar, especially where bones had been exposed. He treated these agonies scornfully and so he was put in a brazier that was already on fire and roasted very slowly until he eventually breathed his last, but remained immovable to the end. Such was the martyrdom of one of the imperial servants, whose name was Peter.

Hadrian

Twenty-three Christians had been brought before Galerius. He was incensed at the way they answered his questions. He called his chief official to note down their names. Then another man, Hadrian, stepped forward and said, "Make a note of my name with theirs."

"Are you mad?" asked Galerius, "do you want to throw away your life as well?"

"I am not mad, sir. Once I was mad, but now I have come into my right mind."

"Do not speak," said Galerius, "but beg my pardon. Say in the presence of everyone that you have made a mistake. Then you answer will be erased from the minutes of this court."

"No," replied Hadrian, "from now on I will ask pardon of God for my evil deeds and for the errors of my past life."

Hadrian was thrown into prison with the other twenty-three Christians. He was visited by his wife, Natalia, whom he had been married to for just over a year. When Hadrian was before Galerius for trial, he carried the hobby- horse on which he was to be tortured. Natalia was there to keep him true to his profession. Hadrian was also beaten. Galerius said to Hadrian, "These other poor creatures are but peasants. You are a noble and are not like them. Acknowledge the gods and you will be freed."

Hadrian would not be separated from his new friends, and said, "I dare say that you know about my home and family and ancestors, but if you knew the family of these holy men, and their wealth, and the home that they are looking for, you would throw yourself instantly at their feet, and beg them to pray for you. Moreover, you would smash your gods with your own hands."

Hadrian was turned over and beaten on his stomach. After a while, the emperor told the beaters to stop. The delicately nurtured body could not bear much more. "You see," said the emperor, "how I wish to spare you. If you will only call on the gods with your voice" [he meant without performing any sacrificial act] "I will have the doctors brought in to attend to your wounds and you will be with me in my palace today."

Hadrian replied that he would do so, if the gods would promise with their own lips to do what Galerius had said they would do for him.

"What," said the emperor, "they cannot speak."

"Why, then," replied the Christian, "do you sacrifice to things which cannot speak?"

Hadrian was thrown back in prison, where, along with some of the other twenty-three confessors, he had his wrists and ankles broken by an iron bar. Natalia held his poor hands on the wooden block while this was done. Mortification set in, and Hadrian died in his prison. Natalia was forced to flee from Byzantium to escape the attentions of the officer of the town, who wanted to marry her. She took with her, as her chief treasure, the hand of her martyred husband, embalmed, and wrapped in a purple covering, which she always kept at the head of her bed.

A. J. Mason, The Historic Martyrs of the Primitive Church, Longmans, 1905, pp 227-8

THEODOTUS

In the reign of Emperor Maximin, Theodotus ran an eating-house in Ancyra, Galatia's capital city. He helped the church and the Christian cause in this way. Theotecnus had ordered that every item of food and drink that was sold in the city should be defiled by being offered to idols, or by coming into contact with something that had been offered. Theotecnus made sure that all bread and wine was treated in this way to hit out at the sacrament which he knew was the church's mainstay. But Theodotus managed to sell food to his Christian customers which had not been polluted, as he bought some of his food from Christian tradesmen.

Theodotus was brought before Theotecnus, who personally helped to torture him. All the usual horrors were tried. Eventually, as blazing torches were held under him, the martyr smelt his own flesh as it burned and tried to turn his nose away from the smell. Theotecnus stood beside him, looking for the slightest sign of weakness. He said, "If you had not blasphemed the gods you would never have suffered like this. You should take my advice, for you are only a shopkeeper, and not say anything against the emperors who have power to shed your blood."

The martyr's reply was enough to make Theotecnus order the executioners to knock out his teeth. Theodotus only answered, "If you cut out my tongue, and all my speech organs, God can still hear a Christian who cannot speak."

Theodotus was remanded in prison. The governor did this deliberately so that as he was led back through the market-place everyone would see how Christians were treated. Theodotus said to the people who crowded round him, "It is fitting for those who believe in Christ to offer to him such sacrifices as I have offered, for he first suffered thus for each of us." After five days in prison, fresh arguments and fresh tortures were applied to him. Theodotus was not insensible to the pain. "O Lord Jesus Christ, hope of the hopeless," he cried out, "hear my prayer and assuage my agony, for it is for thy holy name that I suffer it." He received grace to endure.

At last Theotecnus wrote his sentence of release: "Theodotus, a patron of the Galilaeans, and an enemy of the gods, who will not obey the emperors, and who also treats me with disrespect, is condemned by my authority to undergo the penalty of the sword, and his beheaded body to be burned with fire." Theodotus was executed, praying to God that the violence of the enemy might come to an end in him, and that peace might be restored to the church.

A. J. Mason, The Historic Martyrs of the Primitive Church, Longmans, 1905, pp 238-9

EUSTRATIUS, EUGENIUS, AUXENTIUS, MARDARIUS AND ORESTES

Emperor Diocletian placed turbulent Cappadocia in the hands of two special commissioners, Lysias and Agricola. Eustratius (who was also known as Cyrisices to his friends), as head registrar in Lysias' court, was forced to witness scenes which tormented him. One day it was his duty to cite in court the actions of a presbyter called Auxentius, who had already made a good confession before Lysias. As Eustratius did this, he was so overcome with admiration for the presbyter, that he announced in public that he himself was also a Christian, and had been once since his childhood. Eustratius was tried by fire, but instead of screaming, he merely smiled.

"Would you like me to dream up a different torture?" asked the angry magistrate. Eustratius welcomed the idea. "Then bring some strong brine, mixed with vinegar," ordered Lysias. "scrape his burns with a piece of broken pottery, and pour brine over the wound, until he can stand no more pain." Eustratius bore this quietly.

"Perhaps," said Lysias, "your bodily exhaustion has affected your mind, and made you delirious. Put away your groundless hopes, and accept the salvation I offer you." But Eustratius would have none of it.

His example was contagious. One of his underlings, Eugenius, now stood up and said aloud, "I too am a Christian, and I curse your religion, and am determined to resist your wishes and the command of the emperors, as my superior Eustratius has done." Eugenius was thrown in prison with Eustratius.

That night the magistrate set out for Nicopolis and made the Christian prisoners march along with him, with nails in their shoes. The next day they arrived in Auauraca, which happened to be the birth place of both Eustratius and Eugenius. There, one man, Mardarius, took the opportunity to declare himself a Christian and considered it an honour being numbered with the prisoners.

Auxentius, the presbyter, who lived in Auauraca, was being examined. "Do not trouble me any more, Auxentius," ordered Lysias, "pay yourself the favour of thinking yourself worthy of being saved. Tell us that you have now given up this silly and dangerous obstinacy."

"I will tell you in a very few words," answered the priest, "I swear to you by the justice above us which takes account of all things, that I will not change my mind. I know and worship one God and one only."

Lysias condemned him to be beheaded.

"Now," said Lysias, "bring in the person who has just attached himself to the others. We will soon give him the honour which he courts."

Mardarius asked Eustratius, "Pray for me, Cyrisices, and tell me how to reply to this wolf of a man. I am no scholar, and he will laugh at me."

"Say nothing, brother," replied Eustratius, "except, "I am a Christian"; "I am a servant of Christ."

Mardarius did as he was told. To all questions his answer was the same. The "wolf" of a magistrate had him tied up head downwards, by a rope passed through the tendons of his heels, and hot irons placed on him. After a time, Mardarius expired, with thanksgiving on his lips, and Eugentius soon followed.

Lysias' troubles for the day were not yet over. He went out to review his troops in a nearby field. He was particularly struck by the looks of a tall, handsome soldier called Orestes. He was paying the man a compliment, when accidentally it came out that Orestes was a Christian. His belt was taken away at once and he was dismissed from the army and arrested. Orestes was executed by Lysias' brother-commissioner, Agricola, in Sebastia. Agricola tried to save Eustratius by suggesting that he should pretend in public to worship the gods, and seek forgiveness from his God afterwards. Eustratius naturally rejected this base suggestion with contempt, and died like a good Christian in the fire.

A. J. Mason, The Historic Martyrs of the Primitive Church, Longmans, 1905, pp 245-7

Claudius, Asterius, Neon, Domnina and Theonilla

Lysias, in Cilicia, the neighbouring province of Cappadocia, condemned five Christians to death, including two women.

Lysias, the president of the province of Cilicia, sitting on the judgement-seat in the city of Aegae, said, "Let the Christians who have been delivered by the officials to the magistrates of this city be presented for my judgment."

The warder Euthalius said, "According to your commandment, my lord, the magistrates of this city present the Christians whom they have been able to get hold of. They consist of three boys, brothers, and two women with a baby. One of them is now before your worship. What is your excellency's wish about him?"

There was no need to find out whether the young man was a Christian; that was already ascertained by the magistrate of the city.

LYSIAS: What is your name?

CLAUDIUS: Claudius.

LYSIAS: Do not throw away your young life by mad folly. Come this moment and sacrifice to the gods, according to the commandment of our lord the Augustus, and so escape the horrors prepared for you.

CLAUDIUS: My God does not require such sacrifices, but works of mercy and upright lives. But your gods are unclean devils, and that is why they are pleased with sacrifices of this kind, destroying for ever the souls of those who worship them. You will never persuade me to worship them.

Lysias ordered him to be prepared for the rods.

LYSIAS: "I have instructions from the emperors to offer rewards and promotions to Christians who consent to sacrifice.

CLAUDIUS: Their rewards are temporal, but to confess Christ is everlasting salvation.

Claudius was placed on the hobby-horse and his feet were burnt. Part of his foot was cut off and shown to him.

CLAUDIUS: Fire and tortures cannot hurt those who fear God. It only helps them to everlasting salvation, because they suffer these things for Christ's sake.

The hooked talons tore his sides. Other tortures followed in succession. They only made him assert more confidently that torture was the way of salvation, and at last he was sent to prison, and his brother Asterius was called in.

LYSIAS: Torture his sides, and as you do so say to him, "Even now obey and sacrifice."

ASTERIUS: I am the brother of the one who answered you just now. He and I are of one mind, and make the same confession. Do what you can. You have my body in your power, but not my soul. Fresh tortures were tried.

ASTERIUS: Fool! Madman! Why do you torment me? Do you not care about what the Lord will make you pay for this?

After further tortures, Asterius still did not give way.

ASTERIUS: Blind, completely blind. I only ask you to leave no part of my body untortured.

The third boy, Neon, came into court.

LYSIAS: My son, come and sacrifice to the gods, and escape torture.

NEON: If your gods have any power let them defend themselves from those who deny them, without wanting you to defend them. But if you are as bad as they are, I am much better than your gods and than you. I will not obey you. My God is the true God, who made heaven and earth.

LYSIAS: Hit him on the neck, and as you do that say, "Do not blaspheme the gods."

NEON: Is it a blasphemy to tell the truth?

Neon's feet were stretched on the horse and hot coals were placed on him and his back was lashed.

NEON: What I know to be for my good and profitable for my soul, that I will do. I cannot change my mind.

Lysias then read this sentence from his tablet.

LYSIAS: Let the brothers Claudius, Asterius, Neon, who are Christians, who blaspheme the gods, and refuse to sacrifice, be crucified outside the gate, and let their bodies be left to be torn to pieces by the birds.

The two women remained to be dealt with. Domnina was presented first.

LYSIAS: You see, my good woman, the tortures and the fire prepared for you. If you wish to escape them, come and sacrifice to the gods.

DOMNINA: I do not wish to fall into eternal fire and into everlasting torments. Therefore I worship God, and his Christ, who made heaven and earth and all things that are therein. Your gods are stone and wood, the work of men's hands.

Lysias ordered her to be stripped naked, and laid out flat, and beaten all over. This order was enough to kill her.

EXECUTIONER: By your eminence, Domnina has already died!

LYSIAS: Throw her body into a deep place in the river.

Then came Theonilla. To her the same invitation was made, to which she replied in similar words as Domnina.

LYSIAS: Slap her face; throw her to the ground, tie her feet together and torture her well.

THEONILLA: Whether you think it good to torture a gentlewoman and a stranger like this, you know best. God sees what you do.

LYSIAS: Hang her up by her hair, and slap her face.

THEONILLA: Is it not enough that you have stripped me naked? I am not the only one that you have covered with shame, but your own mother and wife also through me, for all women are of the same nature.

LYSIAS: Are you married or are you a widow?

THEONILLA: I have been a widow for twenty-three years. I have stayed a widow for my God's sake, fasting and watching in prayers ever since I forsook the unclean idols and knew my God.

Lysias responded by ordering the tormentors to shave her head with a razor to see if anything would make her ashamed, to put a girdle of wild briars on her, to tie her to four stakes, and to have her body beaten all over. The final torture was to be burning charcoal placed above and below her so that she could be left to die in these fumes.

But before the charcoal was brought, Theonilla, like Domnina, was mercifully released.

EXECUTIONER: Sir, she is no longer alive.

LYSIAS: Get a sack and put her body in it. Tie it tight and throw it into the sea.

A. J. Mason, The Historic Martyrs of the Primitive Church, Longmans, 1905, pp 252-4

Januarius, Bishop of Benevento

Acts of the Hieromartyr

In the time of Diocletian, emperor, and in the fifth consulate of Constantine [Constantius], and seventh [probably "fifth"] of Maximian, there was a great persecution of the Christians. At that time Diocletian appointed Timothy, a pagan, governor in the province of Campania and ordered him to offer sacrifices to idols and to compel all who believed in Christ to do the same. It happened as he was making the customary round of cities, he came to the city of Nola. There he ordered the officials to present themselves before him and when they were present he began to inquire from them concerning the judgments of his predecessors.

To him the officials related their deeds and among them, when they reached the affairs of the blessed martyrs Sosius, deacon of the church at Miseno and Proculus, deacon of the church at Pozzuoli, and Eutychetes and Acutius, and how they had been tormented by various tortures and had been recast into prison by the order of the judge, he asked the officials what had been done with them. They replied saying that they for a long time were detained in chains and they uttered in addition evil remarks concerning the Blessed Januarius, bishop of Benevento. This most unjust Timothy having heard these remarks regarding Januarius, ordered him to be brought before him and when he was presented before his tribunal at Nola, Timothy the judge said to him: "Januarius, having heard of the reputation of your family I exhort you to sacrifice to the gods in obedience to the decrees of the invincible rulers. But if you are unwilling I shall subject you to horrible torments which the God whom you worship when he shall see them he himself shall fear." St. Januarius however replied: "Be silent, O unhappy man, and do not insult in my hearing Him who created heaven and earth, lest the Lord God may hear such a blasphemy as that which proceeds from your mouth and he may destroy you and you shall be mute and deaf, not hearing and like a blind man not seeing." Having heard these things the tyrant Timothy says to the saint: "Is it in your power that by any enchantments whatever you or your god can prevail against me?" St. Januarius replies: "My power is nothing but there is a God in heaven who can resist you and all who obey and abet you." And when he had said this the tyrant ordered him back to prison. Being very angry he ordered a furnace to be heated for three days and the saint to be cast into it. The holy man made the sign of the cross on his forehead, looked up to heaven sighing and extending his hands, and having entered the fiery furnace he was praising God, saying: "O Lord Jesus Christ for the sake of thy holy name I embrace willingly this suffering and I expect every promise which thou hast promised to those who love Thee. Hear me praying to Thee and deliver me from this flame, thou who wert present with the three children, Ananias, Azarias, Misael in the fiery furnace, and be with me in this my trial to deliver me from the hands of the enemy."

Saying these things, Blessed Januarius began to walk with holy angels in the midst of the fire praising the Father and Son and Holy Ghost. When the soldiers who were around the furnace heard St. Januarius in its depth praising God they feared with a great fear and ran in great haste and told the judge saying, "We beseech thee, sir, not to be angry with us but we have heard the voice of Januarius in the furnace invoking his Lord, and being greatly terrified we fled." Timothy hearing this ordered the furnace to be opened and when it was opened the flames shot out and devoured some incredulous pagans who were around about it. But St. Januarius appeared in the midst glorifying the Lord Jesus Christ so that the fire could not touch either his clothes or his hair. Timothy however when he had heard this ordered him before him and said to him: "Of what avail is it that the magic you exercise is powerful? By various torments I will make you perish." St. Januarius replied: "It will not be well for thee, thou cruel tyrant, to alienate the servant of Christ from the truth of Christ or to cause me to obey through fear. I will hope in the Lord. I will not fear no matter what men may do to me," and thus replying the judge ordered him led back to prison. On another day early in the morning Timothy had Januarius before him: "How long, unhappy man, will you refuse to sacrifice to the immortal gods? Approach now and offer incense. If not I shall order you to be beheaded and if he can, let your God free you from my hands." The saint replied: "You do not know that the power of God is great. Would that you would repent so that my God might pardon you whom you say to be unable to free me from your hands! When you speak thus you are heaping up wrath for yourself on the day of wrath." The judge not liking this speech ordered his shackels to be removed. Januarius prayed God saying: "O Lord Jesus Christ who hast not abandoned me from my mother's womb now hear thy servant crying to thee and command me to depart this world and obtain thy mercy." The judge thinking how he would kill him sent him back to prison. While guarded by soldiers in hard captivity, two of his clergy, the deacon Festus and the reader Desiderius, learned of their bishop's captivity and being moved by the Holy Ghost they immediately set out from Beneventum and came to Nola, and there weeping they cried: "Why is such a man in custody? What crimes did he commit? When did he fail to aid those in trouble? What sick man was visited by him without regaining health? Who approached him weeping and went away not rejoicing?"

Their words were reported to Timothy who ordered them at once to be detained and along with Januarius to be brought before him, whereupon he asked Januarius who were these two and the saint replied: "One is my deacon and the other is my reader." "Do they proclaim themselves Christians?" "Certainly, for if you ask them, I hope in my Lord Jesus Christ that they will not deny themselves to be Christians," and being asked, they said: "We are Christians and we are prepared to die for the love of God."

Then Timothy filled with anger ordered Januarius the bishop, along with Festus the deacon and Desiderius the reader, to be bound in chains and to be dragged before his chariot to the city of Pozzuoli, determining that there along with Sosius, Proculus, Eutyches and Acutius, they should be delivered up to wild beasts. When they were come to Pozzuoli, they were kept in prison until the arena was prepared. On the day appointed they were led into the amphitheatre and Timothy coming ordered the wild beasts to be let loose; and when this was done, St. Januarius cried: "O brethren, seize the shield of faith and let us pray to the Lord our Helper in the name of the Lord who made heaven and earth." And the mercy of God was so present that to the feet of Januarius like sheep with heads down ran the wild beasts. The unbelieving judge had the beasts removed and the saints of God taken from the arena and brought before his tribunal, where sitting in state he dictated their sentence: "We order to be beheaded, Januarius bishop, Sosius, Proculus and Festus deacons, Desiderius reader, Eutyches and Acutius, citizens of Pozzuoli, who have professed themselves Christians and have despised the sacrifices of the gods and the commands of the emperor."

But St. Januarius looking up to heaven said: "Lord Jesus Christ who descended from on high for the redemption of the human race, deliver me and free me from the hand of this enemy and I beg thee my God that you punish Timothy for the things he did against me thy servant and that thou blind his eyes so that he may not see the light of heaven." When he had finished his prayer darkness fell on his [Timothy's] eyes and suddenly he was made blind. Then prayed Januarius to the Lord, and said: "I give thanks to thee, Father of our Lord Jesus Christ, who hast heard thy servant and destroyed the eyes of the impious Timothy because many souls on account of him have been perverted to the evil spirits."

Then Timothy was suffering with his stricken eyes and the pain was increasing. Repentant he began to cry out and say to the officials: "Go, bring Januarius to me." And they going found him lead along by the executioners on the incline that leads to the Solfatara and bringing him back they set him before the judge and a great multitude of people was attracted by the sight.

But Timothy began to cry out with a great cry and to say to St. Januarius: "Januarius, servant of the most high God, pray the Lord, thy God, for me blind that I may recover the sight which I have lost."

Then Januarius raising his eyes to heaven prayed: "God of Abraham, God of Isaac, God of Jacob, hear my prayer and restore to Timothy though unworthy his eyes that all the people present may know that thou art God and there is no other but thee; for we may not return evil for evil." And when St. Januarius had finished his prayer his were opened. The multitude seeing the wonderful things which the Lord wrought by Januarius his martyr, many of the bystanders believed in the Lord Jesus Christ, almost five thousand, and they cried out raising their voices: "Will not the God of such and so great a man be feared? Will he not perhaps take revenge for their sufferings and death and will we not all likewise perish?" Januarius was very beautiful both in body and disposition. Then the impious judge Timothy seeing such a crowd turned toward the Lord was troubled and (lest the servant of the Lord Jesus Christ might be deprived of his crown) fearing the commands of the emperor the judge ordered the soldiers to take him away quickly and to behead him with the holy martyrs. When they were on their way to martyrdom a certain old and very poor man, hoping favor from Januarius placed himself in his way and fell at his feet and besought him that he might receive some of his clothes. But Januarius said to that old man: "When my body has been buried thou wilt see that I myself will give thee my orarium with which I will have bound my eyes."

The mother also of St. Januarius residing at Benevento, three days before her son suffered, saw in a dream that Januarius was flying in the air to heaven and when she was puzzled by the dream and would inquire what it meant, suddenly it was announced to her that her son was imprisoned for the love of God. She however greatly terrified, prostrating herself in prayer before the Lord, gave up her spirit. In the meantime when the saints had arrived at the place where they were to be beheaded, that is at the Solfatara, St. Januarius kneeling prayed: "O Lord, omnipotent God, into thy hands I commend my spirit" and then rising he took his orarium and bound his eyes and kneeling again he placed his hand on his neck and asked the executioner to strike. The executioner struck with great force and cut off at the same time a finger of the saint's hand and his head. The other saints received likewise their crown.

St. Januarius after his execution appeared to the old man and offered him as he had promised the orarium which had bound his eyes and said: "Behold what I promised you, take it as I promised it," and he took it and hid it in his bosom with great reverence. The executioners and two other officials seeing the old man, laughingly asked him: "Have you got what he who was beheaded promised?" But he said, "Yes," and showed them the orarium which they recognized and wondered greatly. On the very same hour at which St. Januarius and the holy martyrs were beheaded the cruel Timothy began to suffer very much and he was exclaiming aloud: "I suffer these pains for having treated Januarius the servant of God so impiously. The angels of God torment [me]." And when he had been long tormented he gave up the ghost. The Christians of various cities were guarding the bodies of the saints that they might carry them off at night to their own cities and they kept a careful though secret watch; and when night was come and all were sleeping, St. Januarius in the silence of the night appeared to one of those who were prepared to take away his body and said to him: "Brother, when you take away my body know that the finger of my hand is missing. Seek it and place it with my body." And so it was done as the saint himself had admonished. The bodies of the saints lay at the Solfatara where later was founded a church worthy of St. Januarius the martyr. Here ends the passion of Januarius Martyr.
The Coptic Church

Christian Martyrdom

To these protracted and cruel persecutions the church opposed no revolutionary violence, no carnal resistance, but the moral heroism of suffering and dying for the truth. But this very heroism was her fairest ornament and staunchest weapon. In this very heroism she proved herself worthy of her divine founder, who submitted to the death of the cross for the salvation of the world, and even prayed that his murderers might be forgiven. The patriotic virtues of Greek and Roman antiquity reproduced themselves here in exalted form, in self-denial for the sake of a heavenly country, and for a crown that fadeth not away. Even boys and girls became heroes, and rushed with a holy enthusiasm to death. In those hard times men had to make earnest of the words of the Lord: "Whosoever doth not bear his cross and come after me, cannot be my disciple." "He, that loveth father and mother more than me, is not worthy of me." But then also the promise daily proved itself true: "Blessed are they, who are persecuted for righteousness' sake; for theirs is the kingdom of heaven." "He, that loseth his life for my sake, shall find it." And it applied not only to the martyrs themselves, who exchanged the troubled life of earth for the blessedness of heaven, but also to the church as a whole, which came forth purer and stronger from every persecution, and thus attested her indestructible vitality. These suffering virtues are among the sweetest and noblest fruits of the Christian religion. It is not so much the amount of suffering which challenges our admiration, although it was terrible enough, as the spirit with which the early Christians bore it.

Men and women of all classes, noble senators and learned bishops, illiterate artisans and poor slaves, loving mothers and delicate virgins, hoary-headed pastors and innocent children approached their tortures in no temper of unfeeling indifference and obstinate defiance, but, like their divine Master, with calm self-possession, humble resignation, gentle meekness, cheerful faith, triumphant hope, and forgiving charity. Such spectacles must have often overcome even the inhuman murderer. "Go on," says Tertullian tauntingly to the heathen governors, "rack, torture, grind us to powder: our numbers increase in proportion as ye mow us down. The blood of Christians is their harvest seed. Your very obstinacy is a teacher. For who is not incited by the contemplation of it to inquire what there is in the core of the matter? And who, after having joined us, does not long to suffer?"

Unquestionably there were also during this period, especially after considerable seasons of quiet, many superficial or hypocritical Christians, who, the moment the storm of persecution broke forth, flew like chaff from the wheat, and either offered incense to the gods (thurificati, sacrificati), or procured false witness of their return to paganism (libellatici, from libellum), or gave up the sacred books (traditores). Tertullian relates with righteous indignation that whole congregations, with the clergy at the head, would at times resort to dishonorable bribes in order to avert the persecution of heathen magistrates. But these were certainly cases of rare exception. Generally speaking the three sorts of apostates (lapsi) were at once excommunicated, and in many churches, through excessive rigor, were even refused restoration. Those who cheerfully confessed Christ before the heathen magistrate at the peril of life, but were not executed, were honored as confessors. Those who suffered abuse of all kind and death itself, for their faith, were called martyrs or blood witnesses. Among these confessors and martyrs were not wanting those in whom the pure, quiet flame of enthusiasm rose into the wild fire of fanaticism, and whose zeal was corrupted with impatient haste, heaven-tempting presumption, and pious ambition; to whom that word could be applied: "Though I give my body to be burned, and have not love, it profiteth me nothing." They delivered themselves up to the heathen officers, and in every way sought the martyr's crown, that they might merit heaven and be venerated on earth as saints.

Thus Tertullian tells of a company of Christians in Ephesus, who begged martyrdom from the heathen governor, but after a few had been executed, the rest were sent away by him with the words: "Miserable creatures, if you really wish to die, you have precipices and halters enough." Though this error was far less discreditable than the opposite extreme of the cowardly fear of man, yet it was contrary to the instruction and the example of Christ and the apostles, and to the spirit of true martyrdom, which consists in the union of sincere humility and power, and possesses divine strength in the very consciousness of human weakness. And accordingly intelligent church teachers censured this stormy, morbid zeal. The church of Smyrna speaks thus: "We do not commend those who expose themselves; for the gospel teaches not so." Clement of Alexandria says: "The Lord himself has commanded us to flee to another city when we are persecuted; not as if the persecution were an evil; not as if we feared death; but that we may not lead or help any to evil doing." In Tertullian's view martyrdom perfects itself in divine patience; and with Cyprian it is a gift of divine grace, which one cannot hastily grasp, but must patiently wait for. But after all due allowance for such adulteration and degeneracy, the martyrdom of the first three centuries still remains one of the grandest phenomena of history, and an evidence of the indestructible divine nature of Christianity.

No other religion could have stood for so long a period the combined opposition of Jewish bigotry, Greek philosophy, and Roman policy and power; no other could have triumphed at last over so many foes by purely moral and spiritual force, without calling any carnal weapons to its aid. This comprehensive and long-continued martyrdom is the peculiar crown and glory of the early church; it pervaded its entire literature and gave it a predominantly apologetic character; it entered deeply into its organization and discipline and the development of Christian doctrine; it affected the public worship and private devotions; it produced a legendary poetry; but it gave rise also, innocently, to a great deal of superstition, and undue exaltation of human merit; and it lies at the foundation of the Catholic worship of saints and relics. Sceptical writers have endeavored to diminish its moral effect by pointing to the fiendish and hellish scenes of the papal crusades against the Albigenses and Waldenses, the Parisian massacre of the Huguenots, the Spanish Inquisition, and other persecutions of more recent date. Dodwell expressed the opinion, which has been recently confirmed by the high authority of the learned and impartial Niebuhr, that the Diocletian persecution was a mere shadow as compared with the persecution of the Protestants in the Netherlands by the Duke of Alva in the service of Spanish bigotry and despotism. Gibbon goes even further, and boldly asserts that "the number of Protestants who were executed by the Spaniards in a single province and a single reign, far exceeded that of the primitive martyrs in the space of three centuries and of the Roman empire." The victims of the Spanish Inquisition also are said to outnumber those of the Roman emperors. Admitting these sad facts, they do not justify any sceptical conclusion. For Christianity is no more responsible for the crimes and cruelties perpetrated in its name by unworthy professors and under the sanction of an unholy alliance of politics and religion, than the Bible for all the nonsense men have put into it, or God for the abuse daily and hourly practised with his best gifts. But the number of martyrs must be judged by the total number of Christians who were a minority of the population. The want of particular statements by contemporary writers leaves it impossible to ascertain, even approximately, the number of martyrs. Dodwell and Gibbon have certainly underrated it, as far as Eusebius, the popular tradition since Constantine, and the legendary poesy of the middle age, have erred the other way. This is the result of recent discovery and investigation, and fully admitted by such writers as Renan. Origen, it is true, wrote in the middle of the third century, that the number of Christian martyrs was small and easy to be counted; God not permitting that all this class of men should be exterminated. But this language must be understood as referring chiefly to the reigns of Caracalla, Heliogabalus, Alexander Severus and Philippus Arabs, who did not persecute the Christians. Soon afterwards the fearful persecution of Decius broke out, in which Origen himself was thrown into prison and cruelly treated. Concerning the preceding ages, his statement must be qualified by the equally valid testimonies of Tertullian, Clement of Alexandria (Origen's teacher), and the still older Irenaeus, who says expressly, that the church, for her love to God, "sends in all places and at all times a multitude of martyrs to the Father."[8] Even the heathen Tacitus speaks of an "immense multitude" (ingens multitudo) of Christians, who were murdered in the city of Rome alone during the Neronian persecution in 64.

To this must be added the silent, yet most eloquent testimony of the Roman catacombs, which, according to the calculation of Marchi and Northcote, extended over nine hundred English miles, and are said to contain nearly seven millions of graves, a large proportion of these including the relics of martyrs, as the innumerable inscriptions and instruments of death testify. The sufferings, moreover, of the church during this period are of course not to be measured merely by the number of actual executions, but by the far more numerous insults, slanders, vexatious, and tortures, which the cruelty of heartless heathens and barbarians could devise, or any sort of instrument could inflict on the human body, and which were in a thousand cases worse than death. Finally, while the Christian religion has at all times suffered more or less persecution, bloody or unbloody, from the ungodly world, and always had its witnesses ready for any sacrifice; yet at no period since the first three centuries was the whole church denied the right of a peaceful legal existence, and the profession of Christianity itself universally declared and punished as a political crime. Before Constantine the Christians were a helpless and proscribed minority in an essentially heathen world, and under a heathen government. Then they died not simply for particular doctrines, but for the facts of Christianity.

Then it was a conflict, not for a denomination or sect, but for Christianity itself. The importance of ancient martyrdom does not rest so much on the number of victims and the cruelty of their sufferings as on the great antithesis and the ultimate result in saving the Christian religion for all time to come. Hence the first three centuries are the classical period of heathen persecution and of Christian martyrdom. The martyrs and confessors of the ante-Nicene age suffered for the common cause of all Christian denominations and sects, and hence are justly held in reverence and gratitude by all.

Dr. Thomas Arnold, who had no leaning to superstitious and idolatrous saint-worship, in speaking of a visit to the church of San Stefano at Rome, remarks: "No doubt many of the particular stories thus painted will bear no critical examination; it is likely enough, too, that Gibbon has truly accused the general statements of exaggeration. But this is a thankless labor. Divide the sum total of the reported martyrs by twenty – by fifty, if you will; after all you have a number of persons of all ages and sexes suffering cruel torment and death for conscience" sake, and for Christ's; and by their sufferings manifestly with God's blessing ensuring the triumph of Christ's gospel. Neither do I think that we consider the excellence of this martyr spirit half enough. I do not think that pleasure is a sin; but though pleasure is not a sin, yet surely the contemplation of suffering for Christ's sake is a thing most needful for us in our days, from whom in our daily life suffering seems so far removed. And as God's grace enabled rich and delicate persons, women and even children, to endure all extremities of pain and reproach, in times past; so there is the same grace no less mighty now; and if we do not close ourselves against it, it might be in us no less glorious in a time of trial." Lecky, a very able and impartial historian, justly censures the unfeeling chapter of Gibbon on persecution.

"The complete absence," he says (*History of European Morals*, I. 494 sqq.), "of all sympathy with the heroic courage manifested by the martyrs, and the frigid, and in truth most unphilosophical severity with which the historian has weighed the words and actions of men engaged in the agonies of a deadly, struggle, must repel every generous nature, while the persistence with which he estimates persecutions by the number of deaths rather than the amount of suffering, diverts the mind from the really distinctive atrocities of the Pagan persecutions .... It is true that in one Catholic country they introduced the atrocious custom of making the spectacle of men burnt alive for their religious opinions an element in the public festivities. It is true, too, that the immense majority of the acts of the martyrs are the transparent forgeries of lying monks; but it is also true that among the authentic records of Pagan persecutions there are histories, which display, perhaps more vividly than any other, both the depth of cruelty to which human nature may sink, and the heroism of resistance it may attain. There was a time when it was the just boast of the Romans, that no refinement of cruelty, no prolongations of torture, were admitted in their stern but simple penal code. But all this was changed. Those hateful games, which made the spectacle of human suffering and death the delight of all classes, had spread their brutalising influence wherever the Roman name was known, had rendered millions absolutely indifferent to the sight of human suffering, had produced in many, in the very centre of an advanced civilisation, a relish and a passion for torture, a rapture and an exultation in watching the spasms of extreme agony, such as an African or an American savage alone can equal. The most horrible recorded instances of torture were usually inflicted, either by the populace, or in their presence, in the arena. We read of Christians bound in chains of red-hot iron, while the stench of their half-consumed flesh rose in a suffocating cloud to heaven; of others who were torn to the very bone by, shells or hooks of iron; of holy virgins given over to the lust of the gladiator or to the mercies of the pander; of two hundred and twenty-seven converts sent on one occasion to the mines, each with the sinews of one leg severed by a red-hot iron, and with an eye scooped from its socket; of fires so slow that the victims writhed for hours in their agonies; of bodies torn limb from limb, or sprinkled with burning lead; of mingled salt and vinegar poured over the flesh that was bleeding from the rack; of tortures prolonged and varied through entire days. For the love of their Divine Master, for the cause they believed to be true, men, and even weak girls, endured these things without flinching, when one word would have freed them from their sufferings, No opinion we may form of the proceedings of priests in a later age should impair the reverence with which we bend before the martyr's tomb. The number of Dutch martyrs under the Duke of Alva amounted, according to Grotius, to over 100,000; according to P. Sarpi, the R. Cath. historian, to 50,000. Motley, in his History of the Rim of the Dutch Republic, vol. II. 504, says of the terrible reign of Alva: "The barbarities committed amid the sack and ruin of those blazing and starving cities are almost beyond belief; unborn infants were torn from the living bodies of their mothers; women and children were violated by the thousands; and whole populations burned and hacked to pieces by soldiers in every mode which cruelty, in its wanton ingenuity, could devise." Buckle and Friedländer (III. 586) assert that during the eighteen years of office of Torquemada, the Spanish Inquisition punished, according to the lowest estimate, 105,000 persons, among whom 8,800 were burnt. In Andalusia 2000 Jews were executed, and 17,000 punished in a single year.

Philip Scaff, History of the Christian Church, chapter 26

Peter, Bishop of Alexandria

St. Peter of Alexandria, noted for the gentleness with which he treated those who had lapsed during the persecutions, became himself in 311 the last great martyr of Egypt under paganism.

The genuine acts of Peter, Bishop of Alexandria and martyr

Were all the limbs of my body to be turned into tongues, and all the joints of my limbs to utter articulate sounds, it would no way be sufficient to express who, how great and how good, was our most blessed Father Peter, Archbishop of Alexandria. Especially incongruous do I consider it to commit to paper what perils he underwent by tyrants, what conflicts he endured with Gentiles and heretics, lest I should seem to make these the subjects of my panegyric rather than that passion to which he manfully submitted to make safe the people of God. Nevertheless, because the office of the narrator must fail in narrating his inmost conversation and wonderful deeds, and language is in no ways sufficient for the task, I have considered it convenient to describe only those exploits of his by which he is known to have attained to the pontificate, and after Arius had been cut off from the unity of the Church, to have been crowned with the martyr's laurel. Yet this do I consider to be a glorious end, and a spectacle of a magnificent contest, sufficient for those who do not doubt of a truthful narration, which is unstained by falsehood. In commencing, therefore, our account of the episcopate of this most holy man, let us call to our aid his own language, in order that we may make it co-operate with our own style.

Alexandria is a city of exceeding magnitude, which holds the first place not only among the Egyptians, but the Thebans also and the Libyans, who are at no great distance from Egypt. A cycle of two hundred and eighty-five years from the incarnation of our Lord and Savior Jesus Christ had rolled round, when the venerable Theonas, the bishop of this city, by an ethereal flight, mounted upwards to the celestial kingdoms. To him Peter, succeeding at the helm of the Church, was by all the clergy and the whole Christian community appointed bishop, the sixteenth in order from Mark the Evangelist, who was also archbishop of the city. He in truth, like the Morning Star rising among the stars, shining forth with the radiance of his sacred virtues, most magnificently governed the citadel of the faith. Inferior to none who had gone before him in his knowledge of Holy Scripture, he nobly applied himself to the advantage and instruction of the Church; being of singular prudence, and in all things perfect, a true priest and victim of God, he watchfully labored night and day in every sacerdotal care.

But because virtue is the mark of the zealot, "it is the tops of the mountains that are struck by lightning," [Horace, Odes, ii, 10 -11]; he hence endured multifarious conflicts with rivals. Why need I say more? He lived in persecution almost the whole of his life. Meanwhile he ordained fifty-five bishops.

Meletius lastly, in mind and name most black, was made the schismatical bishop of the city of Lycopolis, doing many things against the rule of the canons, and surpassing even the bloody soldiery in cruelty who, at the time of the Lord's Passion, feared to rend His coat; he was so hurried on by giving the rein to his madness, that, rending asunder the Catholic Church not only in the cities of Egypt, but even in its villages, he ordained bishops of his own party, nor cared he ought for Peter, nor for Christ, who was in the person of Peter. To him Arius, who was yet a laic, and not marked with the clerical tonsure, adhered, and was to him and his family most dear; and not without reason: every animal, as says the Scripture, loves its like. But upon this coming to his knowledge, the man of God being affected with grief, said that this persecution was worse than the former. And although he was in hiding, yet, so far as his strength permitted, directing everywhere his exhortations, and preaching up the unity of the Church, he strengthened men to withstand the ignorance and nefarious temerity of Meletius. Whence it came to pass that not a few, being influenced by his salutary admonitions, departed from the Meletian impiety.

Nearly about the same time Arius, armed with a viper's craft, as if deserting the party of Meletius, fled for refuge to Peter, who at the request of the bishops raised him to the honors of the diaconate, being ignorant of his exceeding hypocrisy. For he was even as a snake suffused with deadly poison. Yet neither can the imposition of hands upon this false one be imputed as a crime to this holy man, as the simulated magic arts of Simon is not ascribed to Philip. Meanwhile, the detestable wickedness of the Meletians increased beyond measure; and the blessed Peter, fearing lest the plague of heresy should spread over the whole flock committed to his care, and knowing that there is no fellowship with light and darkness, and no concord betwixt Christ and Belial, by letter separated the Meletians from the communion of the Church. And because an evil disposition cannot long be concealed, upon that instant the wicked Arius, when he saw his aiders and abettors cast down from the dignity of the Church, gave way to sadness and lamentation. This did not escape the notice of this holy man. For when his hypocrisy was laid bare, immediately using the evangelical sword, "If thy right eye offend thee, pluck it out and cast it from thee," and cutting off Arius from the body of the Church as a putrid limb, he expelled and banished him from the communion of the faithful.

This done, the storm of persecution suddenly abating, peace, although for a short time, smiled. Then this most choice priest of the Lord shone manifestly before the people, and the faithful began to run in crowds to keep the memory of the martyrs, and to assemble in congregations to the praise of Christ. Whom this priest of the divine law quickened with his holy eloquence, and so roused and strengthened that the multitude of believers increased continually in the Church. But the old enemy of salvation of man did not long remain quiet and look on these things with favoring eyes. For on a sudden the storm-cloud of paganism gave forth its hostile thunder, and like a winter shower struck against the serenity of the Church, and chased it away in flight. But that this may be understood more clearly, we must necessarily turn back to the atrocities of Diocletian, that impious one, and rebel against God, and also to Maximian Galerius, who at that time, with his son Maximin, harassed the regions of the East with his tyrannical sway.

For in the time of this man the fire of Christian persecution so raged, that not only in one region of the universe, but even throughout the whole world, both by land and by sea, the storm of impiety gave forth its thunder. The imperial edicts and most cruel decrees running hither and thither, the worshipers of Christ were put to death now openly, and now by clandestine snares; no day, no night, passed off free from the effusion of Christian blood. Nor was the type of slaughter of one kind alone; some were slain with diverse and most bitter tortures; some again, that they might want the humanity of kinsmen, and burial in their own country, were transported to other climes, and by certain new machinations of punishment, and as yet to the age unknown, were driven to the goal of martyrdom. Oh, the horrible wickedness! So great was their impiety that they even upturned from their foundations the sanctuaries of divine worship, and burned the sacred books in the fire. Diocletian of execrable memory having died, Constantinus Major was elected to administer the kingdom, and in the western parts began to hold the reins of government.

In these days, information was brought to Maximin about the aforesaid archbishop, that he was a leader and holding chief place among the Christians; and he, inflamed with his accustomed iniquity, on the instant ordered Peter to be apprehended and cast into prison. For which purpose he despatched to Alexandria five tribunes, accompanied with their bands of soldiers, who, coming thither as they had been commanded, suddenly seized the priest of Christ and committed him to the custody of a prison. Wonderful was the devotion of the faithful! When it was known that this holy man was shut up in the dungeons of the prison, an incredibly large number ran together, principally a band of monks and of virgins, and with no material arms, but with rivers of tears and the affection of pious minds, surrounded the prison's circuit. And as good sons towards a good father, nay, rather as the Christian members of a most Christian head, adhered to him with all theirs bowels of compassion, and were to him as walls, observing that no pagan might get an opportunity of access to him. One indeed was the vow of all, one their voice, and one their compassion and resolve to die rather than to see any evil happen to this holy man.

Now while the man of God was being kept for a few days in the same stocks, with his body thrust back, the tribunes made a suggestion to the king concerning him, but he, after his ferocious manner, gave his sentence for capitally punishing the most blessed patriarch. And when this got to the ears of the Christians, they all with one mind began to guard the approaches to the prison with groaning and lamentation, and persistently prevented any Gentile from obtaining access to him. And when the tribunes could by no means approach him to put him to death, they held a council, and determined that the soldiers should with drawn swords break in upon the crowd of people, and so draw him forth to behead him; and if any opposed, he should be put to death.

Arius, in the meanwhile, having as yet been endowed only with the dignity of a Levite, and fearing lest, after the death of so great a father, he should noways be able to get reconciled to the Church, came to those who held the chief place amongst the clergy, and, hypocrite that he was, by his sorrowful entreaties and plausible discourse, endeavored to persuade the holy archbishop to extend to him his compassion, and to release him from the ban of excommunication. But what is more deceptive than a feigned heart? What more simple than a holy composure? There was no delay; those who had been requested went in to the priest of Christ, and, after the customary oration, prostrating themselves on the ground, and with groans and tears kissing his hands, implored him, saying, "Thee, indeed most blessed father, for the excellence of thy faith, the Lord hath called to receive the martyr's crown, which we noways doubt does quickly await thee.

Therefore do we think it right that, with thy accustomed piety, thou shouldest pardon Arius, and extend thy indulgence to his lamentations."

Upon hearing this the man of God, moved with indignation, put them aside, and, raising his hands to heaven, exclaimed: "Do ye dare to supplicate me on behalf of Arius? Arius, both here and in the future world, will always remain banished and separate from the glory of the Son of God, Jesus Christ our Lord." He thus protesting, all who were present, being struck with terror, like men dumb, kept silence. Moreover they suspected that he, not without some divine notification, gave forth such a sentence against Arius. But when the merciful father beheld them silent and sad from compunction of heart, he would not persist in austerity, or leave them, as if in contempt, without satisfaction; but taking Achillas and Alexander, who amongst the priests appeared to be the eldest and the most holy, having one of them at his right hand, and the other on his left, he separated them a little from the rest, and at the end of his discourse said to them:

"Do not, my brethren, take me for a man inhuman and stern; for indeed I too am living under the law of sin; but believe my words. The hidden treachery of Arius surpasses all iniquity and impiety, and not asserting this of mine own self, have I sanctioned his excommunication. For in this night, whilst I was solemnly pouring forth my prayers to God, there stood by me a boy of about twelve years, the brightness of whose face I could not endure, for this whole cell in which we stand was radiant with a great light. He was clothed with a linen tunic divided into two parts, from the neck to the feet, and holding in his two hands the rents of his tunic, he applied them to his breast to hide his nakedness. At this vision I was stupefied with astonishment. And when boldness of speech was given to me, I exclaimed: Lord, who hath rent thy tunic? Then said he, Arius hath rent it, and by all means beware of receiving him into communion; behold, to-morrow they will come to entreat you for him. See, therefore, that thou be not persuaded to acquiesce: nay, rather lay thy commands upon Achillas and Alexander the priests, who after thy translation will rule my Church, not by any means to receive him. Thou shalt very quickly fulfil the lot of the martyr. Now there was no other cause of this vision. So now I have satisfied you, and I have declared unto you what I was ordered. But what you will do in consequence of this, must be your own care. Thus much concerning Arius.

"Ye know too, beloved, and ye know well, what has been the manner of my conversation amongst you, and what conflicts I have endured from the idolatrous Gentiles, who, being ignorant of the Lord and Savior, do not cease in their madness to spread abroad the fame of a multitude of gods who are no gods. Ye know likewise how, in avoiding the rage of my persecutors, I wandered an exile from place to place. For long time I lay in hiding in Mesopotamia, and also in Syria amongst the Phoenicians; in either Palestine also I had for a long time to wander; and from thence, if I may so say, in another element, that is, in the islands I tarried no short time. Yet in the midst of all these calamities I did not cease day and night writing to the Lord's flock committed to my poor care, and confirming them in the unity of Christ. For an anxious solicitude for them constantly kept urging my heart, and suffered me not to rest; then only did I think it to be more tolerable to me when I committed them to the Power above.

"Likewise also, on account of those fortunate prelates, Phileus, I mean Hesychius and Theodorus, who of divine grace have received a worthy vocation, what great tribulation agitated my mind. For these, as ye know, for the faith of Christ were with the rest of the confessors wasted with diverse torments. And because in such a conflict they were not only of the clergy but of the laity also the standard-bearers and preceptors, I on this account greatly feared lest they should be found wanting under their long affliction, and lest their defection, which is terrible to speak of, should be to many an occasion of stumbling and of denying the faith, for there were more than six hundred and sixty confined along with them within the precincts of a dungeon. Hence, although oppressed with great labor and toil, I ceased not to write to them with reference to all those predicted passages [of Scripture], exhorting them to earn the martyr's palm with the power of divine inspiration. But when I heard of their magnificent perseverance, and the glorious end of the passion of them all, falling on the ground I adored the majesty of Christ, who had thought fit to count them amongst the throng of the martyrs.

"Why should I speak to you about Meletius of Lycopolis? What persecutions, what treachery, he directed against me, I doubt not but that ye well know. Oh, the horrible wickedness! he feared not to rend asunder the holy Church, which the Son of God redeemed with His precious blood, and to deliver which from the tyranny of the devil He hesitated not to lay down his life. This Church, as I have begun to say, the wicked Meletius rending asunder, ceased not to imprison in dungeons, and to afflict holy bishops even, who have a little before us by martyrdom penetrated to the heavens. Beware therefore of his insidious devices. For I, as ye see, go bound by divine charity, preferring above all things the will of God. I know, indeed, that under their breath the tribunes whisper of my death with eager haste; but I will not from this circumstance open any communication with them, nor will I count my life more precious than myself. Nay, rather, I am prepared to finish the course which my Lord Jesus Christ hath deigned to promise to me, and faithfully render up to Him the ministry which from Him I have received. Pray for me, my brothers; you will not see me longer living in this life with you. Wherefore I testify before God and your brotherhood, that before all of you have I preserved a clean conscience. For I have not shunned to declare unto you the injunctions of the Lord, and I have refused not to make known to you the things which will hereafter be necessary.

"Wherefore take heed unto yourselves, and the whole flock over which the Holy Ghost has appointed you as overseers in succession — thee Achillas in the first place, and next to thee Alexander. Behold with living voice I protest to you, that after my death men will arise in the Church speaking perverse things, and will again divide it, like Meletius, drawing away the people after their madness. So I have told you before. But I pray you, mine own bowels, be watchful; for ye must undergo many tribulations. For we are no better than our fathers.

"Are ye ignorant what things my father endured from the Gentiles, he who brought me up, the most holy bishop Theonas, whose pontifical chair I have undertaken to fill? Would that I had his manners also! Why too should I speak of the great Dionysius his predecessor? Who wandering from place to place sustained many calamities from the frantic Sabellius. Nor will I omit to mention you, ye most holy fathers and high priests of the divine law, Heraclius and Demetrius, for whom Origen, that framer of a perverse dogma, laid many temptations, who cast upon the Church a detestable schism, which to this day is throwing it into confusion. But the grace of God which then protected them, will, I believe, protect you also.

"But why do I delay you longer, my very dear brethren, with the outpouring of my prolix discourse. It remains, that with the last words of the Apostle who thus prayed I address you: And now I commend you to God and the word of His grace, which is powerful to direct both you and His flock." [Cf. Acts 20].

When he had finished, falling on his knees, he prayed with them. And his speech ended, Achillas and Alexander kissing his hands and feet and bursting into tears sobbed bitterly, specially grieving at those words of his which they heard when he said that they should henceforth see him in this life no more. Then this most gentle teacher going to the rest of the clergy, who, as I have said, had come into him to speak in behalf of Arius, spake to them his last consoling words, and such as were necessary; then pouring forth his prayers to God, and bidding them adieu, he dismissed them all in peace.

These things having thus ended, it was

everywhere published far and wide that Arius had not been cut off from the catholic unity without a divine interposition, but that contriver of deceit, and disseminator of all wickedness, ceased not to keep hidden his viper's poison in the labyrinth of his bosom, hoping that he should be reconciled by Achillas and Alexander. This is that Arius the heresiarch, the divider of the consubstantial and indivisible Trinity. This is he who with rash and wicked mouth, was not afraid to blaspheme the Lord and Savior, beyond all other heretics; the Lord, I say, and Savior, who out of pity for our human wanderings, and being sorely grieved that the world should perish in deadly destruction and condemnation, deigned for us all to suffer in the flesh. For it is not to be believed that the Godhead which is impassible was subject to the passion. But because the theologians and fathers have taken care in better style to remove from Catholics' ears the blasphemies of this nature, and another task is ours, let us return to our subject.

This most sagacious pontiff then, perceiving the cruel device of the tribunes, who, in order to bring about his death, were willing to put to the sword the whole Christian multitude that was present, was unwilling that they should together with him taste the bitterness of death, but as a faithful servant imitates his Lord and Savior, whose acts were even as his words, "The good Shepherd giveth His life for the sheep," [John 10:11], prompted by his piety, called to him an elder of those who there waited on his words, and said to him: "Go to the tribunes who seek to kill me, and say to them, Cease ye from all your anxiety, lo! I am ready and willing of mine own accord to give myself to them. Bid them come this night to the rearward of the house of this prison, and in the spot in which they shall hear a signal given on the wall from within, there let them make an excavation, and take me and do with me as they have commanded." The elder, obeying the commands of this most holy man (for so great a father could not be contradicted), departed to the tribunes, and made the intimation to them as he had been commanded.

They, when with them had received it, were exceedingly rejoiced, and taking with them some stonemasons, came about the dawn of the day without their soldiers to the place that had been pointed out to them. The man of God had passed the whole night as a vigil without sleep in prayer and watchfulness. But when he heard their approach, whilst all who were with him were rapt in slumber, with a slow and gentle step he descended to the interior part of the prison, and according to the agreement made, made a sound on the wall; and those outside hearing this, forcing an aperture, received this athlete of Christ armed on all sides with no brazen breastplate, but with the virtue of the cross of the Lord and fully prepared to carry out the Lord's words who said, "Fear not them which kill the body, but are not able to kill the soul: but rather fear Him which is able to destroy both soul and body in hell." [Matt 10:28] Wonderful was the occurrence! Such a heavy whirlwind of wind and rain prevailed during that night, that no one of those who kept the door of the prison could hear the sound of the excavation. This martyr most constant too, kept urging on his murderers, saying, "Do what ye are about to do, before those are aware who are guarding me."

But they took him up and brought him to the place called Bucolia, where the holy St. Mark underwent martyrdom for Christ. Astonishing is the virtue of the saints! As they called him along, and beheld his great constancy and strength of mind when in peril of death, on a sudden a fear and trembling came upon them to such a degree, that none of them could look steadfastly into his face. Moreover, the blessed martyr entreated them to allow him to go to the tomb of St. Mark, for he desired to commend himself to his patronage. But they from confusion, looking down on the ground, said, "Do as you wish, but make haste." Therefore approaching the burial-place of the evangelist, he embraced it, and speaking to him as if he were yet alive in the flesh and able to hear him, he prayed after this manner:

"O father most honorable, thou evangelist

of the only-begotten Savior, thou witness of His passion, thee did Christ choose, who is the Deliverer of us all, to be the first pontiff and pillar of this see; to thee did He commit the task of proclaiming the faith throughout the whole of Egypt and its boundaries. Thou, I say, hast watchfully fulfilled that ministry of our human salvation which was intrusted to thee; as the reward of this labor thou hast doubtless obtained the martyr's palm. Hence, not without justice, are thou counted worthy to be saluted evangelist and bishop. Thy successor was Anianus, and the rest in descending series down to the most blessed Theonas, who disciplined my infancy, and deigned to educate my heart. To whom I, a sinner and unworthy, have been beyond my deservings appointed as successor by an hereditary descent. And, what is best of all, lo! the largeness of the divine bounty has granted me to become a martyr of His precious cross and joyful resurrection, giving to my devotion the sweet and pleasant odor of His passion, that I should be made meet to pour out unto Him the offering of my blood. And, because the time of making this offering is now instant, pray for me that, the divine power assisting me, I may be meet to reach the goal of His agony with a stout heart and ready faith.

"I commend also to thy glorious patronage the flock of Christ's worshipers which was committed to my pastoral care; to thee, I say, I with prayers commend it, who are approved as the author and guardian of all preceding and subsequent occupiers of this pontifical chair, and who, holding its first honors, are the successor not of man, but of the God-man, Christ Jesus."

Saying these words, he went back to a little distance from the sacred tomb, and raising his hands to heaven, prayed with a loud voice, saying:

"O thou Only-begotten, Jesus Christ, Word of the Eternal Father, hear me invoking Thy clemency. Speak peace, I beseech Thee, to the tempest that shakes Thy Church, and with the effusion of my blood, who am Thy servant, make an end to the persecution of Thy people."

Then a certain virgin dedicated to God, who had her cell adjoining to the tomb of the evangelist, as she was spending the night in prayer, heard a voice from heaven, saying: "Peter was the first of the apostles, Peter is the last of the martyred bishops of Alexandria."

Having ended his prayer, he kissed the tomb of the blessed evangelist, and of the other pontiffs who were buried there, and went forth to the tribunes. But they seeing his face as it had been the face of an angel, being terror-stricken, feared to speak to him of his instant agony. Nevertheless, because God does not desert those who trust in Him, He willed not to leave His martyr without consolation in the moment of so great a trial. For lo! an old man and an aged virgin, coming from the smaller towns, were hastening to the city, one of whom was carrying four skins for sale, and the other two sheets of linen. The blessed prelate, when he perceived them, recognized a divine dispensation with reference to himself. He inquired of them on the instant, "Are ye Christians?" And they replied, "Yes." Then said he, "Whither are ye going?" And they replied, "To the market in the city to sell these things that we are carrying." Then the most merciful father answered, "My faithful children, God has marked you out, persevere with me." And they immediately recognizing him, said, "sire, let it be as thou hast commanded."

Then turning to the tribunes, he said, "Come, do what ye are about to do, and fulfil the king's command; for the day is now on the point of breaking." But they, suffering violence as it were on account of the wicked decree of the prince, brought him to the spot opposite to the sanctuary of the evangelist, into a valley near the tombs. Then said the holy man, "spread out, thou aged man, the skins which thou carriest, and thou too, O aged woman, the linen sheets." And when they had been spread out, this most constant martyr, mounting upon them, extended both his hands to heaven, and bending his knees on the ground, and fixing his mind upon heaven, returned his thanks to the Almighty Judge of the contest, and fortifying himself with the sign of the cross, said, "Amen." Then loosening his omophorion from his neck, he stretched it forth, saying, "What is commanded you, do speedily."

Meanwhile the hands of the tribunes were paralyzed, and looking upon one another in turn, each urged his fellow to the deed, but they were all held fast with astonishment and fear. At length they agreed that out of their common stock a reward for the execution should be appointed, and that the man who should venture to perpetrate the deed should enjoy the reward. One of them after the manner of the traitor Judas, emboldened by the desire of money, drew his sword and beheaded the pontiff, on the 25th day of November, after he had held the pontificate twelve years – three of which were before the persecution, but the nine remaining were passed by him under persecutions of diverse kinds. The blood-money being instantly claimed by the executioner, these wicked purchasers, or rather, destroyers, of man's life quickly returned, for they feared the multitude of the people, since, as I have said, they were without military escort. But the body of the blessed martyr, as the fathers affirm who went first to the place of execution, remained erect, as if instant in prayer, until many people, coming together, discovered it standing in the same posture; so that what was his constant practice whilst living, to this his inanimate body testified. They found also the aged man and woman watching with grief and lamentation the most precious relic of the Church. So, honoring him with a triumphal funeral, they covered his body with the linen sheets; but the sacred blood which had been poured forth, they collected reverently in a wallet.

In the meanwhile an innumerable multitude of either sex, flocking together from the populous city, with groans and ejaculations asked each other in turn, being ignorant, in what manner this had happened. In truth, from the least to the greatest, a very great grief was prevalent amongst all. For when the chief men of the city beheld the laudable importunity of the multitude, who were busied in dividing his sacred spoils to keep them as relics, they wrapped him up the tighter in the skins and linen sheets. For the most holy minister of God was always clothed in sacerdotal vestments of a white color – that is, with the tunic, the kolobion, and the omophorion.

Then there arose among them no small contention; for some were for carrying the most sacred limbs to the church which he had himself built, and where he now rests, but others were endeavoring to carry him to the sanctuary of the evangelist, where he attained the goal of martyrdom; and since neither party would yield to the other, they began to turn their religious observance into a wrangling and a fight. In the meanwhile a spirited body of senators of those who are engaged in the public transport service, seeing what had happened, for they were near the sea, prepared a boat, and suddenly seizing upon the sacred relics, they placed them in it, and scaling the Pharos [Lighthouse] from behind, by a quarter which has the name of Leucado, they came to the church of the most blessed mother of God, and Ever-Virgin Mary, which, as we began to say, he had constructed in the western quarter, in a suburb, for a cemetery of the martyrs. Thereupon, the throng of the people, as if the heavenly treasure had been snatched from them, some by straight roads, and others by a more devious route, followed by hasty steps. And when they at length arrived there, there was no longer any altercation where he was to be placed, but by a common and unimpeachable counsel they agreed first to place him in the episcopal chair, and then to bury him.

And this, most prudent reader, I would not have you regard as a wild fancy and superstition, since, if you learn the cause of this novelty, you will admire and approve of the zeal and deed of the populace. For this blessed priest, when he celebrated the sacrament of the divine mysteries, did not, as is the ecclesiastical custom, sit upon his pontifical throne, but upon its footstool underneath, which, when the people beheld, they disliked, and complainingly exclaimed,"Thou oughtest, O father, to sit upon thy chair"; and when they repeated this frequently, the minister of the Lord rising, calmed their complaints with tranquil voice, and again took his seat upon the same stool. So all this seemed to be done by him from motives of humility.

But upon a certain great festival it happened that he was offering the sacrifice of the mass, and wished to do this same thing. Thereupon, not only the people, but the clergy also, exclaimed with one voice, "Take thy seat upon thy chair, bishop." But he, as if conscious of a mystery, feigned not to hear this; and giving the signal for silence (for no one dared pertinaciously to withstand him), he made them all quiet, and yet, nevertheless, sat down on the footstool of the chair; and the solemnities of the mass having been celebrated as usual, each one of the faithful returned to his own home.

But the man of God sending for the clergy, with tranquil and serene mind, charged them with rashness, saying, "How is it that ye blush not for having joined the cry of the laity, and reproaching me? Howbeit, since your reproach flows not from the muddy torrent of arrogance, but from the pure fountain of love, I will unfold to you the secret of this mystery. Very often when I wish to draw near to that seat, I see a virtue as it were sitting upon it, exceeding radiant with the brightness of its light. Then, being in suspense between joy and fear, I acknowledge that I am altogether unworthy to sit upon such a seat, and if I did not hesitate to cause an occasion of offence to the people, without doubt I would not even venture to sit upon the stool itself. Thus it is, my beloved sons, that I seem to you in this to transgress the pontifical rule. Nevertheless, many times when I see it vacant, as ye yourselves are witnesses, I refuse not to sit upon the chair after the accustomed manner. Wherefore do ye, now that ye are acquainted with my secret, and being well assured that, if I shall be indulged, I will sit upon the chair, for I hold not in slight esteem the dignity of my order, cease any further from joining in the exclamations of the populace."

This explanation the most holy father, whilst he was yet alive, was compelled to give to the clergy. The faithful of Christ, therefore, remembering all this with pious devotion, brought his sacred body, and caused it to sit upon the episcopal throne. As much joy and exultation arose then to heaven from the people, as if they were attending him alive and in the body. Then embalming him with sweet spices, they wrapped him in silken coverings; what each one of them could be the first to bring, this he accounted to himself as greatest gain. Then carrying palms, the tokens of victory, with flaming tapers, with sounding hymns, and with fragrant incense, celebrating the triumph of his heavenly victory, they laid down the sacred relics, and buried them in the cemetery which had been long ago constructed by him, where too from henceforth, and even to this day, miraculous virtues cease not to show themselves. Pious vows, forsooth, are received with a propitious hearing; the health of the impotent is restored; the expulsion of unclean spirits testifies to the martyr's merits. These gifts, O Lord Jesus, are Thine, whose wont it is thus magnificently to honor Thy martyrs after death: Thou who with the Father and Holy Consubstantial Spirit livest and reignest for evermore. Amen.

After this, how that wolf and framer of treachery, that is Arius, covered with a sheep's skin, entered into the Lord's fold to worry and torment it, or in what manner he was enabled to attain to the dignity of the priesthood, let us employ ourselves in relating in brief. [Editor's Note: It was Achillas, the successor of Peter, who admitted Arius to the priesthood.]

And this not to annoy those who ventured to recall to the threshing-floor of the Lord those tares of apostasy and contagion that had been winnowed out of the Church by a heavenly fan; for these are without doubt reckoned eminent for sanctity, but thinking it a light thing to believe so holy a man, they transgressed the injunctions of the divine command. What then? Do we reprehend them? By no means. For as long as this corruptible body weighs us down, and this earthly habitation depresses the sense of our infirmity, many are easily deceived in their imaginations, and think that to be just which is unjust, that to be holy which is impure. The Gibeonites who, by the divine threatenings, were to be utterly destroyed, having one thing in their wishes and another in their voice and mien, were able quickly to deceive Joshua, that just distributor of the land of promise. David also, full of prophetic inspiration, when he had heard the words of the deceitful youth, although it was by the inscrutable and just judgment of God, yet acted very differently from what the true nature of the case required. What also can be more sublime than the apostles, who have not removed themselves from our infirmity? For one of them writes, "In many things we offend all;" [James 3:2], and another, "If we say we have no sin, we deceive ourselves, and the truth is not in us." [I John 1:8]. But when we repent of these, so much the more readily do we obtain pardon, when we have sinned not willingly, but through ignorance or frailty. And certainly offences of this sort come not of prevarication, but of the indulgence of compassion. But I leave to others to write an apology for this; let us pursue what is in hand. After that magnificent defender of the faith, Peter, worthy of his name, had by the triumph of martyrdom...

Anastasius the Librarian Apud Maium, Spicilegii, tom. iii. p. 671, translated by Rev. Jas. B. H. Hawkins, 1879

PROCOPIUS

The historian Eusebius, a presbyter and later bishop of the capital of Palestine, recorded the martyrdoms of Caesarea.

The first martyrdom Eusebius records is Procopius'.

Procopius was born in Jerusalem, lived at Scythopolis, the Bethshan of the Bible, where he was reader and exorcist. He had lived an ascetic life from his youth, living on a diet of bread and water, sometimes fasting for seven days. Day and night he studied the scriptures and translated Greek books into Aramaic for the edification of his countrymen.

Along with other Christian confessors he was brought, at the beginning of the persecution to Caesarea. As soon as he arrived at the city gate, without even going to prison, he was brought before the governor and told to sacrifice to the gods. Procopius answered, "There is only one God, the Almighty." The governor did not argue with him but begged him, if he would not acknowledge the gods, to burn incense to the four emperors.

Procopius burst out laughing and replied with a quotation from the Iliad, where Homer says,

It is not good to have lords many;
Let One be Lord, One King.

The governor did not understand the spiritual meaning which the Christian put into this verse. He considered that Procopius' language was treasonable and condemned him to be beheaded.

A. J. Mason, The Historic Martyrs of the Primitive Church, Longmans, 1905, pp 285-6

ALPHAEUS AND ZACCHAEUS

Many leading Christians from the neighbouring churches were soon called on to follow Procopius' example. Some failed from the first. Others passed from torture to torture, were scourged, racked, had their sides crimped, were loaded with heavy irons, so that some of them lost the use of their hands.

In many cases the officials were satisfied with an unreal appearance of success. One man was dragged to the altar, both his hands held fast by attendants on either side; some of the sacrificial meat was placed by force in his right hand, and he was dismissed. Another never even touched the sacrifice, but the bystanders shouted that he had sacrificed and he went free. Another was brought from prison in a fainting condition, and thrown on one side for dead. His chains were taken off and he was deemed to have sacrificed. Some others, who vehemently protested that they had neither sacrificed nor intended to do so, were struck on the mouth, and their cries were drowned by people shouting around them, and they were thus hustled out of court.

Out of all this group of people only two were put to death under governor Flavian, Alphaeus and Zacchaeus. Zacchaeus, a deacon from Gadara, was given his name by his friends because, like the tax collector from Jericho, he was very short and because he earnestly longed to see the Lord. He joyfully bore his testimony before the magistrate under torture, and was thrown into the stocks overnight.

Alphaeus, a reader and exorcist from Caesarea itself, tried hard to convince his feebler brethren not to comply with the command to sacrifice. This quickly brought him before the magistrate. There he spoke freely and eloquently about his beliefs, and after being tortured was thrown into the stocks like Zacchaeus. Three days later the two men were brought into the court. The magistrate told them to sacrifice to the emperors, but they answered, "We know but one King, the King of all." The two men were then sentenced and beheaded.

A. J. Mason, The Historic Martyrs of the Primitive Church, Longmans, 1905, pp 286-7

Habib

Introduction

The following remarkable document tells the story of one of the very last Christians put to death by the pagan Roman authorities before the Edict of Toleration reached the Eastern Provinces. Supposedly based on eyewitness accounts and official court records, its authenticity is generally accepted by secular scholars. While many saints' biographies have a "mythic" timelessness and an abundance of miracles which make them seem unbelievable to the modern reader, this text with its three-dimensional characters and "gritty realism" is startlingly contemporary. The various bureaucrats who preside over Habib's horrible sufferings, for example, are not depicted as satanic monsters but as all-too-ordinary men with ordinary passions and ambitions. The tense, morally confused atmosphere generated by Habib's stubborn and "unnecessary" insistence on civil disobedience is one that modern readers of many political persuasions will instantly recognize. Holy St. Habib, pray to God for us in these times, not so far off from yours!

N. Redington

The martyrdom of Habib the deacon

In the month of Ab, of the year six hundred and twenty of the kingdom of Alexander the Macedonian, in the consulate of Licinius and Constantine, which is the year in which he [name lost in MS?] was born, in the magistracy of Julius and Barak, in the days of Cona bishop of Edessa, Licinius made a persecution against the church and all the people of the Christians, after that first persecution which Diocletian the emperor had made. And Licinius the emperor commanded that there should be sacrifices and libations, and that the altars in every place should be restored, that they might burn sweet spices and frankincense before Zeus. And, when many were persecuted, they cried out of their own accord: We are Christians; and they were not afraid of the persecution, because these who were persecuted were more numerous than those who persecuted [them]. Now Habib, who was of the village of Telzeha and had been made a deacon, went secretly into the churches which were in the villages, and ministered and read the Scriptures, and encouraged and strengthened many by his words, and admonished them to stand fast in the truth of their belief, and not to be afraid of the persecutors; and gave them directions [for their conduct]. And, when many were strengthened by his words, and received his addresses affectionately, being careful not to renounce the covenant they had made, and when the Sharirs of the city, the men who had been appointed with reference to this particular matter, heard of it, they went in and informed Lysanias, the governor who was in the town of Edessa, and said to him: Habib, who is a deacon in the village of Telzeha, goes about and ministers secretly in every place, and resists the command of the emperors, and is not afraid.

And, when the governor heard these things, he was filled with rage against Habib; and he made a report, and sent and informed

Licinius the emperor of all those things which Habib was doing; [he wished] also to ascertain what command would be issued respecting him and [the rest of] those who would not sacrifice. [For] although a command had been issued that every one should sacrifice, yet it had not been commanded what should be done to those who did not sacrifice: because they had heard that Constantine, the commander in Gaul and Spain, was become a Christian and did not sacrifice. And Licinius the emperor [thus] commanded Lysanias the governor: Whoever it is that has been so daring as to transgress our command, our Majesty has commanded that he shall be burned with fire; and that all others who do not consent to sacrifice shall be put to death by the sword. Now, when this command came to the town of Edessa, Habib, in reference to whom the report had been made, was gone across [the river] to the country of the people of Zeugma, to minister there also secretly.

And, when the governor sent and inquired for him in his village, and in all the country round about, and he was not to be found, he commanded that all his family should be arrested, and also the inhabitants of his village; and they arrested them and put them in irons, his mother and the rest of his family, and also some of the people of his village; and they brought them to the city, and shut them up in prison. And, when Habib heard what had taken place, he considered in his mind and pondered anxiously in his thoughts: It is expedient for me, [said he], that I should go and appear before the judge of the country, rather than that I should remain in secret and others should be brought in [to him] and be crowned [with martyrdom] because of me, and that I should find myself in great shame. For in what respect will the name of Christianity help him who flees from the confession of Christianity? Lo! if he flee from this, the death of nature is before him whithersoever he goes, and escape from it he cannot, because this is decreed against all the children of Adam.

And he went immediately to Theotecna, a veteran who was chief of the band of attendants on the governor; and he said to him: I am Habib of Telzeha, whom ye are inquiring for. And Theotecna said to him: If so be that no one saw thee coming to me, hearken to me in what I say to thee, and depart and go away to the place where thou hast been, and remain there in this time [of persecution]; and of this, that thou camest to me and spakest with me and that I advised thee thus, let no one know or be aware. And about thy family and the inhabitants of thy village, be not at all anxious: for no one will at all hurt them, but they will be in prison a few days only, and [then] the governor will let them go: because against them the emperors have not commanded anything serious or alarming. But, if on the contrary thou wilt not be persuaded by me in regard to these things which I have said to thee, I am clear of thy blood: because, if so be that thou appear before the judge of the country, thou wilt not escape from death by fire, according to the command of the emperors which they have issued concerning thee. Habib said to Theotecna: It is not about my family and the inhabitants of my village that I am concerned, but for my own salvation, lest it should be forfeited. About this too I am much distressed, that I did not happen to be in my village on the day that the governor inquired for me, and that on my account lo! many are put in irons, and I have been looked upon by him as a fugitive. Therefore, if so be that thou wilt not consent to my request and take me in before the governor, I will go alone and appear before him. And, when Theotecna heard him speak thus to him, he laid hold of him firmly, and handed him over to his assistants, and they went together to conduct him to the judgment-hall of the governor.

And Theotecna went in and informed the governor, and said to him: Habib of Telzeha, whom thine Excellency was inquiring for, is come.

And the governor said: Who is it that has brought him? and where did they find him? and what did he do where he was?

Theotecna said to him: He came hither himself, of his own accord, and without the compulsion of any one, since no one knew anything about him.

And when the governor heard [this], he was greatly exasperated against him; and thus he spake: This [fellow], who has so acted, has shown great contempt towards me and has despised me, and has accounted me as no judge; and, because he has so acted, it is not meet that any mercy should be shown towards him; nor yet either that I should hasten to pass sentence of death against him, according to the command of the emperors concerning him; but it is meet for me to have patience with him, so that the bitter torments and punishments [inflicted on him] may be the more abundant, and that through him I may terrify many [others] from daring again to flee. And many persons being collected together and standing by him at the door of the judgment-hall, some of whom were members of the body of attendants and some people of the city, there were some of them that said to him: Thou hast done badly in coming and showing thyself to those who were inquiring for thee, without the compulsion of the judge; and there were [others], again, who said to him: Thou hast done well in coming and showing thyself of thine own accord, rather than that the compulsion of the judge should bring thee: for now is thy confession of Christ known to be of thine own will, and not from the compulsion of men. And those things which the Sharirs of the city had heard from those who were speaking to him as they stood at the door of the judgment-hall – and this circumstance also in particular, that he had gone secretly to Theotecna and that [the latter] had not been willing to denounce him, had been heard by the Sharirs of the city – everything that they had heard they made known to the judge.

And the judge was enraged against those who had been saying to Habib: Wherefore didst thou come and show thyself to the judge, without the compulsion of the judge himself? And to Theotecna he said: It is not seemly for a man who has been made chief over his fellows to act deceitfully in this manner towards his superior, and to set at nought the command of the emperors, which they issued against Habib the rebel, that he should be burned with fire.

Theotecna said: I have not acted deceitfully against my fellows, neither was it my purpose to set at naught the command which the emperors have issued: for what am I before thine Excellency, that I should have dared to do this ? But I strictly questioned him as to that for which thine Excellency also has demanded an account at my hands, that I might know and see whether it was of his own free will that he came hither, or whether the compulsion of thine Excellency brought him by the hand of others; and, when I heard from him that he came of his own accord, I carefully brought him to the honorable door of the judgment-hall of thy Worship.

And the governor hastily commanded, and they brought in Habib before him.

The officers said: Lo! he standeth before thine Excellency.

And he began to question him thus, and said to him: What is thy name? And whence art thou? And what art thou?

He said to him: My name is Habib, and I am from the village of Telzeha, and I have been made a deacon.

The governor said: Wherefore hast thou transgressed the command of the emperors, and dost minister in thine office of deacon, which thou art forbidden by the emperors to do, and refusest to sacrifice to Zeus, whom the emperors worship?

Habib said: We are Christians: we do not worship the works of men, who are nothing, whose works also are nothing; but we worship God, who made the men [who made the works].

The governor said: Persist not in that daring mind with which thou art come into my presence, and insult not Zeus, the great boast of the emperors.

Habib said: But this Zeus is an idol, the work of men. It is very well for thee to say that I insult him. But, if the carving of him out of wood and the fixing of him with nails proclaim aloud concerning him that he is made, how sayest thou to me that I insult him? Since lo! his insult is from himself, and against himself.

The governor said: By this very thing, that thou refusest to worship him, thou insultest him.

Habib said: But, if because I do not worship him I insult him, how great an insult, then, did the carpenter inflict on him, who carved him with an axe of iron; and the smith, who smote him and fixed him with nails!

And, when the governor heard him speak thus, he commanded him to be scourged without pity. And, when he had been scourged by five [men], he said to him: Wilt thou now obey the emperors? For, if thou wilt not obey [them], I will tear thee severely with combs, and I will torture thee with all [kinds of] tortures, and then at last I will give command concerning thee that thou be burned with fire.

Habib said: These threats with which lo! thou art seeking to terrify me, are much meaner and paltrier than those which I had already settled it in my mind to endure: then came I and made my appearance before thee.

The governor said: Put him into the iron cask for murderers, and let him be scourged as he deserves. And, when he had been scourged, they said to him: Sacrifice to the gods. But he cried aloud, and said: Accursed are your idols, and so are they who join with you in worshiping them like you. And the governor commanded, and they took him up to the prison; but they refused him permission to speak with his family, or with the inhabitants of his village, according to the command of the judge. On that day was the festival of the emperors.

And on the second of Ilul the governor commanded, and they brought him from the prison. And he said to him: Wilt thou renounce that in which thou standest and obey the command which the emperors issue? For, if thou wilt not obey, with the bitter tearings of combs will I make thee obey them.

Habib said: I have not obeyed them, and moreover it is settled in my mind that I will not obey them – no, not even if thou lay upon me punishments still worse than those which the emperors have commanded.

The governor said: By the gods I swear, that, if thou do not sacrifice, I will leave no harsh and bitter [sufferings untried] with which I will not torture thee: and we shall see whether Christ, whom thou worshippest, will deliver thee.

Habib said: All those who worship Christ are delivered through Christ, because they worship not creatures along with the Creator of creatures.

The governor said: Let him be stretched out and be scourged with whips, until there remain not a place in his body on which he has not been scourged.

Habib said: As for these inflictions, which thou supposest to be so bitter with their lacerations, out of them are plaited crowns of victory for those who endure them.

The governor said: How call ye afflictions ease, and account the torments of your bodies a crown of victory?

Habib said: It is not for thee to ask me concerning these things, because thine unbelief is not worthy to hear the reasons of them. That I will not sacrifice I have said [already], and I say [so still].

The governor said: Thou art subjected to these punishments because thou deservest them: I will put out thine eyes, which look upon this Zeus and are not afraid of him; and I will stop thine ears, which hear the laws of the emperors and tremble not.

Habib said: To the God whom thou deniest here belongs that other world; and there wilt thou [be made to] confess Him with scourgings, thou hast again denied Him.

The governor said: Leave alone that world of which thou hast spoken, and consider anxiously now, that from this punishment to which lo! thou art being subjected there is no one that can deliver thee; unless indeed the gods deliver thee, on thy sacrificing to them.

Habib said: Those who die for the sake of the name of Christ, and worship not those objects that are made and created, will find their life in the presence of God; but those who love the life of time more than that – their torment will be forever.

And the governor commanded, and they

hanged him up and tore him with combs; and, while they were tearing him with the combs, they knocked him about. And he was hanging a long while, until the shoulder-blades of his arms creaked. The governor said to him: Wilt thou comply even now, and put on incense before Zeus there?

Habib said: Prior to these sufferings I did not comply with thy demands: and now that lo! I have undergone them, how thinkest thou that I shall comply, and thereby lose that which I have gained by them?

The governor said: By punishments fiercer and bitterer than these I am prepared to make thee obey, according to the command of the emperors, until thou do their will.

Habib said: Thou art punishing me for not obeying the command of the emperors, when lo! thou thyself also, whom the emperors have raised to greatness and made a judge, hast transgressed their command, in that thou hast not done to me that which the emperors have commanded thee.

The governor said: Because I have had patience with thee, [therefore] has thou spoken thus, like a man that brings an accusation.

Habib said: Hadst thou not scourged me, and bound me, and torn me with combs, and put my feet in fetters, there would have been room to think that thou hadst had patience with me. But, if these things take place in the meanwhile, where is the patience towards me of which thou hast spoken?

The governor said: These things which thou hast said will not help thee, because they all go against thee, and they will bring upon thee inflictions bitterer even than those which the emperors have commanded.

Habib said: Had I not been sensible that they would [indeed] help me, I should not have spoken a single word about them before thee.

The governor said: I will silence thy speeches, and at the same time as regards thee pacify the gods, whom thou hast not worshiped; and I will satisfy the emperors in respect to thee, as regards thy rebellion against their commands.

Habib said: I am not afraid of the death with which thou seekest to terrify me; for, had I been afraid of it, I should not have gone about from house to house and ministered: on which account [it was that] I did so minister.

The governor said: How is it that thou worshippest and honorest a man, but refusest to worship and honor Zeus there?

Habib said: I worship not a man, because the Scripture teaches me, "Cursed is everyone that putteth his trust in man;" but God, who took upon Him a body and became a man, [Him] do I worship, and glorify.

The governor said: Do thou that which the emperors have commanded; and, as for that which is in thy own mind, if thou art willing to give it up, [well]; but, if thou art not willing, [then] do not abandon it.

Habib said: To do both these things [together] is impossible: because falsehood is contrary to truth, and it is impossible that that should be banished from my thought which is firmly fixed in my mind.

The governor said: By inflictions bitter and severe will I make thee dismiss from thy thoughts that of which thou hast said, "It is firmly fixed in my mind."

Habib said: [As for] these inflictions by which thou thinkest that it will be rooted out of my thoughts, by means of these it is that it grows within my thoughts, like a tree which bears fruit.

The governor said: What help will stripes and combs give to that tree of thine? and more especially at the time when I shall command fire against it, to burn it up without pity.

Habib said: It is not on those things at which thou lookest that I look, because I contemplate the things which are out of sight; and therefore I do the will of God, the Maker, and not that of an idol made, which is not sensible of anything whatever.

The governor said: Because he thus denies the gods whom the emperors worship, let him be torn with combs in addition to his former tearings: for, amidst the many questions which I have had the patience to ask him, he has forgotten his former tearings.

And, while they were tearing him, he cried aloud and said: "The sufferings of this time are not equal to that glory which shall be revealed in" [Rom. 8:18] those who love Christ.

And, when the governor saw that even under these inflictions he refused to sacrifice, he said to him: Does your doctrine so teach you, that you should hate your own bodies?

Habib said: Nay, we do not hate our bodies: the Scripture distinctly teaches us, "Whosoever shall lose his life shall find it." But another thing too it teaches us: that we should "not cast that which is holy to dogs, nor cast pearls before swine."

The governor said: I know that in speaking thus thy sole object is that my rage and the wrath of my mind may be excited, and that I may pronounce sentence of death against thee speedily. I am not going, then, to be hurried on to that which thou desirest; but I will have patience: not, indeed, for thy relief, but so that the tortures inflicted on thee may be increased, and that thou mayest see thy flesh falling off before thy face by means of the combs that are passing over thy sides.

Habib said: I myself also am looking for this, that thou shouldst multiply thy tortures upon me, even as thou hast said.

The governor said: Submit to the emperors, who have power to do whatsoever they choose.

Habib said: It is not of men to do whatsoever they choose, but of God, whose power is in the heavens, and over all the dwellers upon earth; "nor is there any that may rebuke His hands and say to Him, "What doest Thou?"

The governor said: For this insolence of thine, death by the sword is too small [a punishment]. I, however, am prepared to command [the infliction] upon thee of a death more bitter than that of the sword.

Habib said: And I, too, am looking for a death which is more lingering than that of the sword, which thou mayest pronounce upon me at any time thou choosest.

And thereupon the governor proceeded to pass sentence of death upon him. And he called out aloud before his attendants, and said, whilst they were listening to him, as were also the nobles of the city: This Habib, who has denied the gods, as ye have also heard from him, and furthermore has reviled the emperors, deserves that his life should be blotted out from beneath this glorious Sun, and that he should not any longer behold this luminary, associate of gods; and, had it not been commanded by former emperors that the corpses of murderers should be buried, it would not be right that the corpse of this fellow either should be buried, because he has been so insolent. I command, that a strap be put into his mouth, as into the mouth of a murderer, and that he be burned by a slow lingering fire, so that the torment of his death may be increased. And he went out from the presence of the governor, with the strap thrust into his mouth; and a multitude of the people of the city ran after him.

And the Christians were rejoicing, forasmuch as he had not turned aside nor quitted his post; but the pagans were threatening him, for refusing to sacrifice. And they led him forth by the western archway, over against the cemetery, which was built by Abshelama, the son of Abgar. And his mother was clad in white, and she went out with him. And, when he was arrived at the place where they were going to burn him, he stood up and prayed, as did all those who came out with him; and he said: O King Christ, since Thine is this world, and Thine the world to come, behold and see, that, while I might have fled from these afflictions, I did not flee, in order that I might not fall into the hands of Thy justice: may this fire, in which I am to be burned, serve me for a recompense before Thee, so that I may be delivered from the fire which is not quenched; and receive Thou my spirit into Thy presence, through Thy Divine Spirit, O glorious Son of the adorable Father!

And, when he had prayed, he turned and blessed them; and they gave him the salutation, weeping as they did so, both men and women; and they said to him: Pray for us in the presence of thy Lord, that He would cause peace among His people, and restoration to His churches which are overthrown. And while Habib was standing, they dug a place, and brought him and set him within it; and they fixed up by him a stake. And they came to bind him to the stake; but he said to them: I will not stir from this place in which ye are going to burn me. And they brought fagots, and set them in order, and placed them on all sides of him. And, when the fire blazed up and the flame of it rose fiercely, they called out to him: Open thy mouth. And the moment he opened his mouth his soul mounted up. And they cried aloud, both men and women, with the voice of weeping. And they pulled and drew him out of the fire, throwing over him fine linen cloths and choice ointments and spices. And they snatched away some of the pieces of wood [which had been put] for his burning, and the brethren and some persons of the laity bore him away. And they prepared him for interment, and buried him by Guria and Shamuna the martyrs, in the same grave in which they were laid, on the hill which is called Baith Allah Cucla, repeating over him psalms and hymns, and conveying his burnt body affectionately and honorably [to the grave]. And even some of the Jews and pagans took part with the Christian brethren in winding up and burying his body. At the time, too, when he was burned, and also at the time when he was buried, there was one spectacle of grief overspreading those within and those without; tears, too, were running down from all eyes: while every one gave glory to God, because for His name's sake he had given his body to the burning of fire. The day on which he was burned was the eve [of the Sabbath], the second of the month Ilul – the day on which the news came that Constantine the Great had set out from the interior of Spain, to proceed to Rome, the city of Italy, that he might carry on war with Licinius, that [emperor] who at this day rules over the eastern portion of the territories of the Romans; and lo! the countries on all sides are in commotion, because no man knows which of them will conquer and continue in [the possession of] his imperial power. And through this report the persecution slackened for a little while from the church. And the notaries wrote down everything which they had heard from the judge; and the Sharirs of the city wrote down all the other things which were spoken outside the door of the judgement-hall, and, according to the custom that existed, they reported to the judge all that they had seen and all that they had heard, and the decisions of the judge were written down in their Acts. I, Theophilus, who have renounced the evil inheritance of my fathers, and confessed Christ, carefully wrote out a copy of these Acts of Habib, even as I had formerly written out [those] of Guria and Shamuna, his fellow-martyrs. And, whereas he had felicitated them upon their death by the sword, he himself also was made like them by the fire in which he was burnt, and received his crown. And, whereas I have written down the year, and the month, and the day, of the coronation of these martyrs, it is not for the sake of those who, like me, were spectators of the deed, but with the view that those who come after us may learn at what time these martyrs suffered, and what manner of men they were; [even as they may learn] also from the Acts of the former martyrs, who [lived] in the days of Domitianus and of all the other emperors who likewise also raised a persecution against the church, and put a great many to death, by stripes and by [tearing with] combs, and by bitter inflictions, and by sharp swords, and by burning fire, and by the terrible sea, and by the merciless mines. And all these things, and things like them, [they suffered] for the hope of the recompense to come. Moreover, the afflictions of these martyrs, and of those of whom I had heard, opened the eyes of me, Theophilus, and enlightened my mind, and I confessed Christ, that He is the Son of God, and is God. And may the dust of the feet of these martyrs, which I received as I was running after them at the time when they were departing to be crowned, procure me pardon for having denied Him, and may He confess me before His worshipers, seeing that I have confessed Him now! And at the twenty-seventh question which the judge put to Habib, he gave sentence against him of death by the burning of fire.

Here endeth the martyrdom of Habib the deacon.

The Coptic Church

Martyrdom of the holy confessors Shamuna, Guria, and Habib

In the six hundredth year from the empire of Alexander the Macedonian, when Diocletian had been nine years sovereign of the Romans, and Maximian was consul for the sixth time, and Augur son of Zoaras was praetor, and Cognatus was bishop of the Edessenes, a great persecution was raised against the churches in all the countries which were under the sway of the Romans. The name of Christian was looked upon as execrable, and was assailed and harassed with abuse; while the priests and the monks, on account of their staunch and unconquerable steadfastness, were-subjected to shocking punishments, and the pious were at their wits' end with sadness and fear. For, desiring as they did to proclaim the truth because of their yearning affection for Christ, they yet shrunk back from doing so for fear of punishment. For those who took up arms against true religion were bent on making the Christians renounce Christianity and embrace the cause of Saturn and Rhea, whilst the faithful on their part labored to prove that the objects of heathen worship had no real existence.

At this period it was that an accusation was preferred before the judge against Guria and Shamuna. The former was a native of Sarcigitua, and the latter of the village of Ganas; they were, however, both brought up at Edessa – which they call Mesopotamia, because it is situated between the Euphrates and the Tigris: a city previously to this but little known to fame, but which after the struggles of its martyrs obtained universal notoriety. These holy men would not by any means spend their lives in the city, but removing to a distance from it, as those who wished to be remote from its turmoils, they made it their aim to be manifest to God only. Guria's purity and lovingness were to him a precious and honorable possession, and from his cultivation of the former the surname of the pure was given him: so that from his name you would not have known who he was, but only when you called him by his surname. Shamuna devoted his body and his youthful and active mind to the service of God, and rivaled Guria in excellence of character. Against these men an indictment was laid before the judge, to the effect that they not only pervaded all the country round about Edessa with their teaching and encouraged the people to hold fast their faith, but also led them to look with contempt on their persecutors, and, in order to induce them to set wholly at nought their impiety, taught them agreeably to that which is written: "Trust not in princes – in the sons of men, in whom is no safety." By these representations the judge was wrought up to a high pitch of madness, and gave orders that all those who held the Christian religion in honor and followed the teaching of Shamuna and Guria, together with those who persuaded them to this, should be apprehended, and shut up in safe keeping. The order was carried into effect; and, seizing the opportunity, he had some of them flogged, and others tortured in various ways, and induced them to obey the emperor's command, and then, as if he were behaving kindly and mercifully, he allowed others to go to their homes; but our two saints, as being the ringleaders and those who bad communicated their piety to others, he ordered to be still further maltreated in prison. They, however, rejoiced in the fellowship of martyrdom. For they heard of many in other provinces who had to pass through the same conflict as themselves: among them Epiphanius and Petrus and the most holy Pamphilus, with many others, at Caesarea in Palestine; Timotheus at Gaza; at Alexandria, Timotheus the Great; Agapetus at Thessalonica; Hesychius at Nicomedia; Philippus at Adrianopolis; at Melitina Petrus; Hermes and his companions in the confines of Martyropolis: all of whom were also encircled with the crown of martyrdom by Duke Heraclianus, along with other confessors too numerous for us to become acquainted with. But we must return to the matters of which we were before speaking.

Antonius, then, the governor of Edessa, having permitted others to return to their homes, had a lofty judgment-seat erected, and ordered the martyrs to be brought before him. The attendants having done as they were bidden, the governor said to the saints: Our most divine emperor commands you to renounce Christianity, of which you are followers, and to pay divine honor to Jupiter by offering incense on the altar. To this Shamuna replied: Far be it from us to abandon the true faith, whereby we hope to obtain immortality, and worship the work of men's hands and an image! The governor said: The emperor's orders must by all means be obeyed. Guria answered: Our pure and divine faith will we never disown, by following the will of men, who are subject to dissolution. For we have a Father in heaven whose will we follow, and He says: "He that shall confess Me before men, him will I also confess before My Father who is in heaven; but he that shall deny Me before men, him will I also deny before My Father and His angels." The judge said: You refuse, then, to obey the will of the emperor? But can you for a moment think, that the purposes of ordinary men and such as have no more power than yourselves are to be really carried into execution, while the commands of those who possess supreme power fall to the ground? They, said the saints, who do the will of the King of kings spurn and reject the will of the flesh. Then, on the governor's threatening them with death unless they obeyed, Shamuna said: We shall not die, O tyrant, if we follow the will of the Creator: nay rather, on the contrary, we shall live; but, if we follow the commands of your emperor, know thou that, even thought thou shouldest not put us to death, we shall perish miserably all the same.

On hearing this, the governor gave orders to Anovitus the jailor to put them in very safe keeping. For the mind which is naturally inclined to evil cannot bear the truth, any more than diseased eyes the bright beams of the sun. And, when he had done as he was commanded, and the martyrs were in prison, where many other saints also had been previously shut by the soldiers, the Emperor Diocletian sent for Musonius the governor of Antioch and ordered him to go to Edessa and see the Christians who were confined there, whether they were of the common or of the sacred class, and question them about their religion, and deal with them as he should see fit. So he came to Edessa; and he had Shamuna and Guria first of all placed before the tribunal of judgment, and said to them: This, arid no less, is the command of the lord of the world, that you make a libation of wine and place incense on the altar of Jupiter. If you refuse to do so, I will destroy you with manifold punishments: for I will tear your bodies to pieces with whips, till I get to your very entrails; and I will not cease pouring boiling lead into your armpits until it reaches even to your bowels; after that, I will hang you up, now by your hands, now by your feet, and I will loosen the fastenings of your joints; and I will invent new and unheard of punishments which you will be utterly unable to endure.

Shamuna answered: We dread "the worm," the threat of which is denounced against those who deny the Lord, and "the fire which is not quenched," more than those tortures which thou hast set before us. For God Himself, to whom we offer rational worship, will, first of all, strengthen us to bear these manifold tortures, and will deliver us out of thy hands; and, after that, will also give us to rest in a place of safety, where is the abode of all those who rejoice. Besides, it is against nothing whatever but the body that thou takest up arms: for what possible harm couldst thou do to the soul? since, as long as it resides in the body, it proves superior to torture; and, when it takes its departure, the body has no feeling whatever left. For, "the more our outward man is destroyed, the more is our inward man renewed day by day; for by means of patience we go through with this contest which is set before us. The governor, however, again, with a kind of protestation, in order that, in case they did not obey, he might with the more justice punish them, said: Give up your error, I beg you, and yield to the command of the emperor: ye will not be able to endure the tortures. The holy Guria answered: We are neither the slaves of error, as thou sayest, nor will we ever obey the command of the emperor: God forbid that we should be so weak-minded and so senseless! For we are His disciples who laid down His life for us, so manifesting the riches of His goodness and His love towards us. We will, therefore, resist sin even to death, nor, come what may, will we be foiled by the stratagems of the adversary, by which the first man was ensnared and plucked death from the tree through his disobedience; and Cain was persuaded, and, after staining his hands with his brother's blood, found the rewards of sin to be wailing and fear. But we, listening to the words of Christ, will "not be afraid of those that kill the body but are not able to kill the soul:" Him rather will we fear "who is able to destroy our soul and body." The tyrant said: It is not to give you an opportunity of disproving my allegations by snatches of your own writings that I refrain from anger and show myself forbearing; but that you may perform the command of the emperor and return in peace to your homes.

These words did not at all shake the resolution of the martyrs; but, approaching nearer: What, said they, does it matter to us, if thou art angry, and nursest thine anger, and rainest tortures upon us like snow-flakes? For then wouldst thou be favoring us all the more, by rendering the proof of our fortitude more conspicuous, and winning for us a greater recompense. For this is the crowning point of our hope, that we shall leave behind our present dwelling, which is but for a time, and depart to one that will last forever. For we have "a tabernacle not made with hands' in heaven, which the Scripture is accustomed also to call "Abraham's bosom," because of the familiar intercourse with God with which he was blessed. The governor, seeing that their firmness underwent no change, forthwith left off speaking and proceeded with the threatened punishments, giving orders to the jailor Anuinus that they should be severally hung up by one hand, and that, when their hands were dislocated by having to bear the entire weight of the body, he should further suspend a heavy stone to their feet, that the sense of pain might be the sharper. This was done, and from the third hour to the eighth they bore this severe torture with fortitude, uttering not a word, nor a groan, nor giving any other indication of a weak or abject mind. You would have said that they were suffering in a body which was not theirs, or that others were suffering and they themselves were nothing more than spectators of what was going on.

In the meantime, whilst they were hanging by their hands, the governor was engaged in trying other cases. Having done with these, he ordered the jailor to inquire of the saints whether or not they would obey the emperor and be released from their torture; and on his putting the question to them, when it was found that they either could not or would not return an answer, he ordered that they should be confined in the inner part of the prison, in a dark dungeon, dark both in name and in reality, and that their feet should be made fast in the stocks. At dawn of day, their feet were loosened from the confinement of the stocks; but their prison was close shut up, so that not a single ray even of sunlight could make its way in; and the jailors were ordered not to give them a bit of bread or a single drop of water for three whole days. So that, in addition to all the rest, the martyrs were condemned to a dark prison and a long privation of food. When the third day arrived, about the beginning of the month of August, the prison was opened to admit light, but they were detained in it stir up to the 10th of November. Then the judge had them brought up before his tribunal: Has not all this time, said he, sufficed to induce you to change your minds and come to some wholesome decision? They answered: We have already several times told thee our mind: do, therefore, what thou hast been commanded. The governor forthwith ordered that Shamuna should be made to kneel down on one side and that an iron chain should be fastened on his knee. This having been done, he hung him up head downwards by the foot with which he had made him kneel; the other he pulled downwards with a heavy piece of iron, which cannot be described in words: thus endeavoring to rend the champion in twain. By this means the socket of the hip-bone was wrenched out of its place and Shamuna became lame. Guria, however, because he was weak and somewhat pale, he left unpunished: not that he regarded him with friendly eyes—not that he had any compassion on his weakness; but rather by way of sparing for another opportunity one whom he was anxious to punish: lest perchance, as he said, through inadvertence on my part he should be worn out before he has undergone the torments in reserve for him.

By this time two hours of the day had passed since Shamuna had been hung up; and the fifth hour had now arrived, and he was still suspended on high – when the soldiers who stood around, taking pity upon him, urged him to obey the emperor's command. But the compassion of sinners had no effect upon the saint. For, although he suffered bitterly from the torture, he vouchsafed them no answer whatever, leaving them to lament at their leisure, and to deem themselves rather, and not him, deserving of pity. But, lifting his eyes to heaven, he prayed to God from the depth of his heart, reminding Him of the wonders done in old time: Lord God, he said, without whom not even a poor little sparrow falls into the snare; who didst cheer the heart of David amid his afflictions; who gavest power to Daniel even against the lions; who madest the children of Abraham victorious over the tyrant and the flame: do Thou now also, O Lord, look on the war which is being waged against us, acquainted as Thou art with the weakness of our nature. For the enemy is trying to turn away the workmanship of Thy right hand from the glory which is with Thee. But regard Thou us with looks of compassion, and maintain within us, against all attempts to extinguish it, the lamp of Thy commandments; and by Thy light guide our paths, and vouchsafe us the enjoyment of that happiness which is in Thee: for Thou art blessed for ever, world without end. Thus did he utter the praise of the Umpire of the strife; and a scribe who was present took down in writing what was said. At length the governor ordered the jailor to release him from his punishment. He did so, and carried him away all faint and exhausted with the pain he suffered, and they bore him back to his former prison and laid him down by the side of the holy Guria. On the 15th of November, however, in the night, about the time of cockcrowing, the judge got up. He was preceded by torches and attendants; and, on arriving at the Basilica, as it is called, where the court was held, he took his seat with great ceremony on the tribunal, and sent to fetch the champions Guria and Shamuna. The latter came in walking between two of the jailors and supported by the hands of both: for he was worn out with hunger and weighed down with age: nothing but his good hope sustained him. Guria, too, had also to be carried in: for he could not walk at all, because his foot had been severely galled by the chain on it. Addressing them both, the advocate of impiety said: In pursuance of the permission which was granted, you have, doubtless, consulted together about what it is expedient for you to do. Tell me, then, whether any fresh resolution has been come to by you, and whether you have in any respect changed your mind in regard to your former purpose; and obey the command of the most divine emperor. For thus will you be restored to the enjoyment of your property and possessions, yea of this most cheering light also. To this the martyrs reply: No one who is wise would make any great account of continuing for a little while in the enjoyment of things which are but transient. Sufficient for us is the time already past for the use and the sight of them; nor do we feel the want of any of them. That death, on the contrary, with which thou art threatening us will convey us to imperishable habitations and give us a participation in the happiness which is yonder.

The governor replied: What you have said has filled my ears with great sadness.

However, I will explain to you what is determined on: if you place incense on the altar and sacrifice to the image of Jupiter, all will be well, and each of you will go away to his home; but, if you still persist in disobeying the command of the emperor, you will most certainly lose your heads: for this is what the great emperor wills and determines. To this the most noble-minded Shamuna replied: If, thou shalt confer upon us so great a favor as to grant us deliverance from the miseries of this life and dismissal to the happiness of the life yonder, so far as in us lies thou shalt be rewarded by Him who lays out our possessions on what is for our good. The governor replied to this somewhat kindly, as it seemed, saying: I have patiently endured hitherto, putting up with those long speeches of yours, in order that by delay you may change your purpose and betake yourselves to what is for your good, and not have to undergo the punishment of death. Those who submit, said he, to death which is only for a time, for the sake of Christ, will manifestly be delivered from eternal death. For those who die to the world live in Christ. For Peter also, who shines so brightly among the band of apostles, was condemned to the cross and to death; and James, the son of thunder was slain by Herod Agrippa with the sword. Moreover, Stephen also was stoned, who was the first to run the course of martyrdom. What, too, wilt thou say of John the Baptist? Thou wilt surely acknowledge his distinguished fortitude and boldness of speech, when he preferred death rather than keep silence about conjugal infidelity, and the adulteress received his head as a reward for her dancing?

Again the governor said: It is not that you may reckon up your saints, as you call them, that I bear so patiently with you, but that, by changing your resolution and yielding to the emperor's commands, you may be rescued from a very bitter death. For, if you behave with such excessive daring and arrogance, what can you expect but that severer punishments are in store for you, under the pressure of which you will be ready even against your will to do what I demand of you: by which time, however, it will be altogether too late to take refuge in compassion? For the cry which is wrung from you by force has no power to challenge pity; whilst, on the other hand, that which is made of your own accord is deserving of compassion. The confessors and martyrs of Christ said: There needs not many words., For lo! we are ready to undergo all the punishments thou mayest lay upon us. What, therefore, has been commanded thee, delay not to perform. For we are the worshipers of Christ the true God, and (again we say it) of Him of whose kingdom there shall be no end; who also is alone able to glorify those in return who glorify His name. In the meantime, whilst these things were being said by the saints, the governor pronounced sentence against them that they should suffer death by the sword. But they, filled with a joy, beyond the power of words to express, exclaimed: To Thee of right belongeth glory and praise, who art God of all, because it hath pleased Thee that we should carry on to its dose the conflict we have entered upon, and that we should also receive at Thy hands the brightness that shah never fade away.

When, therefore, the governor saw their unyielding firmness, and how they had heard the final sentence with exultation of soul, he said to the saints: May God search into what is being done, and be witness that so far as I was concerned it was no wish of mine that you should lose your lives; but the inflexible command of the emperor to me compels me to this. He then ordered a halberdier to take charge of the martyrs, and, putting them in a carriage, to convey them to a distance from the city with some soldiers, and there to end them with the sword. So he, taking the saints out at night by the Roman gate, when the citizens were buried in profound slumber, conveyed them to Mount Bethelabicla on the north of the city. On their arrival at that place, having alighted from the carriage with joy of heart and great firmness of mind, they requested the halberdier and those who were under his orders to give them time to pray; and it was granted. For, just as if their tortures and their blood were not enough to plead for them, they still by reason of their humility deemed it necessary to pray. So they raised their eyes to heaven and prayed earnestly, concluding with the words: God and Father of our Lord Jesus Christ, receive in peace our spirits to Thyself. Then Shamuna, turning to the halberdier, said: Perform that which thou hast been commanded. So he kneeled down along with Guria, and they were beheaded, on the 15th of November. This is the account of what happened to the martyrs.

But forasmuch as the number sought for a third in order that in them the Trinity might be glorified, it found, oh admirable providence! Habib – at a subsequent time indeed: but he also, along with those who had preceded him, had determined to enter on the journey, and on the very day of their martyrdom reached his consummation. Habib, then, great among martyrs, was a native of the same place as they, namely of the village of Thelsaea; and he had the honor of being invested with the sacred office of the diaconate. But, when Licinius swayed the scepter of the Roman empire and Lysanias had appointed governor of Edessa, a persecution was again raised against the Christians, and the general danger threatened Habib. For he would go about the city, teaching the divine Scriptures to all he met with, arid courageously seeking to strengthen them in piety. When this came to the ears of Lysanias, he gave information of it to the Emperor Licinius. For he was anxious to be himself entrusted with the business of bringing the Christians to trial, and especially Habib: for he had never been entrusted with it before. The emperor, then, sent him a letter and commanded him to put Habib to death. So, when Lysanias had received the letter, search was made everywhere for Habib, who on account of his office in the Church lived in some part of the city, his mother and some of his relations residing with him. When he got intelligence of the matter, fearing lest he should incur punishment for quitting the ranks of martyrdom, he went of his own accord and presented himself to a man who was among the chief of the body-guard, named Theotecnus, and presently he said: I am Habib for whom ye are seeking. But he, looking kindly at him, said: No one, my good man, is as yet aware of thy coming to me: so go away, and look to thy safety; and he not concerned about thy mother, nor about thy relations: for they cannot possibly get into any trouble. Thus far Theotecnus.

But Habib, because the occasion was one that called for martyrdom, refused to yield to a weak and cowardly spirit and secure his safety in any underhand way. He replied, therefore: It is not for the sake of my dear mother, nor for the sake of my kinsfolk, that I denounce myself; but I have come for the sake of the confession of Christ. For Io! whether thou consent or no, I will make my appearance before the governor, and I will proclaim my Master Christ before princes and kings. Theotecnus, accordingly, apprehensive that he might go of his own accord to the governor, and that in this way he might himself be in jeopardy for not having denounced him, took Habib and conducted him to the governor: Here, said he, is Habib, for whom search has been made. When Lysanias learned that Habib had come of his own accord to the contest, he concluded that this was a mark of contempt and overweening boldness, as if he set light by the solemn dignity of the judicial seat; and he had him at once put on his trial. He inquired of him his condition of life, his name, and his country. On his answering that he was a native of the village of Thelsaea, and intimating that he was a minister of Christ, the governor immediately charged the martyr with not obeying the emperor's commands. He insisted that a plain proof of this was his refusal to offer incense to Jupiter. To this Habib kept replying that he was a Christian, and could not forsake the true God, or sacrifice to the lifeless works of men's hands which had no sensation. The governor hereupon ordered, that his arms should be bound with ropes, and that he should be raised up high on a beam and torn with iron claws.

The hanging up was far more difficult to bear than the tearing: for he was in danger of being pulled asunder, through the forcible strain with which his arms were stretched out. In the meantime, as he was hanging up in the air, the governor had recourse to smooth words, and assumed the guise of patience. He, however, continued to threaten him with severer punishments unless he should change his resolution. But he said: No man shall induce me to forsake the faith, nor persuade me to worship demons, even though he should inflict tortures more and greater. On the governor's asking him what advantage he expected to gain from tortures which destroyed his whole body, Habib, Christ's martyr, replied: The objects, of our regard do not last merely for the present, nor do we pursue the things that are seen; and, if thou too art minded to turn thy look towards our hope and promised recompense, possibly thou wilt even say with Paul: "The sufferings of this time are not worthy to be compared with the glory which is to be revealed in us." The governor pronounced his words to be the language of imbecility; and, when he saw that, notwithstanding all the efforts he made, by turns using smooth words and assuming the part of patience, and then again threatening him and menacing him with a shocking death, he could not in either way prevail with him, he said, as he pronounced sentence upon him: I will not inflict on thee a sudden and speedy death; I will bring on thy dissolution gradually by means of a slow fire, and in this way make thee lay aside thy fierce and intractable spirit. Thereupon, some wood was collected together at a place outside the city on the northward, and he was led to the pile, followed by his mother, and also by those who were otherwise by blood related to him. He then prayed, and pronounced a blessing on all, and gave them the kiss in the Lord; and after that the wood was kindled by them, and he was cast into the fire; and, when he had opened his mouth to receive the flame, he yielded up his spirit to Him who had given it. Then, when the fire had subsided, his relatives wrapped him in a costly piece of linen and anointed him with unguents; and, having suitably sung psalms and hymns, they laid him by the side of Shamuna and Guria, to the glory of the Father, and of the Son, and of the Holy Spirit, who constitute a Divine Trinity, which cannot be divided: to whom is due honor and worship now and always, and for evermore, Amen. Such was the close of the life of the martyr Habib in the time of Licinius, and thus did he obtain the privilege of being laid with the saints, and thus did he bring to the pious rest from their persecutions. For shortly afterwards the power of Licinius waned, and the rule of Constantine prospered, and the sovereignty of the Romans became his; and he was the first of the emperors who openly professed piety, and allowed the Christians to live as Christians.

The Coptic Church, from Simeon Mataphrartes

A homily on Guria and Shamuna

Shamuna and Guria, martyrs who made
themselves illustrious in their afflictions,
Have in love required of me to tell of their
illustrious deeds.
To champions of the faith the doctrine
calleth me,
That I should go and behold their contests
and their crowns.
Children of the right hand, who have done
battle against the left,
Have called me this day to recite the
marvelous tale of their conflicts: –
Simple old men, who entered into the fight
like heroes,
And nobly distinguished themselves in the
strife of blood:
Those who were the salt of our land, and it
was sweetened thereby,
And its savor was restored, which had
become insipid through unbelief:
Candlesticks of gold, which were full of the
oil of the crucifixion,
By which was lighted up all our region,
which had turned to darkness:
Two lamps, of which, when all the winds
were blowing
Of every kind of error, the lights were not
put out;
Good laborers, who from the spring of day
labored
In the blessed vineyard of the house of God

right duteously:
Bulwarks of our land, who became to us as it were a defense
Against all spoilers in all the wars that surrounded us:
Havens of peace, a place also of retreat for all that were distressed,
And a resting-place for the head of every one that was in need of succor:
Two precious pearls, which were
An ornament for the bride of my lord Abgar, the Aramaean's son.
Teachers they were who practised their teaching in blood,
And whose faith was known by their sufferings.
On their bodies they wrote the story of the Son of God
With the marks of combs and scourges which thickly covered them.
They showed their love, not by words of the mouth alone,
But by tortures and by the rending of their limbs asunder.
For the love of the Son of God they gave up their bodies:
Since it beseemeth the lover that for his love he should give up himself.
Fire and sword proved their love, how true it was;
And more beautiful than silver tried in a furnace of earth were their necks.
They looked on God, and, because they saw His exalted beauties,
Therefore did they look with contempt upon their sufferings for His sake.
The Sun of righteousness had arisen in their hearts;
And they were enlightened by it, and with HIS light chased they away the darkness.
At the idols of vanity, which error had brought in, they laughed,
Instinct with the faith of the Son of God which is full of light.
The love of the Lord was as a fire in their hearts;
Nor could all the brambles of idolatry stand before it.
Fixed was their love on God unchangeably:
And therefore did they look with scorn upon the sword, all athirst as it was for blood.
With guilelessness and yet with wisdom stood they in the judgment- hall,
As they had been commanded by the Teacher of that which is true.
Despising as they did kindred and family, guileless were they;
Forasmuch, also, as possessions and wealth were held in no account by them.
Nor guileless only: for in the judgment-hall with the wisdom of serpents too
They were heedful of the faith of the house of God.
When a serpent is seized and struck, he guards his head,
But gives up and leaves exposed all his body to his captors:
And, so long as his head is kept from harm, his life abideth in him;
But, if the head be struck, his life is left a prey to destruction.
The head of the soul is men's faith;
And, if this be preserved unharmed, by it is also preserved their life:
Even though the whole body be lacerated with blows,
Yet, so long as faith is preserved, the soul is alive;
But, if faith is struck down by unbelief,
Lost is the soul, and life has perished from the man.
Shamuna and Guria of the faith as men
Were heedful, that it should not be struck down by persecutors:
For they knew that, if faith is preserved,
Both soul and body are preserved from destruction.
And, because of this, touching their faith were they solicitous,
That that should not be struck down in which their very life was hidden.
They gave up their bodies both to blows and to dislocation,
Yea to every kind of torture, that their faith should not be stricken down;
And, even as the serpent also hides his head from blows,
So hid they their faith within their hearts;
And the body was smitten, and endured stripes, and bore sufferings:
But overthrown was not their faith which was within their hearts.

The mouth betrayeth the soul to death when it speaks,
And with the tongue, as with a sword, worketh slaughter.
And from it spring up both life and death to men:
Denying a man dies, confessing he lives, and the mouth hath power over it.
Denial is death, and in confession is the soul's life;
And power hath the mouth over them both, like a judge.
The word of the mouth openeth the door for death to enter in;
This, too, calleth for life, and it beameth forth upon the man.
Even the robber by one word of faith
Won him the kingdom, and became heir of paradise, all fraught with blessings.
The wicked judges too, from the martyrs, the sons of the right hand,
Demanded that by word of mouth only they should blaspheme;
But, like true men holding fast the faith,
They uttered not a word by which unbelief might be served.
Shamuna, beauty of our faith, who is adequate to tell of thee?
All too narrow is my mouth for thy praise, too mean for thee to be spoken of by it.
Thy truth is thy beauty, thy crown thy suffering, thy wealth thy stripes,
And by reason of thy blows magnificent is the beauty of thy championship.
Proud of thee is our country, as of a treasury which is full of gold:
Since wealth art thou to us, and a coveted store which cannot be stolen from us.
Guria, martyr, staunch hero of our faith,
Who shall suffice thee, to recount thy beauties divine?
Lo! tortures on thy body are set like gems of beryl,
And the sword on thy neck like a chain of choice gold.
Thy blood upon thy form is a robe of glory full of beauty,
And the scourging of thy back a vesture with which the sun may not compare.
Radiant thou art and comely by virtue of these thy sufferings, so abounding;
And resplendent are thy beauties, because of the pains which are so severe upon thee.
Shamuna, our riches, richer art thou than the rich:
For Io! the rich stand at thy door, that thou mayest relieve them.
Small thy village, poor thy country: who, then, gave thee
That lords of villages and cities should court thy favor?
Lo! judges in their robes and vestments
Take dust from thy threshold, as though it were the medicine of life.
The cross is rich, and to its worshipers increaseth riches;
And its poverty despiseth all the riches of the world.
Shamuna and Guria, sons of the poor, lo! at your doors
Bow down the rich, that they may receive from you supplies for their wants.
The Son of God in poverty and want
Showed to the world that all its riches are as nothing,
His disciples, all fishermen, all poor, all weak,
All men of little note, became illustrious through His faith.
One fisherman, whose "village" too was a home of fishermen,
He made chief over the twelve, yea head of the house.
One a tentmaker, who aforetime was a persecutor,
He seized upon, and made him a chosen vessel for the faith.
Shamuna and Guria came from villages that were not wealthy,
And lo! in a great city became they lords;
And its chief men, its judges also, stand before their doors,
And they solicit their charity to satisfy their wants.
From their confession of the faith of the Son of God
These blessed men acquired. riches beyond compute.
Poor did He Himself become, and the poor made He rich;
And lo! enriched is the whole creation through His poverty.

The chosen martyrs did battle against error,
And in the confession of the Son of God stood they firm like valiant men.
They went in and confessed Him before the judge with look undaunted,
That He too might confess them, even as they confessed Him, before His Father.
There arose against them the war of pagans like a tempest;
But the cross was their helmsman, and steered them on.
They were required to sacrifice to lifeless images,
But they departed not from their confession of the Son of God.
The wind of idolatry blew in their faces,
But they themselves were as rocks piled up against the hurricane.
Like a swift whirlwind, error snatched at them;
But, forasmuch as they were sheltered by the crucifixion, it hurt them not.
The Evil One set on all his dogs to bark, that they might bite them;
But, forasmuch as they had the cross for a staff, they put them all to flight.
But who is sufficient to tell of their contests,
Or their sufferings, or the rending asunder of their limbs?
Or who can paint the picture of their coronation,
How they went up from the contest covered with glory?
To judgment they went in, but of the judge they took no account;
Nor were they anxious what they should say when questioned.
The judge menaced them, and multiplied his words of threatening;
And recounted tortures and all kinds of inflictions, that he might terrify them.
He spake great words, that by fright and intimidation,
By menaces too, he might incline them to sacrifice.
Yet the combatants despised the menaces, and the intimidations,
And the sentence of judgment, and all bodily deaths;
And they prepared themselves for insult and stripes, and for blows,
And for provocation, and to be dragged along, and to be burnt;
For imprisonment also, and for bonds, and for all evil things,
And for all tortures, and for all sufferings, rejoicing all the while.
They were not alarmed nor affrighted, nor dismayed,
Nor did the sharpness of the tortures bend them to sacrifice.
Their body they despised, and as dung upon the ground accounted they it:
For they knew that, the more it was beaten, the more would its beauty increase;
And, the more the judge increased his menaces to alarm them,
The more did they show their contempt of him, having no fear of his threats.
He kept telling them what tortures he had prepared for them;
And they continued telling him about Gehenna which was reserved for him.
By those things which he told them he tried to frighten them to sacrifice;
And they spoke to him about the fearful judgment yonder.
Truth is wiser than wise words,
And very hateful, however much it may be adorned, is falsehood.
Shamuna and Guria went on speaking truth,
While the judge continued to utter falsehood.
And therefore were they not afraid of his threatening,
Because all his menaces against the truth were accounted by them as empty sound.
The intercourse of the world they despised, they contemned and scorned, yea they abandoned;
And to return to it they had no wish, or to enter it again.
From the place of judgment they set their faces to depart
To that meeting-place for them all, the life of the new world.
They cared neither for possessions nor for houses,
Nor for the advantages of this world, so full of evil.
In the world of light was their heart bound captive with God,

And to "that" country did they set their face to depart;
And they looked to the sword, to come and be a bridge
To let them pass over to God, for whom they were longing.
This world they accounted as a little tent,
But that yonder as a city full of beauties;
And they were in haste by the sword to depart hence
To the land of light, which is full of blessing for those who are worthy of it.
The judge commanded to hang them up by their arms,
And without mercy did they stretch them out in bitter agony.
A demon's fury breathed rage into the heart of the judge,
And embittered him against the steadfast ones, inciting him to crush them;
And between the height and the depth he stretched them out to afflict them:
And they were a marvel to both sides, when they saw how much they endured.
At the old men's frame heaven and earth marveled,
To see how much suffering it bore nor cried out for help under their affliction.
Hung up and dragged along are their feeble bodies by their arms,
Yet is there deep silence, nor is there one that cries out for help or that murmurs.
Amazed were all who beheld their contests,
To see how calmly the outstretched forms bore the inflictions laid upon them.
Amazed too was Satan at their spotless frames,
To see what weight of affliction they sustained without a groan. Yea, and
gladdened too were the angels by that fortitude of theirs,
To see how patiently it bore that contest so terrible that was.
But, as combatants who were awaiting their crowns,
There entered no sense of weariness into their minds.
Nay, it was the judge that grew weary; yea, he was astonished:
But the noble men before him felt no weariness in their afflictions.
He asked them whether they would consent to sacrifice;
But the mouth was unable to speak from pain.
Thus did the persecutors increase their inflictions,
Until they gave no place for the word to be spoken.
Silent was the mouth from the inflictions laid on their limbs;
But the will, like that of a hero, was nerved with fortitude from itself.
Alas for the persecutors! how destitute were they of righteousness!
But the children of light – how were they clad in faith!
They demand speech, when there is no place for speaking,
Since the word of the mouth was forbidden them by pain.
Fast bound was the body, and silent the mouth, and it was unable
To utter the word when unrighteously questioned.
And what should the martyr do, who had no power to say,
When he was questioned, that he would not sacrifice?
All silent were the old men full of faith,
And from pain they were incapable of speaking.
Yet questioned they were: and in what way, if a man is silent
When he is questioned, shall he assent to that which is said?
But the old men, that they might not be thought to assent,
Expressed clearly by signs the word which it behoved them to speak.
Their heads they shook, and, instead of speech, by a dumb sign they showed
The resolve of the new man that was within.
Their heads hung down, signifying amidst their pains
That they were not going to sacrifice, and every one understood their meaning.
As long as there was in them place for speech, with speech did they confess;
But, when it was forbidden them by pain, they spake with a dumb sign.
Of faith they spoke both with the voice and

without the voice:
So that, when speaking and also when silent, they were alike steadfast.
Who but must be amazed at the path of life, how narrow it is,
And how straight to him that desires to walk in it?
Who but must marvel to see that, when the will is watchful and ready, It is
very broad and full of light to him that goeth therein?
About the path are ditches; full also is it of pitfalls;
And, if one turn but a little aside from it, a ditch receives him.
That dumb sign only is there between the right and the left,
And on "Yea" and "Nay" stand sin and righteousness.
By a dumb sign only did the blessed men plainly signify that they would not sacrifice,
And in virtue of a single dumb sign did the path lead them to Eden;
And, if this same dumb sign had inclined and turned down but a little
Toward the depth, the path of the old men would have been to Gehenna.
Upwards they made a sign, to signify that upwards were they prepared to ascend;
And in consequence of that sign they ascended and mingled with the heavenly ones.
Between sign and sign were Paradise and Gehenna:
They made a sign that they would not sacrifice, and they inherited the place of the kingdom.
Even while they were Silent they were advocates for the Son of God:
For not in multitude of words doth faith consist.
That fortitude of theirs was a full-voiced confession,
And as though with open mouth declared they their faith by signs;
And every one knew what they were saying, though silent,
And enriched and increased was the faith of the house of God;
And error was put to shame by reason of two old men, who, though they spake not,
Vanquished it; and they kept silence, and their faith stood fast.
And, though tempestuous accents were heard from the judge,
And the commands of the emperor were dreadful, yea violent,
And paganism had a bold face and an open mouth,
And its voice was raised, and silent were the old men with pain,
Yet null and void became the command and drowned was the voice of the judge,
And without speech the mute sign of the martyrs bore off the palm.
Talking and clamor, and the sound of stripes, on the left;
And deep silence and suffering standing on the right;
And, by one mute sign with which the old men pointed above their heads,
The head of faith was lifted up, and error was put to shame.
Worsted in the encounter were they who spoke, and the victory was to the silent:
For, voiceless they uttered by signs the discourse of faith.
They took them down, because they had vanquished while silent;
And they put them in bonds, threatening yet to vanquish them.
Bonds and a dungeon void of light were by the martyrs
Held of no account – yea rather as the light which has no end.
To be without bread, and without water, and without light,
Pleased them well, because of the love of the Son of God.
The judge commanded by their feet to hang them up
With their heads downwards, by a sentence all unrighteous:
Hanged up was Shamuna with his head downwards; and he prayed
In prayer pure and strained clear by pain.
Sweet fruit was hanging on the tree in that judgment-hall,
And its taste and smell made the very denizens of heaven to marvel.

Afflicted was his body, but sound was his faith;
Bound fast was his person, but unfettered was his prayer over his deed.
For, prayer nothing whatsoever turneth aside,
And nothing hindereth it – not even sword, not even fire.
His form was turned upside down, but his prayer was unrestrained,
And straight was its path on high to the abode of the angels.
The more the affliction of the chosen martyr was increased,
The more from his lips was all confession heard.
The martyrs longed for the whetted sword affectionately,
And sought it as a treasure full of riches.
A new work has the Son of God wrought in the world –
That dreadful death should be yearned for by many.
That men should run to meet the sword is a thing unheard of,
Except they were those whom Jesus has enlisted in His service by His crucifixion.
That death is bitter, every one knoweth lo! from earliest time:
To martyrs alone is it not bitter to be slain.
They laughed at the whetted sword when they saw it,
And greeted it with smiles: for it was that which was the occasion of their crowns.
As though it had been something hated, they left the body to be beaten:
Even though loving it, they held it not back from pains.
For the sword they waited, and the sword went forth and crowned them:
Because for it they looked; and it came to meet them, even as they desired.
The Son of God slew death by His crucifixion;
And, inasmuch as death is slain, it caused no suffering to the martyrs.
With a wounded serpent one playeth without fear;
A slain lion even a coward will drag along:
The great serpent our Lord crushed by His crucifixion;
The dread lion did the Son of God slay by His sufferings.
Death bound He fast, and laid him prostrate and trampled on him at the gate of Hades;
And now whosoever will draweth near and mocketh at him, because he is slain.
These old men, Shamuna and Guria, mocked at death,
As at that lion which by the Son of God was slain.
The great serpent, which slew Adam among the trees,
Who could seize, so long as he drank not of the blood of the cross?
The Son of God crushed the dragon by His crucifixion,
And lo! boys and old men mock at the wounded serpent.
Pierced is the lion with the spear which pierced the side of the Son of God;
And whosoever will trampleth on him, yea mocketh at him.
The Son of God – He is the cause of all good things,
And Him doth it behove every mouth to celebrate.
He did Himself espouse the bride with the blood which flowed from His wounds,
And of His wedding-friends He demanded as a nuptial gift the blood of their necks.
The Lord of the wedding-feast hung on the cross in nakedness,
And whosoever came to be a guest, He let fall
His blood upon him.
Shamuna and Guria gave up their bodies for His sake
To sufferings and tomes and to all the various forms of woe.
At Him they looked as He was mocked by wicked men,
And thus did they themselves endure mockery without a groan.
Edessa was enriched by your slaughter, O blessed ones:
For ye adorned her with your crowns and with your sufferings.
Her beauty are ye, her bulwark ye, her salt ye,
Her riches and her store, yea her boast and all her treasure.

Faithful stewards are ye:
Since by your sufferings ye did array the bride in beauty.
The daughter of the Parthians, who was espoused to the cross,
Of you maketh her boast: since by your teaching lo! she was enlightened.
Her advocates are ye; scribes who, though silent, vanquished
All error, whilst its voice was uplifted high in unbelief.
Those old men of the daughter of the Hebrews were sons of Belial,
False witnesses, who killed Naboth, feigning themselves to be true.
Her did Edessa outdo by her two old men full of beauty,
Who were witnesses to the Son of God, and died like Naboth.
Two were there, and two here, old men;
And these were called witnesses, and witnesses those.
Let us now see which of them were witnesses chosen of God,
And which city is beloved by reason of her old men and of her honorable ones.
Lo! the sons of Belial who slew Naboth are witnesses;
And here Shamuna and Guria, again, are witnesses.
Let us now see which witnesses, and which old men,
And which city can stand with confidence before God.
Sons of Belial were those witnesses of that adulterous woman,
And lo! their shame is all portrayed in their names.
Edessa's just and righteous old men, her witnesses,
Were like Naboth, who himself also was slain for righteousness' sake.
They were not like the two lying sons of Belial,
Nor is Edessa like Zion, which also crucified the Lord.
Like herself her old men were false, yea dared
To shed on the ground innocent blood wickedly.
But by these witnesses here lo! the truth is spoken. –
Blessed be He who gave us the treasure-store of their crowns!
Here endeth the Homily on Guria and Shamuna.

Mar Jacob

George, Soldier and Martyr
23 April 303

George is a soldier and martyr who suffered around 303 at Lydda (Diospolis) in Palestine. The earliest surviving record of him is a church inscription in Syria, dated about 346. Commemorations of him are numerous, early, and widespread. However, no details of his life are known. In 495 his name appears on a list of "good men, justly remembered, whose good deeds are known only to God." The best-known story about him is that he rescued a beautiful princess in Libya by killing a dragon. It should be noted that this story is unknown before the appearance in 1265 of a romance called the Golden Legend (Legendum Aureum), translated into English in 1483.

When the soldiers of the First Crusade were besieging Antioch in 1098, they had a vision of George and Demetrius (a deacon of Sirmium in Serbia, martyred under Maximian, and referred to as a "soldier of Christ," from which he was often understood to be a literal soldier) encouraging them to maintain the siege, which ultimately proved successful. Richard I ("the Lion-Heart") of England, who fought in the Holy Land in 1191-1192, placed himself and his army under George's protection, and with the return home of the Crusaders, the popularity of George in England increased greatly. Edward III founded the Order of the Garter in 1348 under his patronage, his banner (a red cross on a white field) began to be used as the English national flag in 1284, and in 1415 Henry V spoke of him to rally the troops before the battle of Agincourt ("Once more unto the breach, dear friends, once more, or close the wall up with our English dead!"), and in the years following George was regarded as the special patron of England, of soldiers, and of the Boy Scouts, as well as of Venice, Genoa, Portugal, and Catalonia. He is also remembered with enthusiasm in many parts of the East Orthodox Church. He is a principal character in Edmund Spenser's allegorical poem *The Faerie Queene*, written in the late 1500's.

James Kiefer, Christian Biographies, By kind permission

St Pancras 290-304

He is said to have suffered at Rome in the fourteenth year of his age. Having been beheaded for the faith, which he had gloriously confessed under Dioclesian in the year 304, he was interred in the cemetery of Calepodius, which afterwards took his name. His old church in that place was repaired in the fifth century by Pope Symmachus, and in the seventh by pope Honorius I. St. Gregory the Great speaks of his relics. St. Gregory of Tours calls him the Avenger of Perjuries, and says that God by a perpetual miracle visibly punished false oaths made before his relics. Pope Vitalian sent a portion of them to king Oswi in 656 Italy, England, France, Spain, &c., abound with churches which bear his name. See D. Jenichen, Diss. de S. Pancratio, urbis et ecclesiae primariae Giessensis patrono titular), in 4to. anno 1758, at Giessen, a university in Upper Hesse, belonging to the landgrave of Hesse Darmstadt.

Alban Butler

Martyrdom of Agnes (1)

Agnes of Rome, Martyr
21 January 304

Agnes is a Christian martyr who died at Rome around 304 in the persecution of Diocletian: the last and fiercest of the persecutions of Christianity by the Roman emperors. The anniversary of her martyrdom is observed on 21 January. Her name means "pure" in Greek and "lamb" in Latin. She is said to have been only about twelve or thirteen when she died, and the remains preserved in St Agnes' Church in Rome are in agreement with this. It is said that her execution shocked many Romans and helped bring an end to the persecutions.

Some said, "It is contrary to Roman law to put a virgin to death. Our leaders say that it is necessary to kill Christians in order to preserve the old Roman ways: but they are themselves scorning those ways in the process."

Others said, "Do young girls constitute such a threat to Rome that it is necessary to kill them?"

Others said, "If this religion can enable a twelve-year-old girl to meet death without fear, it is worth checking out."

There is a narrative poem by Keats, called "The Eve of Saint Agnes." It is a romantic poem with a mediaeval setting, about an elopement the night before St Agnes' Day. The only tie-in with Agnes is that (presumably because she died as a young virgin), Agnes is regarded as the patron of young unmarried girls, and there is a folk-belief that a girl who goes to bed supperless on the eve of St Agnes's Day will dream that night about her husband-to-be.

James Kiefer, Christian Biographies, By kind permission

Martyrdom of Agnes (2)

Agnes (A.D. 304 or 305)

St Jerome says that the tongues and pens of all nations are employed in the praises of this saint, who overcame both the cruelty of the tyrant and the tenderness of her age, and crowned the glory of chastity with that of martyrdom. St. Austin observes that her name signifies chaste in Greek, and a lamb in Latin. She has always been looked upon in the church as a special patroness of purity, with the Immaculate Mother of God and St. Thecla. Rome was the theater of the triumph of St. Agnes; and Prudentius says that her tomb was shown within sight of that city. She suffered not long after the beginning of the persecution of Diocletian, whose bloody edicts appeared in March, in the year of our Lord 303. We learn from St. Ambrose and St. Austin that she was only thirteen years of age at the time of her glorious death. Her riches and beauty excited the young noblemen of the first families in Rome to vie with one another in their addresses who should gain her in marriage. Agnes answered them all that she had consecrated her virginity to a heavenly spouse, who could not be beheld by mortal eyes. Her suitors, finding her resolution impregnable to all their arts and importunities, accused her to the governor as a Christian, not doubting but threats and torments would overcome her tender mind, on which allurements could make no impression. The judge at first employed the mildest expression and most inviting promises, to which Agnes paid no regard, repeating always that she could have no other spouse than Jesus Christ. He then made use of threats, but found her soul endowed with a masculine courage, and even desirous of racks and death. At last terrible fires were made, and iron hooks, racks, and other instruments of torture, displayed before her, with threats of immediate execution. The young virgin surveyed them all with an undaunted eye, and with a cheerful countenance beheld the fierce and cruel executioners surrounding her, and ready to dispatch her at the word of command. She was so far from betraying the least symptom of fear that she even expressed her joy at the sight, and offered herself to the rack. She was then dragged before the idols and commanded to offer incense, "but could by no means be compelled to move her hand, except to make the sign of the cross," says St. Ambrose.

The governor seeing his measures ineffectual, said he would send her to a house of prostitution, where what she prized so highly should be exposed to the insults of the debauchees. Agnes answered that Jesus Christ was too jealous of the purity of his spouses to suffer it to be violated in such a manner, for he was their defender and protector. "You may," said she, "stain your sword with my blood, but will never be able to profane my body, consecrated to Christ." The governor was so incensed at this that he ordered her to be immediately led to the public brothel, with liberty to all persons to abuse her person at pleasure. Many young profligates ran thither, full of the wicked desire of gratifying their lust, but were seized with such awe at the sight of the saint that they durst not approach her-one only excepted, who, attempting to be rude to her, was that very instant, by a flash" as it were, of lightning from heaven, struck blind, and fell trembling to the ground. His companions, terrified, took him up and carried him to Agnes, who was at a distance, singing hymns of praise to Christ, her protector. The virgin by prayer restored him to his sight and health.

The chief prosecutor of the saint, who at first sought to gratify- his lust and avarice, now labored to satiate his revenge by incensing the judge against her, his passionate fondness being changed into anger and rage. The governor wanted not others to spur him on, for he was highly exasperated to see himself baffled and set at defiance by one of her tender age and sex. Therefore, resolved upon her death, he condemned her to be beheaded. Agnes, transported with joy on hearing this sentence, and still more at the sight of the executioner, "went to the place of execution more cheerfully," says St. Ambrose, "than others go to their wedding." The executioner had secret instructions to use all means to induce her to a compliance, but Agnes always answered she could never offer so great an injury to her heavenly spouse, and, having made a short prayer, bowed down her neck to adore God, and received the stroke of death. The spectators wept to see so beautiful and tender a virgin loaded with fetters, and to behold her fearless under the very sword of the executioner, who with a trembling hand cut off her head at one stroke. Her body was buried at a small distance from Rome, near the Nomentan Road. A church was built on the spot in the time of Constantine the Great, and was repaired by Pope Honorius in the seventh century. It is now in the hands of Canon-Regulars, standing without the walls of Rome, and is honored with her relics in a-very rich silver shrine, the gift of Pope Paul V, in whose-time they were found in this church, together with those of St. Emerentiana. The other beautiful rich church of St. Agnes, within the city, built by Pope Innocent X (the right of patronage being vested in the family of Pamphili), stands on the place where her chastity was exposed. The feast of St. Agnes is mentioned in all Martyrologies, both of the East and West, though on different days. It was formerly a holyday for the women in England, as appears from the Council of Worcester, held in the year 1240. St. Ambrose, St. Austin, and other fathers have wrote her panegyric. St. Martin of Tours was singularly devout to her. Thomas à Kempis honored her as his special patroness, as his works declare in many places. He relates many miracles wrought and graces received through her intercession.

Marriage is a holy state, instituted by God, and in the order of providence and nature the general or more ordinary state of those who live in the world. Those, therefore, who upon motives of virtue, and in a Christian and holy manner, engage in this state, do well. Those, nevertheless, who, for the sake of practicing more perfect virtue, by a divine call, prefer a state of perpetual virginity, embrace that which is more perfect and more excellent. Dr. Wells, a learned Protestant, confesses that Christ declares voluntary chastity, for the kingdom of heaven's sake, to be an excellency, and an excellent state of life. This is also the manifest inspired doctrine of St. Paul; and in the revelations of St. John spotless virgins are called, in a particular manner, the companions of the Lamb, and are said to enjoy the singular privilege of following him wherever he goes. The tradition of the church has always been unanimous in this point; and among the Romans, Greeks, Syrians, and barbarians many holy virgins joyfully preferred torments and death to the violation of their integrity, which they bound themselves by vow to preserve without defilement in mind or body. The fathers, from the very disciples of the apostles, are all profuse in extolling the excellency of holy virginity, as a special fruit of the incarnation of Christ, his divine institution, and a virtue which has particular charms in the eyes of God, who delights in chaste minds, and chooses to dwell singularly in them. They often repeat that purity raises men, even in this mortal life, to the dignity of angels-purifies the soul, fits it for a more perfect love of God, and a closer application to heavenly things, and disengages the mind and heart from worldly thoughts and affections: it produces in the soul the nearest resemblance to God. Chastity is threefold-that of virgins, that of widows, and that of married persons; in each state it will receive its crown, as St. Ambrose observes,[9] but in the first is most perfect, so that St. Austin calls it fruit a hundred-fold, and that of marriage sixty-fold; but the more excellent this virtue is, and the higher its glory and reward, the more heroic and the more difficult is its victory; nor is it perfect unless it be embellished with all other virtues in a heroic degree, especially divine charity and the most profound humility.

Alban Butler, The Lives of the Fathers, Martyrs and Other Principal Saints

Vincent of Saragossa, Deacon and Martyr
22 January 304

The title line above states almost all that is certainly known about Vincent, the earliest Spanish martyr whose name is known to us. It is said that he was brought to trial along with his bishop Valerius, and that since Valerius had a speech impediment, Vincent spoke for both, and that his fearless manner so angered the governor that Vincent was tortured and killed, though his aged bishop was only exiled.

James Kiefer, Christian Biographies, By kind permission

Catherine of Alexandria, Martyr
25 November 310

The story of Catherine of Alexandria has caught the popular imagination of many generations (she is, for example, one of the personages from whom Joan of Arc claimed to receive regular visits and messages), although most scholars judge it to be simply a work of fiction with no historical basis. No references to her can be traced earlier than the ninth (or possibly the eighth) century.

It is said that Catherine was a Christian maiden of Alexandria in Egypt, possessed of beauty, brains, and noble birth. She rebuked the heathen emperor Maxentius for his idolatry, and he responded by offering to marry her if she would renounce her faith. She refused. Fifty philosophers were set to refute her in a public debate. She easily won every point, and made them look foolish. The emperor, a sore loser, had them burned alive. The emperor went out of town on business, and when he returned, he discovered that Catherine had converted his queen and the 200 soldiers of the empress's bodyguard. This was too much. He had the Empress and her soldiers put to death. Catherine was sentenced to be tortured on a spiked wheel, but the wheel flew apart and the fragments killed many of her accusers. After this and other marvels, Catherine was beheaded, and from her veins flowed not blood but milk. The angels carried her to Mount Sinai, where St. Catherine's Monastery is now located.

She is depicted carrying a spiked wheel, representing the manner in which it was proposed to put her to death. The "catherine-wheel," a form of fireworks that spins as it burns, is named for her.

Catherine is patron of preachers, philosophers, librarians (probably association with the Library of Alexandria), young girls, and craftsmen working with a wheel (potters, spinners, etc). The Mt. Sinai monastery was built by Justinian in 527, and has borne the name of Catherine since the eighth or ninth century. The monastery survives unmolested by the Moslems (by express command of Mohammed) and has a vast but uncatalogued treasure of ancient manuscripts. One of the earliest known manuscripts of the complete New Testament, the Codex Sinaiaticus, was found there, borrowed by the finder, and never returned to the monastery. Since then, they have been a bit crusty to visiting scholars.

James Kiefer, Christian Biographies, By kind permission

THE FORTY MARTYRS OF SEBASTE

10 March 320

In the year 320, Constantine was Emperor of the West and Licinius of the East. Licinius, under pressure from Constantine, had agreed to legalize Christianity in his territory, and the two made an alliance (cemented by the marriage of Licinius to Constantia the sister of Constantine), but now Licinius broke the alliance and made a new attempt to suppress Christianity. He ordered his soldiers to repudiate it on pain of death. In the "Thundering Legion," stationed near Sebaste in Armenia (now Sivas in Turkey), forty soldiers refused, and when promises, threats, and beatings failed to shake them, they were stripped naked one evening and herded onto the middle of a frozen lake, and told, "You may come ashore when you are ready to deny your faith." To tempt them, fires were built on shore, with warm baths, blankets, clothing, and hot food and drink close by. The mother of the youngest soldier was present and encouraged her son from the bank. As night deepened, thirty-nine men stood firm, while one broke and ran to the shore. However, one of the soldiers standing guard on shore was so moved by the steadfastness of the Christians that he stripped off his clothes and ran out to join them. They welcomed him into their company, and so the number of the martyrs remained at forty, and by morning, all were dead of exposure. (One source says that the few in whom a little life remained were stabbed to death at dawn.)

We still have what some scholars believe to be an authentic eyewitness account of their martyrdom. It includes farewell messages to their family and friends written shortly before their deaths.

James Kiefer, Christian Biographies, By kind permission

AGAPIUS AND THECLA

Urban succeeded Flavian as governor of Palestine and a man, Agapius, and a woman, Thecla, were killed.

As the great festival approached, Urban, was determined to add special interest to the celebration, by announcing, that in addition to horse racing in the circus at Caesarea, a gala performance in the theater, and other interesting spectacles, two Christians, Agapius and Thecla, along with some other Christians, would fight the beasts. The sensation throughout Palestine was immense, for such exhibitions were uncommon there. On the appointed day, six stalwart young men tied one another's hands tight behind their backs, ran as fast as they could up to Urban, just as he was entering the amphitheater, and shouted aloud that they were Christians, and were not afraid of wild beasts.

One of the six, Timolaus , came from the distant province of Pontus; Tionysius came from Tripoli in Phoenicia; Romulus was a sub-deacon from Diospolis; Paesis and Alexander were Egyptians, and another Alexander came from Gaza. As soon as the governor and his attendants had recovered themselves they had the six men thrown into prison. There they were visited by a compassionate brother of the last-named Alexander, another Agapius from Gaza, and by another Christian called Dionysius , who looked after their needs. These two visiting Christians looked after the prisoners so well that Urban had them arrested as well. A few days later, all eight Christians, were brought out together, condemned, and beheaded.

As soon as Thecla was thrown to the wild beasts she died, but Agapius survived. He languished in prison for two and a half years in Caesarea. At least three times during this time he had been led out with criminals to be executed. But, each time, the governor either had pity on him or lived in hope that he would recant, and had him thrown back into prison. But in November 306, the cruel emperor Maximin, came to Caesarea to celebrate his birthday. The place was, of course, in holiday mood. On such occasions it was customary for the emperor to treat the crowds to a fine show of animals from a foreign country, or to acrobats or jugglers. But the only novelty that Maximin had to offer was a pair of criminals to be given to wild beasts. In front of one of them a placard reading, "Christian, Agapius' was carried. The other man was a slave who had murdered his master. No sooner were they presented before Maximin than the emperor, in the middle of shouts and applause crying for his clemency, bestowed a free pardon on the murderer.

Agapius was paraded around the amphitheater and exposed to the derision of the spectators. The emperor asked him if he would abandon his Christianity, in which case he would be set at liberty. Agapius refused, calling on the crowd to witness that he had been condemned without committing any crime, except for his belief in the one Almighty God. For this belief Agapius said that he would gladly die, so that his endurance might encourage younger Christians to despise death for the sake of eternal life. The cages were then opened. Agapius ran and flung himself into the arms of a she-bear, which tore him, but did not kill him. He was returned to prison for one more night. On the following day they tied heavy stones to his feet and dropped him into the sea.

A. J. Mason, The Historic Martyrs of the Primitive Church, Longmans, 1905, pp 289-90

Apphian

Apphian was martyred at Caesarea under Urban.

A similar death [to that of Agapius'] had been inflicted a little earlier in the year upon one in whom the historian Eusebius was more deeply interested. A young man of nineteen, Apphian, who belonged to the distinguished family in Lycia, had been sent by his heathen parents to complete his education in Beirut. That city was famed for its luxurious vices and its schools, but Apphian was proof against the seductions of the society into which he was thrown, and surprised every one who observed him by the purity and severity of his life. When his course at Beirut had finished, he returned to his Lycian home; but during his absence, as it seems, he had embraced the Christian faith, and, finding the heathen atmosphere in which his parents lived intolerable, he determined to run away. Taking no means of subsistence with him, but casing himself wholly upon the providence of God, he found himself at Caesarea. It was the very place for the studious young Christian. There was a vast library of the learned Pamphilus, who had gathered round him a community of students, of whom Eusebius himself was one. Apphian was welcomed into the community, to which a brother of his already belonged, and threw himself with ardor into the teaching of Pamphilus, living, like his master, a life of stern asceticism.

Apphian had been in Caesarea for nearly year, when an edict was received, requiring the attendance of the whole population at sacrificial rites. Criers passed through the streets summoning men, women, and children to the temples, where military officers stood, furnished with lists of the inhabitants, and calling them over, name by name. Urban, the governor, was himself in the very act of pouring a libation, when the young Apphian, who had told no one what he intended to do, slipped through the band of soldiers and officials in attendance upon him, seized the governor by the right hand and bade him desist from the idolatrous proceeding. With gentle earnestness he warned him that it was not well to turn from the one true God and to sacrifice to devils.

Naturally the guards fell upon the audacious youth, and with no very merciful handling carried him off into the darkness of the prison, where they left him for the night with his legs in the torturing stocks. Next day he appeared before Urban. The governor bade him sacrifice, and he refused. Then began a dreadful series of tortures. Again and again the young man's ribs were laid open. Blows fell about his head and neck till his face was so swollen and disfigured that no one could have recognized him. As he still remained firm, Urban told them to soak some rags with oil, and wrap them around his legs, and set fire to them. The juices of his body exuded and dripped with the heat; but Apphian was undaunted. To all questions about himself, he origin, his lodging-place, he only replied from time to time that he was a Christian. They took him back once more to the prison, and next day he was sentenced to death by drowning.

Eusebius eyewitnesses the sequel to this event. An earthquake – no uncommon phenomenon in those parts – shook the city. A violent storm arose in the sea. Amidst the roaring and raging of the elements, the body of the young martyr was thrown up by the waves at the very gate of the city.

A. J. Mason, The Historic Martyrs of the Primitive Church, Longmans, 1905, pp 290-2

Ennatha and Valentina

Under Firmilian, Urban's successor as governor of Palestine, Ennatha and Valentina were martyred.

"No one can have so thorough a sense of the sufferings of Christ as he whom it hath chanced to suffer in the same manner." The Imitation of Christ, ascribed to Thomas à Kempis

A company of Christians were taken into custody at Gaza, where they were busy listening to the Bible being read. Some of them were treated in a way that had now become almost normal – their left feet were disabled, and their right eyes were burned out. Others were tortured in even worse ways. A youth, Ennatha, on being threatened with a horrible fate, could not contain her burning indignation, but shouted out aloud her detestation of the tyrant emperor, who entrusted the government of the province to so barbarous a judge. For this outspoken language Ennatha was first submitted to the lash, and then hoisted upon the torture-block to have her sides laid open. When she had lain there for an hour or so, bearing patiently the thrice-repeated application of the knife or claw, a woman's voice cried aloud to the court's judge, from the crowded court, "How long do you intend to torture my sister in such a barbarous way?"

The speaker was a woman of Caesarea, who had dedicated herself, like Ennatha, to a life of virginity. Her name was Valentina. She was of diminutive stature, and unattractive in appearance; but her feelings were strong and her mind resolute. The sight of what they were doing to Ennatha was more than she could endure. Of course, she was instantly set before Firmilian, and declared herself a Christian. The judge attempted to persuade her to sacrifice, but she refused. They dragged her up to the law altar, upon which a fire was burning.

Valentina saw her opportunity and seized it. Her hands were held, but she deliberately raised her foot, and kicked off the altar the preparations for sacrifice, and the fire that lay on it. The enraged Firmilian had her placed at once on the torture block, and inflicted on her a worse lashing of the sides than anyone present had ever seen inflicted before. Taking her down still alive, he tied her and Ennatha fast to each other and burned them together at the stake.

A. J. Mason, The Historic Martyrs of the Primitive Church, Longmans, 1905, pp 302-3

AGAPE, CHIONE AND IRENE

In Thessalonica, in the province of Macedonia, six women were brought before the governor, Dulcitius, charged with refusing to eat what had been sacrificed to the gods.

DULCITIUS: Why did you go to the sacrifice and yet refuse to partake?

AGAPE: Because I believe in the living God.

IRENE: Because I fear God.

CHIONE: Because I believe in the living God, so I could never do such a thing.

CASSIA: Because I want to save my soul.

EUTYCHIA: I would prefer to die than eat your sacrifices.

PHILIPPA: I say the same. I would rather die than eat your sacrifices.

Dulcitius then singled out Agape and Chione for interrogation, after which he sentenced them. Agape and Chione, for disloyally defying the divine edict of the emperors and Caesars, and for still clinging to the irrational and vain religion of the Christians, which is execrable in the eyes of all devoted men, were to be given over to the flames. The governor added that Agatho and Cassia, and Philippa, and Irene, were to be detained in prison during his good pleasure, because of their youth.

After the martyrdom of Agape and Chione, Irene, their sister, was examined again. This time the scriptures were the main subject of the examination. It had come to the governor's hearing that Irene had kept Christian writings and not surrendered them.

DULCITIUS: Your conduct shows your obstinate madness. You have wilfully kept Christian parchments, books, writing tablets, notes and pages from the writings of the wicked Christians from all ages. Who told you to retain these parchments and writings?

IRENE: It was almighty God, who commanded us to love him even if it meant dying for him. For this reason we did not dare to hand over these books. We chose to be burned alive rather than give them up.

DULCITIUS: Who else knew you had these books?

IRENE: Almighty God, who knows everything, saw them, but nobody else, as God is my witness. We believed our own people to be more dangerous than enemies and thought that they might accuse us. So we showed the books to no one.

Delcitius pronounced sentence on Irene. No rack or claw was used on her, but she was submitted to a moral torture that was far worse. Before she died she was stripped naked and exposed to the abuse of wicked men. Irene's books were then publicly burned. Irene was brought before Dulcitius once more and asked if she persisted in her stupidity. Irene said that she was only doing her duty to God. Dulcitius then ordered paper to be brought and he wrote her final sentence. Like her sisters, Irene was burned alive, on the same spot as they were. It is not known what became of her four companions.

A. J. Mason, The Historic Martyrs of the Primitive Church, Longmans, 1905, pp 340-6

IRENAEUS

Sirmium, a little above its confluence with the Danube, was one of the main seats of the empire during Diocletian's reign. The bishop of Sirmium, at the height of the persecution, was a young man for his station, called Irenaeus. Probus, the governor of Pannonia, summoned him.

PROBUS: Obey the divine ordinances.

IRENAEUS: The person who sacrifices to the god and not to God shall be utterly destroyed.

PROBUS: Our most gracious princes have

ordered sacrifices to be carried out, or torture to be applied.

IRENAEUS: My orders are to submit to torture rather than to deny God and sacrifice to devils.

PROBUS: Sacrifice, or I must have you tortured.

IRENAEUS: I shall rejoice if you do, that I may take part in my Lord's suffering.

The torture was severely inflicted.

PROBUS: What do you say, Irenaeus – will you sacrifice?

IRENAEUS: I am sacrificing to my God by a good confession, as I have always done.

Irenaeus' mother and father, and wife and friends were then brought in and they cried in front of him, pleading with him that he was too young to die.

PROBUS: Let their tears deter you from your madness. Think of your youth and sacrifice. IRENAEUS: I think about my eternal welfare when I decline to sacrifice.

Probus ordered Irenaeus to be thrown into prison where he endured many hardships. In the middle of one night Probus sent for him and ordered him to sacrifice, and so save himself from further troubles.

IRENAEUS: Do as you have been ordered, but you must not expect me to sacrifice. Probus was so annoyed that he ordered Irenaeus to be beaten with sticks.

IRENAEUS: I have a God whom I have learned to worship since I was a child. I adore him. He comforts me in everything, and to him I offer sacrifice, but I cannot worship gods made with hands.

PROBUS: Have you a wife?

IRENAEUS: No.

PROBUS: Have you any children?

IRENAEUS: No.

PROBUS: Have you any mother and father?

IRENAEUS: No.

PROBUS: Then, who were the people crying who were brought into court?

IRENAEUS: One of Jesus Christ's commandments says, "He that loveth father or mother, or wife or children or kinsfolk, more than me, is not worthy of me."

Probus then sentenced Irenaeus to be executed with the sword. Irenaeus was led out to one of the bridges over the Save, where he took off his clothes, stretched out his hands towards heaven and prayed, "O Lord Jesus Christ, who suffered for the salvation of the world, let thy heavens open that the angels may receive the spirit of your servant Irenaeus, who suffers for thy name and for thy people in thy catholic church of Sirmium. I beseech thee, and I entreat thy mercy, that thou receive me and confirm thy faith in them." Then the sword fell and Irenaeus' body was thrown into the Save.

A. J. Mason, The Historic Martyrs of the Primitive Church, Longmans, 1905, pp 349-51

QUIRINUS

Quirinus was bishop of Siscia, in the province of Pannonia. He heard that Christians were being arrested so he left Siscia, seeking refuge elsewhere. But he was caught and brought before the local justice, Maximus.

MAXIMUS: Why are you trying to run away from Siscia?

QUIRINUS: I am only obeying the command, "When they persecute you in one city, flee to another one."

MAXIMUS: Whose commandment is that?

QUIRINUS: The commandment of Christ, the true God.

MAXIMUS: Do you not know that the emperor's commandments would find you wherever you were? He whom you call the true God cannot help you once you are caught, as you are discovering now.

QUIRINUS: The Lord whom we serve is always with us, and wherever we are, he is able to help us. He was with me when I was caught, and he is here to comfort me, and it is he who answers you through my mouth.

MAXIMUS: You talk a great deal and while you do so you are disobeying the orders of the emperors. Read the divine orders and you must.

QUIRINUS: I will not listen to the bidding of your emperors because that is sacrilegious, as they command Christ's servants to sacrifice to your gods. I cannot serve them, as they are nothing. My God, whom I serve, is in heaven and earth, and in the sea and everywhere, but is above everything. Everything was made by him and in him everything lives.

MAXIMUS: You have lived too long and have picked up old wives' tales.

Maximus ordered Quirinus to be beaten with sticks.

MAXIMUS: Acknowledge that the gods whom the Roman empire serves are mighty gods. If you comply, you shall be made a priest of the great god Jupiter. If not, you shall be sent and tried by Amantius, the governor of Pannonia Prima. He will pass the death sentence on you which you deserve.

QUIRINUS: I am now discharging the office of priesthood. I am made a priest indeed, if I am allowed to offer my own body to the true God. As for my body being beaten, I like it. It does not hurt me. I am at your disposal for worse tortures so that others may follow me to eternal life which is easily reached by this road.

MAXIMUS: Put him in heavy chains and return him to prison.

QUIRINUS: I have no horror of prison, as God will be with me there.

Three days later Quirinus was taken in heavy chains from town to town along the Danube until he came to Sabaria where Amantius was governor. Amantius said he was reluctant to have a man of Quirinus' age whipped. He told Quirinus to sacrifice so that he might spend the rest of his days in peace. Quirinus replied that, old as he was, faith would give him strength greater than all his tortures, that he had no great desire to live, and no fear of dying.

Quirinus was sentenced. Quirinus was to have a stone fixed to his neck and thrown into a river. The road to Scarabantia crossed the river Sibaris over a high bridge, from which the bishop was thrown.

A. J. Mason, The Historic Martyrs of the Primitive Church, Longmans, 1905, pp 360-2

Maxima and Donatilla

Christian women and girls in North Africa were as courageous as the Christian men. Anulinus, the proconsul of Africa, visited Thuburbo and sent off two officers to bring all the Christians there before him to sacrifice. When they arrived they were told to sacrifice or be painfully tortured.

A panic seized the unhappy crowd. Husbands who might have been willing to endure something themselves could not bear the thought of what might be done to their wives. Priests, deacons, people in lesser orders, gave way. Even the young men and virgins had not heart to stand out. All bowed down and worshipped the idols.

The proconsul was also told about two Christian girls, Maxima and Donatilla, who were not present. They were found and brought before Anulinus and they were questioned. He delivered them to be whipped.

Maxima told him that it was no great punishment to have their flesh beaten, when the spirit is saved and the soul is redeemed and comforted. Then the poor girls, with their bruised backs, were forced to lie on broken potsherds and glass. They told Anulinus that they had a great Physician who healed their wounds, and that while he, their judge, was being brought low, they were exalted in glory. They were placed on the hobby-horse. "It is God's judgement that men should suffer for their Lord," they said. When it seemed as if they must be exhausted from torture, with their throats parched, Anulinus ordered a drink to be given to them. "You are foolish," they said to him, "have we not our God, the most high, for our refreshment?" The proconsul ordered hot coals to be placed on the hair on their heads. "It is true," they said, "what is written in the law, "We went through fire and water, and came through into a place of refreshment."

At last Anulinus ordered them to the amphitheatre. It was a joyful sound to them. "Now our hour is coming," they said, "give what sentence you will." The proconsul confessed that he was tired, and would be glad to be rid of them. "Tired," cried the undaunted girls, "with one hour of it! You have only just come, and you are tired?" The proconsul gave word for a hungry bear to be let loose on them. "Do as you are bidden," said Donatilla to the keeper, "do not fear."

"In the name of our Lord Jesus Christ we shall conquer you today," they cried to Anulinus. The bear, as so often happened, only growled and licked Maxima's feet. Then Anulinus read the final judgment from his tablet: "We order Maxima and Donatilla, to be punished with the sword."

They answered, "Thanks be to God," and suffered without further delay. Their bodies were buried within the precincts of the amphitheater itself.

A. J. Mason, The Historic Martyrs of the Primitive Church, Longmans, 1905, pp 392-4

Theodota

c 318, Greece

Towards the end of the reign of Licinius a persecution arose in Philippopolis, in Thrace, Greece. Agrippa the prefect, on Apollo's festival, ordered that the whole city should offer a great sacrifice with him. Theodota, who had formerly been a harlot, was accused of refusing to conform, and being called on by the president, answered him, that she had indeed been a grievous sinner, but could not add sin to sin, nor defile herself with a sacrilegious sacrifice. Her constancy encouraged seven hundred and fifty men, probably a troop of soldiers, to step forth, and, professing themselves Christians, to refuse to join in the sacrifice.

Theodota was thrown into prison for twenty days, where she prayed continually. Being brought to the bar she entered the court and burst into tears, and prayed aloud that Christ would pardon the crimes of her past life, and arm her with strength that she might bear with constancy and patience the cruel torments she was to going to suffer. In her answers to the judge she confessed that she had been a harlot, but declared that she had become a Christian, though unworthy to bear that sacred name. Agrippa commanded her to be cruelly scourged. The pagans that stood near her, ceased not to exhort her to free herself from torments by obeying the president but for one moment. But Theodota remained constant, and under the lashes cried out: "I will never abandon the true God, nor sacrifice to lifeless statues."

The president ordered her to be hoisted upon the rack, and her body to be torn with an iron comb. Under these torments she earnestly prayed to Christ, and said: I adore you, O Christ, and thank you, because you have made me worthy to suffer this for your name."

The judge, enraged at her resolution and patience, said to the executioner: Tear her flesh again with the iron comb; then pour vinegar and salt into her wounds."

She said, "so little do I fear your torments, that I entreat you to increase them to the utmost, that I may find mercy and attain to the greater crown."

Agrippa then commanded the executioners to pluck out her teeth, which they violently pulled out one by one with pincers. The judge at length condemned her to be stoned. She was led out of the city, and, during her martyrdom, prayed thus: "O Christ, as you showed favour to Rahab the harlot, and received the good thief; so turn not your mercy from me."

Alban Butler, The Lives of the Saints, Dublin, 1833, volume II, pp 522-23.

Felix

Felix was bishop of Tibiuca, a town near Carthage. The elders of the people were summoned before the curator. It so happened that Felix had gone into Carthage on that day. A priest called Aper, and two readers, Cyrus and Vitalis, were presented. The curator asked them if they had any sacred books. They said that they had. "Give them to be burnt with fire," said the magistrate.

"Our bishop has them with him," was their reply.

"Where is he?" asked the curator. Aper said that he did not know. They were then put under surveillance until they could be sent to the proconsul Anulinus.

Next day the bishop came home. The curator sent an official to fetch him. "Bishop Felix," he said respectfully, "give me any books or parchments you possess."

"I have some," he answered firmly, "but I will not give them."

"What the emperors have commanded," said the curator, "must come before what you say. Give me the books, to be burnt with fire."

The bishop answered, "I would prefer to be burnt with fire myself than have the sacred Scriptures burnt. It is good to obey God rather than men."

The curator could only repeat his saying, that the emperor's command must come before what the bishop chose to say.

"The commandment of the Lord," answered Felix, "comes before the commandment of men."

The magistrate gave him three days to reflect. On the third day he asked him the result of his reflections. "What I said before," Felix answered, "I say again now, and I shall say the same before the proconsul."

"You shall go to the proconsul, then," said the curator, "and shall there give your account."

The bishop was placed under the charge of a member of the local senate. One June 24 he was taken in chains to Carthage, and there thrown into prison. Next morning, very early, he was brought to the bar of the proconsul. Anulinus asked him why he had not given up his "useless books".

Perhaps he intended to give the bishop a hint how to escape from the situation. But Felix was too straightforward to resort to any subterfuge. He replied to Anulinus, as he had done to the local magistrate at Tibiuca, "I have books; but I will not give them."

Anulinus put him into the deepest part of the prison for another sixteen days, and then had him out at ten o"clock at night to ask him the same question. The bishop's "pious obstinacy", as Gibbon calls it, only returned the same answer, "I do not intend to give them."

There was only one end to such determination. "slay Felix with the sword," said Anulinus. Felix cried aloud, "Thanks be to thee, O Lord, who hast vouchsafed to deliver me." At the place of execution, he lifted his eyes to heaven, and said, "Thanks be to thee, O God. I have lived fifty-six years in this world. I have kept my virginity. I have preserved the Gospels. I have preached faith and truth. O Lord God of heaven and earth, O Jesus Christ, I bow my neck as an offering to thee, who abidest for ever, to whom be glory and majesty, for ever and ever. Amen."

A. J. Mason, The Historic Martyrs of the Primitive Church, Longmans, 1905, pp 405-6

Bademus
Abbot, martyr, 376
Feast day: April 10

Bademus was a rich and noble citizen of Bethlapeta, in Persia, who, desiring to devote himself to the service of God out of his estates, founded a monastery near that city, which he governed with great sanctity. The purity of his soul had never been sullied by any crime, and the sweet odour of his sanctity diffused a love of virtue in the hearts of those that approached him. He watched whole nights in prayer, and passed sometimes several days together without eating; bread and water were his usual fare. He conducted his religious in the paths of perfection with sweetness, prudence, and charity. In this amiable retreat he enjoyed a calmness and happiness which the great men of the world would view with envy did they compare with it the unquiet scenes of vice and vanity in which they live. But, to crown his virtue, God permitted him, with seven of his monks, to be apprehended by the pursuivants of King Sapor in the thirty-sixth year of his persecution. He lay four months in a dungeon loaded with chains, during which lingering martyrdom he was every day called out to receive a certain number of stripes. But he triumphed over his torments by the patience and joy with which he suffered them for Christ. At the same time a Christian lord of the Persian court named Nersan, prince of Aria, was cast into prison because he refused to adore the sun. At first he showed some resolution; but at the sight of tortures his constancy failed him and he promised to conform. The king, to try if his change was sincere, ordered Bademus to be brought to Lapeta, with his chains struck off, and to be introduced into the prison of Nersan, which was a chamber in the royal palace. Then his majesty sent word to Nersan by two lords that if, with his own hand, he would despatch Bademus, he should be restored to his liberty and former dignities. The wretch accepted the condition; a sword was put into his hand and he advanced to plunge it into the breast of the abbot. But being seized with a sudden terror, he stopped short and remained some time without being able to lift up his arm to strike. The servant of Christ stood undaunted, and with his eyes fixed upon him said, "Unhappy Nersan, to what a pitch of impiety do you carry your apostasy! With joy I run to meet death; but could wish to fall by some other hand than yours: why must you be my executioner?" Nersan had neither courage to repent nor heart to accomplish his crime. He strove, however, to harden himself, and continued with a trembling hand to aim at the sides of the martyr. Fear, shame, remorse, and respect for the martyr, whose virtue he wanted courage to imitate, made his strokes forceless and unsteady; and so great was the number of the martyr's wounds that they stood in admiration at his invincible patience. At the same time they detested the cruelty and despised the base cowardice of the murderer, who at last, aiming at his neck, after four strokes severed his head from the trunk. Neither did he escape the divine vengeance: for a short time after, falling into public disgrace, he perished by the sword after tortures, and under the maledictions of the people. Such is the treachery of the world towards those who have sacrificed their all in courting it. Though again and again deceived by it, they still listen to its false promises and continue to serve this hard master till their fall becomes irretrievable. The body of St. Bademus was reproachfully cast out of the city by the infidels, but was secretly carried away and interred by the Christians. His disciples were released from their chains four years afterwards, upon the death of King Sapor. St. Bademus suffered on the 10th of the moon of April in the year 376, of King Sapor the sixty-seventh.

Monks were called Mourners by the Syrians and Persians, because by their state they devoted themselves in a particular manner to the most perfect exercises of compunction and penance, which indeed are an indispensable duty of every Christian. The name of angels was often given them over all the East, during several ages, because by making heavenly contemplation and the singing of the divine praises their great and glorious employment, if they duly acquit themselves of it, they may be justly called the seraphim of the earth. The soul which loves God is made a heaven which he inhabits, and in which she converses with him in the midst of her own substance. Though he is infinite and the highest heavenly spirits tremble before him, and how poor and base soever we are, he invites us to converse with him, and declares that it is his delight to be with us. Shall not we look upon it as our greatest happiness and comfort to be with Him and to enjoy the unspeakable sweetness of his presence. Oh! what ravishing delights does a soul taste which is accustomed, by a familiar habit, to converse in the heaven of her own interior with the three persons of the adorable Trinity! Dissipated worldlings wonder how holy solitaries can pass their whole time buried in the most profound solitude and silence of creatures. But those who have had any experience of this happiness are surprised, with far greater reason, how it is possible that any souls which are created to converse eternally with God should here live in constant dissipation, seldom entertaining a devout thought of Him whose charms and sweet conversation eternally ravish all the blessed.

Alban Butler, The Lives of the Fathers, Martyrs and Other Principal Saints, volume 4

Sabas the Goth, 372

The faith of Christ erected its trophies not only over the pride and sophistry of the heathen philosophers, and the united powers of the Roman empire, but also over the kings of barbarous infidel nations; who, though in every other thing the contrast of the Romans, and enemies to their name, yet vied with them in the rage with which they sought, by every human stratagem, and every invention of cruelty, to depress the cross of Christ: but which the finger of God was more visible in the propagation of his faith. Even among the Goths, his name was glorified by the blood of martyrs. Athanaric, king of the Goths, in 370, started to persecute the Christians. The Greeks commemorate fifty-one martyrs who suffered in that nation. The two most illustrious are Nicetas and Sabas.

Sabas was born a Goth, but was converted in his youth and became a faithful imitator of the obedience, mildness, humility, and other virtues of the apostles. He was affable to all men, yet with dignity; a lover of truth, an enemy to all dissimulation or disguise, intrepid and modest. He often spent a whole day or all night in prayer. He burned with an ardent desire in all things to glorify Jesus Christ.

The princes and magistrates of Gothia began, in 370, to persecute the Christians, by compelling them to eat meats which had been sacrificed to idols, out of a superstitious motive, as if they were sanctified. In 371 a commissary of the king arrived at Sabas' town in search of Christians. Some of the inhabitants offered to swear that there were no Christians in the place. Sabas appeared, and stepping up to those who were going to take that oath, said: "Let no man swear for me: for I am a Christian."

The commissary asked the by-standers what wealth he had: and being told he had nothing besides the clothes on his back, the commissary despised him, saying: "such a fellow can do us neither good nor harm."

The next year Atharidus, son of one that enjoyed a petty sovereignty in that country, entered Sabas' town in the middle of the night, and hauled Sabas from his bed without allowing him to put on his clothes, and dragged him naked over thorns and briars, forcing him along with whips and staves. The persecutors did not have a rack so they took the axle-tree of a cart, laid it on Sabas' neck, and stretching out his hands, fastened them to each end. They fastened another in a similar way to his feet. He was tortured through most of the night in this position. The next morning Atharidus had Sabas' hands tied and had him hung up on a beam of the house. Then he ordered meats that had been sacrificed to idols to be served before him, but Sabas said, "This pernicious meat is impure and profane, as is Atharidus himself who sent it." One of the slaves of Atharidus, incensed at these words, struck the point of his javelin against the saint's chest with such force that all present believed that he had been killed.

But Sabas said, "Do you think you have killed me? Know that I felt no more pain than if the javelin had been a lock of wool." Atharidus, being informed of these particulars, gave orders that he should be put to death. Sabas was then thrown into the River Musaeus where he drowned.

Alban Butler, The Lives of the Saints, Dublin, 1833, volume 1, pp 459-60

Martyrdom of Alban (1)

The city of St Albans derives its name from the first English martyr, the proto-martyr. In 304 a Roman soldier, Alban, was stationed at Verulamium, a Roman town which subsequently changed its name to St Albans. The Diocletian persecution, or as modern historians now believe, during earlier persecutions during the reign of Emperor Severus, who was noted for his persecution of Christians, a priest called Amphibalus, from Caerleon, was on the run and arrived in Verulamium looking for shelter. Alban took Amphibalus into his home, even though Alban was not a Christian himself. While he was protecting the fugitive Alban took note of the hours the priest spent in prayer. He then asked Amphibalus to instruct him in his faith and in a short time Alban himself embraced the Christian faith.

He was quickly earmarked as a protector of Christians and was denounced for this. Soldiers were sent to search his house, but Alban heard they were on the way. So he gave Amphibalus his clothes and let him out of his house through a secret door. Alban just had time to put on the priest's clothes before the soldiers arrived. He was taken before a judge where his disguise was quickly unmasked. In an attempt to make Alban deny his new faith he was ordered to make a sacrifice to the gods, by sprinkling a handful of incense on an altar. As a Christian Alban felt he could not do this. When asked to offer sacrifices to Jupiter and Apollo, Alban replied, "I confess Jesus Christ, the son of God, with my whole being. Those whom you call gods are idols; they are made by hands." Alban further enraged the court when he refused to disclose where Amphibalus had escaped to. He was then scourged. Partly because he bore this terrible punishment so patiently he was then sentenced to death.

He was taken across the river Ver, to the top of a nearby hill, which overlooked the city. On the way there the soldier who had been instructed to carry out the execution refused to do this as he himself also followed in Alban's footsteps and embraced Christianity. This resulted in Alban and this Roman soldier both being beheaded. The date for this is now thought to be 22 June 209 and the abbey marks it annually with its Rose Service (on the Sunday after June 22) which is still attended by pilgrims. Rose Sunday gains its name from St Alban being a rose among the martyrs.

Tradition says that Amphibalus (whose name is Greek for cloak) was found in Wales and brought to Redbourne, near Verulamium, where he was subjected to terrible tortures, before being executed.
Editor

Martyrdom of Alban (2)

By the Venerable Bede: Historia Ecclesiastica Gentis Anglorum: The History of the Primitive Church of England. Book One, Chapter Seven

The Martyrdom of St. Alban and his Companions During this persecution, one of the most illustrious of those who suffered death for the faith, was St. Alban, of whom the Priest Fortunatus, in the book which he wrote in commendation of Virgins, speaking of the great number of martyrs who were sent to heaven by it from every part of the world, says,

Albanum egregium fæcunda Britannia profert, (Fruitful Britain holy Alban yields.)

He was yet a Pagan, when the cruel Emperors first published their edicts against the Christians, and when he received a clergyman flying from his persecutors into his house as an asylum. Having observed that his guest spent whole days and nights in continual praying and watching, he felt himself on a sudden inspired by the grace of God, and began to emulate so glorious an example of faith and piety, and being leisurely instructed by his wholesome admonitions, casting off the darkness of idolatry, he became a Christian in all sincerity of heart. – And, when he had exercised his hospitality towards the before-mentioned clergyman, for some days, a report reached the ears of the impious prince, that the confessor of Christ, to whom the glory of martyrdom had not yet been granted, was concealed in Alban's house: upon which, he commanded some soldiers to make a strict search after him. When they came to his house, St. Alban immediately presented himself to them, dressed in the clothes which his guest and instructor usually wore. Now it happened that the Judge, at the time when Alban was carried before him, was standing at the altar, and offering sacrifice to the Dæmons. And, when he saw Alban, being much enraged at his having presumed, of his own accord, to deliver himself into the hands of the soldiers, and incur the danger of being put to death, he ordered him to be dragged to the idols of Devils, before which he stood, saying, "Because you have chosen to conceal a rebellious and sacrilegious person, rather than to deliver him up to the soldiers, that he might suffer the punishment due to him, for despising and blaspheming the gods – you shall undergo all the punishment, which was to have been inflicted on him, if you refuse to comply with the rights of our religion."

But St. Alban, who had before voluntarily professed himself a Christian to the persecutors of the faith, was not the least intimidated at the prince's threats; but, being armed with the armor of the spiritual warfare, plainly told him that, he would not obey his commands. "Then," said the judge, "of what family or descent are you?"

"What does it concern you," answered Alban, "of what family I am? But if you desire to hear the truth of my religion, be it known unto you, that I am now a Christian, and employ my time in the practice of Christian duties."

"I ask your name?" said the judge, "which tell me immediately."

"I am called Alban by my parents," he replied, "and ever worship and adore the true and living God, who created all things."

Then the judge, in a rage, said, "If you will enjoy the happiness of eternal life, do not delay to offer sacrifice to the great gods."

To which Alban answered, "Those sacrifices, which you offer to devils, can neither avail the offerers any thing, nor obtain for them the effect of their petitions; on the contrary, whosoever offers sacrifices to these idols, shall receive the eternal pains of hell for his reward."

The judge, on hearing him say these words, was exasperated even to fury. He therefore ordered the holy confessor of God to be scourged by the executioners, thinking that stripes would shake that constancy of heart which words could not affect. But he bore the greatest torments for our Lord, not only patiently, but joyfully.

When the judge perceived that he was not to be overcome by tortures, or withdrawn from the profession of the Christian religion, he sentenced him to be beheaded. Being led to execution, he came to a river, which was divided at the place where he was to suffer with a wall and sand, and the stream was very rapid. Here he saw a multitude of persons of both sexes, and of all ages and ranks, who were doubtless assembled by a divine impulse, to attend the most blessed confessor and martyr; and had so occupied the bridge on the river, as to render it almost impossible for him and all of them to pass over it that evening. Almost every body flocking out of the city to see the execution, the judge, who remained in it, was left without any attendance.

St. Alban therefore, whose mind was filled with an ardent desire to arrive quickly at his martyrdom, approached to the stream, and, lifting up his eyes to heaven, addressed his prayer to the Almighty; when, behold, he saw the water immediately recede, and leave the bed of the river dry, for them to pass over. The executioner, who was to have beheaded him among the rest, observing this prodigy, hastened to meet him at the place of execution; and, being moved by divine inspiration, threw down the drawn sword which he carried, and prostrated himself at his feet, earnestly desiring that he might rather suffer death, with or for the martyr, than be constrained to take away the life of so holy a man. Whilst he of a persecutor became a companion in the true faith, and the rest of the executioners hesitated to take up the sword from the ground, the most venerable confessor of God ascended a hill with the throng.

This very pleasant place was about half a mile from the river, enamelled with a great variety of flowers, or rather quite covered with them; where there was no part very steep or craggy, but the whole of it was levelled by nature, like the sea when it is calm: which beautiful and agreeable appearance seemed to render it fit and worthy to be enriched and sanctified with the martyr's blood. When St. Alban had reached the summit of this hill, he prayed to God to give him water; and immediately, an ever-flowing spring rose at his feet, the course being confined; so that every one might perceive that the river had been before obedient to the martyr. For it could not be supposed that he would ask for water at the top of the hill, who had not left it in the river below, unless he had been convinced that it was expedient for the glory of God that he should do so. That river, nevertheless, having been made subservient to the martyr's devotion, and performed the office which he enjoined it, returned; and continued to flow in its natural course as before.

Here, therefore, this most valiant martyr, being beheaded, received the crown of life which God has promised to those who love him. But the executioner, who was so wicked as to embrue his sacrilegious hands in the martyr's sacred blood, was not permitted to rejoice at his death; for his eyes dropped to the ground at the same moment as the blessed martyr's head. At the same time was also beheaded there, the soldier, who before, through a divine inspiration, had refused to execute the sentence on the martyr: concerning whom it is evident, that, though he was not baptized at the baptismal font, yet he was cleansed with the laver of his own blood, and made worthy to enter into the kingdom of heaven.

The judge then, astonished at the novelty of so many heavenly miracles, ordered that the persecution should cease immediately, beginning thus to honour the saints for their patience and constancy, in suffering that death by the terrors of which he had expected to have withdrawn them from their adherence to the Christian faith.
The Venerable Bede

Martyrdom of Alban (3)

St. Alban suffered on the 20th of June, near the city of Verulam, now, from him, called St. Alban's; a church of most exquisite workmanship, and suitable to commemorate his martyrdom, having been afterwards erected there as soon as peace was restored to the Christian church; in which place there cease not to this day the miraculous cures of many sick persons, and the frequent working of wonders. At the same time suffered Aaron and Julius, inhabitants of the city of Leicester [or Caerleon], and many others of both sexes, in other places; who, having been tormented on the rack till their members were dislocated, and having endured various other unheard-of cruelties, yielded their souls, after the conflict was over, to the joys of the city above. Alban, while he was yet a heathen, fell in with a poor Christian priest, who was trying to hide himself from the persecutors. Alban took him into his own house, and sheltered him there; and he was so much struck with observing how the priest prayed to God, and spent long hours of the night in religious exercises, that he soon became a believer in Christ. But the priest was hotly searched for, and information was given that he was hidden in Alban's house. And when the soldiers came to look for him there, Alban knew their errand, and put on the priest's dress, so that the soldiers seized him and carried him before the judge. The judge found that they had brought the wrong man, and, in his rage at the disappointment, he told Alban that he must himself endure the punishment which had been meant for the other. Alban heard this without any fear, and on being questioned, he declared that he was a Christian, a worshipper of the one true God, and that he would not sacrifice to idols which could do no good. He was put to the torture, but bore it gladly for his Saviour's sake, and then, as he was still firm in professing his faith, the judge gave orders that he should be beheaded. And when he had been led out to the place of execution, which was a little grassy knoll that rose gently on one side of the town, the soldier, who was to have put him to death, was so moved by the sight of Alban's behaviour, that he threw away his sword, and desired to be put to death with him. They were both beheaded, and the town of Verulam, where they suffered, has since been called St. Alban's, from the name of the first British martyr. This martyrdom took place early in the persecution; but, (as we have seen) Constantius afterwards protected the British Christians, and his son Constantine, who succeeded to his share in the empire, treated them with yet greater favor.
Canon J.C. Robertson, Sketches of Church History, SPCK, 1904

The Edict of Milan

Constantine Augustus and Licinius Augustus

The persecution of Christians ended in 313 when Constantine of the West and Licinius of the East proclaimed the Edict of Milan, which established a policy of religious freedom for all.

This is an English translation of the edict.

When I, Constantine Augustus, as well as I, Licinius Augustus, fortunately met near Mediolanurn (Milan), and were considering everything that pertained to the public welfare and security, we thought, among other things which we saw would be for the good of many, those regulations pertaining to the reverence of the Divinity ought certainly to be made first, so that we might grant to the Christians and others full authority to observe that religion which each preferred; whence any Divinity whatsoever in the seat of the heavens may be propitious and kindly disposed to us and all who are placed under our rule. And thus by this wholesome counsel and most upright provision we thought to arrange that no one whatsoever should be denied the opportunity to give his heart to the observance of the Christian religion, of that religion which he should think best for himself, so that the Supreme Deity, to whose worship we freely yield our hearts) may show in all things His usual favor and benevolence. Therefore, your Worship should know that it has pleased us to remove all conditions whatsoever, which were in the rescripts formerly given to you officially, concerning the Christians and now any one of these who wishes to observe Christian religion may do so freely and openly, without molestation. We thought it fit to commend these things most fully to your care that you may know that we have given to those Christians free and unrestricted opportunity of religious worship. When you see that this has been granted to them by us, your Worship will know that we have also conceded to other religions the right of open and free observance of their worship for the sake of the peace of our times, that each one may have the free opportunity to worship as he pleases; this regulation is made we that we may not seem to detract from any dignity or any religion.

Moreover, in the case of the Christians especially we esteemed it best to order that if it happens anyone heretofore has bought from our treasury from anyone whatsoever, those places where they were previously accustomed to assemble, concerning which a certain decree had been made and a letter sent to you officially, the same shall be restored to the Christians without payment or any claim of recompense and without any kind of fraud or deception, Those, moreover, who have obtained the same by gift, are likewise to return them at once to the Christians. Besides, both those who have purchased and those who have secured them by gift, are to appeal to the vicar if they seek any recompense from our bounty, that they may be cared for through our clemency. All this property ought to be delivered at once to the community of the Christians through your intercession, and without delay. And since these Christians are known to have possessed not only those places in which they were accustomed to assemble, but also other property, namely the churches, belonging to them as a corporation and not as individuals, all these things which we have included under the above law, you will order to be restored, without any hesitation or controversy at all, to these Christians, that is to say to the corporations and their conventicles: providing, of course, that the above arrangements be followed so that those who return the same without payment, as we have said, may hope for an indemnity from our bounty. In all these circumstances you ought to tender your most efficacious intervention to the community of the Christians, that our command may be carried into effect as quickly as possible, whereby, moreover, through our clemency, public order may be secured. Let this be done so that, as we have said above, Divine favor towards us, which, under the most important circumstances we have already experienced, may, for all time, preserve and prosper our successes together with the good of the state. Moreover, in order that the statement of this decree of our good will may come to the notice of all, this rescript, published by your decree, shall be announced everywhere and brought to the knowledge of all, so that the decree of this, our benevolence, cannot be concealed.

From Lactantius, De Mort. Pers., ch. 48. opera, ed. 0. F. Fritzsche, II, p 288 sq. (Bibl Patr. Ecc. Lat. XI). Translated in University of Pennsylvania. Dept. of History: Translations and Reprints from the Original Sources of European history, (Philadelphia, University of Pennsylvania Press [1897?-1907?]), Vol 4:, 1, pp. 28- 30

Rise of the Worship of Martyrs and Relics

In thankful remembrance of the fidelity of this "noble army of martyrs," in recognition of the unbroken communion of saints, and in prospect of the resurrection of the body, the church paid to the martyrs, and even to their mortal remains, a veneration, which was in itself well-deserved and altogether natural, but which early exceeded the scriptural limit, and afterwards degenerated into the worship of saints and relics. The heathen hero-worship silently continued in the church and was baptized with Christian names. In the church of Smyrna, according to its letter of the year 155, we find this veneration still in its innocent, childlike form: "They [the Jews] know not, that we can neither ever forsake Christ, who has suffered for the salvation of the whole world of the redeemed, nor worship another. Him indeed we adore (proskunou"men) as the Son of God; but the martyrs we love as they deserve (ajgapw"men ajxivw") for their surpassing love to their King and Master, as we wish also to be their companions and fellow-disciples." The day of the death of a martyr was called his heavenly birth-day, and was celebrated annually at his grave (mostly in a cave or catacomb), by prayer, reading of a history of his suffering and victory, oblations, and celebration of the holy supper. But the early church did not stop with this.

Martyrdom was taken, after the end of the second century, not only as a higher grade of Christian virtue, but at the same time as a baptism of fire and blood, an ample substitution for the baptism of water, as purifying from sin, and as securing an entrance into heaven. Origen even went so far as to ascribe to the sufferings of the martyrs an atoning virtue for others, an efficacy like that of the sufferings of Christ, on the authority of such passages as 2 Cor. 12:15; Col. 1:24; 2 Tim. 4:6. According to Tertullian, the martyrs entered immediately into the blessedness of heaven, and were not required, like ordinary Christians, to pass through the intermediate state. Thus was applied the benediction on those who are persecuted for righteousness' sake, Matt. 5:10-12. Hence, according to Origen and Cyprian, their prayers before the throne of God came to be thought peculiarly efficacious for the church militant on earth, and, according to an example related by Eusebius, their future intercessions were bespoken shortly before their death. In the Roman Catacombs we find inscriptions where the departed are requested to pray for their living relatives and friends. The veneration thus shown for the persons of the martyrs was transferred in smaller measure to their remains. The church of Smyrna counted the bones of Polycarp more precious than gold or diamonds. The remains of Ignatius were held in equal veneration by the Christians at Antioch. The friends of Cyprian gathered his blood in handkerchiefs, and built a chapel over his tomb. A veneration frequently excessive was paid, not only to the deceased martyrs, but also the surviving confessors. It was made the special duty of the deacons to visit and minister to them in prison. The heathen Lucian in his satire, "De morte Peregrini," describes the unwearied care of the Christians for their imprisoned brethren; the heaps of presents brought to them; and the testimonies of sympathy even by messengers from great distances; but all, of course, in Lucian's view, out of mere good-natured enthusiasm. Tertullian the Montanist censures the excessive attention of the Catholics to their confessors. The libelli pacis, as they were called – intercessions of the confessors for the fallen – commonly procured restoration to the fellowship of the church. Their voice had peculiar weight in the choice of bishops, and their sanction not rarely overbalanced the authority of the clergy. Cyprian is nowhere more eloquent than in the praise of their heroism. His letters to the imprisoned confessors in Carthage are full of glorification, in a style somewhat offensive to our evangelical ideas. Yet after all, he protests against the abuse of their privileges, from which he had himself to suffer, and earnestly exhorts them to a holy walk; that the honor they have gained may not prove a snare to them, and through pride and carelessness be lost. He always represents the crown of the confessor and the martyr as a free gift of the grace of God, and sees the real essence of it rather in the inward disposition than in the outward act. Commodian conceived the whole idea of martyrdom in its true breadth, when he extended it to all those who, without shedding their blood, endured to the end in love, humility, and patience, and in all Christian virtue.

Philip Scaff, History of the Christian Church, chapter 27

Persecution under Julian the Apostate

This emperor was the son of Julius Constantius, and the nephew of Constantine the Great. He studied the rudiments of grammar under the inspection of Mardonius, a eunuch, and a heathen of Constantinople. His father sent him some time after to Nicomedia, to be instructed in the Christian religion, by the bishop of Eusebius, his kinsman, but his principles were corrupted by the pernicious doctrines of Ecebolius the rhetorician, and Maximus the magician.

Constantius, dying the year 361, Julian succeeded him, and had no sooner attained the imperial dignity than he renounced Christianity and embraced paganism, which had for some years fallen into great disrepute. Though he restored the idolatrous worship, he made no public edicts against Christianity. He recalled all banished pagans, allowed the free exercise of religion to every sect, but deprived all Christians of offices at court, in the magistracy, or in the army. He was chaste, temperate, vigilant, laborious, and pious; yet he prohibited any Christian from keeping a school or public seminary of learning, and deprived all the Christian clergy of the privileges granted them by Constantine the Great.

Biship Basil made himself first famous by his opposition to Arianism, which brought upon him the vengeance of the Arian bishop of Constantinople; he equally opposed paganism. The emperor's agents in vain tampered with Basil by means of promises, threats, and racks, he was firm in the faith, and remained in prison to undergo some other sufferings, when the emperor came accidentally to Ancyra. Julian determined to examine Basil himself, when that holy man being brought before him, the emperor did every thing in his power to dissuade him from persevering in the faith. Basil not only continued as firm as ever, but, with a prophetic spirit foretold the death of the emperor, and that he should be tormented in the other life. Enraged at what he heard, Julian commanded that the body of Basil should be torn every day in seven different parts, until his skin and flesh were entirely mangled. This inhuman sentence was executed with rigor, and the martyr expired under its severities, on June 28, A.D. 362.

Donatus, bishop of Arezzo, and Hilarinus, a hermit, suffered about the same time; also Gordian, a Roman magistrate. Artemius, commander in chief of the Roman forces in Egypt, being a Christian, was deprived of his commission, then of his estate, and lastly of his head.

The persecution raged dreadfully about the latter end of the year 363; but, as many of the particulars have not been handed down to us, it is necessary to remark in general, that in Palestine many were burnt alive, others were dragged by their feet through the streets naked until they expired; some were scalded to death, many stoned, and great numbers had their brains beaten out with clubs. In Alexandria, innumerable were the martyrs who suffered by the sword, burning, crucifixion and stoning. In Arethusa, several were ripped open, and corn being put into their bellies, swine were brought to feed therein, which, in devouring the grain, likewise devoured the entrails of the martyrs, and in Thrace, Emilianus was burnt at a stake; and Domitius murdered in a cave, whither he had fled for refuge.

The emperor, Julian the apostate, died of a wound which he received in his Persian expedition, A.D. 363, and even while expiring, uttered the most horrid blasphemies. He was succeeded by Jovian, who restored peace to the Church.

After the decease of Jovian, Valentinian succeeded to the empire, and associated to himself Valens, who had the command in the east, and was an Arian and of an unrelenting and persecuting disposition.

Philip Scaff, History of the Christian Church

Martyrs at Merum in Phrygia, under Julian

Introduction to The Ecclesiastical History

Eusebius, surnamed Pamphilus, writing the History of the Church in ten books, closed it with that period of the emperor Constantine, when the persecution which

Diocletian had begun against the Christians came to an end. Also in writing the life of Constantine, this same author has but slightly treated of matters regarding Arius, being more intent on the rhetorical finish of his composition and the praises of the emperor, than on an accurate statement of facts. Now, as we propose to write the details of what has taken place in the churches since his time to our own day, we begin with the narration of the particulars which he has left out, and we shall not be solicitous to display a parade of words, but to lay before the reader what we have been able to collect from documents, and what we have heard from those who were familiar with will be proper to enter into a brief account of Constantine's conversion to Christianity, making a beginning with this event.

Martyrs at Merum in Phrygia

Amachius governor of Phrygia ordered that the temple at Merum, a city of that province, should be opened, and cleared of the filth which had accumulated there by lapse of time: also that the statues it contained should be polished fresh. This in being put into operation grieved the Christians very much. Now a certain Macedonius and Theodulus and Tatian, unable to endure the indignity thus put upon their religion, and impelled by a fervent zeal for virtue, rushed by night into the temple, and broke the images m pieces. The governor infuriated at what had been done, would have put to death many in that city who were altogether innocent, when the authors of the deed voluntarily surrendered themselves, choosing rather to die themselves in defense of the truth, than to see others put to death in their stead. The governor seized and ordered them to expiate the crime they had committed by sacrificing: on their refusal to do this, their judge menaced them with tortures; but they despising his threats, being endowed with great courage, declared their readiness to undergo any sufferings, rather than pollute themselves by sacrificing. After subjecting them to all possible tortures he at last laid them on gridirons under which a fire was placed, and thus slew them. But even in this last extremity they gave the most heroic proofs of fortitude, addressing the ruthless governor thus: "If you wish to eat broiled flesh, Amachius, turn us on the other side also, lest we should appear but half cooked to your taste." Thus these martyrs ended their life.

Socrates Scholasticus, The Ecclesiastical History, book 1, chapter 1 and book 3, chapter 15

USTHAZANES

When, in course of time, the Christians increased in number, and began to form churches, and appointed priests and deacons, the Magi, who as a priestly tribe had from the beginning in successive generations acted as the guardians of the Persian religion, became deeply incensed against them. The Jews, who through envy are in some way naturally opposed to the Christian religion, were likewise offended. They therefore brought accusations before Sapor, the reigning sovereign, against Symeon, who was then archbishop of Seleucia and Ctesiphon, royal cities of Persia, and charged him with being a friend of the Caesar of the Romans, and with communicating the affairs of the Persians to him. Sapor believed these accusations, and at first, ground the Christians with excessive taxes, although he knew that the generality of them had voluntarily embraced poverty. He entrusted the exaction to cruel men, hoping that, by the want of necessaries, and the atrocity of the exacters, they might be compelled to abjure their religion; for this was his aim. Afterwards, however, be commanded that the priests and conductors of the worship of God should be slain with the sword. The churches were demolished, their vessels were deposited in the treasury, and Symeon was arrested as a traitor to the kingdom and the religion of the Persians. Thus the Magi, with the cooperation of the Jews, quickly destroyed the houses of prayer. Symeon, on his apprehension, was bound with chains, and brought before the king. There the man evinced his excellence and courage; for when Sapor commanded that he should be led away to the torture, he did not fear, and would not prostrate himself. The king, greatly exasperated, demanded why he did not prostrate himself as he had done formerly. Symeon replied, "Formerly I was not led away bound in order that I might abjure the truth of God, and therefore I did not then object to pay the customary respect to royalty; but now it would not be proper for me to do so; for I stand here in defense of godliness and of our opinion." When he ceased speaking, the king commanded him to worship the sun, promising, as an inducement, to bestow gifts upon him, and to hold him in honor; but on the other hand, threatening, in case of non-compliance, to visit him and the whole body of Christians with destruction. When the king found that he neither frightened him by menaces, nor caused him to relax by promises, and that Symeon remained firm and refused to worship the sun, or to betray his religion, he commanded him to be put in bonds for a while, probably imagining that he would change his mind.

When Symeon was being conducted to prison, Usthazanes, an aged eunuch, the foster-father of Sapor and superintendent of the palace, who happened to be sitting at the gates of the palace, arose to do him reverence. Symeon reproachfully forbade him in a loud and haughty voice, averted his countenance, and passed by; for the eunuch had been formerly a Christian, but had recently yielded to authority, and had worshiped the sun. This conduct so affected the eunuch that he wept aloud, laid aside the white garment with which he was robed, and clothed himself, as a mourner, in black. He then seated himself in front of the palace, crying and groaning, and saying, "Woe is me! What must not await me since I have denied God; and on this account Symeon, formerly my familiar friend, does not think me worthy of being spoken to, but turns away and hastens from me."

When Sapor heard of what had occurred, he called the eunuch to him, and inquired into the cause of his grief, and asked him whether any calamity had befallen his family. Usthazanes replied and said, "O king, nothing has occurred to my family; but I would rather have suffered any other affliction whatsoever than that which has befallen me, and it would have been easy to bear. Now I mourn because I am alive, and ought to have been dead long ago; yet I still see the sun which, not voluntarily, but to please thee, I professed to worship. Therefore, on both accounts, it is just that I should die, for I have been a betrayer of Christ, and a deceiver of thee." He then swore by the Maker of heaven and earth, that he would never swerve from his convictions. Sapor, astonished at the wonderful conversion of the eunuch, was still more enraged against the Christians, as if they had effected it by enchantments. Still, he spared the old man, and strove with all his strength, by alternate gentleness and harshness, to bring him over to his own sentiments. But finding that his efforts were useless, and that Usthazanes persisted in declaring that he would never be so foolish as to worship the creature instead of the creator, he became inflamed with passion, and commanded that the eunuch's head should be struck off with a sword. When the executioners came forward to perform their office, Usthazanes requested them to wait a little, that he might communicate something to the king. He then called one of the most faithful eunuchs, and bade him say to Sapor, "From my youth until now I have been well affected, O king, to your house, and have ministered with fitting diligence to your father and yourself. I need no witnesses to corroborate my statements; these facts are well established. For all the matters wherein at divers times I have gladly served you, grant me this reward; let it not be imagined by those who are ignorant of the circumstances, that I have incurred this punishment by acts of unfaithfulness against the kingdom, or by the commission of any other crime; but let it be published and proclaimed abroad by a herald, that Usthazanes loses his head for no knavery that he has ever committed in the palaces, but for being a Christian, and for refusing to obey the king in denying his own God."

The eunuch delivered this message, and Sapor, according to the request of

Usthazanes, commanded a herald to make the desired proclamation; for the king imagined that others would be easily deterred from embracing Christianity, by reflecting that he who sacrificed his aged foster-father and esteemed household servant, would assuredly spare no other Christian. Usthazanes, however, believed that as by his timidity in consenting to worship the sun, he had caused many Christians to fear, so now, by the diligent proclamation of the cause of his sufferings, many might be edified by learning that he died for the sake of religion, and so became imitators of his fortitude.

Sozomen's Memoir, book 2, chapter 9

SYMEON

In this manner the honorable life of Usthazanes was terminated, and when the intelligence was brought to Symeon in the prison, he offered thanksgiving to God on his account. The following day, which happened to be the sixth day of the week, and likewise the day on which, as immediately preceding the festival of the resurrection, the annual memorial of the passion of the Saviour is celebrated, the king issued orders for the decapitation of Symeon; for he had again been conducted to the palace from the prison, had reasoned most nobly with Sapor on points of doctrine, and had expressed a determination never to worship either the king or the sun. On the same day a hundred other prisoners were ordered to be slain. Symeon beheld their execution, and last of all he was put to death. Amongst these victims were bishops, presbyters, and other clergy of different grades. As they were being led out to execution, the chief of the Magi approached them, and asked them whether they would preserve their lives by conforming to the religion of the king and by worshiping the sun. As none of them would comply with this condition, they were conducted to the place of execution, and the executioners applied themselves to the task of slaying these martyrs. Symeon, standing by those who were to be slain, exhorted them to constancy, and reasoned concerning death, and the resurrection, and piety, and showed them from the sacred Scriptures that a death like theirs is true life; whereas to live, and through fear to deny God, is as truly death. He told them, too, that even if no one were to slay them, death would inevitably overtake them; for our death is a natural consequence of our birth. The things after those of this life are perpetual, and do not happen alike to all men; but as if measured by some rule, they must give an accurate account of the course of life here. Each one who did well, will receive immortal rewards and will escape the punishments of those who did the opposite. He likewise told them that the greatest and happiest of all good actions is to die for the cause of God. While Symeon was pursuing such themes, and like a household attendant, was exhorting them about the manner in which they were to go into the conflicts, each one listened and spiritedly went to the slaughter. After the executioner had despatched a hundred, Symeon himself was slain; and Abedechalaas and Anannias, two aged presbyters of his own church, who had been his fellow-prisoners, suffered with him.

Sozomen's Memoir, book 2, chapter 10

PUSICES

Pusices, the superintendent of the king's artisans, was present at the execution; perceiving that Anannias trembled as the necessary preparations for his death were being made, he said to him, "O old man, close your eyes for a little while and be of good courage, for you will soon behold the light of Christ."

No sooner had he uttered these words than he was arrested and conducted before the king; and as he frankly avowed himself a Christian, and spoke with great freedom to the king concerning his opinion and the martyrs, he was condemned to an extraordinary and most cruel death, because it was not lawful to address the king with such boldness. The executioners pierced the muscles of his neck in such a manner as to extract his tongue. On the charge of some persons, his daughter, who had devoted herself to a life of holy virginity, was arraigned and executed at the same time.

The following year, on the day on which the passion of Christ was commemorated, and when preparations were being made for the celebration of the festival commemorative of his resurrection from the dead, Sapor issued a most cruel edict throughout Persia, condemning to death all those who should confess themselves to be Christians. It is hid that a greater number of Christians suffered by the sword; for the Magi sought diligently in the cities and villages for those who had concealed themselves; and many voluntarily surrendered themselves, lest they should appear, by their silence, to deny Christ. Of the Christians who were thus un-sparingly sacrificed, many who were attached to the palace were slain, and amongst these was Azades, (2) a eunuch, who was especially beloved by the king. On hearing of his death, Sapor was overwhelmed with grief, and put a stop to the general slaughter of the Christians; and he directed that the teachers of religion should alone be slain.

Sozomen's Memoir, book 2, chapter 11

Tarbula

About the same period, the queen was attacked with a disease, and Tarbula, the sister of Symeon the bishop, a holy virgin, was arrested with her servant, who shared in the same mode of life, as likewise a sister of Tarbula, who, after the death of her husband, abjured marriage, and led a similar career. The cause of their arrest was the charge of the Jews, who reported that they had injured the queen by their enchantments, on account of their rage at the death of Symeon. As invalids easily give credit to the most repulsive representations, the queen believed the charge, and especially because it emanated from the Jews, since she had embraced their sentiments, and lived in the observance of the Jewish rites, for she had great confidence in their veracity and in their attachment to herself. The Magi having seized Tarbula and her companions, condemned them to death; and after having sawn them asunder, they fastened them up to poles and made the queen pass through the midst of the poles as a medium for turning away the disease. It is said that this Tarbula was beautiful and very stately in form, and that one of the Magi, having become deeply enamored with her, secretly sent a proposal for intercourse, and promised as a reward to save her and her companions if she would consent. But she would give no ear to his licentiousness, and treated the Magi with scorn, and rebuked his lust. She would rather prefer courageously to die than to betray her virginity.

As it was ordained by the edict of Sapor, which we mentioned above, that the Christians should not be slaughtered indiscriminately, but that the priests and teachers of the opinions should be slain, the Magi and Arch-Magi traversed the whole country of Persia, studiously maltreating the bishops and presbyters. They sought them especially in the country of Adiabene, a part of the Persian dominions, because it was wholly Christianized.

Sozomen's Memoir, book 2, chapter 12

Martyrdom of St Acepsimas and His Companions

About this period they arrested Acepsimas the bishop, and many of his clergy. After having taken counsel together, they satisfied themselves with the hunt after the leader only; they dismissed the rest after they had taken away their property. James, however, who was one of the presbyters, voluntarily followed Acepsimas, obtained permission from the Magi to share his prison, and spiritedly ministered to the old man, lightened his misfortunes as far as he was able, and dressed his wounds; for not long after his apprehension, the Magi had injuriously tortured him with raw thongs in forcing him to worship the sun; and on his refusal to do so had retained him again in bonds. Two presbyters named Aithalas and James, and two deacons, by name Azadanes and Abdiesus, after being scourged most injuriously by the Magi, were compelled to live in prison, on account of their opinions. After a long time had elapsed, the great Arch-Magi communicated to the king the facts about them to be punished; and having received permission to deal with them as he pleased, unless they would consent to worship the sun, he made known this decision of Sapor's to the prisoners. They replied openly, that they would never betray the cause of Christ nor worship the sun; he tortured them unsparingly. Acepsimas persevered in the manly confession of his faith, till death put an end to his torments. Certain Armenians, whom the Persians retained as hostages, secretly carried away his body and buried it. The other prisoners, although not less scourged, lived as by a miracle, and as they would not change their judgment, were again put in bonds. Among these was Aithalas, who was stretched out while thus beaten, and his arms were torn out of his shoulders by the very great wrench; and he carried his hands about as dead and swinging loosely, so that others had to convey food to his mouth.

Under this rule, an innumerable multitude of presbyters, deacons, monks, holy virgins, and others who served the churches and were set apart for its dogma, terminated their lives by martyrdom. The following are the names of the bishops, so far as I have been able to ascertain: Barbasymes, Paulus, Gaddiabes, Sabinus, Mareas, Mocius, John, Hormisdas, Papas, James, Romas, Maares, Agas, Bochres, Abdas, Abdiesus, John, Abramins, Agdelas, Sapores, Isaac, and Dausas. The latter had been made prisoner by the Persians, and brought from a place named Zabdaeus. He died about this time in defense of the dogma; and Mareabdes, a chorepiscopus, and about two hundred and fifty of his clergy, who had also been captured by the Persians, suffered with him.

Sozomen's Memoir, book 2, chapter 13

Bishop Milles

About this period Milles suffered martyrdom. He originally served the Persians in a military capacity, but afterwards abandoned that vocation, in order to embrace the apostolical mode of life. It is related that he was ordained bishop over a Persian city, and he underwent a variety of sufferings, and endured wounds and drawings; and that, failing in his efforts to convert the inhabitants to Christianity, he uttered imprecations against the city, and departed. Not long after, some of the principal citizens offended the king, and an army with three hundred elephants was sent against them; the city was utterly demolished and its land was ploughed and sown. Milles, taking with him only his wallet, in which was the holy Book of the Gospels, repaired to Jerusalem in prayer; thence he proceeded to Egypt in order to see the monks. The extraordinary and admirable works which we have heard that he accomplished, are attested by the Syrians, who have written an account of his actions and life.

Sozomen's Memoir, book 2, chapter 13

16,000 Martyrs

For my own part, I think that I have said enough of him and of the other martyrs who suffered in Persia during the reign of Sapor; for it would be difficult to relate in detail every circumstance respecting them, such as their names, their country, the mode of completing their martyrdom, and the species of torture to which they were subjected; for they are innumerable, since such methods are jealously affected by the Persians, even to the extreme of cruelty. I shall briefly state that the number of men and women whose names have been ascertained, and who were martyred at this period, have been computed to be sixteen thousand; while the multitude outside of these is beyond enumeration, and on this account to reckon off their names appeared difficult to the Persians and Syrians and to the inhabitants of Edessa, who have devoted much care to this matter.

Sozomen's Memoir, book 2, chapter 14

Constantine Writes to Sapor Telling Him to Stop Persecuting Christians

The persecution of Christians greatly declined when Constantine became Emperor. After this time martyrdoms gradually changed from being thought of as "bloody" martyrdoms to the "white" martyrdoms of monasticism.

Constantine the Roman emperor was angry, and bore it ill when he heard of the sufferings to which the Christians were exposed in Persia. He desired most anxiously to render them assistance, yet knew not in what way to effect this object. About this time some ambassadors from the Persian king arrived at his court, and after granting their requests and dismissing them, he thought it would be a favorable opportunity to address Sapor in behalf of the Christians in Persia, and wrote to him, confessing that it would be a very great and forever indescribable favor, if he would be humane to those who admired the teaching of the Christians under him. "There is nothing in their religion," said he, "of a reprehensible nature; by bloodless prayers alone do they offer supplication to God, for he delighteth not in the outpouring of blood, but taketh pleasure only in a pure soul devoted to virtue and to religion; so that they who believe these things are worthy of commendation."

The emperor then assured Sapor that God would be propitious to him if he treated the Christians with lenity, and adduced the example of Valerian and of himself in proof thereof. He had himself, by faith in Christ, and by the aid of Divine inclination, come forth from the shores of the Western ocean, and reduced to obedience the whole of the Roman world, and had terminated many wars against foreigners and usurpers; and yet had never had recourse to sacrifices or divinations, but had for victory used only the symbol of the Cross at the head of his own armies, and prayer pure from blood and defilement. The reign of Valerian was prosperous so long as he refrained from persecuting the Church; but he afterwards commenced a persecution against the Christians, and was delivered by Divine vengeance into the hands of the Persians, who took him prisoner and put him to a cruel death."

It was in this strain that Constantine wrote to Sapor, urging him to be well-disposed to this religion; for the emperor extended his watchful care over all the Christians of every region, whether Roman or foreign.

Sozomen's Memoir, book 2, chapter 15

Juventinus and Maximinus

Now Julian, with less restraint, or shall I say, less shame, began to arm himself against true religion, wearing indeed a mask of moderation, but all the while preparing gins and traps which caught all who were deceived by them in the destruction of iniquity. He began by polluting with foul sacrifices the wells in the city and in Daphne, that every man who used the fountain might be partaker of abomination. Then he thoroughly polluted the things exposed in the Forum, for bread and meat and fruit and vegetables and every kind of food were aspersed. When those who were called by the Saviour's name saw what was done, they groaned and bewailed and expressed their abomination; nevertheless they partook, for they remembered the apostolic law, "Everything that is sold in the shambles eat, asking no question for conscience sake." Two officers in the army, who were shield bearers in the imperial suite, at a certain banquet lamented in somewhat warm language the abomination of what was being done, and employed the admirable language of the glorious youths at Babylon, "Thou hast given us over to an impious Prince, an apostate beyond all the nations on the earth." One of the guests gave information of this, and the emperor arrested these right worthy men and endeavoured to ascertain by questioning them what was the language they had used. They accepted the imperial enquiry as an opportunity for open speech, and with noble enthusiasm replied "sir we were brought up in true religion; we were obedient to most excellent laws, the laws of Constantine and of his sons; now we see the world full of pollution, meats and drinks alike defiled with abominable sacrifices, and we lament. We bewail these things at home, and now before thy face we express our grief, for this is the one thing in thy reign which we take ill." No sooner did he whom sympathetic courtiers called most mild and most philosophic hear these words than he took off his mask of moderation, and exposed the countenance of impiety. He ordered cruel and painful scourgings to be inflicted on them and deprived them of their lives; or shall we not rather say freed them from that sorrowful time and gave them crowns of victory? He pretended indeed that punishment was inflicted upon them not for the true religion for sake of which they were really slain, but because of their insolence, for he gave out that he had punished them for insulting the emperor, and ordered this report to be published abroad, thus grudging to these champions of the truth the name and honour or martyrs. The name of one was Juventinus; of the other Maximinus. The city of Antioch honoured them as defenders of true religion, and deposited them in a magnificent tomb, and up to this day they are honoured by a yearly festival. Other men in public office and of distinction used similar boldness of speech, and won like crowns of martyrdom.

The Ecclesiastical History, Theodoret, chapter 11

The persecutions and martyrdoms in Persia

At this time Isdigirdes, King of the Persians, began to wage war against the churches and the circumstances which caused him so to do were as follows. A certain bishop, Abdas by name, adorned with many virtues, was stirred with undue zeal and destroyed a Pyreum, Pyreum being the name given by the Persians to the temples of the fire which they regarded as their God.

On being informed of this by the Magi Isdigirdes sent for Abdas and first in moderate language complained of what had taken place and ordered him to rebuild the Pyreum.

This the bishop, in reply, positively refused to do, and thereupon the king threatened to destroy all the churches, and in the end carried out all his threats, for first be gave orders for the execution of that holy man and then commanded the destruction of the churches. Now I am of opinion that to destroy the Pyreum was wrong and inexpedient, for not even the divine Apostle, when he came to Athens and saw the city wholly given to idolatry, destroyed any one of the altars which the Athenians honoured, but convicted them of their ignorance by his arguments, and made manifest the truth. But the refusal to rebuild the fallen temple, and the determination to choose death rather than so do, I greatly praise and honour, and count to be a deed worthy of the martyr's crown; for building a shrine in honour of the fire seems to me to be equivalent to adoring it.

From this beginning arose a tempest which stirred fierce and cruel waves against the nurslings of the true faith, and when thirty years had gone by the agitation still remained kept up by the Magi, as the sea is kept in commotion by the blasts of furious winds. Magi is the name given by the Persians to the worshippers of the sun and moon but I have exposed their fabulous system in another treatise and have adduced solutions of their difficulties.

On the death of Isdigirdes, Vararanes, his son, inherited at once the kingdom and the war against the faith, and dying in his turn left them both together to his son. To relate the various kinds of tortures and cruelties inflicted on the saints is no easy task. In some cases the hands were flayed, in others the back; of others they stripped the heads of skin from brow to beard; others were enveloped in split reeds with the cut part turned inwards and were surrounded with tight bandages from head to foot; then each of the reeds was dragged out by force, and, tearing away the adjacent portions of the skin, caused severe agony; pits were dug and carefully greased in which quantities of mice were put; then they let down the martyrs, bound hand and foot, so as not to be able to protect themselves from the animals, to be food for the mice, and the the mice, under stress of hunger, little by little devoured the flesh of the victims, causing them long and terrible suffering. By others sufferings were endured even more terrible than these, invented by the enemy of humanity and the opponent of the truth, but the courage of the martyrs was unbroken, and they hastened unbidden in their eagerness to win that death which ushers men into indestructible life.

Of these I will cite one or two to serve as examples of the courage of the rest. Among the noblest of the Persians was one called Hormisdas, by race an Achaemenid and the son of a Prefect. On receiving information that he was a Christian the king summoned him and ordered him to abjure God his Saviour. He replied that the royal orders were neither right nor reasonable, "for he," so he went on, "who is taught to find no difficulty in spurning and denying the God of all, will haply the more easily despise a king who is a man of mortal nature; and if, sir, he who denies thy sovereignty is deserving of the severest punishment, how much more terrible a chastisement is not due to him who denies the Creator of the world?" The king ought to have admired the wisdom of what was said, but, instead of this, he stripped the noble athlete of his wealth and rank, and ordered him to go clad in nothing save a loin cloth, and drive the camels of the army. After some days had gone by, as he looked out of his chamber, he saw the excellent man scorched by the rays of the sun, and covered with dust, and he be thought him of his father's illustrious rank, and sent for him, and told him to put on a tunic of linen. Then thinking the toil he had suffered, and the kindness shewn him, had softened his heart, "Now at least," said he "give over your opposition, and deny the carpenter's son." Full of holy zeal Hormisdas tore the tunic and flung it away saying, "If you think that this will make one give up the true faith, keep your present with your false belief." When the king saw how bold he was he drove him naked from the palace.

One Suenes, who owned a thousand slaves, resisted the King, and refused to deny his master. The King therefore asked him which of his slaves was the vilest, and to this slave handed over the ownership of all the rest, and gave him Suenes to be his slave. He also gave him in marriage Suenes' wife, supposing that thus he could bend the will of the champion of the truth. But he was disappointed, for he had built his house upon the rock.

The king also seized and imprisoned a deacon of the name of Benjamin. After two years there came an envoy from Rome, to treat of other matters, who, when he was informed of this imprisonment, petitioned the king to release the deacon. The king ordered Benjamin to promise that he would not attempt to teach the Christian religion to any of the Magi, and the envoy exhorted Benjamin to obey, but Benjamin, after he heard what the envoy had to say, replied, "It is impossible for me not to impart the light which I have received; for how great a penalty is due for the hiding of our talent is taught in the history of the holy gospels."

Up to this time the King had not been informed of this refusal and ordered him to be set free. Benjamin continued as he was wont seeking to catch them that were held down by the darkness of ignorance, and bringing them to the light of knowledge. After a year information of his conduct was given to the king, and he was summoned and ordered to deny Him whom he worshiped.

He then asked the king "What punishment should be assigned to one who should desert his allegiance and prefer another?"

"Death and torture," said the king.

"How then" continued the wise deacon "should he be treated who abandons his Maker and Creator, makes a God of one of his fellow slaves, and offers to him the honour due to his Lord?"

Then the king was moved with wrath, and had twenty reeds pointed, and driven into the nails of his hands and feet. When he saw that Benjamin took this torture for child's play, he pointed another reed and drove it into his privy part and by working it up and down caused unspeakable agony. After this torture the impious and savage tyrant ordered him to be impaled upon a stout knotted staff, and so the noble sufferer gave up the ghost.

Innumerable other similar deeds of violence were committed by these impious men, but we must not be astonished that the Lord of all endures their savagery and impiety, for indeed before the reign of Constantine the Great all the Roman emperors wreaked their wrath on the friends of the truth, and Diocletian, on the day of the Saviour's passion, destroyed the churches throughout the Roman Empire, but after nine years had gone by they rose again in bloom and beauty many times larger and more splendid than before, and he and his iniquity perished.

These wars and the victory of the church had been predicted by the Lord, and the event teaches us that war brings us more blessing than peace. Peace makes us delicate, easy and cowardly. War whets our courage and makes us despise this present world as passing away. But these are observations which we have often made in other writings.
The Ecclesiastical History of Theodoret, book 5, chapter 38

Persecutions in Persia

The Gospel having spread itself into Persia, the pagan priests, who worshipped the sun, were greatly alarmed, and dreaded the loss of that influence they had hitherto maintained over the people's minds and properties. Hence they thought it expedient to complain to the emperor that the Christians were enemies to the state, and held a treasonable correspondence with the Romans, the great enemies of Persia.

The emperor Sapores, being naturally averse to Christianity, easily believed what was said against the Christians, and gave orders to persecute them in all parts of his empire. On account of this mandate, many eminent persons in the church and state fell martyrs to the ignorance and ferocity of the pagans.

Constantine the Great being informed of the persecutions in Persia, wrote a long letter to the Persian monarch, in which he recounts the vengeance that had fallen on persecutors, and the great success that had attended those who had refrained from persecuting the Christians.

Speaking of his victories over rival emperors of his own time, he said, "I subdued these solely by faith in Christ; for which God was my helper, who gave me victory in battle, and made me triumph over my enemies. He hath likewise so enlarged to me the bounds of the Roman Empire, that it extends from the Western Ocean almost to the uttermost parts of the East: for this domain I neither offered sacrifices to the ancient deities, nor made use of charm or divination; but only offered up prayers to the Almighty God, and followed the cross of Christ. Rejoiced should I be if the throne of Persia found glory also, by embracing the Christians: that so you with me, and they with you, may enjoy all happiness."

In consequence of this appeal, the persecution ended for the time, but it was renewed in later years when another king succeeded to the throne of Persia.
Foxe's Book of Martyrs, Edited by William Byron Forbush

Eusebius, Nestabus, and Zeno

As I have advanced thus far in my history, and have given an account of the death of George and of Theodoritus, I deem it right to relate some particulars concerning the death of the three brethren, Eusebius, Nestabus, and Zeno.

The inhabitants of Gaza, being inflamed with rage against them, dragged them from their house, in which they had concealed themselves and cast them into prison, and beat them. They then assembled in the theater, and cried out loudly against them, declaring that they had committed sacrilege in their temple, and had used the past opportunity for the injury and insult of paganism. By these shouts and by instigating one another to the murder of the brethren, they were filled with fury; and when they had been mutually incited, as a crowd in revolt is wont to do, they rushed to the prison. They handled the men very cruelly; sometimes with the face and sometimes with the back upon the ground, the victims were dragged along, and were dashed to pieces by the pavement. I have been told that even women quilted their distaffs and pierced them with the weaving-spindles, and that the cooks in the markets snatched from their stands the boiling pots foaming with hot water and poured it over the victims, or perforated them with spits. When they had torn the flesh from them and crushed in their skulls, so that the brain ran out on the ground, their bodies were dragged out of the city and flung on the spot generally used as a receptacle for the carcasses of beasts; then a large fire was lighted, and they burned the bodies; the remnant of the bones not consumed by the fire was mixed with those of camels and asses, that they might not be found easily.

But they were not long concealed; for a Christian woman, who was an inhabitant, though not a native of Gaza, collected the bones at night by the direction of God. She put them in an earthen pot and gave them to Zeno, their cousin, to keep, for thus God had informed her in a dream, and also had indicated to the woman where the man lived: and before she saw him, he was shown to her, for she was previously unacquainted with Zeno; and when the persecution had been agitated recently he remained concealed.

He was within a little of being seized by the people of Gaza and being put to death; but he had effected his escape while the people were occupied in the murder of his cousins, and had fled to Anthedon, a maritime city, about twenty stadia from Gaza and similarly favorable to paganism and devoted to idolatry. When the inhabitants of this city discovered that he was a Christian, they beat him terribly on the back with rods and drove him out of the city. He then fled to the harbor of Gaza and concealed himself; and here the woman found him and gave him the remains. He kept them carefully in his house until the reign of Theodosius, when he was ordained bishop; and he erected a house of prayer beyond the wails of the city, placed an altar there, and deposited the bones of the martyrs near those of Nestor, the Confessor.

Nestor had been on terms of intimacy with his cousins, and was seized with them by the people of Gaza, imprisoned, and scourged. But those who dragged him through the city were affected by his personal beauty; and, struck with compassion, they cast him, before he was quite dead, out of the city. Some persons found him, and carried him to the house of Zeno, where he expired during the dressing of his cuts and wounds. When the inhabitants of Gaza began to reflect on the enormity of their crime, they trembled lest the emperor should take vengeance on them.

It was reported that the emperor was filled with indignation, and had determined upon punishing the decuria; but this report was false, and had no foundation save in the fears and self-accusations of the criminals. Julian, far from evincing as much anger against them as he had manifested against the Alexandrians on the murder of George, did not even write to rebuke the people of Gaza. On the contrary, he deposed the governor of the province, and held him as a suspect, and represented that clemency alone prevented his being put to death. The crime imputed to him was, that of having arrested some of the inhabitants of Gaza, who were reported to have begun the sedition and murders, and of having imprisoned them until judgment could be passed upon them in accordance with the laws. "For what right had he," asked the emperor, "to arrest the citizens merely for retaliating on a few Galileans the injuries that had been inflicted on them and their gods?" This, it is said, was the fact in the case.

Sozomen's Memoir, book 4, chapter 9

Mark, Bishop of Arethusa

At the same period the inhabitants of Gaza sought for the monk Hilarion; but he had fled to Sicily. Here he employed himself in collecting wood in the deserts and on the mountains, which he carried on his shoulders for sale in the cities, and, by these means, obtained sufficient food for the support of the body. But as he was at length recognized by a man of quality whom he had dispossessed of a demon, he retired to Dalmatia, where, by the power of God he performed numerous miracles, and through prayer, repressed an inundation of the sea and restored the waves to their proper bounds, and again departed, for it was no joy to him to live among those who praised him; but when he changed his place of abode, he was desirous of being unobserved and by frequent migrations to be rid of the fame which prevailed about him. Eventually he sailed for the island of Cyprus, but touched at Paphos, and, at the entreaty of the bishop of Cyprus, he loved the life there and practiced philosophy at a place called Charburis.

Here he only escaped martyrdom by flight; for he fled in compliance with the Divine precept which commands us not to expose ourselves to persecution; but that if we fall into the hands of persecutors, to overcome by our own fortitude the violence of our oppressors.

The inhabitants of Gaza and of Alexandria were not the only citizens who exercised such atrocities against the Christians as those I have described. The inhabitants of Heliopolis, near Mount Libanus, and of Arethusa in Syria, seem to have surpassed them in excess of cruelty. The former were guilty of an act of barbarity which could scarcely be credited, had it not been corroborated by the testimony of those who witnessed it. They stripped the holy virgins, who had never been looked upon by the multitude, of their garments, and exposed them in a state of nudity as a public spectacle and objects of insult. After numerous other inflictions they at last shaved them, ripped them open, and concealed in their viscera [internal organs] the food usually given to pigs; and since the swine could not distinguish, but were impelled by the need of their customary food, they also tore in pieces the human flesh.

I am convinced that the citizens of Heliopolis perpetrated this barbarity against the holy virgins on account of the prohibition of the ancient custom of yielding up virgins to prostitution with any chance comer before being united in marriage to their betrothed. This custom was prohibited by a law enacted by Constantine, after he had destroyed the temple of Venus at Heliopolis, and erected a church upon its ruins.

Mark, bishop of Arethusa, an old man and venerable for his gray hairs and life, was put to a very cruel death by the inhabitants of that city, who had long entertained inimical feelings against him, because, during the reign of Constantine, he had more spiritedly than persuasively elevated the pagans to Christianity, and had demolished a most sacred and magnificent temple. On the accession of Julian he saw that the people were excited against the bishop; an edict was issued commanding the bishop either to defray the expenses of its re-erection, or to rebuild the temple. Reflecting that the one was impossible and the other unlawful for a Christian and still less for a priest, he at first fled from the city. On hearing, however, that many were suffering on his account, that some were dragged before the tribunals and others tortured, he returned, and offered to suffer whatever the multitude might choose to inflict upon him. The entire people, instead of admiring him the more as having manifested a deed befitting a philosopher, conceived that he was actuated by contempt towards them, and rushed upon him, dragged him through the streets, pressing and plucking and beating whatever member each one happened upon. People of each sex and of all ages joined with alacrity and fury in this atrocious proceeding. His ears were severed by fine ropes; the boys who frequented the schools made game of him by tossing him aloft and rolling him over and over, sending him forward, catching him up, and unsparingly piercing him with their styles. When his whole body was covered with wounds, and he nevertheless was still breathing, they anointed him with honey and a certain mixture, and placing him in a fish-basket made of woven rushes, raised him up on an eminence. It is said that while he was in this position, and the wasps and bees lit upon him and consumed his flesh, he told the inhabitants of Arethusa that he was raised up above them, and could look down upon them below him, and that this reminded him of the difference that would exist between them in the life to come. It is also related that the prefect who, although a pagan, was of such noble conduct that his memory is still honored in that country, admired the self-control of Mark, and boldly uttered reproaches against the emperor for allowing himself to be vanquished by an old man, who was exposed to innumerable tortures; and he added that such proceedings reflected ridicule on the emperor, while the names of the persecuted were at the same time rendered illustrious. Thus did the

blessed one endure all the torments inflicted upon him by the inhabitants of Arethusa with such unshaken fortitude that even the pagans praised him.
Sozomen's Memoir, book 4, chapter 10

Macedonius, Theodulus, Tatian, Busiris, Basil and Eupsychius

About the same period, Macedonius, Theodulus, and Tatian, who were Phrygians by birth, courageously endured martyrdom.

A temple of Misos, a city of Phrygia, having been reopened by the governor of the province, after it had been closed many years, these martyrs entered therein by night, and destroyed the images. As other individuals were arrested, and were on the point of being punished for the deed, they avowed themselves the actors in the transaction. They might have escaped all further punishment by offering sacrifices to idols; but the governor could not persuade them to accept acquittal on these terms. His persuasions being ineffectual, he maltreated them in a variety of forms, and finally extended them on a gridiron, beneath which a fire had been lighted. While they were being consumed, they said to the governor, "Amachus (for that was his name), "if you desire cooked flesh, give orders that our bodies may be turned with the other side to the fire, in order that we may not seem, to your taste, half cooked." Thus did these men nobly endure and lay down their life amid the punishments.

Busiris

It is said that Busiris also obtained renown at Ancyra, a city of Galatia, by his brilliant and most manly confession of religion. He belonged to the heresy denominated by Eucratites; the governor of the province apprehended and designed to maltreat him for ridiculing the pagans. He led him forth publicly to the torture chamber and commanded that he should be elevated. Busiris raised both hands to his head so as to leave his sides exposed, and told the governor that it would be useless for the executioners to lift him up to the instrument of torture and afterwards to lower him, as he was ready without this to yield to the tortures as much as might be desired. The governor was surprised at this proposition; but his astonishment was increased by what followed, for Busiris remained firm, holding up both hands and receiving the blows while his sides were being torn with hooks, according to the governor's direction. Immediately afterwards, Busiris was consigned to prison, but was released not long subsequently, on the announcement of the death of Julian. He lived till the reign of Theodosius, renounced his former heresy, and joined the Catholic Church.

Basil and Eupsychius

It is said that about this period, Basil, presbyter of the church of Ancyra, and Eupsychius, a noble of Caesarea in Cappadocia, who had but just taken to himself a wife and was still a bridegroom, terminated their lives by martyrdom. I believe that Eupsychius was condemned in consequence of the demolition of the temple of Fortune, which, as I have already stated, excited the anger of the emperor against all the inhabitants of Caesarea. Indeed, all the actors in this transaction were condemned, some to death, and others to banishment. Basil had long manifested great zeal in defense of the faith, and had opposed the Arians during the reign of Constantius; hence the partisans of Eudoxius had prohibited him from holding public assemblies. On the accession of Julian, however, he traveled hither and thither, publicly and openly exhorting the Christians to cleave to their own doctrines, and to refrain from defiling themselves with pagan sacrifices and libations. He urged them to account as nothing the honors which the emperor might bestow upon them, such honors being but of short duration, and leading to eternal infamy. His zeal had already rendered him an object of suspicion and of hatred to the pagans, when one day he chanced to pass by and see them offering sacrifice. He sighed deeply, and uttered a prayer to the effect that no Christian might be suffered to fall into similar delusion. He was seized on the spot, and conveyed to the governor of the province. Many tortures were inflicted on him; and in the manly endurance of this anguish he received the crown of martyrdom.

Even if these cruelties were perpetrated contrary to the will of the emperor, yet they serve to prove that his reign was signalized by martyrs neither ignoble nor few.

For the sake of clearness, I have related all these occurrences collectively, although the martyrdoms really occurred at different periods.

Sozomen's Memoir, book 4, chapter 11

Persecutions under the Arian heretics

The author of the Arian heresy was Arius, a native of Lybia, and a priest of Alexandria, who, in A.D. 318, began to publish his errors. He was condemned by a council of Lybian and Egyptian bishops, and that sentence was confirmed by the Council of Nice, A.D. 325. After the death of Constantine the Great, the Arians found means to ingratiate themselves into the favor of the emperor Constantinus, his son and successor in the east; and hence a persecution was raised against the orthodox bishops and clergy. The celebrated Athanasius, and other bishops, were banished, and their sees filled with Arians.

In Egypt and Lybia, thirty bishops were martyred, and many other Christians cruelly tormented; and, A.D. 386, George, the Arian bishop of Alexandria, under the authority of the emperor, began a persecution in that city and its environs, and carried it on with the most infernal severity. He was assisted in his diabolical malice by Catophonius, governor of Egypt; Sebastian, general of the Egyptian forces; Faustinus, the treasurer; and Heraclius, a Roman officer.

The persecutions now raged in such a manner that the clergy were driven from Alexandria, their churches were shut, and the severities practiced by the Arian heretics were as great as those that had been practiced by the pagan idolaters. If a man, accused of being a Christian, made his escape, then his whole family were massacred, and his effects confiscated.

Foxe's Book of Martyrs, Edited by William Byron Forbush

Persecution of the Christians by the Goths and Vandals

Many Scythian Goths having embraced Christianity about the time of Constantine the Great, the light of the Gospel spread itself considerably in Scythia, though the two kings who ruled that country, and the majority of the people continued pagans. Fritegern, king of the West Goths, was an ally to the Romans, but Athanarich, king of the East Goths, was at war with them. The Christians, in the dominions of the former, lived unmolested, but the latter, having been defeated by the Romans, wreaked his vengeance on his Christian subjects, commencing his pagan injunctions in the year 370.

In religion the Goths were Arians, and called themselves Christians; therefore they destroyed all the statues and temples of the heathen gods, but did no harm to the orthodox Christian churches. Alaric had all the qualities of a great general. To the wild bravery of the Gothic barbarian he added the courage and skill of the Roman soldier. He led his forces across the Alps into Italy, and although driven back for the time, returned afterward with an irresistible force.

The Last Roman "Triumph"

After this fortunate victory over the Goths a "triumph," as it was called, was celebrated at Rome. For hundreds of years successful generals had been awarded this great honor on their return from a victorious campaign. Upon such occasions the city was given up for days to the marching of troops laden with spoils, and who dragged after them prisoners of war, among whom were often captive kings and conquered generals. This was to be the last Roman triumph, for it celebrated the last Roman victory. Although it had been won by Stilicho, the general, it was the boy emperor, Honorius, who took the credit, entering Rome in the car of victory, and driving to the Capitol amid the shouts of the populace. Afterward, as was customary on such occasions, there were bloody combats in the Colosseum, where gladiators, armed with swords and spears, fought as furiously as if they were on the field of battle.

The first part of the bloody entertainment was finished; the bodies of the dead were dragged off with hooks, and the reddened sand covered with a fresh, clean layer. After this had been done the gates in the wall of the arena were thrown open, and a number of tall, well- formed men in the prime of youth and strength came forward. Some carried swords, others three-pronged spears and nets. They marched once around the walls, and stopping before the emperor, held up their weapons at arm's length, and with one voice sounded out their greeting, Ave, Caesar, morituri te salutant! "Hail, Caesar, those about to die salute thee!"

The combats now began again; the glatiators with nets tried to entangle those with swords, and when they succeeded mercilessly stabbed their antagonists to death with the three-pronged spear. When a glatiator had wounded his adversary, and had him lying helpless at his feet, he looked up at the eager faces of the spectators, and cried out, Hoc habet! "He has it!" and awaited the pleasure of the audience to kill or spare.

If the spectators held out their hands toward him, with thumbs upward, the defeated man was taken away, to recover if possible from his wounds. But if the fatal signal of "thumbs down" was given, the conquered was to be slain; and if he showed any reluctance to present his neck for the death blow, there was a scornful shout from the galleries, Recipe ferrum! "Receive the steel!" Privileged persons among the audience would even descend into the arena, to better witness the death agonies of some unusually brave victim, before his corpse was dragged out at the death gate.

The show went on; many had been slain, and the people, madly excited by the desperate bravery of those who continued to fight, shouted their applause. But suddenly there was an interruption. A rudely clad, robed figure appeared for a moment among the audience, and then boldly leaped down into the arena. He was seen to be a man of rough but imposing presence, bareheaded and with sun-browned face. Without hesitating an instant he advanced upon two gladiators engaged in a life-and-death struggle, and laying his hand upon one of them sternly reproved him for shedding innocent blood, and then, turning toward the thousands of angry faces ranged around him, called upon them in a solemn, deep-toned voice which resounded through the deep inclosure. These were his words: "Do not requite God's mercy in turning away the swords of your enemies by murdering each other!"

Angry shouts and cries at once drowned his voice: "This is no place for preaching! – the old customs of Rome must be observed! – On, gladiators!" Thrusting aside the stranger, the gladiators would have again attacked each other, but the man stood between, holding them apart, and trying in vain to be heard. "sedition! sedition! down with him!" was then the cry; and the gladiators, enraged at the interference of an outsider with their chosen vocation, at once stabbed him to death. Stones, or whatever missiles came to hand, also rained down upon him from the furious people, and thus he perished, in the midst of the arena.

His dress showed him to be one of the hermits who vowed themselves to a holy life of prayer and self-denial, and who were reverenced by even the thoughtless and combat-loving Romans. The few who knew him told how he had come from the wilds of Asia on a pilgrimage, to visit the churches and keep his Christmas at Rome; they knew he was a holy man, and that his name was Telemachus – no more. His spirit had been stirred by the sight of thousands flocking to see men slaughter one another, and in his simple-hearted zeal he had tried to convince them of the cruelty and wickedness of their conduct. He had died, but not in vain. His work was accomplished at the moment he was struck down, for the shock of such a death before their eyes turned the hearts of the people: they saw the hideous aspects of the favorite vice to which they had blindly

surrendered themselves; and from the day Telemachus fell dead in the Colosseum, no other fight of gladiators was ever held there.
Foxe's Book of Martyrs, Edited by William Byron Forbush

3. Christian writings

A collection of the writings, prayers and the spoken words of the martyrs and about the martyrs and martyrdom and persecution of Christians from the period 284–313

A. Quotations about martyrdom

Augustine

The massacre of the innocents
It is certainly not without reason that the Church exalts to the honorable rank of martyrs those children who were slain when Herod sought our Lord Jesus Christ to put Him to death.
Augustine, Letter 166

Of the adversaries of the Name of Christ, whom the Barbarians for Christ's sake spared when they stormed the city
For to this earthly city belong the enemies against whom I have to defend the city of God. Many of them, indeed, being reclaimed from their ungodly error, have become sufficiently creditable citizens of this city; but many are so inflamed with hatred against it, and are so ungrateful to its Redeemer for His signal benefits, as to forget that they would now be unable to utter a single word to its prejudice, had they not found in its sacred places, as they fled from the enemy's steel, that life in which they now boast themselves. Are not those very Romans, who were spared by the barbarians through their respect for Christ, become enemies to the name of Christ? The reliquaries of the martyrs and the churches of the apostles bear witness to this; for in the sack of the city they were open sanctuary for all who fled to them, whether Christian or Pagan. To their very threshold the blood-thirsty enemy raged; there his murderous fury owned a limit. Thither did such of the enemy as had any pity convey those to whom they had given quarter, lest any less mercifully disposed might fall upon them. And, indeed, when even those murderers who everywhere else showed themselves pitiless came to those spots where that was forbidden which the license of war permitted in every other place, their furious rage for slaughter was bridled, and their eagerness to take prisoners was quenched. Thus escaped multitudes who now reproach the Christian religion, and impute to Christ the ills that have befallen their city; but the preservation of their own life – a boon which they owe to the respect entertained for Christ by the barbarians – they attribute not to our Christ, but to their own good luck. They ought rather, had they any right perceptions, to attribute the severities and hardships inflicted by their enemies, to that divine providence which is wont to reform the depraved manners of men by chastisement, and which exercises with similar afflictions the righteous and praiseworthy, – either translating them, when they have passed through the trial, to a better world, or detaining them still on earth for ulterior purposes. And they ought to attribute it to the spirit of these Christian times, that, contrary to the custom of war, these bloodthirsty barbarians spared them, and spared them for Christ's sake, whether this mercy was actually shown in promiscuous places, or in those places specially dedicated to Christ's name, and of which the very largest were selected as sanctuaries, that full scope might thus be given to the expansive compassion which desired that a large multitude might find shelter there. Therefore ought they to give God thanks, and with sincere confession flee for refuge to His name, that so they may escape the punishment of eternal fire – they who with lying lips took upon them this name, that they might escape the punishment of present destruction. For of those whom you see insolently and shamelessly insulting the servants of Christ, there are numbers who would not have escaped that destruction and slaughter had

they not pretended that they themselves were Christ's servants. Yet now, in ungrateful pride and most impious madness, and at the risk of being punished in everlasting darkness, they perversely oppose that name under which they fraudulently protected themselves for the sake of enjoying the light of this brief life.
Augustine, City of God, book 1, chapter 1

CONCERNING THE NATURE OF THE HONOR WHICH THE CHRISTIANS PAY TO THEIR MARTYRS
But, nevertheless, we do not build temples, and ordain priests, rites, and sacrifices for these same martyrs; for they are not our gods, but their God is our God. Certainly we honor their reliquaries, as the memorials of holy men of God who strove for the truth even to the death of their bodies, that the true religion might be made known, and false and fictitious religions exposed.
Augustine, City of God, chapter 27

MARTYRS MEANS WITNESSES
Thus the name martyrs, which means witnesses, was given to those who, by the will of God, bore this testimony, by their confessions, their sufferings, and their death.
Augustine, Concerning the nature of good, against the Manichaeans, book 21, chapter 75

Eusebius

They are put to death, and they gain new life.
Eusebius

The church of Christ has been founded by shedding its own blood, not that of others; by enduring outrage, not by inflicting it.
Jerome

Jerome

Persecutions have made the church of Christ grow; martyrdoms have crowned it.
Jerome

B. Eusebius' Church History

Eusebius' *Church History* consists of ten books. Most manuscripts also have a document added called *The Martyrs of Palestine*. Chapter 8 from Eusebius' *Church History* is set out below, followed by *The Martyrs of Palestine*.

Introduction

As we have described in seven books the events from the time of the apostles, we think it proper in this eighth book to record for the information of posterity a few of the most important occurrences of our own times, which are worthy of permanent record. Our account will begin at this point.

Chapter 1
The Events Which Preceded the Persecution in Our Times

It is beyond our ability to describe in a suitable manner the extent and nature of the glory and freedom with which the word of piety toward the God of the universe, proclaimed to the world through Christ, was honored among all men, both Greeks and barbarians, before the persecution in our day. The favor shown our people by the rulers might be adduced as evidence; as they committed to them the government of provinces, and on account of the great friendship which they entertained toward their doctrine, released them from anxiety in regard to sacrificing. Why need I speak of those in the royal palaces, and of the rulers over all, who allowed the members of their households, wives and children and servants, to speak openly before them for the Divine word and life, and suffered them almost to boast of the freedom of their faith? Indeed they esteemed them highly, and preferred them to their fellow-servants. Such an one was that Dorotheus, the most devoted and faithful to them of all, and on this account especially honored by them among those who held the most honorable offices and governments. With him was the celebrated Gorgonius, and as many as had been esteemed worthy of the same distinction on account of the word of God.

And one could see the rulers in every church accorded the greatest favor by all officers and governors. But how can any one describe those vast assemblies, and the multitude that crowded together in every city, and the famous gatherings in the houses of prayer; on whose account not being satisfied with the ancient buildings they erected from the foundation large churches in all the cities? No envy hindered the progress of these affairs which advanced gradually, and grew and increased day by day. Nor could any evil demon slander them or hinder them through human counsels, so long as the divine and heavenly hand watched over and guarded his own people as worthy. But when on account of the abundant freedom, we fell into laxity and sloth, and envied and reviled each other, and were almost, as it were, taking up arms against one another, rulers assailing rulers with words like spears, and people forming parties against people, and monstrous hypocrisy and dissimulation rising to the greatest height of wickedness, the divine judgment with forbearance, as is its pleasure, while the multitudes yet continued to assemble, gently and moderately harassed the episcopacy.

This persecution began with the brethren in the army. But as if without sensibility, we were not eager to make the Deity favorable and propitious; and some, like atheists, thought that our affairs were unheeded and ungoverned; and thus we added one wickedness to another. And those esteemed our shepherds, casting aside the bond of piety, were excited to conflicts with one another, and did nothing else than heap up strifes and threats and jealousy and enmity and hatred toward each other, like tyrants eagerly endeavoring to assert their power. Then, truly, according to the word of Jeremiah, "The Lord in his wrath darkened the daughter of Zion, and cast down the glory of Israel from heaven to earth, and remembered not his foot-stool in the day of his anger. The Lord also overwhelmed all the beautiful things of Israel, and threw down all his strongholds."

And according to what was foretold in the Psalms: "He has made void the covenant of his servant, and profaned his sanctuary to the earth, – in the destruction of the churches, – and has thrown down all his strongholds, and has made his fortresses cowardice. All that pass by have plundered the multitude of the people; and he has become besides a reproach to his neighbors. For he has exalted the right hand of his enemies, and has turned back the help of his sword, and has not taken his part in the war. But he has deprived him of purification, and has cast his throne to the ground. He has shortened the days of his time, and besides all, has poured out shame upon him."

Chapter 2
The Destruction of the Churches

All these things were fulfilled in us, when we saw with our own eyes the houses of prayer thrown down to the very foundations, and the Divine and Sacred Scriptures committed to the flames in the midst of the market-places, and the shepherds of the churches basely hidden here and there, and some of them captured ignominiously, and mocked by their enemies. When also, according to another prophetic word, "Contempt was poured out upon rulers, and he caused them to wander in an untrodden and pathless way."

But it is not our place to describe the sad misfortunes which finally came upon them, as we do not think it proper, moreover, to record their divisions and unnatural conduct to each other before the persecution. Wherefore we have decided to relate nothing concerning them except the things in which we can vindicate the Divine judgment. Hence we shall not mention those who were shaken by the persecution, nor those who in everything pertaining to salvation were shipwrecked, and by their own will were sunk in the depths of the flood. But we shall introduce into this history in general only those events which may be useful first to ourselves and afterwards to posterity. Let us therefore proceed to describe briefly the sacred conflicts of the witnesses of the Divine Word. It was in the nineteenth year of the reign of Diocletian, in the month Dystrus, called March by the Romans, when the feast of the Savior's passion was near at hand, that royal edicts were published everywhere, commanding that the churches be leveled to the ground and the Scriptures be destroyed by fire, and ordering that those who held places of honor be degraded, and that the household servants, if they persisted in the profession of Christianity, be deprived of freedom.

Such was the first edict against us. But not long after, other decrees were issued, commanding that all the rulers of the churches in every place be first thrown into prison, and afterwards by every artifice be compelled to sacrifices.

Chapter 3
The Nature of the Conflicts endured in the Persecution

Then truly a great many rulers of the churches eagerly endured terrible sufferings, and furnished examples of noble conflicts. But a multitude of others, benumbed in spirit by fear, were easily weakened at the first onset.

Of the rest each one endured different forms of torture. The body of one was scourged with rods. Another was punished with insupportable rackings and scrapings, in which some suffered a miserable death. Others passed through different conflicts. Thus one, while those around pressed him on by force and dragged him to the abominable and impure sacrifices, was dismissed as if he had sacrificed, though he had not. Another, though he had not approached at all, nor touched any polluted thing, when others said that he had sacrificed, went away, bearing the accusation in silence. Another being taken up half dead, was cast aside as if already dead, and again a certain one lying upon the ground was dragged a long distance by his feet and counted among those who had sacrificed. One cried out and with a loud voice testified his rejection of the sacrifice; another shouted that he was a Christian, being resplendent in the confession of the saving Name. Another protested that he had not sacrificed and never would. But they were struck in the mouth and silenced by a large band of soldiers who were drawn up for this purpose; and they were smitten on the face and cheeks and driven away by force; so important did the enemies of piety regard it, by any means, to seem to have accomplished their purpose. But these things did not avail them against the holy martyrs; for an accurate description of whom, what word of ours could suffice?

Chapter 4
The Famous Martyrs of God, who filled Every Place with their Memory and won Various Crowns in behalf of Religion

For we might tell of many who showed admirable zeal for the religion of the God of the universe, not only from the beginning of the general persecution, but long before that time, while yet peace prevailed. For though he who had received power was seemingly aroused now as from a deep sleep, yet from the time after Decius and Valerian, he had been plotting secretly and without notice against the churches. He did not wage war against all of us at once, but made trial at first only of those in the army. For he supposed that the others could be taken easily if he should first attack and subdue these. Thereupon many of the soldiers were seen most cheerfully embracing private life, so that they might not deny their piety toward the Creator of the universe. For when the commander, whoever he was, began to persecute the soldiers, separating onto tribes an purging those who were enrolled in the army, giving them the choice either by obeying to receive the honor which belonged to them, or on the other hand to be deprived of it if they disobeyed the command, a great many soldiers of Christ's kingdom, without hesitation, instantly preferred the confession of him to the seeming glory and prosperity which they were enjoying. And one and another of them occasionally received in exchange, for their pious constancy, not only the loss of position, but death. But as yet the instigator of this plot proceeded with moderation, and ventured so far as blood only in some instances; for the multitude of believers, as it is likely, made him afraid, and deterred him from waging war at once against all.

But when he made the attack more boldly, it is impossible to relate how many and what sort of martyrs of God could be seen, among the inhabitants of all the cities and countries.

Chapter 5
Those in Nicomedia

Immediately on the publication of the decree against the churches in Nicomedia, a certain man, not obscure but very highly honored with distinguished temporal dignities, moved with zeal toward God, and incited with ardent faith, seized the edict as it was posted openly and publicly, and tore it to pieces as a profane and impious thing; and this was done while two of the sovereigns were in the same city,

the oldest of all, and the one who held the fourth place in the government after him. But this man, first in that place, after distinguishing himself in such a manner suffered those things which were likely to follow such daring, and kept his spirit cheerful and undisturbed till death.

Chapter 6
Those in the Palace

This period produced divine and illustrious martyrs, above all whose praises have ever been sung and who have been celebrated for courage, whether among Greeks or barbarians, in the person of Dorotheus and the servants that were with him in the palace. Although they received the highest honors from their masters, and were treated by them as their own children, they esteemed reproaches and trials for religion, and the many forms of death that were invented against them, as, in truth, greater riches than the glory and luxury of this life.

We will describe the manner in which one of them ended his life, and leave our readers to infer from his case the sufferings of the others. A certain man was brought forward in the above-mentioned city, before the rulers of whom we have spoken. He was then commanded to sacrifice, but as he refused, he was ordered to be stripped and raised on high and beaten with rods over his entire body, until, being conquered, he should, even against his will, do what was commanded. But as he was unmoved by these sufferings, and his bones were already appearing, they mixed vinegar with salt and poured it upon the mangled parts of his body. As he scorned these agonies, a gridiron and fire were brought forward. And the remnants of his body, like flesh intended for eating, were placed on the fire, not at once, lest he should expire instantly, but a little at a time. And those who placed him on the pyre were not permitted to desist until, after such sufferings, he should assent to the things commanded. But he held his purpose firmly, and victoriously gave up his life while the tortures were still going on. Such was the martyrdom of one of the servants of the palace, who was indeed well worthy of his name, for he was called Peter. The martyrdoms of the rest, though they were not inferior to his, we will pass by for the sake of brevity, recording only that Dorotheus and Gorgonius, with many others of the royal household, after varied sufferings, ended their lives by strangling, and bore away the trophies of God-given victory.

At this time Anthimus, who then presided over the church in Nicomedia, was beheaded for his testimony to Christ. A great multitude of martyrs were added to him, a conflagration having broken out in those very days in the palace at Nicomedia, I know not how, which through a false suspicion was laid to our people. Entire families of the pious in that place were put to death in masses at the royal command, some by the sword, and others by fire. It is reported that with a certain divine and indescribable eagerness men and women rushed into the fire. And the executioners bound a large number of others and put them on boats and threw them into the depths of the sea. And those who had been esteemed their masters considered it necessary to dig up the bodies of the imperial servants, who had been committed to the earth with suitable burial and cast them into the sea, lest any, as they thought, regarding them as gods, might worship them lying in their sepulchers.

Such things occurred in Nicomedia at the beginning of the persecution. But not long after, as persons in the country called Melitene, and others throughout Syria, attempted to usurp the government, a royal edict directed that the rulers of the churches everywhere should lye thrown into prison and bonds. What was to be seen after this exceeds all description. A vast multitude were imprisoned in every place; and the prisons everywhere, which had long before been prepared for murderers and robbers of graves, were filled with bishops, presbyters and deacons, readers and exorcists, so that room was no longer left in them for those condemned for crimes. And as other decrees followed the first, directing that those in prison if they would sacrifice should be permitted to depart in freedom, but that those who refused should be harassed with many tortures, how could any one, again, number the multitude of martyrs in every province, and especially of those in Africa, and Mauritania, and Thebais, and Egypt? From this last country many went into other cities and provinces, and became illustrious through martyrdom.

Chapter 7
The Egyptians in Phoenicia

Those of them that were conspicuous in Palestine we know, as also those that were at Tyre in Phoenicia. Who that saw them was not astonished at the numberless stripes, and at the firmness which these truly wonderful athletes of religion exhibited under them? and at their contest, immediately after the scourging, with bloodthirsty wild beasts, as they were cast before leopards and different kinds of bears and wild bears and bulls goaded with fire and red-hot iron? and at the marvelous endurance of these noble men in the face of all sorts of wild beasts?

We were present ourselves when these things occurred, and have put on record the divine power of our martyred Savior Jesus Christ, which was present and manifested itself mightily in the martyrs. For a long time the man-devouring beasts did not dare to touch or draw near the bodies of those dear to God, but rushed upon the others who from the outside irritated and urged them on. And they would not in the least touch the holy athletes, as they stood alone and naked and shook their hands at them to draw them toward themselves for they were commanded to do this. But whenever they rushed at them, they were restrained as if by some diviner power and retreated again. This continued for a long time, and occasioned no little wonder to the spectators. And as the first wild beast did nothing, a second and a third were let loose against one and the same martyr. One could not but be astonished at the invincible firmness of these holy men, and the enduring and immovable constancy of those whose bodies were young. You could have seen a youth not twenty years of age standing unbound and stretching out his hands in the form of a cross, with unterrified and untrembling mind, engaged earnestly in prayer to God, and not in the least going back or retreating from the place where he stood, while bears and leopards, breathing rage and death, almost touched his flesh. And yet their mouths were restrained, I know not how, by a divine and incomprehensible power, and they ran back again to their place. Such an one was he.

Again you might have seen others, for they were five in all, cast before a wild bull, who tossed into the air with his horns those who approached from the outside, and mangled them, leaving them to be token up half dead; but when he rushed with rage and threatening upon the holy martyrs, who were standing alone, he was unable to come near them; but though he stamped with his feet, and pushed in all directions with his horns, and breathed rage and threatening on account of the irritation of the burning irons, he was, nevertheless, held back by the sacred Providence. And as he in nowise harmed them, they let loose other wild beasts upon them. Finally, after these terrible and various attacks upon them, they were all slain with the sword; and instead of being buried in the earth they were committed to the waves of the sea.

Chapter 8
These in Egypt Such was the conflict of those Egyptians who contended nobly for religion in Tyre

But we must admire those also who suffered martyrdom in their native land; where thousands of men, women, and children, despising the present life for the sake of the teaching of our Savior, endured various deaths. Some of them, after scrapings and rackings and severest scourgings, and numberless other kinds of tortures, terrible even to hear of, were committed to the flames; some were drowned in the sea; some offered their heads bravely to those who cut them off; some died under their tortures, and others perished with hunger. And yet others were crucified; some according to the method commonly employed for malefactors; others yet more cruelly, being nailed to the cross with their heads downward, and being kept alive until they perished on the cross with hunger.

Chapter 9
Those in Thebais

It would be impossible to describe the outrages and tortures which the martyrs in Thebais endured. They were scraped over the entire body with shells instead of hooks until they died. Women were bound by one foot and raised aloft in the air by machines, and with their bodies altogether bare and uncovered, presented to all beholders this most shameful, cruel, and inhuman spectacle. Others being bound to the branches and trunks of trees perished. For they drew the stoutest branches together with machines, and bound the limbs of the martyrs to them; and then, allowing the branches to assume their natural position, they tore asunder instantly the limbs of those for whom they contrived this. All these things were done, not for a few days or a short time, but for a long series of years. Sometimes more than ten, at other times above twenty were put to death. Again not less than thirty, then about sixty, and yet again a hundred men with young children and women, were slain in one day, being condemned to various and diverse torments.

We, also being on the spot ourselves, have observed large crowds in one day; some suffering decapitation, others torture by fire; so that the murderous sword was blunted, and becoming weak, was broken, and the very executioners grew weary and relieved each other. And we beheld the most wonderful ardor, and the truly divine energy and zeal of those who believed in the Christ of God. For as soon as sentence was pronounced against the first, one after another rushed to the judgment seat, and confessed themselves Christians. And regarding with indifference the terrible things and the multiform tortures, they declared themselves boldly and undauntedly for the religion of the God of the universe. And they received the final sentence of death with joy and laughter and cheerfulness; so that they sang and offered up hymns and thanksgivings to the God of the universe till their very last breath.

These indeed were wonderful; but yet more wonderful were those who, being distinguished for wealth, noble birth, and honor, and for learning and philosophy, held everything secondary to the true religion and to faith in our Savior and Lord Jesus Christ. Such an one was Philoromus, who held a high office under the imperial government at Alexandria, and who administered justice every day, attended by a military guard corresponding to his rank and Roman dignity. Such also was Phileas, bishop of the church of Thmuis, a man eminent on account of his patriotism and the services rendered by him to his country, and also on account of his philosophical learning.

These persons, although a multitude of relatives and other friends besought them, and many in high position, and even the judge himself entreated them, that they would have compassion on themselves and show mercy to their children and wives, yet were not in the least induced by these things to choose the love of life, and to despise the ordinances of our Savior concerning confession and denial. But with manly and philosophic minds, or rather with pious and God-loving souls, they persevered against all the threats and insults of the judge; and both of them were beheaded.

Chapter 10
The Writings of Phileas the Martyr describing the Occurrences at Alexandria

Since we have mentioned Phileas as having a high reputation for secular learning, let him be his own witness in the following extract, in which he shows us who he was, and at the same time describes more accurately than we can the martyrdoms which occurred in his time at Alexandria:

"Having before them all these examples and models and noble tokens which are given us in the Divine and Sacred Scriptures, the blessed martyrs who were with us did not hesitate, but directing the eye of the soul in sincerity toward the God over all, and having their mind set upon death for religion, they adhered firmly to their calling. For they understood that our Lord Jesus Christ had become man on our account, that he might cut off all sin and furnish us with the means of entrance into eternal life. For "he counted it not a prize to be on an equality with God, but emptied himself taking the form of a servant; and being found in fashion as a man, he humbled himself unto death, even the death of the cross."

Wherefore also being zealous for the greater gifts, the Christ-bearing martyrs endured all trials and all kinds of contrivances for torture; not once only, but some also a second time. And although the guards vied with each other in threatening them in all sorts of ways, not in words only, but in actions, they did not give up their resolution; because "perfect love casteth out fear."

"What words could describe their courage and manliness under every torture? For as liberty to abuse them was given to all that wished, some beat them with clubs, others with rods, others with scourges, yet others with thongs, and others with ropes. And the spectacle of the outrages was varied and exhibited great malignity. For some, with their hands bound behind them, were suspended on the stocks, and every member stretched by certain machines. Then the torturers, as commanded, lacerated with instruments their entire bodies not only their sides, as in the case of murderers, but also their stomachs and knees and cheeks. Others were raised aloft, suspended from the porch by one hand, and endured the most terrible suffering of all, through the distension of their joints and limbs. Others were bound face to face to pillars, not resting on their feet, but with the weight of their bodies bearing on their bonds and drawing them tightly.

And they endured this, not merely as long as the governor talked with them or was at leisure, but through almost the entire day. For when he passed on to others, he left officers under his authority to watch the first, and observe if any of them, overcome by the tortures, appeared to yield. And he commanded to cast them into chains without mercy, and afterwards when they were at the last gasp to throw them to the ground and drag them away. For he said that they were not to have the least concern for us, but were to think and act as if we no longer existed, our enemies having invented this second mode of torture in addition to the stripes.

Some, also, after these outrages, were placed on the stocks, and had both their feet stretched over the four holes, so that they were compelled to lie on their backs on the stocks, being unable to keep themselves up on account of the fresh wounds with which their entire bodies were covered as a result of the scourging. Others were thrown on the ground and lay there under the accumulated infliction of tortures, exhibiting to the spectators a more terrible manifestation of severity, as they bore on their bodies the marks of the various and diverse punishments which had been invented.

As this went on, some died under the tortures, shaming the adversary by their constancy. Others half dead were shut up in prison, and suffering with their agonies, they died in a few days; but the rest, recovering under the care which they received, gained confidence by time and their long detention in prison.

When therefore they were ordered to choose whether they would be released from molestation by touching the polluted sacrifice, and would receive from them the accursed freedom, or refusing to sacrifice, should be condemned to death, they did not hesitate, but went to death cheerfully. For they knew what had been declared before by the Sacred Scriptures. For it is said, "He that sacrificeth to other gods shall be utterly destroyed," and, "Thou shalt have no other gods before me."

Such are the words of the truly philosophical and God-loving martyr, which, before the final sentence, while yet in prison, he addressed to the brethren in his parish, showing them his own circumstances, and at the same time exhorting them to hold fast, even after his approaching death, to the religion of Christ.

But why need we dwell upon these things,

and continue to add fresh instances of the conflicts of the divine martyrs throughout the world, especially since they were dealt with no longer by common law, but attacked like enemies of war?

Chapter 11
Those in Phrygia

A Small town of Phrygia, inhabited solely by Christians, was completely surrounded by soldiers while the men were in it. Throwing fire into it, they consumed them with the women and children while they were calling upon Christ. This they did because all the inhabitants of the city, and the curator himself, and the governor, with all who held office, and the entire populace, confessed themselves Christians, and would not in the least obey those who commanded them to worship idols.

There was another man of Roman dignity named Adauctus, of a noble Italian family, who had advanced through every honor under the emperors, so that he had blamelessly filled even the general offices of magistrate, as they call it, and of finance minister. Besides all this he excelled in deeds of piety and in the confession of the Christ of God, and was adorned with the diadem of martyrdom. He endured the conflict for religion while still holding the office of finance minister.

Chapter 12
Many Others, both Men and Women, who suffered in Various Ways

Why need we mention the rest by name, or number the multitude of the men, or picture the various sufferings of the admirable martyrs of Christ? Some of them were slain with the axe, as in Arabia. The limbs of some were broken, as in Cappadocia. Some, raised on high by the feet, with their heads down, while a gentle fire burned beneath them, were suffocated by the smoke which arose from the burning wood, as was done in Mesopotamia. Others were mutilated by cutting off their noses and ears and hands, and cutting to pieces the other members and parts of their bodies, as in Alexandria. Why need we revive the recollection of those in Antioch who were roasted on grates, not so as to kill them, but so as to subject them to a lingering punishment? Or of others who preferred to thrust their right hand into the fire rather than touch the impious sacrifice? Some, shrinking from the trial, rather than be taken and fall into the hands of their enemies, threw themselves from lofty houses, considering death preferable to the cruelty of the impious.

A certain holy person in soul admirable for virtue, in body a woman ,who was illustrious beyond all in Antioch for wealth and family and reputation, had brought up in the principles of religion her two daughters, who were now in the freshness and bloom of life. Since great envy was excited on their account, every means was used to find them in their concealment; and when it was ascertained that they were away, they were summoned deceitfully to Antioch. Thus they were caught in the nets of the soldiers. When the woman saw herself and her daughters thus helpless, and knew the things terrible to speak of that men would do to them and the most unbearable of all terrible things, the threatened violation of their chastity, she exhorted herself and the maidens that they ought not to submit even to hear of this. For, she said, that to surrender their souls to the slavery of demons was worse than all deaths and destruction; and she set before them the only deliverance from all these things escape to Christ. They then listened to her advice. And after arranging their garments suitably, they went aside from the middle of the road, having requested of the guards a little time for retirement, and cast themselves into a river which was flowing by. Thus they destroyed themselves. But there were two other virgins in the same city of Antioch who served God in all things, and were true sisters, illustrious in family and distinguished in life, young and blooming, serious in mind, pious in deportment, and admirable for zeal. As if the earth could not bear such excellence, the worshipers of demons commanded to cast them into the sea. And this was done to them.

In Pontus, others endured sufferings horrible to hear. Their fingers were pierced with sharp reeds under their nails. Melted lead, bubbling and boiling with the heat, was poured down the backs of others, and they were roasted in the most sensitive parts of the body. Others endured on their bowels and privy members shameful and inhuman and unmentionable torments, which the noble and law-observing judges, to show their severity, devised, as more honorable manifestations of wisdom. And new tortures were continually invented, as if they were endeavoring, by surpassing one another, to gain prizes in a contest. But at the close of these calamities, when finally they could contrive no greater cruelties, and were weary of putting to death, and were filled and satiated with the shedding of blood, they turned to what they considered merciful and humane treatment, so that they seemed to be no longer devising terrible things against us. For they said that it was not fitting that the cities should be polluted with the blood of their own people, or that the government of their rulers, which was kind and mild toward all, should be defamed through excessive cruelty; but that rather the beneficence of the humane and royal authority should be extended to all, and we should no longer be put to death. For the infliction of this punishment upon us should be stopped in consequence of the humanity of the rulers. Therefore it was commanded that our eyes should be put out, and that we should be maimed in one of our limbs. For such things were humane in their sight, and the lightest of punishments for us. So that now on account of this kindly treatment accorded us by the impious, it was impossible to tell the incalculable number of those whose right eyes had first been cut out with the sword, and then had been cauterized with fire; or who had been disabled in the left foot by burning the joints, and afterward condemned to the provincial copper mines, not so much for service as for distress and hardship. Besides all these, others encountered other trials, which it is impossible to recount; for their manly endurance surpasses all description. In these conflicts the noble martyrs of Christ shone illustrious over the entire world, and everywhere astonished those who beheld their manliness; and the evidences of the truly divine and unspeakable power of our Savior were made manifest through them. To mention each by name would be a long task, if not indeed impossible.

Chapter 13
The Bishops of the Church that evinced by their Blood the Genuineness of the Religion which they preached

As for the rulers of the Church that suffered martyrdom in the principal cities, the first martyr of the kingdom of Christ whom we shall mention among the monuments of the pious is Anthimus, bishop of the city of Nicomedia, who was beheaded. Among the martyrs at Antioch was Lucian, a presbyter of that parish, whose entire life was most excellent. At Nicomedia, in the presence of the emperor, he proclaimed the heavenly kingdom of Christ, first in an oral defense, and afterwards by deeds as well. Of the martyrs in Phoenicia the most distinguished were those devoted pastors of the spiritual flocks of Christ: Tyrannion, bishop of the church of Tyre; Zenobius, a presbyter of the church at Sidon; and Silvanus, bishop of the churches about Emesa.

The last of these, with others, was made food for wild beasts at Emesa, and was thus received into the ranks of martyrs. The other two glorified the word of God at Antioch through patience unto death. The bishop was thrown into the depths of the sea. But Zenobius, who was a very skillful physician, died through severe tortures which were applied to his sides.

Of the martyrs in Palestine, Silvanus, bishop of the churches about Gaza, was beheaded with thirty-nine others at the copper mines of Phaeno. There also the Egyptian bishops, Peleus and Nilus, with others, suffered death by fire. Among these we must mention Pamphilus, a presbyter, who was the great glory of the parish of Caesarea, and among the men of our time most admirable. The virtue of his manly deeds we have recorded in the proper place. Of those who suffered death illustriously at Alexandria and throughout Egypt and Thebais, Peter, bishop of Alexandria, one of the most excellent teachers of the religion of Christ, should first be mentioned; and of the presbyters with him

Faustus, Dius and Ammonius, perfect martyrs of Christ; also Phileas, Hesychius, Pachymius and Theodorus, bishops of Egyptian churches, and besides them many other distinguished persons who are commemorated by the parishes of their country and region.

It is not for us to describe the conflicts of those who suffered for the divine religion throughout the entire world, and to relate accurately what happened to each of them. This would be the proper work of those who were eyewitnesses of the events. I will describe for posterity in another work those which I myself witnessed. But in the present book I will add to what I have given the revocation issued by our persecutors, and those events that occurred at the beginning of the persecution, which will be most profitable to such as shall read them.

What words could sufficiently describe the greatness and abundance of the prosperity of the Roman government before the war against us while the rulers were friendly and peaceable toward us? Then those who were highest in the government, and had held the position ten or twenty years, passed their time in tranquil peace, in festivals and public games and most joyful pleasures and cheer. While thus their authority was growing uninterruptedly, and increasing day by day, suddenly they changed their peaceful attitude toward us, and began an implacable war. But the second year of this movement was not yet past, when a revolution took place in the entire government and overturned all things. For a severe sickness came upon the chief of those of whom we have spoken, by which his understanding was distracted; and with him who was honored with the second rank, he retired into private life. Scarcely had he done this when the entire empire was divided; a thing which is not recorded as having ever occurred before. Not long after, the Emperor Constantius, who through his entire life was most kindly and favorably disposed toward his subjects, and most friendly to the Divine Word, ended his life in the common course of nature, and left his own son, Constantine, as emperor and Augustus in his stead. He was the first that was ranked by them among the gods, and received after death every honor which one could pay to an emperor. He was the kindest and mildest of emperors, and the only one of those of our day that passed all the time of his government in a manner worthy of his office. Moreover, he conducted himself toward all most favorably and beneficently. He took not the smallest part in the war against us, but preserved the pious that were under him unharmed and unabused. He neither threw down the church buildings, nor did he devise anything else against us. The end of his life was honorable and thrice blessed. He alone at death left his empire happily and gloriously to his own son as his successor one who was in all respects most prudent and pious.

His son Constantine entered on the government at once, being proclaimed supreme emperor and Augustus by the soldiers, and long before by God himself, the King of all. He showed himself an emulator of his father's piety toward our doctrine. Such an one was he.

But after this, Licinius was declared emperor and Augustus by a common vote of the rulers. These things grieved Maximinus greatly, for until that time he had been entitled by all only Caesar. He therefore, being exceedingly imperious, seized the dignity for himself, and became Augustus, being made such by himself. In the mean time he whom we have mentioned as having resumed his dignity after his abdication, being detected in conspiring against the life of Constantine, perished by a most shameful death. He was the first whose decrees and statues and public monuments were destroyed because of his wickedness and impiety.

Chapter 14
The Character of the Enemies of Religion

Maxentius his son, who obtained the government at Rome, at first feigned our faith, in complaisance and flattery toward the Roman people. On this account he commanded his subjects to cease persecuting the Christians, pretending to religion that he might appear merciful and mild beyond his predecessors. But he did not prove in his deeds to be such a person as was hoped, but ran into all wickedness and abstained from no impurity or licentiousness, committing adulteries and indulging in all kinds of corruption. For having separated wives from their lawful consorts, he abused them and sent them back most dishonorably to their husbands. And he not only practiced this against the obscure and unknown, but he insulted especially the most prominent and distinguished members of the Roman senate. All his subjects, people and rulers, honored and obscure, were worn out by grievous oppression. Neither, although they kept quiet, and bore the bitter servitude, was there any relief from the murderous cruelty of the tyrant. Once, on a small pretense, he gave the people to be slaughtered by his guards; and a great multitude of the Roman populace were slain in the midst of the city, with the spears and arms, not of Scythians and barbarians, but of their own fellow- citizens. It would be impossible to recount the number of senators who were put to death for the sake of their wealth; multitudes being slain on various pretenses. To crown all his wickedness, the tyrant resorted to magic. And in his divinations he cut open pregnant women, and again inspected the bowels of newborn infants. He slaughtered lions, and performed various execrable acts to invoke demons and avert war. For his only hope was that, by these means, victory would be secured to him. It is impossible to tell the ways in which this tyrant at Rome oppressed his subjects, so that they were reduced to such an extreme dearth of the necessities of life as has never been known, according to our contemporaries, either at Rome or elsewhere.

But Maximinus, the tyrant in the East, having secretly formed a friendly alliance with the Roman tyrant as with a brother in wickedness, sought to conceal it for a long time. But being at last detected, he suffered merited punishment. It was wonderful how akin he was in wickedness to the tyrant at Rome, or rather how far he surpassed him in it. For the chief of sorcerers and magicians were honored by him with the highest rank. Becoming exceedingly timid and superstitious, he valued greatly the error of idols and demons. Indeed, without soothsayers and oracles he did not venture to move even a finger, so to speak. Therefore he persecuted us more violently and incessantly than his predecessors. He ordered temples to be erected in every city, and the sacred groves which had been destroyed through lapse of time to be speedily restored. He appointed idol priests in every place and city; and he set over them in every province, as high priest, some political official who had especially distinguished himself in every kind of service, giving him a band of soldiers and a body-guard. And to all jugglers, as if they were pious and beloved of the gods, he granted governments and the greatest privileges. From this time on he distressed and harassed, not one city or country, but all the provinces under his authority, by extreme exactions of gold and silver and goods, and most grievous prosecutions and various fines. He took away from the wealthy the property which they had inherited from their ancestors, and bestowed vast riches and large sums of money on the flatterers about him. And he went to such an excess of folly and drunkenness that his mind was deranged and crazed in his carousals; and he gave commands when intoxicated of which he repented afterward when sober. He suffered no one to surpass him in debauchery and profligacy, but made "himself an instructor in wickedness to those about him, both rulers and subjects. He urged on the army to live wantonly in every kind of revelry and intemperance, and encouraged the governors and generals to abuse their subjects with rapacity and covetousness, almost as if they were rulers with him. Why need we relate the licentious, shameless deeds of the man, or enumerate the multitude with whom he committed adultery? For he could not pass through a city without continually corrupting women and ravishing virgins. And in this he succeeded with all except the Christians. For as they despised death, they cared nothing for his power. For the men endured fire and sword and crucifixion and wild beasts and the depths of the sea, and cutting off of limbs, and burnings, and pricking and digging out of eyes, and mutilations of the entire body, and besides these, hunger and mines and bonds. In all they showed patience in behalf of religion rather than transfer to idols the reverence due to God. And the women were not less manly than the men in behalf of the teaching of the Divine Word, as they endured conflicts with the men, and bore away equal prizes of virtue. And when they were dragged away for corrupt purposes, they surrendered their lives to death rather than their bodies to impurity.

One only of those who were seized for adulterous purposes by the tyrant, a most distinguished and illustrious Christian woman in Alexandria, conquered the passionate and intemperate soul of Maximinus by most heroic firmness. Honorable on account of wealth and family and education, she esteemed all of these inferior to chastity. He urged her many times, but although she was ready to die, he could not put her to death, for his desire was stronger than his anger. He therefore punished her with exile, and took away all her property.

Many others, unable even to listen to the threats of violation from the heathen rulers, endured every form of tortures, and rackings, and deadly punishment.

These indeed should be admired. But far the most admirable was that woman at Rome, who was truly the most noble and modest of all, whom the tyrant Maxentius, fully resembling Maximinus in his actions, endeavored to abuse. For when she learned that those who served the tyrant in such matters were at the house (she also was a Christian), and that her husband, although a prefect of Rome, would suffer them to take and lead her away, having requested a little time for adorning her body, she entered her chamber, and being alone, stabbed herself with a sword. Dying immediately, she left her corpse to those who had come for her. And by her deeds, more powerfully than by any words, she has shown to all men now and hereafter that the virtue which prevails among Christians is the only invincible and indestructible possession.

Such was the career of wickedness which was carried forward at one and the same time by the two tyrants who held the East and the West. Who is there that would hesitate, after careful examination, to pronounce the persecution.

Chapter 15
The Events which happened to the Heathen

During the entire ten years of the persecution, they were constantly plotting and warring against one another. For the sea could not be navigated, nor could men sail from any port without being exposed to all kinds of outrages; being stretched on the rack and lacerated in their sides, that it might be ascertained through various tortures, whether they came from the enemy; and finally being subjected to punishment by the cross or by fire. And besides these things shields and breastplates were preparing, and darts and spears and other warlike accoutrements were making ready, and galleys and naval armor were collecting in every place. And no one expected anything else than to be attacked by enemies any day. In addition to this, famine and pestilence came upon them, in regard to which we shall relate what is necessary in the proper place.

Chapter 16
The Change of Affairs for the Better
Such was the state of affairs during the entire persecution.

But in the tenth year, through the grace of God, it ceased altogether, having begun to decrease after the eighth year. For when the divine and heavenly grace showed us favorable and propitious oversight, then truly our rulers, and the very persons by whom the war against us had been earnestly prosecuted, most remarkably changed their minds, and issued a revocation, and quenched the great fire of persecution which had been kindled, by merciful proclamations and ordinances concerning us. But this was not due to any human agency; nor was it the result, as one might say, of the compassion or philanthropy of our rulers far from it, for daily from the beginning until that time they were devising more and more severe measures against us, and continually inventing outrages by a greater variety of instruments but it was manifestly due to the oversight of Divine Providence, on the one hand becoming reconciled to his people, and on the other, attacking him who instigated these evils, and showing anger toward him as the author of the cruelties of the entire persecution. For though it was necessary that these things should take place, according to the divine judgment, yet the Word saith, "Woe to him through whom the offense cometh." Therefore punishment from God came upon him, beginning with his flesh, and proceeding to his soul. For an abscess suddenly appeared in the midst of the secret parts of his body, and from it a deeply perforated sore, which spread irresistibly into his inmost bowels. An indescribable multitude of worms sprang from them, and a deathly odor arose, as the entire bulk of his body had, through his gluttony, been changed, before his sickness, into an excessive mass of soft fat, which became putrid, and thus presented an awful and intolerable sight to those who came near. Some of the physicians, being wholly unable to endure the exceeding offensiveness of the odor, were slain; others, as the entire mass had swollen and passed beyond hope of restoration, and they were unable to render any help, were put to death without mercy.

Chapter 17
The Revocation of the Rulers

Wrestling with so many evils, he thought of the cruelties which he had committed against the pious. Turning, therefore, his thoughts toward himself, he first openly confessed to the God of the universe, and then summoning his attendants, he commanded that without delay they should stop the persecution of the Christians, and should by law and royal decree, urge them forward to build their churches and to perform their customary worship, offering prayers in behalf of the emperor. Immediately the deed followed the word. The imperial decrees were published in the cities, containing the revocation of the acts against us in the following form:

"The Emperor Caesar Galerius Valerius Maximinus, Invictus, Augustus, Pontifex Maximus, conqueror of the Germans, conqueror of the Egyptians, conqueror of the Thebans, five times conqueror of the Sarmatians, conqueror of the Persians, twice conqueror of the Carpathians, six times conqueror of the Armenians, conqueror of the Medes, conqueror of the Adiabeni, Tribune of the people the twentieth time, Emperor the nineteenth time, Consul the eighth time, Father of his country, Proconsul; and the Emperor Caesar Flavius Valerius Constantinus, Pius, Felix, Invictus, Augustus, Pontifex Maximus, Tribune of the people, Emperor the fifth time, Consul, Father of his country, Proconsul; and the Emperor Caesar Valerius Licinius, Pius, Felix, Invictus, Augustus, Pontifex Maximus, Tribune of the people the fourth time, Emperor the third time, Consul, Father of his country, Proconsul; to the people of their provinces, greeting:

"Among the other things which we have ordained for the public advantage and profit, we formerly wished to restore everything to conformity with the ancient laws and public discipline of the Romans, and to provide that the Christians also, who have forsaken the religion of their ancestors, should return to a good disposition. For in some way such arrogance had seized them and such stupidity had overtaken them, that they did not follow the ancient institutions which possibly their own ancestors had formerly established, but made for themselves laws according to their own purpose, as each one desired, and observed them, and thus assembled as separate congregations in various places. When we had issued this decree that they should return to the institutions established by the ancients, a great many submitted under danger, but a great many being harassed endured all kinds of death.

"And since many continue in the same folly, and we perceive that they neither offer to the heavenly gods the worship which is due, nor pay regard to the God of the Christians, in consideration of our philanthropy and our invariable custom, by which we are wont to extend pardon to all, we have determined that we ought most cheerfully to extend our indulgence in this matter also; that they may again be Christians, and may rebuild the conventicles in which they were accustomed to assemble, on condition that nothing be done by them contrary to discipline. In another letter we shall indicate to the magistrates what they have to observe. Wherefore, on account of this indulgence of ours, they ought to supplicate their God for our safety, and that of the people, and their own, that the public welfare may be preserved in every place, and that they may live securely in their several homes."

Such is the tenor of this edict, translated, as well as possible, from the Roman tongue into the Greek. It is time to consider what took place after these events.

An additional chapter [found in some copies in Book 8]

The author of the edict very shortly after this confession was released from his pains and died. He is reported to have been the original author of the misery of the persecution, having endeavored, long before the movement of the other emperors, to turn from the faith the Christians in the army, and first of all those in his own house, degrading some from the military rank, and abusing others most shamefully, and threatening still others with death, and finally inciting his partners in the empire to the general persecution. It is not proper to pass over the death of these emperors in silence.

As four of them held the supreme authority, those who were advanced in age and honor, after the persecution had continued not quite two years, abdicated the government, as we have already stated, and passed the remainder of their lives in a common and private station. The end of their lives was as follows. He who was first in honor and age perished through a long and most grievous physical infirmity. He who held the second place ended his life by strangling, suffering thus according to a certain demoniacal prediction, on account of his many daring crimes.

Of those after them, the last, of whom we have spoken as the originator of the entire persecution, suffered such things as we have related. But he who preceded him, the most merciful and kindly emperor Constantius, passed all the time of his government in a manner worthy of his office. Moreover, he conducted himself towards all most favorably and beneficently. He took not the smallest part in the war against us, and preserved the pious that were under him unharmed and unabused. Neither did he throw down the church buildings, nor devise anything else against us. The end of his life was happy and thrice blessed. He alone at death left his empire happily and gloriously to his own son as his successor, one who was in all respects most prudent and pious. He entered on the government at once, being proclaimed supreme emperor and Augustus by the soldiers; and he showed himself an emulator of his father's piety toward our doctrine.

Such were the deaths of the four of whom we have written, which took place at different times. Of these, moreover, only the one referred to a little above by us, with those who afterward shared in the government, finally published openly to all the above-mentioned confession, in the written edict which he issued.

Eusebius

c. The Martyrs of Palestine

Introduction

It was in the nineteenth year of the reign of Diocletian, in the month Xanthicus, which is called April by the Romans, about the time of the feast of our Savior's passion, while Flavianus was governor of the province of Palestine, that letters were published everywhere, commanding that the churches be leveled to the ground and the Scriptures be destroyed by fire, and ordering that those who held places of honor be degraded, and that the household servants, if they persisted in the profession of Christianity, be deprived of freedom. Such was the force of the first edict against us. But not long after other letters were issued, commanding that all the bishops of the churches everywhere be first thrown into prison, and afterward, by every artifice, be compelled to sacrifice.

Chapter 1

The first of the martyrs of Palestine was Procopius, who, before he had received the trial of imprisonment, immediately on his first appearance before the governor's tribunal, having been ordered to sacrifice to the so-called gods, declared that he knew only one to whom it was proper to sacrifice, as he himself wills. But when he was commanded to offer libations to the four emperors, having quoted a sentence which displeased them, he was immediately beheaded. The quotation was from the poet: "The rule of many is not good; let there be one ruler and one king."

It was the seventh day of the month Desius, the seventh before the ides of June, as the Romans reckon, and the fourth day of the week, when this first example was given at Caesura in Palestine. Afterwards, in the same city, many rulers of the country churches readily endured terrible sufferings, and furnished to the beholders an example of noble conflicts. But others, benumbed in spirit by terror, were easily weakened at the first onset. Of the rest, each one endured different forms of torture, as scourgings without number, and rackings, and tearings of their sides, and insupportable fetters, by which the hands of some were dislocated. Yet they endured what came upon them, as in accordance with the inscrutable purposes of God. For the hands of one were seized, and he was led to the altar, while they thrust into his right hand the polluted and abominable offering, and he was dismissed as if he had sacrificed. Another had not even touched it, yet when others said that he had sacrificed, he went away in silence. Another, being taken up half dead, was cast aside as if already dead, and released from his bonds, and counted among the sacrificers. When another cried out, and testified that he would not obey, he was struck in the mouth, and silenced by a large band of those who were drawn up for this purpose, and driven away by force, even though he had not sacrificed. Of such consequence did they consider it, to seem by any means to have accomplished their purpose. Therefore, of all this number, the only ones who were honored with the crown of the holy martyrs were Alphaeus and Zacchaeus. After stripes and scrapings and severe bonds and additional tortures and various other trials, and after having their feet stretched for a night and day over four holes in the stocks, on the seventeenth day of the month Dius, -that is, according to the Romans, the fifteenth before the Kalends of December,- having confessed one only God and Christ Jesus as king, as if they had uttered some blasphemy, they were beheaded like the former martyr.

Chapter 2

What occurred to Romanus on the same day at Antioch, is also worthy of record. For he was a native of Palestine, a deacon and exorcist in the parish of Caesarea; and being present at the destruction of the churches, he beheld many men, with women and children, going up in crowds to the idols and sacrificing. But, through his great zeal for religion, he could not endure the sight, and rebuked them with a loud voice. Being arrested for his boldness, he proved a most noble witness of the truth, if there ever was one. For when the judge informed him that he was to die by fire, he received the sentence with cheerful countenance and most ready mind, and was led away. When he was bound to the stake, and the wood piled up around him, as they were awaiting the arrival of the emperor before lighting the fire, he cried, "Where is the fire for me?" Having said this, he was summoned again before the emperor, and subjected to the unusual torture of having his tongue cut out. But he endured this with fortitude and showed to all by his deeds that the Divine Power is present with those who endure any hardship whatever for the sake of religion, lightening their sufferings and strengthening their zeal. When he learned of this strange mode of punishment, the noble man was not terrified, but put out his tongue readily, and offered it with the greatest alacrity to those who cut it off. After this punishment he was thrown into prison, and suffered there for a very long time. At last the twentieth anniversary of the emperor being near, when, according to an established gracious custom, liberty was proclaimed everywhere to all who were in bonds, he alone had both his feet stretched over five holes in the stocks, and while he lay there was strangled, and was thus honored with martyrdom, as he desired. Although he was outside of his country, yet, as he was a native of Palestine, it is proper to count him among the Palestinian martyrs. These things occurred in this manner during the first year, when the persecution was directed only against the rulers of the Church.

Chapter 3

In the course of the second year, the persecution against us increased greatly. And at that time Urbanus being governor of the province, imperial edicts were first issued to him, commanding by a general decree that all the people should sacrifice at once in the different cities, and offer libations to the idols.

In Gaza, a city of Palestine, Timotheus endured countless tortures, and afterwards was subjected to a slow and moderate fire. Having given, by his patience in all his sufferings, most genuine evidence of sincerest piety toward the Deity, he bore away the crown of the victorious athletes of religion. At the same time Agapius and our contemporary, Thecla, having exhibited most noble constancy, were condemned as food for the wild beasts. But who that beheld these things would not have admired, or if they heard of them by report, would not have been astonished? For when the heathen everywhere were holding a festival and the customary shows, it was noised abroad that besides the other entertainments, the public combat of those who had lately been condemned to wild beasts would also take place.

As this report increased and spread in all directions, six young men, namely, Timolaus, a native of Pontus, Dionysius from Tripolis in Phoenicia, Romulus, a sub-deacon of the parish of Diospolis, Paesis and Alexander, both Egyptians, and another Alexander from Gaza, having first bound their own hands, went in haste to Urbanus, who was about to open the exhibition, evidencing great zeal for martyrdom. They confessed that they were Christians, and by their ambition for all terrible things, showed that those who glory in the religion of the God of the universe do not cower before the attacks of wild beasts. Immediately, after creating no ordinary astonishment in the governor and those who were with him, they were cast into prison. After a few days two others were added to them. One of them, named Agapius, had in former confessions endured dreadful torments of various kinds. The other, who had supplied them with the necessaries of life, was called Dionysius. All of these eight were beheaded on one day at Caesarea, on the twenty-fourth day of the month Dystrus, which is the ninth before the Kalends of April. Meanwhile, a change in the emperors occurred, and the first of them all in dignity, and the second retired into private life, and public affairs began to be troubled. Shortly after the Roman government became divided against itself, and a cruel war arose among them. And this division, with the troubles which grew out of it, was not settled until peace toward us had been established throughout the entire Roman Empire. For when this peace arose for all, as the daylight after the darkest and most gloomy night, the public affairs of the Roman government were re-established, and became happy and peaceful, and the ancestral good-will toward each other was revived. But we will relate these things more fully at the proper time. Now let us return to the regular course of events.

Chapter 4

Maximinus Caesar having come at that time into the government, as if to manifest to all the evidences of his reborn enmity against God, and of his impiety, armed himself for persecution against us more vigorously than his predecessors. In consequence, no little confusion arose among all, and they scattered here and there, endeavoring in some way to escape the danger; and there was great commotion everywhere. But what words would suffice for a suitable description of the Divine love and boldness, in confessing God, of the blessed and truly innocent lamb,-I refer to the martyr Apphianus, -who presented in the sight of all, before the gates of Caesarea, a wonderful example of piety toward the only God? He was at that time not twenty years old. He had first spent a long time at Berytus, for the sake of a secular Grecian education, as he belonged to a very wealthy family. It is wonderful to relate how, in such a city, he was superior to youthful passions, and clung to virtue, uncorrupted neither by his bodily vigor nor his young companions; living discreetly, soberly and piously, in accordance with his profession of the Christian doctrine and the life of his teachers. If it is needful to mention his native country, and give honor to it as producing this noble athlete of piety, we will do so with pleasure. The young man came from Pagae, -if any one is acquainted with the place,-a city in Lycia of no mean importance. After his return from his course of study in Berytus, though his father held the first place in his country, he could not bear to live with him and his relatives, as it did not please them to live according to the rules of religion. Therefore, as if he were led by the Divine Spirit, and in accordance with a natural, or rather an inspired and true philosophy, regarding this preferable to what is considered the glory of life, and despising bodily comforts, he secretly left his family. And because of his faith and hope in God, paying no attention to his daily needs, he was led by the Divine Spirit to the city of Caesarea, where was prepared for him the crown of martyrdom for piety. Abiding with us there, and conferring with us in the Divine Scriptures diligently for a short time, and fitting himself zealously by suitable exercises, he exhibited such an end as would astonish any one should it be seen again. Who, that hears of it, would not justly admire his courage, boldness, constancy, and even more than these the daring deed itself, which evidenced a zeal for religion and a spirit truly superhuman? For in the second attack upon us under Maximinus, in the third year of the persecution, edicts of the tyrant were issued for the first time, commanding that the rulers of the cities should diligently and speedily see to it that all the people offered sacrifices. Throughout the city of Caesarea, by command of the governor, the heralds were summoning men, women, and children to the temples of the idols, and besides this, the chiliarchs were calling out each one by name from a roll, and an immense crowd of the wicked were rushing together from all quarters. Then this youth fearlessly, while no one was aware of his intentions, eluded both us who lived in the house with him and the whole band of soldiers that surrounded the governor, and rushed up to Urbanus as he was offering libations, and fearlessly seizing him by the right hand, straightway put a stop to his sacrificing, and skillfully and persuasively, with a certain divine inspiration, exhorted him to abandon his delusion, because it was not well to forsake the one and only true God, and sacrifice to idols and demons. It is probable that this was done by the youth through a divine power which led him forward, and which all but cried aloud in his act, that Christians, who were truly such, were so far from abandoning the religion of the God of the universe which they had once espoused, that they were not only superior to threats and the punishments which followed, but yet bolder to speak with noble and untrammeled tongue, and, if possible, to summon even their persecutors to turn from their ignorance and acknowledge the only true God. Thereupon, he of whom we are speaking, and that instantly, as might have been expected after so bold a deed, was torn by the governor and those who were with him as if by wild beasts. And having endured manfully innumerable blows over his entire body, he was straightway cast into prison. There he was stretched by the tormentor with both his feet in the stocks for a night and a day; and the next day he was brought before the judge. As they endeavored to force him to surrender, he exhibited all constancy under suffering and terrible tortures. His sides were torn, not once, or twice, but many times, to the bones and the very bowels; and he received so many blows on his face and neck that those who for a long time had been well acquainted with him could not recognize his swollen face. But as he would not yield under this treatment, the torturers, as commanded, covered his feet with linen cloths soaked in oil and set them on fire. No word can describe the agonies which the blessed one endured from this. For the fire consumed his flesh and penetrated to his bones, so that the humors of his body were melted and oozed out and dropped down like wax. But as he was not subdued by this, his adversaries being defeated and unable to comprehend his superhuman constancy, cast him again into prison. A third time he was brought before the judge; and having witnessed the same profession, being half dead, he was finally thrown into the depths of the sea. But what happened immediately after this will scarcely be believed by those who did not see it. Although we realize this, yet we must record the event, of which to speak plainly, all the inhabitants of Caesarea were witnesses. For truly there was no age but beheld this marvelous sight. For as soon as they had cast this truly sacred and thrice-blessed youth into the fathomless depths of the sea, an uncommon commotion and disturbance agitated the sea and all the shore about it, so that the land and the entire city were shaken by it. And at the same time with this wonderful and sudden perturbation, the sea threw out before the gates of the city the body of the divine martyr, as if unable to endure it.

Such was the death of the wonderful Apphianus. It occurred on the second day of the month Xanthicus, which is the fourth day before the Nones of April, on the day of preparation

Chapter 5

About the same time, in the city of Tyre, a youth named Ulpianus, after dreadful tortures and most severe scourgings, was enclosed in a raw oxhide, with a dog and with one of those poisonous reptiles, an asp, and cast into the sea. Wherefore I think that we may properly mention him in connection with the martyrdom of Apphianus. Shortly afterwards, Aedesius, a brother of Apphianus, not only in God, but also in the flesh, being a son of the same earthly father, endured sufferings like his, after very many confessions and protracted tortures in bonds, and after he had been sentenced by the governor to the mines in Palestine. He conducted himself through them all in a truly philosophic manner; for he was more highly educated than his brother, and had prosecuted philosophic studies. Finally in the city of Alexandria, when he beheld the judge, who was trying the Christians, offending beyond all bounds, now insulting holy men in various ways, and again consigning women of greatest modesty and even religious virgins to procurers for shameful treatment, he acted like his brother. For as these things seemed insufferable, he went forward with bold resolve, and with his words and deeds overwhelmed the judge with shame and disgrace. After suffering in consequence many forms of torture, he endured a death similar to his brother's, being cast into the sea. But these things, as I have said, happened to him in this way a little later.

Chapter 6

In the fourth year of the persecution against us, on the twelfth day before the Kalends of December, which is the twentieth day of the month Dius, on the day before the Sabbath, while the tyrant Maximinus was present and giving magnificent shows in honor of his birthday, the following event, truly worthy of record, occurred in the city of Caesarea. As it was an ancient custom to furnish the spectators more splendid shows when the emperors were present than at other times, new and foreign spectacles taking the place of the customary amusements, such as animals brought from India or Ethiopia or other places, or men who could astonish the beholders with skillful bodily exercises,-it was necessary at this time, as the emperor was giving the exhibition, to add to the shows something more wonderful. And what should this be? A witness of our doctrine was brought into the midst and endured the contest for the true and only religion. This was Agapius, who, as we have stated a little above, was, with Thecla, the second to be thrown to the wild beasts for food. He had also, three times and more, marched with malefactors from the prison to the arena; and every time, after threats from the judge, whether in compassion or in hope that he might change his mind, had been reserved for other conflicts. But the emperor being present, he was brought out at this time, as if he had been appropriately reserved for this occasion, until the very word of the Savior should be fulfilled in him, which through divine knowledge he declared to his disciples, that they should be brought before kings on account of their testimony unto him.

He was taken into the midst of the arena with a certain malefactor who they said was charged with the murder of his master. But this murderer of his master, when he had been cast to the wild beasts, was deemed worthy of compassion and humanity, almost like Barabbas in the time of our Savior. And the whole theater resounded with shouts and cries of approval, because the murderer was humanely saved by the emperor, and deemed worthy of honor and freedom. But the athlete of religion was first summoned by the tyrant and promised liberty if he would deny his profession. But he testified with a loud voice that, not for any fault, but for the religion of the Creator of the universe, he would readily and with pleasure endure whatever might be inflicted upon him. Having said this, he joined the deed to the word, and rushed to meet a bear which had been let loose against him, surrendering himself most cheerfully to be devoured by him. After this, as he still breathed, he was cast into prison. And living yet one day, stones were bound to his feet, and he was drowned in the depths of the sea. Such was the martyrdom of Agapius.

Chapter 7

Again, in Caesarea, when the persecution had continued to the fifth year, on the second day of the month Xanthicus, which is the fourth before the Nones of April, on the very Lord's day of our Savior's resurrection, Theodosia, a virgin from Tyre, a faithful and sedate maiden, not yet eighteen years of age, went up to certain prisoners who were confessing the kingdom of Christ and sitting before the judgment seat, and saluted them, and, as is probable, besought them to remember her when they came before the Lord. Thereupon, as if she had committed a profane and impious act, the soldiers seized her and led her to the governor. And he immediately, like a madman and a wild beast in his anger, tortured her with dreadful and most terrible torments in her sides and breasts, even to the very bones. And as she still breathed, and withal stood with a joyful and beaming countenance, he ordered her thrown into the waves of the sea. Then passing from her to the other confessors, he condemned all of them to the copper mines in Phaeno in Palestine. Afterwards on the fifth of the month Dius, on the Nones of November according to the Romans, in the same city, Silvanus (who at that time was a presbyter and confessor, but who shortly after was honored with the episcopate and died a martyr), and those with him, men who had shown the noblest firmness in behalf of religion, were condemned by him to labor in the same copper mines, command being first given that their ankles be disabled with hot irons. At the same time he delivered to the flames a man who was illustrious through numerous other confessions. This was Domninus, who was well known to all in Palestine for his exceeding fearlessness After this the same judge, who was a cruel contriver of suffering, and an inventor of devices against the doctrine of Christ, planned against the pious punishments that had never been heard of. He condemned three to single pugilistic combat. He delivered to be devoured by wild beasts Auxentius, a grave and holy old man. Others who were in mature life he made eunuchs, and condemned them to the same mines. Yet others, after severe tortures, he cast into prison. Among these was my dearest friend Pamphilus, who was by reason of every virtue the most illustrious of the martyrs in our time. Urbanus first tested him in rhetorical philosophy and learning; and afterwards endeavored to compel him to sacrifice. But as he saw that he refused and in nowise regarded his threats, being exceedingly angry, he ordered him to be tormented with severest tortures. And when the brutal man, after he had almost satiated himself with these tortures by continuous and prolonged scrapings in his sides, was yet covered with shame before all, he put him also with the confessors in prison. But what recompense for his cruelty to the saints, he who thus abused the martyrs of Christ, shall receive from the Divine judgment, may be easily determined from the preludes to it, in which immediately, and not long after his daring cruelties against Pamphilus, while he yet held the government, the Divine judgment came upon him. For thus suddenly, he who but yesterday was judging on the lofty tribunal, guarded by a band of soldiers, and ruling over the whole nation of Palestine, the associate and dearest friend and table companion of the tyrant himself, was stripped in one night, and overwhelmed with disgrace and shame before those who had formerly admired him as if he were himself an emperor; and he appeared cowardly and unmanly, uttering womanish cries and supplications to all the people whom he had ruled. And Maximinus himself, in reliance upon whose favor Urbanus was formerly so arrogantly insolent, as if he loved him exceedingly for his deeds against us, was set as a harsh and most severe judge in this same Caesarea to pronounce sentence of death against him, for the great disgrace of the crimes of which he was convicted. Let us say this in passing. A suitable time may come when we shall have leisure to relate the end and the fate of those impious men who especially fought against us, both of Maximinus himself and those with him.

Chapter 8

Up to the sixth year the storm had been incessantly raging against us. Before this time there had been a very large number of confessors of religion in the so-called Porphyry quarry in Thebais, which gets its name from the stone found there. Of these, one hundred men, lacking three, together with women and infants, were sent to the governor of Palestine. When they confessed the God of the universe and Christ, Firmilianus, who had been sent there as governor in the place of Urbanus, directed, in accordance with the imperial command, that they should be maimed by burning the sinews of the ankles of their left feet, and that their right eyes with the eyelids and pupils should first be cut out, and then destroyed by hot irons to the very roots. And he then sent them to the mines in the province to endure hardships with severe toil and suffering. But it was not sufficient that these only who suffered such miseries should be deprived of their eyes, but those natives of Palestine also, who were mentioned just above as condemned to pugilistic combat, Since they would neither receive food from the royal storehouse nor undergo the necessary preparatory Exercises. Having been brought on this account not only before the overseers, but also before Maximinus himself, and having manifested the noblest persistence in confession by the endurance of hunger and stripes, they received like punishment with those whom we have mentioned, and with them other confessors in the city of Caesarea. Immediately afterwards others who were gathered to hear the Scriptures read, were seized in Gaza, and some endured the same sufferings in the feet and eyes; but others were afflicted with yet greater torments and with most terrible tortures in the sides. One of these, in body a woman, but in understanding a man, would not endure the threat of fornication, and spoke directly against the tyrant who entrusted the government to such cruel judges. She was first scourged and then raised aloft on the stake, and her sides lacerated. As those appointed for this purpose applied the tortures incessantly and severely at the command of the judge, another, with mind fixed, like the former, on virginity as her aim,- a woman who was altogether mean in forth and contemptible in appearance; but, on the other hand, strong in soul, and endowed with an understanding superior to her body,- being unable to bear the merciless and cruel and inhuman deeds, with a boldness beyond that of the combatants famed among the Greeks, cried out to the judge from the midst of the crowd: "And how long will you thus cruelly torture my sister?" But he was greatly enraged, and ordered the woman to be immediately seized. Thereupon she was brought forward and having called herself by the august name of the Savior, she was first urged by words to sacrifice, and as she refused she was dragged by force to the altar. But her sister continued to maintain her former zeal, and with intrepid and resolute foot kicked the altar, and overturned it with the fire that was on it. Thereupon the judge, enraged like a wild beast, inflicted on her such tortures in her sides as he never had on any one before, striving almost to glut himself with her raw flesh. But when his madness was satiated, he bound them both together, this one and her whom she called sister, and condemned them to death by fire. It is said that the first of these was from the country of Gaza; the other, by name Valentina, was of Caesarea, and was well known to many. But how can I describe as it deserves the martyrdom which followed, with which the thrice-blessed Paul was honored. He was condemned to death at the same time with them, under one sentence. At the time of his martyrdom, as the executioner was about to cut off his head, he requested a brief respite. This being granted, he first, in a clear and distinct voice, supplicated God in behalf of his fellow-Christians, praying for their pardon, and that freedom might soon be restored to them. Then he asked for the conversion of the Jews to God through Christ; and proceeding in order he requested the same things for the Samaritans, and besought that those Gentiles, who were in error and were ignorant of God, might come to a knowledge of him, and adopt the true religion. Nor did he leave neglected the mixed multitude who were standing around. After all these, oh! great and unspeakable forbearance! he entreated the God of the universe for the judge who had condemned him to death, and for the highest rulers, and also for the one who was about to behead him, in his hearing and that of all present, beseeching that their sin toward him should not be reckoned against them. Having prayed for these things with a loud voice, and having, as one who was dying unjustly, moved almost all to compassion and tears, of his own accord he made himself ready, and submitted his bare neck to the stroke of the sword, and was adorned with divine martyrdom. This took place on the twenty-fifth day of the month Panemus, which is the eighth before the Kalends of August. Such was the end of these persons. But not long after, one hundred and thirty admirable athletes of the confession of Christ, from the land of Egypt, endured, in Egypt itself, at the command of Maximinus the same afflictions in their eyes and feet with the former persons, and were sent to the above- mentioned mines in Palestine. But some of them were condemned to the mines in Cilicia.

Chapter 9

After such noble acts of the distinguished martyrs of Christ, the flame of persecution lessened, and was quenched, as it were by their sacred blood, and relief and liberty were granted to those who, for Christ's sake, were laboring in the mines of Thebais, and for a little time we were beginning to breath pure air. But by some new impulse, I know not what, he who held the power to persecute was again aroused against the Christians. Immediately letters from Maximinus against us were published everywhere in every province. The governors and the military prefect urged by edicts and letters and public ordinances the magistrates and generals and notaries in all the cities to carry out the imperial decree, which ordered that the altars of the idols should with all speed be rebuilt; and that all men, women, and children, even infants at the breast, should sacrifice and offer oblations; and that with diligence and care they should cause them to taste of the execrable offerings; and that the things for sale in the market should be polluted with libations from the sacrifices; and that guards should be stationed before the baths in order to defile with the abominable sacrifices those who went to wash in them. When these orders were being carried out, our people, as was natural, were at the beginning greatly distressed in mind; and even the unbelieving heathen blamed the severity and the exceeding absurdity of what was done. For these things appeared to them extreme and burdensome. As the heaviest storm impended over all in every quarter, the divine power of our Savior again infused such boldness into his athletes, that without being drawn on or dragged forward by any one, they spurned the threats. Three of the faithful joining together, rushed on the governor as he was sacrificing to the idols, and cried out to him to cease from his delusion, there being no other God than the Maker and Creator of the universe. When he asked who they were, they confessed boldly that they were Christians. Thereupon Firmilianus, being greatly enraged, sentenced them to capital punishment without inflicting tortures upon them. The name of the eldest of these was Antoninus; of the next, Zebinas, who was a native of Eleutheropolis; and of the third, Germanus. This took place on the thirteenth of the month Dius, the Ides of November.

There was associated with them on the same day Ennathas, a woman from Scythopolis, who was adorned with the chaplet of virginity. She did not indeed do as they had done, but was dragged by force and brought before the judge. She endured scourgings and cruel insults, which Maxys, a tribune of a neighboring district, without the knowledge of the superior authority, dared to inflict upon her. He was a man worse than his name, sanguinary in other respects, exceedingly harsh, and altogether cruel, and censured by all who knew him. This man stripped the blessed woman of all her clothing, so that she was covered only from her loins to her feet and the rest of her body was bare. And he led her through the entire city of Caesarea, and regarded it as a great thing to beat her with thongs while she was dragged through all the market-places. After such treatment she manifested the noblest constancy at the judgment seat of the governor himself; and the judge condemned her to be burned alive. He also carried his rage against the pious to a most inhuman length and transgressed the laws of nature, not being ashamed even to deny burial to the lifeless bodies of the sacred men. Thus he ordered the dead to be exposed in the open air as food for wild beasts and to be watched carefully by night and day. For many days a large number of men attended to this savage and barbarous decree. And they looked out from their post of observation, as if it were a matter worthy of care, to see that the dead bodies should not be stolen. And wild beasts and dogs and birds of prey scattered the human limbs here and there, and the whole city was strewed with the entrails and bones of men, so that nothing had ever appeared more dreadful and horrible, even to those who formerly hated us; though they bewailed not so much the calamity of those against whom these things were done, as the outrage against themselves and the common nature of man. For there was to be seen near the gates a spectacle beyond all description and tragic recital; for not only was human flesh devoured in one place, but it was scattered in every place; so that some said that limbs and masses of flesh and parts of entrails were to be seen even within the gates. After these things had continued for many days, a wonderful event occurred. The air was clear and bright and the appearance of the sky most serene. When suddenly throughout the city from the pillars which supported the public porches many drops fell like tears; and the market places and streets, though there was no mist in the air, were moistened with sprinkled water, whence I know not. Then immediately it was reported everywhere that the earth, unable to endure the abomination of these things, had shed tears in a mysterious manner; and that as a rebuke to the relentless and unfeeling nature of men, stones and lifeless wood had wept for what had happened. I know well that this account may perhaps appear idle and fabulous to those who come after us, but not to those to whom the truth was confirmed at the time.

Chapter 10

On the fourteenth day of the following month Appellaeus, the nineteenth before the Kalends of January, certain persons from Egypt were again seized by those who examined people passing the gates. They had been sent to minister to the confessors in Cilicia. They received the same sentence as those whom they had gone to help, being mutilated in their eyes and feet. Three of them exhibited in Ascalon, where they were imprisoned, marvelous bravery in the endurance of various kinds of martyrdom. One of them named Ares was condemned to the flames, and the others, called Probus and Elias, were beheaded. On the eleventh day of the month Audynaeus, which is the third before the Ides of January, in the same city of Caesarea, Peter an ascetic, also called Apselamus, from the village of Anea, on the borders of Eleutheropolis, like purest gold, gave noble proof by fire of his faith in the Christ of God. Though the judge and those around him besought him many times to have compassion on himself, and to spare his own youth and bloom, he disregarded them, preferring hope in the God of the universe to all things, even to life itself. A certain Asclepius, supposed to be a bishop of the sect of

Marcion, possessed as he thought with zeal for religion, but "not according to knowledge," ended his life on one and the same funeral pyre. These things took place in this manner.

Chapter 11

It is time to describe the great and celebrated spectacle of Pamphilus, a man thrice dear to me, and of those who finished their course with him. They were twelve in all; being counted worthy of apostolic grace and number. Of these the leader and the only one honored with the position of presbyter at Caesarea, was Pamphilus; a man who through his entire life was celebrated for every virtue, for renouncing and despising the world, for sharing his possessions with the needy, for contempt of earthly hopes, and for philosophic deportment and exercise. He especially excelled all in our time in most sincere devotion to the Divine Scriptures and indefatigable industry in whatever he undertook, and in his helpfulness to his relatives and associates. In a separate treatise on his life, consisting of three books, we have already described the excellence of his virtue. Referring to this work those who delight in such things and desire to know them, let us now consider the martyrs in order. Second after Pamphilus, Vales, who was honored for his venerable gray hair, entered the contest. He was a deacon from Aelia, an old man of gravest appearance, and versed in the Divine Scriptures, if any one ever was. He had so laid up the memory of them in his heart that he did not need to look at the books if he undertook to repeat any passage of Scripture. The third was Paul from the city of Jamna, who was known among them as most zealous and fervent in spirit. Previous to his martyrdom, he had endured the conflict of confession by cauterization. After these persons had continued in prison for two entire years, the occasion of their martyrdom was a second arrival of Egyptian brethren who suffered with them. They had accompanied the confessors in Cilicia to the mines there and were returning to their homes. At the entrance of the gates of Caesarea, the guards, who were men of barbarous character, questioned them as to who they were and whence they came. They kept back nothing of the truth, and were seized as malefactors taken in the very act. They were five in number. When brought before the tyrant, being very bold in his presence, they were immediately thrown into prison. On the next day, which was the nineteenth of the month Peritius, according to the Roman reckoning the fourteenth before the Kalends of March, they were brought, according to command, before the judge, with Pamphilus and his associates whom we have mentioned. First, by all kinds of torture, through the invention of strange and various machines, he tested the invincible constancy of the Egyptians. Having practiced these cruelties upon the leader of all, he asked him first who he was. He heard in reply the name of some prophet instead of his proper name. For it was their custom, in place of the names of idols given them by their fathers, if they had such, to take other names; so that you would hear them calling themselves Elijah or Jeremiah or Isaiah or Samuel or Daniel, thus showing themselves inwardly true Jews, and the genuine Israel of God, not only in deeds, but in the names which they bore. When Firmilianus had heard some such name from the martyr, and did not understand the force of the word, he asked next the name of his country. But he gave a second answer similar to the former, saying that Jerusalem was his country, meaning that of which Paul says, "Jerusalem which is above is free, which is our mother," and, "Ye are come unto Mount Sion, and unto the city of the living God, the heavenly Jerusalem."

This was what he meant; but the judge thinking only of the earth, sought diligently to discover what that city was, and in what part of the world it was situated. And therefore he applied tortures that the truth might be acknowledged. But the man, with his hands twisted behind his back, and his feet crushed by strange machines, asserted firmly that he had spoken the truth. And being questioned again repeatedly what and where the city was of which he spoke, he said that it was the country of the pious alone, for no others should have a place in it, and that it lay toward the far East and the rising sun. He philosophized about these things according to his own understanding, and was in nowise turned froth them by the tortures with which he was afflicted on every side. And as if he were without flesh or body he seemed insensible of his sufferings. But the judge being perplexed, was impatient, thinking that the Christians were about to establish a city somewhere, inimical and hostile to the Romans. And he inquired much about this, and investigated where that country toward the East was located. But when he had for a long time lacerated the young man with scourgings, and punished him with all sorts of torments, he perceived that his persistence in what he had said could not be changed, and passed against him sentence of death. Such a scene was exhibited by what was done to this man. And having inflicted similar tortures on the others, he sent them away in the same manner. Then being wearied and perceiving that he punished the men in vain, having satiated his desire, he proceeded against Pamphilus and his companions. And having learned that already under former tortures they had manifested an unchangeable zeal for the faith, he asked them if they would now obey. And receiving from every one of them only this one answer, as their last word of confession in martyrdom, he inflicted on them punishment similar to the others. When this had been done, a young man, one of the household servants of Pamphilus, who had been educated in the noble life and instruction of such a man, learning the sentence passed upon his master, cried out from the midst of the crowd asking that their bodies might be buried. Thereupon the judge, not a man, but a wild beast, or if anything more savage than a wild beast, giving no consideration to the young man's age, asked him only the same question. When he learned that he confessed himself a Christian, as if he had been wounded by a dart, swelling with rage, he ordered the tormentors to use their utmost power against him. And when he saw that he refused to sacrifice as commanded, he ordered them to scrape him continually to his very bones and to the inmost recesses of his bowels, not as if he were human flesh but as if he were stones or wood or any lifeless thing. But after long persistence he saw that this was in vain, as the man was speechless and insensible and almost lifeless, his body being worn out by the tortures. But being inflexibly merciless and inhuman, he ordered him to be committed straightway, as he was, to a slow fire. And before the death of his earthly master, though he had entered later on the conflict, he received release from the body, while those who had been zealous about the others were yet delaying. One could then see. Porphyry, like one who had come off victorious in every conflict, his body covered with dust, but his countenance cheerful, after such sufferings, with courageous and exulting mind, advancing to death. And as if truly filled with the Divine Spirit, covered only with his philosophic robe thrown about him as a cloak, soberly and intelligently he directed his friends as to what he wished, and beckoned to them, preserving still a cheerful countenance even at the stake. But when the fire was kindled at some distance around him in a circle, having inhaled the flame into his mouth, he continued most nobly in silence from that time till his death, after the single word which he uttered when the flame first touched him, and he cried out for the help of Jesus the Son of God. Such was the contest of Porphyry. His death was reported to Pamphilus by a messenger, Seleucus. He was one of the confessors from the army. As the bearer of such a message, he was forthwith deemed worthy of a similar lot. For as soon as he related the death of Porphyry, and had saluted one of the martyrs with a kiss, some of the soldiers seized him and led him to the governor. And he, as if he would hasten him on to be a companion of the former on the way to heaven, commanded that he be put to death immediately. This man was from Cappadocia, and belonged to the select band of soldiers, and had obtained no small honor in those things which are esteemed among the Romans. For in stature and bodily strength, and size and vigor, he far excelled his fellow-soldiers, so that his appearance was matter of common talk, and his whole form was admired on account of its size and symmetrical proportions. At the beginning of the persecution he was prominent in the conflicts of confession, through his patience under scourging. After he left the army he set himself to imitate zealously the religious ascetics, and as if he were their father and guardian he showed himself a bishop and patron of destitute orphans and defenseless widows and of those who were distressed with penury or sickness. It is likely that on this account he was deemed worthy of an extraordinary call to martyrdom by God, who rejoices in such things more than in the smoke and blood of sacrifices. He was the tenth athlete among those whom we have mentioned as meeting their end on one and the same day. On this day, as was fitting, the chief gate was opened, and a ready way of entrance into the kingdom of heaven was given to the martyr Pamphilus and to the others with him. In the footsteps of Seleucus came Theodulus, a grave and pious old man, who belonged to the governor's household, and had been honored by Firmilianus himself more than all the others in his house on account of his age, and because he was a father of the third generation, and also on account of the kindness and most faithful conscientiousness which he had manifested toward him. As he pursued the course of Seleucus when brought before his master, the latter was more angry at him than at those who had preceded him, and condemned him to endure the martyrdom of the Savior on the cross.

As there lacked yet one to fill up the number of the twelve martyrs of whom we have spoken, Julian came to complete it. He had just arrived from abroad, and had not yet entered the gate of the city, when having learned about the martyrs while still on the way, he rushed at once, just as he was, to see them. When he beheld the tabernacles of the saints prone on the ground, being filled with joy, he embraced and kissed them all. The ministers of slaughter straightway seized him as he was doing this and led him to Firmilianus. Acting as was his custom, he condemned him to a slow fire. Thereupon Julian, leaping and exulting, in a loud voice gave thanks to the Lord who had judged him worthy of such things, and was honored with the crown of martyrdom. He was a Cappadocian by birth, and in his manner of life he was most circumspect, faithful and sincere, zealous in all other respects, and animated by the Holy Spirit himself. Such was the company which was thought worthy to enter into martyrdom with Pamphilus. By the command of the impious governor their sacred and truly holy bodies were kept as food for the wild beasts for four days and as many nights. But since, strange to say, through the providential care of God, nothing approached them,-neither beast of prey, nor bird, nor dog,- they were taken up uninjured, and after suitable preparation were buried in the customary manner. When the report of what had been done to these men was spread in all directions, Adrianus and Eubulus, having come from the so-called country of Manganaea to Caesarea, to see the remaining confessors, were also asked at the gate the reason for their coming; and having acknowledged the truth, were brought to Firmilianus. But he, as was his custom, without delay inflicted many tortures in their sides, and condemned them to be devoured by wild beasts. After two days, on the fifth of the month Dystrus, the third before the Nones of March, which was regarded as the birthday of the tutelary divinity of Caesarea, Adrianus was thrown to a lion, and afterwards slain with the sword. But Eubulus, two days later, on the Nones of March, that is, on the seventh of the month Dystrus, when the judge had earnestly entreated him to enjoy by sacrificing that which was considered freedom among them, preferring a glorious death for religion to transitory life, was made like the other an offering to wild beasts, and as the last of the martyrs in Caesarea, sealed the list of athletes. It is proper also to relate here, how in a short time the heavenly Providence came upon the impious rulers, together with the tyrants themselves. For that very Firmilianus, who had thus abused the martyrs of Christ, after suffering with the others the severest punishment, was put to death by the sword. Such were the martyrdoms which took place at Caesarea during the entire period of the persecution.

Chapter 12

I Think it best to pass by all the other events which occurred in the meantime: such as those which happened to the bishops of the churches, when instead of shepherds of the rational flocks of Christ, over which they presided in an unlawful manner, the divine judgment, considering them worthy of such a charge, made them keepers of camels, an irrational beast and very crooked in the structure of its body, or condemned them to have the care of the imperial horses;-and I pass by also the insults and disgraces and tortures they endured from the imperial overseers and rulers on account of the sacred vessels and treasures of the Church; and besides these the lust of power on the part of many, the disorderly and unlawful ordinations, and the schisms among the confessors themselves; also the novelties which were zealously devised against the remnants of the Church by the new and factious members, who added innovation after innovation and forced them in unsparingly among the calamities of the persecution, heaping misfortune upon misfortune. I judge it more suitable to shun and avoid the account of these things, as I said at the beginning. But such things as are sober and praiseworthy, according to the sacred word,-"and if there be any virtue and praise," -I consider it most proper to tell and to record, and to present to believing hearers in the history of the admirable martyrs. And after this I think it best to crown the entire work with an account of the peace which has appeared unto us from heaven.

Chapter 13

The seventh year of our conflict was completed; and the hostile measures which had continued into the eighth year were gradually and quietly becoming less severe. A large number of confessors were collected at the copper mines in Palestine, and were acting with considerable boldness, so far as even to build places of worship. But the ruler of the province, a cruel and wicked man, as his acts against the martyrs showed, having come there and learned the state of affairs, communicated it to the emperor, writing in accusation whatever he thought best. Thereupon, being appointed superintendent of the mines, he divided the band of confessors as if by a royal decree, and sent some to dwell in Cyprus and others in Lebanon, and he scattered others in different parts of Palestine and ordered them to labor in various works. And, selecting the four who seemed to him to be the leaders, he sent them to the commander of the armies in that section. These were Peleus and Nilus, Egyptian bishops, also a presbyter, and Patermuthius, who was well known among them all for his zeal toward all. The commander of the army demanded of them a denial of religion, and not obtaining this, he condemned them to death by fire. There were others there who had been allotted to dwell in a separate place by themselves,- such of the confessors as on account of age or mutilations, or for other bodily infirmities, had been released from service. Silvanus, a bishop from Gaza, presided over them, and set a worthy and genuine example of Christianity. This man having from the first day of the persecution, and throughout its entire continuance, been eminent for his confessions in all sorts of conflicts, had been kept all that time that he might, so to speak, set the final seal upon the whole conflict in Palestine. There were with him many from Egypt, among whom was John, who surpassed all in our time in the excellence of his memory. He had formerly been deprived of his sight. Nevertheless, on account of his eminence in confession he had with the others suffered the destruction of his foot by cauterization. And although his sight had been destroyed he was subjected to the same burning with fire, the executioners aiming after everything that was merciless and pitiless and cruel and inhuman. Since he was such a man, one would not be so much astonished at his habits and his philosophic life, nor would he seem so wonderful for them, as for the strength of his memory. For he had written whole books of the Divine Scriptures, "not in tables of stone" as the divine apostle says, neither on skins of animals, nor on paper which moths and time destroy, but truly "in fleshy tables of the heart," in a transparent soul and most pure eye of the mind, so that whenever he wished he could repeat, as if from a treasury of words, any portion of the Scripture, whether in the law, or the prophets, or the historical books, or the gospels, or the writings of the apostles. I confess that I was astonished when I first saw the man as he was standing in the midst of a large congregation and repeating portions of the Divine Scripture. While I only heard his voice, I thought that, according to the custom in the meetings, he was reading. But when I came near and perceived what he was doing, and observed all the others standing around him with sound eyes while he was using only the eyes of his mind, and yet was speaking naturally like some prophet, and far excelling those who were sound in body, it was impossible for me not to glorify God and wonder. And I seemed to see in these deeds evident and strong confirmation of the fact that true manhood consists not in excellence of bodily appearance, but in the soul and understanding alone. For he, with his body mutilated, manifested the superior excellence of the power that was within him. But as to those whom we have mentioned as abiding in a separate place, and attending to their customary duties in fasting and prayer and other exercises, God himself saw fit to give them a salutary issue by extending his right hand in answer to them. The bitter foe, as they were armed against him zealously through their prayers to God, could no longer endure them, and determined to slay and destroy them from off the earth because they troubled him. And God permitted him to complish this, that he might not be restrained from the wickedness he desired, and that at the same time they might receive the prizes of their manifold conflicts. Therefore at the command of the most accursed Maximinus, forty, lacking one, were beheaded in one day. These martyrdoms were accomplished in Palestine during eight complete years; and of this description was the persecution in our time. Beginning with the demolition of the churches, it increased greatly as the rulers rose up from time to time against us. In these assaults the multiform and various conflicts of those who wrestled in behalf of religion produced an innumerable multitude of martyrs in every province,-in the regions extending from Libya and throughout all Egypt, and Syria, and from the East round about to the district of Illyricum. But the countries beyond these, all Italy and Sicily and Gaul, and the regions toward the setting sun, in Spain, Mauritania, and Africa, suffered the war of persecution during less than two years, and were deemed worthy of a speedier divine visitation and peace; the heavenly Providence sparing the singleness of purpose and faith of those men. For what had never before been recorded in the annals of the Roman government, first took place in our day, contrary to all expectation; for during the persecution in our time the empire was divided into two parts. The brethren dwelling in the part of which we have just spoken enjoyed peace; but those in the other part endured trials without number. But when the divine grace kindly and compassionately manifested its care for us too, then truly our rulers also, those very ones through whom the wars against us had been formerly carried on, changed their minds in a most wonderful manner, and published a recantation; and by favorable edicts and mild decrees concerning us, extinguished the conflagration against us. This recantation also must be recorded.

D. Eusebius of Cæsarea

Eusebius Pamphili, Bishop of Cæsarea in Palestine, the "Father of Church History"; b. about 260; d. before 341.

LIFE

It will save lengthy digression if we at once speak of a document which will often have to be referred to on account of its biographical importance, viz., the letter written by Eusebius to his diocese in order to explain his subscription to the Creed propounded by the Council of Nicæa. After some preliminary remarks, the writer proceeds: "We first transmit to you the writing concerning the faith which was put forward by us, and then the second, which they have published after putting in additions to our expressions. Now the writing presented by us, which when read in the presence of our most religious emperor was declared to have a right and approved character was as follows: [The Faith put forward by us]. As we have received from the bishops before us both in our first catechetical instruction and when we were baptized, and as we have learned from the Divine Scriptures, and as we have believed and taught in the presbyterate and in the office of bishop itself so now likewise believing we offer to you our faith and it is thus." Then follows a formal creed [Theodoret, Hist., I, 11; Socrates, Hist., I, 8; St. Athanasius, de Dec. Syn. Nic. (appendix) and elsewhere. Translated by Newman with notes in the Oxford Library of the Fathers (Select Treatises of St. Athanasius, p. 59) and St. Athanasius, vol. I. The translation given here is Dr. Hort's. The words in brackets are probably genuine though not given by Socrates and St. Athanasius].

Dr. Hort in 1876 ("Two Dissertations', etc., pp. 56 sqq.) pointed out that this creed was presumably that of the Church of Cæsarea of which Eusebius was bishop. This view is widely accepted (cf. Lightfoot, art. "Euseb." in "Dict. of Christ. Biog."

All references to Lightfoot, unless otherwise stated, are to this article.

Sanday, "Journal of Theolog. Studies", vol. I, p. 15; Gwatkin, "studies of Arianism", p. 42, 2nd edition; McGiffert, "Prolog. to C. H. of Euseb." in "select Library of Nic. and post-Nic. Fathers"; Duchesne, "Hist. de l'Eglise", vol. II, p. 149). According to this view it is natural to regard the introduction, "As we have received" etc., as autobiographical, and to infer that Eusebius had exercised the office of priesthood in the city of Cæsarea before he became its bishop, and had received his earliest religious instruction and the sacrament of Baptism there also. But other interpretations of this document are given, one of which destroys, while the other diminishes, its biographical value: (a) According to some the creed proferred by Eusebius was drawn up as a formula to be subscribed by all the bishops. It was they who were to say that it embodied what they had been taught as catechumens and had taught as priests and bishops. This seems to have been the view generally held before Hort, and was Kattenbusch's view in 1804 (Das apostolische Symbol, vol. I, p. 231). One objection to this view may be noted. It makes all the bishops equivalently say that before they received the episcopate they had for some time exercised the duties of the priesthood. (b) Others maintain that this creed was not the local creed of Cæsarea, but one drawn up by Eusebius in his own justification as embodying what he had always believed and taught. According to this interpretation the preliminary statement still remains autobiographical; but it merely informs us that the writer exercised the office of priest before he became a bishop. This interpretation has been adopted by Kattenbusch in his second volume (p. 239) published in 1900. One of the reasons which he gives for his change of view is that when he was preparing his first volume he used Socrates, who does not give the superscription which we have printed in brackets. It is a vital matter with writers of the school of Kattenbusch not to accept what seems the natural interpretation of Eusebius's words, viz., that the creed he read before the council was actually the one he had always used. If this is admitted, "then", to quote Dr. Sanday, "I cannot but think that the theory of Kattenbusch and Harnack [viz. that the Eastern creeds were daughters of the early Roman creed, and this latter did not reach the East till about A. D. 272] breaks down altogether. Bishop Lightfoot puts the birth of Eusebius about 260 A. D., so that he would be something like twelve years old when Aurelian intervened in the affairs of Antioch. In other words he was in all probability already baptized, and had already been catechised in the Cæsarean creed at a time when, in the Kattenbusch-Harnack hypothesis, the parent of that creed had not yet reached Antioch much less Cæsarea or Jerusalem" (Journ. Th. Studies, I, 15).

Concerning Eusebius's parentage we know absolutely nothing; but the fact that he escaped with a short term of imprisonment during the terrible Diocletian persecution, when his master Pamphilus and others of his companions suffered martyrdom, suggests that he belonged to a family of some influence and importance. His relations, later on, with the Emperor Constantine point to the same conclusion. At some time during the last twenty years of the third century he visited Antioch, where he made the acquaintance of the priest Dorotheus, and heard him expound the Scriptures (H. E., VII, 32). By a slip of the pen or the memory , Lightfoot (p. 309) makes Dorotheus a priest of the Church of Cæsarea. In 296 he saw for the first time the future Emperor Constantine, as he passed through Palestine in the company of Diocletian (Vit. Const., I, 19).

At a date which cannot be fixed Eusebius made the acquaintance of Pamphilus, the founder of the magnificent library which remained for several centuries the great glory of the Church of Cæsarea. Pamphilus came from Phonicia, but at the time we are considering resided at Cæsarea, where he presided over a college or school for students. A man of noble birth, and wealthy, he sold his patrimony and gave the proceeds to the poor. He was a great friend to indigent students, supplying them to the best of his ability with the necessaries of life, and bestowing on them copies of the Holy Scriptures. Too humble to write anything himself, he spent his time in preparing accurate copies of the Scriptures and other books, especially those of Origen. Eloquent testimonies to the care bestowed by Pamphilus and Eusebius on the sacred text are found in Biblical MSS. which have reproduced their colophons.

During the persecution Eusebius visited Tyre and Egypt and witnessed numbers of martyrdoms (H. E., VIII, vii and ix). He certainly did not shun danger, and was at one time a prisoner. When, where, or how he escaped death or any kind of mutilation, we do not know. An indignant bishop, who had been one of his fellow-prisoners and "lost an eye for the Truth", demanded at the Council of Tyre how "he came off scathless". To this taunt it was hardly a question made under circumstances of great provocation, Eusebius deigned no reply (Epiphan., Hær., lxviii, 8; cf. St. Athanas., "Apol. c. Arian.", viii, 1). He had many enemies, yet the charge of cowardice was never seriously made the best proof that it could not have been sustained. We may assume that, as soon as the persecution began to relax, Eusebius succeeded Pamphilus in the charge of the college and library. Perhaps he was ordained priest about this time. By 315 he was already a bishop, for he was present in that capacity at the dedication of a new basilica at Tyre, on which occasion he delivered a discourse given in full in the last book of the Church history.

Alexander, Bishop of Alexandria, excommunicated Arius about the year 320. The Arians soon found that for all practical purposes Eusebius was on their side. He wrote to Alexander charging him with misrepresenting the teaching of the Arians and so giving them cause "to attack and misrepresent whatever they please" (see below). A portion of this letter has been preserved in the Acts of the second Council of Nicæa, where it was cited to prove that Eusebius was a heretic. He also took part in a synod of Syrian bishops who decided that Arius should be restored to his former position, but on his side he was to obey his bishop and continually entreat peace and communion with him (Soz., H. E., I, 15). According to Duchesne (Hist. de l"Eglise, II, 132), Arius, like Origen before him, found an asylum at Cæsarea. At the opening of the Council of Nicæa Eusebius occupied the first seat on the right of the emperor, and delivered the inaugural address which was "couched in a strain of thanksgiving to Almighty God on his, the emperor's behalf" (Vit. Const., III, 11; Soz., H. E., I, 19). He evidently enjoyed great prestige and may not unreasonably have expected to be able to steer the council through the via media between the Scylla and Charybdis of "Yes' and "No". But if he entertained such hopes they were soon disappointed. We have already spoken of the profession of faith which he brought forward to vindicate his own orthodoxy, or perhaps in the hope that the council might adopt it. It was, in view of the actual state of the controversy, a colorless, or what at the present day would be called a comprehensive, formula. After some delay Eusebius subscribed to the uncompromising creed drawn up by the council, making no secret, in the letter which he wrote to his own Church, of the non-natural sense in which he accepted it. Between 325 and 330 a heated controversy took place between Eusebius and Eustathius, Bishop of Antioch. Eustathius accused Eusebius of tampering with the faith of Nicæa;

the latter retorted with the charge of Sabellianism. In 331 Eusebius was among the bishops who, at a synod held in Antioch, deposed Eustathius. He was offered and refused the vacant see. In 334 and 335 he took part in the campaign against St. Athanasius at the synods held in Cæsarea and Tyre respectively. From Tyre the assembly of bishops were summoned to Jerusalem by Constantine, to assist at the dedication of the basilica he had erected on the site of Calvary. After the dedication they restored Arius and his followers to communion. From Jerusalem they were summoned to Constantinople (336), where Marcellus was condemned. The following year Constantine died. Eusebius survived him long enough to write his Life and two treatises against Marcellus, but by the summer of 341 he was already dead, since it was his successor, Acacius, who assisted as Bishop of Cæsarea at a synod held at Antioch in the summer of that year.

WRITINGS

We shall take Eusebius's writings in the order given in Harnack's "Altchrist. Lit.", pp. 554 sqq.

A. Historical

(1) The lost Life of Pamphilus, often referred to by Eusebius, of which only a single fragment, describing Pamphilus' liberality to poor students, quoted by St. Jerome (c. Ruffin., I, ix), survives.

(2) A collection of Ancient Martyrdoms, used by the compiler of Wright's Syriac Martyrology, also lost.

(3) On the Martyrs of Palestine. There are two distinct forms of this work, both drawn up by Eusebius. The longer is only extant in a Syriac version which was first edited and translated by Cureton in 1861. The shorter form is found in most MSS. (not, however, in the best) of the Church History, sometimes at the end of the last book, generally between books VIII and IX, also in the middle of book VIII. The existence of the same work in two different forms raises a number of curious literary problems. There is, of course, the question of priority. Here, with two notable exceptions, scholars seem to be agreed in favour of the longer form. Then comes the question, why Eusebius abridged it and, finally, how the abridgment found its way into the Church History. The shorter form lacks some introductory remarks, referred to in c. xiii, which defined the scope of the book. It also breaks off when the writer is about to "record the palinode" of the persecutors. It seems probable that part of the missing conclusion is extant in the form of an appendix to the eighth book of the Church History found in several MSS. This appendix contrasts the miserable fate of the persecutors with the good fortune of Constantine and his father. From these data Lightfoot concludes that what we now possess formed "part of a larger work in which the sufferings of the Martyrs were set off against the deaths of the persecutors". It must, however, be remembered that the missing parts would not add much to the book. So far as the martyrs are concerned, it is evidently complete, and the fate of the persecutors would not take long in the telling. Still, the missing conclusion may explain why Eusebius curtailed his account of the Martyrs. The book, in both forms, was intended for popular reading. It was therefore desirable to keep down the price of copies. If this was to be done, and new matter (i. e. the fate of the persecutors) added, the old matter had to be somewhat curtailed. In 1894, in the Theologische Literaturzeitung (p. 464) Preuschen threw out the idea that the shorter form was merely a rough draft not intended for publication. Bruno Violet, in his "Die Palästinischen Martyrer" (Texte u. Untersuch., XIV, 4, 1896) followed up this idea and pointed out that, whereas the longer form was constantly used by the compilers of Martyrologies, Menologies, and the like, the shorter form was never used. In a review of Violet (Theolog. Litz, 1897, p. 300), Preuschen returns to his original idea, and further suggests that the shorter form must have been joined to the Church History by some copyist who had access to Eusebius's MSS. Harnack (Chronologie, 11, 115) holds to the priority of the longer form, but he thinks that the shorter form was composed almost at the same time for readers of the Church History.

(4) The Chronicle.

(5) The Church History. It would be difficult to overestimate the obligation which posterity is under to Eusebius for this monumental work. Living during the period of transition, when the old order was changing and all connected with it was passing into oblivion, he came forward at the critical moment with his immense stores of learning and preserved priceless treasures of Christian antiquity. This is the great merit of the Church History. It is not a literary work which can be read with any pleasure for the sake of its style. Eusebius's "diction", as Photius said, "is never pleasant nor clear". Neither is it the work of a great thinker. But it is a storehouse of information collected by an indefatigable student. Still, great as was Eusebius's learning, it had its limitations. He is provokingly ill-informed about the West. That he knows very little about Tertullian or St. Cyprian is due, no doubt, to his scant knowledge of Latin; but in the case of a Greek writer, like Hippolytus, we can only suppose that his works somehow failed to make their way to the libraries of the East. Eusebius's good faith and sincerity has been amply vindicated by Lightfoot. Gibbon's celebrated sneer, about a writer "who indirectly confesses that he has related whatever might redound to the glory, and that he has suppressed all that could tend to the disgrace, of religion", can be sufficiently met by referring to the passages (H. E., VIII, ii; Mart. Pal. c. 12) on which it is based. Eusebius does not "indirectly confess', but openly avows, that he passes over certain scandals, and he enumerates them and denounces them. "Nor again", to quote Lightfoot, "can the special charges against his honor as a narrator be sustained. There is no ground whatever for the charge that Eusebius forged or interpolated the passage from Josephus relating to our Lord quoted in H. E., I, 11, though Heinchen is disposed to entertain the charge. Inasmuch as this passage is contained in all our MSS., and there is sufficient evidence that other interpolations (though not this) were introduced into the text of Josephus long before his time (see Orig., c. Cels., I, 47, Delarue's note) no suspicion can justly attach to Eusebius himself. Another interpolation in the Jewish historian, which he quotes elsewhere (11, 23), was certainly known to Origen (l. c.). Doubtless also the omission of the owl in the account of Herod Agrippa's death (H. E., 11, 10) was already in some texts of Josephus (Ant., XIX, 8, 2). The manner in which Eusebius deals with his numerous quotations elsewhere, where we can test his honesty, is a sufficient vindication against this unjust charge" (L., p. 325).

The notices in the Church History bearing on the New Testament Canon are so important that a word must be said about the rule followed by Eusebius in what he recorded and what he left unrecorded. Speaking generally, his principle seems to have been to quote testimonies for and against those books only whose claims to a place in the Canon had been disputed. In the case of undisputed books he gave any interesting information concerning their composition which he had come across in his reading. The subject was most carefully investigated by Lightfoot in an article in "The Contemporary" (January, 1875, reprinted in "Essays on Supernatural Religion"), entitled "The Silence of Eusebius". In regard to the Gospel of St. John, Lightfoot concludes: "The silence of Eusebius respecting early witnesses to the Fourth Gospel is an evidence in its favor." For the episcopal lists in the Church History, see article on the Chronicle. The tenth book of the Church History records the defeat of Licinius in 323, and must have been completed before the death and disgrace of Crispus in 326, for it refers to him as Constantine's "most pious son". The ninth book was completed between the defeat of Maxentius in 312, and Constantine's first rupture with Licinius in 314.

(6) The Life of Constantine, in four books. This work has been most unjustly blamed, from the time of Socrates downwards, because it is a panegyric rather than a history. If ever there was a man under an obligation to respect the maxim, De mortuis nil nisi bonum, this man was Eusebius, writing the Life of Constantine within three years after his death (337). This Life is especially valuable because of the account it gives of the Council of Nicæa and the earlier phases of the Arian controversy. It is well to remember that one of

our chief sources of information for the history of that council is a book written to magnify Constantine.

B. Apologetic

(7) Against Hierocles. Hierocles, who, as governor in Bithynia and in Egypt, was a cruel enemy of the Christians during the persecution, before the persecution had attacked them with the pen. There was nothing original about his work except the use he made of Philostratus's Life of Apollonius of Tyana to institute a comparison between the Lord and Apollonius in favour of the latter. In his reply Eusebius confined himself to this one point.

(8) "Against Porphyry", a work in twenty-five books of which not a fragment survives.

(9) The "Præparatio Evangelica", in fifteen books.

(10) The "Demonstratio Evangelica", in twenty books, of which the last ten, with the exception of a fragment of the fifteenth, are lost. The object of these two treatises, which should be regarded as two parts of one comprehensive work, was to justify the Christian in rejecting the religion and philosophy of the Greeks in favour of that of the Hebrews, and then to justify him in not observing the Jewish manner of life. The "Præparatio" is devoted to the first of these objects. The following summary of its contents is taken from Mr. Gifford's introduction to his translation of the "Præparatio": "The first three books discuss the threefold system of Pagan Theology, Mythical, Allegorical, and Political. The next three, IV-VI, give an account of the chief oracles, of the worship of dæmons, and of the various opinions of Greek Philosophers on the doctrines of Plato and Free Will. Books VII- IX give reasons for preferring the religion of the Hebrews founded chiefly on the testimony of various authors to the excellency of their Scriptures and the truth of their history. In Books X-XII Eusebius argues that the Greeks had borrowed from the older theology and philosophy of the Hebrews, dwelling especially on the supposed dependence of Plato upon Moses. In the last three books the comparison of Moses with Plato is continued, and the mutual contradictions of other Greek Philosophers, especially the Peripatetics and Stoics, are exposed and criticized."

The "Præparatio" is a gigantic feat of erudition, and, according to Harnack (Chronologie, II, p. 120), was, like many of Eusebius's other works, actually composed during the stress of the persecution. It ranks, with the Chronicle, second only to the Church History in importance, because of its copious extracts from ancient authors whose works have perished. The first book of the Demonstratio chiefly deals with the temporary character of the Mosaic Law. In the second the prophecies concerning the vocation of the Gentiles and the rejection of the Jews are discussed. In the remaining eight the testimonies of the prophets concerning Christ are treated of.

We now pass to three books, of which nothing is known save that they were read by Photius, viz. (11), The "Præparatio Ecclesiastica", (12), the "Demonstratio Ecclesiastica", and (13) Two Books of Objection and Defense, of which, from Photius's account, there seem to have been two separate editions.

(14) The "Theophania" or "Divine Manifestation". Except for a few fragments of the original, this work is only extant in a Syriac version discovered by Tattam, edited by Lee in 1842, and translated by the same in 1843. It treats of the cosmic function of the Word, the nature of man, the need of revelation, etc. The fourth and fifth books are particularly remarkable as a kind of anticipation of modern books on Christian evidences. A curious literary problem arises out of the relations between the "Theophania" and the work "De Laudibus Constantini". There are entire passages which are almost verbatim the same in both works. Lightfoot decides in favour of the priority of the first-named work. Gressel, who has edited the "Theophania" for the Berlin edition of the Greek Fathers, takes the opposite view. He compares the parallel passages and argues that they are improved in the "De Laudibus Constantini".

(15) "On the Numerous Progeny of the Ancients". This work is referred to by Eusebius twice, in the "Præp. Ev.", VII, 8, and in the

"Dem. Ev.", VII, 8; and also (Lightfoot and Harnack think) by St. Basil ("De Spir. Sanct.", xxix), where he says, "I draw attention to his [Eusebius's] words in discussing the difficulties started in connexion with ancient polygamy." Arguing from St. Basil's words, Lightfoot thinks that in this treatise Eusebius dealt with the difficulty presented by the Patriarchs possessing more than one wife. But he overlooked the reference in the "Dem. Ev.", from which it would appear that the difficulty dealt with was, perhaps, a more general one, viz., the contrast presented by the desire of the Patriarchs for a numerous offspring and the honour in which continence was held by Christians.

C. Exegetical

(16) Eusebius narrates, in his Life of Constantine (IV, 36, 37), how he was commissioned by the emperor to prepare fifty sumptuous copies of the Bible for use in the Churches of Constantinople. Some scholars have supposed that the Codex Sinaiticus was one of these copies. Lightfoot rejects this view chiefly on the ground that "the Text of the codex in many respects differs too widely from the readings found in Eusebius'.

(17) Sections and Canons. Eusebius drew up ten canons, the first containing a list of passages common to all four Evangelists; the second, those common to the first three and so on. He also divided the Gospels into sections numbered continuously. A number, against a section, referred the reader to the particular canon where he could find the parallel sections or passages.

(18) The labours of Pamphilus and Eusebius in editing the Septuagint have already been spoken of. They "believed (as did St. Jerome nearly a century afterwards) that Origen had succeeded in restoring the old Greek version to its primitive purity". The result was a "mischievous mixture of the Alexandrian version with the versions of Aquila and Theodotion" (Swete, "Introd. to O. T. in Greek", pp. 77, 78). For the labours of the two friends on the text of the N. T. the reader may be referred to Rousset, "Textcritische Studien zum N. T.", c. ii. Whether as in the case of the Old Testament, they worked on any definite critical principles is not known.

(19) (a) Interpretation of the ethnological terms in the Hebrew Scriptures; (b) Chronography of Ancient Judaea with the Inheritances of the Ten Tribes; (c) A plan of Jerusalem and the Temple; (d) on the Names of Places in the Holy Scriptures. These four works were written at the request of Eusebius's friend Paulinus. Only the fourth is extant. It is known as the "Topics," or the "Onomasticon".

(20) On the nomenclature of the Book of the Prophets. This work gives a short biography of each Prophet and an account of his prophecies.

(21) Commentary on the Psalms. There are many gaps in the MSS. of this work, and they end in the 118th Psalm. The missing portions are in part supplied by extracts from the Catenae. An allusion to the discovery of the Holy Sepulchre fixes the date at about 330. Lightfoot speaks very highly of this commentary.

(22) Commentary on Isaiah, written after the persecution.

(23 to 28) Commentaries on other books of Holy Scripture, of some of which what may be extracts are preserved.

(29) Commentary on St. Luke, of which what seem to be extracts are preserved.

(30) Commentary on I Cor., the existence of which seems to be implied by St. Jerome (Ep. xlix).

(31) Commentary on Hebrews. A passage that seems to belong to such a commentary was discovered and published by Mai.

(32) On the Discrepancies of the Gospels, in two parts. An epitome, very probably from the hand of Eusebius, of this work was discovered and published by Mai in 1825. Extracts from the original are preserved. Of the two parts, the first, dedicated to a certain Stephen, discusses questions respecting the genealogies of Christ; the second, dedicated to one Marinus, questions concerning the Resurrection. The Discrepancies were largely borrowed from by St. Jerome and St. Ambrose, and have thus indirectly exercised a considerable influence on Biblical studies.

(33) General Elementary Introduction, consisting of ten books, of which VI-IX are

extant under the title of "Prophetical Extracts". These were written during the persecution. There are also a few fragments of the remaining books. "This work seems to have been a general introduction to theology, and its contents were very miscellaneous as the extant remains show" (L., p. 339).

D. Dogmatic

(34) The Apology for Origen. This work has already been mentioned in connexion with Pamphilus. It consisted of six books, the last of which was added by Eusebius. Only the first book is extant, in a translation by Rufinus.

(35) "Against Marcellus, Bishop of Ancyra", and (36) "On the Theology of the Church", a refutation of Marcellus. In two articles in the "Zeitschrift für die Neutest. Wissenschaft" (vol. IV, pp. 330 sqq. and vol. VI, pp. 250 sqq.), written in English, Prof. Conybeare has maintained that our Eusebius could not have been the author of the two treatises against Marcellus. His arguments are rejected by Prof. Klostermann, in his introduction to these two works published in 1905 for the Berlin edition of the Greek Fathers. The "Contra Marcellum" was written after 336 to justify the action of the synod held at Constantinople when Marcellus was deposed; the "Theology" a year or two later.

(37) "On the Paschal Festival" (a mystical interpretation). This work was addressed to Constantine (Vit. Const., IV, 35, 3l6). A long fragment of it was discovered by Mai.

(38) A treatise against the Manichæans is perhaps implied by Epiphanius (Hær., lxvi, 21).

E. Orations and Sermons

(39) At the Dedication of the Church in Tyre (see above).

(40) At the Vicennalia of Constantine. This seems to have been the opening address delivered at the Council of Nicæa. It is not extant.

(41) On the Sepulchre of the Saviour, A. D. 325 (Vit. Const., IV, 33) not extant.

(42) At the Tricennalia of Constantine. This work is generally known as the "De Laudibus Constantini". The second part (11-18) seems to have been a separate oration joined on to the Tricennalia.

(43) "In Praise of the Martyrs". This oration is preserved in the same MS. as the "Theophania" and "Martyrs of Palestine". It was published and translated in the "Journal of Sacred Literature" by Mr. H. B. Cowper (New Series, V, pp. 403 sqq., and ibid. VI, pp. 129 sqq.).

(44) On the Failure of Rain, not extant.

F. Letters

The history of the preservation of the three letters, (45) to Alexander of Alexandria, (46) to Euphrasion, or Euphration, (47) to the Empress Constantia, is sufficiently curious. Constantia asked Eusebius to send her a certain likeness of Christ of which she had heard; his refusal was couched in terms which centuries afterwards were appealed to by the Iconoclasts. A portion of this letter was read at the Second Council of Nicæa, and against it were set portions from the letters to Alexander and Euphrasion to prove that Eusebius "was delivered up to a reprobate sense, and of one mind and opinion with those who followed the Arian superstition" (Labbe, "Conc.", VIII, 1143-1147; Mansi, "Conc.", XIII, 313-317). Besides the passage quoted in the council, other parts of the letter to Constantia are extant.

(48) To the Church of Cæsarea after the Council of Nicæa.

F.J. Bacchus, The Catholic Encyclopedia

Part Five

Martyrs from the Fifth to the Fifteenth Centuries

Contents

1. Introduction

Persecution

General persecution may be defined in general as the unlawful coercion of another's liberty or his unlawful punishment, for not every kind of punishment can be regarded as persecution. For our purpose it must be still further limited to the sphere of religion, and in that sense persecution means unlawful coercion or punishment for religion's sake.

The Church has suffered many kinds of persecution. The growth and the continued existence of Christianity have been hindered by cultured paganism and by savage heathenism. And in more recent times agnosticism has harassed the Church in the various states of America and Europe. But most deplorable of all persecutions have been those that Catholicism has suffered from other Christians. With regard to these it has to be considered that the Church herself has appealed to force, and that, not only in her own defence, but also, so it is objected, in unprovoked attack. Thus by means of the Inquisition (q. v.) or religious wars she was herself the aggressor in many instances during the Middle Ages and in the time of the Reformation. And even if the answer be urged that she was only defending her own existence, the retort seems fairly plausible that pagan and heathen powers were only acting in their own defence when they prohibited the spread of Christianity. The Church would therefore seem to be strangely inconsistent, for while she claims toleration and liberty for herself she has been and still remains intolerant of all other religions.

In answer to this objection, we may admit the fact and yet deny the conclusion. The Church claims to carry a message or rather a command from God and to be God's only messenger. In point of fact it is only within recent years, when toleration is supposed to have become a dogma, that the other "champions of Revelation" have abandoned their similar claims. That they should abandon their right to command allegiance is a natural consequence of Protestantism; whereas it is the Church's claim to be the accredited and infallible ambassador of God which justifies her apparent inconsistency. Such intolerance, however, is not the same as persecution, by which we understand the unlawful exercise of coercion. Every corporation lawfully constituted has the right to coerce its subjects within due limits. And though the Church exercises that right for the most part by spiritual sanctions, she has never relinquished the right to use other means. Before examining this latter right to physical coercion, there must be introduced the important distinction between pagans and Christians. Regularly, force has not been employed against pagan or Jew: "For what have I to do to judge them that are without?" (I Cor., v, 12).

Instances of compulsory conversions such as have occurred at different periods of the Church's history must be ascribed to the misplaced zeal of autocratic individuals. But the Church does claim the right to coerce her own subjects. Here again, however, a distinction must be made. The non-Catholic Christians of our day are, strictly speaking, her subjects; but in her legislation she treats them as if they were not her subjects. The "Ne temere", e. g., of Pius X (1907), recognizes the marriages of Protestants as valid, though not contracted according to Catholic conditions: and the laws of abstinence are not considered to be binding on Protestants. So, with regard to her right to use coercion, the Church only exercises her authority over those whom she considers personally and formally apostates. A modern Protestant is not in the same category with the Albigenses or Wyclifites. These were held to be personally responsible for their apostasy; and the Church enforced her authority over them: It is true that in many cases the heretics were rebels against the State also; but the Church's claim to exercise coercion is not confined to such cases of social disorder. And what is more, her purpose was not only to protect the faith of the orthodox, but also to punish the apostates. Formal apostasy was then looked upon as treason against God a much more heinous crime than treason against a civil ruler, which, until recent times, was punished with great severity. It was a poisoning of the life of the soul in others (St. Thomas Aquinas, II-II, Q. xi, articles 3, 4.) There can be no doubt, therefore, that the Church claimed the right to use physical coercion against formal apostates. Not, of course, that she would exercise her authority in the same way to-day, even if there were a Catholic State in which other Christians were personally and formally apostates. She adapts her discipline to the times and circumstances in order that it may fulfil its salutary purpose. Her own children are not punished by fines, imprisonment, or other temporal punishments, but by spiritual pains and penalties, and heretics are treated as she treated pagans: "Fides suadenda est, non imponenda" (Faith is a matter of persuasion, not of compulsion) a sentiment that roes back to St. Basil ("Revue de l'Orient Chrétien", 2nd series, XIV, 1909, 38) and to St. Ambrose, in the fourth century, the latter applying it even to the treatment of formal apostates. It must also be remembered that when she did use her right to exercise physical coercion over formal apostates, that right was then universally admitted. Churchmen had naturally the ideas of their time as to why and how penalties should be inflicted. Withal, the Roman Inquisition (q. v.) was very different from that of Spain, and the popes did not approve the harsh proceedings of the latter. Moreover, such ideas of physical coercion in matters spiritual were not peculiar to Catholics. The Reformers were not less, but, If anything, more, intolerant. If the intolerance of Churchmen is blamable, then that of the Reformers is doubly so. From their own standpoint, it was unjustifiable. First, they were in revolt against the established authority of the Church, and secondly they could hardly use force to compel the unwilling to conform to their own principle of private judgment. With this clear demarcation of the Reformer's private judgment from the Catholic's authority, it hardly serves our purpose to estimate the relative violence of Catholic and Protestant Governments during the times of the Reformation. And yet it is well to remember that the methods of the maligned Inquisition in Spain and Italy were far less destructive of life than the religious wars of France and Germany. What is, however, more to our purpose is to notice the outspoken intolerance of the Protestant leaders; for it gave an additional right to the Church to appeal to force. She was punishing her defaulting subjects and at the same time defending herself against their attacks.

Such compulsion, therefore, as is used by legitimate authority cannot be called persecution, nor can its victims be called martyrs. It is not enough that those who are condemned to death should be suffering for their religious opinions. A martyr is a witness to the truth; whereas those who suffered the extreme penalty of the Church were at the most the witnesses to their own sincerity, and therefore unhappily no more than pseudo-martyrs. We need not dwell upon the second objection which pretends that a pagan government might be justified in harassing Christian missionaries in so far as it considered Christianity to be subversive of established authority. The Christian revelation is the supernatural message of the Creator to His creatures, to which there can be no lawful resistance. Its missionaries have the right and the duty to preach it everywhere. They who die in the propagation or maintenance of the Gospel are God's witnesses to the truth, suffering persecution for His sake.

Outline of principal persecutions

The brief outline here given of persecutions directed against the Church follows the chronological order, and is scarcely more than a catalogue of the principal formal and public onslaughts against Catholicism. Nor does it take into account other forms of attack, e. g., literary and social persecution, some form of suffering for Christ's sake being a sure note of the True Church (John, xv, 20; II Tim., iii, 12; Matt., x, 23). For a popular general account of persecutions of Catholics previous to the nineteenth century.

ROMAN PERSECUTIONS (52-312)

Under Julian the Apostate (361-63)

Constantine's edict of toleration had accelerated the final triumph of Christianity. But the extreme measures passed against the ancient religion of the empire, and especially by Constans, even though they were not strictly carried out, roused considerable opposition. And when Julian the Apostate (361-63) came to the throne, he supported the defenders of paganism, though he strove to strengthen the old religion by recommending works of charity and a priesthood of Strictly moral lives which, a thing unheard of, should preach and instruct. State protection was withdrawn from Christianity, and no section of the Church favoured more than another, so that the Donatists and Arians were enabled to return.

All the privileges formerly granted to clerics were repealed; civil jurisdiction taken from the bishops, and the subsidies to widows and virgins stopped. Higher education, also, was taken out of the hands of Christians by the prohibition of anyone who was not a pagan from teaching classical literature. And finally, the tombs of martyrs were destroyed. The emperor was afraid to proceed to direct persecution, but he fomented the dissensions among the Christians, and he tolerated and even encouraged the persecutions raised by pagan communities and governors, especially in Alexandria, Heliopolis, Maiouma, the port of Gaza, Antioch, Arethusa, and Cæsarea in Cappadocia. Many, in different places, suffered and even died for the Faith, though another pretext was found for their death, at least by the emperor. Of the martyrs of this period mention may be made of John and Paul (q. v.), who suffered in Rome; the soldiers Juventinus and Maximian (cf. St. John Chrysostom's sermon on them in P. G., L, 571-77); Macedonius, Tatian, and Theodulus of Meros in Phrygia (Socrates, III, 15; Sozomen, V, 11); Basil, a priest of Ancyra (Sozomen, V, 11). Julian himself seems to have ordered the executions of John and Paul, the steward and secretary respectively of Constantia, daughter of Constantine. However, he reigned only for two years, and his persecution was, in the words of St. Athanasius, "but a passing cloud".

Persia

When the persecution of Christianity was abandoned by the Roman Government, it was taken up by Rome's traditional enemy, the Persians, though formerly they had been more or less tolerant of the new religion. On the outbreak of war between the two empires, Sapor II (310-80), under the instigation of the Persian priests, initiated a severe persecution of the Christians in 339 or 340. It comprised the destruction or confiscation of churches and a general massacre, especially of bishops and priests. The number of victims, according to Sozomen (Hist. Eccl., II, 9-14), was no less than 16,000, among them being Symeon, Bishop of Seleucia; there was a respite from the general persecution, but it was resumed and with still greater violence by Bahram V (420-38), who persecuted savagely for one year, and was not prevented from causing numerous individual martyrdoms by the treaty he made (422) with Theodosius II, guaranteeing liberty of conscience to the Christians. Yezdegerd II (438-57), his successor, began a fierce persecution in 445 or 446, traces of which are found shortly before 450. The persecution of Chosroes I from 541 to 545 was directed chiefly against the bishops and clergy. He also destroyed churches and monasteries and imprisoned Persian noblemen who had become Christians. The last persecution by Persian kings was that of Chosroes II (590-628), who made war on all Christians alike during 627 and 628. Speaking generally, the dangerous time for the Church in Persia was when the kings were at war with the Roman Empire.

Among the Goths

Christianity was introduced among the Goths about the middle of the third century, and "Theophilus Episcopus Gothiæ" was present at the Council of Nicæa (325). But, owing to the exertions of Bishop Ulfilas (340, died 383), an Arian, Arianism was professed by the great majority of the

Visigoths of Dacia (Transylvania and West Hungary), converts from paganism; and it passed with them into Lower Mysia across the Danube, when a Gothic chieftain, after a cruel persecution drove Ulfilas and his converts from his lands, probably in 349. And subsequently, when in 370 the Visigoths, pressed by the Huns, crossed the Danube and entered the Roman Empire, Arianism was the religion practised by the Emperor Valens. This fact, along with the national character given to Arianism by Ulfilas (q. v.), made it the form of Christianity adopted also by the Ostrogoths, from whom it spread to the Burgundians, Suevi, Vandals, and Lombards.

The first persecution we hear of was that directed by the pagan Visigoth King Athanaric. begun about 370 and lasting for two, or perhaps six, years after his war with Valens. St. Sabas was drowned in 372, others were burnt, sometimes in a body in the tents which were used as churches. When, in the fifth and sixth centuries, the Visigoths invaded Italy, Gaul, and Spain, the churches were plundered, and the Catholic bishops and clergy were often murdered; but their normal attitude was one of toleration, Euric (483), the Visigoth King of Toulouse, is especially mentioned by Sidonius Apollinaris (Ep. vii, 6) as a hater of Catholicism and a persecutor of the Catholics, though it is not clear that he persecuted to death. In Spain there was persecution at least from time to time during the period 476-586, beginning with the aforesaid Euric, who occupied Catalonia in 476. We hear of persecution by Agila (549-554) also, and finally by Leovigild (573-86). Bishops were exiled and church goods seized. His son Hermenigild, a convert to the Catholic Faith, is described in the seventh century (e. g. by St. Gregory the Great) as a martyr. A contemporary chronicler, John of Biclaro, who had himself suffered for the Faith, says that the prince was murdered in prison by an Arian, Sisibert; but he does not say that Leovigild approved of the murder. With the accession of Reccared, who had become a Catholic, Arianism ceased to be the creed of the Spanish Visigoths.

As for the Ostrogoths, they seem to have been fairly tolerant, after the first violences of the invasion. A notable exception was the persecution of Theodoric (524-26). It was prompted by the repressive measures which Justin I had issued against the Arians of the Eastern Empire, among whom Goths would of coarse be included. One of the victims of the persecution was Pope John I who died in prison.

Among the Lombards

St. Gregory the Great, in parts of his "Dialogues", describes the sufferings which Catholics had to endure at the time of the Lombard invasion under Alboin (568) and afterwards. But on the whole, after Autharis's death (590) the Lombards were not troublesome, except perhaps in the Duchies of Benevento and Spoleto. Autharis's queen, Theudelinda, a Catholic princess of Bavaria, was able to use her influence with her second husband, Agilulf, Autharis's successor, so that he, although probably remaining an Arian, was friendly to the Church and allowed his son to be baptized a Catholic.

Among the Vandals

The Vandals, Arians like the Visigoths and the others, were the most hostile of all towards the Church. During the period of their domination in Spain (422-29) the Church suffered persecution, the details of which are unknown. In 429, under the lead of Genseric, the Goths crossed over to Africa, and by 455 had made themselves masters of Roman Africa. In the North, the bishops were driven from their sees into exile. When Carthage was taken in 439 the churches were given over to the Arian clergy, and the bishop Quodvultdeus (a friend of St. Augustine) and the greater part of the Catholic clergy were stripped of what they had, put on board unseaworthy ships, and carried to Naples. Confiscation of church property and exile of the clergy was the rule throughout the provinces of the North, where all public worship was forbidden to Catholics. In the provinces of the South, however, the persecution was not severe. Some Catholic court officials, who had accompanied Genseric from Spain, were tortured, exiled, and finally put to death because they refused to apostatize. No Catholic, in fact, was allowed to hold any office.

Genseric's son, Huneric, who succeeded in 477, though at first somewhat tolerant, arrested and banished under circumstances of great cruelty nearly five thousand Catholics, including bishops and clergy, and finally by an edict of 25 Feb., 484, abolished the Catholic worship, transferred all churches and church property to the Arians, exiled the bishops and clergy, and deprived of civil rights all those who would not receive Arian baptism. Great numbers suffered savage treatment, many died, others were mutilated or crippled for life. His successor, Guntamund (484-96), did not relax the persecution until 487. But in 494 the bishops were recalled, though they had afterwards to endure some persecution from Trasamund (496-523). And complete peace came to the Church at the accession of Genseric's son Hilderic, with whom the Vandal domination ended.

In Arabia

Christianity penetrated into South Arabia (Yemen) in the fourth century. In the sixth century the Christians were brutally persecuted by the Jewish King Dunaan, no less than five thousand, including the prince, Arethas, being said to have suffered execution in 523 after the capture of Nagra. The Faith was only saved from utter extinction at this period by the armed intervention of the King of Abyssinia. And it did in fact disappear before the invading forces of Islam.

Under the Muslims

With the spread of Mohammedanism in Syria, Egypt, Persia, and North Africa, there went a gradual subjugation of Christianity. At the first onset of invasion, in the eighth Century, many Christians were butchered for refusing to apostatize; afterwards they were treated as helots, subject to a special tax, and liable to suffer loss of goods or life itself at the caprice of the caliph or the populace. In Spain the first Mohammedan ruler to institute a violent persecution of the Christians was the viceroy Abderrahman II (821-52). The persecution was begun in 850, was continued by Mohammed (852-87) and lasted with interruptions till 960, when the Christians were strong enough to intimidate their persecutors. The number of martyrs was small, Eulogius, Archbishop of Toledo (11 March, 859), who has left us an account of the persecution, being himself the most famous.

Under the Iconoclasts

The troubles brought on the Church of the East by the Iconoclastic emperors cover a period of one hundred and twenty years. Leo III (the Isaurian) published two edicts against images about 726 and 730. The execution of the edicts was strenuously resisted. Popes Gregory II and III protested in vigorous language against the autocratic reformer, and the people resorted to open violence. But Constantine V (Copronymus, 741-75) continued his father's policy, summoning a council at Constantinople in 754 and then persecuting the orthodox party. The monks formed the especial object of his attack. Monasteries were demolished, and the monks themselves shamefully maltreated and put to death. Under Constantine VI (780-97), through the influence of his mother, the regent Irene, the Seventh ecumenical Council was summoned in 787, and rescinded the decrees of Copronymus's Council. But there was a revival of the persecution under Leo V (813-20), the bishops who stood firm, as well as the monks, being the special objects of his attack, while many others were directly done to death or died as a result of cruel treatment in prison. This persecution, which was continued under Michael II (820-29), reached its most fierce phase under Theophilus (829-42). Great numbers of monks were put to death by this monarch; but at his decease the persecutions ended (842).

Modern period

We have reviewed the persecutions undergone by the Church during the first millennium of her existence. During her second millennium she has continued to suffer persecution in her mission of spreading the Gospel, and especially in Japan and China. She has also had to face the attacks of her own children, culminating in the excesses and religious wars of the Reformation.

POLAND

Within the last century, Poland has suffered what is perhaps the most notable of recent persecutions. Catholicism had continued to be the established religion of the country until the intervention of Catherine II of Russia (1762-96). By means of political intrigues and open hostility, she first of all secured a position of political suzerainty over the country, and then effected the separation of the Ruthenians from the Holy See, and incorporated them with the Orthodox Church of Russia. Nicholas I (1825-55), and Alexander II (1855-81), resumed her policy of intimidation and forcible suppression. The latter monarch especially showed himself a violent persecutor of the Catholics, the barbarities that were committed in 1863 being so savage as to call forth a joint protest from the Governments of France, Austria, and Great Britain. After his death the Catholics were granted a certain measure of toleration, and in 1905 Nicholas II granted them full liberty of worship.

LIBERALISM

A new spirit of opposition appears in the so-called "Liberalism" and in Free Thought, whose influence has been felt in Catholic as well as Protestant countries. Its origin is to be traced back to the infidel philosophy of the eighteenth century. At the end of that century it had grown so strong that it could menace the Church with armed violence. In France six hundred priests were murdered by Jourdan, "the Beheader", in 1791, and in the next year three hundred ecclesiastics, including an archbishop and two bishops, were cruelly massacred in the prisons of Paris. The Reign of Terror ended in 1795. But the spirit of infidelity which triumphed then has ever since sought and found opportunities for persecution. And it has been assisted by the endeavours of even so-called Catholic governments to subordinate the Church to the State, or to separate the two powers altogether. In Switzerland the Catholics were so incensed by the attacks of the Liberal party on their religious freedom that they resolved on an appeal to arms. Their Sonderbund (q. v.) or "Separate League" was at first successful in the war of 1843, and in spite of its final defeat by the forces of the Diet in 1847 the result has been to secure religious liberty throughout Switzerland. Since that time the excitement caused by the decree on Papal Infallibility found vent in another period of hostile legislation; but the Catholics have been strong enough to maintain and reinforce their position in the country.

In other countries Liberalism has not issued in such direct warfare against the Church; though the defenders of the Church have often been ranged against revolutionaries who were attacking the altar along with the throne. But the history of the nineteenth century reveals a constant opposition to the Church. Her influence has been straitened by adverse legislation, the monastic orders have been expelled and their property confiscated, and, what is perhaps most characteristic of modern persecution, religion has been excluded from the schools and universities. The underlying principle is always the same, though the form it assumes and the occasion of its development are peculiar to the different times and places. Gallicanism in France, Josephinism in Austria, and the May Laws of the German Empire have all the same principle of subordinating the Church to the Government, or separating the two powers by a secularist and unnatural divorce. But the solidarity of Catholics and the energetic protests of the Holy See succeeded often in establishing Concordats to safeguard the independent rights of the Church. The terms of these concessions have not always been observed by Liberal or Absolutist Governments. Still they saved the Church in her time of peril. And the enforced separation of Church from State which followed the renunciation of the Concordats has taught the Catholics in Latin countries the dangers of Secularism (q. v.) and how they must defend their rights as members of a Church which transcends the limits of states and nations, and acknowledges an authority beyond the reach of political legislation. In the Teutonic countries, on the other hand, the Church does not loom so large a target for the missiles of her enemies. Long years of persecution have done their work, and left the Catholics with a greater need and a greater sense of solidarity. There is less danger of confusing friend and foe, and the progress of the Church is made more apparent.

James Bridge, The Catholic Encyclopedia, Volume 11

Martyr

The Greek word *martus* signifies a witness who testifies to a fact of which he has knowledge from personal observation. It is in this sense that the term first appears in Christian literature; the Apostles were "witnesses" of all that they had observed in the public life of Christ, as well as of all they had learned from His teaching, "in Jerusalem, and in all Judea, and Samaria, and even to the uttermost part of the earth" (Acts, i, 8). St. Peter, in his address to the Apostles and disciples relative to the election of a successor to Judas, employs the term with this meaning: "Wherefore, of these men who have companied with us all the time that the Lord Jesus came in and went out among us, beginning from the baptism of John until the day he was taken up from us, one of these must be made witness with us of his resurrection" (Acts, i, 22). In his first public discourse the chief of the Apostles speaks of himself and his companions as "witnesses" who saw the risen Christ and subsequently, after the miraculous escape of the Apostles from prison, when brought a second time before the tribunal, Peter again alludes to the twelve as witnesses to Christ, as the Prince and Saviour of Israel, Who rose from the dead; and added that in giving their public testimony to the facts, of which they were certain, they must obey God rather than man (Acts, v, 29 sqq.). In his First Epistle St. Peter also refers to himself as a "witness of the sufferings of Christ" (I Pet., v. 1).

But even in these first examples of the use of the word martus in Christian terminology a new shade of meaning is already noticeable, in addition to the accepted signification of the term. The disciples of Christ were no ordinary witnesses such as those who gave testimony in a court of justice. These latter ran no risk in bearing testimony to facts that came under their observation, whereas the witnesses of Christ were brought face to face daily, from the beginning of their apostolate, with the possibility of incurring severe punishment and even death itself. Thus, St. Stephen was a witness who early in the history of Christianity sealed his testimony with his blood. The careers of the Apostles were at all times beset with dangers of the gravest character, until eventually they all suffered the last penalty for their convictions. Thus, within the lifetime of the Apostles, the term martus came to be used in the sense of a witness who at any time might be called upon to deny what he testified to, under penalty of death. From this stage the transition was easy to the ordinary meaning of the term, as used ever since in Christian literature: a martyr, or witness of Christ, is a person who, though he has never seen nor heard the Divine Founder of the Church, is yet so firmly convinced of the truths of the Christian religion, that he gladly suffers death rather than deny it. St. John, at the end of the first century, employs the word with this meaning; Antipas, a convert from paganism, is spoken of as a "faithful witness (martus) who was slain among you, where Satan dwelleth" (Apoc., ii, 13). Further on the same Apostle speaks of the "souls of them that were slain for the Word of God and for the testimony (martyrian) which they held" (Apoc., vi, 9). Yet, it was only by degrees, in the course of the first age of the Church, that the term martyr came to be exclusively applied to those who had died for the faith. The grandsons of St. Jude, for example, on their escape from the peril they underwent when cited before Domitian were afterwards regarded as martyrs (Euseb., "list. eccl", III, xx, xxxii). The famous confessors of Lyons, who endured so bravely awful tortures for their belief, were looked upon by their fellow-Christians as martyrs, but they themselves declined this title as of right belonging only to those who had actually died: "They are already martyrs whom Christ has deemed worthy to be taken up in their confession, having sealed their testimony by their departure; but we are confessors mean and lowly" (Euseb., op. cit., V, ii).

This distinction between martyrs and confessors is thus traceable to the latter part of the second century: those only were martyrs who had suffered the extreme penalty, whereas the title of confessors was given to Christians who had shown their willingness to die for their belief, by bravely enduring imprisonment or torture, but were not put to death. Yet the term martyr was still sometimes applied during the third century to persons still living, as, for instance, by St. Cyprian, who gave the title of martyrs to a number of bishops, priests, and laymen condemned to penal servitude in the mines (Ep. 76). Tertullian speaks of those arrested as Christians and not yet condemned as martyres designati. In the fourth century, St. Gregory of Nazianzus alludes to St. Basil as "a martyr", but evidently employs the term in the broad sense in which the word is still sometimes applied to a person who has borne many and grave hardships in the cause of Christianity. The description of a martyr given by the pagan historian Ammianus Marcellinus (XXII, xvii), shows that by the middle of the fourth century the title was everywhere reserved to those who had actually suffered death for their faith. Heretics and schismatics put to death as Christians were denied the title of martyrs (St. Cyprian, "De Unit.", xiv; St. Augustine, Ep. 173; Euseb., "Hist. Eccl.", V, xvi, xxi). St. Cyprian lays down clearly the general principle that "he cannot be a martyr who is not in the Church; he cannot attain unto the kingdom who forsakes that which shall reign there." St. Clement of Alexandria strongly disapproves (Strom., IV, iv) of some heretics who gave themselves up to the law; they "banish themselves without being martyrs".

The orthodox were not permitted to seek martyrdom. Tertullian, however, approves the conduct of the Christians of a province of Asia who gave themselves up to the governor, Arrius Antoninus (Ad. Scap., v). Eusebius also relates with approval the incident of three Christians of C'sarea in Palestine who, in the persecution of Valerian, presented themselves to the judge and were condemned to death (Hist. Eccl., VII, xii). But while circumstances might sometimes excuse such a course, it was generally held to be imprudent. St. Gregory of Nazianzus sums up in a sentence the rule to be followed in such cases: it is mere rashness to seek death, but it is cowardly to refuse it (Orat. xlii, 5, 6). The example of a Christian of Smyrna named Quintus, who, in the time of St. Polycarp, persuaded several of his fellow believers to declare themselves Christians, was a warning of what might happen to the over- zealous: Quintus at the last moment apostatized, though his companions persevered. Breaking idols was condemned by the Council of Elvira (306), which, in its sixtieth canon, decreed that a Christian put to death for such vandalism would not be enrolled as a martyr. Lactantius, on the other hand, has only mild censure for a Christian of Nicomedia who suffered martyrdom for tearing down the edict of persecution (Do mort. pers., xiii). In one case St. Cyprian authorizes seeking martyrdom. Writing to his priests and deacons regarding repentant lapsi who were clamouring to be received back into communion, the bishop after giving general directions on the subject, concludes by saying that if these impatient personages are so eager to get back to the Church there is a way of doing so open to them. "The struggle is still going forward", he says, "and the strife is waged daily. If they (the lapsi) truly and with constancy repent of what they have done, and the fervour of their faith prevails, he who cannot be delayed may be crowned" (Ep. xiii).

Legal basis of the persecutions

Acceptance of the national religion in antiquity was an obligation incumbent on all citizens; failure to worship the gods of the

State was equivalent to treason. This universally accepted principle is responsible for the various persecutions suffered by Christians before the reign of Constantine; Christians denied the existence of and therefore refused to worship the gods of the state pantheon. They were in consequence regarded as atheists. It is true, indeed, that the Jews also rejected the gods of Rome, and yet escaped persecution. But the Jews, from the Roman standpoint, had a national religion and a national God, Jehovah, whom they had a full legal right to worship. Even after the destruction of Jerusalem, when the Jews ceased to exist as a nation, Vespasian made no change in their religious status, save that the tribute formerly sent by Jews to the temple at Jerusalem was henceforth to be paid to the Roman exchequer. For some time after its establishment, the Christian Church enjoyed the religious privileges of the Jewish nation, but from the nature of the case it is apparent that the chiefs of the Jewish religion would not long permit without protest this state of things. For they abhorred Christ's religion as much as they abhorred its Founder. At what date the Roman authorities had their attention directed to the difference between the Jewish and the Christian religion cannot be determined, but it appears to be fairly well established that laws proscribing Christianity were enacted before the end of the first century. Tertullian is authority for the statement that persecution of the Christians was institutum Neronianum an institution of Nero (Ad nat., i, 7). The First Epistle of St. Peter also Clearly alludes to the proscription of Christians, as Christians, at the time it was written (I, St. Peter, iv, 16). Domitian (81-96) also, is known to have punished with death Christian members of his own family on the charge of atheism (Suetonius, "Domitianus", xv). While it is therefore probable that the formula: "Let there be no Christians" (Christiani non sint) dates from the second half of the first century, yet the earliest clear enactment on the subject of Christianity is that of Trajan (98-117) in his famous letter to the younger Pliny, his legate in Bithynia.

Pliny had been sent from Rome by the emperor to restore order in the Province of Bithynia-Pontus. Among the difficulties he encountered in the execution of his commission one of the most serious concerned the Christians. The extraordinarily large number of Christians he found within his jurisdiction greatly surprised him: the contagion of their "Superstition", he reported to Trajan, affected not only the cities but even the villages and country districts of the province (Pliny, Ep., x, 96). One consequence of the general defection from the state religion was of an economic order: so many people had become Christians that purchasers were no longer found for the victims that once in great numbers were offered to the gods. Complaints were laid before the legate relative to this state of affairs, with the result that some Christians were arrested and brought before Pliny for examination. The suspects were interrogated as to their tenets and those of them who persisted in declining repeated invitations to recant were executed. Some of the prisoners, however, after first affirming that they were Christians, afterwards, when threatened with punishment, qualified their first admission by saying that at one time they had been adherents of the proscribed body but were so no longer. Others again denied that they were or ever had been Christians. Having never before had to deal with questions concerning Christians Pliny applied to the emperor for instructions on three points regarding which he did not see his way clearly: first, whether the age of the accused should be taken into consideration in meting out punishment; secondly, whether Christians who renounced their belief should be pardoned; and thirdly, whether the mere profession of Christianity should be regarded as a crime, and punishable as such, independent of the fact of the innocence or guilt of the accused of the crimes ordinarily associated with such profession.

To these inquiries Trajan replied in a rescript which was destined to have the force of law throughout the second century in relation to Christianity. After approving what his representative had already done, the emperor directed that in future the rule to be observed in dealing with Christians should be the following: no steps were to be taken by magistrates to ascertain who were or who were not Christians, but at the same time, if any person was denounced, and admitted that he was a Christian, he was to be punished evidently with death. Anonymous denunciations were not to be acted upon, and on the other hand, those who repented of being Christians and offered sacrifice to the gods, were to be pardoned. Thus, from the year 112, the date of this document, perhaps even from the reign of Nero, a Christian was ipso facto an outlaw. That the followers of Christ were known to the highest authorities of the State to be innocent of the numerous crimes and misdemeanors attributed to them by popular calumny, is evident from Pliny's testimony to this effect, as well as from Trajan's order: conquirendi non sunt. And that the emperor did not regard Christians as a menace to the State is apparent from the general tenor of his instructions. Their only crime was that they were Christians, adherents of an illegal religion. Under this regime of proscription the Church existed from the year 112 to the reign of Septimius Severus (193-211). The position of the faithful was always one of grave danger, being as they were at the mercy of every malicious person who might, without a moment's warning, cite them before the nearest tribunal. It is true indeed, that the delator was an unpopular person in the Roman Empire, and, besides, in accusing a Christian he ran the risk of incurring severe punishment if unable to make good his charge against his intended victim. In spite of the danger, however, instances are known, in the persecution era, of Christian victims of delation.

The prescriptions of Trajan on the subject of Christianity were modified by Septimius Severus by the addition of a clause forbidding any person to become a Christian. The existing law of Trajan against Christians in general was not, indeed, repealed by Severus, though for the moment it was evidently the intention of the emperor that it should remain a dead letter. The object aimed at by the new enactment was, not to disturb those already Christians, but to check the growth of the Church by preventing conversions. Some illustrious convert martyrs, the most famous being Sts. Perpetua and Felicitas, were added to the roll of champions of religious freedom by this prohibition, but it effected nothing of consequence in regard to its primary purpose. The persecution came to an end in the second year of the reign of Caracalla (211-17). From this date to the reign of Decius (250-53) the Christians enjoyed comparative peace with the exception of the short period when Maximinus the Thracian (235-38) occupied the throne. The elevation of Decius to the purple began a new era in the relations between Christianity and the Roman State. This emperor, though a native of Illyria, was nevertheless profoundly imbued with the spirit of Roman conservatism. He ascended the throne with the firm intention of restoring the prestige which the empire was fast losing, and he seems to have been convinced that the chief difficulty in the way of effecting his purpose was the existence of Christianity. The consequence was that in the year 250 he issued an edict, the tenor of which is known only from the documents relating to its enforcement, prescribing that all Christians of the empire should on a certain day offer sacrifice to the gods. This new law was quite a different matter from the existing legislation against Christianity. Proscribed though they were legally, Christians had hitherto enjoyed comparative security under a regime which clearly laid down the principle that they were not to be sought after officially by the civil authorities. The edict of Decius was exactly the opposite of this: the magistrates were now constituted religious inquisitors, whose duty it was to punish Christians who refused to apostatize. The emperor's aim, in a word, was to annihilate Christianity by compelling every Christian in the empire to renounce his faith. The first effect of the new legislation seemed favourable to the wishes of its author. During the long interval of peace since the reign of Septimius Severus nearly forty years a considerable amount of laxity had crept into the Church's discipline, one consequence of which was, that on the publication of the edict of persecution, multitudes of Christians besieged the magistrates everywhere in their eagerness to comply with its demands. Many other nominal Christians procured by bribery certificates stating that they had complied with the law, while still others apostatized under torture. Yet after this first throng of weaklings had put themselves outside the pale of Christianity there still remained, in every part of the empire, numerous Christians worthy of their religion, who endured all manner of torture, and death itself, for their convictions. The persecution lasted about eighteen months, and wrought incalculable harm. Before the Church had time to repair the damage thus caused, a new conflict with the State was inaugurated by an edict of Valerian published in 257. This enactment was directed against the clergy, bishops priests, and deacons, who were directed under pain of exile to offer sacrifice. Christians were also forbidden, under pain of death, to resort to their cemeteries. The results of this first edict were of so little moment that the following year, 258, a new edict appeared requiring the clergy to offer sacrifice under penalty of death. Christian senators, knights, and even the ladies of their families, were also affected by an order to offer sacrifice under penalty of confiscation of their goods and reduction to plebeian rank. And in the event of these severe measures proving ineffective the law prescribed further punishment: execution for the men, for the women exile. Christian slaves and freedmen of the emperor's household also were punished by confiscation of their possessions and reduction to the lowest ranks of slavery. Among the martyrs of this persecution were Pope Sixtus II and St. Cyprian of Carthage. Of its further effects little is known, for want of documents, but it seems safe to surmise that, besides adding many new martyrs to the Church's roll, it must have caused enormous suffering to the Christian nobility. The persecution came to an end with the capture (260) of Valerian by the Persians; his successor, Gallienus (260-68), revoked the edict and restored to the bishops the cemeteries and meeting places.

From this date to the last persecution inaugurated by Diocletian (284-305) the Church, save for a short period in the reign of Aurelian (270-75), remained in the same legal situation as in the second century. The first edict of Diocletian was promulgated at Nicomedia in the year 303, and was of the following tenor: Christian assemblies were forbidden; churches and sacred books were ordered to be destroyed, and all Christians were commanded to abjure their religion forthwith. The penalties for failure to comply with these demands were degradation and civil death for the higher classes, reduction to slavery for freemen of the humbler sort, and for slaves incapacity to receive the gift of freedom. Later in the same year a new edict ordered the imprisonment of ecclesiastics of all grades, from bishops to exorcists. A third edict imposed the death-penalty for refusal to abjure, and granted freedom to those who would offer sacrifice; while a fourth enactment, published in 304, commanded everybody without exception to offer sacrifice publicly. This was the last and most determined effort of the Roman State to destroy Christianity. It gave to the Church countless martyrs,, and ended in her triumph in the reign of Constantine.

Number of martyrs

Of the 249 years from the first persecution under Nero (64) to the year 313, when Constantine established lasting peace, it is calculated that the Christians suffered persecution about 129 years and enjoyed a certain degree of toleration about 120 years. Yet it must be borne in mind that even in the years of comparative tranquillity Christians were at all times at the mercy of every person ill-disposed towards them or their religion in the empire. Whether or not delation of Christians occurred frequently during the era of persecution is not known, but taking into consideration the irrational hatred of the pagan population for Christians, it may safely be surmised that not a few Christians suffered martyrdom through betrayal. An example of the kind related by St. Justin Martyr shows how swift and terrible were the consequences of delation. A woman who had been converted to Christianity was accused by her husband before a magistrate of being a Christian. Through influence the accused was granted the favour of a brief respite to settle her worldly affairs, after which she was to appear in court and put forward her defence. Meanwhile her angry husband caused the arrest of the catechist, Ptolom'us by name, who had instructed the convert. Ptolom'us, when questioned, acknowledged that he was a Christian and was condemned to death. In the court, at the time this sentence was pronounced, were two persons who protested against the iniquity of inflicting capital punishment for the mere fact of professing Christianity. The magistrate in reply asked if they also were Christians, and on their answering in the affirmative both were ordered to be executed. As the same fate awaited the wife of the delator also, unless she recanted, we have here an example of three, possibly four, persons suffering capital punishment on the accusation of a man actuated by malice, solely for the reason that his wife had given up the evil life she had previously led in his society (St. Justin Martyr, II, Apol., ii).

As to the actual number of persons who died as martyrs during these two centuries and a half we have no definite information. Tacitus is authority for the statement that an immense multitude (ingens multitudo) were put to death by Nero. The Apocalypse of St. John speaks of "the souls of them that were slain for the word of God" in the reign of Domitian, and Dion Cassius informs us that "many" of the Christian nobility suffered death for their faith during the persecution for which this emperor is responsible. Origen indeed, writing about the year 249, before the edict of Decius, states that the number of those put to death for the Christian religion was not very great, but he probably means that the number of martyrs up to this time was small when compared with the entire number of Christians (cf. Allard, "Ten Lectures on the Martyrs", 128). St. Justin Martyr, who owed his conversion largely to the heroic example of Christians suffering for their faith, incidentally gives a glimpse of the danger of professing Christianity in the middle of the second century, in the reign of so good an emperor as Antoninus Pius (138-61). In his "Dialogue with Trypho" (cx), the apologist, after alluding to the fortitude of his brethren in religion, adds, "for it is plain that, though beheaded, and crucified, and thrown to wild beasts, and chains, and fire, and all other kinds of torture, we do not give up our confession; but, the more such things happen, the more do others in larger numbers become faithful. . . . Every Christian has been driven out not only from his own property, but even from the whole world; for you permit no Christian to live." Tertullian also, writing towards the end of the second century, frequently alludes to the terrible conditions under which Christians existed ("Ad martyres", "Apologia", "Ad Nationes", etc.): death and torture were ever present possibilities.

But the new regime of special edicts, which began in 250 with the edict of Decius, was still more fatal to Christians. The persecutions of Decius and Valerian were not, indeed, of long duration, but while they lasted, and in spite of the large number of those who fell away, there are clear indications that they produced numerous martyrs. Dionysius of Alexandria, for instance, in a letter to the Bishop of Antioch tells of a violent persecution that took place in the Egyptian capital, through popular violence, before the edict of Decius was even published. The Bishop of Alexandria gives several examples of what Christians endured at the hands of the pagan rabble and then adds that "many others, in cities and villages, were torn asunder by the heathen" (Euseb., "Hist. eccl.", VI, xli sq.). Besides those who perished by actual violence, also, a "multitude wandered in the deserts and mountains, and perished of hunger and thirst, of cold and sickness and robbers and wild beasts" (Euseb., l. c.). In another letter, speaking of the persecution under Valerian, Dionysius states that "men and women, young and old, maidens and matrons, soldiers and civilians, of every age and race, some by scourging and fire, others by the sword, have conquered in the strife and won their crowns" (Id., op. cit., VII, xi). At Cirta, in North Africa, in the same persecution, after the execution of Christians had continued for several days, it was resolved to expedite matters. To this end the rest of those condemned were brought to the bank of a river and made to kneel in rows. When all was ready the executioner passed along the ranks and despatched all without further loss of time (Ruinart, p. 231).

But the last persecution was even more severe than any of the previous attempts to extirpate Christianity. In Nicomedia "a great multitude" were put to death with their bishop, Anthimus; of these some perished by the sword, some by fire, while others were drowned. In Egypt "thousands of men, women and children, despising the present life, . . . endured various deaths" (Euseb., "Hist. eccl.", VII, iv sqq.), and the same happened in many other places throughout the East. In the West the persecution came to an end at an earlier date than in the East, but, while it lasted, numbers of martyrs, especially at Rome, were added to the calendar (cf. Allard, op. cit., 138 sq.). But besides those who actually shed their blood in the first three centuries account must be taken of the numerous confessors of the Faith who, in prison, in exile, or in penal servitude suffered a daily martyrdom more difficult to endure than death itself. Thus, while anything like a numerical estimate of the number of martyrs is impossible, yet the meagre evidence on the subject that exists clearly enough establishes the fact that countless men, women and even children, in that glorious, though terrible, first age of Christianity, cheerfully sacrificed their goods, their liberties, or their lives, rather than renounce the faith they prized above all.

Trial of the martyrs

The first act in the tragedy of the martyrs was their arrest by an officer of the law. In some instances the privilege of custodia libera, granted to St. Paul during his first imprisonment, was allowed before the accused were brought to trial; St. Cyprian, for example, was detained in the house of the officer who arrested him, and treated with consideration until the time set for his examination. But such procedure was the exception to the rule; the accused Christians were generally cast into the public prisons, where often, for weeks or months at a time, they suffered the greatest hardships. Glimpses of the sufferings they endured in prison are in rare instances supplied by the Acts of the Martyrs. St. Perpetua, for instance, was horrified by the awful darkness, the intense heat caused by overcrowding in the climate of Roman Africa, and the brutality of the soldiers (Passio SS. Perpet., et Felic., i). Other confessors allude to the various miseries of prison life as beyond their powers of description (Passio SS. Montani, Lucii, iv). Deprived of food, save enough to keep them alive, of water, of light and air; weighted down with irons, or placed in stocks with their legs drawn as far apart as was possible without causing a rupture; exposed to all manner of infection from heat, overcrowding, and the absence of anything like proper sanitary conditions these were some of the afflictions that preceded actual martyrdom. Many naturally, died in prison under such conditions, while others, unfortunately, unable to endure the strain, adopted the easy means of escape left open to them, namely, complied with the condition demanded by the State of offering sacrifice.

Those whose strength, physical and moral, was capable of enduring to the end were, in addition, frequently interrogated in court by the magistrates, who endeavoured by persuasion or torture to induce them to recant. These tortures comprised every means that human ingenuity in antiquity had devised to break down even the most courageous; the obstinate were scourged with whips, with straps, or with ropes; or again they were stretched on the rack and their bodies torn apart with iron rakes. Another awful punishment consisted in suspending the victim, sometimes for a whole day at a time, by one hand; while modest women in addition were exposed naked to the gaze of those in court. Almost worse than all this was the penal servitude to which bishops, priests, deacons, laymen and women, and even children, were condemned in some of the more violent persecutions; these refined personages of both sexes, victims of merciless laws, were doomed to pass the remainder of their days in the darkness of the mines, where they dragged out a wretched existence, half naked, hungry, and with no bed save the damp ground. Those were far more fortunate who were condemned to even the most disgraceful death, in the arena, or by crucifixion.

Honors paid to the martyrs

It is easy to understand why those who endured so much for their convictions should have been so greatly venerated by their co-regionists from even the first days of trial in the reign of Nero. The Roman officials usually permitted relatives or friends to gather up the mutilated remains of the martyrs for interment, although in some instances such permission was refused. These relics the Christians regarded as "more valuable than gold or precious stones" (Martyr. Polycarpi, xviii). Some of the more famous martyrs received special honours, as for instance, in Rome, St. Peter and St. Paul, whose "trophies", or tombs, are spoken of at the beginning of the third century by the Roman priest Caius (Eusebius, "Hist. eccl.", II, xxi, 7). Numerous crypts and chapels in the Roman catacombs, some of which, like the capella gr ca, were constructed in sub-Apostolic times, also bear witness to the early veneration for those champions of freedom of conscience who won, by dying, the greatest victory in the history of the human race. Special commemoration services of the martyrs, at which the holy Sacrifice was offered over their tombs the origin of the time honoured custom of consecrating altars by enclosing in them the relics of martyrs were held on the anniversaries of their death; the famous Fractio Panis fresco of the capella gr ca, dating from the early second century, is probably a representation in miniature, of such a celebration. From the age of Constantine even still greater veneration was accorded the martyrs. Pope Damasus (366-84) had a special love for the martyrs, as we learn from the inscriptions, brought to light by de Rossi, composed by him for their tombs in the Roman catacombs. Later on veneration of the martyrs was occasionally exhibited in a rather undesirable form; many of the frescoes in the catacombs have been mutilated to gratify the ambition of the faithful to be buried near the saints (retro sanctos), in whose company they hoped one day to rise from the grave. In the Middle Ages the esteem in which the martyrs were held was equally great; no hardships were too severe to be endured in visiting famous shrines, like those of Rome, where their relics were contained.

Maurice M. Hassatt, Catholic Encyclopedia, 1909

An Old English Martyrology

From an early period, the Christian church endeavoured to keep alive and to celebrate the memory of its martyrs. They compiled martyrologies and remembered martyrs, usually on the anniversary of their death. This English Martyrology is compiled from manuscripts in the libraries of the British Museum and of Corpus Christi College, Cambridge. The figures in brackets are the age of the martyrs.

DECEMBER

25 Anastasia* Rome
A glorious martyrdom

26 Eugenia Rome
Died in prison

26 Stephen Jerusalem
Stoned to death

JANUARY

3 Anteros Rome
Suffered martyrdom for Christ

20 Faianus Rome
Suffered martyrdom for Christ

20 Marius Rome
Suffered martyrdom for Christ

21 Agnes* Rome
Suffered martyrdom for Christ (13)

22 Anastasius* Persia
Beheaded
23 Emerentiana* Rome Beheaded
24 Babyllas* Antochia Beheaded
[A gap now appears in the manuscript.]

MARCH
7 Perpetua* & Felicitas* Carthage
Suffered martyrdom for Christ
23 Theodoretus Antioch Beheaded

APRIL
9 Seven Women* Sirmium
Suffered martyrdom for Christ
14 Valerianus & Tiburtius* Rome
Beheaded
18 Eleutherius & Anthia* Rome
Killed with a sword
25 Mark Alexandria
Dragged by a rope around his neck
28 Vitalis* Vicolongo Burned alive
28 Christophorus Samos Beheaded

MAY
3 Alexander* Rome
Stabbed to death
8 Victor* Milan Beheaded
12 Pancratius* Rome Beheaded (15)
14 Victor* & Corona* Rome Beheaded
20 Basilla Rome Killed with the sword

JUNE
2 Marcellinus & Petrus Rome
Beheaded
2 Arthemius Rome
Killed with the sword
16 Ferreolus & Ferrucius Besançon
Killed with the sword
17 Nicander & Blastus Rome
Burned to death
18 Marcus & Marcellinus* Rome
Beheaded
19 Gervasius & Protasius Milan
Beaten to death; beheaded
22 James the Less* Jerusalem
Killed by a weaver's beam
22 Alban St Albans Beheaded

JULY
7 Procopius Caesarea Beheaded
7 Marina Antioch Beheaded
10 Seven brothers* Rome
Killed by different tortures
10 Rufina & Secunda Rome
Drowned in River Tiber
14 Phocas Pontus
Thrown into a burning oven
17 Speratus Carthage Beheaded
19 Christina Tyrus Drowned at sea

AUGUST
2 Theodota Nicea Burned to death
9 Romanus Rome
Suffered martyrdom for Christ
10 Lawrence* Rome Roasted alive
12 Euplius* Catania Beheaded
13 Hipploytus Rome
Dragged behind wild horses
17 Mommos Caesarea Stoned to death
22 Symphorianus Autun Beheaded
25 Bartholomew* India Flayed alive
29 John the Baptist Beheaded
30 Felix* Venusia Beheaded

SEPTEMBER
11 Protus* & Hyacinthus* Rome
Beheaded
21 Matthew the apostle
Stabbed with a sword from behind
24 Andochius & Thyrsus Gaul
Necks broken with cudgels

OCTOBER
8 Dionysius Paris Beheaded
24 Sixteen soldiers Fidenae Beheaded
31 Quintinus Rome Beheaded

NOVEMBER
8 Quattuor Coronati Rome
Drowned in a locked lead chest
28 Saturninus* Toulouse
Dragged by a wild bull
30 Andrew Patras Crucified

DECEMBER
13 Lucia Rome Beheaded
21 Thomas India
Stabbed with sword, pierced with
spears

George Herzfeld, An Old English Martyrology, Kegan Paul, Trench, Trubner, London, 1900

** The following entries give details about some of the people featured in this Old-English Martyrology.*

DECEMBER 25

Anastasia On the same day as Christ's birth the churches of God celebrate the birth of St Anastasia the holy lady. She was very noble in the sight of the world and much better before God. The heathen emperor Diocletianus delivered her to his prefect that he might terrify her with tortures, so that she abjured Christ and sacrificed to the idols. The prefect ordered her to be locked up in the dungeon sixty days and nights. After a glorious martyrdom she gave up this present life, and her body rests now in the town of Rome.

JANUARY 21

Agnes The passion of the holy virgin St Agnes is on the twenty-first of January. She suffered martyrdom for Christ when she was thirteen years old. Symphronius, a prefect of the town of Rome, tried to compel the virgin by threats to become his son's wife. When she refused this, he commanded her to be led naked to a brothel. When the son of the town prefect was about to ravish her he died, and so the Romans said that she was an enchantress and a sorceress, and a sword was thrust into her throat. Thus she yielded up her spirit to God, and her body rests near the town of Rome on the road called Numentana.

JANUARY 22

Anastasius The holy man Anastasius was at first a sorcerer in the country of Persia, but afterwards he believed in Christ. Cosroas, king of Persia, ordered him to be hung up by one hand and urged him to forswear the belief in God. As he would not consent to this, the king ordered him to be beheaded.

JANUARY 23

Emerentiana Emerentiana was brought up by Agnes, and very boldly reproached the pagans at Rome with their folly, and she was stoned by them, until she sent forth her spirit.

JANUARY 24

Babyllas Babyllas was holy bishop in the town of Antiochia. This bishop defended the door of the church with Christian folks against Numerianus, the heathen emperor. Babyllas said to the emperor, "Do thou not enter into the house of God, thou hast polluted hands and thou art a devilish wolf." The emperor commanded him to be beheaded and his three servants with him, one of whom was twelve years, the second nine years, and the third seven years; the names of the servants were Urbanus, Prilidianus, and Epolonius.

MARCH 7

Perpetua and Felicitas Perpetua's and Felicitas' bodies rest in the large town of Carthage in Africa. Perpetua dreamt when she was in her girlhood that she had the appearance of a man and that she had a sword in her hand and that she fought with it valiantly. All this was afterwards fulfilled at her martyrdom, when she overcame the devil and the heathen persecutors with manly determination.

Then there was Felicitas, a Christian woman, and she was with child as she was sent to prison for Christ's sake. When therefore the persecutors were about to dismiss her, she wept and prayed to God to rid her of the child, and then she brought it forth on the same night in the seventh month of her pregnancy, and she suffered martyrdom for Christ's sake.

APRIL 9

Seven Women Seven women suffered martyrdom for Christ at Sirmium in Pannonia. Their names are:

Saturnina, Hilarina, Dominando, Rogantina, Serotina, Donata, Paulina.

APRIL 14

Valerianus and Tiburtius

The brothers Valerianus and Tiburtius were urged under tortures by Almachius, prefect of Rome, to abjure Christ. As they would not submit to this, he commanded them to be beheaded. The man who saw them beheaded believed in God, and he was scourged to death for Christ's sake; his name was Maximus.

April 18

Eleutherius and Anthia Eleutherius was bishop of Mechania in Apulia, but later suffered martyrdom at Rome for Christ's sake. The emperor Hadrianus urged him by threats to renounce Christ. As he refused to do this, the emperor ordered four horses to be hitched to a cart, and for Eleutherius to be placed in fetters and dragged behind the cart, so that the wild horses might run over rough paths in the desert and break all his limbs. Then the emperor ordered him to be killed with a sword. Then Eleutherius' mother, Anthia, threw herself on to her son's body. The emperor ordered Anthia to be martyred also, and praising God she gave up her spirit.

April 28

Vitalis The body of Vitalis rests at Vicolongo, that is, in the long town. Vitalis was first a soldier of the emperor under the consul Paulinus in the town of Ravenna, but then he believed in Christ and converted other people to the Christian faith. The consul grew angry at this and forced him to worship idols. As he would not submit to it, the consul commanded men to dig a deep hole and to put him into it alive, and to fill it from above with earth and stones, until he gave up his spirit.

May 3

Alexander On the third day of the month is the martyrdom of the young pope Alexander in Rome and of two priests with him who were called Eventius and Theodolus. The prefect Aurelianus who killed the Christians there urged them to forswear Christ. As they would not submit to this, he commanded them all three to be thrown into a burning oven. As the fire would not burn them, he ordered the priests to be beheaded and the pope to be stabbed to death.

May 8

Victor This Victor was of Moorish descent, and he was a soldier of the heathen emperor Maximianus, but he was a Christian. The emperor advised him to give up the faith of Christ. As he would not agree to this he was threatened with tortures. He commanded molten lead to be poured on him, but that did not harm him any more than cold water. Then he bade his jesters lead him to a wood and behead him there.

May 12

Pancratius The noble youth Pancratius was only fifteen years old when he suffered death for the Christian faith. He was born in the country of Phrygia of an illustrious family, his father's name was Clendonius, and his mother's name Cyriada, and he was baptised at Rome by the pope Cornelius. Then the pagan emperor Diocletianus advised him to forswear Christ, and declared that he then would make him as wealthy as if he were his own son. As he would not consent to this, he ordered him to be beheaded on the road at Rome called Aurelia.

May 14

Victor and Corona This Victor came from the country of Cilicia. He was a soldier of the emperor Antoninus, yet he believed in Christ. Sebastian, the heathen prefect of Egypt, tried to compel him to worship idols. As he would not assent to this, he bade a certain sorcerer give him meat that was poisoned with the strongest poison, and that did not hurt him. Then he ordered him to be flayed alive.

There was the wife of another soldier, Corona by name, who was young and had been married one year and four months. She said to Victor, "Blessed art thou, Victor, and thy holy works are blessed. I see two crowns coming from heaven, the larger one is thine, and the smaller mine." On account of this apparition the woman believed in Christ, and then the prefect ordered them both to be martyred.

June 18

Marcus and Marcellinus These illustrious men were brothers and both were Christians. The emperor Diocletian commanded that they should sacrifice to the idols, or else be beheaded. As they went to the execution, their father and mother and their two wives with many children came to meet them and implored them to forsake the faith of Christ. When their mind turned to the worship of idols, St Sebastian, the Christian hero, heard of this and began to show them how insignificant and how shameful a man's life is in this world, and how long and how fearful the eternal punishment, and how glorious the eternal happiness, until their hearts turned to Christ again; and they kissed each other and were martyred for Christ's sake.

JUNE 22

James the Less On the twenty-second day of the month is the commemoration of the apostle and messenger of God who in Scripture is called James the son of Alpheus. After the Lord's ascension he was bishop in Jerusalem. He never ate meat nor drank wine nor used woollen garments, but only linen ones, nor did he care for bathing, nor did he shorten his locks with scissors nor clip his beard with a knife; but he always earnestly prayed to God, so that his skin grew hard on the knees as the knees of a camel are. This James was killed by the Jewish scribes with a weaver's beam because they hated Christ.

JULY 10

Seven brothers

These seven brothers suffered martyrdom for Christ's sake in the days of the emperor Antoninus. They were the sons of the noble widow Felicitas. Publius, the town-reeve of Rome, tried to turn these brothers aside from the Christian faith with great tortures, but they did not consent to it. Then he killed them by different tortures, and their spirits flew to heaven together. The names of these brothers were Januarius and Felix, Philippus and Sylvanus, Alexander, Vitalis and Martialis.

AUGUST 10

Lawrence Lawrence restored the sight of many a blind man, and he distributed all the treasures that were in God's churches at Rome to poor men and foreigners; and therefore the pagan emperor Decius afflicted him with unspeakable tortures. At last he commanded him to be stretched out on an iron bed and to roast and broil him there alive; and the more he was roasted, the fairer he was to look at. Then Lawrence raised his eyes and said to the emperor: "Look here now, thou poor one, eat this side that is roasted and turn me on the other." After this he offered God thanks and sent forth his spirit to heaven.

AUGUST 12

Euplius Euplius carried Christ's gospel in a case on his shoulders wherever he went. He came into the town of Catania and went into the courthouse, where the judge Calvisianus was in a large assembly with heathen folks. There Euplius uncovered Christ's gospel and told the people what the four evangelists said about the terrible judgement of God. For that reason the judge became angry and ordered him to be beheaded, and when he was led to his martyrdom, heaven was opened, and he saw our Lord in his glory.

AUGUST 25

Bartholomew The apostle Bartholomew was Christ's messenger in India. In this country he destroyed the images that had been worshipped before. The king of that nation received baptism and his queen and all the people that belonged to his dominion. The heathen bishops then went and complained about this to the king's brother, who was in another kingdom and was older than he was. The older brother therefore ordered Bartholomew, the servant of Christ, to be flayed alive. Then the believing king came with a strong army and took his body and brought it away with great glory and buried it in a wonderful large church.

AUGUST 30

Felix Felix lived in the town of Tubsoc. The emperor Diocletianus bade the reeve to take away from the bishop all the books of God and burn them. Then the bishop would not give up the books, but said: "It is better that I be burnt myself rather than the holy scriptures." Then the judge ordered him to be sent with his priests to another fiercer judge. Thus he was sent to many parts to different judges, and every one threatened him about the books of God, until he came to the town of Venusia, in the province of Aulia. There the town-reeve threatened him about the books: he said, "I have them, but I will not give them up." After this he was ordered to be executed, and two of his disciples, Fortunatus and Septimus, suffered with him.

SEPTEMBER 11

Protus and Hyacinthus Protus and Hyacinthus were servants of the noble virgin Eugenia, and they received baptism with her. In the days of Gallienus, Nicetius, the town-reeve of Rome, ordered them to be brought to the idol of Mars and bade them worship it. When they offered a prayer to God, the idol fell down at their feet and was entirely broken. The reeve ordered them to be beheaded for this, and they were made Christ's martyrs.

NOVEMBER 28

Saturninus Saturninus lived in Toulouse and because of the bishop's sanctity all the idols that were worshipped in the town were silent. Therefore the heathen townspeople became angry with him and bound the holy bishop by his feet to a bull and made it fierce, so that it rushed over stony ground and crushed the bishop's head: all his limbs were torn, and he gave up his spirit to Christ.

These entries and the Old English Martyrology were compiled from the following four manuscripts: British Museum, Add. MS. 23211 and Cod. Cotton. Julius A X; Corpus Christi College, Cambridge, Nos. 196 and 41. They illustrate the details of the martyr's life and martyrdom which were originally thought worth remembering.

2. Martyrdoms

BENJAMIN, MARTYR, DEACON, 424

Feast day: March 31

Isdegerdes, son of Sapor III, put a stop to the cruel persecution against the Christians in Persia, which had been begun by Sapor II, and the church had enjoyed twelve years' peace in that kingdom when, in 420, it was disturbed by the indiscreet zeal of one Abdas, a Christian bishop, who burned down the Pyraeum, or temple of fire, the great divinity of the Persians. King Isdegerdes threatened to demolish all the churches of the Christians unless he would rebuild it. Abdas had done ill in destroying the temple, but did well in refusing to rebuild it; for nothing can make it lawful to contribute to any act of idolatry, or to the building a temple, as Theodoret observes. Isdegerdes therefore demolished all the Christian churches in Persia, put to death Abdas, and raised a general persecution against the church, which continued forty years with great fury. Isdegerdes died the year following, in 421. But his son and successor, Varanes, carried on the persecution with greater inhumanity. The very description which Theodoret, a contemporary writer, and one that lived in the neighbourhood, gives of the cruelties he exercised on the Christians strikes us with horror: some were flayed alive in different parts of the body, and suffered all kinds of torture that could be invented: others, being stuck all over with sharp reeds, were hauled and rolled about in that condition; others were tormented divers other ways, such as nothing but the most hellish malice was capable of suggesting. Amongst these glorious champions of Christ was St. Benjamin, a deacon. The tyrant caused him to be beaten and imprisoned. He had lain a year in the dungeon when an ambassador from the emperor obtained his enlargement on condition he should never speak to any of the courtiers about religion.

The ambassador passed his word in his behalf that he would not; but Benjamin, who was a minister of the gospel, declared that he could not detain the truth in captivity, conscious to himself of the condemnation of the slothful servant for having hid his talent. He therefore neglected no opportunity of announcing Christ. The king, being informed that he still preached the faith in his kingdom, ordered him to be apprehended; but the martyr made no other reply to his threats than by putting this question to the king: What opinion he would have of any of his subjects who should renounce his allegiance to him, and join in war against him? The enraged tyrant caused reeds to be run in between the nails and the flesh both of his hands and feet, and the same to be thrust into other most tender parts, and drawn out again, and this to be frequently repeated with violence. He lastly ordered a knotty stake to be thrust into his bowels, to rend and tear them, in which torment he expired in the year 424. The Roman Martyrology places his name on the 31st of March.

Alban Butler, The Lives of the Fathers, Martyrs and Other Principal Saints

Martyrs of Najran

While Jews and Christians were battling for control over Arabia, before the rise of Islam, a widespread persecution of Christians by Jews took place from about 520, which was centred on the Arab city of Najran. When Ethiopia conquered South Arabia it resulted in its Christian evangelization.

The following extracts are summaries of a "Letter" by Simeon of Beth-Arsham, regarded as a primary source, recording these persecutions and martyrdoms.

Paul

After the Jews captured the Christians in the city of Najran they ordered them to show them the bones of their martyrs. They brought the bones of their bishop, Paul, who had been consecrated the first bishop of Najran by Philoxenos, the bishop of Hierapolis. Paul had won his martyr's crown by being stoned by Jews from Tiberias.

Martyrs and church burnt

The Jews made a great heap of all the bones of Christian martyrs in the centre of the church. Then they crammed the church full of two thousand Christians, including readers, deacons, sons of the covenant and daughters of the covenant, presbyters and subdeacons. The Jews then encircled the church with wood and set fire to the wood and to the inside of the church.

Some women who had not been caught, but who were companions to those inside the church, saw the church on fire. They ran to the church, shouting to each other, "Come, companions," as they ran into the fire and were also burnt.

Elizabeth

Elizabeth, the sister of the former bishop Paul, had been hidden in a house by Christians. When she found out that the church, the bones of her brother and the sons of the covenant were being burnt, she left her place of hiding and went to the burning church, saying, "I go with you all to Christ." With that she went into the church's court where the Jews saw her and seized her. The Jews thought that she had escaped from the burning church and concluded that she must be a witch. Elizabeth protested that she came from outside the church and that she wanted to die inside the church with her companions, saying, "I want to be burnt in the church where I served, along with my brother's bones and with my companions." She was forty-seven years old.

But the Jews tied her up with thin ropes after making her bend her head and knees like a camel. They tortured her with ropes on her legs, arms, breasts and temples. Then they placed a crown of mud on her head, and mocked her, saying, "Take your crown, servant of the carpenter's son." Then they poured boiling oil on her head, before taking her outside the city, where they stripped her naked and tied her legs with ropes which were then attached to a wild camel. These ropes had wooden bells on them so the camel ran off into the desert, and so the blessed Elizabeth received her crown.

A child of eight

An eight-year-old boy was found by the Jews wandering among the corpses from the burnt church. They took him to their king who asked the boy, "Who were you looking for among the corpses?" The boy replied that he was searching for his father, so that he might die with him. He said, "I am not going to leave you until you kill me as you killed my father and my mother. I do not want them to go to Christ without me." The king responded by ordering the boy's execution by being beheaded.

Irfan Shahid, The Martyrs of Najran: New Documents, Société des Bollandistes, Brussels, pp 46, 47, 49-51, 61

Martin

665 Italy

But the emperor, through his representative, Theodore Calliopa, the exarch of Ravenna, deposed the pope as a rebel and heretic, and removed him from Rome (June, 653). He imprisoned him with common criminals in Constantinople, exposed him to cold, hunger, and all sorts of injuries, and at last sent him by ship to a cavern in Cherson on the Black Sea (March, 655). Martin bore this cruel treatment with dignity, and died Sept. 16, 655, in exile, a martyr to his faith in the doctrine of two wills.

Maximus was likewise transported to Constantinople (653), and treated with even greater cruelty. He was (with two of his disciples) confined in prison for several years, scourged, deprived of his tongue and right hand, and thus mutilated sent, in his old age, to Lazica in Colchis on the Pontus Euxinus, where he died of these injuries, Aug. 13, 662. His two companions likewise died in exile.

The persecution of these martyrs prepared the way for the triumph of their doctrine. In the meantime province after province was conquered by the Saracens.

Philip Scaff, The History of the Church

Germany 753

In 753 Lull or Lullus became archbishop of Mainz. Laying aside his dignities, he became once more an humble missionary, and returned with about fifty devoted followers to the field of the baffled labors of his youth among the Friesians, where a reaction in favor of heathenism had taken place since the death of Willibrord. He planted his tents on the banks of the river Borne near Dockum (between Franecker and Groningen), waiting for a large number of converts to be confirmed. But, instead of that, he was assailed and slain, with his companions, by armed pagans. He met the martyr's death with calmness and resignation, June 5, 754 or 755. His bones were deposited first at Utrecht, then at Mainz, and at last in Fulda.

Philip Scaff, The History of the Church

Persecutions from About the Middle of the Fifth, to the Conclusion of the Seventh Century

Proterius was made a priest by Cyril, bishop of Alexandria, who was well acquainted with his virtues, before he appointed him to preach. On the death of Cyril, the see of Alexandria was filled by Discorus, an inveterate enemy to the memory and family of his predecessor. Being condemned by the council of Chalcedon for having embraced the errors of Eutyches, he was deposed, and Proterius chosen to fill the vacant see, who was approved of by the emperor. This occasioned a dangerous insurrection, for the city of Alexandria was divided into two factions; the one to espouse the cause of the old, and the other of the new prelate. In one of the commotions, the Eutychians determined to wreak their vengeance on Proterius, who fled to the church for sanctuary: but on Good Friday, A.D. 457, a large body of them rushed into the church, and barbarously murdered the prelate; after which they dragged the body through the streets, insulted it, cut it to pieces, burnt it, and scattered the ashes in the air.

Hermenigildus, a Gothic prince, was the eldest son of Leovigildus, a king of the Goths, in Spain. This prince, who was originally an Arian, became a convert to the orthodox faith, by means of his wife Ingonda. When the king heard that his son had changed his religious sentiments, he stripped him of the command at Seville, where he was governor, and threatened to put him to death unless he renounced the faith he had newly embraced. The prince, in order to prevent the execution of his father's menaces, began to put himself into a posture of defence; and many of the orthodox persuasion in Spain declared for him. The king, exasperated at this act of rebellion, began to punish all the orthodox Christians who could be seized by his troops, and thus a very severe persecution commenced: he likewise marched against his son at the head of a very powerful army. The prince took refuge in Seville, from which he fled, and was at length besieged and taken at Asieta. Loaded with chains, he was sent to Seville, and at the feast of Easter refusing to receive the Eucharist from an Arian bishop, the enraged king ordered his guards to cut the prince to pieces, which they punctually performed, April 13, A.D. 586.

Martin, bishop of Rome, was born at Todi, in Italy. He was naturally inclined to virtue, and his parents bestowed on him an admirable education. He opposed the heretics called Monothelites, who were patronized by the emperor Heraclius. Martin was condemned at Constantinople, where he was exposed in the most public places to the ridicule of the people, divested of all episcopal marks of distinction, and treated with the greatest scorn and severity. After lying some months in prison, Martin was sent to an island at some distance, and there cut to pieces, A.D. 655.

John, bishop of Bergamo, in Lombardy, was a learned man, and a good Christian. He did his utmost endeavors to clear the Church from the errors of Arianism, and joining in this holy work with John, bishop of Milan, he was very successful against the heretics, on which account he was assassinated on July 11, A.D. 683.

Killien was born in Ireland, and received from his parents a pious and Christian education. He obtained the Roman pontiff's license to preach to the pagans in Franconia, in Germany. At Wurtzburg he converted Gozbert, the governor, whose example was followed by the greater part of the people in two years after. Persuading Gozbert that his marriage with his brother's widow was sinful, the latter had him beheaded, A.D. 689.

Foxe's Book of Martyrs, Edited by William Byron Forbush

Anastasius, Persia, 628

St Anastasius was a trophy of the holy cross of Christ, when it was carried away into Persia by Chosroes, in 614, after he had taken and plundered Jerusalem. The martyr was a Persian, son of a Magian, instructed in the sciences of that sect, and a young soldier in the Persian troops. Upon hearing the news of the taking of the cross by his king, he became very inquisitive concerning the Christian religion. Its sublime truths made such an impression on his mind, that when he returned to Persia from an expedition into the Roman empire, he left the army and went to Hierapolis. In Hierapolis he stayed with a devout Christian, who was a silversmith. He went to Jerusalem to be baptised and changed his Persian name of Magundat, to that of Anastasius, meaning according to the signification of that Greek word, that he was raised from death to a new and spiritual life. In 621 he became a monk in a monastery five miles from Jerusalem, where the abbot, Justin, had his hair cut off, and put him in monastic habit.

On a visit to Garizim, seven years later, which was then under the control of the Persians, Anastasius saw Persian soothsayers from the garrison occupied in their abominable superstitions in the streets. Anastasius spoke boldly against them and was arrested by the Persian magistrate, on suspicion of being a spy. Anastasius informed them that he had once enjoyed the dignity of Magian with them, and had renounced it to become a humble follower of Christ. Upon this confession he was thrown into prison. Marzabanes, the governor of the city commanded him to be chained by the foot to another criminal, and his neck and one foot to be also linked together by a heavy chain, and condemned him in this condition to carry heavy stones.

Anastasius was later transferred to Barsaloe in Assyria, six miles from Discartha, near the Euphrates, where the king was. There he was beaten with staves for three days, then laid on his back, and a heavy beam placed on his legs, which crushed his flesh and bones. Then he was hung up for two hours by one hand, with a great weight at his feet. The judge, despairing to overcome him, went to the king for his orders, which were, that Anastasius should be executed. The sixty-eight other Christian prisoners were strangled one after another, on the banks of the river, in front of Athanasius. All the time the judge urged Athanasius to return to Persian worship, and to escape so disgraceful a death, promising, in case of compliance, that he should be made one of the greatest men in the court. Anastasius, with his eyes lifted up to heaven, gave thanks to God for bringing his life to so happy a conclusion. He was accordingly strangled, and after his death he head was cut off. This was in 628, the seventeenth of the emperor Heraclius, on the 22nd of January.

Alban Butler, The Lives of the Saints, Dublin, 1833, volume I, pp 95-96

Persecutions from the Early Part of the Eighth, to Near the Conclusion of the Tenth Century

Boniface, archbishop of Mentz, and father of the German church, was an Englishman, and is, in ecclesiastical history, looked upon as one of the brightest ornaments of this nation. Originally his name was Winfred, or Winfrith, and he was born at Kirton, in Devonshire, then part of the West-Saxon kingdom. When he was only about six years of age, he began to discover a propensity to reflection, and seemed solicitous to gain information on religious subjects. Wolfrad, the abbot, finding that he possessed a bright genius, as well as a strong inclination to study, had him removed to Nutscelle, a seminary of learning in the diocese of Winchester, where he would have a much greater opportunity of attaining improvements than at Exeter.

After due study, the abbot seeing him qualified for the priesthood, obliged him to receive that holy order when he was about thirty years old. From which time he began to preach and labor for the salvation of his fellow creatures; he was released to attend a synod of bishops in the kingdom of West-Saxons. He afterwards, in 719, went to Rome, where Gregory II who then sat in Peter's chair, received him with great friendship, and finding him full of all virtues that compose the character of an apostolic missionary, dismissed him without commission at large to preach the Gospel to the pagans wherever he found them. Passing through Lombardy and Bavaria, he came to Thuringia, which country had before received the light of the Gospel, he next visited Utrecht, and then proceeded to Saxony, where he converted some thousands to Christianity.

During the ministry of this meek prelate, Pepin was declared king of France. It was that prince's ambition to be crowned by the most holy prelate he could find, and Boniface was pitched on to perform that ceremony, which he did at Soissons, in 752. The next year, his great age and many infirmities lay so heavy on him, that, with the consent of the new king, and the bishops of his diocese, he consecrated Lullus, his countryman, and faithful disciple, and placed him in the see of Mentz. When he had thus eased himself of his charge, he recommended the church of Mentz to the care of the new bishop in very strong terms, desired he would finish the church at Fuld, and see him buried in it, for his end was near. Having left these orders, he took boat to the Rhine, and went to Friesland, where he converted and baptized several thousands of barbarous natives, demolished the temples, and raised churches on the ruins of those superstitious structures. A day being appointed for confirming a great number of new converts, he ordered them to assemble in a new open plain, near the river Bourde. Thither he repaired the day before; and, pitching a tent, determined to remain on the spot all night, in order to be ready early in the morning. Some pagans, who were his inveterate enemies, having intelligence of this, poured down upon him and the companions of his mission in the night, and killed him and fifty-two of his companions and attendants on June 5, A.D. 755. Thus fell the great father of the Germanic Church, the honor of England, and the glory of the age in which he lived.

Forty-two persons of Armorian in Upper Phyrgia, were martyred in the year 845, by the Saracens, the circumstances of which transactions are as follows:

In the reign of Theophilus, the Saracens ravaged many parts of the eastern empire, gained several considerable advantages over the Christians, took the city of Armorian, and numbers suffered martyrdom.

Flora and Mary, two ladies of distinction, suffered martyrdom at the same time.

Perfectus was born at Corduba, in Spain, and brought up in the Christian faith. Having a quick genius, he made himself master of all the useful and polite literature of that age; and at the same time was not more celebrated for his abilities than admired for his piety. At length he took priest's orders, and performed the duties of his office with great assiduity and punctuality. Publicly declaring Mahomet an impostor, he was sentenced to be beheaded, and was accordingly executed, A.D. 850; after which his body was honorably interred by the Christians.

Adalbert, bishop of Prague, a Bohemian by birth, after being involved in many troubles, began to direct his thoughts to the conversion of the infidels, to which end he repaired to Dantzic, where he converted and baptized many, which so enraged the pagan priests, that they fell upon him, and despatched him with darts, on April 23, A.D. 997.

Foxe's Book of Martyrs, Edited by William Byron Forbush

ADALBERT
Poland, 997

Adalbert, archbishop of Prague, from 983 to 997, preached against polygamy, the trade in Christian slaves, chiefly carried on by the Jews, but in vain. Twice he left his see, disgusted and discouraged; finally he was martyred by the Prussian Wends. Not until 1038 archbishop Severus succeeded in enforcing laws concerning marriage, the celebration of the Lord's Day, and other points of Christian morals.

Philip Scaff, The History of the Church

PERSECUTIONS IN THE ELEVENTH CENTURY

Alphage, archbishop of Canterbury, was descended from a considerable family in Gloucestershire, and received an education suitable to his illustrious birth. His parents were worthy Christians, and Alphage seemed to inherit their virtues.

The see of Winchester being vacant by the death of Ethelwold, Dunstan, archbishop of Canterbury, as primate of all England, consecrated Alphage to the vacant bishopric, to the general satisfaction of all concerned in the diocese.

Dustain had an extraordinary veneration for Alphage, and, when at the point of death, made it his ardent request to God that he might succeed him in the see of Canterbury; which accordingly happened, though not until about eighteen years after Dunstan's death in 1006.

After Alphage had governed the see of Canterbury about four years, with great reputation to himself, and benefit to his people, the Danes made an incursion into England, and laid siege to Canterbury. When the design of attacking this city was known, many of the principal people made a flight from it, and would have persuaded Alphage to follow their example. But he, like a good pastor, would not listen to such a proposal. While he was employed in assisting and encouraging the people, Canterbury was taken by storm; the enemy poured into the town, and destroyed all that came in their way by fire and sword. He had the courage to address the enemy, and offer himself to their swords, as more worthy of their rage than the people: he begged they might be saved, and that they would discharge their whole fury upon him. They accordingly seized him, tied his hands, insulted and abused him in a rude and barbarous manner, and obliged him to remain on the spot until his church was burnt, and the monks massacred. They then decimated all the inhabitants, both ecclesiastics and laymen, leaving only every tenth person alive; so that they put 7236 persons to death, and left only four monks and 800 laymen alive, after which they confined the archbishop in a dungeon, where they kept him close prisoner for several months.

During his confinement they proposed to him to redeem his liberty with the sum of 3000 pounds, and to persuade the king to purchase their departure out of the kingdom, with a further sum of 10,000 pounds. As Alphage's circumstances would not allow him to satisfy the exorbitant demand, they bound him, and put him to severe torments, to oblige him to discover the treasure of the church; upon which they assured him of his life and liberty, but the prelate piously persisted in refusing to give the pagans any account of it. They remanded him to prison again, confined him six days longer, and then, taking him prisoner with them to Greenwich, brought him to trial there. He still remained inflexible with respect to the church treasure; but exhorted them to forsake their idolatry, and embrace Christianity. This so greatly incensed the Danes, that the soldiers dragged him out of the camp and beat him unmercifully. One of the soldiers, who had been converted by him, knowing that his pains would be lingering, as his death was determined on, actuated by a kind of barbarous compassion, cut off his head, and thus put the finishing stroke to his martyrdom, April 19, A.D. 1012. This transaction happened on the very spot where the church at Greenwich, which is dedicated to him, now stands. After his death his body was thrown into the Thames, but being found the next day, it was buried in the cathedral of St. Paul's by the bishops of London and Lincoln; from whence it was, in 1023, removed to Canterbury by Ethelmoth, the archbishop of that province.

Gerard, a Venetian, devoted himself to the service of God from his tender years: entered into a religious house for some time, and then determined to visit the Holy Land. Going into Hungary, he became acquainted with Stephen, the king of that country, who made him bishop of Chonad.

Ouvo and Peter, successors of Stephen, being deposed, Andrew, son of Ladislaus, cousin-german to Stephen, had then a tender of the crown made him upon condition that he would employ his authority in extirpating the Christian religion out of Hungary. The ambitious prince came into the proposal, but Gerard being informed of his impious bargain, thought it his duty to remonstrate against the enormity of Andrew's crime, and persuade him to withdraw his promise. In this view he undertook to go to that prince, attended by three prelates, full of like zeal for religion. The new king was at Alba Regalis, but, as the four bishops were going to cross the Danube, they were stopped by a party of soldiers posted there. They bore an attack of a shower of stones patiently, when the soldiers beat them unmercifully, and at length despatched them with lances. Their martyrdoms happened in the year 1045.

Stanislaus, bishop of Cracow, was descended from an illustrious Polish family. The piety of his parents was equal to their opulence, and the latter they rendered subservient to all the purposes of charity and benevolence. Stanislaus remained for some time undetermined whether he should embrace a monastic life, or engage among the secular clergy. He was at length persuaded to the latter by Lambert Zula, bishop of Cracow, who gave him holy orders, and made him a canon of his cathedral. Lambert died on November 25, 1071, when all concerned in the choice of a successor declared for Stanislaus, and he succeeded to the prelacy.

Bolislaus, the second king of Poland, had, by nature, many good qualities, but giving away to his passions, he ran into many enormities, and at length had the appellation of Cruel bestowed upon him. Stanislaus alone had the courage to tell him of his faults, when, taking a private opportunity, he freely displayed to him the enormities of his crimes. The king, greatly exasperated at his repeated freedoms, at length determined, at any rate, to get the better of a prelate who was so extremely faithful. Hearing one day that the bishop was by himself, in the chapel of St. Michael, at a small distance from the town, he despatched some soldiers to murder him. The soldiers readily undertook the bloody task; but, when they came into the presence of Stanislaus, the venerable aspect of the prelate struck them with such awe that they could not perform what they had promised. On their return, the king, finding that they had not obeyed his orders, stormed at them violently, snatched a dagger from one of them, and ran furiously to the chapel, where, finding Stanislaus at the altar, he plunged the weapon into his heart. The prelate immediately expired on May 8, A.D. 1079.

Foxe's Book of Martyrs, Edited by William Byron Forbush

Kilien

A name remarkable in the roll of martyrs is now brought before our notice; it is that of Kilien. He was born in Ireland, and received from his parents a pious and Christian education. In the course of time he crossed the sea, with eleven other people, in order to make converts on the Continent. On landing, they directed their route to the circle of Franconia, in Germany. On arriving at the city of Wurtzburg, they found the people in general, with their governor Gozbert, to be pagans, but conceived great hopes of converting them to the gospel faith. Gozbert directed the attention of his heathen subjects to the preaching of the prelate; and the greater part of them became Christians in less than two years.

Gozbert had married his brother's widow; but Kilien, though he had the sinfulness of the thing, did not consider it wise to rebuke him till he was confirmed in his faith. When deemed him established in the truth, he entreated him, as the proof of his sincerity, to quit the person whom he had looked up as his wife, as he could not retain her without sin. Gozbert, surprised at the proposal, told the bishop this was the hardest test he had ever exacted from him. "But," he said, "since I have renounced my own inclinations and pleasures in so many particulars for the love of God, I will make the work complete by complying with your advice in this too."

His wife, however, determined to take revenge on those who had persuaded Gozbert to adopt such a resolution. She accordingly sent to the place where they were assembled, and had them all beheaded. Kilien and his companions submitted without resistance, the former telling them that they need not fear those who had no power over the soul, but could only kill the body, which in a short time would perish in the course of nature. This happened in 689, and the martyrs were privately buried in the night, together with their books, clothes, and all that they had.

John Foxe, The Book of Martyrs, revised with notes and an appendix by W. Bramley-Moore, London, 1869, pp 54-5

The Hewalds

Bede records that after Willibrord preached in Frisia many people were converted to Christ resulting in his companions, the Hewalds, being martyred, in 692.

Egbert, the man of God, perceived that God did not wish him to go and preach to the heathen, so he sent Willibrord and twelve of his companions to preach in western Frisia. Many turned from worshipping idols to believing in Christ. Two more English priests followed in their wake and preached in the province of the Old Saxons. These priests both had the same name, but due to their very different coloured hair, one was called Hewald the Black, and the other Hewald the White. Both men were devout and religious and sang psalms and said prayers and brought holy cups and a consecrated table to serve as an altar for their daily sacrifice of the Saviour to God.

When the Old Saxons realised that the Hewalds practiced a different religion from them they began to fear them. They were afraid that they might ask their God to convert them to their religion and so the whole province would go over to the new religion. They suddenly attacked them. They put Hewald the White to the sword at once, but made Hewald the Black suffer a lingering death, as they tore him apart, limb by limb. Their bodies were then thrown into the Rhine, on October 3.

The English Martyrs under Henry VIII and Elizabeth 1535-1583, Catholic Truth Society, 1901, pp 280-2

Martyrdom of Boniface (1)

Boniface, Bishop, Missionary, Martyr 5 June 754

Wynfrith, nicknamed Boniface ("good deeds"), was born around 680 near Crediton in Devonshire, England. When he was five, he listened to some monks who were staying at his father's house. They had returned from a mission to the pagans on the continent, and Boniface was so impressed by them that he resolved to follow their example. Although his father had intended him for a secular career, he gave way to his son's entreaties and sent him at the age of seven to a monastery school. He eventually became director of the school at Nursling, in Winchester, where he wrote the first Latin grammar in England, and gave lectures that were widely copied and circulated.

At thirty, he was ordained and set out to preach in Friesland (overlaps with modern Holland), whence he was soon expelled because of war between its heathen king and Charles Martel of France. Boniface, after a brief withdrawal, went into Hesse and Bavaria, having secured the support of the Pope and of Charles Martel for his work there. In Hesse, in the presence of a large crowd of pagans, he cut down the Sacred Oak of Geismar, a tree of immense age and girth, sacred to the god Thor. It is said that after only a few blows of his axe, the tree tottered and crashed to the ground, breaking into four pieces and revealing itself to be rotted away within. It was the beginning of a highly successful missionary effort, and the planting of a vigorous Christian church in Germany, where Boniface was eventually consecrated bishop. He asked the Christian Saxons of England to support his work among their kinsmen on the continent, and they responded with money, books, supplies, and above all, with a steady supply of monks to assist him in teaching and preaching.

Boniface did not confine his attentions to Germany. He worked to establish cooperation between the Pope and others in Italy on the one hand and Charles and his successors in France on the other. He persuaded Carloman and Pepin, the sons of Charles, to call synods for the reform of the church in their territories, where under previous rulers bishoprics had often been sold to the highest bidder. He never forgot his initial failure in Friesland, and in old age resigned his bishopric and returned to work there. Many Frisians had been converted earlier by Willibrord (another Saxon missionary from England—see 7 Nov), but had lapsed after his death. Boniface preached among them with considerable success. On June 5, the eve of Pentecost, 754, he was preparing a group of Frisians for confirmation when they were attacked and killed by heathen warriors.

The historian Christopher Dawson estimates that he has had a greater influence on the history of Europe than any other Englishman.

James Kiefer, Christian Biographies, By kind permission

Martyrdom of Boniface (2)

Apostle of Germany, date of birth unknown; martyred 5 June, 755 (754); emblems: the oak, axe, book, fox, scourge, fountain, raven, sword. He was a native of England, though some authorities have claimed him for Ireland or Scotland. The place of his birth is not known, though it was probably the south-western part of Wessex. Crediton (Kirton) in Devonshire is given by more modern authors. The same uncertainty exists in regard to the year of his birth. It seems, however, safe to say that he was not born before 672 or 675, or as late as 680. Descended from a noble family, from his earliest years he showed great ability and received a religious education. His parents intended him for secular pursuits, but, inspired with higher ideals by missionary monks who visited his home, Winfrid felt himself called to a religious state. After much difficulty he obtained his father's permission and went to the monastery of Adescancastre on the site of the present city of Exeter, where, under the direction of Abbot Wolfhard, he was trained in piety and learning. About seven years later he went to the Abbey of Nhutscelle (Nutshalling) between Winchester and Southampton. Here, leading an austere and studious life under Abbot Winbert, he rapidly advanced in sanctity and knowledge, excelling especially in the profound understanding of scriptures, of which he gives evidence in his letters. He was also well educated in history, grammar, rhetoric, and poetry. He made his profession as a member of the Benedictine Order and was placed in charge of the monastic school. At the age of thirty he was ordained priest. Through his abbot the fame of Winfrid's learning soon reached high civil and ecclesiastical circles. He also had great success as a preacher. With every prospect of a great career and the highest dignities in his own country, he had no desire for human glory, for the thought of bringing the light of the Gospel to his kindred, the Old Saxons, in Germany, had taken possession of his mind. After many requests Winfrid at last obtained the permission of his abbot.

In 716 he set out for the mission in Friesland. Since the Faith had already been preached there by Wigbert, Willibrord, and others, Winfrid expected to find a good soil for his missionary work, but political disturbances caused him to return temporarily to England. Towards the end of 717 Abbot Winbert died, and Winfrid was elected to succeed him, but declined and induced Daniel, Bishop of Winchester, to influence the monks to elect another. Winfrid was left free to follow out his intentions, but before going back to his apostolic work he wished to visit Rome and to obtain from the pope the apostolic mission and the necessary faculties. Bishop Daniel gave him an open letter of recommendation to kings, princes, bishops, abbots, and priests, and a private letter to the pope. On Winfrid s arrival in Rome, in the fall of 718, Pope Gregory II received him kindly, praised his resolutions, and having satisfied himself in various conferences as to the orthodoxy of Winfrid, his morals, and the purity of his motives, on 15 May, 719, he gave him full authority to preach the Gospel to the heathens in Germany to the right of the Rhine, ordering him at the same time to adhere to the Roman practice in the administration of the Sacrament of Baptism, and to consult with the Holy See in case of difficulties.

Having received instructions to make to make his first journey through the country, only a tour of inspection, he travelled through Bavaria and found the Church flourishing, with a number of churches and monasteries. In Alamannia, which he crossed on his way to Thuringia, he found similar conditions. Thuringia was considered by Rome as Christian, and the mission of Winfrid was supposed to be that of an authorized reformer. He found the country, however, in a bad condition, St. Kilian had laboured with energy, but without success. Duke Gotzbert and some years later his son, Hethan II, both converts of St. Kilian had been murdered, perhaps on account of their injudicious zeal in trying to spread Christianity. Great numbers of their rebellious subjects had lapsed into heathenism, or a mixture of Christianity and idolatry. Winfrid tried to enkindle a missionary spirit in the priests and to make the people live up to the pure precepts of the Christian religion. Though he converted some of the heathens, he did not meet with the success which he had anticipated. On his way to the court of Charles Martel, possibly to interest that prince in the matter, he received news of the death of the Frisian King Radbod, and went to Friesland. Here he spent three years under the aged St. Willibrord, traveling about with tireless energy and preaching fearlessly as he went. Multitudes of Christians who had fallen away during the persecution of Radbod were brought to repentance and thousands of pagans accepted the Faith. Many of the converts were brought together to lead a religious life under the Rule of St. Benedict. St. Willibrord, feeling the weight of his years, wished to make Winfrid his assistant and successor in the See of Utrecht. Winfrid refused, giving as his main reason that the pope had sent him for missionary work. He therefore left and followed in the wake of the army of Charles Martel as far as Trier. Near this city was the Abbey of Pfalzel (Palatiolum). From there he took with him as a disciple and companion Gregory, a boy of about fourteen or fifteen, afterwards abbot in Utrecht, and continued his journey to Thuringia, where he converted many. He then went into Hessia, where many more were brought into the fold of Christ. With the assistance of two chiefs whom he had converted he established a monastic cell at Amneburg at the River Ohm (then called Amana) in Upper Hessia, as a kind of missionary centre in which native clergy were to be educated.

While Winfrid was under the jurisdiction of St. Willibrord he had no special reason for reporting to the Holy See, but, now working independently, he considered it his duty to do so. He therefore sent Bynnan, one of his disciples, with a letter to Gregory recounting his labours of the past years and asking for further directions. Bynnan promptly executed his commission and soon returned with the pope's answer, expressing satisfaction with what had been done and a desire to confer with Winfrid personally. Winfrid accordingly set out for Rome, taking his course through France and Burgundy. He was warmly welcomed by the pope, who questioned him carefully, made him take the usual oath of allegiance, received from him a profession of faith, and on 30 November, 722 (723), consecrated him a regional bishop, with the name Boniface. Some say that Winfrid had taken this name at the time of his religious profession; others, that he received it on his first visit to Rome. The same discrepancy of opinion exists in derivation from bonum facere or bonum fatum; perhaps it is only an approximate Latinization of Wyn-frith. Pope Gregory then sent Boniface back with letters to his diocesans in Thuringia and Hessia demanding obedience for their new bishop. A letter was also addressed to Charles Martel asking his protection. Boniface himself had received a set of ecclesiastical canons for his guidance.

Boniface returned to Upper Hessia and repaired the losses which occurred during his absence, many having drifted back into paganism; he also administered everywhere the Sacrament of Confirmation. He continued his work in Lower Hessia. To show the heathens how utterly powerless were the gods in whom they placed their confidence, Boniface felled the oak sacred to the thunder-god Thor, at Geismar, near Fritzlar. He had a chapel built out of the wood and dedicated it to the prince of the Apostles. The heathens were astonished that no thunderbolt from the hand of Thor destroyed the offender, and many were converted. The fall of this oak marked the fall of heathenism. Tradition tells us that Boniface now passed on to the River Werra and there erected a Church of St. Vitus, around which sprang up a town which to the present day bears the name of Wannfried. At Eschwege he is said to have destroyed the statue of the idol Stuffo. Thence he went into Thuringia.

The difficulties that confronted him here were very great Christianity had indeed made great progress, but it had become mixed up with heretical tenets and pagan customs. This was due to a great extent to some Celtic missionaries, several of whom had never been ordained, while others had been raised to the priesthood by non-Catholic bishops, though all performed priestly functions. These taught doctrines and made use of ceremonies at variance with the teaching and use of the Roman Church, especially in regard to the celebration of Easter, the conferring of baptism, celibacy, the papal and episcopal authority. Besides, many were wanting in education, some scarcely able to read or write, and equally ready to hold services for the Christians and to offer sacrifices to the idols for the heathens. A neighbouring bishop (probably of Cologne) also gave trouble, by laying claim to a part of the district under Boniface's jurisdiction and treating his authority as an intrusion, thereby indirectly strengthening the party of the heretics. All this caused him great anxiety and suffering as may be seen from his letters to England. He overcame all, thanks to his episcopal dignity and to his own personality, full of courage and zeal in the cause which he defended, and supported by the authority of the pope and of Charles Martel. His friends helped him not only by their prayers, but also by material aid. Many valuable books, ecclesiastical articles and the like were sent to him with words of encouragement. Numbers of men and women went to Germany at different times to be his helpers. Among them were Lullus, Denehard, Burchard, Wigbert, Sola, Witta (called also Wizo and Albinus), Wunibald, Willibald and the pious women Lioba, Chunihild, Chunitrude, Berthgit, Walburga, and Thecla. With these, and others recruited in Thuringia and elsewhere in Germany, he continued his labours. The number of the faithful increased wonderfully, including many of the nobility and the educated of the country.

These assisted him in the building of churches and chapels. Boniface took care to have institutions in which religious life would be fostered. In Thuringia he built the first monastery Ohrdruf on the River Ohrn near Altenberga. He appointed Thecla Abbess of Kitzingen, Lioba of Bischofsheim, and Walburga of Heidenheim.

Pope Gregory II died 11 February, 731, and was succeeded on 18 March by Gregory III. Boniface hastened to send a delegation to the new pontiff, to pay his respects and to assure him of his fidelity. The answer to this seems to be lost. In 732 Boniface wrote again and stated among other things that the work was becoming too much for one man. Gregory III congratulated him on his success and praised his zeal, in recognition sending him the pallium, and making him an archbishop, but still without a fixed see. He gave him instructions to appoint bishops wherever he thought it necessary. Boniface now enlarged the monastery of Ameneburg and built a church, dedicating it to St. Michael. Another monastery he founded at Fritzlar near the River Eder, which was completed in 734. The church, a more magnificent structure, was not finished before 740. In 738 Boniface made his third journey to Rome, intending to resign his office and devote himself exclusively to the mission among the Saxons. He was accompanied by a number of his disciples, who were to see true Christian life in the centre of Christianity. Gregory III received him graciously and was rejoiced at the result of Boniface's LABOURT, but would not allow him to resign. Boniface remained in Rome for about a year and then returned to his mission invested with the authority of a legate of the Holy See. His first care on his return was the Church in Bavaria.

In 715 (716) Duke Theodo had come to Rome out of devotion, but probably also to secure ecclesiastical order in his provinces. Gregory II sent three ecclesiastics with instructions to do away with abuses. Their work, however, was rendered futile by the death of Theodo in 717 and the subsequent political quarrels. Boniface had twice passed through the country. Now with the help of Duke Odilo and of the nobles he began the work of reorganization acting entirely according to the instructions of Gregory II. He examined the orders of the clergy, deposed the obstinate, reordained those whose ordination he found invalid, provided they had erred through ignorance and were willing to submit to authority. He made a new circumscription of the dioceses and appointed bishops for the vacant sees, viz., the Abbot John to the See of Salzburg, vacant since the death of St. Rupert in 718; Erembert to Freising, vacant since the death of his brother, St. Corbinian, in 730; Gaubald for Ratisbon. Passau had been established and provided for by the pope himself through the nomination of Vivilo. About this time Boniface founded the new Diocese of Buraburg, and named Witta as its bishop. This diocese existed for only a short time, during the administration of two bishops, and was then joined to Augsburg. Somewhat later the dioceses of Eichstőtt and Erfurt (Erphesfurt) were formed, and Willibald was consecrated bishop for the former about October, 741; for the latter Boniface appointed as first (and last) bishop Adalar, who, it seems, never received episcopal consecration, as he is continually spoken of as a priest.

Charles Martel had died 22 October, 741, at Quiercy on the Oise and was succeeded by his sons Carloman and Pepin. In Rome Pope Gregory III died 28 November, 741, and was followed by Zachary. Carloman asked Boniface, his former preceptor, to a consultation. The result of this was a letter to the pope in which Boniface reported his actions in Bavaria and asked advice in various matters. He also stated the wish of Carloman that a synod be held. In answer Pope Zachary, 1 April, 742, confirmed the erection of the dioceses, sanctioned the holding of the synod, and gave the requested information. The synod, partly ecclesiastical and partly secular, was held 21 April, 742, but the place cannot be ascertained. The bishops appointed by Boniface were present and several others, but it was mainly the authority of Boniface and the power of Carloman that gave weight to the first

German synod. Among its decrees the most noteworthy are those ordaining the subjection of the clergy to the bishop of the diocese and forbidding them to take any active part in wars, to carry arms, or to hunt. Very strict regulations were made against carnal sins on the part of priests and religious. The Rule of St. Benedict was made a norm for religious. Laws were also enacted concerning marriage within the forbidden degrees of kindred. A second national synod was held 1 March, 743, at Liptina in Hainault, and another at Soissons, 2 March, 744. In this synod a sentence of condemnation was passed against two heretics, Adalbert and Clement, the former a native of Gaul, the latter of Ireland. They were strain condemned in 745 and also at a synod held in Rome. Several other synods were held in Germany to strengthen faith and discipline. At the request of Carloman and Pepin the authority of Boniface over Bavaria was confirmed and extended over Gaul.

In 744 St. Willibrord, Bishop of Utrecht, died, and Boniface took the diocese under his charge, appointed an assistant or chorepiscopus. About the same time the See of Cologne became vacant through the death of Ragenfried, and it was the intention of Boniface as well as the wish of Pope Zachary to make this his archiepiscopal see, but the clergy opposed. Before the project could be carried out the Diocese of Mainz lost its bishop through the deposition of Gewilieb who led a very irregular life and had killed the slayer of his father, who was his predecessor in the episcopal office. Pope Zachary, 1 May, 748 (747), appointed Boniface Archbishop of Mainz and Primate of Germany. The new archdiocese comprised the dioceses of Tongem, Cologne, Worms, Speyer, Utrecht, and the dioceses erected by Boniface himself: Buraburg, Eichstött, Erfurt, and Werzburg. Of Augsburg, Coire, and Constance the decree does not speak, but they are shortly afterwards mentioned as belonging to the province. After a few years Boniface was able to reconcile his enemies with the Holy See, so that the supremacy of the pope was acknowledged in Great Britain, Germany, and Gaul, as well as in Italy.

In 747 Carloman resigned his share of the government to his brother Pepin and left to spend the remainder of his days as a monk. He built a monastery in honour of St. Silvester at Soracte near Rome, and later retired to Monte Cassino. His motives for this are not known, but perhaps he was frightened at the severity of the measures he had felt himself obliged to use in order to obtain a union among the German tribes. Pepin, now the sole ruler, became the founder of the Carlovingian dynasty. That Boniface had anything to do with the disestablishment of the old royal family and the introduction of a new one cannot be proved. He did not mingle in the politics of the country, except in this, that he did all in his power to convert the people to the true Faith, and to bring them into spiritual subjection to the Roman pontiff. It is generally stated that Boniface anointed and crowned Pepin by order of the pope, though this is denied by some.

The rest of his life Boniface spent in confirming what he had achieved in Germany. This he did by frequently holding synods and by enforcing the sacred canons. He did much for true religious life in the monasteries, especially at Fulda, which had been established under his supervision by St. Sturm, and into which Boniface returned yearly to train the monks and to spend some days in prayer and meditation. At his request Pope Zachary exempted the abbey from all episcopal jurisdiction and placed it under the immediate care of the Holy See. This was something new for Germany, though already known and practised in Italy and England. It seems that Boniface's last act as Archbishop of Mainz was the repudiation of the claim of the Archbishop of Cologne to the diocese of Utrecht. The matter was laid before Pepin, who decided against Cologne. The same decision must have been given by Pope Stephen II (III) who had become the successor of Zachary, 26 March, 752, for after that time no further claim was made by Cologne. No change was made until the ninth century, when Cologne was made an archdiocese and Utrecht one of its suffragan sees. Boniface appointed Abbot Gregory as administrator of Utrecht, and Eoban, who had been assistant, he took as his companion.

When Boniface saw that all things had been properly taken care of, he took up the work he had dreamed of in early manhood, the conversion of the Frisians. With royal consent, and with that of the pope previously given, he in 754 resigned the Archdiocese of Mainz to his disciple Lullus, whom in 752 he had consecrated bishop, again commenced a missionary tour, and laboured with success to the East of the Zuider Zee. Returning in the following year, he ordered the new converts to assemble for confirmation at Dorkum on the River Borne. The heathens fell upon them and murdered Boniface and fifty-two companions (according to some, thirty-seven). Soon afterwards, the Christians, who had scattered at the approach of the heathens, returned and found the body of the martyr and beside him the bloodstained copy of St. Ambrose on the "Advantage of Death". The body was taken to Utrecht, afterwards through the influence of Lullus removed to Mainz, and later, according to a wish expressed by the saint himself during his lifetime, to the Abbey of Fulda. Portions of his relics are at Louvain, Mechlin, Prague, Bruges, and Erfurt. A considerable portion of an arm is at Eichfeld. His grave soon became a sanctuary, to which the faithful came in crowds especially on his feast and during the Octave. England is supposed to have been the first place where his martyrdom was celebrated on a fixed day. Other countries followed. On 11 June, 1874, Pope Pius IX extended the celebration to the entire world. Brewers, tailors, and file-cutters have chosen St. Boniface as their patron, also various cities in Germany. The writings of St. Boniface which have been preserved are: "Collection of Letters"; "Poems and Riddles"; "Poenitentiale"; "Compendium of the Latin Language"; "Compendium of Latin Prosody"; "Sermons" (doubtful).

Francis Mershman, The Catholic Encyclopedia, Volume 2

Christian martyrs in Muslim Spain

Between 850 and 859 forty-eight Christians were decapitated in the Spanish town of Cordoba for religious offences against Islam. All these martyrdoms were recorded by Eulogius, a Cordoban priest, so that he could write up passions which would perpetuate the memory of these Christian martyrs through his martyrology.

Isaac

The first of these forty-eight martyrs was Isaac. Due to his noble birth he rose to the highest rank in the local government that a non-Muslim was allowed, that of secretary of the covenant (*katib adh-dhimam*). He gave all this up and went to live in a monastery close to Cordoba, in Tabanos. Isaac visited Cordoba three years later to ask a judge about some details of Islamic law. This official spoke about Muhammad's life and this launched Isaac into a full scale attack on Islam in which he affirmed that its prophet was being tormented in hell for misleading the Arabs.

The judge was amazed at this outburst and concluded that Isaac must be either drunk or mad. But Isaac assured the judge that he was compelled to so outspoken because of the "zeal of righteousness". Isaac was promptly arrested, sentenced. His decapitated body was left hanging for all to see.

Sanctius

Two days after Isaac's martyrdom Sanctius, a young Christian soldier, was also decapitated, for the same reason. It is not clear if Isaac's example had inspired Sanctius, but it is known that six more Christians were so greatly influenced by Sanctius' example that Cordoba had six more dead Christians within forty-eight hours of Sanctius' death.

Six more martyrs

The deacon Walabonsus and the priest Petrus came to study in Cordoba. Two monks, Sabinianus and Wistremundus from the monastery at St Zoylus, were also visiting Cordoba.

Habentius, who came from Cordoba and the founder of a monastery at Tabanos, and Hieremia, made up the last two of this group of six Christians. All six went before the judge together and made their intentions very plain when they said that they confessed the same faith as Isaac and Sanctius. They boldly stated that Christ was God and that Muhammad was the antichrist. They were speedily executed.

Helios, Paulus and Isidorus

On April 16, 856, a priest from western Spain, Helias, and two monks, Paulus and Isidorus, committed blasphemy in the eyes of the Muslims and were also speedily dispatched.

Aurea

Aurea's father was a Muslim, but Aurea had lived with her mother as a nun in a convent, without any of her Muslim relatives finding out. Aurea had witnessed the martyrdom of her two brothers, Joannes and Adulphus, as well as three people from her convent, Maria, Walabonsus and Petrus. When some of Aurea's relatives discovered Aurea they brought her before the judge. Aurea was given the choice of renouncing her Christian faith or being executed. Aurea chose the former. But her conscience plagued her and she continued to live as a Christian, until she met up with her family, who ensured that she was imprisoned and executed for being a follower of Christ.

Five Friars Minor, 1220

Berardus, Peter, Acursius, Adjutus, and Otto were sent by St Francis to preach to the Muslims in the west, while he went in person to those of the east. They preached first to the Moors of Seville, where they suffered much for their zeal, and were banished. Passing on from there to Morocco, they began to preach Christ there, and being banished returned again. The infidel judge had them scourged until their ribs appeared bare. He then ordered burning oil and vinegar to be poured into their wounds, and their bodies to be rolled over sharp stones and potsherds. At length the king brought them before him, and taking his scimitar, clove their heads asunder in the middle of their fore heads, on the 16th of January, 1220.

Alban Butler, The Lives of the Saints, Dublin, 1833, volume I, p 72.

NUNILO AND ALODIA

Martyrs in Spain, beheaded at Huesca in 851

Roderic having dethroned and pulled out the eyes of Vitiza, the Gothic Icing of Spain, and excluded his children from the crown, usurped himself the throne, in 711. Count Julian, the most powerful nobleman in Spain, and governor of that part which was contiguous to the Straits, out of revenge for an insult which Roderic had offered his daughter, whom the tyrant had ravished, invited the Moors or Saracens from Africa into Spain. Mousa, who was governor of those Saracens, having obtained the consent of the caliph Miramolin, sent first only twelve thousand men under a general named Tarif, who easily possessed themselves of Mount Calpe, and the town Heraclea, which these Moors called from that time, Gibraltar, or Mouth, of Tarif, from this general, and the word Gibel, which in Arabic signifies mountain; whence Aetna in Sicily was called by the Saracens, Gibel These Moors maintained their ground in this fortress, and being reinforced from Africa, defeated the Spaniards in Andalusia. King Roderic was no more heard of after this battle; but two hundred years after, his tomb was discovered in a country church in Portugal; from which circumstance it is conjectured that he fled, and hid himself in that country. Tarif made himself master of Mantesa, Malaga, Murcia, and Toledo, the capital of the Gothic empire. Mousa, jealous of his success, crossed the Straits with another army, took Seville, Merida, and other places, and in three years time the Moors or Saracens were masters of all Spain, in 716, and carried away an immense booty. A misunderstanding arising between Tarif and Mousa, they were both recalled by Miramolin, and Mousa's son Abdalasisa left governor of Spain, and Seville made the capital, though Tarif had resided at Cordova. The Spanish Goths chose Pelagius, the sole surviving prince of the blood royal, king of Spain, in 716, who assembled an army in the mountains of Asturias, recovered that country, Galicia, and Biscay, and afterwards Leon; and erected the Christian kingdom, called first of Asturias afterwards of Leon. This prince gave great proofs of his valor and piety as did his successor, Alphonsus the Catholic. The Saracen governors, especially the third, called Abderamene, ruled with great cruelty, and often carried their arms into the southern parts of France, but were repulsed by Charles Martel. This governor Abderamene, surnamed Adahil, in 759 shook off all dependence upon the sultans of Egypt, took the title of king and fixed his court at Cordova; and the other Moorish governors in Spain imitated his example. After the first desolation of war many of these princes tolerated the Christians in their dominions, and allowed them to build new churches and monasteries under certain conditions, and according to the laws of a polity established by them. But, in the ninth century, a most cruel persecution was raised at Cordova, by king Abderamene the Second, and his son Mahomet.

Among the numberless martyrs who in those days sealed their fidelity to the law of God with their blood, two holy virgins were most illustrious. They were sisters, of noble extraction, and their names were Nunilo and Alodia. Their father was a Mahometan, and their mother a Christian, and after the death of her first husband, she was so unhappy as to take a second husband who was also a Mahometan. Her two daughters, who had been brought up in the Christian faith, had much to suffer in the exercise of their religion from the brutality of this step-father, who was a person of high rank in Castile. They were also solicited by many suitors to marry, but resolving to serve God in the state of holy virginity, they obtained leave to go to the house of a devout Christian aunt, where, enjoying an entire liberty as to their devotions, they strove to render themselves every day more agreeable to their divine Spouse. Their fasts were severe, and almost daily, and their devotions were only interrupted by necessary duties or other good works. The town where they lived, named Barbite, or Vervete, (which seems to be that which is now called Castro Viejo, near Najara in Castile, upon the borders of Navarre,) being subject to the Saracens, when the laws of king Abderamene were published against the Christians, they were too remarkable by their birth and the reputation of their zeal and piety not to be soon apprehended by the king's officers. They appeared before the judge not only undaunted, but with a holy joy painted on their countenances. He employed the most flattering caresses and promises to work them into a compliance, and at length proceeded to threats. When these artifices failed him, he put them into the hands of impious women, hoping these instruments of the devil would be able by their crafty address to insinuate themselves into the hearts of the virgins. But Christ enlightened and protected his spouses, and those wicked women after many trials were obliged to declare to the judge that nothing could conquer their resolution. He therefore condemned them to be beheaded in their prison; which was executed on the 22nd of October, 851, or, according to Morales, in 840. Their bodies were buried in the same place: the greatest part of their relics is now kept in the abbey of St. Savior of Leger, in Navarre. Their festival is celebrated with an extraordinary concourse of people at Huesca in Aragon, and at Bosca, where a portion of their relics is preserved. See St. Eulogius Memorial, 1. 2, c. 7; Ambr. Morales, in schol. ad Eulog. p 286; Mariana, &c.
Alban Butler, The Lives of the Saints, Dublin, 1833, volume 1, p 82.

Edmund of East Anglia, King and Martyr
20 November 870

When the heathen Anglo-Saxons invaded Christian Britain in the 400's, they eventually established seven kingdoms: Essex, Wessex, Sussex (East Saxons, West Saxons, and South Saxons), Mercia, Northumbria, and East Anglia (three kingdoms of the Angles), and the Jute kingdom of Kent. (The borders between these ancient kingdoms are still borders between regions speaking English with different accents today.) Under the influence of missionaries from the Celts and from continental Europe, these peoples became Christian, only to be faced themselves by a wave of heathen invaders.

Edmund was born about 840, became King of East Anglia in about 855, and in 870 faced a horde of marauding Danes, who moved through the countryside, burning churches and slaughtering villages wholesale. On reaching East Anglia, their leaders confronted Edmund and offered him peace on condition that he would rule as their vassal and forbid the practice of the Christian faith. Edmund refused this last condition, fought, and was captured. He was ill-treated and killed. His burial place is the town of Bury St. Edmunds.

James Kiefer, Christian Biographies, By kind permission

Gellért

Hungary

Martyrdom of Bishop Gellért

The Hungarian Pagan Revolt of 1046 and the Martyrdom of Bishop Gellért

A few years after the death of Stephen I, the first Christian Hungarian king, an uprising against King Peter turned into a pagan revolt to restitute paganism. Many Christians were killed, among them the famous bishop Gellért.

King Stephen I of Hungary died on August 15, 1038. Before his death, he designated Peter Orseolo, the son of his sister and the doge of Venice, her husband, as his successor. Peter became king of Hungary after Stephen's death. He laid heavy taxes on the people and oppressed them as a tyrant, as a result Hungarian nobles deposed him in 1041. Peter left the country and fled to Germany, but returned in 1044, and took over the throne again with the help of Emperor Henry III. Peter then subordinated Hungary to the emperor, ending its independence. The common people and the nobles joined together to overthrow his reign. They sent messengers to Kiev in 1046, to recall András (Andrew) and Levente from Russian soil and install them into power.

András (Andrew), Levente and Béla were the sons of King Stephen's cousin. They fled the country before Stephen's death to avoid a possible attempt on their life, and went to Bohemia, then to Poland, where Béla married the daughter of the Polish monarch. András and Levente continued their way to Russia and settled in the court of Yaroslav the Wise in Kiev. András married Princess Anastasia and they both became faithful Christians, while Levente remained pagan. Many Hungarians planned to use the return of Andrew and Levente for the abolishment of Christianity, and to revert to the pagan faith. The uprising turned into a pagan revolt. The pagans led by a noble called Vata started raging campaigns to destroy churches and kill Christians. As a result of the horrible slaughter, a multitude of Christians were martyred, among them the bishops Gellért (Gerard), Besztrik and Buldi.

The pagan Levente and the Christian András joined the rebels for a short time, but when the pagans started a war against Christians and killed the bishops on the banks of the Danube River, András turned against them, helped by the Christians and the Russians in his escort. The revolt was suppressed, Peter was killed and András crowned king (reigned 1046 1060).

Bishop Gellért (Gerard) was a nobleman from Venice, his original name being Gerard di Sagredo. As a boy he became very sick and his parents took him to a Benedictine monastery where he was taken care of and later regained his health. He became a Benedictine, and after his studies at Bologna, he was chosen abbot of the monastery, but left for the Holy Land in AD 1015. On his journey he met the abbot of Pannonhalma, called Rasian, who invited him to Hungary and Gellért accepted the invitation. King Stephen I of Hungary was so impressed by the preaching of the talented young Gellért, that he entrusted him with the tutoring of the 8 year-old Prince Imre. Gellért trained him for 7 years, Imre becoming a noble minded, exceptional young Christian prince.

Gellért spent the next 7 years in solitude in the Bakony Mountains, where he studied the Holy Scriptures and wrote his commentaries. His book, entitled Deliberatio, is probably the first collection of Hungarian Bible commentaries. Gellért went on a missionary journey to the region of the Maros River in Transylvania (the western part of modern Romania). He preached the Gospel, baptized the converted, and founded schools, churches, presbyteries. Gellért was martyred on the shore of the Danube River, in the area of modern Budapest, in 1046.

Seeing the affliction of their nation, the Hungarian nobles gathered together at Csanád for counsel. In the name of the whole country, they sent messengers to András and Levente in Russia, asking them to come home to Hungary and defend the people from the angry Germans, assuring them that the whole Hungary is waiting for them and will follow them whole-heartedly. The nobles swore that when András and Levente enter Hungary, all Hungarians will gather around them and accept them as their leaders. 82. Being afraid of a trap, András and Levente sent messengers in secret to Hungary. But when they later arrived to Újvár a city built by King Aba , a multitude of Hungarians gathered around them. The people being led by demonic impulses demanded that András and Levente let them live according to pagan customs, let them kill the priests and bishops, destroy the churches, cast away the Christian faith and worship idols. András and Levente let the people follow their hearts and become lost as their ancestors were, otherwise they would not have fought by their side against King Peter.

A man called Vata from the fortress of Belus was the first to dedicate himself to the devil. He shaved off his hair leaving three tails of hair on his head according to pagan customs. After some time, his son, János (John) also followed in the steps of his father. He gathered around himself many magicians, fortune-tellers and shamans and became very influential among the rich. His priestess called Rasdi was later imprisoned by the Christian King Béla for such a long time, that she ate her own legs and perished. According to the old books on the deeds of the Hungarians, it was absolutely forbidden for Christians to take wives from the family of Vata and János, as these men turned away the Hungarian people from the Gospel of Christ during the time of grace, the same way as Dathan and Abiram stirred rebellion against God during Old Testament times.

At the cursed and damnable instigation of Vata, all the people dedicated themselves to the devil, eating horse meat and doing many wicked things. They killed the Christians and the priests, destroyed many churches, revolted against King Peter and wickedly killed the Germans and Italians all over Hungary who held different offices. During the night, they sent three messengers to Peter's camp to announce the commands of András and Levente, that bishops, priests and tax collectors should be killed, pagan customs are to be followed and even the memory of Peter and his Germans and Italians should vanish. The following morning King Peter heard all these things and found out that the two brothers returned and at their commands the Hungarians had killed his officers, but he concealed his dismay, trying to appear cheerful. He broke up his camp and crossed the Danube River at Zsitvatõ, planning to go to Székesfehérvár. But the Hungarians found out about his intentions, arrived before him into the city, occupied the bastions and the towers, shut the gates and did not let the king enter the city.

In the meantime, András and Levente advanced with the multitude and arrived to the crossing place on the Danube River in central Hungary which is commonly called Pest. When bishops Gellért, Besztrik, Buldi and Beneta and governor Szolnok heard this, they left the city of Székesfehérvár and went to meet princes András and Levente and welcome them with respect.

When they arrived to the above mentioned crossing point, the wicked Vata and his accomplices, possessed by the demons to whom they had dedicated themselves, attacked the bishops and their companions and stoned them. Bishop Saint Gellért showed the sign of the cross constantly to those who stoned him, which angered them even more. They overthrew the cart of the bishop, put him on a trundle and hurled him down the cliffs of Kelenföld. Since he was still breathing, they thrust a spear through his chest and dashed his brain on a stone. This is how Christ's glorious martyr left the ills of this world for eternal bliss. Many times the Danube River overflew its banks and covered the stone on which Saint Gellért's head was crushed; but not even in seven years could its waters wash the blood off. Finally, the priests took the stone and carried it to Csanád, and it is now placed above Gellért's altar. A church built in memory of the blessed martyr Gellért now stands on the place where his head was crushed, at the foot of the cliff. Gellért was a Benedictine born in Venice, he came to Pannonia, lived as a hermit in Bél at first, then he became the bishop of the Church at Csanád.

Bishop Buldi was stoned to death and moved to the glorious afterlife. Besztrik and Beneta crossed the Danube in a boat to András and Levente. The pagans on the other side of the river inflicted a wound upon bishop Besztrik; he died on the third day. In the meantime Prince András arrived there and delivered bishop Beneta from the hands of the pagans. Saint Gellért's prophecy came to pass, as all of them were martyred except Beneta. Governor Szolnok jumped in the Danube with his horse and as he was drifting, a boat came and saved him from certain death. The boat was of a man called Murtmur, who was baptized by Szolnok. When Murtmur tried to save the governor, the pagans threatened him with death if he would not kill governor Szolnok. Murtmur became terrified and killed the governor with a sword in his own boat. So many priests and other Christians were martyred for Christ that day, that only God and the angels know their number.

Diognetus

Germany, Christian Missions among the Wends, 1066

Charlemagne was the first who attempted to introduce Christianity among the Slavic tribes which, under the collective name of Wends, occupied the Northern part of Germany, along the coast of the Baltic, from the mouth of the Elbe to the Vistula: Wagrians in Holstein, Obotrites in Mecklenburg, Sorbians on the Saxon boundary, Wilzians in Brandenburg, etc. But in the hands of Charlemagne, the Christian mission was a political weapon; and to the Slavs, acceptation of Christianity became synonymous with political and national subjugation. Hence their fury against Christianity which, time after time, broke forth, volcano-like, and completely destroyed the work of the missionaries. The decisive victories which Otto I. gained over the Wends, gave him an opportunity to attempt, on a large scale, the establishment of the Christian church among them. Episcopal sees were founded at Havelberg in 946, at Altenburg or Oldenburg in 948, at Meissen, Merseburg, and Zeitz in 968, and in the last year an archiepiscopal see was founded at Magdeburg. Boso, a monk from St. Emmeran, at Regensburg, who first had translated the formulas of the liturgy into the language of the natives, became bishop of Merseburg, and Adalbert, who first had preached Christianity in the island of Rügen, became archbishop.

But again the Christian church was used as a means for political purposes, and, in the reign of Otto II., a fearful rising took place among the Wends under the leadership of Prince Mistiwoi. He had become a Christian himself; but, indignant at the suppression which was practiced in the name of the Christian religion, he returned to heathenism, assembled the tribes at Rethre, one of the chief centers of Wendish heathendom, and began, in 983, a war which spread devastation all over Northern Germany. The churches and monasteries were burnt, and the Christian priests were expelled. Afterwards Mistiwoi was seized with remorse, and tried to cure the evil he had done in an outburst of passion. But then his subjects abandoned him; he left the country, and spent the last days of his life in a Christian monastery at Bardewick. His grandson, Gottschalk, whose Slavic name is unknown, was educated in the Christian faith in the monastery of St. Michael., near Lüneburg; but when he heard that his father, Uto, had been murdered, 1032, the old heathen instincts of revenge at once awakened within him. He left the monastery, abandoned Christianity, and raised a storm of persecution against the Christians, which swept over all Brandenburg, Mecklenburg, and Holstein. Defeated and taken prisoner by Bernard of Lower Saxony, he returned to Christianity; lived afterwards at the court of Canute the Great in Denmark and England; married a Danish princess, and was made ruler of the Obotrites. A great warrior, he conquered Holstein and Pommerania, and formed a powerful Wendish empire; and on this solid political foundation, he attempted, with considerable success, to build up the Christian church. The old bishoprics were re-established, and new ones were founded at Razzeburg and Mecklenburg; monasteries were built at Leuzen, Oldenburg, Razzeburg, Lübeck, and Mecklenburg; missionaries were provided by Adalbert, archbishop of Hamburg-Bremen; the liturgy was translated into the native tongue, and revenues were raised for the support of the clergy, the churches, and the service.

But, as might have been expected, the deeper Christianity penetrated into the mass of the people, the fiercer became the resistance of the heathen. Gottschalk was murdered at Lentz, June 7, 1066, together with his old teacher, Abbot Uppo, and a general rising now took place. The churches and schools were destroyed; the priests and monks were stoned or killed as sacrifices on the heathen altars; and Christianity, was literally swept out of the country. It took several decades before a new beginning could be made, and the final Christianization of the Wends was not achieved until the middle of the twelfth century.

Philip Scaff

Elphage, Archbishop of Canterbury, Martyr

Elphage was born of noble and virtuous parents, who gave him a good education. Fearing the snares of riches, he renounced the world whilst he was still very young; and though most dutiful to his parents in all other things, he in this courageously overcame the tears of his tender mother. He served God first in the monastery of Deerhurst in Gloucestershire.

His desire of greater perfection taught him always to think that he had not yet begun to live to God. After some years he left Deerhurst, and built himself a cell in a desert place of the abbey of Bath, where he shut himself up, unknown to men, but well known to God, for whose love he made himself a voluntary martyr of repentance. His virtue, after some time, shone to men the brighter through the veils of his humility, and many noblemen and others addressed themselves to him for instruction in the paths of perfection, and he was at length obliged to take upon himself the direction of the great abbey of Bath.

Perfection is more difficult to maintain in monastic houses with large communities. St. Elphege lamented bitterly the irregularities of the tepid among the brethren, especially little junketings, from which he in a short time reclaimed them; and God, by the sudden death of one, opened the eyes of all the rest. The good abbot would not tolerate the least relaxation in his community, being sensible how small a breach may totally destroy the regularity of a house. He used to say that it would have been much better for a man to have stayed in the world than to be an imperfect monk; and that to wear the habit of a saint without having the spirit, was a perpetual lie, and an hypocrisy which insults, but can never impose upon, Almighty God.

When St. Ethelwold, bishop of Winchester died in 984, St. Dunstan, being admonished by St. Andrew in a vision, obliged our holy abbot to quit his solitude and accept episcopal consecration. The virtues of Elphege became more conspicuous in this high station, though he was no more than thirty years of age when he was first placed in it. In winter, howsoever cold it was, he always rose at midnight, went out, and prayed a long time barefoot, and without his upper garment. He never eat meat unless on extraordinary occasions. He was no less remarkable for charity to his neighbor than severity to himself. He accordingly provided so liberally for the needs of the poor, that during his time there were no beggars in the whole diocese of Winchester.

The holy prelate had governed the see of Winchester for twenty-two years with great edification, when, after the death of Archbishop Altrie, in 1006, he was translated to that of Canterbury, being then fifty-two years of age. He who trembled under his former burden was much more terrified at the thought of the latter: but was compelled to acquiesce. Saving visited Rome to receive his pallium, on his return he held a great national council at Oenham, in 1009, in which 32 canons were published for the reform of errors and abuses, and the establishment of discipline; and, among other things, the then ancient law, commanding the fast on Friday, was confirmed.

The Danes at that time were making the most dreadful havoc in England. They landed where they pleased, and not only plundered the country, but committed excessive barbarities on the natives, with little or no opposition from the weak King Ethelred. Their army being joined by the traitorous Earl Edric, they marched out of the West into Kent, and pitched camp before Canterbury. But before it was besieged, however, the English nobility, perceiving the danger the place was in, desired the archbishop, then in the city, to provide for his security by flight, which he refused to do, saying that it was the part only of a hireling to abandon his flock in the time of danger.

During the siege he often sent out to the enemies asking them to spare his innocent sheep, whom he endeavoured to animate against the worst that could happen. And having prepared them, by his zealous I exhortations, rather to suffer the utmost than renounce their faith, he gave them the blessed eucharist, and recommended them to the divine Protection

Whilst he was thus employed in assisting and encouraging his people, Canterbury was taken by storm. The infidels on entering the city made a dreadful slaughter of all that came in their way, without distinction of sex or age. As soon as the holy prelate learned of the barbarity of the enemy, he broke from the monks, who would have detained him in the church, where they thought he might be safe. He pressed through the Danish troop and made his way to the place of slaughter. Then turning to the enemy, he desired them to forbear the massacre of his people, and rather discharge their fury upon him, crying out to the murderers: "Spare these innocent persons. There is no glory in spilling their blood. Turn your indignation rather against me. 1 have reproached you for your cruelties; I have fed, clothed, and ransomed these your captives." The archbishop talking with this freedom was immediately seized, and treated by the Danes with all manner of barbarity. Not content with making him watch the burning of his cathedral, and the decimation of his monks and of the citizens, they tore his face, beat and kicked him unmercifully, laid him in irons, and confined him several months in a filthy dungeon.

But being afflicted with an epidemic of fatal dysentery in their army, and attributing this scourge to their cruel usage of the saint, they drew him out prison. He prayed for them, and gave their sick bread which he had blessed. When the sick ate this, they recovered, and the calamity ceased. Their chiefs returned thanks to the servant of God, and discussed setting him free. Covetousness, however, prevailed in their councils, and they exacted for his ransom 3,000 marks of gold.

Elphage pointed out that the country had all been laid waste; moreover, that patrimony of the poor was not to be squandered. He therefore was bound once again, and on Easter Sunday he was brought before the commander of the Danish fleet, which then lay at Greenwich. He was threatened with torments and death until he paid the ransom demanded. He answered them that the only gold he had to offer them was that of true wisdom which consists in the knowledge and worship of the living God, and if they refused to listen to it, it would fare worse with them than with Sodom; adding that their empire would not last long in England.

His answer enraged the barbarians. They knocked him down with the backs of their battle-axes, then stoned him.

Like St Stephen, the holy man prayed to God to forgive them and to receive his soul. In the end, raising himself up a little, he said: "O good Shepherd! O incomparable Shepherd! Look with compassion on the children of your church, which I, dying, commend to you."

At this point a Dane that had been lately baptized by the saint, perceiving him agonizing and under torture, grieved to see him suffer in so slow and painful a manner. To put an end to his pain, the Dane clove his head with his battle-axe, and gave the finishing stroke to his martyrdom.

Thus died St. Elphege, on the l9th of April, 1012, in the 59th year of his age. He was solemnly interred in the cathedral of St. Paul in London. In 1023, his body was found intact, and translated with honour to Canterbury; Knut, the Danish king, and Agelnoth, the archbishop, went with it from St. Paul's to the river. It was carried by monks down a narrow street to the water-side, and put on board a vessel. The King held the stern. Queen Emma also attended with great presents; and an incredible multitude of people followed the procession from London. The church of Canterbury, on the occasion, was most magnificently adorned. This translation was made on the 8th of June, on which it was annually commemorated. His relics lay near the high altar till the dispersion of relics under Henry VIII. Hakon, Thorkill, and the other Danish commanders, perished miserably soon after, and their numerous fleet of above two hundred sail was almost all lost in violent storms. St. Elphege is named in the Roman Martyrology.

Saint Elphage is also known as Alphage, Aelphage and Alfheah.

Alban Butler

Eirk

Sweden, 1160

Erik IX Jedvardsson was ruler of much of Sweden from 1150 to 1160. He was the head of a Christian kingdom with nearby pagan kingdoms, all sharing an old tradition of fighting. Around 1155, he headed an expedition into Finland, then loosely under Swedish rule, to consolidate Swedish authority there and to establish a protected Christian mission, headed by Henry of Uppsala, now considered the founder of the Church in Finland. Erik is also known for undertaking to provide Sweden with fair laws and fair courts, and for measures designed to assist the poor and the infirm. As he was in church on 18 May 1, the day after Ascension Day, he was told that a pagan Danish army was approaching to kill him. He replied, "Let us at least finish the sacrifice. The rest of the feast I shall keep elsewhere." As he was leaving the church, the pagans rushed upon him and killed him.

Erik was honored both as an upholder of the Christian faith and as a national hero, the ancestor of a long line of Swedish kings. Within thirty years after his death his name appeared on the Swedish Calendar, and he is accounted the principal patron of Sweden, as (for example) Patrick is of Ireland. The silver casket with his remains still rests in the cathedral at Uppsala.

James E. Kiefer, Sketches in Church History, by kind permission

Martyrdom of Thomas à Becket (1)

1170 saw the fateful killing of Archbishop Thomas Becket by Henry II's knights, on the steps leading up to the cathedral's high altar. Less than three years later Becket was declared a saint and pilgrims flocked to his grave in their thousands. Today the spot of Becket's murder is marked by a six inch square stone. On a wall nearby the following words are carved:

Thomas Becket
Archbishop. Saint. Martyr.
Died here
Tuesday 29th December
1170

In the struggle between State and Church it was not possible for Becket to be neutral. From the moment of his consecration all

Becket's efforts were directed against the power of the King, Henry II. By 1164 the breach was complete and Becket went into exile in France for six years, calling himself Brother Dearlove. Henry took out his rage on Becket's friends and followers and it was probably this, more than anything else, which brought all England to Becket's side.

Early in 1170, the King and the Archbishop patched up their quarrel near Freteval and on December 1 Becket returned to England. But Becket knew that his life was in danger. The day after his return Becket preached in the chapter house on the text, "Here we have no abiding city, but we seek one to come." On Christmas Day, he preached his famous sermon in Canterbury Cathedral, using the familiar text, "I come to die among you". The clash between monarch and archbishop over the immunity of the clergy from secular jurisdiction could not be resolved. In Becket's absence Henry II had arranged for his son Henry to be crowned as his successor and colleague by the Archbishop of York, assisted by the Bishops of London and Salisbury. Since Augustine's day the crowning of monarchs had always been performed by the Archbishop of Canterbury, so Becket procured letters from the Pope against the these three men. They went to see Henry in France and told him, "As long as Thomas Becket lives you will have neither good days, nor peaceful kingdom, nor quiet life." These words produced the following outcry from Henry, "A fellow that I have loaded with benefits; a fellow who came to court on a lame horse, with a cloak for a saddle, sits without hindrance on the throne itself. What sluggard wretches, what cowards have I brought up in my court! Not one will deliver me from this low-born priest." Henry then rushed from the room. Among the courtiers to hear this outburst were four knights, Hugh de Moreville, Richard de Bret, Reginal Fitzurse and Sir William Tracy. The crossed over to England and surprised Becket by suddenly appearing in his room in Canterbury on the morning of December 29, 1170. They felt repulsed by the determined words of the archbishop and they withdrew to arm themselves so they could arrest him. The primate's servants then locked all the gates, but Randulf del Broc, whom the four knights were staying with, being the King's custos of the see of Canterbury, was able to guide the knights back to Becket's rooms, by way of the orchard. Becket's monks had advised him to flee, but as he would not, they hastily guided the archbishop into the church, by way of the cloisters. But the knights caught up with Becket as he passed the north transept and was going up the steps leading to the choir. The presence of the four armed knights made everyone except three men desert Becket's side: Robert Canon of Merton, William Fitzstephen the historian, and Edward Grim, a clerk who later wrote up an accurate account of the event.

Reginald Fitzure seized Becket by his pall, intending to drag him back across the church, but the archbishop managed to cling to a pillar, so one of the other knights struck him with the flat of his sword. Then Becket shouted: "Touch me not Reginald Fitzurse! Why should you treat me thus? I have granted you many favours. You are my man, and owe fealty and obedience-you are your fellows." Fitzurse replied, "I owe you no fealty inconsistent with that I owe to my lord the King." Becket was then wounded in the head by a blow that might have killed him had not his faithful clerk, Edward Grim, cushioned the blow by using his own arm. Richard le Bret then struck Becket with such force that the point of his sword, after striking Becket, was broken off. (This broken piece of sword was later preserved as a relic of the martyrdom.)

Richard le Bret's thrust proved fatal, but was followed by a despicable deed, carried out by Hugh of Horsea, a subdeacon. He placed his own foot on the neck of the archbishop, as he lay on the ground, and with his sword drew out Becket's brains scattering them over the pavement, exclaiming, "Let us be off. He will rise no more!" Only one of the four knights had struck no blow, Hugh de Moreville, a man of gentle disposition, who kept the crowds from becoming involved by preventing they from going beyond the transept where the murder took place. The knights then left "with a savage burst of triumph they ran shouting as if in battle, the watchword of the kings of England 'The king's men, the king's men!' wounding a servant of the archdeacon of Sens for lamenting this horrific murder."

When Becket's body was finally lifted it was discovered that he was wearing an extremely coarse horse-hair shirt. The medieval people were quick to respond to the tragedy. Becket had been the first Englishman to defy autocratic power. His supporters knew that they were fighting against evil actions. Because Becket stood out as a burning light in the dark struggle against tyranny tens of thousands of people visited his shrine from all over the world.
Editor

Martyrdom of Thomas à Becket (2)

Thomas of Canterbury, archbishop and martyr

29 December 1170

On December 29, we remember Thomas a Becket, Archbishop of Canterbury, slain in his own cathedral in 1170, for his defiance of King Henry II. The death of Thomas reminds us that a Christian, even when safe from pagans, can be in danger from his fellow-Christians. It also reminds us that one can be martyred in a cause where the merits of the particular issue at hand are not obvious to all men of good will. The issue here, or one of the issues, was one of court jurisdiction. King Henry claimed that a cleric accused of an ordinary crime ought to be tried in the King's Courts like any layman. Thomas, who was Henry's Chancellor and his close friend, vigorously upheld the king's position. However, when he was made Archbishop of Canterbury with the king's support, he reversed himself completely and upheld the right of clergy to be tried only in Church courts, which could not inflict capital punishment. (This reversal does not imply fickleness or treachery. As Chancellor, Thomas was bound to serve the king. Now, as Archbishop, he was bound to defend the Church.) Henry wanted an arrangement by which (for example) a priest accused of murder would be tried by a Church Court, which if it found him guilty would degrade him to the rank of a layman, whereupon a King's Court would try him, and if it found him guilty would order him hanged. Thomas objected that a man could not be tried and punished twice for the same offense.

Henry, being angered at opposition from someone whom he had counted on for support, was heard to exclaim in anger, "This fellow who has eaten my bread has lifted up his heel against me [see Psalm 41:9]. Have I no friend who will rid me of this upstart priest?" Four of his knights promptly rode to Canterbury, where they confronted the Archbishop and demanded that he back down. When he did not, they killed him. Public reaction was immediate and vigorous, and reckoned Thomas as a saint and a martyr, and Henry as a blaspheming murderer. Henry swore that he had not intended his remark to be taken seriously, and had himself publicly whipped at the tomb of Thomas. Thomas was very soon canonized, and his tomb was one of the most popular places of pilgrimage in Europe for the next three-and-a-half centuries. During a war between England and France, a King of France obtained a cease-fire to enable him to make a pilgrimage to Canterbury. Chaucer's Canterbury Tales is concerned with a group of pilgrims on their way to the tomb of Thomas.

The chief moral that I draw from Thomas's life and death is that when a man seeks to serve God, God graciously accepts that service, even if the man is quite wrong about what it is that God expects of him.
James Kiefer, Christian Biographies, By kind permission

Martyrdom of Thomas à Becket (3)

The writer of this extract was the monk of Canterbury, Gervase, who died in 1205.

But on the fifth day of the nativity, which was the third day of the week, there arrived four courtiers, who desired to speak with the archbishop, thinking by this to discover the weak points [of the monastery]. These were Reginald Fitz-Urse, Hugh de Morville, William de Traci, and Richard Brito. After a long discussion, they began to employ threats; and at length rising up hastily, they went out into the courtyard; and under the spreading branches of a mulberry-tree, they cast off the garments with which they had covered their breastplates, and, accompanied by those persons whom they bad summoned from the province, they returned into the archbishop's palace. Yet he, unmoved by the exhortations, the prayers, and the tears of his followers, remained firm in his place, until the time had arrived for the performance of the evening service in the church; towards which he advanced with a slow and deliberate step, like one who of his own free-will prepares himself for death. Having entered the church, he paused at the threshold; and he asked his attendants of what they were afraid. When the clerks began to fall into disorder, be said, "Depart, ye cowards! Let these blind madmen go on in their career. We command you, in virtue of your obedience, not to shut the door."

While he was thus speaking, behold! the executioners having ransacked the bishop's palace, rushed together through the cloisters; three of whom carried hatchets in their left bands, and one an axe or a two-edged glaive, while all of them brandished drawn swords in their right hands. But after they had rushed through the open door, they separated from each other, Fitz-Urse turning to the left, while the three others took to the right. The archbishop had already ascended a few steps, when Fitz-Urse, as he hurried onwards, asked one whom he met, "Where is the archbishop?"

Hearing this, he turned round on the step, and, with a slight motion of the head, he was the first to answer, "Here am I, Reginald. I have conferred many a benefit on you, Reginald; and do you now come to me with arms in your hands?"

"You shall soon find that out," was the reply. "Are not you that notorious traitor to the king?" And, laying hold on his pall, he said, "Depart hence;" and he struck the pall with his sword.

The archbishop replied, "I am no traitor; nor will I depart, wretched man!" and he plucked the fringe of his pall from out the knight's hand. The other repeated the words, "Flee hence!"

The reply was, " I will not flee; here your malice shall be satisfied."

At these words the assassin stepped back, as if smitten by a blow. In the meantime the other three assailants had arrived; and they exclaimed, " Now you shall die!"

" If," said the archbishop, "you seek my life, I forbid you, under the threat of an anathema, from touching any one of my followers. As for me, I willingly embrace death, provided only that the church obtain liberty and peace at the price of my blood."

When he had said these words, he stretched forth his head to the blows of the murderers. Fitz-Urse hastened forward, and with his whole strength lie planted a blow upon the extended head; and he cried out, as if in triumph over his conquered enemy, "Strike! strike!" Goaded on by the author of confusion, these butchers, adding wound to wound, dashed out his brains; and one of them, following up the martyr, (who at this time was either in the act of falling, or had already fallen) struck the pavement with his sword but the point of the weapon broke off short.

They now returned through the cloister, crying out, "Knights of the king, let us go; he is dead!" And then they pillaged whatever they found in the archbishop's residence. See here a wonder. While he was yet alive, and could speak, and stand on his feet, men called him a traitor to the king; but when he was laid low, with his brains dashed out, he was called the holy Thomas, even before the breath had left his body.

This blessed martyr suffered death in the ninth year of his patriarchate, on the fourth of the calends of January [29th Dec.], being the third day of the week, A.D. 1170, while the monks were singing their vespers. His dead body was removed and placed in the shrine before the altar of Christ. On the morrow it was carried by the monks and deposited in a tomb of marble within the crypt. Now, to speak the truth – that which

I saw with my eyes, and handled with my hands – he wore hair-cloth next his skin, then stamin, over that a black cowl, then the white cowl in which he was consecrated; he also wore his tunic and dalmatic, his chasuble, pall, and miter; Lower down, he had drawers of sack-cloth, and over these others of linen; his socks were of wool, and he had on sandals. If any one (as he ought) desires to know more of this martyr, let him read those books or writers which I have mentioned above, namely, Herbert, John, William, Benedict, and Gervase: and let him not omit the letters of the same saint. Others there are who probably have written respecting him; but even if it be so, they cannot tell all that ought to be known about him.

After his martyrdom the church of Canterbury was vacant for two years and five months. That he is alive in Christ is proved by the miracles which are performed throughout the whole world.

Gervase of Canterbury, History of the Archbishops of Canterbury, quoted in The Church Historians of England, volume V, part 1, pp. 329-336. Translated by Joseph Stevenson. London: Seeley's, 1853

Martyrdom of Thomas à Becket (4)

Life of Saint Thomas, martyr, of Canterbury

Thomas is as much to say as abisme or double, or trenched and hewn, he was an abisme profound in humility, as it appeared in the hair that he wore, and in washing of the feet of the poor people, double in prelation that was in word and in ensample, and hewn and trenched in his passion. Saint Thomas the martyr was son to Gilbert Beckett, a burgess of the city of London, and was born in the place where as now standeth the church called Saint Thomas of Acre. And this Gilbert was a good devout man, and took the cross upon him, and went on pilgrimage into the Holy Land, and had a servant with his knees. And on a Trinity Sunday received he his dignity, and there was at that time the king with many a great lord and sixteen bishops. And from thence was sent the abbot of Evesham to the pope with other clerks for the pall which he gave and brought to him, and he full meekly received it. And under his habit he ware the habit of a monk, and so was he under within forth a monk, and outward a clerk, and did great abstinence making his body lean and his soul fat. And he used to be well served at his table, and took but little refection thereof, and lived holily in giving good ensample.

After this, many times the king went over into Normandy, and in his absence always Saint Thomas had the rule of his son and of the realm, which was governed so well that the king could him great thanks, and then abode long in this realm. And when so was that the king did any thing against the franchise and liberties of holy church, Saint Thomas would ever withstand it to his power. And on a time when the sees of London and of Winchester were vacant and void, the king kept them both long in his hand for to have the profits of them; wherefore Saint Thomas was heavy, and came to the king and desired him to give those two bishopricks to some virtuous men. And anon the king granted to him his desire and ordained one master Roger, bishop of Winchester, and the Earl of Gloucester's son, bishop of London, named Sir Robert. And anon after Saint Thomas hallowed the abbey of Reading, which the first Henry founded. And that same year he translated Saint Edward, king and confessor at Westminster, where he was laid in a rich shrine. And in some short time after, by the enticement of the devil, fell great debate, variance, and strife, between the king and Saint Thomas, and the king sent for all the bishops to appear tofore him at Westminster at a certain day, at which day they assembled tofore him, whom he welcomed, and after said to them how that the archbishop would destroy his law, and not suffer him to enjoy such things as his predecessors had used tofore him. Whereto Saint Thomas answered that he never intended to do thing that should displease the king as far as it touched not the franchise and liberties of holy church. Then the king rehearsed how he would not suffer clerks that were thieves to have the execution of the law; to which Saint Thomas said, that he ought not to execute them, but they longeth to the correction of holy church, and other divers points; to which Saint Thomas would not agree. To the which the king said: Now I see well that thou wouldest foredo the laws of this land which have been used in the days of my predecessors, but it shall not lie in thy power, and so the king being wroth departed. Then the bishops all counseled Saint Thomas to follow the king's intent, or else the land should be in great trouble; and in like wise the lords temporal that were his friends counseled him the same, and Saint Thomas said: I take God to record it was never mine intent to displease the king, or to take any thing that longeth to his right or honor. And then the lords were glad and brought him to the king to Oxenford, and the king deigned not to speak to him. And then the king called all the lords spiritual and temporal tofore him, and said he would have all the laws of his forefathers there new confirmed, and there they were confirmed by all the lords spiritual and temporal. And after this the king charged them for to come to him to Clarendon to his parliament at a certain day assigned, on pain to run in his indignation, and at that time so departed. And this parliament was holden at Clarendon, the eleventh year of the king's reign, and the year of our Lord eleven hundred and sixty-four. At this parliament were many lords which all were against Saint Thomas. And then the king sitting in his parliament, in the presence of all his lords, demanded them if they would abide and keep the laws that had been used in his forefathers' days.

Then Saint Thomas spake for the part of holy church, and said: All old laws that be good and rightful, and not against our mother holy church, I grant with good will to keep them. And then the king said that he would not leave one point of his law, and waxed wroth with Saint Thomas. And then certain bishops required Saint Thomas to obey to the king's desire and will, and Saint Thomas desired respite to know the laws, and then to give him an answer. And when he understood them all, to some he consented, but many he denied and would never be agreeable to them, wherefore the king was wroth and said he would hold and keep them like as his predecessors had done before him, and would not minish one point of them.

Then Saint Thomas said to the king with full great sorrow and heavy cheer, Now, my most dear lord and gracious king, have pity on us of holy church, your bedemen, and give to us respite for a certain time. And thus departed each man. And Saint Thomas went to Winchester, and there prayed our Lord devoutly for holy church, and to give him aid and strength for to defend it, for utterly he determined to abide by the liberties and franchise, and fell down on his knees and said, full sore weeping: O good Lord, I acknowledge that I have offended, and for mine offence and trespass this trouble cometh to holy church, I purpose, good Lord, to go to Rome for to be assoiled of mine offences; and departed towards Canterbury. And anon the king sent his officers to his manors and despoiled them, because he would not obey the king's statutes. And the king commanded to seize all his lands and goods into his hands, and then his servants departed from him, and he went to the seaside for to have gone over sea, but the wind was against him, and so thrice he took his ship and might not pass. And then he knew that it was not our Lord's will that he should yet depart, and returned secretly to Canterbury, of whose coming his men made great joy. And on the morn came the king's officers for to seize all his goods, for the noise was that Saint Thomas had fled the land; wherefore they had despoiled all his manors and seized them into the king's hand. And when they came they found him at Canterbury, whereof they were sore abashed, and returned to the king informing him that he was yet at Canterbury, and anon after Saint Thomas came to the king to Woodstock for to pray him to be better disposed towards holy church. And then said the king to him in scorn: May not we two dwell both in this land? Art thou so sturdy and hard of heart? To whom Saint Thomas answered: Sire, that was never my thought, but I would fain please you, and do all that you desire so that ye hurt not the liberties of holy church, for them will I maintain while I live, ever to my power. With which words the king was sore moved, and swore that he would have them kept, and especial if a clerk were a thief he should be judged and executed by the king's law, and by no spiritual law, and said he would never suffer a clerk to be his master in his own land, and charged Saint Thomas to appear before him at Northampton, and to bring all the bishops of this land with him, and so departed. Saint Thomas besought God of help and succor, for the bishops which ought to be with him were most against him.

After this Saint Thomas went to Northampton where the king had then his great council in the castle with all his lords, and when he came tofore the king he said: I am come to obey your commandment, but before this time was never bishop of Canterbury thus entreated, for I am head of the Church of England, and am to you, Sir King, your ghostly father, and it was never God's law that the son should destroy his father which hath charge of his soul. And by your striving have you made all the bishops that should abide by the right of the church to be against holy church and me, and ye know well that I may not fight, but am ready to suffer death rather than I should consent to lose the right of holy church. Then said the king, Thou speakest as a proud clerk, but I shall abate thy pride ere I leave thee, for I must reckon with thee. Thou understandest well that thou wert my chancellor many years, and once I lent to thee 500 coins which thou never yet hast repaid, which I will that thou pay me again or else incontinent thou shalt go to prison. And then Saint Thomas answered: Ye gave me that 500 coins, and it is not fitting to demand that which ye have given. Notwithstanding he found surety for the said 500 coins and departed for that day. And after this, the next day the king demanded 30,000 coins that he had surmised on him to have stolen, he being chancellor, whereupon he desired day to answer; at which time he said that when he was archbishop he set him free therein without any claim or debt before good record, wherefore he ought not to answer unto that demand. And the bishops desired Saint Thomas to obey the king but in no wise he would not agree to such things as should touch against the liberties of the church. And then they came to the king, and forsook Saint Thomas, and agreed to all the king's desire, and the proper servants of Saint Thomas fled from him and forsook him, and then poor people came and accompanied him. And on the night came to him two lords and told to him that the king's men had emprised to slay him. And the next night after he departed in the habit of a brother of Sempringham, and so chevissed that he went over sea.

And in the meanwhile certain bishops went to Rome for to complain on him to the pope, and the king sent letters to the king of France not to receive him. And the King Louis said that, though a man were banished and had committed there trespasses, yet should he be free in France. And so after when this holy Saint Thomas came, he received him well, and gave him licence to abide there and do what he would. In this meanwhile the king of England sent certain lords into the pope complaining on the Archbishop Thomas, which made grievous complaints, which when the pope had heard said, he would give none answer till that he had heard the Archbishop Thomas speak, which would hastily come thither. But they would not abide his coming, but departed without speeding of their intents, and came into England again. And anon after, S Thomas came to Rome on Saint Mark's day at afternoon, and when his caterer should have bought fish for his dinner because it was fasting day, he could get none for no money, and came and told to his lord Saint Thomas so, and he bade him buy such as he could get, and then he bought flesh and made it ready for their dinner. And Saint Thomas was served with a capon roasted, and his men with boiled meat. And so it was that the pope heard that he was come, and sent a cardinal to welcome him, and he found him at his dinner eating flesh, which anon returned and told to the pope how he was not so perfect a man as he had supposed, for contrary to the rule of the church he eateth this day flesh. The pope would not believe him, but sent another cardinal which for more evidence took the leg of the capon in his kerchief and affirmed the same, and opened his kerchief tofore the pope, and he found the leg turned into a fish called a carp. And when the pope saw it, he said, they were not true men to say such things of this good bishop. They said faithfully that it was flesh that he ate. After this Saint Thomas came to the pope and did his reverence and obedience, whom the pope welcomed, and after communication he demanded him what meat he had eaten, and he said: Flesh as ye have heard tofore, because he could find no fish and very need compelled him thereto. Then the pope understood of the miracle that the capon's leg was turned into a carp, and of his goodness granted to him and to all them of the diocese of Canterbury licence to eat flesh ever after on Saint Mark's day when it falleth on a fish day, and pardon withal, which is kept and accustomed unto this day. And then Saint Thomas informed the pope how the king of England would have him consent to divers articles against the liberties of holy church, and what wrongs he did to the same, and that for to die he would never consent to them. And when the pope had heard him he wept for pity, and thanked God that he had such a bishop under him that had so well defended the liberties of holy church, and anon wrote out letters and bulls commanding all the bishops of Christendom to keep and observe the same.

And then Saint Thomas offered to the pope his bishopric up into the pope's hand, and his miter with the cross and ring, and the pope commanded him to keep it still, and said he knew no man more able than he was. And after Saint Thomas said mass tofore the pope in a white chasuble; and after mass he said to the pope that he knew by revelation that he should suffer death for the right of holy church, and when it should fall that chasuble should be turned from white into red. And after he departed from the pope and came down into France unto the abbey of Pontigny, and there he had knowledge that when the lords spiritual and temporal which had been at Rome were come home and had told the king that they might in no wise have their intent, that the king was greatly wroth, and anon banished all the kinsmen that were longing to Saint Thomas that they should incontinent void his land, and made them swear that they should go to him and tell to him that for his sake they were exiled, and so they went over sea to him at Pontigny and he being there was full sorry for them. And after there was a great chapter in England of the monks of Citeaux and there the king desired them to write to Pontigny that they should no longer keep ne sustain Thomas the Archbishop, for if they did, he would destroy them of that order being in England. And, for fear thereof they wrote so over to Pontigny that he must depart thence with his kinsmen, and so he did, and was then full heavy, and remitted his cause to God.

And anon after, the king of France sent to him that he should abide where it pleased him, and dwell in his realm and he would pay for the costs of him and his kinsmen. And he departed and went to Sens, and the abbot brought him on the way. And Saint Thomas told him how he knew by a vision that he should suffer death and martyrdom for the right of the church, and prayed him to keep it secret during his life. After this the king of England came into France, and there told the king how Saint Thomas would destroy his realm, and then there told how he would foredo such laws as his elders had used tofore him, wherefore Saint Thomas was sent for, and they were brought together. And the king of France labored sore for to set them at accord, but it would not be, for that one would not minish his laws and accustoms, and Saint Thomas would not grant that he should do England against Saint Thomas, and was wroth with him and commanded him to void his realm with all his kinsmen. And then Saint Thomas wist not whither to go; but comforted his kinsmen as well as he might, and purposed to have gone in to Provence for to have begged his bread. And as he was going, the king of France sent for him again, and when he came he cried him mercy and said he had offended God and him, and bade him abide in his realm where he would, and he would pay for the dispenses of him and his kin. And in the meanwhile the king of England ordained his son king, and made him to be crowned by the Archbishop of York, and other bishops, which was against the statutes of the land, for the Archbishop of Canterbury should have consented and also have crowned him, wherefore Saint Thomas gat a bull for to do accurse them that so did against him, and also on them that occupied the goods longing to him. And yet after this the king labored so much that he accorded the king of England and Saint Thomas which accord endured not long, for the king varied from it afterward. But Saint Thomas, upon this accord, came home to Canterbury, where he was received worshipfully, and sent for them that had trespassed against him, and by the authority of the pope's bull openly denounced them accursed unto the time they come to amendment. And when they knew this they came to him and would have made him to assoil them by force; and sent word over to the king how he had done, whereof the king was much wroth and said: If he had men in his land that loved him they would not suffer such a traitor in his land alive.

And forthwith four knights took their counsel together and thought they would do to the king a pleasure, and emprised to slay Saint Thomas, and suddenly departed and took their shipping towards England. And when the king knew of their departing he was sorry and sent after them, but they were on the sea and departed ere the messengers came, wherefore the king was heavy and sorry.

These be the names of the four knights: Sir Reginald Fitzurse, Sir Hugh de Morville, Sir William de Tracy, Sir Richard le Breton. On Christmas day Saint Thomas made a sermon at Canterbury in his own church, and weeping, prayed the people to pray for him, for he knew well his time was nigh, and there executed the sentence on them that were against the right of holy church. And that same day as the king sat at meat all the bread that he handled waxed anon moldy and hoar, that no man might eat of it, and the bread that they touched not was fair and good for to eat.

And these four knights aforesaid came to Canterbury on the Tuesday in Christmas week about Evensong time, and came to Saint Thomas and said that the king commanded him to make amends for the wrongs that he had done, and also that he should assoil all them that he had accursed anon, or else they should slay him. Then said Thomas: All that I ought to do by right, that will I with a good will do, but as to the sentence that is executed I may not undo, but that they will submit them to the correction of holy church, for it was done by our holy father the pope and not by me. Then said Sir Reginald: But if thou assoil the king and all other standing in the curse, it shall cost thee thy life. And Saint Thomas said: Thou knowest well enough that the king and I were accorded on Mary Magdalene day, and that this curse should go forth on them that had offended the church.

Then one of the knights smote him as he kneeled before the altar on the head. And one Sir Edward Grim, that was his crossier put forth his arm with the cross to bear off the stroke, and the stroke smote the cross asunder and his arm almost off, wherefore he fled for fear, and so did all the monks, that were that time at compline. And then smote each at him, that they smote off a great piece of the skull of his head, that his brain fell on the pavement. And so they slew and martyred him, and were so cruel that one of them brake the point of his sword against the pavement. And thus this holy and blessed Archbishop Saint Thomas suffered death in his own church for the right of all holy church. And when he was dead they stirred his brain, and after went in to his chamber and took away his goods, and his horse out of his stable, and took away his bulls and writings, and delivered them to Sir Robert Broke to bear into France to the king. And as they searched his chamber they found in a chest two shirts of hair made full of great knots, and then they said: Certainly he was a good man; and coming down into the churchward they began to dread and fear that the ground would not have borne them, and were marvelously aghast, but they supposed that the earth would have swallowed them all quick. And then they knew that they had done amiss. And anon it was known all about, how that he was martyred, and anon after took this holy body, and unclothed him, and found bishop's clothing above, and the habit of a monk under. And next his flesh he wore hard hair, full of knots, which was his shirt. And his breech was of the same, and the knots slicked fast within the skin, and all his body full of worms; he suffered great pain. And he was thus martyred the year of our Lord one thousand one hundred and seventy-one, and was fifty-three years old. And soon after tidings came to the king how he was slain, wherefore the king took great sorrow, and sent to Rome for his absolution.

Now after that Saint Thomas departed from the pope, the pope would daily look upon the white chasuble that Saint Thomas had said mass in, and the same day that he was martyred he saw it turned into red, whereby he knew well that that same day he suffered martyrdom for the right of holy church, and commanded a mass of requiem solemnly to be sung for his soul. And when the quire began to sing requiem, an angel on high above began the office of a martyr: Letabitur justus, and then all the quire followed singing forth the mass of the office of a martyr. And the pope thanked God that it pleased him to show such miracles for his holy martyr, at whose tomb by the merits and prayers of this holy martyr our blessed Lord hath showed many miracles. The blind have recovered their sight, the dumb their speech, the deaf their hearing, the lame their limbs, and the dead their life. If I should here express all the miracles that it hath pleased God to show for this holy saint it should contain a whole volume, therefore at this time, I pass over unto the feast of his translation, where I propose with the grace of God to recite some of them. Then let us pray to this glorious martyr to be our advocate, that by his petition we may come to everlasting bliss. Amen.

The Golden Legend or Lives of the Saints; compiled by Jacobus de Voragine, Archbishop of Genoa, 1275. First Edition Published 1470. Englished by William Caxton, First Edition 1483, Edited by F.S. Ellis, Temple Classics, 1900

Martyrdom of Thomas à Becket (5)

The Martyrdom of Thomas Becket. Dec. 29, 1170

On the murder of Becket we have the reports of five eye-witnesses, Edward Grim (a Saxon monk of Cambridge), William Fitz-Stephen (Becket's chaplain), John of Salisbury (his faithful friend), William of Canterbury, and the anonymous author of a Lambeth MS. Two other biographers, Herbert of Bosham and Roger of Pontigny, though absent from England at that time, were on intimate terms with Becket, and took great pains to ascertain the facts to the minutest details.

Four warlike knights of high birth and large estate, chamberlains to the king, Sir Reginald Fitz-Urse ("Son of the Bear," whom Becket had originally introduced to the court), Sir William. de Tracy (of royal blood), Hugh de Moreville (judiciary of Northumberland and Cumberland), and Sir Richard le Bret or Breton (commonly known as Brito), eagerly caught at the king's suggestion, and resolved to carry it out in the spirit of passionate loyalty, at their own risk, as best they could, by imprisonment, or exile, or, if necessary, by murder. They seem to have had no premeditated plan except that of signal vengeance. Without waiting for instructions, they at once departed on separate routes for England, and met at the castle of Saltwood, which belonged to the see of Canterbury, but was then occupied by Randulf of Broc. They collected a band of about a dozen armed men, and reached St. Augustine's abbey outside of the walls of Canterbury, early on the 29th of December, which was a Tuesday.

On the morning of that fatal day, Becket

had forebodings of his death, and advised the clergy to escape to Sandwich before daylight. He attended mass in the cathedral, confessed to two monks, and received three scourgings, as was his custom. At the banquet he drank more freely than usual, and said to the cupbearer, "He who has much blood to shed, must drink much." After dinner he retired to his private room and sat on his bed, talking to his friends, John of Salisbury, William Fitz-Stephen, and Edward Grim. He was then still in full vigor, being in the fifty-third year of his age, retaining his dignified aspect and the luster of his large eyes.

At about four that afternoon, the knights went to the archbishop's palace, leaving their weapons behind, and concealing their coats of mail by the ordinary cloak and gown. They demanded from him, in the name of the king, the absolution of the excommunicated bishops and courtiers. He refused, and referred them to the pope, who alone could absolve them. He declared: "I will never spare a man who violates the canons of Rome or the rights of the Church. My spirituals I hold from God and the pope; my temporals, from the king. Render unto Caesar the things that are Caesar's, and unto God the things that are God's." The knights said, "You speak in peril of your life." Becket replied: "Come ye to murder me in my own house? You cannot be more ready to kill me than I am to die. You threaten me in vain; were all the swords in England hanging over my head, you could not terrify me from my obedience to God and my lord the pope. I defy you, and will meet you foot to foot in the battle of the Lord." During the altercation, Becket lost command over his fiery temper. His friend, John of Salisbury, gently censured him for his exasperating tone. The knights quitted the room and called their men to arms.

A few minutes before five the bell tolled for vespers. Urged by his friends, the archbishop, with his cross carried before him, went through the cloisters to the cathedral. The service had begun, the monks were chanting the psalms in the choir, the church was filled with people, when two boys rushed up the nave and created a panic by announcing that armed men were breaking into the cloister. The attendants of Becket, who had entered the church, shut the door and urged him to move into the choir for safety. "Away, you cowards!" he said, "by virtue of your obedience, I command you not to shut the door; the church must not be turned into a fortress." He was evidently prepared and eager for martyrdom. He himself reopened the door, and dragged the excluded monks into the building, exclaiming, "Come in, come in faster, faster!" The monks and priests were terror-stricken and fled in every direction, to the recesses and side-chapels, to the roof above, and the crypt below. Three only remained faithful, Canon Robert of Merton, Chaplain William Fitz-Stephen, and the clerk Edward Grim. One of the monks confesses that he ran with clasped hands up the steps as fast as his feet would carry him.

Becket proceeded to the high altar and archiepiscopal chair, in which he and all his predecessors from time immemorial had been enthroned. There, no doubt, he wished to gain the crown of martyrdom. It was now about five in the winter evening; the shades of night were gathering, and the lamps on the altars shed only a dim light in the dark cathedral. The tragedy which followed was finished in a few minutes.

In the meantime the knights, clad in mail which covered their faces up to their eyes, and with drawn swords, followed by a motley group of ruffians, provided with hatchets, rushed into the cathedral and shouted: "Where is the traitor? Where is the archbishop?" Becket replied, descending the steps of the altar and facing his enemies, "Behold me, no traitor, but a priest of God!" They again demanded the absolution of the bishops and his surrender to the king's justice. "I cannot do otherwise than I have done," he said, and turning to Fitz-Urse, who was armed with a sword and an axe, he added; "Reginald, you have received many favors at my hands: come you to me and into my church armed!" The knights tried to drag him out of the sanctuary, not intending to kill him there; but he braced himself against the pillar between the altars of the Virgin, his special patroness, and St. Benedict, whose rule he followed, and said: "I am ready to die. May the Church through my blood obtain peace and liberty! I charge you in the name of God Almighty that you hurt no one here but me." In the struggle, he grappled with De Tracy and threw him to the pavement. He called Fitz-Urse (who had seized him by the collar of his long cloak) a miserable wretch, and wrenched the cloak from his grasp, saying, "Off, thou pander, thou!" The soldier, maddened by the foul epithet, waving the sword over his head, struck the first blow, and dashed off his cap. Tracy, rising from the pavement, aimed at his head; but Edward Grim, standing by, interposed his arm, which was almost severed, and then he sank back against the wall. Becket received blow after blow in an attitude of prayer. As he felt the blood trickling down his face, he bowed his neck for the death-blow, clasped his hands, and said in a low voice: "I commend my cause and the cause of the Church to God, to St. Denis, the martyr of France, to St. Alfege, and to the saints of the Church. In the name of Christ and for the defense of his Church, I am ready to die. Lord, receive my spirit."

These were his last words. The next blow felled him to his knees, the last laid him on the floor at the foot of the altar of St. Benedict. His hands were still joined as if in prayer. Richard the Breton cut off the upper part of his skull, which had received the sacred oil. Hugh of Horsea, the subdeacon, trampled upon his neck, thrust his sword into the ghastly wound, and scattered the blood and the brains over the pavement. Then he said, "Let us go, let us go; the traitor is dead; he will rise no more."

The murderers rushed from the church through the cloisters into the palace for plunder; while a violent thunder-storm broke over the cathedral. They stole about two thousand marks in gold and silver, and rode off on Becket's fine horses in the thick darkness of the night.

The body of Thomas was buried in the crypt. The remains of his blood and brains were sacredly kept. His monkish admirers discovered, to their amazement and delight, that the martyr, who had once been arrayed in purple and fine linen, wore on his skin under his many garments the coarsest haircloth abounding with vermin. This seemed to betray the perfection of ascetic sanctity according to mediaeval notions. The spot of his "martyrdom" is still shown close to the entrance of the cathedral from the cloister.

The results of Becket's murder

The atrocious murder sent a thrill of horror throughout the Christian world. The moment of Becket's death was his triumph. His exalted station, his personal virtues, the sacrilege, all contributed to deepen the impression. At first opinion was divided, as he had strong enemies, even at Canterbury. A monk declared that Becket paid a just penalty for his obstinacy others said, "He wished to be king and more than king; the archbishop of York dared to preach that Becket "perished, like Pharaoh, in his pride."

But the torrent of public admiration soon silenced all opposition. Miracles took place at his tomb, and sealed his claim to the worship of a saint and martyr. "The blind see, the deaf hear, the dumb speak, the lame walk, the lepers are cleansed, the devils are cast out, even the dead are raised to life." Thus wrote John of Salisbury, his friend. Remarkable cures, no doubt, took place; credulity and fraud exaggerated and multiplied them. Within a few years after the murder, two collections of his miracles were published, one by Benedict, prior of Canterbury (afterwards abbot of Peterborough), and one by William, monk of Canterbury. According to these reports, the miracles began to occur the very night of the archbishop's death. His blood had miraculous efficacy for those who drank it.

Two years after his death, Feb. 21, 1173, Becket was solemnly canonized by Alexander III., who had given him only a lukewarm support in his contest with the king. There is scarcely another example of such an early recognition of saintship; but public sentiment had anticipated it. At a council in Westminster the papal letters of canonization were read. All the bishops who had opposed Becket were present, begged pardon for their offence, and acquiesced in the pope's decision. The 29th of December was set apart as the feast of "St. Thomas of Canterbury."

King Henry II., as the supposed author of the monstrous crime, was branded with a popular excommunication. On the first news, he shut himself up for three days in his chamber, rolled himself in sackcloth and ashes, and obstinately refused food and comfort. He lived secluded for five weeks, exclaiming again and again, "Alas, alas that it ever happened!" He issued orders for the apprehension of the murderers, and despatched envoys to the pope to exculpate, himself and to avert the calamity of excommunication and, an interdict. After long delay a reconciliation took place in the cathedral of Avranches in Normandy, before the papal legates, the archbishop of Rouen, and many bishops and noblemen, May 22, 1172.171 Henry swore on the holy Gospels that he had neither commanded nor desired the death of Becket, that it caused him more grief than the death of his father or his mother, and that he was ready to make full satisfaction. He pledged himself to abrogate the Statutes of Clarendon; to restore the church of Canterbury to all its rights and possessions; to undertake, if the pope should require it, a three years' crusade to Jerusalem or Spain, and to support two hundred knights in the Holy Land. After these pledges he said aloud: "Behold, my lord legates, my body is in your hands; be assured that whatever you order, whether to go to Jerusalem or to Rome or to St. James [at Compostella in Spain], I am ready to obey." He was led by the bishops into the church and reconciled. His son, who was present, promised Cardinal Albert to make good his father's pledges. This penance was followed by a deepest humiliation at Canterbury.

Two years later, July 12, 1174, the king, depressed by disasters and the rebellion of his wife and his sons, even made a pilgrimage to the tomb of Becket. He dismounted from his horse as he came in sight of the towers of Canterbury, walked as a penitent pilgrim in a woollen shirt, with bare and bleeding feet, through the streets, knelt in the porch of the cathedral, kissed the sacred stone on which the archbishop had fallen, threw himself prostrate before the tomb in the crypt, and confessed to the bishops with groans and tears his deep remorse for the hasty words which had led to the murder. Gilbert Foliot, bishop of London, once Becket's rival and enemy, announced to the monks and bystanders the king's penitence and intention to restore the rights and property of the Church, and to bestow forty marks yearly on the monastery to keep lamps burning at the martyr's tomb. The king, placing his head and shoulders on the tomb, submitted to the degrading punishment of scourging, and received five stripes from each bishop and abbot, and three stripes from each of the eighty monks. Fully absolved, he spent the whole night on the bare ground of the crypt in tears and prayers, imploring the forgiveness of the canonized saint in heaven whom he had persecuted on earth.

No deeper humiliation of king before priest is recorded in history. It throws into the shade the submission of Theodosius to Ambrose, of Edgar to Dunstan, of Barbarossa to Alexander, and even the scene at Canossa.

Fifty years after the martyrdom, Becket's relics were translated with extraordinary solemnity from the tomb in the crypt to the costly shrine of Becket, which blazed with gold and jewels, in the reconstructed Canterbury cathedral (1220). And now began on the largest scale that long succession of pilgrimages, which for more than three hundred years made Canterbury the greatest sacred resort of Western Christendom, next to Jerusalem and Rome. It was more frequented than Loreto in Italy and Einsiedeln in Switzerland. No less than a hundred thousand pilgrims were registered at Canterbury in 1420. From all parts of England, Scotland, Wales, and Ireland, from France and the far north, men and women flocked to the shrine: priests, monks, princes, knights, scholars, lawyers, merchants, mechanics, peasants. There was scarcely an English king, from Henry II. to Henry VIII., who did not from motives of piety or policy pay homage to the memory of the saint. Among the last distinguished visitors were John Colet, dean of St. Paul's, and Erasmus, who visited the shrine together between the years 1511 and 1513, and King Henry VIII. and Emperor Charles V., who attended the last jubilee in 1520. Plenary indulgences were granted to the pilgrims. Some went in December, the month of his martyrdom; a larger number in July, the month of the translation of his relics. Every fiftieth year a jubilee lasting fifteen days was celebrated in his honor. Six such jubilees were celebrated: 1270, 1320, 1370, 1420, 1470, 1520. The offerings to St. Thomas exceeded those given to any other saint, even to the holy Virgin.

Geoffrey Chaucer, the father of English poetry, who lived two centuries after Becket' martyrdom, has immortalized these pilgrimages in his Canterbury Tales, and given us the best description of English society at that time. The pilgrimages promoted piety, social intercourse, superstition, idleness, levity, and immorality, and aroused moral indignation among many serious and spiritually minded men.

The superstitious idolatry of St. Thomas was continued down to the time of the Reformation, when it was rudely but forever crushed out. Henry VIII. cited Becket to appear in court to answer to the charges of treason and rebellion. The case was formally argued at Westminster. His guilt was proved, and on the 10th of June, 1538, St. Thomas was condemned as a "rebel and a traitor to his prince." The rich shrine at Canterbury was pillaged; the gold and jewels were carried off in two strong coffers, and the rest of the treasure in twenty-six carts. The jewels went into the hands of Henry VIII., who wore the most precious of them, a diamond, the "Regale of France," in the ring on his thumb; afterwards it glittered in the golden, "collar" of his daughter, the bigoted Queen Mary. A royal proclamation explained the cause and mode of Becket's death, and the reasons for his degradation. All festivals, offices, and prayers in his name were forbidden. The site of his shrine has remained vacant to this day.

The Reformation prepared the way for a more spiritual worship of God and a more just appreciation of the virtues and faults of Thomas Becket than was possible in the age in which he lived and died – a hero and a martyr of the papal hierarchy, but not of pure Christianity, as recorded in the New Testament. To the most of his countrymen, as to the English-speaking people at large, his name has remained the synonym for priestly pride and pretension, for an arrogant invasion of the rights of the civil estate. To a certain class of English High Churchmen he remains, like Laud of a later age, the martyr of sacerdotal privilege, the unselfish champion of the dowered rights of the Church. The atrocity of his taking-off no one will choose to deny. But the haughty assumption of the high prelate had afforded pretext enough for vehement indignation and severe treatment. Priestly robes may for a time conceal and even protect pride from violence, but sooner or later it meets its just reward. The prelate's superiority involved in Becket's favorite expression, "saving the honor of my order," was more than a king of free blood could be expected to bear.

This dramatic chapter of English history may be fitly closed with a scene from Lord Tennyson's tragedy which presents the personal quality that brought about Thomas à Becket's fall.

JOHN OF SALISBURY:
Thomas, I would thou hadst returned to England
Like some wise prince of this world from his wars,
With more of olive-branch and amnesty
For foes at home thou hast raised the world against thee.

BECKET:
Why, John, my kingdom is not of this world.

JOHN OF SALISBURY:
If it were more of this world it might be
More of the next. A policy of wise pardon

Wins here as well as there. To bless thine
enemies.

BECKET:
Ay, mine, not Heaven's.

JOHN OF SALISBURY:
And may there not be something
Of this world's leaven in thee too, when
crying
On Holy Church to thunder out her rights
And thine own wrong so piteously. Ah,
Thomas,
The lightnings that we think are only
Heaven's
Flash sometimes out of earth against the
heavens.
The soldier, when he lets his whole self go
Lost in the common good, the common
wrong,
Strikes truest ev'n for his own self. I crave
Thy pardon I have still thy leave to speak.
Thou hast waged God's war against the
King; and yet
We are self-uncertain creatures, and we may,
Yea, even when we know not, mix our spites
And private hates with our defence of
Heaven.
Philip Scaff

AN ACCOUNT OF THE PERSECUTIONS IN ITALY, UNDER THE PAPACY

We shall now enter on an account of the persecutions in Italy, a country which has been, and still is,

1. The center of popery.
2. The seat of the pontiff.
3. The source of the various errors which have spread themselves over other countries, deluded the minds of thousands, and diffused the clouds of superstition and bigotry over the human understanding.

In pursuing our narrative we shall include the most remarkable persecutions which have happened, and the cruelties which have been practiced,

1. By the immediate power of the pope.
2. Through the power of the Inquisition.
3. By the bigotry of the Italian princes.

Arnold of Brescia

In the twelfth century, the first persecutions under the papacy began in Italy, at the time that Adrian, an Englishman, was pope, being occasioned by the following circumstances:

A learned man, and an excellent orator of Brescia, named Arnold, came to Rome, and boldly preached against the corruptions and innovations which had crept into the Church. His discourses were so clear, consistent, and breathed forth such a pure spirit of piety, that the senators and many of the people highly approved of, and admired his doctrines.

This so greatly enraged Adrian that he commanded Arnold instantly to leave the city, as a heretic. Arnold, however, did not comply, for the senators and some of the principal people took his part, and resisted the authority of the pope.

Adrian now laid the city of Rome under an interdict, which caused the whole body of clergy to interpose; and, at length he persuaded the senators and people to give up the point, and suffer Arnold to be banished. This being agreed to, he received the sentence of exile, and retired to Germany, where he continued to preach against the pope, and to expose the gross errors of the Church of Rome.

Adrian, on this account, thirsted for his blood, and made several attempts to get him into his hands; but Arnold, for a long time, avoided every snare laid for him. At length, Frederic Barbarossa arriving at the imperial dignity, requested that the pope would crown him with his own hand. This Adrian complied with, and at the same time asked a favor of the emperor, which was, to put Arnold into his hands. The emperor very readily delivered up the unfortunate preacher, who soon fell a martyr to Adrian's vengeance, being hanged, and his body burnt to ashes, at Apulia. The same fate attended several of his old friends and companions.

Encenas, a Spaniard

Encenas, a Spaniard, was sent to Rome, to be brought up in the Roman Catholic faith; but having conversed with some of the reformed, and having read several treatises which they put into his hands, he became a Protestant. This, at length, being known, one of his own relations informed against him, when he was burnt by order of the pope, and a conclave of cardinals. The brother of Encenas had been taken up much about the same time, for having a New Testament in the Spanish language in his possession; but before the time appointed for his execution, he found means to escape out of prison, and retired to Germany.

Faninus

Faninus, a learned layman, by reading controversial books, became of the reformed religion. An information being exhibited against him to the pope, he was apprehended, and cast into prison. His wife, children, relations, and friends visited him in his confinement, and so far wrought upon his mind, that he renounced his faith, and obtained his release. But he was no sooner free from confinement than his mind felt the heaviest of chains; the weight of a guilty conscience. His horrors were so great that he found them insupportable, until he had returned from his apostasy, and declared himself fully convinced of the errors of the Church of Rome. To make amends for his falling off, he now openly and strenuously did all he could to make converts to Protestantism, and was pretty successful in his endeavors. These proceedings occasioned his second imprisonment, but he had his life offered him if he would recant again. This proposal he rejected with disdain, saying that he scorned life upon such terms. Being asked why he would obstinately persist in his opinions, and leave his wife and children in distress, he replied, "I shall not leave them in distress; I have recommended them to the care of an excellent trustee." "What trustee?" said the person who had asked the question, with some surprise: to which Faninus answered, "Jesus Christ is the trustee I mean, and I think I could not commit them to the care of a better." On the day of execution he appeared remarkably cheerful, which one observing, said, "It is strange you should appear so merry upon such an occasion, when Jesus Christ himself, just before his death, was in such agonies, that he sweated blood and water." To which Faninus replied: "Christ sustained all manner of pangs and conflicts, with hell and death, on our accounts; and thus, by his sufferings, freed those who really believe in him from the fear of them." He was then strangled, his body was burnt to ashes, and then scattered about by the wind.

Dominicus, an educated soldier

Dominicus, a learned soldier, having read several controversial writings, became a zealous Protestant, and retiring to Placentia, he preached the Gospel in its utmost purity, to a very considerable congregation. One day, at the conclusion of his sermon, he said, "If the congregation will attend to-morrow, I will give them a description of Antichrist, and paint him out in his proper colors."

A vast concourse of people attended the next day, but just as Dominicus was beginning his sermon, a civil magistrate went up to the pulpit, and took him into custody. He readily submitted; but as he went along with the magistrate, he made use of this expression: "I wonder the devil hath let me alone so long." When he was brought to examination, this question was put to him: "Will you renounce your doctrines?" To which he replied: "My doctrines! I maintain no doctrines of my own; what I preach are the doctrines of Christ, and for those I will forfeit my blood, and even think myself happy to suffer for the sake of my Redeemer." Every method was taken to make him recant for his faith, and embrace the errors of the Church of Rome; but when persuasions and menaces were found ineffectual, he was sentenced to death, and hanged in the market place.

Galeacius

Galeacius, a Protestant gentleman, who resided near the castle of St. Angelo, was apprehended on account of his faith. Great endeavors being used by his friends he recanted, and subscribed to several of the superstitious doctrines propogated by the Church of Rome. Becoming, however, sensible of his error, he publicly renounced his recantation. Being apprehended for this, he was condemned to be burnt, and agreeable to the order was chained to a stake, where he was left several hours before the fire was put to the fagots, in order that his wife, relations, and friends, who surrounded him, might induce him to give up his opinions. Galeacius, however, retained his constancy of mind, and entreated the executioner to put fire to the wood that was to burn him. This at length he did, and Galeacius was soon consumed in the flames, which burnt with amazing rapidity and deprived him of sensation in a few minutes.

Soon after this gentleman's death, a great number of Protestants were put to death in various parts of Italy, on account of their faith, giving a sure proof of their sincerity in their martyrdoms.

Foxe's Book of Martyrs, Chapter 6, Edited by William Byron Forbush

Seven Friars Minor, 1221

Seven zealous priests from the Franciscan order, Daniel, the provincial of Calabria, Samuel, Angelus, Donulus, Leo, Nicholas, and Hugolin, sailed to Africa in 1221, to announce Christ to the Muslims. They arrived at Ceuta where they preached for three days in the suburbs of the city, where Christians lived. Then they went into the heart of the city where the infidels lived and preached Christ to them. The populace hearing them immediately took fire, covered them with mire and filth, and carried them before the king, whose name was Mahomet. From their rough habits and shorn heads he took them for madmen, but sent them to the governor of the town. By him, after a long examination, they were remanded to the king, who condemned them to be beheaded. They suffered with great joy in 1221, on the 10th of October.

Alban Butler, The Lives of the Saints, Dublin, 1833, volume 2, p 655.

Antony, John and Eustachius, Lithuania, 1342

Antony, John and Eustachius were three noblemen from Lithuania. Antony and John were brothers. In Lithuania they were called Kukley, Mihley, and Nizilo. They were all chamberlains to Olgerd, the great duke of Lithuania, who governed there from 1329 to 1381. They also attended on the great duchess, and were worshippers of fire, according to the idolatrous superstition of that country, till they had the happiness to be converted to the Christian faith, and baptised by a priest called Nestorius.

For refusing to eat forbidden meats on fast days, they were cast into prison, and, after many trials, put to death by order of Olgerd, the great duke: John, the eldest, on April 24, his brother Antony on June 14, and the youngest Eustachius, on December 13. Eustachius endured many tortures before his execution. He was beaten with clubs, had his legs broken, the hair and skin of his head violently torn off, because he would not allow his hair to be shaved, according to the custom of the heathen. They suffered at Vilna, about 1342, and were buried in the church of the Holy Trinity, of the Russian-Greek rite, united in communion to the Roman Catholic church.

Alban Butler, The Lives of the Saints, Dublin, 1833, volume 1, p 467.

Martyrdom of Ramon Lull (Raymundus Lullus) (1)
North Africa

Raymundus Lullus, 1235?-1315, devoted his life to the conversion of Mohammedans and attested his zeal by a martyr's death. He was one of the most noteworthy figures produced during the Middle Ages in Southwestern Europe. He made three missionary tours to Africa and originated the scheme for establishing chairs at the universities to teach the Oriental languages and train missionaries. He also wrote many tracts with the aim of convincing unbelievers of the truth of Christianity.

Lullus was born in Palma on the island of Majorca. His father had gained distinction by helping to wrest the Balearic islands from the Saracens. The son married and had children, but led a gay and licentious life at court and devoted his poetic gifts to erotic sonnets. At the age of thirty-one he was arrested in his wild career by the sight of a cancer on the breast of a woman, one of the objects of his passion, whom he pursued into a church, and who suddenly exposed her disease. He made a pilgrimage to Campostella, and retired to Mt. Randa on his native island. Here he spent five years in seclusion, and in 1272 entered the third order of St. Francis. He became interested in the conversion of Mohammedans and other infidels and studied Arabic under a Moor whom he had redeemed from slavery. A system of knowledge was revealed to him which he called "the Universal Science," ars magna or ars generalis. With the aid of the king of Aragon he founded, in 1276 on Majorca, a college under the control of the Franciscans for the training of missionaries in the Arabic and Syriac tongues.

Lullus went to Paris to study and to develop his Universal Science. At a later period he returned and delivered lectures there. In 1286 he went to Rome to press his missionary plans, but failed to gain the pope's favor. In 1292 he set sail on a missionary tour to Africa from Genoa. In Tunis he endeavored in vain to engage the Mohammedan scholars in a public disputation. A tumult arose and Lullus narrowly escaped with his life. Returning to Europe, he again sought to win the favor of the pope, but in vain. In 1309 he sailed the second time for Tunis, and again he sought to engage the Mohammedans in disputation. Offered honors if he would turn Mohammedan, he said, "And I promise you, if you will turn and believe on Jesus Christ, abundant riches and eternal life."

Again violently forced to leave Africa, Lullus laid his plans before Clement V. and the council of Vienne, 1311. Here he presented a refutation of the philosophy of Averrhoes and pressed the creation of academic chairs for the Oriental languages. Such chairs were ordered erected at Avignon, Paris, Oxford, Salamanca, and Bologna to teach Greek, Hebrew, Chaldee, and Arabic.

Although nearly eighty years old the indefatigable missionary again set out for Tunis. His preaching at Bougia led, as before, to tumults, and Lullus was dragged outside of the city and stoned. Left half dead, he was rescued by Christian seamen, put on board a ship, and died at sea. His bones are preserved at Palma.

Philip Scaff, The History of the Church

Martyrdom of Ramon Lull (2)

"I desire to be a fool that I may give honour and glory to God, and I will have no art nor device in my words by reason of the greatness of my love."

Ramon Lull, who delighted to call himself the Fool of Love, was an influential writer and missionary in the Middle Ages. He was martyred in 1315 or 1316.

The aged 83-year-old "white-bearded old apostle" was more successful in his third African mission in Tunis than his previous two. One chronicler relates that among his converts were some of the most influential and learned Moors of the city. This may have been the reason why people stopped being tolerant towards him. Lull went to Bugia from Tunis, where, throwing caution to the winds, the Fool of Love went out boldly into the streets, proclaiming in a loud voice the truth of the religion for which he had spent his life. A hostile crowd gathered round him. Without putting up any resistance the aged Lover of Christ allowed the cruel stones to crash into his frail body. The moment of his departure had come, a moment which he had looked forward to since as a young convert he had written in his Book of Contemplation, "Thy servant and subject, O Lord has very great fear of dying a natural death for he would fain have his death the noblest that is, namely, death for thy love." Lull had his wish and he died a Christian martyr.

Editor

France, 1317

In the decretal Quorumdam exegit, and in the bull Sancta romana et universalis ecclesia, Dec. 30, 1317, John XXII took a positive position against the Spirituals. A few weeks later, he condemned a formal list of their errors and abolished all the convents under Spiritual management. From this time on dates the application of the name

Fraticelli1 to the Spirituals. They refused to submit, and took the position that even a pope had no right to modify the Rule of St. Francis. Michael of Cesena, the general of the order, defended them. Sixty-four of their number were summoned to Avignon. Twenty-five refused to yield, and passed into the hands of the Inquisition. Four were burnt as martyrs at Marseilles, May 7, 1318. Others fled to Sicily.

Philip Scaff, The History of the Church

LOLLARDS

From about 1390 to 1425, we hear of the Lollards in all directions, so that the contemporary chronicler was able to say that of every two men found on the roads, one was sure to be a Lollard. With the accession of Henry IV. of Lancaster (1399–1413), a severe policy was adopted. The culminating point of legislation was reached in 1401, when parliament passed the act for the burning of heretics, the first act of the kind in England. The statute referred to the Lollards as a new sect, damnably thinking of the faith of the Church in respect to the sacraments and, against the law of God and the Church, usurping the office of preaching. It forbade this people to preach, hold schools and conventicles and issue books. The violators were to be tried in the diocesan courts and, if found guilty and refusing to abjure, were to be turned over to the civil officer and burnt. The burning, so it was stipulated, was to be on a high place where the punishment might be witnessed and the onlookers be struck with fear.

The most prominent personages connected with the earliest period of Wycliffism, Philip Repyngdon, John Ashton, Nicolas Hereford and John Purvey, all recanted. The last three and Wyclif are associated by Knighton as the four arch-heretics.

Repyngdon, who had boldly declared himself at Oxford for Wyclif and his view of the sacrament, made a full recantation, 1382. Subsequently he was in high favor, became chancellor of Oxford, bishop of Lincoln and a cardinal, 1408. He showed the ardor of his zeal by treating with severity the sect whose views he had once espoused.

John Ashton had been one of the most active of Wyclif's preachers. In setting forth his heretical zeal, Knighton describes him as "leaping up from his bed and, like a dog, ready to bark at the slightest sound." He finally submitted in Courtenay's court, professing that he "believed as our modur, holy kirke, believes," and that in the sacrament the priest has in his hand Christ's very body. He was restored to his privileges as lecturer in Oxford, but afterwards fell again into heretical company.

Hereford, Wyclif's fellow-translator, appealed to Rome, was condemned there and cast into prison. After two years of confinement, he escaped to England and, after being again imprisoned, made his peace with the Church and died a Carthusian.

In 1389, nine Lollards recanted before Courtenay, at Leicester. The popular preacher, William Swynderby, to whose sermons in Leicester the people flocked from every quarter, made an abject recantation, but later returned to his old ways, and was tried in 1891 and convicted. Whether he was burnt or died in prison, Foxe says, he could not ascertain.

The number suffering death by the law of 1401 was not large in the aggregate. The victims were distributed through the 125 years down to the middle of Henry VIII.'s reign. There were among them no clergymen of high renown like Ridley and Latimer. The Lollards were an humble folk, but by their persistence showed the deep impression Wyclif's teachings had made. The first martyr, the poor chaplain of St. Osythe, William Sawtrae, died March 2, 1401, before the statute for burning heretics was passed. He abjured and then returned again to his heretical views. After trying him, the spiritual court ordered the mayor or sheriff of London to "commit him to the fire that he be actually burnt." The charges were that he denied the material presence, condemned the adoration of the cross and taught that preaching was the priesthood's most important duty.

Among other cases of burnings were John Badby, a tailor of Evesham, 1410, who met his awful fate chained inside of a cask; two

London merchants, Richard Turming and John Claydon at Smithfield, 1415; William Taylor, a priest, in 1423 at Smithfield; William White at Norwich, 1428; Richard Hoveden, a London citizen, 1430; Thomas Bagley, a priest, in the following year; and in 1440, Richard Wyche, who had corresponded with Huss. Peter Payne, the principal of St. Edmund's College, Oxford, took refuge in flight, 1417, and became a leader among the Hussites, taking a prominent part as their representative at the Council of Basel. According to Foxe there were, between 1424–1480, 100 prosecutions for heresy in Norwich alone. The menace was considered so great that, in 1427, Richard Flemmyng, bishop of Lincoln, founded Lincoln College, Oxford, to counteract heresy. It was of this college that John Wesley was a fellow, the man who made a great breach in the Church in England.

The case of William Thorpe, who was tried in 1397 and again before Arundel, 1407, is of interest not only in itself, but for the statements that were made in the second trial about Wyclif. The archbishop, after accusing Thorpe of having travelled about in Northern England for 20 years, spreading the infection of heresy, declared that he was called of God to destroy the false sect to which the prisoner belonged, and pledged himself to "punish it so narrowly as not to leave a slip of you in this land." Thorpe's assertion that Wyclif was the greatest clerk of his time evoked from Arundel the acknowledgment that he was indeed a great clerk and, by the consent of many, "a perfect liver," but that many of the conclusions of his learning were damned, as they ought to be.

Up to the close of the 14th century, a number of laymen in high position at court had favored Wycliffism, including Sir Lewis Clifford, Sir Richard Stury and Sir John Clanvowe, all of the king's council, Sir John Cheyne, speaker of the lower house, the Lord Chancellor, Sir Thomas Erpingham and also the earl of Salisbury. This support was for the most part withdrawn when persecution took an active form. With Sir John Oldcastle, otherwise known as Lord Cobham from his marriage with the heiress of the Cobham estate, it was different. He held firm to the end, encouraged the new preachers on his estates in Kent, and condemned the mass, auricular confession and the worship of images. Arundel's court, before which he appeared after repeated citations, turned him over to the secular arm "to do him to death." Oldcastle was imprisoned in the Tower, but made his escape and was at large for four years. In 1414, he was charged with being a party to an uprising of 20,000 Lollards against the king. Declared an outlaw, he fled to Wales, where he was seized three years later and taken to London to be hanged and burnt as a traitor and heretic, Dec. 15, 1417. John Foxe saw in him "the blessed martyr of Christ, the good Lord Cobham."

Philip Scaff, The History of the Church

MARTYRDOM OF JOAN OF ARC (1)

Joan of Arc, Visionary
30 May 1431

Joan of Arc (Jeanne d'Arc, Jeanne la Pucelle) was born in France, near the border of Burgundy, on 6 January 1412. In her time the King of England claimed the crown of France by the laws of inheritance, and English troops were fighting in France to support that claim. (The English King inherited through a woman, and the French claimants, the House of Valois, asserted that French law did not allow the crown to be inherited by or through a woman.) Henry V of England won a decisive victory at the Battle of Agincourt in 1415 (see Shakespeare's play Henry V, filmed in 1944 starring Laurence Olivier and in 1993 starring Kenneth Branagh, who emphasizes the darker aspects of war), and signed an agreement with the Valois monarch Charles VI, providing that Charles should keep his crown during his lifetime, that his daughter Catherine should marry Henry, and that Henry should be the next king. Charles VI had a son (the Dauphin), but the Queen took an oath that she had been unfaithful to her husband, and that the Dauphin was not the King's son, and therefore had no right to inherit the throne. In 1422, Henry V died, leaving an infant son who became Henry VI of England. England claimed the throne of France in his name. The Duke of Burgundy supported the English claim, and was allied with England. The French claimant, the Dauphin (later Charles VII), had not been crowned. Since many Frenchmen thought that his mother the Queen might be telling the truth about his illegitimacy, the story largely paralyzed the national will to fight for Charles.

Into this situation came Joan. When she was thirteen, she began to hear voices telling her that she was called to save France. Eventually she identified these voices as those of Michael the Archangel (mentioned in the Bible in Daniel and Jude and Revelation), and Catherine of Alexandria and Margaret of Antioch, two early virgin martyrs about whom little is known historically (the accounts of their lives as we have them contain many blatant improbabilities, and even among thoroughly conservative Roman Catholics, they are widely thought to be fictional persons), but who were popular in France at that time. Acting, as she said, under direction from her voices, she persuaded a local baron to send her to the castle of Charles at Chinon, where she spoke with the Dauphin (French word for the heir to the throne until he is officially crowned king), and convinced him that her message was genuine. The city of Orleans was under siege by the English. Joan and an army marched to the scene and raised the siege (8 May 1429). She then proceeded to win other battles, and to bring Charles to Rheims to be crowned king. However, the king refused to take her advice that he should press the military advantage. When she attempted to recapture Paris from the English, he denied her adequate support, and the attempt failed. In May 1430 she was taken prisoner in battle, and tried on an accusation of sorcery and heresy. Charles made no effort to ransom her or rescue her, although her first captors would almost certainly have accepted a ransom. She was convicted and burned at the stake on 30 May 1431, being then a little less than nineteen and a half years old. The French, however, eventually went on to win the war and to expel the English from France. King Charles, perhaps because it was not to his advantage to have it said that he had been crowned by a witch and a heretic, and that he owed his victories and his kingdom to a pact with the Devil, pressured the Church courts for a review of the verdict against Joan, and got her condemnation annulled in 1456. She came to be regarded as a French national hero, and was eventually canonized by the Pope in May 1920. Her day (or a Sunday close to it) is a French national holiday. She is ranked with Denis of Paris and Remi of Rheims as one of France's three great national saints. She is honored by the Church, not for winning military victories, or even because her visions were necessarily authentic, but because, being persuaded of the will of God for her life, she responded in faith and obedience to that will as she understood it.

James Kiefer, Christian Biographies, By kind permission

Martyrdom of Joan of Arc (2)

Joan of Arc was burned by the British on May 29, 1431 at Rouen, and while not officially recognised as "a martyr of the church" in the Roman Catholic calendar, is regarded as the national saint of France, and 489 years after her death, was canonised, in 1920.

"If I were to say that God had not sent me, I would be damning myself, for it is true that God did send me." Joan of Arc

On May 8th 1429, Joan of Arc, dressed in white armour, successfully led the French army against the English siege of Orleans. A few days later Joan inflicted a crushing defeat on the English on the Loire, resulting in Charles being crowned king on July 17th at Rheims, flanked by Joan, holding her standard. However, when Joan was captured by the Burgundians at Compiègne on 23 May, 1430, King Charles never lifted a finger to help her, even after she had been sold by the Duke of Burgundy to the English on 21 November.

All the English wanted to do with Joan of Arc was to pass sentence on her as a heretic and a sorceress. Joan endured six public and nine private sessions which all amounted to a most unfair trial. Joan admitted quite categorically during her trial that "God sent a voice to guide me". Her voices, inner convictions, and visions were seized on. She was told they all emanated from the devil and that only a heretic like her would place her voices above the teaching and wisdom of the church. Wearing men's clothes was used as corroborating evidence that Joan was evil.

Joan suffered a terrible imprisonment. She was denied all the comforts of the Church as she was denied a place in the ecclesiastical prison and was thrown into a common cell, where she was chained to a block of wood, and denied a bed. Joan was condemned for being apostate, a heretic and a sorceress. But, just after she was excommunicated and pronounced a heretic, Joan broke down. For a brief time, she agreed to follow the Church in everything and she no longer insisted that she had received visions and revelations and heard voices. Joan's relapse was short-lived. When Bishop Cauchon visited her cell she told him that her voices had started again. "They told me that through them God sent me his pity of the betrayal to which I consented in making the abjuration and revocation to save my life and that in saving my life I was damning myself. If I were to say that God had not sent me, I would be damning myself, for it is true that God did send me." This statement sent Joan to her death. On 29 May, 1431, Joan was condemned as a relapsed heretic and on Wednesday 30 May at 8.00am was burned by the British at the stake at Rouen. Joan died a teenager, nineteen years of age.
Editor

WALDENSES

Summary of their persecution

Pope Innocent VIII, in 1488, determined to persecute the Waldenses (named after Peter Waldo of Lyons who opposed some of the teachings of the Pope). To this end he sent Albert de Capitaneis, Archdeacon of Cremona, to France; who, on arriving in Dauphiny, asked for the assistance of the king's lieutenant to exterminate the Waldenses from the valley of Loyse. The lieutenant readily granted his assistance, and marched a body of troops to the place; but when they arrived in the valley, they found that it had been deserted by the inhabitants, who had fled to the mountains, and hid themselves in dens and caves of the earth. The archdeacon and lieutenant immediately followed them with their troops, and catching many, threw them over precipices, resulting in them being dashed to pieces. Several, however, hid in the innermost parts of the caverns, where they were able to remain concealed. The archdeacon and lieutenant not being able to find them, ordered the mouths of the caves to be filled with faggots, which being lighted, those inside were suffocated. On searching the caves, numerous children were found suffocated, either in their cradles or in their mothers" arms; and a total of about 3,000 men, women, and children were destroyed in this persecution.
John Foxe, The Book of Martyrs, revised with notes and an appendix by W. Bramley-Moore, London, 1869, pp 60-1

PAPAL PERSECUTIONS

Thus far our history of persecution has been confined principally to the pagan world. We come now to a period when persecution, under the guise of Christianity, committed more enormities than ever disgraced the annals of paganism. Disregarding the maxims and the spirit of the Gospel, the papal Church, arming herself with the power of the sword, vexed the Church of God and wasted it for several centuries, a period most appropriately termed in history, the "dark ages." The kings of the earth, gave their power to the "Beast," and submitted to be trodden on by the miserable vermin that often filled the papal chair, as in the case of Henry, emperor of Germany. The storm of papal persecution first burst upon the Waldenses in France.

Persecution of the Waldenses in France

Popery having brought various innovations into the Church, and overspread the Christian world with darkness and superstition, some few, who plainly perceived the pernicious tendency of such errors, determined to show the light of the Gospel in its real purity, and to disperse those clouds which artful priests had raised about it, in order to blind the people, and obscure its real brightness.

The principal among these was Berengarius, who, about the year 1000, boldly preached Gospel truths, according to their primitive purity. Many, from conviction, assented to his doctrine, and were, on that account, called Berengarians. To Berengarius succeeded Peer Bruis, who preached at Toulouse, under the protection of an earl, named Hildephonsus; and the whole tenets of the reformers, with the reasons of their separation from the Church of Rome, were published in a book written by Bruis, under the title of "Antichrist."

By the year of Christ 1140, the number of the reformed was very great, and the probability of its increasing alarmed the pope, who wrote to several princes to banish them from their dominions, and employed many learned men to write against their doctrines.

In A.D. 1147, because of Henry of Toulouse, deemed their most eminent preacher, they were called Henericians; and as they would not admit of any proofs relative to religion, but what could be deduced from the Scriptures themselves, the popish party gave them the name of apostolics. At length, Peter Waldo, or Valdo, a native of Lyons, eminent for his piety and learning, became a strenuous opposer of popery; and from him the reformed, at that time, received the appellation of Waldenses or Waldoys.

Pope Alexander III being informed by the bishop of Lyons of these transactions, excommunicated Waldo and his adherents, and commanded the bishop to exterminate them, if possible, from the face of the earth; hence began the papal persecutions against the Waldenses.

The proceedings of Waldo and the reformed, occasioned the first rise of the inquisitors; for Pope Innocent III authorized certain monks as inquisitors, to inquire for, and deliver over, the reformed to the secular power. The process was short, as an accusation was deemed adequate to guilt, and a candid trial was never granted to the accused.

The pope, finding that these cruel means had not the intended effect, sent several learned monks to preach among the Waldenses, and to endeavor to argue them out of their opinions. Among these monks was one Dominic, who appeared extremely zealous in the cause of popery. This Dominic instituted an order, which, from him, was called the order of Dominican friars; and the members of this order have ever since been the principal inquisitors in the various inquisitions in the world. The power of the inquisitors was unlimited; they proceeded against whom they pleased, without any consideration of age, sex, or rank. Let the accusers be ever so infamous, the accusation was deemed valid; and even anonymous informations, sent by letter, were thought sufficient evidence. To be rich was a crime equal to heresy; therefore many who had money were accused of heresy, or of being favorers of heretics, that they might be obliged to pay for their opinions. The dearest friends or nearest kindred could not, without danger, serve any one who was imprisoned on account of religion. To convey to those who were confined, a little straw, or give them a cup of water, was called favoring of the heretics, and they were prosecuted accordingly. No lawyer dared to plead for his own brother, and their malice even extended beyond the grave; hence the bones of many were dug up and burnt, as examples to the living. If a man on his deathbed was accused of being a follower of Waldo, his estates were confiscated, and the heir to them defrauded of his inheritance; and some were sent to the Holy Land, while the Dominicans took possession of their houses and properties, and, when the owners returned, would often pretend not to know them. These persecutions were continued for several centuries under different popes and other great dignitaries of the Catholic Church. Persecutions of the Albigenses

The Albigenses were a people of the

reformed religion, who inhabited the country of Albi. They were condemned on the score of religion in the Council of Lateran, by order of Pope Alexander III. Nevertheless, they increased so prodigiously, that many cities were inhabited by persons only of their persuasion, and several eminent noblemen embraced their doctrines. Among the latter were Raymond, earl of Toulouse, Raymond, earl of Foix, the earl of Beziers, etc.

A friar, named Peter, having been murdered in the dominions of the earl of Toulouse, the pope made the murder a pretense to persecute that nobleman and his subjects. To effect this, he sent persons throughout all Europe, in order to raise forces to act coercively against the Albigenses, and promised paradise to all that would come to this war, which he termed a Holy War, and bear arms for forty days. The same indulgences were likewise held out to all who entered themselves for the purpose as to such as engaged in crusades to the Holy Land. The brave earl defended Toulouse and other places with the most heroic bravery and various success against the pope's legates and Simon, earl of Montfort, a bigoted Catholic nobleman. Unable to subdue the earl of Toulouse openly, the king of France, and the queen mother, and three archbishops raised another formidable army, and had the art to persuade the earl of Toulouse to come to a conference, when he was treacherously seized upon, made a prisoner, forced to appear barefooted and bareheaded before his enemies, and compelled to subscribe an abject recantation. This was followed by a severe persecution against the Albigenses; and express orders that the laity should not be permitted to read the sacred Scriptures. In the year 1620 also, the persecution against the Albigenses was very severe. In 1648 a heavy persecution raged throughout Lithuania and Poland. The cruelty of the Cossacks was so excessive that the Tartars themselves were ashamed of their barbarities. Among others who suffered was the Rev. Adrian Chalinski, who was roasted alive by a slow fire, and whose sufferings and mode of death may depict the horrors which the professors of Christianity have endured from the enemies of the Redeemer.

The reformation of papistical error very early was projected in France; for in the third century a learned man, named Almericus, and six of his disciples, were ordered to be burnt at Paris for asserting that God was no otherwise present in the sacramental bread than in any other bread; that it was idolatry to build altars or shrines to saints and that it was ridiculous to offer incense to them.

The martyrdom of Almericus and his pupils did not, however, prevent many from acknowledging the justness of his notions, and seeing the purity of the reformed religion, so that the faith of Christ continually increased, and in time not only spread itself over many parts of France, but diffused the light of the Gospel over various other countries.

In the year 1524, at a town in France, called Melden, one John Clark set up a bill on the church door, wherein he called the pope Antichrist. For this offence he was repeatedly whipped, and then branded on the forehead. Going afterward to Mentz, in Lorraine, he demolished some images, for which he had his right hand and nose cut off, and his arms and breast torn with pincers. He sustained these cruelties with amazing fortitude, and was even sufficiently cool to sing the One hundredth and fifteenth Psalm, which expressly forbids idolatry; after which he was thrown into the fire, and burnt to ashes.

Many persons of the reformed persuasion were, about this time, beaten, racked, scourged, and burnt to death, in several parts of France, but more particularly at Paris, Malda, and Limosin.

A native of Malda was burnt by a slow fire, for saying that Mass was a plain denial of the death and passion of Christ. At Limosin, John de Cadurco, a clergyman of the reformed religion, was apprehended and ordered to be burnt.

Francis Bribard, secretary to cardinal de Pellay, for speaking in favor of the reformed, had his tongue cut out, and was then burnt,

A.D. 1545. James Cobard, a schoolmaster in the city of St. Michael, was burnt, A.D. 1545, for saying "That Mass was useless and absurd"; and about the same time, fourteen men were burnt at Malda, their wives being compelled to stand by and behold the execution.

A.D. 1546, Peter Chapot brought a number of Bibles in the French tongue to France, and publicly sold them there; for which he was brought to trial, sentenced, and executed a few days afterward. Soon after, a cripple of Meaux, a schoolmaster of Fera, named Stephen Poliot, and a man named John English, were burnt for the faith.

Monsieur Blondel, a rich jeweler, was, in A.D. 1548, apprehended at Lyons, and sent to Paris; there he was burnt for the faith by order of the court, A.D. 1549. Herbert, a youth of nineteen years of age, was committed to the flames at Dijon; as was also Florent Venote in the same year.

In the year 1554, two men of the reformed religion, with the son and daughter of one of them, were apprehended and committed to the castle of Niverne. On examination, they confessed their faith, and were ordered to execution; being smeared with grease, brimstone, and gunpowder, they cried, "Salt on, salt on this sinful and rotten flesh." Their tongues were then cut out, and they were afterward committed to the flames, which soon consumed them, by means of the combustible matter with which they were besmeared. The Bartholomew Massacre at Paris, etc.

On the twenty second day of August, 1572, commenced this diabolical act of sanguinary brutality. It was intended to destroy at one stroke the root of the Protestant tree, which had only before partially suffered in its branches. The king of France had artfully proposed a marriage, between his sister and the prince of Navarre, the captain and prince of the Protestants. This imprudent marriage was publicly celebrated at Paris, August 18, by the cardinal of Bourbon, upon a high stage erected for the purpose. They dined in great pomp with the bishop, and supped with the king at Paris. Four days after this, the prince (Coligny), as he was coming from the Council, was shot in both arms; he then said to Maure, his deceased mother's minister, "O my brother, I do now perceive that I am indeed beloved of my God, since for His most holy sake I am wounded." Although the Vidam advised him to fly, yet he abode in Paris, and was soon after slain by Bemjus; who afterward declared he never saw a man meet death more valiantly than the admiral.

The soldiers were appointed at a certain signal to burst out instantly to the slaughter in all parts of the city. When they had killed the admiral, they threw him out at a window into the street, where his head was cut off, and sent to the pope. The savage papists, still raging against him, cut off his arms and private members, and, after dragging him three days through the streets, hung him by the heels without the city. After him they slew many great and honorable persons who were Protestants; as Count Rochfoucault, Telinius, the admiral's son-in-law, Antonius, Clarimontus, marquis of Ravely, Lewes Bussius, Bandineus, Pluvialius, Burneius, etc., and falling upon the common people, they continued the slaughter for many days; in the three first they slew of all ranks and conditions to the number of ten thousand. The bodies were thrown into the rivers, and blood ran through the streets with a strong current, and the river appeared presently like a stream of blood. So furious was their hellish rage, that they slew all papists whom they suspected to be not very staunch to their diabolical religion. From Paris the destruction spread to all quarters of the realm.

At Orleans, a thousand were slain of men, women, and children, and six thousand at Rouen.

At Meldith, two hundred were put into prison, and later brought out by units, and cruelly murdered.

At Lyons, eight hundred were massacred. Here children hanging about their parents, and parents affectionately embracing their children, were pleasant food for the swords and bloodthirsty minds of those who call themselves the Catholic Church. Here three hundred were slain in the bishop's house; and the impious monks would suffer none to be buried.

At Augustobona, on the people hearing of the massacre at Paris, they shut their gates that no Protestants might escape, and searching diligently for every individual of the reformed Church, imprisoned and then barbarously murdered them. The same cruelty they practiced at Avaricum, at Troys, at Toulouse, Rouen and many other places, running from city to city, towns, and villages, through the kingdom.

As a corroboration of this horrid carnage, the following interesting narrative, written by a sensible and learned Roman Catholic, appears in this place, with peculiar propriety.

"The nuptials (says he) of the young king of Navarre with the French king's sister, was solemnized with pomp; and all the endearments, all the assurances of friendship, all the oaths sacred among men, were profusely lavished by Catharine, the queen-mother, and by the king; during which, the rest of the court thought of nothing but festivities, plays, and masquerades. At last, at twelve o'clock at night, on the eve of St. Bartholomew, the signal was given. Immediately all the houses of the Protestants were forced open at once. Admiral Coligny, alarmed by the uproar jumped out of bed, when a company of assassins rushed in his chamber. They were headed by one Besme, who had been bred up as a domestic in the family of the Guises. This wretch thrust his sword into the admiral's breast, and also cut him in the face. Besme was a German, and being afterwards taken by the Protestants, the Rochellers would have brought him, in order to hang and quarter him; but he was killed by one Bretanville. Henry, the young duke of Guise, who afterwards framed the Catholic league, and was murdered at Blois, standing at the door until the horrid butchery should be completed, called aloud, "Besme! is it done?" Immediately after this, the ruffians threw the body out of the window, and Coligny expired at Guise's feet.

"Count de Teligny also fell a sacrifice. He had married, about ten months before, Coligny's daughter. His countenance was so engaging, that the ruffians, when they advanced in order to kill him, were struck with compassion; but others, more barbarous, rushing forward, murdered him.

"In the meantime, all the friends of Coligny were assassinated throughout Paris; men, women, and children were promiscuously slaughtered and every street was strewed with expiring bodies. Some priests, holding up a crucifix in one hand, and a dagger in the other, ran to the chiefs of the murderers, and strongly exhorted them to spare neither relations nor friends.

"Tavannes, marshal of France, an ignorant, superstitious soldier, who joined the fury of religion to the rage of party, rode on horseback through the streets of Paris, crying to his men, 'Let blood! let blood! bleeding is as wholesome in August as in May.' In the memories of the life of this enthusiastic, written by his son, we are told that the father, being on his deathbed, and making a general confession of his actions, the priest said to him, with surprise, 'What! no mention of St. Bartholomew's massacre?' to which Tavannes replied, 'I consider it as a meritorious action, that will wash away all my sins.' Such horrid sentiments can a false spirit of religion inspire!

"The king's palace was one of the chief scenes of the butchery; the king of Navarre had his lodgings in the Louvre, and all his domestics were Protestants. Many of these were killed in bed with their wives; others, running away naked, were pursued by the soldiers through the several rooms of the palace, even to the king's antechamber. The young wife of Henry of Navarre, awaked by the dreadful uproar, being afraid for her consort, and for her own life, seized with horror, and half dead, flew from her bed, in order to throw herself at the feet of the king her brother. But scarce had she opened her chamber door, when some of her Protestant domestics rushed in for refuge. The soldiers immediately followed, pursued them in sight of the princess, and killed one who crept under her bed. Two others, being wounded with halberds, fell at the queen's feet, so that she was covered with blood.

"Count de la Rochefoucault, a young nobleman, greatly in the king's favor for his comely air, his politeness, and a certain peculiar happiness in the turn of his conversation, had spent the evening until eleven o'clock with the monarch, in pleasant familiarity; and had given a loose, with the utmost mirth, to the sallies of his imagination. The monarch felt some remorse, and being touched with a kind of compassion, bid him, two or three times, not to go home, but lie in the Louvre. The count said he must go to his wife; upon which the king pressed him no farther, but said, 'Let him go! I see God has decreed his death.' And in two hours after he was murdered.

"Very few of the Protestants escaped the fury of their enthusiastic persecutors. Among these was young La Force (afterwards the famous Marshal de la Force) a child about ten years of age, whose deliverance was exceedingly remarkable. His father, his elder brother, and he himself were seized together by the Duke of Anjou's soldier. These murderers flew at all three, and struck them at random, when they all fell, and lay one upon another. The youngest did not receive a single blow, but appearing as if he was dead, escaped the next day; and his life, thus wonderfully preserved, lasted four score and five years.

"Many of the wretched victims fled to the water side, and some swam over the Seine to the suburbs of St. Germaine. The king saw them from his window, which looked upon the river, and fired upon them with a carbine that had been loaded for that purpose by one of his pages; while the queen-mother, undisturbed and serene in the midst of slaughter, looking down from a balcony, encouraged the murderers and laughed at the dying groans of the slaughtered. This barbarous queen was fired with a restless ambition, and she perpetually shifted her party in order to satiate it.

"Some days after this horrid transaction, the French court endeavored to palliate it by forms of law. They pretended to justify the massacre by a calumny, and accused the admiral of a conspiracy, which no one believed. The parliament was commended to proceed against the memory of Coligny; and his dead body was hanged in chains on Montfaucon gallows. The king himself went to view this shocking spectacle. So one of his courtiers advised him to retire, and complaining of the stench of the corpse, he replied, 'A dead enemy smells well.' The massacres on St. Bartholomew's day are painted in the royal saloon of the Vatican at Rome, with the following inscription: Pontifex, Coligny necem probat, i.e., 'The pope approves of Coligny's death.'

"The young king of Navarre was spared through policy, rather than from the pity of the queen-mother, she keeping him prisoner until the king's death, in order that he might be as a security and pledge for the submission of such Protestants as might effect their escape.

"This horrid butchery was not confined merely to the city of Paris. The like orders were issued from court to the governors of all the provinces in France; so that, in a week's time, about one hundred thousand Protestants were cut to pieces in different parts of the kingdom! Two or three governors only refused to obey the king's orders. One of these, named Montmorrin, governor of Auvergne, wrote the king the following letter, which deserves to be transmitted to the latest posterity.

"SIRE: I have received an order, under your majesty's seal, to put to death all the Protestants in my province. I have too much respect for your majesty, not to believe the letter a forgery; but if (which God forbid) the order should be genuine, I have too much respect for your majesty to obey it."

At Rome the horrid joy was so great, that they appointed a day of high festival, and a jubilee, with great indulgence to all who kept it and showed every expression of gladness they could devise! and the man who first carried the news received 1000 crowns of the cardinal of Lorraine for his ungodly message. The king also commanded the day to be kept with every demonstration of joy, concluding now that the whole race of Huguenots was extinct.

Many who gave great sums of money for

their ransom were immediately after slain; and several towns, which were under the king's promise of protection and safety, were cut off as soon as they delivered themselves up, on those promises, to his generals or captains.

At Bordeaux, at the instigation of a villainous monk, who used to urge the papists to slaughter in his sermons, two hundred and sixty-four were cruelly murdered; some of them senators. Another of the same pious fraternity produced a similar slaughter at Agendicum, in Maine, where the populace at the holy inquisitors' satanical suggestion, ran upon the Protestants, slew them, plundered their houses, and pulled down their church.

The duke of Guise, entering into Blois, suffered his soldiers to fly upon the spoil, and slay or drown all the Protestants they could find. In this they spared neither age nor sex; defiling the women, and then murdering them; from whence he went to Mere, and committed the same outrages for many days together. Here they found a minister named Cassebonius, and threw him into the river.

At Anjou, they slew Albiacus, a minister; and many women were defiled and murdered there; among whom were two sisters, abused before their father, whom the assassins bound to a wall to see them, and then slew them and him.

The president of Turin, after giving a large sum for his life, was cruelly beaten with clubs, stripped of his clothes, and hung feet upwards, with his head and breast in the river: before he was dead, they opened his belly, plucked out his entrails, and threw them into the river; and then carried his heart about the city upon a spear.

At Barre great cruelty was used, even to young children, whom they cut open, pulled out their entrails, which through very rage they gnawed with their teeth. Those who had fled to the castle, when they yielded, were almost hanged. Thus they did at the city of Matiscon; counting it sport to cut off their arms and legs and afterward kill them; and for the entertainment of their visitors, they often threw the Protestants from a high bridge into the river, saying, "Did you ever see men leap so well?"

At Penna, after promising them safety, three hundred were inhumanly butchered; and five and forty at Albia, on the Lord's Day. At Nonne, though it yielded on conditions of safeguard, the most horrid spectacles were exhibited. Persons of both sexes and conditions were indiscriminately murdered; the streets ringing with doleful cries, and flowing with blood; and the houses flaming with fire, which the abandoned soldiers had thrown in. One woman, being dragged from her hiding place with her husband, was first abused by the brutal soldiers, and then with a sword which they commanded her to draw, they forced it while in her hands into the bowels of her husband.

At Samarobridge, they murdered above one hundred Protestants, after promising them peace; and at Antsidor, one hundred were killed, and cast part into a jakes, and part into a river. One hundred put into a prison at Orleans, were destroyed by the furious multitude.

The Protestants at Rochelle, who were such as had miraculously escaped the rage of hell, and fled there, seeing how ill they fared who submitted to those holy devils, stood for their lives; and some other cities, encouraged thereby, did the like. Against Rochelle, the king sent almost the whole power of France, which besieged it seven months; though by their assaults, they did very little execution on the inhabitants, yet by famine, they destroyed eighteen thousand out of two and twenty. The dead, being too numerous for the living to bury, became food for vermin and carnivorous birds. Many took their coffins into the church yard, laid down in them, and breathed their last. Their diet had long been what the minds of those in plenty shudder at; even human flesh, entrails, dung, and the most loathsome things, became at last the only food of those champions for that truth and liberty, of which the world was not worthy. At every attack, the besiegers met with such an intrepid reception, that they left one hundred and thirty-two captains, with a proportionate number of men, dead in the field. The siege at last was broken up at the request of the duke of Anjou, the king's brother, who was proclaimed king of Poland, and the king, being wearied out, easily complied, whereupon honorable conditions were granted them.

It is a remarkable interference of Providence, that, in all this dreadful massacre, not more than two ministers of the Gospel were involved in it.

The tragical sufferings of the Protestants are too numerous to detail; but the treatment of Philip de Deux will give an idea of the rest. After the miscreants had slain this martyr in his bed, they went to his wife, who was then attended by the midwife, expecting every moment to be delivered. The midwife entreated them to stay the murder, at least till the child, which was the twentieth, should be born. Notwithstanding this, they thrust a dagger up to the hilt into the poor woman. Anxious to be delivered, she ran into a corn loft; but hither they pursued her, stabbed her in the belly, and then threw her into the street. By the fall, the child came from the dying mother, and being caught up by one of the Catholic ruffians, he stabbed the infant, and then threw it into the river. From the Revocation of the Edict of Nantes, to the French Revolution, in 1789

The persecutions occasioned by the revocation of the edict of Nantes took place under Louis XIV. This edict was made by Henry the Great of France in 1598, and secured to the Protestants an equal right in every respect, whether civil or religious, with the other subjects of the realm. All those privileges Louis the XIV confirmed to the Protestants by another statute, called the edict of Nismes, and kept them inviolably to the end of his reign.

On the accession of Louis XIV the kingdom was almost ruined by civil wars. At this critical juncture, the Protestants, heedless of our Lord's admonition, "They that take the sword shall perish with the sword," took such an active part in favor of the king, that he was constrained to acknowledge himself indebted to their arms for his establishment on the throne. Instead of cherishing and rewarding that party who had fought for him, he reasoned that the same power which had protected could overturn him, and, listening to the popish machinations, he began to issue out proscriptions and restrictions, indicative of his final determination. Rochelle was presently fettered with an incredible number of denunciations. Montauban and Millau were sacked by soldiers. Popish commissioners were appointed to preside over the affairs of the Protestants, and there was no appeal from their ordinance, except to the king's council. This struck at the root of their civil and religious exercises, and prevented them, being Protestants, from suing a Catholic in any court of law. This was followed by another injunction, to make an inquiry in all parishes into whatever the Protestants had said or done for twenty years past. This filled the prisons with innocent victims, and condemned others to the galleys or banishment.

Protestants were expelled from all offices, trades, privileges, and employs; thereby depriving them of the means of getting their bread: and they proceeded to such excess in this brutality, that they would not suffer even the midwives to officiate, but compelled their women to submit themselves in that crisis of nature to their enemies, the brutal Catholics. Their children were taken from them to be educated by the Catholics, and at seven years of age, made to embrace popery. The reformed were prohibited from relieving their own sick or poor, from all private worship, and divine service was to be performed in the presence of a popish priest. To prevent the unfortunate victims from leaving the kingdom, all the passages on the frontiers were strictly guarded; yet, by the good hand of God, about 150,000 escaped their vigilance, and emigrated to different countries to relate the dismal narrative.

All that has been related hitherto were only infringements on their established charter, the edict of Nantes. At length the diabolical revocation of that edict passed on the eighteenth of October, 1685, and was registered the twenty-second, contrary to all form of law. Instantly the dragoons were quartered upon the Protestants throughout the realm, and filled all France with the like news, that the king would no longer suffer any Huguenots in his kingdom, and therefore they must resolve to change their religion. Hereupon the intendants in every parish (which were popish governors and spies set over the Protestants) assembled the reformed inhabitants, and told them they must, without delay, turn Catholics, either freely or by force. The Protestants replied, that they "were ready to sacrifice their lives and estates to the king, but their consciences being God's they could not so dispose of them."

Instantly the troops seized the gates and avenues of the cities, and placing guards in all the passages, entered with sword in hand, crying, "Die, or be Catholics!" In short, they practiced every wickedness and horror they could devise to force them to change their religion.

They hanged both men and women by their hair or their feet, and smoked them with hay until they were nearly dead; and if they still refused to sign a recantation, they hung them up again and repeated their barbarities, until, wearied out with torments without death, they forced many to yield to them.

Others, they plucked off all the hair of their heads and beards with pincers. Others they threw on great fires, and pulled them out again, repeating it until they extorted a promise to recant.

Some they stripped naked, and after offering them the most infamous insults, they stuck them with pins from head to foot, and lanced them with penknives; and sometimes with red-hot pincers they dragged them by the nose until they promised to turn. Sometimes they tied fathers and husbands, while they ravished their wives and daughters before their eyes. Multitudes they imprisoned in the most noisome dungeons, where they practised all sorts of torments in secret. Their wives and children they shut up in monasteries.

Such as endeavored to escape by flight were pursued in the woods, and hunted in the fields, and shot at like wild beasts; nor did any condition or quality screen them from the ferocity of these infernal dragoons: even the members of parliament and military officers, though on actual service, were ordered to quit their posts, and repair directly to their houses to suffer the like storm. Such as complained to the king were sent to the Bastile, where they drank the same cup. The bishops and the intendants marched at the head of the dragoons, with a troop of missionaries, monks, and other ecclesiastics to animate the soldiers to an execution so agreeable to their Holy Church, and so glorious to their demon god and their tyrant king.

In forming the edict to repeal the edict of Nantes, the council were divided; some would have all the ministers detained and forced into popery as well as the laity; others were for banishing them, because their presence would strengthen the Protestants in perseverance: and if they were forced to turn, they would ever be secret and powerful enemies in the bosom of the Church, by their great knowledge and experience in controversial matters. This reason prevailing, they were sentenced to banishment, and only fifteen days allowed them to depart the kingdom.

On the same day that the edict for revoking the Protestants' charter was published, they demolished their churches and banished their ministers, whom they allowed but twenty-four hours to leave Paris. The papists would not suffer them to dispose of their effects, and threw every obstacle in their way to delay their escape until the limited time was expired which subjected them to condemnation for life to the galleys. The guards were doubled at the seaports, and the prisons were filled with the victims, who endured torments and wants at which human nature must shudder.

The sufferings of the ministers and others, who were sent to the galleys, seemed to exceed all. Chained to the oar, they were exposed to the open air night and day, at all seasons, and in all weathers; and when through weakness of body they fainted under the oar, instead of a cordial to revive them, or viands to refresh them, they received only the lashes of a scourge, or the blows of a cane or rope's end. For the want of sufficient clothing and necessary cleanliness, they were most grievously tormented with vermin, and cruelly pinched with the cold, which removed by night the executioners who beat and tormented them by day. Instead of a bed, they were allowed sick or well, only a hard board, eighteen inches broad, to sleep on, without any covering but their wretched apparel; which was a shirt of the coarsest canvas, a little jerkin of red serge, slit on each side up to the armholes, with open sleeves that reached not to the elbow; and once in three years they had a coarse frock, and a little cap to cover their heads, which were always kept close shaved as a mark of their infamy. The allowance of provision was as narrow as the sentiments of those who condemned them to such miseries, and their treatment when sick is too shocking to relate; doomed to die upon the boards of a dark hold, covered with vermin, and without the least convenience for the calls of nature. Nor was it among the least of the horrors they endured, that, as ministers of Christ, and honest men, they were chained side by side to felons and the most execrable villains, whose blasphemous tongues were never idle. If they refused to hear Mass, they were sentenced to the bastinado, of which dreadful punishment the following is a description. Preparatory to it, the chains are taken off, and the victims delivered into the hands of the Turks that preside at the oars, who strip them quite naked, and stretching them upon a great gun, they are held so that they cannot stir; during which there reigns an awful silence throughout the galley. The Turk who is appointed the executioner, and who thinks the sacrifice acceptable to his prophet Mahomet, most cruelly beats the wretched victim with a rough cudgel, or knotty rope's end, until the skin is flayed off his bones, and he is near the point of expiring; then they apply a most tormenting mixture of vinegar and salt, and consign him to that most intolerable hospital where thousands under their cruelties have expired.

Martyrdom of John Calas

We pass over many other individual martyrdoms to insert that of John Calas, which took place as recently as 1761, and is an indubitable proof of the bigotry of popery, and shows that neither experience nor improvement can root out the inveterate prejudices of the Roman Catholics, or render them less cruel or inexorable to Protestants.

John Calas was a merchant of the city of Toulouse, where he had been settled, and lived in good repute, and had married an English woman of French extraction. Calas and his wife were Protestants, and had five sons, whom they educated in the same religion; but Lewis, one of the sons, became a Roman Catholic, having been converted by a maidservant, who had lived in the family about thirty years. The father, however, did not express any resentment or ill-will upon the occasion, but kept the maid in the family and settled an annuity upon the son. In October, 1761, the family consisted of John Calas and his wife, one woman servant, Mark Antony Calas, the eldest son, and Peter Calas, the second son. Mark Antony was bred to the law, but could not be admitted to practice, on account of his being a Protestant; hence he grew melancholy, read all the books he could procure relative to suicide, and seemed determined to destroy himself. To this may be added that he led a dissipated life, was greatly addicted to gaming, and did all which could constitute the character of a libertine; on which account his father frequently reprehended him and sometimes in terms of severity, which considerably added to the gloom that seemed to oppress him.

On the thirteenth of October, 1761, Mr. Gober la Vaisse, a young gentleman about 19 years of age, the son of La Vaisse, a celebrated advocate of Toulouse, about five o'clock in the evening, was met by John Calas, the father, and the eldest son Mark Antony, who was his friend. Calas, the father, invited him to supper, and the family and their guest sat down in a room up one pair of stairs; the whole company, consisting of Calas the father, and his wife, Antony and Peter Calas, the sons, and La Vaisse the guest, no other person being in the house, except the maidservant who has been already mentioned.

It was now about seven o'clock. The supper was not long; but before it was over, Antony left the table, and went into the kitchen, which was on the same floor, as he was accustomed to do. The maid asked him if he was cold? He answered, "Quite the contrary, I burn"; and then left her. In the meantime his friend and family left the room they had supped in, and went into a bed- chamber; the father and La Vaisse sat down together on a sofa; the younger son Peter in an elbow chair; and the mother in another chair; and, without making any inquiry after Antony, continued in conversation together until between nine and ten o'clock, when La Vaisse took his leave, and Peter, who had fallen asleep, was awakened to attend him with a light.

On the ground floor of Calas's house was a shop and a warehouse, the latter of which was divided from the shop by a pair of folding doors. When Peter Calas and La Vaisse came downstairs into the shop, they were extremely shocked to see Antony hanging in his shirt, from a bar which he had laid across the top of the two folding doors, having half opened them for that purpose. On discovery of this horrid spectacle, they shrieked out, which brought down Calas the father, the mother being seized with such terror as kept her trembling in the passage above. When the maid discovered what had happened, she continued below, either because she feared to carry an account of it to her mistress, or because she busied herself in doing some good office to her master, who was embracing the body of his son, and bathing it in his tears. The mother, therefore, being thus left alone, went down and mixed in the scene that has been already described, with such emotions as it must naturally produce. In the meantime Peter had been sent for La Moire, a surgeon in the neighborhood. La Moire was not at home, but his apprentice, Mr. Grosle, came instantly. Upon examination, he found the body quite dead; and by this time a papistical crowd of people were gathered about the house, and, having by some means heard that Antony Calas was suddenly dead, and that the surgeon who had examined the body, declared that he had been strangled, they took it into their heads he had been murdered; and as the family was Protestant, they presently supposed that the young man was about to change his religion, and had been put to death for that reason.

The poor father, overwhelmed with grief for the loss of his child, was advised by his friends to send for the officers of justice to prevent his being torn to pieces by the Catholic multitude, who supposed he had murdered his son. This was accordingly done and David, the chief magistrate, or capitol, took the father, Peter the son, the mother, La Vaisse, and the maid, all into custody, and set a guard over them. He sent for M. de la Tour, a physician, and MM. la Marque and Perronet, surgeons, who examined the body for marks of violence, but found none except the mark of the ligature on the neck; they found also the hair of the deceased done up in the usual manner, perfectly smooth, and without the least disorder: his clothes were also regularly folded up, and laid upon the counter, nor was his shirt either torn or unbuttoned.

Notwithstanding these innocent appearances, the capitol thought proper to agree with the opinion of the mob, and took it into his head that old Calas had sent for La Vaisse, telling him that he had a son to be hanged; that La Vaisse had come to perform the office of executioner; and that he had received assistance from the father and brother.

As no proof of the supposed fact could be procured, the capitol had recourse to a monitory, or general information, in which the crime was taken for granted, and persons were required to give such testimony against it as they were able. This recites that La Vaisse was commissioned by the Protestants to be their executioner in ordinary, when any of their children were to be hanged for changing their religion: it recites also, that, when the Protestants thus hang their children, they compel them to kneel, and one of the interrogatories was, whether any person had seen Antony Calas kneel before his father when he strangled him: it recites likewise, that Antony died a Roman Catholic, and requires evidence of his catholicism.

But before this monitory was published, the mob had got a notion that Antony Calas was the next day to have entered into the fraternity of the White Penitents. The capitol therefore caused his body to be buried in the middle of St. Stephen's Church. A few days after the interment of the deceased, the White Penitents performed a solemn service for him in their chapel; the church was hung with white, and a tomb was raised in the middle of it, on the top of which was placed a human skeleton, holding in one hand a paper, on which was written "Abjuration of heresy," and in the other a palm, the emblem of martyrdom. The next day the Franciscans performed a service of the same kind for him.

The capitol continued the persecution with unrelenting severity, and, without the least proof coming in, thought fit to condemn the unhappy father, mother, brother, friend, and servant, to the torture, and put them all into irons on the eighteenth of November.

From these dreadful proceedings the sufferers appealed to the parliament, which immediately took cognizance of the affair, and annulled the sentence of the capitol as irregular, but they continued the prosecution, and, upon the hangman deposing it was impossible Antony should hang himself as was pretended, the majority of the parliament were of the opinion, that the prisoners were guilty, and therefore ordered them to be tried by the criminal court of Toulouse. One voted him innocent, but after long debates the majority was for the torture and wheel, and probably condemned the father by way of experiment, whether he was guilty or not, hoping he would, in the agony, confess the crime, and accuse the other prisoners, whose fate, therefore, they suspended.

Poor Calas, however, an old man of sixty-eight, was condemned to this dreadful punishment alone. He suffered the torture with great constancy, and was led to execution in a frame of mind which excited the admiration of all that saw him, and particularly of the two Dominicans (Father Bourges and Father Coldagues) who attended him in his last moments, and declared that they thought him not only innocent of the crime laid to his charge, but also an exemplary instance of true Christian patience, fortitude, and charity. When he saw the executioner prepared to give him the last stroke, he made a fresh declaration to Father Bourges, but while the words were still in his mouth, the capitol, the author of this catastrophe, who came upon the scaffold merely to gratify his desire of being a witness of his punishment and death, ran up to him, and bawled out, "Wretch, there are fagots which are to reduce your body to ashes! speak the truth." M. Calas made no reply, but turned his head a little aside; and that moment the executioner did his office.

The popular outcry against this family was so violent in Languedoc, that every body expected to see the children of Calas broke upon the wheel, and the mother burnt alive.

Young Donat Calas was advised to fly into Switzerland: he went, and found a gentleman who, at first, could only pity and relieve him, without daring to judge of the rigor exercised against the father, mother, and brothers. Soon after, one of the brothers, who was only banished, likewise threw himself into the arms of the same person, who, for more than a month, took every possible precaution to be assured of the innocence of the family. Once convinced, he thought himself, obliged, in conscience, to employ his friends, his purse, his pen, and his credit, to repair the fatal mistake of the seven judges of Toulouse, and to have the proceedings revised by the king's council. This revision lasted three years, and it is well known what honor Messrs. de Grosne and Bacquancourt acquired by investigating this memorable cause. Fifty masters of the Court of Requests unanimously declared the whole family of Calas innocent, and recommended them to the benevolent justice of his majesty. The Duke de Choiseul, who never let slip an opportunity of signalizing the greatness of his character, not only assisted this unfortunate family with money, but obtained for them a gratuity of 36,000 livres from the king.

On the ninth of March, 1765, the arret was signed which justified the family of Calas, and changed their fate. The ninth of March, 1762, was the very day on which the innocent and virtuous father of that family had been executed. All Paris ran in crowds to see them come out of prison, and clapped their hands for joy, while the tears streamed from their eyes.

This dreadful example of bigotry employed the pen of Voltaire in deprecation of the horrors of superstition; and though an infidel himself, his essay on toleration does honor to his pen, and has been a blessed means of abating the rigor of persecution in most European states. Gospel purity will equally shun superstition and cruelty, as the mildness of Christ's tenets teaches only to comfort in this world, and to procure salvation in the next. To persecute for being of a different opinion is as absurd as to persecute for having a different countenance: if we honor God, keep sacred the pure doctrines of Christ, put a full confidence in the promises contained in the Holy Scriptures, and obey the political laws of the state in which we reside, we have an undoubted right to protection instead of persecution, and to serve heaven as our consciences, regulated by the Gospel rules, may direct.

Foxe's Book of Martyrs, Chapter 5, Edited by William Byron Forbush

TORTURES AND TORMENTS OF THE CHRISTIAN MARTYRS

A large number of books were published in the seventeenth century which graphically illustrated the numerous ways in which Christian martyrs were tortured and killed.

Of Crosses and Stakes

A. Martyrs suspended by one foot.
B. Suspended by both feet.
C. Raised on the cross, head uppermost.
D. nailed to the cross, head downwards.
E. Hung up by both arms, heavy weights being attached to the feet.
F. Christian woman suspended by the hair.
G. Martyrs hung up by one arm only, ponderous stones being fastened to their feet.

Divers Modes of Suspension

A. Martyr suspended by both feet, and a great stone fastened to his neck.
B. Sometimes the Blessed Martyrs, after being smeared with honey were bound to stakes fixed in the ground, and so exposed to the rays of the sun to be tortured by the stings of flies and bees.
C. Martyr suspended by one foot; one leg is bent at the knee, which is constricted by means of an iron ring, the other being weighted with a heavy mass of iron.

More suspensions

A. Martyr suspended by the feet, and his head at the same time pounded with hammers.
B. Martyr suspended by the hands, which are tied behind his back, heavy weights being fastened to his feet and around his neck.

The Great Wheel

A. Sometimes martyrs were bound to the circumference of great wheels, and so hurled from a height over stony places.

Wheels of a Second Sort

A. Martyr whose limbs are interwoven in the spokes of a wheel, on which he is left exposed for days, till he dies.
B. Martyr bound to a narrow wheel, which is revolved, so that his body is horribly mangled on iron spikes fixed underneath.

Wherein Bodies were Racked and Stretched

A. A pulley.
B. martyrs racked at the pulleys.

C. Crushed in the press, just as grapes and olives are pressed in making wine and oil.
D. Capstan or windlass.

Raised on a Pulley

A. Martyr, with his hands tied behind his back, hoisted in the air by a rope.
B. Pulley.
C. Spikes, or sometimes, sharp flints, on to which the Martyr was let fall.

On the use of Cudgels

A. Martyr bound to four stakes and beaten with cudgels.
B. Martyr laid naked on iron spikes and violently beaten with a cudgel.
C. Martyr bound hand and foot and similarly beaten with a cudgel.

Buffeted, Stoned and Crushed

A. Martyr buffeted, kicked, and pounded with the fists.
B. Martyr being stoned.
C. Martyr whose face and jaws are bruised and broken with a stone.
D. Martyr crushed under a huge stone.

Of Currycombs and Pincers

A. Martyr tortured by means of the iron claw or pincers.
B. Torn with the hooks.
C. Mangled with the iron currycombs.

Scorched on the Wooden Horse

A. Martyr hung from the wooden horse and scorched with the flame of torches.
B. Martyr suspended by his feet from a pulley and tortured in a like fashion.

Frying-pans and Pots

A. Martyr thrown head-first into a caldron full of molten lead or boiling oil.
B. Martyr in a hot frying-pan.
C. martyr plunged into a boiling pot.

The Brazen Bull and Iron Bed

A. Martyr's dismembered limbs put in a frying-pan.
B. Martyr in the brazen bull.
C. Laid on the iron bed and broiled.

Other Instruments of Martyrdom

A. Martyr whose hand is filled with incense mingled with live coals, and who being constrained by the pain to scatter the incense, is said to have made sacrifice to the idol.
B. Martyr clad in the iron tunic and shod with the red-hot shoes, which consume the flesh off his bones.
C. Martyr seated in the iron chair, while a red-hot helmet, or morion, is set on his head.

Burning Coals, Molten Substances

A. Martyr compelled to walk over burning coals, while molten lead, boiling pitch, or like substances, are poured over his head.

Some Uses of Fires

A. Martyr cast into a burning fiery furnace.
B. Martyrs set in a tun, or cask, and burned therein.
C. Martyr burned in a room, or chamber, that hath been set on fire.
D. Bound hand and foot and set on a blazing pile.
E. Bound to four pegs fixed in the ground, with a fire burning underneath.
F. Bound with ropes drenched in oil and consumed by a fire lighted under him.
G. Thrown into a pit full of live coals.
H. Iron shovel for stirring and rousing the fire.

Stabbed by Styles, and Amputated

A. Martyr stabbed to death by boys with their writing styles.
B. Martyr whose limbs are amputated one by one.

Beating and Piercing

A. Martyr stabbed in the throat with a dagger.

B. Short to death with arrows.
C. Beaten over the head with an axe.
D. Beheaded with a sword.
E. Transfixed with a spear.

Sawn in Two

A. Martyr struck with a club or cudgel.
B. Sawn in two with an iron saw.
C. Hands and feet cut off.

Piercing the Inwards

A. Martyr pierced through with a sharp-pointed stake.
B. Martyr whose belly has been cut open and the liver torn out, which the heathen used sometimes to eat.

Martyrs being Flayed Alive

A. Martyrs being flayed alive.

Legs Torn, and Sharp Reeds

A. Martyr bound by either leg to the tops of two neighboring trees, which have been bent down and forcibly drawn together, and will presently be suddenly let go again.
B. Martyr tortured by having sharp reeds stuck under his finger and toe nails.

Condemned to the Wild Beasts

A. Martyr imprisoned in a net, and so exposed to be tossed by a wild bull.
B. Thrown down naked to be devoured by wild beasts.
C. Wrapped in a wild beast's hie, and so left to be torn by animals.
D. His feet fixed in a great stone, and with red-hot brad-awls stuck under his fingernails, the martyr is given over to be worried by starving dogs.

Cast Down from a Height

A. Martyrs cast down headlong from a height.
B. Thrown into a lime kiln.

Shut Up in a Box and Drowned

A. Martyr shut up in a leaden box and drowned in a river.
B. Sewn up in a bag, together with a cock, a viper, an ape, and a dog, and thrown into the nearest sea or stream.
Author Unknown: Tortures and Torments of the Christian Martyrs, William Brendon & Son, 1904

3. Christian writers

A selection from the writings, and the spoken words of the martyrs and about the martyrs and martyrdom and persecution of Christians from the 5th to the 15th centuries.

A. Of martyrdom, Thomas Aquinas

We must now consider martyrdom, under which head there are five points of inquiry:
(1) Whether martyrdom is an act of virtue?
(2) Of what virtue is it the act?
(3) Concerning the perfection of this act;
(4) The pain of martyrdom;
(5) Its cause.

1 Whether martyrdom is an act of virtue?

Objection 1: It seems that martyrdom is not an act of virtue. For all acts of virtue are voluntary. But martyrdom is sometimes not voluntary, as in the case of the Innocents who were slain for Christ's sake, and of whom Hillary says (Super Matth. i) that "they attained the ripe age of eternity through the glory of martyrdom." Therefore martyrdom is not an act of virtue.

Objection 2: Further, nothing unlawful is an act of virtue. Now it is unlawful to kill oneself, and yet martyrdom is achieved by so doing: for Augustine says (De Civ. Dei i) that "during persecution certain holy women, in order to escape from those who threatened their chastity, threw themselves into a river, and so ended their lives, and their martyrdom is honored in the Catholic Church with most solemn veneration." Therefore martyrdom is not an act of virtue.

Objection 3: Further, it is praiseworthy to offer oneself to do an act of virtue. But it is not praiseworthy to court martyrdom, rather would it seem to be presumptuous and rash. Therefore martyrdom is not an act of virtue.

On the contrary, The reward of beatitude is not due save to acts of virtue. Now it is due to martyrdom, since it is written (Mt. 5:10): "Blessed are they that suffer persecution for justice' sake, for theirs is the kingdom of heaven." Therefore martyrdom is an act of virtue. I answer that, As stated above, it belongs to virtue to safeguard man in the good of reason. Now the good of reason consists in the truth as its proper object, and in justice as its proper effect, as shown above (Question [109], Articles [1],2; Question [123], Article [12]). And martyrdom consists essentially in standing firmly to truth and justice against the assaults of persecution. Hence it is evident that martyrdom is an act of virtue.

Reply to Objection 1: Some have said that in the case of the Innocents the use of their free will was miraculously accelerated, so that they suffered martyrdom even voluntarily.

Since, however, Scripture contains no proof of this, it is better to say that these babes in being slain obtained by God's grace the glory of martyrdom which others acquire by their own will. For the shedding of one's blood for Christ's sake takes the place of Baptism. Wherefore just as in the case of baptized children the merit of Christ is conducive to the acquisition of glory through the baptismal grace, so in those who were slain for Christ's sake the merit of Christ's martyrdom is conducive to the acquisition of the martyr's palm. Hence Augustine says in a sermon on the Epiphany (De Diversis lxvi), as though he were addressing them: "A man that does not believe that children are benefited by the baptism of Christ will doubt of your being crowned in suffering for Christ. You were not old enough to believe in Christ's future sufferings, but you had a body wherein you could endure suffering of Christ Who was to suffer."

Reply to Objection 2: Augustine says (*De Civ. Dei* i) that "possibly the Church was induced by certain credible witnesses of Divine authority thus to honor the memory of those holy women."

Reply to Objection 3: The precepts of the Law are about acts of virtue. Now it has been stated that some of the precepts of the Divine Law are to be understood in reference to the preparation of the mind, in the sense that man ought to be prepared to do such and such a thing, whenever expedient. In the same way certain things belong to an act of virtue as regards the preparation of the mind, so that in such and such a case a man should act according to reason. And this observation would seem very much to the point in the case of martyrdom, which consists in the right endurance of sufferings unjustly inflicted. Nor ought a man to give another an occasion of acting unjustly: yet if anyone act unjustly, one ought to endure it in moderation.

Whether martyrdom is an act of fortitude?

Objection 1: It seems that martyrdom is not an act of fortitude. For the Greek (*martyr*) signifies a witness. Now witness is borne to the faith of Christ. according to Acts 1:8, "You shall be witnesses unto Me," etc. and Maximus says in a sermon: "The mother of martyrs is the Catholic faith which those glorious warriors have sealed with their blood." Therefore martyrdom is an act of faith rather than of fortitude.

Objection 2: Further, a praiseworthy act belongs chiefly to the virtue which inclines thereto, is manifested thereby, and without which the act avails nothing. Now charity is the chief incentive to martyrdom: Thus Maximus says in a sermon: "The charity of Christ is victorious in His martyrs." Again the greatest proof of charity lies in the act of martyrdom, according to Jn. 15:13, "Greater love than this no man hath, that a man lay down his life for his friends." Moreover without charity martyrdom avails nothing, according to 1 Cor. 13:3, "If I should deliver my body to be burned, and have not charity, it profiteth me nothing." Therefore martyrdom is an act of charity rather than of fortitude.

Objection 3: Further, Augustine says in a sermon on St. Cyprian: "It is easy to honor a martyr by singing his praises, but it is a great thing to imitate his faith and patience."

Now that which calls chiefly for praise in a virtuous act, is the virtue of which it is the act. Therefore martyrdom is an act of patience rather than of fortitude.

On the contrary, Cyprian says (*Ep. ad Mart. et Conf.* ii): "Blessed martyrs, with what praise shall I extol you? Most valiant warriors, how shall I find words to proclaim the strength of your courage?" Now a person is praised on account of the virtue whose act he performs. Therefore martyrdom is an act of fortitude.

I answer that it belongs to fortitude to strengthen man in the good of virtue, especially against dangers, and chiefly against dangers of death, and most of all against those that occur in battle. Now it is evident that in martyrdom man is firmly strengthened in the good of virtue, since he cleaves to faith and justice notwithstanding the threatening danger of death, the imminence of which is moreover due to a kind of particular contest with his persecutors. Hence Cyprian says in a sermon (Ep. ad Mart. et Conf. ii): "The crowd of onlookers wondered to see an unearthly battle, and Christ's servants fighting erect, undaunted in speech, with souls unmoved, and strength divine." Wherefore it is evident that martyrdom is an act of fortitude; for which reason the Church reads in the office of Martyrs: They "became valiant in battle" (Heb. 11:34).

Reply to Objection 1: Two things must be considered in the act of fortitude. one is the good wherein the brave man is strengthened, and this is the end of fortitude; the other is the firmness itself, whereby a man does not yield to the contraries that hinder him from achieving that good, and in this consists the essence of fortitude. Now just as civic fortitude strengthens a man's mind in human justice, for the safeguarding of which he braves the danger of death, so gratuitous fortitude strengthens man's soul in the good of Divine justice, which is "through faith in Christ Jesus," according to Rm. 3:22. Thus martyrdom is related to faith as the end in which one is strengthened, but to fortitude as the eliciting habit.

Reply to Objection 2: Charity inclines one to the act of martyrdom, as its first and chief motive cause, being the virtue commanding it, whereas fortitude inclines thereto as being its proper motive cause, being the virtue that elicits it. Hence martyrdom is an act of charity as commanding, and of fortitude as eliciting. For this reason also it manifests both virtues. It is due to charity that it is meritorious, like any other act of virtue: and for this reason it avails not without charity.

Reply to Objection 3: The chief act of fortitude is endurance: to this and not to its secondary act, which is aggression, martyrdom belongs. And since patience serves fortitude on the part of its chief act, viz. endurance, hence it is that martyrs are also praised for their patience.

Whether martyrdom is an act of the greatest perfection?

Objection 1: It seems that martyrdom is not an act of the greatest perfection. For seemingly that which is a matter of counsel and not of precept pertains to perfection, because, to wit, it is not necessary for salvation. But it would seem that martyrdom is necessary for salvation, since the Apostle says (Rm. 10:10), "With the heart we believe unto justice, but with the mouth confession is made unto salvation," and it is written (1 Jn. 3:16), that "we ought to lay down our lives for the brethren." Therefore martyrdom does not pertain to perfection.

Objection 2: Further, it seems to point to greater perfection that a man give his soul to God, which is done by obedience, than that he give God his body, which is done by martyrdom: wherefore Gregory says (*Moral.* xxxv) that "obedience is preferable to all sacrifices." Therefore martyrdom is not an act of the greatest perfection.

Objection 3: Further, it would seem better to do good to others than to maintain oneself in good, since the "good of the nation is better than the good of the individual," according to the Philosopher (*Ethic.* i, 2). Now he that suffers martyrdom profits himself alone, whereas he that teaches does good to many. Therefore the act of teaching and guiding subjects is more perfect than the act of martyrdom.

On the contrary, Augustine (*De Sanct.*

Virgin. xlvi) prefers martyrdom to virginity which pertains to perfection. Therefore martyrdom seems to belong to perfection in the highest degree.

I answer that, We may speak of an act of virtue in two ways. First, with regard to the species of that act, as compared to the virtue proximately eliciting it. In this way martyrdom, which consists in the due endurance of death, cannot be the most perfect of virtuous acts, because endurance of death is not praiseworthy in itself, but only in so far as it is directed to some good consisting in an act of virtue, such as faith or the love of God, so that this act of virtue being the end is better.

A virtuous act may be considered in another way, in comparison with its first motive cause, which is the love of charity, and it is in this respect that an act comes to belong to the perfection of life, since, as the Apostle says (Col. 3:14), that "charity . . . is the bond of perfection." Now, of all virtuous acts martyrdom is the greatest proof of the perfection of charity: since a man's love for a thing is proved to be so much the greater, according as that which he despises for its sake is more dear to him, or that which he chooses to suffer for its sake is more odious. But it is evident that of all the goods of the present life man loves life itself most, and on the other hand he hates death more than anything, especially when it is accompanied by the pains of bodily torment, "from fear of which even dumb animals refrain from the greatest pleasures," as Augustine observes. And from this point of view it is clear that martyrdom is the most perfect of human acts in respect of its genus, as being the sign of the greatest charity, according to Jn. 15:13: "Greater love than this no man hath, that a man lay down his life for his friends."

Reply to Objection 1: There is no act of perfection, which is a matter of counsel, but what in certain cases is a matter of precept, as being necessary for salvation. Thus Augustine declares (De Adult. Conjug. xiii) that a man is under the obligation of observing continency, through the absence or sickness of his wife. Hence it is not contrary to the perfection of martyrdom if in certain cases it be necessary for salvation, since there are cases when it is not necessary for salvation to suffer martyrdom; thus we read of many holy martyrs who through zeal for the faith or brotherly love gave themselves up to martyrdom of their own accord. As to these precepts, they are to be understood as referring to the preparation of the mind.

Reply to Objection 2: Martyrdom embraces the highest possible degree of obedience, namely obedience unto death; thus we read of Christ (Phil. 2:8) that He became "obedient unto death." Hence it is evident that martyrdom is of itself more perfect than obedience considered absolutely.

Reply to Objection 3: This argument considers martyrdom according to the proper species of its act, whence it derives no excellence over all other virtuous acts; thus neither is fortitude more excellent than all virtues.

Whether death is essential to martyrdom?

Objection 1: It seems that death is not essential to martyrdom. For Jerome says in a sermon on the Assumption (*Epist. ad Paul et Eustoch.*): "I should say rightly that the Mother of God was both virgin and martyr, although she ended her days in peace": and Gregory says (*Hom. iii in Evang.*): "Although persecution has ceased to offer the opportunity, yet the peace we enjoy is not without its martyrdom, since even if we no longer yield the life of the body to the sword, yet do we slay fleshly desires in the soul with the sword of the spirit." Therefore there can be martyrdom without suffering death.

Objection 2: Further, we read of certain women as commended for despising life for the sake of safeguarding the integrity of the flesh: wherefore seemingly the integrity of chastity is preferable to the life of the body. Now sometimes the integrity of the flesh has been forfeited or has been threatened in confession of the Christian faith, as in the case of Agnes and Lucy. Therefore it seems that the name of martyr should be accorded to a woman who forfeits the integrity of the flesh for the sake of Christ's faith, rather than if she were to forfeit even the life of the body:

wherefore also Lucy said: "If thou causest me to be violated against my will, my chastity will gain me a twofold crown."

Objection 3: Further, martyrdom is an act of fortitude. But it belongs to fortitude to brave not only death but also other hardships, as Augustine declares (Music. vi). Now there are many other hardships besides death, which one may suffer for Christ's faith, namely imprisonment, exile, being stripped of one's goods, as mentioned in Heb. 10:34, for which reason we celebrate the martyrdom of Pope Saint Marcellus, notwithstanding that he died in prison. Therefore it is not essential to martyrdom that one suffer the pain of death.

Objection 4: Further, martyrdom is a meritorious act. Now it cannot be a meritorious act after death. Therefore it is before death; and consequently death is not essential to martyrdom.

On the contrary, Maximus says in a sermon on the martyrs that "in dying for the faith he conquers who would have been vanquished in living without faith."

I answer that a martyr is so called as being a witness to the Christian faith, which teaches us to despise things visible for the sake of things invisible, as stated in Heb. 11. Accordingly it belongs to martyrdom that a man bear witness to the faith in showing by deed that he despises all things present, in order to obtain invisible goods to come. Now so long as a man retains the life of the body he does not show by deed that he despises all things relating to the body. For men are wont to despise both their kindred and all they possess, and even to suffer bodily pain, rather than lose life. Hence Satan testified against Job (Job 2:4): "Skin for skin, and all that a man hath he will give for his soul" [Douay: 'life'] i.e. for the life of his body. Therefore the perfect notion of martyrdom requires that a man suffer death for Christ's sake.

Reply to Objection 1: The authorities quoted, and the like that one may meet with, speak of martyrdom by way of similitude.

Reply to Objection 2: When a woman forfeits the integrity of the flesh, or is condemned to forfeit it under pretext of the Christian faith, it is not evident to men whether she suffers this for love of the Christian faith, or rather through contempt of chastity. Wherefore in the sight of men her testimony is not held to be sufficient, and consequently this is not martyrdom properly speaking. In the sight of God, however, Who searcheth the heart, this may be deemed worthy of a reward, as Lucy said.

Reply to Objection 3: Fortitude regards danger of death chiefly, and other dangers consequently; wherefore a person is not called a martyr merely for suffering imprisonment, or exile, or forfeiture of his wealth, except in so far as these result in death.

Reply to Objection 4: The merit of martyrdom is not after death, but in the voluntary endurance of death, namely in the fact that a person willingly suffers being put to death. It happens sometimes, however, that a man lives for some time after being mortally wounded for Christ's sake, or after suffering for the faith of Christ any other kind of hardship inflicted by persecution and continued until death ensues. The act of martyrdom is meritorious while a man is in this state, and at the very time that he is suffering these hardships.

Whether faith alone is the cause of martyrdom?

Objection 1: It seems that faith alone is the cause of martyrdom. For it is written (1 Pt. 4:15,16): "Let none of you suffer as a murderer, or a thief, or a railer, or a coveter of other men's things. But if as a Christian, let him not be ashamed, but let him glorify God in this name." Now a man is said to be a Christian because he holds the faith of Christ.

Therefore only faith in Christ gives the glory of martyrdom to those who suffer.

Objection 2: Further, a martyr is a kind of witness. But witness is borne to the truth alone. Now one is not called a martyr for bearing witness to any truth, but only for witnessing to the Divine truth, otherwise a man would be a martyr if he were to die for confessing a truth of geometry or some other speculative science, which seems ridiculous. Therefore faith alone is the cause of martyrdom.

Objection 3: Further, those virtuous deeds

would seem to be of most account which are directed to the common good, since "the good of the nation is better than the good of the individual," according to the Philosopher (*Ethic.* i, 2). If, then, some other good were the cause of martyrdom, it would seem that before all those would be martyrs who die for the defense of their country. Yet this is not consistent with Church observance, for we do not celebrate the martyrdom of those who die in a just war. Therefore faith alone is the cause of martyrdom.

On the contrary, It is written (Mt. 5:10): "Blessed are they that suffer persecution for justice' sake," which pertains to martyrdom, according to a gloss, as well as Jerome's commentary on this passage. Now not only faith but also the other virtues pertain to justice. Therefore other virtues can be the cause of martyrdom.

I answer that martyrs are so called as being witnesses, because by suffering in body unto death they bear witness to the truth; not indeed to any truth, but to the truth which is in accordance with godliness, and was made known to us by Christ: wherefore Christ's martyrs are His witnesses. Now this truth is the truth of faith. Wherefore the cause of all martyrdom is the truth of faith.

But the truth of faith includes not only inward belief, but also outward profession, which is expressed not only by words, whereby one confesses the faith, but also by deeds, whereby a person shows that he has faith, according to James 2:18, "I will show thee, by works, my faith." Hence it is written of certain people (Titus 1:16): "They profess that they know God but in their works they deny Him." Thus all virtuous deeds, inasmuch as they are referred to God, are professions of the faith whereby we come to know that God requires these works of us, and rewards us for them: and in this way they can be the cause of martyrdom. For this reason the Church celebrates the martyrdom of Blessed John the Baptist, who suffered death, not for refusing to deny the faith, but for reproving adultery.

Reply to Objection 1: A Christian is one who is Christ's. Now a person is said to be Christ's, not only through having faith in Christ, but also because he is actuated to virtuous deeds by the Spirit of Christ, according to Rm. 8:9, "If any man have not the Spirit of Christ, he is none of His"; and again because in imitation of Christ he is dead to sins, according to Gal. 5:24, "They that are Christ's have crucified their flesh with the vices and concupiscences." Hence to suffer as a Christian is not only to suffer in confession of the faith, which is done by words, but also to suffer for doing any good work, or for avoiding any sin, for Christ's sake, because this all comes under the head of witnessing to the faith.

Reply to Objection 2: The truth of other sciences has no connection with the worship of the Godhead: hence it is not called truth according to godliness, and consequently the confession thereof cannot be said to be the direct cause of martyrdom. Yet, since every lie is a sin, avoidance of a lie, to whatever truth it may be contrary, may be the cause of martyrdom inasmuch as a lie is a sin against the Divine Law.

Reply to Objection 3: The good of one's country is paramount among human goods: yet the Divine good, which is the proper cause of martyrdom, is of more account than human good. Nevertheless, since human good may become Divine, for instance when it is referred to God, it follows that any human good in so far as it is referred to God, may be the cause of martyrdom.

Thomas Aquinas, The Summa Theologica

B. Quotations about Martyrdom

I have committed my cause to the great judge of all mankind, so I am not moved by threats, nor are your swords more ready to strike than is my soul for martyrdom.

Thomas à Beckett

Part Six

Martyrs from the Reformation era

Contents

Walter Mill	
Religious Intolerance and Liberty in England and America:	Philip Scaff
Thomas Bilney:	John Foxe
The Reformation: Protestant Martyrs:	Philip Scaff
Thomas Harding:	John Foxe
Hitten:	John Foxe
William Letton:	John Foxe
John Frith:	John Foxe
John Lambert:	John Foxe
William Tyndale:	James Kiefer
	John Foxe
Four views on the Holy Communion:	John Foxe
John Fisher:	James Kiefer
	E. H. Burton and J. H. Pollen
Bishop John Fisher's reply:	
Thomas More:	James Kiefer
	The English Martyrs under Henry VIII and Elizabeth
Twelve Carthusian monks:	E. H. Burton and J. H. Pollen
Faith of sixteenth-century monks:	E. H. Burton and J. H. Pollen
The martyrs of Meaux:	H.M. Bower
Thomas Cromwell:	John Foxe
Dr. Cuthbert Barnes, Thomas Garnet, and William Jerome:	
Thomas Bainard, and James Moreton:	
Anthony Parsons:	
The Duke of Somerset:	Henry Machyn
	John Foxe
Persecutions in England during Queen Mary's reign:	John Foxe
Lady Jane Grey	
John Hooper:	
Thomas Tomkins:	John Foxe
John Rogers:	John Foxe
Rowland Taylor:	John Foxe
William Hunter:	John Foxe
Robert Farrar:	John Foxe
John Bradford:	John Foxe
Laurence Saunders:	Editor
George Marsh:	John Foxe
William Flower:	John Foxe
The Rev. John Cardmaker and John Warne:	John Foxe

John Simpson and John Ardeley:	John Foxe
Thomas Haukes:	John Foxe
Thomas Watts:	John Foxe
Dirick Carver and John Launder:	John Foxe
James Abbes:	John Foxe
John Denley, John Newman, and Patrick Packingham:	John Foxe
Elizabeth Warne:	John Foxe
George Tankerfield:	John Foxe
Rev. Robert Samuel:	John Foxe
John Philpot:	John Foxe
John Lomas, Agnes Snoth, Anne Wright, Joan Sole, and Joan Catmer:	John Foxe
The vision of three ladders:	John Foxe
Hugh Laverick and John Aprice:	John Foxe
Thomas Dowry:	John Foxe
Executions at Stratford-le-Bow:	John Foxe
Rev. Julius Palmer:	John Foxe
Joan Waste and Others:	John Foxe
Persecutions in the Diocese of Canterbury:	John Foxe
Seven more martyrs at Canterbury:	John Foxe
Alice Benden:	John Foxe
Matthew Plaise:	John Foxe
Rev. John Hullier:	John Foxe
Simon Miller and Elizabeth Cooper:	John Foxe
Executions at Colchester:	John Foxe
George Eagles:	John Foxe
Mrs. Joyce Lewes:	John Foxe
Executions at Islington:	John Foxe
James Austoo's letter:	John Foxe
John Noyes:	John Foxe
Mrs. Cicely Ormes:	John Foxe
Rev. John Rough:	John Foxe
Cuthbert Symson:	John Foxe
Thomas Hudson, Thomas Carman, and William Seamen:	John Foxe
The Story of Roger Holland:	John Foxe
John Willes:	John Foxe
Rev. Richard Yeoman:	John Foxe
Thomas Benbridge:	John Foxe
Mrs. Prest:	John Foxe
Richard Sharpe, Thomas Banion, and Thomas Hale:	John Foxe

Edmund Campion:	The English Martyrs Under Henry VIII and Elizabeth
Illustrations of persecution of Catholics:	J. H. Pollen
Mary Queen of Scots:	Editor
John Amias and Robert Dalby:	Martyrs Omitted by John Foxe, compiled by a member of the English Church
Forty Martyrs of England and Wales:	James Keifer
Forty Martyrs of England and Wales:	S. Anselm Parker
Nicholas Owen:	S. Anselm Parker
Roman Catholics persecuted:	Martyrs Omitted by John Foxe, compiled by a member of the English Church
Richard Barry:	Martyrs Omitted by John Foxe, compiled by a member of the English Church
A True Confession of Faith of the Brownists:	Albert Peel
English martyrs, 1535–83:	The English Martyrs under Henry VIII and Elizabeth
The martyrs of Japan:	James Kiefer
John Ogilvie:	C. J. Karslake
Pursuivants and the harrying of Catholics:	Annual Letters of the English Mission
A layman's exhortation to Catholic priests:	John Heigham
Edmund Arrowsmith:	The Life of Edmund Arrowsmith
Peter O'Higgins:	Martyrs Omitted by John Foxe, compiled by a member of the English Church
Hugh Green:	Douai Diary
Brabant and the Gospellers:	Peter Wright
Charles I:	James Kiefer Editor
The Martyr's King:	John Keble
Charles I's last words	
Persecution in the valleys of Piedmont in the seventeenth century:	John Foxe
Rawlins White:	John Foxe
Christopher Waid:	John Foxe
Rise and Progress of the Protestant Religion in Ireland; with an Account of the Barbarous Massacre of 1641:	John Foxe
Catholic intolerance:	Philip Scaff

1. Introduction

An Account of the Inquisition

When the reformed religion began to diffuse the Gospel light throughout Europe, Pope Innocent III entertained great fear for the Romish Church. He accordingly instituted a number of inquisitors, or persons who were to make inquiry after, apprehend, and punish, heretics, as the reformed were called by the papists.

The head inquisitor: Dominic

At the head of these inquisitors was one Dominic, who had been canonized by the pope, in order to render his authority the more respectable. Dominic, and the other inquisitors, spread themselves into various Roman Catholic countries, and treated the Protestants with the utmost severity. In process of time, the pope, not finding these roving inquisitors so useful as he had imagined, resolved upon the establishment of fixed and regular courts of Inquisition. After the order for these regular courts, the first office of Inquisition was established in the city of Toulouse, and Dominic became the first regular inquisitor, as he had before been the first roving inquisitor.

The Spanish Inquisition

Courts of Inquisition were now erected in several countries; but the Spanish Inquisition became the most powerful, and the most dreaded of any. Even the kings of Spain themselves, though arbitrary in all other respects, were taught to dread the power of the lords of the Inquisition; and the horrid cruelties they exercised compelled multitudes, who differed in opinion from the Roman Catholics, carefully to conceal their sentiments.

Frederic II

In 1244, their power was further increased by the emperor Frederic II, who declared himself the protector and friend of all the inquisitors, and published the cruel edicts, viz.,

1. That all heretics who continue obstinate, should be burnt.
2. That all heretics who repented, should be imprisoned for life.

Merciless torture

Upon all occasions the inquisitors carry on their processes with the utmost severity, and punish those who offend them with the most unparalleled cruelty. A Protestant has seldom any mercy shown him, and a Jew, who turns Christian, is far from being secure.

The inquisitors allow torture to be used only three times, but during those times it is so severely inflicted, that the prisoner either dies under it, or continues always after a cripple, and suffers the severest pains upon every change of weather. We shall give an ample description of the severe torments occasioned by the torture, from the account of one who suffered it the three respective times, but happily survived the cruelties he underwent.

The first torture

At the first time of torturing, six executioners entered, stripped him naked to his drawers, and laid him upon his back on a kind of stand, elevated a few feet from the floor. The operation commenced by putting an iron collar round his neck, and a ring to each foot, which fastened him to the stand. His limbs being thus stretched out, they wound two ropes round each thigh; which ropes being passed under the scaffold, through holes made for that purpose, were all drawn tight at the same instant of time, by four of the men, on a given signal.

It is easy to conceive that the pains which immediately succeeded were intolerable; the ropes, which were of a small size, cut through the prisoner's flesh to the bone, making the blood to gush out at eight different places thus bound at a time. As the prisoner persisted in not making any confession of what the inquisitors required, the ropes were drawn in this manner four times successively.

The second torture

The manner of inflicting the second torture was as follows: they forced his arms backwards so that the palms of his hands were turned outward behind him; when, by means of a rope that fastened them together at the wrists, and which was turned by an engine, they drew them by degrees nearer each other, in such a manner that the back of each hand touched, and stood exactly parallel to each other. In consequence of this violent contortion, both his shoulders became dislocated, and a considerable quantity of blood issued from his mouth. This torture was repeated thrice; after which he was again taken to the dungeon, and the surgeon set the dislocated bones.

The third torture

Two months after the second torture, the prisoner being a little recovered, was again ordered to the torture room, and there, for the last time, made to undergo another kind of punishment, which was inflicted twice without any intermission. The executioners fastened a thick iron chain round his body, which crossing at the breast, terminated at the wrists. They then placed him with his back against a thick board, at each extremity whereof was a pulley, through which there ran a rope that caught the end of the chain at his wrists. The executioner then, stretching the end of his rope by means of a roller, placed at a distance behind him, pressed or bruised his stomach in proportion as the ends of the chains were drawn tighter. They tortured him in this manner to such a degree, that his wrists, as well as his shoulders, were quite dislocated. They were, however, soon set by the surgeons; but the barbarians, not yet satisfied with this species of cruelty, made him immediately undergo the like torture a second time, which he sustained (though, if possible, attended with keener pains,) with equal constancy and resolution. After this, he was again remanded to the dungeon, attended by the surgeon to dress his bruises and adjust the part dislocated, and here he continued until their auto da fe, or jail delivery, when he was discharged, crippled and diseased for life.

An Account of the Cruel Handling and Burning of Nicholas Burton, an English Merchant, in Spain

The fifth day of November, about the year of our Lord 1560, Mr. Nicholas Burton, citizen sometime of London, and merchant, dwelling in the parish of Little St. Bartholomew, peaceably and quietly, following his traffic in the trade of merchandise, and being in the city of Cadiz, in the party of Andalusia, in Spain, there came into his lodging a Judas, or, as they term them, a familiar of the fathers of Inquisition; who asking for the said Nicholas Burton, feigned that he had a letter to deliver into his own hands; by which means he spake with him immediately. And having no letter to deliver to him, then the said promoter, or familiar, at the motion of the devil his master, whose messenger he was, invented another lie, and said he would take lading for London in such ships as the said Nicholas Burton had freighted to lade, if he would let any; which was partly to know where he loaded his goods, that they might attach them, and chiefly to protract the time until the sergeant of the Inquisition might come and apprehend the body of the said Nicholas Burton; which they did incontinently.

He then well perceiving that they were not able to burden or charge him that he had written, spoken, or done any thing there in that country against the ecclesiastical or temporal laws of the same realm, boldly asked them what they had to lay to his charge that they did so arrest him, and bade them to declare the cause, and he would answer them. Notwithstanding they answered nothing, but commanded him with threatening words to hold his peace, and not speak one word to them.

"He instructed the poor prisoners"

And so they carried him to the filthy common prison of the town of Cadiz where he remained in irons fourteen days amongst thieves.

All which time he so instructed the poor prisoners in the Word of God, according to the good talent which God had given him in that behalf, and also in the Spanish tongue to utter the same, that in that short space he had well reclaimed several of those superstitious and ignorant Spaniards to embrace the Word of God, and to reject their popish traditions.

Which being known unto the officers of the Inquisition, they conveyed him laden with irons from thence to a city called Seville, into a more cruel and straiter prison called Triana, where the said fathers of the Inquisition proceeded against him secretly according to their customary cruel tyranny, that never after he could be suffered to write or speak to any of his nation: so that to this day it is unknown who was his accuser.

Afterward, the twentieth of December, they brought the said Nicholas Burton, with a great number of other prisoners, for professing the true Christian religion, into the city of Seville, to a place where the said inquisitors sat in judgment which they called auto, with a canvas coat, whereupon in divers parts was painted the figure of a huge devil, tormenting a soul in a flame of fire, and on his head a copping tank of the same work.

His tongue was forced out of his mouth with a cloven stick fastened upon it, that he should not utter his conscience and faith to the people, and so he was set with another Englishman of Southampton, and divers other condemned men for religion, as well Frenchmen as Spaniards, upon a scaffold over against the said Inquisition, where their sentences and judgments were read and pronounced against them.

"Most cruelly burned"

And immediately after the said sentences given, they were carried from there to the place of execution without the city, where they most cruelly burned them, for whose constant faith, God is praised.

This Nicholas Burton by the way, and in the flames of fire, had so cheerful a countenance, embracing death with all patience and gladness, that the tormentors and enemies which stood by, said, that the devil had his soul before he came to the fire; and therefore they said his senses of feeling were past him.

The Story of Galileo

The most eminent men of science and philosophy of the day did not escape the watchful eye of this cruel despotism. Galileo, the chief astronomer and mathematician of his age, was the first who used the telescope successfully in solving the movements of the heavenly bodies. He discovered that the sun is the center of motion around which the earth and various planets revolve. For making this great discovery Galileo was brought before the Inquisition, and for a while was in great danger of being put to death.

After a long and bitter review of Galileo's writings, in which many of his most important discoveries were condemned as errors, the charge of the inquisitors went on to declare, "That you, Galileo, have upon account of those things which you have written and confessed, subjected yourself to a strong suspicion of heresy in this Holy Office, by believing, and holding to be true, a doctrine which is false, and contrary to the sacred and divine Scripture— viz., that the sun is the center of the orb of the earth, and does not move from the east to the west; and that the earth moves, and is not the center of the world."

In order to save his life. Galileo admitted that he was wrong in thinking that the earth revolved around the sun, and swore that— "For the future, I will never more say, or assert, either by word or writing, anything that shall give occasion for a like suspicion." But immediately after taking this forced oath he is said to have whispered to a friend standing near, "The earth moves, for all that."

Summary of the Inquisition

Of the multitudes who perished by the Inquisition throughout the world, no authentic record is now discoverable. But wherever popery had power, there was the tribunal. It had been planted even in the east, and the Portuguese Inquisition of Goa was, until within these few years, fed with many an agony. South America was partitioned into provinces of the Inquisition; and with a ghastly mimicker of the crimes of the mother state, the arrivals of viceroys, and the other popular celebrations were thought imperfect without an auto da fe. The Netherlands were one scene of slaughter from the time of the decree which planted the Inquisition among them. In Spain the calculation is more attainable. Each of the seventeen tribunals during a long period burned annually, on an average, ten miserable beings! We are to recollect that this number was in a country where persecution had for ages abolished all religious differences, and where the difficulty was not to find the stake, but the offering. Yet, even in Spain, thus gleaned of all heresy, the Inquisition could still swell its lists of murders to thirty-two thousand! The numbers burned in effigy, or condemned to penance, punishments generally equivalent to exile, confiscation, and taint of blood, to all ruin but the mere loss of worthless life, amounted to three hundred and nine thousand. But the crowds who perished in dungeons of torture, of confinement, and of broken hearts, the millions of dependent lives made utterly helpless, or hurried to the grave by the death of the victims, are beyond all register; or recorded only before HIM, who has sworn that "He that leadeth into captivity, shall go into captivity: he that killeth with the sword must be killed with the sword."

Such was the Inquisition, declared by the Spirit of God to be at once the offspring and the image of the popedom. To feel the force of the parentage, we must look to the time. In the thirteenth century, the popedom was at the summit of mortal dominion; it was independent of all kingdoms; it ruled with a rank of influence never before or since possessed by a human scepter; it was the acknowledged sovereign of body and soul; to all earthly intents its power was immeasurable for good or evil. It might have spread literature, peace, freedom, and Christianity to the ends of Europe, or the world. But its nature was hostile; its fuller triumph only disclosed its fuller evil; and, to the shame of human reason, and the terror and suffering of human virtue, Rome, in the hour of its consummate grandeur, teemed with the monstrous and horrid birth of the INQUISITION!

Foxe's Book of Martyrs, Chapter 5, Edited by William Byron Forbush

The tortures of the Inquisition

A stunning blow

The re-establishment of the Inquisition decided the question of the Reformation of Italy. The country, struck with this blow as it was lifting itself up, instantly fell back into the old gulf. It had become suddenly apparent that religious reform must be won with a great fight of suffering, and Italy had not strength to press on through chains, and dungeons, and scaffolds to the goal she wished to reach. The prize was glorious, she saw, but the price was great. Pallavicino has confessed that it was the Inquisition that saved Italy from lapsing into Protestantism.

Three classes in Italy

The religious question had divided the Italians of that day into three classes. The bulk of the nation had not thought on the question at all, and harbored no purpose of leaving the Church of Rome. To them the restoration of the Inquisition had no terrors. There was another and large class who had abandoned Rome, but who had not clearness to advance to the open profession of Protestantism. They were most to be pitied of all should they fall into the hands of the inquisitors, seeing they were too undecided either to decline or to face the horrors of the Holy Office. The third class were in no doubt as to the course they must pursue. They could not return to a Church which they held to be superstitious, and they had no alternative before them but provide for their safety by flight, or await death amid the fires of the Inquisition. The consternation was great; for the Protestants had not dreamed of their enemies having recourse to such violent measures. Numbers fled, and these fugitives were to be found in every city of Switzerland and Germany.

Among these was Bernardino Ochino, on whose eloquent orations all ranks of his countrymen had been hanging but a few months before, and in whose audience the emperor himself might be seen when he visited Italy. Not, however, till he had been served with a citation from the Holy Office at Rome did Ochino make his escape. Flight was almost as bitter as death to the orator. He was leaving behind him the scene of those brilliant triumphs which he could not hope to renew on a foreign soil. Pausing on the summit of the Great St. Bernard, he devoted a few moments to those feelings of regret which were so natural on abandoning so much that he could not hope ever again to enjoy. He then went forward to Geneva. But, alas! the best days of the eloquent monk were past. At Geneva, Ochino's views became tainted and obscured with the new philosophy, which was beginning to air itself at that young school of pantheism.

Flight of Peter Martyr Vermigli of Ochino

Peter Martyr Vermigli soon followed. He was presiding over the convent of his order in Lucca, when the storm came with such sudden violence. He set his house in order and fled; but it was discovered after he was gone that the heresy remained although the heretic had escaped, his opinions having been embraced by many of the Luccese monks. The same was found to be the case with the order to which Ochino belonged, the Capuchins namely, and the Pope at first meditated, as the only cure, the suppression of both orders. Peter Martyr went ultimately to Strasburg, and a place was found for him in its university, where his lamp continued to burn clearly to the close. Juan di Valdez died before the tempest burst, which drove beyond the Alps so many of the distinguished group that had formed itself around him at Pausilippo, and saw not the evil days which came on his adopted country. But the majority of those who had embraced the Protestant faith were unable to escape. They were immured in the prisons of the various Holy Offices throughout Italy; some were kept in dark cells for years, in the hope that they would recant, others were quickly relieved by martyrdom.

Caraffa made Pope

The restorer of the Inquisition, the once reforming Caraffa, mounted the Papal chair, under the name of Paul IV. The rigors of the Holy Office were not likely to be relaxed under the new Pope; but twenty years were needed to enable the torture and the stake to annihilate the Protestants of Italy.

The Martyrs, Mollio and Tisserano

Of those who suffered martyrdom we shall mention only two Mollio, a Bolognese professor, renowned throughout Italy for his learning and his pure life; and Tisserano, a native of Perugia. On the 15th of September, 1553, an assembly of the Inquisition, consisting of six cardinals with their episcopal assessors, was held with great pomp at Rome. A train of prisoners, with burning tapers in their hands, was led in before the tribunal. All of them recanted save Mollio and Tisserano. On leave being given them to speak, Mollio broke out, says McCrie, "in a strain of bold and fervid invective, which chained them to their seats, at the same time that it cut them to the quick." He rebuked his judges for their lewdness, their avarice, and their blood-thirsty cruelty, and concluded as follows: "Wherefore I appeal from your sentence, and summon you, cruel tyrants and murderers, to answer before the judgment-seat of Christ at the last day, where your pompous titles and gorgeous trappings will not dazzle, nor your guards and torturing apparatus terrify us. And in testimony of this, take back that which you have given me." In saying this, he threw the flaming torch which he held in his hand on the ground, and extinguished it. Galled, and gnashing upon him with their teeth, like the persecutors of the first Christian martyrs, the cardinals ordered Mollio, together with his companion, who approved of the testimony he had borne, to instant execution. They were conveyed, accordingly, to the Campo del Flor, where they died with the most pious fortitude."

Italian Protestantism Crushed

The eight years that elapsed between 1534 and 1542 are notable ones in the annals of

Protestant Christianity. That epoch witnessed the birth of three movements, Which were destined to stamp a character upon the future of Europe, and powerfully to modify the conflict then in progress in Christendom. In 1534 the Jesuits recorded their first vow in the Church of Montmartre, in Paris. In 1540 their society was regularly launched by the Papal edict. In 1542, Paul III issued the bull for the re-establishment of the Inquisition; and in 1541 Calvin returned to Geneva, to prepare that spiritual army that was to wage battle with Jesuitism backed by the Inquisition. The meeting of these dates the contemporaneous rise of these three instrumentalities, is sufficiently striking, and is one of the many proofs which we meet in history that there is an Eye watching all that is done on earth, and that never does an agency start up to destroy the world, but there is set over against it a yet more powerful agency to convert the evil it would inflict into good.

A Notable Epoch

It is one of these great epochs at which we have arrived. Jesuitism, the consummation of error the Inquisition, the maximum of force, stand up and array themselves against a now fully developed Protestantism. In following the steps of the combatants, we shall be led in succession to the mountains of the Waldenses, to the cities of France, to the swamps of Holland, to the plains of Germany, to Italy, to Spain, to England and Scotland. Round the whole of Christendom will roll the tide of this great battle, casting down one nation into the darkness of slavery, and lifting up another into the glory of freedom, and causing the gigantic crimes of the persecutor and the despot to be forgotten in the excelling splendor of the patriot and the martyr. This is the struggle with the record of which we shall presently be occupied. Meanwhile we proceed to describe one of those few Inquisitions that remain to this day in almost the identical state in which they existed when the Holy Office was being vigorously worked. This will enable us to realize more vividly the terror of that weapon which Paul III prepared for the hands of the Jesuits, and the Divine power of that faith which enabled the confessors of the Gospel to withstand and triumph over it.

The Inquisition at Nuremberg

Turn we now to the town of Nuremberg, in Bavaria. The zeal with which Duke Albert, the sovereign of Bavaria, entered into the restoration of Roman Catholicism, we have already narrated. To further the movement, he provided every one of the chief towns of his dominions with a Holy Office, and the Inquisition of Nuremberg still remains an anomalous and horrible monument in the midst of a city where the memorials of an exquisite art, and the creations of an unrivaled genius, meet one at every step. We shall first describe the Chamber of Torture.5

The Torture-Chamber

The house so called immediately adjoins the Imperial Castle, which from its lofty site looks down on the city, whose Gothic towers, sculptured fronts, and curiously ornamented gables are seen covering both banks of the Pegnitz, which rolls below. The house may have been the guard-room of the castle. It derives its name, the Torture-chamber, not from the fact that the torture was here inflicted, but because into this one chamber has been collected a complete set of the instruments of torture gleaned from the various Inquisitions that formerly existed in Bavaria. A glance suffices to show the whole dreadful apparatus by which the adherents of Rome sought to maintain her dogmas. Placed next to the door, and greeting the sight as one enters, is a collection of hideous masks. These represent creatures monstrous of shape, and malignant and fiendish of nature, It is in beholding them that we begin to perceive how subtle was the genius that devised this system of coercion, and that it took the mind as well as the body of the victim into account. In gazing on them, one feels as if he had suddenly come into polluting and debasing society, and had sunk to the same moral level with the creatures here figured before him. He suffers a conscious abatement of dignity and fortitude. The persecutor had calculated, doubtless, that the effect produced upon the mind of his victim by these dreaded apparitions, would be that he would become morally relaxed, and less able to sustain his cause. Unless of strong mind, indeed, the unfortunate prisoner, on entering such a place, and seeing himself encompassed with such unearthly and hideous shapes, must have felt as if he were the vile heretic which the persecutor styled him, and as if already the infernal den had opened its portals, and sent forth its venomous swarms to bid him welcome. Yourself accursed, with accursed beings are you henceforth to dwell such was the silent language of these abhorred images.

Its Furnishings

We pass on into the chamber, where more dreadful sights meet our gaze. It is hung round and round with instruments of torture, so numerous that it would take a long while even to name them, and so diverse that it would take a much longer time to describe them. We must take them in groups, for it were hopeless to think of going over them one by one, and particularizing the mode in which each operated, and the ingenuity and art with which all of them have been adapted to their horrible end. There were instruments for compressing the fingers till the bones should be squeezed to splinters. There were instruments for probing below the finger-nails till an exquisite pain, like a burning fire, would run along the nerves. There were instruments for tearing out the tongue, for scooping out the eyes, for grubbing-up the ears. There were bunches of iron cords, with a spiked circle at the end of every whip, for tearing the flesh from the back till bone and sinew were laid bare. There were iron cases for the legs, which were tightened upon the limb placed in them by means of a screw, till flesh and bone were reduced to a jelly. There were cradles set full of sharp spikes, in which victims were laid and rolled from side to side, the wretched occupant being pierced at each movement of the machine with innumerable sharp points. There were iron ladles with long handles, for holding molten lead or boiling pitch, to be poured down the throat of the victim, and convert his body into a burning cauldron. There were frames with holes to admit the hands and feet, so contrived that the person put into them had his body bent into unnatural and painful positions, and the agony grew greater and greater by moments, and yet the man did not die. There were chestfuls of small but most ingeniously constructed instruments for pinching, probing, or tearing the more sensitive parts of the body, and continuing the pain up to the very verge where reason or life gives way. On the floor and walls of the apartment were other and larger instruments for the same fearful end lacerating, mangling, and agonizing living men; but these we shall meet in other dungeons we are yet to visit.

The first impression on entering the chamber was one of bewildering horror; a confused procession of mangled, mutilated, agonizing men, speechless in their great woe, the flesh peeled from off their livid sinews, the sockets where eyes had been, hollow and empty, seemed to pass before one. The most dreadful scenes which the great genius of Dante has imagined, appeared tame in comparison with the spectral groups which this chamber summoned up. The first impulse was to escape, lest images of pain, memories of tormented men, who were made to die a hundred deaths in one, should take hold of one's mind, never again to be effaced from it.

The things we have been surveying are not the mere models of the instruments made use of in the Holy Office; they are the veritable instruments themselves. We see before us the actual implements by which hundreds and thousands of men and women, many of them saints and confessors of the Lord Jesus, were torn, and mangled, and slain. These terrible realities the men of the sixteenth century had to face and endure, or renounce the hope of the life eternal. Painful they were to flesh and blood nay, not even endurable by flesh and blood unless sustained by the Spirit of the mighty God.

The Max Tower

We leave the Torture-chamber to visit the Inquisition proper. We go eastward, about half a mile, keeping close to the northern wall of the city, till we come to an old tower, styled in the common parlance of Nuremberg the Max Tower. We pull the bell, the iron handle and chain of which are seen suspended beside the door-post. The cicerone appears, carrying a bunch of keys, a lantern, and some half-dozen candles. The lantern is to show us our way, and the candles are for the purpose of being lighted and stuck up at the turnings in the dark underground passages which we are about to traverse. Should mischance befall our lantern, these tapers, like beacon-lights in a narrow creek, will pilot us safely back into the day. The cicerone, selecting the largest from the bunch of keys, inserts it in the lock of the massy portal before which we stand, bolt after bolt is turned, and the door, with hoarse heavy groan as it turns on its hinge, opens slowly to us. We begin to descend. We go down one flight of steps; we go down a second flight; we descend yet a third. And now we pause a moment. The darkness is intense, for here never came the faintest glimmer of day; but a gleam thrown forward from the lantern showed us that we were arrived at the entrance of a horizontal, narrow passage. We could see, by the flickering of the light upon its sides and roof, that the corridor we were traversing was hewn out of the rock. We had gone only a few paces when we were brought up before a massy door. As far as the dim light served us, we could see the door, old, powdery with dust, and partly worm-eaten. Passing in, the corridor continued, and we went forward other three paces or so, when we found ourselves before a second door. We opened and shut it behind us as we did the first. Again we began to thread our way: a third door stopped us. We opened and closed it in like manner. Every step was carrying us deeper into the heart of the rock, and multiplying the barriers between us and the upper world. We were shut in with the thick darkness and the awful silence. We began to realize what must have been the feelings of some unhappy disciple of the Gospel, surprised by the familiars of the Holy Office, led through the midnight streets of Nuremberg, conducted to Max Tower, led down flight after flight of stairs, and along this horizontal shaft in the rock, and at every few paces a massy door, with its locks and bolts, closing behind him! He must have felt how utterly he was beyond the reach of human pity and human aid. No cry, however piercing, could reach the ear of man through these roofs of rock. He was entirely in the power of those who had brought him thither.

The Chamber of Question

At last we came to a side-door in the narrow passage. We halted, applied the key, and the door, with its ancient mold, creaking harshly as if moving on a hinge long disused, opened to let us in. We found ourselves in a rather roomy chamber, it might be about twelve feet square. This was the Chamber of Question. Along one side of the apartment ran a low platform. There sat of old the inquisitors, three in number the first a divine, the second a casuist, and the third a civilian. The only occupant of that platform was the crucifix, or image of the Savior on the cross, which still remained. The six candles that usually burned before the "holy Fathers" were, of course, extinguished, but our lantern supplied their place, and showed us the grim furnishings of the apartment. In the middle was the horizontal rack or bed of torture, on which the victim was stretched till bone started from bone, and his dislocated frame became the seat of agony, which was suspended only when it had reached a pitch that threatened death.

The various Instruments of Torture

Leaning against the wall of the chamber was the upright rack, which is simpler, but as an instrument of torture not less effectual, than the horizontal one. There was the iron chain which wound over a pulley, and hauled up the victim to the vaulted roof; and there were the two great stone weights which, tied to his feet, and the iron cord let go, brought him down with a jerk that dislocated his limbs, while the spiky rollers, which he grazed in his descent, cut into and excoriated his back, leaving his body a bloody, dislocated mass.6 Here, too, was the cradle of which we have made mention above, amply garnished within with cruel knobs, on which the sufferer, tied hand and foot, was thrown at every movement of the machine, to be bruised all over, and brought forth discolored, swollen, bleeding, but still living. All round, ready to hand, were hung the minor instruments of torture. There were screws and thumbkins for the fingers, spiked collars for the neck, iron boots for the legs, gags for the mouth, cloths to cover the face, and permit the slow percolation of water, drop by drop, down the throat of the person undergoing this form of torture. There were rollers set round with spikes, for bruising the arms and back; there were iron scourges, pincers, and tongs for tearing out the tongue, slitting the nose and ears, and otherwise disfiguring and mangling the body till it was horrible and horrifying to look upon it. There were other things of which an expert only could tell the name and the use. Had these instruments a tongue, and could the history of this chamber be written, how awful the tale!

We shall suppose that all this has been gone through; that the confessor has been stretched on the bed of torture; has been gashed, broken, mangled, and yet, by power given him from above, has not denied his Savior: he has been "tortured not accepting deliverance:" what further punishment has the Holy Office in reserve for those from whom its torments have failed to extort a recantation? These dreadful dungeons furnish us with the means of answering this question.

The Subterranean Dungeons

We return to the narrow passage, and go forward a little way. Every few paces there comes a door, originally strong and massy, and garnished with great iron knobs but now old and moldy, and creaking when opened with a noise painfully loud in the deep stillness. The windings are numerous, but at every turning of the passage a lighted candle is placed, lest peradventure the way should be missed, and the road back to the living world be lost for ever. A few steps are taken downwards, very cautiously, for a lantern can barely show the ground. Here there is a vaulted chamber, entirely dug out of the living rock, except the roof, which is formed of hewn stone. It contains an iron image of the Virgin; and on the opposite wall, suspended by an iron hook, is a lamp, which when lighted shows the goodly proportions of "Our Lady." On the instant of touching a spring the image flings open its arms, which resemble the doors of a cupboard, and which are seen to be stuck full on the inside with poignards, each about a foot in length. Some of these knives are so placed as to enter the eyes of those whom the image enfolded in its embrace, others are set so as to penetrate the ears and brain, others to pierce the breast, and others again to gore the abdomen.

The Iron Virgin

The person who had passed through the terrible ordeal of the Question- chamber, but had made no recantation, would be led along the tortuous passage by which we had come, and ushered into this vault, where the first object that would greet his eye, the pale light of the lamp falling on it, would be the iron Virgin. He would be bidden to stand right in front of the image. The spring would be touched by the executioner the Virgin would fling open her arms, and the wretched victim would straightway be forced within them. Another spring was then touched the Virgin closed upon her victim; a strong wooden beam, fastened at one end to the wall by a movable joint, the other placed against the doors of the iron image, was worked by a screw, and as the beam was pushed out, the spiky arms of the Virgin slowly but irresistibly closed upon the man, cruelly goring him.

The Burial of the Dead

When the dreadful business was ended, it needed not that the executioner should put himself to the trouble of making the Virgin unclasp the mangled carcass of her victim; provision had been made for its quick and secret disposal. At the touching of a third spring, the floor of the image would slide aside, and the body of the victim drop down the mouth of a perpendicular shaft in the rock. We look down this pit, and can see, at a great depth, the shimmer of water. A canal had been made to flow underneath the vault where stood the iron Virgin, and when she had done her work upon those who were delivered over to her tender mercies, she let them fall, with quick descent and sullen plunge, into the canal underneath, where they were floated to the Pegnitz, and from the Pegnitz to the Rhine, and by the Rhine to the ocean, there to sleep beside the dust of Huss and Jerome.

J.A. Wylie, History of the Jesuits, 1878, chapter 11

An overview of the Inquisition

Inquisition

(Lat. *inquirere,* to look to). By this term is usually meant a special ecclesiastical institutional for combating or suppressing heresy. Its characteristic mark seems to be the bestowal on special judges of judicial powers in matters of faith, and this by supreme ecclesiastical authority, not temporal or for individual cases, but as a universal and permanent office. Moderns experience difficulty in understanding this institution, because they have, to no small extent, lost sight of two facts. On the one hand they have ceased to grasp religious belief as something objective, as the gift of God, and therefore outside the realm of free private judgment; on the other they no longer see in the Church a society perfect and sovereign, based substantially on a pure and authentic Revelation, whose first most important duty must naturally be to retain unsullied this original deposit of faith. Before the religious revolution of the sixteenth century these views were still common to all Christians; that orthodoxy should be maintained at any cost seemed self-evident.

However, while the positive suppression of heresy by ecclesiastical and civil authority in Christian society is as old as the Church, the Inquisition as a distinct ecclesiastical tribunal is of much later origin. Historically it is a phase in the growth of ecclesiastical legislation, whose distinctive traits can be fully understood only by a careful study of the conditions amid which it grew up. Our subject may, therefore, be conveniently treated as follows:

I. The Suppression of Heresy during the first twelve Christian centuries;

II. The Suppression of Heresy by the Institution known as the Inquisition under its several forms:

(A) The Inquisition of the Middle Ages;

(B) The Inquisition in Spain;

(C) The Holy Office at Rome.

I. The suppression of heresy during the first twelve centuries

Though the Apostles were deeply imbued with the conviction that they must transmit the deposit of the Faith to posterity undefiled, and that any teaching at variance with their own, even if proclaimed by an angel of Heaven, would be a culpable offense, yet St. Paul did not, in the case of the heretics Alexander and Hymeneus, go back to the Old Covenant penalties of death or scourging (Deut., xiii, 6 sqq.; xvii, 1 sqq.), but deemed exclusion from the communion of the Church sufficient (1 Tim., i, 20; Tit., iii, 10). In fact to the Christians of the first three centuries it could scarcely have occurred to assume any other attitude towards those who erred in matters of faith. Tertullian (*Ad. Scapulam,* c. ii) lays down the rule: Humani iuris et naturalis potestatis, unicuique quod putaverit colere, nec alii obest aut prodest alterius religio. Sed nec religionis est religionem colere, quae sponte suscipi debeat, non vi. In other words, he tells us that the natural law authorized man to follow only the voice of individual conscience in the practice of religion, since the acceptance of religion was a matter of free will, not of compulsion. Replying to the accusation of Celsus, based on the Old Testament, that the Christians persecuted dissidents with death, burning, and torture, Origen (*C. Cels.,* VII, 26) is satisfied with explaining that one must distinguish between the law which the Jews received from Moses and that given to the Christians by Jesus; the former was binding on the Jews, the latter on the Christians. Jewish Christians, if sincere, could no longer conform to all of the Mosaic law; hence they were no longer at liberty to kill their enemies or to burn and stone violators of the Christian Law.

St. Cyprian of Carthage, surrounded as he was by countless schismatics and undutiful Christians, also put aside the material sanction of the Old Testament, which punished with death rebellion against priesthood and the Judges. "Nunc autem, quia circumcisio spiritalis esse apud fideles servos Dei coepit, spiritali gladio superbi et contumaces necantur, dum de Ecclesia ejiciuntur" (*Ep. lxxii, ad Pompon.*, n. 4) religion being now spiritual, its sanctions take on the same character, and excommunication replaces the death of the body. Lactantius was yet smarting under the scourge of bloody persecutions, when he wrote this Divine Institutes in A.D. 308. Naturally, therefore, he stood for the most absolute freedom of religion. He writes: "Religion being a matter of the will, it cannot be forced on anyone; in this matter it is better to employ words than blows [verbis melius quam verberibus res agenda est]. Of what use is cruelty? What has the rack to do with piety? Surely there is no connection between truth and violence, between justice and cruelty . . . . It is true that nothing is so important as religion, and one must defend it at any cost . . . It is true that it must be protected, but by dying for it, not by killing others; by long-suffering, not by violence; by faith, not by crime. If you attempt to defend religion with bloodshed and torture, what you do is not defense, but desecration and insult. For nothing is so intrinsically a matter of free will as religion." (*Divine Institutes* V:20)

The Christian teachers of the first three centuries insisted, as was natural for them, on complete religious liberty; furthermore, they not only urged the principle that religion could not be forced on others a principle always adhered to by the Church in her dealings with the unbaptized but, when comparing the Mosaic Law and the Christian religion, they taught that the latter was content with a, spiritual punishment of heretics (i.e. with excommunication), while Judaism necessarily proceeded against its dissidents with torture and death.

However, the imperial successors of Constantine soon began to see in themselves Divinely appointed "bishops of the exterior", i.e. masters of the temporal and material conditions of the Church. At the same time they retained the traditional authority of "Pontifex Maximus", and in this way the civil authority inclined, frequently in league with prelates of Arian tendencies, to persecute the orthodox bishops by imprisonment and exile. But the latter, particularly St. Hilary of Poltiers (*Liber contra Auxentium*, c. iv), protested vigorously against any use of force in the province of religion, whether for the spread of Christianity or for preservation of the Faith. They repeatedly urged that in this respect the severe decrees of the Old Testament were abrogated by the mild and gentle laws of Christ. However, the successors of Constantine were ever persuaded that the first concern of imperial authority was the protection of religion and so, with terrible regularity, issued many penal edicts against heretics. In the space of fifty seven years sixty-eight enactments were thus promulgated. All manner of heretics were affected by this legislation, and in various ways, by exile, confiscation of property, or death. A law of 407, aimed at the traitorous Donatists, asserts for the first time that these heretics ought to be put on the same plane as transgressors against the sacred majesty of the emperor, a concept to which was reserved in later times a very momentous role. The death penalty however, was only imposed for certain kinds of heresy; in their persecution of heretics the Christian emperors fell far short of the severity of Diocletian, who in 287 sentenced to the stake the leaders of the Manichaeans, and inflicted on their followers partly the death penalty by beheading, and partly forced labor in the government mines.

So far we have been dealing with the legislation of the Christianized State. In the attitude of the representatives of the Church towards this legislation some uncertainty is already noticeable. At the close of the forth century, and during the fifth, Manichaeism, Donatism, and Priscillianism were the heresies most in view. Expelled from Rome and Milan, the Manichaeism sought refuge in Africa. Though they were found guilty of abominable teachings and misdeeds (St. Augustine, De haeresibus, no. 46), the Church refused to invoke the civil power against them; indeed, the great Bishop of Hippo explicitly rejected the use force. He sought their return only through public and private acts of submission, and his efforts seem to have met with success. Indeed, we learn from him that the Donatists themselves were the first to appeal to the civil power for protection against the Church. However, they fared like Daniels accusers: the lions turned upon them. State intervention not answering to their wishes, and the violent excesses of the Circumcellions being condignly punished, the Donatists complained bitterly of administrative cruelty. St. Optatus of Mileve defended the civil authority (*De Schismate Donntistarum*, III, Christianity. 6-7) as follows:

> . . . as though it were not permitted to come forward as avengers of God, and to pronounce sentence of death! . . . But, say you, the State cannot punish in the name of God. Yet was it not in the name of God that Moses and Phineas consigned to death the worshipers of the Golden calf and those who despised the true religion?

This was the first time that a Catholic bishop championed a decisive cooperation of the State in religious questions, and its right to inflict death on heretics. For the first time, also, the Old Testament was appealed to, though such appeals had been previously rejected by Christian teachers.

St. Augustine, on the contrary, was still opposed to the use of force, and tried to lead back the erring by means of instruction; at most he admitted the imposition of a moderate fine for refractory persons. Finally, however, he changed his views, whether moved thereto by the incredible excesses of the Circumcellions or by the good results achieved by the use of force, or favoring force through the persuasions of other bishops. Apropos of his apparent inconsistency it is well to note carefully whom he is addressing. He appears to speak in one way to government officials, who wanted the existing laws carried out to their fullest extent, and in another to the Donatists, who denied to the State any right of punishing dissenters. In his correspondence with state officials he dwells on Christian charity and toleration, and represents the heretics as straying lambs, to be sought out and perhaps, if recalcitrant chastised with rods and frightened with threats of severer but not to be driven back to the fold by means of rack and sword . On the other hand, in his writings against the Donatists he upholds the rights of the State: sometimes, he says, a salutary severity would be to the interest of the erring ones themselves and likewise protective of true believers and the community at large (*Vacandard*, 1. c., pp. 17-26)

As to Priscillianism, not a few points remain yet obscure, despite recent valuable researches. It seems certain, however, that Priscillian, Bishop of Avilia in Spain, was accused of heresy and sorcery, and found guilty by several councils. St. Ambrose at Milan and St. Damascus at Rome seem to have refused him a hearing. At length he appealed to Emperor Maximus at Trier, but to his detriment, for he was there condemned to death. Priscillian himself, no doubt in full consciousness of his own innocence, had formerly called for repression of the Manichaeans by the sword. But the foremost Christian teachers did not share these sentiments, and his own execution gave them occasion for a solemn protest against the cruel treatment meted out to him by the imperial government. St. Martin of Tours, then at Trier, exerted himself to obtain from the ecclesiastical authority the abandonment of the accusation, and induced the emperor to promise that on no account would he shed the blood of

Priscillian, since ecclesiastical deposition by the bishops would be punishment enough, and bloodshed would be opposed to the Divine Law. After the execution he strongly blamed both the accusers and the emperor, and for a long time refused to hold communion with such bishops as had been in any way responsible for Priscillians death. The great Bishop of Milan, St. Ambrose, described that execution as a crime.

Priscillianism, however, did not disappear with the death of its originator; on the contrary, it spread with extraordinary rapidly, and, through its open adoption of Manichaeism, became more of a public menace than ever. In this way the severe judgments of St. Augustine and St. Jerome against Priscillianism become intelligible. In 447 Leo the Great had to reproach the Priscillianists with loosening the holy bonds of marriage, treading all decency under foot, and deriding all law, human and Divine. It seemed to him natural that temporal rulers should punish such sacrilegious madness, and should put to death the founder of the sect and some of his followers. He goes on to say that this redounded to the advantage of the Church: "quae etsi sacerdotali contenta iudicio, cruentas refugit ultiones, severis tamen christianorum principum constitutionibus adiuratur, dum ad spiritale recurrunt remedium, qui timent corporale supplicium" -though the Church was content with a spiritual sentence on the part of its bishops and was averse to the shedding of blood, nevertheless it was aided by the imperial severity, inasmuch as the fear of corporal punishment drove the guilty to seek a spiritual remedy.

The ecclesiastical ideas of the first five centuries may be summarized as follows: the Church should for no cause shed blood (St. Augustine, St. Ambrose, St. Leo I, and others); other teachers, however, like Optatus of Mileve and Priscillian, believed that the State could pronounce the death penalty on heretics in case the public welfare demanded it; the majority held that the death penalty for heresy, when not civilly criminal, was irreconcilable with the spirit of Christianity.

St. Augustine (Ep. c, n. 1), almost in the name of the western Church, says: "Corrigi eos volumus, non necari, nec disciplinam circa eos negligi volumus, nec suppliciis quibus dignisunt exerceri" we wish them corrected, not put to death; we desire the triumph of (ecclesiastical) discipline, not the death penalties that they deserve. St. John Chrysostom says substantially the same in the name of the Eastern Church: "To consign a heretic to death is to commit an offence beyond atonement"; and in the next chapter he says that God forbids their execution, even as He forbids us to uproot cockle, but He does not forbid us to repel them, to deprive them of free speech, or to prohibit their assemblies. The help of the "secular arm" was therefore not entirely rejected; on the contrary, as often as the Christian welfare, general or domestic, required it, Christian rulers sought to stem the evil by appropriate measures. As late the seventh century St. Isidore of Seville expresses similar sentiments. How little we are to trust the vaunted impartiality of Henry Charles Lea, the American historian of the Inquisition, we may here illustrate by an example. In his History of the Inquisition in the Middle Ages", He closes this period with these words: It was only sixty-two years after the slaughter of Priscillian and his followers had excited so much horror, that Leo I, when the heresy seemed to be reviving in 447, not only justified the act, but declared that, if the followers of a heresy so damnable were allowed to live, there would be an end to human and Divine law. The final step had been taken and the church was definitely pledged to the suppression of heresy at any cost. It is impossible not to attribute to ecclesiastical influence the successive edicts by which, from the time of Theodosius the Great, persistence in heresy was punished with death. In these lines Lee has transferred to the pope words employed by the emperor. Moreover, it is simply the exact opposite of historical truth to assert that the imperial edicts punishing heresy with death were due to ecclesiastical influence, since we have shown that in this period the more influential ecclesiastical authorities declared that the death penalty was contrary to the spirit of the Gospel, and themselves opposed its execution. For centuries this was the ecclesiastical attitude both in theory and in practice. Thus, in keeping with the civil law, some Manichaeans were executed at Ravenna in 556. On the other hand. Elipandus of Toledo and Felix of Urgel, the chiefs of Adoptionism anti Predestinationism, were condemned by and councils, but were otherwise left unmolested. We may note, however, that the monk Gothescalch, after the condemnation of his false doctrine that Christ had not died for all mankind, was by the Synods of Mainz in 848 and Quiercy in 849 sentenced to flogging and imprisonment, punishments then common in monasteries for various infractions of the rule.

(3) About the year 1000 Manichaeans from Bulgaria, under various names, spread over Western Europe. They were numerous in Italy, Spain, Gaul and Germany. Christian popular sentiment soon showed itself adverse to these dangerous sectaries, and resulted in occasional local persecutions, naturally in forms expressive of the spirit of the age. In 1122 King Robert the Pious (regis iussu et universae plebis consensu), "because he feared for the safety of the kingdom and the salvation of souls" had thirteen distinguished citizens, ecclesiastic and lay, burnt alive at Orléans. Elsewhere similar acts were due to popular outbursts. A few years later the Bishop of Chalons observed that the sect was spreading in his diocese, and asked of Wazo, Bishop of Liège, advice as to the use of force: "An terrenae potestatis gladio in eos sit animadvertendum necne". Wazo replied that this was contrary to the spirit of the Church and the words of its Founder, Who ordained that the tares should be allowed to grow with the wheat until the day of the harvest, lest the wheat be uprooted with the tares; those who today were tares might to-morrow be converted, and turn into wheat; let them therefore live, and let mere excommunication suffice St. Chrysostom, as we have seen, had taught similar doctrine. This principle could not be always followed. Thus at Goslar, in the Christmas season of 1051, and in 1052, several heretics were hanged because Emperor Henry III wanted to prevent the further spread of "the heretical leprosy." A few years later, In 1076 or 1077, a Catharist was condemned to the stake by the Bishop of Cambrai and his chapter. Other Catharists, in spite of the archbishops intervention, were given their choice by the magistrates of Milan between doing homage to the Cross and mounting the pyre. By far the greater number chose the latter. In 1114 the Bishop of Soissons kept sundry heretics in durance in his episcopal city. But while he was gone to Beauvais, to ask advice of the bishops assembled there for a synod the"believing folk, fearing the habitual soft-heartedness of ecclesiatics (clericalem verensmollitiem), stormed the prison took the accused outside of town, and burned them. The people disliked what to them was the extreme dilatoriness of the clergy in pursuing heretics. In 1144 Adalerbo II of Liège hoped to bring some imprisoned Catharists to better knowledge through the grace of God, but the people, less indulgent, assailed the unhappy creatures and only with the greatest trouble did the bishop succeed in rescuing some of them from death by fire. A like drama was enacted about the same time at Cologne. while the archbishop and the priests earnestly sought to lead the misguided back into the Church, the latter. were violently taken by the mob (a populis nimio zelo abreptis) from the custody of the clergy and burned at the stake. The best-known heresiarchs of that time, Peter of Bruys and Arnold of Brescia, met a similar fate the first on the pyre as a victim of popular fury, and the latter under the henchmans axe as a victim of his political enemies. In short, no blame attaches to the Church for her behavior towards heresy in those rude days. Among all the bishops of the period, so far as can be ascertained, Theodwin of Liège, successor of the aforesaid Wazo and predecessor of Adalbero II, alone appealed to the civil power for the punishment of heretics, and even he did not call for the death penalty, which was rejected by all. who were more highly respected in

the twelfth century than Peter Canter, the most learned man of his time, and St. Bernard of Clairvaux? The former says ("*Verbum abbreviatum*", c. lxxviii, in P.L., CCV, 231): Whether they be convicted of error, or freely confess their guilt, Catharists are not to be put to death, at]east not when they refrain from armed assaults upon the Church. For although the Apostle said, A man that is a heretic after the third admonition, avoid, he certainly did not say, Kill him. Throw them into prison, if you will, but do not put them to death. So far was St. Bernard from agreeing with the methods of the people of Cologne, that he laid down the axiom: Fides suadenda, non imponenda (By persuasion, not by violence, are men to be won to the Faith). And if he censures the carelessness of the princes, who were to blame because little foxes devastated the vineyard, yet he adds that the latter must not be captured by force but by arguments (capiantur non armis, sed argumentis); the obstinate were to be excommunicated, and if necessary kept in confinement for the safety of others (aut corrigen disunt ne pereant, aut, ne perimant, coercendi). The synods of the period employ substantially the same terms, e.g. the synod at Reims in 1049 under Leo IX, that at Toulouse in 1119, at which Callistus II presided, and finally the Lateran Council of 1139.Hence, the occasional executions of heretics during this period must be ascribed partly to the arbitrary action of individual rulers, partly to the fanatic outbreaks of the over zealous populace, and in no wise to ecclesiastical law or the ecclesiastical authorities. There were already, it is true, canonists who conceded to the Church the right to pronounce sentence of death on heretics; but the question was treated as a purely academic one, and the theory exercised virtually no influence on real life. Excommunication, proscription, imprisonment, etc., were indeed inflicted, being intended rather as forms of atonement than of real punishment, but never the capital sentence. The maxim of Peter Cantor was still adhered to: "Catharists, even though divinely convicted in an ordeal, must not be punished by death." In the second half of the twelfth century, however, heresy in the form of Catharism spread in truly alarming fashion, and not only menaced the Church's existence, but undermined the very foundations of Christian society. In opposition to this propaganda there grew up a kind of prescriptive law at least throughout Germany, France, and Spain which visited heresy with death by the flames. England on the whole remained untainted by heresy.

When, in 1166, about thirty sectaries made their way thither, Henry II ordered that they be burnt on their foreheads with red-hot iron, be beaten with rods in the public square, and then driven off. Moreover, he forbade anyone to give them shelter or otherwise assist them, so that they died partly from hunger and partly from the cold of winter. Duke Philip of Flanders, aided by William of the White Hand, Archbishop of Reims, was particularly severe towards heretics. They caused many citizens in their domains, nobles and commoners, clerics, knights, peasants, spinsters, widows, anti married women, to be burnt alive, confiscated their property, and divided it between them. This happened in 1183. Between 1183 and 1206 Bishop Hugo of Auxerre acted similarly towards the neo-Mainchaeans. Some he despoiled; the other she either exiled or sent to the stake. King Philip Augustus of France had eight Catharists burnt at Troyes in 1200 one at Nevers in 1201, several at Braisne-sur-Vesle in 1204, and many at Paris "priests, clerics, laymen, and women belonging to the sect". Raymund V of Toulouse (1148-94) promulgated a law which punished with death the followers of the sect and their favorers. Simon de Montfort's men-at-arms believed in 1211 that they were carrying out this law when they boasted how they had burned alive many, and would continue to do so (unde multos combussimus et adhuc cum invenimus idem facere non cessamus).

In 1197 Peter II, King of Aragon and Count of Barcelona, issued an edict in obedience to which the Waldensians and all other schismatics were expelled from the land; whoever of this sect was still found in his kingdom or his county after Palm

Sunday of the next year was to suffer death by fire, also confiscation of goods. Ecclesiastical legislation was far from this severity. Alexander III at the Lateran Council of 1179 renewed the decisions already made as to schismatics in Southern France, and requested secular sovereigns to silence those disturbers of public order if necessary by force, to achieve which object they were at liberty to imprison the guilty and to appropriate their possessions, According to the agreement made by Lucius III and Emperor Frederick Barbarossa at Verona (1148), the heretics of every community were to be sought out, brought before the episcopal court, excommunicated, and given up to the civil power to he suitably punished. The suitable punishment(debita anim adversio, ultio) did not, however, as yet mean capital punishment, hut the proscriptive ban, though even this, it is true, entailed exile, expropriation, destruction of the culprits dwelling, infamy, debarment from public office, and the like. The *Continuatio Zwellensis altera, ad ann. 1184* accurately describes the condition of heretics at this time when it says that the pope excommunicated them, and put them under the civil ban, while he confiscated their goods Under Innocent III nothing was done to intensify or add to the extant statutes against heresy, though this pope gave them a wider range by the action of his legates and through the Forth Lateran Council (1215). But this act was indeed a relative service to the heretics, for the regular canonical procedure thus introduced did much to abrogate the arbitrariness, passion, and injustice of the Civil courts in Spain, France and Germany. In so far as, and so long as, his prescriptions remained in force, no summary condemnations or executions en masse occurred, neither stake nor rack were set up; and, if, on one occasion during the first year of his pontificate, to justify confiscation, he appealed to the Roman Law and its penalties for crimes against the sovereign power, yet he did not draw the extreme conclusion that heretics deserved to be burnt. His reign affords many examples showing how much of the vigor he took away in practice from the existing penal code. II.

The suppression of heresy by the institution known as the Inquisition

A. The Inquisition of The Middle Ages

(1) Origin During the first three decades of the thirteenth century the Inquisition, as the institution, did not exist. But eventually Christian Europe was so endangered by heresy, and penal legislation concerning Catharism had gone so far, that the Inquisition seemed to be a political necessity. That these sects were a menace to Christian society had been long recognized by the Byzantine rulers. As early as the tenth century Empress Theodora had put to death a multitude of Paulicians, and in 1118 Emperor Alexius Comnenus treated the Bogomili with equal severity, but this did not prevent them from pouring over all Western Europe. Moreover these sects were in the highest degree aggressive, hostile to Christianity itself, to the Mass, the sacraments, the ecclesiastical hierarchy and organization; hostile also to feudal government by their attitude towards oaths, which they declared under no circumstances allowable. Nor mere their views less fatal to the continuance of human society, for on the one hand they forbade marriage and the propagation of the human race. and on the other hand they made a duty of suicide through the institution of the Endura. It has been said that more perished through the Endura (the Catharist suicide code) than through the Inquisition. It was, therefore, natural enough for the custodians of the existing order in Europe, especially of the Christian religion, to adopt repressive measures against such revolutionary teachings. In France Louis VIII decreed in 1226 that persons excommunicated by the diocesan bishop, or his delegate, should receive "meet punishment". In 1249 Louis IX ordered barons to deal with heretics according to the dictates of duty. A decree of the Council of Toulouse (1229) makes it appear probable that in France death at the stake was already comprehended as in keeping with the aforesaid debita animadversio. To seek to trace in these measures the influence of imperial or papal ordinances is vain, since the burning of heretics had already come to be regarded as prescriptive. The *Etablissements de St. Louis etcoutumes de Beauvaisis*, compiled about 1235, embodies as a law sanctioned by custom the execution of unbelievers at the stake. In Italy Emperor Frederick II, as early as 22 November, 1220, issued a rescript against heretics, conceived, however quite in the spirit of Innocent III, and Honorius III commissioned his legates to see to the enforcement in Italian cities of both the canonical decrees of 1215 and the imperial legislation of 1220. From the foregoing it cannot be doubted that up to 1224 there was no imperial law ordering, or presupposing as legal, the burning of heretics. The rescript for Lombardy of 1224 is accordingly the first law in which death by fire is contemplated. That Honorius III was in any way concerned in the drafting of this ordinance cannot be maintained; indeed the emperor was all the less in need of papal inspiration as the burning of heretics in Germany was then no longer rare; his legists, moreover, would certainly have directed the emperors attention to the ancient Roman Law that punished high treason with death, and Manichaeism in particular with the stake. The imperial rescripts of 1220 and 1224 were adopted into ecclesiastical criminal law in 1231, and were soon applied at Rome. It was then that the Inquisition of the Middle Ages came into being. What was the immediate provocation? Contemporary sources afford no positive answer. Bishop Douais, who perhaps commands the original contemporary material better than anyone, has attempted in his latest work to explain its appearance by a supposed anxiety of Gregory IX to forestall the encroachments of Frederick II in the strictly ecclesiastical province of doctrine. For this purpose it would seem necessary for the pope to establish a distinct and specifically ecclesiastical court. From this point of view, though the hypothesis cannot be fully proved, much is intelligible that otherwise remains obscure. There was doubtless reason to fear such imperial encroachments in an age yet filled with the angry contentions of the Imperium and the Sacerdotium. We need only recall the trickery of the emperor and his Pretended eagerness for the purity of the Faith, his Increasingly rigorous legislation against heretics, the numerous executions of his personal rivals on the pretext of heresy, the hereditary passion of the Hohenstaufen for supreme control over Church and State, their claim of God-given authority over both, of responsibility in both domains to God and God only etc. What was more natural than that the Church should strictly reserve to herself her own sphere, while at the same time endeavoring to avoid giving offence to the emperor? A purely spiritual or papal religious tribunal would secure ecclesiastical liberty and authority for this court could be confided to men of expert knowledge and blameless reputation, and above all to independent men in whose hands the Church could safely trust the decision as to the orthodoxy or heterodoxy of a given teaching. On the other hand, to meet the emperors wishes as far as allowable, the penal code of the empire could be taken over as it stood.

(2) The New Tribunal

(a) Its essential characteristic The pope did not establish the Inquisition as a distinct and separate tribunal; what he did was to appoint special but permanent judges, who executed their doctrinal functions In the name of the pope. Where they sat, there was the Inquisition. It must he carefully noted that the characteristic feature of the Inquisition was not its peculiar procedure, nor the secret examination of witnesses and consequent official indictment: this procedure was common to all courts from the time of Innocent III. Nor was it the pursuit of heretics in all places: this had been the rule since the Imperial Synod of Verona under Lucius III and Frederick Barbarossa. Nor again was it the torture, which was not prescribed or even allowed for decades after the beginning of the Inquisition, nor, finally, the various sanctions, imprisonment,

confiscation, the stake, etc., all of which punishments were usual long before the Inquisition. The Inquisitor, strictly speaking, was a special but permanent judge, acting in the name of the pope and clothed by him with the right and the duty to deal legally with offences against the Faith; he had, however, to adhere to the established rules of canonical procedure and pronounce the customary penalties. Many regarded it, as providential that just at this time sprang up two new orders, the Dominicans and the Franciscans, whose members, by their superior theological training and other characteristics, seemed eminently fitted to perform the inquisitorial task with entire success. It was safe to assume that they were not merely endowed with the requisite knowledge, but that they would also, quite unselfishly and uninfluenced by worldly motives, do solely what seemed their duty for the Good of the Church. In addition, there was reason to hope that, because of their great popularity, they would not encounter too much opposition. It seems, therefore, not unnatural that the inquisitors should have been chosen by the popes prevailingly from these orders, especially from that of the Dominicans. It is to he noted, however, that the inquisitors were not chosen exclusively from the mendicant orders, though the Senator of Rome no doubt meant such when in his oath of office (1231) he spoke of inquisitores datos ab ecclesia. In his decree of 1232 Frederick II calls them inquisitores ab apostolica sede datos. The Dominican Alberic, in November of 1232, went through Lombardy as inquisitor haereticae pravitatis. The prior and sub-prior of the Dominicans at Friesbach were given a similar commission as early as 27 November, 1231; on 2 December, 1232, the convent of Strasburg, and a little later the convents of Würzburg, Ratisbon, and Bremen, also received the commission. In 1233 a rescript of Gregory IX, touching these matters, was sent simultaneously to the bishops of Southern France and to the priors of the Dominican Order. We know that Dominicans were sent as inquisitors in 1232 to Germany along the Rhine, to the Diocese of Tarragona in Spain and to Lombardy; in 1233 to France, to the territory of Auxerre, the ecclesiastical provinces of Bourges, Bordeaux, Narbonne, and Auch, and to Burgundy; in 1235 to the ecclesiastical province of Sens. In fine, about 1255 we find the Inquisition in full activity in all the countries of Central and Western Europe in the county of Toulouse, in Sicily, Aragon, Lombardy, France, Burgundy, Brabant, and Germany. That Gregory IX, through his appointment of Dominicans and Franciscans as inquisitors, withdrew the suppression of heresy from the proper courts (i.e. from the bishops), is a reproach that in so general a form cannot be sustained. So little did he think of displacing episcopal authority that, on the contrary he provided explicitly that no inquisitional tribunal was to work anywhere without the diocesan bishops co-operation. And if, on the strength of their papal jurisdiction, inquisitors occasionally manifested too great an inclination to act independently of episcopal authority it was precisely the popes who kept them within right bounds. As early as 1254 Innocent IV prohibited anew perpetual imprisonment or death at the stake without the episcopal consent. Similar orders were issued by Urban IV in 1262, Clement IV in 1265, and Gregory X in 1273, until at last Boniface VIII and Clement V solemnly declared null and void all judgments issued in trials concerning faith, unless delivered with the approval anti co-operation of the bishops. The popes always upheld with earnestness the episcopal authority, and sought to free the inquisitional tribunals from every kind of arbitrariness and caprice. It was a heavy burden of responsibility almost too heavy for a common mortal which fell upon the shoulders of an inquisitor, who was obliged, at least indirectly, to decide between life and death. The Church was bound to insist that he should possess, in a pre-eminent degree, the qualities of a good judge; that he should be animated with a glowing zeal for the Faith, the salvation of souls, and the extirpation of heresy; that amid all difficulties and dangers he should never yield to anger or passion;

that he should meet hostility fearlessly, but should not court it; that he should yield to no inducement or threat, and yet not be heartless; that, when circumstances permitted, he should observe mercy in allotting penalties; that he should listen to the counsel of others, and not trust too much to his own opinion or to appearances, since often the probable is untrue, and the truth improbable. Some what thus did Bernard Gui (or Guldonis) and Eymeric, both of them inquisitors for years, describe the ideal inquisitor. Of such an inquisitor also was Gregory IX doubtlessly thinking when he urged Conrad of Marburg: "not to punish the wicked so as to hurt the innocent". History shows us how far the inquisitors answered to this ideal. Far from being inhuman, they were, as a rule, men of spotless character and sometimes of truly admirable sanctity, and not a few of them have been canonized by the Church. There is absolutely no reason to look on the medieval ecclesiastical judge as intellectually and morally inferior to the modern judge. No one would deny that the judges of today, despite occasional harsh decisions and the errors of a, few, pursue a highly honorable profession. Similarly, the medieval inquisitors should be judged as a whole. Moreover, history does not justify the hypothesis that the medieval heretics were prodigies of virtue, deserving our sympathy in advance.

(b) Procedure This regularly began with a months "term of grace", proclaimed by the inquisitor whenever he came to a heresy-ridden district. The inhabitants mere summoned to appear before the inquisitor. On those who confessed of their own accord a suitable penance (e.g. a pilgrimage) was imposed, but never as severe punishment like incarceration or surrender to the civil power. However, these relations with the residents of a, place often furnished important indications, pointed out the proper quarter for investigation, and sometimes much evidence was thus obtained against individuals. These mere then cited before the judges usually by the parish priest, although occasionally by the secular authorities and the trial began. If the accused at once made full and free confession, the affair was soon concluded, and not to the disadvantage of the accused. But in most instances the accused entered denial even after swearing on the Four Gospels, and this denial was stubborn in the measure that the testimony was incriminating. David of Augsburg pointed out to the inquisitor four methods of extracting open acknowledgment: fear of death, i.e. by giving the accused to understand that the stake awaited him if he would not confess; more or less close confinement, possibly emphasized by curtailment of food; visits of tried men, who would attempt to induce free confession through friendly persuasion; torture, which will be discussed below.

(c) The Witnesses When no voluntary admission was made, evidence was adduced. Legally, there had to be at least two witnesses, although conscientious judges rarely contended themselves with that number. The principle had hitherto been held by the Church that the testimony of a heretic, an excommunicated person, a perjurer, in short, of an "infamous", was worthless before the courts. But in its destination of unbelief the Church took the further step of abolishing this long established practice, and of accepting a heretics evidence at nearly full value in trials concerning faith. This appears as early as the twelfth century in the "Decretum Gratiani". While Frederick II readily assented to this new departure, the inquisitors seemed at first uncertain as to the value of the evidence of an "infamous"person. It was only in 1261, after Alexander IV had silenced their scruples, that the new principle was generally adopted both in theory and in practice. This grave modification seems to have been defended on the ground that the heretical conventicles took place secretly, and were shrouded in great obscurity, so that reliable information could be obtained from none but themselves. Even prior to the establishment of the Inquisition the names of the witnesses were sometimes withheld

from the accused person, and this usage was legalized by Gregory IX, Innocent IV, and Alexander IV. Boniface VIII, however, set it aside by his Bull *Ut commissi vobis officii* and commanded that at all trials, even inquisitorial, the witnesses must be named to the accused. There was no personal confrontation of witnesses, neither was there any cross-examination. Witnesses for the defense hardly ever appeared, as they would almost infallibly be suspected of being heretics or favorable to heresy. For the same reason those impeached rarely secured legal advisers, and mere therefore obliged to make personal response to the main points of a charge. This, however, was also no innovation, for in 1205 Innocent III, by the Bull "Si adversus vos" forbade any legal help for heretics: "We strictly prohibit you, lawyers and notaries, from assisting in any way, by council or support, all heretics and such as believe In them, adhere to them, render them any assistance or defend them in any way. But this severity soon relaxed, and even in Eymerics day it seems to have been the universal custom to grant heretics a legal adviser, who, however, had to be in every way beyond suspicion, "upright, of undoubted loyalty, skilled in civil and canon law, and zealous for the faith." Meanwhile, even in those hard times, such legal severities were felt to be excessive, and attempts were made to mitigate them in various ways, so as to protect the natural rights of the accused. First he could make known to the judge the names of his enemies: should the charge originate with them, they would be quashed without further ado. Furthermore, it was undoubtedly to the advantage of the accused that false witnesses were punished without mercy. The aforesaid inquisitor, Bernard Gui, relates an instance of a father falsely accusing his son of heresy. The sons innocence quickly coming to light, the false accuser was apprehended, and sentenced to prison for life.

In addition he was pilloried for five consecutive Sundays before the church during service, with bare head and bound hands. Perjury in those days was accounted an enormous offence, particularly when committed by a false witness. Moreover, the accused had a considerable advantage in the fact that the inquisitor had to conduct the trial in co-operation with the diocesan bishop or his representatives, to whom all documents relating to the trial had to submitted. Both together, inquisitor and bishop, were also made to summon and consult a number of upright and experienced men (boni viri), and to decide in agreement with their decision (vota).Innocent IV (11 July. 1254), Alexander IV (15 April, 1255, and 27 April, 1260), and Urban IV (2 August, 1264) strictly prescribed this institution of the boni viri i.e. the consultation in difficult cases of experienced men, well versed in theology and canon law, and in every way irreproachable. The documents of the trial were either in their entirety handed to them, or a least an abstract drawn up by a public notary was furnished; they were also made acquainted with the witnesses names, and their first duty was to decide whether or not the witnesses were credible. The boni viri were very frequently called on. Thirty, fifty, eighty, or more persons laymen and priests; secular and regular would be summoned, all highly respected and independent men, and singly sworn to give verdict upon the cases before them accordingly to the best of their knowledge and belief. Substantially they were always called upon to decide two questions: whether and what guilt lay at hand, and what punishment was to be inflicted. That they might be influenced by no personal considerations, the case would be submitted to them somewhat in the abstract, i.e., the name of the person inculpated was not given. Although, strictly speaking, the boni viri were entitled only to an advisory vote, the final ruling was usually in accordance with their views, and, whether their decision was revised, it was always in the direction of clemency, the mitigation of the findings being indeed of frequent occurrence.

The judges were also assisted by a consilium permanens, or standing council, composed of other sworn judges. In these dispositions surely lay the most valuable guarantees for all objective, impartial, and just operation of the inquisition courts. Apart from the conduct of his own defense the accused disposed of other legal means for safeguarding his rights: he could reject a judge who had shown prejudice, and at any stage of the trial could appeal to Rome. Eymeric leads one to infer that in Aragon appeals to the Holy See were not rare. He himself as inquisitor had on one occasion to go to Rome to defend in person his own position, but he advises other inquisitors against that step, as it simply meant the loss of much time and money; it were wiser, he says, to try a case in such a manner that no fault could be found. In the event of an appeal the documents of the case were to be sent to Rome under seal, and Rome not only scrutinized them, but itself gave the final verdict. Seemingly, appeals to Rome were in great favor; a milder sentence, it was hoped, would be forthcoming, or at least some time would be gained.

(d) Punishments The present writer can find nothing to suggest that the accused were imprisoned during the period of inquiry. It was certainly customary to grant the accused person his freedom until the sermo generalis, were he ever so strongly inculpated through witnesses or confession; he was not yet supposed guilty, though he was compelled to promise under oath always to be ready to come before the inquisitor, and in the end to accept with good grace his sentence, whatever its tenor. The oath was assuredly a terrible weapon in the hands of the medieval judge. If the accused person kept it, the judge was favorably inclined; on the other hand, if the accused violated it, his credit grew worse. Many sects, it was known, repudiated oaths on principle; hence the violation of an oath caused the guilty party easily to incur suspicion of heresy. Besides the oath, the inquisitor might secure himself by demanding a sum of money as bail, or reliable bondsmen who would stand surety for the accused. It happened, too, that bondsmen undertook upon oath to deliver the accused "dead or alive" It was perhaps unpleasant to live under the burden of such an obligation, but, at any rate, it was more endurable than to await a final verdict in rigid confinement for months or longer. Curiously enough torture was not regarded as a mode of punishment, but purely as a means of eliciting the truth. It was not of ecclesiastical origin, and was long prohibited in the ecclesiastical courts. Nor was it originally an important factor in the inquisitional procedure, being unauthorized until twenty years after the Inquisition had begun. It was first authorized by Innocent IV in his Bull *Adex stirpanda* of 15 May, 1252, which was confirmed by Alexander IV on 30 November, 1259, and by Clement IV on 3 November, 1265. The limit placed upon torture was *citra membri diminutionem etmortis periculum* i.e, it was not to cause the loss of life or limb or imperil life. Torture was to applied only once, and not then unless the accused were uncertain in his statements, and seemed already virtually convicted by manifold and weighty proofs. In general, this violent testimony (quaestio) was to be deferred as long as possible, and recourse to it was permitted in only when all other expedients were exhausted. Conscientiousness and sensible judges quite properly attached no great importance to confessions extracted by torture. After long experience Eymeric declared: The torture is deceptive and ineffectual. Had this papal legislation been adhered to in practice, the historian of the Inquisition would have fewer difficulties to satisfy. In the beginning, torture was held to be so odious that clerics were forbidden to be present under pain of irregularity. Sometimes it had to be interrupted so as to enable the inquisitor to continue his examination, which, of course, was attended by numerous inconveniences. Therefore on 27 April, 1260, Alexander IV authorized inquisitors to absolve one another of this irregularity. Urban IV on 2 August, 1262, renewed the permission, and this was soon interpreted as formal licence to continue the examination in the torture chamber itself. The inquisitors manuals faithfully noted and approved this usage. The general rule ran that torture was to be resorted to only once. But this was

sometimes circumvented first, by assuming that with every new piece of evidence the rack could be utilized afresh, and secondly, by imposing fresh torments on the poor victim (often on different days), not by way of repetition, but as a continuation (non ad modumiterationis sed continuationis), as defended by Eymeric; "quia, iterari non debent [tormenta], nisinovis super venitibus indiciis, continuari non prohibentur." But what was to be done when the accused, released from the rack, denied what he had just confessed? Some held with Eymeric that the accused should be set at liberty; others, however, like the author of the *Sacro Arsenale* held that the torture should be continued. because the accused had too seriously incriminated himself by his previous confession.

When Clement V formulated his regulations for the employment of torture, he never imagined that eventually even witnesses would be put on the rack, although not their guilt, but that of the accused, was in question. From the popes silence it was concluded that a witness might be put upon the rack at the discretion of the inquisitor. Moreover, if the accused was convicted through witnesses, or had pleaded guilty, the torture might still he used to compel him to testify against his friends and fellow-culprits. It would be opposed to all Divine and human equity so one reads in the *Sacro Arsenale, oero Pratica dell Officio della Santa Inquisizione* (Bologna, 1665) to inflict torture unless the judge were personally persuaded of the guilt of the accused. But one of the difficulties of the procedure is why torture was used as a means of learning the truth. On the one hand, the torture was continued until the accused confessed or intimated that he was willing to confess, On the other hand, it was not desired, as in fact it was not possible, to regard as freely made a confession wrung by torture. It is at once apparent how little reliance may be placed upon the assertion so often repeated in the minutes of trials, *confessionem esse veram, non factam vi tormentorum* (the confession was true and free), even though one had not occasionally read in the preceding pages that, after being taken down from the rack, he freely confessed this or that. However, it is not of greater importance to say that torture is seldom mentioned in the records of inquisition trials but once, for example in 636 condemnations between 1309 and 1323; this does not prove that torture was rarely applied. Since torture was originally inflicted outside the court room by lay officials, and since only the voluntary confession was valid before the judges, there was no occasion to mention in the records the fact of torture. On the other hand it, is historically true that the popes not only always held that torture must not imperil life or but also tried to abolish particularly grievous abuses, when such became known to them. Thus Clement V ordained that inquisitors should not apply the torture without the consent of the diocesan bishop.

From the middle of the thirteenth century, they did not disavow the principle itself, and, as their restrictions to its use were not always heeded, its severity, though of tell exaggerated, was in many cases extreme. The consuls of Carcassonne in 1286 complained to the pope, the King of France, and the vicars of the local bishop against the inquisitor Jean Garland, whom they charged with inflicting torture in an absolutely inhuman manner, and this charge was no isolated one. The case of Savonarola has never been altogether cleared up in this respect. The official report says he had to suffer three and a half *tratti da fune* (a sort of *strappado*). When Alexander VI showed discontent with the delays of the trial, the Florentine government excused itself by urging that Savonarola was a man of extraordinary sturdiness and endurance, and that he had been vigorously tortured on many days but with little effect. It is to be noted that torture was most cruelly used, where the inquisitors were most exposed to the pressure of civil authority. Frederick II, though always boasting of his zeal for the purity of the Faith, abused both rack and Inquisition to put out of the way his personal enemies. The tragical ruin of the Templars is ascribed to the abuse of torture by Philip the

Fair and his henchmen. At Paris, for instance, thirty-six, and at Sens twenty-five, Templars died as the result of torture.

Blessed Joan of Arc could not have been sent to the stake as a heretic and a recalcitrant, if her judges had not been tools of English policy. And the excesses of the Spanish Inquisition are largely due to the fact that in its administration civil purposes overshadowed the ecclesiastical. Every reader of the "Cautio criminalis" of the Jesuit Father Friedrich Spee knows to whose account chiefly must be set down the horrors of the witchcraft trials. Most of the punishments that were properly speaking inquisitional were not inhuman, either by their nature or by the manner of their infliction. Most frequently certain good works were ordered, e.g. the building of a church, the visitation of a church, a pilgrimage more or less distant, the offering of a candle or a chalice, participation in a crusade, and the like. Other works partook more of the character of real and to some extent degrading punishments, e.g. fines, whose proceeds were devoted to such public purposes as church-building, road-making, and the like; whipping with rods during religious service; the pillory; the wearing of colored crosses, and soon. The hardest penalties were imprisonment in its various degrees exclusion from the communion of the Church, and the usually consequent surrender to the civil power. *Cum ecclesia* ran the regular expression, *ultra non habeat quod faciat pro suis demeritis contra ipsum, id circo, eundum reliquimus brachio et iudicio saeculari* i.e. since the Church can no farther punish his misdeeds, she leaves him to the civil authority. Naturally enough, punishment as a legal sanction is always a hard and painful thing, whether decreed by civil of ecclesiastical justice. There is, however, always an essential distinction between civil and ecclesiastical punishment. While chastisement inflicted by secular authority aims chiefly at punishment violation of the law, the Church seeks primarily the correction of the delinquent; indeed his spiritual welfare frequently so much in view that the element of punishment is almost entirely lost sight of. Commands to hear Holy Mass on Sundays and holidays, to frequent religious services, to abstain from manual labor, to receive Communion at the chief festivals of the year, to forbear from soothsaying and usury, etc., can be efficacious as helps toward the fulfillment of Christian duties. It being furthermore incumbent on the inquisitor to consider not merely the external sanction, but also the inner change of heart, his sentence lost the quasi-mechanical stiffness so often characteristic of civil condemnation. Moreover, the penalties incurred were on numberless occasions remitted, mitigated, or commuted. In the records of the Inquisition we very frequently read that because of old age, sickness, or poverty in the family, the in the family, the due punishment was materially reduced owing to the inquisitor sheer pity, or the petition of a good Catholic. Imprisonment for life was altered to a fine, and this to an alms; participation in a crusade was commuted into a pilgrimage, while a distant and costly pilgrimage became a visit to a neighboring shrine or church, and so on. If the inquisitors leniency were abused, he was authorized to revive in full the original punishment. On the whole, the Inquisition was humanely conducted. Thus we read that a son obtained his fathers release by merely asking for it, without putting forward any special reasons. Licence to leave risen for three weeks, three months, or an unlimited period-say until the recovery or decease of sick parents was not infrequent.

Rome itself censured inquisitioners or deposed them because they were too harsh, but never because they mere too merciful. Imprisonment was not always accounted punishment in the proper sense: it was rather looked on as an opportunity for repentance, a preventive against backsliding or the infection of others. It was known as *immuration* (from the Latin *murus*, a wall), or incarceration, and was inflicted for a definite time or for life. Immuration for life was the lot of those who had failed to profit by the aforesaid term of grace, or had perhaps recanted only from fear of death, or had once before abjured heresy. Themurus strictus seu arctus, or carcer strictissimus, implied close and solitary confinement, occasionally aggravated by fasting or chains. In practice, however, these regulations were not always enforced literally. We read of immured persons receiving visits rather freely, playing games, or dining with their jailors. On the other hand, solitary confinement was at times deemed insufficient, and then the immured were put in irons or chained to the prison wall. Members of a religious order, when condemned for life, were immured in their own convent nor ever allowed to speak with any of their fraternity.

The dungeon or cell was euphemistically called *In Pace* it was, indeed, the tomb of a man buried alive. It was looked upon as a remarkable favor when, in 1330, through the good offices of the Archbishop of Toulouse, the French king permitted a dignitary of a certain order to visit the *In Pace* twice a month and comfort his imprisoned brethren, against which favor the Dominicans lodged with Clement VI a fruitless protest. Though the prison cells were directed to be kept in such a way as to endanger neither the life nor the health of occupants, their true condition was sometimes deplorable. In some cells the unfortunates were bound in stocks or chains, unable to move about, and forced to sleep on the ground . . . . There was little regard for cleanliness. In some cases there was no light or ventilation, and the food was meager and very poor. Occasionally the popes had to put an end through their legates to similarly atrocious conditions. After inspecting the Carcassonne and Albi prisons in 1306, the legates Pierre de la Chapelle and Béranger de Frédol dismissed the warden, removed the chains from the captives, and rescued some from their underground dungeons. The local bishop was expected to provide food from the confiscated property of the prisoner. For those doomed to close confinement, it was meager enough, scarcely more than bread and water. It was, not long, however, before prisoners were allowed other victuals, wine and money also from outside, and this was soon generally tolerated. Officially it was not the Church that sentenced unrepenting heretics to death, more particularly to the stake. As legate of the Roman Church even Gregory IV never went further than the penal ordinances of Innocent III required, nor ever inflicted a punishment more severe than excommunication. Not until four years after the commencement of his pontificate did he admit the opinion, then prevalent among legists, that heresy should be punished with death, seeing that it was confessedly no less serious an offence than high treason. Nevertheless he continued to insist on the exclusive right of the Church to decide in authentic manner in matters of heresy; at the same time it was not her office to pronounce sentence of death.

The Church, thenceforth, expelled from her bosom the impenitent heretic, whereupon the state took over the duty of his temporal punishment. Frederick II was of the same opinion; in his Constitution of 1224 he says that heretics convicted by an ecclesiastical court shall, on imperial authority, suffer death by fire. In this way Gregory IX may be regarded as having had no share either directly or indirectly in the death of condemned heretics. Not so the succeeding popes. In the Bull *Ad exstirpanda* (1252) Innocent IV says: When those adjudged guilty of heresy have been given up to the civil power by the bishop or his representative, or the Inquisition, the podestà or chief magistrate of the city shall take them at once, and shall, within five days at the most, execute the laws made against them. Moreover, he directs that this Bull and the corresponding regulations of Frederick II be entered in every city among the municipal statutes under pain of excommunication, which was also visited on those who failed to execute both the papal and the imperial decrees. Nor could any doubt remain as to what civil regulations were meant, for the passages which ordered the burning of impenitent heretics were inserted in the papal decretals from the imperial constitutions *Commissis nobis* and *Inconsutibilem tunicam*. The aforesaid Bull

Ad exstirpanda remained thenceforth a fundamental document of the Inquisition, renewed or reinforced by several popes, Alexander IV (1254-61), Clement IV (1265-68), Nicholas IV (1288-02), Boniface VIII (1294-1303), and others. The civil authorities, therefore, were enjoined by the popes, under pain of excommunication to execute the legal sentences that condemned impenitent heretics to the stake. It is to he noted that excommunication itself was no trifle, for, if the person excommunicated did not free himself from excommunication within a year, he was held by the legislation of that period to be a heretic, and incurred all the penalties that affected heresy.

The Number of Victims. How many victims were handed over to the civil power cannot be stated with even approximate accuracy. We have nevertheless some valuable information about a few of the Inquisition tribunals, and their statistics are not without interest. At Pamiers, from 1318 to 1324, out of twenty-four persons convicted but five were delivered to the civil power, and at Toulouse from 1308 to 1323, only forty-two out of nine hundred and thirty bear the ominous note "relictus culiae saeculari". Thus, at Pamiersone in thirteen, and at Toulouse one in forty-two seem to have been burnt for heresy although these places were hotbeds of heresy and therefore principal centers of the Inquisition. We may add, also, that this was the most active period of the institution. These data and others of the same nature bear out the assertion that the Inquisition marks a substantial advance in the contemporary administration of justice, and therefore in the general civilization of mankind. A more terrible fate awaited the heretic when judged by a secular court. In 1249 Count Raylmund VII of Toulouse caused eighty confessed heretics to be burned in his presence without permitting them to recant. It is impossible to imagine any such trials before the Inquisition courts. The large numbers of burnings detailed in various histories are completely unauthenticated, and are either the deliberate invention of pamphleteers, or are based on materials that pertain to the Spanish Inquisition of later times or the German witchcraft trials. Once the Roman Law touching the crimen laesae majestatis had been made to cover the case of heresy, it was only natural that the royal or imperial treasury should imitate the Roman fiscus, and lay claim to the property of persons condemned. was fortunate, though inconsistent and certainly not strict justice, that this penalty did not affect every condemned person, but only those sentenced to perpetual confinement or the stake. Even so, this circumstance added not a little to the penalty, especially as in this respect innocent people, the culprits wife and children, were the chief sufferers. Confiscation was also decreed against persons deceased, and there is a relatively high number of such judgments. Of the six hundred and thirty-six cases that came before the inquisitor Bernard Gui, eighty-eight pertained to dead people.

(e) The Final Verdict The ultimate decision was usually pronounced with solemn ceremonial at the sermo generalis orauto-da-fé (act of faith), as it was later called. One or two days prior to this sermo everyone concerned had the charges read to him again briefly, and in the vernacular; the evening before he was told where and when to appear to hear the verdict. The sermo, a short discourse or exhortation, began very early in the morning; then followed the swearing in of the secular officials, who were made to vow obedience to the inquisitor in all things pertaining to the suppression of heresy. Then regularly followed the so-called "decrees of mercy" (i.e. commutations, mitigations, and remission of previously imposed penalties), and finally due punishments were assigned to the guilty, after their offences had been again enumerated. This announcement began with the minor punishments, and went on to the most severe, i.e., perpetual imprisonment or death. Thereupon the guilty were turned over to the civil power, and with this act the sermo generalis closed, and the inquisitional proceedings were at an end.

(3) The chief scene of the Inquisitions activity was Central and Southern Europe.
The Scandinavian countries were spared altogether. It appears in England only on the occasion of the trial of the Templars, nor was it known in Castile and Portugal until the accession of Ferdinand and Isabella. It was introduced into the Netherlands with the Spanish domination, while in Northern France it was relatively little known. On the other hand, the Inquisition, whether because of the particularly perilous sectarianism there prevalent or of the greater severity of ecclesiastical and civil rulers, weighed heavily on Italy (especially Lombardy), on Southern France (in particular the country of Toulouse and on Languedoc) and finally on the Kingdom of Aragon and on Germany. Honorius IV (1285-87) introduced it into Sardinia, and in the fifteenth century it displayed excessive zeal in Flanders and Bohemia. The inquisitors were, as a rule, irreproachable, not merely in personal conduct, but in the administration of their office. Some, however, like Robert le Bougre, a Bulgarian (Catharist) convert to Christianity and subsequently a Dominican, seem to have yielded to a blind fanaticism and deliberately to have provoked executions en masse. On 29 May, 1239, at Montwimer in Champagne, Robert consigned to the flames at one time about a hundred and eighty persons, whose trial had begun and ended within one week. Later, when Rome found that the complaints against him were justified, he was first deposed and then incarcerated for life.

(4) How are we to explain the Inquisition in the light of its own period?
For the true office of the historian is not to defend facts and conditions, but to study and understand them in their natural course and connection. It is indisputable that in the past scarcely any community or nation vouchsafed perfect toleration to those who set up a creed different from that of the generality. A kind of iron law would seem to dispose mankind to religious intolerance. Even long before the Roman State tried to check with violence the rapid encroachments of Christianity, Plate had declared it one of the supreme duties of the governmental authority in his ideal state to show no toleration towards the "godless" that is, towards those who denied the state religion even though they were content to live quietly and without proselytizing; their very example, he said would be dangerous. They were to be kept in custody; "in a place where one grew wise", as the place of incarceration was euphemistically called; they should be relegated thither for five years, and during this time listen to religious instruction every day. The more active and proselytizing opponents of the state religion were to be imprisoned for life in dreadful dungeons, and after death to be deprived of burial. It is thus evident what little justification there is for regarding intolerance as a product of the Middle Ages. Everywhere and always in the past men believed that nothing disturbed the commonweal and public peace so much as religious dissensions and conflicts, and that, on the other hand, a uniform public faith was the surest guarantee for the States stability and prosperity. The more thoroughly religion had become part of the national life, and the stronger the general conviction of its inviolability and Divine origin, the more disposed would men be to consider every attack on it as an intolerable crime against the Deity and a highly criminal menace to the public peace. The first Christian emperors believed that one of the chief duties of an imperial ruler was to place his sword at the service of the Church and orthodoxy, especially as their titles of "Pontifex Maximus" and "Bishop of the Exterior" seemed to argue in them Divinely appointed agents of Heaven. Nevertheless the principal teachers of the Church held back for centuries from accepting in these matters the practice of the civil rulers; they shrank particularly from such stern measures against heresy as punishment, both of which they deemed inconsistent with the spirit of Christianity. But, In the Middle Ages, the Catholic Faith became alone dominant, and the welfare of the Commonwealth came to be closely bound up with the cause of religious unity King Peter of Aragon,

therefore, but voiced the universal conviction when he said: "The enemies of the Cross of Christ and violators of the Christian law are likewise our enemies and the enemies of our kingdom, and ought therefore to be dealt with as such." Emperor Frederick II emphasized this view more vigorously than any other prince, and enforced it in his Draconian enactments against heretics. The representative of the Church were also children of their own time, and in their conflict with heresy accepted the help that their age freely offered them, and indeed often forced upon them. Theologians and canonists, the highest and the saintliest, stood by the code of their day, and sought to explain and to justify it. The learned and holy Raymund of Pennafort, highly esteemed by Gregory IX, was content with the penalties that dated from Innocent III, viz.. the ban of the empire, confiscation of property, confinement in prison, etc. But before the end of the century, St. Thomas Aquinas (*Summa Theol.,* II-II:11:3 and II-II:11:4) already advocated capital punishment for heresy though it cannot be said that his arguments altogether compel conviction. The Angelic Doctor, however speaks only in a general way of punishment by death, and does not specify more nearly the manner of its infliction. This the jurists did in a positive way that was truly terrible. The celebrated Henry of Segusia (Susa), named Hostiensis after his episcopal See of Ostia (d. 1271), and the no less eminent Joannes Andreae (d.1345), when interpreting the Decree *Ad abolendam* of Lucius III, take *debita anim adversio* (due punishment) as synonymous with *ignis crematio* (death by fire), a meaning which certainly did not attach to the original expression of 1184.

Theologians and jurists based their attitude to some extent on the similarity between heresy and high treason, a suggestion that they owed to the Law of Ancient Rome. They argued, moreover, that if the death penalty could be rightly inflicted on thieves and forgers, who rob us only of worldly goods, how much more righteously on those who cheat us out of supernatural goods out of faith, the sacraments, the life of the soul. In the severe legislation of the Old Testament (Deut., xiii, 6-9; xvii, 1-6) they found another argument. And lest some should urge that those ordinances were abrogated by Christianity, the words of Christ were recalled: "I am not come to destroy, but to fulfill" (Matt., v. 17); also His other saying (John, xv.6): "If any one abide not in me, he shall be cast forth as a branch, and shall wither, and they shall gather him up, and cast him into the fire, and he burneth". It is well known that belief in the justice of punishing heresy with death was so common among the sixteenth century reformers Luther, Zwingli, Calvin, and their adherents that we may say their toleration began where their power ended. The Reformed theologian, Hieronymus Zanchi, declared in a lecture delivered at the University of Heidlelberg: We do not now ask if the authorities may pronounce sentence of death upon heretics; of that there can be no doubt, and all learned and right-minded men acknowledge it. The only question is whether the authorities are bound to perform this duty. And Zanchi answers this second question in the affirmative, especially on the authority of "all pious and learned men who have written on the subject in our day" (*Historisch-politische Blatter*, CXL, (1907), p. 364). It may be that in modern times men judge more leniency the views of others, but does this forthwith make their opinions objectively more correct than those of their predecessors? Is there no longer any inclination to persecution? As late as 1871 Professor Friedberg wrote in Holtzendorffs *Jahrbuch fur Gesetzebung*: "If a new religious society were to be established today with such principles as those which, according to the Vatican Council, the Catholic Church declares a matter of faith, we would undoubtedly consider it a duty of the state to suppress, destroy, and uproot it by force". Do these sentiments indicate an ability to appraise justly the institutions and opinions of former centuries, not according to modern feelings, but to the standards of their age? In forming an estimate of the Inquisition, it is necessary to distinguish clearly between principles and historical fact on the one hand, and on the other those exaggerations or rhetorical descriptions which reveal bins and an obvious determination to injure Catholicism, rather than to encourage the spirit of tolerance and further its exercise. It is also essential to note that the Inquisition, in its establishment and procedure, pertained not to the sphere of belief, but to that of discipline. The dogmatic teaching of the Church is in no way affected by the question as to whether the Inquisition was justified in its scope, or wise in its methods, or extreme in its practice. The Church established by Christ, as a perfect society, is empowered to make laws and inflict penalties for their violation. Heresy not only violates her law but strikes at her very life, unity of belief; and from the beginning the heretic had incurred all the penalties of the ecclesiastical courts.

When Christianity became the religion of the Empire, and still more when the peoples of Northern Europe became Christian nations, the close alliance of Church and State made unity of faith essential not only to the ecclesiastical organization, but also to civil society. Heresy, in consequence, was & crime which secular rulers were bound in duty to punish. It was regarded as worse than any other crime, even that of high treason; it was for society in those times what we call anarchy. Hence the severity with which heretics were treated by the secular power long before the Inquisition was established. As regards the character of these punishments, it should be considered that they were the natural expression not only of the legislative power, but also of the popular hatred for heresy in an age that dealt both vigorously and roughly with criminals of every type. The heretic, in a word, was simply an outlaw whose offence, in the popular mind, deserved and sometimes received a punishment as summary as that which is often dealt out in our own day by an infuriated populace to the authors of justly detested crimes. That such intolerance was not peculiar to Catholicism, but was the natural accompaniment of deep religious conviction in those, also, who abandoned the Church, is evident from the measures taken by some of the Reformers against those who differed from them in matters of belief. As the learned Dr. Schaff declares in his *History of the Christian Church* (vol. V, New York, 1907, p. 524), To the great humiliation of the Protestant churches, religious intolerance and even persecution unto death were continued long after the Reformation. In Geneva the pernicious theory was put into practice by state and church, even to the use of torture and the admission of the testimony of children against their parents, and with the sanction of Calvin. Bullinger, in the second Helvetic Confession, announced the principle that heresy could be punished like murder or treason. Moreover, the whole history of the Penal Laws against Catholics in England and Ireland, and the spirit of intolerance prevalent in many of the American colonies during the seventeenth and eighteenth centuries may be cited in proof thereof. It would obviously be absurd to make the Protestant religion as such responsible for these practices. But having set up the principle of private judgment, which, logically applied, made heresy impossible, the early Reformers proceeded to treat dissidents as the medieval heretics had been treated. To suggest that this was inconsistent is trivial in view of the deeper insight it affords into the meaning of a tolerance which is often only theoretical and the source of that intolerance which men rightly show towards error, and which they naturally though not rightly, transfer to the erring.

B. The Inquisition in Spain

(1) Historical Facts Religious conditions similar to those in Southern France occasioned the establishment of the Inquisition in the neighboring Kingdom of Aragon. As early as 1226 King James I had forbidden the Catharists his kingdom, and in 1228 had outlawed both them and their friends. A little later, on the advice of his confessor, Raymond of Pennafort, he asked Gregory IX to establish the Inquisition in Aragon. By the Bull Declinante jam mundi of 26 May, 1232, Archbishop Esparrago and his suffragans were instructed to search, either personally or by enlisting the services of the Dominicans or other suitable agents, and condignly punish the heretics in their dioceses. At the Council of Léridain 1237 the Inquisition was formally confided to the Dominicans and the Franciscans. At the Synod of Tarragona in 1242, Raymund of Pennafort defined the terms haereticus, receptor, fautor, defensor, etc., and outlined the penalties to be inflicted. Although the ordinances of Innocent IV, Urban IV, and Clement VI were also adopted and executed with strictness by the Dominican Order, no striking success resulted. The Inquisitor Fray Pence de Planes was poisoned, and Bernardo Travasser earned the crown of martyrdom at the hands of the heretics. Aragons best-known inquisitor is the Dominican Nicolas Eymeric. His *Directorium Inquisitionis* (written in Aragon 1376; printed at Rome 1587, Venice 1595 and 1607), based on forty-four years experience, is an original source and a document of the highest historical value. The Spanish Inquisition, however, properly begins with the reign of Ferdinand the Catholic and Isabella. The Catholic faith was then endangered by pseudo converts from Judaism and Mohammedanism. On 1 November, 1478, Sixtus IV empowered the Catholic sovereigns to set up the Inquisition. The judges were to be at least forty years old, of unimpeachable reputation, distinguished for virtue and wisdom, masters of theology, or doctors or licentiates of canon law, and they must follow the usual ecclesiastical rules and regulations. On 17 September, 1480, Their Catholic Majesties appointed, at first for Seville, the two Dominicans Miguel de Morillo and Juan de San Martin as inquisitors, with two of the secular clergy assistants. Before long complaints of grievous abuses reached Rome, and were only too well founded. In a Brief of Sixtus IV of 29 January 1482, they were blamed for having, upon the alleged authority of papal Briefs, unjustly imprisoned many people, subjected them to cruel tortures, declared them false believers, and sequestrated the property of the executed. They were at first admonished to act only in conjunction with, the bishops, and finally were threatened with deposition, and would indeed have been deposed had not Their Majesties interceded for them. Fray Tomás Torquemada (b. at Valladolid In 1420, d. at Avila, 16 September, 1498) was the true organizer of the Spanish Inquisition. At the solicitation of their Spanish Majesties Sixtus IV bestowed on Torquemada the office of grand inquisitor, the institution of which indicates a decided advance in the development of the Spanish Inquisition. Innocent VIII approved the act of his predecessor, and under date of 11 February, 1486, and 6 February, 1487, Torquemada was given dignity of grand inquisitor for the kingdoms of Castile, Leon, Aragon, Valencia, etc. The institution speedily ramified from Seville to Cordova, Jaen, Villareal, and Toledo, About 1538 there were nineteen courts, to which three were afterwards added in Spanish America (Mexico, Lima, and Cartagena). Attempts at introducing it into Italy failed, and the efforts to establish it in the Netherlands entailed disastrous consequences for the mother country. In Spain, however, it remained operative into the nineteenth century. Originally called into being against secret Judaism and secret Islam, it served to repel Protestantism in the sixteenth century, but was unable to expel French Rationalism and immorality of the eighteenth. King Joseph Bonaparte abrogated it in 1808, but it was reintroduced by Ferdinand VII in 1814 and approved by Pius VII on certain conditions, among others the abolition of torture. It was definitely abolished by the Revolution of 1820.

(2) **Organization** At the head of the Inquisition, known as the Holy Office, stood the grand inquisitor, nominated by the king and confirmed by the pope. By virtue of his papal credentials he enjoyed authority to delegate his powers to other suitable persons, and to receive appeals from all Spanish courts. He was aided by a High Council (*Consejo Supremo*) consisting of five members the so-called Apostolic inquisitors, two secretaries, two relatores, one advocatus fiscalis and several consulters and

qualificators. The officials of the supreme tribunal were appointed by the grand inquisitor after consultation with the king. The former could also freely appoint, transfer, remove from office, visit, and inspect or call to account all inquisitors and officials of the lower courts. Philip III, on 16 December, 1618, gave the Dominicans the privilege of having one of their order permanently a member of the Consejo Supremo. All power was really concentrated in this supreme tribunal. It decided important or disputed questions, and heard appeals; without its approval no priest, knight, or noble could be imprisoned, and no *auto-da-fé* held; an annual report was made to it concerning the entire Inquisition, and once a month a financial report. Everyone was subject to it, not excepting priests, bishops, or even the sovereign. The Spanish Inquisition is distinguished from the medieval its monarchical constitution and a greater consequent centralization, as also by the constant and legally provided-for influence of the crown on all official appointments and the progress of trials.

(3) **Procedure** The procedure, on the other hand, was substantially the same as that already described. Here, too, a "term of grace" of thirty to forty days was invariably granted, and was often prolonged. Imprisonment resulted only when unanimity had been arrived at, or the offence had been proved. Examination of the accused could take place only in the presence of two disinterested priests, whose obligation it was to restrain any arbitrary act in their presence the protocol had to be read out twice to the accused. The defense lay always in the hands of a lawyer. The witnesses although unknown to the accused, were sworn, and very severe punishment, even death, awaited false witnesses. Torture was applied only too frequently and to cruelly, but certainly not more cruelly than under Charles V's system of judicial torture in Germany.

(4) **Historical Analysis** The Spanish Inquisition deserves neither the exaggerated praise nor the equally exaggerated vilification often bestowed on it. The number of victims cannot be calculated with even approximate accuracy; the much maligned autos-da-fé were in reality but a religious ceremony (*actus fidei*); the San Benito has its counterpart in similar garbs elsewhere; the cruelty of St. Peter Arbues, to whom not a single sentence of death can be traced with certainty, belongs to the realms of fable. However, the predominant ecclesiastical nature of the institution can hardly be doubted. The Holy See sanctioned the institution, accorded to the grand inquisitor canonical installation and therewith judicial authority concerning matters of faith, while from the grand inquisitor jurisdiction passed down to the subsidiary tribunals under his control. Joseph de Maistre introduced the thesis that the Spanish Inquisition was mostly a civil tribunal; formerly, however, theologians never questioned its ecclesiastical nature. Only thus, indeed, can one explain how the Popes always admitted appeals from it to the Holy See, called to themselves entire trials and that at any stage of the proceedings, exempted whole classes of believers from its jurisdiction, intervened in the legislation, deposed grand inquisitors, and so on.

C. The Holy Office at Rome

The great apostasy of the sixteenth century, the filtration of heresy into Catholic lands, and the progress of heterodox teachings everywhere, prompted Paul III to establish the *Sacra Congregatio Romanae et universalis Inquisitionis seu sancti officii* by the Constitution *Licetab initio* of 21 July, 1542. This inquisitional tribunal, composed of six cardinals, was to be at once the final court of appeal for trials concerning faith, and the court of first instance for cases reserved to the pope. The succeeding popes especially Pius IV and Pius V made further provision for the procedure and competency of this court. By his Constitution *Immensa aeterni* of 23 January, 1587, Sixtus V became the real organizer, or rather reorganizer of this congregation. The Holy Office is first among the Roman congregations. Its personnel includes judges, officials, consulters, and qualificators. The real judges are cardinals nominated by the pope, whose original number of six was raised by Pius IV to eight and by Sixtus V to thirteen. Their actual number depends on the reigning pope. This congregation differs from the others, inasmuch as it has no cardinal-prefect: the pope always presides in person when momentous decisions are to be announced. The solemn plenary session on Thursdays is always preceded by a session of the cardinals on Wednesdays, at the church of Santa Maria sopra Minerva, and a meeting of the consultors on Mondays at the palace of the Holy Office. The highest official is the *commissarius sancti oficii*, a Dominican of the Lombard province, to whom two coadjutors are given from the same order. He acts as the proper judge throughout the whole case until the plenary session exclusive, thus conducting it up to the verdict. The assessor *sancti officii*, always one of the secular clergy, presides at the plenary sessions. The *promotor fiscalis* is at once prosecutor and fiscal representative, while the advocatus reorum undertakes the defense of the accused. The duty of the consultors is to afford the cardinals expert advice. They may come from the secular clergy or the religious orders, but the General of the Dominicans, the magister sacri palatii, and a third member of the same order are always *ex-officio* consultors. The qualificators are appointed for life, but give their opinions only when called upon. The Holy Office has jurisdiction over all Christians and, according to Pius IV, even over cardinals. In practice, however, the latter are held exempt.

Joseph Blötzer, The Catholic Encyclopedia, Volume 8

The Spanish Inquisition

Torquemada's name, with clouds o'ercast,
Looms in the distant landscape of the past
Like a burnt tower upon a blackened heath,
Lit by the fires of burning woods beneath.
Longfellow

The Inquisition of Spain is one of the bywords of history. The horrors it perpetrated have cast a dark shadow over the pages of Spanish annals. Organized to rid the Spanish kingdoms of the infection of heresy, it extended its methods to the Spanish dependencies in Europe, Sicily and Holland and to the Spanish colonies of the new world. After the marriage of Philip II with Mary Tudor it secured a temporary recognition in England. In its bloody sacrifices, Jews, Moors, Protestants and the practitioners of the dark arts were included. No country in the world was more concerned to maintain the Catholic faith pure than was Spain from the 15th to the 18th century, and to no Church organization was a more unrestricted authority given than to the Spanish Inquisition. Agreeing with the papal Inquisition established by Innocent III in its ultimate aim, the eradication of heresy, it differed from that earlier institution by being under the direction of a tribunal appointed by the Spanish sovereign, immediately amenable to him and acting independently of the bishops. The papal Inquisition was controlled by the Apostolic see, which appointed agents to carry its rules into effect and whose agency was to a certain extent subject to the assent of the bishops. Engaged in the wars for the dispossession of the Pagan Moors, the Spanish kingdoms had shown little disposition to yield to the intrusion of Catharan and other heresy from the North.

The menace to its orthodox repose came from the Jews, Jews who held firmly to their ancestral faith and Jews who had of their own impulse or through compulsion adopted the Christian rites. In no part of Europe was the number of Jews so large and nowhere had they been more prosperous in trade and reached such positions of eminence as physicians and as counselors at court. The Jewish literature of mediaeval Spain forms a distinct and notable chapter in Hebrew literary history. To rid the land of the Jews who persisted in their ancestral belief was not within the jurisdiction of the Church. That belonged to the state, and, according to the canon law, the Jew was not to be molested in the practice of his religion. But the moment Jews or Moors submitted to baptism they became amenable to ecclesiastical discipline. Converted Jews in Spain were called conversos, or maranos – the newly converted – and it was with them, in its first period, that the Spanish Inquisition had chiefly to do. After Luther's doctrines began to spread it addressed itself to the extirpation of Protestants, but, until the close of its history, in 1834, the Jewish Christians constituted most of its victims. From an early time Spanish legislation was directed to the humiliation of the Jews and their segregation from the Christian population.

The ecumenical Council of Vienne, 1312, denounced the liberality of the Spanish law which made a Jewish witness necessary to the conviction of a Jew. Spanish synods, as those of Valladolid and Tarragona, 1322, 1329, gave strong expression to the spirit of intolerance with which the Spanish church regarded the Jewish people. The sacking and wholesale massacre of their communities, which lived apart in quarters of their own called Juderias, were matters of frequent occurrence, and their synagogues were often destroyed or turned into churches. It is estimated that in 1391, 50,000 Jews were murdered in Castile, and the mania spread to Aragon. The explanation of this bitter feeling is to be sought in the haughty pride of the descendants of Abraham according to the flesh, their persistent observance of their traditions and the exorbitant rates of usury which they charged. Not content with the legal rate, which in Aragon was 20% and in Castile 33 % they often compelled municipalities to pay even higher rates. The prejudice and fears of the Christian population charged them with sacrilege in the use of the wafer and the murder of baptized children, whose blood was used in preparations made for purposes of sorcery. Legislation was made more exacting. The old rules were enforced enjoining a distinctive dress and forbidding them to shave their beards or to have their hair cut round. All employment in Christian households, the practice of medicine and the occupation of agriculture were denied them. Scarcely any trade was left to their hand except the loaning of money, and that by canon law was illegal for Christians.

The joint reign of Ferdinand, 1452–1516, and Isabella, 1451–1504, marked an epoch in the history of the Jews in Spain, both those who remained true to their ancestral faith and the large class which professed conversion to the Christian Church. In conferring the title "Catholic" upon Ferdinand and Isabella, 1495, Alexander VI gave as one of the reasons the expulsion of the Jews from Spain, 1492. The institution of the Spanish Inquisition, which began its work twelve years before, was directed primarily against the conversos, people of Jewish blood and members of the Church who in heart and secret usage remained Jews. The papal Inquisition was never organized in Castile, and in Aragon it had a feeble existence. With the council of Tortosa, 1429, complaints began to be made that the conversos neglected to have their children baptized, and by attending the synagogues and observing the Jewish feasts were putting contempt upon their Christian faith. That such hypocrisy was practiced cannot be doubted in view of the action of the Council of Basel which put its brand upon it. In 1451 Juan II applied to the papal court to appoint a commission to investigate the situation. At the same time the popular feeling was intensified by the frantic appeals of clerics such as Friar Alfonso de Espina who in his Fortalicium fidei – the Fortification of the Faith – brought together a number of alleged cases of children murdered by Jews and argued for the Church's right to baptize Jewish children in the absence of the parents' consent.

The story ran that before Isabella's accession her confessor Torquemada, that hammer of heretics, secured from her a vow to leave no measure untried for the extirpation of heresy from her realm. Sometime later, listening to this same ecclesiastic's appeal, Ferdinand and his consort applied to the papal see for the establishment of the Inquisition in Castile. Sixtus IV, who was then occupying the chair of St. Peter, did not hesitate in a matter so important, and on Nov. 1, 1478, issued the bull sanctioning the fell Spanish tribunal. It authorized the Spanish sovereigns to appoint three bishops or other ecclesiastics to proceed against heretics and at the same time empowered them to remove and replace these officials as they thought fit. After a delay of two years, the commission was constituted, 1480, and consisted of two Dominican theologians, Michael de Morillo and John of St. Martin, and a friar of St. Pablo, Seville. A public reception was given to the commission by the municipal council of Seville. The number of prisoners was soon too large for the capacity of St. Pablo, where the court first established itself, and it was removed to the chief stronghold of the city, the fortress of Triana, whose ample spaces and gloomy dungeons were well fitted for the dark work for which it had been chosen.

Once organized, the Inquisition began its work by issuing the so-called Edict of Grace which gave heretics a period of 30 or 40 days in which to announce themselves and, on making confession, assured them of pardon. Humane as this measure was, it was also used as a device for detecting other spiritual criminals, those confessing, called penitentes, being placed under a vow to reveal the names of heretics. The humiliations to which the penitents were subjected had exhibition at the first auto de fe held in Toledo, 1486, when 750 penitents of both sexes were obliged to march through the city carrying candles and bare-headed; and, on entering the cathedral, were informed that one-fifth of their property had been confiscated, and that they were thenceforth incapacitated to hold public office.

The first auto de fe was held in Seville, Feb. 6, 1481, six months after the appointment of the tribunal, when six men and women were cremated alive. The ghastly spectacle was introduced with a sermon, preached by Friar Alfonso de Hojeda. A disastrous plague, which broke out in the city, did not interrupt the sittings of the tribunal, which established itself temporarily at Aracena, where the first holocaust included 23 men and women. According to a contemporary, by Nov. 4, 1491, 298 persons had been committed to the flames and 79 condemned to perpetual imprisonment. The tribunal established at Ciudad Real, 1483, burnt 52 heretics within two years, when it was removed, in 1485, to Toledo. In Avila, from 1490–1500, 75 were burnt alive, and 26 dead bodies exhumed and cast into the flames. In cases, the entire conversos population was banished, as in Guadalupe, by the order of the inquisitor-general, Deza, in 1500.

From Castile, the Inquisition extended its operations to Aragon, where its three chief centers were Valencia, Barcelona and Saragossa, and then to the Balearic Islands, where it was especially active. The first burning in Saragossa took place, 1484, when two men were burnt alive and one woman in effigy, and at Barcelona in 1488, when four persons were consumed alive. The interest of Sixtus IV continued to follow the tribunal he had authorized and, in a letter addressed to Isabella, Feb. 13, 1483, he assured the queen that its work lay close to his heart. The same year, to render the tribunal more efficient, it was raised by Ferdinand to the dignity of the fifth council of the state with the title, Concejo de la Suprema y General Inquisicion. Usually called the suprema, this body was to have charge of the Holy Office throughout the realm. The same end was promoted by the creation of the office of inquisitor-general, 1483, to which the power was consigned of removing and appointing inquisitorial functionaries.

Thomas de Torquemada

The first incumbent was Thomas de Torquemada, at that time prior of Santa Cruz in Segovia. This fanatical ecclesiastic, whose name is a synonym of uncompromising religious intolerance and heartless cruelty, had already been appointed, in 1482, an inquisitor by the pope. He brought to his duties a rare energy and formulated the rules characteristic of the Spanish Inquisition. With Torquemada at its head, the Holy Office became, next to royalty itself, the strongest power in Spain. Its decisions fell like the blow of a great iron hammer, and there was no power beneath the sovereign that dared to offer them resistance. In 1507, at the death of Deza, third inquisitor-general, Castile and Aragon were placed under distinct tribunals. Cardinal Ximenes, 1436–1517, a member of the Franciscan order and one of the foremost figures in Spanish church history, was elevated to the office of supreme inquisitor of Castile. His distinction as archbishop of Toledo pales before his fame as a scholar and patron of letters. He likewise was unyielding in the prosecution of the work of ridding his country of the taint of heresy, but he never gave way to the temptation of using his office for his own advantage and enriching himself from the sequestrated property of the conversos, as Torquemada was charged with doing.

Under Adrian of Utrecht, at first inquisitor-general of Aragon, the tribunals of the two kingdoms were again united in 1518, and, by the addition of Navarre, which Ferdinand had conquered, the whole Iberian peninsula, with the exception of Portugal, came under the jurisdiction of a single supreme official. Adrian had acted as tutor to Charles V, and was to succeed Leo X on the papal throne. From his administration, the succession of inquisitors-general continued unbroken till 1835, when the last occupant of the office died, Geronimo Castellan y Salas, bishop of Tarazona. The interesting question has been warmly discussed, whether the Inquisition of Spain was a papal institution or an institution of the state, and the attempt has been made to lift the responsibility for its organization and administration from the supreme pontiff. The answer is, that it was predominantly an ecclesiastical institution, created by the authority of Sixtus IV and continuously supported by pontifical sanction. On the other hand, its establishment was sought after by Ferdinand and Isabella, and its operations, after the papal authorization had been secured, was under the control of the Spanish sovereign. So far as we know, the popes never uttered a word in protest against the inhuman measures which were practiced by the Spanish tribunals. Their only dissent arose from the persistence with which Ferdinand kept the administrative agency in his own hands and refused to allow any interference with his disposition of the sequestrated estates.

The hearty approbation of the Apostolic see is vouched for in many documents, and the responsibility for the Spanish tribunal was distinctly assumed by Sixtus V, Jan. 22, 1588, as an institution established by its authority. Sixtus IV and his successors sought again and again to get its full management into their own hands, but were foiled by the firmness of Ferdinand. When, for example, in a bull dated April 18, 1482, the pope ordered the names of the witnesses and accusers to be communicated to the suspects, that the imprisonments should be in episcopal gaols, that appeal might be taken to the Apostolic chair and that confessions to the bishop should stop all prosecution, Ferdinand sharply resented the interference and hinted that the suggestion had started with the use of conversos gold in the curia. This papal action was only a stage in the battle for the control of the Holy Office. Ferdinand was ready to proceed to the point of rupture with Rome rather than allow the principle of appeals which would have reduced the power of the suprema to impotence. Sixtus wrote a compromising reply, and a year later, October, 1483, Ferdinand got all he asked for, and the appointment of Torquemada was confirmed.

The royal management of the Inquisition was also in danger of being fatally hampered by letters of absolution, issued according to custom by the papal penitentiary, which were valid not only in the court of conscience but in stopping public trials. Ferdinand entered a vigorous protest against their use in Spain, when Sixtus, 1484, confirmed the penitentiary's right; but here also Sixtus was obliged to retreat, at least in part, and Alexander VI and later Clement VII, 1524, made such letters invalid when they conflicted with the jurisdiction of the Spanish tribunal. Spain was bent on doing things in its own way and won practical independence of the curia. The principle, whereby in the old Inquisition the bishops were co-ordinate in authority with the inquisitors or superior to them, had to be abandoned in Spain in spite of the pope's repeated attempts to apply it. Innocent VIII, 1487, completely subjected the bishops to the inquisitorial organization, and when Alexander, 1494, annulled this bull and required the inquisitors to act in conjunction with the bishop, Ferdinand would not brook the change and, under his protection, the suprema and its agents asserted their independence to Ferdinand. Likewise, in the matter of confiscations of property, the sovereign claimed the right to dictate their distribution, now applying them for the payment of salaries to the inquisitors and their agents, now appropriating them for the national exchequer, now for his own use or for gifts to his favorites. No concern of his reign, except the extension of his dominions, received from Ferdinand more constant and sympathetic attention than the deletion of heresy. With keen delight he witnessed the public burnings as adapted to advance the Catholic faith. He scrutinized the reports sent him by inquisitors and, at times, he expressed his satisfaction with their services by gifts of money. In his will, dated the day before his death, he enjoined his heir, Charles V, to be strenuous in supporting the tribunal. As all other virtues, so this testament ran, "are nothing without faith by which and in which we are saved, we command the illustrious prince, our grandson, to labor with all his strength to destroy and extirpate heresy from our kingdoms and lordships, appointing ministers, God-fearing and of good conscience, who will conduct the Inquisition justly and properly for the service of God and the exaltation of the Catholic faith, and who will also have a great zeal for the destruction of the sect of Mohammed." Without doubt, the primary motive in the establishment of the tribunal was with Ferdinand, and certainly with Isabella, religious. There seems at no time to have been any widespread revolt against the procedure of the Inquisition. In Aragon, some mitigation of its rigors and rules was proposed by the Cortes of Barcelona, 1512, such as the withdrawal from the inquisitors of the right to carry weapons and the exemption of women from the seizure of their property, in cases where a husband or father was declared a heretic, but Ferdinand and Bishop Enguera, the Aragonese inquisitor-general, were dispensed by Leo X, 1514, from keeping the oath they had taken to observe the rules. At Charles V's accession, an effort was made to have some of the more offensive evils abolished, such as the keeping of the names of witnesses secret, and in 1520 the Cortes of Valladolid and Corunna made open appeal for the amendment of some of the rules. Four hundred thousand ducats were offered, presumably by conversos, to the young king if he would give his assent, and, as late as 1528, the kingdom of Granada, in the same interest, offered him 50,000 ducats. But the appeals received no favorable action and, under the influence of Ximines, in 1517, the council of Castile represented to Charles that the very peace of Spain depended upon the maintenance of the Inquisition. The cardinal wrote a personal letter to the king, declaring that interference on his part would cover his name with infamy.

The most serious attempt to check the workings of the Inquisition occurred in Saragossa and resulted in the assassination of the chief inquisitor, Peter Arbues, an act of despair laid at the door of the conversos. Arbues was murdered in the cathedral Jan. 25, 1485, the fatal blow being struck from behind, while the priest was on his knees engaged in prayer. He knew his life was threatened and not only wore a coat of mail and cap of steel, but carried a lance. He lingered twenty-four hours. Miracles wrought at the coffin vouched for the sanctity of the murdered ecclesiastic. The sacred bell of Villela tolled unmoved by hands. Arbues' blood liquefied on the cathedral floor two weeks after the deed. Within two years, the popular veneration showed itself in the erection of a splendid tomb to the martyr's memory and the Catholic Church, by the bull of Pius IX, June 29, 1867, has given him the honors of canonization. As the assassination of the papal delegate, Peter of Castelnau, at the opening of the crusade against the Albigenses, 1208, wrought to strengthen Innocent in his purpose to wipe out heresy, even with the sword, likewise the taking off of Arbues only tightened the grip of the Spanish Inquisition in Aragon. His murderers and all in any way accessory to the crime were hunted down, their hands were cut off at the portal of the cathedral and their bodies dragged to the market-place, where they were beheaded and quartered or burnt alive. Next to the judicial murders perpetrated by the Inquisition, its chief evil was the confiscation of estates. The property of the conversos offered a tempting prize to the cupidity of the inquisitors and to the crown. The tribunal was expected to live from the spoils of the heretics. Torquemada's Instructions of 1484 contained specific rules governing the disposition of goods held by heretics. There was no limit put upon their despoilment, except that lands transferred before 1479 were exempted from seizure, a precaution to avoid the disturbance of titles. The property of dead heretics, though they had lain in their graves fifty years, was within the power of the tribunal. The dowries of wives were mercifully exempted whose husbands were adjudged heretical, but wives whose fathers were found to be heretics lost their dowries. The claims of the children of heretic fathers might have been expected to call for merciful consideration, but the righteousness of their dispossession had no more vigorous advocates than the clergy. To such property, as the bishop of Simancas argued, the old Christian population had a valid moral claim.

The Instructions of 1484 direct that, if the children were under age at the time of the confiscation, they were to be distributed among pious families, and announced it as the king's intention, in case they grew up good Christians, so to endow them with alms, especially the girls, that they might marry or enter religion. The practice of confiscation extended to the bedding and wearing apparel of the victims. One gracious provision was that the slaves of condemned heretics should receive freedom. Lands were sold at auction 30 days after their sequestration, but the low price which they often brought indicates that purchasers enjoyed special privileges of acquisition. Ferdinand and his successor, Charles, were profuse in their disposition of such property. Had the moneys been used for the wars against the Moors, as at first proposed by Torquemada, the plea might be made that the tribunal was moved by unselfish considerations, but they were not. Not only did Ferdinand take money for his bankrupt treasury, but he appropriated hunting horses, pearls and other objects for his own use. The Flemish favorites of Charles V, in less than ten months, sent home 1,100,000 ducats largely made up of bequests derived from the exactions of the sacred court. Dr. Lea, whose merit it is to have shown the vast extent to which the sequestration of estates was carried, describes the money transactions of the Inquisition as "a carnival of plunder." It was even found to be not incompatible with a purpose to maintain the purity of the faith to enter into arrangements whereby, for a sufficient consideration, communities received protection from inquisitorial charges. The first such bargain was made at Valencia, 1482. The king, however, did not hesitate on occasion to violate his pact and allow unfortunate conversos, who had paid for exemption, to be arraigned and condemned. No law existed requiring faith to be kept with a heretic. It also happened that condemned conversos purchased freedom from serving in the galleys or wearing the badge of heresy, the sanbenito.

As early as 1485, Ferdinand and Isabella were able to erect a royal palace at Guadalupe, costing 2,732,333 maravedis, with the proceeds of sequestrated property and, in a memorial address to Charles X, 1524, Tristan de Leon asserted that these sovereigns had received from the possessions of heretics no less than 10,000,000 ducats. Torquemada also was able to spend vast sums upon his enterprises, such as the conventual building of St. Thomas at Avila, which it was supposed were drawn from the victims whom his religious fervor condemned to the loss of their goods and often of their lives.

When the heretical mine was showing signs of exhaustion in Spain, the Spanish colonies of Mexico and Peru poured in their spoils to enable the Holy Office to maintain the state to which it had been accustomed. At an early period, it began to take care for its own perpetuation by making investments on a large scale. After Ferdinand's death, the suprema's power increased, and it demanded a respect only less than that which was yielded to the crown. Its arrogance and insolence in administration kept pace with the high pretension it made to sacredness of aim and divine authority. The institution was known as the Holy Office, the building it occupied was the holy house, casa santa, and the public solemnity at which the tribunal appeared officially before the public and announced its decisions was called the act of faith, auto de fe. The suprema acted upon the principle started by Paramo, that the inquisitor was the chief personage in his district. He represented both the pope and king. On the one hand, he claimed the right to arrest at will and without restriction from the civil authority; on the other, he demanded freedom for his officials from all arrest and violence. In trading and making exports, the Holy Office claimed exemption from the usual duties levied upon the people at large. Immunity from military service and the right to carry deadly weapons by day and night were among other privileges to which it laid claim. A deliverance of the Apostolic see, 1515, confirmed it in its right to arrest the highest noble in the land who dared to attack its prerogatives or agents and, in case of need, to protect itself by resort to bloodshed. Its jurisdiction extended not only to the lower orders of the clergy, but also to members of the orders, a claim which, after a long struggle, was confirmed by the edicts of Pius IX and X, 1559, 1561. A single class was exempted from the rules of its procedure, the bishops. However, the exemption was rather apparent than real, for the Holy Office exercised the right of arraigning bishops under suspicion before the papal chair. The first cases of this kind were prelates of Jewish extraction, Davila of Segovia, 1490, and Aranda of Calahorra, 1498. Both were tried in Rome, the former being exonerated, and Aranda kept in prison in S. Angelo, where he is supposed to have died, 1500. The most famous of the episcopal suspects, the archbishop of Toledo, Bartholomew of Carranza, 1503–1576, was kept in prison for 17 years, partly in Spain and partly in Rome. The case enjoyed a European reputation. Carranza had the distinction of administering the last rites to Charles X and was for a time a favorite of Philip II, but that sinister prince turned against him. Partly from jealousy of Carranza's honors, as has been surmised, and chiefly on account of his indiscretions of speech, the inquisitor-general Valdes decided upon the archbishop's prosecution, and when his Commentary on the Catechism appeared in Spanish, he was seized under authorization from the Apostolic see, 1559. For two years the prelate was kept in a secret prison and then brought to trial. After delay, Pius IX, 1564, appointed a distinguished commission to investigate the case and Pius X forced his transfer in 1567 to Rome, where he was confined in S. Angelo for nine years. Under Pius X's successor, Gregory XIII, Carranza was compelled to abjure alleged errors, suspended from his seat for five years and remanded to confinement in a Roman convent, where he afterwards died. The boldness and vast power of the Inquisition could have no better proof than the indignity and punishment placed upon a primate of Spain.

The procedure of the Holy Office followed the rules drawn by Torquemada, 1484, 1485, called the Instructions of Seville, and the Instructions of Valladolid prepared by the same hand, 1488 and 1498. These early codes were afterwards known as the Instructiones antiguas, and remained in force until superseded by the code of 1561 prepared by the inquisitor-general, Valdes. Torquemada lodged the control of the Inquisition in the suprema, to which all district tribunals were subordinated. Permanent tribunals were located at Seville, Toledo, Valladolid, Madrid (Corte),

Granada, Cordova, Murcia Llerena, Cuenca, Santiago, Logro and the Canaries under the crown of Castile and at Saragossa, Valencia, Barcelona and Majorca under the crown of Aragon. The officials included two inquisitors an assessor or consulter on modes of canonical procedure, an alguazil or executive officer, who executed the sentences of the tribunal, notaries who kept the records, and censors or califadores who pronounced elaborate opinions on points of dispute. To these was added an official who appraised and took charge of confiscated property. A large body of subordinates, such as the familiars or confidential agents, complete the list of officials. Laymen were eligible to the office of inquisitor, provided they were unmarried, and a condition made for holding any of these places was parity of blood, limpieza, freedom from all stain of Morisco, Jewish or heretic parentage and of ancestral illegitimacy.

This peculiar provision led to endless investigation of genealogical records before appointments were made. Each tribunal had a house of its own, containing the audience chamber, rooms for the inquisitors, a library for the records, le secreto de la Inquisicion, – a chamber of torture and secret prisons. The familiars have a dark fame. They acted as a body of spies to detect and report cases of heresy. Their zeal made them the terror of the land, and the Cortes of Monzon, 1512, called for the reduction of their number. In its procedure, the Inquisition went on the presumption that a person accused was guilty until he had made out his innocence. The grounds of arrest were rumor or personal denunciation. Informing on suspects was represented to the people as a meritorious act and inculcated even upon children as a duty. The instructions of 1484 prescribed a mitigated punishment for minors who informed on heretical fathers, and Bishop Simancas declared it to be the sacred obligation of a son to bring his father, if guilty, to justice. The spiritual offender was allowed an advocate. Secrecy was a prime feature in the procedure. After his arrest, the prisoner was placed in one of the secret prisons, – carceres secretas, – and rigidly deprived of all intercourse with friends. All papers bearing upon his case were kept from him. The names of his accusers and of witnesses for his prosecution were withheld. In the choice of its witnesses the Inquisition allowed itself great liberty, even accepting the testimony of persons under the Church's sentence of excommunication, of Jews who remained in the Hebrew faith and of heretics. Witnesses for the accused were limited to persons zealous for the orthodox faith, and none of his relatives to the fourth generation were allowed to testify. Heresy was regarded as a desperate disorder and to be removed at all costs. On the other hand, the age of amenability was fixed at 12 for girls and 14 for boys. The age of fourscore gave no immunity from the grim rigors of the exacting tribunal. The charges, on which victims were arraigned, included the slightest deflection in word or act from strict Catholic usage, such as the refusal to eat pork on a single occasion, visiting a house where Moorish notions were taught, as well as saying that the Virgin herself and not her image effected cures, and that Jews and Moors would be saved if they sincerely believed the Jewish and the Moorish doctrines to be true. Recourse was had to torture, not only to secure evidence of guilt. Even when the testimony of witnesses was sufficient to establish guilt, resort was had to torture to extract a confession from the accused that thereby his soul might be delivered from the burden of secret guilt, to extract information of accomplices, and that a wholesome influence might be exerted in deterring others from heresy by giving them an example of punishment.

Torture

The modes of torture most in use were the water ordeal and the garruche. In the water-cure, the victim, tightly bound, was stretched upon a rack or bed, and with the body in an inclined position, the head downward. The jaws were distended, a linen cloth was thrust down the victim's throat and water from a quart jar allowed to trickle through it into his inward parts. On occasion, seven or eight such jars were slowly emptied. The garrucha, otherwise known as the strappade, has already been described. In its application in Spain it was customary to attach weights to the feet and to suspend the body in such a manner that the toes alone touched the ground, and the Spanish rule required that the body be raised and lowered leisurely so as to increase the pain. The final penalties for heresy included, in addition to the spiritual impositions of fasting and pilgrimage, confiscation of goods, imprisonment, public scourging, the galleys, exile and death. Confiscation and burning extended to the dead, against whom the charge of heresy could be made out. At Toledo, July 25, 1485, more than 400 dead were burnt in effigy. Frequently at the autos no living victims suffered. In cases of the dead their names were effaced from their tombstones, that "no memory of them should remain on the face of the earth except as recorded in our sentence." Their male descendants, including the grandchildren, were incapacitated from occupying benefices and public positions, from riding on horseback, carrying weapons and wearing silk or ornaments.

The penalty of scourging was executed in public on the bodies of the victims, bared to the waist, by the public executioner. Women of 86 to girls of 13 were subjected to such treatment. Galley labor as a mode of punishment was sanctioned by Alexander VI, 1503. The sentence of perpetual imprisonment was often relaxed, either from considerations of mercy or for financial reasons. Up to 1488, there had been 5000 condemnations to lasting imprisonment. The saco bendito, or sanbenito, another characteristic feature of the Spanish Inquisition, was a jacket of gray or yellow texture, furnished before and behind with a large cross as prescribed by Torquemada. This galling humiliation was aggravated by the rule that, after they were laid aside, the sanbenitos should be hung up in the churches, together with a record of the wearer's name inscribed and his sentence. To avoid the shame of this public display, descendants often sought to change their names, a practice the law soon checked. The precedent for the sanbenito was found in the covering our first parents wore to hide their nakedness, or in the sackcloth worn in the early Church as a mark of penance.

Auto de fe

The *auto de fe*, the final act in the procedure of the Inquisition, shows the relentlessness of this tribunal, and gave the spectators a foretaste of the solemnities of the day of judgment. There heretics, after being tried by the inquisitorial court, were exposed to public view, and received the first official notice of their sentence. The ceremonial took place on the public squares, where platforms and staging were erected at municipal expense, and such occasions were treated as public holidays. On the day appointed, the prisoners marched in procession, led by Dominicans and others bearing green and white crosses, and followed by the officials of the Holy Office. Arrived at the square, they were assigned seats on benches. A sermon was then preached and an oath taken from the people and also from the king, if present, to support the Inquisition. The sentences were then announced. Unrepentant heretics were turned over to the civil officers. Wearing benitos, inscribed with their name, they were conducted on asses to the brasero, or place of burning, which was usually outside the city limits, and consigned to the flames. The other heretics were then taken back to the prisons of the Inquisition. Inquisitorial agents were present at the burnings and made a record of them for the use of the religious tribunal.

The solemnities of the *auto de fe* were usually begun at 6 in the morning and often lasted into the afternoon. Theoretically, the tribunal did not pass the sentence of blood. The ancient custom of the Church and the canon law forbade such a decision. Its authority ceased with the abandonment – or, to use the technical expression, the relaxation – of the offender to the secular arm. By an old custom in passing sentence of incorrigible heresy, it even prayed the secular officer to avoid the spilling of blood and to exercise mercy. The prayer was an empty form. The state well understood its duty, and its failure to punish with death heretics convicted by the spiritual court was punishable with excommunication. It did not presume to review the case, to take new evidence or even to require a statement of the evidence on which the sentence of heresy was reached. The duty of the secular officer was ministerial, not judicial. The sentence of heresy was synonymous with burning at the stake. The Inquisition, however, did not stop with turning heretics over to the state, but, as even Vacandard admits, at times pronounced the sentence of burning. So honorable to the state and to religion were the autos de fe regarded that kings attended them and they were appointed to commemorate the marriage of princes or their recovery from sickness.

Ferdinand was in the habit of attending them. On the visit of Charles X to Valencia, 1528, public exhibition was given at which 13 were relaxed in person and 10 in effigy. Philip II's marriage, in 1560, to Isabella of Valois was celebrated by an auto in Toledo and, in 1564, when this sovereign was in Barcelona, a public exhibition was arranged in his honor, at which eight were sentenced to death. Such spectacles continued to be witnessed by royal personages till 1701, when Philip X set an example of better things by refusing to be present at one. The last case of an execution by the Spanish Inquisition was a schoolmaster, Cayetano Ripoll, July 26, 1826. His trial lasted nearly two years. He was accused of being a deist, and substituting in his school the words "Praise be to God" for "Ave Maria purissima." He died calmly on the gibbet after repeating the words, "I die reconciled to God and to man."

The Index

Not satisfied with putting heretical men out of the world, the Inquisition also directed its attention to noxious writings. At Seville, in 1490, Torquemada burnt a large number of Hebrew copies of the Bible, and a little later, at Salamanca, he burnt 6000 copies. Ten years later, 1502, Ferdinand and Isabella promulgated a law forbidding books being printed, imported and sold which did not have the license of a bishop or certain specified royal judges. All Lutheran writings were ordered by Adrian, in 1521, delivered up to the Inquisition. Thenceforth the Spanish tribunal proved itself a vigorous guardian of the purity of the press. The first formal Index, compiled by the University of Louvain, 1546, was approved by the inquisitor-general Valdes and the suprema, and ordered printed with a supplement. This was the first Index Expurgatorius printed in Spain. All copies of the Scriptures in Spanish were seized and burnt, and the ferocious law of 1558 ordered booksellers keeping or selling prohibited books punished with confiscation of goods or death. Strict inquisitorial supervision was had over all libraries in Spain down into the 19th century. Of the effect of this censorship upon Spanish culture, Dr. Lea says: "The intellectual development which in the 16th century promised to render Spanish literature and learning the most illustrious in Europe was stunted and starved into atrophy, the arts and sciences were neglected, and the character which Spain acquired among the nations was tersely expressed in the current saying that Africa began at the Pyrenees."

14,344 burnt alive

The "ghastly total" of the victims consigned by the Spanish Inquisition to the flames or other punishments has been differently stated. Precise tables of statistics are of modern creation, but that it was large is beyond question. The historian, Llorente, gives the following figures: From 1480–1498, the date of Torquemada's death, 8800 were burnt alive, 6500 in effigy and 90,004 subjected to other punishments. From 1499–1506, 1664 were burnt alive, 832 in effigy and 32,456 subjected to other punishments. From 1507–1517, during the term of Cardinal Ximines, 2536 were burnt alive, 1368 in effigy and 47,263 subjected to other penalties. This writer gives the grand totals up to 1524 as 14,344 burnt alive, 9372 in effigy and 195,937 condemned to other penalties or released as penitents. In 1524, an inscription was placed on the fortress of Triana Seville, running: "In the year 1481, under the pontificate of Sixtus IX and the rule of Ferdinand and Isabella, the Inquisition was begun here. Up to 1524, 20,000 heretics and more abjured their awful crime on this spot and nearly 1000 were burnt." From records still extant, the victims in Toledo before 1501 are found to have numbered 297 burnt alive and 600 in effigy, and 5400 condemned to other punishment or reconciled. The documents, however, are not preserved or, at any rate, not known from which a full estimate could be made. In any case the numbers included thousands of victims burnt alive and tens of thousands subjected to other punishments.

The rise of the Spanish Inquisition was contemporary with Spain's advance to a foremost place among the nations of Europe. After eight centuries, her territory was for the first time completely free from the government of the Mohammedan. The renown of her regiments was soon to be unequaled. Spanish ships opened the highways of the sea and returned from the New World freighted with its wealth. Spanish diplomacy was in the ascendant in Italy. But the decay of her vital forces her religious zeal did not check. Spain's Catholic orthodoxy was assured, but Spain placed herself outside the current of modern culture and progress. By her policy of religious seclusion and pride, she crushed independence of thought and virility of moral purpose. One by one, she lost her territorial acquisitions, from the Netherlands and Sicily to Cuba and the Philippines in the far Pacific. Heresy she consumed inside of her own precincts, but the paralysis of stagnation settled down upon her national life and institutions, and peoples professing Protestantism, which she still calls heresy, long since have taken her crown in the world of commerce and culture, invention and nautical enterprise. The present map of the world has faint traces of that empire on which it was the boast of the Spaniard of the 16th century that the sun never set. This reduction of territory and resources calls forth no spirit of denunciation. Nay, it attracts a sympathetic consideration which hopes for the renewed greatness of the land of Ferdinand and Isabella, through the introduction of that intellectual and religious freedom which has stirred the energies of other European peoples and kept them in the path of progress and new achievement.

Philip Scaff, The History of the Church

2. The martyrdoms

John Huss

Under the story of John Huss Bunyan wrote in his copy of Foxe's Book of Martyrs that he had with him during his own 12-year imprisonment:

Heare is John Hus that you may see,
Uesed in deed with all crulity;
But now leet us follow and look one him,
whear he is full field in deed to the brim.

Letter from Huss to two of his friends

Christianity has stayed faithful, with no pope – who is only a man, because it has Jesus Christ at its head. Christ is its guide. The life of grace is its heartbeat, from which flow the seven gifts of the Holy Spirit. It is to Christ, wretched though I am, that I flee, in the sure hope that he will guide me with his life and help. I trust that he will deliver me from my sins and from my existing wretched life and will give me the reward of infinite joy.

John Huss was a Bohemian by birth, and born in the village of Hussinetz, in about 1380. His parents gave him the best education they could bestow, and, having acquired a tolerable knowledge of the classics at a private school, he was then sent to Prague University, where he soon became conspicuous by his talents and industry.

Trithemius speaks of him as "a man of very great note for his judgement, subtlety, eloquence, and knowledge of the Scriptures." And the Jesuit Balbinus, who was certainly not inclined in his favor, says of him in his Epitome of the History of

Bohemia: "John Huss was more subtle than eloquent: but the modesty and severity of his manners; his unpolished, austere, and entirely blameless life; his pale, thin visage; his good nature, and his affability to all, even to the meanest people, were more persuasive than the greatest eloquence."

As pastor of the church of Bethlehem in Prague, and rector of the university, Huss soon became famous for his preaching and bold proclamation of the truth which quickly attracted the notice and excited the malignity of the Pope and his followers.

The principal reason which aroused Huss's indignation was a bull published by Pope John XXIII which promised remission of sins to everyone who joined his forces against Ladislaus, King of Naples. When the bull was published in Prague Huss did not refrain from preaching against it as repugnant to the spirit of the Christian faith. The Pope summoned Huss to Rome, and, upon his refusing to comply, excommunicated him, and forbade divine service to be performed in all the churches in Prague, except for one, so long as Huss remained in the city. To avoid disturbances, Huss moved to Hussinetz.

The teachings of the English reformer, Wycliffe, were eagerly received in Bohemia by many people, especially by John Huss and his friend and fellow- martyr, Jerome of Prague. The Pope summoned Huss to appear before the court at Rome to answer the accusations leveled against him about his preaching. Eventually three proctors appeared for Dr Huss before Cardinal Colonna: they pleaded an excuse for Huss's absence, and said they were ready to answer on his behalf. But the cardinal declared him contumacious, and, accordingly, excommunicated him. Notwithstanding such a severe decree, and an expulsion from his church in Prague, he moved again to Hussinetz, where he continued to promulgate the truth, both from the pulpit and with the pen.

In November 1414 a general council assembled at Constance in Germany to resolve the dispute between three people contesting for the papal throne: John, supported by the Italians; Gregory, supported by the French, and Benedict supported by the Spaniards. John Huss was summoned to appear before this council together with a certificate of safe conduct which said, "You shall let John Huss pass, stop, stay, and return freely, without any hindrance whatever." Notwithstanding the promise of the emperor to give him safe conduct to and from Constance, no attention was paid to the imperial pledge; but, according to the maxim of this same council, that "faith is not to be kept with heretics," when Huss entered the city he was arrested, and imprisoned in the palace.

While Huss was in prison the council acted like the inquisitors. They condemned all the teaching of Wycliffe and ordered his remains to be exhumed, and burned to ashes, which was carried out.

When Huss was brought before the council he was accused of twenty-six heresies. The council pronounced him a heretic condemning him to be burned as such, unless he recanted. Huss was then thrown into a filthy prison, where, during the day, he was so laded with chains that he could hardly move, and at night was fastened by his hands to a ring on the prison wall. Soon after Huss had been condemned four bishops and two lords were sent by the emperor to the prison, in order to prevail on Huss to recant. But Huss called God to witness, with tears in his eyes, that he was not conscious of having preached or written anything against God's truth, or against the faith of his orthodox church. The deputies then represented the great wisdom and authority of the council: to which Huss replied, "Let them send the meanest person of that council, who can convince me by argument from the word of God, and I will submit my judgement to him." The deputies, finding they could not make any impression on him, departed, greatly astonished at the strength of his resolve.

On 4th July Huss, for the last time, was brought before the council. After a long examination he was commanded to abjure, which, without hesitation, he refused to do. The Bishop of Lodi then preached a sermon concerning the destruction of heretics, from the text, "Let the body of sin be destroyed." The council then censured him for being obstinate and incorrigible, and ordained that he should be degraded from the priesthood, his books publicly burnt, and himself delivered to the secular powers.

Huss received the sentence without the slightest emotion; and then knelt down, lifted up his eyes towards heaven, exclaiming, with the magnanimity of a primitive martyr, "May thy infinite mercy, O my God! pardon this injustice of mine enemies. Thou knowest the injustice of my accusations: how deformed with crimes I have been represented; how I have been oppressed with worthless witnesses, and a false condemnation; yet, O my God! let that mercy of thine, which no tongue can express, prevail with thee not to avenge my wrongs."

But these excellent sentences were received as so many expressions of treason, and only tended to inflame his adversaries. Accordingly, the bishops appointed by the council stripped him of his priestly garments, degraded him, and put a paper miter on his head, on which they painted three devils, with this inscription: "Heresiarch" [Heretic]. This mockery was received by the martyr with an air of unconcern, and seemed to give him dignity rather thank disgrace. A serenity appeared in his looks, which indicated that his soul was approaching the realms of everlasting happiness; and when the bishop urged him to recant, he turned to the people and addressed them thus."These lords and bishops do counsel me that I should confess before you all that I have erred; which thing, if it might be done with the infamy and reproach of many only, they might, peradventure, easily persuade me to do; but now I am in the sight of the Lord my God, without whose great displeasure I could not do that which they require. For I well know that I never taught any of those things which they have falsely accused me of, but I have always preached, taught, written, and thought contrary thereunto. Should I by this my example trouble so many consciences, endued with the most certain knowledge of the Scriptures and of the gospel of our Lord Jesus Christ? I will never do it, neither commit any such offence, that I should seem to esteem this vile carcass appointed unto death more than their health and salvation." At this most godly word he was forced again to hear that he did obstinately persevere in his pernicious errors.

After the ceremony of degradation the bishops delivered him to the emperor, who handed him over to the Duke of Bavaria. His books were burnt at the gates of the church; and on July 6th he was led to the suburbs of Constance to be burnt alive.

Having reached the place of execution, he fell on his knees, sung several portions from the Psalms, and looked steadfastly towards heaven, saying, "Into thy hands, O Lord! do I commit my spirit: thou hast redeemed me, O most good and faithful God."

As soon as the chain was put around him at the stake, he said, with a smiling countenance, "My Lord Jesus Christ was bound with a harder chain than this for my sake: why, then, should I be ashamed of this old rusty one?" Then he prayed: "Lord Jesus Christ, it is for the sake of the gospel and the preaching of the word that I patiently undergo this ignominious death."

When the faggots were piled around him, the Duke of Bavaria was officious as to desire him to abjure. "No," he said, "I never preached any doctrine of an evil tendency; and what I taught with my lips I now seal with my blood." He then said to the executioner, "You are now going to burn a goose (the meaning of Huss's name in Bohemian), but in a century you will have a swan whom you can neither roast nor boil." If this were spoken in prophecy, he must have alluded to Martin Luther, who came about a hundred years after him, and had a swan for his arms.

As soon as the faggots were lighted, the martyr sang a hymn, with so cheerful a voice, that he was heard above the cracklings of the fire and the noise of the multitude. At length his voice was interrupted by the flames, which soon put an end to his existence. His ashes were collected, and, by order of the council, thrown into the Rhine, lest his adherents should honor them as relics.

John Foxe, The Book of Martyrs, revised with notes and an appendix by W. Bramley-Moore, London, 1869, pp 152-159

A PAPAL APOLOGY

On Friday, 17 December, 1999, Pope John Paul II expressed his deep regret over the fate of Czech religious reformer Jan Hus, who was burnt at the stake in 1415 for heresy. He said, "Today, on the eve of the Great Jubilee, I feel the need to express deep regret for the cruel death inflicted on Jan Hus and for the consequent wound of conflict and division which was thus imposed on the minds and hearts of the Bohemian people."

Pope John Paul II

JEROME OF PRAGUE

This hero in the cause of truth was born and educated at Prague, where he soon became distinguished for his learning and eloquence. Having completed his studies, he traveled over a great part of Europe, and visited many of the seats of learning, particularly the universities of Paris, Heidelberg, Cologne, and Oxford. At Oxford he became acquainted with the works of Wycliffe, and being a person of uncommon application, he translated many of them into his own language, having made himself master of English. On his return to Prague, Jerome openly professed the doctrines of Wycliffe, and finding that they had made considerable progress in Bohemia, from the industry and zeal of Huss, he became his assistant in the work of reformation.

On April 4th, 1415, Jerome went to Constance, about three months before Huss's death. He entered the town privately, and consulting with some of the leaders of his party, was convinced that he could render his friend no service. The council at Constance wanted to seize Jerome, so he left there for Bohemia, but at Hirsaw, on officer under the command of the Duke of Sultzbach seized Huss. The Duke of Sultzbach immediately wrote to the council in Constance who told him to send his prisoner to them. The Duke of Sultzbach then put Huss in iron and set off for Constance. On his way he met the Elector Palatine who had a long chain fastened to Jerome, by which he was then pulled along, like a wild beast, to the cloister, where, after some insults and examinations, he was taken to a tower and tied to a block, with his legs in stocks. He remained like this for eleven days and nights until he became so dangerously ill that he had to be untied. He remained in prison until the martyrdom of his friend Huss. Then he was brought out and threatened with torture, and, in a moment of weakness, he forgot his resolution, abjured his doctrines, and confessed that Huss deserved his fate, and that both he and Wycliffe were heretics. As a result of this his chains were taken off and his harsh treatment was suspended. He was kept in prison, but hoped to be released every day. But his enemies suspected his sincerity and proposed another form of recantation to him. He refused to answer this, except in public, and was accordingly brought before the council, when, to the astonishment of his hearers he renounced his recantation and asked permission to plead his own cause. This was refused and he vented his indignation thus.

"What barbarity is this? For 340 days have I been confined in a variety of prisons. The cause I now plead is not my own, it is the cause of men: it is the cause of Christians: it is a cause which is to affect the rights of posterity, however the experiment is to be made in my person."

At the end of Jerome's trial Jerome received the same sentence as had been passed on Huss, and was, delivered over the secular power; but, being a layman, had not to undergo the ceremony of degradation. They had, however, prepared for him a paper cap painted with red devils, which, being put on his head, he said, "Our Lord Jesus Christ, when he suffered death for me, a most miserable sinner, did wear a crown of thorns upon his head; and I, for his sake, will wear this cap."

They delayed his execution for two days, hoping that he would recant; during which time the Cardinal of Florence used all his powers to win him over, but all proved ineffective. Jerome had resolved to seal his teaching with his blood.

On his way to the place of execution he sang several hymns; and on arriving at the place where Huss had suffered, the knelt down and prayed fervently. He embraced the stake with great cheerfulness; and when the executioner went behind him to set fire to the faggots, he said, "Come here and kindle it before my eyes; for had I been afraid of it, I would not have come here, having had so many opportunities to escape." When the flames enveloped him he sang a hymn; and the last words he was heard to say were: "Hanc animam in flammis affero, Christe, tibi!" ("This soul in flames I offer, Christ, to thee!')

The contemporary writers – namely, Eneas Sylvius, afterwards Pope Pius II; Theodoric de Niem, then on the council; Theodoric Urie, and Poggius, the Florentine, who was an eyewitness to Jerome's end – all agree in extolling the heroic constancy and firmness with which he underwent his dreadful death. Poggius, after giving an account of his death, in a letter to Leonardo of Arezzo, added, in a kind of rapture, "Thus died this man, eminent beyond all belief. Oh, glorious man, truly worthy of immortal memory! I was an eyewitness of his end. Whether he was guilty of insincerity or obstinacy I know not; but his death was most philosophical. Mutius did not with so constant resolution endure the burning of one member as he did the burning of his whole body, nor did Socrates more cheerfully drink of the poisonous draught, than he embraced the stake."

John Foxe, The Book of Martyrs, revised with notes and an appendix by W. Bramley-Moore, London, 1869, pp 159-65

Persecution in Bohemia

Emperor Ferdinand instituted a high court of reformers, upon the plan of the Inquisition, with this difference, that the reformers were to remove from place to place, and always to be attended by a body of troops. The greater part of this court consisted of Jesuits, from whose decisions there was no appeal. This bloody court, attended by its military guard, made the tour of Bohemia, and seldom examined or saw a prisoner; but suffered the soldiers to murder the Protestants as they pleased, and then to report the matter in their own fashion.

Not long afterwards a secret order was issued by the emperor for apprehending all noblemen and gentlemen who had been principally concerned in supporting the Protestant cause, and in nominating Frederick, Elector Palatine of the Rhine, to be King of Bohemia. Fifty of these were suddenly seized in one night, and brought to the castle of Prague; while the estates of those who were absent were confiscated, themselves made outlaws, and their names fixed upon a gallows as a mark of public ignominy.

The high court of the reformers later tried those who had been apprehended, and two apostate Protestants were appointed to examine them. As none of the prisoners would renounce their faith, or acknowledge themselves in error, they were all pronounced guilty; the sentence was, however, referred to the emperor. When that monarch had read their names, and the accusations against them, he passed judgment on all, but in a different manner; his sentences being of our kinds: death, banishment, imprisonment for life, and imprisonment during pleasure.

Twenty of them being ordered for execution. The morning of the execution having arrived, a cannon was fired as a signal to bring the prisoners from the castle to the principal market-place, in which scaffolds were erected, and a body of troops drawn up to attend. The prisoners left the castle, and passed with dignity the cheerfulness through soldiers, Jesuits, priests, executioners, and a prodigious concourse of people assembled to see the exit of these martyrs. The following are among the principal who suffered on this occasion.

Lord Schilik

Lord Schilik, a nobleman about 50 years old. On being told that he was to be quartered, and his parts scattered in different places, he smiled, and said, "The loss of a sepulcher is but a trifling consideration." A gentleman who stood by, crying, "Courage, my lord." Lord Schilik replied, "I possess the favor of God, which is sufficient to inspire anyone with courage: the fear of death does not trouble me. I have faced him in fields of battle to oppose Antichrist." After repeating a short prayer, he told the executioner he was ready, who cut off his right hand and head, and then quartered him. His hand and head were placed on the high tower of Prague, and his quarters distributed in different parts of the city.

Viscount Winceslaus

Another victim was Viscount Winceslaus. This venerable 70-year-old nobleman was noted equally for his piety, learning and hospitality. He was so little affected by the loss of worldly riches, that on his house being broken open, his property seized, and his estates confiscated, he only said, with great composure, "The Lord hath given, and the Lord hath taken away." As he approached the block, he stroked his grey beard, and said, "Venerable hairs, the greater honor now attends you; a crown of martyrdom is your portion." Then laying down his head, it was severed from his body, and afterwards placed upon a pole in a conspicuous part of the town.

Sir Gasper Kaplitz

This 86-year-old nobleman, as he came to the place of execution, addressed the principal officer thus: "Behold a miserable ancient man, who hath often entreated God to take him out of this wicked world, but could not till now obtain his desire; for God reserved me till these years to be a spectacle to the world, and a sacrifice to himself; therefore God's will be done."

An officer told him, that out of consideration of his great age, if he would only ask pardon, he would immediately receive it. "Ask pardon!" he exclaimed. "I will ask pardon from God, whom I have frequently offended, but not of the emperor, whom I never offended. No. I die innocent, with a clear conscience. I would not be separated from my noble companions in the faith." So saying, he cheerfully resigned his neck to the block.

Simon Sussickey

Simon Sussickey, not being of noble birth, was ordered to be hanged. He appeared impatient to go, saying, "Every moment delays me from entering the kingdom of Christ."

Nathaniel Wodnianskey

This gentleman was hanged for having supported the Protestant cause. At the gallows the Jesuits used all their persuasions to make him renounce his faith, but without effect. His own son then approached the gallows, and said, "Sir, if life should be offered to you on condition of apostasy, I entreat you to remember Christ."

To this the father replied, "It is very acceptable, my son, to be exhorted to constancy by you, but suspect me not; rather endeavor to confirm in their faith your brothers, sisters, and children, and teach them to imitate my constancy." He had no sooner concluded these words than he received his fate with great fortitude.

John Foxe, The Book of Martyrs, revised with notes and an appendix by W. Bramley-Moore, London, 1869, pp 147-51

Great Britain and Ireland, before Queen Mary

A brief history

Gildas, the most ancient British writer extant, who lived about the time that the Saxons left the island of Great Britain, has drawn a most shocking instance of the barbarity of those people. The Saxons, on their arrival, being heathens like the Scots and Picts, destroyed the churches and murdered the clergy wherever they came: but they could not destroy Christianity, for those who would not submit to the Saxon yoke, went and resided beyond the Severn. Neither have we the names of those Christian sufferers transmitted to us, especially those of the clergy. The most dreadful instance of barbarity under the Saxon government, was the massacre of the monks of Bangor, A.D. 586. These monks were in all respects different from those men who bear the same name at present. In the eighth century, the Danes, a roving crew of barbarians, landed in different parts of Britain, both in England and Scotland. At first they were repulsed, but in A.D. 857, a party of them landed somewhere near Southampton, and not only robbed the people but burned down the churches, and murdered the clergy. In A.D. 868, these barbarians penetrated into the center of England, and took up their quarters at Nottingham; but the English, under their king, Ethelred, drove them from their posts, and obliged them to retire to Northumberland. In 870, another body of these barbarians landed at Norfolk, and engaged in battle with the English at Hertford. Victory declared in favor of the pagans, who took Edmund, king of the East Angles, prisoner, and after treating him with a thousand indignities, transfixed his body with arrows, and then beheaded him.

In Fifeshire, in Scotland, they burned many of the churches, and among the rest that belonging to the Culdees, at St. Andrews. The piety of these men made them objects of abhorrence to the Danes, who, wherever they went singled out the Christian priests for destruction, of whom no less than two hundred were massacred in Scotland. It was much the same in that part of Ireland now called Leinster, there the Danes murdered and burned the priests alive in their own churches; they carried destruction along with them wherever they went, sparing neither age nor sex, but the clergy were the most obnoxious to them, because they ridiculed their idolatry, and persuaded their people to have nothing to do with them. In the reign of Edward III the Church of England was extremely corrupted with errors and superstition; and the light of the Gospel of Christ was greatly eclipsed and darkened with human inventions, burthensome ceremonies and gross idolatry.

The followers of Wickliffe, then called Lollards, were become extremely numerous, and the clergy were so vexed to see them increase; whatever power or influence they might have to molest them in an underhand manner, they had no authority by law to put them to death. However, the clergy embraced the favorable opportunity, and prevailed upon the king to suffer a bill to be brought into parliament, by which all Lollards who remained obstinate, should be delivered over to the secular power, and burnt as heretics. This act was the first in Britain for the burning of people for their religious sentiments; it passed in the year 1401, and was soon after put into execution.1400–1529

Lord Cobham

Soon after this, Sir John Oldcastle, Lord Cobham, in consequence of his attachment to the doctrines of Wickliffe, was accused of heresy, and being condemned to be hanged and burnt, was accordingly executed in Lincoln's Inn Fields, A.D. 1419. In his written defense Lord Cobham said: "As for images, I understand that they be not of belief, but that they were ordained since the belief of Christ was given by sufferance of the Church, to represent and bring to mind the passion of our Lord Jesus Christ, and martyrdom and good living of other saints: and that whoso it be, that doth the worship to dead images that is due to God, or putteth such hope or trust in help of them, as he should do to God, or hath affection in one more than in another, he doth in that, the greatest sin of idol worship. Also I suppose this fully, that every man in this earth is a pilgrim toward bliss, or toward pain; and that he that knoweth not, we will not know, we keep the holy commandments of God in his living here (albeit that he go on pilgrimages to all the world, and he die so), he shall be damned: he that knoweth the holy commandments of God, and keepeth them to his end, he shall be saved, though he never in his life go on pilgrimage, as men now use, to Canterbury, or to Rome, or to any other place." Upon the day appointed, Lord Cobham was brought out of the Tower with his arms bound behind him, having a very cheerful countenance. Then was he laid upon a hurdle, as though he had been a most heinous traitor to the crown, and so drawn forth into St. Giles's field. As he was come to the place of execution, and was taken from the hurdle, he fell down devoutly upon his knees, desiring Almighty God to forgive his enemies. Then stood he up and beheld the multitude, exhorting them in most godly manner to follow the laws of God written in the Scriptures, and to beware of such teachers as they see contrary to Christ in their conversation and living. Then was he hanged up by the middle in chains of iron, and so consumed alive in the fire, praising the name of God, so long as his life lasted; the people, there present, showing great dolor. And this was done A.D. 1418. How the priests that time fared, blasphemed, and accursed, requiring the people not to pray for him, but to judge him damned in hell, for that he departed not in the obedience of their pope, it were too long to write. Thus resteth this valiant Christian knight, Sir John Oldcastle, under the altar of God, which is Jesus Christ, among that godly company, who, in the kingdom of patience, suffered great tribulation with the death of their bodies, for His faithful word and testimony.

Thomas Granter

In August, 1473, one Thomas Granter was apprehended in London; he was accused of professing the doctrines of Wickliffe, for which he was condemned as an obstinate heretic. This pious man, being brought to the sheriff's house, on the morning of the day appointed for his execution, desired a little refreshment, and having ate some, he said to the people present, "I eat now a very good meal, for I have a strange conflict to engage with before I go to supper"; and having eaten, he returned thanks to God for the bounties of His all-gracious providence, requesting that he might be instantly led to the place of execution, to bear testimony to the truth of those principles which he had professed. Accordingly he was chained to a stake on Tower-hill, where he was burnt alive, professing the truth with his last breath.

Badram: to the stake at Norwich

In the year 1499, one Badram, a pious man, was brought before the bishop of Norwich, having been accused by some of the priests, with holding the doctrines of Wickliffe. He confessed he did believe everything that was objected against him. For this, he was condemned as an obstinate heretic, and a warrant was granted for his execution; accordingly he was brought to the stake at Norwich, where he suffered with great constancy.

Burnt alive

In 1506, one William Tilfrey, a pious man, was burnt alive at Amersham, in a close called Stoneyprat, and at the same time, his daughter, Joan Clarke, a married women, was obliged to light the fagots that were to burn her father.

Convicted of being a Lollard

This year also one Father Roberts, a priest, was convicted of being a Lollard before the bishop of Lincoln, and burnt alive at Buckingham.

Thomas Norris

In 1507 one Thomas Norris was burnt alive for the testimony of the truth of the Gospel, at Norwich. This man was a poor, inoffensive, harmless person, but his parish priest conversing with him one day, conjectured he was a Lollard. In consequence of this supposition he gave information to the bishop, and Norris was apprehended.

Lawrence Guale, burnt alive at Salisbury

In 1508, one Lawrence Guale, who had been kept in prison two years, was burnt alive at Salisbury, for denying the real presence in the Sacrament. It appeared that this man kept a shop in Salisbury, and entertained some Lollards in his house; for which he was informed against to the bishop; but he abode by his first testimony, and was condemned to suffer as a heretic.

William Succling and John Bannister

October 18, 1511, William Succling and John Bannister, who had formerly recanted, returned again to the profession of the faith, and were burnt alive in Smithfield.

John Brown

In the year 1517, one John Brown (who had recanted before in the reign of Henry VII and borne a fagot round St. Paul's,) was condemned by Dr. Wonhaman, archbishop of Canterbury, and burnt alive at Ashford. Before he was chained to the stake, the archbishop Wonhaman, and Yester, bishop of Rochester, caused his feet to be burnt in a fire until all the flesh came off, even to the bones. This was done in order to make him again recant, but he persisted in his attachment to the truth to the last.

John Stilincen: "believed the opinion of Wickliffe"

September 24, 1518, John Stilincen, who had before recanted, was apprehended, brought before Richard Fitz-James, bishop of London, and on the twenty-fifth of October was condemned as a heretic. He was chained to the stake in Smithfield amidst a vast crowd of spectators, and sealed his testimony to the truth with his blood. He declared that he was a Lollard, and that he had always believed the opinions of Wickliffe; and although he had been weak enough to recant his opinions, yet he was now willing to convince the world that he was ready to die for the truth.

Thomas Mann and Robert Celin

In the year 1519, Thomas Mann was burnt in London, as was one Robert Celin, a plain, honest man for speaking against image worship and pilgrimages.

James Brewster

Much about this time, was executed in Smithfield, in London, James Brewster, a native of Colchester. His sentiments were the same as the rest of the Lollards, or those who followed the doctrines of Wickliffe; but notwithstanding the innocence of his life, and the regularity of his manners, he was obliged to submit to papal revenge.

Christopher the shoemaker

During this year, one Christopher, a shoemaker, was burnt alive at Newbury, in Berkshire, for denying those popish articles which we have already mentioned. This man had gotten some books in English, which were sufficient to render him obnoxious to the Romish clergy.

Robert Silks

Robert Silks, who had been condemned in the bishop's court as a heretic, made his escape out of prison, but was taken two years afterward, and brought back to Coventry, where he was burnt alive. The sheriffs always seized the goods of the martyrs for their own use, so that their wives and children were left to starve.

Foxe's Book of Martyrs, Edited by William Byron Forbush, chapter 14

SCOTLAND

Heresy also penetrated into Scotland, James Resby, one of Wyclif's poor priests, being burnt at Perth, 1407, and another at Glasgow, 1422. In 1488, a Bohemian student at St. Andrews, Paul Craw, suffered the same penalty for heresy.639 The Scotch parliament of 1425 enjoined bishops to make search for heretics and Lollards, and in 1416 every master of arts at St. Andrews was obliged to take an oath to defend the Church against them.

Between 1450–1517, Lollardy was almost wholly restricted to the rural districts, and little mention is made of it in contemporary records. At Amersham, one of its centers, four were tried in 1462, and some suffered death, as William Barlowe in 1466, and John Goose a few years later. In 1507, three were burnt there, including William Tylsworth, the leading man of the congregation. At the crucial moment he was deserted by the members, and sixty of them joined in carrying fagots for his burning. This time of recantation continued to be known in the district as the Great Abjuration. The first woman to suffer martyrdom in England, Joan Broughton, was burnt at Smithfield, 1494, as was also her daughter, Lady Young. Nine Lollards made public penance at Coventry, 1486, but, as late as 1519, six men and one woman suffered death there. Foxe also mentions William Sweeting and John Brewster as

being burnt at Smithfield, 1511, and John Brown at Ashford the same year. How extensively Wyclif's views continued to be secretly held and his writings read is a matter of conjecture. Not till 1559 was the legislation directed against Lollardy repealed.
Philip Scaff, The History of the Church

Persecutions in Scotland during King Henry VIII's reign

Patrick Hamilton

Like as there was no place, either of Germany, Italy, or France, wherein there were not some branches sprung out of that most fruitful root of Luther; so likewise was not this isle of Britain without his fruit and branches. Amongst whom was Patrick Hamilton, a Scotchman born of high and noble stock, and of the king's blood, of excellent towardness, twenty-three years of age, called abbot of Ferne. Coming out of his country with three companions to seek godly learning, he went to the University of Marburg in Germany, which university was then newly erected by Philip, Landgrave of Hesse. During his residence here, he became intimately acquainted with those eminent lights of the Gospel, Martin Luther and Philip Melancthon; from whose writings and doctrines he strongly attached himself to the Protestant religion. The archbishop of St. Andrews (who was a rigid papist) learning of Mr. Hamilton's proceedings, caused him to be seized, and being brought before him, after a short examination relative to his religious principles, he committed him a prisoner to the castle, at the same time ordering him to be confined in the most loathsome part of the prison. The next morning Mr. Hamilton was brought before the bishop, and several others, for examination, when the principal articles exhibited against him were, his publicly disapproving of pilgrimages, purgatory, prayers to saints, for the dead, etc. These articles Mr. Hamilton acknowledged to be true, in consequence of which he was immediately condemned to be burnt; and that his condemnation might have the greater authority, they caused it to be subscribed by all those of any note who were present, and to make the number as considerable as possible, even admitted the subscription of boys who were sons of the nobility. So anxious was this bigoted and persecuting prelate for the destruction of Mr. Hamilton, that he ordered his sentence to be put in execution on the afternoon of the very day it was pronounced. He was accordingly led to the place appointed for the horrid tragedy, and was attended by a prodigious number of spectators.

The greatest part of the multitude would not believe it was intended he should be put to death, but that it was only done to frighten him, and thereby bring him over to embrace the principles of the Romish religion. When he arrived at the stake, he kneeled down, and, for some time prayed with great fervency. After this he was fastened to the stake, and the fagots placed round him. A quantity of gunpowder having been placed under his arms was first set on fire which scorched his left hand and one side of his face, but did no material injury, neither did it communicate with the fagots. In consequence of this, more powder and combustible matter were brought, which being set on fire took effect, and the fagots being kindled, he called out, with an audible voice: "Lord Jesus, receive my spirit! How long shall darkness overwhelm this realm? And how long wilt Thou suffer the tyranny of these men?"

The fire burning slow put him to great torment; but he bore it with Christian magnanimity. What gave him the greatest pain was, the clamor of some wicked men set on by the friars, who frequently cried, "Turn, thou heretic; call upon our Lady; say, Salve Regina, etc."

To whom he replied, "Depart from me, and trouble me not, ye messengers of Satan."

One Campbell, a friar, who was the ringleader, still continuing to interrupt him by opprobrious language; he said to him, "Wicked man, God forgive thee." After which, being prevented from further speech by the violence of the smoke, and the rapidity of the flames, he resigned up his soul into the hands of Him who gave it.

This steadfast believer in Christ suffered martyrdom in the year 1527.

Henry Forest

One Henry Forest, a young inoffensive Benedictine, being charged with speaking respectfully of the above Patrick Hamilton, was thrown into prison; and, in confessing himself to a friar, owned that he thought Hamilton a good man; and that the articles for which he was sentenced to die, might be defended. This being revealed by the friar, it was received as evidence; and the poor Benedictine was sentenced to be burnt. Whilst consultation was held, with regard to the manner of his execution, John Lindsay, one of the archbishop's gentlemen, offered his advice, to burn Friar Forest in some cellar; "for," said he, "the smoke of Patrick Hamilton hath infected all those on whom it blew."

This advice was taken, and the poor victim was rather suffocated, than burnt.

David Stratton and Norman Gourlay

The next who fell victims for professing the truth of the Gospel, were David Stratton and Norman Gourlay. When they arrived at the fatal spot, they both kneeled down, and prayed for some time with great fervency. They then arose, when Stratton, addressing himself to the spectators, exhorted them to lay aside their superstitious and idolatrous notions, and employ their time in seeking the true light of the Gospel. He would have said more, but was prevented by the officers who attended. Their sentence was then put into execution, and they cheerfully resigned up their souls to that God who gave them, hoping, through the merits of the great Redeemer, for a glorious resurrection to life immortal. They suffered in the year 1534.

Thomas Forret; Killor and Beverage, two blacksmiths; Duncan Simson, a priest; and Robert Forrester, a gentleman

The martyrdoms of the two before-mentioned persons, were soon followed by that of Mr. Thomas Forret, who, for a considerable time, had been dean of the Romish Church; Killor and Beverage, two blacksmiths; Duncan Simson, a priest; and Robert Forrester, a gentleman. They were all burnt together, on the Castle-hill at Edinburgh, the last day of February, 1538.

Jerome Russell and Alexander Kennedy

The year following the martyrdoms of the before-mentioned persons, viz. 1539, two others were apprehended on a suspicion of heresy; namely, Jerome Russell and Alexander Kennedy, a youth about eighteen years of age. These two persons, after being some time confined in prison, were brought before the archbishop for examination. In the course of which Russell, being a very sensible man, reasoned learnedly against his accusers; while they in return made use of very opprobrious language. The examination being over, and both of them deemed heretics, the archbishop pronounced the dreadful sentence of death, and they were immediately delivered over to the secular power in order for execution. The next day they were led to the place appointed for them to suffer; in their way to which, Russell, seeing his fellow-sufferer have the appearance of timidity in his countenance, thus addressed him: "Brother, fear not; greater is He that is in us, than He that is in the world. The pain that we are to suffer is short, and shall be light; but our joy and consolation shall never have an end. Let us, therefore, strive to enter into our Master and Savior's joy, by the same straight way which He hath taken before us. Death cannot hurt us, for it is already destroyed by Him, for whose sake we are now going to suffer."

When they arrived at the fatal spot, they both kneeled down and prayed for some time; after which being fastened to the stake, and the fagots lighted, they cheerfully resigned their souls into the hands of Him who gave them, in full hopes of an everlasting reward in the heavenly mansions.

George Wishart

An Account of the Life, Sufferings, and Death of Mr. George Wishart, Who Was Strangled and Afterward Burned, in Scotland, for Professing the Truth of the Gospel

About the year of our Lord 1543, there was, in the University of Cambridge, one Master George Wishart, commonly called Master George of Benet's College, a man of tall stature, polled-headed, and on the same a round French cap of the best; judged to be of melancholy complexion by his physiognomy, black-haired, long-bearded, comely of personage, well spoken after his country of Scotland, courteous, lowly, lovely, glad to teach, desirous to learn, and well traveled; having on him for his clothing a frieze gown to the shoes, a black millian fustian doublet, and plain black hosen, coarse new canvas for his shirts, and white falling bands and cuffs at his hands.

He was a man modest, temperate, fearing God, hating covetousness; for his charity had never end, night, noon, nor day; he forbare one meal in three, one day in four for the most part, except something to comfort nature. He lay hard upon a puff of straw and coarse, new canvas sheets, which, when he changed, he gave away. He had commonly by his bedside a tub of water, in the which (his people being in bed, the candle put out and all quiet) he used to bathe himself. He loved me tenderly, and I him. He taught with great modesty and gravity, so that some of his people thought him severe, and would have slain him; but the Lord was his defense. And he, after due correction for their malice, by good exhortation amended them and went his way. Oh, that the Lord had left him to me, his poor boy, that he might have finished what he had begun! for he went into Scotland with divers of the nobility, that came for a treaty to King Henry.

In 1543, the archbishop of St. Andrews made a visitation into various parts of his diocese, where several persons were informed against at Perth for heresy. Among those the following were condemned to die, viz. William Anderson, Robert Lamb, James Finlayson, James Hunter, James Raveleson, and Helen Stark.

The accusations laid against these respective persons were as follow: The four first were accused of having hung up the image of St. Francis, nailing ram's horns on his head, and fastening a cow's tail to his rump; but the principal matter on which they were condemned was having regaled themselves with a goose on fast day. James Reveleson was accused of having ornamented his house with the three crowned diadem of Peter, carved in wood, which the archbishop conceived to be done in mockery to his cardinal's cap. Helen Stark was accused of not having accustomed herself to pray to the Virgin Mary, more especially during the time she was in childbed. On these respective accusations they were all found guilty, and immediately received sentence of death; the four men, for eating the goose, to be hanged; James Raveleson to be burnt; and the woman, with her sucking infant, to be put into a sack and drowned. The four men, with the woman and the child, suffered at the same time, but James Raveleson was not executed until some days after. The martyrs were carried by a great band of armed men (for they feared rebellion in the town except they had their men of war) to the place of execution, which was common to all thieves, and that to make their cause appear more odious to the people. Every one comforting another, and assuring themselves that they should sup together in the Kingdom of Heaven that night, they commended themselves to God, and died constantly in the Lord.

The woman desired earnestly to die with her husband, but she was not suffered; yet, following him to the place of execution, she gave him comfort, exhorting him to perseverance and patience for Christ's sake, and, parting from him with a kiss, said, "Husband, rejoice, for we have lived together many joyful days; but this day, in which we must die, ought to be most joyful unto us both, because we must have joy forever; therefore I will not bid you good night, for we shall suddenly meet with joy in the Kingdom of Heaven." The woman, after that, was taken to a place to be drowned, and albeit she had a child sucking on her breast, yet this moved nothing in the unmerciful hearts of the enemies. So, after she had commended her children to the neighbors of the town for God's sake, and the sucking bairn was given to the nurse, she sealed up the truth by her death.

Being desirous of propagating the true Gospel in his own country George Wishart left Cambridge in 1544, and on his arrival in Scotland he first preached at Montrose, and afterwards at Dundee. In this last place he made a public exposition of the Epistle to the Romans, which he went through with such grace and freedom, as greatly alarmed the papists. In consequence of this, (at the instigation of Cardinal Beaton, the archbishop of St. Andrews) one Robert Miln, a principal man at Dundee, went to the church where Wishart preached, and in the middle of his discourse publicly told him not to trouble the town any more, for he was determined not to suffer it.

This sudden rebuff greatly surprised Wishart, who, after a short pause, looking sorrowfully on the speaker and the audience, said: "God is my witness, that I never minded your trouble but your comfort; yea, your trouble is more grievous to me than it is to yourselves: but I am assured to refuse God's Word, and to chase from you His messenger, shall not preserve you from trouble, but shall bring you into it: for God shall send you ministers that shall fear neither burning nor banishment. I have offered you the Word of salvation. With the hazard of my life I have remained among you; now you yourselves refuse me; and I must leave my innocence to be declared by my God. If it be long prosperous with you, I am not lede by the Spirit of truth; but if unlooked-for troubles come upon you, acknowledge the cause and turn to God, who is gracious and merciful. But if you turn not at the first warning, He will visit you with fire and sword." At the close of this speech he left the pulpit, and retired. After this he went into the west of Scotland, where he preached God's Word, which was gladly received by many.

A short time after this Mr. Wishart received intelligence that the plague had broken out in Dundee. It began four days after he was prohibited from preaching there, and raged so extremely that it was almost beyond credit how many died in the space of twenty-four hours. This being related to him, he, notwithstanding the importunity of his friends to detain him, determined to go there, saying: "They are now in troubles, and need comfort. Perhaps this hand of God will make them now to magnify and reverence the Word of God, which before they lightly esteemed."

Here he was with joy received by the godly. He chose the east gate for the place of his preaching; so that the healthy were within, and the sick without the gate. He took his text from these words, "He sent His word and healed them," etc. In this sermon he chiefly dwelt upon the advantage and comfort of God's Word, the judgments that ensue upon the contempt or rejection of it, the freedom of God's grace to all His people, and the happiness of those of His elect, whom He takes to Himself out of this miserable world. The hearts of his hearers were so raised by the divine force of this discourse, as not to regard death, but to judge them the more happy who should then be called, not knowing whether he should have such comfort again with them. After this the plague abated; though, in the midst of it, Wishart constantly visited those that lay in the greatest extremity, and comforted them by his exhortations. When he took his leave of the people of Dundee, he said that God had almost put an end to that plague, and that he was now called to another place. He went from thence to Montrose; where he sometimes preached, but he spent most of his time in private meditation and prayer.

It is said that before he left Dundee, and while he was engaged in the labors of love to the bodies as well as to the souls of those poor afflicted people, Cardinal Beaton engaged a desperate popish priest, called John Weighton, to kill him; the attempt to execute which was as follows: one day, after Wishart had finished his sermon, and the people departed, a priest stood waiting at the bottom of the stairs, with a naked dagger in his hand under his gown. But Mr. Wishart, having a sharp, piercing eye, and seeing the priest as he came from the pulpit, said to him, "My friend, what would you have?" and immediately clapping his hand upon the dagger, took it from him. The priest being terrified, fell to his knees, confessed his intention, and craved pardon. A noise was hereupon raised, and it coming to the ears of those who were sick, they cried, "Deliver the traitor to us, we will take him by force"; and they burst in at the gate. But Wishart, taking the priest in his arms, said, "Whatsoever hurts him shall hurt me; for he hath done me no mischief, but much good, by teaching more heedfulness for the time to come." By this conduct he appeased the people and saved the life of the wicked priest.

Soon after his return to Montrose, the cardinal again conspired his death, causing a letter to be sent him as if it had been from his familiar friend, the laird of Kennier, in which it was desired with all possible speed to come to him, as he was taken with a sudden sickness. In the meantime the cardinal had provided sixty men armed to lie in wait within a mile and a half of Montrose, in order to murder him as he passed that way. The letter came to Wishart's hand by a boy, who also brought him a horse for the journey. Wishart, accompanied by some honest men, his friends, set forward; but something particular striking his mind by the way, he returned, which they wondering at, asked him the cause; to whom he said, "I will not go; I am forbidden of God; I am assured there is treason. Let some of you go to yonder place, and tell me what you find." Which doing, they made the discovery; and hastily returning, they told Mr. Wishart; whereupon he said, "I know I shall end my life by that bloodthirsty man's hands, but it will not be in this manner."

A short time after this he left Montrose, and proceeded to Edinburgh, in order to propagate the Gospel in that city. By the way he lodged with a faithful brother, called James Watson of Inner-Goury. In the middle of the night he got up, and went into the yard, which two men hearing they privately followed him. While in the yard, he fell on his knees, and prayed for some time with the greatest fervency, after which he arose, and returned to his bed. Those who attended him, appearing as though they were ignorant of all, came and asked him where he had been. But he would not answer them. The next day they importuned him to tell them, saying "Be plain with us, for we heard your mourning, and saw your gestures."

On this he with a dejected countenance, said, "I had rather you had been in your beds." But they still pressing upon him to know something, he said, "I will tell you; I am assured that my warfare is near at an end, and therefore pray to God with me, that I shrink not when the battle waxeth most hot."

Soon after, Cardinal Beaton, archbishop of St. Andrews, being informed that Mr. Wishart was at the house of Mr. Cockburn, of Ormistohn, in East Lothian, applied to the regent to cause him to be apprehended; with which, after great persuasion, and much against his will, he complied. In consequence of this the cardinal immediately proceeded to the trial of Wishart, against whom no less than eighteen articles were exhibited. Mr. Wishart answered the respective articles with great composure of mind, and in so learned and clear a manner as greatly surprised most of those who were present. After the examination was finished, the archbishop endeavored to prevail on Mr. Wishart to recant; but he was too firmly fixed in his religious principles and too much enlightened with the truth of the Gospel, to be in the least moved. On the morning of his execution there came to him two friars from the cardinal; one of whom put on him a black linen coat, and the other brought several bags of gunpowder, which they tied about different parts of his body. As soon as he arrived at the stake, the executioner put a rope round his neck and a chain about his middle, upon which he fell on his knees and thus exclaimed:

"O thou Savior of the world, have mercy upon me! Father of heaven, I commend my spirit into Thy holy hands."

After this he prayed for his accusers, saying, "I beseech thee, Father of heaven, forgive them that have, from ignorance or an evil mind, forged lies of me: I forgive them with all my heart. I beseech Christ to forgive them that have ignorantly condemned me."

He was then fastened to the stake, and the fagots being lighted immediately set fire to the powder that was tied about him, which blew into a flame and smoke. The governor of the castle, who stood so near that he was singed with the flame, exhorted the martyr, in a few words, to be of good cheer, and to ask the pardon of God for his offences. To which he replied, "This flame occasions trouble to my body, indeed, but it hath in nowise broken my spirit. But he who now so proudly looks down upon me from yonder lofty place (pointing to the cardinal) shall, ere long, be ignominiously thrown down, as now he proudly lolls at his ease." Which prediction was soon after fulfilled. The hangman, that was his tormentor, sat down upon his knees, and said, "Sir, I pray you to forgive me, for I am not guilty of your death." To whom he answered, "Come hither to me." When that he was come to him, he kissed his cheek, and said: "Lo, here is a token that I forgive thee. My heart, do thine office." And then he was put upon the gibbet and hanged, and burned to powder. When that the people beheld the great tormenting, they might not withhold from piteous mourning and complaining of this innocent lamb's slaughter. It was not long after the martyrdom of this blessed man of God, Master George Wishart, who was put to death by David Beaton, the bloody archbishop and cardinal of Scotland, A.D. 1546, the first day of March, that the said David Beaton, by the just revenge of God's mighty judgment, was slain within his own castle of St. Andrews, by the hands of one Leslie and other gentlemen, who, by the Lord stirred up, brake in suddenly upon him, and in his bed murdered him the said year, the last day of May, crying out, "Alas! alas! slay me not! I am a priest!" And so, like a butcher he lived, and like a butcher he died, and lay seven months and more unburied, and at last like a carrion was buried in a dunghill.

Walter Mill

The last who suffered martyrdom in Scotland, for the cause of Christ, was one Walter Mill, who was burnt at Edinburgh in the year 1558. This person, in his younger years, had traveled in Germany, and on his return was installed a priest of the Church of Lunan in Angus, but, on an information of heresy, in the time of Cardinal Beaton, he was forced to abandon his charge and abscond. But he was soon apprehended, and committed to prison. Being interrogated by Sir Andrew Oliphant, whether he would recant his opinions, he answered in the negative, saying that he would "sooner forfeit ten thousand lives, than relinquish a particle of those heavenly principles he had received from the suffrages of his blessed Redeemer."

In consequence of this, sentence of condemnation was immediately passed on him, and he was conducted to prison in order for execution the following day. This steadfast believe in Christ was eighty-two years of age, and exceedingly infirm; whence it was supposed that he could scarcely be heard. However, when he was taken to the place of execution, he expressed his religious sentiments with such courage, and at the same time composure of mind, as astonished even his enemies. As soon as he was fastened to the stake and the fagots lighted, he addressed the spectators as follows: "The cause why I suffer this day is not for any crime, (though I acknowledge myself a miserable sinner) but only for the defense of the truth as it is in Jesus Christ; and I praise God who hath called me, by His mercy, to seal the truth with my life; which, as I received it from Him, so I willingly and joyfully offer it up to His glory. Therefore, as you would escape eternal death, be no longer seduced by the lies of the seat of Antichrist: but depend solely on Jesus Christ, and His mercy, that you may be delivered from condemnation." And then added that he trusted he should be the last who would suffer death in Scotland upon a religious account. Thus did this pious Christian cheerfully give up his life in defense of the truth of Christ's Gospel, not doubting but he should be made partaker of his heavenly Kingdom.

Foxe's Book of Martyrs, Edited by William Byron Forbush, chapter 15

Religious Intolerance and Liberty in England and America

Sixteenth and seventeenth century England and America

The history of the Reformation in England and Scotland is even more disfigured by acts of intolerance and persecution than that of the Continent, but resulted at last in greater gain for religious freedom. The modern ideas of well regulated, constitutional liberty, both civil and religious, have grown chiefly on English soil. At first it was a battle between persecution and mere toleration, but toleration once legally secured prepared the way for full religious liberty. All parties when persecuted, advocated liberty of conscience, and all parties when in power, exercised intolerance, but in different degrees. The Episcopalians before 1689 were less intolerant than the Romanists under Queen Mary; the Presbyterians before 1660 were less intolerant than the Episcopalians; the Independents less intolerant (in England) than the Presbyterians (but more intolerant in New England); the Baptists, Quakers, Socinians and Unitarians consistently taught freedom of conscience, and were never tempted to exercise intolerance. Finally all became tolerant in consequence of a legal settlement in 1689, but even that was restricted by disabling clauses. The Romanists used fire and sword; the Episcopalians fines, prisons, pillories, nose-slittings, ear-croppings, and cheek-burnings; the Presbyterians tried depositions and disabilities; the Independents in New England exiled Roger Williams, the Baptist (1636), and hanged four Quakers (two men and two women, 1659, 1660 and 1661) in Boston, and nineteen witches in Salem (1692). But all these measures of repression proved as many failures and made persecution more hateful and at last impossible.

The first act of the English Reformation, under Henry VIII, was simply the substitution of a domestic for a foreign popery and tyranny; and it was a change for the worse. No one was safe who dared to dissent from the creed of the despotic monarch who proclaimed himself "the supreme head of the Church of England." At his death (1547), the six bloody articles were still in force; but they contained some of the chief dogmas of Romanism which he held in spite of his revolt against the pope. Under the brief reign of Edward VI (1547–1553), the Reformation made decided progress, but Anabaptists were not tolerated; two of them, who held some curious views on the incarnation, were burnt as obstinate heretics, Joan Bocher, commonly called Joan of Kent, May 2, 1550, and George Van Pare, a Dutchman April 6, 1551. The young king refused at first to sign the death-warrant of the woman, correctly thinking that the sentence was "a piece of cruelty too like that which they had condemned in papists;" at last he yielded to Cranmer's authority, who argued with him from the law of Moses against blasphemy, but he put his hand to the warrant with tears in his eyes and charged the archbishop with the responsibility for the act if it should be wrong. The reign of the bloody Queen Mary (1553–1558) was a fearful retaliation, but sealed the doom of popery by the blood of Protestant martyrs, including the Reformers, Cranmer, Latimer, and Ridley, who were burnt in the market place at Oxford. Queen Elizabeth (1558–1603), by virtue of her office, as "Defender of the Faith, and supreme governor of the Church" in her dominions, permanently established the Reformed religion, but to the exclusion of all dissent. Her penal code may have been a political necessity, as a protection against domestic treason and foreign invasion, but it aimed systematically at the annihilation of both Popery and Puritanism. It acted most severely upon Roman Catholic priests, who could only save their lives by concealment or exile.

Conformity to the Thirty-nine Articles and the Book of Common Prayer was rigidly enforced; attendance upon the Episcopal service was commanded, while the mass and every other kind of public worship were forbidden under severe penalties. The rack in the tower was freely employed against noblemen suspected of disloyalty to the queen-pope. The statute de haereticis comburendis from the reign of Henry IX

(1401) remained in force, and two Anabaptists were burnt alive under Elizabeth, and two Arians under her successor. The statute was not formally abolished till 1677. Ireland was treated ecclesiastically as well as politically as a conquered province, and England is still suffering from that cruel polity, which nursed a hereditary hatred of the Catholic people against their Protestant rulers, and made the removal of the Irish grievances the most difficult problem of English statesmanship. Popery disappeared for a while from British soil, and the Spanish Armada was utterly defeated. But Puritanism, which fought in the front rank against the big pope at Rome, could not be defeated by the little popes at home. It broke out at last in open revolt against the tyranny of the Stuarts, and the cruelties of the Star Chamber and High-Commission Court, which were not far behind the Spanish Inquisition, and punished freedom of speech and of the press as a crime against society. Puritanism ruled England for about twenty years (1640 to 1660), which form the most intensely earnest and excited period in her history. It saved the rights of the people against the oppression of their rulers, but it punished intolerance with intolerance, and fell into the opposite error of enforcing Puritan, in the place of Episcopal, uniformity, though with far less severity. The Long Parliament abolished the Episcopal hierarchy and liturgy (Sept. 10, 1642), expelled about two thousand royalist clergymen from their benefices, and executed on the block Archbishop Laud (1644) and King Charles I (1649), as traitors; thus crowning them with the glory of martyrdom and preparing the way for the Restoration. Episcopalians now became champions of toleration, and Jeremy Taylor, the Shakespeare of the English pulpit, raised his eloquent voice for the Liberty of Prophesying (1647), which, however, he afterward recalled in part when he was made a bishop by Charles II (1661).

The Westminster Assembly of Divines (1643–1652), which numbered one hundred and twenty-one divines and several lay-deputies and is one of the most important ecclesiastical meetings ever held, was intrusted by Parliament with the impossible task of framing a uniform creed, discipline and ritual for three kingdoms. The extraordinary religious commotion of the times gave rise to all sorts of religious opinions from the most rigid orthodoxy to deism and atheism, and called forth a lively pamphlet war on the subject of toleration, which became an apple of discord in the Assembly. Thomas Edwards, in his Gangraena (1645), enumerated, with uncritical exaggeration, no less than sixteen sects and one hundred and seventy-six miscellaneous "errors, heresies and blasphemies," exclusive of popery and deism. There were three theories on toleration, which may be best stated in the words of George Gillespie, one of the Scottish commissioners of the Assembly. The theory of the "Papists who hold it to be not only no sin, but good service to God to extirpate by fire and sword all that are adversaries to, or opposers of, the Church and Catholic religion."

Under this theory John Hus and Jerome of Prague were burnt at the Council of Constance. Gillespie calls it., in the Preface, "the black devil of idolatry and tyranny." "The second opinion doth fall short as far as the former doth exceed: that is, that the magistrate ought not to inflict any punishment, nor put forth any coercive power upon heretics and sectaries, but on the contrary grant them liberty and toleration." This theory is called "the white devil of heresy and schism," and ascribed to the Donatists (?), Socinians, Arminians and Independents. But the chief advocate was Roger Williams, the Baptist, who became the founder of Rhode Island.90 He went to the root of the question, and demanded complete separation of politics from religion. Long before him, the Puritan Bishop Hooper, and Robert Browne, the renegade founder of Congregationalism had taught the primitive Christian principle that the magistrates had no authority over the church and the conscience, but only over civil matters. Luther expressed the same view in

1523. "The third opinion is that the magistrate may and ought to exercise his coercive power in suppressing and punishing heretics and sectaries less or more, according as the nature and degree of the error, schism, obstinacy, and danger of seducing others may require." For this theory Gillespie quotes Moses, St. Augustin, Calvin, Beza, Bullinger, John Gerhard, and other Calvinistic and Lutheran divines. It was held by the Presbyterians in England and Scotland, including the Scottish commissioners in the Assembly, and vigorously advocated by Dr. Samuel Rutherford, Professor of Divinity in St. Andrews, and most zealously by Thomas Edwards, a Presbyterian minister in London.

It had a strong basis in the national endorsement of the Solemn League and Covenant, and triumphed in the Westminster Assembly. It may therefore be called the Presbyterian theory of the seventeenth century. But it was never put into practice by Presbyterians, at least not to the extent of physical violence, against heretics and schismatics either in England or Scotland. The Westminster Confession of Faith, in its original shape, declares, on the one hand, the great principle of religious liberty, that "God alone is Lord of the conscience," but also, on the other hand, that dangerous heretics "may lawfully be called to account, and proceeded against by the censures of the church, and by the power of the civil magistrate." And it assigns to the civil magistrate the power and duty to preserve "unity and peace in the church," to suppress "all blasphemies and heresies," to prevent or reform "all corruptions and abuses in worship and discipline," and for this purpose "to call synods and be present at them.". The five Independent members of the Assembly under the lead of Dr. Goodwin protested against the power given to the civil magistrate and to synods. The obnoxious clauses of the Confession were therefore omitted or changed in the Congregational recension called "the Savoy Declaration" (1658). But the toleration of the Independents, especially after they obtained the ascendancy under Cromwell's protectorate differed very little from that of the Presbyterians. They were spoiled by success. They excluded from their program Popery, Prelacy, and Socinianism.

Dr. Owen, their most distinguished divine, who preached by command a sermon before Parliament on the day after the execution of Charles I, entitled "Righteous Zeal encouraged by Divine Protection" (Jer. 15:19, 20), and accepted the appointment as Dean of Christ Church and Vice-Chancellor of the University at Oxford, laid down no less than sixteen fundamentals as conditions of toleration. He and Dr. Goodwin served on the Commission of the forty-three Triers which, under Cromwell's protectorate, took the place of the Westminster Assembly. Cromwell himself, though the most liberal among the English rulers and the boldest protector of Protestantism abroad, limited toleration to Presbyterians, Independents, Baptists and Quakers, all of whom recognized the sacred Scriptures and the fundamental articles of Christianity; but he had no toleration for Romanists and Episcopal Royalists, who endangered his reign and who were suspected of tolerating none but themselves. His great foreign secretary, John Milton, the most eloquent advocate of liberty in the English language, defended the execution of the king, and was intolerant to popery and prelacy. Had Cromwell reigned longer, the Triers and the Savoy Conference which he reluctantly appointed, would probably have repeated the vain attempt of the Westminster Assembly to impose a uniform creed upon the nation, only with a little more liberal "accommodation" for orthodox dissenters except "papists" and "prelatists"). Their brethren in New England where they had full sway, established a Congregational theocracy which had no room even for Baptists and Quakers.

Cromwell's reign was a brief experiment. His son was incompetent to continue it. Puritanism had not won the heart of England, but prepared its own tomb by its excesses and blunders. Royalty and Episcopacy, which struck their roots deep in the past, were restored with the powerful aid of the Presbyterians. And now followed a reaction in favor of political and ecclesiastical despotism, and public and private immorality, which for a time ruined all the good which Puritanism had done. Charles II, who "never said a foolish thing and never did a wise one," broke his solemn pledges and took the lead in intolerance and licentiousness. The Act of Uniformity was re-enacted May 19, 1662, and went into operation on St. Bartholomew's Day, August 24, 1662, made hideous by the St. Bartholomew Massacre, nearly a hundred years before. "And now came in," says Baxter, one of the most moderate as well as most learned and pious of the Nonconformists, "the great inundation of calamities, which in many streams overwhelmed thousands of godly Christians, together with their pastors." All Puritan ministers were expelled from their livings and exposed to starvation, their assemblies forbidden, and absolute obedience to the king and conformity to episcopacy were enforced, even in Scotland. The faithful Presbyterians in that country (the Covenanters) were subjected by the royal dragonnades to all manner of indignities and atrocities. "They were hunted" – says an English historian – like criminals over the mountains; their ears were torn from their roots; they were branded with hot irons; their fingers were wrenched asunder by the thumbkins; the bones of their legs were shattered in the boots; women were scourged publicly through the streets; multitudes were transported to the Barbadoes; an infuriated soldiery was let loose upon them, and encouraged to exercise all their ingenuity in torturing them.

The period of the Restoration is, perhaps, the most immoral and disgraceful in English history. But it led at last to the final overthrow of the treacherous and semi-popish dynasty of the Stuarts, and inaugurated a new era in the history of religious liberty. Puritanism was not dead, but produced some of its best and most lasting works – Milton's Paradise Lost, and Bunyan's Pilgrim's Progress – in this period of its deepest humiliation and suffering.8. The act of Toleration under the reign of William and Mary, 1689, made an end to violent persecutions in England. And yet it is far from what we now understand by religious liberty. Toleration is negative, liberty positive; toleration is a favor, liberty a right; toleration may be withdrawn by the power which grants it, liberty is as inalienable as conscience itself; toleration is extended to what cannot be helped and what may be in itself objectionable, liberty is a priceless gift of the Creator. The Toleration of 1689 was an accommodation to a limited number of Dissenters – Presbyterians, Independents, Baptists and Quakers, who were allowed liberty of separate organization and public worship on condition of subscribing thirty-six out of the Thirty-Nine Articles of the Church of England. Roman Catholics and Unitarians were excluded, and did not acquire toleration in England till the nineteenth century, the former by the Act of Emancipation passed April 13, 1829. Even now the Dissenters in England labor under minor disabilities and social disadvantages, which will continue as long as the government patronizes an established church. They have to support the establishment, in addition to their own denomination.

Practically, however, there is more religious liberty in England than anywhere on the Continent, and as much as in the United States. The last and most important step in the progress of religious liberty was taken by the United States of America in the provision of the Federal Constitution of 1787, which excludes all religious tests from the qualifications to any office or public trust. The first amendment to the Constitution (1789) enacts that "Congress shall make no law respecting an establishment of religion, or prohibiting the free exercise thereof." Thus the United States government is by its own free act prevented from ever establishing a state-church, and on the other hand it is bound to protect freedom of religion, not only as a matter of opinion, but also in its public exercise, as one of the inalienable rights of an American citizen, like the freedom of speech and of the press. History had taught the framers of the

Constitution that persecution is useless as well as hateful, and that it has its root in the unholy alliance of religion with politics. Providence had made America a hospitable home for all fugitives from persecution, – Puritans, Presbyterians, Huguenots, Baptists, Quakers, Reformed, Lutherans, Roman Catholics, etc. – and foreordained it for the largest development of civil and religious freedom consistent with order and the well-being of society. When the colonies, after a successful struggle for independence, coalesced into one nation they could not grant liberty to one church or sect without granting it to all. They were thus naturally driven to this result. It was the inevitable destiny of America. And it involved no injustice or injury to any church or sect.

The modern German empire forms in some measure a parallel. When it was formed in 1870 by the free action of the twenty or more German sovereignties, it had to take them in with their religion, and abstain from all religious and ecclesiastical legislation which might interfere with the religion of any separate state. The constitutional provision of the United States in regard to religion is the last outcome of the Reformation in its effect upon toleration and freedom, not foreseen or dreamed of by the Reformers, but inevitably resulting from their revolt against papal tyranny. It has grown on Protestant soil with the hearty support of all sects and parties. It cuts the chief root of papal and any other persecution, and makes it legally impossible. It separates church and state, and thus prevents the civil punishment of heresy as a crime against the state. It renders to Caesar the things that are Caesar's, and renders to God the things that are God's. It marks a new epoch in the history of legislation and civilization. It is the American contribution to church history. No part of the federal constitution is so generally accepted and so heartily approved as that which guarantees religious liberty, the most sacred and most important of all liberties. It is regarded almost as an axiom which needs no argument. Religious liberty has thus far been fully justified by its effects. It has stimulated the fullest development of the voluntary principle. The various Christian churches can live in peace and harmony together, and are fully able to support and to govern themselves without the aid of the secular power. This has been proven by the experience of a century, and this experience is the strongest argument in favor of the separation of church and state. Christianity flourishes best without a state-church. The separation, however, is peaceful, not hostile, as it was in the Ante-Nicene age, when the pagan state persecuted the church. Nor is it a separation of the nation from Christianity. The government is bound to protect all forms of Christianity with its day of rest, its churches, its educational and charitable institutions. Even irreligion and infidelity are tolerated within the limits of the law of self-preservation. Religious liberty may, of course, be abused like any other liberty. It has its necessary boundary in the liberty of others and the essential interests of society.

The United States government would not tolerate, much less protect, a religion which requires human sacrifices, or sanctions licentious rites, or polygamy, or any other institution inconsistent with the laws and customs of the land, and subversive of the foundation of the state and the order of Christian civilization. Hence the recent prohibition of polygamy in the Territories, and the unwillingness of Congress to admit Utah into the family of States unless polygamy is abolished by the Mormons. The majority of the population decides the religion of a country, and, judged by this test, the American people are as Christian as any other on earth, only in a broader sense which recognizes all forms of Christianity. While Jews and infidels are not excluded from the enjoyment of any civil or political right on account of their religion or irreligion, they cannot alter the essentially Christian character of the sentiments, habits and institutions of the nation. There are three important institutions in which church and state touch each other even in the United States, and where a collision of interests may take place: education in the public schools, marriage, and Sunday as a day of civil and sacred rest. The Roman Catholics are opposed to public schools unless they can teach in them their religion which allows no compromise with any other; the Mormons are opposed to monogamy, which is the law of the land and the basis of the Christian family; the Jews may demand the protection of their Sabbath on Saturday, while infidels want no Sabbath at all except perhaps for amusement and dissipation. But all these questions admit of a peaceful settlement and equitable adjustment, without a relapse into the barbarous measures of persecution. The law of the United States is supreme in the Territories and the District of Columbia, but does not forbid any of the States to establish a particular church, or to continue a previous establishment. The Colonies began with the European system of state-churchism, only in a milder form, and varying according to the preferences of the first settlers.

In the New England Colonies – except Rhode Island founded by the Baptist Roger Williams – orthodox Congregationalism was the established church which all citizens were required to support; in Virginia and the Southern States, as also in New York, the Episcopal Church was legally established and supported by the government. Even those Colonies which were professedly founded on the basis of religious toleration, as Maryland and Pennsylvania, enacted afterwards disabling clauses against Roman Catholics, Unitarians, Jews and infidels. In Pennsylvania, the Quaker Colony of William Penn, no one could hold office, from 1693 to 1775, without subscribing a solemn declaration of belief in the orthodox doctrine of the Holy Trinity and condemning the Roman Catholic doctrine of transubstantiation and the mass as idolatrous. The great revolution of legislation began in the Colony of Virginia in 1776, when Episcopacy was disestablished, and all other churches freed from their disabilities. The change was brought about by the combined efforts of Thomas Jefferson (the leading statesman of Virginia, and a firm believer in absolute religious freedom on the ground of philosophic neutrality), and of all dissenting denominations, especially the Presbyterians, Baptists and Quakers. The other Colonies or States gradually followed the example, and now there is no State in which religious freedom is not fully recognized and protected. The example of the United States exerts a silent, but steady and mighty influence upon Europe in raising the idea of mere toleration to the higher plane of freedom, in emancipating religion from the control of civil government, and in proving the advantages of the primitive practice of ecclesiastical self-support and self-government. The best legal remedy against persecution and the best guarantee of religious freedom is a peaceful separation of church and state; the best moral remedy and guarantee is a liberal culture, a comprehensive view of the many-sidedness of truth, a profound regard for the sacredness of conscientious conviction, and a broad and deep Christian love as described by the Apostle Paul.

Philip Scaff, The History of the Church

THOMAS BILNEY

Thomas Bilney was brought up at Cambridge. On leaving the university, he went to several places and preached; and in his sermons spoke with great boldness against the pride and insolence of the clergy. This was during Cardinal Wolsey's ministry, who upon hearing of Bilney's attacks, imprisoned him. Overcome with fear, Bilney abjured, was pardoned, and returned to Cambridge in 1530. Here he fell into great horror of mind in consequence of his denial of the truth. He became overwhelmed with shame, and bitterly repenting of his sin, resolved to make some atonement by a public confession of his sentiments. To prepare himself for the task, he studied the Scriptures with deep attention for two years, at the end of which he left the university and went to Norfolk, where he preached up and down that country against idolatry and superstition. He openly confessed his own sin of denying the faith; and, taking no precautions as he traveled, was soon seized by the bishop's officers, condemned as a relapse, and degraded. Parker, later

Archbishop of Canterbury, was an eyewitness of his sufferings, which he bore with great fortitude and resignation, and continued very cheerful after his sentence. He ate up the poor provisions that he was given, saying he must keep up a ruinous cottage till it fell. He often quoted these words from Isaiah: "When thou walkest through the fire, thou shalt not be burned." By burning his finger in a candle, he prepared himself for the fire, and said it would only consume the stubble of his body, and would purify his soul.

On November 10th he was taken to the stake, where he repeated the Creed, as a testimony that he was a true Christian. He then prayed earnestly, and with the deepest feeling repeated these words, "Enter not into judgment with thy servant." Dr Warner, who attended, embraced him, shedding many tears, and wishing he might die in as good a frame of mind as Bilney then was. The friars requested him to inform the people that they were not instrumental to his death, which he did, so that the his last act was full of charity.

The officers then put the reeds and faggots around his body, and set first to the first, which made a great flame and disfigured his face; he held up his hands, and struck his chest, crying sometimes, "Jesus!', sometimes, "Credo!'. But the flame was blown away from him several times, by a strong wind, until eventually the wood caught fire and the flame grew stronger and he gave up his spirit.

His body shrank and leaned down on the chain, until one of the officers with his halbert struck out the staple from the chain behind him, so that his body fell down to the base of the fire, where they heaped wood over it to consume it.

John Foxe, The Book of Martyrs, revised with notes and an appendix by W. Bramley-Moore, London, 1869, pp 227-29

The Reformation: Protestant Martyrs

No great cause in church or state, in religion or science, has ever succeeded without sacrifice. Blood is the price of liberty. "The blood of martyrs is the seed of Christianity." Persecution develops the heroic qualities of human nature, and the passive virtues of patience and endurance under suffering. Protestantism has its martyrs as well as Catholicism. In Germany it achieved a permanent legal existence only after the Thirty Years' War. The Reformed churches in France, Holland, England, and Scotland, passed through the fiery ordeal of persecution. It has been estimated that the victims of the Spanish Inquisition outnumber those of heathen Rome, and that more Protestants were executed by the Spaniards in a single reign, and in a single province of Holland, than Christians in the Roman empire during the first three centuries. Jews and heathens have persecuted Christians, Christians have persecuted Jews and heathens, Romanists have persecuted Protestants, Protestants have persecuted Romanists, and every state-church has more or less persecuted dissenters and sects. It is only within a recent period that the sacred rights of conscience have been properly appreciated, and that the line is clearly and sharply drawn between church and state, religious and civil offenses, heresy and crime, spiritual and temporal punishments.

The persecution of Protestants began at the Diet of Worms in 1521. Charles X issued from that city the first of a series of cruel enactments, or "placards," for the extermination of the Lutheran heresy in his hereditary dominion of the Netherlands. In 1523 two Augustinian monks, Henry Voes and John Esch, were publicly burnt, as adherents of Luther, at the, stake in Brussels. After the fires were kindled, they repeated the Apostles' Creed, sang the "Te Deum laudamus," and prayed in the flames, "Jesus, thou Son of David, have mercy upon us." The heroic death of these Protestant proto-martyrs inspired Luther's first poem, which begins, – "Ein neues Lied wir heben an."

The prior of their convents Lampert Thorn, was suffocated in prison. Adolph Klarenbach and Peter Flysteden suffered at the stake in Cologne with constancy and triumphant joy, Sept. 28, 1529. George Winkler, a preacher in Halle, was cited by the Archbishop of Cologne to Aschaffenburg for distributing the communion in both kinds, and released, but murdered by unknown hands on his return, May, 1527. Duke George of Saxony persecuted the Lutherans, not by death, but by imprisonment and exile.

John Herrgott, a traveling book-peddler, was beheaded (1527) for revolutionary political opinions, rather than for selling Lutheran books. In Southern Germany the Edict of Worms was more rigidly executed. Many executions by fire and sword, accompanied by barbarous mutilations, took place in Austria and Bavaria. In Vienna a citizen, Caspar Tauber, was beheaded and burnt, because he denied purgatory and transubstantiation, Sept. 17, 1524.813 In Salzburg a priest was secretly beheaded without a trial, by order of the archbishop, for Lutheran heresy.

George Wagner, a minister at Munich, was burnt Feb. 8, 1527. Leonard Kōser (or Kaiser) shared the same fate, Aug. 18, 1527, by order of the bishop of Passau. Luther wrote him, while in prison, a letter of comfort. But the Anabaptists had their martyrs as well, and they died with the same heroic faith. Hōtzer was burnt in Constance, Hebmaier in Vienna. In Passau thirty perished in prison. In Salzburg some were mutilated, others beheaded, others drowned, still others burnt alive.

The burning of Servetus

Unfortunately, the Anabaptists were not much better treated by Protestant governments; even in Zürich several were drowned in the river under the eyes of Zwingli. The darkest blot on Protestantism is the burning of Servetus for heresy and blasphemy, at Geneva, with the approval of Calvin and all the surviving Reformers, including Melanchthon (1553). He had been previously condemned, and burnt in effigy, by a Roman-Catholic tribunal in France. Now such a tragedy would be impossible in any church. The same human passions exist, but the ideas and circumstances have changed.

Philip Scaff, The History of the Church

THOMAS HARDING

In 1532, Thomas Harding, who with his wife, had been accused of heresy, was brought before the bishop of Lincoln, and condemned for denying the real presence in the Sacrament. He was then chained to a stake, erected for the purpose, at Chesham in the Pell, near Botely; and when they had set fire to the fagots, one of the spectators dashed out his brains with a billet. The priests told the people that whoever brought fagots to burn heretics would have an indulgence to commit sins for forty days.

Foxe's Book of Martyrs, Edited by William Byron Forbush, chapter 14

HITTEN: BURNT ALIVE IN FRONT OF HIS PARISH CHURCH

During the latter end of this year, Worham, archbishop of Canterbury, apprehended one Hitten, a priest at Maidstone; and after he had been long tortured in prison, and several times examined by the archbishop, and Fisher, bishop of Rochester, he was condemned as a heretic, and burnt alive before the door of his own parish church. William Letton, a monk of great age. At the same time was condemned William Letton, a monk of great age, in the county of Suffolk, who was burned at Norwich for speaking against an idol that was carried in procession; and for asserting, that the Sacrament should be administered in both kinds.

Foxe's Book of Martyrs, Edited by William Byron Forbush, chapter 14

JOHN FRITH

Frith was a young man well known for his learning and the first in England to write against the bodily presence in the sacrament. He followed Zuinglius's teaching on these grounds: Christ received in the sacrament gave eternal life, but this was given only to those who believed, from which he inferred that he was received only by faith. These reasons he put in writing, which falling into the hands of Sir Thomas More, were answered by him; but Frith never saw his publication until he was in prison; and then, though he was loaded with irons, and had no books, he replied. For these offences he was seized in May, 1533, and brought before Stokesly, Gardiner, and Longland. They accused him with not believing in purgatory and transubstantiation. He gave his reasons that made him see neither of these as articles of faith; but thought that neither the affirming nor the denying them ought to be determined positively. The bishops seemed unwilling to proceed to sentence; but he continuing resolute, Stokesly pronounced it, and delivered him to the secular power, at the same time desiring that his punishment might be moderated, so that the rigor might not be too extreme, nor yet the gentleness of it too much mitigated – a piece of hypocrisy which deceived no one. Frith, with fellow martyr Hewitt, were taken to the stake at Smithfield on July 4th 1533. On arriving there, Frith expressed great joy, and hugged the faggots with sheer delight. A priest called Cook, who stood by, told the people not to pray for them more than they would do for a dog: at this Frith smiled, and prayed God to forgive him. The fire was then kindled, and consumed the martyrs to ashes.

John Foxe, The Book of Martyrs, revised with notes and an appendix by W. Bramley-Moore, London, 1869, p 231

John Lambert

I answer with Augustine, "That this is the body of Christ after a certain manner." John Lambert was born in Norfolk and educated at Cambridge university. After being converted by Bilney he became disgusted at the corruption of the church; and apprehensive of persecution, he crossed the sea and joined Tyndale and Frith. He was appointed chaplain to the English at Antwerp. But the persecuting spirit of Sir Thomas More reached him, and on the accusation of a man called Barlow, was taken from Antwerp to London. He was put on trial in Lambeth and then in Oxford before Archbishop Warham. Warham died the following year and Lambert was released.

Lambert argued that when Christ said, "This cup is the new testament," these words do not change either the cup nor the wine corporeally into the new testament. Using the same argument he said that Christ's words spoken about the bread do not turn it corporeally into the body of Christ.

On account of this teaching he was summoned for trial by Archbishop Cranmer and forced to defend himself, for Cranmer, who later became a fervent believer in the reformed doctrines on the sacrament, still favored the Roman view. At his trial King Henry VIII asked him, "Answer as touching the sacrament of the altar. Dost thou say that it is the body of Christ, or dost thou deny it?'

LAMBERT: I answer with Augustine, "That this is the body of Christ after a certain manner."

THE KING: Answer me neither out of Augustine nor any other authority; but tell me plainly, do you believe it is the body of Christ or not?

LAMBERT: Then I deny that it is the body of Christ.

THE KING: Mark well, for now thou shalt be condemned by Christ's own words: "Hoc est corpus meum." ("This is my body.")

On the appointed day Lambert was taken to Smithfield to be executed. The manner of his death was dreadful; for after his legs were burned up to the stumps, and his wretched tormentors had withdrawn the fire from him, so that only a small one was left under him, two soldiers who stood on either side of him hoisted him on their halberts as far as the chain would go, while he, lifting up such hands as he had, cried unto the people: "None but Christ, none but Christ." Then he was let down again from the soldiers' pikes, fell into the fire, where he expired.

John Foxe, The Book of Martyrs, revised with notes and an appendix by W. Bramley-Moore, London, 1869, pp 238-240

Martyrdom of William Tyndale (1)

William Tyndale, priest, scholar, martyr 6 October 1536

William Tyndale was born about 1495 at Slymbridge near the Welsh border. He received his degrees from Magdalen College, Oxford, and also studied at Cambridge. He was ordained to the priesthood in 1521, and soon began to speak of his desire, which eventually became his life's obsession, to translate the Scriptures into English. It is reported that, in the course of a dispute with a prominent clergyman who disparaged this proposal, he said, "If God spare my life, ere many years I will cause a boy that driveth the plow to know more of the Scriptures than thou dost." The remainder of his life was devoted to keeping that vow, or boast. Finding that the King, Henry VIII, was firmly set against any English version of the Scriptures, he fled to Germany (visiting Martin Luther in 1525), and there traveled from city to city, in exile, poverty, persecution, and constant danger. Tyndale understood the commonly received doctrine — the popular theology — of his time to imply that men earn their salvation by good behavior and by penance. He wrote eloquently in favor of the view that salvation is a gift of God, freely bestowed, and not a response to any good act on the part of the receiver. His views are expressed in numerous pamphlets, and in the introductions to and commentaries on various books of the Bible that accompanied his translations. He completed his translation of the New Testament in 1525, and it was printed at Worms and smuggled into England. Of 18,000 copies, only two survive. In 1534, he produced a revised version, and began work on the Old Testament. In the next two years he completed and published the Pentateuch and Jonah, and translated the books from Joshua through Second Chronicles, but then he was captured (betrayed by one he had befriended), tried for heresy, and put to death. He was burned at the stake, but, as was often done, the officer strangled him before lighting the fire. His last words were, "Lord, open the King of England's eyes." Miles Coverdale continued Tyndale's work by translating those portions of the Bible (including the Apocrypha) which Tyndale had not lived to translate himself, and publishing the complete work. In 1537, the "Matthew Bible" (essentially the Tyndale-Coverdale Bible under another man's name to spare the government embarrassment) was published in England with the Royal Permission. Six copies were set up for public reading in Old St. Paul's Church, and throughout the daylight hours the church was crowded with those who had come to hear it. One man would stand at the lectern and read until his voice gave out, and then he would stand down and another would take his place. All English translations of the Bible from that time to the present century are essentially revisions of the Tyndale-Coverdale work.

James Kiefer, Christian Biographies, By kind permission

Martyrdom of William Tyndale (2)

"Lord, open the King of England's eyes!"

William Tyndale, although he did not suffer in England, ought to rank with the martyrs of our country, of which, from his great zeal, perseverance, and dispersing of truth, he may rightly be esteemed the apostle.

William Tyndale was born around the borders of Wales, and brought up in the University of Oxford, where he studied the liberal arts and the Scriptures. He then moved to Cambridge, and then to Gloucestershire where he became tutor to a knight called Welch. To this gentleman's table several abbots, deans, and other beneficed men used to go, with whom Tyndale talked about learned men, especially Luther and Erasmus, and about questions concerning the Scriptures.

Not long after, Tyndale happened to be in the company of a certain divine, and in their discussion pressed him so hard that the doctor burst out with these blasphemous words: "We were better to be without God's laws than the Pope'.

Tyndale, full of godly zeal, replied: "I defy the Pope and all his laws." He added that if God spared him life, ere many years, he would cause a boy who drives the plough to know more of the Scriptures than he did.

Tyndale left Mr Welch's service, under pressure from disapproving priests, and on arriving in London he was recommended to Tunstall, Bishop of London, by Sir Henry

Guildford. But Tyndale found no favor in the bishop's eyes. He remained in London for nearly a year, greatly distressed with the pomp, pride, and ignorance of the clergy, so that he realized that not only was there no room in the bishop's house for him to translate the New Testament, but that there was no room for him to do this in all England.

He left for Germany and then moved on to the Netherlands and stayed most of the time in Antwerp. There he pondered how he might best help his countrymen understand God's word. He realized that the cause for people's blindness in England, and the reason for the errors and superstitions of the church was ignorance of the Scriptures. The truth was entombed in a dead language, while the priests spent their energy on preventing people from enquiring about the oracles of God. With these considerations in mind Tyndale felt moved, by God's Spirit, to translate the Scriptures into his mother tongue for the benefit of the uneducated people in England. He started with the New Testament in around 1527. His books were published and sent over to England, and became like holy fire from the altar, to give light in the night season.

Tyndale then translated the first five books of the Old Testament and sailed to Hamburg, intending to print them in that city, when one of those mysterious providences happened to him which are beyond human reason. On his voyage he was shipwrecked, and lost all his manuscripts, and almost everything he possessed. However, he started his work again in Hamburg with a man called Coverdale, in a house belonging to Miss Emmerson, in 1529. The English church leaders had persuaded the king to issue a proclamation which condemned and forbad Tyndale's translation of the New Testament. Not content with this they plotted to see how they could kill the author.

Tyndale had returned to Antwerp and was betrayed there by a man called Philips. Tyndale was taken to Filford castle, eighteen miles from Antwerp, where he remained until his death.

At last, after eighteen months, and must fruitless arguments, Tyndale was condemned by a decree issued from Augsburg by the emperor. Tyndale was taken to be executed and as he was being tied to the stake, he cried with a loud and earnest voice, "Lord, open the King of England's eyes!" He was then strangled, and his remains burnt to ashes. Such was the power and excellence of this truly good man, that during his imprisonment he converted the jailor, and his daughter, and others in his employment. Several of them who came into contact with him during his imprisonment said of him, that if he were not a good Christian, they did not know whom to trust; and the procurator-general left this testimony about him, that he was "a learned, a good, and a godly man."

John Foxe, The Book of Martyrs, revised with notes and an appendix by W. Bramley-Moore, London, 1869, pp 278-84

Four views on the Holy Communion

The four views which have unhappily divided the Christian world on the subject of the sacrament [i.e., Holy Communion, the Lord's Supper or the Mass] are the following:

1. The Romish doctrine, or transubstantiation. This maintains the absolute change of the elements into the actual body and blood of Christ; so that though the elements of bread and wine remain present to the senses, they are no longer what they seem, being changed into the body, blood, and divinity of Christ.

2. The Lutheran view, called consubstantiation. This maintains that after consecration the body and blood of Christ are substantially present, but nevertheless that the bread and wine are present, unchanged.

3. The Anglican view – that Christ is present in the sacrament only after the spiritual manner, and that his body and blood are eaten by the faithful after a spiritual, and not after a carnal manner, to the maintenance of their spiritual life and their growth in grace.

4. The Zwinglian, which declares the sacrament to be no channel of grace, but only a commemorative feast, admitting only a

figurative presence of Christ's body and blood.

Alas! that prisons should have been peopled, and thousands immolated on the pyre, for the sake of opinions; and that nothing but death could atone for the horrible crime of individual judgment, instead of allowing each to stand or fall to their own master.

John Foxe, The Book of Martyrs, revised with notes and an appendix by W. Bramley-Moore, London, 1869, pp 369

Martyrdom of John Fisher (1)

John Fisher, bishop, martyr 22 June 1535

John Fisher was born in 1469, enrolled at Cambridge University in 1483, ordained in 1491, and in 1502 became chaplain to Lady Margaret Beaufort, mother of King Henry VII. With her money and his ideas, they greatly altered Cambridge, restoring the teaching of Greek and Hebrew, bringing Erasmus over as a lecturer, and endowing many chairs and scholarships. In 1504 Fisher was made Chancellor of Cambridge and Bishop of Rochester. In 1527 he became chaplain to the new king, Henry VIII, and confessor to the queen, Catherine of Aragon. He stood high in the favor of Henry, who proclaimed that no other realm had any bishop as learned and devout.

James Kiefer, Christian Biographies, By kind permission

Martyrdom of John Fisher (2)

John Fisher, Cardinal and Bishop, takes the first place among the martyrs of the sixteenth century in dignity, example, and the influence of his name. He was born in 1459, at Beverley, and studied when young with a priest of that collegiate church. Afterwards he spent many years at Cambridge with distinction, and was made Bishop of Rochester in 1504, being forty-five years of age. No one was more vigilant against the poison of Luther's doctrines creeping into England. The book which earned for Henry VIII from the Pope the title of Defender of the Faith was written by his advice, if not indeed by his hand. Fisher was considered the most learned, pious and inflexible of the English bishops, and Cardinal Pole regards him as the model of a perfect prelate.

The time, however, came when his virtue and adherence to the faith were imputed to him as crimes. The king, tired of his wife, and in love with Anne Boleyn, affected to have scruples about his marriage. Wolsey, from political motives, wished a divorce, and knew that if Fisher could be gained over, little opposition need be feared from the clergy. But the holy bishop, being sent for, at once advised his majesty with all speed to lay aside those thoughts: "and for any peril," he added, "that may happen to your soul thereby, let the guilt rest on mine." When after long delay, the cause of divorce was before the Papal Legates' Court, as Queen Catherine's chief defender "there stood forth John Fisher, the light not only of England, but of Christendom, to demonstrate that their marriage could not be dissolved by any power, divine or human. He declared that for this opinion he was ready to lay down his life, adding that as John the Baptist, in olden times, regarded death glorious in a cause of matrimony, and it was not so holy then as it has now become by the shedding of Christ's blood, he could not encourage himself more, or face any peril with greater confidence than by taking the Baptist for his own example."

Fisher was brought before Cranmer, the Archbishop of Canterbury, who told him, "You must answer directly, whether you will, or you will not subscribe" [to the supremacy of the Church of England being vested in the king of England, his heirs and successors].

Then said the Bishop of Rochester, "If you will needs have me answer directly, my answer is, that, forasmuch as my own conscience cannot be satisfied, I absolutely refuse the oath." Upon this he was immediately committed to the Tower, where he suffered many privations. Mr Richard Rich, the Solicitor- General, was the sole witness brought against the sick prelate. In front of a jury Mr Rich retold a supposed conversation he had had with the venerable prisoner in the Tower, in which Bishop Fisher spoke his mind plainly about the statue. A verdict of guilty was soon recorded, and the Lord Chancellor asked the bishop if he had any more to say for himself. The persecuted bishop replied, "Truly, my lord, if that which I have before spoken be not sufficient, I have no more to say, but only to desire Almighty God to forgive them that have thus condemned me, for I think they know not what they have done."

Bishop John Fisher's reply

The Lord Chancellor pronounced sentence on Bishop John Fisher, as in the cases of high treason. In reply the godly bishop said:

"My lords, I am here condemned before you of high treason for denial of the king's supremacy over the Church of England, but by what order of justice I leave to God, who is the searcher both of the king his majesty's conscience and yours; nevertheless, being found guilty, as it is termed, I am and must be contented with all that God shall send, to those who I wholly refer and submit myself. And now to tell you more plainly my mind, touching this matter of the king's supremacy, I think indeed, and always have thought, and do now lastly affirm, that his grace cannot justly claim any such supremacy over the church of God, as he now taketh upon him; neither has it ever been, or heard of, that any temporal prince, before his days, hath presumed to that dignity; wherefore, if the king will now adventure himself in proceeding in this strange and unwonted case, so no doubt but he shall deeply incur the grievous displeasure of the almighty, to the great damage of his own soul, and of many others, and to the utter ruin of this realm committed to his charge, whereof will ensue some sharp punishment at his hands; wherefore, I pray god his grace may remember himself in good time, and hearken to good counsel for the preservation of himself and his realm, and the quietness of all Christendom." On June 22, 1535, he was upon the scaffold at about ten of the clock, when the executioner, being ready to do his office, kneeled down to him, as the fashion is, and asked him forgiveness. "I forgive thee," said he, "with all my heart, and I trust thou shalt see me overcome this storm lustily."

Then was his gown and tippet taken from him, and he stood in his doublet and hose, in sight of all the people, whereof was no small number assembled to see his execution. There was to be seen a long, lean, and slender body, having on it little other substance besides skin and bones, insomuch as most part of the beholders marveled much to see a living man so far consumed, for he seemed a very image of death; and as it were death in a man's shape, using a man's voice; and therefore it was thought the king was something cruel to put such a man to death, being near his end, and to kill that which was dying already, except it were for pity sake to rid him of his pain. When the innocent and holy man was come upon the scaffold, he spake to the people to the following effect: "Christian people, I am come hither to die for the faith of Christ's holy Catholic church, and I thank God hitherto my stomach hath served very well thereunto, so that yet I have not feared death; wherefore I desire you all to help and assist with your prayers, that at the very stroke and instant of death's stroke, I may stand steadfast, without fainting in any one point of the Catholic faith, free from any fear."

Then he knelt down and prayed the Te Deum Laudamus, ending with the words, "In Thee, O Lord, have I hoped." Then came the executioner, and bound a handkerchief about his eyes; and so this holy Father, lifting up his hands and heart towards heaven, said a few prayers, which were not long, but fervent and devout; which being ended, he laid his head down on the middle of a little block, when the executioner, being ready with a sharp and heavy axe, cut asunder his slender neck at one blow, which bled so abundantly that many wondered to see so much blood issue out of so slender and lean a body.

E. H. Burton and J. H. Pollen, Lives of the English Martyrs, Vol 1, 1583-1588, Longman, 1914, pp 10-15

Martyrdom of Thomas More (1)

Thomas More, scholar, martyr 6 July 1535

Thomas More was born in London, 6 February 1478, the son of a judge. He was sent to Oxford for two years, then studied law and was called to the Bar in 1501. He spent four years at the London Charterhouse (monastery of the Carthusian monks), hoping to become a priest or monk or friar. Leaving the Charterhouse, he entered Parliament. In 1505 he married Jane Colt, who eventually bore him three daughters and a son, but died in 1511. A few weeks after her death, More married a widow, Alice Middleton, with a son and a daughter of her own. The second marriage produced no offspring, but Alice made a good home for the six children already there, plus others whom More took in as students or as foster children. He was noted for giving his daughters far more education than most women, even in the upper classes, received. His friends included Desiderius Erasmus and John Colet, and other scholars who desired moderate reforms in the Church but were set against any break with the Papacy. Henry VIII, who became king in 1509, recognized More's learning and integrity, enjoyed his intelligent and cheerful conversation and ready wit, became his friend, and appointed him to numerous public offices, including finally that of Lord Chancellor of England.

Henry wrote a book *On The Seven Sacraments*, a defense of traditional doctrines against the teachings of Martin Luther. (The Pope rewarded him with the title, "Defender of the Faith," a title born to this day by English monarchs.) More, discussing the book with Henry while it was still in rough draft, said, "I am troubled, because the book seems to me to give too much honor to the Pope." Henry replied, "There is no such thing as giving too much honor to the Pope."

More himself was pressed into service by the Bishop of London to write pamphlets arguing against the writings of Luther and Tyndale. More undertook to show that Tyndale's translation of the Scriptures is so full of errors that it deserves to be suppressed. Tyndale replied, defending the verses that More had specified, and so on. More and Tyndale exchanged several broadsides, and it can reasonably be maintained that the attacks on both sides were directed against positions that the other side did not really hold, that neither really understood completely the position that the other was defending. (On the other hand, Tyndale's denunciations of what he took to be the doctrines taught by Rome would have fallen on deaf ears if they had not in fact described doctrines that many men believed they had heard from the pulpit, and had found utterly unacceptable. And, mutatis mutandis, the converse holds.)

Thus, for many years, More and Fisher prospered and enjoyed the King's favor. Then the political winds changed. Henry (for reasons that I have discussed at length elsewhere) declared that his marriage to Queen Catharine was null and void. He was opposed in this, by More and Fisher, by Tyndale, and (less promptly and vigorously) by the Pope. Henry broke off relations with the Pope, and proceeded to set Catharine aside and take another wife, Anne Boleyn. Fisher, as a Bishop and as a member of the House of Lords, was called on to ratify this decision, and dramatically refused. More, who by this time was Lord Chancellor of England, resigned his position and retired to private life, hoping that he would be allowed to remain silent, neither supporting the king nor opposing him. But the king required him to take a loyalty oath which recognized the King as the earthly head of the Church in England. This Thomas could not do. He did not believe that the authority of the Pope was a matter of Divine decree — he thought that it was a matter of usage and custom, and expedient for the unity and peace of the Church. He believed that there were many practices in the Church of his day that needed to be reformed, but he did not trust Tyndale, or Luther, or above all Henry, to steer reform in the right direction. So he refused the oath, and was thrown into the Tower of London. While in prison, he wrote *A Dialogue of Comfort Against*

Tribulation, a work still in print, and well worth reading. It is deeply moving to see the contrast between the generally gloomy atmosphere of some of the devotional works that More wrote when he had health, riches, honors, high office, the comfort of a devoted family... and the serene cheerfulness of the Dialogue of Comfort, written when he had none of these, and had every reason to expect that he would eventually be executed for treason. (The penalty for treason was to be hanged, drawn, and quartered. This meant that the convicted traitor was hanged by the neck (not dropped through a trapdoor as in a modern hanging, which is supposed to kill instantly, but slowly lifted off his feet) until he lost consciousness, then taken down and revived, then castrated, then disemboweled and his intestines burned in a fire, then finally put out of his misery by beheading, after which his head was placed on a pike on London Bridge and his body was cut into four quarters to be sent to four parts of the kingdom and displayed there as a warning against treason. This penalty, though not always enforced, was on the English law books from 1305 until at least 1805. I seem to recall that it was carried out once and only once in what is now the United States.) Writing with this fate hanging over him, More faces the prospect straightforwardly. He does not deny that he is terrified, but he maintains that God gives strength to those who ask for it and need it, and that, where the sufferings of martyrdom are concerned, any Christian will be glad tomorrow to have suffered so today.

Thomas More was put to death on 6 July 1536. The Roman calendar commemorates him on 22 June together with John Fisher, Bishop of Rochester, who was beheaded on that date a fortnight before More, also for refusing to take the king's oath. Both of them, though convicted of treason, were simply beheaded (a relatively clean and quick death). In Anglican circles, More is often remembered on 6 October together with William Tyndale. Although they disputed bitterly in print, they were in agreement on far more important matters, and curiously alike in many ways. As C.S. Lewis has pointed out, both expected death by torture, and both were mercifully disappointed. Both opposed the annulment of the King's marriage to Katherine of Aragon, both were disdainful of the Middle Ages and eager partisans of the New Learning of the Renaissance, both were vehement opponents of the New Economics, and, most important of all, both of them, while loyal subjects of the King, were prepared to defy him to the death, in the service, as they saw it, of their Lord and Savior Jesus Christ. Incidentally, it would be a mistake to suppose that Henry killed Tyndale in his earlier, Romanist days, and then killed Fisher and More in his later, Protestant days. Tyndale was killed fifteen months after More and Fisher. It would also be a mistake to say (as I have heard it said) that the Church of England killed More. He died, if I may make the distinction, for religious reasons, but was killed by Henry for political reasons, and his death was opposed most strenuously by Archbishop Cranmer.

I close this account with Thomas More's closing words to the court that sentenced him to death. "More I have not to say, my lords, but that like as the blessed Apostle St. Paul, as we read in the Acts of the Apostles, was present and consented to the death of St. Stephen, and kept their clothes that stoned him to death, and yet they be now both twain holy saints in Heaven, and shall continue there friends for ever, so I verily trust, and shall right heartily pray, that though your lordships have now here in earth been Judges to my condemnation, we may yet hereafter in Heaven right merrily all meet together, to our everlasting salvation. And thus I desire Almighty God to preserve and defend the King's Majesty, and to send him good counsel."

James Kiefer, Christian Biographies, By kind permission

Martyrdom of Sir Thomas More (2)

"I die the King's good servant, but God's first." More, from the scaffold

Acts of Parliament, passed in November

1534, sealed More's fate. Firstly, the Act of Supremacy rejected any foreigners having any authority in ecclesiastic matters and declared that the King was the supreme head of the English Church. Secondly, the Treason Act now made it a treasonable offence to deny any of his titles, specifically being Supreme Head of the English Church. Thirdly, Fisher, along with five other non-juring clergymen, and More were cited in the Act of Attainder.

More still refused to say whether or not he accepted the King as supreme head in religious matters. So at his state trial in Westminster Hall a false witness had to be resorted to. He declared that he had heard More say in prison, "No more than Parliament could make a law that God were not God could Parliament make the King Supreme Head of the Church." This was enough to convict More. Lord Chancellor Audley, More's successor, asked More if he wanted to say anything. More replied, "I verily trust that though your Lordships have now here on earth been judges to my condemnation, we yet in heaven merrily all meet together to our everlasting salvation." Later, More stated his true position about the king being the Supreme Head of the Church. He said, "In as much as this indictment is based on an Act of Parliament directly repugnant to the laws of God and his holy Church, the supreme Government of which, or of any part whereof, may no temporal Prince presume by any law to take upon him, as rightfully belonging to the See of Rome, a spiritual preeminence by the mouth of our Savior himself, personally present on earth, only to St Peter and his successors, bishops of the same See, by special prerogative granted, it is therefore in law, amongst Christian men, insufficient to charge any Christian man."

More's Trial and Execution

When at last the Judge called on the jury, they brought in a verdict of death against him. Thereupon he said, frankly, "I have by the grace of God been always a Catholic, never out of the communion of the Roman Pontiff, but I had heard it said at times that the authority of the Roman Pontiff was certainly lawful and to be respected, but still an authority derived from human law, and not standing on a divine prescription. Then when I observed that public affairs were so ordered that the sources of the power of the Roman Pontiff would necessarily be examined, I gave myself up to a most diligent examination of that question for the space of seven years, and found that the authority of the Roman Pontiff, which you rashly – I will not use stronger language – have set aside, is not only lawful, to be respected, and necessary, but also grounded on the divine law and prescription. That is my opinion, that is the belief in which by the grace of God I shall die." He had hardly ended his answer when they all cried out that More was a traitor and a rebel.

Sentence was therefore passed upon him, and he was led back to the Tower. He was met at the Old Swan Stairs by his son who with tears in his eyes asked his blessing. His daughter Margaret placed herself at the Tower wharf and received his blessing upon her knees; then she forced her way through the guard, and embracing her father, ceased not for some time from kissing him, and exclaiming "My father! O my father!" Sir Thomas comforted her, and they separated. But a second time she rushed through the throng, and hung upon his neck; Sir Thomas then shed some tears; all around were overcome, and even the guards could not refrain from weeping.

As More was led to the scaffold he had a joke with the Master Lieutenant, and said to him, "I pray you, Master Lieutenant, see me safe up, and for my coming down, let me shift for myself." More was allowed to say little. He simply asked for the prayers of the spectators, and that they should pray for the King, recited Psalm 51, and assured the crowd that he died for the Catholic faith and that he died "the King's good servant, but God's first." To the executioner he said, "Thou wilt do me this day a greater benefit than ever any mortal man can be able to do me; pluck up thy spirit, man, and be not afraid to do thy office; my neck is very short, take heed therefore that thou strike not awry, for saving they honesty." The executioner severed More's head from his body in a single blow.

The English Martyrs under Henry VIII and Elizabeth, The Catholic Truth Society 1891, pp 20-21

Twelve Carthusian Monks

Every means which dissimulation and cruelty could devise had been ineffectually resorted to in order to induce the religious of the Charterhouse Priory to stifle the dictates of their consciences, subscribe to the oath of supremacy, and in fine, acknowledge the legality of all the king's proceedings. Lay governors were appointed over them, who treated them with the utmost severity and daily insults. They were scarcely allowed sufficient food for the sustenance of life, while the intruders feasted and drank.

All these means, however, failing, four of these holy men, who were considered to have the greatest influence in the house, were removed to distant convents in the country, where the monks had conformed to the will of the king and his Vicar-General, Cromwell. Blessed John Rochester was one of the four monks who were forcibly removed from the Charterhouse. He was sent to a convent of his Order, near Hull, in Yorkshire, on the 4th of May, 1536. Blessed James Walworth was the companion of Rochester in all his sufferings. Like Rochester he resisted every overture to break his monastic vows, or to swerve from the faith of his forefathers. A nobleman, who resided in the neighborhood of the monastery, informed Cromwell of their constancy, and the impracticability of overcoming their resolution. Whereupon the Vicar-General gave him authority to proceed against their lives. They were accordingly conducted to York, and in the presence of the Duke of Norfolk, the nobleman commanded them to be put to death. So little were the forms of law and justice attended to by the men who professed to bring about a reformation in religion.

The command was immediately put into execution, and the courageous champions of the faith were suspended upon a gallows, in chains, where their bodies were left hanging until, after the lapse of many years, their bodies fell to the ground.

Ten more names were yet to be added to the roll of Carthusian martyrs. Of these three were priests, Blessed Richard Bere, Blessed Thomas Johnson, and Blessed Thomas Green. One was a deacon, Blessed John Davy, and six were lay- brothers, BB. William Greenwood, Thomas Scryven, Robert Salt, Walter Pierson, Thomas Redyng, and William Horne. It was judged impolitic to put these ten monks publicly to death, so they were dragged, towards the end of May, 1537, from their convent, and committed close prisoners to Newgate. The king's intention was to destroy them privately by severe treatment; and to effect his purpose, they were confined, with their hands tied behind them to the walls of their dungeon, so that they could in no way render any service to each other, or even assist themselves. All communication with them was strictly forbidden, and their prison was rendered insupportable by the stench and filth which surrounded them.

In this deplorable condition they must have perished in a few days had their sufferings not come to the knowledge of the virtuous and intrepid Margaret Clement. This lady was the wife of a learned and pious physician, the friend of Sir Thomas More. She bribed the gaolers and so obtained daily entrance into the prison, disguised as a milk woman, with a pail upon her head, and supported the famishing religious, with the milk that she brought with her. She also cleansed, as far as she was able, their place of confinement, and carried away the filth in her pail. This charitable office she pursued for some days, until the king inquired if the monks were all dead? Being answered in the negative, he expressed his surprise, and gave orders that their confinement should be rendered still more rigorous. The keeper, being then fearful for his own personal safety, would no longer permit Mrs Clement to gain admittance into the prison. How long each of these persecuted men were able to bear such inhuman treatment is not known, but it

appears that they died by mid June, 1537.
E. H. Burton and J. H. Pollen, Lives of the English Martyrs, Vol 1, 1583-1588, Longman, 1914, pp 146-48

Faith of sixteenth-century monks

There entered others to pry into the liberty of the monks, searching forth the cause of their courage and constancy, and inquiring how they, above all others, durst stoutly resist the king's command, and what the weapons were wherewith they feared not to bid combat unto such a king. And when they found that the weapons, wherewith they defended themselves and their doctrine, were the sword of the spirit, which is the Word of God, and the frequent reading of the divine Scriptures and ancient fathers, being always ready to give satisfaction to every one that demanded an account of the faith and hope which was in them, therefore they took away all the books they could find in their cells, that by this means disarmed, they might be the more easily overcome. But neither could they thus prevail, for, although some armed with shield of learning did fight valiantly, notwithstanding others more confounded and pierced the hearts of the adversaries with their innocent simplicity; wherewith being well armed they would by no means pass over the bounds which their forefathers had set down for them, nor depart from the doctrine of our holy mother the church.

Then the time of trial came to show how every man's affections were inclined; whether to God or the devil, or the flesh and the world; because every one might do what he would, and the liberty of the one might do what he would, and the liberty of the flesh, which is the very slavery and thraldom of the devil, was granted to all that would depart out of the house. But thanks be to God, there was so much holiness of life, such constancy of mind, such modesty of words, such gladness in their countenance, such joy in their doings, and the moderation in all things, that all were troubled and confounded that saw them; for although they were deprived of a Prior, and made orphans without a father, yet every one was a prior unto himself, directing and instructing themselves prudently in all things.
E. H. Burton and J. H. Pollen, Lives of the English Martyrs, Vol 1, 1583-1588, Longman, 1914, pp 146-48

The martyrs of Meaux

The earliest "Reformed Church" inside France was organized by Estienne Mangin and Pierre LeClerc, who with twelve others were martyred in 1546.

Among the many cities of the kingdom of France, which were by the word of God made sharers and partakers in heavenly grace, the town of Meaux should be given first place. It is situated in Brie, on the river Marne, ten leagues from Paris. They celebrated once or twice the holy Supper as it had been established by Christ the Lord. Soon the little church increased so much that three to four hundred people of both sexes and of all ages were flocking to it, from as far as six leagues away. This caused them to be forthwith discovered and watched by some mischievous persons. They were indeed warned by certain friends and kind people to be on their guard against the crafty devices in preparation for them.

In 1546, on the 8th of September, a day consecrated by the Papists for celebrating the nativity of the virgin Mary, there came to the magistrate at the seventh hour of the morning an informer, who declared that the congregation had already begun to collect. As the magistrate and Provost arrived Pierre LeClerc was in the middle of expounding a passage from 1 Corinthians. The officers' attendants, who entered the building, stood for some time in a silent group as if thunderstruck. Then LeClerc was arrested and bound and tied, as he said, "Let us go, as God has thought fit." His gentleness was imitated by all the rest, both men and women, sixty-two people in total. This was indeed a sight to wonder at, when so many people of both sex were led away by so few, and showed such docility and willingness. The people were taken off to prison as they sang psalms, especially Psalm 72, "O God, the heathen are come."

As soon as they were shut up in prison a

very grave charge was brought against them: that they had ventured to perform the Supper of the Lord. And as to this matter it would be vain indeed to ask what offence and exasperation the mere phrase would have aroused in the whole order of monks and priests. So they were quickly placed in carriages, without so much as straw litter to give them a chance of repose, and taken to Paris. The judgement of the Parlement de Paris was that the fourteen should be condemned to death. These were Pierre LeClerc, Estienne Mangin, Jacques Bouchebec, Jean Brissebarre, Henry Hutinot, Thomas Honnore, Jean Boudouin, Jean Flesche, Jean Piquery, Jean Matheflon, Philippe Petit, Michel Caillon, and François LeClerc, who were all condemned to be first drawn on a hurdle to the place of execution and then burnt alive in the great market place at Meaux close to the house of Mangin.

Punishments of less severity, but still various in degree, were ordained for the rest, who were less conspicuous for their firmness and constancy in the pious doctrine they had adopted. These cases included both sexes. Some were beaten with rods and sent into exile; and it was ordained that others should be spectators of the bitter punishment suffered by those fourteen we have named, being themselves stationed in the greatest ignominy. One among them was ordered to be hung up by the armpits, his neck in a noose, and in that posture made a spectator of their extreme punishment. Indeed some women were condemned to look on in disgrace while the execution of the men was carried out.

Finally it was decreed and ordained by the same court that the house of Mangin, which it was said had been used for their meetings, should be entirely razed to the ground, for a perpetual mark of their impiety, as it was pronounced to be. On that spot a chapel was to be reared, wherein the Mass should be celebrated on each Thursday, a service instituted for the adoration of that chief god of the Papists which they falsely pretend is in the sacrament.

H. M. Bower, The Fourteen of Meaux, Longmans, 1894, pp 36-40

Thomas Cromwell

On July 28, 1540, or 1541, (for the chronology differs) Thomas Cromwell, earl of Essex, was brought to a scaffold on Tower-hill, where he was executed with some striking instances of cruelty. He made a short speech to the people, and then meekly resigned himself to the axe. It is, we think, with great propriety, that this nobleman is ranked among the martyrs; for although the accusations preferred against him, did not relate to anything in religion, yet had it not been for his zeal to demolish popery, he might have to the last retained the king's favor. To this may be added, that the papists plotted his destruction, for he did more towards promoting the Reformation, than any man in that age, except the good Dr. Cranmer.

Dr. Cuthbert Barnes, Thomas Garnet, and William Jerome

Soon after the execution of Cromwell, Dr. Cuthbert Barnes, Thomas Garnet, and William Jerome, were brought before the ecclesiastical court of the bishop of London, and accused of heresy. Being before the bishop of London, Dr. Barnes was asked whether the saints prayed for us? To this he answered, that "he would leave that to God; but (said he) I will pray for you."

On the thirteenth of July, 1541, these men were brought from the Tower to Smithfield, where they were all chained to one stake; and there suffered death with a constancy that nothing less than a firm faith in Jesus Christ could inspire.

Thomas Bainard and James Moreton: burnt alive at Buckingham

Dreadful persecutions were at this time carried on at Lincoln, under Dr. Longland, the bishop of that diocese. At Buckingham, Thomas Bainard, and James Moreton, the one for reading the Lord's Prayer in English, and the other for reading St. James' Epistles ion English, were both condemned and burnt alive.

Anthony Parsons

Anthony Parsons, a priest, together with two

others, was sent to Windsor, to be examined concerning heresy; and several articles were tendered to them to subscribe, which they refused. This was carried on by the bishop of Salisbury, who was the most violent persecutor of any in that age, except Bonner. When they were brought to the stake, Parsons asked for some drink, which being brought him, he drank to his fellow-sufferers, saying, "Be merry, my brethren, and lift up your hearts to God; for after this sharp breakfast I trust we shall have a good dinner in the Kingdom of Christ, our Lord and Redeemer." At these words Eastwood, one of the sufferers, lifted up his eyes and hands to heaven, desiring the Lord above to receive his spirit. Parsons pulled the straw near to him, and then said to the spectators, "This is God's armor, and now I am a Christian soldier prepared for battle: I look for no mercy but through the merits of Christ; He is my only Savior, in Him do I trust for salvation;" and soon after the fires were lighted, which burned their bodies, but could not hurt their precious and immortal souls. Their constancy triumphed over cruelty, and their sufferings will be held in everlasting remembrance.

Reading the Bible in English banned

Thus were Christ's people betrayed every way, and their lives bought and sold. For, in the said parliament, the king made this most blasphemous and cruel act, to be a law forever: that whatsoever they were that should read the Scriptures in the mother-tongue (which was then called "Wickliffe's learning"), they should forfeit land, cattle, body, life, and goods, from their heirs for ever, and so be condemned for heretics to God, enemies to the crown, and most arrant traitors to the land.

Foxe's Book of Martyrs, Edited by William Byron Forbush, chapter 14

Martyrdom of The Duke of Somerset (1)

The execution of the Duke of Somerset, 1552

On 22 January, soon after 8 o'clock in the morning, the duke of Somerset was beheaded on Tower Hill. There was as great a company as has been seen... the king's guard being there with their halberds and a thousand more with halberds of the privilege of the Tower, Ratcliffe, Limehouse, Whitechapel, St Katherine's and Stratford Bow, as well as Hoxton and Shoreditch; and the two sheriffs being present there, seeing the execution of my lord, and his head being cut off, and shortly after his body was put into a coffin and carried into the Tower, and there buried in the church, on the northside of the choir of St Peter's, and I beseech God to have mercy on his soul, amen! And there was a sudden rumbling a little before he died, as if it had been guns shooting and great horses coming, so that a thousand fell to the ground for fear, for they who were at one side thought no other but that one was killing another, so that they fell down to the ground, one upon another with their halberds, some fell into the ditch of the Tower and other places, and a hundred into the Tower ditch, and some ran away for fear.

Recorded by Henry Machyn, a London undertaker

Martyrdom of The Duke of Somerset (2)

At this time a great creation of peers took place. Warwick was made Duke of Northumberland, the Percies being then under an attainder: Paulet was made Marquis of Winchester; and Herbert, Earl of Pembroke. There was none so likely to take the king out of Northumberland's hands as the Duke of Somerset, who was beginning to form a new party. Therefore, upon some informations, the Duke of Somerset, Sir Ralph Vane, Sir Thomas Palmer, Sir Thomas Arundel and several others were committed to the Tower. The Duke of Somerset was brought to trial on December 1st and charged with a plot to seize the king, to imprison Northumberland and to raise the city of London. The unfortunate duke was condemned to be executed. Mr Foxe, who was present at the scene, has left an account of the execution which we cannot do better than quote.

On 22nd January, 1552, King Edward's uncle, the Duke of Somerset, was brought out of the Tower of London, and delivered up to the sheriffs of the city, who were accompanied by a great number of armed men and guards. When brought upon the scaffold, he maintained the utmost serenity; and kneeling down, he lifted up his hands, and commended his soul to God.

After having offered up a few short prayers, he arose and turned round, apparently quite undismayed at the sight of the executioner and his axe; but with the most perfect cheerfulness and composure addressed the people, in almost the following words:

"Dearly beloved friends, I am brought here to suffer death, although I have never offended, by word or deed, against the king; and have been as true and faithful a subject as any man in this realm. Nevertheless, as the law has sentenced me to death, I acknowledge that I, as well as any other man, have no appeal from it. Therefore, to show my obedience to the laws, I have come here to die, heartily thanking God for having allowed me this time for repentance, instead of cutting me off by sudden death.

"There is yet something, beloved friends, regarding the Christian religion, which I must put you in mind of; and which, when I was in authority, I always set forth to the utmost of my power. Not only do I not repent of my actions, but I rejoice in them, since now the forms of our Christian religion have come nearer to the order of the primitive church; which I look upon as a great benefit unto you and me, and exhort you all with thankfulness to accept and embrace what is so purely set forth before you, and to show the same in your lives, which, if you do not, greater calamity and mischief will surely follow."

Just as he concluded these words, the assembly was suddenly alarmed by a loud and extraordinary noise. To some it appeared as the sound of a great tempest, to others as the explosion of gunpowder, and to others as if a multitude of horsemen were rapidly approaching; but though all heard the noise, no one could see any cause for it. The terrified people ran in all directions; some falling into ditches and puddles, other hastening into the houses; other, falling down upon the ground, cried out to Jesus to save them. Those who remained in their places scarcely knew where they were, so great was the general panic. I, among the rest, was so alarmed by this hurbly, that I stood still amazed. During this commotion the people espied Sir Anthony Brown riding under the scaffold, which raised a fresh tumult, for all hoped that the king had sent his uncle pardon by this messenger; and throwing their caps up in the air, with great rejoicings, they cried, "Pardon, pardon is come; God save the king!" Thus the duke saw before his death what a popular favorite he was, and few dukes ever had more tears shed for them, for all men saw in his fall the ruin of England.

Somerset meanwhile remained standing quietly in his place, without displaying any excitement or emotion, though it must have given him comfort in these last dying moments to see how universal was the love and respect felt for him by the large mass of the people, though they were powerless to save him from the machinations of his enemies, whose rank and influence placed them beyond the pale of justice. At length, making a sign to the crowd with his hand to maintain silence, he thus addressed them:

"Dearly beloved friends, there is no such matter here in hand as you vainly hope or believe. It seemeth thus good unto Almighty God, whose ordinance it is meet and necessary that we all be obedient unto. Wherefore I pray you all to be quiet, and to be contented with my death, which I am most willing to suffer. And let us now join in prayer unto the Lord for the preservation of the king's majesty, unto whom, hitherto, I have always showed myself a most faithful and true subject. I have always been most diligent about his majesty, in his affairs both at home and abroad, and no less diligent in seeking the common good of the whole realm."

At which words all the people cried out it was most true.

Then the duke proceeding, said, "Unto whose majesty I wish continual health, and will all felicity, and all prosperous success."

Whereunto the people again cried out, "Amen."

"Moreover, I do wish unto all his councillors the grace and favor of God, whereby they may rule in all things uprightly with justice; unto whom I exhort you all in the Lord to show yourselves obedient, as it is your bounden duty, under the pain of condemnation, and also most profitable for the preservation and safeguard of the king's majesty.

"Moreover, as heretofore I have had oftentimes affairs with divers men, and hard it is to please every man, therefore, if there be any who hath been offended and injured by me, I most humbly require and ask him forgiveness; but especially Almighty God, whom throughout all my life I have most grievously offended. And all other, whatsoever they be, that have offended me, I do with my whole heart forgive them. Now I once again require you, dearly beloved in the Lord, that you will keep yourselves quiet and still, lest through your quietness I shall be much more composed."

After this, he again knelt down, when Dr Cox, who had accompanied him in order to let him have the benefit of his counsel and advice, if needed, presented him with a scroll of paper, on which was written a brief confession to God. The duke, after hearing it, again stood up, without any appearance of emotion, and bade farewell to the sheriffs, the Lieutenant of the Tower, and all others who were on the scaffold; then, giving some money to the executioner, he took off his gown, and, kneeling down, untied his shirt strings. The executioner removed his collar and other things, which would have proved a hindrance; and the duke, lying down, called out, "Lord Jesus, save me!" As the name of Jesus was on his lips, the fatal blow was struck, and in a moment he was freed for ever from all the cares and anxieties of this troubled world.

John Foxe, The Book of Martyrs, revised with notes and an appendix by W. Bramley-Moore, London, 1869, pp 288-294

PERSECUTIONS IN ENGLAND DURING QUEEN MARY'S REIGN

The premature death of that celebrated young monarch, Edward VI, occasioned the most extraordinary and wonderful occurrences, which had ever existed from the times of our blessed Lord and Savior's incarnation in human shape. This melancholy event became speedily a subject of general regret. The succession to the British throne was soon made a matter of contention; and the scenes which ensued were a demonstration of the serious affliction in which the kingdom was involved. As his loss to the nation was more and more unfolded, the remembrance of his government was more and more the basis of grateful recollection. The very awful prospect, which was soon presented to the friends of Edward's administration, under the direction of his counselors and servants, was a contemplation which the reflecting mind was compelled to regard with most alarming apprehensions. The rapid approaches which were made towards a total reversion of the proceedings of the young king's reign, denoted the advances which were thereby represented to an entire resolution in the management of public affairs both in Church and state. Alarmed for the condition in which the kingdom was likely to be involved by the king's death, an endeavor to prevent the consequences, which were but too plainly foreseen, was productive of the most serious and fatal effects. The king, in his long and lingering affliction, was induced to make a will, by which he bequeathed the English crown to Lady Jane, the daughter of the duke of Suffolk, who had been married to Lord Guilford, the son of the duke of Northumberland, and was the granddaughter of the second sister of King Henry, by Charles, duke of Suffolk. By this will, the succession of Mary and Elizabeth, his two sisters, was entirely superseded, from an apprehension of the returning system of popery; and the king's council, with the chief of the nobility, the lord-mayor of the city of London, and almost all the judges and the principal lawyers of the realm, subscribed their names to this regulation, as a sanction to the measure. Lord Chief Justice Hale, though a true Protestant and an upright judge, alone declined to unite his name in favor of the Lady Jane, because he had already signified his opinion that Mary was entitled to assume the reins of government. Others objected to Mary's being placed on the throne, on account of their fears that she might marry a foreigner, and thereby bring the crown into considerable danger. Her partiality to popery also left little doubt on the minds of any, that she would be induced to revive the dormant interests of the pope, and change the religion which had been used both in the days of her father, King Henry, and in those of her brother Edward: for in all his time she had manifested the greatest stubbornness and inflexibility of temper, as must be obvious from her letter to the lords of the council, whereby she put in her claim to the crown, on her brother's decease.

When this happened, the nobles, who had associated to prevent Mary's succession, and had been instrumental in promoting, and, perhaps, advising the measures of Edward, speedily proceeded to proclaim Lady Jane Gray, to be queen of England, in the city of London and various other populous cities of the realm. Though young, she possessed talents of a very superior nature, and her improvements under a most excellent tutor had given her many very great advantages. Her reign was of only five days' continuance, for Mary, having succeeded by false promises in obtaining the crown, speedily commenced the execution of her avowed intention of extirpating and burning every Protestant. She was crowned at Westminster in the usual form, and her elevation was the signal for the commencement of the bloody persecution which followed. Having obtained the sword of authority, she was not sparing in its exercise. The supporters of Lady Jane Gray were destined to feel its force. The duke of Northumberland was the first who experienced her savage resentment. Within a month after his confinement in the Tower, he was condemned, and brought to the scaffold, to suffer as a traitor. From his varied crimes, resulting out of a sordid and inordinate ambition, he died unpitied and unlamented. The changes, which followed with rapidity, unequivocally declared that the queen was disaffected to the present state of religion. Dr. Poynet was displaced to make room for Gardiner to be bishop of Winchester, to whom she also gave the important office of lord-chancellor. Dr. Ridley was dismissed from the see of London, and Bonne introduced. J. Story was put out of the bishopric of Chichester, to admit Dr. Day. J. Hooper was sent prisoner to the Fleet, and Dr. Heath put into the see of Worcestor. Miles Coverdale was also excluded from Exeter, and Dr. Vesie placed in that diocese. Dr. Tonstall was also promoted to the see of Durham. These things being marked and perceived, great heaviness and discomfort grew more and more to all good men's hearts; but to the wicked great rejoicing. They that could dissemble took no great care how the matter went; but such, whose consciences were joined with the truth, perceived already coals to be kindled, which after should be the destruction of many a true Christian.

Lady Jane Gray

The Words and Behavior of the Lady Jane upon the Scaffold

The next victim was the amiable Lady Jane Gray, who, by her acceptance of the crown at the earnest solicitations of her friends, incurred the implacable resentment of the bloody Mary. When she first mounted the scaffold, she spoke to the spectators in this manner: "Good people, I am come hither to die, and by a law I am condemned to the same. The fact against the queen's highness was unlawful, and the consenting thereunto by me: but, touching the procurement and desire thereof by me, or on my behalf, I do wash my hands thereof in innocency before God, and the face of you, good Christian people, this day:" and therewith she wrung her hands, wherein she had her book. Then said she, "I pray you all, good Christian people, to bear me witness, that I die a good Christian woman, and that I do look to be saved by no other mean, but only by the mercy of God in the blood of His only Son Jesus Christ: and I confess that when I did know the Word of God, I neglected the same, loved myself and the world, and therefore this plague and punishment is happily and worthily happened unto me for my sins; and yet I thank God, that of His goodness He hath thus given me a time and a respite to repent. And now, good people, while I am alive, I pray you assist me with your prayers."

And then, kneeling down, she turned to Feckenham, saying, "Shall I say this Psalm?" and he said, "Yea." Then she said the Psalm of Miserere mei Deus, in English, in a most devout manner throughout to the end; and then she stood up, and gave her maid, Mrs. Ellen, her gloves and handkerchief, and her book to Mr. Bruges; and then she untied he gown, and the executioner pressed upon her to help her off with it: but she, desiring him to let her alone, turned towards her two gentlewomen, who helped her off therewith, and also with her frowes, paaft, and neckerchief, giving to her a fair handkerchief to put about her eyes.

Then the executioner kneeled down, and asked her forgiveness, whom she forgave most willingly. Then he desired her to stand upon the straw, which doing, she saw the block. Then she said, "I pray you, despatch me quickly." Then she kneeled down, saying, "Will you take it off before I lay me down?" And the executioner said, "No, madam." Then she tied a handkerchief about her eyes, and feeling for the block, she said, "What shall I do? Where is it? Where is it?" One of the standers-by guiding her thereunto, she laid her head upon the block, and then stretched forth her body, and said, "Lord, into Thy hands I commend my spirit;" and so finished her life, in the year of our Lord 1554, the twelfth day of February, about the seventeenth year of her age.

Thus died Lady Jane; and on the same day Lord Guilford, her husband, one of the duke of Northumberland's sons, was likewise beheaded, two innocents in comparison with them that sat upon them. For they were both very young, and ignorantly accepted that which others had contrived, and by open proclamation consented to take from others, and give to them.

Touching the condemnation of this pious lady, it is to be noted that Judge Morgan, who gave sentence against her, soon after he had condemned her, fell mad, and in his raving cried out continually to have the Lady Jane taken away from him, and so he ended his life. On the twenty-first day of the same month, Henry, duke of Suffolk, was beheaded on Tower-hill, the fourth day after his condemnation: about which time many gentlemen and yeomen were condemned, whereof some were executed at London, and some in the country. In the number of whom was Lord Thomas Gray, brother to the said duke, being apprehended not long after in North Wales, and executed for the same. Sir Nicholas Throgmorton, also, very narrowly escaped.

John Hooper

When Mary ascended the throne Hooper was one of the first who were summoned to London. His friends, warning him of his danger, entreated him to leave the country, but he refused, saying, "Once did I flee, and take me to my feet, but now, because I am called to this place and vocation, I am thoroughly persuaded to remain, and to live and die with my sheep." He was ordered to appear before Dr Heath, who had been deprived of his bishopric in King Edward's time, and before Dr Bonner, Bishop of London, because he had, in the previous reign, been one of his accusers. On arriving in London, before he saw Bonner and Heath, he was intercepted, and commanded to appear before the queen and her council. On coming before them, Gardiner received him very opprobriously, railing at him, and accusing him of his religion. He answered boldly and freely, but was, notwithstanding, committed to ward, being told that it was not for his religion, but for certain sums of money which he owed the queen, that he was imprisoned. In March following, he was again called before Gardiner, and deprived of both his bishoprics (Worcester and Gloucester), not being permitted to plead his own cause.

On the 4th February, 1555, Bonner degraded Hooper, with all the usual pomp and pride of the Romish church. The same night his keeper gave him a hint that he would probably be sent to Gloucester to be burned. This greatly rejoiced Hooper, who, raising his hands to heaven, praised God for sending him to suffer death among the people over whom he was pastor. Immediately he sent word to his servant, to bring him his boots, spurs, cloak, that he might be in readiness to ride whenever the order came. At four o'clock the following morning, the keeper, accompanied by some others, came and searched him, to see whether he had concealed any papers. He was then led by the sheriff to a place previously appointed, where he was met by six of the queen's guard, who had orders to take him to Gloucester. The guard took him first to the Angel Inn, where he breakfasted. At break of day he cheerfully mounted his horse to proceed on the journey to Gloucester. His head was covered with a hood, placed under his hat, that he might not be recognized, and care was taken always to stop to bait or lodge at a different inn to the one the bishop was accustomed to stay at when he traveled. On Thursday they reached Cirencester, a town fifteen miles from Gloucester. Here the party halted at the house of a woman who knew the bishop, and had always hated him and the truths he had so boldly declared. When she saw the manner in which he was now being led to death, she lamented his case with tears, confessing that she had always believed that if put on his trial he would remain firm. After dining at Cirencester, they proceeded on their journey to Gloucester, which they reached about five o'clock the same evening. About a mile from the town great numbers of people had congregated to meet their bishop, and they loudly bewailed his sad fate, insomuch that one of the guard rode on with speed to the town, to ask aid from the mayor and sheriffs, lest the prisoner should be released by force. Accordingly a strong body of men were sent to the gate, with weapons, and the people were ordered to remain in their houses. Hooper was lodged at the house of a Mr Ingram, in the city. During the first part of the night he slept soundly, and afterwards remained engaged in prayer until the morning.

Sir Anthony Kingston, a former friend of the bishop's, had been appointed to attend at his execution. As soon as he saw the bishop he burst into tears. Hooper did not at first recognize him, when Sir Anthony said:

"Why, my lord, do not you know me – an old friend of yours – Anthony Kingston?"

"Yes, Sir Anthony, I do know you well, and am glad to see you in health, and praise God for the same."

"But I am sorry, my lord, to see you in this case, for, as I understand, you are come hither to die. But, alas! Consider that life is sweet, and death is bitter; therefore, seeing life may be had, desire to live, for life hereafter may do good."

"Indeed, it is true, Sir Anthony; I am come hither to end this life, and to suffer death here, because I will not gainsay the truth that I have heretofore taught among you in this diocese and elsewhere; and I thank you for your friendly counsel, although it be not as I could have wished it."

Sir Anthony then took leave of him, not without shedding bitter tears, and tears also ran down the face of the good bishop. At eight the next morning, the commissioners who were appointed to witness the execution arrived, accompanied by a large band of men. On seeing such a strongly-armed guard, Hooper said, "I am no traitor, neither needed you to have made such a business to bring me to the place where I must suffer; for if you had allowed me, I would have gone alone to the stake, and troubled none of you." Having been strictly forbidden to speak, he went in silence to the appointed place, smiling cheerfully on any whom he knew; he walked with difficulty, as he was suffering much from sciatica, which he had caught in prison. Upwards of 7,000 people congregated to see the last scene, the boughs of the trees in the square being used as seats. Three iron hoops had been prepared to fasten him to the stake, and he had three bags of gunpowder tied to him. When he had been secured, he pointed out how the faggots should be placed, and even arranged some with his own hands. There was a strong wind, and the greater part of the faggots being green, it was a long time before they caught fire. Three times were they lighted before they really began to burn up, and even when the gunpowder exploded it did him no good. He was heard to pray aloud, "Lord Jesus, have mercy upon me! Lord Jesus, receive my spirit!" These were the last words he was heard to utter; but when he was black in the mouth, and his tongue so swollen that he could not speak, yet his lips were seen to move. In three quarters of an hour his body fell forwards, and he was released from his sufferings.

John Foxe, The Book of Martyrs, revised with notes and an appendix by W. Bramley-Moore, London, 1869, pp 379-83

THOMAS TOMKINS

This plain honest Christian was by trade a weaver, and lived in the parish of Shoreditch, till he was summoned before the inhuman Bishop Bonner, and, with many others who had renounced the errors of Popery, was confined in a prison in that tyrant's house at Fulham.

During his confinement, the treatment which he received at the bishop's hands was not only disgraceful to the character of the latter as a prelate, but even as a man; for Bonner's violence was such, because Tomkins would not assent to the erroneous doctrine of transubstantiation, that his lordship struck him in the face, and plucked out the greatest part of his beard. Alas! that the outrages of Caiaphas' hall, Herod's palace, and Pilate's praetorium, should thus have been reproduced in modern times by those who called themselves the disciples of the lowly Jesus.

On another occasion, because our martyr remained inflexible, and would not deviate in the least point from the uncorrupted truths of the gospel, Bonner, in the presence of several of his visitors at his seat at Fulham, took the poor weaver by the fingers, and held his hand over the flame of wax candle, having three or four wicks, supposing that, being terrified by the smart of the fire, he would abjure the doctrine which he then maintained.

Tomkins, expecting nothing but immediate death, commended himself unto the Lord, saying, "O Lord, into thy hands I commend my spirit." When relating the incident to one James Hinse, Tomkins declared that his spirit was so entranced in God, that he did not feel the pain. And yet that burning was so severe, that the veins shrunk, and the sinews burst, and the water spurted in Mr Harpsfield's face, insomuch that Harpsfield, moved with pity, desired the bishop to stay, saying that he had tried him enough.

When he had been in prison for half a year, about the 8th of February he was brought with several others before Bishop Bonner, in his consistory, to be examined; to whom first was brought forth a certain bill or schedule, subscribed (as appeareth) with his own hand, and fifth day of the same month, containing these words:

"Thomas Tomkins, of Shoreditch, and of the diocese of London, hath believed and doth believe, that in the sacrament of the altar, under the forms of bread and wine there is not the very body and blood of our Savior Jesus Christ in substance, but only a token and remembrance thereof, the very body and blood of Christ being only in heaven and nowhere else.

By me, THOMAS TOMKINS

Whereupon he was asked whether he acknowledged the same subscription to be his own. He admitted it to be so. The bishop then endeavored to persuade him with fair words, rather than with reasons, to relinquish his opinions, and to return to the unity of the Catholic Church, promising, if he would do so, to absolve him from the past. But he constantly refused.

Having been declared an obstinate heretic by the bloody tribunal of bishops, they delivered him up to the secular power, and he was burned in Smithfield, March 6th, 1555, triumphing in the middle of the flames, and adding to the noble company of martyrs who had preceded him through the path of the fiery trial to the realms of immortal glory.

John Foxe, The Book of Martyrs, revised with notes and an appendix by W. Bramley-Moore, London, 1869, pp 85-88

John Rogers

Jesus said, "No-one who has left home or wife or brothers or parents or children for the sake of the kingdom of God will fail to receive many times as much in this age and, in the age to come, eternal life" (Luke 18:29-30 NIV). While Mr Rogers remained in prison, he expressed his sentiments, in a bold and manly strain, upon the evils and abuses brought into the country, and threatened its rulers with the vengeance that had fallen, in different ages, upon the enemies of truth.

"I am an Englishman born," said he, "and, God knoweth, do naturally wish well to my country. I have often proved that the things which I have much feared should come to pass have indeed followed. I pray God I may fail of my guessing in this behalf.

"And as touching your rejoicing, although God had set you aloft to punish us by miracle (for so you report and brag openly of yourself), and to minister justice, if we will not receive your holy father's mercy, and thereby do declare your church to be true, and ours false; to that I answer thus: God's works are wonderful, and are not to be comprehended and perceived by man's wisdom, nor by the wit of the most wise and prudent.

"But here they will cry out, "Lo! these men will be still John Baptist, the apostles, and prophets."

"I answer, We make not ourselves like unto them, in the singular virtues and gifts of God given unto them; as of doing miracles, and of many other things. The similitude and likeness of them and us consisteth not in all things, but only in this, that is, that we be like then in doctrine, and in the suffering of persecution and infamy for the same. The apostles were beaten for their boldness, and they rejoiced that they suffered for Christ's cause. Ye have also provided rods for us, and bloody whips; yet when ye have done that which God's hand and counsel hath determined that ye shall do, be it life or death, I trust that God will so assist us by his Spirit and grace, that we shall patiently suffer, and praise God for it. And whatsoever become of me and others, which now suffer for speaking and professing the truth, yet be ye sure that God's Word will prevail and have the upper hand, when your bloody laws and wicked devices, for want of sure foundation, shall fall in the dust. Of what force, I pray you, may a man think these Parliaments to be, which scantily can stand a year in strength? or what credit is to be given to these law makers, who are not ashamed to establish contrary laws, and to condemn that for evil which before they affirmed and decreed to be good? Truly ye are so ready, contrary to all right, to change and turn for the pleasure of man, that at length, I fear, God will use you like changelings, and both turn you forth of his kingdom and out of your own country."

Mr Rogers was confined for a long time, lodged in Newgate among thieves, and often harshly examined by Gardiner and others. He was at length condemned by the Bishop of Winchester. The keeper of Newgate's wife was sent to tell him to prepare for the fire. When she came to him, she found him sleeping so profoundly, that she had some difficulty in awaking him. At length, being aroused and fairly awaked, he was told to make haste.

He was then led to Bishop Bonner to be degraded, which being done, he craved one petition of the bishop – that he might speak a few words to his wife before he was burnt. Even this was denied him. "Then," said he, "you declare what your charity is."

The sheriffs now led him away to Smithfield. Here he was asked if he would recant his opinion. He answered that what he had preached he would seal with his blood. "Then," said the sheriff, "thou art a heretic."

To which the unshaken hero of God replied, "That shall be known at the day of judgement."

"Well," said the sheriff, "I will never pray for thee."

"But I will pray for you," said Mr Rogers.

All the way to the stake he was singing psalms; all the people were rejoicing at his constancy. On the way he was met by his wife and his eleven children, one an infant in her arms. This sad sight did not move him, but he cheerfully and patiently went on his way to Smithfield, where he was burnt to ashes in the presence of a great number of people, and his soul ascended in a chariot of fire to that Redeemer of whom he was worthy, inasmuch as he loved him more than wife and children, yea, even than his own life also.

John Foxe, The Book of Martyrs, revised with notes and an appendix by W. Bramley-Moore, London, 1869, pp 326-27

Rowland Taylor

The little town of Hadley first heard the pure gospel of Christ from the lips of Thomas Bilney, who preached there with great earnestness, and whose work was greatly blessed, with many men and women gladly embracing the faith as it is in Christ Jesus. After Bilney's martyrdom Dr Rowland Taylor was appointed vicar of the parish.

When Mary succeeded to the crown, dark clouds gathered round Taylor and all others who were like-minded, and an opportunity was soon seized of bringing him into trouble. Two men in Hadley, Clark and Foster, the one a tradesman and the other a lawyer, determined to have mass publicly performed in the parish church, according to the rites of the Romish priests. They accordingly persuaded the minister from a neighboring parish to come over and perform the service during Passion week. Dr Taylor, hearing the bells ringing at an unusual hour, hastened to the church to inquire the cause. Finding the large doors fastened, he entered through the chancel, and was astonished to see a priest in Romish vestments preparing to celebrate mass, and guarded by a body of armed men. Dr Taylor, as vicar, demanded of him what right he had to be there without his consent, to which the lawyer, Foster, insolently replied, "Thou traitor! how darest thou to intercept the execution of the queen's orders?" But the doctor undauntedly denied the charge of traitor, and asserted his mission as a minister of Christ, and delegation to that part of his flock, commanding the priest, as a wolf in sheep's clothing, to depart, nor infect the pure church of God with Popish idolatry.

In January, 1555, Dr Taylor was summoned to appear before the Bishops of London, Durham, Norwich, Salisbury, and Winchester, and required to give a determinate answer to the charge of heresy made against him, either to abjure his errors or receive the sentence of condemnation. He boldly answered that he would not depart from the truth he had preached nor submit to the authority of the Pope, and that he thanked God for his graciousness in counting him worthy to suffer for his name. On this the bishops at once proceeded to read the sentence of death on him, and committed him to the Compter.

At Chelmsford Dr Taylor was delivered to the sheriff of Suffolk, and conducted by him to Hadley. When they arrived there, and were riding over the bridge, there was a poor man waiting with five children: and when he saw Dr Taylor, he and his children fell down upon their knees, and holding up their hands, cried with a loud voice, "Oh, dear father and good shepherd, God help and succor thee, as thou hast many a time succored me and my poor children!' Such witness had this servant of God of his virtuous and charitable life. The streets of Hadley were crowded with men and women of the town and country, who waited to see him; and on beholding him led to death, with weeping eyes and lamentable voices they cried one to another, "Ah, good Lord! There goeth our good shepherd from us, who so faithfully hath taught us, so fatherly hath cared for us, and so religiously hath governed us!'

Coming to the alms-houses, which he well knew, he cast money to the poor people, which remained out of what had been given him during his imprisonment. As for his living, they took it from him at his first committal to prison, so that he was supported all the time of his confinement by the alms of his visitors.

On arriving at Aldham Common, the place where he should suffer, seeing a great multitude, he asked, "What place is this, and what meaneth it that so much people are gathered hither?'

It was answered, "It is Aldham Common, the place where you must suffer: and the people are come to behold you."

Then, said he, "Thanked be God, I am even at home."

On alighting, he desired leave of the sheriff to speak; but the latter refused it. Dr Taylor, perceiving that he would not be allowed to speak, sat down, and seeing one named Soyce, he called him, and said, "Soyce, I pray thee come and pull off my boots, and take them for thy labor: thou hast long looked for them, now take them." Then he rose up and pulled off his clothes unto his shirt, and gave them away; which done, he said with a loud voice, "Good people, I have taught you nothing but God's holy Word, and those lessons that I have taken out of God's blessed book, the Holy Bible: and I am come hither this day to seal it with my blood."

With that Holmes, yeoman of the guard, who had used Dr Taylor very cruelly all the way, gave him a great stroke upon the head. Then, seeing that they would not allow him to speak, Dr Taylor knelt down and prayed, and a poor woman who was among the people stepped in and prayed with him; but they thrust her away, and threatened to tread her down with their horses: notwithstanding this, she would not move, but remained and prayed with him. When he had prayed he went to the stake and kissed it, and placed himself in a pitch-barrel, which they had set for him to stand in, and so stood with his back upright against the stake, with his hands folded together, and his eyes towards heaven, and kept praying continually.

Sir John Shelton standing by, as Dr Taylor was saying the psalm Miserere in English, struck him on the lips. "You knave,' said he, "speak Latin; I will make thee." At last they kindled the fire; when the martyr, holding up his hands, called upon God, and said, "Merciful Father of heaven, for Jesus Christ my Savior's sake, receive my soul into thy hands." He then folded his hands together, and bore his sufferings without a murmur. Soyce, seizing a halbert, struck him such a blow on the head, that his brains were knocked out, and his body fell lifeless into the flames.

John Foxe, The Book of Martyrs, revised with notes and an appendix by W. Bramley-Moore, London, pp 334-337

Martyrdom of William Hunter

William Hunter had been trained to the doctrines of the Reformation from his earliest youth, being descended from religious parents, who carefully instructed him in the principles of true religion. Hunter, then nineteen years of age, refusing to receive the communion at Mass, was threatened to be brought before the bishop; to whom this valiant young martyr was conducted by a constable. Bonner caused William to be brought into a chamber, where he began to reason with him, promising him security and pardon if he would recant. Nay, he would have been content if he would have gone only to receive and to confession, but William would not do so for all the world. Upon this the bishop commanded his men to put William in the stocks in his gate house, where he sat two days and nights, with a crust of brown bread and a cup of water only, which he did not touch.

At the two days' end, the bishop came to him, and finding him steadfast in the faith, sent him to the convict prison, and commanded the keeper to lay irons upon him as many as he could bear. He continued in prison three quarters of a year, during which time he had been before the bishop five times, besides the time when he was condemned in the consistory in St. Paul's, February 9, at which time his brother, Robert Hunter, was present. Then the bishop, calling William, asked him if he would recant, and finding he was unchangeable, pronounced sentence upon him, that he should go from that place to Newgate for a time, and thence to Brentwood, there to be burned. About a month afterward, William was sent down to Brentwood, where he was to be executed. On coming to the stake, he knelt down and read the Fifty-first Psalm, until he came to these words, "The sacrifices of God are a broken spirit; a broken and a contrite heart, O God, Thou wilt not despise."

Steadfast in refusing the queen's pardon, if he would become an apostate, at length one Richard Ponde, a bailiff, came, and made the chain fast about him. William now cast his psalter into his brother's hand, who said, "William, think on the holy passion of Christ, and be not afraid of death." "Behold," answered William, "I am not afraid." Then he lifted up his hands to heaven, and said, "Lord, Lord, Lord, receive my spirit;" and casting down he head again into the smothering smoke, he yielded up his life for the truth, sealing it with his blood to the praise of God.

Foxe's Book of Martyrs, Edited by William Byron Forbush, chapter 16

Robert Farrar

Robert Farrar was bishop of St David's and was burned at Carmarthen, March 30, 1555.

This excellent and learned prelate had been promoted to his bishopric by the Lord Protector, in the reign of Edward; but after the fall of is patron, he also had fallen into disgrace, through the malice and false accusations of several enemies, among whom was George Constantine, his own servant. Fifty-six articles were preferred against him, in which he was charged with many negligences and contumacies of the church government. These he answered and denied. But so many and so bitter were his enemies, that they prevailed, and he was in consequence thrown into prison. He was now prosecuted on different charges – namely, such as related to doctrine; and he had been called up in company with the glorious martyrs, Hooper, Rogers, Bradford, and Saunders, on the 4th of February, and with them would have been condemned; but from the want of leisure, where he remained till the 14th of February. As much of the examination and answers as could be collected we here present to our readers.

At his first appearance before the lord chancellor, Stephen Gardiner, Bishop of Winchester, and the Bishops of Durham, Bath (Dr Bourne) and Worcester, the lord chancellor said unto him, "Now, sir, have you heard how the world goeth here?'

FARRAR: If it please your honor, I know not.

WINCHESTER: What say you? Do you not know things abroad, notwithstanding you are a prisoner?

FARRAR: No, my lord, I know not.

WINCHESTER: Lo! what froward fellow is this!

FARRAR: If it please your lordship, how should I know anything abroad, being a prisoner?

WINCHESTER: Have you not heard of the coming in of the lord cardinal?

FARRAR: I know not my lord cardinal; but I have heard that a cardinal was come in, but I did not believe it, and I believe it not yet.

WORCESTER: I pray your lordship tell him yourself, that he may know what is done.

WINCHESTER: The queen's majesty and the Parliament hath restored religion to the same state it was in at the beginning of the reign of our King Henry VIII. Ye are in the queen's debt, and her majesty will be good unto you, if you will return to the Catholic Church.

FARRAR: In what state I am concerning my debts to the queen's majesty, in the Court of Exchequer, my lord treasurer knoweth: and the last time that I was before your honor, and the first time also, I showed you that I had made an oath never to consent nor agree that the Bishop of Rome should have any power or jurisdiction within this realm: and further I need not rehearse to your lordship; you know it well enough.

BOURNE: You were once abjured for heresy at Oxford.

FARRAR: That was I not.

BOURNE: You were.

FARRAR: I never was; it is not true.

BOURNE: You went from St David's to Scotland.

FARRAR: That I did not.

BOURNE: You did.

FARRAR: That did I never; but I went from York to Scotland.

BOURNE: Ah! so said I; you went with Barlow.

FARRAR: That is true, but never from St David's.

BOURNE: You carried books out of Oxford, to the Archbishop of York, L. Lee.

FARRAR: I did not; but I carried old books from St Oswald's to the Bishop of York.

BOURNE: You supplanted your master.

FARRAR: That did I never in my life.

BOURNE: By my faith you did.

FARRAR: Forsooth, I did not, never in my life; but did shield and save my master from danger, and that obtained of King Henry VIII, for my true service, I thank God therefore.

BOURNE: (To my lord chancellor) My lord, he hath an ill name in Wales, as ever had any.

FARRAR: That is not so. Whosoever saith so, they shall never be able to prove it.

BOURNE: He hath deceived the queen in diverse sums of money.

FARRAR: That is utterly untrue; I never deceived the king nor queen of one penny in my life, and you shall never be able to prove that you say.

WINCHESTER: Thou art a false knave. Then Farrar stood up unbidden, for all that while he kneeled, and said, "No, my lord; I am a true man, I thank God for it. I was born under King Henry VII, I served King Henry VIII and King Edward VI truly, and have served the queen's majesty that now is, truly with my poor heart and word: more I could not do, and I was never false, nor shall be, by the grace of God."

WINCHESTER: How sayest thou? wilt thou be reformable?

FARRAR: My lord, I have an oath to God, and to King Henry VIII, and also to King Edward, and in that to the queen's majesty, the which I can never break while I live, to die for it.

DURHAM: You have made another oath before.

FARRAR: No, my lord, I never made another oath before.

DURHAM: You made a vow.

FARRAR: That did I not.

WINCHESTER: You made a profession to live without a wife.

FARRAR: No, my lord, that did I never: I made a profession to live chastely; but not without a wife.

WORCESTER: You were sworn to him that was master of your house.

FARRAR: That was I never.

WINCHESTER: Well, you are a froward knave: we will have no more to do with you, seeing that you will not come; we will be short with you, and that you shall know within this seven-night.

FARRAR: I am as it pleaseth your honor to call me; but I cannot break my oath, which your lordship yourself made before me, and gave in example, the which confirmed my conscience. Then I can never break the oath whilst I live, to die for it.

DURHAM: Well, saith he, he standeth upon his oath; call another. My lord chancellor then rang a little bell; and Mr Farrar said, "I pray God save the king and queen's majesties long to continue in honor to God's glory and their comfort, and the comfort of the whole realm; and I pray God save all your honors,' and so departed.

After these examinations, Bishop Farrar remained in prison uncondemned, till the 14th of February, and then was sent down to Wales, to receive sentence of condemnation.

On the appointed day this true servant of God appeared before Henry, the pretended bishop of St David's, and was asked whether he would renounce his heresies, schisms, and errors which hitherto he had maintained, and if he would subscribe to the Catholic articles.

Upon this Bishop Farrar did exhibit a certain schedule written in English; appealing withal by express word of mouth from the bishop, as from an incompetent judge, to Cardinal Poole.

Notwithstanding this, Morgan, proceeding in his rage, pronounced the definitive sentence against him, contained in writing: by which sentence he denounced him as a heretic excommunicate, and to be given up forthwith to the secular power – namely, to the sheriff of the town of Carmarthen, Mr Leyson; after which his degradation followed as a matter of course.

Thus this godly bishop, being condemned and degraded, was committed to the secular power, and not long after was brought to the place of execution in the town of Carmarthen, where he, in the market-place on the south side of the cross, on the 30th of March, most patiently sustained the torments of fire.

John Foxe, The Book of Martyrs, revised with notes and an appendix by W. Bramley-Moore, London, 1869, pp 338-341

JOHN BRADFORD

"I pray you stretch out your gentleness that I may feel it, for hitherto I have not."

John Bradford determined to devote his life to the Scriptures, and the ministry of the Word. In order to carry out his plan, he went to Cambridge University, where he applied himself with such diligence, that in a few years the degree of Master of Arts was conferred on him. He was then made a Fellow of Pembroke College, and was befriended by Martin Bucer, who strongly urged him to use his talents in preaching. Bradford replied that he could not preach, ask he did not consider himself qualified for such an office; to which his friend would answer, "If thou hast not fine wheat bread, yet give the poor people barely bread, or whatsoever else the Lord hath committed unto thee."

Bradford was appointed by Dr Ridley as a prebendary of St Paul's, where he labored diligently for three years, after which he was called upon to show his allegiance to his Savior by following him to prison and to death.

It was in the first year of Queen Mary's reign that the Bishop of Bath, Dr Bourne, preached at Paul's Cross on the merits of Popery, which raised the indignation of the people to such a pitch, that they would have pulled him out from the pulpit by force, had not the bishop, seeing the danger, called to Mr Bradford, who was standing near, to come forward and take his place. Bradford obeyed the request, and so greatly was he respected and beloved, that he soon quelled the rising tumult, and dismissed the people quietly to their homes. Within three days he was summoned before the queen's council, and accused of having saved Bourne's life, and having put himself forward to preach in the bishop's stead; being found guilty, he was committed to the Tower.

For two years he remained closely confined there; and then he was brought before the lord chancellor, and other councillors, to be examined on the accusation of seditious behavior at Paul's Cross.

On entering the council room, the chancellor told him he had been justly imprisoned for his arrogancy in preaching without authority; "but now,' he said, "the time for mercy has come, and the queen's highness hath by us sent for you, to declare and give the same, if you will with us return; and if you will do as we have done, you shall find as we have found."

To this Bradford answered, "My lords, I know that I have been long imprisoned, and – with humble reverence be it spoken – unjustly, for that I did nothing seditiously, falsely, or arrogantly, in word or fact, by preaching or otherwise, but rather sought truth, peace, and all godly quietness, as an obedient and faithful subject, both in going about to serve the present Bishop of Bath, then Mr Bourne, the preacher at the Cross, and in preaching for quietness accordingly."

The chancellor angrily made answer: I know thou hast a glorious tongue, and goodly shows thou makest; but all is lies thou speakest. And again, I have not forgot how stubborn thou wast when thou wast before us in the Tower, whereupon thou wast committed to prison concerning religion."

The conversation continued as follows:

BRADFORD: My lord, I stand as before you, so before God, and one day we shall all stand before him; the truth then will be the truth, though now ye will not take it so. Yea, my lord, I dare say that my lord of Bath, Mr Bourne, will witness with me, that I sought his safeguard with the peril of mine own life. I thank God, therefore.

BISHOP BONNER: That is not true, for I myself did see thee take upon thee too much.

BRADFORD: No; I took nothing upon me undesired, and that of Mr Bourne himself, as, were he present, I dare say he would affirm. For he desired me both to help him to pacify the people, and also not to leave him until he was in safety. The councillors and bishops then began to question him on religious opinions, that they might find some reason to sentence him to death; and after much argument, the lord chancellor again offered him mercy, to which Bradford nobly and simply answered that mercy with God's mercy would be welcome, but otherwise he would have none. On this the chancellor rang a bell, and when the under-marshal entered, said to him, "You shall take this man with you, and keep him close, without conference with any man but by your knowledge, and suffer him not to write any letters, for he is of another manner of charge to you now than he was before." And so the first examination ended, Bradford testifying by his looks, as well as his words, that he was ready and willing, yea, even desirous, to lay down his life in confirmation of his faith and doctrine.

In about a week he was again brought before the council, when the chancellor having made a long speech, Bradford thus answered: "My lords, as I now stand in your sight before you, so I humbly beseech your honors to consider that you sit in the seat of the Lord, who, as David doth witness, is in the congregation of judges, and sitteth in the midst of them judging: and as you would have your place to be by us taken as God's place, so demonstrate yourselves to follow him in your sitting; that is, seek not guiltless blood, neither hunt by questions to bring into a snare them which are out of the same. At this present I stand before you guilty or guiltless; then proceed and give sentence accordingly: if guiltless, then give me the benefit of a subject, which hitherto I could not have."

Here the lord chancellor said that Bradford began with a true sentence, saying that the Lord is in the midst of them that judge: "But,' said he, "this and all thy gesture declareth but hypocrisy and vain-glory." He then continued, endeavoring to clear himself from the charge of seeking to shed innocent blood, stating that Bradford's act at Paul's Cross was arrogant and presumptuous, and a taking upon himself to lead the people, which could not but tend to much disquietness. He then accused him of having written seditious letters when in the Tower, and of having endeavored to pervert the people, and finally questioned him closely as to his belief in the presence of Christ in the sacrament.

To this Bradford replied, "My lord, I have now been a year and almost three quarters in prison, and in all this time you have never questioned my hereabouts, when I might have spoke my conscience frankly without peril; but now you have a law to hang up and put to death, if a man answer freely and not to your liking, and so now you come to demand this question. Ah! my lord, Christ used not this way to bring men to faith; nor did the prophets nor apostles."

Here the lord chancellor, affecting astonishment and horror, replied that neither did he use such means, that he had ofttimes been charged with showing too much gentleness and forbearance. The Bishop of London, and nearly all the rest of the audience, the broke out into affirmations of his gentleness and mildness.

Mr Bradford answered, "Then, my lord, I pray you stretch out your gentleness that I may feel it, for hitherto I have not."

The lord chancellor being now informed that his dinner was ready, arose, and Bradford was again led to his prison.

At seven the next morning, Mr Thomas Hussey came into the room where he was confined, and, saying that he came to see and speak to him through love, said, "So wonderfully did you behave yourself before chancellor and other bishops yesterday, that even the greatest enemies you have say they have no matter against you; therefore I advise you to desire a time, and men to confer with, so by that means you may escape danger, which is otherwise nearer to you than you suppose."

Bradford refused to make any such request, which would give occasion to people to think that he doubted the doctrine he confessed. While they were still talking Dr Seton entered the room, and began to speak of Ridley and Latimer, who, he said, were unable to answer anything, and had desired to confer with others, hinting that Bradford had better follow their example. Bradford, however, refused his suggestions as he had Mr Hussey's, whereupon they both became enraged, calling him arrogant and vain-glorious.

Soon after they had quitted his cell, the prisoner was again brought before his judges, when, after a long discussion, during which he displayed as much gentleness as they did ferocity, the sentence of excommunication was read, when he knelt down an thanked God that he was thought worthy to suffer for his sake. It was proposed that he should be sent to Manchester, his native town, to be burnt; and while they were settling whether or not it should be so, he was once again committed to prison.

He remained there nearly five months; when one afternoon the keeper's wife came to him, and in much trouble, said, "Oh, Mr Bradford, I come to bring you heavy news."

"What is that?' asked he.

"Tomorrow,' she replied, "you must be burnt; and your chain is now a- buying, and you must soon go to Newgate."

Bradford, taking off his cap, and lifting up his eyes to heaven, exclaimed, "I thank God for it."

Then, after thanking the woman for the kindness she had always shown him, he went to his room, and remained in private prayer for some time. At midnight he was removed to Newgate, and the next morning conducted by a large body of armed men to Smithfield, where he suffered death by being burnt alive, in company with a young man only twenty years of age, being joyful to the last moment of his life that he was thought worthy to die for his Savior.

John Foxe, The Book of Martyrs, revised with notes and an appendix by W. Bramley-Moore, London, 1869, pp 339-346

LAURENCE SAUNDERS

Laurence Saunders was one of the Puritans executed in 1555 as part of Queen Mary's great persecution of Protestants.

"If the Devil were wise enough and would stand by in silence and let the Gospel be preached, he would suffer less harm. For when there is no battle for the Gospel it rusts and it finds no cause and no occasion to show its vigor and power. Therefore, nothing better can befall the Gospel than that the world should fight it with force and cunning."
Martin Luther

Baron Mourdaunt asked Laurence where he was going. "I have a cure in London," he replied, and "I go to instruct my people according to my duty."

"I would advise you not to preach,"'said Mourdaunt.

"If you forbid me by lawful authority, then I must obey," said Laurence.

"No, I will not forbid you but I give you counsel."

After they parted Mordaunt rode at once to inform Edmund Bonner, Bishop of London, that Saunders would preach to his congregation next day.

The following morning Laurence preached and in the afternoon returned to the church to deliver the customary second sermon. But the Bishop's officer arrived to escort him to Fulham Palace where he was charged with "treason for breaking the Queen's proclamation, heresy and sedition for his sermon." The bishop ordered him to write out his rejection of the Catholic doctrine of the mass. Laurence did so, realizing that he was writing his own death warrant. "My Lord, you do seek my blood," Laurence said as he handed the paper to Bonner, "and you shall have it. I pray God that you may be so baptized in it that you may thereafter loathe blood-sucking and become a better man."

After a fifteen-month imprisonment, Laurence was taken to Coventry, where he arrived on 7 February, 1555. He spent the night in the common gaol among other prisoners, where he passed the time praying. Next morning he was led to the place of execution outside the city, dressed in an old gown and a shirt, barefooted. Near the stake an officer asked Laurence to recant his heresies in exchange for a royal pardon: "If not, yonder fire is prepared for you."

Laurence remained steadfast. "It is not I nor my fellow-preachers of God's truth that have hurt the Queen's realm, but yourself and such as you are, which have always resisted God's holy word. I hold no heresies; but the blessed gospel of Christ, that I hold; that have I taught, and that will I never revoke."

With that the tormentor cried, "Away with him!"

"And away," Foxe wrote, "went Saunders with a merry courage towards the fire. He fell to the ground and prayed; he rose up again and took the stake in his arms and kissed it saying, Welcome the cross of Christ. Welcome everlasting life.

And being fastened to the stake and fire put to him, full sweetly he slept in the Lord. ***Editor***

The Rev George Marsh

George Marsh, born in the parish of Deane, in the county of Lancaster, received a good education and trade from his parents; about his twenty-fifth year he married, and lived, blessed with several children, on his farm until his wife died. He then went to study at Cambridge, and became the curate of Rev. Lawrence Saunders, in which duty he constantly and zealously set forth the truth of God's Word, and the false doctrines of the modern Antichrist. Being confined by Dr. Coles, the bishop of Chester, within the precincts of his own house, he was dept from any intercourse with his friends during four months; his friends and mother, earnestly wished him to have flown from "the wrath to come;" but Mr. Marsh thought that such a step would ill agree with that profession he had during nine years openly made. He, however, secreted himself, but he had much struggling, and in secret prayer begged that God would direct him, through the advice of his best friends, for his own glory and to what was best. At length, determined by a letter he received, boldly to confess the faith of Christ, he took leave of his mother-in-law and other friends, recommending his children to their care and departed for Smethehills, whence he was, with others, conducted to Lathum, to undergo examination before the earl of Derby, Sir William Nores, Mr. Sherburn, the parson of Garpnal, and others. The various questions put to him he answered with a good conscience, but when Mr. Sherburn interrogated him upon his belief of the Sacrament of the altar, Mr. Marsh answered like a true Protestant that the essence of the bread and wine was not at all changed, hence, after receiving dreadful threats from some, and fair words from others, for his opinions, he was remanded to ward, where he lay two nights without any bed. On Palm Sunday he underwent a second examination, and Mr. Marsh much lamented that his fear should at all have induced him to prevaricate, and to seek his safety, as long as he did not openly deny Christ; and he again cried more earnestly to God for strength that he might not be overcome by the subtleties of those who strove to overrule the purity of his faith. He underwent three examinations before Dr. Coles, who, finding him steadfast in the Protestant faith, began to read his sentence; but he was interrupted by the chancellor, who prayed the bishop to stay before it was too late. The priest then prayed for Mr. Marsh, but the latter, upon being again solicited to recant, said he durst not deny his Savior Christ, lest he lose His everlasting mercy, and so obtain eternal death. The bishop then proceeded in the sentence. He was committed to a dark dungeon, and lay deprived of the consolation of any one (for all were afraid to relieve or communicate with him) until the day appointed came that he should suffer. The sheriffs of the city, Amry and Couper, with their officers, went to the north gate, and took out Mr. George Marsh, who walked all the way with the Book in his hand, looking upon the same, whence the people said, "This man does not go to his death as a thief, nor as one that deserveth to die."

When he came to the place of execution

without the city, near Spittal-Boughton, Mr. Cawdry, deputy chamberlain of Chester, showed Mr. Marsh a writing under a great seal, saying that it was a pardon for him if he would recant. He answered that he would gladly accept the same did it not tend to pluck him from God. After that, he began to speak to the people showing the cause of his death, and would have exhorted them to stick unto Christ, but one of the sheriffs prevented him. Kneeling down, he then said his prayers, put off his clothes unto his shirt, and was chained to the post, having a number of fagots under him, and a thing made like a firkin, with pitch and tar in it, over his head. The fire being unskillfully made, and the wind driving it in eddies, he suffered great extremity, which notwithstanding he bore with Christian fortitude.

When he had been a long time tormented in the fire without moving, having his flesh so broiled and puffed up that they who stood before him could not see the chain wherewith he was fastened, and therefore supposed that he had been dead, suddenly he spread abroad his arms, saying, "Father of heaven have mercy upon me!" and so yielded his spirit into the hands of the Lord. Upon this, many of the people said he was a martyr, and died gloriously patient. This caused the bishop shortly after to make a sermon in the cathedral church, and therein he affirmed, that the said "Marsh was a heretic, burnt as such, and is a firebrand in hell." Mr. Marsh suffered April 24, 1555.

William Flower

William Flower, otherwise Branch, was born at Snow-hill, in the county of Cambridge, where he went to school some years, and then came to the abby of Ely. After he had remained a while he became a professed monk, was made a priest in the same house, and there celebrated and sang Mass. After that, by reason of a visitation, and certain injunctions by the authority of Henry VIII he took upon him the habit of a secular priest, and returned to Snow-hill, where he was born, and taught children about half a year. He then went to Ludgate, in Suffolk, and served as a secular priest about a quarter of a year; from thence to Stoniland; at length to Tewksbury, where he married a wife, with whom he ever after faithfully and honestly continued. After marriage he resided at Tewksbury about two years, and thence went to Brosley, where he practiced physic and surgery; but departing from those parts he came to London, and finally settled at Lambeth, where he and his wife dwelt together. However, he was generally abroad, excepting once or twice in a month, to visit and see his wife. Being at home upon Easter Sunday morning, he came over the water from Lambeth into St. Margaret's Church at Westminster; when seeing a priest, named John Celtham, administering and giving the Sacrament of the alter to the people, and being greatly offended in his conscience with the priest for the same, he struck and wounded him upon the head, and also upon the arm and hand, with his wood knife, the priest having at the same time in his hand a chalice with the consecrated host therein, which became sprinkled with blood. Mr. Flower, for this injudicious zeal, was heavily ironed, and put into the gatehouse at Westminster; and afterward summoned before bishop Bonner and his ordinary, where the bishop, after he had sworn him upon a Book, ministered articles and interrogatories to him. After examination, the bishop began to exhort him again to return to the unity of his mother the Catholic Church, with many fair promises. These Mr. Flower steadfastly rejecting, the bishop ordered him to appear in the same place in the afternoon, and in the meantime to consider well his former answer; but he, neither apologizing for having struck the priest, nor swerving from his faith, the bishop assigned him the next day, April 20, to receive sentence if he would not recant. The next morning, the bishop accordingly proceeded to the sentence, condemning and excommunicating him for a heretic, and after pronouncing him to be degraded, committed him to the secular power.

On April 24, St. Mark's eve, he was brought to the place of martyrdom, in St. Margaret's churchyard, Westminster, where the fact was committed: and there coming to the stake, he prayed to Almighty God, made a confession of his faith, and forgave all the world. This done, his hand was held up against the stake, and struck off, his left hand being fastened behind him. Fire was then set to him, and he burning therein, cried with a loud voice, "O Thou Son of God receive my soul!" three times. His speech being now taken from him, he spoke no more, but notwithstanding he lifted up the stump with his other arm as long as he could. Thus he endured the extremity of the fire, and was cruelly tortured, for the few fagots that were brought being insufficient to burn him they were compelled to strike him down into the fire, where lying along upon the ground, his lower part was consumed in the fire, whilst his upper part was little injured, his tongue moving in his mouth for a considerable time.

The Rev John Cardmaker and John Warne

May 30, 1555, the Rev John Cardmaker, otherwise called Taylor, prebendary of the Church of Wells, and John Warne, upholsterer, of St. John's, Walbrook, suffered together in Smithfield. Mr. Cardmaker, who first was an observant friar before the dissolution of the abbeys, afterward was a married minister, and in King Edward's time appointed to be a reader in St. Paul's; being apprehended in the beginning of Queen Mary's reign, with Dr. Barlow, bishop of Bath, he was brought to London, and put in the Fleet prison, King Edward's laws being yet in force. In Mary's reign, when brought before the bishop of Winchester, the latter offered them the queen's mercy, if they would recant.

Articles having been preferred against Mr. John Warne, he was examined upon them by Bonner, who earnestly exhorted him to recant his opinions, to whom he answered, "I am persuaded that I am in the right opinion, and I see no cause to recant; for all the filthiness and idolatry lies in the Church of Rome."

The bishop then, seeing that all his fair promises and terrible threatenings could not prevail, pronounced the definitive sentence of condemnation, and ordered May 30, 1555, for the execution of John Cardmaker and John Warne, who were brought by the sheriffs to Smithfield. Being come to the stake, the sheriffs called Mr. Cardmaker aside, and talked with him secretly, during which Mr. Warne prayed, was chained to the stake, and had wood and reeds set about him.

The people were greatly afflicted, thinking that Mr. Cardmaker would recant at the burning of Mr. Warne. At length Mr. Cardmaker departed from the sheriffs, and came towards the stake, knelt down, and made a long prayer in silence to himself. He then rose up, put off his clothes to his shirt, and went with a bold courage unto the stake and kissed it; and taking Mr. Warne by the hand, he heartily comforted him, and was bound to the stake, rejoicing. The people seeing this so suddenly done, contrary to their previous expectation, cried out, "God be praised! the Lord strengthen thee, Cardmaker! the Lord Jesus receive thy spirit!" And this continued while the executioner put fire to them, and both had passed through the fire to the blessed rest and peace among God's holy saints and martyrs, to enjoy the crown of triumph and victory prepared for the elect soldiers and warriors of Christ Jesus in His blessed Kingdom, to whom be glory and majesty forever. Amen.

John Simpson and John Ardeley

John Simpson and John Ardeley were condemned on the same day with Mr. Carmaker and John Warne, which was the twenty-fifth of May. They were shortly after sent down from London to Essex, where they were burnt in one day, John Simpson at Rochford, and John Ardeley at Railey, glorifying God in His beloved Son, and rejoicing that they were accounted worthy to suffer.

Thomas Haukes

Thomas Haukes, with six others, was condemned on the ninth of February, 1555.

In education he was erudite; in person, comely, and of good stature; in manners, a gentleman, and a sincere Christian. A little before death, several of Mr. Hauke's friends, terrified by the sharpness of the punishment he was going to suffer, privately desired that in the midst of the flames he should show them some token, whether the pains of burning were so great that a man might not collectedly endure it. This he promised to do; and it was agreed that if the rage of the pain might be suffered, then he should lift up his hands above his head towards heaven, before he gave up the ghost.

Not long after, Mr. Haukes was led away to the place appointed for slaughter by Lord Rich, and being come to the stake, mildly and patiently prepared himself for the fire, having a strong chain cast about his middle, with a multitude of people on every side compassing him about, unto whom after he had spoken many things, and poured out his soul unto God, the fire was kindled. When he had continued long in it, and his speech was taken away by violence of the flame, his skin drawn together, and his fingers consumed with the fire, so that it was thought that he was gone, suddenly and contrary to all expectation, this good man being mindful of his promise, reached up his hands burning in flames over his head to the living God, and with great rejoicings as it seemed, struck or clapped them three times together. A great shout followed this wonderful circumstance, and then this blessed martyr of Christ, sinking down in the fire, gave up his spirit, June 10, 1555.

Thomas Watts

Thomas Watts, of Billerica, in Essex, of the diocese of London, was a linen draper. He had daily expected to be taken by God's adversaries, and this came to pass on the fifth of April, 1555, when he was brought before Lord Rich, and other commissioners at Chelmsford, and accused for not coming to the church. Being consigned over to the bloody bishop, who gave him several hearings, and, as usual, many arguments, with much entreaty, that he would be a disciple of Antichrist, but his preaching availed not, and he resorted to his last revenge – that of condemnation. At the stake, after he had kissed it, he spake to Lord Rich, charging him to repent, for the Lord would revenge his death. Thus did this good martyr offer his body to the fire, in defense of the true Gospel of the Savior.

Dirick Carver and John Launder

The twenty-second of July, 1555, Dirick Carver, brewer, of Brighthelmstone, aged forty, was burnt at Lewes. And the day following John Launder, husbandman, aged twenty-five, of Godstone, Surrey, was burnt at Stening.

Dirick Carver was a man whom the Lord had blessed as well with temporal riches as with his spiritual treasures. At his coming into the town of Lewes to be burnt, the people called to him, beseeching God to strengthen him in the faith of Jesus Christ; and, as he came to the stake, he knelt down, and prayed earnestly. Then his Book was thrown into the barrel, and when he had stripped himself, he too, went into a barrel. As soon as he was in, he took the Book, and threw it among the people, upon which the sheriff commanded, in the name of the king and queen, on pain of death, to throw in the Book again. And immediately the holy martyr began to address the people. After he had prayed a while, he said, "O Lord my God, Thou hast written, he that will not forsake wife, children, house, and every thing that he hath, and take up Thy cross and follow Thee, is not worthy of Thee! but Thou, Lord, knowest that I have forsaken all to come unto Thee. Lord, have mercy upon me, for unto Thee I commend my spirit! and my soul doth rejoice in Thee!" These were the last words of this faithful servant of Christ before enduring the fire. And when the fire came to him, he cried, "O Lord, have mercy upon me!" and sprang up in the fire, calling upon the name of Jesus, until he gave up the ghost.

James Abbes

James Abbes, a young man, wandered about to escape apprehension, but was at last informed against, and brought before the bishop of Norwich, who influenced him to recant; to secure him further in apostasy, the bishop afterward gave him a piece of money; but the interference of Providence is here remarkable. This bribe lay so heavily upon his conscience, that he returned, threw back the money, and repented of his conduct. Like Peter, he was contrite, steadfast in the faith, and sealed it with his blood at Bury, August 2, 1555, praising and glorifying God.

John Denley, John Newman, and Patrick Packingham

Mr. Denley and Newman were returning one day to Maidstone, the place of their abode, when they were met by E. Tyrrel, Esq., a bigoted justice of the peace in Essex, and a cruel persecutor of the Protestants. He apprehended them merely on suspicion. On the fifth of July, 1555, they were condemned, and consigned to the sheriffs, who sent Mr. Denley to Uxbridge, where he perished, August eighth, 1555. While suffering in agony, and singing a Psalm, Dr. Story inhumanly ordered one of the tormentors to throw a fagot at him, which cut his face severely, caused him to cease singing, and to raise his hands to his face. Just as Dr. Story was remarking in jest that he had spoiled a good song, the pious martyr again changed, spread his hands abroad in the flames, and through Christ Jesus resigned his soul into the hands of his Maker.

Mr. Packingham suffered at the same town on the twenty-eighth of the same month. Mr. Newman, pewterer, was burnt at Saffron Waldon, in Essex, August 31, for the same cause, and Richard Hook about the same time perished at Chichester.

Elizabeth Warne

Elizabeth Warne, widow of John Warne, upholsterer, martyr, was burnt at Stratford-le-bow, near London, at the end of August, 1555.

George Tankerfield

George Tankerfield, of London, cook, born at York, aged twenty-seven, in the reign of Edward VI had been a papist; but the cruelty of bloody Mary made him suspect the truth of those doctrines which were enforced by fire and torture. Tankerfield was imprisoned in Newgate about the end of February, 1555, and on August 26, at St. Alban's, he braved the excruciating fire, and joyfully died for the glory of his Redeemer.

Rev Robert Samuel

This gentleman was minister of Bradford, Suffolk, where he industriously taught the flock committed to his charge, while he was openly permitted to discharge his duty. He was first persecuted by Mr. Foster, of Copdock, near Ipswich, a severe and bigoted persecutor of the followers of Christ, according to the truth in the Gospel. Notwithstanding Mr. Samuel was ejected from his living, he continued to exhort and instruct privately; nor would he obey the order for putting away his wife, whom he had married in King Edward's reign; but kept her at Ipswich, where Foster, by warrant, surprised him by night with her. After being imprisoned in Ipswich jail, he was taken before Dr. Hopton, bishop of Norwich, and Dr. Dunnings, his chancellor, two of the most sanguinary among the bigots of those days. To intimidate the worthy pastor, he was in prison chained to a post in such a manner that the weight of his body was supported by the points of his toes: added to this his allowance of provision was reduced to a quantity so insufficient to sustain nature that he was almost ready to devour his own flesh. From this dreadful extremity there was even a degree of mercy in ordering him to the fire. Mr. Samuel suffered August 31, 1555.

John Philpot

This martyr was the son of a knight, born in Hampshire, and brought up at New College, Oxford, where for several years he studied the civil law, and became eminent in the Hebrew tongue. He was a scholar and a gentleman, zealous in religion, fearless in disposition, and a detester of flattery. After visiting Italy, he returned to England, affairs in King Edward's days wearing a more promising aspect. During this reign he continued to be archdeacon of Winchester under Dr. Poinet, who succeeded Gardiner. Upon the accession of Mary, a convocation was summoned, in which Mr. Philpot defended the Reformation against his ordinary, Gardiner, again made bishop of Winchester, and soon was conducted to Bonner and other commissioners for examination, October 2, 1555, after being eighteen months' imprisoned. Upon his demanding to see the commission, Dr. Story cruelly observed, "I will spend both my gown and my coat, but I will burn thee! Let him be in Lollard's tower, (a wretched prison,) for I will sweep the king's Bench and all other prisons of these heretics!"

Upon Mr. Philpot's second examination, it was intimated to him that Dr. Story had said that the lord chancellor had commanded that he should be made away with. It is easy to foretell the result of this inquiry. He was committed to Bonner's coal house, where he joined company with a zealous minister of Essex, who had been induced to sign a bill of recantation; but afterward, stung by his conscience, he asked the bishop to let him see the instrument again, when he tore it to pieces; which induced Bonner in a fury to strike him repeatedly, and tear away part of his beard. Mr. Philpot had a private interview with Bonner the same night, and was then remanded to his bed of straw like other prisoners, in the coal house. After seven examinations, Bonner ordered him to be set in the stocks, and on the following Sunday separated him from his fellow-prisoners as a sower of heresy, and ordered him up to a room near the battlements of St. Paul's, eight feet by thirteen, on the other side of Lollard's tower, and which could be overlooked by any one in the bishop's outer gallery. Here Mr. Philpot was searched, but happily he was successful in secreting some letters containing his examinations.

In the eleventh investigation before various bishops, and Mr. Morgan, of Oxford, the latter was so driven into a corner by the close pressure of Mr. Philpot's arguments, that he said to him, "Instead of the spirit of the Gospel which you boast to possess, I think it is the spirit of the buttery, which your fellows have had, who were drunk before their death, and went, I believe, drunken to it." To this unfounded and brutish remark, Mr. Philpot indignantly replied, "It appeareth by your communication that you are better acquainted with that spirit than the Spirit of God; wherefore I tell thee, thou painted wall and hypocrite, in the name of the living God, whose truth I have told thee, that God shall rain fire and brimstone upon such blasphemers as thou art!" He was then remanded by Bonner, with an order not to allow him his Bible nor candlelight.

On December 4, Mr. Philpot had his next hearing, and this was followed by two more, making in all, fourteen conferences, previous to the final examination in which he was condemned; such were the perseverance and anxiety of the Catholics, aided by the argumentative abilities of the most distinguished of the papal bishops, to bring him into the pale of their Church. Those examinations, which were very long and learned, were all written down by Mr. Philpot, and a stronger proof of the imbecility of the Catholic doctors, cannot, to an unbiased mind, be exhibited.

On December 16, in the consistory of St. Paul's Bishop Bonner, after laying some trifling accusations to his charge, such as secreting powder to make ink, writing some private letters, etc., proceeded to pass the awful sentence upon him, after he and the other bishops had urged him by every inducement to recant. He was afterward conducted to Newgate, where the avaricious Catholic keeper loaded him with heavy irons, which by the humanity of Mr. Macham were ordered to be taken off. On December 17, Mr. Philpot received intimation that he was to die next day, and the next morning about eight o'clock, he joyfully met the sheriffs, who were to attend him to the place of execution.

Upon entering Smithfield, the ground was so muddy that two officers offered to carry him to the stake, but he replied: "Would you make me a pope? I am content to finish my journey on foot." Arriving at the stake, he said, "Shall I disdain to suffer at the stake, when my Redeemer did not refuse to suffer the most vile death upon the cross for me?" He then meekly recited the One hundred and seventh and One hundred and eighth Psalms, and when he had finished his prayers, was bound to the post, and fire applied to the pile. On December 18, 1555, perished this illustrious martyr, reverenced by man, and glorified in heaven!

John Lomas, Agnes Snoth, Anne Wright, Joan Sole, and Joan Catmer

These five martyrs suffered together, January 31, 1556. John Lomas was a young man of Tenterden. He was cited to appear at Canterbury, and was examined January 17. His answers being adverse to the idolatrous doctrine of the papacy, he was condemned on the following day, and suffered January 31.

Agnes Snoth, widow, of Smarden Parish, was several times summoned before the Catholic Pharisees, and rejecting absolution, indulgences, transubstantiation, and auricular confession, she was adjudged worthy to suffer death, and endured martyrdom, January 31, with Anne Wright and Joan Sole, who were placed in similar circumstances, and perished at the same time, with equal resignation.

Joan Catmer, the last of this heavenly company, of the parish Hithe, was the wife of the martyr George Catmer.

Seldom in any country, for political controversy, have four women been led to execution, whose lives were irreproachable, and whom the pity of savages would have spared. We cannot but remark here that, when the Protestant power first gained the ascendency over the Catholic superstition, and some degree of force in the laws was necessary to enforce uniformity, whence some bigoted people suffered privation in their person or goods, we read of few burnings, savage cruelties, or poor women brought to the stake, but it is the nature of error to resort to force instead of argument, and to silence truth by taking away existence, of which the Redeemer himself is an instance. The above five persons were burnt at two stakes in one fire, singing hosannahs to the glorified Savior, until the breath of life was extinct. Sir John Norton, who was present, wept bitterly at their unmerited sufferings.

The vision of three ladders

When Robert Samuel was brought forth to be burned, certain there were that heard him declare what strange things had happened unto him during the time of his imprisonment; to wit, that after he had famished or pined with hunger two or three days together, he then fell into a sleep, as it were one half in a slumber, at which time one clad all in white seemed to stand before him, who ministered comfort unto him by these words: "Samuel, Samuel, be of good cheer, and take a good heart unto thee: for after this day shalt thou never be either hungry or thirsty."

No less memorable it is, and worthy to be noted, concerning the three ladders which he told to divers he saw in his sleep, set up toward heaven; of the which there was one somewhat longer than the rest, but yet at length they became one, joining (as it were) all three together. As this godly martyr was going to the fire, there came a certain maid to him, which took him about the neck, and kissed him, who, being marked by them that were present, was sought for the next day after, to be had to prison and burned, as the very party herself informed me: howbeit, as God of His goodness would have it, she escaped their fiery hands, keeping herself secret in the town a good while after. But as this maid, called Rose Nottingham, was marvelously preserved by the providence of God, so there were other two honest women who did fall into the rage and fury of that time. The one was a brewer's wife, the other was a shoemaker's wife, but both together now espoused to a new husband, Christ. With these two was this maid aforesaid very familiar and well acquainted, who, on a time giving counsel to the one of them, that she should convey herself away while she had time and space, had this answer at her hand again: "I know well," saith she, "that it is lawful enough to fly away; which remedy you may use, if you list. But my case standeth otherwise. I am tied to a husband, and have besides young children at home; therefore I am minded, for the love of Christ and His truth, to stand to the extremity of the matter."

And so the next day after Samuel suffered, these two godly wives, the one called Anne Potten, the other called Joan Trunchfield, the wife of Michael Trunchfield, shoemaker, of Ipswich, were apprehended, and had both into one prison together. As they were both by sex and nature somewhat tender, so were they at first less able to endure the straitness of the prison; and especially the brewer's wife was cast into marvelous great agonies and troubles of mind thereby. But Christ, beholding the weak infirmity of His servant, did not fail to help her when she was in this necessity; so at the length they both suffered after Samuel, in 1556, February 19. And these, no doubt, were those two ladders, which, being joined with the third, Samuel saw stretched up into heaven. This blessed Samuel, the servant of Christ, suffered the thirty-first of August, 1555.

The report goeth among some that were there present, and saw him burn, that his body in burning did shine in the eyes of them that stood by, as bright and white as new-tried silver. When Agnes Bongeor saw herself separated from her prison-fellows, what piteous moan that good woman made, how bitterly she wept, what strange thoughts came into her mind, how naked and desolate she esteemed herself, and into what plunge of despair and care her poor soul was brought, it was piteous and wonderful to see; which all came because she went not with them to give her life in the defense of her Christ; for of all things in the world, life was least looked for at her hands. For that morning in which she was kept back from burning, had she put on a smock, that she had prepared only for that purpose. And also having a child, a little young infant sucking on her, whom she kept with her tenderly all the time that she was in prison, against that day likewise did she send away to another nurse, and prepared herself presently to give herself for the testimony of the glorious Gospel of Jesus Christ. So little did she look for life, and so greatly did God's gifts work in her above nature, that death seemed a great deal better welcome than life. After which, she began a little to stay herself, and gave her whole exercise to reading and prayer, wherein she found no little comfort. In a short time came a writ from London for the burning, which according to the effect thereof, was executed.

Hugh Laverick and John Aprice

Here we perceive that neither the impotence of age nor the affliction of blindness, could turn aside the murdering fangs of these Babylonish monsters. The first of these unfortunates was of the parish of Barking, aged sixty-eight, a painter and a cripple. The other was blind, dark indeed in his visual faculties, but intellectually illuminated with the radiance of the everlasting Gospel of truth. Inoffensive objects like these were informed against by some of the sons of bigotry, and dragged before the prelatical shark of London, where they underwent examination, and replied to the articles propounded to them, as other Christian martyrs had done before. On the ninth day of May, in the consistory of St. Paul's, they were entreated to recant, and upon refusal, were sent to Fulham, where Bonner, by way of a dessert after dinner, condemned them to the agonies of the fire. Being consigned to the secular officers, May 15, 1556, they were taken in a cart from Newgate to Stratford-le-Bow, where they were fastened to the stake. When Hugh Laverick was secured by the chain, having no further occasion for his crutch, he threw it away saying to his fellow-martyr, while consoling him, "Be of good cheer my brother; for my lord of London is our good physician; he will heal us both shortly – thee of thy blindness, and me of my lameness." They sank down in the fire, to rise to immortality!

Thomas Dowry

Thomas Dowry. We have again to record an act of unpitying cruelty, exercised on this lad, whom Bishop Hooper, had confirmed in the Lord and the knowledge of his Word. How long this poor sufferer remained in prison is uncertain. By the testimony of one John Paylor, register of Gloucester, we learn that when Dowry was brought before Dr. Williams, then chancellor of Gloucester, the usual articles were presented him for subscription. From these he dissented; and, upon the doctor's demanding of whom and where he had learned his heresies, the youth replied, "Indeed, Mr. Chancellor, I learned from you in that very pulpit. On such a day (naming the day) you said, in preaching upon the Sacrament, that it was to be exercised spiritually by faith, and not carnally and really, as taught by the papists." Dr. Williams then bid him recant, as he had done; but Dowry had not so learned his duty. "Though you," said he, "can so easily mock God, the world, and your own conscience, yet will I not do so."

Executions at Stratford-le-Bow

At this sacrifice, which we are about to detail no less than thirteen were doomed to the fire. Each one refusing to subscribe contrary to conscience, they were condemned, and the twenty-seventh of June, 1556, was appointed for their execution at Stratford-le-Bow. Their constancy and faith glorified their Redeemer, equally in life and in death.

Rev Julius Palmer

This gentleman's life presents a singular instance of error and conversion. In the time of Edward, he was a rigid and obstinate papist, so adverse to godly and sincere preaching, that he was even despised by his own party; that this frame of mind should be changed, and he suffer persecution and death in Queen Mary's reign, are among those events of omnipotence at which we wonder and admire. Mr. Palmer was born at Coventry, where his father had been mayor. Being afterward removed to Oxford, he became, under Mr. Harley, of Magdalen College, an elegant Latin and Greek scholar. He was fond of useful disputation, possessed of a lively wit, and a strong memory. Indefatigable in private study, he rose at four in the morning, and by this practice qualified himself to become reader in logic in Magralen College. The times of Edward, however, favoring the Reformation, Mr. Palmer became frequently punished for his contempt of prayer and orderly behavior, and was at length expelled the house. He afterwards embraced the doctrines of the Reformation, which occasioned his arrest and final condemnation. A certain nobleman offered him his life if he would recant. "If so," said he, "thou wilt dwell with me. And if thou wilt set thy mind to marriage, I will procure thee a wife and a farm, and help to stuff and fit thy farm for thee. How sayst thou?"

Palmer thanked him very courteously, but very modestly and reverently concluded that as he had already in two places renounced his living for Christ's sake, so he would with God's grace be ready to surrender and yield up his life also for the same, when God should send time. When Sir Richard perceived that he would by no means relent: "Well, Palmer," saith he, "then I perceive one of us twain shall be damned: for we be of two faiths, and certain I am there is but one faith that leadeth to life and salvation."

Palmer: "O sir, I hope that we both shall be saved."

Sir Richard: "How may that be?"

Palmer: "Right well, sir. For as it hath pleased our merciful Savior, according to the Gospel's parable, to call me at the third hour of the day, even in my flowers, at the age of four and twenty years, even so I trust He hath called, and will call you, at the eleventh hour of this your old age, and give you everlasting life for your portion.

Sir Richard: "Sayest thou so? Well, Palmer, well, I would I might have thee but one month in my house: I doubt not but I would convert thee, or thou shouldst convert me."

Then said Master Winchcomb, "Take pity on thy golden years, and pleasant flowers of lusty youth, before it be too late."

Palmer: "Sir, I long for those springing flowers that shall never fade away."

He was tried on the fifteenth of July,

1556, together with one Thomas Askin, fellow prisoner. Askin and one John Guin had been sentenced the day before, and Mr. Palmer, on the fifteenth, was brought up for final judgment. Execution was ordered to follow the sentence, and at five o'clock in the same afternoon, at a place called the Sand-pits, these three martyrs were fastened to a stake. After devoutly praying together, they sung the Thirty-first Psalm. When the fire was kindled, and it had seized their bodies, without an appearance of enduring pain, they continued to cry, "Lord Jesus, strengthen us! Lord Jesus receive our souls!" until animation was suspended and human suffering was past. It is remarkable, that, when their heads had fallen together in a mass as it were by the force of the flames, and the spectators thought Palmer as lifeless, his tongue and lips again moved, and were heard to pronounce the name of Jesus, to whom be glory and honor forever!

Joan Waste and Others

This poor, honest woman, blind from her birth, and unmarried, aged twenty-two, was of the parish of Allhallows, Derby. Her father was a barber, and also made ropes for a living: in which she assisted him, and also learned to knit several articles of apparel. Refusing to communicate with those who maintained doctrines contrary to those she had learned in the days of the pious Edward, she was called before Dr. Draicot, the chancellor of Bishop Blaine, and Peter Finch, official of Derby.

With sophistical arguments and threats they endeavored to confound the poor girl; but she proffered to yield to the bishop's doctrine, if he would answer for her at the Day of Judgment, (as pious Dr. Taylor had done in his sermons) that his belief of the real presence of the Sacrament was true. The bishop at first answered that he would; but Dr. Draicot reminding him that he might not in any way answer for a heretic, he withdrew his confirmation of his own tenets; and she replied that if their consciences would not permit them to answer at God's bar for that truth they wished her to subscribe to, she would answer no more questions. Sentence was then adjudged, and Dr. Draicot appointed to preach her condemned sermon, which took place August 1, 1556, the day of her martyrdom.

His fulminating discourse being finished, the poor, sightless object was taken to a place called Windmill Pit, near the town, where she for a time held her brother by the hand, and then prepared herself for the fire, calling upon the pitying multitude to pray with her, and upon Christ to have mercy upon her, until the glorious light of the everlasting Sun of righteousness beamed upon her departed spirit.

In November, fifteen martyrs were imprisoned in Canterbury castle, of whom all were either burnt or famished. Among the latter were J. Clark, D. Chittenden, W. Foster of Stone, Alice Potkins, and J. Archer, of Cranbrooke, weaver. The two first of these had not received condemnation, but the others were sentenced to the fire. Foster, at his examination, observed upon the utility of carrying lighted candles about on Candlemas-day, that he might as well carry a pitchfork; and that a gibbet would have as good an effect as the cross.

We have now brought to a close the sanguinary proscriptions of the merciless Mary, in the year 1556, the number of which amounted to above EIGHTY-FOUR!

Persecutions in the Diocese of Canterbury

In the month of February, the following persons were committed to prison: R. Coleman, of Waldon, laborer; Joan Winseley, of Horsley Magna, spinster; S. Glover, of Rayley; R. Clerk, of Much Holland, mariner; W. Munt, of Much Bentley, sawyer; Marg. Field, of Ramsey, spinster; R. Bongeor, currier; R. Jolley, mariner; Allen Simpson, Helen Ewire, C. Pepper, widow; Alice Walley (who recanted), W. Bongeor, glazier, all of Colchester; R. Atkin, of Halstead, weaver; R. Barcock, of Wilton, carpenter; R. George, of Westbarhonlt, laborer; R. Debnam of Debenham, weaver; C. Warren, of Cocksall, spinster; Agnes Whitlock, of Dover-court, spinster; Rose Allen, spinster; and T.

Feresannes, minor; both of Colchester.

These persons were brought before Bonner, who would have immediately sent them to execution, but Cardinal Pole was for more merciful measures, and Bonner, in a letter of his to the cardinal, seems to be sensible that he had displeased him, for he has this expression: "I thought to have them all hither to Fulham, and to have given sentence against them; nevertheless, perceiving by my last doing that your grace was offended, I thought it my duty, before I proceeded further, to inform your grace."

This circumstance verifies the account that the cardinal was a humane man; and though a zealous Catholic, we, as Protestants, are willing to render him that honor which his merciful character deserves. Some of the bitter persecutors denounced him to the pope as a favorer of heretics, and he was summoned to Rome, but Queen Mary, by particular entreaty, procured his stay. However, before his latter end, and a little before his last journey from Rome to England, he was strongly suspected of favoring the doctrine of Luther.

Seven more martyrs at Canterbury

As in the last sacrifice four women did honor to the truth, so in the following auto da fe we have the like number of females and males, who suffered June 30, 1557, at Canterbury, and were J. Fishcock, F. White, N. Pardue, Barbary Final, widow, Bardbridge's widow, Wilson's wife, and Benden's wife.

Alice Benden

Of this group we shall more particularly notice Alice Benden, wife of Edward Bender, of Staplehurst, Kent. She had been taken up in October, 1556, for non-attendance, and released upon a strong injunction to mind her conduct. Her husband was a bigoted Catholic, and publicly speaking of his wife's contumacy, she was conveyed to Canterbury Castle, where knowing, when she should be removed to the bishop's prison, she should be almost starved upon three farthings a day, she endeavored to prepare herself for this suffering by living upon twopence halfpenny per day.

On January 22, 1557, her husband wrote to the bishop that if his wife's brother, Roger Hall, were to be kept from consoling and relieving her, she might turn; on this account, she was moved to a prison called Monday's Hole. Her brother sought diligently for her, and at the end of five weeks providentially heard her voice in the dungeon, but could not otherwise relieve her, than by putting soe money in a loaf, and sticking it on a long pole. Dreadful must have been the situation of this poor victim, lying on straw, between stone walls, without a change of apparel, or the meanest requisites of cleanliness, during a period of nine weeks!

On March 25 she was summoned before the bishop, who, with rewards, offered her liberty if she would go home and be comfortable; but Mrs. Benden had been inured to suffering, and, showing him her contracted limbs and emaciated appearance, refused to swerve from the truth. She was however removed from this black hole to the West Gate, whence, about the end of April, she was taken out to be condemned, and then committed to the castle prison until the nineteenth of June, the day of her burning. At the stake, she gave her handkerchief to one John Banks, as a memorial; and from her waist she drew a white lace, desiring him to give it to her brother, and tell him that it was the last band that had bound her, except the chain; and to her father she returned a shilling he had sent her. The whole of these seven martyrs undressed themselves with alacrity, and, being prepared, knelt down, and prayed with an earnestness and Christian spirit that even the enemies of the cross were affected. After invocation made together, they were secured to the stake, and, being encompassed with the unsparing flames, they yielded their souls into the hands of the living Lord.

Matthew Plaise

Matthew Plaise, weaver, a sincere and shrewd Christian, of Stone, Kent, was brought before Thomas, bishop of Dover, and other inquisitors, whom he ingeniously teased by his indirect answers, of which the following is a specimen.

Dr. Harpsfield. Christ called the bread His body; what dost thou say it is?

Plaise. I do believe it was that which He gave them.

Dr. H. What as that?

P. That which He brake.

Dr. H. What did He brake?

P. That which He took.

Dr. H. What did He take?

P. I say, what He gave them, that did they eat indeed.

Dr. H. Well, then, thou sayest it was but bread which the disciples did eat.

P. I say, what He gave them, that did they eat indeed.

A very long disputation followed, in which Plaise was desired to humble himself to the bishop; but this he refused. Whether this zealous person died in prison, was executed, or delivered, history does not mention.

Rev John Hullier

Rev John Hullier was brought up at Eton College, and in process of time became curate of Babram, three miles from Cambridge, and went afterward to Lynn; where, opposing the superstition of the papists, he was carried before Dr. Thirlby, bishop of Ely, and sent to Cambridge castle: here he lay for a time, and was then sent to Tolbooth prison, where, after three months, he was brought to St. Mary's Church, and condemned by Dr. Fuller. On Maunday Thursday he was brought to the stake: while undressing, he told the people to bear witness that he was about to suffer in a just cause, and exhorted them to believe that there was no other rock than Jesus Christ to build upon. A priest named Boyes, then desired the mayor to silence him. After praying, he went meekly to the stake, and being bound with a chain, and placed in a pitch barrel, fire was applied to the reeds and wood; but the wind drove the fire directly to his back, which caused him under the severe agony to pray the more fervently. His friends directed the executioner to fire the pile to windward of his face, which was immediately done. A quantity of books were now thrown into the fire, one of which (the Communion Service) he caught, opened it, and joyfully continued to read it, until the fire and smoke deprived him of sight; then even, in earnest prayer, he pressed the book to his heart, thanking God for bestowing on him in his last moments this precious gift

The day being hot, the fire burnt fiercely; and at a time when the spectators supposed he was no more, he suddenly exclaimed, "Lord Jesus, receive my spirit," and meekly resigned his life. He was burnt on Jesus Green, not far from Jesus College. He had gunpowder given him, but he was dead before it became ignited. This pious sufferer afforded a singular spectacle; for his flesh was so burnt from the bones, which continued erect, that he presented the idea of a skeleton figure chained to the stake. His remains were eagerly seized by the multitude, and venerated by all who admired his piety or detested inhuman bigotry.

Simon Miller and Elizabeth Cooper

In the following month of July, received the crown of martyrdom. Miller dwelt at Lynn, and came to Norwich, where, planting himself at the door of one of the churches, as the people came out, he requested to know of them where he could go to receive the Communion. For this a priest brought him before Dr. Dunning, who committed him to ward; but he was suffered to go home, and arrange his affairs; after which he returned to the bishop's house, and to his prison, where he remained until the thirteenth of July, the day of his burning. Elizabeth Cooper, wife of a pewterer, of St. Andrews, Norwich, had recanted; but tortured for what she had done by the worm which dieth not, she shortly after voluntarily entered her parish church during the time of the popish service, and standing up, audibly proclaimed that she revoked her former recantation, and cautioned the people to avoid her unworthy example. She was taken from her own house by Mr. Sutton the sheriff, who very reluctantly complied with the letter of the law, as they had been servants and in friendship together. At the stake, the poor sufferer, feeling the fire, uttered the cry of "Oh!" upon which Mr. Miller, putting his hand behind him towards her, desired her to be of a good courage, "for (said he) good sister, we shall have a joyful and a sweet supper." Encouraged by this example and exhortation, she stood the fiery ordeal without flinching, and, with him, proved the power of faith over the flesh.

Executions at Colchester

It was before mentioned that twenty-two persons had been sent up from Colchester, who upon a slight submission, were afterward released. Of these, William Munt, of Much Bentley, husbandman, with Alice, his wife, and Rose Allin, her daughter, upon their return home, abstained from church, which induced the bigoted priest secretly to write to Bonner. For a short time they absconded, but returning again, March 7, one Edmund Tyrrel, (a relation of the Tyrrel who murdered King Edward and his brother) with the officers, entered the house while Munt and his wife were in bed, and informed them that they must go to Colchester Castle. Mrs. Munt at that time being very ill, requested her daughter to get her some drink; leave being permitted, Rose took a candle and a mug; and in returning through the house was met by Tyrrel, who cautioned her to advise her parents to become good Catholics. Rose briefly informed him that they had the Holy Ghost for their adviser; and that she was ready to lay down her own life for the same cause. Turning to his company, he remarked that she was willing to burn; and one of them told him to prove her, and see what she would do by and by. The unfeeling wretch immediately executed this project; and, seizing the young woman by the wrist, he held the lighted candle under her hand, burning it crosswise on the back, until the tendons divided from the flesh, during which he loaded her with many opprobrious epithets. She endured his rage unmoved, and then, when he had ceased the torture, she asked him to begin at her feet or head, for he need not fear that his employer would one day repay him. After this she took the drink to her mother.

This cruel act of torture does not stand alone on record. Bonner had served a poor blind harper in nearly the same manner, who had steadily maintained a hope that if every joint of him were to be burnt, he should not fly from the faith. Bonner, upon this, privately made a signal to his men, to bring a burning coal, which they placed in the poor man's hand, and then by force held it closed, until it burnt into the flesh deeply.

George Eagles

George Eagles, tailor, was indicted for having prayed that "God would turn Queen Mary's heart, or take her away'; the ostensible cause of his death was his religion, for treason could hardly be imagined in praying for the reformation of such an execrable soul as that of Mary. Being condemned for this crime, he was drawn to the place of execution upon a sledge, with two robbers, who were executed with him. After Eagles had mounted the ladder, and been turned off a short time, he was cut down before he was at all insensible; a bailiff, named William Swallow, then dragged him to the sledge, and with a common blunt cleaver, hacked off the head; in a manner equally clumsy and cruel, he opened his body and tore out the heart. In all this suffering the poor martyr repined not, but to the last called upon his Savior. The fury of these bigots did not end here; the intestines were burnt, and the body was quartered, the four parts being sent to Colchester, Harwich, Chelmsford, and St. Rouse's. Chelmsford had the honor of retaining his head, which was affixed to a long pole in the market place. In time it was blown down, and lay several days in the street, until it was buried at night in the churchyard. God's judgment not long after fell upon Swallow, who in his old age became a beggar, and who was affected with a leprosy that made him obnoxious even to the animal creation; nor did Richard Potts, who troubled Eagles in his dying moments, escape the visiting hand of God.

MRS. JOYCE LEWES

This lady was the wife of Mr. T. Lewes, of Manchester. She had received the Romish religion as true, until the burning of that pious martyr, Mr. Saunders, at Coventry. Understanding that his death arose from a refusal to receive the Mass, she began to inquire into the ground of his refusal, and her conscience, as it began to be enlightened, became restless and alarmed. In this inquietude, she resorted to Mr. John Glover, who lived near, and requested that he would unfold those rich sources of Gospel knowledge he possessed, particularly upon the subject of transubstantiation. He easily succeeded in convincing her that the mummery of popery and the Mass were at variance with God's most holy Word, and honestly reproved her for following too much the vanities of a wicked world. It was to her indeed a word in season, for she soon became weary of her former sinful life and resolved to abandon the Mass and dilatrous worship. Though compelled by her husband's violence to go to church, her contempt of the holy water and other ceremonies was so manifest, that she was accused before the bishop for despising the sacramentals.

A citation, addressed to her, immediately followed, which was given to Mr. Lewes, who, in a fit of passion, held a dagger to the throat of the officer, and made him eat it, after which he caused him to drink it down, and then sent him away. But for this the bishop summoned Mr. Lewes before him as well as his wife; the former readily submitted, but the latter resolutely affirmed, that, in refusing holy water, she neither offended God, nor any part of his laws. She was sent home for a month, her husband being bound for her appearance, during which time Mr. Glover impressed upon her the necessity of doing what she did, not from self-vanity, but for the honor and glory of God. Mr. Glover and others earnestly exhorted Lewes to forfeit the money he was bound in, rather than subject his wife to certain death; but he was deaf to the voice of humanity, and delivered her over to the bishop, who soon found sufficient cause to consign her to a loathsome prison, whence she was several times brought for examination. At the last time the bishop reasoned with her upon the fitness of her coming to Mass, and receiving as sacred the Sacrament and sacramentals of the Holy Ghost.

"If these things were in the Word of God," said Mrs. Lewes, "I would with all my heart receive, believe, and esteem them."

The bishop, with the most ignorant and impious effrontery, replied, "If thou wilt believe no more than what is warranted by Scriptures, thou art in a state of damnation!" Astonished at such a declaration, this worthy sufferer ably rejoined that his words were as impure as they were profane.

After condemnation, she lay a twelvemonth in prison, the sheriff not being willing to put her to death in his time, though he had been but just chosen. When her death warrant came from London, she sent for some friends, whom she consulted in what manner her death might be more glorious to the name of God, and injurious to the cause of God's enemies. Smilingly, she said: "As for death, I think but lightly of. When I know that I shall behold the amiable countenance of Christ my dear Savior, the ugly face of death does not much trouble me." The evening before she suffered, two priests were anxious to visit her, but she refused both their confession and absolution, when she could hold a better communication with the High Priest of souls. About three o'clock in the morning, Satan began to shoot his fiery darts, by putting into her mind to doubt whether she was chosen to eternal life, and Christ died for her. Her friends readily pointed out to her those consolatory passages of Scripture which comfort the fainting heart, and treat of the Redeemer who taketh away the sins of the world. About eight o'clock the sheriff announced to her that she had but an hour to live; she was at first cast down, but this soon passed away, and she thanked God that her life was about to be devoted to His service. The sheriff granted permission for two friends to accompany her to the stake – an indulgence for which he was afterward severely handled. Mr. Reniger and Mr. Bernher led her to the place of execution; in going to which, from its distance, her great weakness, and the press of the people, she had nearly fainted. Three times she prayed fervently that God would deliver the land from popery and the idolatrous Mass; and the people for the most part, as well as the sheriff, said Amen.

When she had prayed, she took the cup, (which had been filled with water to refresh her,) and said, "I drink to all them that unfeignedly love the Gospel of Christ, and wish for the abolition of popery." Her friends, and a great many women of the place, drank with her, for which most of them afterward were enjoined penance. When chained to the stake, her countenance was cheerful, and the roses of her cheeks were not abated. Her hands were extended towards heaven until the fire rendered them powerless, when her soul was received int o the arms of the Creator. The duration of her agony was but short, as the under-sheriff, at the request of her friends, had prepared such excellent fuel that she was in a few minutes overwhelmed with smoke and flame. The case of this lady drew a tear of pity from everyone who had a heart not callous to humanity.

Executions at Islington

About the seventeenth of September, suffered at Islington the following four professors of Christ: Ralph Allerton, James Austoo, Margery Austoo, and Richard Roth. James Austoo and his wife, of St. Allhallows, Barking, London, were sentenced for not believing in the presence. Richard Roth rejected the seven Sacraments, and was accused of comforting the heretics by the following letter written in his own blood, and intended to have been sent to his friends at Colchester

James Austoo's letter

O dear Brethren and Sisters,

How much reason have you to rejoice in God, that He hath given you such faith to overcome this bloodthirsty tyrant thus far! And no doubt He that hath begun that good work in you, will fulfill it unto the end. O dear hearts in Christ, what a crown of glory shall ye receive with Christ in the kingdom of God! O that it had been the good will of God that I had been ready to have gone with you; for I lie in my lord's Little-ease by day, and in the night I lie in the Coalhouse, apart from Ralph Allerton, or any other; and we look every day when we shall be condemned; for he said that I should be burned within ten days before Easter; but I lie still at the pool's brink, and every man goeth in before me; but we abide patiently the Lord's leisure, with many bonds, in fetters and stocks, by which we have received great joy of God. And now fare you well, dear brethren and sisters, in this world, but I trust to see you in the heavens face to face.

O brother Munt, with your wife and my sister Rose, how blessed are you in the Lord, that God hath found you worthy to suffer for His sake! with all the rest of my dear brethren and sisters known and unknown. O be joyful even unto death. Fear it not, saith Christ, for I have overcome death. O dear heart, seeing that Jesus Christ will be our help, O tarry you the Lord's leisure. Be strong, let your hearts be of good comfort, and wait you still for the Lord. He is at hand. Yea, the angel of the Lord pitcheth his tent round about them that fear him, and delivereth them which way he seeth best. For our lives are in the Lord's hands; and they can do nothing unto us before God suffer them. Therefore give all thanks to God.

O dear hearts, you shall be clothed in long white garments upon the mount of Sion, with the multitude of saints, and with Jesus Christ our Savior, who will never forsake us. O blessed virgins, ye have played the wise virgins' part, in that ye have taken oil in your lamps that ye may go in with the Bridegroom, when he cometh, into the everlasting joy with Him. But as for the foolish, they shall be shut out, because they made not themselves ready to suffer with Christ, neither go about to take up His cross. O dear hearts, how precious shall your death be in the sight of the Lord! for dear is the death of His saints. O fare you well, and pray. The grace of our Lord Jesus Christ be with you all. Amen, Amen. Pray, pray, pray!

Written by me, with my own blood,

Richard Roth

This letter, so justly denominating Bonner the "bloodthirsty tyrant," was not likely to excite his compassion. Roth accused him of bringing them to secret examination by night, because he was afraid of the people by day. Resisting every temptation to recant, he was condemned, and on September 17, 1557, these four martyrs perished at Islington, for the testimony of the Lamb, who was slain that they might be of the redeemed of God.

John Noyes

John Noyes, a shoemaker, of Laxfield, Suffolk, was taken to Eye, and at midnight, September 21, 1557, he was brought from Eye to Laxfield to be burned. On the following morning he was led to the stake, prepared for the horrid sacrifice. Mr. Noyes, on coming to the fatal spot, knelt down, prayed, and rehearsed the Fiftieth Psalm. When the chain enveloped him, he said, "Fear not them that kill the body, but fear him that can kill both body and soul, and cast it into everlasting fire!" As one Cadman placed a fagot against him, he blessed the hour in which he was born to die for the truth; and while trusting only upon the all-sufficient merits of the Redeemer, fire was set to the pile, and the blazing fagots in a short time stifled his last words, "Lord, have mercy on me! Christ, have mercy upon me!" The ashes of the body were buried in a pit, and with them one of his feet, whole to the ankle, with the stocking on.

Mrs. Cicely Ormes

This young martyr, aged twenty-two, was the wife of Mr. Edmund Ormes, worsted weaver of St. Lawrence, Norwich. At the death of Miller and Elizabeth Cooper, before mentioned, she had said that she would pledge them of the same cup they drank of. For these words she was brought to the chancellor, who would have discharged her upon promising to go to church, and to keep her belief to herself. As she would not consent to this, the chancellor urged that he had shown more lenity to her than any other person, and was unwilling to condemn her, because she was an ignorant foolish woman; to this she replied, (perhaps with more shrewdness than he expected,) that however great his desire might be to spare her sinful flesh, it could not equal her inclination to surrender it up in so great a quarrel. The chancellor then pronounced the fiery sentence, and September 23, 1557, she was brought to the stake, at eight o'clock in the morning.

After declaring her faith to the people, she laid her hand on the stake, and said, "Welcome, thou cross of Christ." Her hand was sooted in doing this, (for it was the same stake at which Miller and Cooper were burnt,) and she at first wiped it; but directly after again welcomed and embraced it as the "sweet cross of Christ." After the tormentors had kindled the fire, she said, "My soul doth magnify the Lord, and my spirit doth rejoice in God my Savior." Then crossing her hands upon her breast, and looking upwards with the utmost serenity, she stood the fiery furnace. Her hands continued gradually to rise until the sinews were dried, and then they fell. She uttered no sigh of pain, but yielded her life, an emblem of that celestial paradise in which is the presence of God, blessed forever.

It might be contended that this martyr voluntarily sought her own death, as the chancellor scarcely exacted any other penance of her than to keep her belief to herself; yet it should seem in this instance as if God had chosen her to be a shining light, for a twelve-month before she was taken, she had recanted; but she was wretched until the chancellor was informed, by letter, that she repented of her recantation from the bottom of her heart. As if to compensate for her former apostasy, and to convince the Catholics that she meant to more to compromise for her personal security, she boldly refused his friendly offer of permitting her to temporize. Her courage in such a cause deserves commendation – the cause of Him who has said, "Whoever is ashamed of me on earth, of such will I be ashamed in heaven."

Rev John Rough

This pious martyr was a Scotchman. At the age of seventeen, he entered himself as one of the order of Black Friars, at Stirling, in Scotland. He had been kept out of an inheritance by his friends, and he took this step in revenge for their conduct to him. After being there sixteen years, Lord Hamilton, earl of Arran, taking a liking to him, the archbishop of St. Andrew's induced the provincial of the house to dispense with his habit and order; and he thus became the earl's chaplain. He remained in this spiritual employment a year, and in that time God wrought in him a saving knowledge of the truth; for which reason the earl sent him to preach in the freedom of Ayr, where he remained four years; but finding danger there from the religious complexion of the times, and learning that there was much Gospel freedom in England, he traveled up to the duke of Somerset, then Lord Protector of England, who gave him a yearly salary of twenty pounds, and authorized him, to preach at Carlisle, Berwick, and Newcastle, where he married. He was afterward removed to a benefice at Hull, in which he remained until the death of Edward VI.

In consequence of the tide of persecution then setting in, he fled with his wife to Friesland, and at Nordon they followed the occupation of knitting hose, caps, etc., for subsistence. Impeded in his business by the want of yarn, he came over to England to procure a quantity, and on November 10, arrived in London, where he soon heard of a secret society of the faithful, to whom he joined himself, and was in a short time elected their minister, in which occupation he strengthened them in every good resolution.

On December 12, through the information of one Taylor, a member of the society, Mr. Rough, with Cuthbert Symson and others, was taken up in the Saracen's Head, Islington, where, under the pretext of coming to see a play, their religious exercises were holden. The queen's vice-chamberlain conducted Rough and Symson before the Council, in whose presence they were charged with meeting to celebrate the Communion. The Council wrote to Bonner and he lost no time in this affair of blood. In three days he had him up, and on the next (the twentieth) resolved to condemn him. The charges laid against him were, that he, being a priest, was married, and that he had rejected the service in the Latin tongue. Rough wanted not arguments to reply to these flimsy tenets. In short, he was degraded and condemned. Mr. Rough, it should be noticed, when in the north, in Edward VI's reign, had saved Dr. Watson's life, who afterward sat with Bishop Bonner on the bench. This ungrateful prelate, in return for the kind act he had received, boldly accused Mr. Rough of being the most pernicious heretic in the country. The godly minister reproved him for his malicious spirit; he affirmed that, during the thirty years he had lived, he had never bowed the knee to Baal; and that twice at Rome he had seen the pope born about on men's shoulders with the false-named Sacrament carried before him, presenting a true picture of the very Antichrist; yet was more reverence shown to him than to the wafer, which they accounted to be their God. "Ah?" said Bonner, rising, and making towards him, as if he would have torn his garment, "Hast thou been at Rome, and seen our holy father the pope, and dost thou blaspheme him after this sort?" This said, he fell upon him, tore off a piece of his beard, and that the day might begin to his own satisfaction, he ordered the object of his rage to be burnt by half-past five the following morning.

Cuthbert Symson

Few professors of Christ possessed more activity and zeal than this excellent person. He not only labored to preserve his friends from the contagion of popery, but he labored to guard them against the terrors of persecution. He was deacon of the little congregation over which Mr. Rough presided as minister.

Mr. Symson has written an account of his own sufferings, which he cannot detail better than in his own words:

"On the thirteenth of December, 1557, I

was committed by the Council to the Tower of London. On the following Thursday, I was called into the ward-room, before the constable of the Tower, and the recorder of London, Mr. Cholmly, who commanded me to inform them of the names of those who came to the English service. I answered that I would declare nothing; in consequence of my refusal, I was set upon a rack of iron, as I judge for the space of three hours!

"They then asked me if I would confess: I answered as before. After being unbound, I was carried back to my lodging. The Sunday after I was brought to the same place again, before the lieutenant and recorder of London, and they examined me. As I had answered before, so I answered now. Then the lieutenant swore by God I should tell; after which my two forefingers were bound together, and a small arrow placed between them, they drew it through so fast that the blood followed, and the arrow brake.

"After enduring the rack twice again, I was retaken to my lodging, and ten days after the lieutenant asked me if I would not now confess that which they had before asked of me. I answered, that I had already said as much as I would. Three weeks after I was sent to the priest, where I was greatly assaulted, and at whose hand I received the pope's curse, for bearing witness of the resurrection of Christ. And thus I commend you to God, and to the Word of His grace, with all those who unfeignedly call upon the name of Jesus; desiring God of His endless mercy, through the merits of His dear Son Jesus Christ, to bring us all to His everlasting Kingdom, Amen. I praise God for His great mercy shown upon us. Sing Hosanna to the Highest with me, Cuthbert Symson. God forgive my sins! I ask forgiveness of all the world, and I forgive all the world, and thus I leave the world, in the hope of a joyful resurrection!"

If this account be duly considered, what a picture of repeated tortures does it present! But even the cruelty of the narration is exceeded by the patient meekness with which it was endured. Here are no expressions of malice, no invocations even of God's retributive justice, not a complaint of suffering wrongfully! On the contrary, praise to God, forgiveness of sin, and a forgiving all the world, concludes this unaffected interesting narrative.

Bonner's admiration was excited by the steadfast coolness of this martyr. Speaking of Mr. Symson in the consistory, he said, "You see what a personable man he is, and then of his patience, I affirm, that, if he were not a heretic, he is a man of the greatest patience that ever came before me. Thrice in one day has he been racked in the Tower; in my house also he has felt sorrow, and yet never have I seen his patience broken."

The day before this pious deacon was to be condemned, while in the stocks in the bishop's coal-house, he had the vision of a glorified form, which much encouraged him. This he certainly attested to his wife, to Mr. Austen, and others, before his death.

With this ornament of the Christian Reformation were apprehended Mr. Hugh Foxe and John Devinish; the three were brought before Bonner, March 19, 1558, and the papistical articles tendered. They rejected them, and were all condemned. As they worshiped together in the same society, at Islington, so they suffered together in Smithfield, March 28; in whose death the God of Grace was glorified, and true believers confirmed!

Thomas Hudson, Thomas Carman, and William Seamen

Thomas Hudson, Thomas Carman, and William Seamen were condemned by a bigoted vicar of Aylesbury, named Berry. The spot of execution was called Lollard's Pit, without Bishopsgate, at Norwich. After joining together in humble petition to the throne of grace, they rose, went to the stake, and were encircled with their chains. To the great surprise of the spectators, Hudson slipped from under his chains, and came forward. A great opinion prevailed that he was about to recant; others thought that he wanted further time. In the meantime, his companions at the stake urged every promise and exhortation to support him. The hopes of the enemies of the cross, however, were disappointed: the good man, far from fearing the smallest personal terror at the approaching pangs of death, was only alarmed that his Savior's face seemed to be hidden from him. Falling upon his knees, his spirit wrestled with God, and God verified the words of His Son, "Ask, and it shall be given." The martyr rose in an ecstasy of joy, and exclaimed, "Now, I thank God, I am strong! and care not what man can do to me!" With an unruffled countenance he replaced himself under the chain, joined his fellow-sufferers, and with them suffered death, to the comfort of the godly, and the confusion of Antichrist.

Berry, unsatiated with this demoniacal act, summoned up two hundred persons in the town of Aylesham, whom he compelled to kneel to the cross at Pentecost, and inflicted other punishments. He struck a poor man for a trifling word, with a flail, which proved fatal to the unoffending object. He also gave a woman named Alice Oxes, so heavy a blow with his fist, as she met him entering the hall when he was in an ill-humor, that she died with the violence. This priest was rich, and possessed great authority; he was a reprobate, and, like the priesthood, he abstained from marriage, to enjoy the more a debauched and licentious life. The Sunday after the death of Queen Mary, he was reveling with one of his concubines, before vespers; he then went to church, administered baptism, and in his return to his lascivious pastime, he was smitten by the hand of God. Without a moment given for repentance, he fell to the ground, and a groan was the only articulation permitted him. In him we may behold the difference between the end of a martyr and a persecutor.

The Story of Roger Holland

In a retired close near a field, in Islington, a company of decent persons had assembled, to the number of forty. While they were religiously engaged in praying and expounding the Scripture, twenty-seven of them were carried before Sir Roger Cholmly. Some of the women made their escape, twenty-two were committed to Newgate, who continued in prison seven weeks. Previous to their examination, they were informed by the keeper, Alexander, that nothing more was requisite to procure their discharge, than to hear Mass. Easy as this condition may seem, these martyrs valued their purity of conscience more than loss of life or property; hence, thirteen were burnt, seven in Smithfield, and six at Brentford; two died in prison, and the other seven were providentially preserved. The names of the seven who suffered were, H. Pond, R. Estland, R. Southain, M. Ricarby, J. Floyd, J. Holiday, and Roger Holland. They were sent to Newgate, June 16, 1558, and executed on the twenty-seventh.

This Roger Holland, a merchant-tailor of London, was first an apprentice with one Master Kemption, at the Black Boy in Watling Street, giving himself to dancing, fencing, gaming, banqueting, and wanton company. He had received for his master certain money, to the sum of thirty pounds; and lost every groat at dice. Therefore he purposed to convey himself away beyond the seas, either into France or into Flanders.

With this resolution, he called early in the morning on a discreet servant in the house, named Elizabeth, who professed the Gospel, and lived a life that did honor to her profession. To her he revealed the loss his folly had occasioned, regretted that he had not followed her advice, and begged her to give his master a note of hand from him acknowledging the debt, which he would repay if ever it were in his power; he also entreated his disgraceful conduct might be kept secret, lest it would bring the gray hairs to his father with sorrow to a premature grave.

The maid, with a generosity and Christian principle rarely surpassed, conscious that his imprudence might be his ruin, brought him the thirty pounds, which was part of a sum of money recently left her by legacy. "Here," said she, "is the sum requisite: you shall take the money, and I will keep the note; but expressly on this condition, that you abandon all lewd and vicious company; that you neither swear nor talk immodestly, and game no more; for, should I learn that you do, I will immediately show this note to your master. I also require, that you shall promise me to attend the daily lecture at Allhallows, and the sermon at St. Paul's every Sunday; that you cast away all your books of popery, and in their place substitute the Testament and the Book of Service, and that you read the Scriptures with reverence and fear, calling upon God for his grace to direct you in his truth. Pray also fervently to God, to pardon your former offences, and not to remember the sins of your youth, and would you obtain his favor ever dread to break his laws or offend his majesty. So shall God have you in His keeping, and grant you your heart's desire." We must honor the memory of this excellent domestic, whose pious endeavors were equally directed to benefit the thoughtless youth in this life and that which is to come. God did not suffer the wish of this excellent domestic to be thrown upon a barren soil; within half a year after the licentious Holland became a zealous professor of the Gospel, and was an instrument of conversion to his father and others whom he visited in Lancashire, to their spiritual comfort and reformation from popery.

His father, pleased with his change of conduct, gave him forty pounds to commence business with in London.

Then Roger repaired to London again, and came to the maid that lent him the money to pay his master withal, and said unto her, "Elizabeth, here is thy money I borrowed of thee; and for the friendship, good will, and the good counsel I have received at thy hands, to recompense thee I am not able, otherwise than to make thee my wife." And soon after they were married, which was in the first year of Queen Mary.

After this he remained in the congregations of the faithful, until, the last year of Queen Mary, he, with the six others aforesaid, were taken.

And after Roger Holland there was none suffered in Smithfield for the testimony of the Gospel, God be thanked.

John Willes

John Willes was another faithful person, on whom the scourging hand of Bonner fell. He was the brother of Richard Willes, before mentioned, burnt at Brentford. Hinshaw and Willes were confined in Bonner's coal house together, and afterward removed to Fulham, where he and Hinshaw remained during eight or ten days, in the stocks. Bonner's persecuting spirit betrayed itself in his treatment of Willes during his examinations, often striking him on the head with a stick, seizing him by the ears, and filliping him under the chin, saying he held down his head like a thief. This producing no signs of recantation, he took him into his orchard, and in a small arbor there he flogged him first with a willow rod, and then with birch, until he was exhausted. This cruel ferocity arose from the answer of the poor sufferer, who, upon being asked how long it was since he had crept to the cross, replied, "Not since he had come to years of discretion, nor would he, though he should be torn to pieces by wild horses." Bonner then bade him make the sign of the cross on his forehead, which he refused to do, and thus was led to the orchard.

One day, when in the stocks, Bonner asked him how he liked his lodging and fare. "Well enough," said Willes, "might I have a little straw to sit or lie upon." Just at this time came in Willes' wife, then largely pregnant, and entreated the bishop for her husband, boldly declaring that she would be delivered in the house, if he were not suffered to go with her. To get rid of the good wife's importunity, and the trouble of a lying-in woman in his palace, he bade Willes make the sign of the cross, and say, In nomine Patris, et Filii, et Spiritus Sancti, Amen. Willes omitted the sign, and repeated the words, "in the name of the Father, and of the Son, and of the Holy Ghost, Amen." Bonner would have the words repeated in Latin, to which Willes made no objection, knowing the meaning of the words. He was then permitted to go home with his wife, his kinsman Robert Rouze being charged to bring him to St. Paul's the next day, whither he himself went, and subscribing to a Latin instrument of little importance, was liberated. This is the last of the twenty-two taken at Islington.

Rev Richard Yeoman

This devout aged person was curate to Dr. Taylor, at Hadley, and eminently qualified for his sacred function. Dr. Taylor left him the curacy at his departure, but no sooner had Mr. Newall gotten the benefice, than he removed Mr. Yeoman, and substituted a Romish priest. After this he wandered from place to place, exhorting all men to stand faithfully to God's Word, earnestly to give themselves unto prayer, with patience to bear the cross now laid upon them for their trial, with boldness to confess the truth before their adversaries, and with an undoubted hope to wait for the crown and reward of eternal felicity. But when he perceived his adversaries lay wait for him, he went into Kent, and with a little packet of laces, pins, points, etc., he traveled from village to village, selling such things, and in this manner subsisted himself, his wife, and children.

At last Justice Moile, of Kent, took Mr. Yeoman, and set him in the stocks a day and a night; but, having no evident matter to charge him with, he let him go again. Coming secretly again to Hadley, he tarried with his poor wife, who kept him privately, in a chamber of the town house, commonly called the Guildhall, more than a year. During this time the good old father abode in a chamber locked up all the day, spending his time in devout prayer, in reading the Scriptures, and in carding the wool which his wife spun. His wife also begged bread for herself and her children, by which precarious means they supported themselves. Thus the saints of God sustained hunger and misery, while the prophets of Baal lived in festivity, and were cosily pampered at Jezebel's table.

Information being at length given to Newall, that Yeoman was secreted by his wife, he came, attended by the constables, and broke into the room where the object of his search lay in bed with his wife. He reproached the poor woman with being a whore, and would have indecently pulled the clothes off, but Yeoman resisted both this act of violence and the attack upon his wife's character, adding that he defied the pope and popery. He was then taken out, and set in stocks until day.

In the cage also with him was an old man, named John Dale, who had sat there three or four days, for exhorting the people during the time service was performing by Newall and his curate. His words were, "O miserable and blind guides, will ye ever be blind leaders of the blind? Will ye never amend? Will ye never see the truth of God's Word? Will neither God's threats nor promises enter into your hearts? Will the blood of the martyrs nothing mollify your stony stomachs? O obdurate, hard-hearted, perverse, and crooked generation! to whom nothing can do good."

These words he spake in fervency of spirit against the superstitious religion of Rome; wherefore Newall caused him forthwith to be attached, and set in the stocks in a cage, where he was kept until Sir Henry Doile, a justice, came to Hadley.

When Yeoman was taken, the parson called earnestly upon Sir Henry Doile to send them both to prison. Sir Henry Doile as earnestly entreated the parson to consider the age of the men, and their mean condition; they were neither persons of note nor preachers; wherefore he proposed to let them be punished a day or two and to dismiss them, at least John Dale, who was no priest, and therefore, as he had so long sat in the cage, he thought it punishment enough for this time. When the parson heard this, he was exceedingly mad, and in a great rage called them pestilent heretics, unfit to live in the commonwealth of Christians.

Sir Henry, fearing to appear too merciful, Yeoman and Dale were pinioned, bound like thieves with their legs under the horses' bellies, and carried to Bury jail, where they were laid in irons; and because they continually rebuked popery, they were carried into the lowest dungeon, where John Dale, through the jail-sickness and evil-keeping, died soon after: his body was thrown out, and buried in the fields. He was a man of sixty-six years of age, a weaver by occupation, well learned in the holy Scriptures, steadfast in his confession of the true doctrines of Christ as set forth in King Edward's time; for which he joyfully suffered prison and chains, and from this worldly dungeon he departed in Christ to eternal glory, and the blessed paradise of everlasting felicity.

After Dale's death, Yeoman was removed to Norwich prison, where, after strait and evil keeping, he was examined upon his faith and religion, and required to submit himself to his holy father the pope. "I defy him, (quoth he), and all his detestable abomination: I will in no wise have to do with him." The chief articles objected to him, were his marriage and the Mass sacrifice. Finding he continued steadfast in the truth, he was condemned, degraded, and not only burnt, but most cruelly tormented in the fire. Thus he ended this poor and miserable life, and entered into that blessed bosom of Abraham, enjoying with Lazarus that rest which God has prepared for His elect.

Thomas Benbridge

Mr. Benbridge was a single gentleman, in the diocese of Winchester. He might have lived a gentleman's life, in the wealthy possessions of this world; but he chose rather to enter through the strait gate of persecution to the heavenly possession of life in the Lord's Kingdom, than to enjoy present pleasure with disquietude of conscience. Manfully standing against the papists for the defense of the sincere doctrine of Christ's Gospel, he was apprehended as an adversary to the Romish religion, and led for examination before the bishop of Winchester, where he underwent several conflicts for the truth against the bishop and his colleague; for which he was condemned, and some time after brought to the place of martyrdom by Sir Richard Pecksal, sheriff.

When standing at the stake he began to untie his points, and to prepare himself; then he gave his gown to the keeper, by way of fee. His jerkin was trimmed with gold lace, which he gave to Sir Richard Pecksal, the high sheriff. His cap of velvet he took from his head, and threw away. Then, lifting his mind to the Lord, he engaged in prayer.

When fastened to the stake, Dr. Seaton begged him to recant, and he should have his pardon; but when he saw that nothing availed, he told the people not to pray for him unless he would recant, no more than they would pray for a dog.

Mr. Benbridge, standing at the stake with his hands together in such a manner as the priest holds his hands in his Memento, Dr. Seaton came to him again, and exhorted him to recant, to whom he said, "Away, Babylon, away!" One that stood by said, "Sir, cut his tongue out"; another, a temporal man, railed at him worse than Dr. Seaton had done.

When they saw he would not yield, they bade the tormentors to light the pile, before he was in any way covered with fagots. The fire first took away a piece of his beard, at which he did not shrink. Then it came on the other side and took his legs, and the nether stockings of his hose being leather, they made the fire pierce the sharper, so that the intolerable heat made him exclaim, "I recant!" and suddenly he trust the fire from him. Two or three of his friends being by, wished to save him; they stepped to the fire to help remove it, for which kindness they were sent to jail. The sheriff also of his own authority took him from the stake, and remitted him to prison, for which he was sent to the Fleet, and lay there sometime. Before, however, he was taken from the stake, Dr. Seaton wrote articles for him to subscribe to. To these Mr. Benbridge made so many objections that Dr. Seaton ordered them to set fire again to the pile. Then with much pain and grief of heart he subscribed to them upon a man's back.

This done, his gown was given him again, and he was led to prison. While there, he wrote a letter to Dr. Seaton, recanting those words he had spoken at the stake, and the articles which he had subscribed, for he was grieved that he had ever signed them. The same day he was again brought to the stake, where the vile tormentors rather broiled than burnt him. The Lord give his enemies repentance!

Mrs. Prest

From the number condemned in this fanatical reign, it is almost impossible to obtain the name of every martyr, or to embellish the history of all with anecdotes and exemplifications of Christian conduct. Thanks be to Providence, our cruel task begins to draw towards a conclusion, with the end of the reign of papal terror and bloodshed. Monarchs, who sit upon thrones possessed by hereditary right, should, of all others, consider that the laws of nature are the laws of God, and hence that the first law of nature is the preservation of their subjects. Maxims of persecutions, of torture, and of death, they should leave to those who have effected sovereignty by fraud or by sword; but where, except among a few miscreant emperors of Rome, and the Roman pontiffs, shall we find one whose memory is so "damned to everlasting fame" as that of Queen Mary? Nations bewail the hour which separates them forever from a beloved governor, but, with respect to that of Mary, it was the most blessed time of her whole reign. Heaven has ordained three great scourges for national sins – plague, pestilence, and famine. It was the will of God in Mary's reign to bring a fourth upon this kingdom, under the form of papistical persecution. It was sharp, but glorious; the fire which consumed the martyrs has undermined the popedom; and the Catholic states, at present the most bigoted and unenlightened, are those which are sunk lowest in the scale of moral dignity and political consequence. May they remain so, until the pure light of the Gospel shall dissipate the darkness of fanaticism and superstition! But to return.

Mrs. Prest for some time lived about Cornwall, where she had a husband and children, whose bigotry compelled her to frequent the abominations of the Church of Rome. Resolving to act as her conscience dictated, she quitted them, and made a living by spinning. After some time, returning home, she was accused by her neighbors, and brought to Exeter, to be examined before Dr. Troubleville, and his chancellor Blackston. As this martyr was accounted of inferior intellect, we shall put her in competition with the bishop, and let the reader judge which had the most of that knowledge conducive to everlasting life. The bishop bringing the question to issue, respecting the bread and wine being flesh and blood, Mrs. Prest said, "I will demand of you whether you can deny your creed, which says, that Christ doth perpetually sit at the right hand of His Father, both body and soul, until He come again; or whether He be there in heaven our Advocate, and to make prayer for us unto God His Father? If He be so, He is not here on earth in a piece of bread. If He be not here, and if He do not dwell in temples made with hands, but in heaven, what! shall we seek Him here? If He did not offer His body once for all, why make you a new offering? If with one offering He made all perfect, why do you with a false offering make all imperfect? If He be to be worshiped in spirit and in truth, why do you worship a piece of bread? If He be eaten and drunken in faith and truth, if His flesh be not profitable to be among us, why do you say you make His flesh and blood, and say it is profitable for body and soul? Alas! I am a poor woman, but rather than to do as you do, I would live no longer. I have said, Sir."

Bishop. I promise you, you are a jolly Protestant. I pray you in what school have you been brought up?

Mrs. Prest. I have upon the Sundays visited the sermons, and there have I learned such things as are so fixed in my breast, that death shall not separate them.

B. O foolish woman, who will waste his breath upon thee, or such as thou art? But how chanceth it that thou wentest away from thy husband? If thou wert an honest woman, thou wouldst not have left thy husband and children, and run about the country like a fugitive.

Mrs. P. Sir, I labored for my living; and as my Master Christ counselleth me, when I was persecuted in one city, I fled into another.

B. Who persecuted thee?

Mrs. P. My husband and my children. For when I would have them to leave idolatry, and to worship God in heaven, he would not hear me, but he with his children rebuked me, and troubled me. I fled not for whoredom, nor for theft, but because I would be no partaker with him and his of that foul idol the Mass; and wheresoever I was, as oft as I could, upon Sundays and holydays. I made excuses not to go to the popish Church.

B. Belike then you are a good housewife, to fly from your husband the Church.

Mrs. P. My housewifery is but small; but God gave me grace to go to the true Church.

B. The true Church, what dost thou mean?

Mrs. P. Not your popish Church, full of idols and abominations, but where two or three are gathered together in the name of God, to that Church will I go as long as I live.

B. Belike then you have a church of your own. Well, let this mad woman be put down to prison until we send for her husband.

Mrs. P. No, I have but one husband, who is here already in this city, and in prison with me, from whom I will never depart.

Some persons present endeavoring to convince the bishop she was not in her right senses, she was permitted to depart. The keeper of the bishop's prisons took her into his house, where she either spun worked as a servant, or walked about the city, discoursing upon the Sacrament of the altar. Her husband was sent for to take her home, but this she refused while the cause of religion could be served. She was too active to be idle, and her conversation, simple as they affected to think her, excited the attention of several Catholic priests and friars. They teased her with questions, until she answered them angrily, and this excited a laugh at her warmth.

"Nay," said she, "you have more need to weep than to laugh, and to be sorry that ever you were born, to be the chaplains of that whore of Babylon. I defy him and all his falsehood; and get you away from me, you do but trouble my conscience. You would have me follow your doings; I will first lose my life. I pray you depart."

"Why, thou foolish woman," said they, "we come to thee for thy profit and soul's health." To which she replied, "What profit ariseth by you, that teach nothing but lies for truth? how save you souls, when you preach nothing but lies, and destroy souls?"

"How provest thou that?" said they.

"Do you not destroy your souls, when you teach the people to worship idols, stocks, and stones, the works of men's hands? and to worship a false God of your own making of a piece of bread, and teach that the pope is God's vicar, and hath power to forgive sins? and that there is a purgatory, when God's Son hath by His passion purged all? and say you make God and sacrifice Him, when Christ's body was a sacrifice once for all? Do you not teach the people to number their sins in your ears, and say they will be damned if they confess not all; when God's Word saith, Who can number his sins? Do you not promise them trentals and dirges and Masses for souls, and sell your prayers for money, and make them buy pardons, and trust to such foolish inventions of your imaginations? Do you not altogether act against God? Do you not teach us to pray upon beads, and to pray unto saints, and say they can pray for us? Do you not make holy water and holy bread to fray devils? Do you not do a thousand more abominations? And yet you say, you come for my profit, and to save my soul. No, no, one hath saved me. Farewell, you with your salvation."

During the liberty granted her by the bishop, before-mentioned, she went into St. Peter's Church, and there found a skillful Dutchman, who was affixing new noses to certain fine images which had been disfigured in King Edward's time; to whom she said, "What a madman art thou, to make them new noses, which within a few days shall all lose their heads?" The Dutchman accused her and laid it hard to her charge. And she said unto him, "Thou art accursed, and so are thy images." He called her a whore. "Nay," said she, "thy images are whores, and thou art a whore-hunter; for doth not God say, "You go a whoring after strange gods, figures of your own making? and thou art one of them." After this she was ordered to be confined, and had no more liberty.

During the time of her imprisonment, many visited her, some sent by the bishop, and some of their own will, among these was one Daniel, a great preacher of the Gospel, in the days of King Edward, about Cornwall and Devonshire, but who, through the grievous persecution he had sustained, had fallen off. Earnestly did she exhort him to repent with Peter, and to be more constant in his profession.

Mrs. Walter Rauley and Mr. William and John Kede, persons of great respectability, bore ample testimony of her godly conversation, declaring, that unless God were with her, it were impossible she could have so ably defended the cause of Christ. Indeed, to sum up the character of this poor woman, she united the serpent and the dove, abounding in the highest wisdom joined to the greatest simplicity. She endured imprisonment, threatenings, taunts, and the vilest epithets, but nothing could induce her to swerve; her heart was fixed; she had cast anchor; nor could all the wounds of persecution remove her from the rock on which her hopes of felicity were built.

Such was her memory, that, without learning, she could tell in what chapter any text of Scripture was contained: on account of this singular property, one Gregory Basset, a rank papist, said she was deranged, and talked as a parrot, wild without meaning. At length, having tried every manner without effect to make her nominally a Catholic, they condemned her. After this, one exhorted her to leave her opinions, and go home to her family, as she was poor and illiterate. "True, (said she) though I am not learned, I am content to be a witness of Christ's death, and I pray you make no longer delay with me; for my heart is fixed, and I will never say otherwise, nor turn to your superstitious doing."

To the disgrace of Mr. Blackston, treasurer of the church, he would often send for this poor martyr from prison, to make sport for him and a woman whom he kept; putting religious questions to her, and turning her answers into ridicule. This done, he sent her back to her wretched dungeon, while he battened upon the good things of this world.

There was perhaps something simply ludicrous in the form of Mrs. Prest, as she was of a very short stature, thick set, and about fifty-four years of age; but her countenance was cheerful and lively, as if prepared for the day of her marriage with the Lamb. To mock at her form was an indirect accusation of her Creator, who framed her after the fashion He liked best, and gave her a mind that far excelled the transient endowments of perishable flesh. When she was offered money, she rejected it, "because (said she) I am going to a city where money bears no mastery, and while I am here God has promised to feed me."

When sentence was read, condemning her to the flames, she lifted up her voice and praised God, adding, "This day have I found that which I have long sought." When they tempted her to recant, "That will I not, (said she) God forbid that I should lose the life eternal, for this carnal and short life. I will never turn from my heavenly husband to my earthly husband; from the fellowship of angels to mortal children; and if my husband and children be faithful, then am I theirs. God is my father, God is my mother, God is my sister, my brother, my kinsman; God is my friend, most faithful."

Being delivered to the sheriff, she was led by the officer to the place of execution, without the walls of Exeter, called Sothenhey, where again the superstitious priests assaulted her. While they were tying her to the stake, she continued earnestly to exclaim "God be merciful to me, a sinner!" Patiently enduring the devouring conflagration, she was consumed to ashes, and thus ended a life which in unshaken fidelity to the cause of Christ, was not surpassed by that of any preceding martyr.

Richard Sharpe, Thomas Banion, and Thomas Hale

Mr. Sharpe, weaver, of Bristol, was brought the ninth day of March, 1556, before Dr. Dalby, chancellor of the city of Bristol, and after examination concerning the Sacrament of the altar, was persuaded to recant; and on the twenty-ninth, he was enjoined to make his recantation in the parish church. But, scarcely had he publicly avowed his backsliding, before he felt in his conscience such a tormenting fiend, that he was unable to work at his occupation; hence, shortly after, one Sunday, he came into the parish church, called Temple, and after high Mass, stood up in the choir door, and said with a loud voice, "Neighbors, bear me record that yonder idol (pointing to the altar) is the greatest and most abominable that ever was; and I am sorry that ever I denied my Lord God!" Notwithstanding the constables were ordered to apprehend him, he was suffered to go out of the church; but at night he was apprehended and carried to Newgate. Shortly after, before the chancellor, denying the Sacrament of the altar to be the body and blood of Christ, he was condemned to be burned by Mr. Dalby. He was burnt the seventh of May, 1558, and died godly, patiently, and constantly, confessing the Protestant articles of faith. With him suffered Thomas Hale, shoemaker, of Bristol, who was condemned by Chanallor Dalby. These martyrs were bound back to back.

Thomas Banion, a weaver, was burnt on August 27, of the same year, and died for the sake of the evangelical cause of his Savior.

J. Corneford, of Wortham; C. Browne, of Maidstone; J. Herst, of Ashford; Alice Snoth, and Catharine Knight, an Aged Woman

With pleasure we have to record that these five martyrs were the last who suffered in the reign of Mary for the sake of the Protestant cause; but the malice of the papists was conspicuous in hastening their martyrdom, which might have been delayed until the event of the queen's illness was decided. It is reported that the archdeacon of Canterbury, judging that the sudden death of the queen would suspend the execution, traveled post from London, to have the satisfaction of adding another page to the black list of papistical sacrifices.

The articles against them were, as usual, the Sacramental elements and the idolatry of bending to images. They quoted St. John's words, "Beware of images!" and respecting the real presence, they urged according to St. Paul, "the things which are seen are temporal." When sentence was about to be read against them, and excommunication to take place in the regular form, John Corneford, illuminated by the Holy Spirit, awfully turned the latter proceeding against themselves, and in a solemn impressive manner, recriminated their excommunication in the following words: "In the name of our Lord Jesus Christ, the Son of the most mighty God, and by the power of His Holy Spirit, and the authority of His holy Catholic and apostolic Church, we do here give into the hands of Satan to be destroyed, the bodies of all those blasphemers and heretics that maintain any error against His most holy Word, or do condemn His most holy truth for heresy, to the maintenance of any false church or foreign religion, so that by this Thy just judgment, O most mighty God, against Thy adversaries, Thy true religion may be known to Thy great glory and our comfort and to the edifying of all our nation. Good Lord, so be it. Amen."

This sentence was openly pronounced and registered, and, as if Providence had awarded that it should not be delivered in vain, within six days after, Queen Mary died, detested by all good men and accursed of God!

Though acquainted with these circumstances, the archdeacon's implacability exceeded that of his great exemplary, Bonner, who, though he had several persons at that time under his fiery grasp, did not urge their deaths hastily, by which delay he certainly afforded them an opportunity of escape. At the queen's decease, many were in bonds: some just taken, some examined, and others condemned. The writs indeed were issued for several burnings, but by the death of the three instigators of Protestant murder – the chancellor, the bishop, and the queen, who fell nearly together, the condemned sheep were liberated, and lived many years to praise God for their happy deliverance.

These five martyrs, when at the stake, earnestly prayed that their blood might be the last shed, nor did they pray in vain. They died gloriously, and perfected the number God had selected to bear witness of the truth in this dreadful reign, whose names are recorded in the Book of Life; though last, not least among the saints made meet for immortality through the redeeming blood of the Lamb!

Catharine Finlay, alias Knight, was first converted by her son's expounding the Scriptures to her, which wrought in her a perfect work that terminated in martyrdom. Alice Snoth at the stake sent for her grandmother and godfather, and rehearsed to them the articles of her faith, and the Commandments of God, thereby convincing the world that she knew her duty. She died calling upon the spectators to bear witness that she was a Christian woman, and suffered joyfully for the testimony of Christ's Gospel.

Unfeeling Bonner

Among the numberless enormities committed by the merciless and unfeeling Bonner, the murder of this innocent and unoffending child may be ranged as the most horrid. His father, John Fetty, of the parish of Clerkenwell, by trade a tailor, and only twenty-four years of age, had made blessed election; he was fixed secure in eternal hope, and depended on Him who so builds His Church that the gates of hell shall not prevail against it. But alas! the very wife of his bosom, whose heart was hardened against the truth, and whose mind was influenced by the teachers of false doctrine, became his accuser. Brokenbery, a creature of the pope, and parson of the parish, received the information of this wedded Delilah, in consequence of which the poor man was apprehended. But here the awful judgment of an ever-righteous God, who is "of purer eyes than to behold evil," fell upon this stone-hearted and perfidious woman; for no sooner was the injured husband captured by her wicked contriving, than she also was suddenly seized with madness, and exhibited an awful and awakening instance of God's power to punish the evil-doer. This dreadful circumstance had some effect upon the hearts of the ungodly hunters who had eagerly grasped their prey; but, in a relenting moment, they suffered him to remain with his unworthy wife, to return her good for evil, and to comfort two children, who, on his being sent to prison, would have been left without a protector, or have become a burden to the parish. As bad men act from little motives, we may place the indulgence shown him to the latter account.

We have noticed in the former part of our narratives of the martyrs, some whose affection would have led them even to sacrifice their own lives, to preserve their husbands; but here, agreeable to Scripture language, a mother proves, indeed, a monster in nature! Neither conjugal nor maternal affection could impress the heart of this disgraceful woman.

Although our afflicted Christian had experienced so much cruelty and falsehood from the woman who was bound to him by every tie both human and divine, yet, with a mild and forbearing spirit, he overlooked her misdeeds, during her calamity endeavoring all he could to procure relief for her malady, and soothing her by every possible expression of tenderness: thus she became in a few weeks nearly restored to her senses. But, alas! she returned again to her sin, "as a dog returneth to his vomit." Malice against the saints of the Most High was seated in her heart too firmly to be removed; and as her strength returned, her inclination to work wickedness returned with it. Her heart was hardened by the prince of darkness; and to her may be applied these afflicting and soul-harrowing words, "Can the Ethiopian change his skin, or the leopard his spots? then may ye also do good, that are accustomed to do evil." Weighing this text duly with another, "I will have mercy on whom I will have mercy," how shall we presume to refine away the sovereignty of God by arrainging Jehovah at the bar of human reason, which, in religious matters, is too often opposed by infinite wisdom? "Broad is the way, that leadeth to destruction, and many there be which go in thereat. Narrow is the way, which leadeth unto life, and few there be that find it." The ways of heaven are indeed inscrutable, and it is our bounden duty to walk ever dependent on God, looking up to Him with humble confidence, and hope in His goodness, and ever confess His justice; and where we "cannot unravel, there learn to trust." This wretched woman, pursuing the horrid dictates of a heart hardened and depraved, was scarcely confirmed in her recovery, when, stifling the dictates of honor, gratitude, and every natural affection, she again accused her husband, who was once more apprehended, and taken before Sir John Mordant, knight, and one of Queen Mary's commissioners.

Upon examination, his judge finding him fixed in opinions which militated against those nursed by superstition and maintained by cruelty, he was sentenced to confinement and torture in Lollard's Tower. Here he was put into the painful stocks, and had a dish of water set by him, with a stone put into it, to what purpose God knoweth, except it were to show that he should look for little other subsistence: which is credible enough, if we consider their like practices upon divers before mentioned in this history; as, among others, upon Richard Smith, who died through their cruel imprisonment touching whom, when a godly woman came to Dr. Story to have leave she might bury him, he asked her if he had any straw or blood in his mouth; but what he means thereby, I leave to the judgment of the wise.

On the first day of the third week of our martyr's sufferings, an object presented itself to his view, which made him indeed feel his tortures with all their force, and to execrate, with bitterness only short of cursing, the author of his misery. To mark and punish the proceedings of his tormentors, remained with the Most High, who noteth even the fall of a sparrow, and in whose sacred Word it is written, "Vengeance is mine; I will repay." This object was his own son, a child of the tender age of eight years. For fifteen days, had its hapless father been suspended by his tormentor by the right arm and left leg, and sometimes by both, shifting his positions for the purpose of giving him strength to bear and to lengthen the date of his sufferings. When the unoffending innocent, desirous of seeing and speaking to its parent, applied to Bonner for permission to do so, the poor child being asked by the bishop's chaplain the purport of his errand, he replied he wished to see his father. "Who is thy father?" said the chaplain. "John Fetty," returned the boy, at the same time pointing to the place where he was confined. The interrogating miscreant on this said, "Why, thy father is a heretic!" The little champion again rejoined, with energy sufficient to raise admiration in any breast, except that of this unprincipled and unfeeling wretch – this miscreant, eager to execute the behests of a remorseless queen – "My father is no heretic: for you have Balaam's mark."

Irritated by reproach so aptly applied, the indignant and mortified priest concealed his resentment for a moment, and took the undaunted boy into the house, where having him secure, he presented him to others, whose baseness and cruelty being equal to his own, they stripped him to the skin, and applied their scourges to so violent a degree, that, fainting beneath the stripes inflicted on his tender frame, and covered with the blood that flowed from them, the victim of their ungodly wrath was ready to expire under his heavy and unmerited punishment.

In this bleeding and helpless state was the suffering infant, covered only with his shirt, taken to his father by one of the actors in the horrid tragedy, who, while he exhibited the heart-rending spectacle, made use of the vilest taunts, and exulted in what he had done. The dutiful child, as if recovering strength at the sight of his father, on his knees implored his blessing. "Alas! Will," said the afflicted parent, in trembling amazement, "who hath done this to thee!" the artless innocent related the circumstances that led to the merciless correction which had been so basely inflicted on him; but when he repeated the reproof bestowed on the chaplain, and which was prompted by an undaunted spirit, he was torn from his weeping parent, and conveyed again to the house, where he remained a close prisoner.

Bonner, somewhat fearful that what had been done could not be justified even among the bloodhounds of his own voracious pack, concluded in his dark and wicked mind, to release John Fetty, for a time at least, from the severities he was enduring in the glorious cause of everlasting truth! whose bright rewards are fixed beyond the boundaries of time, within the confines of eternity; where the arrow of the wicked cannot wound, even "where there shall be no more sorrowing for the blessed, who, in the mansion of eternal bliss shall glorify the Lamb forever and ever." He was accordingly by order of Bonner, (how disgraceful to all dignity, to say bishop!) liberated from the painful bonds, and led from Lollard's Tower, to the chamber of that ungodly and infamous butcher, where he found the bishop bathing himself before a great fire; and at his first entering the chamber, Fetty said, "God be here and peace!" "God be here and peace, (said Bonner,) that is neither God speed nor good morrow!" "If ye kick against this peace, (said Fetty), then this is not the place that I seek for."

A chaplain of the bishop, standing by, turned the poor man about, and thinking to abash him, said, in mocking wise, "What have we here – a player!" While Fetty was thus standing in the bishop's chamber, he espied, hanging about the bishop's bed, a pair of great black beads, whereupon he said, "My Lord, I think the hangman is not far off: for the halter (pointing to the beads) is here already!"

At which words the bishop was in a marvelous rage. Then he immediately after espied also, standing in the bishop's chamber, in the window, a little crucifix. Then he asked the bishop what it was, and he answered, that it was Christ. "Was He handled as cruelly as He is here pictured!" said Fetty.

"Yea, that He was," said the bishop.

"And even so cruelly will you handle such as come before you; for you are unto God's people as Caiaphas was unto Christ!"

The bishop, being in a great fury, said, "Thou art a vile heretic, and I will burn thee, or else I will spend all I have, unto my gown."

"Nay, my Lord, (said Fetty) you were better to give it to some poor body, that he may pray for you."

Bonner, notwithstanding his passion, which was raised to the utmost by the calm and pointed remarks of this observing Christian, thought it most prudent to dismiss the father, on account of the nearly murdered child. His coward soul trembled for the consequences which might ensue; fear is inseparable from little minds; and this dastardly pampered priest experienced its effects so far as to induce him to assume the appearance of that he was an utter stranger to, namely, MERCY.

The father, on being dismissed, by the tyrant Bonner, went home with a heavy heart, with his dying child, who did not survive many days the cruelties which had been inflicted on him.

How contrary to the will of our great King and Prophet, who mildly taught His followers, was the conduct of this sanguinary and false teacher, this vile apostate from his God to Satan! But the archfiend had taken entire possession of his heart, and guided every action of the sinner he had hardened; who, given up to terrible destruction, was running the race of the wicked, marking his footsteps with the blood of the saints, as if eager to arrive at the goal of eternal death.

Foxe's Book of Martyrs, Edited by William Byron Forbush, chapter 16

Martyrdoms of Ridley and Latimer

"Be of good comfort, Mr Ridley, and play the man! We shall this day light such a candle, by God's grace, in England, as I trust never shall be put out." Latimer's words to Ridley as a faggot was set on fire at his feet

Ridley

On the 17th October, 1555, those two pillars of Christ's church, Dr Nicholas Ridley, Bishop of London, and Mr Hugh Latimer, sometime Bishop of Worcester, were burnt in one fire at Oxford – men ever memorable for their piety, learning, and incomparable ornaments and gifts of grace, joined with no less commendable sincerity of life.

Dr Ridley, born in Northumberland, entered the Cambridge university, where, in a short time, he became famed for his singular aptness, and was called to higher offices in the university, and was then made head of Pembroke Hall, and there made doctor of divinity. Then he went to Paris, and on his return was made chaplain to King Henry VIII, and later promoted to the bishopric of Rochester, and from there, in King Edward's days, translated to that of London.

Dr Ridley was first brought to a knowledge of Christ and his gospel by reading Bertram's book on the sacrament; and his conference with Archbishop Cranmer, and with Peter Martyr, did much to confirm him in that belief. Being now, by the grace of God, thoroughly converted to the true way, he was as constant and faithful in the right knowledge which the Lord had revealed unto him, as he was before blind and zealous in his old ignorance, and so long as the power and authority of the state defended the gospel, and supported the happiness of the church, his influence was mighty for spiritual good. But after it pleased God (in his wise providence) to bereave us of our stay, it taking from us King Edward, the whole state of the Church of England was left desolate and open to the enemy's hand: so that Bishop Ridley, after the accession of Queen Mary, was one of the first upon whom they laid their hands, and sent to prison: first in the Tower, and from there conveyed, with the Archbishop of Canterbury [Cranmer] and Mr Latimer, to Oxford, and with them con fined in the common prison of Bocardo.

Letter from Bishop Ridley

Letter from Bishop Ridley and his fellow-prisoners to Mr Bradford and his fellow-prisoners, in the King's bench, in Southwark, anno 1554.Well beloved in Christ our Savior, we all with one heart wish to you, with all those that love God in deed and truth, grace an health, and especially to our dearly-beloved companions which are in Christ's cause, and the cause both of their brethren and of their own salvation, to put their neck willingly under the yoke of Christ's cross. How joyful it was to us to hear the report of Dr Taylor, and of his godly confession, I assure you it is hard for me to express.

Blessed be God, which was and is the giver of that, an of all godly strength and support in the time of adversity. As for the rumors that have or do go abroad, either of our relenting or massing, we trust that they which know God and their duty towards their brethren in Christ, will not be too light of belief. For it is not the slanderer's evil tongue, but a man's evil deed, that can with God defile a man; and, therefore, with God's grace, you shall never have cause to do otherwise than you say you do, that is, not to doubt but that we will, by God's grace, continue. Like rumors as you have heard of our coming to London have been here spread of coming of certain learned men prisoners hither from London; but as yet we know no certainty which of these rumors is or shall be more true. Know you that we have your in our daily remembrance, and wish you and all the rest of our foresaid companies well in Christ.

My lord of Worcester passed through Oxford, but he did not visit us. The same day our restraint began to be more close, and the book of the communion was taken from us by the bailiffs, at the mayor's command, as the bailiffs did report to us. No man is licensed to come unto us; before they might, that would see us upon the wall, but that is so grudged at, and so evil reported, that we are now restrained. Sir, blessed be God, with all our evil reports, grudges, and restraints, we are merry in God; all our care is and shall be, by God's grace, to please and serve him, of whom we look and hope, after there temporal and momentary miseries, to have eternal joy and perpetual felicity with Abraham, Isaac, and Jacob, Peter and Paul, and all the heavenly company of the angels in heaven, through Jesus Christ our Lord. As yet there has not learned man, nor any scholar, been to visit us since we came into Bocardo, which now in Oxford may be called a college of quondams [people who had previously held office]. For as you know we are no fewer than three, and I dare say every one well contented with his portion, which I do reckon to be our heavenly Father's fatherly, good, and gracious gift. Thus fare you well. We shall, by God's grace, one day meet together, and be merry. That day assuredly approacheth apace; the Lord grant that it may shortly come. For before that day come, I fear the world will wax worse and worse. But then all our enemies shall be overthrown and trodden under foot; righteousness and truth then shall have the victory, and bear the bell away, whereof the Lord grant us to be partakers, and all that love truly the truth.

We all pray you, as we can, to cause all our commendations to be made unto all such as you know did visit us and you when we were in the Tower, with their friendly remembrances and benefits. Mrs Wilkson and Mrs Warcup have not forgotten us, but ever since we came to Bocardo, with their charitable and friendly benevolence, have comforted us: not that else we did lack (for God be blessed, he hath always sufficiently provided for us), but that is a great comfort, and an occasion for us to bless God, when we see that he maketh them so friendly to tender us, whom some of us were never familiarly acquainted withal.

Yours in Christ.

Nicholas Ridley.

Latimer

At the age of fourteen he was sent to Cambridge university. Latimer, like St Paul, was both zealous and misguided. He confesses that as a priest he was so servile an observer of the Romish decrees, that in the celebration of mass his conscience was much troubled lest he had insufficiently mingled his wine with water; and, moreover, he believed that he should never be damned if he became a professed friar, with many other like superstitions. Mr Thomas Bilney, perceiving that Latimer had a great zeal, although, like that of some of the Judaising teachers, not according to knowledge, felt a brotherly pity towards him, and began to consider by what means he might expound to this ignorant brother the way of God more perfectly, even as Aquila and Priscilla did to Apollos. Impressed with these feelings, after a short time he came to Mr Latimer's study, and asked him to hear his own confession; the result of which interview was, that Latimer's understanding was so enlightened by God's good Spirit, that immediately he forsook the study of the school doctors, and other such philosophers falsely so called, and became an earnest student of the Bible, and of that divinity which centers in the cross of Christ. He was a changed character, for he hated that which he had loved, and he now loved that which he had hated. Jesus, the Son of God, had been revealed to him, and, like the apostle, in faith and obedience he was now ready to ask, "Lord, what wilt thou have me to do?'

After Latimer preached he gave the people certain cards out of the 5th, 6th, and 7th chapters of St Matthew, in the study of which they might, not only then, but at all other times, occupy their time. For the chief triumph [the word "trump', as now used, is a corruption of "triumph' – the "triumph card'] in the cards he selected the heart, as the principal thing with which they should serve God, whereby he quite overthrew all hypocritical and external ceremonies, not tending to the furtherance of God's holy Word and sacraments. He added, moreover, to the praise of that triumph, that though it were ever so small, yet it would take up the best court card beside in the bunch, yea, though it were the king of clubs, meaning thereby how the Lord would be worshiped and served in simplicity of heart and verity, wherein consisteth true Christian religion, and not in the outward deeds of the letter only, or in the glittering show of man's traditions, or pardons, pilgrimages, ceremonies, vows, devotions, voluntary works, and works of supererogation, foundations, oblations, the Pope's supremacy, and "other such like things'. For the better attaining hereof, he wished the Scriptures to be in English, in order that the common people might be enabled to learn their duty to God and to their neighbors. As Latimer's sermons were so important in their consequences, we here present the reader with the following beautiful extract from one of them.

Extract from a sermon of Mr Latimer, in Cambridge, about the year 1529.

"Tue quis es?' Which words are as much to say in English, "Who art thou?' These be the words of the Pharisees, which were sent by the Jews unto St John the Baptist in the wilderness, to have knowledge of him who he was; which words they spake unto him of an evil intent, thinking that he would have taken on him to be Christ, and so they would have had him done by their good wills, because they knew that he was more carnal and given to their laws than Christ indeed should be, as they perceived by their old prophecies: and also, because they marveled much at his great doctrine, preaching, and baptizing, they were in doubt whether he was Christ or not; wherefore they said unto him, "Who art thou?' Then answered St John, an confessed that he was not Christ.

Now then, according to the preacher, let every man and woman, of a good and simple mind, contrary to the Pharisees' intent, ask this question, "Who art thou?' This question must be moved to themselves, what they be of themselves, on this fashion: "What art thou of thy only and natural generation between father and mother, when thou camest into the world? What substance, what virtue, what goodness art thou of thyself?' Which question, if thou rehearse oftentimes to thyself, thou shalt well perceive and understand how thou shalt reply, which must be made like this: "I am of myself, and by myself, coming from my natural father and mother, the child of anger and indignation of God, the true inheritor of hell, a lump of sin, and working nothing of myself, but all towards hell, except I have better help of another than I have of myself." Now we may see in what state we enter into this world, that we be of ourselves the true and just inheritors of hell, the children of the ire and indignation of Christ, working all towards hell, whereby we deserve of ourselves perpetual damnation by the right judgement of God, and the true claim of ourselves: which unthrifty state that we be born unto is come unto us for our own deserts, as proveth well this example following:

"Let it be admitted for the probation of this, that it might please the king's grace now being, to accept into his favor a mean man of simple degree and birth, not born to any possession; whom the king's grace favoureth, not because this person hath of himself deserved any such favor, but that the king casteth his favor unto him of his own mere motion and fancy: and because the king's grace will more declare his favor unto him, he giveth unto this said man a thousand pounds in lands, to him and his heirs, on this condition, that he shall take upon him to be the chief captain and defender of his town of Calais, and to be true and faithful to him in the custody of the same, against the Frenchmen especially above all other enemies.

This man taketh on him this charge, promising this fidelity thereunto. It chanceth in process of time, that by the singular acquaintance and frequent familiarity of this captain with the Frenchman, these Frenchmen give unto the said captain of Calais a great sum of money, so that he will be but content and agreeable that they may enter into the said town of Calais by force of arms, and so thereby possess the same unto the crown of France. Upon this agreement the Frenchman do invade the said town of Calais, only by the negligence of this captain.

Now the king hearing of this invasion, cometh with a great puissance to defend this his said town, and so by good policy of war overcometh the said Frenchmen, and entereth again into his town of Calais. Then he being desirous to know how these enemies of his came tither, maketh strict search and inquiry by whom this treason was conspired; but this search it was known, and found by his own captain to be the very author and the beginner of the betraying of it. The king, seeing the great infidelity of this person, dischargeth this man of his office, and taketh from him and his heirs this thousand pounds' possession. Think you not that the king doth use justice unto him, and all his posterity and heirs? Yes truly; the said captain cannot deny himself but that he had true justice, considering how unfaithfully he behaved himself to his prince, contrary to his own fidelity and promise. So likewise it was of our first father Adam: he had given him the spirit and science of knowledge, to work all goodness therewith; this said spirit was not given only to him, but unto all his heirs and posterity. He had also delivered him the town of Calais, that is to say, Paradise in earth, the most strong and fairest town in the world, to be in his custody: he, nevertheless, by the instigation of these Frenchmen, that is, the temptation of the fiend, did consent unto their desire, and so he broke his promise and fidelity, the commandment of the everlasting King, his master, in eating of the apple by him prohibited.

Now then, the King, seeing this great treason in his captain, dispossessed him of the thousand pounds of lands, that is to say, from everlasting life and glory, and all his heirs and posterity: for likewise as he had the spirit of science and knowledge for him and his heirs, so in like manner when he lost the same, his heirs also lost it by him, and in him. So now this example proveth that by our father Adam we had once in him the very inheritance of everlasting joy; and by him and in him again we lost the same.

And now the world standing in this damnable state, cometh in the occasion of the incarnation of Christ; the Father in heaven perceiving the frail nature of man, that he by himself and of himself could do nothing for himself, by his prudent wisdom sent down the second person in the Trinity, his Son Jesus Christ, to declare unto man his pleasure and commandment: and so at the Father's will Christ took on him human nature, being willing to deliver man out of this miserable way, and was content to suffer cruel passion in shedding his blood for all mankind; and so left behind, for our safeguard, laws and ordinances, to keep us always in the right path to everlasting life, as the gospels, the sacraments, the commandments etc, which if we keep and observe according to our profession, we shall answer better the question "Who art thou?' that we did before: for before thou didst enter into the sacrament of baptism, thou wert but a natural man, or a natural woman; as I might say, a man, a woman; but after thou takest on thee Christ's religion, thou hast a longer name, for then thou art a Christian man, a Christian woman. Now then, seeing thou art a Christian man, what shall be the answer to this question, "Who art thou?'

The answer to this question is, when I ask it of myself, I must say that I am a Christian man, a Christian woman, the child of everlasting joy, through the merits of the bitter passion of Christ. This is a joyful answer. Here we may see how much we are bound and indebted to God, that hath revived us from death to life, and saved us that were damned: which great benefit we cannot well consider, unless we remember what we were of ourselves before we meddled with him or his laws: and the more we know our feeble nature, and set less by it, the more we shall conceive and know in our hearts what God hath done for us; and the more we know what God hath done for us, the less we shall set by ourselves, and the more we shall love and please God; so that in no condition we shall either know ourselves of God, except we utterly confess ourselves to be mere vileness and corruption. Well, now it is come to this point, that we are Christian men, Christian women, I pray you, what does Christ require of a Christian man, or of a Christian woman? Christ requireth nothing else of a Christian man or woman but that they will observe his rule."

To relate the noise and alarm the preaching of these sermons occasioned at Cambridge would require too much time and space.

First came out the prior of Black Friars, named Buckenham, who attempted to prove that it was not expedient for the Scriptures to be in English, lest the ignorant and vulgar sort might be running into some inconvenience: as for example:

"The ploughman, when he heareth this in the gospel, "No man that layeth his hand on the plough and looketh back, is meet for the kingdom of God," might, peradventure, cease from his plough. Likewise a baker, when he hears that a little leaven corrupteth a whole lump of dough, may perchance leave our bread unleavened, and so our bodies shall be unseasoned. Also the simple man, when he heareth in the Gospel, "If thine eye offend thee, pluck it out, and cast if from thee," may make himself blind, and so fill the world with beggars." Mr Latimer, being thus persecuted by the friars, doctors, and masters of that university, about the year 1529, continued, notwithstanding the malice of these adversaries, preaching in Cambridge for about three years. Mr Latimer and Mr Bilney conferred together so frequently, that the field wherein they walked was called "The Heretics' Hill'.

Mr Latimer was, at length, cited before the cardinal for heresy. He was brought to London, where he was greatly molested, and detained a long time from his cure, being summoned thrice every week before the said bishops, to vindicate his preaching, and to subscribe to certain articles or propositions, devised by the instigation of his enemies. The following curious incident was related by himself, in a sermon preached at Stamford, October 9, 1550, and the following are his words:

"I was once in examination before five or six bishops, where I had much trouble: thrice every week I cam to examinations, and many snares and traps were laid to get something. Now God knoweth I was ignorant of the law, but that God gave me wisdom what I should speak; it was God indeed, or else I had never escaped them. At last I was brought forth to be examined into a chamber hung with arras, where I was wont to be examined; but now at this time the chamber was somewhat altered. For now the fire was taken away, and an arras hung over the chimney, and the table stood near the fireplace.

There was among the bishops who examined me one with whom I have been very familiar, and took him for my great friend, an aged man, and he sat next to the table's end.

Then among all other questions, he put forth a very subtle and crafty one, and such a one, indeed, as I could not think so great danger in. And when I should make answer, "I pray you, Mr Latimer,' said one, "speak out; I am very thick of hearing, and here may be many that sit far off." I marveled at this, that I was bid to speak out, and began to suspect, and give an ear to the chimney; and there I heard a pen writing in the chimney behind the cloth. They had appointed one there to write all mine answers, for they made sure that I should not start from them; and there was no starting from them. God was my good Lord, and gave me answer, else I could never have escaped."

Mr Latimer continued in his laborious episcopal functions until the passing of the Six Articles. Being then much distressed through the straitness of the times, he felt that the must either sacrifice a good conscience or else forsake his bishopric; accordingly he did the latter. When he visited London, he was imprisoned in the Tower, where he remained until King Edward came to the crown, when the golden mouth of this English Chrysostom was opened again. He often affirmed that the preaching of the Gospel would cost him his life, for which he was cheerfully prepared; for after the death of King Edward, and not long after Mary had been proclaimed queen, Mr Latimer was arrested and brought to London.

When Mr Latimer entered Smithfield, he merrily said that Smithfield had long groaned for him. He was then brought before the council, where he patiently bore all the mocks and taunts of the scornful Papists, and was again sent to the Tower.

Examination of Dr Ridley, in September, 1555

After the appearing of Dr Cranmer, Archbishop of Canterbury, before the Pope's delegate and the Queen's Commissioners in St Mary's Church at Oxford, about the 12th of September, on the 28th of the said month another commission was sent down to Oxford from Cardinal Pole, to John White, Bishop of Lincoln, Dr Brooks, Bishop of Gloucester, and Dr Holyman, Bishop of Bristol, saying that they should examine and judge Mr Latimer and Dr Ridley, for sundry erroneous opinions that Hugh Latimer and Nicholas Ridley did maintain in open disputations held in Oxford, in the months of May, June, and July, in the year 1554. Dr Ridley appeared first of all before the Lords

Commissioners, in the Divinity School at Oxford.

The Bishop of Lincoln, in a long oration, exhorted Dr Ridley to recant, and submit himself to the universal faith of Christ, endeavoring to prove the right of supremacy in the Church of Rome, charging him also with having formerly been favorable to their doctrine, and adducing many other arguments.

RIDLEY: I most heartily thank your lordship, as well for your gentleness as for your good and favorable zeal in this learned exhortation, in which I have marked especially three points, by which you sought to persuade me to leave my religion, which I perfectly know to be grounded, not upon man's imaginations and decrees, but upon the infallible truth of Christ's gospel.

The first point is this, That the see of Rome, taking its beginning from Peter, upon whom you say Christ hath built his Church, hath in all ages, lineally, from bishop to bishop, been brought to this time.

Secondly, That even the holy fathers from time to time have confessed the same.

Thirdly, That in that I was once of the same opinion, and together with you I did acknowledge the same

First, as touching the saying of Christ, from whence your lordship gathereth the foundation of the Church upon Peter, truly the place is not to be understood as you take it, as the circumstance of the place will declare. For after Christ had asked his disciples whom men judged him to be, and they answered that some had said he was a prophet, some Elias, some one thing, some another, then he said, "Whom say ye that I am?' Then Peter answered, "I say that thou art Christ, the Son of God." To whom Christ answered, "I say thou art Peter, and upon this stone I will build my Church;' that is to say, Upon this stone, not meaning Peter himself, as though he would have constituted a mortal man so frail and brittle a foundation of his stable and infallible Church; but upon this rock-stone, that is, this confession of thine, that I am the Son of God, I will build my Church. For this is the foundation and beginning of all Christianity, with word, heart, and mind, to confess that Christ is the Son of God.

Here you see upon what foundation Christ's Church is built, not upon the frailty of men, but upon the infallible Word of God.

Now as touching the lineal descent of the bishops in the see of Rome, true it is that the patriarchs of Rome in the apostles' time, and long after, were great maintainers of Christ's glory, in which, above all other countries and regions, there especially was preached the true gospel, the sacraments most duly administered; and as, before Christ's coming, it was a city so valiant in power and martial affairs, that all the world was in a manner subject to it, and after Christ's passion diverse of the apostles there suffered persecution for the Gospel's sake, so after that the emperors, their hearts being illuminated, received the Gospel, and became Christians, the Gospel there, as well for the fame of the place, flourished most, whereby the bishops of that place were had in more reverence and honor, most esteemed in all councils and assemblies, not because they acknowledged them to be their head, but because the place was most reverenced and spoken of, for the great power and strength of the same. As now here in England, the Bishop of Lincoln, in sessions and sittings. As long as Rome continued to set forth God's glory I cannot but commend it. But after the bishops of the see, seeking their own pride, and not God's honor, began to set themselves above kings and emperors, challenging to them the title of God's vicars, the dominion and supremacy over all the world, I cannot but with St Gregory, a Bishop of Rome also, confess that place is the very true Antichrist, where St John speaketh by name of the whore of Babylon, and say, with the said St Gregory, "He that maketh himself a bishop over all the world is worse than Antichrist."

Now where you say I was once of the same religion as you are of, the truth is, I cannot but confess, the same. Yet so was St Paul a persecutor of Christ.

LINCOLN: Mr Ridley, we came here,

not to dispute with you but only to take your answer to certain articles. These articles you shall now hear, and tomorrow, at eight o'clock, in St Mary's Church, we will require and take your answer, and then according to the same proceed.

The Articles which condemned Ridley and Latimer

In the name of God, Amen. We, John of Lincoln, James of Gloucester, and John of Bristol, bishops, etc.

1. We do object to thee, Nicholas Ridley, and to thee, Hugh Latimer, jointly and severally, first, that thou, Nicholas Ridley, in this high University of Oxford, in the year 1554, hast affirmed, and openly defended and maintained, and in many other times and places besides, that the true and natural body of Christ, after the consecration of the priest, is not really present in the sacrament of the altar.
2. That thou hast publicly affirmed and defended that in the sacrament of the altar remaineth still the substance of bread and wine.
3. That thou hast openly affirmed, and obstinately maintained, that in the mass is no propitiatory sacrifice for the living and the dead.

After examination upon the above articles, the Bishop of Lincoln concluded: "Mr Ridley, I am sorry to see such stubbornness in you, that by no means you will be persuaded to acknowledge your errors, and receive the truth: but seeing it is so, because you will not suffer us to persist in the first, we must of necessity proceed to the other part of our commission. Therefore, I pray you, hearken to what I shall say." And forthwith he read the sentence of condemnation, which was written in a long process; the substance of which was, that the said Nicholas Ridley did affirm, maintain, and stubbornly defend certain opinions, assertions, and heresies, contrary to the Word of God, and the received faith of the Church, and could by no means be turned from these heresies. They therefore condemned him as an obstinate heretic, and adjudged him presently, both by word and in deed, to be degraded from the degree of a bishop, from the priesthood, and all the ecclesiastical orders; declaring him, moreover, to be no member of the Church, and therefore they committed him to the secular powers, of them to receive the due punishment according to the temporal laws.

The last examination of Bishop Latimer before the Commissioners

LINCOLN: Recant, revoke your errors and turn to the catholic Church.

LATIMER: Your lordship often repeats the "catholic Church', as though I should deny the same. No, my lord, I confess there is a catholic Church, to the determination of which I will stand, but not the church which you call catholic, which ought rather to be termed diabolic.

Christ made one oblation and sacrifice for the sins of the whole world, and that a perfect sacrifice; neither needeth there to be, nor can there be, any other propitiatory sacrifice.

LINCOLN: Recant, revoke your errors and false assertions.

LATIMER: I will not deny my Master, Christ.

The bishop then committed Mr Ridley to the mayor, saying, "Now he is your prisoner, Mr Mayor."

Ridley and Latimer's martyrdom, 16th October, 1555

The place for their execution was chosen on the north side of Oxford, in the ditch over against Balliol College; and for fear of any tumult that might arise to hinder the burning of the servants of Christ, the Lord Williams and the householders of the city were commanded by the queen's letters to be prepared to assist if required.

Dr Ridley had on a black gown, furred and faced with foins, such as he used to wear when he was a bishop; a tippet of velvet, furred likewise, about his neck; a velvet night-cap upon his head, with a corner cap; and slippers on his feet. He walked to the stake between the mayor and the alderman.

After him came Mr Latimer, in a poor

Bristow frieze frock, much worn, with his buttoned cap and kerchief on his head, and a new long shroud hanging down to his feet. The sight of these two martyrs stirred men's hearts to rue upon them, beholding, on the one hand, the honor they sometimes had, and on the other, the calamity into which they had fallen. They came to the stake. Dr Ridley, earnestly holding up both his hands, looked towards heaven; then shortly after, seeing Mr Latimer, with a cheerful look he ran to him and embraced him, saying, "Be of good heart, brother, for God will either assuage the fury of the flame, or else strengthen us to abide it."

He then went to the stake, and, kneeling down, prayed with great fervor, while Mr Latimer following, kneeled also, and prayed with like earnestness. After this, they arose and conversed together, and, while thus employed, Dr Smith began his sermon from Paul's epistle to the Corinthians, chapter 13: "If I yield my body to the fire to be burnt, and have not charity, I shall gain nothing thereby." Strange paradox, that this panegyric of on love, in its mortality so heavenly, in its originality so sublime – and which, if it had occurred in Plato or Seneca, would have challenged the admiration of the world, with its Voltaires and Gibbons, as a masterpiece of classical beauty – should have been so prostituted on this occasion.

At the conclusion of the sermon, which only lasted a quarter of an hour, Ridley said to Latimer, "Will you answer, or shall I?'

Mr Latimer said, "Begin you first, I pray you."

"I will,' said Dr Ridley.

He then, with Mr Latimer, kneeled to my Lord Williams, the Vice-Chancellor of Oxford, and the other commissioners, who sat upon a form, and said, "I beseech you, my lord, even for Christ's sake, that I may speak but two or three words."

And while my lord bent his head to the mayor and vice-Chancellor, to know whether he might have leave to speak, the bailiffs and Dr Marshal, the vice-chancellor, ran hastily to him, and, with their hands stopping his mouth, said, "Mr Ridley, if you will revoke your erroneous opinions, you shall not only have liberty so to do, but also your life."

"Not otherwise?' said Dr Ridley.

"No,' answered Dr Marshal; "therefore, if you will not do so, there is no remedy: you must suffer for your deserts."

"Well,' said the martyr, "so long as the breath is in my body, I will never deny my Lord Christ and his known truth. God's will be done in me." With that he rose, and said, with a loud voice, "I commit our cause to Almighty God, who will indifferently judge all."

To which Mr Latimer added his old saying, "Well, there is nothing hid but it shall be opened." They were then commanded to prepare immediately for the stake.

They accordingly obeyed with all meekness. Dr Ridley gave his gown and tippet to his brother-in-law, Mr Shipside, who all the time of his imprisonment, although he was not suffered to come to him, lay there, at his own charges, to provide him necessaries, which he sent him by the sergeant in charge. Some other of his apparel he also gave away; the others the bailiffs took.

He likewise made presents of other small things to gentlemen standing by, divers of whom were weeping pitifully. To Sir Henry Lea he gave a new groat; to my Lord Williams' gentleman, some napkins; some nutmegs, some pieces of ginger, his watch dial, and all that he had about him, he gave to those who stood near. Some plucked the points off his hose, and happy was he who could get the least rag for a remembrance of this good man.

Mr Latimer quietly suffered his keeper to pull off his hose and his other apparel, which was very simple; and being stripped to his shroud, he seemed as comely a person as one could well see.

Then Dr Ridley, standing as yet in his truss, or trousers, said to his brother, "It were best for me to go in my trousers still."

"No,' said Mr Latimer, "it will put you to more pain; and it will do a poor man good."

Whereunto Dr Ridley said, "Be it, in the name of God,' and so unlaced himself.

Then, being in his shirt, he held up his hand, and said, "Oh, heavenly Father, I give unto thee most hearty thanks that thou hast called me to be a professor of thee, even unto death. I beseech thee, Lord God, have mercy on this realm of England, and deliver it from all her enemies."

Then the smith took an iron chain and placed it about both their waists; and as he was knocking in the staple, Dr Ridley took the chain in his hand, and, looking aside to the smith, said, "Good fellow, knock it in hard, for the flesh will have its course."

Then Dr Ridley's brother (Shipside) brought him a bag of gunpowder and tied it about his neck. Dr Ridley asked him what it was. He answered, "Gunpowder."

Then he said, "I will take it to be sent of God, therefore I will receive it. And have you any,' said he, "for my brother?' (meaning Mr Latimer).

"Yea, sir, that I have,' said he.

"Then give it him,' said he, "in time, lest you come too late."

So his brother went and carried it to Mr Latimer.

They then brought a lighted faggot, and laid it at Dr Ridley's feet; upon which Mr Latimer said, "BE OF GOOD COMFORT, MR RIDLEY, AND PLAY THE MAN! WE SHALL THIS DAY LIGHT SUCH A CANDLE, BY GOD'S GRACE, IN ENGLAND, AS I TRUST NEVER SHALL BE PUT OUT."

When Dr Ridley saw the fire flaming up towards him, he cried out, with an amazing loud voice, "Into thy hands, O Lord, I commend my spirit: Lord, receive my spirit!' and continued often to repeat, "Lord, Lord, receive my spirit!'

Mr Latimer cried as vehemently, "O Father of heaven, receive my soul!' after which he soon died, seemingly with little pain.

But Dr Ridley, owing to the bad arrangement of the fire (the faggots being green, and piled too high, so that the flames were kept down by the green wood, and burned fiercely beneath), was put to such exquisite pain, that he desired them, for God's sake, to let the fire come to him; which his brother-in-law heard, but did not very well understand; so to rid him out of his pain (for which cause he gave attendance), and not well knowing what he did, in his own sorrow, he heaped faggots upon him, so that he quite covered him, which made the fire so vehement beneath, that it burned all Ridley's lower pars before it touched his upper, and made him struggle under the faggots. Ridley, in his agony, often desired the spectators to let the fire come to him, saying, "I cannot burn." Yet in all his torment he did not forget always to call upon God, "Lord, have mercy upon me!' yet intermingling his cry with "Let the fire come unto me, I cannot burn;' in which pain he labored till one of the bystanders pulled the faggots from above with his bill, and where Ridley saw the fire flame up, he leaned himself to that side. As soon as the fire touched the gunpowder, he was seen to stir no more, but burned on the other side, falling down at Mr Latimer's feet, his body being divided.

The dreadful sight filled almost every eye with tears, for some pitied their persons, who thought their souls had no need thereof.

John Foxe, The Book of Martyrs, revised with notes and an appendix by W. Bramley-Moore, London, 1869, pp 413-71

Thomas Cranmer
Martyred 21st March 1556

Archbishop of Canterbury and compiler of the Book of Common Prayer. In Queen Mary's reign he was tried and condemned to be executed for being a heretic. Before his execution, he signed recantations of the beliefs which were really his.

"I recant of my recantations"

Thomas Cranmer was born at Aslacton, in Nottinghamshire, on the 2nd July, 1489. His family, who traced their descent from the time of the Norman Conquest, had resided in that town for many generations. On his father's death, in 1503, his mother placed him at Jesus College, in Cambridge, where he applied himself with great diligence to his studies, particularly to those of Greek, Hebrew, and theology. In 1510 he was chosen a fellow of his college, but in consequence of his marriage taking place shortly afterwards, he lost his fellowship. On this he became a reader in Buckingham College [now known as Magdalen College].

While Cranmer was at Cambridge, the vexed question of King Henry VIII's divorce with Lady Catherine of Aragon arose. The cardinals Campeggio and Wolsey had been appointed as Papal commissioners to decide the knotty point, but finding themselves beset with difficulties, from Henry's urgency on the one hand, and from the fact that Catherine was aunt to the Emperor Charles V, on the other, procrastinated matters, in the usual hope that time and the chapter of accidents would befriend them, and bring the desired solution. The king, however, became enraged at the delay. He accordingly dismissed Cardinal Campeggio, and visited Waltham Abbey, in Essex, where Cranmer was staying, because of the plague. At Waltham, Dr Gardiner, later Bishop of Winchester, and Fox, subsequently Bishop of Hereford, who were in attendance on the king, met Cranmer, and the conversation turned upon the pending controversy of the time.

In the course of conversation Cranmer suggested the expediency of "trying the question by the Word of God;' and that the matter might be as well settled in England by the universities as in Rome, or in any foreign court. When Fox, who was Royal almoner, repeated the substance of the conversation to the king, the king swore "that that man had the right sow by the ear." Cranmer was accordingly summoned to court, received into favor, and, on the disgrace of Wolsey, promoted to the see of Canterbury.

It is not for us to enter into a minute analysis of the difficulties of the archbishop's position, or of the motives which influenced his conduct at certain critical junctures. Candour obliges us to admit that there are many passages in his life which a faithful biographer would desire to treat with charity. At the same time, allowance must be made for the dilemmas of a giant mind struggling to free itself from the shackles of association, education, and prejudice, and for its gradual advance towards the goal of truth. Cranmer's opinions passed through various transition states; and his mind was extricated from erroneous doctrines on the sacramental presence only by slow degrees. His conduct, with reference to his oath of consecration, the divorce of Anne Boleyn, the condemnation of John Frith and Joan of Kent, is open to the apologies of the casuist or the censure of the rigid moralist; but, considering that he was educated in the Church of Rome, we may well wonder at his grasp of truth and his advance towards the light. To him, as much as to any other, is England indebted for the legacy of an open Bible, and his master mind advanced the reformation of the Church of England to almost her present position, and molded her with a wisdom full of homage to truth, yet with a deference to antiquity, when adjudged blameless.

We now pass over those events of his public career and come to the close of his eventful life. In September, 1555, Dr Brooks, Bishop of Gloucester, came with authority from Cardinal Pole to judge Cranmer. Brooke required Cranmer to appear before the Pope within eighty days. In February, 1556, Bonner and Thirleby were sent to degrade him for his contumacy in not going to Rome, although he was all the while kept in prison. Cranmer denied that the Pope had any authority over him, and appealed from his sentence to a free general council.

But now many devices were set on foot to make him recant: both English and Spanish divines had many conferences with him, and great hopes were given him, not only of life, but of preferment, if he would do it; and these, at last, had a fatal effect upon him, for he signed a recantation of all his former opinions, and concluded it with a protestation that he had done it freely, for the discharge of his conscience. The queen, however, was resolved to sacrifice him to her resentments; and, she said, it was good for his own soul that he repented; but since he had been the chief spreader of heresy over the nation, it was necessary to make him a public example. Accordingly the writ was sent down to burn him, and, after some stop had been made in the execution of it, new orders came for doing it suddenly. This was kept from Cranmer's knowledge, for they intended to carry him to the stake without giving him any notice, and so hoped to make him die in despair; yet he, suspecting somewhat, wrote a long paper, containing a confession of his faith, such as his conscience, and not his fears, had dictated.

He was carried to St Mary's on 21st March, where Dr Cole preached, and vindicated the queen's justice in condemning Cranmer; but magnified his conversion much, and ascribed it to God's Spirit. He gave him great hopes of heaven, and promised him all the relief that masses could bring.

All this time, with great grief, Cranmer stood hearing his sermon: one while lifting up his hands and eyes unto heaven, and then again, for shame, letting them down to earth, while the tears gushed from his eyes. Great commiseration and pity moved all men's hearts, that beheld so heavy a countenance, and such abundance of tears in an old man of so reverend dignity.

After Cole had ended his sermon, he called back the people to prayers that were ready to depart. "Brethren,' he said, "lest any man should doubt of this man's earnest conversion and repentance, you shall hear him speak before you, and, therefore, I pray you, Mr Cranmer, to perform that now which you promised not long ago – namely, that you would openly express the true and undoubted profession of your faith, that you may take away all suspicion from men, and that all men may understand that you are a catholic indeed."

"I will do it,' said the archbishop, "and that with a good will;' and rising up, and putting off his cap, he began to speak thus unto the people:

Cranmer's last words

"Good people – my dearly beloved brethren in Christ, I beseech you most heartily to pray for me to Almighty God, that he will forgive me all my sins and offences, which are without number, and great above measure. But yet one thing grieveth my conscience more than all the rest, whereof, God willing, I intend to speak more hereafter. But how great and how many soever my sins be, I beseech you to pray to God of his mercy to pardon and forgive them all." And here, kneeling down, he said the following prayer:

"O Father of heaven, O Son of God, Redeemer of the world, O Holy Ghost, three persons and one God, have mercy upon me, most wretched caitiff and miserable sinner. I have offended both against heaven and earth more than my tongue can express. Whither, then, may I go, or whither shall I flee? To heaven I may be ashamed to lift up mine eyes, and in earth I find no place of refuge or succor. To thee, therefore, O Lord, do I run; to thee do I humble myself, saying, O Lord my God, my sins be great, but yet have mercy upon me for thy great mercy. The great mystery that God became man was not wrought for little or few offences. Thou didst not give thy Son, O heavenly Father, unto death for small sins only, but for all the greatest sins of the world, so that the sinner return to thee with his whole heart, as I do at this present. Wherefore have mercy on me, O God, whose property is always to have mercy; have mercy upon me, O Lord, for they great mercy. I crave nothing for mine own merits, but for thy name's sake. And now, O Father of heaven, hallowed be thy name." And after repeating the Lord's Prayer, he continued:

"Every man, good people, desireth at the time of his death to give some good exhortation, that others may remember the same before their death, and be the better thereby; so I beseech God grant me that I may speak something at this my departing, whereby God may be glorified, and you edified.

"First, it is a heavy cause to see that so many folk so much dote upon the love of this false world, and be so careful for it, that of the love of God, or the world to come, they seem to care very little or nothing. Therefore, this shall be my first exhortation: That you set not your minds over much upon this deceitful world, but upon God, and upon the world to come, and to learn to know what this lesson meaneth which St John teacheth, that the love of this world is hatred against God."

"The second exhortation is, That next unto God you obey your King and Queen, willingly and gladly."

"The third exhortation is, That you love altogether like brethren and sisters."

"The fourth exhortation shall be to them that have great substance and riches of this world, That they will well consider and weigh Luke 18:24, 1 John 3:17 and James 5:1-3. Let them that be rich ponder well these three sentences; for if they ever had occasion to show their charity, they have it now at this present, the poor people being so many, and victuals so dear."

"And now, forasmuch as I am come to the last end of my life, whereupon hangeth all my life past and all my life to come, either to live with my master Christ for ever in joy, or else to be in pain for ever with wicked devils in hell, and I see before my eyes presently either heaven ready to receive me, or else hell ready to swallow me up; I shall therefore declare to you my very faith how I believe, without any color of dissimulation, for now is no time to dissemble, whatsoever I have said or written in times past.

"First, I believe in God the Father Almighty, maker of heaven and earth etc. And I believe every article of the catholic faith, every word and sentence taught by our Savior Jesus Christ, his apostles and prophets, in the New and Old Testament.

"And now I come to the great thing, that so much troubleth my conscience, more than any thing that ever I did or said in my whole life; and this is the setting abroad of a writing contrary to the Truth; which now here I renounce and refuse, as things written with my hand, contrary to the truth which I thought in my heart, and written for fear of death, and to save my life, if it might be; and that is, all such bills and papers which I have written or signed with my hand since my degradation, wherein I have written many things untrue. And forasmuch as my hand offended, writing contrary to my heart, my hand shall first be punished therefore; for, may I come to the fire it shall be first burned.

[In two sentences that followed he abjured the Pope and stood by his former book on the sacrament.]

There was an immediate outcry at this unexpected recantation of his recantations, and he was pulled down from the stage and hustled along the street to the ditch opposite Balliol College, where Latimer and Ridley had been burned.

[After kneeling in prayer he stripped himself of his shirt, bared his head and feet, shook hands with some of the bystanders and so went to the stake.]

And when the wood was kindled, and the fire began to burn near him, stretching out his arm, he put his right hand into the flame, which he held so steadfast and immovable that all men might see his hand burned before his body was touched. His body did so abide the burning of the flame, with such constancy and steadfastness, that standing always in one place, without moving his body, he seemed to move no more than the stake to which he was bound: he eyes were lifted up unto heaven, and often times he repented his unworthy right hand, so long as his voice would suffer him: and using often the words of Stephen, "Lord Jesus receive my spirit'; in the greatness of the flame he gave up the ghost.

John Foxe, The Book of Martyrs, revised with notes and an appendix by W. Bramley-Moore, London, 1869, pp 401-415

March 1556 – The execution of Archbishop Thomas Cranmer

This account of Cranmer's execution was recorded by an anonymous bystander.

Imprisoned by Mary I, Cranmer wrote a recantation of Protestantism, but he denied that recantation before he died. But that I know for our great friendships, and long continued love, you look even of duty that I should signify to you of the truth of such things as here chanceth among us; I would not at this time have written to you the unfortunate end, and doubtful tragedy, of Thomas Cranmer late bishop of Canterbury: because I little pleasure take in beholding of such heavy sights. And, when they are once overpassed, I like not to rehearse them again; being but a renewing of my woe, and doubling my grief. For although his former, and wretched end, deserves a greater misery, (if any greater might have chanced than chanced unto him), yet, setting aside his offenses to God and his country, and beholding the man without his faults, I think there was none that pitied not his case, and bewailed not his fortune, and feared not his own chance, to see so noble a prelate, so grave a counselor, of so long continued honor, after so many dignities, in his old years to be deprived of his estate, adjudged to die, and in so painful a death to end his life. I have no delight to increase it. Alas, it is too much of itself, that ever so heavy a case should betide to man, and man to deserve it. But to come to the matter: on Saturday last, being 21 of March, was his day appointed to die. And because the morning was much rainy, the sermon appointed by Mr Dr Cole to be made at the stake, was made in St Mary's church: whither Dr Cranmer was brought by the mayor and aldermen, and my lord Williams: with whom came divers gentlemen of the shire, sir T A Bridges, sir John Browne, and others. Where was prepared, over against the pulpit, a high place for him, that all the people might see him. And, when he had ascended it, he kneeled him down and prayed, weeping tenderly: which moved a great number to tears, that had conceived an assured hope of his conversion and repentance.... When praying was done, he stood up, and, having leave to speak, said, "Good people, I had intended indeed to desire you to pray for me; which because Mr Doctor hath desired, and you have done already, I thank you most heartily for it. And now will I pray for myself, as I could best devise for mine own comfort, and say the prayer, word for word, as I have here written it." And he read it standing: and after kneeled down, and said the Lord's Prayer; and all the people on their knees devoutly praying with him.... And then rising, he said, "Every man desireth, good people, at the time of their deaths, to give some good exhortation, that other may remember after their deaths, and be the better thereby. So I beseech God grant me grace, that I may speak something, at this my departing, whereby God may be glorified, and you edified.... And now I come to the great thing that troubleth my conscience more than nay other thing that ever I said or did in my life: and that is, the setting abroad of writings contrary to the truth. Which here now I renounce and refuse, as things written with my hand, contrary to the truth which I thought in my heart, and written for fear of death, and to save my life, if it might be: and that is, all such bills, which I have written or signed with mine own hand since my degradation: wherein I have written many things untrue. And forasmuch as my hand offended in writing contrary to my heart, therefore my hand shall first be punished: for if I may come to the fire, it shall be first burned. And as for the pope, I refuse him, as Christ's enemy and Antichrist, with all his false doctrine." And here, being admonished of his recantation and dissembling, he said, "Alas, my lord, I have been a man that all my life loved plainness, and never dissembled till now against the truth; which I am most sorry for it." He added hereunto, that, for the sacrament, he believed as he had taught in his book against the bishop of Winchester. And here he was suffered to speak no more....

Then was he carried away; and a great number, that did run to see him go so wickedly to his death, ran after him, exhorting him, while time was, to remember himself. And one Friar John, a godly and well learned man, all the way traveled with him to reduce him. But it would not be. What they said in particular I cannot tell, but the effect appeared in the end: for at the stake he professed, that he died in all such opinions as he had taught, and oft repented him of his recantation. Coming to the stake with a cheerful countenance and willing mind, he put off his garments with haste, and stood upright in his shirt: and bachelor of divinity, named Elye, of Brazen-nose college, labored to convert him to his former recantation, with the two Spanish friars. And when the friars saw his constancy, they said in Latin to one another "Let us go from him: we ought not to be nigh him: for the devil is with him." But the bachelor of divinity was more earnest with him: unto whom he answered, that, as concerning his recantation, he repented it right sore, because he knew it was against the truth; with other words more. Whereby the Lord Williams cried, "Make short, make short." Then the bishop took certain of his friends by the hand. But the bachelor of divinity refused to take him by the hand, and blamed all the others that so did, and said, he was sorry that ever he came in his company. And yet again he required him to agree to his former recantation. And the bishop answered, (showing his hand), "This was the hand that wrote it, and therefore shall it suffer first punishment."

Fire being now put to him, he stretched out his right hand, and thrust it into the flame, and held it there a good space, before the fire came to any other part of his body; where his hand was seen of every man sensibly burning, crying with a loud voice, "This hand hath offended." As soon as the fire got up, he was very soon dead, never stirring or crying all the while. His patience in the torment, his courage in dying, if it had been taken either for the glory of God, the wealth of his country, or the testimony of truth, as it was for a pernicious error, and subversion of true religion, I could worthily have commended the example, and matched it with the fame of any father of ancient time: but, seeing that not the death, but cause and quarrel thereof, commendeth the sufferer, I cannot but much dispraise his obstinate stubbornness and sturdiness in dying, and specially in so evil a cause. Surely his death much grieved every man; but not after one sort. Some pitied to see his body so tormented with the fire raging upon the silly carcass, that counted not of the folly. Other that passed not much of the body, lamented to see him spill his soul, wretchedly, without redemption, to be plagued for ever. His friends sorrowed for love; his enemies for pity; strangers for a common kind of humanity, whereby we are bound one to another. Thus I have enforced myself, for your sake, to discourse this heavy narration, contrary to my mind: and, being more than half weary, I make a short end, wishing you a quieter life, with less honor; and easier death, with more praise.

Author unknown

A complete list of the English martyrs who suffered under Queen Mary, 1555-58

Compiled by John Foxe

1555

John Rogers	Anglican clergyman	Smithfield	Feb 4	Burnt
Laurence Saunders	Anglican clergyman	Coventry	Feb 8	Burnt
Dr John Hooper	Bishop	Gloucester	Feb 9	Burnt
Dr Rowland Taylor	Anglican clergyman	Aldham	Feb 9	Burnt
Thomas Tomkins	Weaver	Smithfield	Mar 16	Burnt
Thomas Higbed	Gentleman	Hordon-on-Hill	Mar 26	Burnt
Thomas Causton	Gentleman	Raleigh, Essex	Mar 26	Burnt
William Hunter	Apprentice	Brentwood	Mar 27	Burnt
William Pygot	Butcher	Braintree	Mar 28	Burnt
Stephen Knight	Barber	Maldon	Mar 28	Burnt
J. Laurence	Anglican clergyman	Colchester	Mar 29	Burnt
Dr R. Farrar	Bishop	Carmarthan	Mar 30	Burnt
Rawlins White	Fisherman	Cardiff	Mar 30	Burnt
George Marsh	Anglican clergyman	Chester	Apr 24	Burnt
William Flower	Monk	Westminster	Apr 24	Burnt
John Simson	Husbandman	Rochford	May 25	Burnt
John Ardeley	Husbandman	Raleigh	May 29	Burnt

John Cardmaker	Prebendary	Smithfield	May 30	Burnt
John Warne	Upholsterer	Smithfield	May 30	Burnt
Thomas Haukes	Gentleman	Coxhall	June 10	Burnt
Thomas Watts	Draper	Chelmsford	June 10	Burnt
N. Chamberlain	Weaver	Colchester	June 14	Burnt
Thomas Osmond	Fuller	Manningtree	June 15	Burnt
William Bamford	Weaver	Harwich	June 15	Burnt
John Bradford	Anglican clergyman	Smithfield	July 9	Burnt
John Leaf	Apprentice	Smithfield	July 9	Burnt
William Minge		Maidstone	July 9	Burnt
John Bland	Anglican clergyman	Canterbury	July 12	Burnt
John Frankesh	Anglican clergyman	Canterbury	July 12	Burnt
Nicholas Shetterden	Canterbury	July 12	Burnt	
Humphry Middleton	Canterbury	July 12	Burnt	
N. Hall	Bricklayer	Rochester	July 19	Burnt
Christopher Waid	Weaver	Dartford	July 19	Burnt
Cirick Carver	Brewer	Lewes	July 22	Burnt
John Launder	Husbandman	Steyning	July 23	Burnt
Elizabeth Warne	Widow	Startford	July 23	Burnt
Thomas Iveson	Carpenter	Chichester	July 23	Burnt
Margery Polley		Rochester	July 23	Burnt
John Aleworth		Reading	July 23	Died in prison
James Abbes		Bury	Aug 2	Burnt
Thomas Denley	Gentleman	Uxbridge	Aug 8	Burnt
Robert Smith	Gentleman	Uxbridge	Aug 8	Burnt
George Tankerfield	Cook	St Albans	Aug 26	Burnt
Patrick Packingham		Uxbridge	Aug 28	Burnt
Stephen Harwood		Stratford	Aug 28	Burnt
Thomas Fust		Ware	Aug 28	Burnt
William Hale		Barnet	Aug 28	Burnt
George King		London	Aug 28	Burnt
Thomas Leyes		London	Aug 28	Died in prison
John Wade		London	Aug 28	Died in prison
William Andrew	Carpenter	Newgate	Aug 28	Died in prison
Robert Samuel	Anglican clergyman	Ipswich	Aug 28	Burnt
John Newman	Pewterer	Saffron Walden	Aug 31	Burnt
Richard Hook		Chichester	Aug 31	Burnt
William Coker		Canterbury	Aug 31	Burnt
Henry Laurence		Canterbury	Aug 31	Burnt
Richard Wright		Canterbury	Aug 31	Burnt
William Hopper		Canterbury	Aug 31	Burnt
Richard Collier		Canterbury	Aug 31	Burnt
William Store		Canterbury	Aug 31	Burnt
William Allen	Laborer	Walsingham	Sept 6	Burnt
Roger Cox		Yoxford	Sept 6	Burnt
Thoms Cob	Butcher	Thetford	Sept 6	Burnt
George Catmer		Canterbury	Sept 6	Burnt
Robert Streater		Canterbury	Sept 6	Burnt
Anthony Burward		Canterbury	Sept 6	Burnt
George Bradbridge		Canterbury	Sept 6	Burnt
James Tutty		Canterbury	Sept 6	Burnt

Thomas Hayward		Lichfield	Sept 6	Burnt
John Gareway		Lichfield	Sept 6	Burnt
Robert Glover	Gentleman	Coventry	Sept 20	Burnt
Cornelius Bungey		Coventry	Sept 20	Burnt
William Wolsey	Constable	Ely	Oct 16	Burnt
Robert Pygot	Painter	Ely	Oct 16	Burnt
Dr Nicholas Ridley	Bishop	Oxford	Oct 16	Burnt
Dr Hugh Latimer	Bishop	Oxford	Oct 16	Burnt
George Roper	Gentleman	Canterbury	Oct 16	Burnt
John Webb	Gentleman	Canterbury	Oct 16	Burnt
Gregory Parke	Gentleman	Canterbury	Oct 16	Burnt
William Wiseman	Cloth-worker	Lollard's Tower	Dec 13	Died in prison
James Gore		Colchester	Dec 13	Died in prison
John Philpot	Archdeacon	Smithfield	Dec 18	Burnt

1556

Thomas Whittle	Anglican clergyman	Smithfield	Jan 27	Burnt in one fire
Bartlet Green	Gentleman	Smithfield	Jan 27	Burnt in one fire
John Tudson	Artificer	Smithfield	Jan 27	Burnt in one fire
John Went	Artificer	Smithfield	Jan 27	Burnt in one fire
Thomas Browne		Smithfield	Jan 27	Burnt in one fire
Isabel Foster		Smithfield	Jan 27	Burnt in one fire
Joan Warne		Smithfield	Jan 27	Burnt in one fire
John Lomas		Canterbury	Jan 31	Burnt
Anne Wright		Canterbury	Jan 31	Burnt
Joan Catmer		Canterbury	Jan 31	Burnt
Agnes Snoth		Canterbury	Jan 31	Burnt
Joan Sole		Canterbury	Jan 31	Burnt
Thomas Cranmer	Archbishop	Oxford	Mar 21	Burnt
Agnes Potten		Oxford	Mar 21	Burnt
Joan Trunchfield		Ipswich	Mar 23	Burnt
Joan Maundrall	Farmer	Salisbury	Mar 23	Burnt
William Coberley	Tailor	Salisbury	Mar 23	Burnt
John Spicer	Mason	Salisbury	Mar 23	Burnt
John Hullier	Minister	Cambridge	Apr 2	Burnt
Robert Drakes	Minister	Smithfield	Apr 23	Burnt
William Tyms	Curate	Smithfield	Apr 23	Burnt
Richard Spurge	Sheerman	Smithfield	Apr 23	Burnt
Thomas Spurge	Fuller	Smithfield	Apr 23	Burnt
Joan Beach		Rochester	Apr 23	Burnt
John Harpole		Rochester	Apr 23	Burnt
Christopher Lyster	Husbandman	Colchester	Apr 28	Burnt
John Mace	Apothecary	Colchester	Apr 28	Burnt
John Spencer	Weaver	Colchester	Apr 28	Burnt
Simon Joyne	Sawyer	Colchester	Apr 28	Burnt
Richard Nichols	Weaver	Colchester	Apr 28	Burnt
John Hammond	Tanner	Colchester	Apr 28	Burnt
Thomas Dowry	A blind boy	Gloucester	May 5	Burnt
Thomas Croker	Bricklayer	Gloucester	May 5	Burnt
Hugh Laverick	A cripple	Stratford-le-Bow	May 15	Burnt
John Aprice	Blind	Stratford-le-Bow	May 15	Burnt

Katherine Hut	Widow	Smithfield	May 16	Burnt
Joan Horns		Smithfield	May 16	Burnt
Elizabeth Thackvel		Smithfield	May 16	Burnt
Margaret Ellis		Newgate	May 16	Died in prison
Thomas Spicer	Laborer	Beccles	May 21	Burnt
John Denny	Laborer	Beccles	May 21	Burnt
Edmund Poole	Laborer	Beccles	May 21	Burnt
Thomas Harland	Carpenter	Lewes	June 6	Burnt
John Oswald	Husbandman	Lewes	June 6	Burnt
Thomas Avington	Turner	Lewes	June 6	Burnt
Thomas Read	Laborer	Lewes	June 6	Burnt
Thomas Wood	Anglican clergyman	Lewis	June 20	Burnt
Thomas Mills		Lewis	June 20	Burnt
William Adherhall	Anglican clergyman	King's Bench	June 24	Died in prison
John Clement	Wheelwright	King's Bench	June 24	Died in prison
Thomas Moor	Merchant's servant	Leicester	June 26	Burnt
Henry Adlington	Sawyer	Stratford	June 27	Burnt
Laurence Parman	Smith	Stratford	June 27	Burnt
Henry Wye	Brewer	Stratford	June 27	Burnt
William Hallywel	Smith	Stratford	June 27	Burnt
George Searles	Tailor	Stratford	June 27	Burnt
Edmund Hurst	Laborer	Stratford	June 27	Burnt
Lyon Cawch	Broker	Stratford	June 27	Burnt
Ralph Jackson	Servant	Stratford	June 27	Burnt
John Derifall	Laborer	Stratford	June 27	Burnt
John Routh	Laborer	Stratford	June 27	Burnt
Elizabeth Pepper		Stratford	June 27	Burnt
Agnes George		Stratford	June 27	Burnt
Thomas Parret		Southwark	June 27	Burnt
Martin Hunt		Southwark	June 27	Burnt
John Norice		Southwark	June 27	Burnt
Robert Bernard	Laborer	Bury, Suffolk	June 27	Burnt
Adam Foster	Husbandman	Bury, Suffolk	June 27	Burnt
Robert Lawson	Weaver	Bury, Suffolk	June 27	Burnt
John Fortune	Blacksmith	Norwich	June 27	Died in prison
John Careless	Weaver	King's Bench	July 1	Died in prison
Julius Palmer	Scholar	Newbury	July 16	Burnt
John Gwin		Newbury	July 16	Burnt
Thomas Askim		Newbury	July 16	Burnt
Catherine Cawches		Guernsey	July 18	Burnt
Guillemme Gilbert		Guernsey	July 18	Burnt
Perotine Massey		Guernsey	July 18	Burnt
Thomas Dungate		Grinstead	July 18	Burnt
John Foreman		Grinstead	July 18	Burnt
Mother Tree	Widow	Grinstead	July 18	Burnt
Joan Waste	Blind girl	Derby	Aug 1	Burnt
Edward Sharp		Bristol	Sept 8	Burnt
John Hart	Shoemaker	Bristol	Sept 8	Burnt
Thomas Ravensdale	Currier	Mayfield	Sept 24	Burnt
	A carpenter	Bristol	Sept 25	Burnt
John Horn		Wooton-under-Edge	Sept 27	Burnt

A woman		Wooton-under-Edge	Sept 27	Burnt
A shoemaker		Northampton	Oct	Burnt
– Hooke		Chester	Oct	Burnt
Three people		Chichester	Oct	Died in prison
John Clark		Canterbury Castle	Nov	Starved to death
Duston Chittenden		Canterbury Castle	Nov	Starved to death
William Foster		Canterbury Castle	Nov	Starved to death
Alice Potkins		Canterbury Castle	Nov	Starved to death
John Archer	Weaver	Canterbury Castle	Nov	Starved to death
1557				
Stephen Kempe		Canterbury	Jan 15	Burnt
William Waterer		Canterbury	Jan 15	Burnt
William Prowting		Canterbury	Jan 15	Burnt
W. Lowick		Canterbury	Jan 15	Burnt
Thomas Hudson		Canterbury	Jan 15	Burnt
William Hay		Canterbury	Jan 15	Burnt
N. Final		Ashford	Jan 16	Burnt
M. Bradbridge		Ashford	Jan 16	Burnt
T. Stephens		Wye	Jan 16	Burnt
J. Philpot		Wye	Jan 16	Burnt
Thomas Loseby		Smithfield	Apr 12	Burnt
Henry Ramsey		Smithfield	Apr 12	Burnt
Thomas Thirtell		Smithfield	Apr 12	Burnt
Margaret Hale		Smithfield	Apr 12	Burnt
Agnes Stanley		Smithfield	Apr 12	Burnt
William Morant		Southwark	May	Burnt
Stephen Gratwick		Southwark	May	Burnt
– King		Southwark	May	Burnt
John Bradbridge		Maidstone	June 18	Burnt
Walter Appleby		Maidstone	June 18	Burnt
Petronil Appleby	His wife	Maidstone	June 18	Burnt
Edmund Allin	Miller	Maidstone	June 18	Burnt
Catherine Allin	His wife	Maidstone	June 18	Burnt
John Manning's wife		Maidstone	June 18	Burnt
Elizabeth	A blind girl	Maidstone	June 18	Burnt
John Fishcock		Canterbury	June 30	Burnt
Nicholas White		Canterbury	June 30	Burnt
Nicholas Pardue		Canterbury	June 30	Burnt
Barbara Final	Widow	Canterbury	June 30	Burnt
Bradbridge's widow		Canterbury	June 30	Burnt
Wilson's widow		Canterbury	June 30	Burnt
Benden's wife		Canterbury	June 30	Burnt
Matthew Plaise		Date unknown		
Richard Woodman	Ironmonger	Lewes	June 22	Burnt
George Stevens		Lewes	June 22	Burnt
William Mainard		Lewes	June 22	Burnt
Alex. Hosman	Servant	Lewes	June 22	Burnt
Thomasine Wood		Lewes	June 22	Burnt
James Morris		Lewes	June 22	Burnt
Denis Burgis		Lewes	June 22	Burnt

Ashdon's wife		Lewes	June 22	Burnt
Grove's wife		Lewes	June 22	Burnt
– Ambrose		Miadstone	June	Died in prison
R. Lush		Bath	June	Died in prison
Simon Miller		Norwich	July 13	Burnt
Elizabeth Cooper		Norwich	July 13	Burnt
William Munt		Colchester	Aug 2	Burnt
Rose Allin		Colchester	Aug 2	Burnt
John Thurston		Colchester	Aug 2	Died in prison
John Johnson		Colchester	Aug 2	Burnt
William Bongeor		Colchester	Aug 2	Burnt
Thomas Benold		Colchester	Aug 2	Burnt
William Purcas		Colchester	Aug 2	Burnt
Agnes Silverside T		Colchester	Aug 2	Burnt
Helen Ewring		Colchester	Aug 2	Burnt
Elizabeth Folkes		Colchester	Aug 2	Burnt
John Kurde	Shoemaker	Northampton	Aug	Burnt
George Eagles	Tailor	Chelmsford	Aug	Burnt
Richard Crashfield		Norwich	Aug	Burnt
– Fryer		Norwich	Aug	Burnt
George Eagles' sister		Rochester	Aug	Burnt
Mrs Joyce Lewes		Lichfield	Aug	Burnt
Ralph Allerton		Islington	Sept 17	Burnt
James Austoo		Islington	Sept 17	Burnt
Richard Roth		Islington	Sept 17	Burnt
Agnes Bongeor		Colchester	Sept 17	Burnt
Margaret Thurston		Colchester	Sept 17	Burnt
John Noyes	Shoemaker	Laxfield	Sept 22	Burnt
Cicely Ormes		Norwich	Sept 23	Burnt
John Foreman		Chichester	Oct	Burnt
John Warner		Chichester	Oct	Burnt
Christian Graver		Chichester	Oct	Burnt
Thomas Athoth		Chichester	Oct	Burnt
Thomas Avington		Chichester	Oct	Burnt
Dennis Burgis		Chichester	Oct	Burnt
Thomsa Ravensdale		Chichester	Oct	Burnt
John Milles		Chichester	Oct	Burnt
Nicholas Holden		Chichester	Oct	Burnt
John Hart		Chichester	Oct	Burnt
Anne Fry		Chichester	Oct	Burnt
John Oseward		Chichester	Oct	Burnt
Thomas Harland		Chichester	Oct	Burnt
James Moris		Chichester	Oct	Burnt
Thomas Dougate		Chichester	Oct	Burnt
John Ashedon		Chichester	Oct	Burnt
Thomas Spurdance		Bury	Nov	Burnt
John Hallingdale		Smithfield	Nov 18	Burnt
William Sparrow		Smithfield	Nov 18	Burnt
Richard Gibson		Smithfield	Nov 18	Burnt
John Rough	Anglican clergyman	Smithfield	Dec 22	Burnt
Margaret Mearing		Smithfield	Dec 22	Burnt

1558

Cuthbert Symson	Deacon	Smithfield	Mar 28	Burnt
Hugh Foxe		Smithfield	Mar 28	Burnt
John Devenish		Smithfield	Mar 28	Burnt
William Nichol		Wales	Apr 9	Burnt
William Seaman		Norwich	May 19	Burnt
Thomas Carman		Norwich	May 19	Burnt
Thomas Hudson		Norwich	May 19	Burnt
William Harris		Colchester	May	Burnt
Richard Day		Colchester	May	Burnt
Christian George		Colchester	May	Burnt
Henry Pond		Smithfield	May	Burnt
Rainol Eastland		Smithfield	May	Burnt
Robert Southam		Smithfield	May	Burnt
Matthew Ricarby		Smithfield	May	Burnt
John Floyd		Smithfield	May	Burnt
John Holliday		Smithfield	May	Burnt
Roger Holland		Smithfield	May	Burnt
Robert Mills		Smithfield	May	Burnt
Stephen Cotton		Brentford	July 14	Burnt
Robert Dynes		Brentford	July 14	Burnt
Stephen Wright		Brentford	July 14	Burnt
John Slade		Brentford	July 14	Burnt
William Pikes		Brentford	July 14	Burnt
Richard Yoeman	Curate	Norwich	July 14	Burnt
John DaleWeaver		Bury	July	Died in prison
John Alcock	Sheerman	Newgate	July	Died in prison
Thomas Benbridge	Gentleman	Smithfield	July	Burnt
John CookeSawyer				
Bury St Edmunds	Aug	Burnt		
Robert Miles	Sheerman	Bury St Edmunds	Aug	Burnt
Alexander Lane	Wheelwright	Bury St Edmunds	Aug	Burnt
James Ashely	Batchelor	Bury St Edmunds	Aug	Burnt
Alexander Gouch		Ipswich	Nov 4	Burnt
Alice Driver		Ipswich	Nov 4	Burnt
Philip Humfrey		Bury	Nov 4	Burnt
John David		Bury	Nov 4	Burnt
Henry David		Bury	Nov	Burnt
Mrs Prest		Exeter	Nov	Burnt
John Cornford		Canterbury	Nov 10	Burnt
Christopher Brown		Canterbury	Nov 10	Burnt
John Herst		Canterbury	Nov 10	Burnt
Alice Snoth		Canterbury	Nov 10	Burnt
Catherine Tynley		Canterbury	Nov 10	Burnt

Persecutions in Venice

While the state of Venice was free from inquisitors, a great number of Protestants fixed their residence there, and many converts were made by the purity of the doctrines they professed, and the inoffensiveness of the conversation they used.

The pope being informed of the great increase of Protestantism, in the year 1542 sent inquisitors to Venice to make an inquiry into the matter, and apprehend such as they might deem obnoxious persons. Hence a severe persecution began, and many worthy persons were martyred for serving God with purity, and scorning the trappings of idolatry.

Death by drowning

Various were the modes by which the Protestants were deprived of life; but one particular method, which was first invented upon this occasion, we shall describe; as soon as sentence was passed, the prisoner had an iron chain which ran through a great stone fastened to his body. He was then laid flat upon a plank, with his face upwards, and rowed between two boats to a certain distance at sea, when the two boats separated, and he was sunk to the bottom by the weight of the stone.

Rotted in jail

If any denied the jurisdiction of the inquisitors at Venice, they were sent to Rome, where, being committed purposely to damp prisons, and never called to a hearing, their flesh mortified, and they died miserably in jail.

Anthony Ricetti

A citizen of Venice, Anthony Ricetti, being apprehended as a Protestant, was sentenced to be drowned in the manner we have already described. A few days previous to the time appointed for his execution, his son went to see him, and begged him to recant, that his life might be saved, and himself not left fatherless. To which the father replied, "A good Christian is bound to relinquish not only goods and children, but life itself, for the glory of his Redeemer: therefore I am resolved to sacrifice every thing in this transitory world, for the sake of salvation in a world that will last to eternity." The lords of Venice likewise sent him word, that if he would embrace the Roman Catholic religion, they would not only give him his life, but redeem a considerable estate which he had mortgaged, and freely present him with it. This, however, he absolutely refused to comply with, sending word to the nobles that he valued his soul beyond all other considerations; and being told that a fellow-prisoner, named Francis Sega, had recanted, he answered, "If he has forsaken God, I pity him; but I shall continue steadfast in my duty." Finding all endeavors to persuade him to renounce his faith ineffectual, he was executed according to his sentence, dying cheerfully, and recommending his soul fervently to the Almighty.

What Ricetti had been told concerning the apostasy of Francis Sega, was absolutely false, for he had never offered to recant, but steadfastly persisted in his faith, and was executed, a few days after Ricetti, in the very same manner.

Francis Spinola

Francis Spinola, a Protestant gentleman of very great learning, being apprehended by order of the inquisitors, was carried before their tribunal. A treatise on the Lord's Supper was then put into his hands and he was asked if he knew the author of it. To which he replied, "I confess myself to be the author of it, and at the same time solemnly affirm, that there is not a line in it but what is authorized by, and consonant to, the holy Scriptures." On this confession he was committed close prisoner to a dungeon for several days.

Being brought to a second examination, he charged the pope's legate, and the inquisitors, with being merciless barbarians, and then represented the superstitions and idolatries practiced by the Church of Rome in so glaring a light, that not being able to refute his arguments, they sent him back to his dungeon, to make him repent of what he had said.

On his third examination, they asked him if he would recant his error. To which he answered that the doctrines he maintained were not erroneous, being purely the same as those which Christ and his apostles had taught, and which were handed down to us in the sacred writings. The inquisitors then sentenced him to be drowned, which was executed in the manner already described. He went to meet death with the utmost serenity, seemed to wish for dissolution, and declaring that the prolongation of his life did but tend to retard that real happiness which could only be expected in the world to come.

An Account of Several Remarkable Individuals, Who Were Martyred in Different Parts of Italy, on Account of Their Religion

John Mollius

John Mollius was born at Rome, of reputable parents. At twelve years of age they placed him in the monastery of Gray Friars, where he made such a rapid progress in arts, sciences, and languages that at eighteen years of age he was permitted to take priest's orders.

He was then sent to Ferrara, where, after pursuing his studies six years longer, he was made theological reader in the university of that city. He now, unhappily, exerted his great talents to disguise the Gospel truths, and to varnish over the error of the Church of Rome. After some years residence in Ferrara, he removed to the university of Behonia, where he became a professor. Having read some treatises written by ministers of the reformed religion, he grew fully sensible of the errors of popery, and soon became a zealous Protestant in his heart.

He now determined to expound, accordingly to the purity of the Gospel, St. Paul's Epistle to the Romans, in a regular course of sermons. The concourse of people that continually attended his preaching was surprising, but when the priests found the tenor of his doctrines, they despatched an account of the affair to Rome; when the pope sent a monk, named Cornelius, to Bononia, to expound the same epistle, according to the tenets of the Church of Rome. The people, however, found such a disparity between the two preachers that the audience of Mollius increased, and Cornelius was forced to preach to empty benches.

Cornelius wrote an account of his bad success to the pope, who immediately sent an order to apprehend Mollius, who was seized upon accordingly, and kept in close confinement. The bishop of Bononia sent him word that he must recant, or be burnt; but he appealed to Rome, and was removed thither.

At Rome he begged to have a public trial, but that the pope absolutely denied him, and commanded him to give an account of his opinions, in writing, which he did under the following heads: Original sin. Free-will. The infallibility of the church of Rome. The infallibility of the pope. Justification by faith. Purgatory. Transubstantiation. Mass. Auricular confession. Prayers for the dead. The host. Prayers for saints. Going on pilgrimages. Extreme unction. Performing services in an unknown tongue, etc., etc.

All these he confirmed from Scripture authority. The pope, upon this occasion, for political reasons, spared him for the present, but soon after had him apprehended, and put to death, he being first hanged, and his body burnt to ashes, A.D. 1553.

Francis Gamba

The year after, Francis Gamba, a Lombard, of the Protestant persuasion, was apprehended, and condemned to death by the senate of Milan. At the place of execution, a monk presented a cross to him, to whom he said, "My mind is so full of the real merits and goodness of Christ that I want not a piece of senseless stick to put me in mind of Him." For this expression his tongue was bored through, and he was afterward burnt. Algerius, a man of great learning, A.D. 1555, Algerius, a student in the university of Padua, and a man of great learning, having embraced the reformed religion, did all he could to convert others. For these proceedings he was accused of heresy to the pope, and being apprehended, was committed to the prison at Venice.

The pope, being informed of Algerius's great learning, and surprising natural abilities, thought it would be of infinite service to the Church of Rome if he could induce him to forsake the Protestant cause. He, therefore, sent for him to Rome, and tried, by the most profane promises, to win him to his purpose. But finding his endeavors ineffectual, he ordered him to be burnt, which sentence was executed accordingly."I tremble at the manner of putting to death"A.D. 1560, Pope Pius the Fourth, ordered all the Protestants to be severely persecuted throughout the Italian states, when great numbers of every age, sex, and condition, suffered martyrdom. Concerning the cruelties practiced upon this occasion, a learned and humane Roman Catholic thus spoke of them, in a letter to a noble lord: "I cannot, my lord, forbear disclosing my sentiments, with respect to the persecution now carrying on: I think it cruel and unnecessary; I tremble at the manner of putting to death, as it resembles more the slaughter of calves and sheep, than the execution of human beings. I will relate to your lordship a dreadful scene, of which I was myself an eye witness: seventy Protestants were cooped up in one filthy dungeon together; the executioner went in among them, picked out one from among the rest, blindfolded him, led him out to an open place before the prison, and cut his throat with the greatest composure. He then calmly walked into the prison again, bloody as he was, and with the knife in his hand selected another, and despatched him in the same manner; and this, my lord, he repeated until the whole number were put to death. I leave it to your lordship's feelings to judge of my sensations upon this occasion; my tears now wash the paper upon which I give you the recital. Another thing I must mention—the patience with which they met death: they seemed all resignation and piety, fervently praying to God, and cheerfully encountering their fate. I cannot reflect without shuddering, how the executioner held the bloody knife between his teeth; what a dreadful figure he appeared, all covered with blood, and with what unconcern he executed his barbarous office."A young Englishman A young Englishman who happened to be at Rome, was one day passing by a church, when the procession of the host was just coming out. A bishop carried the host, which the young man perceiving, he snatched it from him, threw it upon the ground, and trampled it under his feet, crying out, "Ye wretched idolaters, who neglect the true God, to adore a morsel of bread." This action so provoked the people that they would have torn him to pieces on the spot; but the priests persuaded them to let him abide by the sentence of the pope.

When the affair was represented to the pope, he was so greatly exasperated that he ordered the prisoner to be burnt immediately; but a cardinal dissuaded him from this hasty sentence, saying that it was better to punish him by slow degrees, and to torture him, that they might find out if he had been instigated by any particular person to commit so atrocious an act.

This being approved, he was tortured with the most exemplary severity, notwithstanding which they could only get these words from him, "It was the will of God that I should do as I did." The pope then passed this sentence upon him.

1. That he should be led by the executioner, naked to the middle, through the streets of Rome.

2. That he should wear the image of the devil upon his head.

3. That his breeches should be painted with the representation of flames.

4. That he should have his right hand cut off.

5. That after having been carried about thus in procession, he should be burnt.

When he heard this sentence pronounced, he implored God to give him strength and fortitude to go through it. As he passed through the streets he was greatly derided by the people, to whom he said some severe things respecting the Romish superstition. But a cardinal, who attended the procession, overhearing him, ordered him to be gagged.

When he came to the church door, where he trampled on the host, the hangman cut off his right hand, and fixed it on a pole. Then two tormentors, with flaming torches, scorched and burnt his flesh all the rest of the way. At the place of execution he kissed the chains that were to bind him to the stake. A monk presenting the figure of a saint to him, he struck it aside, and then being chained to the stake, fire was put to the fagots, and he was soon burnt to ashes.

A venerable old man

A little after the last-mentioned execution, a venerable old man, who had long been a prisoner in the Inquisition, was condemned to be burnt, and brought out for execution. When he was fastened to the stake, a priest held a crucifix to him, on which he said, "If you do not take that idol from my sight, you will constrain me to spit upon it." The priest rebuked him for this with great severity; but he bade him remember the First and Second Commandments, and refrain from idolatry, as God himself had commanded. He was then gagged, that he should not speak any more, and fire being put to the fagots, he suffered martyrdom in the flames.

Foxe's Book of Martyrs, Chapter 6, Edited by William Byron Forbush

Persecutions in Germany

The general persecutions in Germany were principally occasioned by the doctrines and ministry of Martin Luther. Indeed, the pope was so terrified at the success of that courageous reformer, that he determined to engage the emperor, Charles V, at any rate, in the scheme to attempt their extirpation.

To this end:

1. He gave the emperor two hundred thousand crowns in ready money.

2. He promised to maintain twelve thousand foot, and five thousand horse, for the space of six months, or during a campaign.

3. He allowed the emperor to receive one half the revenues of the clergy of the empire during the war.

4. He permitted the emperor to pledge the abbey lands for five hundred thousand crowns, to assist in carrying on hostilities against the Protestants.

Thus prompted and supported, the emperor undertook the extirpation of the Protestants, against whom, indeed, he was particularly enraged himself; and, for this purpose, a formidable army was raised in Germany, Spain, and Italy.

The Protestant princes, in the meantime, formed a powerful confederacy, in order to repel the impending blow. A great army was raised, and the command given to the elector of Saxony, and the landgrave of Hesse. The imperial forces were commanded by the emperor of Germany in person, and the eyes of all Europe were turned on the event of the war.

At length the armies met, and a desperate engagement ensued, in which the Protestants were defeated, and the elector of Saxony and the landgrave of Hesse both taken prisoners. This fatal blow was succeeded by a horrid persecution, the severities of which were such that exile might be deemed a mild fate, and concealment in a dismal wood pass for happiness. In such times a cave is a palace, a rock a bed of down, and wild roots delicacies.

Those who were taken experienced the most cruel tortures that infernal imaginations could invent; and by their constancy evinced that a real Christian can surmount every difficulty, and despite every danger acquire a crown of martyrdom.

Henry Voes and John Esch

Henry Voes and John Esch, being apprehended as Protestants, were brought to examination. Voes, answering for himself and the other, gave the following answers to some questions asked by a priest, who examined them by order of the magistracy.

Priest. Were you not both, some years ago, Augustine friars?

Voes. Yes.

Priest. How came you to quit the bosom of the Church at Rome?

Voes. On account of her abominations.

Priest. In what do you believe?

Voes. In the Old and New Testaments.

Priest. Do you believe in the writings of the fathers, and the decrees of the Councils?

Voes. Yes, if they agree with Scripture.

Priest. Did not Martin Luther seduce you both?

Voes. He seduced us even in the very same manner as Christ seduced the apostles; that is, he made us sensible of the frailty of our bodies, and the value of our souls.

This examination was sufficient. They were both condemned to the flames, and soon after suffered with that manly fortitude which becomes Christians when they receive a crown of martyrdom.

Henry Sutphen, arrested at night

Henry Sutphen, an eloquent and pious preacher, was taken out of his bed in the middle of the night, and compelled to walk barefoot a considerable way, so that his feet were terribly cut. He desired a horse, but his conductors said, in derision, "A horse for a heretic! no, heretics may go barefoot." When he arrived at the place of his destination, he was condemned to be burnt; but, during the execution, many indignities were offered him, as those who attended not content with what he suffered in the flames, cut and slashed him in a most terrible manner.

Peter Spengler, drowned

Many were murdered at Halle; Middleburg being taken by storm all the Protestants were put to the sword, and great numbers were burned at Vienna.

Peter Spengler, a pious divine, of the town of Schalet, was thrown into the river, and drowned. Before he was taken to the banks of the stream which was to become his grave, they led him to the market place that his crimes might be proclaimed; which were, not going to Mass, not making confession, and not believing in transubstantiation. After this ceremony was over, he made a most excellent discourse to the people, and concluded with a kind hymn, of a very edifying nature.

His head was struck off at a single blow

A Protestant gentleman being ordered to lose his head for not renouncing his religion, went cheerfully to the place of execution. A friar came to him, and said these words in a low tone of voice, "As you have a great reluctance publicly to abjure your faith, whisper your confession in my ear, and I will absolve your sins."

To this the gentleman loudly replied, "Trouble me not, friar, I have confessed my sins to God, and obtained absolution through the merits of Jesus Christ."

Then turning to the executioner, he said, "Let me not be pestered with these men, but perform your duty," on which his head was struck off at a single blow.

Foxe's Book of Martyrs, Edited by William Byron Forbush, chapter 10

Persecution of the Anabaptists

We pass now to the measures taken against the separatists. At first Zwingli tried to persuade them in private conferences, but in vain. Then followed a public disputation, which took place by order of the magistracy in the council hall, Jan. 17, 1525. Grebel was opposed to it, but appeared, together with Manz and Reubli. They urged the usual arguments against infant baptism, that infants cannot understand the gospel, cannot repent and exercise faith. Zwingli answered them, and appealed chiefly to circumcision and 1 Cor. 7:14, where Paul speaks of the children of Christian parents as "holy." He afterwards published his views in a book, "On Baptism, Rebaptism, and Infant Baptism" (May 27, 1525). Bullinger, who was present at the disputation, reports that the Anabaptists were unable to refute Zwingli's arguments and to maintain their ground. Another disputation was held in March, and a third in November, but with no better result. The magistracy decided against them, and issued an order that infants should be baptized as heretofore, and that parents who refuse to have their children baptized should leave the city and canton with their families and goods.

The Anabaptists refused to obey, and ventured on bold demonstrations. They arranged processions, and passed as preachers of repentance, in sackcloth and girdled, through the streets of Zurich, singing, praying, exhorting, abusing the old dragon (Zwingli) and his horns, and exclaiming, "Woe, woe unto Zurich!"

The leaders were arrested and shut up in a room in the Augustinian convent. A commission of ministers and magistrates were sent to them to convert them. Twenty-four professed conversion, and were set free. Fourteen men and seven women were retained and shut up in the Witch Tower, but they made their escape April 5.

Grebel, Manz, and Blaurock were rearrested, and charged with communistic and revolutionary teaching. After some other excesses, the magistracy proceeded to threaten those who stubbornly persisted in their error, with death by drowning. He who dips, shall be dipped, – a cruel irony.

It is not known whether Zwingli really consented to the death sentence, but he certainly did not openly oppose it. Six executions in all took place in Zurich between 1527 and 1532. Manz was the first victim. He was bound, carried to a boat, and thrown into the river Limmat near the lake, Jan. 5, 1527. He praised God that he was about to die for the truth, and prayed with a loud voice, "Into thy hands, O Lord, I commend my spirit!" Bullinger describes his heroic death. Grebel had escaped the same fate by previous death in 1526. The last executions took place March 23, 1532, when Heinrich Karpfis and Hans Herzog were drowned. The foreigners were punished by exile, and met death in Roman Catholic countries. Blaurock was scourged, expelled, and burnt, 1529, at Clausen in the Tyrol. Hōtzer, who fell into carnal sins, was beheaded for adultery and bigamy at Constance, Feb. 24, 1529. John Zwick, a Zwinglian, says that "a nobler and more manful death was never seen in Constance." Thomas Blaurer bears a similar testimony. Hübmaier, who had fled from Waldshut to Zurich, December, 1525, was tried before the magistracy, recanted, and was sent out of the country to recant his recantation. He labored successfully in Moravia, and was burnt at the stake in Vienna, March 10, 1528. Three days afterwards his faithful wife, whom he had married in Waldshut, was drowned in the Danube.

Other Swiss cantons took the same measures against the Anabaptists as Zurich. In Zug, Lorenz Fürst was drowned, Aug. 17, 1529. In Appenzell, Uliman and others were beheaded, and some women drowned. At Basle, Oecolampadius held several disputations with the Anabaptists, but without effect; whereupon the Council banished them, with the threat that they should be drowned if they returned. The Council of Berne adopted the same course.

In Germany and in Austria the Anabaptists fared still worse. The Diet of Speier, in April, 1529, decreed that "every Anabaptist and rebaptized person of either sex be put to death by sword, or fire, or otherwise." The decree was severely carried out, except in Strassburg and the domain of Philip of Hesse, where the heretics were treated more leniently. The most blood was shed in Roman Catholic countries. In Görz the house in which the Anabaptists were assembled for worship was set on fire. "In Tyrol and Görz," says Cornelius, "the number of executions in the year 1531 reached already one thousand; in Ensisheim, six hundred. At Linz seventy-three were killed in six weeks. Duke William of Bavaria, surpassing all others, issued the fearful decree to behead those who recanted, to burn those who refused to recant....

Throughout the greater part of Upper Germany the persecution raged like a wild chase.... The blood of these poor people flowed like water so that they cried to the Lord for help.... But hundreds of them of all ages and both sexes suffered the pangs of torture without a murmur, despised to buy their lives by recantation, and went to the place of execution joyfully and singing psalms."The blood of martyrs is never shed in vain.

The Anabaptist movement was defeated, but not destroyed; it revived among the Mennonites, the Baptists in England and America, and more recently in isolated congregations on the Continent. The questions of the subjects and mode of baptism still divide Baptist and Pedobaptist churches, but the doctrine of the salvation of unbaptized infants is no longer condemned as a heresy; and the principle of religious liberty and separation of Church and State, for which the Swiss and German Anabaptists suffered and died, is making steady progress. Germany and Switzerland have changed their policy, and allow to Baptists, Methodists, and other Dissenters from the state-church that liberty of public worship which was formerly denied them; and the state-churches reap the benefit of being stirred up by them to greater vitality. In England the Baptists are one of the leading bodies of Dissenters, and in the United States the largest denomination next to the Methodists and Roman Catholics.

Philip Scaff, The History of the Church

MARTYRS' MIRROR

Martyrs' Mirror of the Defenseless Christians who baptized only upon confession of faith, and who suffered and died for the testimony of Jesus, their Savior, from the time of Christ to the year A.D. 1660.

The Martyrs' Mirror is a history book that was first published in 1660 in Dutch by Thielman J. van Braght. It was translated from the original Dutch by Joseph F. Sohm. The book contains many chronicles, memorials and testimonies of Christians who were baptized only on confession of faith and so were persecuted for their faith in Jesus Christ. The aim of the book was to put into writing accounts of Christians who were faithful to death to Jesus Christ.

Leonhard Keyser, A.D. 1527

Leonhard Keyser, a priest, burned as a heretic at Scharding, AD 1527

When the believers greatly increased under persecution and the cross, there was, in Bavaria, a learned priest of the mass, named Leonhard Keyser, who examined the writings of Zwingli and Luther, and also went to Wittenberg, where he conferred with the doctors and commemorated the Supper with them.

Having returned to Bavaria, he examined the fruits and doctrines of the Anabaptists, as well as Zwingli and Luther, and joined himself under the cross to the separated cross-bearing church of the Anabaptists, in the year 1525, and forthwith continued in his ministry, with great power and zeal, undaunted by all the tyranny which arose over the believers, in the way of drowning, burning and putting to death. Acts 9:20. In the second year of his ministry, Leonhard Keyser was apprehended at Scharding, in Bavaria, and condemned by the bishop of Passau and other priests and capitulars, to be burned on Friday before St. Lawrence day, in August of the same year. Having bound him on a cart, they took him to the fire, the priests going alongside, and speaking Latin to him, but he, on account of the people, answered them in German; even as they had refused to speak to him in German before the court, which he had frequently requested. When he came out into the field, and was approaching the fire, he, bound, as he was, leaned down at the side of the cart, and plucked a flower with his hand, saying to the judge, who rode on horseback along side of the cart: "Lord judge, here I pluck a flower; if you can burn this flower and me, you have justly condemned me; but, on the other hand, if you cannot burn me and this flower in my hand, consider what you have done and repent," Thereupon the judge and the three executioners threw an extraordinary quantity of wood into the fire, in order to burn him immediately to ashes by the great fire. But when the wood was entirely burned up, his body was taken from the fire uninjured. Then the three executioners and their assistants built another great fire of wood, which when it was consumed, his body still remained uninjured, only his hair and his nails were somewhat burnt brown, and, the ashes having been removed from his body, the latter was found smooth and clear, and the flower in his hand, not withered, or burnt in the least, the executioners then cut his body into pieces, which they threw into a new fire. When the wood was burned up, the pieces lay unconsumed in the fire. Finally they took the pieces and threw them into the river Inn. This judge was so terrified by this occurrence that he resigned his office, and moved to another place. His chief servant, who was with the judge, and saw and heard all this, came to us in Moravia, became our brother and lived and died piously. That it might not be forgotten our teachers have recorded this as it came from his own lips, and now cause it to be promulgated and made known.

Edited by Tiffany Sullivan, from The Martyrs' Mirror, by kind permission

FELIX MANTZ, A.D. 1526

Felix Mantz was also an originator of the Reformation of the faith, in Germany, and when he, with great zeal, practiced, taught, and preached, the recognized truth of the Gospel, he was envied, accused and imprisoned by his adversaries, and finally drowned at Zurich for the evangelical truth, thus becoming a witness of the sufferings of Christ. This occurred in the year of our Lord 1526. He left the following admonition to his fellow brethren, for their comfort: "My heart rejoices in God, who gives me much knowledge and wisdom, that I may escape the eternal, and never ending death. Therefore I praise Thee, O Lord Christ from heaven, that Thou dost turn away my sorrow and sadness; Thou whom God has sent me as a Savior, and for an example and a light, and who has called me into His heavenly Kingdom, already before my end has come, that I should have eternal joy with Him, and should love Him and all His righteousness, which exists here, and which shall endure forever hereafter, and without which nothing avails or subsists; hence so many who do not have this in truth, are deceived by a vain opinion. But alas! how many are found at the present who boast of the Gospel and speak, teach, and preach much about it, but are full of hatred and envy, and who have not the love of God in them, whose deceit is known to all the world, as we have experienced in these latter days, that those who have come to us in sheep's clothing are ravening wolves, who hate the pious on the earth, and obstruct the way to life and to the true sheepfold. Thus do the false prophets and hypocrites of this world, who curse and pray with the same mouth, and whose life is disorderly. They call upon the authorities to kill us, by which they destroy the very essence of Christianity. But I will praise the Lord Christ, who exercises all patience towards us; for He instructs us with His divine graces, and shows love to all men, according to the nature of God His heavenly Father, which none of the false prophets are able to do.

"Here we must observe this difference, that the sheep of Christ seek the praise of God; this is their choice, and they do not suffer themselves to be hindered either by possessions or temporal good, for they are in the keeping of Christ. The Lord Christ compels no one to come to His glory; only those that are willing and prepared attain unto it by true faith and baptism. Whenever a person brings forth genuine fruits of repentance, the heaven of eternal joys is, through grace, purchased and obtained for him by Christ, through the shedding of His innocent blood, which He so willingly poured out; thereby showing us His love, and enduing us with the power of His Spirit, and whoever receives and uses it grows and is made perfect in God. Only love to God through Christ shall stand and prevail; not boasting, denouncing, or threatening. It is love alone that is pleasing to God: he that cannot show love shall not stand in the sight of God. The true love of Christ shall not destroy the enemy; he that would be an heir with Christ is taught that he must be merciful, as the Father in heaven is merciful. Christ never accused any one, as do the false teachers of the present day; from which it is evident that they do not have the love of Christ, nor understand His Word; and still they would be shepherds and teachers; but at last they will have to despair, when they shall find, that everlasting pain shall be their recompense, if they do not reform. Christ also never hated any one; neither did His true servants, but they continued to follow Christ in the true way, as He went before them. This Light of life they have before them, and are glad to walk in it; but those who are hateful and envious, and do thus wickedly betray, accuse, smite and quarrel, cannot be Christians. They are those who run before Christ as thieves and murderers, and under a false pretense shed innocent blood. By this we may know them that are not on the side of Christ; for they, as children of Belial, prompted by envy, destroy the ordinances of Jesus Christ; even as Cain slew his brother Abel, when God accepted the offerings of Abel."

With this I will finish my discourse, desiring that all the pious be mindful of the fall of Adam, who when he accepted the advice of the serpent, and became disobedient to God, the punishment of death came upon him. Thus it shall also happen to those who do not accept Christ, but resist Him, love this world, and have not the love of God. And this I close with this that I will firmly adhere to Christ, and trust

in Him, who is acquainted with all my needs, and can deliver me out of it. Amen.
Edited by Tiffany Sullivan, from The Martyrs' Mirror, by kind permission

Hendrick Pruyt, A.D. 1574

Hendrick Pruyt tarred and tied to his ship and set afire outside Workum, AD 1574

About the year 1574 there was another pious brother, named Hendrick Pruyt, born at Harder-wijck, in Guelderland, and a seaman by occupation, who came and sailed in the Zuyder Zee, on the coast of Friesland. And as a Spanish colonel was stationed at Wurckom, who was a zealous servant of the King of Spain, and a great war was carried on at that time between Holland and the King of Spain, the soldiers of the latter came in a yacht, on board of said Hendrick Pruyt's vessel. And as he saw no way of escape, he said to his wife: "Trijnt-jen Jans, lamb, there comes the wolf;" exhorting her to boldness and to answer without dissimulation to whatever she might be asked.

When these robbers came on board they asked: "Where does this craft hail from?"

They answered: "From Har-derwijck." Though that place was at that time at peace with the king, they nevertheless had to go on shore with them, and Hendrick Pruyt was put in prison at Wurckom. His wife, who came to him, was greatly concerned how to obtain his release, for they were young people who greatly loved each other: and as Hendrick Pruyt had little hope of being released, he asked his wife not to go to much trouble on his account, but that she should travel to her brother and friends, who were principally interested in the vessel, that they might see how to get the vessel released, which was also done. While she went home, they in the meantime examined Hendrick Pruyt and found that he was a brother of the Mennistic persuasion.

On account of this they dealt with him so cruelly and tyrannically, that they could not wait until the return of his wife, whom they might then also have made to tread this way of suffering. But they took this pious man and cast him into a boat which they had well smeared with tar. They also tarred the prisoner's body, and bound his outstretched hands to the ends of the mast-thwart, and took him thus without the harbor, set fire to the boat, and started him burning seaward. But as his hands through the fire had become loosed or disengaged from their bonds, it seemed probable that he might yet deliver himself from the fire; but these murderers, seeing this, hastened to him, and thrust him through, and ended his life. Thus this friend of God passed valiantly through the conflict, and the seed of God, which he had received in his heart through the preaching of the divine Word, remained in him un-to the end, whereby he through patience overcame his enemies, kept the faith, and through God's grace obtained the crown of eternal glory.

When this colonel perceived that Trijn Jans, his wife, hearing this report, would not readily be willing to run into the hands of these wolves, he was very much dissatisfied with it; saying: "If I had her here, she would have to go the same route;" and that if he could at any time get hold of this woman, though she were buried somewhere in a city, he would nevertheless dig up her dead body and burn it.

Consider, beloved reader, how such awful blood-thirstiness and tyranny accord with the Word, spirit and example of Christ and His apostles, whose followers, they, without shame, still dare call themselves.
Edited by Tiffany Sullivan, from The Martyrs' Mirror, by kind permission

Dirk Willems

Dirk Willems here turns around to save his persecutor's life; was then captured, imprisoned, and burned outside Asperen, AD 1569

In the year 1569 a pious, faithful brother and follower of Jesus Christ, named Dirk Willems. was apprehended at Asperen, in Holland, and had to endure severe tyranny from the papist. But as he had founded his faith not upon the drifting sand of human commandments, but upon the firm foundation stone, Christ Jesus, he, notwithstanding all evil winds of human doctrine, and heavy showers of tyrannical and severe persecution, remained immovable and steadfast unto the end; wherefore, when the chief Shepherd shall appear in the clouds of heaven and gather together His elect from all the ends of the earth, he shall also through grace hear the words: "Well done, good and faithful servant; thou hast been faithful over a few things, I will make thee ruler over many things; enter thou into the joy of thy Lord." I Pet. 5:4; Matt. 24 :31; 25:23.

Concerning his apprehension, it is stated by trustworthy persons, that when he fled he was hotly pursued by a thief-catcher, and as there had been some frost, said Dirk Willems ran before over the ice, getting across with considerable peril. The thief-catcher following him broke through, when Dirk Willems, perceiving that the former was in danger of his life, quickly returned and aided him in getting out, and thus saved his life. The thief-catcher wanted to let him go, but the burgomaster, very sternly called to him to consider his oath, and thus he was again seized by the thief-catcher, and, at said place, after severe imprisonment and great trials proceeding from the deceitful papists, put to death at a lingering fire by these bloodthirsty, ravening wolves, enduring it with great steadfastness, and confirming the genuine faith of the truth with his death and blood, as an instructive example to all pious Christians of this time, and to the everlasting disgrace of the tyrannous papists.

In this connection, it is related as true from the trustworthy memoirs of those who were present at the death of this pious witness of Jesus Christ, that the place where this offering occurred was without Asperen, on the side of Leerdam, and that, a strong east wind blowing that day, the kindled fire was much driven away from the upper part of his body, as he stood at the stake; in consequence of which this good man suffered a lingering death, insomuch that in the town of Leerdam, towards which the wind was blowing, he was heard to exclaim over seventy times: "0 my Lord; my God," etc., for which cause the judge or bailiff, who was present on horseback, filled with sorrow and regret at the man's sufferings, wheeled about his horse, turning his back toward the place of execution, and said to the executioner: "Dispatch the man with a quick death." But how or in what manner the executioner then dealt with this pious witness of Jesus, I have not been able to learn, except only, that his life was consumed by the fire, and that he passed through the conflict with great steadfastness, having commended his soul into the hands of God.

As we have come into possession of the sentence which these rulers of darkness passed upon this friend of God, we have deemed it well, to add it here for the benefit of the readers, in order that reading the same, they may be able to perceive the truth of this matter.

Copy of judgment

Whereas, Dirk Willems, born at Asperen, at present a prisoner, has, without torture and iron bonds (or otherwise) before the bailiff and us judges, confessed, that at the age of fifteen, eighteen or twenty years, he was rebaptized in Rotterdam, at the house of one Pieter Willems, and that he, further, in Asperen, at his house, at divers hours, harbored and admitted secret conventicles and prohibited doctrines, and that he also has permitted several persons to be rebaptized in his aforesaid house; all of which is contrary to our holy Christian faith, and to the decrees of his royal majesty, and ought not to be tolerated, but severely punished, for an example to others; therefore, we the aforesaid judges, having, with mature deliberation of council, examined and considered all that was to be considered in this matter, have condemned and do condemn by these presents in the name, and in the behalf, of his royal majesty, as Count of Holland, the aforesaid Dirk Willems, prisoner, persisting obstinately in his opinion, that he shall be executed with fire, until death ensues; and declare all his property confiscated, for the benefit of his royal majesty. So done this 16th of May, in presence of the judges, Cornelis Goverts, Jan van Stege Jans, Adnaen Gerritts, Adnaen Jans, Lucas Rutgers, Jan Jans, and Jan Roefelofs, A. D., 1569.

Extracted from the records of the town of Asperen, and after collation this copy was found to agree [with the original], the 15th of October 1606. Acknowledged by me, the town clerk of Asperen. T'Sheerenbergh.
Edited by Tiffany Sullivan, from The Martyrs' Mirror, by kind permission

Pelagius A.D. 925

It is stated that about A.D. 925, a lad of thirteen years, called Pelagius, was put to death for the name of Christ, in Cordova, which occurred as follows: His uncle, Ermoigus (who by some writers is called a bishop), having been apprehended and imprisoned at Cordova, by the Arabian King Habarrhaghman, said Ermoigus, in order to be released, left his nephew, who was then only about thirteen years old, in his stead, as a pledge, which for more than three years was not redeemed, either through the neglect of his friends, or because the King would not let go the youth, who was now very comely and well-mannered. In the meantime, this lad exercised himself diligently in the Christian religion, to prepare himself for his martyrdom, which seemed to him to be drawing near. When he was about thirteen and a half years old, he was brought before the King, and, standing there, immediately began to confess his faith, declaring that he was ready to die for it [ie: for the name of Christ.] But the King, having in view something else than to hear the confession of the son of God, or of the Christian faith, proposed to the youth, who was quite innocent in evil, some improper things, which this hero of Christ valiantly and in a Christian manner refused, willing rather, to die an honorable death for the name of Christ, than to live shamefully with the devil, and pollute both soul and body with such an abominable sin. The King, hoping that he could yet be persuaded, commanded his servants to ply him with fair promises, to the effect, that, if he would apostatize, he should be brought up with royal splendor at the court of the King. But the Lord, in whom he trusted, strengthened him against all the allurements of this world, so that he said:" I am a Christian, and will remain a Christian, and obey only Christ's commands all the days of my life." The King, seeing that he remained steadfast, was filled with rage, and commanded his guards to take him, suspend him by iron tongs, and pinch him and haul him up and down until he should either die of renounce Christ as his Lord. But having undergone all this, he was as fearless as ever, and refused not to suffer still more tortures, even until death.

When the tyrant perceived the immovable steadfastness of this youth, he commanded that they should cut him limb from limb, and throw the pieces in the river. As he thus stood before the King, dripping with blood, from his previous tortures, he prayed to none than Jesus Christ our Lord, saying: "O Lord, deliver me out of the hands of my enemies." When he lifted up his hands to God [in prayer], The executioners pulled them apart and cut off first one arm, and then the other; thus also his legs, and lastly, his head. When this was done, the pieces were thrown in the river. Thus this young hero and pious witness of Jesus Christ ended his life, on the 29th of June, A.D. 925, his martyrdom having lasted from seven o'clock in the morning until evening.
Edited by Tiffany Sullivan, from The Martyrs' Mirror, by kind permission

Elizabeth A.D. 1549

Elizabeth was apprehended on the 15th of January, 1549. When those who had come to apprehend her entered the house in which she lived, they found a Latin Testament. Having secured Elizabeth, they said: "We have gotten the right man; We have now the teacheress;" adding: " Where is your husband, Menno Simons, The teacher?" They then brought her to the town-house. The following day two beadles took her between them to prison.

She was then arraigned before the council, and asked upon oath, whether she had a husband.

Elizabeth answered: "We ought not to swear, but our words should be, Yea, yea, and Nay, nay; I have no husband."

Lords: "We say you are a teacher, and that you seduce many. We have been told this, and we want to know who your friends are."

Elizabeth: "My God has commanded me to Love my Lord and my God, and to honor my parents; for what I suffer for the name of Christ is a reproach to my friends."

Lords: "We will let you alone in regard to this, but we want to know whom you have taught."

Elizabeth: "Oh, no, my lords, let me in peace with this, but interrogate me concerning my faith, which I will gladly tell you."

Lords: "We shall make you so afraid, that you will tell us."

Elizabeth: "I hope through the grace of God, that He will keep my tongue, so that I shall not become a traitoress, a deliver my brother into death."

Lords: "What persons were present when you were baptized?"

Elizabeth: "Christ said: ask them that were present, or who heard it." John 18:21.

Lords: "Now we perceive that you are a teacher; for you compare yourself to Christ."

Elizabeth: "No, my lords, far be it from me; for I do not esteem my self above the off scourings which are swept out from the house of the Lord."

Lords: "What then do you hold concerning the house of God? Do you not regard our church as the house of God?"

Elizabeth: "No, my lords, for it is written: "Ye are the temple of the living God: as God hath said, I will dwell in them, and walk in them." 2 Corinthians 6:16.

Lords: "What do you hold concerning our mass?"

Elizabeth: "My lords, of your mass I think nothing at all; but I highly esteem all that accords with the word of God."

Lords: "What are your views with regard to the most adorable, holy sacrament?"

Elizabeth: "I have never in my life read in the Holy scriptures of a holy sacrament, but of the Lords supper." (She also quoted the Scripture relating to this.)

Lords: "Be silent, for the devil speaks through your mouth."

Elizabeth: "Yea, my lords, this is a small matter for the servant is not better than his lord."

Lords: "You speak from a spirit of pride."

Elizabeth: "No, my lords, I speak with frankness."

Lords: "What did the Lord say, when He gave His disciples the Supper?"

Elizabeth: "What did He give them, flesh or bread?"

Lords: "He gave them bread."

Elizabeth: " Did not the Lord remain sitting there? Who then would eat the flesh of the Lord?"

Lords: "What are your views concerning infant baptism, seeing you have been rebaptized?"

Elizabeth: "No, my lords, I have not been rebaptized. I have been baptized once upon my faith; for it is written that baptism belongs to believers."

Lords: "Are our children damned then, because the are baptized?"

Elizabeth: "No, my lords, God forbid, that I should judge the children."

Lords: "Do you not seek your salvation in baptism?"

Elizabeth: "No, my lords, all the water in the sea could not save me; but salvation is in Christ (Acts 4:10), and He has commanded me to love God my Lord above all things, and my neighbor as myself."

Lords: "Have the priests power to forgive sins?"

Elizabeth: "No, my lords; how should I believe this? I say that Christ is the only priest through whom sins are forgiven." Heb. 7:21.

Lords: "You say that you believe everything that accords with the Holy Scriptures; do you not believe the words of James?"

Elizabeth: "Yea, my lords, why should I not believe them?"

Lords: "Does he not say: "go to the elder of the church, that he may anoint you, and pray over you?" James 5:14.

Elizabeth: "Yea, my lords; but do you mean to say that you are of this church?"

Lords: "The Holy Ghost has saved you already; you need neither confession nor sacrament?"

Elizabeth: "No, my lords, I acknowledge that I have transgressed the ordinance of the pope, which the Emperor has confirmed by decrees, But prove to me that I have transgressed in any article against my Lord and my God, and I will cry woe over me, miserable being."

The foregoing is the first confession.

Afterwards she was again brought before the council, and led into the torture chamber, Hans, the executioner, being present. The lords then said: "We have thus long dealt with you in kindness; but if you will not confess, we will resort to severity with you." The Procurator General said: "master Hans, seize her."

Master Hans answered: "Oh, no, my lords, She will voluntarily confess."

But as she would not voluntarily confess, he applied the thumbscrews to her thumbs and forefingers, so that the blood squirted out at the nails.

Elizabeth said: "Oh! I cannot endure it any longer."

The lords said: " Confess, and we will relieve your pain. "

But she cried to the Lord her God: " Help me, O Lord, Thy poor handmaiden! for Thou art a helper in time of need."

The lords all exclaimed: "Confess, and we will relieve you your pain; for we told you to confess, not to cry to God the Lord."

But she steadfastly adhered to God her Lord, as related above; and the Lord took away her pain, so that she said to the lords: "Ask me, and I shall answer you: for I no longer feel the least pain in my flesh, as I did before."

Lords: "Will you not yet confess?"

Elizabeth: " No, my lords."

They then applied the screws to her shins, one on each.

She said: "O my lords, do not put me to shame; for never a man touched my bare body."

The Procurator General said: "Miss Elizabeth, we shall not treat you dishonorably."

She then fainted away. They said to one another, "Perhaps she is dead." But waking up, she said: "I live, and am not dead."

Then they took of the screws, and plied her with entreaties.

Elizabeth: "Why do you thus entreat me? This is the way to do with children."

Thus they obtained not one word from her, detrimental to her brethren in the Lord. Or to any other person.

Lords: "Will you revoke all that you have previously confessed here?"

Elizabeth: "No, my lords, but I will seal it with my death."

Lords: " We will try you no more; will you voluntarily tell us, who baptized you?"

Elizabeth: "Oh, no, my lords; I have certainly told you, I will not confess this."

Sentence was then passed upon Elizabeth, on the 27th of March, 1549; she was condemned to death-to be drowned in a bag, and thus offered up her body to God.

Edited by Tiffany Sullivan, from The Martyrs' Mirror, by kind permission

Claudine Le Vettre, and with her a Brother A.D. 1568

Meenen is a beautiful little town in Fanders, three leagues from Rijssel, on the road to Bruges, built on the edge of the Leye. In this town there lived a God-fearing man, Piersom des Muliers, with his wife Claudine le Vettre, who through the preaching of Leenaert Bouwens, and by reading and studying the word of God, were turned from papal idolatry. Learning if this, Titelmannus, Dean of Ronse, and inquisitor of the faith, came thither with bailiffs, thinking to apprehend the afore said Piersom in his house, But a pious man of the council of Meenen had warned Piersom to flee from the inquisitor, which he did, betaking himself into a certain piece of woods not far from his house. But his wife Claudine being engaged with her four children, tarried a little too long, and had just left the house, with a child in one arm, when the bailiffs entered, who tumultuously asked the children and the neighbors where the husband was; and when they could not learn it they prepared to leave. Perceiving this, one of the neighbors, kindled with an evil and perverse zeal, said: "Men, there goes the wife with a child on her arm." They therefore forthwith caught her, and delivered her into the hands of the aforesaid inquisitor. This happened in the year of 1567, a few months before the Duke of Alva's arrival in the Netherlands. She was taken from Meenen to Ypres, where many lay in prison for the faith that is because they could not understand that there was another Mediator and Savior than Jesus Christ alone, who was offered up for our sins on the tree of the cross (1 Timothy 2:5; Romans 4:25); and could not believe that God had any pleasure in images of wood and stone, or silver and gold, but believed rather that such worship was prohibited in the word of God (Exodus 20:4; Deuteronomy 4:16). And because they also did not believe that dead men can hear our prayers and help us; but much rather that we are to call upon no one but God alone, who is the discerner of our hearts and thought, and knows what we shall pray for, even before we have poured out our prayer; who exclaimed with a loud voice: "Come unto me, all ye that labor and are heavy laden, and I will give you rest," etc.; "to whom all the prophets and apostles point us, and not to one of the departed saints." Matthew 4:10; Revelations 2:13; Hebrews 4:12; Matthew 6:8; Romans 8:26; Matthew 11:28; Acts 10:43; Acts 4:12; Jeremiah 23:5; Jeremiah 33:15.

All who held such faith were by Titelmannus declared heretics, and delivered to the secular authorities, to be dealt with according to the decrees, namely, the men to be burnt alive, and the women to be buried alive. This severe death greatly terrified some, so that many apostatized, in order to save their lives. For at one time a large number broke out of prison and escaped, so that Claudine also could have made her escape, but she would not leave her child; so also a pious brother, who remained with her in prison unto the end, and would not leave her, dying with her for the truth, at said place. But Claudine did not apostatize, notwithstanding manifold assaults, continuing one year, but remained steadfast in the faith, refuting, from the Word of God, all that the priests and monks were able to bring forward against her, as appeared from divers letters which she wrote to her husband from prison.

Finally, when they could not prevail upon her, they endeavored to move her by her maternal love for her infant, which hitherto had been nourished at it's mother's breast in prison. The child therefore was taken from her and put out to a wet nurse, which was the greatest affliction she suffered during her imprisonment, and on account of which she wept many a tear, constantly praying God for power and strength against such temptation and assault of the flesh, in order that she might not fall, even as many as her fellow believers fell in her presence. God Almighty heard her prayer, for the duke of Alva, having in the meantime entered the country, and commanded to clear all prisons from heretics, she also was crowned with the crown of the godly, without Ypres, A.D. 1568; and with her a brother, who was also burnt for the truth, at said place.

Edited by Tiffany Sullivan, from The Martyrs' Mirror, by kind permission

Persecutions in the Netherlands

In 1568 Scobland, Hues and Coomans were arrested in Antwerp. In a letter from prison they wrote:"Since it is the will of the Almighty that we should suffer for his name, we patiently submit; though the flesh may rebel against the spirit, yet the truths of the gospel shall support us, and Christ shall bruise the serpent's head. We are comforted, for we have faith; we fear not affliction, for we have hope; we forgive our enemies, for we have charity. Do not worry about us, we are happy because of God's promises and exult in being thought worthy to suffer for Christ's sake. We do not desire release, but fortitude; we ask not for liberty, but for the power of perseverance; we wish for no change but that which places a crown of victory on our heads."

Such were the noble sentiments of these three servants of God when subjected too the fiery furnace of martyrdom; the secret of their strength was because there was a fourth with them, even the Son of God.

Scoblant was the first to be put on trial. He persisted in his faith and was sentenced to death. On his return to prison he asked his jailor not to allow any friar to visit him, saying, "They can do me no good, but may greatly disturb me; I trust that my salvation is already sealed in heaven, and that the blood of Christ, in which I firmly trust, has washed away my sins. I now throw off this mantle of clay, for robes of eternal glory. May I be the last martyr to Papal tyranny, that the church of Christ may have rest on earth, as she will hereafter."

On the day of execution he sang Psalm 40 and repeated the Lord's Prayer with great fervency as he was bound to the stake. Having commended his soul to God, the martyr soon perished in the flames.

Shortly after this Hues died in prison.

After the loss of Hues, Coomans wrote to his friends: "I am now deprived of my companions: Scobland is martyred, and Hues is dead; yet I am not alone: the God of Israel is with me, who is my shield and my exceeding great reward." When brought to trial, Coomans readily acknowledged himself to be of the reformed religion; and to every charge leveled against him explained his doctrine from the gospel.

"But,' said the judge, "will you die for the faith you profess?'

"I am not only willing to die for the truth,' replied Coomans, "but also to suffer the utmost stretch of inventive cruelty for the gospel's sake; after which my soul shall be received by God himself in the midst of eternal glory." After this Coomans was sentenced to death. He went cheerfully to his execution, and perished with a holy resignation, as a result of an enlightened faith.

John Foxe, The Book of Martyrs, revised with notes and an appendix by W. Bramley-Moore, London, 1869, pp 165-67

London Separatists, 1569

In 1569 John Nash was released from prison and on behalf of the London Separatists (members of the first Congregational churches) he wrote the following letter complaining about Christians being imprisoned.

In this your tyranye, you maynteyne and extoll them [the ceremonies] above the worde of God, in that you persecute and imprison some, to the death of the faythful servaunts of the Lord, those names here followe.

1. Randall Partrag
2. Giles Fowler
3. Thomas Bowland
4. Mr Pattenson, preacher
5. John Kynge
6. Mr Fitz, preacher
7. John Lernarde
8. Margrett Racye
9. the wyffe of Mr Causlen

All thees were godlye and zealous Christians and dyed by your tyrannous imprisonment and cruel tyrannye. These with all their companye abhorred all false sects and schismes, errors, herecyes, and all papistry, and all false and fayned religion and stoode faste to Chrystes institution and holye religion to the death, those that dyed departed constant Christians, even in your persecution.

Albert Peel, The Noble Army of Congregational Martyrs, Independent Press, 1928, pp 25-6

The Huguenots, 1572

Our attention is now turned to one of those more appalling massacres which dares claim a fiendish prominence in the annals of slaughter. We allude to the massacre of St Bartholomew. Charles IX of France and his mother Catherine, finding open persecution only excited the Huguenots to more obstinate resistance, determined to gain by subtlety what they failed to obtain by force. To make themselves more sure of their prey, they fixed on two plans: first, the king commanded Coligny to take his army into the Low Countries, so that he might find out the number and names of his followers: secondly, a marriage was proposed between the king's sister, Marguerite de Valois, and Henry of Navarre, the head of the Huguenot princes and the heir to the crown. All the leading Huguenot nobles were invited to Paris for this marriage which took place on 18th August, 1572. The 24th August was fixed for the massacre. At 2am the bell of St Germain l'Auxerrois tolled, at which signal the Duke of Guise led his followers to Coligny's house: the duke remained below while his servants, headed by a young man named Besme, ascended to the admiral's room. On their entering his apartment, Coligny said, "You ought to respect my grey hairs; but, do what you will, you can but shorten my life by a few days." The admiral, on being wounded in both arms, immediately said to Maure, preacher to the Queen of Navarre, "Oh, my brother! I now perceive that I am beloved of my God, seeing that for this most name's sake I do suffer these wounds." After stabbing him several times they threw him out of the window; when his head and arms were cut off by the rabble, and the body hung up by the feet on a gibbet. Besme later declared that he had never seen any person suffer death more courageously.

The martyrdom of this virtuous man had no sooner taken place than the armed soldiers ran about slaying all the Protestants they could find within the walls of the city. This continued for several days; but the greatest slaughter took place during the first three days, in which over 100,000 men and women, of all ages are said to have perished.

These brutal deeds were not confined within the walls of Paris, but extended into other cities and quarters of the realm, especially to Lyons, Orleans, Toulouse, and Rouen, where the cruelties were unparalleled. Within one month 60,000 Protestants are said to have been slain in France alone. When news of the massacre was received in Rome, the greatest of rejoicings took place, and a medal was struck to commemorate this victory of the faith.

The following are the detailed records of the above enormities.

2,000 were murdered in the city of Poitiers in one day.

At Meldis 200 were thrown into prison, and being brought out as sheep to the slaughter, were pitilessly cut to pieces.

At Orleans 1,000 men, women and children were slain.

At Lyons 800 perished most miserably; the children hanging on their fathers' necks, and the fathers embracing their children.

At Toulouse 200 were murdered.

At Albia of Cahors, upon the Lord's day, the 16th December, the Papists, at the ringing of the bell, broke open the doors where the Protestants were assembled, and killed, without distinction, all they could find, among whom was one Guacerius, a rich merchant, whom they took into his own house, and murdered with his wife and children.

John Foxe, The Book of Martyrs, revised with notes and an appendix by W. Bramley-Moore, London, 1869, pp 130-32

WILLIAM LAUD

William Laud, born in 1573, was Archbishop of Canterbury from 1633 to 1645 in the days of King Charles I. It was a turbulent time throughout, one of violent divisions in the Church of England, eventually culminating in the English Civil War.

An example is the surplice controversy. We have all encountered Christians who are opposed to celebrating Christmas on the grounds that:

(a) the Bible nowhere commands us to celebrate Christmas, and does not mention the 25th of December; and

(b) the pagans had a festival in December at which they built fires and feasted and exchanged gifts, from which it follows that those who celebrate Christmas are participating in pagan rites.

Similarly, in the late 1500's and early 1600's, there were Christians in England who objected to the garment called the surplice. When participating in the services of Morning and Evening Prayer in Church, clergy, including choir members, normally wore a cassock (a black, floor-length, fairly tight-fitting garment) covered by a surplice (a white, knee-length, fairly loose garment with loose sleeves).

The Puritans objected to the surplice:

(a) as not mentioned in the Bible, and

(b) as something that the Roman Catholics had worn before the Reformation, which made it one of the props of idolatrous worship, and marked anyone who wore it as an idolater.

Archbishop Laud regarded it as a seemly, dignified, garment, an appropriate response to the Apostle Paul's injunction, "Let all things be done decently and in order." The

Puritans thought differently, and violently interrupted services at which the surplice was worn. On one occasion, a group of Puritans broke into an Oxford chapel the night before a service and stole the surplices, which they thrust into a the dung-pit of a privy. Again, a woman marched into Lichfield Cathedral, accompanied by the town clerk and his wife, and ruined the altar hangings with a bucket of pitch.

Under English Law, it was part of Laud's office as Archbishop to maintain order and to punish offences against the peace of the Church. He made it his practice to proceed not only against poor and obscure offenders, but also, perhaps especially, against rich and powerful ones. It is well that men should be equal before the law, but his integrity on this point ultimately cost Laud his life.

Laud was also the prosecutor of record in the trials of those who published seditious or violent and abusive attacks on the doctrine and discipline of the Church, and the Puritans produced an abundance of scurrilous attacks on those who disagreed with them, which were duly punished, with Laud taking the responsibility. When in 1630 (note, before Laud became Archbishop), Alexander Leighton published Zion's Plea Against Prelacy, a violent attack on the Bishops as tools of Antichrist, he was sentenced to be publicly whipped and branded, and to have his ears cut off. He was sixty years old and a Doctor of Divinity, and the sentence aroused great public indignation. (It is not certain that it was actually carried out.)

Laud made enemies chiefly in three ways.

(1) He punished those who attacked the Church, both those who vandalized and those who confined themselves to verbal abuse.

(2) He upheld various customs in public worship (such as the wearing of the surplice) that were harmless in themselves, but which aroused the suspicion and fury of those who feared a return to power of Roman Catholicism.

(3) He sought the financial independence of the clergy, so that a preacher was not dependent on what support the local squire was pleased to give him. His proposed means to this end was to restore to the Church some of the Church lands that had been seized by Henry VIII and given or sold to various nobles and gentlemen. The proposal never reached the stage of discussion about details, so it was not clear how compensation would be handled, but the mere whisper of such a proposal was enough to make every landholder in the country feel personally threatened.

In 1637 an attempt was made to introduce the Book of Common Prayer into general use in Scotland, and it immediately caused rioting. In February of 1638, Scottish leaders signed the National Covenant, by which they pledged themselves to uphold the Puritan position by force, and by the end of the year they had voted to depose and excommunicate every bishop in Scotland. The unrest spread to England, and in 1640 Laud was arrested on a charge of high treason. He was kept in the Tower for four years, and tried in 1644, at the age of seventy-one. He was found guilty, not because there was any evidence of his guilt, but because the House of Commons was determined that he should die. On the scaffold he prayed: "The Lord receive my soul, and have mercy on me, and bless this kingdom with peace and charity, that there may not be this effusion of Christian blood amongst them."

James E. Kiefer, By kind permission

Thomas Sherwood

Blessed Thomas Sherwood was born in London, of pious and Catholic parents, and by them brought up in the true faith and in the fear of God. Mr Sherwood frequented the house of Lady Tregony, a virtuous Catholic, who had a son named Martin, whose faith and manners were widely distant from those of his mother. This young spark suspected that Mass was sometimes privately said in his mother's house, and this as he imagined, by the means of Mr Sherwood; which was the occasion of his conceiving an implacable hatred against him; insomuch that, one day meeting him in the streets, he cried out, "Stop the traitor! Stop the traitor!'

and so causing him to be apprehended, had him before the next Justice of Peace. Where, when they were come, Mr Tregony could allege nothing else against Mr Sherwood, but that he suspected him to be a Papist. Upon which the Justice examined him concerning his religion; and in particular, what his sentiments were concerning the Queen's Church-headship, and the Pope's supremacy. To which Mr Sherwood candidly answered, "That he did not believe the Queen to be the head of the Church of England; and that this preeminence belonged to the Pope." Upon which he was immediately committed, and cast into a dungeon in the Tower.

In the Tower he was most cruelly racked, in order to make him discover where he had heard Mass. But he suffered all their tortures with a greatness of soul not unequal to that of the primitive martyrs, and would not be induced to betray or bring any man into danger. After this, he was thrust into a dark, filthy hole, where he endured very much from hunger, stench and cold, and the general want of all things, no one being allowed to visit him or afford him any comfort.

In fine, after about six months' suffering in this manner, with invincible patience, and gloriously triumphing over chains, dungeons, and torments, during which he often repeated these words, "Lord Jesu, O! I am not worthy that I should suffer these things for Thee! much less am I worthy of those rewards which thou hast promised to give to such as confess thee:' he was brought to his trial, and condemned for denying the Queen's supremacy; and was executed according to sentence, being cut down while he was yet alive, dismembered, bowelled, and quartered. He suffered at Tyburn, February 7, 1578, at the age of fourteen.

E. H. Burton and J. H. Pollen, Lives of the English Martyrs, Vol 1, 1583-1588, Longman, 1914, pp 78-9

Maxims of English Catholic Martyrs, 1583-1588

[Before he came to the hurdle, on of the underkeepers said to him: "O Mr Towsham, if I were in the like danger as you are, and might avoid it as easily as you may by going to church, surely I would soon yield to that."]

The happy priest answered: "I pray thee be contented, good friend; within this hour I shall conquer the world, the flesh and the devil."

[He was so laid on the hurdle that one of his legs draggled on the ground as he was drawn, and being urged by a schismastic woman to draw it up, he replied,]

"No, all is too little for Christ's sake."

Venerable Stephen Rowsham, martyred York, 23 March, 1587

[As Sir William Fleetwood, the Recorder of London, in a white hot rage, was about to hit him:]

"Use your might, for I will gladly suffer anything for the Catholic faith."

Venerable George Haydock, Tyburn, 12 February, 1584

"He was a man of extraordinary Christian simplicity and sincerity, in a word, a true Israelite in whom there is no guile."

[Dr Champney speaking about the three years' imprisonment the Venerable John Robinson, martyred at Ipswich, 1 October, 1588, underwent.]

[On being sentenced to execution] "What is all this? Is it any more than one death?'

Venerable Richard White, martyred at Revham, 15 October, 1584

"I have received this night greater consolation than I deserved."

Said on the morning of his martyrdom by Venerable Robert Sutton, at Stafford, 27 July, 1587

". . . our school of patience . . ."[Referring to prison]

Venerable John Body, martyred at Andover, 2 November, 1583

[Sheriff Fawcet wanted her to confess that she died because of treason.]

"No, no, Mr Sheriff, I die for the love of my Lord Jesu."

[On receiving her death sentence]

"God be thanked, all that he shall send me shall be welcome; I am not worthy of so good a death as this."

Venerable Margaret Clitherow, martyred at York, 26 March, 1586

[On being sentenced to death on a

Thursday, expecting it to be carried out, as was usual, on the Saturday, Mr Taylor said on Friday, having said Mass and his office:]

"How happy should I be, if on this day, on which Christ died for me, I might encounter death for him." [Scarcely had he said this than the officer unexpectedly came and took him to his execution.]

The Venerable Hugh Taylor, York, 26 November, 1585

E. H. Burton and J. H. Pollen, Lives of the English Martyrs, Vol 1, 1583-1588, Longman, 1914

Edmund Campion

Blessed Edmund Campion was born in London; he was first taught in Christ Church Hospital, and later at Oxford, in St John's College, where, after he had passed with great applause though the University by the persuasions of some of his friends he suffering himself to be made a deacon after the new fashion. He went to the new seminary at Douay, then chose to become a member of the Society of Jesus, and was, in Rome, admitted in 1573. In 1580, the day after midsummer he happily landed at Dover, being by God's great goodness delivered out of the searchers' and officers' hands, who detained him upon suspicion for some hours.

After he had labored, often preaching three times a day, in God's harvest near thirteen months, being betrayed by one George Eliot, after long search he fell into the persecutors' hands on July 17, 1581, being found in a secret closet, in a Catholic gentleman and confessor's house called Mr Yates, of Lyford.

After he had been two days in the custody of the Sheriff of Berkshire, he was carried to London. At dinner Eliot said to him, "Mr Campion, you look cheerfully upon everybody but me; I know you are very angry with me in your heart for this work."

"God forgive thee, Eliot,' said he, "for so judging of me; I forgive thee, and in token thereof, I drink to thee; yea, and if thou wilt repent and come to confession, I will absolve thee; but large penance thou must have."

In his way to London, besides the tying of his legs under his horse, and the binding his arms behind him, the Council appointed a paper to be set upon his hat with large capital letters, CAMPION, THE SEDITIOUS JESUIT; and gave orders so to parade him through the streets at the most crowded part of the day, which was executed accordingly, all London, almost, beholding the spectacle; the mob gazing, and with delight beholding the novelty; but the wiser sort lamenting to see our country so fallen. And thus on the 22nd of July he was delivered up to the Lieutenant of the Tower.

Here, besides the ordinary miseries of imprisonment, he was divers times racked to force out of him, by torments, whose houses he had frequented, by whom he was relieved, whom he had reconciled, when, which way, and for what purpose and by what commission, he came into the realm; how, where, and by whom he printed and dispersed his books and such like.

At his first racking, they went no further with him; but afterwards, when they saw he would not give way in religion, which was the thing they most desired, they forged matter of treason against him, and framed their demands accordingly; about which he was so cruelly torn and rent upon the torture, the two last times, that he thought they meant to make him away in that manner. Before he went to the rack, he used to fall down at the rack-house door, upon both knees, to commend himself to God's mercy; and upon the rack he called continually upon God, repeating often the holy name of Jesus. He most charitably forgave his tormentors. His keeper asking him the next day, how he felt his hands and feet, he answered, "Not ill, because not at all."

The poor jury did that which they understood was looked for at their hands, and pronounced Father Campion to be "Guilty." Mr Popham, the Attorney-General, sentenced him to be hanged, drawn, and quartered, as in cases of high treason. On 1st December Campion was taken to Tyburn on a hurdle, from which he cried to the crowds, "God save you all, God bless you, and make you all good Catholics."

Father Campion was brought into the cart, where, after some little pause, he began to speak upon that text of St Paul, "We are made a spectacle to the world' (1 Corinthians 4:9), but was interrupted by Sir Francis Knowles and the Sheriffs urging him to confess his treason. To whom he answered, "For the treason which has been laid to my charge and I am come here to suffer for; I desire you all to bear witness with me, that thereof I am altogether innocent."

Whereupon answer was made to him by one of the Council, that he might not deny what had been proved by sufficient evidence. "Well, my lord,' said he, "I am a Catholic man, and a priest; in that faith have I lived, and in that faith do I intend to die: and if you esteem my religion treason, then am I guilty; as for any other treason I never committed, God is my judge: but you have now what you desire."

And the cart being drawn away, he meekly and sweetly yielded his soul unto his Savior, protesting that he died a perfect Catholic. His mild death, and former sincere protestations of his innocency, moved the people to such compassion and tears, that the adversaries "were glad to excuse the matter."

He suffered at Tyburn, December 1, 1581, being forty-two years of age.

The English Martyrs Under Henry VIII and Elizabeth, 1535-1583, Catholic Truth Society, 1901, pp 80-88

ILLUSTRATIONS OF PERSECUTION OF CATHOLICS

Six striking engravings, made from copper plates in the first edition of the Italian translation of William Allen's book Campion and his Companions, show how Catholics were arrested, mocked, led off to prison, examined, tortured, drawn and executed. These engravings give the earliest representations of the sufferings of the [Catholic] English martyrs, and as Allen's book was the seed, as it were, of the subsequent martyrologies, so these pictures became the models for later artists. The following captions to the pictures give a rare insight into the tortures of Catholic martyrs.

1 APPREHENSION

The priest, in secular disguise, is recognized in the street by a spy or priest-catcher, and on the cry being raised "a traitor! a traitor!' the men and boys take up stones to throw at him. He is arrested, bound, and led away to prison amidst the jeers of the people.

2 THE ROAD TO PRISON

The priest has been taken at Mass, and is led away to prison through the streets in his sacred vestments, accompanied as fellow prisoners by the devout people who have heard his Mass. Other priests are brought in on horseback from the country, men with torches leading the way at night. One of the priests, who is riding with his feet tied together, has on his hat, "Edmund Campion, the seditious Jesuit."

3 EXAMINATION WITH TORMENT

A man is being whipped at the cart's tail, and on his return from this punishment an official heats an iron with which his ears are to be pierced and he is to be branded as a rogue. Two ministers are looking on.

4 THE RACK

When a man was examined on the rack, cords were tied on his wrists and ankles, and by means of windlasses these were tightened as the examiners directed. Other prisoners were sometimes brought to witness the torture or to hear the groans of the victims, to induce them to say what was required of them.

5 TO TYBURN

The hurdle is dragged through the streets at a horse's heels, the sheriff and other officials accompanying it, and the poor "traitor' is worried with controversy when he would prepare himself for death. The gallows, the cart, the fire and cauldron are all in readiness for his arrival.

6 EXECUTION

There have been three victims. One is just cut down, one is stripped and his bowels are thrown into the fire, the third is already cut up, his head is on the pole and parts of him are in the cauldron of boiling pitch preparatory to being hung over the city gates.

J. H. Pollen, Father Edmund Campion and his companions, Burns and Oates, 1908, pp 120-125

Mary Queen of Scots

Mary Queen of Scots was beheaded in Elizabeth I's reign, as a Roman Catholic threat to the English throne, on February 8, 1587

Mary conducted her own defense, but it was clear from the start of her trial that the Star Chamber would only reach one verdict. Mary was declared a dangerous instrument for the restoration of the Roman Church.

Mary wrote the following letter to Elizabeth: "Madame, for the sake of that Jesus to whose name all powers bow, I require you to ordain that when my enemies have slaked their black thirst for my innocent blood, you will permit my poor desolated servants altogether to carry away my corpse, to bury it in holy ground with the other queens of France. As they tell me that you will in nothing force my conscience nor my religion, and have even conceded me a priest, refuse me not this my last request, that you will permit free sepulcher to this body when the soul is departed, which, when united, could never obtain liberty to live in repose, such as you would procure for yourself; against which repose – before God I speak – I never aimed a blow: but God will let you see the truth of all after my death.

". . . To conclude, I pray God, the just Judge, of his mercy that he will enlighten you with his Holy Spirit, and that he will give you his grace to die in the perfect charity I am disposed to do, and to pardon all those who have caused, or who have co-operated in, my death. Such will be my last prayer to my end, which I esteem myself happy will precede the persecution which I foresee menaces, and that I desire that my blood and my country may be remembered in that time."

On February 7th, 1587, the Earls of Kent and Shrewsbury arrived at Fotheringay with a warrant for Mary's execution. That night Jan Kennedy read to her from her Book of Hours. In the morning her ladies dressed her in a magnificent black satin gown with long sleeves, over a petticoat of crimson satin, a long white veil and shoes made of Spanish leather.

Guards and a crowd of spectators filled the great hall. The scaffold, the chair, and the block were draped in black. The Queen, in matching black, sat while the warrant was read and the Dean of Peterborough preached an interminable sermon. Mary interrupted him. They argued about the teaching of their respective churches, and ended up denouncing the other in their prayers. Mary's black gown was removed to leave a figure standing in crimson on the scaffold.

Mary knelt clumsily, as she was stiff from lack of exercise and illness. She held the block with her hands until one of the executioners took them into his own hands. The other executioner took aim, struck and missed. His third blow severed Mary's head. The Dean of Peterborough was heard to say, "So perish all the Queen's enemies."

Editor

John Amias and Robert Dalby

"Martyrdom is an honor, and Carmelites do not seek honors." Bernanos

John Amias, born in Yorkshire, was alumnus of Douay College, where he was priested in 1581 and sent on the English mission with Mr Edmund Sykes. In 1588 Robert Dalby, who was born in Durham, and who had also been an alumnus and priest at Douay College, was sent on the English mission. Both Amias and Dalby fell into the hands of the Protestant persecutors, and were condemned to die the death of traitors, on account of their priestly character. Dr Champney, gives the following account of them:

"This year, on the 15th of March, John Amias and Robert Dalby, suffered at York, as in cases of high treason, for no other cause but they were priests, ordained by the authority of the See of Rome, and had returned to England, and exercised their priestly functions for the benefit of the souls of their neighbors. I was myself an eye-witness of the glorious combat of these holy men, being at that time a young man, 20 years old, and I returned home confirmed, by the sight of their constancy and meekness, in the Catholic faith, which by God's grace I then followed; for they visibly appeared to be like lambs led to the slaughter.

"They were drawn about a mile out of the city to the place of execution, where, being arrived and taken off the hurdle, they prostrated themselves upon their faces to the ground, and then employed some time in prayer, till Mr Amias, being called by the sheriff, rose up, and, with a serene countenance, walked to the gallows and kissed it. Then kissing the ladder, went up. The hangman, after fitting the rope to his neck, bade him ascend a step or two, affirming that thus he would suffer the less. He then turned to the people, and declared that the cause of his death was not treason, but religion. But here he was interrupted and not allowed to go on. Therefore composing himself for death, with his eyes and hands lifted up to heaven, forgiving all who had anyways procured his death, and praying for his persecutors, he recommended his soul to God, and being flung off the ladder, he quietly expired; for he was suffered to hang so long, till he seemed to be quite dead. Then he was cut down, dismembered and disemboweled, his head cut off and the trunk of his body quartered.

"All this while, his companion, Mr Dalby, was most intent in prayer; who, being called upon, immediately followed the footsteps of him that had gone before him, and obtained the like victory."

Martyrs Omitted by Foxe, compiled by a member of the English Church, 1870, pp 86-8

Forty Martyrs of England and Wales (1)

Forty Martyrs (RC) of England and Wales, 25 October 1570

In the years following the quarrel between Henry VIII of England and the Pope of Rome, questions of religious faith became entangled with questions of political loyalty. Henry when young had married his brother's widow, Catharine of Aragon (Spain), who bore him a daughter, Mary. Marriage with one's brother's widow was not permitted in those days, and Henry's marriage had taken place by special permission of the Pope. Later, Henry claimed that the Pope had no right to make an exception, and that the marriage was null and void. He set Catharine aside, and married Anne Boleyn, who bore him a daughter, Elizabeth. Henry later accused Anne of adultery, had her beheaded, and married Jane Seymour, who bore him a son, Edward, and died shortly after giving birth. Roman Catholics held that Mary was born in wedlock, but that Elizabeth was not and had no right to inherit the throne. Protestants held the reverse opinion. (There were exceptions on both sides.) Not surprisingly, Mary grew up Roman Catholic, and her half-sister Elizabeth grew up Protestant. After Henry's death, Edward ruled from 1547 to 1553 (aged 10 to 16), and was (or his advisors were) Protestant. After his death, Mary (born 1516) ruled from 1553 to 1558, and was vigorously Roman Catholic, trying to undo all the changes of the previous reigns, but by methods that lost her support she might otherwise have had. After her death, Elizabeth (born 1533) ruled from 1558 to 1601, and was a moderate Protestant, attempting so far as possible to avoid conflict with either side. For some years, she succeeded fairly well, and then the Pope decreed that:

(1) Roman Catholics in England, who had hitherto been attending the English-language services in their parish churches, must instead receive the sacraments from priests smuggled in from the mainland to say Mass in Latin; and

(2) Elizabeth was no lawful monarch, and Roman Catholics had a duty to depose her and replace her with her Roman Catholic cousin, Mary of Scotland.

The English government reacted by declaring that the saying of Mass in Latin was treason. The stage was set for more than a hundred years of religious martyrdoms with political undercurrents.

In 1970, the Vatican selected as representatives of a larger group (totaling perhaps three hundred) forty Roman Catholic men and women, both clergy and laity, who suffered death for conscience' sake during the years from 1535 to 1679. Their names are given below, with years of death. Those marked with an asterisk (*) are Welsh, the others English. Religious Orders (monks, friars, etc.).

CARTHUSIANS:
John Houghton, Augustine Webster, Robert Lawrence, 1535

BRIGITTINE:
Richard Reynolds; 1535

AUGUSTINIAN FRIAR:
John Stone; 1539

JESUITS:
Edmund Campion, 1581; Robert Southwell, Henry Walpole, 1595; Nicholas Owen, Jesuit lay brother, 1606; Thomas Garnet, 1608; Edmund Arrowsmith, 1628; Henry Morse, 1645; Philip Evans*, David Lewis*, 1679

BENEDICTINES:
John Roberts*, 1610; Ambrose Barlow, 1641; Alban Roe, 1642

FRIAR OBERVANT:
John Jones*, 1598

FRANCISCAN:
John Wall, 1679

SECULAR CLERGY (PARISH PRIESTS NOT IN MONASTIC ORDERS):
Cuthbert Mayne, 1577; Ralph Sherwin, Alexander Briant, 1581; John Pain, Luke Kirby, 1582; Edmund Gennings, Eustace White, Polydore Plasden, 1591; John Boste, 1594; John Almond, 1612; John Southworth, 1654; John Lloyd*, John Plessington, John Kemble, 1679.

LAYMEN:
Richard Gwyn*, poet and schoolmaster 1584; Swithun Wells*, schoolmaster, 1591; Philip Howard, Earl of Arundel and Surrey, died in prison (poisoned?) 1595; John Rigby, household retainer of the Huddleston family, 1600

LAYWOMEN:
Margaret Clitherow, wife, mother, and schoolmistress, 1586; Margaret Ward, for managing a priest's escape from prison, 1588; Anne Line, widow, "harborer of priests", 1601.

James Kiefer, Christian Biographies, By kind permission

FORTY MARTYRS OF ENGLAND AND WALES (2)

The following Catholic martyrs were all killed in the 16th and 17th centuries.

They were all persecuted for continuing to profess the Catholic faith following King Henry VIII's promulgation of the Act of Supremacy, which declared that the king of England was the head of the Church of England.

Most of them were hanged, drawn, and quartered. This barbaric execution meant that the individual was hanged on a gallows until he was just about to become unconscious. So, while the individuals were still alive, and conscious, they were ripped open and eviscerated. The hangman searched the entrails until he found the heart. This he then tore out, showed it to the watching crowd, before throwing it onto the fire.

Alban Bartholomew Roe: Benedictine priest (born in Suffolk; died at Tyburn, 1642) (f.d. [feast day] January 21).

Alexander Briant: priest (born in Somerset, England; died at Tyburn, 1851) (f.d. December 1).

Ambrose Edward Barlow: Benedictine priest (born in Manchester, England, 1585; died at Lancaster, 1641) (f.d. September 10).

Anne Higham Line: widow, for harboring priests (born at Dunmow, Essex, England; died at Tyburn, 1601) (f.d. February 27).

Augustine Webster: Carthusian priest (died at Tyburn, 1535) (f.d. May 4).

Cuthbert Mayne: Priest (born in Youlston, Devonshire, England, 1544; died at Launceston, 1577) (f.d. November 30).

David Lewis: Jesuit priest, (born at Abergavenny, Monmouthshire, Wales, in 1616; died at Usk 1679) (f.d. August 27).

(Brian) Edmund Arrowsmith: Jesuit priest (born Haydock, England, 1584; died at Lancaster in 1628) (f.d. August 28).

Edmund Campion: Jesuit priest (born in London, England, c. 1540; died at Tyburn, 1581) (f.d. December 1).

Edmund Jennings (Genings, Gennings):

priest (born at Lichfield, England, in 1567; died at Tyburn 1591) (f.d. December 10).

Eustace White: priest (born at Louth, Lincolnshire, England; died at Tyburn, 1591) (f.d. December 10).

Henry Morse: Jesuit priest (born at Broome, Suffolk, England, in 1595; died at Tyburn, 1645) (f.d. February 1).

Henry Walpole: Jesuit priest (born at Docking, Norfolk, England, 1558; died at York in 1595) (f.d. April 7).

John Almond: priest (born at Allerton, near Liverpool, England, 1577; died at Tyburn, 1612) (f.d. December 5).

John Boste: priest (born in Dufton, Westmorland, England, c. 1544; died at Dryburn near Durham, 1594) (f.d. July 24).

John Houghton: Carthusian priest (born in Essex, England, in 1487; died at Tyburn, 1535) (f.d. May 4).

John Jones (alias Buckley): Friar Observant (born in Clynog Fawr, Carnavonshire, Wales; died at Southwark, London, in 1598) (f.d. July 12).

John Kemble: priest (born at Saint Weonard's, Herefordshire, England, in 1599; died at Hereford in 1679) (f.d. August 22).

John Lloyd: priest, Welshman (born in Brecknockshire, Wales; died in Cardiff, Wales, in 1679) (f.d. July 22).

John Paine (Payne): priest (born at Peterborough, England; died at Chelmsford, 1582) (f.d. April 2).

John Plessington (a.k.a. William Pleasington): priest (born at Dimples Hall, Lancashire, England; died at Barrowshill, Boughton outside Chester, England, 1679) (f.d. July 19).

John Rigby: household retainer of the Huddleston family (born near Wigan, Lancashire, England, c. 1570; died at Southwark in 1601) (f.d. June 21).

John Roberts: Benedictine priest, Welshman (born near Trawsfynydd Merionethshire, Wales, in 1577; died at Tyburn, 1610) (f.d. December 10).

John Southworth: priest (born in Lancashire, England, in 1592; died at Tyburn 1654) (f.d. June 28).

John Stone: Augustinian friar (born in Canterbury, England; died at Canterbury, c. 1539) (f.d. December 27).

John Wall: Franciscan priest (born in Lancashire, England, 1620; died at Redhill, Worcester, in 1679) (f.d. August 22).

Luke Kirby: priest (born at Bedale, Yorkshire, England; died at Tyburn, 1582) (f.d. May 30).

Margaret Middleton Clitherow: wife, mother, and school mistress (born in York, England, c. 1555; died at York in 1586) (f.d. March 25).

Margaret Ward: gentlewoman who engineered a priest's escape from jail (born in Congleton, Cheshire, England; died at Tyburn in 1588) (f.d. August 30).

Nicholas Owen: Jesuit lay brother (born at Oxford, England; died in the Tower of London in 1606) (f.d. March 2).

Philip Evans: Jesuit priest, (born in Monmouthshire, Wales, in 1645; died in Cardiff, Wales, in 1679) (f.d. July 22).

Philip Howard: Earl of Arundel and Surrey (born in 1557; died in the Tower of London, believed to have been poisoned, 1595) (f.d. October 19).

Polydore Plasden: priest (born in London, England; died at Tyburn, in 1591) (f.d. December 10).

Ralph Sherwin: priest (born at Rodsley, Derbyshire, England; died at Tyburn, 1851) (f.d. December 1).

Richard Gwyn: poet and schoolmaster; protomartyr of Wales (born at Llanidloes, Montgomeryshire, Wales, in 1537; died at WRevham, Wales, in 1584) (f.d. October 17).

Richard Reynolds: Brigittine priest (born in Devon, England, c. 1490; died Tyburn in 1535) (f.d. May 4).

Robert Lawrence: Carthusian priest (died at Tyburn in 1535) (f.d. May 4).

Robert Southwell: Jesuit priest (born at Horsham Saint, Norfolk, England, c. 1561; died at Tyburn in 1595) (f.d. February 21).

Swithun Wells: schoolmaster (born at Bambridge, Hampshire, England, in 1536; died at Gray's Inn Fields, London, 1591) (f.d. December 10).

Mrs. Wells was also condemned to death, but was reprieved and died in prison, 1600).

Thomas Garnet: Jesuit priest (born at

Southwark, England; died at Tyburn, in 1608) (f.d. June 23).

S. Anselm Parker, The Catholic Encyclopedia, Volume 11

Nicholas Owen

A Jesuit lay-brother, martyred in 1606. There is no record of his parentage, birthplace, date of birth, or entrance into religion. Probably a carpenter or builder by trade, he entered the Society of Jesus before 1580, and had previously been the trusty servant of the missionary fathers. More (1586-1661) associates him with the first English lay-brothers. He was imprisoned on the death of [St.] Edmund Campion for openly declaring that martyr's innocence, but afterwards served Fathers Henry Garnett and John Gerard for eighteen years, was captured again with the latter, escaped from the Tower, and is said to have contrived the escape of Father Gerard. He was finally arrested at Hindlip Hall, Worcestershire, while impersonating Father Garnett. "It is incredible", writes Cecil, "how great was the joy caused by his arrest . . . knowing the great skill of Owen in constructing hiding places, and the innumerable quantity of dark holes which he had schemed for hiding priests all through England." Not only the Secretary of State but Waade, the Keeper of the Tower, appreciated the importance of the disclosures which Owen might be forced to make. After being committed to the Marshalsea and thence removed to the Tower, he was submitted to most terrible "examinations" on the Topcliffe rack, with both arms held fast in iron rings and body hanging, and later on with heavy weights attached to his feet, and at last died under torture. It was given out that he had committed suicide, a calumny refuted by Father Gerard in his narrative. As to the day of his death, a letter of Father Garnett's shows that he was still alive on 3 March; the "Menology" of the province puts his martyrdom as late as 12 Nov. He was of singularly innocent life and wonderful prudence, and his skill in devising hiding-places saved the lives of many of the missionary fathers.

S. Anselm Parker, The Catholic Encyclopedia, Volume 11

Roman Catholics persecuted

In Hallam's *Constitutional History of England*, we are told that "the rack seldom stood idle for all the latter part of Queen Elizabeth's reign." The Roman Catholic martyrs under her amounted to 204 according to Milner. Many others died of hardships in prison; many, deprived of their property, were banished, mutilated, condemned to be burnt, and reprieved. Dr Bridgewater names over 1,200 who suffered in this way before 1588, that is, before the greatest heat of the persecution. He lists:

3 Archbishops
1 Abbot
4 whole convents of religious
13 deans
14 archdeacons
60 prebendaries
530 priests
49 doctors of divinity
18 doctors of the law
15 masters of colleges
1 queen
18 peers
26 knights
326 gentlemen
60 peeresses and gentlewomen

Many of these died in prison, several under sentence of death.

In Stowe's *Chronicles*, we find that 4,000 peasants were massacred for not accepting Protestantism, under Lord John Russell, in Devonshire.

Hume says that:

645 monasteries
90 colleges
2,374 chantries and free chapels
110 hospitals
were ruined under Henry VIII.

Martyrs Omitted by Foxe, compiled by a member of the English Church, 1870, pp 1-2

Richard Barry

Let us now turn to one of the blackest pages in our English history, and give a few examples of Puritan intolerance in Ireland. With the wholesale butcheries, such as that at Drogheda, where Roman Catholics were slain without an offer of mercy, through apostatizing from their faith, a butchery lasting in that town for five days, the blood of fellow-Christians – man, woman, and child – running in the streets like rivers; with these we need not to trouble the reader. It is only of martyrdoms wherein death was willingly submitted to for conscience's sake, that we shall treat; for his and for our own edification.

At Cashel, when all resistance of the people to their barbarous invaders had ceased, the priests, together with very aged men and women (some stated to have been in their hundredth year), took refuge at the foot of the altar in the cathedral; among whom was Father Theobald Stapleton, who, crucifix in hand, and in his sacred vestments, was cut to pieces; and when all the rest had fallen in the same way, Richard Barry, of the order of St Dominic, alone survived.

Struck by his noble and sanctified appearance, the captain said to him, "Your life is your own, provided you fling off that habit. But if you cling to such a banner, verily you peril life itself."

To this Barry replied, "My habit is an emblem of the passion of the Redeemer, and more dear to me than life."

"Think more wisely,' rejoined the captain. "Indulge not this blind passion for martyrdom; for, if you comply not with my orders, death awaits you."

"But if so,' replied the devoted man, "your cruelties will be to me a blessing, and death itself a great gain."

Infuriated, they bound the holy man to a stone chair, kindled a slow fire under his feet and legs, and, "after two hours of torture, his eyes flashed their last upon that heaven which he was about to enter."

Martyrs Omitted by Foxe, compiled by a member of the English Church, 1870, pp 181-82

A True Confession of Faith of the Brownists

Robert Browne formed a "gathered church' in Norwich in 1580 and published three books in 1582, one entitled, A Treatise upon the 23 of Matthew, both for an order of studying and handling the Scriptures, and also avoyding the Popish disorders, and ungodly communion of all false Christians, and especially of wicked Preachers and hirelings. *By 1583 a royal proclamation ordered the destruction of all of Browne's books. Browne's followers became known as the "Brownists."*

An extract from *A True Confession of Faith of the Brownists* (1596) states: "We have been miserably entreated by the Prelates and cheef of the Clergie: some of us cast into most vile and noisome prisons and dungeons, laden with irons, and there, without all pitie, deteyned many years, as the cities of London, Norwich, Gloucester, Bury, and many other places of the land can testify. Yet here the malice of Satan stayed not it self, but raised up against us more grievous persecution, even unto the violent death of some, and lamentable exile of us all.

"So that through their barbarous crueltie 24 souls have perished in their prisons, with in the Citie of London only (besides other places of the land).

"Margin: In Newgate Mr Crane a man about 60 years of age; Richard Jacson, Thomas Stevens, William Howton, Thomas Drewet, John Gwalter, Roger Ryppon, Robert Awoburne, Scipio Bellot, Robert Bowle, John Barnes being sick unto death, was carried forth and departed this life shortly after. Mother Maner of 60 years, Mother Roe of 60 years, Anna Tailour, Judeth Myller, Margaret Farrer beeing sick unto death was carried forth, and ended her life within a day or two after. John Purdy in brydwel, Mr Denford in the Gatehouse about 60 years of age. Father Debnham, about 70 years, George Bryty in Counter wood street, Henry Thomson in the clink, John Chandler in the Count. Poultry, being sick unto death was carried forth, and died within few days. Walter Lane in the Fleet, Thomas Hewet in Counter Woodstreet."

Albert Peel, The Noble Army of Congregational Martyrs, Independent Press, 1928, pp 42-44

English Martyrs, 1535–83

Decree confirming official martyrs

Decree [of the congregation of sacred rites] confirming the honor given to the blessed martyrs John Cardinal Fisher, Thomas More, and others, put to death in England for the faith from the year 1535 to 1583. England, once called the Island of Saints and the Dowry of the Virgin Mother of God, as even from the first ages of the Church it had been renowned for the sufferings of many Martyrs, so also, when it was torn by the fearful schism of the sixteenth century from the obedience and communion of the Roman See, was not without the testimony of those who, for the dignity of this See, and for the truth of the orthodox Faith, did not hesitate to lay down their lives by the shedding of their blood.

In this noble band of Martyrs nothing whatever is wanting to its completeness or its honor: neither the grandeur of the Roman purple, nor the venerable dignity of Bishops, nor the fortitude of the Clergy both secular and regular, nor the invincible firmness of the weaker. Eminent amongst them is John Fisher, Bishop of Rochester and Cardinal of the Holy Roman Church, whom Paul III speaks of in his Letters as "conspicuous for sanctity, celebrated for learning, venerable by age, an honor and an ornament to the kingdom, and to the Clergy of the whole world."

With him must be named the layman Thomas More, Chancellor of England, whom the same Pontiff deservedly extols, as "excelling in sacred learning, and courageous in the defense of truth." The most authoritative ecclesiastical historians, therefore, are unanimously of opinion that they all shed their blood for the defense, restoration, and preservation of the Catholic Faith.

Names of martyrs of the Church of England, both of ancient and of more recent times have been engraved at Rome on copper-plate with the title:

Sufferings of the Holy Martyrs who, in ancient and more recent times of persecution, have been put to death in England for Christ, and for professing the truth of the Catholic Faith.

Those who suffered death under King Henry VIII: John Fisher, Bishop of Rochester, Cardinal of the Holy Roman Church; Thomas More, Chancellor of England; Margaret Pole, Countess of Salisbury, mother of Cardinal Pole; Richard Reynolds, of the Order of St Bridget; John Haile, Priest; eighteen Carthusians, namely: John Houghton, Augustine Webster, Robert Laurence, William Exnew, Humphrey Middelmore, Sebastian Newdigate, John Rochester, James Walworth, William Greenwood, John Davy, Robert Salt, Walter Pierson, Thomas Green, Thomas Scryven, Thomas Redyng, Thomas Johnson, Richard Bere and William Horne; John Forest, Priest of the Order of St Francis; John Stone, of the Order of St Augustine; for Secular Priests: Thomas Abel, Edward Powel, Richard Fetherson, John Larke; and German Gardiner, a layman.

Those who suffered under Elizabeth: Priests, Cuthbert Mayne, John Nelson, Everard Hanse, Rodolph Sherwin, John Payne, Thomas Ford, John Shert, Robert Johnson, William Fylby, Luke Kirby, Laurence Richardson, William Lacy, Richard Kirdman, James Hudson, or Tompson, William Hart, Richard Thirkeld, Thomas Woodhouse, and Plumtree. Also three Priests of the Society of Jesus: Edmund Campion, Alexander Briant, and Thomas Cottam. Lastly, John Storey, Doctor of Laws; John Felton, and Thomas Sherwood, laymen.

The present Decree was issued on this 29th day of December, sacred to the Martyr Thomas Archbishop of Canterbury, whose faith and constancy these Blessed Martyrs so strenuously imitated.

D. Cardinal Bartoloni, Prefect of the Congregation of Sacred Rites, Laurence Salvati, Secretary

The English Martyrs under Henry VIII and Elizabeth, Catholic Truth Society, 1901, i-iv

The Martyrs of Japan
5 February 1597

The Christian faith was first introduced into Japan in the sixteenth century by Jesuit and later by Franciscan missionaries. By the end of that century, there were probably about 300,000 baptized believers in Japan.

Unfortunately, this promising beginning met reverses, brought about by rivalries between different groups of missionaries and political intrigues by the Spanish and Portuguese governments, along with power politics among factions in the Japanese government itself. The result was a suppression of Christians.

The first victims were six Franciscan friars and twenty of their converts, who were crucified as Nagasaki on 5 February 1597. After a short interval of relative tolerance, many other Christians were arrested, imprisoned for life, or tortured and killed; and the Church was totally driven underground by 1630. However, when Japan was re-opened to Western contacts 250 years later, it was found that a community of Japanese Christians had survived underground, without clergy, without Scriptures, with only very sketchy instructions in the doctrines of the faith, but with a firm commitment to Jesus as Lord.
James Kiefer, Christian Biographies, By kind permission

JOHN OGILVIE
Scotland 1615

In these more enlightened and less intolerant days [1877] it is not easy even to imagine the wretched sort of life which was the lot of those amongst the Scotch who at the beginning of the sixteenth century still clung to the faith of their fathers. Still less easy is it to picture all the hardships and perils to which Scotch missionary priests were exposed. The Catholic religion had been declared no longer the religion of Scotland, as the great monument to John Knox in the Necropolis of Glasgow triumphantly, but rather suggestively, informs the Protestant passer-by. The cruellest laws had been passed against the Catholics, and their faith was continually made the subject of the foulest misrepresentations and the bitterest ridicule.

According to popular ideas, carefully nourished by the instructions of the preachers, all Catholics were idolaters, traitors, parricides, everything that is bad. The Pope's jurisdiction had been abolished from Scotland in 1560 and a further act of Parliament declared that to say Mass, or even to hear Mass, was a criminal offence. The first time this law was broken it was punished with the confiscation of goods, the second time by banishment, and the third time by death. As Dr Gordon wrote in his *Scotichronicon*, "It appears hardly credible that the wanton barbarities which Father Ogilvie had to endure could have been directed and sanctioned by the constituted authorities. They are scarcely to be paralleled by the refined cruelty of the persecutions of Christians during the first three centuries of the church, or of the Indian savages and cannibals."

It was towards the end of 1613 that Father Ogilvie succeeded with Father Moffet in getting back into Scotland. He would of course have come disguised, to avoid being captured by the Presbyterians, who were ever watching for any one having the least appearance of being a Catholic priest. He devoted himself with unflagging energy and with a zeal truly apostolic as he sought out the faithful, exhorting them to be courageous and in administering to them the holy sacraments. However, Father Ogilvie was captured in October 1614. Within six months of his arrest he was condemned to death, and within three hours from his condemnation had won, at the early age of thirty-four, a martyr's crown.

During his trial Father Ogilvie said: "If I should be exiled for any evil deed committed, I should certainly take care not to come back, but if I were exiled for this cause which I sustain, I should not fail to retrace my steps to the country. And would that every hair of my head might convert a thousand to the orthodox faith, and you, Archbishop, in the first place. I do not consider that consciences are bound by these iniquitous statutes of yours enacted without law and without authority."

The judges soon pronounced on him sentence of death, which was of this kind, viz., that he should be conducted to a gibbet erected for him in the public street, and having been there hanged, his head should be cut off, and the four quartered parts of his body should be left exposed to sight, in four different public places. . . . After the repeated commands of the sheriff to throw

him off the ladder, the executioner at last reluctantly, and with great compassion, cast him down from the step. When this was done, there arose a tumult and murmur, every sex and age regretting his unjust death, and expressing their detestation of the cruelty of the ministers and especially the archbishop. The cord by which the most holy soul of the martyr had been released from the prison-house of the body was cut, and the holy body, having nothing to retain it, fell with a great fall on the boards below."
C. J. Karslake, An Account of the Imprisonment and Martyrdom of Father John Ogilvie, Burns and Oates, 1877, pp 40-49

Pursuivants and the harrying of Catholics

During the reigns of James I and Charles I priest-hunters or pursuivants often forced magistrates to enforce laws against priests, and even have them executed. Many of the pursuivants were "the riff-raff of the population' who stood to personally benefit from their operations.

King James' laws, adding to those of Queen Elizabeth's are most severe and cunningly planned to bring about the ruin of the Catholics. Lest they should prove a dead letter, informers are encouraged by the prospect of ample rewards. The most inveterate enemies of our religion among the ministers and the laity have been appointed inquisitors and judges, who, to win the approval of the King and Parliament, set no limits to their vexations and extortions. In this they are fully supported by their underlings, known as pursuivants, who for the most part are men of damaged reputation, thieves, suspected or rather known coiners, or those guilty of other felonies. These miscreants ply their trade not only in London, but have the country parceled out among them, with full licence to act as if in an enemy's territory.

They visit at any hour of the night that suits them the dwellings of Catholics, and those of Protestants also, if there exists the slightest suspicion of their containing Catholic inmates, taking the precaution to surround them with musketeers or soldiers, to prevent any one escaping. If not admitted at once, they break down the doors, then, as it may suit their pleasure, confine the members of the household to their rooms, while they go over the house, prying into every corner, chest and cupboard. If the keys are not forthcoming, they force the locks; expostulation or resistance, they answer with abuse or blows; if they find any money they seize it without hope of recovery, under the pretext that it is stored up for the support of priests and Jesuits, or for the seminaries, Colleges or Religious Houses beyond the seas. As for books, sacred vessels, vestments, especially such as are marked with a cross, and other church stuff, they profane and confiscate them, and by dint of threats compel the owners to satisfy their insatiable greed. It is needless to mention the demolition of walls, the tearing up of floors and pavement in order to discover some lurking priest or Jesuit. Decency forbids us to particularize their treatment of gentle and virtuous women, in order to discover books, rosaries, Agnus Deis and the like. Suffice it to say that when they have searched and plundered to their heart's content, they take bill of the master of the house for his appearance at the assizes, and lest they should be called to account for their misdeeds, they bring him before a Justice of the Peace, who tenders the oath of allegiance, thus forcing him to choose between apostasy and utter ruin.

The tragic fate of a certain priest, who, though not a Jesuit, should yet be mentioned in this annual report, shows how dangerous it is to await the arrival of the pursuivants and to flee by night. A few weeks since, the mansion of a noble lady was surrounded in the dead of night in consequence of information given by a false brother, of a priest being there. As they began their search, the priest jumped out of bed, and without waiting to dress, snatched up his coat, and sought to escape by the roof of the house, but his foot slipped and he fell headlong. It is thought that he was slain by the posses of armed men posted round the house, for his death was caused by a wound in the head, not by the fracture of his limbs, and not only

did the marks on the ground show that he alighted on his feet, but he was heard by some people to cry out, "Where are you dragging me to? What are you going to do to me? Do you want to murder me? The heretics, taking up the corpse, buried it at a cross-road, driving a stake through the stomach, the usual way in this country of burying suicides, as they reported him to be."
Annual Letters of the English Mission, 1614. Foley, Records, vol. 6, part ii, 1061

A LAYMAN'S EXHORTATION TO CATHOLIC PRIESTS

And you, religious fathers and reverend priests, to whom is committed the care of this devastated vineyard, and who are unto us in our distress the sole dispensers of the divine sacrament, venture still, I beseech you, as hereto you have done, the loss of your lives, to distribute unto us this divine food and to break unto us this celestial bread. For in your hands only it is, in this time of dearth, to preserve the lives of your brethren, lest they perish by famine. And we again, my Catholic brethren, let us boldly adventure our lives to give them harbor and entertainment. Imitating herein our noble patron and proto-martyr of England, blessed St Alban, who presented himself, yea gave his own life, to preserve the life of his priest Amphibalus.

Even so, when either foolish heretics or foolish friends shall condemn you of folly for losing your goods or exposing your lives for to harbor priests, consider with yourselves that you harbor him who bringeth unto you the body and blood of Jesus Christ, and that if you shed your blood to receive him who consecrateth in your house the blood of Christ, what else do you do but render blood for blood, and spend your blood for the blood of Christ. You, therefore, the right honorable and worshipful of the English nation, which have brought this holy sacrifice at a hundred marks, and such as were poorer with the utter deprivation of all the poor little they had in the world, and further, such as have not had so much money, have laid to pawn their very carcasses into sundry prisons, goals and loathsome dungeons, and with what great and unspeakable reward will our Savior one day repay and requite your charity! In a word, all the sufferances, all the ignominies, all the injuries, all the damages and all the detriments which you shall endure for the defense of this sacrifice, will minister matter to all ensuring posterity of your most noble and heroical acts, which, though you die, will ever live to future memory, resound to your own immortal glory and to the everlasting renown of our English nation.
John Heigham, A Devout Exposition of the Holy Mass, 1614, Preface

EDMUND ARROWSMITH 1628

Between the accession of James I and the death of Cromwell, 39 priests, 2 Jesuit brothers and 6 laymen were executed under the penal statutes. Only Edmund Arrowsmith, a priest, and a laborer Richard Herst were martyred in Charles I's reign.

Arrowsmith, ordained at Arras in 1612, having studied at Douai, was sent on the English mission in 1613, became a member of the Society of Jesus in 1623, before being arrested and executed at Lancaster in 1628.

Various were the affections of the persons who assisted at this tragedy and beheld B. Edmund Arrowsmith's exit. Many Protestants, moved by his fortitude and patience, wished their souls with his, who then died. Some judged it very laudable to be constant to their religion, but thought it too great a stretch of obligation to die for that cause. Some touched with compassion, esteemed it barbarous to use a person thus for his religion. Mr Leigh [who had shouted at the martyr during his trial and called on him to recant just before his execution] and some of his malicious temper seemed the only people pleased with this inhumanity.

The Catholics who in great numbers had attended this last scene of his apostolical life were comforted and confirmed in the truth of that religion, which he recommended efficaciously by his example. They praised God, who in their days had raised Fr. Arrowsmith and placed before their eyes this pattern of patience, humility, constancy, charity, incessant zeal for souls, which shone forth with luster in the triumphant martyr.

The behavior of the sanguinary judge [Sir Henry Yelverton] increased the martyr's glory, and in that respect, must be allowed a place in the Acts of the martyr. Pleased with the success of his illegal and barbarous proceedings, he had anticipated the day of execution to see with satisfaction the death of Fr. Arrowsmith, whom he condemned without regard even to the known laws of civilized nations. He was ashamed to appear at the place of execution, perhaps to indulge his cruel temper more, in seeing the butchery at a distance through a prospective glass, without any constraint from the spectators who would justly be surprised at this extraordinary procedure in an administrator of justice. Thus he sated his eyes with blood, having first taken an oath not to sit down to table till Arrowsmith was dead.

Dinner was ordered up in a kind of triumph when his oath was discharged; here he seemed religious, to be more cruel. After dinner some venison came in, a present to the judge; while he admired the venison, Fr. Arrowsmith's quarters were brought in, that he might enjoy the bloody act of which he was the author. To glut himself with horror he barbarously handled the quarters of the deceased, laid them by the venison and was not ashamed inhumanly to compare them together.

The Life of Edmund Arrowsmith

Peter O'Higgins

Peter O'Higgins, of the order of St Dominic, was led to the scaffold in the courtyard of Dublin Castle in 1641, a pious and an eloquent man. He was arrested and brought before the lords-justices on a charge of endeavoring to seduce Protestants from their religion. Failing to sustain any capital charge against him, he was informed by those in authority that, if he abandoned his faith, he should have many and great privileges, but that all depended on his embracing Protestantism.

It was on the morning fixed for his death that this message was sent to him. In reply, O'Higgins desired to have this proposal under the signature of the justices, and that it should be handed to him when in sight of the gibbet. Hearing this, the justices sent the written document for pardon on the before-named conditions, together with the warrant for his execution.

O'Higgins had just ascended the first step of the ladder leading to the gibbet, when the executioner placed the paper in his hand. He bowed courteously on receiving it. There was a loud demonstration of exultation on the part of the mob at the supposed apostasy of the martyr from his faith. Standing yet on the scaffold, he exhibited the document he had received, and commented warmly on the avowed iniquity of his judges.

Addressing the members of his own faith among the crowd, he said: "My brethren, God has so willed that I should fall into the hands of our relentless persecutors; they have not been able, however, to convict me of any crime against the laws of the realm. But my religion is an abomination in their sight; and I am here today to protest, in the sight of God and man, that I am condemned for my faith. For some time I was in doubt as to the charge on which they would ground my condemnation; but, thanks to heaven, it is no longer so; and I am about to die for my attachment to the Catholic faith. See you here the condition on which I might save my life? Apostasy is all they require; but, before high heaven, I spurn their offers, and with my last breath will glorify God for the honor he had done me, in allowing me thus to suffer for his name."

He then cast the conditional reprieve into the crowd, and bade the executioner perform his office; the bystanders hearing him give thanks to God with his last breath.

Martyrs Omitted by Foxe, compiled by a member of the English Church, 1870, pp 184-85

Hugh Green 1642

Hugh Green, 1584-1642, born in London, was trained at Douai, where he was ordained in 1612. He then worked for the next thirty years on the English mission, before being executed at Dorchester.

On Friday, 19 August, the Reverend Hugh Green, alias Ferdinand Browne, of London,

an alumnus of this College, bravely suffered at Dorchester an illustrious martyrdom or, rather, an unheard-of butchery on account of his priesthood. For when his belly was cut open by the executioner and his abdomen placed on his breast, he gazed at it, and with his left hand touched his bowels, while with his right hand he fortified himself with the sign of our redemption. And while the executioner was tearing out his liver and, disturbing his entrails, was searching for his heart, he distinctly pronounced several times the saving name of Jesus. His forehead was bathed with sweat, and blood and water flowed from his eyes and nose. And when on account of the gushing streams of blood his tongue could no longer pronounce the saving name of Jesus, his lips moved, and the frequent groans which he uttered from his inmost heart were proof of the most bitter pain and torture which, with his eyes lifted to heaven, he bore with an unconquered soul for half an hour and more. He suffered in the fifty-seventh year of his age, the cause of his death being that he was a Roman priest.
Douai Diary, 1642

Brabant and the Gospellers

To speak nothing of the infinite dissensions, hurliburlies, massacres, murders, wars, treasons which have been caused in the Christian world by these new Gospellers and their gospel, for they are patent to the eye, and France, Germany, England, Scotland, the Low Countries and wheresoever these Gospellers come, do find it by woeful experience too true. To omit thousands of examples which are well known to every man, I will only mention that unheard-of villainous cruelty of their exercised not many years since upon the poor citizens of Tuelmont, a village in Brabant, where what cruelty soever hath been committed by any tyrant, what rape or beastliness by any savage or brutish men, what sacrilege soever by Jew, Turk or infidel what these also committed by the followers of these new Gospellers. To lock up hospitals and burn both lame, maimed and sick alive was nothing, to pluck young infants from their mothers' breasts and by the legs fling them up in the air and catch them on their dagger's point was common: to kill young and old, little and great, of all sexes and ages was their sport. They had no horror or scruple to ravish chaste matrons and violate sacred virgins publicly in the churches and chapels, and after they had by the multiplicity of those obscene acts killed them, afterwards brutishly to abuse their bodies. Yea, which makes me even tremble to think of it, they dreaded not in the most vile manner which could be invented to abuse Christ our Lord in the Blessed Sacrament, and all this not by the private soldier alone or upon the sudden, or in the height of fury, but in the cold blood, after three days consult, by approbation of all their officers.
Peter Wright

Martyrdom of Charles I (1)
King of England and Scotland, Martyr

Charles was born in 1600, second son of James VI of Scotland (who upon the death of Queen Elizabeth in 1603 became James I of England as well). At his birth, he was not expected to live, and at the age of four, he could still neither speak nor walk. Since he had an elder brother Henry, he was not expected to inherit the throne. But just before he turned twelve, his brother died, making Charles the heir. He responded by undertaking a program of training, physical and otherwise, with the result that his speech difficulties were reduced to a slight stammer, and he could speak several languages and fence and ride and in general qualify as a suitable heir to the throne. By the time he did inherit the throne in 1625, he inherited troubles with it. His father, by arrogance and tactlessness, by a disreputable private life, by enriching his favorites at the expense of the public welfare, by an unpopular foreign policy, had largely depleted the popular good will toward the monarchy that his predecessor had accumulated. Charles inherited his father's largely unpopular advisors, an unsuccessful war with Spain, and the beginnings of an unsuccessful war with France. The reign of Charles was largely occupied with a struggle against his Parliament, chiefly over two issues, taxation and the Church.

By ancient tradition, most taxes could be levied only by Parliament. Certain fees, however, had special status. It was customary for Parliament, at the beginning of every reign, to grant the new monarch authority for life to assess and collect customs duties ("tonnage and poundage"), and the King could levy "Ship Money" for the maintenance of the Royal Navy. Traditionally, only five seacoast cities (the Cinque Ports), all with large shipping industries, and therefore all obviously benefitting from Naval protection, were subject to the levy. Charles pointed out, truly enough, that every Englishman benefitted from Naval protection, and claimed the right to collect money to support the Navy from all England. This Parliament would not concede.

Parliament contained many Puritans, who wished to "purify" the Church of England by making it conformable to the practices of Calvin's church in Geneva. This meant abolishing bishops and the use of the Book of Common Prayer. This Charles believed to be wrong.

Immediately upon his accession, Charles found Parliament suspicious of him. Instead of the customary bill giving him lifetime authority to collect tariffs, they gave him a grant for two years only. Charles, who had inherited the belief that kings rule by Divine Right, responded to what he regarded as the outrageous behavior of Parliament, by confrontation rather than, as a more cunning man might have done, by manipulation. The results were not good. He finally dissolved Parliament.

Charles, by avoiding war, and otherwise reducing government expenditures, managed to run the government on customs duties and Ship Money and revenues from Crown lands, and so on, from 1629 to 1640. But in 1639 he attempted to install the English Book of Common Prayer in Scotland, and an armed insurrection followed, so that Charles, needing money to pay his troops, called what became known as the Long Parliament. This Parliament, considering that it had the King at its mercy, refused him any tax revenues unless he would agree to renounce his right to levy customs duties and Ship Money, and they took from him other immemorial royal prerogatives, and ordered the execution of some of his supporters. Charles went to the North of England and gathered an army to fight against Parliament. This was the First Civil War, which lasted about from 1642 to 1646. Charles lost. He entrusted himself to the Scottish Army, which promptly sold him to the English Parliament, which held him prisoner.

Here one of Charles's principal faults, and a disastrous one, became obvious. He firmly believed in his own God-given right to rule, and considered that in dealing with those who were trying to take his status from him by force, he had the right to make whatever promises expediency dictated, and to break them when expedient. (Just so, many persons otherwise extremely honest, if confronted with the kidnaping of a child and consequent ransom demands, would think it quite justifiable to promise the kidnappers anything, and to break the promise by marking the bills, staking out the drop site, and so forth. They would say that it is not dishonest to thwart a robber and a potential murderer, by lies and broken promises if necessary, since you are taking from him nothing that he has a right to.) The result was, that when Charles was finally defeated and backed into a corner, he had no credibility left to bargain with. In this connection, his defenders point out that, at the end, when he was being held prisoner on the Isle of Wight, he had the opportunity to save his life by escaping, and refused it, since it involved breaking his word. He would break his promise in order, as he believed, to save his country from disaster, but not if the only thing to be gained was his personal life and liberty.

Not even his worst enemies thought Charles less than a good man in private life. Unlike his predecessor and his successor, he was faithful to his marriage vows; and his marriage (though it got off to a slow start, being a political alliance to a bride he had never seen) was remarkable among royal marriages for its happiness and mutual devotion. When his accusers wished to say something against his moral character, the worst charge they could find to bring was that he read Shakespeare.

In 1647, Charles signed a secret agreement with a group of Scots that brought about the Second Civil War, in which the Royalists were again defeated.

A war which was, in one sense, about taxation, was in another sense about religion. The Parliamentary armies were led by Oliver Cromwell, a staunch Puritan and a military genius. (He is said to be a collateral descendant of Henry VIII's advisor Thomas Cromwell. However, a correspondent who has researched his life doubts this. He says that Oliver's family moved from Wales to England at a time when last names were not common in Wales, and adopted the Cromwell name because T. Cromwell then stood high in the king's favor.) He began by opposing Charles in the name of liberty, but soon his battle cry became the Puritan faith. Wherever his troops went, they smashed stained-glass windows and pictures and statues, stabled their horses in churches, and burned vestments and Prayer Books. (The same correspondent says that this was not Cromwell's original policy, although it was that of some of his soldiers. He says that Cromwell eventually suppressed traditional Anglican usages because they were rallying points for royalists. Another correspondent, from Ely, informs me that Ely Cathedral was spared desecration when Cromwell took Ely, by Cromwell's personal command.) At the end, when Charles was Cromwell's prisoner, he was required to assent to a law abolishing bishops in the Church of England. He had previously given his consent to such an abolition in Scotland, where the Puritans were in the majority, but here he dug in his heels and declared that Bishops were part of the Church as God had established it, and that he could not in conscience assent to Cromwell's demand. His refusal sealed his doom, and it is for this that he is accounted a martyr, since he could have saved his life by giving in on this question. He was brought to trial before Parliament, found guilty of treason, and beheaded 30 January 1649. On the scaffold, he said (I quote from memory and may not have the exact words):

No man in England is a better friend to liberty than myself, but I must tell you plainly that the liberty of subjects consists not in having a hand in the government, but in having that government, and those laws, whereby their lives and their goods may be most their own. That is to say, one may reasonably ask of a government that it establish justice in the land; so that judges do not take bribes, so that innocent men are not convicted of crimes, while the guilty are convicted and punished, so that honest men need fear neither robbers nor the sheriff. One may further ask that taxes be not excessive, and that punishments be not disproportionate to the crime. Charles would have said, "Do not ask whether the laws were made by men whom you elected. Ask whether they are reasonable and good laws, upholding justice and the public weal." He would have invited comparison of his record in this respect with that of the Long Parliament (which sat for twenty years without an election, and whose members came to think of themselves as rulers for life, accountable to no one) and Cromwell (who eventually dissolved Parliament and ruled as a military dictator, under whose rule the ordinary Englishman had far less liberty than under Charles).

In his struggle with his opponents, Charles considered himself to be contending for two things: the good of the realm and the liberty and well-being of the people, which he believed would be better served by the monarch ruling according to ancient precedent, maintaining the traditional rights of the people as enshrined in the common law, than by a Parliament that ended up denying that it was either bound by the law or accountable to the people; and the Church of England, preaching the doctrine of the undivided Church of the first ten centuries, administering sacraments regarded not as mere psychological aids to devotion but as vehicles of the presence and activity of God in his Church, governed by bishops who had been consecrated by bishops who had been consecrated by bishops... back certainly to the second century, and, as many have believed, back to the Twelve Apostles and to the command of Christ himself.

In his Declaration at Newport, in the last year of his life, he said: I conceive that Episcopal government is most consonant to the Word of God, and of an apostolical institution, as it appears by the Scripture, to have been practiced by the Apostles themselves, and by them committed and derived to particular persons as their substitutes or successors therein and hath ever since to these last times been exercised by Bishops in all the Churches of Christ, and therefore I cannot in conscience consent to abolish the said government. In prison, Charles wrote a letter, which he gave to the Bishop of London to give to his son, the Prince of Wales. I quote a few extracts.

With God, I would have you begin and end, who is King of Kings, the sovereign disposer of the kingdoms of the world, who pulleth down one and setteth up another. The best government and highest sovereignty you can attain to is to be subject to Him, that the scepter of his word and spirit may rule in your heart. The true glory of princes consists in advancing God's glory, in the maintenance of true religion and the Church's good; also in the dispensation of civil power, with justice and honor to the public peace. Above all, I would have you, as I hope you are already, well grounded and settled in your religion, the best profession of which I have ever esteemed that of the Church of England, in which you have been educated; yet I would have your own judgement and reason now sealed to that sacred bond which education hath written, that it may be judiciously your own religion, and not other men's custom or tradition which you profess. In this I charge you to persevere, as coming nearest to God's word for doctrine, and to the primitive examples for government, with some little amendment which I have otherwise expressed, and often offered, though in vain. Your fixation in matters of religion will not be more necessary for your soul's than your kingdom's peace, when God shall bring you to them. When you have done justice to God, your own soul and his Church in the profession and preservation of truth and unity in religion, the next main hinge on which your prosperity will depend and move, is that of civil justice, wherein the settled laws of these kingdoms, to which you are rightly heir, are the most excellent rules you can govern by, which by an admirable temperament give very much to subjects industry, liberty, and happiness; and yet reserve enough to the majesty and prerogative of any king who owns his people as subjects, not as slaves, whose subjection as it preserves their property, peace, and safety, so it will never diminish their rights, nor their ingenious liberties, which consist in the enjoyment of the fruits of their industry and the benefit of those laws to which themselves have consented. Your prerogative is best showed and exercised in remitting rather than in exacting the rigor of the laws; there being nothing worse than legal tyranny. I have offered acts of indemnity and oblivion....

I would have you always propense to the same way, whenever it shall be desired and accepted, let it be granted, not only as an act of state policy and necessity, but of Christian charity and choice. It is all I have now left me, a power to forgive those that have deprived me of all; and I thank God I have a heart to do it, and joy as much in this grace, which God hath given me, as in all my former enjoyments; for this is a greater argument of God's love to me than any prosperity can be. Be confident (as I am) that the most of all sides, who have done amiss, have done so, not out of malice, but misinformation, or misapprehension of things. The more conscious you shall be to your own merits upon your people, the more prone you will be to expect all love and loyalty from them, and to inflict no punishment upon them for former miscarriages; and you will have more inward complacency in pardoning one, than in punishing a thousand. I do require and entreat you, as your father and your King, that you never suffer your heart to receive the least check against or disaffection from the true religion established in the Church of England. I tell you I have tried it, and after much search and many disputes, have concluded it to be the best in the world, not only in the community, as Christian, but also in the special notion, as reformed, keeping the middle way between the pomp of superstitious tyranny, and the meanness of fantastic anarchy. Nor would I have you to entertain any aversion of dislike of Parliaments, which, in their right constitution with freedom and honor, will never hinder or diminish your greatness, but will rather be an interchanging of love, loyalty, and confidence, between a prince and his people. Nothing can be more happy for all than, in fair, grave, and honorable ways, to contribute their counsels in common, enacting all things by public consent, without tyranny or tumults. We must not starve ourselves, because some have surfeited of wholesome food. I know God can – I hope he will – restore me to my rights. I cannot despair, either of his mercy, or of my people's love and pity. At worst, I trust I shall but go before you to a better kingdom, which God hath prepared for me, and me for it, through my Savior Jesus Christ, to whose mercy I commend you, and all mine. Farewell, till we meet, if not on earth, yet in Heaven.

On the day before he was to die, Charles's two youngest children were brought to him. The Princess Elizabeth, at that time twelve years old, later wrote as follows of their meeting: ... He wished me not to grieve and torment myself for him, for that would be a glorious death that he should die, it being for the laws and liberties of this land and for maintaining the true Protestant religion. He bid me read Bishop Andrewes' sermons, Hooker's Ecclesiastical Polity, and Bishop Laud's books against Fisher, which would ground me against popery. He told me he had forgiven all his enemies and hoped God would forgive them also, and commanded all the rest of my brothers and sister to forgive them.

On the day of his death, he rose early and dressed with great care, saying that he was going to his Savior as a bride to a bridegroom, and must dress as befitted such a joyful occasion. He was attended by Bishop Juxton, who read to him from the Scriptures the appointed reading for that day, (Matthew 27, the Passion of Our Lord). Afterwards he was conducted to Whitehall, the place of execution. There, in the building, he received the Holy Communion from the bishop. Afterward, he was offered a meal. He refused, saying that it was fitting that the Holy Communion should be his last food. However, the bishop intervened, pointing out that he had already fasted many hours, that it would be more time yet till he was put to death, and that if he fainted his enemies would say that it was from terror. He yielded to this argument and ate and drank a little. At one o'clock, he came out to the block, and made a speech to the crowd, declaring his innocency of the charges against him, but acknowledging his guilt in that, fearing for his own life and that of his queen, he had not pardoned Thomas Wentworth when Parliament passed a Bill of Attander against him, although he believed him innocent. He declared that he forgave those by whom he was brought to death, and he offered a prayer for the people of the realm. He made a profession of faith, and then knelt at the block. He said to the executioner: "I shall make a short prayer. When I put out my hands, then strike." A minute later he was dead.

After his death, the realm was ruled, first by the Parliament, then by the Army, and then by Cromwell personally, as Lord Protector. Cromwell's military abilities held him in power for ten years, and when he died, his son Richard Cromwell inherited his post, but lacked the ability to maintain control. Within a year, the country invited the late king's son, then in exile in France, to assume the throne as Charles II. Soon after, he remarked, "I see that it is my own fault that I remained so long in exile, for since coming to England I have not met a single man that has not long desired my return." Charles II heeded his father's advice and sought no revenge on those who had put his father to death. However, the new Parliament was of a different mind, and had the principal surviving leaders of the plan to kill the king put to death for treason.

In a day when religious toleration was not widespread, King Charles I was noteworthy for his reluctance to engage in religious persecution of any kind, whether against Romanists or Anabaptists.

His attitude toward accusations of witchcraft is noteworthy. His father, King James I, had written a book on witchcraft, and considered himself an expert on the subject. Under his reign, persecutions of witches were frequent. Public hysteria brought many suspects to the stake. It was Charles's practice to have women accused of witchcraft brought before him, and in most cases, he concluded that they were old and sick or wandering in their wits, and he gave them money and sent them home.

Charles was never a Roman Catholic, and firmly refused all urgings to become one, saying that he believed the Church of England to be more truly Catholic than the Church of Rome. However, there were many Roman Catholics in his family. His mother, Anne of Denmark, had converted to Rome. His own wife, Henrietta Maria, a French princess whom he had married in what was originally a political alliance but ended as a love match, was a Roman Catholic. It was accordingly not surprising that the Puritans accused him of being secretly disposed toward Rome, and that they regarded all his moves toward religious toleration as part of a Roman Catholic plan to seize the government.

James Kiefer, Christian Biographies, By kind permission

MARTYRDOM OF CHARLES I (2)

"The chief arms left me were those only which the ancient Christians were wont to use against their persecutors, prayers and tears. These may serve a good man's turn, if not to conquer as a soldier yet to suffer as a martyr." Charles I, Eikon Basilike

As everything turned against Charles he increasingly saw himself cast in the role of a martyr. He wrote, "The chief arms left me were those only which the ancient Christians were wont to use against their persecutors, prayers and tears. These may serve a good man's turn, if not to conquer as a soldier yet to suffer as a martyr,' in Eikon Basilike.

Charles, dressed in black, refused to plead when put on trial, rather preferring to question the right a few members of the House of Commons had to try at all. After adjourning three times the court then decided that Charles would not be allowed to speak and they said they found him guilty of treason against the people and that he was condemned to death.

Soldiers lined the streets Charles walked through on his way to the scaffold. No one was supposed to hear his last words. Nevertheless two newspaper reporters managed to take down the following words from the martyr-king which were subsequently published in the London newspapers."The people's liberty and freedom consist in having government, in having those laws by which their lives and their goods may be most their own. It is not their having a share in the government. If I would have given way to an arbitrary way, to have all laws changed by the power of the sword, I needed not to have come here; and therefore I tell you that I am the martyr of the people." At this point he said words to Bishop Jexon which subsequently become very famous, "I go from a corruptible to an incorruptible crown, where no disturbance can be."

THE MARTYR'S KING

"True son of our dear Mother, early taught
With her to worship, and for her to die,
Nurs'd in her aisles to more than kingly
  thought,
Oft in her solemn hours we dream thee nigh.
And yearly now, before the Martyr's King,
For thee she offers her maternal tears,
Calls us, like thee, to His dear feet to cling,
And bury in his wounds our earthly fears."

John Keble, The Christian Year

LAST WORDS OF CHARLES I STUART, KING AND MARTYR

"I go from a Corruptible to an Incorruptible Crown"

30 January 1649

"I shall be very little heard of anybody here; I shall therefore speak a word unto you here; indeed I could hold my peace very well, if I did think that holding my peace would make some men think that I submit to the guilt, as well as to the punishment; but I think it is duty to God first and then to my country for to clear myself both as an honest man and a good king and a good Christian. I shall begin with my innocency. In troth I think it not very needful for me to insist long upon this, for all the world knows that I never did begin a with the two Houses of Parliament, and I call God to witness, to whom I must shortly make my account, that I never did intend for to encroach upon their privileges; they began upon me, it is the militia, they be upon, they contest that the militia was mine, but they thought it fit to have it from me; and to be short, if anybody will look to the date the commissions, of their commissions and mine, and likewise to declarations, will see clearly that they began these unhappy troubles, I; so that as the guilt of these enormous crimes that are laid against me hope in God that God will clear me of it, I will not, I am in charity; God forbid that I should lay it upon the two Houses of Parliament there is no necessity of either, I hope they are free of this guilt, for I do believe that ill instruments between them and me has been the chief cause of all this bloodshed; so that by way of speaking as I find my' clear of this, I hope (and pray God) that they may too: yet for all to God forbid that I should be so ill a Christian as not to say that God's judgements are just upon me: many times he does pay justice by unjust sentence, that is ordinary; I will only say this, that an unjust sentence that I suffered for to take effect is punished now, by an unjust sentence upon me; that is, so far I have said, to show you that I am innocent man.

Now for to show you that I am a good Christian: I hope there is a good man that will bear me witness, that I have forgiven all the world: even those in particular that have been the chief causes of my death who they are, God knows, I do not desire to know, I pray God forgive them. But this is not all; my charity must go farther, I wish that they may repent, for indeed they have committed a great sin in that particular; I pray God with Saint Stephen that they may take the right way to peace of the kingdom, for my charity commands me not only to forgive particular men, but my charity commands me to endeavor to the last gasp the peace of the kingdom: so, sirs, I do with all my soul, and I do hope (there is some here will carry it further) that they may endeavor the peace of the kingdom. Now, sirs, I must show you both how you are out of the way and will put you in a way; first, you are out of the way, for certainly all the way you ever had yet as I could find by anything is in the way of conquest; certainly this is an ill way; for conquest, sir, in my opinion is never just, except there be a good just cause, either for the matter of wrong or just title, and then if you go beyond it, the first quarrel that you have to it, that makes it unjust at the end, that was just as first: But if it be only matter of conquest, then it is a great robbery; as a pirate said to Alexander, that he was the great robber, he was but a petty robber; and so, sir, I do think the way that you are in, is much out of the way.

Now, sir, for to put you in the way, believe it you will never do right, nor God will never prosper you, until you give God his due, the King his due (that is, my successor), and the people their due; I am as much for them as any of you; you must give. God his due by regulating rightly his church according to his Scripture which is now out of order: for to set you in a way particularly now I cannot, but only this, a national synod freely called, freely debating among themselves, must settle this, when that every opinion is freely and clearly heard.

For the king, indeed I will not. . . [At this point a gentleman touched the axe and the King said, "Hurt not the axe that may hurt me."] For the King: the laws of the land will clearly instruct you for that; therefore because it concerns my own particular, I only give you a touch of it. For the people. And truly I desire their liberty and freedom, as much as anybody whomsoever; but I must tell you that their liberty and their freedom consists in having of government those laws by which their life and their goods may he most their own. It is not for having share in government, sir, that is nothing pertaining to them. A subject and a sovereign are clean different things; and therefore, until they do that, I mean, that you do put the people in that liberty as I say, certainly they will never enjoy themselves.

Sirs, it was for this that now I am come here: if I would have given way to an arbitrary way, for to have all laws changed according to the power of the sword, I needed not to have come here; and therefore, I tell you (and I pray God it be not laid to your charge) that I am the martyr of the people.

In troth, sirs, I shall not hold you much longer; for I will only say this to you, that in truth I could have desired some little time longer, because that I would have put this I have said in a little more order, and a little better digested, than I have done; and therefore I hope you excuse me.

I have delivered my conscience, I pray God, that you do take those courses that are best for the kingdom, and your own salvation.

[Dr Juxon: will Your Majesty (though it may be very well known Your Majesty's affections to religion, yet it may be expected that you should) say somewhat to the world's satisfaction.]

I thank you very heartily, my lord, for that; I had almost forgotten it. In troth, sirs, my conscience in religion, I think, is very well known to the world; and therefore I declare before you all that I die a Christian according to the profession of the Church of England, as I found it left me by my father; and this honest man [pointing to Dr Juxon] will witness it, Sirs, excuse me for this same. I have a good cause, and I have a gracious God; I will say no more. I go from a corruptible to an incorruptible crown, where no disturbance can be, no disturbance in the world."

Persecution in the Valleys of Piedmont in the Seventeenth Century

Pope Clement VIII sent missionaries into the valleys of Piedmont, to induce the Protestants to renounce their religion. One of the first people who attracted the attention of the Papists was Mr Sebastian Basan, a zealous Protestant, who was seized by the missionaries, imprisoned, tortured for fifteen months, and then burnt alive.

Before the persecution began, the missionaries used kidnappers to steal the Protestants' children, so that they could be brought up Roman Catholics. Later, they took these children away by force, and killed any parents who objected.

This was followed by a most cruel ordeal, which was sanctioned by Duke Andrew Gastaldo on 25th January 1655. This order set out that the head of every family, with the members of that family, of the reformed religion, living in Lucerne, St Giovanni, Bibiana, Campiglione, St Secondo, Lucernetta, La Torre, Fenile and Bricherassio, should, within three days, leave. If they refused to do this they would be killed and their goods and property confiscated, unless they became Roman Catholics.

The suddenness of the order affected everyone. Notwithstanding this the Papists drove them from their homes and many people perished on the mountains through the severity of the winter or from lack of food. Those who remained behind were murdered by the Popish inhabitants or shot by the troops. These cruelties are described in a letter from a Protestant who managed to escape:"The army, having got footing, became very numerous by the addition of a multitude of the neighboring Popish inhabitants, who, finding that we were the destined prey of the plunderers, fell upon us with impetuous fury. As well as the Duke of Savoy's troops, and the Roman Catholic inhabitants, there were several regiments of French auxiliaries, some companies belonging to the Irish brigades, and several bands formed from outlaws, smugglers, and prisoners, who had been promised pardon and liberty in this world; and absolution in the next, for assisting to exterminate the Protestants from Piedmont.

"This armed multitude being encouraged by the Roman Catholic bishops and monks fell upon the Protestants in a most furious manner. All now was horror and despair: blood stained the floors of the houses, dead bodies bestrewed the streets, and groans and cried shocked the ears of humanity from every quarter. In one village they vented their cruelty on 150 women and children after the men had fled, beheading the women, and dashing out the brains of the children."

It was with reference to this persecution that Milton wrote the following well-known sonnet:

Avenge, O Lord, thy slaughtered saints, whose bones
Lie scattered on the Alpine mountains cold;
Even them who kept thy truth so pure of old;
When all our fathers worshiped stocks and stones,
Forget not; in thy book record their groans,
Who were thy sheep, and in thine ancient fold,
Slain by the bloody Piedmontese, that rolled
Mother with infant down the rocks. Their moans
The vales redoubled to the hills, and they
To heaven. Their martyr'd blood and ashes sow
O'er all the Italian fields, where still doth sway
The triple tyrant: that from these may grow
A hundredfold, who, having learned thy way
Early, may fly the Babylonian woe.

John Foxe, The Book of Martyrs, revised with notes and an appendix by W. Bramley-Moore, London, 1869, pp 207-11

Rawlins White

Among the more humble people who suffered martyrdom was Rawlins White, a fisherman, from Cardiff. He was brought before the Bishop of Llandaff and the bishop declared that he had been sent for because of his heretical opinions and because through his instruction he had led many people into error. In conclusion, he exhorted him to consider how own state, and offered him favor if he recanted.

When the bishop had finished, Rawlins boldly replied, "My lord, I thank God I am a Christian man, and I hold no opinions contrary to the Word of God; and if I do, I desire to be reformed out of the Word of God, as a Christian ought to be."

The bishop then told him plainly that he must proceed against him according to law, and condemn him as a heretic.

"Proceed in your law, in God's name,' said the fearless Rawlins; "but for a heretic you shall never condemn me while the world stands."

"But,' said the bishop to his company, "before we proceed any further with him, let us pray to God that he would send some spark of grace upon him, and it may so chance that God, through our prayers, will here turn his heart." Accordingly, having prayed, the bishop said, "Now, Rawlins, wilt thou revoke thy opinions or not?'

The man of truth replied, "Surely, my lord, Rawlins you left me, Rawlins you find me, and, by God's grace, Rawlins I will continue."

The bishop then had the definitive sentence read. Rawlins was then dismissed and taken to Cardiff, where he was put into the prison of the town, called Cockmarel, a very dark and loathsome dungeon.

The day being at hand whereon the servant of God should crown his faith by martyrdom, he spent the night before in solemn preparation.

On perceiving that his time was near, he sent to his wife, and desired her by the messenger that she should make ready and send him his wedding garment, meaning his shirt in which he should be burned. This request, or rather commandment, his wife performed with grief of heart, and sent it to him early in the morning.

The hour of his execution having come, the martyr was brought out of prison, having on his body the long shirt, which he called his wedding garment, and an old russet-coat which he was wont to wear. Besides this, he had upon his legs an old pair of leather buskins. And being thus equipped, he was accompanied, or rather guarded, with a great number of bills and weapons, which sight when he beheld, "Alas!' said he, "what meaneth all this? By God's grace, I will not run away: with all my heart and mind I give God most hearty thanks that he hath made me worthy to abide all this for his holy name's sake."

He now came to a place where his poor wife and children stood weeping and making great lamentation, the sudden sight of whom so pierced his heart, that the tears trickled down his face. But soon afterwards, as though he were ashamed of this infirmity of his flesh, he began to be, as it were, angry with himself; insomuch that, striking his chest with his hand, he said, "Ah, flesh, hinderest thou me so? Well, I tell thee, do what thou canst, thou shalt not, by God's grace, have the victory."

But this time he approached the stake that had been set up, and was surrounded with some wood for the fire, which, when he beheld, he went forward boldly; but in going towards the stake, he fell down upon his knees, and kissed the ground; and, in rising, a little earth stuck to his nose, when he said, "Earth unto earth, and dust unto dust; thou art my mother, and unto thee I shall return."

Then he went cheerfully, and set his back close to the stake. A smith then came with a great chain of iron, whom when he saw, he cast up his hand, and, with a loud voice, gave God great thanks.

When the smith had fastened him to the stake, the officers began to lay on more wood, with a little straw and reeds, wherein the good old man was no less occupied than the rest; for as far as he could reach his hands, he would pluck the straw and reeds, and lay it about him in places most convenient for his speedy dispatch.

When all things were ready, directly over against the stake in the face of Rawlins White, there was a stand erected, which a priest mounted and addressed the people, who were numerous, because it was market day. When Rawlins perceived him, and considered why he came, he, reaching a little straw unto himself, made two little stays, and set them under his elbows. The priest proceeded with the sermon, and began to inveigh against Rawlins' opinions, in which harangue he cited the place of Scripture whereby the idolatrous mass is commonly defended. When Rawlins perceived that he went about not only to preach and teach the people false doctrine, but also to confirm it by Scripture, he suddenly started up, and beckoned his hands to the people, saying twice, "Come hither, good people, and hear not a false prophet preaching." Then said he unto the preacher, "Ah, thou wicked hypocrite! Dost thou presume to prove thy false doctrine by Scripture?'

Upon this, fearing the effects of his truth upon the people, some that stood by cried out, "Put fire! Put fire!' which being done, the straw and reeds cast up a great and sudden flame. While the martyr was being consumed, which was a somewhat long process, he cried with a loud voice, "O Lord, receive my spirit!' until he could not open his mouth. At last, the extremity of the fire was so vehement against his legs, that they were wasted before the rest of his body was hurt, which made his body fall over the chain into the fire sooner than it would have done. So perished a fisherman, one of the noble army of martyrs, whose brightest ornaments are some of the rough fishermen who mended their nets, in old time, on the shore of Gennesaret.

John Foxe, The Book of Martyrs, revised with notes and an appendix by W. Bramley-Moore, London, 1869, pp 482-87

Christopher Waid

"Show some good upon me, O Lord, that they which hate me may see it, and be ashamed: because thou, Lord, hast helped me, and comforted me." Psalm 86:17

Christopher Waid, a linen-weaver, was condemned for heresy, by Maurice, Bishop of Rochester, and sentenced to be burnt at Dartford, which was his native town. The usual spot for executions was a place called the Brimth, a gravel pit, about a quarter of a mile out of the town; and it was decided that Waid should suffer there. Accordingly, on the morning appointed for his death, a cart was sent early from Dartford with the stake, a load of faggots and tall wood, and a good supply of reeds, that all might be in readiness for the arrival of the martyr. About ten o'clock Christopher Waid and one Margaret Polley (a widow who had been previously condemned for heresy) arrived, both riding pinioned, and accompanied by the sheriff, with a large retinue, and many other gentlemen.

When Mrs Polley saw in the distance the large crowd assembled round the gravel pit where they were to suffer, she said, cheerfully, to Waid, "You may rejoice to see such a company gathered to celebrate your marriage this day."

The procession passed the place, and proceeded down the town, where Mrs Polley was left until the sheriff returned from Waid's execution. Christopher had his clothes taken off in an inn, where he put on a long white shirt, which was sent for him by his wife, and being again pinioned, he proceeded on foot to the place of execution. When he reached the stake, he put his arms round it and kissed it, he then put his back against it, and stood in a pitch barrel, brought for that purpose; a smith brought a hoop of iron, and fastening two staples under his arms, made him fast to the stake. When he was settled, he lifted up his eyes and hands to heaven, and repeated the last verse of the 86th Psalm: "Show some good upon me, O Lord, that they which hate me may see it, and be ashamed: because thou, Lord, hast helped me, and comforted me." A pulpit had been erected on a little hillock near the stake, which a friar entered with a book in his hand. Immediately Waid espied him, he called earnestly to the people to take heed of the doctrine of the whore of Babylon, and to embrace the gospel as preached in King Edward's time. While he was thus speaking, the sheriff interrupted him, saying, "Be quiet, Ward, and die patiently."

"I am quiet,' said he, "I thank God, Mr Sheriff, and so trust to die." During this time the friar stood still, making as though he was going to speak, but whether astonished at Waid's earnestness, or thinking it hopeless to make the people listen to him, he suddenly came down, and went away to the town. The reeds were then piled about Waid, who arranged them himself, so as to leave an opening for his face, that his voice might be heard. His enemies, perceiving that, kept throwing faggots at his face, but as long as he could he pushed them aside again, though his face was much hurt by the end of one which struck him. When the fire was applied he showed no signs of fear or impatience, but often cried out, "Lord Jesus, receive my soul." At length his voice could no longer be heard, but even after he was dead his hands remained clasped over his head, as if in the act of prayer; and it pleased God to show him this token for good, vindicating his own character as a hearer and an answerer of prayer, to the encouragement of the martyr, and to the confusion and shame of the enemy, which is the due promotion of fools.

John Foxe, The Book of Martyrs, revised with notes and an appendix by W. Bramley-Moore, London, 1869, pp 543-44

Rise and Progress of the Protestant Religion in Ireland; with an Account of the Barbarous Massacre of 1641

The gloom of popery had overshadowed Ireland from its first establishment there until the reign of Henry VIII when the rays of the Gospel began to dispel the darkness, and afford that light which until then had been unknown in that island. The abject ignorance in which the people were held, with the absurd and superstitious notions they entertained, were sufficiently evident to many; and the artifices of their priests were so conspicuous, that several persons of distinction, who had hitherto been strenuous papists, would willingly have endeavored to shake off the yoke, and embrace the Protestant religion; but the natural ferocity of the people, and their strong attachment to the ridiculous doctrines which they had been taught, made the attempt dangerous. It was, however, at length undertaken, though attended with the most horrid and disastrous consequences.

The introduction of the Protestant religion into Ireland may be principally attributed to George Browne, an Englishman, who was consecrated archbishop of Dublin on the nineteenth of March, 1535. He had formerly been an Augustine friar, and was promoted to the miter on account of his merit.

After having enjoyed his dignity about five years, he, at the time that Henry VIII was suppressing the religious houses in

England, caused all the relics and images to be removed out of the two cathedrals in Dublin, and the other churches in his diocese; in the place of which he caused to be put up the Lord's Prayer, the Creed, and the Ten Commandments.

A short time after this he received a letter from Thomas Cromwell, lord-privy seal, informing him that Henry VIII having thrown off the papal supremacy in England, was determined to do the like in Ireland; and that he thereupon had appointed him (Archbishop Browne) one of the commissioners for seeing this order put in execution. The archbishop answered that he had employed his utmost endeavors at the hazard of his life, to cause the Irish nobility and gentry to acknowledge Henry as their supreme head, in matters both spiritual and temporal; but had met with a most violent opposition, especially from George, archbishop of Armagh; that this prelate had, in a speech to his clergy, laid a curse on all those who should own his highness' supremacy: adding, that their isle, called in the Chronicles Insula Sacra, or the Holy Island, belonged to none but the bishop of Rome, and that the king's progenitors had received it from the pope. He observed likewise, that the archbishop and clergy of Armagh had each despatched a courier to Rome; and that it would be necessary for a parliament to be called in Ireland, to pass an act of supremacy, the people not regarding the king's commission without the sanction of the legislative assembly. He concluded with observing, that the popes had kept the people in the most profound ignorance; that the clergy were exceedingly illiterate; that the common people were more zealous in their blindness than the saints and martyrs had been in the defense of truth at the beginning of the Gospel; and that it was to be feared that Shan O'Neal, a chieftain of great power in the northern part of the island, was decidedly opposed to the king's commission.

In pursuance of this advice, the following year a parliament was summoned to meet at Dublin, by order of Leonard Grey, at that time lord-lieutenant. At this assembly Archbishop Browne made a speech, in which he set forth that the bishops of Rome used, anciently, to acknowledge emperors, kings, and princes, to be supreme in their own dominions; and, therefore, that he himself would vote King Henry VIII as supreme in all matters, both ecclesiastical and temporal. He concluded with saying that whosoever should refuse to vote for this act, was not a true subject of the king. This speech greatly startled the other bishops and lords; but at length, after violent debates, the king's supremacy was allowed.

Two years after this, the archbishop wrote a second letter to Lord Cromwell, complaining of the clergy, and hinting at the machinations which the pope was then carrying on against the advocates of the Gospel. This letter is dated from Dublin, in April, 1538; and among other matters, the archbishop says, "A bird may be taught to speak with as much sense as many of the clergy do in this country. These, though not scholars, yet are crafty to cozen the poor common people and to dissuade them from following his highness orders. The country folk here much hate your lordship, and despitefully call you, in their Irish tongue, the Blacksmith's Son. As a friend, I desire your lordship to look well to your noble person. Rome hath a great kindness for the duke of Norfolk, and great favors for this nation, purposely to oppose his highness." A short time after this, the pope sent over to Ireland (directed to the archbishop of Armagh and his clergy) a bull of excommunication against all who had, or should own the king's supremacy within the Irish nation; denouncing a curse on all of them, and theirs, who should not, within forty days, acknowledge to their confessors, that they had done amiss in so doing.

Archbishop Browne gave notice of this in a letter dated, Dublin, May, 1538. Part of the form of confession, or vow, sent over to these Irish papists, ran as follows: "I do further declare him or here, father or mother, brother or sister, son or daughter, husband or wife, uncle or aunt, nephew or niece, kinsman or kinswoman, master or mistress, and all others, nearest or dearest relations, friend or acquaintance whatsoever, accursed, that either do or shall hold, for the time to come, any ecclesiastical or civil power above the authority of the Mother Church; or that do or shall obey, for the time to come, any of her, the Mother of Churches' opposers or enemies, or contrary to the same, of which I have here sworn unto: so God, the Blessed Virgin, St. Peter, St. Paul, and the Holy Evangelists, help me," etc. is an exact agreement with the doctrines promulgated by the Councils of Lateran and Constance, which expressly declare that no favor should be shown to heretics, nor faith kept with them; that they ought to be excommunicated and condemned, and their estates confiscated, and that princes are obliged, by a solemn oath, to root them out of their respective dominions.

How abominable a church must that be, which thus dares to trample upon all authority! How besotted the people who regard the injunctions of such a church! In the archbishop's last-mentioned letter, dated May, 1538, he says: "His highness' viceroy of this nation is of little or no power with the old natives. Now both English and Irish begin to oppose your lordship's orders, and to lay aside their national quarrels, which I fear will (if anything will) cause a foreigner to invade this nation." Not long after this, Archbishop Browne seized one Thady O'Brian, a Franciscan friar, who had in his possession a paper sent from Rome, dated May, 1538, and directed to O'Neal. In this letter were the following words: "His Holiness, Paul, now pope, and the council of the fathers, have lately found, in Rome, a prophecy of one St. Lacerianus, an Irish bishop of Cashel, in which he saith that the Mother Church of Rome falleth, when, in Ireland, the Catholic faith is overcome. Therefore, for the glory of the Mother Church, the honor of St. Peter, and your own secureness, suppress heresy, and his holiness' enemies." This Thady O'Brian, after further examination and search made, was pilloried, and kept close prisoner until the king's orders arrived in what manner he should be further disposed of. But order coming over from England that he was to be hanged, he laid violent hands on himself in the castle of Dublin. His body was afterwards carried to Gallows-green, where, after being hanged up for some time, it was interred.

After the accession of Edward VI to the throne of England, an order was directed to Sir Anthony Leger, the lord-deputy of Ireland, commanding that the liturgy in English be forthwith set up in Ireland, there to be observed within the several bishoprics, cathedrals, and parish churches; and it was first read in Christ-church, Dublin, on Easter day, 1551, before the said Sir Anthony, Archbishop Browne, and others. Part of the royal order for this purpose was as follows: "Whereas, our gracious father, King Henry VIII taking into consideration the bondage and heavy yoke that his true and faithful subjects sustained, under the jurisdiction of the bishop of Rome; how several fabulous stories and lying wonders misled our subjects; dispensing with the sins of our nations, by their indulgences and pardons, for gain; purposely to cherish all evil vices, as robberies, rebellions, thefts, whoredoms, blasphemy, idolatry, etc., our gracious father hereupon dissolved all priories, monasteries, abbeys, and other pretended religious houses; as being but nurseries for vice or luxury, more than for sacred learning," etc.

On the day after the Common Prayer was first used in Christchurch, Dublin, the following wicked scheme was projected by the papists: In the church was left a marble image of Christ, holding a reed in his hand, with a crown of thorns on his head. Whilst the English service (the Common Prayer) was being read before the lord-lieutenant, the archbishop of Dublin, the privy-council, the lord-mayor, and a great congregation, blood was seen to run through the crevices of the crown of thorns, and trickle down the face of the image. On this, some of the contrivers of the imposture cried aloud, "See how our Savior's image sweats blood! But it must necessarily do this, since heresy is come into the church." Immediately many of the lower order of people, indeed the vulgar of all ranks, were terrified at the sight of so miraculous and undeniable an evidence of the divine displeasure; they hastened from the church, convinced that the doctrines of Protestantism emanated from an infernal source, and that salvation was only to be found in the bosom of their own infallible Church.

This incident, however ludicrous it may appear to the enlightened reader, had great influence over the minds of the ignorant Irish, and answered the ends of the impudent impostors who contrived it, so far as to check the progress of the reformed religion in Ireland very materially; many persons could not resist the conviction that there were many errors and corruptions in the Romish Church, but they were awed into silence by this pretended manifestation of Divine wrath, which was magnified beyond measure by the bigoted and interested priesthood.

We have very few particulars as to the state of religion in Ireland during the remaining portion of the reign of Edward VI and the greater part of that of Mary. Towards the conclusion of the barbarous sway of that relentless bigot, she attempted to extend her inhuman persecutions to this island; but her diabolical intentions were happily frustrated in the following providential manner, the particulars of which are related by historians of good authority.

Mary had appointed Dr. Pole (an agent of the bloodthirsty Bonner) one of the commissioners for carrying her barbarous intentions into effect. He having arrived at Chester with his commission, the mayor of that city, being a papist, waited upon him; when the doctor taking out of his cloak bag a leathern case, said to him, "Here is a commission that shall lash the heretics of Ireland." The good woman of the house being a Protestant, and having a brother in Dublin, named John Edmunds, was greatly troubled at what she heard. But watching her opportunity, whilst the mayor was taking his leave, and the doctor politely accompanying him downstairs, she opened the box, took out the commission, and in its stead laid a sheet of paper, with a pack of cards, and the knave of clubs at top. The doctor, not suspecting the trick that had been played him, put up the box, and arrived with it in Dublin, in September, 1558.

Anxious to accomplish the intentions of his "pious" mistress, he immediately waited upon Lord Fitz-Walter, at that time viceroy, and presented the box to him; which being opened, nothing was found in it but a pack of cards. This startling all the persons present, his lordship said, "We must procure another commission; and in the meantime let us shuffle the cards." Dr. Pole, however, would have directly returned to England to get another commission; but waiting for a favorable wind, news arrived that Queen Mary was dead, and by this means the Protestants escaped a most cruel persecution. The above relation as we before observed, is confirmed by historians of the greatest credit, who add, that Queen Elizabeth settled a pension of forty pounds per annum upon the above mentioned Elizabeth Edmunds, for having thus saved the lives of her Protestant subjects.

During the reigns of Elizabeth and James I, Ireland was almost constantly agitated by rebellions and insurrections, which, although not always taking their rise from the difference of religious opinions, between the English and Irish, were aggravated and rendered more bitter and irreconcilable from that cause. The popish priests artfully exaggerated the faults of the English government, and continually urged to their ignorant and prejudiced hearers the lawfulness of killing the Protestants, assuring them that all Catholics who were slain in the prosecution of so pious an enterprise, would be immediately received into everlasting felicity. The naturally ungovernable dispositions of the Irish, acted upon by these designing men, drove them into continual acts of barbarous and unjustifiable violence; and it must be confessed that the unsettled and arbitrary nature of the authority exercised by the English governors, was but little calculated to gain their affections. The Spaniards, too, by landing forces in the south, and giving every encouragement to the discontented natives to join their standard, kept the island in a continual state of turbulence and warfare. In 1601, they disembarked a body of four thousand men at Kinsale, and commenced what they called "the Holy War for the preservation of the faith in Ireland;" they were assisted by great numbers of the Irish, but were at length totally defeated by the deputy, Lord Mountjoy, and his officers.

This closed the transactions of Elizabeth's reign with respect to Ireland; an interval of apparent tranquillity followed, but the popish priesthood, ever restless and designing, sought to undermine by secret machinations that government and that faith which they durst no longer openly attack. The pacific reign of James afforded them the opportunity of increasing their strength and maturing their schemes, and under his successor, Charles I, their numbers were greatly increased by titular Romish archbishops, bishops, deans, vicars-general, abbots, priests, and friars; for which reason, in 1629, the public exercise of the popish rites and ceremonies was forbidden.

But notwithstanding this, soon afterwards, the Romish clergy erected a new popish university in the city of Dublin. They also proceeded to build monasteries and nunneries in various parts of the kingdom; in which places these very Romish clergy, and the chiefs of the Irish, held frequent meetings; and from thence, used to pass to and fro, to France, Spain, Flanders, Lorraine, and Rome; where the detestable plot of 1641 was hatching by the family of the O'Neals and their followers.

A short time before the horrid conspiracy broke out, which we are now going to relate, the papists in Ireland had presented a remonstrance to the lords-justice of that kingdom, demanding the free exercise of their religion, and a repeal of all laws to the contrary; to which both houses of parliament in England solemnly answered that they would never grant any toleration to the popish religion in that kingdom.

This further irritated the papists to put in execution the diabolical plot concerted for the destruction of the Protestants; and it failed not of the success wished for by its malicious and rancorous projectors.

The design of this horrid conspiracy was that a general insurrection should take place at the same time throughout the kingdom, and that all the Protestants, without exception, should be murdered. The day fixed for this horrid massacre, was the twenty-third of October, 1641, the feast of Ignatius Loyola, founder of the Jesuits; and the chief conspirators in the principal parts of the kingdom made the necessary preparations for the intended conflict.

In order that this detested scheme might the more infallibly succeed, the most distinguished artifices were practiced by the papists; and their behavior in their visits to the Protestants, at this time, was with more seeming kindness than they had hitherto shown, which was done the more completely to effect the inhuman and treacherous designs then meditating against them.

The execution of this savage conspiracy was delayed until the approach of winter, that sending troops from England might be attended with greater difficulty. Cardinal Richelieu, the French minister, had promised the conspirators a considerable supply of men and money; and many Irish officers had given the strongest assurances that they would heartily concur with their Catholic brethren, as soon as the insurrection took place.

The day preceding that appointed for carrying this horrid design into execution was now arrived, when, happily, for the metropolis of the kingdom, the conspiracy was discovered by one Owen O'Connelly, an Irishman, for which most signal service the English Parliament voted him 500 pounds and a pension of 200 pounds during his life.

So very seasonably was this plot discovered, even but a few hours before the city and castle of Dublin were to have been surprised, that the lords-justice had but just time to put themselves, and the city, in a proper posture of defense. Lord M'Guire, who was the principal leader here, with his accomplices, was seized the same evening in the city; and in their lodgings were found swords, hatchets, pole-axes, hammers, and such other instruments of death as had been prepared for the destruction and extirpation of the Protestants in that part of the kingdom.

Thus was the metropolic happily preserved; but the bloody part of the intended tragedy was past prevention. The conspirators were in arms all over the kingdom early in the morning of the day appointed, and every Protestant who fell in their way was immediately murdered. No age, no sex, no condition, was spared. The wife weeping for her butchered husband, and embracing her helpless children, was pierced with them, and perished by the same stroke. The old, the young, the vigorous, and the infirm, underwent the same fate, and were blended in one common ruin. In vain did flight save from the first assault, destruction was everywhere let loose, and met the hunted victims at every turn. In vain was recourse had to relations, to companions, to friends; all connections were dissolved; and death was dealt by that hand from which protection was implored and expected. Without provocation, without opposition, the astonished English, living in profound peace, and, as they thought, full security, were massacred by their nearest neighbors, with whom they had long maintained a continued intercourse of kindness and good offices. Nay, even death was the slightest punishment inflicted by these monsters in human form; all the tortures which wanton cruelty could invent, all the lingering pains of body, the anguish of mind, the agonies of despair, could not satiate revenge excited without injury, and cruelly derived from no just cause whatever. Depraved nature, even perverted religion, though encouraged by the utmost license, cannot reach to a greater pitch of ferocity than appeared in these merciless barbarians. Even the weaker sex themselves, naturally tender to their own sufferings, and compassionate to those of others, have emulated their robust companions in the practice of every cruelty. The very children, taught by example and encouraged by the exhortation of their parents, dealt their feeble blows on the dead carcasses of the defenseless children of the English.

Nor was the avarice of the Irish sufficient to produce the least restraint on their cruelty. Such was their frenzy, that the cattle they had seized, and by repine had made their own, were, because they bore the name of English, wontonly slaughtered, or, when covered with wounds, turned loose into the woods, there to perish by slow and lingering torments.

The commodious habitations of the planters were laid in ashes, or leveled with the ground. And where the wretched owners had shut themselves up in the houses, and were preparing for defense, they perished in the flames together with their wives and children.

Such is the general description of this unparalleled massacre; but it now remains, from the nature of our work, that we proceed to particulars.

The bigoted and merciless papists had no sooner begun to imbrue their hands in blood than they repeated the horrid tragedy day after day, and the Protestants in all parts of the kingdom fell victims to their fury by deaths of the most unheard-of cruelty.

The ignorant Irish were more strongly instigated to execute the infernal business by the Jesuits, priests, and friars, who, when the day for the execution of the plot was agreed on, recommended in their prayers, diligence in the great design, which they said would greatly tend to the prosperity of the kingdom, and to the advancement of the Catholic cause. They everywhere declared to the common people, that the Protestants were heretics, and ought not to be suffered to live any longer among them; adding that it was no more sin to kill an Englishman than to kill a dog; and that the relieving or protecting them was a crime of the most unpardonable nature.

The papists having besieged the town and castle of Longford, and the inhabitants of the latter, who were Protestants, surrendering on condition of being allowed quarter, the besiegers, the instant the townspeople appeared, attacked them in a most unmerciful manner, their priest, as a signal for the rest to fall on, first ripping open the belly of the English Protestant minister; after which his followers murdered all the rest, some of whom they hanged, others were stabbed or shot, and great numbers knocked on the head with axes provided for the purpose.

The garrison at Sligo was treated in like manner by O'Connor Slygah; who, upon the Protestants quitting their holds, promised them quarter, and to convey them safe over the Curlew mountains, to Roscommon. But he first imprisoned them in a most loathsome jail, allowing them only grains for their food. Afterward, when some papists were merry over their cups, who were come to congratulate their wicked brethren for their victory over these unhappy creatures, those Protestants who survived were brought forth by the White-friars, and were either killed, or precipitated over the bridge into a swift river, where they were soon destroyed. It is added, that this wicked company of White-friars went, some time after, in solemn procession, with holy water in their hands, to sprinkle the river; on pretense of cleansing and purifying it from the stains and pollution of the blood and dead bodies of the heretics, as they called the unfortunate Protestants who were inhumanly slaughtered at this very time.

At Kilmore, Dr. Bedell, bishop of that see, had charitably settled and supported a great number of distressed Protestants, who had fled from their habitations to escape the diabolical cruelties committed by the papists. But they did not long enjoy the consolation of living together; the good prelate was forcibly dragged from his episcopal residence, which was immediately occupied by Dr. Swiney, the popish titular bishop of Kilmore, who said Mass in the church the Sunday following, and then seized on all the goods and effects belonging to the persecuted bishop.

Soon after this, the papists forced Dr. Bedell, his two sons, and the rest of his family, with some of the chief of the Protestants whom he had protected, into a ruinous castle, called Lochwater, situated in a lake near the sea. Here he remained with his companions some weeks, all of them daily expecting to be put to death. The greatest part of them were stripped naked, by which means, as the season was cold, (it being in the month of December) and the building in which they were confined open at the top, they suffered the most severe hardships. They continued in this situation until the seventh of January, when they were all released. The bishop was courteously received into the house of Dennis O'Sheridan, one of his clergy, whom he had made a convert to the Church of England; but he did not long survive this kindness. During his residence here, he spent the whole of his time in religious exercises, the better to fit and prepare himself and his sorrowful companions for their great change, as nothing but certain death was perpetually before their eyes. He was at this time in the seventy-first year of his age, and being afflicted with a violent ague caught in his late cold and desolate habitation on the lake, it soon threw him into a fever of the most dangerous nature. Finding his dissolution at hand, he received it with joy, like one of the primitive martyrs just hastening to his crown of glory. After having addressed his little flock, and exhorted them to patience, in the most pathetic manner, as they saw their own last day approaching, after having solemnly blessed his people, his family, and his children, he finished the course of his ministry and life together, on the seventh day of February 1642.

His friends and relations applied to the intruding bishop for leave to bury him, which was with difficulty obtained; he, at first telling them that the churchyard was holy ground, and should be no longer defiled with heretics: however, leave was at last granted, and though the church funeral service was not used at the solemnity, (for fear of the Irish papists) yet some of the better sort, who had the highest veneration for him while living, attended his remains to the grave. At this interment they discharged a volley of shot, crying out, Requiescat in pace ultimus Anglorum, that is, "May the last of the English rest in peace." Adding, that as he was one of the best so he should be the last English bishop found among them. His learning was very extensive; and he would have given the world a greater proof of it, had he printed all he wrote. Scarce any of his writings were saved; the papists having destroyed most of his papers and his library. He had gathered a vast heap of critical expositions of Scripture, all which with a great trunk full of his manuscripts, fell into the hands of the Irish. Happily his great Hebrew manuscript was preserved, and is now in the library of Emanuel College, Oxford.

In the barony of Terawley, the papists, at the instigation of the friars, compelled above forty English Protestants, some of whom were women and children, to the hard fate of either falling by the sword, or of drowning in the sea. These choosing the latter, were accordingly forced, by the naked weapons of their inexorable persecutors, into the deep, where, with their children in their arms, they first waded up to their chins, and afterwards sunk down and perished together.

In the castle of Lisgool upwards of one hundred and fifty men, women, and children, were all burnt together; and at the castle of Moneah not less than one hundred were all put to the sword. Great numbers were also murdered at the castle of Tullah, which was delivered up to M'Guire on condition of having fair quarter; but no sooner had that base villain got possession of the place than he ordered his followers to murder the people, which was immediately done with the greatest cruelty.

Many others were put to deaths of the most horrid nature, and such as could have been invented only by demons instead of men. Some of them were laid with the center of their backs on the axle-tree of a carriage, with their legs resting on the ground on one side, and their arms and head on the other. In this position, one of the savages scourged the wretched object on the thighs, legs, etc., while another set on furious dogs, who tore to pieces the arms and upper parts of the body; and in this dreadful manner were they deprived of their existence. Great numbers were fastened to horses' tails, and the beasts being set on full gallop by their riders, the wretched victims were dragged along until they expired. Others were hung on lofty gibbets, and a fire being kindled under them, they finished their lives, partly by hanging, and partly by suffocation.

Nor did the more tender sex escape the least particle of cruelty that could be projected by their merciless and furious persecutors. Many women, of all ages, were put to deaths of the most cruel nature. Some, in particular, were fastened with their backs to strong posts, and being stripped to their waists, the inhuman monsters cut off their right breasts with shears, which, of course, put them to the most excruciating torments; and in this position they were left, until, from the loss of blood, they expired.

Such was the savage ferocity of these barbarians, that even unborn infants were dragged from the womb to become victims to their rage. Many unhappy mothers were hung naked in the branches of trees, and their bodies being cut open, the innocent offsprings were taken from them, and thrown to dogs and swine. And to increase the horrid scene, they would oblige the husband to be a spectator before suffering himself.

At the town of Issenskeath they hanged above a hundred Scottish Protestants, showing them no more mercy than they did to the English. M'Guire, going to the castle of that town, desired to speak with the governor, when being admitted, he immediately burnt the records of the county, which were kept there. He then demanded 1000 pounds of the governor, which, having received, he immediately compelled him to hear Mass. and to swear that he would continue to do so. And to complete his horrid barbarities, he ordered the wife and children of the governor to be hanged before his face; besides massacring at least one hundred of the inhabitants. Upwards of one thousand men, women, and children, were driven, in different companies, to Portadown bridge, which was broken in the middle, and there compelled to throw themselves into the water, and such as attempted to reach the shore were knocked on the head.

In the same part of the country, at least four thousand persons were drowned in different places. The inhuman papists, after first stripping them, drove them like beasts to the spot fixed on for their destruction; and if any, through fatigue, or natural infirmities, were slack in their pace, they pricked them with their swords and pikes; and to strike terror on the multitude, they murdered some by the way. Many of these poor wretches, when thrown into the water, endeavored to save themselves by swimming to the shore but their merciless persecutors prevented their endeavors taking effect, by shooting them in the water.

In one place one hundred and forty English, after being driven for many miles stark naked, and in the most severe weather, were all murdered on the same spot, some being hanged, others burnt, some shot, and many of them buried alive; and so cruel were their tormentors that they would not suffer them to pray before they robbed them of their miserable existence.

Other companies they took under pretense of safe conduct, who, from that consideration, proceeded cheerfully on their journey; but when the treacherous papists had got them to a convenient spot, they butchered them all in the most cruel manner.

One hundred and fifteen men, women, and children, were conducted, by order of Sir Phelim O'Neal, to Portadown bridge, where they were all forced into the river, and drowned. One woman, named Campbell, finding no probability of escaping, suddenly clasped one of the chief of the papists in her arms, and held him so fast that they were both drowned together.

In Killyman they massacred forty-eight families, among whom twenty-two were burnt together in one house. The rest were either hanged, shot, or drowned.

In Kilmore, the inhabitants, which consisted of about two hundred families, all fell victims to their rage. Some of them sat in the stocks until they confessed where their money was; after which they put them to death. The whole county was one common scene of butchery, and many thousands perished, in a short time, by sword, famine, fire, water, and others the most cruel deaths, that rage and malice could invent.

These bloody villains showed so much favor to some as to despatch them immediately; but they would by no means suffer them to pray. Others they imprisoned in filthy dungeons, putting heavy bolts on their legs, and keeping them there until they were starved to death.

At Casel they put all the Protestants into a loathsome dungeon, where they kept them together, for several weeks, in the greatest misery. At length they were released, when some of them were barbarously mangled, and left on the highways to perish at leisure; others were hanged, and some were buried in the ground upright, with their heads above the earth, and the papists, to increase their misery, treating them with derision during their sufferings. In the county of Antrim they murdered nine hundred and fifty-four Protestants in one morning; and afterwards about twelve hundred more in that county.

At a town called Lisnegary, they forced twenty-four Protestants into a house, and then setting fire to it, burned them together, counterfeiting their outcries in derision to the others.

Among other acts of cruelty they took two children belonging to an Englishwoman, and dashed out their brains before her face; after which they threw the mother into a river, and she was drowned. They served many other children in the like manner, to the great affliction of their parents, and the disgrace of human nature.

In Kilkenny all the Protestants, without exception, were put to death; and some of them in so cruel a manner, as, perhaps, was never before thought of.

They beat an Englishwoman with such savage barbarity, that she had scarce a whole bone left; after which they threw her into a ditch; but not satisfied with this, they took her child, a girl about six years of age, and after ripping up its belly, threw it to its mother, there to languish until it perished. They forced one man to go to Mass, after which they ripped open his body, and in that manner left him. They sawed another asunder, cut the throat of his wife, and after having dashed out the brains of their child, an infant, threw it to the swine, who greedily devoured it.

After committing these, and several other horrid cruelties, they took the heads of seven Protestants, and among them that of a pious minister, all of which they fixed up at the market cross. They put a gag into the minister's mouth, then slit his cheeks to his ears, and laying a leaf of a Bible before it, bid him preach, for his mouth was wide enough. They did several other things by way of derision, and expressed the greatest satisfaction at having thus murdered and exposed the unhappy Protestants.

It is impossible to conceive the pleasure these monsters took in exercising their cruelty, and to increase the misery of those who fell into their hands, when they butchered them they would say, "Your soul to the devil." One of these miscreants would come into a house with his hands imbued in blood, and boast that it was English blood, and that his sword had pricked the white skins of the Protestants, even to the hilt. When any one of them had killed a Protestant, others would come and receive a gratification in cutting and mangling the body; after which they left it exposed to be devoured by dogs; and when they had slain a number of them they would boast, that the devil was beholden to them for sending so many souls to hell. But it is no wonder they should thus treat the innocent Christians, when they hesitated not to commit blasphemy against God and His most holy Word.

In one place they burnt two Protestant Bibles, and then said they had burnt hell-fire. In the church at Powerscourt they burnt the pulpit, pews, chests, and Bibles belonging to it. They took other Bibles, and after wetting them with dirty water, dashed them in the faces of the Protestants, saying, "We know you love a good lesson; here is an excellent one for you; come to-morrow, and you shall have as good a sermon as this." Some of the Protestants they dragged by the hair of their heads into the church, where they stripped and whipped them in the most cruel manner, telling them, at the same time, that if they came tomorrow, they should hear the like sermon.

In Munster they put to death several ministers in the most shocking manner. One, in particular, they stripped stark naked, and driving him before them, pricked him with swords and darts until he fell down, and expired.

In some places they plucked out the eyes, and cut off the hands of the Protestants, and in that manner turned them into the fields, there to wander out their miserable existence. They obliged many young men to force their aged parents to a river, where they were drowned; wives to assist in hanging their husbands; and mothers to cut the throats of their children.

In one place they compelled a young man to kill his father, and then immediately hanged him. In another they forced a woman to kill her husband, then obliged the son to kill her, and afterward shot him through the head.

At a place called Glaslow, a popish priest, with some others, prevailed on forty Protestants to be reconciled to the Church of Rome. They had no sooner done this than they told them they were in good faith, and that they would prevent their falling from it, and turning heretics, by sending them out of the world, which they did by immediately cutting their throats.

In the county of Tipperary upwards of thirty Protestants, men, women, and children, fell into the hands of the papists, who, after stripping them naked, murdered them with stones, pole-axes, swords, and other weapons.

In the county of Mayo about sixty Protestants, fifteen of whom were ministers, were, upon covenant, to be safely conducted to Galway, by one Edmund Burke and his soldiers; but that inhuman monster by the way drew his sword, as an intimation of his design to the rest, who immediately followed his example, and murdered the whole, some of whom they stabbed, others were run through the body with pikes, and several were drowned.

In Queen's County great numbers of Protestants were put to the most shocking deaths. Fifty or sixty were placed together in one house, which being set on fire, they all perished in the flames. Many were stripped naked, and being fastened to horses by ropes placed round their middles, were dragged through bogs until they expired. Some were hung by the feet to tenterhooks driven into poles; and in that wretched posture left until they perished. Others were fastened to the trunk of a tree, with a branch at top. Over this branch hung one arm, which principally supported the weight of the body; and one of the legs was turned up, and fastened to the trunk, while the other hung straight. In this dreadful and uneasy posture did they remain as long as life would permit, pleasing spectacles to their bloodthirsty persecutors.

At Clownes seventeen men were buried alive; and an Englishman, his wife, five children, and a servant maid, were all hanged together, and afterward thrown into a ditch. They hung many by the arms to branches of trees, with a weight to their feet; and others by the middle, in which posture they left them until they expired. Several were hanged on windmills, and before they were half dead, the barbarians cut them in pieces with their swords. Others, both men, women, and children, they cut and hacked in various parts of their bodies, and left them wallowing in their blood to perish where they fell. One poor woman they hanged on a gibbet, with her child, an infant about a twelve-month old, the latter of whom was hanged by the neck with the hair of its mother's head, and in that manner finished its short but miserable existence.

In the county of Tyrone no less than three hundred Protestants were drowned in one day; and many others were hanged, burned, and otherwise put to death. Dr. Maxwell, rector of Tyrone, lived at this time near Armagh, and suffered greatly from these merciless savages. This person, in his examination, taken upon oath before the king's commissioners, declared that the Irish papists owned to him, that they, at several times, had destroyed, in one place, 12,000 Protestants, whom they inhumanly slaughtered at Glynwood, in their flight from the county of Armagh.

As the river Bann was not fordable, and the bridge broken down, the Irish forced thither at different times, a great number of unarmed, defenseless Protestants, and with pikes and swords violently thrust about one thousand into the river, where they miserably perished.

Nor did the cathedral of Armagh escape the fury of those barbarians, it being maliciously set on fire by their leaders, and burnt to the ground. And to extirpate, if possible, the very race of those unhappy Protestants, who lived in or near Armagh, the Irish first burnt all their houses, and then gathered together many hundreds of those innocent people, young and old, on pretense of allowing them a guard and safe conduct to Colerain, when they treacherously fell on them by the way, and inhumanly murdered them.

The like horrid barbarities with those we have particularized, were practiced on the wretched Protestants in almost all parts of the kingdom; and, when an estimate was afterward made of the number who were sacrificed to gratify diabolical souls of the papists, it amounted to one hundred and fifty thousand. But it now remains that we proceed to the particulars that followed.

These desperate wretches, flushed and grown insolent with success, (though by methods attended with such excessive barbarities as perhaps not to be equaled) soon got possession of the castle of Newry, where the king's stores and ammunition were lodged; and, with as little difficulty, made themselves masters of Dundalk. They afterward took the town of Ardee, where they murdered all the Protestants, and then proceeded to Drogheda. The garrison of Drogheda was in no condition to sustain a siege, notwithstanding which, as often as the Irish renewed their attacks they were vigorously repulsed by a very unequal number of the king's forces, and a few faithful Protestant citizens under Sir Henry Tichborne, the governor, assisted by the Lord Viscount Moore. The siege of Drogheda began on the thirtieth of November, 1641, and held until the fourth of March, 1642, when Sir Phelim O'Neal, and the Irish miscreants under him were forced to retire.

In the meantime ten thousand troops were sent from Scotland to the remaining Protestants in Ireland, which being properly divided in the most capital parts of the kingdom, happily eclipsed the power of the Irish savages; and the Protestants for a time lived in tranquillity.

In the reign of King James II they were again interrupted, for in a parliament held at Dublin in the year 1689, great numbers of the Protestant nobility, clergy, and gentry of Ireland, were attainted of high treason. The government of the kingdom was, at that time, invested in the earl of Tyrconnel, a bigoted papist, and an inveterate enemy to the Protestants. By his orders they were again persecuted in various parts of the kingdom. The revenues of the city of Dublin were seized, and most of the churches converted into prisons. And had it not been for the resolution and uncommon bravery of the garrisons in the city of Londonderry, and the town of Inniskillin, there had not one place remained for refuge to the distressed Protestants in the whole kingdom; but all must have been given up to King James, and to the furious popish party that governed him.

The remarkable siege of Londonderry was opened on the eighteenth of April, 1689, by twenty thousand papists, the flower of the Irish army. The city was not properly circumstanced to sustain a siege, the defenders consisting of a body of raw undisciplined Protestants, who had fled thither for shelter, and half a regiment of Lord Mountjoy's disciplined soldiers, with the principal part of the inhabitants, making it all only seven thousand three hundred and sixty-one fighting men.

The besieged hoped, at first, that their stores of corn and other necessaries, would be sufficient; but by the continuance of the siege their wants increased; and these became at last so heavy that for a considerable time before the siege was raised a pint of coarse barley, a small quantity of greens, a few spoonfuls of starch, with a very moderate proportion of horse flesh, were reckoned a week's provision for a soldier. And they were, at length, reduced to such extremities that they ate dogs, cats, and mice.

Their miseries increasing with the siege, many, through mere hunger and want, pined and languished away, or fell dead in the streets. And it is remarkable, that when their long-expected succors arrived from England, they were upon the point of being reduced to this alternative, either to preserve their existence by eating each other, or attempting to fight their way through the Irish, which must have infallibly produced their destruction.

These succors were most happily brought by the ship Mountjoy of Derry, and the Phoenix of Colerain, at which time they had only nine lean horses left with a pint of meal to each man. By hunger, and the fatigues of war, their seven thousand three hundred and sixty-one fighting men were reduced to four thousand three hundred, one fourth part of whom were rendered unserviceable.

As the calamities of the besieged were great, so likewise were the terrors and sufferings of their Protestant friends and relations; all of whom (even women and children) were forcibly driven from the country thirty miles round, and inhumanly reduced to the sad necessity of continuing some days and nights without food or covering, before the walls of the town; and were thus exposed to the continual fire both of the Irish army from without and the shot of their friends from within.

But the succors from England happily arriving put an end to their affliction; and the siege was raised on the thirty-first of July, having been continued upwards of three months.

The day before the siege of Londonderry was raised the Inniskillers engaged a body of six thousand Irish Roman Catholics, at Newton, Butler, or Crown-Castle, of whom near five thousand were slain. This, with the defeat at Londonderry, dispirited the papists, and they gave up all farther attempts to persecute the Protestants.

The year following, viz. 1690, the Irish took up arms in favor of the abdicated prince, King James II but they were totally defeated by his successor King William the Third. That monarch, before he left the country, reduced them to a state of subjection, in which they have ever since continued.

But notwithstanding all this, the Protestant interest at present stands upon a much stronger basis than it did a century ago. The Irish, who formerly led an unsettled and roving life, in the woods, bogs, and mountains, and lived on the depredation of their neighbors, they who, in the morning seized the prey, and at night divided the spoil, have, for many years past, become quiet and civilized. They taste the sweets of English society, and the advantages of civil government. They trade in our cities, and are employed in our manufactories. They are received also into English families; and treated with great humanity by the Protestants.

Foxe's Book of Martyrs, Edited by William Byron Forbush, chapter 17

Catholic Intolerance

This is the place to present the chief facts on the subject of religious toleration and intolerance, which gives to the case of Servetus its chief interest and importance in history. His theological opinions are of far less consequence than his connection with the theory of persecution which caused his death.

Persecution and war constitute the devil's chapter in history; but it is overruled by Providence for the development of heroism, and for the progress of civil and religious freedom. Without persecutors, there could be no martyrs. Every church, yea, every truth and every good cause, has its martyrs, who stood the fiery trial and sacrificed comfort and life itself to their sacred convictions. The blood of martyrs is the seed of toleration; toleration is the seed of liberty; and liberty is the most precious gift of God to every man who has been made in his image and redeemed by Christ.

Of all forms of persecution, religious persecution is the worst because it is enacted in the name of God. It violates the sacred rights of conscience, and it rouses the strongest and deepest passions. Persecution by word and pen, which springs from the hatred, envy, and malice of the human heart, or from narrowness and mistaken zeal for truth, will continue to the end of time; but persecution by fire and sword contradicts the spirit of humanity and Christianity, and is inconsistent with modern civilization. Civil offences against the State deserve civil punishment, by fine, imprisonment, confiscation, exile, and death, according to the degree of guilt. Spiritual offences against the Church should be spiritually judged, and punished by admonition, deposition, and excommunication, with a view to the reformation and restoration of the offender. This is the law of Christ. The temporal punishment of heresy is the legitimate result of a union of Church and State, and diminishes in rigor as this union is relaxed. A religion established by law must be protected by law. Hence the Constitution of the United States in securing full liberty of religion, forbids Congress to establish by law any religion or church. The two were regarded as inseparable. An established church must in self-defense persecute dissenters, or abridge their liberties; a free church cannot persecute. And yet there may be as much individual Christian kindness and charity in an established church, and as much intolerance and bigotry in a free church. The ante-Nicene Fathers had the same zeal for orthodoxy and the same abhorrence of heresy as the Nicene and post-Nicene Fathers, the mediaeval popes and schoolmen, and the Reformers; but they were confined to the spiritual punishment of heresy. In the United States of America persecution is made impossible, not because the zeal for truth or the passions of hatred and intolerance have ceased, but because the union between Church and State has ceased.

The theory of religious persecution was borrowed from the Mosaic law, which punished idolatry and blasphemy by death. "He that sacrificeth unto any god, save unto Jehovah only, shall be utterly destroyed." He that blasphemeth the name of Jehovah, he shall surely be put to death; all the congregation shall certainly stone him: as well the stranger, as the home-born, when he blasphemeth the name of Jehovah, shall be put to death." The Mosaic theocracy was superseded in its national and temporal provisions by the kingdom of Christ, which is "not of this world." The confounding of the Old and New Testaments, of the law of Moses and the gospel of Christ, was the source of a great many evils in the Church.

The New Testament furnishes not a shadow of support for the doctrine of persecution. The whole teaching and example of Christ and the Apostles are directly opposed to it. They suffered persecution, but they persecuted no one. Their weapons were spiritual, not carnal. They rendered to God the things that are God's, and to Caesar the things that are Caesar's. The only passage which St. Augustin could quote in favor of coercion, was the parabolic "Constrain them to come in" (Luke 14:23), which in its literal acceptation would teach just the reverse, namely, a forced salvation. St. Thomas Aquinas does not quote any passage from the New Testament in favor of intolerance, but tries to explain away those passages which commend toleration (Matt. 13:29, 30; 1 Cor. 11:19; 2 Tim. 2:24). The Church has never entirely forgotten this teaching of Christ and always, even in the darkest ages of persecution, avowed the principle, "Ecclesia non sitit sanguinem"; but she made the State her executor. In the first three centuries the Church had neither the power nor the wish to persecute. Justin Martyr, Tertullian, and Lactantius were the earliest advocates of the liberty of conscience. The Toleration Edict of Constantine (313) anticipated the modern theory of the right of every man to choose his religion and to worship according to his conviction. But this was only a step towards the union of the empire with the Church, when the Church assumed the position and power of the heathen state religion.

The era of persecution within the Church began with the first Ecumenical Council, which was called and enforced by Constantine. This Council presents the first instance of a subscription to a creed, and the first instance of banishment for refusing to subscribe. Arius and two Egyptian bishops, who agreed with him, were banished to Illyria. During the violent Arian controversies, which shook the empire between the first and second Ecumenical Councils (325–381), both parties when in power freely exercised persecution by imprisonment, deposition, and exile. The Arians were as intolerant as the orthodox. The practice furnished the basis for a theory and public law.

The penal legislation against heresy was inaugurated by Theodosius the Great after the final triumph of the Nicene Creed in the second Ecumenical Council. He promulgated during his reign (379–395) no less than fifteen severe edicts against heretics, especially those who dissented from the doctrine of the Trinity. They were deprived of the right of public worship, excluded from public offices, and exposed, in some cases, to capital punishment.[1000] His rival and colleague, Maximus, put the theory into full practice, and shed the first blood of heretics by causing Priscillian, a Spanish bishop of Manichaean tendency, with six adherents, to be tortured, condemned, and executed by the sword.

The better feeling of the Church raised in Ambrose of Milan and Martin of Tours a protest against this act of inhumanity. But public sentiment soon approved of it. Jerome seems to favor the death penalty for heresy on the ground of Deut. 13:6–10. The great Augustin, who had himself been a Manichaean heretic for nine years, justified forcible measures against the Donatists, in contradiction to his noble sentiment: "Nothing conquers but truth, the victory of truth is love." The same Christian Father who ruled the thinking of the Church for many centuries, and molded the theology of the Reformers, excluded all unbaptized infants from salvation, though Christ emphatically included them in the kingdom of heaven. Leo I., the greatest of the early popes, advocated the death penalty for heresy and approved of the execution of the Priscillianists. Thomas Aquinas, the master theologian of the Middle Ages, lent the weight of his authority to the doctrine of persecution, and demonstrated from the Old Testament and from reason that heretics are worse criminals than debasers of money, and ought to be put to death by the civil magistrate.[1002] Heresy was regarded as the greatest sin, and worse than murder, because it destroyed the soul. It took the place of idolatry in the Mosaic law.

The Theodosian Code was completed in the Justinian Code (527–534); the Justinian Code passed into the Holy Roman Empire, and became the basis of the legislation of Christian Europe. Rome ruled the world longer by law and by the cross than she had ruled it by the sword. The canon law likewise condemns to the flames persons convicted of heresy. This law was generally accepted on the Continent in the thirteenth century. England in her isolation was more independent, and built society on the foundation of the common law; but Henry IX and his Parliament devised the sanguinary statute de haeretico comburendo, by, which William Sawtre, a parish priest, was publicly burnt at Smithfield (Feb. 26, 1401) for denying the doctrine of transubstantiation, and the bones of Wiclif were burnt by Bishop Fleming of Lincoln (in 1428). The statute continued in force till 1677, when it was formally abolished.

On this legal and theological foundation the mediaeval Church has soiled her annals with the blood of an army of heretics which is much larger than the army of Christian martyrs under heathen Rome. We need only refer to the crusades against the Albigenses and Waldenses, which were sanctioned by Innocent III., one of the best and greatest of popes; the tortures and autos-da-fé of the Spanish Inquisition, which were celebrated with religious festivities; the fifty thousand or more Protestants who were executed during the reign of the Duke of Alva in the Netherlands (1567–1573); the several hundred martyrs who were burned in Smithfield under the reign of the bloody Mary; and the repeated wholesale persecutions of the innocent Waldenses in France and Piedmont, which cried to heaven for vengeance.

It is vain to shift the responsibility upon the civil government. Pope Gregory XIII. commemorated the massacre of St. Bartholomew not only by a Te Deum in the churches of Rome, but more deliberately and permanently by a medal which represents "The Slaughter of the Huguenots" by an angel of wrath. The French bishops, under the lead of the great Bossuet, lauded Louis XIX as a new Constantine, a new Theodosius, a new Charlemagne, a new exterminator of heretics, for his revocation of the Edict of Nantes and the infamous dragoonades against the Huguenots. Among the more prominent individual cases of persecution, we may mention the burning of Hus (1415) and Jerome of Prague (1416) by order of the Council of Constance, the burning of Savonarola in Florence (1498), the burning of the three English Reformers at Oxford (1556), of Aonio Paleario at Rome (1570), and of Giordano Bruno (1600) in the same city and on the same spot where (1889) the liberals of Italy have erected a statue to his memory. Servetus was condemned to death at the stake, and burnt in effigy, by a Roman Catholic tribunal before he fell into the hands of Calvin. The Roman Church has lost the power, and to a large extent also the disposition, to persecute by fire and sword. Some of her highest dignitaries frankly disown the principle of persecution, especially in America, where they enjoy the full benefit of religious freedom. But the Roman curia has never officially disowned the theory on which the practice of persecution is based. On the contrary, several popes since the Reformation have indorsed it. Pope Clement VIII. denounced the Toleration Edict of Nantes as "the most accursed that can be imagined, whereby liberty of conscience is granted to everybody; which is the worst thing in the world." Pope Innocent I "condemned, rejected, and annulled" the toleration articles of the Westphalian Treaty of 1648, and his successors have ever protested against it, though in vain. Pope Pius II, in the Syllabus of 1864, expressly condemned, among the errors of this age, the doctrine of religious toleration and liberty.1006 And this pope has been declared to be officially infallible by the Vatican decree of 1870, which embraces all his predecessors (notwithstanding the stubborn case of Honorius I.) and all his successors in the chair of St. Peter. Leo XIII. has moderately and cautiously indorsed the doctrine of the Syllabus.

Philip Scaff, The History of the Church

Irish Confessors and Martyrs, 1540-1713

The period covered by this article embraces that between the years 1540 and (approximately) 1713.

Religious persecution in Ireland began under Henry VIII, when the local Parliament adopted acts establishing the king's ecclesiastical supremacy, abolishing the pope's jurisdiction, and suppressing religious houses. The act against the pope came into operation 1 November, 1537. Its penalties were sufficiently terrible, but the licence of those enforcing it was still more terrible. When they had been at work little over a year the Bishop of Derry wrote to Pope Paul III that the King of England's deputy and his adherents, refusing to acknowledge the pope, were burning houses, destroying churches, ravishing maids, robbing and killing unoffending persons. They kill, he said, all priests who pray for the pope or refuse to erase his name from the canon of the Mass, and they torture preachers who do not repudiate his authority. It would fill a book to detail their cruelty. Intolerable as these evils seemed, they were aggravated beyond measure, three years later, when the general suppression of religious houses was superadded. Then ensued the persecution which the Four Masters likened to that of the early Church under the pagan emperors, declaring that it was exceeded by no other, and could be described only by eyewitnesses. The extirpation was so thorough that even remembrance of the victims was effaced. In the published catalogue of Irish martyrs submitted recently to the Congregation of Rites, there are but two cases belonging to Henry's reign. The absence of records for this period is easily explained. The destruction of all kinds of ecclesiastical property, and documents especially, accounts for much, since few but churchmen could make such records; but it is perhaps a more probable explanation that scarcely any were made, as it was neither sage nor practicable to have or transmit what reflected upon government under Tudor despotism. Few memorials could be committed to paper before places of refuge had been secured in foreign countries. Then they were taken down from the lips of aged refugees, and as might be expected they exhibit the vagueness and confusion of dates and incidents to which personal reminiscences are subject when spread over long and unsettled periods.

For the time of the suppression there is a partial narrative in the recital of an old Trinitarian friar, written down by one of his brethren, Father Richard Goldie or Goold (Goldæus), an Irish professor at the University of Alcalá. According to this account, on the first announcement of the king's design, Theobald (Burke?), provincial of the order, came to Dublin with eight other doctors to maintain the pope's supremacy. They were cast into prison; Theobald's heart was torn from his living body; Philip, a writer, was scourged, put into boots filled with oil and salt, roasted till the flesh came away from the bone, and then beheaded; the rest were hanged or beheaded; Cornelius, Bishop of Limerick, was beheaded there; Cormac was shot and stoned to death at Galway; Maurice and Thomas, brothers-german, hanged on their way to Dublin; Stephen, stabbed near Wexford; Peter of Limerick and Geoffrey, beheaded; John Macabrigus, lay brother, drowned; Raymond, ex-superior, dragged at a horse's tail in Dublin; Tadhg O'Brien of Thomond, torn to pieces in the viceroy's presence at Bombriste bridge between Limerick and Kilmallock; the Dublin community, about fifty, put to various deaths; those of Adare, cut down, stabbed, or hanged; those of Galway, twenty, burned to death in their convent or, by another account, six were thrown into a lime-kiln, the rest weighted with stones and cast into the sea; those of Drogheda, forty, slain, hanged, or thrown into a pit; at Limerick, over fifty butchered in choir or thrown with weights into the Shannon; at Cork and Kilmallock, over ninety slain by the sword or dismembered, including William Burke, John O'Hogan, Michael, Richard, and Giollabrighde. This is the earliest narrative as regards period. It deals only with the Trinitarians. It had the misfortune to be worked up by Lopez, a fanciful Spanish writer, and consequently has incurred perhaps more discredit than it deserves. The promoters of the cause of the Irish martyrs have not extracted any names from it. Nevertheless, the version given by O'Sullevan Bearr in his "Patriciana Decas", despite many apparent inaccuracies and exaggerations, contains in its main statements a not improbable picture of the experiences of this single order when the agents of rapine and malignity were let loose upon the members. It is as a cry from the torture chamber, expressing the agony of a victim who loses the power to detail accurately the extent of his sufferings or the manner of their infliction.

The first general catalogue is that of Father John Houling, S.J., compiled in Portugal between 1588 and 1599. It is styled a very brief abstract of certain cases and is directed towards canonization of the eleven bishops, eleven priests, and forty-four lay persons whom it commemorates as sufferers for the Faith by death, chains, or exile under Elizabeth. Cornelius O'Devany, the martyred Bishop of Down and Connor, took up the record about the point where Houling broke off, and he continued it until his own imprisonment in 1611. Shortly before that time he forwarded a copy to Father Holywood, S.J., desiring him to take steps to have the lives of those noted therein illustrated at length and preserved from oblivion. O'Devany's catalogue was in David Rothe's hands while he was preparing the "Processus Martyrialis", published, in 1619, as the third part of his "Analecta", which still remains a most important contribution to the subject. During the next forty years Copinger (1620), O'Sullevan Bearr (1621 and 1629), Molanus (1629), Morison (1659), and others sent forth from the press works devoted either wholly or in part to advancing the claims of Irish martyrs to recognition and veneration. In 1669 Antony Bruodin, O.S.F., published at Prague a thick octavo volume of about 800 pages, entitled "Propugnaculum Catholicæ Veritatis", a catalogue of Irish martyrs under Henry VIII, Edward VI, Elizabeth, and James, containing notices of about 200 martyrs, with an index of 164 persons whose Christian names come first as in a martyrology. Bruodin based his work on Rothe's "Analecta", but he made large additions from other writers, as Good, Bourchier, Gonzaga, Baressus, Sanders, Wadding, Alegambe, and Nadasi, and in particular from a manuscript ascribed to Matthew Creagh, Vicar-General of Killaloe, which had been brought to the Irish Franciscans of Prague in 1660.

Practically nothing was done for about two centuries after Bruodin's publication. A proposal to take up the cause of Primate Oliver Plunket within a few years of his martyrdom was discountenanced by the Holy See, lest at that critical juncture such action should become an occasion of political trouble in England. After the English Revolution and the commencement of the new era of oppression that succeeded the capitulation of Limerick, it was manifest that any movement towards canonization of the victims of laws still in force would result in merciless reprisals on the part of the ascendancy. At length, in 1829, the last political hindrances were removed by Catholic Emancipation, but over thirty years were allowed to pass unmarked by any action, either because more immediate demands pressed upon the energies of the Catholic community or because, during the long period for which the matter had been laid aside, the sources of trustworthy information had become so inaccessible or forgotten that the task of accumulating evidence seemed too formidable to undertake. In 1861 Dr. Moran, then Vice-Rector of the Irish College, Rome, and subsequently in succession Bishop of Ossory and Cardinal Archbishop of Sydney, reopened the question by his life of Oliver Plunket, the first of a series of important historical publications, in which he covered the whole period of Irish persecutions from Henry VIII to Charles II. All these publications were effectively, if not professedly, directed towards hastening the Church's solemn recognition of the martyrs. The first of these writings (1861) expressed the hope that the day was not far distant when the long afflicted Church of Ireland would be consoled by the canonization of Oliver Plunket. In 1884, when the last of them, a reissue of Rothe's "Analecta", was published, the intermediate advance had been so great that the editor, then Rothe's successor in Ossory, noted the expression of a wish both in Ireland and abroad "that, although our whole people might justly be regarded as a nation of martyrs, yet some few names, at least, among the most remarkable for constancy and heroism would be laid before the Sacred Congregation of Rites and, if found worthy, be enrolled among the privileged martyrs of Holy Church." While Dr. Moran was thus engaged, Major Myles O'Reilly also entered the long neglected field, and in 1868 he published a collection of memorials in which he brought together, from all the original sources his great industry could reach, biographies of those who suffered for the Faith in the sixteenth, seventeenth, and eighteenth centuries. This collection was made with both zeal and discrimination; it was the first general compilation since Bruodin's, and, coming down to a later date, it contained twice the number of notices in the former one. As a result, in great measure, of these several publications, the case was brought to such a point, about ten years after the reissue of Rothe's "Analecta", that the ecclesiastical authorities were in a position to make preparations for holding the processus ordinarius informativus, the diocesan inquiry which is a preliminary in the process of canonization. The work of collecting evidence, greatly facilitated by the previous labors of Moran and O'Reilly, was entrusted to Father Denis Murphy, S.J. He, unhappily, did not live to submit his testimony; but before his death he had reduced to order a great mass of materials extracted from a larger number of writers than had been used by O'Reilly. The number of individual notices is, however, much less, since Father Murphy excluded, with one or two exceptions, all those whose trials did not culminate in death. His materials were published in 1896, under the title of "Our Martyrs", and the record begun by Father Houling was thus, after three hundred years, completed by his brother Jesuit in form to be submitted in a regular process of canonization.

The usual practice of conducting the preliminary process in the diocese where the martyrs suffered would have entailed the erecting of a tribunal in every diocese in Ireland, a course attended with no advantages. The Archbishop of Dublin, therefore, at the united request of all the Irish bishops, accepted the responsibility of conducting a general investigation for the whole country. But, before further progress could be made, certain unforeseen causes of delay arose which were not removed until the end of the year 1903. In December of that year the vice-postulator issued his requests for the attendance of witnesses in the February following. The initial session was opened by the Archbishop of Dublin, 15 February, 1904. Between that date and 3 August, when the taking of evidence in Ireland was completed, sixty sessions had been held. The testimony of Cardinal Moran was taken by commission in Sydney. When it arrived in Ireland meetings were resumed, 23 October, and continued for some twenty further sessions to complete the return, a transcript of the evidence with exhibits of books and documents. This work was brought to a conclusion at Christmas, and on 5 February, 1905, the full return of the inquiry was delivered to the Congregation of Rites. The number of sessions held was about eighty, in all of which the Archbishop of Dublin presided. Evidence was taken in respect of about three hundred and forty persons, with a view to establish the existence of a traditional belief among learned and pious Catholics that many persons suffered death for the Catholic Faith in Ireland under the penal laws; that these persons did, in fact, suffer martyrdom in defense of the Catholic Faith and of the pope's spiritual authority as Vicar of Christ; and that there is a sincere desire among Irish Catholics, in Ireland and elsewhere, to see these martyrs solemnly recognized by the Church. The chief portion of the evidence was necessarily that derived from records, printed or written. In addition, witnesses testified to the public repute of martyrdom, and traditions to that effect preserved in families, religious orders, various localities, and the country at large, with a particular statement in every case as to the source of the information furnished by the witness. Subsequent to this inquiry the further minor process (processiculus), to collect writings attributed to some of the martyrs, was held January-March, 1907.

The investigation of the claims to the title of martyr made for those who suffered under the Irish penal enactments since 1537, is attended by difficulties that do not arise in the case of their fellow-sufferers in England, difficulties due to the historical situation and to the character of the available evidence. Not more than one-third of Ireland was subject to the rule of Henry VIII when he undertook to detach the island from the Catholic Church. The remainder was governed by hereditary lords under native institutions. The king's deputy at times obtained acknowledgment of the overlordship supposed to be conferred by the Bull Laudabiliter; but the acknowledgment was so little valued that the population was commonly classified as the king's subjects and the Irish enemies, not, as yet, the Irish rebels. The Church, however, was the Church of Ireland, not the Church of the English Pale, and the claim to Supreme Headship of the Church entailed the effective reduction of the whole island to civil obedience, which, as then understood, required acceptance of the whole English system of laws and manners. Hence, it is not always easy to discern how far the fate of an individual resulted from his fidelity to religion, and how far from defense of ancestral institutions. Again, the evidence is not always satisfactory, for reasons already mentioned. The public records are very defective, as in a country that has experienced two violent revolutions, but the loss so caused might possibly be overestimated. No large proportion of those put to death had been brought before a regular court. There was a general immunity from consequences which encouraged captains of roving bands and stationary garrisons, provost-martials, and all that class, to carry out the intention of the law without its forms. In such cases there are no records. During the year of the Armada a Spanish ship made prize of a Dublin vessel bound for France. A Cistercian monk and a Franciscan friar were found on board. They said they were the sole survivors of two large monasteries in the North of Ireland which had been burned with the rest of the inmates. There seems to be no other mention of this atrocity.

The list which follows (p. signifying priest; l. layman) includes the names of those persons only in respect of whom evidence was taken at the inquiry held in Dublin. The case of Primate Oliver Plunket has already been conducted successfully through the Apostolic Process by Cardinal Logue, his successor.

(1) Under King Henry VIII

1540: The guardian and friars, Franciscan Convent, Monaghan: beheaded.

1541: Robert and other Cistercian monks, St. Mary's Abbey, Dublin: imprisoned and put to death; as the Cistercians of Dublin surrendered their house and its possessions peaceably, there is possibly confusion as to this instance.

(2) Under Queen Elizabeth

1565: Conacius Macuarta (Conn McCourt) and Roger MacCongaill (McConnell), Franciscans: flogged to death, Armagh, 16 December, for refusing to acknowledge the queen's supremacy.

1575: John Lochran, Donagh O'Rorke, and Edmund Fitzsimon, Franciscans: hanged, 21 January, Downpatrick; 1575: Fergall Ward, Franciscan guardian, Armagh: hanged, 28 April, with his own girdle.

1577: Thomas Courcy, vicar-general at Kinsale: hanged, 30 March; William Walsh, Cistercian, Bishop of Meath: died, 4 January, in exile at Alcalá.

1578: Patrick O'Hely, Bishop of Mayo, and Cornelius O'Rorke, Franciscans: tortured and hanged, 22 August, Kilmallock; 1578: David Hurley, dean of Emly: died in prison; 1578: Thomas Moeran, dean of Cork: taken in the exercise of his functions and executed.

1579: Thaddæus Daly and his companion, O.S.F.: hanged, drawn, and quartered at Limerick, 1 January. The bystanders reported that his head when cut off distinctly uttered the words: "Lord, show me Thy ways." 1579: Edmund Tanner, S.J., Bishop of Cork: died, 4 June, in prison at Dublin; 1579: John O'Dowd, O.S.F.: refused to reveal a confession, put to death at Elphin by having his skull compressed with a twisted cord; 1579: Thomas O'Herlahy, Bishop of Ross.

1580: Edmund MacDonnell, S.J.: 16 March, Cork (but the year should be 1575 and the name perhaps O'Donnell); 1580: Laurence O'Moore, Oliver Plunkett, gentleman, and William Walsh or Willick, an Englishman: tortured and hanged, 11 November, after the surrender of Dun-an-oir in Kerry; 1580: Daniel O'Neilan p., O.S.F.: fastened round the waist with a rope and thrown with weights tied to his feet from one of town-gates at Youghal, finally fastened to a mill-wheel and torn to pieces, 28 March. He is obviously the person whom Mooney commemorates under the name O'Duillian, assigning the date, 22 April, 1569, from hearsay; 1580: Daniel Hanrichan, Maurice O'Scanlan, and Philip O'Shee (O'Lee), priests, O.S.F.: beaten with sticks and slain, 6 April, before the altar of Lislachtin monastery, Co. Kerry; 1580: the prior at the Cistercian monastery of Graeg, and his companions. Murphy, quoting O'Sullevan, says the monastery was Graiguenamanagh; O'Sullevan names the place Seripons, Jerpoint.

1581: Nicholas Nugent, chief justice, David Sutton, John Sutton, Thomas Eustace, John Eustace, William Wogan, Robert Sherlock, John Clinch, Thomas Netherfield, or Netterville, Robert Fitzgerald, gentleman of the Pale, and Walter Lakin (Layrmus): executed on a charge of complicity in rebellion with Lord Baltinglass; 1581: Matthew Lamport, described as a parish priest (pastor) of Dublin Diocese, but more probably a baker (pistor) of Wexford: executed for harboring Baltinglass and Father Rochford, S.J.

1581: Robert Meyler, Edward Cheevers, John O'Lahy, and Patrick Canavan, sailors of Wexford: hanged, drawn, and quartered, 5 July, for conveying priests, a Jesuit, and laymen out of Ireland; 1581: Patrick Hayes, shipowner of Wexford, charged with aiding bishops, priests, and others: died in prison; 1581: Richard French, Ferns Diocese: died in prison; 1581: Nicholas Fitzgerald, Cistercian: hanged, drawn, and quartered, September, at Dublin.

1582: Phelim O'Hara and Henry Delahoyde, O.S.F., of Moyne, Co. Mayo: hanged and quartered, 1 May; 1582: Thaddæus O'Meran, or O'Morachue, O.S.F., guardian of Enniscorthy; 1582: Phelim O'Corra (apparently Phelim O'Hara, above); 1582: Æneas Penny, parish priest of Killatra (Killasser, Co. Mayo): slain by soldiers while saying Mass, 4 May; 1582: Roger O'Donnellan, Cahill McGoran, Peter McQuillan, Patrick O'Kenna, James Pillan, priests, and Roger O'Hanlon (more correctly McHenlea, in Curry), lay brother, O.S.F.: died, 13 February, Dublin Castle, but the date can scarcely be correct for all; 1582: Henry O'Fremlamhaidh (anglicized Frawley); 1582: John Wallis, priest: died, 20 January, in prison at Worcester; 1582: Donagh O'Reddy, parish priest of Coleraine: hanged and transfixed with swords, 12 June, at the altar of his church.

1584: Dermot O'Hurley, Archbishop of Cashel; 1584: Gelasius O'Cullenan, O.Cist., Abbot of Boyle, and his companion, variously named Eugene Cronius and Hugh or John Mulcheran (? Eoghan O'Maoilchiarain), either Abbot of Trinity Island, Co. Roscommon, or a secular priest: hanged, 21 November, at Dublin; 1584: John O'Daly, O.S.F.: trampled to death by cavalry; 1584: Eleanor Birmingham, widow of Bartholomew Ball: denounced by her son, Walter Ball, Mayor of Dublin, died in prison; 1584: Thaddæus Clancy, 15 September, near Listowel.

1585: Richard Creagh, Archbishop of Armagh: poisoned, 14 October, in the Tower of London. 1585: Maurice Kenraghty;

Patrick O'Connor and Malachy O'Kelly, O.Cist.: hanged and quartered, 19 May, at Boyle.

1586: Maurice, or Murtagh, O'Brien, Bishop of Emly: died in prison at Dublin; Donagh O'Murheely (O'Murthuile, wrongly identified with O'Hurley) and a companion, O.S.F. stoned and tortured to death at Muckross, Killarney.

1587: John Cornelius, O.S.F., of Askeaton; another John Cornelius, S.J., surnamed O'Mahony, born in England of Irish parents from Kinelmeky, Co. Cork, is included among the venerables of the English list; 1587: Walter Farrell, O.S.F., Askeaton: hanged with his own girdle.

1588: Dermot O'Mulrony, O.S.F., Brother Thomas, and another Franciscan of Galbally, Co. Limerick: put to death there 21 March; 1588: Maurice Eustace, Jesuit novice: hanged and quartered, 9 June, Dublin; 1588: John O'Molloy, Cornelius O'Dogherty, and Geoffrey Farrell, Franciscan priests: hanged, drawn, and quartered, 15 December, at Abbeyleix; 1588: Patrick Plunkett, knight: hanged and quartered, 6 May, Dublin; 1588: Peter Miller, B.D., Diocese of Ferns: tortured, hanged, and quartered, 4 October, 1588; 1588: Peter (or Patrick) Meyler: executed at Galway; notwithstanding the different places of martyrdom assigned, these two names may be those of the same person, a native of Wexford executed at Galway; 1588: Patrick O'Brady, O.S.F., prior at Monaghan: Murphy, on slender grounds, supposes him to be the guardian put to death in 1540, but Copinger and after him Curry, in his "Civil Wars in Ireland", state that six friars were slain in the monastery of Moynihan (Monaghan) under Elizabeth, Thaddæus O'Boyle, guardian of Donegal, slain there, 13 April, by soldiers.

1590: Matthew O'Leyn, O.S.F.: 6 March, Kilcrea; 1590: Christopher Roche, l.: died, 13 December, under torture, Newgate, London.

1591: Terence Magennis, Magnus O'Fredliney or O'Todhry, Loughlin og Mac O'Cadha (? Mac Eochadha, Keogh), Franciscans of Multifarnham: died in prison.

1594: Andrew Strich, Limerick: died in Dublin Castle.

1597: John Stephens, Dublin province, apparently chaplain to the O'Byrnes of Wicklow: hanged and quartered, 4 September, for saying Mass; 1597: Walter Fernan: torn on the rack, 12 March, at Dublin.

1599: George Power, Vicar-General of Ossory: died in prison.

1600: John Walsh, Vicar-General of Dublin: died in prison at Chester; 1600: Patrick O'Hea: charged with harboring priests, died in prison, 4 December, Dublin: probably the Patrick Hayes of 1581 (supra); 1600: James Dudall (Dowdall): died either 20 November or 13 August, Exeter; 1600: Nicholas Young, died, Dublin Castle.

1601: Redmond O'Gallagher, Bishop of Derry: slain by soldiers, 15 March, near Dungiven; 1601: Daniel, or Donagh, O'Mollony, Vicar-General of Killaloe: died of torture, 24 April, Dublin Castle; 1601: John O'Kelly: died, 15 May, in prison; 1601: Donagh O'Cronin, clerk: hanged and disemboweled, Cork; 1601: Bernard Moriarty, dean of Ardagh and Vicar-General of Dublin: having his thighs broken by soldiers, died in prison, Dublin.

1602: Dominic Collins, lay brother, S.J.: hanged, drawn, and quartered, 31 October, Youghal.

1602: To this year seems to belong the death of Eugene MacEgan, styled Bishop-designate of Ross, of which he was vicar Apostolic, mortally wounded while officiating in the Catholic army. There was no Catholic army on foot in 1606, at which date his name appears in the official list. He was buried at Timoleague.

The following Dominicans suffered under Elizabeth (1558-1603), but the dates are uncertain: Father MacFerge, prior, and twenty-four friars of Coleraine, thirty-two members of the community of Derry, slain there the same night, two priests and seven novices of Limerick and Kilmallock, assembled in 1602 with forty Benedictine, Cistercian, and other monks, at Scattery Island in the Shannon to be deported under safe conduct in a man-of-war, were cast overboard at sea.

(3) Under James I and Charles I (1604-1648)

1606: Bernard O'Carolan: executed by martial law, Good Friday; 1606: Eugene O'Gallagher, abbot, and Bernard O'Trevir, prior, of the Cistercians of Assaroe, Ballyshannon: slain there by soldiers; 1606: Sir John Burke of Brittas, County Limerick: for rescuing and defending with arms a priest seized by soldiers, executed at Limerick, 20 Dec., 1606. The date is accurately known from contemporary letters printed in Hogan's "Ibernia Ignatiana".

1607: Niall O'Boyle, O.S.F.: beheaded or hanged, 15 Jan., Co. Tyrone; 1607: John O'Luin, O.P.: hanged at Derry; 1607: Patrick O'Derry, O.S.F.: hanged, drawn, and quartered at Lifford (but according to Bruodin, 6 January, 1618); 1607: Francis Helam or Helan, O.S.F.: apprehended saying Mass in Drogheda, and imprisoned; 1607: Dermot Bruodin, O.S.F., tortured at Limerick: released at the intervention of the Earl of Thomond, he died of years and labors at Ennis (9 August, 1617, according to Bruodin).

1608: Donagh (in religion, William) O'Luin, O.P., prior of Derry: hanged and quartered there.

1610: John Lune, Ferns Diocese: hanged and quartered, 12 November, Dublin.

1612: Cornelius O'Devany, O.S.F., Bishop of Down and Connor: executed with Patrick O'Lochran, Cork Diocese, 1 February, Dublin.

1614: William McGillacunny (MacGiolla Coinigh), O.P.: executed at Coleraine.

1617: Thomas Fitzgerald, O.S.F.: died in prison, 12 July, Dublin.

1618: John Honan, O.S.F.: tortured, hanged, and quartered, 14 October, Dublin.

1621: Francis Tailler, alderman, Dublin: died a prisoner in the Castle, 30 January; 1621: James Eustace, O.Cist.: hanged and quartered, 6 September.

1628: Edmund Dungan, Bishop of Down and Connor: died, 2 November, Dublin Castle.

1631: Paul (Patrick) Fleming, O.S.F.: put to death by heretics, 13 November, at Benesabe, Bohemia, with his companion, Matthew Hore.

1633: Arthur MacGeoghegan, O.P.: hanged, drawn, and quartered, 27 November, Tyburn.

1639: John Meagh, S.J.: shot, 31 May, by the Swedish army near Guttenberg, Bohemia.

1641: Peter O'Higgin, O.P., prior at Naas: hanged, 24 March, Dublin.

1642: Philip Clery; 1642: Hilary Conroy, O.S.F.: but most probably this is the Hilary Conroy, O.S.F., chaplain to Ormond's regiment, hanged at Gowran in 1650 by the Cromwellians; 1642: Fergal Ward, O.S.F., and Cornelius O'Brien: hanged on board ship in the Shannon, by parliamentarians, October; 1642: Francis O'Mahony, O.S.F., guardian at Cork: tortured and hanged, regaining consciousness, he was again hanged with his girdle; 1642: Thomas Aquinas of Jesus, O.D.C., hanged, 6 July, Drogheda; 1642: Angelus of St. Joseph, O.D.C.; Robert (in religion, Malachy) O'Shiel, O.Cist.: hanged, 4 May, Newry; 1642: Edmund Hore and John Clancy, priests, Waterford Diocese: put to death, March, at Dungarvan; 1642: Raymund Keogh, O.P., Stephen Petit, O.P., prior at Mullingar: shot while hearing confessions on the battlefield; 1642: Cormac Egan, lay brother, O.P.

1643: Peter of the Mother of God, lay brother, O.D.C.

1644: Cornelius O'Connor and Eugene O'Daly, O.SS.T.: drowned at sea by a Parliamentarian commander, 11 January; 1644: Christopher Ultan or Donlevy, O.S.F., died in Newgate, London.

1645: Hugh MacMahon, l., and Conor Maguire, Baron of Enniskillen: executed for complicity in the outbreak of the Confederate War; 1645: Henry White: hanged at Rathconnell, Co. Meath (but before this year, if by Sir C. Coote, as stated); 1645: Edmund Mulligan, O.Cist., in July, near Clones, slain by Parliamentarians; 1645: Malachy O'Queely, Archbishop of Tuam; 1645: Thaddæus O'Connell, O.S.A.: executed by Parliamentarians after the battle of Sligo; 1645: John Flaverty, O.P.

1647: At the storming of the Rock of

Cashel by Inchiquin, 15 September, Richard Barry,, O.P., William Boyton, S.J., Richard Butler, O.S.F., James Saul, lay brother, O.S.F., Elizabeth Carney, Sister Margaret, a Dominican tertiary, Theobald Stapleton, Edward Stapleton, Thomas Morrissey and many others, priests and women, were slain in the church.

1648: Gerald FitzGibbon, cleric, and David Fox, lay brother at Kilmallock, Dominic O'Neaghten, lay brother, Roscommon, Peter Costello, sub-prior, Straid, Co. Mayo, all Dominicans; Andrew Hickey, O.S.F.: hanged near Adare.

(4) Commonwealth (1649-1659)

1649: Robert Netterville, S.J.: died at Drogheda, 19 June, of a severe beating with sticks; 1649: John Vath, S.J., and his brother Thomas, secular priest, Dominic Dillon, O.P., prior at Urlar, Richard Oveton, O.P., prior at Athy, Peter Taaffe, O.S.A., prior at Drogheda: slain in Drogheda massacre; 1649: Bernard Horumley (? Gormley), O.S.F.: hanged, Drogheda; 1649: Raymund Stafford, Paul Synnott, John Esmond, Peter Stafford, Didacus Cheevers and Joseph Rochford, lay brothers, Franciscans: slain in Wexford massacre; 1649: James O'Reilly, O.P.: slain near Clonmel; 1649: William Lynch, O.P.: hanged.

1650: Boetius Egan, O.S.F., Bishop of Ross, celebrated for exhorting the garrison of Carrigadrehid Castle to maintain their post against Broghill: dismembered and hanged; 1650: Miler Magrath (Father Michael of the Rosary), O.P.: hanged, Clonmel; 1650: Francis Fitzgerald, O.S.F.: hanged, Cork; 1650: Walter de Wallis, O.S.F., and Antony Musæus (? Hussey), O.S.F.: hanged, Mullingar; 1650: John Dormer, O.S.F.: died in prison, Dublin; 1650: Nicholas Ugan, or Ulagan, O.S.F.: hanged with his girdle; 1650: Thomas Plunkett and twelve other Franciscans, Eugene O'Teman, O.S.F.: flogged and cut to pieces by soldiers.

1651: Franciscans: Denis O'Neilan, hanged, Inchicronan, Co. Clare; Thaddæus O'Carrighy, hanged near Ennis; Hugh McKeon, died in prison, Athlone; Roger de Mara (MacNamara), shot and hanged, Clare Castle; Daniel Clanchy and Jeremiah O'Nerehiny (Nerny), lay brothers, Quin, hanged; Philip Flasberry, hanged near Dublin; Francis Sullivan,, shot in a cave, Co. Kerry, December; William Hickey, hanged; 1651: Dominicans: Terence Albert O'Brien, O.P., Bishop of Emly; John Wolfe, hanged, Limerick; John O'Cuilin (Collins), beheaded; William O'Connor, prior at Clonmel, beheaded, and Thomas O'Higgin, hanged, Clonmel; Bernard O'Ferrall, slain, his brother Laurence, hanged, Longford; Vincent Gerald Dillon, chaplain to Irish troops in England, died in prison, York; Ambrose Æneas O'Cahill, cut to pieces by cavalry, Cork; Donagh Dubh (Black) and James Moran, lay brothers; laymen: Louis O'Farrall, died in prison, Athlone; Charles O'Dowd, hanged; Donagh O'Brien, burned alive; Sir Patrick Purcell, Sir Geoffrey Galway, Thomas Strich, mayor, Dominic Fanning, ex-mayor, Daniel O'Higgin, hanged after surrender of Limerick; Henry O'Neill, Theobald de Burgo.

1652: Secular priests: Roger Ormilius (? Gormley) and Hugh Garrighy: hanged, Co. Clare; 1652: Cornelius MacCarthy, Co. Kerry; 1652: Bernard Fitzpatrick, Ossory Diocese; 1652: Franciscans hanged: Eugene O'Cahan, guardian at Ennis, Sliabh Luachra, Anthony Broder, deacon, near Tuam, Bonaventure de Burgo, Nielan Locheran, Derry. 1652: Anthony O'Ferrall, Tulsk, John O'Ferrall; Edmund O'Bern, O.P.: beheaded after torture, Jamestown; 1652: Laymen hanged: Thaddæus O'Connor Sligo, Boyle; John O'Conor Kerry, Tralee; Thaddæus O'Conor of Bealnamelly in Connaught; Bernard McBriody; Edmund Butler, Dublin; Brigid D'Arcy, wife of Florence Fitzpatrick; Conn O'Rorke: slain after quarter given.

1653: Dominicans: Thaddæus Moriarty, prior at Tralee, hanged, Killarney; Bernard O'Kelly or lay brother, Galway; David Roche, sold into slavery, St. Kitts; Honoria Burke and her maid, Honoria Magan, tertiaries, Burrishoole; Daniel Delany, Arklow, hanged, Gorey.

1654: Bernard Conney, O.S.F., died in Galway jail; Mary Roche, Viscountess Fermoy, Cork; William Tirry, Augustinian hermit, probably in Co. Cork. V1655: Daniel O'Brien, dean of Ferns, Luke Bergin, O.Cist., and James Murchu: hanged, 14 April.

The Restoration Onwards

1665: Raymund O'Moore, O.P., Dublin; 1679: Felix O'Conor, O.P., Sligo; 1691: Gerald Fitzgibbon, O.P., Listowel; 1695: John O'Murrough, O.P., Cork; 1704: Clement O'Colgan, O.P., Derry; 1707: Daniel McDonnell, O.P., Galway; 1707: Felix McDowell, O.P., Dublin; 1711 (or thereabouts): James O'Hegarty, Derry Diocese; 1713: Dominic McEgan, O.P., Dublin.

Uncertain Dates

Forty Cistercians of Monasternenagh, Co. Limerick may be the monks mentioned at 1602, though the manner of death is stated differently; Daniel O'Hanan, l., died in prison; Donagh O'Kennedy, Donagh Serenan, Fulgentius Jordan, Raymund O'Malley, John Tullis, and Thomas Deir, Augustinians, Cork, 1654; James Chevers, O.S.F., James Roche, O.S.F., John Mocleus (? Mockler), O.S.F., John O'Loughlin, O.P., two Dominican fathers, Kilmallock. VApparently the lay brothers Fitzgibbon and Fox, 1648; Michael Fitzsimon, l., Conn O'Kiennan, hanged, drawn, and quartered, 1615; Daniel O'Boyle, O.S.F.; Dermot MacCarrha (MacCarthy); Donchus O'Falvey, perhaps the Daniel Falvey, friar, remanded at Kerry Lent Assizes, 1703; John MacConnan, possibly the John Oonan (Conan) of Copinger, executed by martial law, Dublin, 1618, and the John Honan, O.S.F., 1617; John O'Grady; Thomas Fleming, l,; Lewis O'Laverty, hanged, drawn, and quartered, 1615.

Robert B. Olson, The Catholic Encyclopedia, Volume 8

Protestant Intolerance

Judgments of the Reformers on Servetus

The Reformers inherited the doctrine of persecution from their mother Church, and practiced it as far as they had the power. They fought intolerance with intolerance. They differed favorably from their opponents in the degree and extent, but not in the principle, of intolerance. They broke down the tyranny of popery, and thus opened the way for the development of religious freedom; but they denied to others the liberty which they exercised themselves. The Protestant governments in Germany and Switzerland excluded, within the limits of their jurisdiction, the Roman Catholics from all religious and civil rights, and took exclusive possession of their churches, convents, and other property. They banished, imprisoned, drowned, beheaded, hanged, and burned Anabaptists, Antitrinitarians, Schwenkfeldians, and other dissenters. In Saxony, Sweden, Norway, and Denmark no religion and public worship was allowed but the Lutheran. The Synod of Dort deposed and expatriated all Arminian ministers and school-teachers. The penal code of Queen Elizabeth and the successive acts of Uniformity aimed at the complete extermination of all dissent, whether papal or protestant, and made it a crime for an Englishman to be anything else than an Episcopalian. The Puritans when in power ejected two thousand ministers from their benefices for non-conformity; and the Episcopalians paid them back in the same coin when they returned to power. "The Reformers," says Gibbon, with sarcastic severity, "were ambitious of succeeding the tyrants whom they had dethroned. They imposed with equal rigor their creeds and confessions; they asserted the right of the magistrate to punish heretics with death. The nature of the tiger was the same, but he was gradually deprived of his teeth and fangs." Protestant persecution violates the fundamental principle of the Reformation. Protestantism has no right to exist except on the basis of freedom of conscience.

How, then, can we account for this glaring inconsistency? There is a reason for everything. Protestant persecution was necessary in self-defense and in the struggle for existence. The times were not ripe for toleration. The infant Churches could not have stood it. These Churches had first to be consolidated and fortified against surrounding foes. Universal toleration at that time would have resulted in universal confusion and upset the order of society. From anarchy to absolute despotism is but one step. The division of Protestantism into two rival camps, the Lutheran and the Reformed, weakened it; further divisions within these camps would have ruined it and prepared an easy triumph for united Romanism, which would have become more despotic than ever before. This does not justify the principle, but it explains the practice, of intolerance.

The Reformers and the Protestant princes and magistrates were essentially agreed on this intolerant attitude, both towards the Romanists and the heretical Protestants, at least to the extent of imprisonment, deposition, and expatriation. They differed only as to the degree of severity. They all believed that the papacy is anti-Christian and the mass idolatrous; that heresy is a sin against God and society; that the denial of the Trinity and the divinity of Christ is the greatest of heresies, which deserves death according to the laws of the empire, and eternal punishment according to the Athanasian Creed (with its three damnatory clauses); and that the civil government is as much bound to protect the first as the second table of the Decalogue, and to vindicate the honor of God against blasphemy. They were anxious to show their zeal for orthodoxy by severity against heresy. They had no doubt that they themselves were orthodox according to the only true standard of orthodoxy – the Word of God in the Holy Scriptures. And as regards the dogmas of the Trinity and Incarnation, they were fully agreed with their Catholic opponents, and equally opposed to the errors of Servetus, who denied those dogmas with a boldness and contempt unknown before.

Let us ascertain the sentiments of the leading Reformers with special reference to the case of Servetus. They form a complete justification of Calvin as far as such a justification is possible.

Luther

Luther, the hero of Worms, the champion of the sacred rights of conscience, was, in words, the most violent, but in practice, the least intolerant, among the Reformers. He was nearest to Romanism in the condemnation of heresy, but nearest to the genius of Protestantism in the advocacy of religious freedom. He was deeply rooted in mediaeval piety, and yet a mighty prophet of modern times. In his earlier years, till 1529, he gave utterance to some of the noblest sentiments in favor of religious liberty. "Belief is a free thing," he said, "which cannot be enforced." "If heretics were to be punished by death, the hangman would be the most orthodox theologian." "Heresy is a spiritual thing which no iron can hew down, no fire burn, no water drown." To burn heretics is contrary to the will of the Holy Spirit." False teachers should not be put to death; it is enough to banish them."But with advancing years he became less liberal and more intolerant against Catholics, heretics, and Jews. He exhorted the magistrates to forbid all preaching of Anabaptists, whom he denounced without discrimination as false prophets and messengers of the devil, and he urged their expulsion. He raised no protest when the Diet of Speier, in 1529, passed the cruel decree that the Anabaptists be executed by fire and sword without distinction of sex, and even without a previous hearing before the spiritual judges. The Elector of Saxony considered it his duty to execute this decree, and put a number of Anabaptists to death in his dominions. His neighbor, Philip of Hesse, who had more liberal instincts than the contemporary princes of Germany, could not find it in his conscience to use the sword against differences of belief. But the theologians of Wittenberg, on being consulted by the Elector John Frederick about 1540 or 1541, gave their judgment in favor of putting the Anabaptists to death, according to the laws of the empire. Luther approved of this judgment under his own name, adding that it was cruel to punish them by the sword, but more cruel that they should damn the ministry of the Word and suppress the true doctrine, and attempt to destroy the kingdoms of the world. If we put a strict construction on this sentence, Luther must be counted with the advocates of the death-penalty for heresy. But he made a distinction between two classes of Anabaptists – those who were seditious or revolutionary, and those who were mere fanatics. The former should be put to death, the latter should be banished. In a letter to Philip of Hesse, dated November 20, 1538, he urgently requested him to expel from his territory the Anabaptists, whom he characterizes as children of the devil, but says nothing of using the sword. We should give him, therefore, the benefit of a liberal construction. At the same time, the distinction was not always strictly observed, and fanatics were easily turned into criminals, especially after the excesses of Münster, in 1535, which were greatly exaggerated and made the pretext for punishing innocent men and women. The whole history of the Anabaptist movement in the sixteenth century has to be rewritten and disentangled from the odium theologicum.

As regards Servetus, Luther knew only his first work against the Trinity, and pronounced it, in his Table Talk (1532), an "awfully bad book." Fortunately for his fame, he did not live to pronounce a judgment in favor of his execution, and we must give him the benefit of silence.

His opinions on the treatment of the Jews changed for the worse. In 1523 he had vigorously protested against the cruel persecution of the Jews, but in 1543 he counseled their expulsion from Christian lands, and the burning of their books, synagogues, and private houses in which they blaspheme our Savior and the Holy Virgin. He repeated this advice in his last sermon, preached at Eisleben a few days before his death.

Melanchthon

Melanchthon's record on this painful subject is unfortunately worse than Luther's. This is all the more significant because he was the mildest and gentlest among the Reformers. But we should remember that his utterances on the subject are of a later date, several years after Luther's death. He thought that the Mosaic law against idolatry and blasphemy was as binding upon Christian states as the Decalogue, and was applicable to heresies as well. He therefore fully and repeatedly justified the course of Calvin and the Council of Geneva, and even held them up as models for imitation! In a letter to Calvin, dated Oct. 14, 1554, nearly one year after the burning of Servetus, he wrote: – "Reverend and dear Brother: I have read your book, in which you have clearly refuted the horrid blasphemies of Servetus; and I give thanks to the Son of God, who was the awarder of your crown of victory in this your combat. To you also the Church owes gratitude at the present moment, and will owe it to the latest posterity. I perfectly assent to your opinion. I affirm also that your magistrates did right in punishing, after a regular trial, this blasphemous man." A year later, Melanchthon wrote to Bullinger, Aug. 20, 1555: – "Reverend and dear Brother: I have read your answer to the blasphemies of Servetus, and I approve of your piety and opinions. I judge also that the Genevese Senate did perfectly right, to put an end to this obstinate man, who could never cease blaspheming. And I wonder at those who disapprove of this severity." Three years later, April 10, 1557, Melanchthon incidentally (in the admonition in the case of Theobald Thamer, who had returned to the Roman Church) adverted again to the execution of Servetus, and called it, a pious and memorable example to all posterity."1025 It is an example, indeed, but certainly not for imitation.

This unqualified approval of the death penalty for heresy and the connivance at the bigamy of Philip of Hesse are the two dark spots on the fair name of this great and good man. But they were errors of judgment. Calvin took great comfort from the endorsement of the theological head of the Lutheran Church.

Martin Bucer

Bucer, who stands third in rank among the Reformers of Germany, was of a gentle and conciliatory disposition, and abstained from persecuting the Anabaptists in Strassburg. He knew Servetus personally, and treated him at first with kindness, but after the publication of his work on the Trinity, be refuted it in his lectures as a "most pestilential book." He even declared in the pulpit or in the lecture-room that Servetus deserved to be disemboweled and torn to pieces. From this we may infer how fully he would have approved his execution, had he lived till 1553.

The Swiss Churches

The Swiss Reformers ought to have been in advance of those of Germany on this subject, but they were not. They advised or approved the exclusion of Roman Catholics from the Reformed Cantons, and violent measures against Anabaptists and Antitrinitarians. Six Anabaptists were, by a cruel irony, drowned in the river Limmat at Zürich by order of the government (between 1527 and 1532). Other cantons took the same severe measures against the Anabaptists. Zwingli, the most liberal among the Reformers, did not object to their punishment, and counseled the forcible introduction of Protestantism into the neutral territories and the Forest Cantons. Ochino was expelled from Zürich and Basel (1563).As regards the case of Servetus, the churches and magistrates of Zürich, Schaffhausen, Basel, and Bern, on being consulted during his trial, unanimously condemned his errors, and advised his punishment, but without committing themselves to the mode of punishment. Bullinger wrote to Calvin that God had given the Council of Geneva a most favorable opportunity to vindicate the truth against the pollution of heresy, and the honor of God against blasphemy. In his Second Helvetic Confession (ch. XXI) he teaches that it is the duty of the magistrate to use the sword against blasphemers. Schaffhausen fully agreed with Zürich. Even the authorities of Basel, which was the headquarters of the skeptical Italians and enemies of Calvin, gave the advice that Servetus, whom their own Oecolampadius had declared a most dangerous man, be deprived of the power to harm the Church, if all efforts to convert him should fail. Six years afterwards the Council of Basel, with the consent of the clergy and the University, ordered the body of David Joris, a chiliastic Anabaptist who had lived there under a false name (and died Aug. 25, 1556), to be dug from the grave and burned, with his likeness and books, by the hangman before a large multitude (1559).

Bern, which had advised moderation in the affair of Bolsec two years earlier, judged more severely in the case of Servetus, because he "had reckoned himself free to call in question all the essential points of our religion," and expressed the wish that the Council of Geneva might have prudence and strength to deliver the Churches from "this pest." Thirteen years after the death of Servetus, the Council of Bern executed Valentino Gentile by the sword (Sept. 10, 1566) for an error similar to but less obnoxious than that of Servetus, and scarcely a voice was raised in disapproval of the sentence.

The Reformers of French Switzerland went further than those of German Switzerland. Farel defended death by fire, and feared that Calvin in advising a milder punishment was guided by the feelings of a friend against his bitterest foe. Beza wrote a special work in defense of the execution of Servetus, whom he characterized as "a monstrous compound of mere impiety and horrid blasphemy." Peter Martyr called him "a genuine son of the devil," whose "pestiferous and detestable doctrines" and "intolerable blasphemies" justified the severe sentence of the magistracy.

Cranmer

The English Reformers were not behind those of the continent in the matter of intolerance. Several years before the execution of Servetus, Archbishop Cranmer had persuaded the reluctant young King Edward VI. to sign the death-warrant of two Anabaptists – one a woman, called Joan Becher of Kent, and the other a foreigner from Holland, George Van Pare; the former was burnt May 2, 1550, the latter, April 6, 1551.The only advocates of toleration in the sixteenth century were Anabaptists and

Antitrinitarians, who were themselves sufferers from persecution. Let us give them credit for their humanity.

Gradual Triumph of Toleration and Liberty

The reign of intolerance continued to the end of the seventeenth century. It was gradually undermined during the eighteenth century, and demolished by the combined influences of Protestant Dissenters, as the Anabaptists, Socinians, Arminians, Quakers, Presbyterians, Independents, of Anglican Latitudinarians, and of philosophers, like Bayle, Grotius, Locke, Leibnitz; nor should we forget Voltaire and Frederick the Great, who were unbelievers, but sincere and most influential advocates of religious toleration; nor Franklin, Jefferson, and Madison in America. Protestant Holland and Protestant England took the lead in the legal recognition of the principles of civil and religious liberty, and the Constitution of the United States completed the theory by putting all Christian denominations on a parity before the law and guaranteeing them the full enjoyment of equal rights.

Hand in hand with the growth of tolerance went the zeal for prison reform, the abolition of torture and cruel punishments, the abrogation of the slave trade, serfdom, and slavery, the improvement of the condition of the poor and miserable, and similar movements of philanthropy, which are the late but genuine outgrowth of the spirit of Christianity.

Philip Scaff, The History of the Church

English Confessors and Martyrs (1534-1729)

Though the resistance of the English as a people to the Reformation compares very badly with the resistance offered by several other nations, the example given by those who did stand firm is remarkably interesting and instructive.

(1) They suffered the extreme penalty for maintaining the unity of the Church and the Supremacy of the Apostolic See, the doctrines most impugned by the reformation in all lands, and at all times.

(2) They maintained their faith almost entirely by the most modern methods, and they were the first to so maintain it, i.e., by education of the clergy in the seminaries, and of Catholic youth in colleges, at the risk, and often at the cost of life.

(3) The tyranny they had to withstand was, as a rule, not the sudden violence of a tyrant, but the continuous oppression of laws, sanctioned by the people in Parliament, passed on the specious plea of political and national necessity, and operating for centuries with an almost irresistible force which the law acquires when acting for generations in conservative and law-abiding counties.

(4) The study of their causes and their acts is easy. The number of martyrs are many; their trials are spread over a long time. We have in many cases the papers of the prosecution as well as those of the defense, and the voice of Rome is frequently heard pronouncing on the questions of the debate, and declaring that this or that matter is essential, on which no compromise can be permitted; or by her silence she lets it be understood that some other formula may pass.

The cause of the beatification

The cause of the beatification of the English Martyrs is important not for England only, but for all missionary countries, where its precedents may possibly be followed. The English cause is a very ancient one. Pope Gregory XIII, between 1580 and 1585, made several important viva voce concessions. Relics of these, martyrs might, in default of others, be used to consecrate altars, a Te Deum might be publically sung on the receipt of the news of their martyrdoms, and their pictures, and their pictures with their names attached might be placed in the church of the English College, Rome. These permissions were given without any systematic inquiry that we know of Pope Urban VII, in 1642, commenced such an inquiry, and though the outbreak of the civil war in 1642 postponed indefinitely the public progress of the cause, a list was drawn up by the vicar Apostolic,

Dr. Richard Smith, Bishop of Chalcedon, which was subsequently amplified and published by Dr. Richard Challoner. It was not until 1855 that the cause was revived, when Canon John Morris (a Jesuit after 1866) became its apostle. After several unsuccessful petitions, as that of the Third Synod of Westminster in 1859, to obtain an immediate sanction for their cultus by papal decree, a formal "ordinary process" was held in London, June to September, 1874. The work was one of much difficulty, first because nothing of the sort had been attempted in England before, and secondly because of the multitude of the martyrs. Largely, however, through the public spirit of the Fathers of the London Oratory, who devoted themselves to it unitedly, success was achieved, both in gathering together a body of evidence, and in fulfilling the multifarious ceremonial precautions on which the Roman jurists so strongly insist. After the cause had been for twelve years in the Roman courts, two decrees were issued which, broadly speaking, gave full force and efficacy to the two ancient papal ordinations before mentioned.

Thus Pope Gregory's concession resulted in the equivalent beatification of sixty-three martyrs mentioned by name in the pictures (at first, in 1888, fifty-four were admitted; in 1895, eight more were added, with one not in the Roman pictures), while the lists drawn up by Bishops Smith and Challoner led to the "admission of the cause" of two hundred and forty-one martyrs (all but twelve post-Gregorian), who are therefore called "Venerables". Forty-four were left with their fate still in suspense, and are called Dilati. Except seven, these are all "Confessors", who certainly died in prison for their faith, though it is not yet proven that they died precisely because of their imprisonment. There is yet another class to be described. While the foregoing cause was pending, great progress was being made with the arrangement of papers in the Public record Office of London, so that we now know immeasurably more of the persecution and its victims than before the cause began. In short, over 230 additional sufferers seem possibly worthy of being declared martyrs. They are called Prætermissi, because they were passed over in the first cause. A new cause was therefore held at Westminster (September, 1888, to August, 1889), and the proceedings have been sent to Rome. For reasons which it is not necessary to touch upon here, it was thought best to include every possible claimant, even those of whom there was very little definite information, and the far-reaching cause of Queen Mary Stuart. This, however, proved a tactical mistake. An obscure cause needs as much attention as a clear cause, or more. Moreover, the Roman courts are, on the one hand, so short-handed, that they grudge giving men to a work which will lead to little result, and on the other hand they are overwhelmed with causes which certainly need attention. In order to facilitate progress, therefore, the cause has been split up; the case of Queen Mary has been handed over to the hierarchy of Scotland, and other simplifications have been attempted; nevertheless the cause of the Prætermissi so far hangs fire. Apostolic letters for a Processus de Scriptus were issued by the Sacred Congregation on Rites on 24 March, 1899, ordering the then Archbishop of Westminster to gather up copies of all the extant writings of the martyrs declared Venerable. This proved a lengthy task, and when complete, the collection comprised nearly 500 scripta, and over 2000 pages. It was not completed till 17 June, 1904. Then, by special concession, four censors were appointed to draw up a special censura in England, and this was forwarded to Rome, where, after further consideration, a decree was drawn up and confirmed by the Pope on 2 March, 1906, declaring that none of the writings produced would hinder the cause of the martyrs now under discussion. In the course of the same year a further decree was obtained allowing altars for the beati, but not without many restrictions.

I. BEATI

The sixty-three are here arranged in companies when they were tried or died together.

(1) UNDER KING HENRY VIII
Cardinal: John Fisher, Bishop of Rochester, 22 June, 1535.
Lord Chancellor: Sir Thomas More, 6 July, 1535.
Carthusians: John Houghton, Robert Lawrence, Augustine Webster, 4 May, 1535; Humphrey Middlemore, William Exmew, Sebastian Newdigate, 19 June, 1535; John Rochester, James Walworth, 11 May, 1537; Thomas Johnson, William Greenwood, John Davye, Robert Salt, Walter Pierson, Thomas Green, Thomas Scryven, Thomas Redyng, Richard Bere, June-September, 1537; Robert Horne, 4 August, 1540.
Benedictines: Richard Whiting, Hugh Farringdon, abbots, 15 November, 1539; Thomas Marshall (or John Beche), 1 December, 1539; John Thorne, Richard James, William Eynon, John Rugg, 15 Nov, 1539
Doctors of Divinity: Thomas Abel, Edward Powell, Richard Fetherstone, 30 July, 1540.
Other secular priests: John Haile, 4 May 1535; John Larke, 7 March, 1544.
Other religious orders: Richard Reynold, Brigittine (4 May, 1535); John Stone, O.S.A., 12 May, 1538; John Forrest, O.S.F., 22 May, 1538.
Laymen and women: Adrian Fortescue, Knight of St. John, 9 July, 1539; Margaret Pole, Countess of Salisbury, 28 May, 1541; German Gardiner, 7 March, 1544.

(2) UNDER QUEEN ELIZABETH
Martyrs connected with the Excommunication: John Felton, 8 Aug., 1570; Thomas Plumtree, 4 Jan., 1571; John Storey, D.C.L., 1 June, 1571; Thomas Percy. Earl of Northumberland, 22 Aug., 1572; Thomas Woodhouse, 13 June, 1573.
First martyrs from the seminaries: Cuthbert Mayne, Protomartyr of Douai College, 29 Nov, 1577; John Nelson, and S.J. before death, 3 Feb., 1578; Thomas Nelson, church student, 7 Feb., 1578; Everard Hanse p., 31 July, 1581.
Martyrs of the Catholic Revival: Edmund Campion, S.J., Ralph Sherwin, Protomartyr of the English College, Rome, Alexander Briant p., and S.J. before death, 1 Dec., 1581; John Payne, 2 April, 1582; Thomas Ford p., John Shert p., Robert Johnson p., 28 May, 1582; William Firby p., Luke Kirby p., Lawrence Richardson p., Thomas Cottom p., and S.J. before death, 30 May, 1582.
York martyrs: William Lacey p., Richard Kirkman p., 22 Aug., 1582; James Thomson p., 28 Nov, 1582; William Hart p., 15 March, 1583; Richard Thirkeld p., 29 May, 1583.

II. VENERABLES

Separate notices will be given of the more notable martyrs and groups of martyrs. But, though they all died heroically, their lives were so retired and obscure that there is generally but little known about them. It may, however, be remarked that, being educated in most cases in the same seminaries, engaged in the same work, and suffering under the same procedures and laws, the details which we know about some of the more notable martyrs (of whom special biographies are given) are generally also true for the more obscure. The authorities, too, will be the same in both cases.

(1) UNDER KING HENRY VIII (12) 1537-38
Anthony Brookby, Thomas Belchiam, Thomas Cort, Franciscans, thrown into prison for preaching against the king's supremacy. Brookby was strangled with his own girdle, the others died of ill treatment.
1539: Friar Waire, O.S.F., and John Griffith p. (generally known as Griffith Clarke), Vicar of Wandsworth, for supporting the papal legate, Cardinal Pole, drawn and quartered, (8 July) at St. Thomas Waterings; Sir Thomas Dingley, Knight of St. John, beheaded, 10 July, with Bl. Adrian Fortescue. John Travers, Irish Augustinian, who had written against the supremacy; before execution his hand was cut off and burnt, but the writing fingers were not consumed, 30 July.
1540-1544: Edmund Brindholme p., of London, and Clement Philpot l., of Calais, attainted for having "adhered to the Pope of Rome", hanged and quartered at Tyburn, 4

Aug., 1540; Sir David Gonson (also Genson and Gunston), Knight of St. John, son of Vice-Admiral Gonson, attainted for "adhering" to Cardinal Pole, hanged and quartered at St. Thomas Waterings, 1 July, 1541; John Ireland p., once a chaplain to More, condemned and executed with Bl. John Larke, 1544; Thomas Ashby, 29 March, 1544.

(2) Under Queen Elizabeth

1583: John Slade, 30 Oct., Winchester, with John Bodley, 2 Nov, Andover.

1584: William Carter, 11 Jan., Tyburn; George Haydock p., with James Fenn p., Thomas Hemerford p., John Nutter p., John Munden p., 12 Feb., Tyburn; James Bell p., with John Finch, 20 April, Lancaster; Richard White, 17 Oct., Revham.

1585: Thomas Alfield p., with Thomas Webley l., 6 July, Tyburn; Hugh Taylor p., with Marmaduke Bowes l., 26 Nov, York. From this time onwards almost all the priests suffered under the law of 27 Elizabeth, merely for their priestly character.

1586: Edward Stransham p., with Nicholas Woodfen p., 21 Jan., Tyburn; Margaret Clitherow, 25 March, York; Richard Sergeant p., with William Thompson p., 20 April, Tyburn; Robert Anderton p., with William Marsden p., 25 April, Isle of Wight; Francis Ingleby p., 3 June, York; John Finglow p., 8 Aug., York; John Sandys p., 11 Aug., Gloucester; John Adams p., with John Lowe p., 8 Oct., Tyburn, and Richard Dibdale p., 8 Oct; Tyburn; Robert Bickerdike p., 8 Oct., York; Richard Langley l., 1 Dec., York.

1587: Thomas Pilchard p., 21 March, Dorchester; Edmund Sykes p., 23 March, York; Robert Sutton p., 27 July, Stafford; Stephen Rowsham p., July or earlier, Gloucester; John Hambley p., about same time, Chard in Somerset; George Douglas p., 9 Sept., York; Alexander Crowe, 13 Nov, York.

1588: Nicholas Garlick p., with Robert Ludlum p. and Richard Sympson p., 24 July, Derby; Robert Morton p., and Hugh Moor l., in Lincoln's Inn Fields; William Gunter p., Theater, Southwark; Thomas Holford p., Clerkenwell; William Dean p., and Henry Webley l., Mile End Green; James Claxton p.; Thomas Felton, O.S.F., Hounslow. These eight were condemned together and suffered on the same day, 28 Aug. Richard Leigh p., Edward Shelly l., Richard Martin l., Richard Flower (Floyd or Lloyd) l., John Roche l., Mrs. Margaret Ward, all condemned with the last, and all suffered 30 Aug., Tyburn. William Way p., 23 Sept., Kingston-on-Thames; Robert Wilcox p., with Edward Campion p., Christopher Buxton p., Robert Windmerpool l., 1 Oct., Canterbury; Robert Crocket p., with Edward James p., 1 Oct., Chichester; John Robertson p., 1 Oct., Ipswich; William Hartley p. Theatre, Southwark, with John Weldon p., Mile End Green, Robert Sutton l., Clerkenwell, and Richard Williams (Queen Mary priest, who was more probably executed in 1592, and his name, erroneously transferred here, seems to have pushed out that of John Symons, or Harrison), 5 Oct., Halloway; Edward Burden p., 29 Nov, York; William Lampley l., Gloucester, day uncertain.

1589: John Amias p., with Robert Dalby p., 16 March, York; George Nichols p., with Richard Yaxley p., Thomas Belson l., and Humphrey Pritchard l., 5 July, Oxford; William Spenser p., with Robert Hardesty l., 24 Sept., York.

1590: Christopher Bayles p., Fleet Street, with Nicholas Horner l., Smithfield, and Alexander Blake, l., 4 March, Gray's Inn Lane; Miles Gerard p., with Francis Dicconson p., 30 April, Rochester; Edward Jones p., Conduit, Fleet Street, and Anthony Middleton p., 6 May, Clerkenwell; Edmund Duke p., with Richard Hill p., John Hogg p., and Richard Holliday p., 27 May, Durham.

1591: Robert Thorpe p., with Thomas Watkinson l., 31 May, York; Monford Scott p., q.

X, with George Beesley p., 2 July, Fleet Street, London; Roger Dicconson p., with Ralph Milner l., 7 July, Winchester; William Pikes l., day not known, Dorchester; Edmund Jennings p., with Swithin Wells l., Gray's Inn Fields; Eustace White p., with Polydore Plasden p., Brian Lacey l., John

Masson l., Sydney Hodgson l., all seven, 10 Dec., Tyburn.
1592: William Patenson p., 22 Jan., Tyburn; Thomas Pormort p., 20 Feb., St. Paul's Churchyard. London; Roger Ashton, 23 June, Tyburn.
1593: Edward Waterson p., 7 Jan. (but perhaps of the next year), Newcastle-on-Tyne; James Bird l., hanged 25 March, Winchester; Joseph Lampton p., 27 July, Newcastle-on-Tyne; William Davies p., 21 July, Beaumaris.
1594: John Speed l., condemned for receiving a priest, 4 Feb., Durham; William Harrington p., 18 Feb., Tyburn; John Cornelius, S.J., with Thomas Bosgrave l., John Carey l., Patrick Salmon l., 4 July, Dorchester; John Boste p., Durham, with John Ingram p., Newcastle-on-Tyne, and George Swallowell, a convert minister, tried together, they suffered 24, 25, and 26 July, Darlington; Edward Osbaldeston p., 16 Nov, York.
1595: Robert Southwell p., S.J., 21 Feb., Tyburn; Alexander Rawlins p., with Henry Walpole p., S.J., 7 April, York; William Freeman p., 13 Aug., Warwick; Philip Howard, Earl of Arundel, 19 Oct., Tower of London.
1596: George Errington, gentleman, William Knight l., William Gibson l., Henry Abbott l., 29 Nov, York.
1597: William Andleby p., with Thomas Warcop l., Edward Fulthrop l., 4 July, York.
1598: John Britton, 1 April, York; Peter Snow p., with Ralph Gromston l., 15 June, York; John Buckley O.S.F., 12 July, St. Thomas Waterings; Christopher Robertson p., 19 Aug., Carlisle; Richard Horner p., 4 Sept., York; 1599: John Lion, l., 16 July, Oakham; James Dowdal, l., 13 Aug., Exeter.
1600: Christopher Wharton p., 28 March, York; John Rigby, 21 June, St. Thomas Waterings; Thomas Sprott p., with Thomas Hunt p., 11 July, Lincoln; Robert Nutter p., with Edward Thwing p., 26 July, Lancaster; Thomas Palasor p., with John Norton l., and John Talbot l., 9 Aug., Durham.
1601: John Pibush p., 18 Feb., St. Thomas Waterings; Mark Barkworth, O.S.B., with Roger Filcock, S.J., and Anne Linne 27 Feb., Tyburn; Thurstan Hunt p., with Robert Middleton p., 31 March Lancaster; Nicholas Tichborne, with Thomas Hackshot l., 24 Aug., Tyburn; 1602: James Harrison p., with Anthony Battie or Bates l., 22 March, York; James Duckett, 19 April, Tyburn; Thomas Tichborne p., with Robert Watkinson p., and Francis Page, S. J., 20 April, Tyburn.
1603: William Richardson p., 17 Feb., Tyburn.

(3) Under James I and Charles

1604: John Sugar p., with Robert Grissold l., 16 July, Warwick; Lawrence Bailey l., 16 Sept., Lancaster; 1605: Thomas Welborne l., with John Fulthering l., 1 Aug., York; William Brown l., 5 Sept., Ripon; 1606: Martyrs at the time of the Powder Plot: Nicholas Owen, S.J., day unknown, Tower; Edward Oldcorne, S. J., with Robert Ashley, S. J., 7 April, Worcester. From this time to the end of the reign the martyrs might have saved their lives had they taken the condemned oath of allegiance. 1607: Robert Drury p., 26 Feb., Tyburn; 1608: Matthew Flathers p., 21 March, York; George Gervase, O.S.B., 11 April, Tyburn; Thomas Garnet, S.J., 23 June, Tyburn. 1610: Roger Cadwallador p., 27 Aug., Leominster; George Napper p., 9 No., Oxford; Thomas Somers p., 10 Dec., Tyburn; John Roberts, O.S.B., 10 Dec., Tyburn; 1612: William Scot, O.S.B., with Richard Newport p., 30 May, Tyburn; John Almond p., 5 Dec., Tyburn; 1616: Thomas Atkinson p., 11 March, York; John Thouless p., with Roger Wrenno l., 18 March, Lancaster; Thomas Maxfield p., 1 July, Tyburn; Thomas Tunstall p., 13 July, Norwich; 1618: William Southerne p., 30 April, Newcastle-under-Lyne. 1628: Edmund Arrowsmith, S. J., (see Edmund Arrowsmith) with Richard Herst l., 20 and 21 Aug., Lancaster.

(4) Commonwealth

All these suffered before the death of Oliver Cromwell. -1641: William Ward p., 26 July, Tyburn; Edward Barlow, O.S.B., 10 Sept., Lancaster; 1642: Thomas Reynolds p., with Bartholomew Roe, O.S.B., 21 January, Tyburn; John Lockwood p., with Edmund

Catherick p., 13 April, York; Edward Morgan p., 26 April, Tyburn; Hugh Green p., 19 Aug., Dorchester; Thomas Bullaker, O.S.F., 12 Oct., Tyburn; Thomas Holland, S.J., 12 Dec., Tyburn. 1643: Henry Heath, O.S.F., 17 April, Tyburn; Brian Cansfield, S.J., 3 Aug., York Castle; Arthur Bell, 11 Dec., Tyburn; 1644: Richard Price, colonel, 7 May, Lincoln; John Duckett p., with Ralph Corbin, S.J., 7 Sept., Tyburn; 1645: Henry Morse, S.J., 1 Feb., Tyburn; John Goodman p., 8 April, Newgate; 1646: Philip Powell, O.S.B., 30 June, Tyburn; John Woodcock, O.S.F., with Edward Bamber p., and Thomas Whitaker p., 7 Aug., Lancaster. 1651: Peter Wright, S.J., 19 May, Tyburn. 1654: John Southworth p., 28 June, Tyburn.

(5) The Oates Plot

1678: Edward Coleman, 3 Dec., Tyburn; Edward Mico, S.J., 3 Dec., in Newgate; Thomas Beddingfeld, 21 Dec., in Gatehouse Prison; 1679: William Ireland, S.J., with John Grove l., 24 Jan, Tyburn; Thomas Pickering O.S.B., 9 May, Tyburn; Thomas Whitbread S.J., with William Harcourt, S.J., John Fenwick, S.J., John Gavin or Green S.J., and Anthony Turner, S.J., 20 June, Tyburn; Francis Nevil, S.J. , Feb., in Stafford Gaol; Richard Langhorne, 14 July, Tyburn; William Plessington p., 19 July, Chester; Philip Evans, S.J., 22 July, with John Lloyd p., 22 July, Cardiff; Nicholas Postgate p., 7 Aug., York; Charles Mahoney, 12 Aug., Ruthin; John Wall, O.S.F., 29 Aug., Worcester; Francis Levinson, O.S.F., 11 Feb., in prison; John Kemble p., 22 Aug., Hereford; David Lewis, S.J., 27 Aug., Usk. 1680: Thomas Thwing p., 23 Oct., York; William Howard, Viscount Stafford, 29 Dec., Tower Hill. The cause of Irish martyr Oliver Plunkett, 1 July, Tower hill, was commenced with the above martyrs. The cause of his beatification is now being actively proceeded with by the Cardinal Archbishop of Armaugh.

VIII. THE FORTY-FOUR DILATI

These are those "put off" for further proof. Of these, the majority were confessors, who perished after a comparatively short period of imprisonment, though definite proof of their death *ex oerumnis* is not forthcoming.

(1) Under Queen Elizabeth (18)

Robert Dimock, hereditary champion of England, was arrested at Mass, and perished after a few weeks' imprisonment at Lincoln, 11 Sept., 1580; John Cooper, a young man, brought up by the writer, Dr. Nicholas Harpsfield, and probably a distributor of Catholic books, arrested at Dover and sent to the Tower, died of "hunger, cold, and stench", 1580; Mr. Ailworth (Aylword), probably of Passage Castle, Waterford, who admitted Catholics to Mass at his house, was arrested, and died after eight days, 1580; William Chaplain p., Thomas Cotesmore p., Roger Holmes p., Roger Wakeman p., James Lomax p., perished in 1584. Cotesmore was a bachelor of Oxford in 1586; of Wakeman's suffering several harrowing details are on record. Thomas Crowther p., Edward Pole p., John Jetter p., and Laurence Vaux p., perished in 1585; John Harrison p., 1586; Martin Sherson p., and Gabriel Thimelby p., 1587; Thomas Metham S.J., 1592; Eleanor Hunt and Mrs. Wells, gentlewomen, on unknown days in 1600 and 1602.

(2) Under the Commonwealth (8)

Edward Wilkes p., died in York Castle before execution in 1642; Boniface Kempe (or Francis Kipton) and Idlephonse Hesketh (or William Hanson) O.S.B., professed of Montserrat, seized by Puritan soldiery in Yorkshire, and worried to death, 26 July (?), 1644; Richard Bradley S.J., b. at Bryning Hall, Lancs, 1605, of a well-known Catholic family, seized, imprisoned, but died before trial at Manchester, 20 Jan, 1640; John Felton, S.J., visiting another Father in Lincoln, was seized and so badly used that, when released (for no one appeared against him) he died within a month, 17 Feb., 1645; Thomas Vaughan of Cortfield p., and Thomas Blount p., imprisoned at Shrewsbury, d. at unknown date; Robert Cox, O.S.B., died at the Clink Prison, 1650.

(3) During the Oates Plot (10)

Thomas Jennison S.J., d. after twelve

months' imprisonment, 27 Sept., 1679. he had renounced a handsome inheritance in favor of his brother, who, nevertheless, having apostatized, turned king's evidence against him. William Lloyd, d. under sentence of death, Brecknock, 1679. Placid Aldham or John Adland (O.S.B.), a convert clergyman, chaplain to Queen Catherine of Braganza, d. under sentence in 1679. William Atkins, S.J., condemned at Stafford, was too deaf to hear the sentence. When it was shouted in his ear he turned and thanked the judge; he was reprieved and died in bonds, 7 March, 1681. Richard Birkett p., d. 1680 under sentence in Lancaster Castle; but our martyrologists seem to have made some confusion between him and John Penketh, S.J., a fellow prisoner (see Gillow, Cath. Rec. Soc., IV, pp. 431-440). Richard Lacey (Prince), S.J., Newgate, 11 March, 1680; William Allsion p., York Castle, 1681; Edward Turner, S.J., 19 March, 1681, Gatehouse; Benedict Counstable, O.S.B., professed at Lamspring, 1669, 11 Dec., 1683, Durham Gaol; Willaim Bennet (Bentney), S.J., 30 Oct., 1692, Leicester Gaol under William III.

(4) Others Put Off for Various Causes (8)

John Mawson, 1614, is not yet sufficiently distinguished from John Mason, 1591; there is a similar difficulty between Matthias Harrison, assigned to 1599, and James Harrison, 1602; William Tyrrwhit, named by error for his brother Robert; likewise the identity of Thomas Dyer, O.S.B., has been fully proved; James Atkinson, killed under torture by Topcliffe, but evidence is wanted of his consistency to the end. Fr. Henry Garnet, S.J., was he killed ex odio fidei, or was he believed to be guilty of the Powder Plot, by merely human misjudgment, not through religious prejudice? The case of Lawrence Hill and Robert Green at the time of the Oates Plot is similar. Was it due to odium fidei, or an unprejudiced error?

IX THE PRÆTERMISSI (242)

(1) Martyrs on the Scaffold

1534: Elizabeth Barton, (The Holy Maid of Kent), with five companions; John Dering, O.S.B., Edward Bocking, O.S.B., Hugh Rich, O.S.F., Richard Masters p., Henry Gold p., 1537. Monks, 28.

After the pilgrimage of grace and the rising of Lincolnshire many, probably several hundred, were executed, of whom no record remains. The following names, which do survive, are grouped under their respective abbeys or priories.

Barling: Matthew Mackerel, abbot and Bishop of Chalcedon, Ord. Præm. Bardney: John Tenent, William Cole, John Francis, William Cowper, Richard Laynton, Hugh Londale, monks.

Bridlington: William Wood, Prior.

Fountains: William Thyrsk, O. Cist.

Guisborough: James Cockerel, Prior.

Jervaulx: Adam Sedbar, Abbot; George Asleby, monk.

Kirkstead: Richard Harrison, Abbott, Richard Wade, William Swale, Henry Jenkinson, monks.

Lenten: Nicholas Heath, Prior; William Gylham, monk.

Sawlet: William Trafford, Abbott; Richard Eastgate, monk.

Whalley: John Paslew, Abbott; John Eastgate, William Haydock, monks.

Woburn: Robert Hobbes, Abbott; Ralph Barnes, sub-prior; Laurence Blonham, monk.

York: John Pickering, O.S.D., Prior.

Place unknown: George ab Alba Rose, O.S.A. Priests: William Burraby, Thomas Kendale, John Henmarsh, James Mallet, John Pickering, Thomas Redforth. Lords: Darcy and Hussey. Knights: Francis Bigod, Stephen Hammerton, Thomas Percy. Laymen (11): Robert Aske, Robert Constable, Bernard Fletcher, George Hudswell, Robert Lecche, Roger Neeve, George Lomley, Thomas Moyne, Robert Sotheby, Nicholas Tempest, Philip Trotter. 1538 (7): Henry Courtney, the Marquess of Exeter; Henry Pole, Lord Montague; Sir Edward Nevell and Sir Nicholas Carew; George Croft p., and John Collins p.; Hugh Holland l.. Their cause was "adhering to the Pope, and his Legate, Cardinal Pole". 1540 (6): Lawrence Cook O. Carm., Prior of Doncaster; Thomas Empson, O.S.B.; Robert Bird p.; William Peterson p.; William

Richardson p.; Giles Heron l. 1544 (3): Martin de Courdres, O.S.A., and Paul of St. William, O.S.A.; Darby Genning l. 1569, 1570 (8): Thomas Bishop, Simon Digby, John Fulthrope, John Hall, Christopher Norton, Thomas Norton, Robert Pennyman, Oswald Wilkinson, Laymen, who suffered, like Blessed Thomas Percy, Earl of Northumberland, on the occasion of the Northern Rising. Various Years (6): Thomas Gabyt, O. Cist., 1575; William Hambleton p., 1585; Roger Martin p., 1592; Christopher Dixon, O.S.A., 1616; James Laburne, 1583; Edward Arden, 1584.

(2) Martyrs in Chains

Bishops (2): Richard Creagh, Archbishop of Armaugh, in Tower of London; Thomas Watson, Bishop of Lincoln, in Wisbeach Castle. Priests in London Prisons (18): Austin Abbott, Richard Adams, Thomas Belser, John Boxall, D.D., James Brushford, Edmund Cannon, William Chedsey, D.D., Henry Cole, D.D., Anthony Draycott, D.D., Andrew Fryer,: Gretus, Richard Hatton, Nicholas Harpsfield,: Harrison, Francis Quashet, Thomas Slythurst, William Wood, John Young, D.D. Laymen in London Prisons (35): Alexander Bales, Richard Bolbet, Sandra Cubley, Thomas Cosen, Mrs. Cosen, Hugh Dutton, Edward Ellis, Gabriel Empringham, John Fitzherbert, Sir Thomas Fitzherbert, John Fryer, Anthony Fugatio (Portuguese),: Glynne, David Gwynne, John Hammond (alias Jackson). Richard Hart, Robert Holland, John Lander, Anne Lander, Peter Lawson, Widow Lingon, Phillipe Lowe,: May, John Molineaux, Henry Percy, Earl of Northumberland, Richard Reynolds, Edmund Sexton, Robert Shelly, Thomas Sommerset, Francis Spencer, John Thomas, Peter Tichborne, William Travers, Sir Edward Waldegrave, Richard Weston. Priests in York (12): John Ackridge, William Baldwin, William Bannersly, Thomas Bedal, Richard Bowes, Henry Comberford, James Gerard, Nicholas Grene, Thomas Harwood, John Pearson, Thomas Ridall, James Swarbrick. Laymen in York (31): Anthony Ash, Thomas Blinkensop, Stephen Branton, Lucy Budge, John Chalmer, Isabel Chalmer, John Constable, Ralph Cowling, John Eldersha, Isabel Foster,: Foster, Agnes Fuister, Thomas Horsley, Stephen Hemsworth, Mary Hutton, Agnes Johnson, Thomas Layne, Thomas Luke, Alice Oldcorne,: Reynold,: Robinson, John Stable, Mrs. Margaret Stable, Geoffrey Stephenson, Thomas Vavasour, Mrs. Dorothy Vavasour, Margaret Webster, Frances Webster, Christopher Watson, Hercules Welborn, Alice Williamson. In Various Prisons: Benedictines (11): James Brown, Richard Coppinger, Robert Edmonds, John Feckinham, Lawrence Mabbs, William Middleton, Placid Peto, Thomas Preston, Boniface Wilford, Thomas Rede, Sister Isabel Whitehead. Brigittine: Thomas Brownel (lay brother). Cistercians (2): John Almond, Thomas Mudde. Dominican: David Joseph Kemys. Franciscans: Thomas Ackridge, Paul Atkinson, q. X (the last of the confessors in chains, died in Hurst Castle, after thirty years' imprisonment, 15 Oct., 1729), Laurence Collier, Walter Coleman, Germane Holmes. Jesuits (12): Matthew Brazier (alias Grimes), Humphrey Browne, Thomas Foster, William Harcourt, John Hudd, Cuthbert Prescott, Ignatius Price, Charles Pritchard, Francis Simeon, Nicholas Tempest, John Thompson, Charles Thursley. Priests (4): William Baldwin, James Gerard, John Pearson, James Swarbick. Laymen (22): Thurstam Arrowsmith, Humphrey Beresford, William Bredstock, James Clayton, William Deeg, Ursula Foster,: Green, William Griffith, William Heath, Richard Hocknell, John Jessop, Richard Kitchin, William Knowles, Thomas Lynch, William Maxfield,: Morecock, Alice Paulin, Edmund Rookwood, Richard Spencer,: Tremaine, Edmund Vyse, Jane Vyse.

X THE ELEVEN BISHOPS

Since the process of the Prætermissi has been held, strong reasons have been shown for including on our list of suffers, whose causes ought to be considered, the eleven bishops whom Queen Elizabeth deprived and left to die in prison, as Bonner, or under some form of confinement. their names are:

Cuthbert Turnstall, b. Durham, died 18 Nov 1559;
Ralph Bayle b. Lichfield, d. 18 Nov, 1559;
Owen Ogle Thorpe, b. Carlisle, d. 31 Dec., 1559;
John White, b. Winchester, d. 12 Jan., 1560;
Richard pate, b. Worcester, d. 23 Nov, 1565;
David Poole, b. Peterborough, d, May, 1568;
Edward Bonner, b. London, d. 5 Sept., 1569;
Gilbert Bourne, b. Bath and Wells, d. 10 Sept., 1569;
Thomas Thurlby, b. Ely, d. 26 Aug., 1570;
James Thurberville, b. Exeter, d. 1 Nov, 1570;
Nicholas Heath, Archbishop of York, d. Dec. 1578.

J.H. Pollen, The Catholic Encyclopedia, Volume 5

The Martyrs of Gorkum

The year 1572, Luther and Calvin had already wrested from the Church a great part of Europe. The iconoclastic storm had swept through the Netherlands, and was followed by a struggle between Lutheranism and Calvinism in which the latter was victorious. In 1571 the Calvinists held their first synod, at Embden. On 1 April of the next year the Watergeuzen (Sea-beggars) conquered Briel and later Vlissingen and other places. In June, Dortrecht and Gorkum fell into their hands and at Gorkum they captured nine Francisans.

These were: Nicholas Pieck, guardian of Gorkum, Hieronymns of Weert, vicar, Theodorus van der Eem, of Amersfoort, Nicasius Janssen, of Heeze, Willehad of Denmark, Godefried of Mervel, Antonius Of Weert, Antonius of Hoornaer, and Franciseus de Roye, of Brussels. To these were added two lay brothers from the same monastery, Petrus of Assche and Cornelius of Wyk near Duurstede. Almost at the same time the Calvinists laid their hands on the learned parish priest of Gorkum, Leonardus Vechel of Bois-le-Duc, who had made distinguished studies in Louvain, and also has assistant Nicolaas Janssen, surnamed Poppel, of Welde in Belgium.

With the above, were also imprisoned Godefried van Duynsen, of Gorkum who was active as a priest in his native city, and Joannes Lenartz of Oisterwljk, an Augustinian and director of the convent of Augustinian nuns in Gorkum. To these fifteen, who from the very first underwent all the sufferings and torments of the persecution, were later added four more companions: Joannes van Hoornaer, a Dominican of the Cologne province and parish priest not far from Gorkum, who, when apprized of the incarceration of the clergy Old Testament Gorkum, hastened to the city in order to administer the sacraments to them and was seized and imprisoned with the rest, Jacobus Lacops of Oudenaar, a Norbertine, who after leading a frivolous life, being disobedient to his order, and neglectful of his religious duties, reformed, became a curate in Monster, Holland and was imprisoned in 1572; Adrianus Janssen of Hilvarenbeek, at one time a Premonstratensian and parish priest in Monster, who was sent to Brielle with Jacobus Lacops; and lastly Andreas Wouters of Heynoord, whose conduct was not edifying up to the time of his arrest, but who made ample amends by his martyrdom. After enduring much suffering and abuse in the prison at Gorkum (26 June-6 July) the first fifteen martyrs were transferred to Brielle. On their way to Dortrecht they were exhibited for money to the curious and arrived at Brielle 13 July. On the following day, Lumey, the commander of the Watergeuzen, caused the martyrs to be interrogated and ordered a sort of disputation. In the meantime the four other martyrs also arrived. It was exacted of each that he abandon his belief in the Blessed Sacrament and in papal supremacy. All remained firm in their faith. Meanwhile there came a letter from William of Orange which enjoined all those in authority to leave priests and religious unmolested. Nevertheless Lumey caused the martyrs to be hanged in the night of 9 July, amid cruel mutilations. Their beatification took place on 14 Nov, 1675, and their canonization on 29 June, 1865. For many years the place of their martyrdom in Brielle has been the scene of numerous pilgrimages and processions.

P. Albers, The Catholic Encyclopedia, Volume 6

Martyrs of Cuncolim, India

On Monday, 25 July, 1583 (N.S.), the village of Cuncolim in the district of Salcete, territory of Goa, India, was the scene of the martyrdom of five religious of the Society of Jesus: Fathers Rudolph Acquaviva, Alphonsus Pacheco, Peter Berno, and Anthony Francis, also Francis Aranha, lay brother.

Rudolph Acquaviva was born 2 October, 1550, at Atri in the Kingdom of Naples. He was the fifth child of the Duke of Atri, and nephew of Claudius Acquaviva, the fifth General of the Society of Jesus, while on his mother's side he was a cousin of St. Aloysius Gonzaga. Admitted into the Society of Jesus 2 April, 1568, he landed in Goa 13 September, 1578. Shortly after his arrival he was selected for a very important mission to the court of the Great Mogul Akbar, who had sent an embassy to Goa with a request that two learned missionaries might be sent to Fatehpir-Sikri, his favoureth residence near Agra. After spending three years at the Mogul court, he returned to Goa, much to the regret of the whole Court and especially of the emperor. On his return to Goa, he was appointed superior of the Salcete mission, which post he held until his martyrdom.

Alphonsus Pacheco was born about 1551, of a noble family of New Castile, and entered the Society on 8 September, 1567. In September, 1574, he arrived in Goa, where he so distinguished himself by his rare prudence and virtue that in 1578 he was sent to Europe on important business. Returning to India in 1581, he was made rector of Rachol. He accompanied two punitive expeditions of the Portuguese to the village of Cuncolim, and was instrumental in destroying the pagodas there.

Peter Berno was born of humble parents in 1550 at Ascona, a Swiss village at the foot of the Alps. After being ordained priest in Rome, he entered the Society of Jesus in 1577, arrived in Goa in 1579, and was soon appointed to Salcete. He accompanied the expeditions to Cuncolim, and assisted in destroying the pagan temples, destroyed an ant-hill which was deemed very sacred, and killed a cow which was also an object of pagan worship. He used to say constantly that no fruit would be gathered from Cuncolim and the hamlets around it till they were bathed in blood shed for the Faith. His superiors declared that he had converted more pagans than all the other fathers put together.

Anthony Francis, born in 1553, was a poor student of Coimbra in Portugal. He joined the Society in 1571, accompanied Father Pacheco to India in 1581, and was shortly afterwards ordained priest in Goa. It is said that whenever he said Mass, he prayed, at the Elevation, for the grace of martyrdom; and that on the day before his death, when he was saying Mass at the church of Orlim, a miracle prefigured the granting of this prayer.

Brother Francis Aranha was born of a wealthy and noble family of Braga in Portugal, about 1551, and went to India with his uncle, the first Archbishop of Goa, Dom Gaspar. There he joined the Society of Jesus, 1 November, 1571. Being a skilled draughtsman and architect, he built several fine chapels in Goa.

These five religious met in the church of Orlim on the 15 of July, 1583, and thence proceeded to Cuncolim, accompanied by some Christians, with the object of erecting a cross and selecting ground for building a church. Seeing an opportunity of doing away with these enemies of their pagodas, the pagan villagers, after holding a council, advanced in large numbers, armed with swords, lances, and other weapons, towards the spot where the Christians were. Gonpalo Rodrigues one of the party, leveled his gun, but Father Pacheco stopped him, saying: "Come, come, Senhor Gonphalo, we are not here to fight." Then, speaking to the crowd, he said in Konkani, their native language, "Do not be afraid". The Pagans then fell upon them; Father Rudolph received five cuts from a scimitar and a spear and died praying God to forgive them, and pronouncing the Holy Name. Father Berno was next horribly mutilated, and Father Pacheco, wounded with a spear, fell on his knees extending his arms in the form of a cross, and praying God to forgive his murderers and send other missionaries to them. Father Anthony Francis was pierced with arrows, and his head was split open with a sword. Brother Aranha, wounded at the outset by a Scimitar and a lance, fell down a deep declivity into the thick crop of a rice-field, where he lay until he was discovered. He was then carried to the idol, to which he was bidden to bow his head. Upon his refusal to do this, he was tied to a tree and, like St. Sebastian was shot to death with arrows. The spot where this tree stood is marked with an octagonal monument surmounted by a cross, which was repaired by the Patriarch of Goa in 1885.

The bodies of the five martyrs were thrown into a well, water of which was afterwards sought by people from all parts of Goa for its miraculous healing. The bodies themselves, when found, after two and a half days, allowed no signs of decomposition. They were solemnly buried in the church of Our Lady of the Snows at Rachol, and remained there until 1597, when they were removed to the college of St. Paul in Goa, and in 1862 to the cathedral of Old Goa. Some of these relics have been sent to Europe at various times. All the bones of the entire right arm of Blessed Rudolph were taken to Rome in 1600, and his left arm was sent from Goa as a present to the Jesuit college at Naples. In accordance with the request of the Pacheco family, an arm and leg of Blessed Alphonsus were sent to Europe in 1609. The process of canonization began in 1600, but it was only in 1741 that Benedict XI declared the martyrdom proved. On the 16th of April, 1893, the solemn beatification of the five martyrs was celebrated at St. Peter's in Rome. It was celebrated in Goa in 1894, and the feast has ever since then been kept with great solemnity at Cuncolim, even by the descendants of the murderers. The Calendar of the Archdiocese of Goa has fixed 26 July as their feast day. Along with the five religious were also killed Gonphalo Rodrigues, a Portuguese, and fourteen native Christians. Of the latter, one was Dominic, a boy of Cuncolim, who was a student at Rachol, and had accompanied the fathers on their expeditions to Cuncolim and pointed out to them the pagan temples. His own heathen uncle dispatched him. Alphonsus, an altar-boy of Father Pacheco had followed him closely, carrying his breviary, which he would not part with. The pagans therefore cut off his hands and cut through his knee-joints to prevent his escape. In this condition he lived till the next day, when he was found and killed. This boy, a native of either Margao or Verna, was buried in the church of the Holy Ghost at Margao.

Francis Rodrigues, who was also murdered, used to say, when he was reproached by the fathers for slight faults, that he hoped to atone for them by shedding his blood as a martyr. Paul da Costa, another of those who died at the hands of the pagans, was an inhabitant of Rachol, and had been distinguished by his desire of dying for the Faith. Speaking of these fifteen courageous Christians, Father Goldie says: For reasons which we have now no means of judging, the Cause of these companions of the five Martyrs was not brought forward before the Archbishop of the time, nor since then has any special cultus, or the interposition of God by miracle, called the attention of the Church to them. But we may hope that their blood was in the odor of sweetness before God.

A.I. D'Souza, The Catholic Encyclopedia, Volume 4

Venerable Robert Southwell

Poet, Jesuit, martyr; born at Horsham St. Faith's, Norfolk, England, in 1561; hanged at Tyburn, 21 February, 1595. His grandfather, Sir Richard Southwell, had been a wealthy man and a prominent courtier in the reign of Henry VIII. It was Richard Southwell who in 1547 had brought the poet Henry Howard, Earl of Surrey, to the block, and Surrey had vainly begged to be allowed to "fight him in his shirt". Curiously enough their respective grandsons, Father Southwell and Philip, Earl of Arundel, were to be the most devoted of friends and fellow-prisoners for the Faith. On his mother's side the Jesuit was descended from the Copley and Shelley families, whence a remote connexion may be established between him an the poet Percy Bysshe Shelley. Robert Southwell was brought up a Catholic, and at a very early age was sent to be educated at Douai, where he was the pupil in philosophy of a Jesuit of extraordinary austerity of life, the famous Leonard Lessius. After spending a short time in Paris he begged for admission into the Society of Jesus – a boon at first denied. This disappointment elicited from the boy of seventeen some passionate laments, the first of his verses of which we have record. On 17 Oct., 1578, however, he was admitted at Rome, and made his simple vows in 1580. Shortly after his noviceship, during which he was sent to Tournai, he returned to Rome to finish his studies, was ordained priest in 1584, and became prefect of studies in the English College. In 1586 he was sent on the English mission with Father Henry Garnett, found his first refuge with Lord Vaux of Harrowden, and was known under the name of Cotton. Two years afterwards he became chaplain to the Countess of Arundel and thus established relations with her imprisoned husband, Philip, Earl of Arundel, the ancestor of the present ducal house of Norfolk, as well as with Lady Margaret Sackville, the earl's half-sister. Father Southwell's prose elegy, "Triumphs over Death", was addressed to the earl to console him for this sister's premature death, and his "Hundred Meditations on the love of God", originally written for her use, were ultimately transcribed by another hand, to present to her daughter Lady Beauchamp. Some six years were spent in zealous and successful missionary work, during which Father Southwell lay hidden in London, or passed under various disguises from one Catholic house to another. For his better protection he affected an interest in the pursuits of the country gentlemen of his day (metaphors taken from hawking are common in his writings), but his attire was always sober and his tastes simple. His character was singularly gentle, and he has never been accused of taking any part either in political intrigues or in religious disputes of a more domestic kind.

In 1592 Father Southwell was arrested at Uxendon Hall, Harrow, through the treachery of an unfortunate Catholic girl, Anne Bellamy, the daughter of the owner of the house. The notorious Topcliffe, who effected the capture, wrote exultingly to the queen: "I never did take so weighty a man, if he be rightly used". But the atrocious cruelties to which Southwell was subjected did not shake his fortitude. He was examined thirteen times under torture by members of the Council, and was long confined in a dungeon swarming with vermin. After nearly three years in prison he was brought to trial and the usual punishment of hanging and quartering was inflicted.

Father Southwell's writings, both in prose and verse, were extremely popular with his contemporaries, and his religious pieces were sold openly by the booksellers though their authorship was known. Imitations abounded, and Ben Jonson declared of one of Southwell's pieces, "The Burning Babe", that to have written it he would readily forfeit many of his own poems. "Mary Magdalene's Tears", the Jesuit's earliest work, licensed in 1591, probably represents a deliberate attempt to employ in the cause of piety the euphuistic prose style, then so popular. "Triumphs over Death", also in prose, exhibits the same characteristics; but this artificiality of structure is not so marked in the "Short Rule of Good Life", the "Letter to His Father", the "Humble Supplication to Her Majesty", the "Epistle of Comfort" and the "Hundred Meditations". Southwell's longest poem, "St. Peter's Complaint" (132 six-line stanzas), is imitated, though not closely, from the Italian "Lagrime di S. Pietro" of Luigi Tansillo. This with some other smaller pieces was printed, with license, in 1595, the year of his death. Another volume of short poems appeared later in the same year under the title of "Maeoniae". The early editions of these are scarce, and some of them command high prices. A poem called "A Foure-fold Meditation", which was printed as Southwell's in 1606, is not his, but was written by his friend the Earl of Arundel. Perhaps no higher testimony can be found of the esteem in which Southwell's verse was held by his contemporaries than the fact that, while it is probable that Southwell had read Shakespeare, it is practically certain that Shakespeare had read Southwell and imitated him.

Herbert Thurston, The Catholic Encyclopedia, Volume 14

An Account of the Persecutions of Friends, Commonly Called Quakers, in the United States

In about the middle of the seventeenth century, much persecution and suffering were inflicted on a sect of Protestant dissenters, commonly called Quakers: a people which arose at that time in England some of whom sealed their testimony with their blood. The principal points upon which their conscientious nonconformity rendered them obnoxious to the penalties of the law, were:

1. The Christian resolution of assembling publicly for the worship of God, in a manner most agreeable to their consciences.

2. Their refusal to pay tithes, which they esteemed a Jewish ceremony, abrogated by the coming of Christ.

3. Their testimony against wars and fighting, the practice of which they judged inconsistent with the command of Christ: "Love your enemies," Matt. 5:44

4. Their constant obedience to the command of Christ: "Swear not at all," Matt. 5:34.

5. Their refusal to pay rates or assessments for building and repairing houses for a worship which they did not approve.

6. Their use of the proper and Scriptural language, "thou," and "thee," to a single person: and their disuse of the custom of uncovering their heads, or pulling off their hats, by way of homage to man.

7. The necessity many found themselves under, of publishing what they believed to be the doctrine of truth; and sometimes even in the places appointed for the public national worship.

Their conscientious noncompliance in the preceding particulars, exposed them to much persecution and suffering, which consisted in prosecutions, fines, cruel beatings, whippings, and other corporal punishments; imprisonment, banishment, and even death. To relate a particular account of their persecutions and sufferings, would extend beyond the limits of this work: we shall therefore refer, for that information, to the histories already mentioned, and more particularly to Besse's Collection of their sufferings; and shall confine our account here mostly to those who sacrificed their lives, and evinced, by their disposition of mind, constancy, patience, and faithful perseverance, that they were influenced by a sense of religious duty. Numerous and repeated were the persecutions against them; and sometimes for transgressions or offences which the law did not contemplate or embrace. Many of the fines and penalties exacted of them, were not only unreasonable and exorbitant, but as they could not consistently pay them, were sometimes distrained to several times the value of the demand; whereby many poor families were greatly distressed, and obliged to depend on the assistance of their friends. Numbers were not only cruelly beaten and whipped in a public manner, like criminals, but some were branded and others had their ears cut off. Great numbers were long confined in loathsome prisons; in which some ended their days in consequence thereof. Many were sentenced to banishment; and a considerable number were transported. Some were banished on pain of death; and four were actually executed by the hands of the hangman, as we shall here relate, after inserting copies of some of the laws of the country where they suffered.

At a General Court Held at Boston, the Fourteenth of October, 1656

"Whereas, there is a cursed sect of heretics, lately risen up in the world, which are commonly called Quakers, who take upon them to be immediately sent from God, and infallibly assisted by the Spirit, to speak and write blasphemous opinions, despising government, and the order of God, in the Church and commonwealth, speaking evil of dignities, reproaching and reviling magistrates and ministers, seeking to turn the people from the faith, and gain proselytes to their pernicious ways: this court taking into consideration the premises, and to prevent the like mischief, as by their means is wrought in our land, doth hereby order, and by authority of this court, be it ordered and enacted, that what master or commander of any ship, bark, pink, or ketch, shall henceforth bring into any harbor, creek, or cove, within this jurisdiction, any Quaker or Quakers, or other blasphemous heretics, shall pay, or cause to be paid, the fine of one hundred pounds to the treasurer of the country, except it appear he want true knowledge or information of their being such; and, in that case, he hath liberty to clear himself by his oath, when sufficient proof to the contrary is wanting: and, for default of good payment, or good security for it, shall be cast into prison, and there to continue until the said sum be satisfied to the treasurer as foresaid."

"And the commander of any ketch, ship, or vessel, being legally convicted, shall give in sufficient security to the governor, or any one or more of the magistrates, who have power to determine the same, to carry them back to the place whence he brought them; and, on his refusal so to do, the governor, or one or more of the magistrates, are hereby empowered to issue out his or their warrants to commit such master or commander to prison, there to continue, until he give in sufficient security to the content of the governor, or any of the magistrates, as aforesaid."

"And it is hereby further ordered and enacted, that what Quaker soever shall arrive in this country from foreign parts, or shall come into this jurisdiction from any parts adjacent, shall be forthwith committed to the House of Correction; and, at their entrance, to be severely whipped, and by the master thereof be kept constantly to work, and none suffered to converse or speak with them, during the time of their imprisonment, which shall be no longer than necessity requires. "And it is ordered, if any person shall knowingly import into any harbor of this jurisdiction, any Quakers' books or writings, concerning their devilish opinions, shall pay for such book or writing, being legally proved against him or them the sum of five pounds; and whosoever shall disperse or conceal any such book or writing, and it be found with him or her, or in his or her house and shall not immediately deliver the same to the next magistrate, shall forfeit or pay five pounds, for the dispersing or concealing of any such book or writing."

"And it is hereby further enacted, that if any persons within this colony shall take upon them to defend the heretical opinions of the Quakers, or any of their books or papers, shall be fined for the first time forty shillings; if they shall persist in the same, and shall again defend it the second time, four pounds; if notwithstanding they again defend and maintain the said Quakers' heretical opinions, they shall be committed to the House of Correction until there be convenient passage to send them out of the land, being sentenced by the court of Assistants to banishment."

"Lastly, it is hereby ordered, that what person or persons soever, shall revile the persons of the magistrates or ministers, as is usual with the Quakers, such person or persons shall be severely whipped or pay the sum of five pounds."

This is a true copy of the court's order, as attests, EDWARD RAWSON, SEC.

At a General Court Held at Boston, the Fourteenth of October, 1657

"As an addition to the late order, in reference to the coming or bringing of any of the cursed sect of the Quakers into this jurisdiction, it is ordered that whosoever shall from henceforth bring, or cause to be brought, directly, or indirectly, any known Quaker or Quakers, or other blasphemous heretics, into this jurisdiction, every such person shall forfeit the sum of one hundred pounds to the country, and shall by warrant from any magistrate be committed to prison, there to remain until the penalty be satisfied and paid; and if any person or persons within this jurisdiction, shall henceforth entertain and conceal any such Quaker or Quakers, or other blasphemous heretics, knowing them so to be, every such person shall forfeit to the country forty shillings for every hour's entertainment and concealment of any Quaker or Quaker, etc., as aforesaid, and shall be committed to prison as aforesaid, until the forfeiture be fully satisfied and paid. "And it is further ordered, that if any Quaker or Quakers shall presume, after they have once suffered what the law requires, to come into this jurisdiction, every such male Quaker shall, for the first offence, have one of his ears cut off, and be kept at work in the House of Correction, until he can be sent away at his own charge; and for the second offence, shall have his other ear cut off; and every woman Quaker, that has suffered the law here, that shall presume to come into this jurisdiction, shall be severely whipped, and kept at the House of Correction at work, until she be sent away at her own charge, and so also for her coming again, she shall be alike used as aforesaid. "And for every Quaker, he or she, that shall a third time herein again offend, they shall have their tongues bored through with a hot iron, and be kept at the House of Correction close to work, until they be sent away at their own charge. "And it is further ordered, that all and every Quaker arising from among ourselves, shall be dealt with, and suffer the like punishment as the law provides against foreign Quakers."

EDWARD RAWSON, Sec.

An Act Made at a General Court, Held at Boston, the Twentieth of October, 1658

Whereas, there is a pernicious sect, commonly called Quakers, lately risen, who by word and writing have published and maintained many dangerous and horrid tenets, and do take upon them to change and alter the received laudable customs of our nation, in giving civil respects to equals, or reverence to superiors; whose actions tend to undermine the civil government, and also to destroy the order of the churches, by denying all established forms of worship, and by withdrawing from orderly Church fellowship, allowed and approved by all orthodox professors of truth, and instead thereof, and in opposition thereunto, frequently meeting by themselves, insinuating themselves into the minds of the simple, or such as are at least affected to the order and government of church and commonwealth, whereby divers of our inhabitants have been infected, notwithstanding all former laws, made upon the experience of their arrogant and bold obtrusions, to disseminate their principles amongst us, prohibiting their coming into this jurisdiction, they have not been deferred from their impious attempts to undermine our peace, and hazard our ruin."

"For prevention thereof, this court doth order and enact, that any person or persons, of the cursed sect of the Quakers, who is not an inhabitant of, but is found within this jurisdiction, shall be apprehended without warrant, where no magistrate is at hand, by any constable, commissioner, or selectman, and conveyed from constable to constable, to the next magistrate, who shall commit the said person to close prison, there to remain (without bail) until the next court of Assistants, where they shall have legal trial. "And being convicted to be of the sect of the Quakers, shall be sentenced to banishment, on pain of death. And that every inhabitant of this jurisdiction, being convicted to be of the aforesaid sect, either by taking up, publishing, or defending the horrid opinions of the Quakers, or the stirring up mutiny, sedition, or rebellion against the government, or by taking up their abusive and destructive practices, viz. denying civil respect to equals and superiors, and withdrawing from the Church assemblies; and instead thereof, frequenting meetings of their own, in opposition to our Church order; adhering to, or approving of any known Quaker, and the tenets and practices of Quakers, that are opposite to the orthodox received opinions of the godly; and endeavoring to disaffect others to civil government and Church order, or condemning the practice and proceedings of this court against the Quakers, manifesting thereby their complying with those, whose design is to overthrow the order established in Church and state: every such person, upon conviction before the said court of Assistants, in manner aforesaid, shall be committed to close prison for one month, and then, unless they choose voluntarily to depart this jurisdiction, shall give bond for their good behavior and appear at the next court, continuing obstinate, and refusing to retract and reform the aforesaid opinions, they shall be sentenced to banishment, upon pain of death. And any one magistrate, upon information given him of any such person, shall cause him to be apprehended, and shall commit any such person to prison, according to his discretion, until he come to trial as aforesaid."

It appears there were also laws passed in both of the then colonies of New Plymouth and New Haven, and in the Dutch settlement at New Amsterdam, now New York, prohibiting the people called Quakers, from coming into those places, under severe penalties; in consequence of which, some underwent considerable suffering. The two first who were executed were William Robinson, merchant, of London, and Marmaduke Stevenson, a countryman, of Yorkshire. These coming to Boston, in the beginning of September, were sent for by the court of Assistants, and there sentenced to banishment, on pain of death. This sentence was passed also on Mary Dyar, mentioned hereafter, and Nicholas Davis, who were both at Boston. But William Robinson, being looked upon as a teacher, was also condemned to be whipped severely; and the constable was commanded to get an able man to do it. Then Robinson was brought into the street, and there stripped; and having his hands put through the holes of the carriage of a great gun, where the jailer held him, the executioner gave him twenty stripes, with a threefold cord whip.

Then he and the other prisoners were shortly after released, and banished, as appears from the following warrant: "You are required by these, presently to set at liberty William Robinson, Marmaduke Stevenson, Mary Dyar, and Nicholas Davis, who, by an order of the court and council, had been imprisoned, because it appeared by their own confession, words, and actions, that they are Quakers: wherefore, a sentence was pronounced against them, to depart this jurisdiction, on pain of death; and that they must answer it at their peril, if they or any of them, after the fourteenth of this present month, September, are found within this jurisdiction, or any part thereof."

EDWARD RAWSON, Boston, September 12, 1659.

Though Mary Dyar and Nicholas Davis left that jurisdiction for that time, yet Robinson and Stevenson, though they departed the town of Boston, could not yet resolve (not being free in mind) to depart that jurisdiction, though their lives were at stake. And so they went to Salem, and some places thereabouts, to visit and build up their friends in the faith. But it was not long before they were taken and put again into prison at Boston, and chains locked to their legs. In the next month, Mary Dyar returned also. And as she stood before the prison, speaking with one Christopher Holden, who was come thither to inquire for a ship bound for England, whither he intended to go, she was also taken into custody. Thus, they had now three persons, who, according to their law, had forfeited their lives. And, on the twentieth of October, these three were brought into court, where John Endicot and others were assembled. And being called to the bar, Endicot commanded the keeper to pull off their hats; and then said, that they had made several laws to keep the Quakers from amongst them, and neither whipping, nor imprisoning, nor cutting off ears, nor banishment upon pain of death, would keep them from amongst them. And further, he said, that he or they desired not the death of any of them. Yet, notwithstanding, his following words, without more ado were, "Give ear, and hearken to your sentence of death." Sentence of death was also passed upon Marmaduke Stevenson, Mary Dyar, and William Edrid. Several others were imprisoned, whipped, and fined.

We have no disposition to justify the Pilgrims for these proceedings, but we think, considering the circumstances of the age in which they lived, their conduct admits of much palliation. The fathers of New England, endured incredible hardships in providing for themselves a home in the wilderness; and to protect themselves in the undisturbed enjoyment of rights, which they had purchased at so dear a rate, they sometimes adopted measures, which, if tried by the more enlightened and liberal views of the present day, must at once be pronounced altogether unjustifiable. But shall they be condemned without mercy for not acting up to principles which were unacknowledged and unknown throughout the whole of Christendom? Shall they alone be held responsible for opinions and conduct which had become sacred by antiquity, and which were common to Christians of all other denominations? Every government then in existence assumed to itself the right to legislate in matters of religion; and to restrain heresy by penal statutes. This right was claimed by rulers, admitted by subjects, and is sanctioned by the names of Lord Bacon and Montesquieu, and many others equally famed for their talents and learning. It is unjust, then, to "press upon one poor persecuted sect, the sins of all Christendom."

The fault of our fathers was the fault of the age; and though this cannot justify, it certainly furnishes an extenuation of their conduct. As well might you condemn them for not understanding and acting up to the principles of religious toleration. At the same time, it is but just to say, that imperfect as were their views of the rights of conscience, they were nevertheless far in advance of the age to which they belonged; and it is to them more than to any other class of men on earth, the world is indebted for the more rational views that now prevail on the subject of civil and religious liberty.

Foxe's Book of Martyrs, Edited by William Byron Forbush, chapter 18

Persecution of the Quakers in New England, 1661

The persecution of the Quakers in New England, by the Puritans and Independents, who had themselves fled from home to enjoy religious liberty, formed a dreadful scene, the very recital of which is revolting to humanity. Some they caused to have their ears cut off; and, among many other cruelties, which would fill a volume, they ordered three Quaker women to be stripped to the waist, and flogged through eleven towns, a distance of eighty miles, in all the severity of the frost and snow. But, as if this was not enough, they actually hanged three men and one woman for Christ's sake, who all acquitted themselves, at their awful exit, with that firmness and submission which a Christian martyr is enabled to sustain at such an hour of nature's extremity, giving full proof of their sincerity and trust in the goodness and support of him, who had called them to make a public profession of his name before a wicked and perverse generation. Their names were William Robinson, Marmaduke Stevenson, William Leddra, and Mary Dyer.

On the day appointed for the execution of these innocent victims, they were led to the gallows by military officers, accompanied by a band of about 200 armed men, besides many horsemen – a measure which plainly indicated that some fear of popular indignation was feared; and, that no appeal might be made to the feelings of the crowd, a drummer was appointed to march in front of the condemned people, to beat the drum, especially when any of them attempted to speak.

Glorious signs of heavenly joy and gladness were visible in the countenances o these holy martyrs, who walked hand in hand to the place where they were to suffer. "This is to me an hour of greatest joy,' exclaimed Mary Dyer; adding that no eye could see, no ear could hear, no tongue could utter, no heart could understand, the sweet refreshings of the Spirit of the Lord which she then felt.

Coming to the ladder, and having taken leave of each other with tender affection, they yielded up their lives into the hands of their enemies. Robinson's last words were, "I suffer for Christ, in whom I live, and for whom I die." Stevenson's last words were, "This day shall we be at rest with the Lord."

William Leddra's last words were, "I commit my righteous cause unto thee, O God." As he took his last breath he said, "Lord Jesus, receive my spirit!' When Mary Dyer climbed the ladder, some of the crowd told her that she would be reprieved if only she would do as they said. But this magnanimous sufferer did not shrink from her doom, knowing well for whom and in whom she was about to die. She was content to lay down her life, as she said, "In obedience to the will of the Lord, I abide faithful unto death."

We, too, have had our martyrs. Such wert thou,
Illustrious woman! though the starry crown
Of martyrdom has sat on many a brow,
In the world's eye, of far more wide renown.
Yet the same spirit graced thy fameless end,
Which shone in Latimer and his compeers;
Upon whose hallowed memories still attend
Manhood's warm reverence, childhood's guileless tears.
Well did they win them; may they keep them long!
Their names require not praise obscure as mine,
Nor does my muse their cherish'd memories wrong,
By this imperfect aim to honor thine.
Heroic martyr of a sect despised!
Thy name and memory to my heart are dear:
Thy fearless zeal (in artless childhood prized)
The lapse of years has taught me to revere.
Thy Christian worth demands no poet's lay,
Historian's pen, nor sculptor's boasted art;
What could the proudest tribute these can pay
To thy immortal spirit, now impart?
Yet seems it like a sacred debt to give
The brief memorial thou mayst well supply;
Whose life display'd how Christians ought to live.
Whose death – how Christian martyrs calmly die.

George Fox, Journal, London, 1852, vol i, pp 389-90

Quakers in prison in England and Wales

"Remember those in prison as if you were their fellow-prisoners' (Hebrews 13:3 NIV)

Now there being very many Friends in prison in the nation, Richard Hubbertorn and I drew up a paper concerning them, and got it delivered to the king, that he might understand how we were dealt with by his officers.

About this time, 1661, persecution was very hot, and from estimates deduced from documents of the period, it is probably that, in 1661 or 1662, there were no less than 4,500 Friends in prison, in England and Wales, at one time, for meeting to worship God, refusing to swear etc. And in such prisons too! Little is known about the savage persecution they underwent and their firmness and patience in their suffering.

In 1662, 20 died in different prisons in London and 7 more after they were freed, as a result of their ill-treatment. In 1664, 25 died, and in 1665, 52 died. The number of Quakers who died in this way in the whole kingdom, amounted 339.

The interruption of family ties, the breaking up of households, the loss to many of all means of support, were hard and cruel sufferings for conscience' sake, but they were grievously aggravated at this time by the damp and filthy condition of the prisons, holes, and dungeons in which the sufferers were confined, as well as by their very crowded condition. And to all these circumstances of trial, must be added those of personal abuse, fines, distraints, and, it may be strictly be said, of wholesale robberies they endured. Some died of the beatings which they received in the breaking up of their meetings, and many from the filthy and close state of the prisons, in some of which they were so closely packed that they had to take it by turns to stand up, while others sat or lay down. There were also often overrun with lice and other vermin.

Oliver Atherton

Among those who were in prison were four Friends for tithes, who had been sent at the suit of the Countess of Derby, and had laid there for nearly two and a half years. One of these, Oliver Atherton, a man of weakly constitution, was, through his long and hard imprisonment in the cold, raw, unwholesome place, brought so low and weak in his body, that there appeared no hope of his life, unless he might be removed. So a letter was written on his behalf to the Countess of Derby, and sent by his son Godfrey Atherton, wherein were laid before her the reasons why he and the rest could not pay tithes; because if they did, they should deny Christ come in the flesh, who by his coming had put an end to tithes, and to the priesthood to which they had been given, and to the commandment by which they had been paid under the law. His weak condition of the body was also laid before her, and the apparent likelihood of his death if she continued to hold him there; that she might be moved to pity and compassion, and also warned not to draw the guilt of innocent blood upon herself.

When his son went to her with his father's letter, a servant of her's abused him, plucked off his cap, and threw it away, and put him out of the gate. Nevertheless the letter was delivered into her own hand, but she shut out all pity and tenderness, and continued him in prison till death. When his son returned to his father in prison, and told him, as he lay on his dying bed, that the Countess denied his liberty, he only said, "She hath been the cause of shedding much blood, but this will be the heaviest blood that ever she spilt." Soon after this he died. Friends having his body delivered to them to bury, as they carried it from the prison to Ormskirk, the parish wherein he had lived, they struck up papers upon the crosses at Garstang, Preston, and other towns, through which they passed, with this inscription: "This is Oliver Atherton, of Ormskirk parish, persecuted to death by the Countess of Derby for good conscience' sake towards God and Christ, because he could not give her tithes." It set out in detail the reasons for him refusing to pay tithes, the length of his imprisonment, the hardships he had undergone, her hard-heartedness towards him, and the manner of his death.

George Fox, Journal, London, 1852, vol i, p 399; vol ii, pp 16, 22

James Renwick

Reverend James Renwick, minister of the Gospel, was martyred on February 17, 1688, in the Grassmarket of Edinburgh.

His last words upon the scaffold

Before he went out of the Tolbooth, he was at dinner with his mother, sisters, and some Christian friends, when the drum beat the first warning of his execution; which so soon as he heard, he leapt up in a ravishment of heavenly joy, saying, "Let us be glad and rejoice, for the marriage of the Lamb is come"' and I can say, in some measure, "The bride, the Lamb's wife, hath made himself ready." And, till dinner was over, he enlarged upon the parallel of a marriage, and invited all of them to come to the wedding, meaning his execution. When he was come to the scaffold, the drums being beat all the while, none of the distant spectators could hear anything that he said; only some very few, that were close by him, did hear it; whereof one has collected the following account. He delivered himself to this effect:

"Spectators, I must tell you I am come here this day to lay down my life for adhering to the truths of Christ, for which I am neither afraid nor ashamed to suffer; nay, I bless the Lord that ever he counted my worthy, or enabled me to suffer anything for him; and I desire to praise his grace that he hath not only kept me free from the gross pollutions of the time, but also from many ordinary pollutions of children; and such as I have been stained with, he hath washen from them in his own blood. I am this day to lay down my life for these three things:

1. For disowning the usurpations of the tyranny of James Duke of York.

2. For preaching that it was unlawful to pay the cess expressly exacted for bearing down the Gospel.

3. For preaching that it was lawful for people to carry arms for defending themselves in their meetings for receiving the persecuted Gospel ordinances.

I think a testimony for these is worth many lives, and if I had ten thousand I would think it little enough to lay them all down for the same.

Dear friends, spectators, I must tell you

that I die a Presbyterian Protestant.

I own the Word of God as the rule of Faith and manners; I own the Confession of Faith, Larger and Shorter Catechisms, Sum of Saving Knowledge, Directory for Worship, etc.; Covenants, National and Solemn League; Acts of General Assemblies, – and all the faithful contendings that have been for the work of reformation.

I leave my testimony approving the preaching of the Gospel in the fields, and the defending the same by arms.

I adjoin my testimony to all that hath been sealed by blood, shed either on scaffolds, fields, or seas, for the cause of Christ.

I leave my testimony against Popery, Prelacy, Erastianism, etc.; against all profanity, and everything contrary to sound doctrine; particularly against all usurpations made upon Christ's right, who is the Prince of the kings of the earth, who alone must bear the glory of ruling his own kingdom, the church; and, in particular, against the absolute power usurped by this usurper, that belongs to no mortal, but is the incommunicable prerogative of Jehovah, and against this toleration flowing from that absolute power."

Upon this, he was bid have done. He answered, "I have near done."

Then he said, "Ye that are the people of God, do not weary in maintaining the testimony of the day, in your stations and places; and whatever ye do, make sure an interest in Christ, for there is a storm coming that shall try your foundation. Scotland must be rid of Scotland before the delivery come. And you that are strangers to God, break off from your sins by repentance, else I will be a witness against you in the day of the Lord."

Here they caused him desist. Upon the scaffold he sung a part of Psalm 103, from the beginning and read chapter 19 of the Revelation.

In prayer he said: "Lord, I die in the faith that thou wilt not leave Scotland, but that thou wilt make the blood of thy witnesses the seed of thy church, and return again, and be glorious in our land. And now, Lord, I am ready – "the bride, the Lamb's wife, hath made herself ready."'

The napkin then being tied about his face, he said to his friend attending him – "Farewell. Be diligent in duty. Make your peace with God, through Christ. There is a great trial coming. As to the remnant I leave, I have committed them to God. Tell them from me not to weary, nor be discouraged in maintaining the testimony. Let them not quit nor forego one of these despised truths. Keep your ground, and the Lord will provide you teachers and ministers, and when he comes, he will make these despised truths glorious upon the earth."

Then he turned over the ladder, with these words in his mouth: "Lord, into they hands I commit my spirit, for thou has redeemed me, Lord God of truth."

And having thus finished his course, served his generation, and witnessed a good confession for his Lord and Master, before many witnesses, by the will of God, ye yielded up his spirit into the hands of God who gave it.

He was the last that sealed the testimony of this suffering period in a public way upon a scaffold.

John H. Thomson (ed.), A Cloud of Witnesses, Edinburgh, 1781, pp 489-91

On a monument in Greyfriars churchyard, Edinburgh

Upon the head of the tomb there is the effigies of an open Bible, drawn with these Scripture citations:

"And when he had opened the first seal, I saw under the altar the souls of them that had been slain for the Word of God, and for the testimony which they held. And they cried with a loud voice, saying, How long, O Lord, holy and true, dost thou not judge and avenge our blood on them that dwell on the earth? And white robes were given unto every one of them, and it was said unto them, that they should rest yet for a little season, until their fellow-servants also, and their brethren, that should be killed as they were, should be fulfilled" (Revelation 6:9-11).

"These are they which have come out of

great tribulation, and have washed their robes, and made them white in the blood of the Lamb" (Revelation 7:4).

Halt, passenger, take heed what thou dost
see:
This tomb doth shew for what some men
did die.
Here lies interred the dust of those who
stood'
Gainst perjury, resisting unto blood;
Adhering to the Covenants and Laws,
Establishing the same, which was the cause
Their lives were sacrificed unto the lust
Of prelatists abjured. Though here their dust
Lies mixt with murderers', and other crew,
Whom justice justly did to death pursue;
But as for this, in them no cause was found
Worthy of death; but only they were found
Constant and steadfast, zealous, witnessing
For the prerogatives of Christ their King.
Which truths were sealed by famous
Guthrie's head,
And all along to Master Renwick's blood,
They did endure the wrath of enemies,
Reproaches, torments, deaths, and injuries.
But yet they're these two from such troubles
came,
And now triumph in glory with the Lamb.

John H. Thomson (ed.)., A Cloud of Witnesses, Edinburgh, 1781, pp 563-4

3. Christian writings

A collection of the writings, of the martyrs and about the martyrs and martyrdom and persecution of Christians from the Reformation era.

An Exhortation to the Patient Suffering of Trouble and Affliction for Christ's Cause Written to all the unfeigned professors of the gospel throughout the realm of England, by John Bradford, at the beginning of his imprisonment, A. D. 1554.

May the Holy Spirit of God, who is the earnest and pledge of God given to his people for their comfort and consolation, be poured into our hearts by the mighty power and mercies of our only Savior Jesus Christ, now and for ever. Amen.

Because I perceive plainly, that to the evils fallen upon us who profess Christ's gospel, greater are most likely to ensue, and after them greater, till the measure of iniquity is heaped up, except we shrink, and having put our hands to the plough look back, and with Lot's wife, and the Israelites desiring to return into Egypt, fall into God's heavy displeasure incurable, Gen. xil Luke il; all which God forbid; and because I am persuaded of you, my dearly beloved brethren and sisters, throughout the realm of England, which have professed unfeignedly the gospel of our Lord and Savior Jesus Christ, (for unto such do I write this epistle,) that as ye have begun to take part with God's gospel and truth, so through his grace ye will persevere, and go on forwards, notwithstanding the storms which have risen and are to arise; I cannot but write something unto you, to go on forwards with earnestness in the way of the Lord, and not to become as the faint-hearted or fearful, whose place St. John appoints (Rev xxi.) with the unbelievers, murderers, and idolaters in eternal perdition, but cheerfully to take the Lord's Cup, and drink of it before it draw towards the dregs and bottom, whereof at length they shall drink with the wicked to eternal destruction, who will not receive it at first with God's children, and with whom God begins his judgment, that as the wicked world rejoices when they lament, so they may rejoice when the wicked world shall mourn, and finds woe intolerable without end.

First therefore, my dearly beloved in the Lord, I beseech you to consider, that though you are in the world, yet you are not of the world. You are not of them which look for their portion in this life, (Psa. xvii.) whose captain is the god of this world, even Satan, who now ruffles it apace, because his time on earth is not long. But you are of them that look for a city of God's own blessing. You are of them that know yourselves to be here but pilgrims and strangers; for here you have no dwelling-place. (Heb xi. xii. xiii., I Pet. ii.) You are of them whose portion is the Lord, and which have their hope in heaven whose captain is Christ Jesus, the Son of God, and governor of heaven and earth. Unto him is given all power, yea, he is God Almighty, with the Father and the Holy Ghost, praiseworthy for ever. (Matt. xxviii., Rom il) You are not of them which receive the beast's mark, which here rejoice, laugh, and have their heart's ease, joy, paradise, and pleasure; but you are of them which have received the angels mark, yea, God's mark, which here lament, mourn, sigh, sob, weep, and have your wilderness to wander in, your purgatory, and even hell to purge and burn up your sins. (Rev xiii., Luke, vi., Ezek. il) You are not of them which cry, Let us eat and drink, for tomorrow we shall die. You are not of that number which say, they have made a covenant with death and hell not to hurt them. You are not of them which take it for a vain thing to serve the Lord. You are not of the number of them which say, Tush, God is in heaven, and sees us not, nor cares for what we do. (Ps. lxxiii.) You are not of the number of them which will fall down for the muck of the world to worship the fiend, or for fear of displeasing men worship the golden image.

Finally, you are not of the number of them which set more by your swine than by Christ, (Matt. viii.) which, for ease and rest in this life, say and do as Antiochus bids you do or say, (Maccabees,) and will follow the multitude to do evil, with Zedechias and the three hundred false prophets; yea, Ahab, Jezebel, and the whole court and country. (Matt. viii., 1 Kings, xxii.)

But you are of the number of them which are dead already, or at least are dying daily to yourselves and to this world. You are of them which have made a covenant with God, to forsake yourselves in this world, and Satan also. You are of them which say, Nay, the Lord has all things written in his memorial book, for such as fear him, and remember his name. (Rom. vi. vii., Col. iii., Luke, xii., Mal. iii.) You are of them which have their loins girded about, and their lights burning in their hands, like unto men that wait for their Lord's coming. (Luke, xii.) You are in the number of them that say, The Lord looks down from heaven, and beholds the children of men: from the habitation of his dwelling, he considers all them that dwell upon the earth. You are of the number of them which will worship the Lord God only, and will not worship the work at man's hands, though the oven burn never so hot. You are of the number of them to whom Christ is precious and dear, which cry out rather because your habitation is prolonged here, as David did. (1 Pet. ii., Ps. cxl) You are of them which follow Mattathias and the godly Jews, which knew the way to life to be a strait way, and that few go through it, which will not stick to follow poor Micaiah, although he is racked and cast into prison, having the sun, moon, seven stars, and all against him. (Matt. vii, 1 Kings, xxii.)

Thus therefore, dearly beloved, remember, first, that, as I said, you are not of this world; that Satan is not your captain: your joy and paradise is not here; your companions are not the multitude of worldlings, and such as seek to please men, and live here at ease in the service of Satan. But you are of another world; Christ is your captain, your joy is in heaven, where your conversation is; your companions are the fathers, patriarchs, prophets, apostles, martyrs, virgins, confessors, and the dear saints of God, which follow the Lamb whithersoever he goes; dipping their garments in his blood, knowing this life and world to be full of evil, a warfare, a smoke, a shadow, a vapor, replenished and environed with all kinds of miseries. This is the first thing which I would have you often and diligently with yourselves consider and muse well upon, namely, what you are, and where you are.

Now, secondly, forget not to call to mind that you ought not to think it a strange thing if misery, trouble, adversity, persecution, and displeasure come upon you. For how can it be otherwise, but that trouble and persecution must come upon you. Can the world love you, which are none of his? Can worldly men, which are your chief enemy's soldiers, regard you? Can Satan suffer you to be at rest, who will do no homage unto him? Can this way be chosen by any that account it so narrow and strait as they do? Will you look to travel, and to have no foul way or rain? Will shipmen shrink, or sailors on the sea give over, if storms arise? Do they not look for such? and, dearly beloved, did not we enter into God's ship and ark of baptism at the first? will you then count it strange, if perils come or tempests blots? Are not you traveling to your heavenly city of

Jerusalem, were is all joy and felicity, and will you tarry by the way for storms and showers? The mart and fair will then be past; the night will so come upon you, that you cannot travel; the door will be barred, and the bride will be at supper. Therefore away with dainty niceness.

Will you think that the Father of heaven will deal more gently with you in this age than he has done with others, his dearest friends, in other ages? What way, yea, what storms and tempests, what troubles and disquietness Abel, Noah, Abraham, Isaac, Jacob, and good Joseph found! Which of these had so fair a life, and such restful times, as we have had? Moses, Aaron, Samuel, David the king, and all the good kings, priests, and prophets in the Old Testament, at one time or other, if not throughout their lives, felt a thousand times more misery than we have felt hitherto.

As for the New Testament, how great was the affliction of Mary, of Joseph, of Zacharias, of Elizabeth, of John the Baptist, of all the apostles and evangelists, yea, of Jesus Christ our Lord, the dear Son and darling of God! And since the time of the apostles, how many and great are the numbers of martyrs, confessors, and such as have suffered the shedding of their blood in this life, rather than they would be stayed in their journey, or lodge in any of Satan's inns, lest the storms or winds which fell in their traveling might have touched them! And, dearly beloved, let us think what we are, and how far unfit to be matched with these, with whom yet we expect we are to be placed in heaven. But with what face can we look for this, who are so fearful and unwilling to leave that, we must leave, and so shortly that we know not the time when? Where is our renouncing and forsaking of the world and the flesh, which we solemnly took upon us in baptism? Ah! shameless cowards that we are, which will not follow the trace of so many fathers, patriarchs, kings, priests, prophets, apostles, evangelists, and saints of God, yea, even of the very Son of God! How many now go with you heartily, as I and all your brethren in bonds and exile for the gospel! Pray for us, for, God willing, we will not leave you now. We will go before you; ye shall see in us, by God's grace, that we preached no lies nor idle tales, but even the very true word of God. For the confirmation whereof we by God's grace, and the help of your prayers, willingly and joyfully give our blood to be shed, as already we have given our livings, goods, friends, and natural country. For now we are certain that we are in the highway to heaven's bliss; as St. Paul says, By many tribulations and persecutions we must enter into God's kingdom.

And because we would go thither ourselves and bring you thither also, therefore the devil stirs up the coals. And forasmuch as we all loitered in the way, he has therefore received power of God to overcast the weather, and to stir up storms, that we, God's children, might more speedily go on forwards, and make more haste, as the counterfeits and hypocrites will tarry and linger till the storms are past; and so when they come, the market will be done, and the doors barred, as it is to be feared. This wind will blow God's children forward, and the devil's darlings backward. Therefore, like God's children, let us go on forward apace, the wind is on our backs, hoist up the sails, lift up your hearts and hands unto God in prayer, and keep your anchor of faith to cast out in time of trouble on the rock of God's word and mercy in Christ, by the cable of God's verity, and I warrant your safely. And thus much for you secondly to consider, that affliction, persecution, and trouble are no strange thing to God's children, and therefore it should not dismay, discourage, or discomfort us, for it is no other thing than all God's dear friends have tasted in their journey heavenwards.

As I would in this troublesome time that ye would consider what you are by the goodness of God in Christ – even citizens of heaven, though you are at present in the flesh, even in a strange region on every side file of fierce enemies, – and what weather and way the dearest friends of God have found; even so would I have you, thirdly, to consider for your further comfort, that if you shrink not, but go on forwards, pressing to the mark appointed, all the power of your enemies shall not overcome you, nor in any point hurt you. (Phil. iii.) But this you must not consider according to the judgment of reason, and the sense of old Adam, but according to the judgment of

God's word and the experience of faith and the new man, for else you mar all. For to reason, and to the experience of our sense, or of the outward man, we poor souls which stick to God's word, to serve him as he requires, are only accounted to be vanquished and to be overcome; for we are cast into prison, lose our livings, friends, goods, country, and life also at length, as concerns this world. But, dearly beloved, God's word teaches otherwise, and faith feels accordingly. Is it not written, Who shall separate us from the love of God? Shall tribulation, or anguish, or persecution, or hunger, or nakedness, or peril, or sword? (Rom. viii.) As it is written, For thy sake are we killed all the day long, and are counted as sheep appointed to be slain.

Nevertheless, in all these things we overcome through Him that loved us: for I am sure that neither death, nor life, neither angels, nor rule, nor power, neither things present, nor things to come, neither high nor low, neither any creature, shall be able to part us from that love wherewith God loves us in Christ Jesus our Lord. Thus spake one who was in affliction, as I am, for the Lord's gospel sake; his holy name be praised therefore, and may he grant me grace with the same to continue in like suffering unto the end. This (I say) one spoke who was in affliction for the gospel, but yet so far from being overcome, that he rejoiced rather for the victory which the gospel had. For though he was bound, yet the gospel was not bound (2 Tim. ii.,) and therefore he gives thanks unto God which always gives the victory in Christ, and opens the savor of his knowledge by us, and such as suffer for his truth, although they shut us up nearer so much, and drive us never so far out of our own natural country in every place. (2 Cor. ii.) The world for a time may deceive itself, thinking it has, the victory, but the end will try the contrary.

Did not Cain think he had the victory when Abel was slain? Thought not the old world and men then living, that they were wise and well, and Noah a fool, who would creep into an ark, leaving his house, lands, and possessions, for I think he was in an honest state for the world. But I pray you who was wise when the flood came? Abraham was considered a fool to leave his own country, friends, and kin, because of God's word; but, dearly beloved, we know it proved otherwise. (Gen. xii.) I will leave all the patriarchs, and come to Moses, and the children of Israel. Tell me, were not they thought to be overcome and stark mad, when for fear of Pharaoh, at God's word, they ran into the Red Sea? Did not Pharaoh and the Egyptians think themselves sure of the victory? But it proved clean contrary. Saul was thought to be well, but David in an evil case, and most miserable, because he had no hole to hide him in; yet at length Saul's misery was seen, and David's felicity began to appear. (1 Sam. xvi. xvii. xviii. xil) The prophet Micaiah being cast into prison for telling Ahab the truth was thought to be overcome by Zedekiah and the other false prophets; but, my good brethren and sisters, the holy history tells otherwise. (I Kings, xxii.) Who did not think the prophets happy in their time? For they were slain, prisoned, laughed to scorn, and jested at of every man. (Jer. xl, Isa. viii., 2 Kings, ii.) And so were all the apostles, yea, the dearly beloved friend of God, than whom among the children of women none arose greater, I mean, John Baptist, who was beheaded, and that in prison, even for a dancing damsel's desire. As all these by the judgment of reason were then counted heretics, runagates, unlearned fools, fishers, publicans, &c., so now were they unhappy and overcome indeed, if God's word and faith did not show the contrary. (Rom. viii.)

But what speak I of these? Look upon Jesus Christ, to whom we must be like fashioned here, if we will be like him elsewhere. Now, say you, was not he taken for a fool, a seditious person, a new fellow, a heretic, and one overcome of every body; yea, even forsaken, both of God and men? But the end told them, and tells us another tale; for now is he in majesty and glory unspeakable. When he was led to Pilate or Herod, or when he was in prison in Caiaphas' house, did not their reason think that he was overcome? When he was beaten, buffeted, scourged, crowned with thorns, banged upon the cross, and utterly left by all his disciples, taunted by the high-priests and elders, cursed by the commons, railed on by the magistrates, and laughed to scorn by the lewd (ignorant, editor) heathen, would not a man then have thought that he had been out of the way, and that his disciples were fools to follow him, and believe him? Think you, that whilst he lay in his grave, men did not point with their fingers, when they saw any that had followed and loved him, or believed in him and his doctrine, saying, "Where is their master and teacher now? What! is he gone? Forsooth, if they had not been fools, they might have well known that the learning he taught could not long continue." Our doctors and Pharisees are no fools now, they may see." On this sort men either spoke, or might have spoken, against all such as loved Christ or his doctrine; but yet at length they and all such were proved fools and wicked wretches. For our Savior arose, maugre their beards (in spite of their opposition, editor), and published his gospel plentifully, in spite of their heads, and the heads of all the wicked world, with the great powers of the same; always overcoming, and then most of all, when he and his doctrine were thought to have had the greatest fall.

As now, dearly beloved, the wicked world rejoices, the papists are puffed up against Christ and his people after their own kind, now they cry out, Where are these new-found preachers? Are they not in the Tower, Marshalsea, Fleet, and beyond the seas? Who would have thought that our old bishops, doctors, and deans, were fools, as they would have made us to believe, and indeed have persuaded some already, which are not of the wisest, especially if they come not home again to the holy church? These and such-like words they have, to cast in our teeth, as triumphers and conquerors; but, dearly beloved, short is their joy; they beguile themselves, this is but a lightening before their death. As God, after he had given the Jews a time to repent, visited them by Vespasian and Titus, most horribly to their utter subversion, delivering first all his people from among them, even so, my dear brethren, will he do with this age, when he has tried his children from amongst them, as now he begins to do, and, by suffering, has made us like to his Christ, and, by being overcome, to overcome indeed, to our eternal comfort. Then will he, if not otherwise, come himself in the clouds: I mean, our dear Lord, whom we confess, preach, and believe on; he will come (I say) with the blast of a trump, and shout of an archangel, and so shall we be caught up in the clouds to meet him in the air: the angels gathering together the wicked wretches, which now welter and wallow as the world and wind blows, to be tied in bundles and cast into the fire, which burns for ever most painfully. (Matt. xiii.) There and then shall they see who has the victory, they or we, when they shall see us afar ok in Abraham's bosom. (Luke, xvi.) Then will they say, "Oh! we thought these folks fools, and had them in derision; we thought their life madness, and their end to be without honor: but look how they are counted among the children of God, and their portion is with the saints.

Oh! we have gone amiss, and would not hearken." Such words as these shall the wicked say one day in hell, whereas now they triumph as conquerors. And thus much for you, thirdly, to look often upon; namely, that whatsoever is done unto you, yea, even death itself, shall not hurt you, any more than it did Abel, David, Daniel, John Baptist, Jesus Christ our Lord with other dear saints of God, who suffered for his name's sake. Let not reason therefore be judge in this matter, nor present sense, but faith and God's word, as I have shown; in the which, let us set before our eyes the shortness of this present time wherein we suffer, and consider the eternity to come, when our enemies and persecutors shall be in intolerable pains, helpless; and we, if we persevere to the end, shall be in such felicity and joys, dangerless, as the very heart of man in no point is able to conceive. If we consider this, (1 say,) we cannot but contemn and set nothing by the sorrows of the cross, and lustily go through thick and thin with good courage.

Thus have I declared unto you, things necessary to be mused on by every one who will abide by Christ and his gospel in this troublesome time, as I trust you all will. Namely, first to consider that we are not of this world, nor of the number of the worldlings, or retainers to Satan; that we are not at home in our own country, but of another world, of the congregation of the saints, and retainers to

Christ, although in a region replete and full of untractable enemies. Secondly, that we may not think it a strange thing to be persecuted for God's gospel, from which the dearest friends of God were in no age free, as indeed it is impossible that they should for any long time be, their enemies being always about them to destroy them if they could. And thirdly, that the assaults of our enemies, be they never so many and fierce, in no point shall be able to prevail against our faith, albeit to reason it seems otherwise, where through we ought to conceive good courage and comfort; for who will be afraid when he knows the enemies cannot prevail? Now I will, for the more encouraging you to the cross, give you a further memorandum, namely, of the advantages which come by the trouble and affliction now risen and to arise to us, which are God's children, elect through Jesus Christ. But look not here to have repeated all the commodities which come by the cross to such as are well exercised therein, for that were more than I can do; I will only speak of a few, thereby to occasion you to gather and at the length to feel and perceive more. First, That there is no cross which comes upon any of us without the counsel of our heavenly Father; for as to the fancy about Fortune, it is wicked, as many places of the Scriptures do teach. And we must needs, to the commendation of God's justice (for in all his doings he is just,) acknowledge in ourselves that we have deserved at the hands of our heavenly Father this his cross or rod which is fallen upon us, – we have deserved it, if not by our unthankfulness, slothfulness, negligence, intemperance, uncleanness, and other sins committed often by us, whereof our consciences can and will accuse us if we call them to counsel, with the examination of our former life, yet at least by our original and birth sin.

Also by doubling of the greatness of God's anger and mercy; by self-love, concupiscence, and such-like sins, which as we brought them with us into this world, so the same always abide in us, and even as a spring always bring something forth in act with us, notwithstanding the continual fight of God's Spirit in us against it.

The first advantage therefore that the cross brings is knowledge, and that both of God and of ourselves. Of God, that he is just, pure, and hates sin. Of ourselves, that we are born in sin, and are from top to toe defiled with concupiscence and corruption, out of which have sprung all the evils that ever at any time we have spoken and done. (Ps. li., Gen. viii., Jer. xvii.) The greatest and most special whereof we are occasioned by the cross to call to mind, as the brethren of Joseph did their evil deed against him when the cross once came upon them. (Gen. xiii.) And so by it we come to the first step to get health for our souls, that is, we are driven to know our sins, original and actual, by God's justice declared in the cross.

Secondly, the end wherefore God declares his justice against our sin both original and actual; and would by his cross have us consider the same, and call to mind our former evil deeds, the end whereof is this, that we might lament, be sorry, sigh, and pray for pardon, that so doing we might obtain the same by means of faith in the merits of Jesus Christ his dear Son. And further, that we, being humbled because of the evil that dwells in us, might become thankful for God's goodness and love, in continual watching and wariness to suppress the evil which lies in us, that it bring not forth fruit to death at any time. (James, i.) This second advantage of the cross therefore we must not count to be a simple knowledge only, but a great gain of God's mercy, with wonderful, rich, and precious virtues of faith, repentance, remission of sins, humility, thankfulness, mortification, and diligence in doing good. Not that properly the cross works these things of itself, but because the cross is the mean and way by which God works the knowledge and feeling of these things in his children; as many, both testimonies and examples in the Scriptures, are easily found of them that diligently weigh what they read therein.

To these two advantages of the cross, join the third of God's singular wisdom that it may be coupled with his justice and mercy. On this sort therefore let us conceive when we see the gospel of God and his church persecuted and troubled, as now it is with us, that because the great, learned, and wise men of the world use not their wisdom to love and serve God, though he opens himself manifestly by his visible creatures to natural wisdom and reason, (Rom. i.,) therefore God both justly infatuates and makes them foolish, giving them up to insensibleness especially herein; for on this manner they reason concerning the affliction which comes for the gospel: "If", say they "this were God's word, if these people were God's children, surely God would then bless and prosper them and their doctrine. But now since there is no doctrine so much hated, no people so much persecuted as they are, therefore it cannot be of God. Rather this is of God which our Queen and old bishops have professed, for how has God preserved them and kept them! What a notable victory has God given unto her, where it seemed impossible that things should have come to pass so as they have done! And did not the great captain confess his fault, that he was out of the way, and not of the faith which these gospellers profess? How many are come again, from that which they professed to be God's word? The most part of this realm, notwithstanding the diligence of preachers to persuade them concerning this new learning, which now is persecuted, never consented to it in heart, as experience teaches. And what plagues have come upon this realm since this gospel, as they call it, came in amongst us? Before, we had plenty, but now there is nothing like as it was. Moreover, all the houses of the parliament have overthrown the laws made for the stablishing of this gospel and religion, and new laws are erected for the continuance of the contrary. How miraculously God confounds their doctrine, and confirms ours! For how was Wyat overthrown! How prosperously came in our King! How has God blessed our Queen with fruit of womb! How is the Pope's Holiness restored again to his right! All these things teach plainly that this their doctrine is not God's word."

Thus reason the worldly wise, which see not God's wisdom; for else, if they considered that there was with us unthankfulness for the gospel, no amendment of life, but all kind of contempt of God, and that all kind of shameless sinning ensued the preaching of the gospel; they must needs see that God could not but chastise and correct; and as he let Satan loose, after he had bound him a certain time for unthankfulness of men, so he let these champions of Satan run abroad, by them to plague us for our unthankfulness. (Rev xl) Great was God's anger against Ahab, because he saved Benhadad, king of Syria, after God had given him into his hands, and afterwards it turned to his own destruction. (1 Kings, xl) God would that double sorrow should have been repaid to them, because of the sorrow they did to the saints of God. Read the 18th of the Revelation. As for the victory given to the Queen's Highness, if men had any godly understanding, they might see many things in it. First, God has done it to win her heart to the gospel. Again, he has done it, as well because they that went against her put their trust in horses and power of men, and not in God, as because in their doing they sought not the propagation of God's gospel, which thing is now plainly seen. Therefore no marvel why God fought against them, seeing they were hypocrites, and under the cloak of the gospel would have debarred the Queen's Highness of her right, but God would not so cloak them.

Now for the relenting, returning, and recanting of some, from that which they once professed or preached. Alas! who would wonder at it? for they never came to the gospel, but for commodity and gain's sake, and now for gain they leave it. The multitude, is no good argument to move a wise man; for who knows not how to love this world better than heaven, and themselves better than their neighbors? "Wide is the gate, says Christ, (Matt. vii.,) and broad is the way that leads to destruction, and many there be that go in thereat; but strait is the gate and narrow is the way which leads unto life, and few there be that find it." All the whole multitude cried out upon Jesus, Crucify him, Crucify him, but they were not to be believed because they were the bigger part.

All Chaldea followed still their false gods, Abraham alone followed the true God. (Gen. xii.) And where they say that greater plagues are fallen upon the realm, in poverty and such other things, than before, it is no argument to move others, except such as love their swine better than Christ, (Matt. viii.;) for the devil chiefly desires his seat to be in religion. If it is there, then he will meddle with nothing we have, all shall be quiet enough; but if he be raised (driven, editor) thence, then will he beg leave to have at our swine. Read Matt. viii. of the Gergesites. As long as with us he had the ruling of religion, which now he has gotten again, then was he Robin Goodfellow, he would do no hurt: but when he was tumbled out of his throne by preaching of the gospel, then he ranged about as he has done, but secretly. Finally, effectual he has not been, but in the children of unbelief. (Eph. ii.) Them indeed has he stirred up to be covetous, oppressors, blasphemers, usurers, whoremongers, thieves, murderers, tyrants, and yet perchance he suffers them to profess the gospel, the more thereby to hinder it, and cause it to be slandered. How many now appear to have been true gospellers? As for the parliament and statutes thereof, no man of wisdom can think otherwise, but that, look what the rulers will, the same must there be enacted; for it goes not in those houses by the better part, but by the bigger part. And it is a common saying, and no less true, that the greater part overcomes the better; so they did in condemning Christ, not regarding the counsel of Nicodemus. (John, vii.) So they did also in many general councils; but all wise men know that acts of parliament are not for God's law in respect of God's law, but in respect of the people. Now what we are God knows, and all the world is more pleased a great deal, to have the devil's decrees than God's religion, so great is our contempt of it. And therefore justly for our sins (as Job says) God has set hypocrites to reign over us, which can no more abide God's true religion, than the owl the light, or bleared eyes the bright sun; for it will have them to do their duties, and walk in diligent doing of the works of their vocation.

If God's word had place, bishops could not play chancellors and idle prelates as they do; priests should be otherwise known than by their shaven crowns and tippets: but enough of this. As for miracles of success against Wyat and others, of the king's coming in, &c., I would men would consider there are two kinds of miracles, one to prepare and confirm men in the doctrine which they have received, and another to prove and try men how they have received it, and how they will stick unto it. Of the former kind, these are not miracles; but of the second, by this success given to the queen, God tries whether we will stick to his truth, simply for his truth sake, or no. This is a mighty illusion, which God sends to prove his people, and to deceive the hypocrites, which receive not God's truth simply, but in respect of gain, praise, estimation. Read how Ahab was deceived, 1 Kings, xxii., 2 Thess. ii., Dent. xiii. But I will now return to the third advantage coming by the cross. Here let us see the wisdom of God in making foolish the wisdom of the world, which knows little of man's corruption; how foul it is in the sight of God, and how it displeases him. Which knows little what the portion of God's people is in another world. Which knows little of the Pattern of Christians, Christ Jesus. Which knows little of the general judgment of God, the greater malice of Satan to God's people, and the price and estimation of the gospel; and therefore in the cross it sees not, as God's wisdom would we should see; namely, that God, in punishing them which sin least, would have his anger against sin seen most, and to be better considered and feared. In punishing his people here, he kindles their desire towards their celestial home. In punishing his servants in this life, he conforms and makes them like to Christ, that, as they are like in suffering, so shall they be in reigning. (Phil. i.) In punishing his church in the world, he gives a demonstration of his judgment which shall come on all men, when the godless shall there find rest, though now they are afflicted, and the wicked now wallowing in wealth shall be wrapped in woe and smart. In punishing the professors of his gospel in earth, he sets forth the malice of Satan against the gospel and his people; for the more confirming of their faith, and the gospel to be God's word indeed, and that they are God's people, for else the devil would let them alone. (Acts, xvi.) In punishing the lovers of his truth more than others, which care not for it, he puts them in mind how they have not valued, as they should have done, the jewel of his word and gospel. Before such trial and experience came, perchance they thought they had believed and had faith, which now they see was but a lip-faith, a mock faith, or an opinion; all which things we see are occasions for us to take better heed by means of the cross.

Therefore, thirdly, let us consider the cross to be commodious for us to learn God's wisdom, and what is man's foolishness, God's displeasure at sin, and desire to be with God, the conformity with Christ, the general judgment, the malice of Satan, hatred of sin, that the gospel is God's word, and how it is to be esteemed, &c. Thus much for this. Now will I, fourthly, briefly show you, that the cross or trouble is profitable for us to learn and behold better the providence, presence, and power of God, that all these may be coupled together as in a chain to hang about our necks, I mean God's justice, mercy, wisdom, power, presence, and providence. When all things are at rest, and men are not in trouble, then they commonly are forgetful of God, and attribute too much to their own wisdom, policy, providence, And diligence, as though they were the procurers of their own fortune, and workers of their own weal. But when the cross comes, and that in such sort as their wits, policies, and friends cannot help, though the wicked despair, run from God to saints, and such other unlawful means, yet the godly therein behold the presence, the providence, and power of God. For the Scripture teaches that all things come from God, both weal and woe, and that the same should be looked upon as God's work, although Satan, the devil, be often an instrument by whom God works justly and mercifully; justly to the wicked, and mercifully to the godly; as by the examples of wicked Saul and godly Job we may easily see God's work by Satan, his instrument in them both.

The children of God, therefore, which before forget God in prosperity, now in adversity are awakened to see God in his work, and no more depend on their own forecast, power, friends, wisdom, riches, &;c., but learn to cast themselves on God's providence and power, whereby they are so preserved and governed, and very often miraculously delivered, that the very wicked cannot but see God's providence, presence, and power, in the cross and affliction of his children, as they (his children I mean) to their joy do feel, thereby learning to know God to be the governor of all things. He it is that gives peace, he it is that sends war, he gives plenty and poverty, he sets up and casts down, he brings to death and afterwards gives life. His presence is everywhere, his providence is within and without, his power is the pillar whereby the godly stand, and to it they lean, as no less able to set up than to cast down. Which the apostle saw in his afflictions, find therefore rejoiced greatly in them, that God's power might singularly be seen therein. Concerning this, I might bring forth innumerable examples of the addiction of God's children, both in the Old and New Testament, wherein we may see how they felt God's presence, providence, and power, plentifully.

But I will omit examples, because every one of us, that has been or is in trouble, cannot but by the same remember God's presence, which we feel by his hand upon us; his providence which leaves us not unprovided for, without any of our own provisions, and his power which both preserves us from many other evils, which else would come upon us, and also makes us able to bear more than we thought we could have done. So very often he delivers us by such means, as have been thought most foolish, and to have been little regarded; and therefore we shake off our sleep of security, and forgetting of God, our trust and shift are in our own policies, our hanging on men, or on our own power. So the cross, you see, is advantageous, fourthly, for to see God's presence, providence, and power, and our negligence, forgetfulness of God, security, self-love, trust, and confidence in ourselves, and that the things in this life are to be cast off, as the others are to be taken hold on. And this shall suffice for the commodities which come by the cross, where through we may be in love with it for the commodities' sake, which at length we shall find, though at present in sense we feel them not. No castigation or punishment is sweet for the present instant, says the apostle, but afterward the end and work of the thing is otherwise. (Heb. xii.) As we see in medicines, the more wholesome they are, the more unpleasant is the taste thereof, as in pills, potions, and such like bitter stuff, yet we will, on the physician's word, drink them gladly for the benefit which comes of them. And, dearly beloved, although to lose life, and goods, or friends, for God's gospel sake seems a bitter and sour thing, yet in that our Physician, which cannot lie, Jesus Christ I mean, tells us, that it is very wholesome, howsoever it be loathsome, let us with good cheer take the cup at his hand, and drink it cheerfully. If the cup seem unpleasant, and the drink too bitter, let us put some sugar therein, even a piece of that which Moses cast into the bitter water, and made the same pleasant: I mean an ounce, yea, a dram of Christ's afflictions and cross, which he suffered for us. If we call this to mind, and cast of them into our cup, considering what he was, what he suffered, of whom, for whom, to what end, and what came thereof, surely we cannot loath our medicine, but we shall wink and drink it lustily (heartily, editor). Lustily, therefore, drink the cup which Christ gives, and will give unto you, my good brethren and sisters; I mean, prepare yourselves to suffer whatever God will lay upon you for the confessing of his holy name. If not, because of these three things, that ye are not of the world, ye suffer not alone, your trouble shall not hurt you, yet for the commodities which come of the cross, I beseech you heartily to embrace it. The fight is but short, the joy is exceeding great.

We must pray always; (Luke, xviii.) then shall we undoubtedly be directed in all things by God's Holy Spirit, which Christ has promised to be our doctor, teacher, and comforter; and, therefore, we need not fear what man or devil can do unto us, either by false teaching or cruel persecution; for our Pastor is such a one that none can take his sheep out of his hands. Thus much, my dear brethren and sisters in our dear Lord and Savior Jesus Christ, I thought good to write unto you for your comfort. From which, if ye, for fear of man, loss of goods, friends, or life, swerve or depart, then you depart and swerve from Christ, and so snare yourselves in Satan's sophistry to your utter subversion. Therefore, as St. Peter says, "Watch, be sober; for as a roaring lion, he seeks to devour you." Be strong in faith; that is, hesitate not, waver not in God's promises, but believe certainly that they pertain to you; that God is with you in trouble; that he will deliver you, and glorify you.

But yet see that you call upon him, specially, that you enter not into temptation, as he taught his disciples even at such time as he saw Satan desire to sift them, as now he has done to sift us. (Ps. xciii, Matt. xxvi., Luke, xxii.) O dear Savior, prevent him now as thou did then, with thy prayer, I beseech thee, and grant that our faith faint not, but strengthen us to confirm the weak, that they deny not thee and thy gospel, that they return not to their vomit, stumbling on those sins from which there is no recovery, causing thee to deny them before thy Father, making their latter end worse than the beginning, as was the case with Lot's wife, Judas Iscariot, Francis Spira, and many others. But rather strengthen them and us all in thy grace, and in those things which thy word teaches, that we may here hazard our life for thy sake, and so shall we be sure to save it, as if we seek to save it, we cannot but lose it; and that being lost, what profit can we have, if we win the whole world? (2 Pet. ii., Matt. I, Heb. vi. I, Mark, viii., Luke, xi., Matt. vi.)

Oh, set thou always before our eyes, not as reason does, this life, the pleasure of the same, death of the body, imprisonment, &c. but everlasting life, and those unspeakable joys which undoubtedly they shall have, which take up the cross and follow thee; and they must needs at length fall into eternal hell fire and destruction of soul and body for evermore, which are afraid for the hoar frost of adversity that man or the devil stirs up to stop or hinder us from going forwards our journey to heaven's bliss to which do thou bring us for thy name's sane. Amen.

Your own in the Lord,
John Bradford

John Bradford's prayers

Daily Prayers of Master John Bradford

A Confession of Sins and Prayer for the Mitigation of God's Wrath and Punishment for the same

O Almighty God, King of all kings, and Governor of all things, whose power no creature is able to resist, to whom it belongs justly to punish sinners, and to be merciful unto them that truly repent; we confess that thou dost most justly punish us, for we have grievously sinned against thee. And we acknowledge, that in punishing us thou declares thyself to be our most merciful Father, as well because thou dost not punish us in any thing as we have deserved, as also because, by punishing us thou dost call us and (as it were) draw us to increase in repentance, in faith, in prayer, in contemning of the world, and in hearty desires for everlasting life, and thy blessed presence; grant us, therefore, gracious Lord, thankfully to acknowledge thy great mercy, who has thus favorably dealt with us, in punishing us, not to our confusion, but to our amendment. And seeing thou hast sworn that thou wills not the death of a sinner, but that he turn and live, have mercy upon us, and turn us unto thee for thy dearly beloved Son Jesus Christ's sake; whom thou would should be made a slain sacrifice for our sins, thereby declaring thy great and unspeakable anger against sin, and thine infinite mercy towards us sinful wretches. And forasmuch as the dullness of our hearts, blindness and corruption are such, that we are not able to rise up unto thee by faithful anal hearty prayer, according to our great necessity, without thy singular grace and assistance; grant unto us, gracious Lord, thy holy and sanctifying Spirit to work in us this good work with a pure and clean mind, with a humble and lowly heart, with grace to weigh and consider the need and greatness of that which we desire, and with an assured faith and trust that thou wilt grant us our requests;—because thou art good and gracious even to young ravens calling upon thee, much more then to us for whom thou hast made all things; yea, and hast not spared thine own dear Son; – because thou hast commanded us to call upon thee; – because thy throne whereunto we come is a throne of grace and mercy; – because thou hast given us a mediator Christ, to bring us unto thee, being the way by whom we come, being the door by whom we enter, and being the head on whom we hang, and hope that our poor petitions shall not be in vain, through and for his name's sake.

We beseech thee, therefore, of thy rich mercy, wherein thou art plentiful to all them that call upon thee, to forgive us our sins, namely, our unthankfulness, unbelief, self-love, neglect of thy word, security, hypocrisy, contempt of thy long suffering, omission of prayer, doubting of thy power, presence, mercy, and good will towards us, insensibleness of thy grace, impatience, &c. And to this thy benefit of correcting us, add these thy gracious gifts, repentance, faith, the spirit of prayer, the contempt of this world, and hearty desires of everlasting life.

Endue us with thy Holy Spirit, according to thy covenant and mercy, as well to assure us of pardon, and that thou dost accept us into thy favor as thy dear children in Christ and for his sake, as to write thy law in our hearts, and so to work in us that we may now begin, and go forwards in believing loving, fearing, obeying, praying, hoping, and serving thee as thou dost require most fatherly and most justly of us, accepting us as perfect through Christ and by imputation. And moreover, when it shall be thy good pleasure, and most to thy glory, deliver us, we beseech thee, out of the hands of thine adversaries, by such means, be it death or life, as may most make to our comfort in Christ. In the mean season, and for ever, save us and govern us with thy Holy Spirit and his eternal consolation.

And concerning thine adversaries, which for thy sake are become our adversaries, so many of them as are to be converted, we beseech thee to show thy mercy upon them, and to convert them. But those that are not to be converted, which thou only dost know, most mighty God and terrible Lord, confound, and get thy name a glory over them, abate their pride, assuage their malice, bring to nought their devilish devices, and grant that we and all thine afflicted children may be armed with thy defense, weaponed with thy wisdom, and guided with thy grace and Holy Spirit, to be preserved for ever from all giving of offence to thy people, and from all perils, to glorify thee, who art the only Giver of all victory, through the merits of thy only Son, Jesus Christ our Lord. Amen.

Another Confession of Sins

As David, seeing thine angel with his sword ready drawn, most righteous Lord, to plague

Jerusalem, cried out unto thee, "It is I, Lord, that have sinned, and that have done wickedly; thine hand, Lord, be on me, and not on thy poor sheep;" where through thou was moved to mercy, and bade thine angel put up his sword, thou having taken punishment enough. Even so we, gracious Lord, seeing thy fearful sword of vengeance ready drawn, and now striking against this common weal and thy church in the same, we have occasion every man now to cast off our eyes from beholding and narrowly spying out other men's faults, and to set our own only in sight, that with the same David thy servant, and with Jonah in the ship, we may cry, "It is we, O Lord, who have sinned, and procured this thy grievous wrath." And this we now, gathered together in Christ's name, do acknowledge, confessing ourselves guilty of horrible ingratitude for our good king for thy gospel and pure religion, and for the peace of thy church, and quietness of the common weal besides our negligences and our many other grievous sins, where through we have deserved not only these but much more grievous plagues, if even at present thou did not, as thou art wont, remember thy mercy.

Hereupon, since thou in thine anger remembers thy mercy before we seek and sue for it, we take boldness, as thou commands us to do, in our trouble, to come and call upon thee, to be merciful unto us; and of thy goodness now we humbly in Christ's name pray thee to hold thy hand and cease thy wrath; or at least so to mitigate it, that this realm may be quietly governed, and the same shortly become a harbor for thy church and true religion; which do thou restore to us again, according to thy great power and mercy, and we shall praise thy name for ever, through Jesus Christ our only Mediator and Savior. Amen.

A Prayer for the Remission of Sins

Oh! Lord God and dear Father, what shall I say, that feel all things to be in a manner with me as in the wicked! Blind is my mind, crooked is my will, and perverse concupiscence is in me, as a spring or stinking puddle. Oh! how faint is faith in me! how little love is there to thee or thy people, how great is self-love, how hard is my heart, &c. By reason whereof I am moved to doubt of thy goodness towards me, whether thou art my Father or not, and whether I am thy child or not. Indeed justly might I doubt it, if the having of these were the causes and not rather the fruits of being thy children. The cause why thou art my Father, is, thy mercy, goodness, grace, and truth in Christ Jesus, which cannot but remain for ever. In respect whereof thou hast borne me this good will, to accept me into the number of thy children, that I might be holy, faithful, obedient, innocent, &c. And therefore thou would not only make me a creature after thy image, enduing me with sight, limbs, shape, form, memory, wisdom, &c., whereas thou might have made me a beast, a maimed creature, lame, blind, frantic, &c.; but also thou would that I should be born of Christian parents, brought into thy church by baptism, and called divers times by the ministry of thy word into thy kingdom, besides the innumerable other benefits always hitherto poured upon me. All this thou hast done of thy good will which thou of thine own mercy bare to me in Christ and for Christ before the world was made; which thou requires straitly that I should believe without doubting, so that in all my needs I should come unto thee as a Father, and make my moan without mistrust of being heard, in thy good time, as most shall make to my comfort. Lo! therefore to thee, dear Father, I come through thy Son our Lord, our Mediator and Advocate, Jesus Christ, who sits on thy right hand, making intercession for me, and I pray thee of thy great goodness and mercy in Christ to be merciful unto me, that I may feel indeed thy sweet mercy, as thy child. The time, O dear Father, I appoint not, but I pray thee that I may with hope still expect and look for thy help. I hope that as thou hast left me for a little while, thou wilt come and visit me, and that in thy great mercy, whereof I have need by reason of my great misery. Thou art wont for a little season in thine anger to hide thy face from those whom thou loves, but surely O Redeemer, in eternal mercies thou wilt show thy compassions. For when thou leaves us, O Lord, thou dost not leave us very long, neither dost thou leave us to our loss, but to out gain and advantage: even that thy

Holy Spirit, with a greater portion of thy power and virtue, may lighten and cheer us, that the want of feeling, to our sorrow, may be recompensed plentifully with the lively sense of having thee, to our eternal joy.

And therefore thou swears, that in thine everlasting mercy thou wilt have compassion on us: of which mercy that we might be most assured, thine oath is to be marked, for thou says, "As I have sworn that I will not bring any more the waters to drown the world; so have I sworn, that I will never more be angry with thee, nor reprove thee. The mountains shall remove, and the hills shall fall down, but my loving kindness shall not move, and the bond of my peace shall not fail thee;" thus says thou the Lord, our merciful Redeemer. Dear Father, therefore; I pray thee, remember, even for thine own truth and mercy's sake, this promise and everlasting covenant, which in thy good time I pray thee to write in my heart, that I may know thee to be the only true God, and Jesus Christ whom thou hast sent: that I may love thee with all my heart for ever, that I may love thy people for thy sake; that I may be holy in thy sight through Christ; that I may always not only strive against sin, but also overcome the same, daily more and more, as thy children do. Above all things desiring the sanctification of thy name, them coming of thy kingdom, the doing of thy will here on earth as it is in heaven, &c, through Jesus Christ our Redeemer, Mediator, and Advocate. Amen.

Another Prayer for Remission of Sins

O gracious God! who seeks by all means to bring thy children into the feeling and sure sense of thy mercy, and therefore when prosperity will not serve, thou sends adversity, graciously correcting them here, whom thou wilt shall live with thee elsewhere for ever: – we poor, wretched creatures give humble praises and thanks unto thee, dear Father, that thou hast vouched us worthy of thy correction at this present time, hereby to work that which we in prosperity and liberty did neglect. For which neglecting and our many other grievous sins, whereof we now accuse ourselves before thee, most merciful Lord, thou might most justly have given us over, and destroyed us both in souls and bodies. But such is thy goodness towards us in Christ, that thou seems to forget all our offences; and as though we were far otherwise than we are indeed, thou wilt that we should suffer this cross now laid upon us for thy truth and gospel's sake, and so be thy witnesses with the prophets, apostles, martyrs, and confessors, yea, with thy dearly beloved Son Jesus Christ, to whom thou dost now here begin to fashion us like, that in his glory we may be like him also.

O good God! what are we on whom thou dost show this great mercy! O loving Lord! forgive us our unthankfulness and sins. O faithful Father! give us thy Holy Spirit now to cry in our hearts, Abba, dear Father – to assure us of our eternal election in Christ – to reveal more and more thy truth unto us – to confirm, strengthen, and establish us so in the same, that we may live and die in it as vessels of thy mercy, to thy glory and to the advantage of thy church. Endue us with the Spirit of thy wisdom, that with good conscience we may always so answer the enemies of thy cause, as may turn to their conversion or confusion, and our unspeakable consolation in Jesus Christ; for whose sake we beseech thee henceforth to keep us, to give us patience, and to will none otherwise for deliverance or mitigation of our misery, than may stand always with thy good pleasure and merciful will towards us. Grant this, dear Father, not only to us in this place, but also to all others elsewhere afflicted for thy name's sake, through the death and merits of Jesus Christ our Lord. Amen.

A Prayer for Deliverance from Sin, and to be Restored to God's Grace and Favour Again

O almighty and everlasting Lord God, who hast made heaven, earth, and all things. O incomprehensible Unity! O always to be worshiped, most blessed Trinity! I humbly beseech thee and pray thee, by the assumption and crucified humanity of our Lord Jesus Christ, that thou would incline and bow down thy Deity to pity my vileness, to drive from me all kinds of vice, wickedness, and sin, and to make in me a new and clean heart, and to renew in me a light spirit, for thy holy name's sake. O Lord Jesus! I beseech thy goodness, for the exceeding great love which drew thee out of thy Father's bosom into the womb of the holy virgin, and for the assumption of man's nature, wherein it pleases thee to save me, and to deliver me from eternal death. – I beseech thee, I say, that thou would draw me out of myself into thee, my Lord God, and grant that thy love may recover again thy grace to me, to increase and make perfect in me that which is wanting, to raise up in me that which is fallen, to restore to me that which I have lost, and to quicken in me that which is dead and should live, so that I may become conformable unto thee in all my life and conversation, thou dwelling in me and I in thee, my heart being supplied with thy grace, and settled in thy faith for ever.

O thou my God! loose and set at liberty my spirit from all inferior things, govern my soul, and so work, that both in soul and body I may be holy, and live to thy glory, world without end. Amen.

A Prayer for the Obtaining of Faith

O merciful God and dear Father of our Lord and Savior Jesus Christ! in whom as thou art well pleased, so hast thou commanded us to hear him. Forasmuch as he often bids us to ask of thee, and promises that thou wilt hear us, and grant us that which in his name we shall ask of thee; lo! gracious Father, I am bold to beg of thy mercy, through thy Son Jesus Christ, one sparkle of true faith and certain persuasion of thy goodness and love towards me in Christ; where through I, being assured of the pardon of all my sins by the mercies of Christ thy Son, may be thankful to thee, love thee, and serve thee in holiness and righteousness all the days of my life. Amen.

A Prayer for Repentance

Most gracious God and merciful Father of our Savior Jesus Christ; – because I have sinned and done wickedly, and through thy goodness have received a desire of repentance, whereto thy long-suffering draws my hard heart; I beseech thee, for thy great mercies sake in Christ, to work the same repentance in me; and by thy Spirit, power, and grace, to humble, mortify, and make my conscience afraid for my sins, to salvation; that in thy good time thou may comfort and quicken me, through Jesus Christ, thy dearly beloved Son. So be it.

A Godly Meditation and Prayer

O almighty and everlasting Lord God! the dear Father of our Savior Jesus Christ, who hast made heaven and earth, the sea, and all that therein is, who art the only ruler, governor, preserver, and keeper of all things, together with thy dearly beloved Son Christ Jesus our Lord, and with thy Holy Ghost the Comforter. O holy, righteous, and wise! O strong, terrible, mighty, and fearful Lord God! Judge of all men, and Governor of all the whole world! O exorable, patient, and most gracious Father! whose eyes are upon the ways of all men, and are so clean that they cannot abide impiety; thou searches the hearts, and tries the very thoughts and reins of all men; thou hates sin, and abhorrent iniquity; for sin's sake thou hast grievously punished mankind, thy most dear creature, as thou hast declared by the penalty of death laid upon all the children of Adam, by the casting out Adam and his offspring forth from paradise. Also by the cursing of the earth; by the drowning of the world; by the burning up of Sodom and Gomorrah; by the hardening the heart of Pharaoh, so that no miracle could convert him; by the drowning of him and his people with him in the Red Sea; by the overthrowing of the Israelites in the wilderness, so that of six hundred thousand only two entered into the land of promise; by rejecting king Saul; by the great punishment upon thy servant David, notwithstanding his hearty repentance; by grievously afflicting Solomon in himself and in his posterity; by the captivity of the ten tribes, and by the thraldom of the Jews, wherein until this present day they continue a notable spectacle to the world of thy wrath against and for sin. But of all the spectacles of thy anger against sin, the greatest and most notable is the death and bloody passion of thy dearly beloved Son Jesus Christ.

Great is thy anger against sin, when in heaven and earth nothing could be found which might appease thy wrath, save the blood- shedding of thine only and most dearly beloved Son, in whom was and is all thy delight. Great is the sore of sin, that needs such a salve. Mighty was the malady that needs such a medicine. If in Christ, in whom was no sin, thy wrath was so fierce for our sin that he was constrained to cry, "My God, my God, why hast thou forsaken me?" how great and insupportable must be thine anger against us, who are nothing but sinful! They that are thy children, through the contemplation of thine anger against sin, most evidently set forth in the death of Christ, do tremble and are afraid, lamenting themselves to him, and heartily crying for mercy; whereas the wicked are altogether careless and contemptuous, nothing lamenting their iniquities nor crying to thee heartily for mercy and pardon, among whom we are rather to be placed, than among thy children. For we are shameless for our sin, and careless for thy wrath; which we may well say, is most grievous against us, and evidently set forth in the taking away of our good king and thy true religion, in the exile of thy servants, imprisonment of thy people, misery of thy children, and death of thy saints. Also by the placing thy enemies in authority over us, by the success thou gives them in all they take in hand, by the returning again of antichrist the pope into our country.

All these, as they declare thy grievous wrath unto all the world, but specially unto us, so they set before our eyes our iniquities and sins, which have deserved the same. For thou art just and holy in all thy works, thy judgments are righteous altogether; it is we, it is we that have sinned, and procured these plagues; we have been unthankful wretches, and most carnal gospellers; therefore to us pertains shame, and nothing else is due, but confession. For we have done very wickedly, we have heaped sin upon sin, so that the measure has overflowed and ascended up to heaven, and brought these plagues, which are but earnests for greater to ensue; and yet, alas, we are altogether careless in manner! What shall we do? What shall we say? Who can give us penitent hearts? Who can open our lips, that our mouths may make acceptable confession unto thee? Alas! of ourselves we cannot think any good, much less wish it, and least of all do it. As for angels or any other creatures, they have nothing but what they have received, and they are made to minister unto us, so that where it passes the power of the master, the minister must needs want. Alas! then, what shall we do? Thou art holy, and we unholy; thaw art good, and we nothing but evil; thou art pure, we altogether impure; thou art light, and we most dark, darkness; how then can there be any convenience or agreement betwixt us? Oh! what may we now do? Despair? No; for thou art God, and therefore good; thou art merciful, and therefore thou forgives sins; with thee is mercy and propitiation, and therefore thou art worshiped. When Adam had sinned, thou gave him mercy before he desired it, and wilt thou deny us mercy, who now desire the same? Adam excused his fault, and accused thee, but we accuse ourselves, and excuse thee; and shall we be sent empty away? Noah found favor when thy fury abounded; and shall we, seeking grace, be frustrated? Abraham was pulled out of idolatry when the world was drowned therein; and art thou his God only? Israel in captivity in Egypt was graciously visited and delivered; and, dear God, the same good Lord, shall we always be forgotten? How often in the wilderness did thou defer, and spare thy plagues, at the request of Moses, when the people themselves made no petition to thee?

And seeing we not only now make our petitions unto thee through thy goodness, but also we have a Mediator for us far above Moses, even Jesus Christ; should we, I say, dear Lord, depart ashamed? So soon as David said, "I have sinned," thou did forthwith answer him, that he should not die, thou had taken away his sins. And, gracious God, even the self- same God, shall not we, who now with David gladly confess that we have sinned, shall not we, I say, hear by thy good Spirit that our sins are pardoned? Oh! grant that with Manasseh we may find favor and mercy; remember that thou hast not spared thine own only dear Son Jesus Christ, but hast given him for us all, to die for our sins, to rise for our righteousness, to ascend for our taking possession of heaven, and to appear before thee for us for ever, a high priest after the order of Melchisedec, that through him we might have free access to come to thy throne, now rather a throne of grace than of justice. Remember that thou by him hast bidden us to ask, and promised that we should receive, saying, "Ask, and ye shall have, and ye shall find; knock, and it shall be opened unto you." O thou dear God, and most mild and merciful Father! we heartily beseech thee to be merciful unto us. For this thy Christ's sake, for his death's sake, for thy promise, truth, and mercy's sake, have mercy upon us; pardon and forgive us all our sins, iniquities, and trespasses, whatsoever we have committed against thee, in thought, word, or deed, ever or at any time hitherto, by any means.

Dear Father, have mercy upon us; though we are poor, yet our Christ is rich; though we are sinners, yet he is righteous; though we are fools, yet he is wise; though we are impure, yet he is pure and holy; for his sake therefore be merciful unto us. Call to mind how thou hast promised that thou wilt pour out thy clean waters, and wash us from our filth, and cleanse us from our evils; forget not that thou hast promised to take from us our stony hearts, and dost promise to give us soft hearts, new hearts, and to put right spirits into the midst of us. Remember thy covenant, namely, how thou wilt be our God, and we shall be thy people; forget not the parts of it, that is, to put out of thy memory for ever all our unrighteousness, and to write in our minds and hearts thy law and testimonies. Remember that thou dost strictly charge us to have none others gods but thee, saying, that thou art the Lord our God. Oh! then declare the same to us all, we now heartily beseech thee; forgive us our sins, forget our iniquities, cleanse us from our filthiness, wash us from our wickedness, pour out thy Holy Spirit upon us, take from us our hard hearts, our stony hearts, our impenitent hearts, ours distrusting and doubtful hearts, our carnal, our secure, our idle, our brutish hearts, our impure, malicious, arrogant, envious, wrathful, impatient, covetous, hypocritical, and selfish hearts; and in place thereof give us new hearts, soft hearts, faithful hearts, merciful hearts, loving, obedient, chaste, pure, holy, righteous, true, simple, lowly, and patient hearts, to fear thee, to love thee, and triumph in thee for ever. Write thy law in our hearts, engrave it in our minds, we heartily beseech thee; give us the spirit of prayer, make us diligent and happy in the works of our vocation, take into thy custody and governance our souls and bodies for ever, our lives, and all that ever we have. Tempt us not further than thou wilt make us able to bear; and whatsoever thou knows we have need of, in soul or body, dear God and gracious Father, vouchsafe to give us that same in thy good time, and guide us always as thy children, so that our life may please thee, and our death praise thee, through Jesus Christ our Lord. For whose sake we heartily pray thee to grant these things thus asked, and all other things necessary for soul and body; not only to us, but to all others also, for whom thou would that we should pray; especially for thy children that are in thraldom, in exile, in prison, misery, heaviness, poverty and sickness.

Be merciful to the whole realm of England; grant us all true repentance, mitigation of our misery, and, if it be thy good will, thy holy word and religion among us once again; pardon our enemies, persecutors, and slanderers, and if it be thy pleasure, turn their hearts; be merciful unto our parents, brethren and sisters, friends, kinsfolks and families, neighbors, and such as by any means thou hast coupled and linked us to, by love or otherwise. And unto us, poor sinners, here gathered together in thy holy name, grant thy blessing and thy Holy Spirit to sanctify us, and dwell in us as thy dear children, to keep us, this day and for ever, from all evil, to thy eternal glory, and our everlasting comfort, and the profit of thy church; which mercifully maintain, cherish, and comfort; strengthening them that stand, so that they may never fall; lifting up them that are fallen; – and keep us from falling from thy truth; through the merits of thy dearly beloved Son Jesus Christ, our only Savior, who lives and reigns with thee and the Holy Ghost, to whom be all praise and honor, both now and for ever. Amen.

C. Prayers of Martyrs as They Faced Death

O Lord Jesu, who art the only health of all men living, and the everlasting life of those who die in thy faith: I give myself wholly unto thy will, being sure that the thing cannot perish whichis committed unto thy mercy.

Thomas Cromwell, before his execution

O eternal God and merciful Father, look down upon me in mercy; in the riches and fullness of all Thy mercies, look down upon me: but not till Thou hast nailed my sins to the Cross of Christ, not till Thou has bathed me in the Blood of Christ, not till I have hid myself in the wounds of Christ, that so the punishment due unto my sins may pass over me. And since Thou art pleased to try me to the utmost, I humbly beseech Thee, give me now, in this great instant, full patience, proportionable comfort, and a heart ready to die for Thine honour, the Kings's happiness, and the Church's preservation.

I am coming, O Lord, as quickly as I can. I know I must pass through death before I can come to see Thee. But it is only the mere shadow of death; a little darkness upon nature. Thou, by Thy merits, hast broken through the jaws of death. The Lord receive my soul, and have mercy upon me, and bless this kingdom with peace and plenty, and with brotherly love and charity, that there may not be this effusion of Christian blood among them: for Jesus Christ's sake, if it be Thy will.

Lord, receive my soul.

William Laud, martyred on Tower Hill, January 10, 1645

O Father of heaven, O Son of God, Redeemer of the world, O Holy Ghost, three persons and one God, have mercy upon me, most wretched caitiff and miserable sinner. I have offended both against heaven and earth more than my tongue can express. Whither, then, may I go, or whither shall I flee? To heaven I may be ashamed to lift up mine eyes, and in earth I find no place of refuge or succour. To thee, therefore, O Lord, do I run; to thee do I humble myself, saying, O Lord my God, my sins be great, but yet have mercy upon me for thy great mercy. The great mystery that God became man was not wrought for little or few offences. Thou didst not give thy Son, O heavenly Father, unto death for small sins only, but for all the greatest sins of the world, so that the sinner return to thee with his whole heart, as I do at this present. Wherefore have mercy on me, O God, whose property is always to have mercy; have mercy upon me, O Lord, for thy great mercy. I crave nothing for mine own merits, but for thy name's sake.

Thomas Cranmer. His last words, before going to the stake, 21 March 1556

O Lord my God, I have hope in thee;
O my dear Jesus, set me free.
Though hard the chains that fasten me
And sore my lot, yet I long for thee.
I languish and groaning bend my knee,
Adoring, imploring, O set me free.

Mary Queen of Scots, on the eve of her execution

O loving Christ, draw me, a weakling, after yourself; for if you do not draw me I cannot follow you. Give me a brave spirit that it may be ready alert. If the flesh is weak, may your grace go before me, come along side me and follow me; for without you I cannot do anything, and especially, for your sake I cannot go to a cruel death. Grant me a ready spirit, a fearless heart, a right faith, a firm hope, and a perfect love, that for your sake I may lay down my life with patience and joy.

John Hus, as he lay chained in prison

Give me, good Lord, a full faith, a firm hope and a fervent love, a love for you incomparably above the love of myself.

Give me your grace, good Lord, to make death no stranger to me.

Lord, give me patience in tribulation and grace in everything to conform my will to yours.

Give me, good Lord, a longing to be with you, not to avoid the calamities of this wretched world, nor so much for the attaining of the joys of heaven, as for a true love of you.

And give me, good Lord, your love and favour, which my love of you, however great, could not deserve, were it not for your great goodness.

These things, good Lord, that I pray for, give me your grace also to work for.

Thomas More, after he had been condemned to death

D. Quotations about Martyrdom

Against the persecution of a tyrant the godly have no remedy but prayer.
John Calvin

When your enemies see that you are so determined that neither sickness, fancies, poverty, life, death, nor sins discourage you, but that you will continue to seek the love of Jesus and nothing else, by continuing your prayer and other spiritual works, they will grow enraged and will not spare you the most cruel abuse.
Walter Hilton

If it were an art to overcome heresy with fire, the executioners would be the most learned doctors on earth.
Martin Luther

If the Devil were wise enough and would stand by in silence and let the Gospel be preached, he would suffer less harm. For when there is no battle for the Gospel it rusts and it finds no cause and no occasion to show its vigor and power. Therefore, nothing better can befall the Gospel than that the world should fight it with force and cunning.
Martin Luther

Part Seven

Martyrs from the Seventeenth to the Twenty-First Centuries

Contents

Jesuit martyrs in Canada	
Anthony Daniel:	Edward P. Spillane
Gabriel Lalemant:	T.J. Campbell
St. Isaac Jogues:	T.J. Campbell
Jean de Brébeuf:	T.J. Campbell
Noel Chabanel:	T.J. Campbell
René Goupil:	Lionel Lindsay
USA	
Kund Iverson:	S.B. Shaw
Constance and Her Companions, The Martyrs of Memphis	James Kiefer
Martin Luther King, Jr:	Editor
Cassie Bernall:	Editor
Hawaii	
Damien, Priest, Missionary, and Martyr:	James Kiefer
The Far East	
Melanasia, New Hebrides	
Martyr's Isle:	Editor
New Guinea	
James Chalmers:	Editor
The martyrs of New Guinea:	James Kiefer
East Asia	
North Korea	
Twentieth century martyrs:	Editor
South East Asia	
Indonesia	
1966	Editor
1997-1999	Editor
108 Christians massacred in Moluccas:	Editor
Thailand	
Roy Orpin:	Editor
Vietnam	
Catechist Andrew:	Editor
Japan	
Martyrs in Japan:	Louis Delplace
Martyrs of 1597:	Alban Butler
Martyrs of 1602-22:	Alban Butler
20,000 massacred, 1662:	John Foxe
Martyrs of 1660-1673:	Editor
Fate of hundreds of people of Matsudaira Yamato-no-kami:	Editor
Manchurian martyrs:	Editor

South America	
Bolivia	
The Ayore Indians:	Editor
Ecuador	
The Martyrs of the Ecuador Mission:	James Kiefer
Jim Elliot:	Editor
Update on the Auca Indians:	Wycliffe Bible Translators
Columbia	
Señor Juan P. Coy:	Pat and Helen Symes
More twentieth century martyrs:	Editor
San Salvador	
Archbishop Romero:	Editor
Africa	
Algeria	
Over one hundred killed:	International Christian Concern
Egypt	
Two young Christian men, 1998:	International Christian Concern
Coptic Christian Fakhri Ayyad Mus'ad, 2000:	International Christian Concern
Mozambique	
Bernard Mizeki, Catechist and Martyr in Africa:	James Kiefer
Ruanda	
500,000 Christian martyrs:	Global Monitor
Uganda	
Catholic and Protestant martyrs:	Editor
The twenty-six Catholic and Protestant martyrs of Uganda:	Editor
James Hannington:	Editor
James Hannington and the Martyrs of Uganda:	James Kiefer
The martyrs of Uganda:	James Kiefer
Archbishop Luwum:	James Kiefer Editor
Madagascar	
Persecutions in the 19th century:	John Foxe
Swaziland	
Swazi Tidings:	The South African Pioneer
Liberia	
Tom and June Jackson:	Worldwide

Congo	
Winnie Davies, 1967:	Editor
Report on the death of a Protestant missionary by a Dutch Roman Catholic missionary:	Len Moules
Senegal	
Pierre Senghor, 1959:	Worldwide
Indian Subcontinent	
Kashmir	
Ron Davies, 1947:	World Conquest
India	
Graham Stewart Stains, 58, and his two sons, Philip, 10, and Timothy, 8; 1999:	Newspaper report
More 20th century martyrdoms in India:	Newspaper reports
The Rev Ashish Prabash Masih	
Mr. Yesu Dasu	
Victor Crasta, and three missionaries	
Ashish Prabash	
Vijay Ekka	
George Kuzhikandum	
Pakistan	
Nine martyrs butchered:	Newspaper reports
More 20th century martyrdoms in Pakistan:	Newspaper reports
Russian and Eastern Europe	
Albania	
Savage campaign against Catholic Church:	Editor
Grave violations of religious rights in Albania:	Palok Plaku
Armenia	
The martyrs of Armenia:	James Kiefer
Russia	
After the 1917 Revolution:	Charles Karner
Ukraine	
Yakim Bely and Iosyf Tyshkevich:	Editor
Soviet Union	
8,100 martyrs:	Editor
General Registers of martyrs, 1917-22:	Keston College

1. Introduction

A LIST OF MARTYRS FROM THE 20TH CENTURY

Countless martyrdoms have taken place in the last hundred years. As in the first nineteen centuries of the Christian era, there seem to be two extreme views about martyrdoms. Either people concentrate on them as if nothing else worthwhile is happening in the world, or, people just ignore the martyrdoms and live as if they were not happening.

The following list of modern martyrs helps to raise our awareness that martyrdoms have been happening in many different parts of the world, even when they are not reported by the news media.

Graham Staines and his sons (1999)

Australian missionary Staines and his two sons, 8 and 10, were attacked while they were sleeping in a jeep. Graham Staines, 58, and his sons Philip and Timothy were burned alive by a mob of Hindu extremists.

Sister Aloysius Maria (1999)

Sr. Aloysius Maria, a Missionary of Charity working in Sierra Leone, was killed in cold blood by the rebels on January 22. Her missionary companion, Father Girolamo Pistoni, was wounded by the kidnappers but abandoned, because they thought he was dead.

Albino Saluhaku (1999)

Father Albino Saluhaku, of the diocese of Huambo, Angola, was killed on January 6, along with two catechists who had been working with him.

Jan Czuba (1998)

This Polish missionary priest was killed by unidentified armed men at a site west of Brazzaville. He was ordained in the diocese of Tarnow, and began his work in the Congo in 1988. He had been serving as pastor of a parish in Loulombo, in the Pool region (the fourth Polish priest to die in that region).

Missionary Sisters of Charity, Yemen (1998)

Three nuns of the Missionaries of Charity religious order were killed as they left their medical clinic in Hodeida on Monday, July 27th, by gunmen wielding automatic weapons. The gunmen fired on the nuns from a passing car.

Daughters of the Resurrection (1998)

Five women religious of the Daughters of the Resurrection congregation, were assassinated in Busasamana on January 8th. The five sisters were Tutsis from the Congo. The assassins were armed with rifles, machetes, and axes. The Vatican Observer newspaper wrote on January 13, that "The sad chapter of the Martyrology of the Church has been opened again in the African region of the Great Lakes."

Thomas Edward Gafney (1997)

Father Gafney was a Jesuit missionary in Nepal, where he had worked for 30 years. He worked among the poor, particularly orphans and drug addicts. December 14, 1997, he was killed in his sleep, struck in the neck with a curved machete-style knife.

Bishop Benjamin de Jesus (1997)

Bishop de Jesus, O.M.I., of the diocese of Jolo, the Philippines, was killed outside his cathedral. He was gunned down early on February 4th by three masked gunmen.

Servando Mayor Garcia and companions (1996)

Marist Brothers Servando Mayor Garcia, Miguel Angel Isla Lucio, Fernando de la Fuente and Julio Rodriguez Jorge were murdered on October 31, 1995 in Eastern Zaire by Rwandan militants. The four missionaries were all from Spain and were working on behalf of the many Rwandan refugees in that war-torn district.

Archbishop Christopher Munzihirwa Mwene Ngabo (1996)

October 29, 1996, Archbishop Ngabo of Bukavu, a Zairian Jesuit who was killed during attacks on his city by Tutsi

Banyamulenge rebels. Also killed in the unrest were a number of Catholic priests, doctors and missionaries, along with their Protestant counterparts.

Archbishop Joachim Ruhuna (1996)
Archbishop Ruhuna, an ethnic Tutsi who presided over the central Diocese of Gitega, Burundi, was ambushed on September 9. His car was fired on and torched. Sister Concessa Ndacikiriwe, Sister Irene Gakobwa, and an unnamed woman church accountant were also killed.

Trappist Martyrs in Algeria (1996)
Seven French Trappist monks were executed by Islamic extremists in Algeria, after being used as political pawns.

Archbishop Pierre Claverie (1996)
This Algerian archbishop lost his life after speaking out against the senseless deaths of the seven French Trappists.

Sudanese Martyrs (1995)
In August five Nuban young women were sentenced to death for apostasy, because they had converted to Christianity from Islam. These unnamed victims are representative of the thousands of converts from Islam who have been condemned to death for their faith in Jesus Christ.

Lay and Religious Martyrs in Burundi (1995)
Saverian fathers Ottorino Maule and Aldo Merchiol, and lay aid worker Katina Gubert were executed doing missionary work in Burundi on October 1, 1995

Cardinal Posadas Ocampo (1993)
On May 23, 1993, Cardinal Posadas Ocampo, accompanied by his driver, was at Guadalajara airport to welcome a fellow bishop. As the cardinal stepped out of the car, two men ran up and shot both the cardinal and his driver; both died instantly. According to Mexican government investigators, the cardinal was the victim of a "crossfire" between two rival drug-trading gangs. However, a post-mortem examination confirmed that the cardinal and his driver had been shot at point-blank range.

Chinese Bishops (1989)
In 1989, the underground bishops of Mainland China decided to organize themselves openly into the National Conference of Roman Catholic Bishops, in contrast to the Government-controlled Patriotic Bishop's Conference. Within a few months, they were all arrested in different parts of China and held for varying lengths of time. Three of the arrested bishops died in custody: Shi Chunjie, Auxiliary Bishop of Baoding; Fan Xueyan, Bishop of Baoding, and Liu di Fen, Bishop of An Guo.

James Carney (1983)
Father James "Guadelupe" Carney was a Jesuit priest who "disappeared" in Honduras during September 1983. Evidence suggests he was thrown from a military helicopter into the Honduran jungle because of his work on behalf of the poor.

Missionary Martyrs of El Salvador (1980)
On December 2nd, 1980, four women, Maryknoll Sisters Ita Ford and Maureen Clarke, Ursuline Sister Dorothy Kazel and Lay missioner Jean Donovan, were stopped on the road in the jungle of El Salvador while doing work on behalf of the poor. The soldiers who had stopped them, under orders from the Salvadoran government, murdered all four and a companion without trial, by taking them to an isolated spot where they were shot dead at close range. The U.N.-sponsored report of the Commission on the Truth for El Salvador concluded that the abductions were planned in advance and the men responsible had carried out the murders on orders from above. It further stated that the head of the National Guard and two officers assigned to investigate the case had concealed the facts to harm the judicial process.

Archbishop Janani Luwum (1977)
Janani Luwum was the Anglican Archbishop

of Uganda during Idi Amin's bloody reign. After a series of provocations, the Archbishop called on President Amin to deliver a note of protest at the policies of arbitrary killings and the unexplained disappearances. He was arrested for treason and his body was riddled with bullets.

Rutilio Grande (1977)

Fr. Grande was a parish priest working with the campesinos in El Salvador. He was murdered by government troops for his outspoken calls for justice.

Francis Xavier Ford (1952)

A missionary priest in China since 1918, Bishop Ford was the first bishop of Kaying when he was arrested by the communists. He died in prison in 1952 in the Canton provence. After his arrest he told a companion, "We are going to prison in honor of Christ. It is no disgrace."

Maria Agneta Chang (1950)

Maria Chang was born to an influential Korean family. Her brother John served as the president of Korea. Yet Maria joined the Maryknoll Sisters in 1928. During the Japanese occupation all foreign religious and clergy were expelled from Korea. Maria chose to stay in the north as superior of a new community of Korean nuns. In 1950 she was arrested and executed by the communists and buried in a mass grave with other victims.

Patrick Bryne (1950)

Bishop Byrne was a missionary to Japan and Korea. During the Second World War he was under house arrest in Kyoto. Following his release he was named the Vatican's Apostolic Delegate to Korea in 1949. He was soon arrested again by Korean communists. He died of pneumonia during a forced march of prisoners during the winter of 1950, reportedly on Nov. 25.

Peter To Rot (1945)

Peter To Rot was born in 1912 in what is now Papua New Guinea, the son of Catholic converts. As an adult he served his village as a lay catechist. In 1942, under Japanese military occupation, all Christian missionaries were imprisoned. Peter worked alone to oppose a series of anti-Christian laws put forward at Japanese instigation. In 1945, he was arrested and murdered by "medical personnel."

Blessed Maria Skobtsova (1945)

Mother Maria was a Russian Orthodox nun who fled to France to escape the Bolsheveks. Arrested later by the Nazis in wartime Paris, she was sent to Ravensbrück concentration camp (1943), where she brought Christian light and hope despite appalling conditions. She was gassed in 1945, reportedly going voluntarily "in order to help her companions to die".

Dietrich Bonhoeffer (1945)

Rev. Bonhoeffer was a Lutheran minister who was arrested for his part in an alleged plot to kill Adolf Hitler. He was executed by the Nazis just days before the end of the war.

Mary Hyacinth Kunkel (1944)

Sister Kunkel, a Maryknoll missionary from New York, was working with the Igorot people in northern Luzon. When American troops landed in 1944 to drive the Japanese from the Phillippines, she and her people were caught in the middle of intense fighting. She was last seen fleeing on foot along a mountain trail with around 500 other displaced persons. Subsequent searches for her found no trace and she was presumed killed.

Maria Restituta (1943)

Maria Restituta was a Moravian religious killed "out of hatred of the Faith" in Vienna in 1943.

Blessed Edith Stein (1942)

Edith Stein was a convert to the Catholic Faith. Born to a devout Jewish family, she embraced the Lord as a adult and joined the Church, eventually professing vows as a Carmelite nun. She was killed in the Holocaust, dying in the gas chamber at Auschwitz.

Titus Brandsma (1942)
Another victim of the Nazis, Fr. Brandsma was a Dutch Carmelite. He was arrested and taken to a concentration camp where, after suffering several days as a victim of "medical experiments", he was given a lethal injection and died July 26, 1942.

Maximilian Kolbe (1941)
Father Maximilian Kolbe died in a Nazi concentration camp at Auschwitz after willingly giving his life that another man might be spared. He was canonized in 1982.

Robert Cairns (1941)
Robert "Sandy" Cairns was a native of Scotland. Ordained a Maryknoll priest in 1918, he went to China as a missionary in 1923. He was a pastor on Sancian Island in December 1941 when the Japanese invaded. Fr. Cairns was bound by soldiers and forced into a boat, along with a native helper. The two men were never seen again.

Jesuit Martyrs of the Holocaust, Germany (1939-1943)
In addition to Edith Stein and Maximillian Kolbe, more than 100 German Jesuits went to their death in prisons and concentration camps. The Holy Cross Holocaust Collection lists them by name along with the names of martyrs who have been beatified as "Blessed."

Victims of The Spanish Civil War (1936-1939)
The Spanish Civil War was marked by violent anti-clericalism. Around 10,000 priests and religious lost their lives because of their identity as Faithful.

Gerard Donovan (1938)
In October 1937, Fr. Donovan was kidnaped while praying with his parishioners in Fushun, Manchuria. His five captors demanded $50,000 for his release. When no ransom was received the bandits murdered him. His remains were found on February 11, 1938, frozen on a mountainside.

Carlos Erana Gurceta and Companions (1936)
Carlos Erana Gurceta was born in Aozaraza-Arechavaleta, Guipuzcoa, Spain, in 1884. He and his two companions, Fidel Fuido and Jesus Hita, were imprisoned and executed in Ciudad Real on September 18,1936.

Victoria Diez y Bustos de Molina (1936)
As a young teacher in Hornachuelos, Spain during the early days of the Spanish Civil War, Victoria Diez was arrested along with 17 others for their Christian witness. After being held overnight they were murdered and dumped in a mine shaft on August 12, 1936.

Dionisio Pamplona and Companions (1936)
Fr. Pamplona along with 12 others, was arrested in Buenos Aires, Spain during the Spanish Civil War. He was tortured and executed by firing squad.

Ceferino Jimenez Malla (1936)
"El Pele", as he was known, lived in Barbastro, Spain during the Civil War. Although he was nearly illiterate, his natural intelligence was enough to bring him to prominence; he became a member of the city council, and the bishop regularly consulted him for advice. At a time when the militia was hunting down priests, Pele was arrested for harboring a young cleric, and eventually shot by a firing squad.

Blessed Louis Versiglia And Callistus Carabario (1930)
Fathers Versiglia and Carabario were Salesian missionaries to China in the 1920's. They were murdered trying to protect some young women in their charge from marauders.

Blessed Miguel Pro (1926)
Miguel Pro was a young seminarian when the Mexican Revolutionary government moved violently to crush the Church in 1914. He fled to the U.S. to continue his studies, returning to Mexico after his ordination. As active priests, Fr. Pro and his

allies were enemies of the State. In 1926 he, along with his brother and two others, were arrested on false charges of conspiracy. They were executed on Saturday, August 14, 1926. As they were about to be killed, the prisoners shouted "Viva Cristo Rey!" – "Long Live Christ the King!"

Fr. Pro is representative of the thousands of Faithful and hundreds of priests and religious who lost their lives in the Mexican government's campaign against the Church.

Russian Martyrs of the Bolshevik Revolution (1918-?)

Reports from Russia's own government reveal that 200,000 clergy, Orthodox, Catholic and Protestant, were brutally killed in Lenin's suppression of the Church.

Charles de Foucauld (1919)

Charles Eugene, viscount of Foucauld, was a notorious Parisian playboy. In 1886 he underwent a religious conversion, and in 1890 he joined a Trappist monastery, but soon left to become a solitary hermit in Palestine. In 1901 he went to Algeria, where he eventually settled at Tamanrasset and there lived the life of a missionary priest and prepared a Taureg dictionary. He was killed in an anti-French uprising on 1 December 1916, by those who said that his goodness tended to create friendly feelings toward the French.

Blessed Isidore Bakanja (1909)

Isidore was brutally beaten because of his evangelizing and died as a result of his wounds in Colonial Africa in 1909.

WESTMINSTER ABBEY'S NEW STATUES

The view of the West Front of Westminster Abbey, London, is one of the best known in the world. The gothic lower part was completed in the fifteenth century; the towers, designed by Nicholas Hawksmoor in a more classical style, were added at the beginning of the eighteenth century.

Both parts of this imposing facade had niches which were evidently intended for statues but were never filled. The comprehensive restoration of the exterior of the Abbey (a twenty-five-year program completed in 1995) provided the opportunity for their original purpose to be fulfilled. In 1992 the six niches high up on the towers were filled with conventional figures of saints. In 1995 four allegorical figures were placed in the niches on either side of the Great West Door: Mercy, Truth, Righteousness and Peace. These traditional virtues (from Psalm 85 verse 10) represent the values for which countless innocent men and women have been prepared to give their lives.

There remained the row of ten niches immediately over the door. It was decided to use these, not just to commemorate saintly or worthy figures from the past, but to proclaim a message of which too few people are aware: the twentieth century has been a century of Christian martyrdom. The cost of Christian witness, and the number of Christians willing to die for what they believed, has been greater in this century than in any previous period in the history of the church.

These ten statues are of individual martyrs; but they are intended to represent all those others who have died (and continue to die) in similar circumstances of oppression and persecution. They are drawn from every continent and many Christian denominations. They include victims of the struggle for human rights in North and South America, of the Soviet and Nazi persecutions in Europe, of religious prejudice and dictatorial rule in Africa, of fanaticism in the Indian subcontinent, of the brutalities of the Second World War in Asia and of the Cultural Revolution in China. In these and other similar circumstances during this most violent of centuries thousands of men and women have paid with their lives for their faith and their convictions. Those represented here have left their testimony to the ultimate cost of Christian witness and to its enduring significance.

The ten martyrs are:

Maximilian Kolbe
Manche Masemola
Janani Luwum
Elizabeth of Russia

Martin Luther King
Oscar Romero
Dietrich Bonhoeffer
Esther John
Lucian Tapiedi
Wang Zhiming

Models for the statues were carefully designed by Tim Crawley from such records and photographs as exist of each of the martyrs and the figures have been carved from French Richemont limestone by him and, under his general direction, by Neil Simmons, John Roberts and Andrew Tanser. Two of these sculptors had already worked on some 300 pieces of stone carving which needed replacement during the restoration of Henry VII Chapel in 1990-95. With these ten statues of modern figures in gothic niches they have now fulfilled one of the most demanding and important sculptural commissions of our time.

The statues were unveiled by the Archbishop of Canterbury, in the presence of H.M. The Queen, H.R.H. The Duke of Edinburgh and church leaders and representatives from many parts of the world on 9 July 1998.

Anthony Harvey, Sub-Dean of Westminster, July 1998

Quotations from the ten martyrs

MAXIMILIAN KOLBE
I want to die in place of this prisoner.

MANCHE MASEMOLA
I shall be baptized with my own blood.

JANANI LUWUM
I am prepared to die in the army of Jesus.

While the opportunity is there, I preach the Gospel with all my might, and my conscience is clear before God that I have not sided with the present government which is utterly self-seeking. I have been threatened many times. Whenever I have the opportunity I have told the president the things the churches disapprove of. God is my witness.

GRAND DUCHESS ELIZABETH
I am leaving a glittering world where I had a glittering position, but with all of you I am descending into a greater world – the world of the poor and the suffering.

MARTIN LUTHER KING
If physical death is the price I must pay to free my brothers and sisters from the permanent death of the spirit, then nothing could be more redemptive.

OSCAR ROMERO
I must tell you, as a Christian, I do not believe in death without resurrection. If I am killed, I shall arise in the Salvadoran people.

DIETRICH BONHOEFFER
The church is the church only when it exists for others.

Suffering then is the badge of true discipleship. The disciple is not above his master. That is why Luther reckoned suffering among the marks of the true Church.

Discipleship means allegiance to the suffering Christ.

ESTHER JOHN
Leave all other ties, Jesus is calling.

LUCIAN TAPIEDI
I will stay with the Fathers and Sisters.

WANG ZHIMING
You should follow the words from above, and repent again.

INTERNET

Christian persecution sites

The following Internet sites provide specific examples of Christian persecution around the world.

www.persecution.com

This is the web site of Voice of the Martyrs, a Christian missionary organization dedicated to serving today's persecuted church. The Voice of the Martyrs works in over 25 countries, providing assistance and encouragement to those who risk all for Christ. The five main purposes of Voice of the Martyrs are:

To give Christians Bibles, literature, and broadcasts in their own language in Communist countries and other restricted areas of the world where Christians are persecuted.

To give relief to the families of Christian martyrs in these areas of the world.

To undertake projects of encouragement to help believers rebuild their lives and witness in countries that have suffered Communist oppression.

To win to Christ those who are opposed to the gospel.

To inform the world about acts committed against Christians and about the courage and faith of the persecuted.

www.persecution.org

This is the web site of International Christian Concern (ICC), a coalition of concerned Christians who believe that we must reach out and help Christians persecuted for their faith. ICC believes that Christians should demonstrate love and support for persecuted Christians by:

writing letters of encouragement
writing protests to government leaders
raising public awareness
soliciting our government's support
offering practical assistance to the persecuted
remembering the persecuted in prayer

www.fica.org

This is the web site for the Fellowship of Indonesian Christians in America. A page on this site (www.fica.org/hr) deals specifically with Christian persecution in Indonesia.

www.indiagospel.net

This is the web site of the India Gospel Network, a full gospel organization, dedicated to provide a forum for Indian Christian believers around the globe for exchange of ideas and information. This site has a link to persecuted Christians in India through

www.pha.jhu.edu/~brink/persec.html

Contains over one hundred links to other sites about Christian persecution.

Quotations about twentieth century martyrdoms

When I see something like this, my heart aches because the believers here don't even know about it, don't care. We're not expressing moral outrage; we're not indignant of the indifference of the United States government towards this. And we ought to be marching in the streets because our brethren are being persecuted, imprisoned, beaten, sold into slavery, and butchered and we don't seem to care in this country.
Chuck Colson, quoted in Focus on the Family, September 16, 1996

More than an estimated 160,000 believers were martyred in 1996, and countless others were subjected to unimaginable horrors.
James Dobson

1996
Christians are being sold into slavery. Some are being thrown into prison. Some are tortured. Many are killed. We must do everything we can in our dealings with other countries to end these practices.
Sen. Don Nickles

Martyr: A Christian believer who dies in a situation of witness as a result of human hostility.
Mission AD 2000

The Church of the first millennium was born of the blood of the martyrs. At the end of the second millennium, the church has once again become a church of martyrs.
Pope John Paul II

There is little disputing the fact that this, above all others, has been the century of Christian martyrdom. Yet that reality receives curiously little attention among contemporary Christians.
Richard John Neuhaus

A State Department report states that Christians have become the most persecuted group in the world and that over 250 million Christians have been attacked, threatened and even murdered for just wanting to live as Christians. In some countries of the Middle East Christians have been murdered.
Based on a report in The Washington Times, August 18, 1997

Two Thirds of All Martyrs Killed in 20th Century

In the 2000 years of the Church's history, it has been estimated that nearly two thirds of all the martyrs died in the 20th century. In the "Christian World Encyclopedia," scholar David B. Barrett maintains that during the last 20 centuries there have been close to 40 million "martyrs," 26,685,000 of them in the 20th century. Barrett uses the term "martyr" in a very broad sense. He writes: "This century has seen very numerous martyrs, especially because of Nazism, communism, and racial and tribal conflicts."

There is more religious persecution in the 21st century than at any other in history. Brutal religious persecution is going on around the world today. Thousands of religious believers were martyred in the last few years. Many others have suffered imprisonment, torture, burning, enslavement and starvation. Christians are the most persecuted group in the world.
Family Research Council

Commission of New Martyrs of the Vatican Jubilee Committee

Bishop Michel Hrynchyshyn, Exarch of the Ukrainians of the Byzantine rite in France, is President of the Commission of New Martyrs of the Vatican Jubilee Committee, a group of 10 experts established a few years ago by the Pope, with the task of gathering information on the martyrs of our century from the Churches of all the different Christian confessions.

An average of some 425 Christian believers are being murdered daily for their faith.
Fair Dinkum, 2,000

U.S. report of religious freedom

The U.S. State Department released its first report on religious freedom around the world. The 1,000-page report documents the status of religious rights in 194 countries. Iran, Afghanistan, China, Iraq, Saudi Arabia, and Sudan were singled out as nations that severely repress the religious freedoms of their citizens.
The Baptist Vision, February 2000

The twenty worst countries for persecuting Christians

(In descending order of level of persecution) Saudi Arabia, Afghanistan, Sudan, China, Yemen, Morocco, Iran, Libya, Tunisia, Egypt, Uzbekistan, Vietnam, Chechnya, Pakistan, Laos, Maldives, Qatar, Turkmenistan, North Korea, and Somalia.
This is Brother Andrew's top 20 list, 1999, published in Open Doors The World Watch

Today Christians are routinely persecuted in about 40 countries around the world.
The Ottawa Citizen, December 23, 1998

More Christians have been martyred for their faith in this century alone than in the previous nineteen centuries combined. More than followers of any other faith, Christians around the world are suffering brutal persecution.
Nina Shea, director of Freedom House, a human rights organization
[Nina Shea, is an international human rights lawyer who has investigated the persecution of Christians for over ten years and has documented the abduction and death of more than 1 million Sudanese, mostly Christians and non-Muslims, at the hands of the country's Islamic fundamentalist government.]

Christians are in fact the most persecuted religious group in the world today, with the greatest number of victims.
Nina Shea, director of Freedom House

FRIAR MARTYRS IN THE 20TH CENTURY

The Union of Major Superiors (UISG and USG – Union of Superiors General) has gathered data about various Religious families.

For the Order of the Friars Minor (OFM) this data has been prepared by the Postulator General. He has conducted this survey in February of 1996 on a worldwide level with the following results. These responses come from 34 of the 128 Provinces of the Order. Of entities or nations in which one assumes that there have been martyrs in this century, the following have not responded: Albania, China, Israel (Holy Land), Lithuania, Romania, Russia, Ukraine, Hungary, Vietnam.

There are reports of about 342 Friars Minors killed "in odium Fidei" in the various parts of the globe.

The martyrs in different countries

Spain 216
Germany 7
Kenya 2
Poland 40
France 6
Canada 1
Croatia 32
Belgium 3
Czech Rep 1
Italy 20
Mexico 3
Slovakia 1
Dalmatia 7
Austria 2
USA 1
U.S.G.

A Jesuit Martyrology of the 20th Century

More than 300 Jesuits died during the 20th century for love of God and their fellow human bings. Some of them were murdered; others died as a result of maltreatment; others were simply made to "disappear" by terrorist regimes who regularly hide their victims. All of them form part of our martyrology for the twentieth century.

The Second Vatican Council declared that the excellence of martyrdom was rooted in the degree of identification with Jesus Christ which motivates a person to give his life for others. At the end of the millennium Pope John Paul II commissioned a Martyrology for the 20th century, so that we might not forget the witness of love of God and neighbor which so many men and women of our time have given with their lives and with their deaths.

Catholic missionaries killed in Africa in 1996

The number of known missionaries around the world killed in 1996 is about 46. Of these, 40 died on the African soil in the following countries:

19 in Zaire
8 in Algeria
7 in Burundi
3 in Rwanda
2 in Ghana
1 in Tanzania

Catholic missionaries killed in 1997

Violence against Catholic missionaries rose in 1997, when compared with 1996 according to the Vatican Congregation for Evangelization. Fides, a news service sponsored by that Congregation, reported that 68 missionaries were killed in 1997.

1997 martyrs

1 bishop
19 priests (15 diocesan priests and 4 members of religious orders)
1 monk
7 nuns
40 seminarians.

The seminarians were slaughtered on April 30, 1997, at the minor seminary in Buta, Burundi.

Country of origin of martyrs

8 from Rwanda
6 from Congo
1 from Nigeria
40 seminarians from Burundi
3 from India
2 from Brazil

Other victims were from Canada, Colombia, the Philippines, Belgium, France, Italy, Ireland, and the United States.

Country where martyrdoms took place
12 in Congo
4 in Rwanda
41 in Burundi
1 each in Chad, Kenya, and Nigeria.
2 in India
2 in Brazil
1 each in Colombia, Peru, the Philippines, and Nepal
Source: Fides, by kind permission

32 Catholic personnel were killed in mission territories in 1999
17 priests (10 diocesan, 7 religious)
9 Sisters (of 4 congregations)
4 seminarians
2 catechists

Grouped according to origin by continent
10 Africans (Angola 5, Burundi 2, Democratic Congo 2, Kenya 1)
12 Asians (Timor 6, India 3, Bangladesh 1, Indonesia 1, Lebanon 1)
5 Americans (Colombia 5)
5 Europeans (Italy 2, Belgium 1, Germany 1, Spain1)

Grouped according to country of martyrdom
15 in Africa (6 in Angola, 3 in Sierra Leone, 2 in Burundi, 2 in Democratic Congo, 1 in Guinea, 1 in South Africa)
11 in Asia (9 in East Timor, 1 in India, 1 in Lebanon)
6 in America (4 in Colombia, 1 in Ecuador, 1 in the Dominican Republic)
Source: Fides, with kind permission

2. Martyrdoms by country

CHINA

MARTYRS IN CHINA

The first Christian martyrs in China appear to have been the missionaries of Ili Böliq in Central Asia, Khan-Bölig (Peking), and Zaitun (Fu-kien), in the middle of the fourteenth century. Islam had been introduced into Central Asia, and in China, the native dynasty of Ming, replacing the Mongol dynasty of Yuan, had not followed the policy of toleration of their predecessors; the Hungarian, Matthew Escandel, being possibly the first martyr.

With the revival of the missions in China with Matteo Ricci, who died at Peking in 1610, the blood of martyrs was soon shed to fertilize the evangelical field; the change of the Ming dynasty to the Manchu dynasty, giving occasion for new prosecution. Andrew Xavier (better known as Andrew Wolfgang) Koffler (b. at Krems, Austria, 1603), a Jesuit, and companion of Father Michel Boym, in the Kwang-si province, who had been very successful during the Ming dynasty, was killed by the Manchu invaders on 12 December, 1651. On 9 May, 1665, the Dominican, Domingo Coronado, died in prison at Peking. Sometime before, a Spanish Dominican, Francisco Fernandez, of the convent of Valladolid, had been martyred on 15 January, 1648. Among the martyrs must be reckoned the celebrated Jesuit Johann Adam Schall von Bell (T'ang Jo-wang), who was imprisoned and ill-treated during the Manchu conquest. They were the first victims in modern times.

After publication by a literato, of a libel against the Christians of Fu-ngan, in Fu-kien, the viceroy of the province gave orders to inquire into the state of the Catholic religion, the result of which was that a dreadful prosecution broke out in 1746, during the reign of Emperor K'ien lung, the victims of which were all Spanish Dominicans; the following were arrested: Juan Alcober (b. at Girone in 1649); Francisco Serrano, Bishop of Tipasa, and coadjutor the vicar Apostolic; and Francisco Diaz (b. in 1712, at Ecija); finally the vicar Apostolic; Pedra Martyr Sanz (b. in 1680, at Asco, Tortosa), Bishop of Mauricastra, and Joachim Royo (b. at Tervel in 1690) surrendered. After they had been cruelly tortured, the viceroy sentenced them to death on 1 November, 1746; Sanz was martyred on 26 May, 1747; his companions shared his fate; the five Dominican martyrs were beatified by Leo XIII, on 14 May, 1893. Shortly after, a fresh prosecution broke out in the Kiang-nan province, and the two Jesuit fathers, Antoine-Joseph Henriquez (b. 13 June, 1707), and Tristan de Attimis (b. in Friuli, 28 July, 1707), were thrown into prison with a great number of Christians, including young girls, who were ill-treated; finally the viceroy of Nan-king sentenced to death the two missionaries, who were strangled on 12 September, 1748. In 1785, the Franciscan brother, Atto Biagini (b. at Pistoia, 1752), died in prison at Peking.

Persecution was very severe during the Kia K'ing period (1796-1820); Louis-Gabriel-Taurin Dufresse (b. at Ville de Lüzoux, Bourbonnais, 1751), of the Paris Foreign Missions, Bishop of Tabraca (24 July, 1800, and Vicar Apostolic of Sze ch'wan, was beheaded in this province on 14 September, 1815. In 1819, a new prosecution took place in the Hu-pe Province; Jean-François-Regis Clet (b. at Grenoble, 19 April, 1748), and aged Lazarist, was betrayed by a renegade, arrested in Ho-nan, and thrown in prison at Wu ch'ang in Oct., 1819; he was strangled on 18 Feb., 1820, and twenty-three Christians were, at the same time, sentenced to perpetual banishment; another Lazarist, Lamiot, who had also been arrested, being the emperor's interpreter, was sent back to Peking; the Emperor Kia K'ing died shortly after; Father Clet was beatified in 1900.

Under the reign of Emperor Tas Kwang, another Lazarist was also the victim of the Mandarin of Hu-pe; also betrayed by a Chinese renegade, Jean-Gabriel Perboyre (b. at Puech, Cahors, on 6 Jan., 1802), was transferred to Wu ch'ang like Clet; during several months, he endured awful tortures, and was finally strangled on 11 September, 1870; he was beatified on 10 November, 1889. Father daddies has written in Chinese, in 1887, a life of Perboyre; full bibliographical details are given of these two martyrs in "Bibliotheca Sinica".

Just after the French treaty of 1844, stipulating free exercises of the Christian religion, the Franciscan Vicar Apostolic of Hu-pe, Giuseppe Rizzolati, was expelled, and Michel Navarro (b. at Granada, 4 June, 1809, was arrested; a Lazarist missionary, Laurent Carayon was taken back from Chi-li to Macao (June, 1846), while Huc and Gabet were compelled to leave Lhasa, the capital of Tibet, on 26 February, 1846, and forcibly conducted to Canton. The death of Father August Chapdelaine, of the Paris Foreign Missions (b. at La Rochelle, Diocese of Coutances, 6 Jan., 1814, beheaded on 29 Feb., 1856, at Si-lin-hien, in the Kwang-si province), was the pretext chosen by France, to join England in a war against China; when peace was restored by a treaty signed at Tien-tsin in June, 1858, it was stipuated by a separate article that the Si-lin mandarin guilty of the murder of the French missionary should be degraded, and disqualified for any office in the future. On 27 Feb., 1857, Jean-Victor Muller, of the Paris Foreign Missions, was arrested in Kwang-tung; an indemnity of 200 dollars was paid to him; he was finally murdered by the rebels at Hing-yi-fu, on 24 April, 1866. On 16 August, 1860, the T'ai-p'ing rebel chief, the Chung Wang, accompanied by the Kan Wang, marched upon Shanghai; on 17th, his troops entered the village of Tsa ka wei, where the orphanage of the Jesuit Luigi de Massa (b. at Naples, 3 March, 1827) was situated; the father was killed with a number of Christians; they were no less than five brothers belonging to the Napolitan family of Massa, all Jesuit missionaries in China: Augustin (b. 16 March, 1813; d. 15 August, 1856), Nicolas (b. 30 Jan., 1815; d. 3 June, 1876), Renü (b. 14 May, 1817; d. 28 April, 1853), Gaetano (b. 31 Jan., 1821; d. 28 April, 1850), and Luigi. Two years later, another Jesuit father, Victor Vuillaume (b. 26 Dec., 1818), was put to death on 4 March, 1862, at Ts'ien Kia, Kiangsu province, by order of the Shanghai authorities.

At the beginning of 1861, Jean-Joseph Fenouil (b. 18 Nov., 1821 at Rudelle, Cahors), later Bishop of Tenedos, and Vicar Apostolic of Yun-nan, was captured by the Lolo savages of Ta Leang Shan, and ill-treated being mistaken for a Chinaman. On 1 Sept., 1854, Nicolas-Michel Krick (b. 2 March, 1819, at Lixheim), of the Paris Foreign Missions, missionary to Tibet, was murdered, with Fater Bourry, in the country of the Abors. On 18 Feb., 1862, Jean-Pierre Nüel (b. at Sainte-Catherine-sur-Rivürie, Diocese of Lyons, June, 1832), Paris Foreign Missions, was beheaded at Kaichou (Kweichou). Gabriel-Marie Piere Durand (b. at Lunel, on 31 Jan., 1835), of the same order, missionary to Tibet, in trying to escape his prosecutors, fell into the Salwein river and was drowned on 28 Sept., 1865.

On 29 August, 1865, Francois Mabileau (b. 1 March, 1829, at Paimboeuf), of the Paris Foreign Missions, was murdered at Yew yang chou, in Eastern Sze Chw'an; four years later, Jean-Francois Rigaud (b. at Arc-et-Senans) was killed on 2 Jan., 1869, at the same place. Redress was obtained for these crimes by the French Legation at Peking. In Kwang-tung, Fathers Verchüre (1867), Dejean (1868), Delavay (1869), were prosecuted; Gilles and Lebrun were ill-treated (1869-1870). Things came to a climax in June, 1870: rumors had been afloat that children had been kidnaped by the missionaries and the sisters at Ts'ien-tsin; the che-fu, instead of calming the people, was exciting them by posting bills hostile to foreigners; the infuriated mob rose on 20 June, 1870: the French consul, Fontainer, and his chancellor Simon, were murdered at the Yamun of the imperial commissioner, Ch'ung Hou; the church of the Lazarists was pillaged and burnt down: Father Chevrier was killed with a Cantonese priest, Vincent Hu, the French interpreter, Thomassin and his wife, a French merchant, Challemaison and his wife; inside the native town, ten sisters of St. Vincent of Paul were put to death in the most cruel manner, while on the other side of the river, the Russian merchants, Bassof and Protopopoff with his wife, were also murdered.

Throughout China there was an outcry from all the foreign communities. It may be said that this awful crime were never punished; France was involved in her gigantic struggle with Germany, and she had to be content with the punishment of the supposed murderers, and with the apology brought to St-Germain by the special embassy of Ch'ung hou, who at one time had been looked upon as one of the instigators of the massacre. Jean Hue (b. 21 Jan., 1837), was massacred with a Chinese priest on 5 Sept., 1873, at Kien-Kiang in Sze chw'an; another priest of the Paris Foreign Missions, Jean-Joseph-Marie Baptifaud (b. 1 June, 1845), was murdered at Pienkio, in the Yun-nan province during the night of 16-17 September, 1874. The secretary of the French legation, Guilaume de Roquette, was sent to Sze ch'wan, and after some protracted negotiations, arranged that two murderers should be executed, and indemnity paid and some mandarins punished (1875).

In the article CHINA we have related the Korean massacres of 1839, and 1866; on 14 May, 1879, Victor Marie Deguette, of the Paris Foreign Missions, was arrested in the district of Kung-tjyou, and taken to Seoul; he was released at the request of the French minister at Peking; during the preceding year the Vicar Apostolic of Korea, Mgr Ridel, one of the survivors of the massacre of 1866, had been arrested and sent back to China. On Sunday, 29 July, 1894, Father Jean-Mo´se Jozeau (b. 9 Feb., 1866), was murdered in Korea. There priests of the Paris Foreign Missions were the next victims: Jean-Baptiste-Honoré Brieux was murdered near Ba-t'ang, on 8 Sept., 1881; in April, 1882, Eugphane Charles Brugnon was imprisoned; Jean-Antoine Louis Terrasse (b. at Lantriac, Haute-Loire) was murdered with seven Christians at Chang In-Yun'nan province, during the night of 27-28 March, 1883; the culprits were flogged and banished, and an indemnity of 50,000 taels was paid. Some time before, Louis-Dominique Conraux, of the same order (b. 1852) was arrested and tortured in Manchuria at Hou Lan. On 1 November, 1897, at eleven o'clock in the evening, a troop of men belonging to the Ta Tao Hwei, the great "Knife Association", an anti-foreign secret society, attacked the German mission (priest of Steyl), in the village of Chang Kia-chwang (Chao-chou prefecture), where Fathers Francis-Xavier Nies (b. 11 June, 1859, at Recklinghausen, Paderborn), Richard Henley (b. 21 July, 1863, at Stetten, near Kaigerloch,

Sigmaringen), and Stenz were asleep; the latter escaped, but the other two were killed. This double murder led to the occupation of Kiao-chou, on 14 Nov., 1897, by the German fleet: the Governor of Shan-tung, Li Peng-heng was replaced by the no less notorious Yu Hien. On 21 April, 1898, Mathieu Bertholet (b. at Charbonnier, Puy de Dome, 12 June, 1865), was murdered in the Kwang-si province at Tong-Kiang chou; he belonged to the Paris Foreign Missions.

In July, 1898, two French missionaries were arrested at Yung chang in Sza-ch'wan, by the bandit Yu Man-tze already sentenced to death in Jan., 1892, at the request of the French legation; one of the missionaries escaped wounded; but the other, Fleury (b. 1869), was set at liberty only on 7 Jan., 1899. On 14 October, 1898, Henri Chanés (b. 22 Sept., 1865, at Coubon-sur-Loire), of the Paris Foreign Missions, was murdered at Pak-tung (Kwang-tung), with several native Christians; the Chinese had to pay 80,000 dollars. In the same year, on 6 Dec., the Belgian Franciscan, Jean Delbrouck (brother Victorin, b. at Boirs, 14 May, 1870), was arrested and beheaded on 11 Dec., his body being cut to pieces; by an agreement signed on 12 Dec., 1899, by the French consul at Hankou, 10,000 taels were paid for the murder, and 44,500 tales for the destruction of churches, buildings, etc. in the prefectures of I-ch'ang and Sha-nan. The most appalling disaster befell the Christian Church in 1900 during the Boxer rebellion: at Peking, the Lazarist, Jules Garrigues (b. 23 June, 1840), was burnt with his church, the Tung-Tang; Doré (b. at Paris, 15 May, 1862) was murdered, and his church the Si Tang, destroyed; two Marist brethren were killed at Sha-la-eul; Father daddies (b. at Brescia, 19 Dec., 1835), who left the French legation to look after the foreign troops who had entered Peking, was caught by the Boxers, and put to death; another priest, Chavanne (b. at St. Chamond, 20 August, 1862), wounded by a shot during the siege, died of smallpox on 26 July.

In the Chi-li province, the following Jesuits suffered for their faith: Modeste Andlauer (b. at Rosheim, Alsace, 1847); Remis Isoré (b. 22 Jan., 1852, at Bambecque, Nord); Paul Denn (b. 1 April, 1847, at Lille); Ignace Mangin (b. 30 July, 1857, at Verny, Lorraine). In the Hu-nan province, the Franciscan: Antonio Fantosati, Vicar Apostolic and Bishop of Adra (b. 16 Oct., 1842, at Sta. Maria in Valle, Trevi); Cesada; and Joseph: in the Hu-pe province, the Franciscan Ebert; in the Shan-si province, where the notorious Yu hien, subsequently beheaded, ordered a wholesale massacre of missionaries both Catholic and Protestant, at T'ai yuan: Gregorio Grassi (b. at Castellazzo, 13 Dec., 1833, vicar apostolic; his coadjutor, Francisco Fogolla (b. at Motereggio, 4 Oct., 1839), Bishop of Bagi; Fathers Facchini, Saccani, Theodoric Balat, Egide, and Brother Andrew Bauer, all Franciscans. In Manchuria: Laurent Guillon (b. 8 Nov., 1854, at Chindrieux, burnt at Mukden, 3 July, 1900), Vicar Apostolic and Bishop of Eumenia; Marie Emonet (b. at Massingy, canton of Rumilly, burnt at Mukden, 2 July, 1900); Jean-Marie Viaud (b. 5 June, 1864; murdered 11 July, 1900); Edouard Agnius (b. at Haubourdin, Nord, 27 Sept., 1874; Murdered 11 July, 1900); Jules-Joseph Bayart (b. 31 March, 1877; murdered 11 July, 1900); Louis-Marie-Joseph Bourgeois (b. 21 Dec., 1863, at La Chapelle-des-Bois, Doubs; murdered 15 July, 1900); Louis Marie Leray (b. at Ligné, 8 Oct., 1872; murdered 16 July, 1900); Auguste Le Guevel (b. at Vannes, 21 March, 1875; murdered, 15 July, 1900); Franpois Georjon (b. at Marlhes, Loire, 3 August, 1869; murdered 20 July, 1900); Jean-Francois Régis Souvignet (b. 22 Oct., 1854, at Monistrol-sur-Loire; murdered 30 July, 1900), all priests of the Paris Foreign Missions.

The Belgian Missions (Congregation of Scheut), numbered also many martyrs: Ferdinant Hamer (b. at Nimegue, Holland, 21 August, 1840; burnt to death in Kan-su), the first Vicar Apostolic of the province; in Mongolia: Joseph Segers (b. at Saint Nicolas, Waes, 20 Oct., 1869); Herman; Mallet; Jaspers; Zylmans; Abbeloos, Dobbe. The cemeteries, at Peking especially, were desecrated, the graves opened and, the remains scattered abroad. Seven cemeteries (one British, five French, and one mission), situated in the neighborhood of Peking has been desecrated. By Article IV of the Protocol signed at Peking, 7 Sept., 1901, it was stipulated: "The Chinese government has agreed to erect an expiatory monument in each of the foreign or international cemeteries, which were desecrated, and in which the tombs were destroyed. It has been agreed with the Representatives of the Powers, that the Legations interested shall settle the details for the erection of these monuments, China bearing all the expenses thereof, estimated at ten thousand taels for the cemeteries at Peking and in its neighborhood, and at five thousand taels for the cemeteries in the provinces." The amounts have been paid. Notwithstanding these negotiations, Hippolyte Julien (b. 16 July, 1874) of the Paris Foreign Missions was murdered on 16 Jan., 1902, at Ma-tze-hao, in the Kwang Tung province.

In 1904, Mgr. Theotime Verhaegen, Franciscan Vicar Apostolic of Southern Hu-pe (b. 1867), was killed with his brother, at Li-Shwan. A new massacre of several missionaries of the Paris Foreign Missions including Father Jean-André Soulia (b. 1858), took place in 1905 in the Mission of Tibet (western part of the province of Sze-chw'an). Finally we shall record the death of the Marist Brother, Louis Maurice, murdered at Nan ch'ang on 25 Feb., 1906.

A long and sad list, to which might be added the names of many others, whose sufferings for the Faith of Christ have not been recorded.

Henri Cordier, The Catholic Encyclopedia, Volume 9

Martyrs in the eighteenth century in China

In 1732, the emperor by an edict banished all missionaries. Peter Sanz went to Macao, but returned to Fokieu, in 1738, and founded several new churches for his numerous converts. The viceroy, provoked at this, arrested him in the middle of his flock, together with four Dominican friars, who labored with him. They were beaten with clubs, buffeted on the face with gauntlets made of several pieces of leather, and at length condemned to lose their heads. The bishop was beheaded on the same day, May 26, 1747.

These four fellow-martyrs of the Order of St Dominic were, Francis Serranus, fifty-two years old, who had labored nineteen years in the Chinese mission, and became bishop of Tipasa: Joachim Roio, fifty-six years old, who had preached in that empire thirty-three years: John Alcomber, forty-two years old, who had spent eighteen years in that mission: and Francis Diaz, thirty- three years old, of which he had employed nine in the same vineyard.

The martyrs of Tonquin, 1744

In Tonquin, a kingdom south-west of China, in which the king and mandarins follow the Chinese religion, though various sects of idolatry and superstition reign among the people, a persecution was raised against the Christians in 1713. In this storm one hundred and fifty churches were demolished, many converts were beaten with a hammer on their knees, and tortured various other ways, and two Spanish missionary priests from the order of St Dominic, suffered martyrdom for the faith, Francis Gil de Federick, and Matthew Alfonso Leziniana.

F. Gil arrived there in 1735, and found more than 20,000 Christians in the west of the kingdom. This vineyard he began assiduously to cultivate; but was arrested in 1737 and condemned to die the following year. The Tonquinese usually execute condemned people only in the last moon of the year. The confessor was often pressed to save his life, by saying that he came into Tonquin as a merchant; but this would have been a lie, and he would not suffer any other to give in such an answer for him. F. Matthew had preached for ten years in Tonquin and after he was arrested and refused to trample on a crucifix, was condemned to die in 1743 and in May, 1741, was taken into the prison where F. Gil was kept.

The idolaters were so astonished to see their ardor to die, and the sorrow of the

latter upon an offer of his life, that they cried out: "Others desire to live, but these men to die." They were both beheaded together on January 22, 1744.
Alban Butler, The Lives of the Saints, Dublin, 1833, volume 1, p 204

The Boxers

It is now estimated that over 32,000 Chinese Christians, 30,000 Catholics and 2,000 Protestants, were killed by the Boxers, as they stormed through China, chanting their imperial command, "Exterminate the Christian religion! Death to the foreign devils!" Never had so many Protestant missionaries been killed in the field in one year. In 1900, 135 missionaries and 53 missionary children were killed in China, of whom 79 were linked to the China Inland Mission (CIM).

Thirteen missionaries from the American Board, which sponsored and supported Congregationalists from America to be missionaries China, were killed in the Boxer uprising of 1900 in North China. The following letter from Mrs Atwater, also published in The Times on 15 October, 1900, bears partial testimony to the thousands of Chinese Christians were massacred in 1900.

> ". . . For Boxers were sweeping through the city, massacring the native Christians and burning them alive in their homes. . . . As the patrol was passing a Taoist temple on the way, a noted Boxer meeting-place, cries were heard within. The temple was forcibly entered. Native Christians were found there, their hands tied behind their backs, awaiting execution and torture; some had already been put to death, and their bodies were still warm and bleeding. All were shockingly mutilated. Their fiendish murderers were at their incantations burning incense before their gods, offering Christians in sacrifice to their angered deities."

The following letter from Mrs Atwater which she wrote home, before she was herself martyred on her own mission station at Fenchow on 15 August, 1900 is dated 3 August, 1900:

> "I have tried to gather courage to write to you once more. How am I to write all the horrible details of these days? I would rather spare you. The dear ones at Shouyang, seven in all, including our lovely girls, were taken prisoners and brought to T'aiyuan in irons, and there by the Governor's orders beheaded, together with the T'aiyuan friends, thirty-three souls. The following day the Roman Catholic priests and nuns from T'aiyuan were also beheaded, ten souls yesterday. Three weeks after these had perished, our Mission at Taku was attacked, and our six friends there were beheaded. We are now waiting our call home. We have tried to get away to the hills, but the plans do not work. Our things are being stolen right and left, for the people know that we are condemned. Why our lives have been spared we cannot tell. The Proclamation says that whoever kills us will be doing the Governor a great service. Our Magistrate has kept peace so far, but if these men come from Taku, there is not much hope, and there seems none any way we turn. The foreign soldiers are in Pao-ting-fu, and it is said that peace is made. This would save us in any civilized land, no matter what people may say. The Governor seems to be in no haste to finish his bloody work, for which there is little doubt he was sent to Shansi.
>
> "Dear one, I long for a sight of your dear faces, but I fear we shall not meet on earth. I have loved you all so much, and I know you will not forget the one who lies in China. There never were sisters and brothers like mine. I am preparing for the end very quietly and calmly. The Lord is wonderfully near, and he will not fail me. I was very restless and excited while there seemed a chance of life, but God has taken away that feeling, and now I just pray for grace to meet the terrible end bravely. The pain will soon be over, and oh the sweetness of the welcome above.
>
> "My little baby will go with me. I think God will give it to me in Heaven, and my dear mother will be so glad to see us. I cannot imagine the Savior's welcome. Oh,

that will compensate for all these days of suspense. Dear ones, live near to God and cling less closely to earth. There is no other way by which we can receive that peace from God which passeth all understanding. I would like to send a special message to each of you, but it tries me too much. I must keep calm and still these hours. I do not regret coming to China, but I am sorry I have done so little. My married life, two precious years, has been so full of happiness. We will die together, my dear husband and I.

"I used to dread separation. If we escape now it will be a miracle. I send my love to you all, and the dear friends who remember me.
Your loving sister,
Lizzie"

Blind Chang

Chang Men was one example of the many thousands of Chinese Christians who died during the Boxer uprising of 1900. Chang became blind in his thirties and his character was then accurately summed up by his nickname "Wu so pu wei te", meaning, "one without a particle of good in him". He neighbors believed that he had been struck blind as a judgement on his evil way of life, He threw his wife and daughter out of his home, gambled, stole and became a womanizer.

When Chang learnt that blind people were being cured at a mission hospital he went there. As a result he received both physical and spiritual sight. He longed to be baptized as a Christian and was told that if he went home and told his village about Jesus Christ, that a missionary would visit him and then baptize him. When James Webster visited Chang five months later he discovered that God had been greatly blessing Chang as a faithful evangelist. Webster was inundated with over four hundred people wanting to become Christians.

Later Chang lost his eyesight again, after a Chinese doctor operated on him, trying to improve his partial sight. However, this did not deter Chang, who became well-known as the itinerant blind Christian evangelist, able to quote nearly all of the New Testament by heart, as well as many complete chapters from the Old Testament. The Boxer rebels came across blind Chang in Tsengkow, in Manchuria. The Boxers captured fifty Christians there but were told that for every one they killed a further ten would appear, and that they needed to deal with the ring leader of the Christian, blind Chang. The Boxers said that they would free their fifty Christian prisoners if one of them would tell them where blind Chang was. No one betrayed blind Chang, but one of the fifty managed to escape and went and told blind Chang what was happening.

Blind Chang went to the Boxers at once. But he refused to worship the god of war in the temple. Chang was herded into an open cart and paraded through the town to a cemetery outside the city. As he went through the crowds blind Chang sang a song he had learned in the Christian hospital:

Jesus loves me, He who died
Heaven's gate to open wide;
He will wash away my sin,
Let His little child come in.
Jesus loves me, He will stay,
Close beside me all the way;
If I love Him when I die,
He will take me home on high.

The last words blind Chang uttered, as the Boxer's sword gleamed in the sun on its way to decapitating Chang's head, were, "Heavenly Father, receive my spirit."
Editor

THE POCKET TEXT-BOOK OF A MISSIONARY MARTYR

China, 1900

A most pathetic little memento of our martyred sister, Miss Georgiana Hurn, has recently reached us from China. It is a copy of Bagster's "Daily Light" – a well-worn little volume, redolent with the odor of the loess soil and the damp, dark mountain caves of Shan-si. Many of the leaves are soiled and loose – the result of frequent handling. It is deeply interesting to turn over the pages of this little text-book and to read the notes which our sister wrote, in the margin, from day to day during their flight.

JULY 10TH
Heard that the Boxers had begun to practice. Things looked dark. See Nov. 8th eve; also July 11th.
Daily Light texts:
(Nov 8th: "The children of Israel pitched before them like two little flocks of kids; but the Syrians filled the country" (1 Kings 20:27); July 11: "I am with thee to save thee" (Jeremiah 15:20).

JULY 21ST
Left Sih-chan to escape to a village, Saturday.
[Evening] Stayed in a village

JULY 22ND
[Morning] Went on to Pao-tsi's home.
("Forasmuch . . . as Christ hath suffered for us in the flesh, arm yourselves likewise with the same mind" 1 Peter 4:1.)
[Evening] Love of God manifested in a special way. Want came in to escort us to further hiding in the hills.
Daily Light texts:
"Keep yourselves in the love of God" (Jude 21).
"As the Father hath loved me, so have I loved you" (John 15:9).

JULY 23
[Morning] Left early for a deserted place in the hills.
[Evening] Very tired after a rush over the hills. Had a trying night with mosquitoes.
Daily Light texts:
"Brethren pray for us" (1 Thessalonians 5:25).
"The effectual fervent prayer of a righteous man availeth much" (James 5:16).

JULY 24TH
[Morning] Stayed in the same [hiding place] Yao-uen-tsi, li-hai. Mosquitoes very troublesome. God's word very comforting.
Daily Light texts:
"Patient in tribulation" (Romans 12:12).
[Evening] Slept in the same place as last night.
Daily Light texts:
"He staggered not at the promise of God through unbelief" (Romans 4:20).
"Is anything too hard for the Lord?" (Genesis 18:14)

JULY 25TH
[Morning] Towards afternoon went to another place.
[Evening] Slept in the open-air by the rocks. 1900.
Daily Light texts:
"In my Father's house are many mansions: if it were not so, I would have told you. I go to prepare a place for you" (John 14:2).
"Thou wilt show me the path of life" (Psalm 16:11).

JULY 26TH
Went further into the hills to a most secluded spot.
Daily Light texts:
"We walk by faith, not by sight" (2 Corinthians 5:7).
This was the last entry.
China's Millions, China Inland Mission, 1901, p 82

A MARTYR-YEAR, 1900

The year 1900 – the last year of the century, has been a sadly memorable one in the history of our thirty-four and a half years' work in China. It has been the Martyr-year of our beloved mission. No fewer than 52 adults and 16 children have, during its latter half, laid down their lives for Christ's sake. Nor does this number – great as it is – we fear, include all who have been put to death. At the time of writing little hope is entertained of the survival of our six beloved workers with four children who were stationed at Ta-tong, Shan-si. In this province alone, of the ninety-one missionaries who were happily at work there in June last, forty-one are known to have suffered martyrdom.

Other missions have suffered in like manner, though not to the same extent.

The Baptist Missionary Society has lost thirteen Missionaries
The Sheo-yang Mission, eleven
The Society for the Propagation of the

Gospel, three
The British and Foreign Bible Society, two
Other missions, including American, forty-six

Making the total of Protestant Missionary Martyrs one hundred and thirty- three.

One of the saddest and most touching features of these sad days has been the death of so many little children, most of whom have suffered with their parents, while others have succumbed to the privations and hardships during the long and perilous journey to the coast.

The church in China, slowly built up through years of toil and struggle, has been in some districts well-nigh wiped out; hundreds of native converts have been cruelly killed, and others relentlessly persecuted because of their fidelity to Christ and his gospel.

China's Millions, China Inland Mission, 1901

A Boxer Placard

From a government Blue-book, No 3 (1900) Placard posted in West City, Peking (Translation) In a certain street in Peking some worshipers of the I-ho ch'uan (Boxers) at midnight suddenly saw a spirit descend in their midst. The spirit was silent for a long time, and all the congregation fell upon their knees and prayed. Then a terrible voice was heard saying:

"I am none other than the Great Yu Ti (God of the unseen world) come down in person. Well knowing that ye are all of devout mind, I have just now descended to make known to you that these are times of trouble in the world, and that it is impossible to set aside the decrees of fate. Disturbances are to be dreaded from the foreign devils; everywhere they are starting Missions, erecting telegraphs, and building railway. They do not believe in the sacred doctrine, and they speak evil of the gods. Their sins are numberless as the hairs of the head.

"So soon as the practice of the I-ho ch'uan has been brought to perfection then shall the devils meet their doom. The will of heaven is that the telegraph wires be first cut, then the railways torn up, and then shall the foreign devils be decapitated. In that day shall the hour of their calamities come. The time for rain to fall is yet afar off, and all on account of the devils.

"I hereby make known these commands to all your righteous folk, that ye may strive with one accord to exterminate all foreign devils, and so turn aside the wrath of heaven. This shall be accounted unto you for well doing; and on the day when it is done the wind and rain shall be according to your desire.

"Therefore I expressly command you make this known in every place."

This I saw with my own eyes, and therefore I make bold to take my pen and write what happened. They who believe it shall have merit; they who do not believe it shall have guilt. The wrath of the spirit was because of the destruction of the Temple of Yu Ti. He sees that the men of the I-ho ch'uan are devout worshipers, and pray to him.

If my tidings are false, may I be destroyed by the five thunderbolts.

4th moon, 1st day (April 29, 1900)

M. Broomhall, Martyred Missionaries of China Inland Mission, China Inland Mission, 1901, pp 304-5

Ten Swedish Holiness Union Missionaries

In Memoriam – "Martyrs of Jesus"

The blood of Christ's faithful witnesses in China "speaketh better" than anything else for the extreme need of Chian's evangelization. Among a painfully large number of martyrs, there was a group of ten who had to lay down their lives for their brethren, when they – so far as we know – were gathered together in conference in the city of Soh-p'ing Fu. They all belonged to the Swedish Holiness Union, and were associated with the China Inland Mission.

Soh-p'ing Fu tragedy

Mr Mills, at Tien-tsin, has been able to gather the following particulars of the massacre at Soh-p'ing, from a native evangelist, who has been in the employ of the Holiness Union friends for some eight years. The trouble first arose because of the excessive drought. In Hwen-yuen Chau prayers and processions for rain were unceasing. The foreigners were reported to sweep away the approaching clouds with yellow paper broom. Also it was said that the meetings held were for the purpose of praying to God that it should not rain. On June 19th there was a great annual fair at Hwen-yen Chau, and on that day the mob came battering at the doors of the Mission house. They eventually broke in, and the foreigners fled to the Ya-men, where they were effectually protected and treated with great kindness.

The Mandarin said, however, that it would be impossible to protect them if rain did not fall, and advised their going on to Ying-chau. He gave them Tls. 300, probably as compensation for loss of property, and they went under escort to Yingchau. There they found Mr G. E. Karlberg. He did not at first think it well to go on to the approaching conference at Soh-p'ing Fu, as he feared the rowdy element at Ying-chau would take the opportunity of his absence to loot and destroy the Mission House. About that time the Boxers appeared in the city, and began to post up threatening placards. Matters became worse, and the Magistrate, who was very friendly to the missionaries, advised their leaving for a time, and they went on to Soh-p'ing Fu.

Two days later the mob attacked the mission premises, but the Magistrate succeeded in preventing their doing much damage, and ordered the native evangelist who was left in charge to pack six or seven boxes, which were afterwards put in the Ya-men for security. The evangelist himself then started for Soh-p'ing Fu. He arrived at Tso-yuin in time to see the Mission House there in flames. Some church members were in the Ya-men, being protected by the Mandarin, who was supplying them with food.

On arrival at Soh-p'ing Fu he found thirteen foreigners and one child: of the Holiness Union, S.A. and Mrs Persson, O.A.L. Larsson, Miss J. Lundell, Miss J. Engvall, E. Pettersson, G. E. Karlberg, N. Carleson, Miss M. Hedlund and Miss A. Johansson; and of the Christian and Missionary Alliance – Mr and Mrs C. Blomberg and child, and a man whose name he did not know. There were also many native Christians gathered for the annual conference which is held yearly at the same time as one in the Mother Church in Sweden, namely, June 24.

Everything was still quiet but Boxer placards were being widely posted up and there was much excitement. After full discussion, the missionaries decided that as danger similar to that experienced in their other stations seemed increasingly imminent, they had better all go to Kalgan if they could get an escort from the Mandarin. This was agreed to by him, but before they could get away the mob gathered and burst into the house. The missionaries all escaped to the Hsien Ya-men by back ways. Their house was looted and burned. After the work of destruction the mob went to the Ya-men and demanded that the foreigners be given up to them that they might kill them. This the Hsien Magistrate refused to do, but to pacify the mob he declared that he had orders to send them to Peking to be killed there, and to give color to his words he had manacles made by the blacksmith and five of the men of the party were handcuffed. The mob seemed happy and dispersed. About 10 pm that same evening the evangelist was taken out of the Ya-men by Manchu soldiers and Boxers and beaten and left for dead.

Before daylight, however, he recovered, and two men finding him helped him to escape from the city. When he was about forty li from the city he was told that on the same night all the foreigners had been killed by Manchu soldiers and Boxers, and that their heads had been put up on the city wall. The church members and servants suffered in like manner at the hands of these same ruffians. This was on the 3rd day of the 6th moon, i.e. June 29.

On the previous day at Ying-chau, the Mandarin had tried to save the Christians, and had given them carts to take them to Soh-p'ing Fu. The Boxers, however, turned them back into the mission premises with the carts and carters, and they were all burned together. Among those who suffered at Ying-chau were the evangelist's mother and little daughter.

At Hwen-yuen Chau he heard that none of the native Christians had suffered martyrdom, but that they had lost everything they had. At Tsoyuin it was reported that all the Christians had been taken to Ta-t'ung Fu, and there, with one hundred others, natives and foreigners, Protestants and Catholics, had been put to death. While he was being detained at Fu-ping, it was commonly reported that all the foreigners at Kwei-hua-ch'eng had been killed, and so fierce were the Boxers against everything foreign, that even vendors of matches were said to have been killed, and no one was allowed to wear anything of foreign made material.

China's Millions, China Inland Mission, 1901, pp 4-6

Canadian martyrs: Miss Hattie Jane Rice and Miss Mary Elizabeth Huston

Hattie Rice and Mary Huston were two of six Canadian workers killed in China in 1900. Miss Huston was directed to proceed to the station of Lu-Ch'eng where she became associated with Miss H. J. Rice. This arrangement proved to be a most suitable and happy one, and a friendship was formed between Miss Huston and Miss Rice which ripened more and more, and became ever increasingly helpful to each. Through varying changes of station life, these two sisters went on in their service, but always in the joy of the Lord. The work at Lu-ch'eng was strengthened in 1898, by the location there of Mr and Mrs E. Cooper, two devoted servants of God.

Then there fell suddenly upon them the heavy stroke of persecution, and in the terrible heat of summer, when the workers would vain have sought something of quiet and rest, Miss Huston and her companions were forced to flee southward, with the hope of escaping into Ho-nan and Hu-peh, and thus into the treaty port of Han-kow. However, a Boxer band was met before they escaped out of Shan-si, between the cities of Kao-p'ing Hsien and Tseh-chau Fu, and the sudden and unexpected attack of these poor, misguided men, resulted in the separation of Miss Huston and Miss Rice from the rest of the party.

Miss Rice, previous to this, had become so exhausted by the sufferings which she had passed through, that she declared to her missionary companions that she could go no further; and now both she and Miss Huston told their persecutors that they were quite prepared to die, but that they could not proceed. At this their enemies became so enraged that they fell upon the two missionaries, striking them down in the public highway, and beating them with the intention of killing them on the spot. Happily, Miss Rice did not suffer long, for as her heart was weak she soon succumbed to the treatment which she was receiving. Thus, the spirit which had longed for so many years to be wholly surrendered to Christ and to obtain God's best, was granted its highest desire in being made a member of that glorious martyr-band which serves above. With her it was "very far better"; but poor China in that hour lost a friend whose prayers and service had meant for its salvation not less than infinite good.

Miss Huston was beaten at the roadside until almost no life was left in her body. The members of the party who had been driven on, and who thus had not been able to do anything for the two young ladies left behind, finally reached the city of Tseh-Chow Fu, where they begged the official to send a cart back for the two missionaries, and to bring them on their way, so that they all might be united once more and thus proceed on their journey to Han- kow. The official promised to fulfil this request, and kept his word as far as he was able to. Ten days after this his bearers arrived, bringing Miss Huston in a litter, who then reported that Miss Rice was dead. Miss Huston herself was in a terrible physical condition. She informed her friends that she had not lost consciousness while being beaten; that she had known when Miss Rice passed away, and that after her tormentors left her, she had lain all night alongside the body of her friend, not leaving her until the morning had come, when she crept away to a place of shelter to die; she had been found there by the official, and had thus been brought on to join her companions in travel. Miss Huston, in spite of her serious and pitiable condition, lived on for nearly a month, often in great pain, but still managed to testify to the peace which guarded her heart. The body, however, had been too severely strained, and just two days before reaching Han-kow, the gentle spirit took its flight heavenwards and homeward.

China's Millions, China Inland Mission, 1901, pp 15-16

South Central Shan-si

The report of this district unhappily is awful. Of the missionaries of the China Inland Mission laboring here thirty-one have been called upon to suffer the loss of their lives, while nineteen have escaped to Han-kow.

Concerning the Ho-tsin friends, there follows information received from Miss Olliff regarding Mr and Mrs McConnell and child, Mr and Mrs J. Young, with Misses Burton and King, and a native servant.

During the 5th Chinese moon (May 28-June 26) Mr and Mrs McConnell, accompanied by Misses Burton and King, left Ho-tsin to spend the summer among the hills, at a place called San-heo, about 20 li from Ki-chan. About the 16th of the 7th moon (July 12), Mr McConnell and family decided they had better leave the hills, and so they prepared to return to Ho-tsin, and cross over into the Shen-si border. It is presumed that they were joined by Mr and Mrs John Young.

Anticipating trouble they did not enter Ho-tsin, but passed on their way toward the Yellow River. They had only gone a short distance when a band of mounted soldiers overtook them, and led Mr McConnell to understand that they had been sent as escort from the Yamen. They advised that instead of taking the main road to Yu-men-k'eo, a quieter road, and a nearer, should be taken to a place called Ts'ing-kia-uan, where a ferry-boat would be provided. Mr McConnell, knowing that the Yu-men-k'eo people occasionally were turbulent, acceded to the suggestion. Arriving at Ts'ing-kia-uan, the soldiers said they had not come to protect them, but to murder them, except they desisted from worshiping God and preaching against idolatry.

Mr McConnell was then dragged from his mule and dispatched with a sword, his wife and child, it is said, meeting with a similar fate. Mr McConnell's little boy Kenneth was heard to say, "Papa puh chuen shah siao Kennie" (Papa does not allow you to kill little Kennie). Miss King besought the murderers, Boxers hired by three military graduates, to desist, saying, "We have come to do you good"; and seeing that the men were relentless, she embraced Miss Burton, and, clasped in one another's arms, they were put to death. At the same time a man and his wife (believed to be Mr and Mrs Young) were seen to clasp one another, as they were put to death in a similar way. The native servant, K'eh-Ts'ien-hsuen, declining to recant, also met with a violent death. Thus perished in all eight people, seven foreigners and one native.

M. Broomhall, Martyred Missionaries of China Inland Mission, China Inland Mission, 1901, pp 30-31

Extracts from Martyrs' Last Letters

Miss Edith Searell (Martyred June 30, 1900)

"You speak in your letter of the possibility of one place being safer than another; I think, dear Eva, from the human standpoint all are equally unsafe, from the point of view of those whose lives are hid with Christ in God all are equally safe! His children shall have a place of refuge, and that place is the secret place of the Most High.

"A mighty fortress is our God", and in him we are safe for time and for eternity. Shall we murmur if we have less of time than we expected?

"The less of time, the more of heaven."

"The briefer life, earlier immortality."

Mr George McConnel (Martyred July 16, 1900)

This text was mentioned in his last letter: "I

trusted in thee, O Lord: I said, Thou art my God. My times are in thy hand: deliver me from the hand of mine enemies, and from them that persecute me" (Psalm 31:14-15).

Mrs Young, letter dated July 5 (Martyred July 16, 1900)

"I feel I must write you a few words at this time. We are so quiet here that we can scarcely realize the trouble you are having down on the plain. But I know that the God of Peace will keep your hearts and minds. The winds may blow, and the waves may roll high; if we keep our eyes off them to the Lord we shall be all right. May God bless and keep you all."

Mrs Kay (Martyred August 30, 1900)

"Mr Kay will not leave here till he is driven out. The natives are so good and have declared that they will stand by us till death, if needs be. We have had many friends from the street to comfort us and to tell us not to be afraid. It is from outsiders we fear. Our trust is in God. I want to give you my home address in case we should be taken home to glory. If anything should happen to us, God will make a way for our children at Chefoo. I have a desire in my heart towards them – that is to be spared for their sake – but His will be done."

Miss Francis Edith Nathan (Martyred August or September, 1900)

"If 'the very hairs of our head are all numbered,' then no man can touch us unless our Father willeth. From earthly powers we shall get very little help, if the Empress Dowager is secretly using these men to rid China of the foreigners. Yet we know the Lord removeth kings. May He indeed keep our hearts in peace, His own perfect peace."

Mr W. G. Peat (Martyred August or September, 1900)

"The 15th of the Chinese month is mentioned here as the date of our destruction. But we are in God's hands, and can say, "I will fear no evil, for thou art with me."

Mr David Barratt (Martyred summer 1900)

"Our blood may be as a true cement (for the foundation), and God's kingdom will increase over this land. Extermination is but exaltation. God guide and bless us! 'Fear not them which kill,' He says, 'are ye not of much more value than many sparrows.' 'Peace, perfect peace,' to you, brother, and all at Lu- ch'eng. 'We may meet in the glory in a few hours or days.' Let us be true till death. 'Be thou faithful unto death, and I will give thee a crown of life.'"

M. Broomhall, Martyred Missionaries of China Inland Mission, China Inland Mission, 1901, pp 29, 33, 35, 41, 43, 53, 57

CIM's Diary of Events, 1900

1899

Dec 31
Murder of Rev S. P. Books of the SPG (Society for the Propagation of the Gospel).

1900

Jan 17
Sir Claude Macdonald sends a protest to the Tsung-li-yamen saying, "The whole of the present difficulty can be traced to the late Governor of Shan-tong, Yh-hsien, who secretly encouraged the seditious society known as 'The Boxers.'"

May 14
Elder Si of Hung-tung, Shan-si, stabbed by Boxers.

May 17
Sir Claude Macdonald reports Boxers destroyed three villages and killed sixty-one Roman Catholic converts near Pao-ting-fu.

May 18
Sir Claude reports Boxers destroyed LMS (London Missionary Society) chapel at King-ts'un, and killed preacher forty miles S.W. of Peking.

MAY 23
Boxers plunder Pastor Hsi's home (Shan-si)

MAY 29
Railway between Peking and Ts'ien-tsin torn up.

JUNE 1
Mr Robinson murdered and Mr Norman carried off.

JUNE 2
Mr Norman murdered.

JUNE 7
Imperial decree issued justifying action of the Boxers.

JUNE 8
Massacre of native Christians at Tung-chau.

JUNE 13
Boxers enter Peking. Hundreds of converts killed.

JUNE 27
Mrs Coombs killed.

JUNE 29
Massacre of thirteen Swedish missionaries at Soh-p'ing, Shan-si.

JUNE 30
Miss Whitchurch and Miss Searell murdered at Hiao-i.

JULY 1
Massacre at south side of Pao-ting-fu, including Mr and Mrs Bagnall and child, and Mr William Cooper.

JULY 2
Imperial edict ordering expulsion of all foreigners and persecution of Christians.

JULY 9
Massacre at T'ai-yuan-fu, including Mrs W. Millar Wilson, Miss Stevens, and Miss Clarke.

JULY 13
Miss Rice murdered.

JULY 16
Murder of the Ho-tsin party, including Mr and Mrs Young, Miss King, and Miss Burton.

JULY 21
Murder of Mr and Mrs Thompson and Miss Desmond, inside K'u-chau city, Cheh- kiang.

JULY 22
Murder of Mr and Mrs Ward and Miss Thirgood, outside K-u-chau.

JULY 24
Murder of Miss Sherwood and Miss Manchester in K'u-chau city.

AUGUST 15
Murder of Fen-chau party, including Mr and Mrs Lundgren and Miss Eldred.

AUGUST 30
Mr and Mrs Kay and child put to death, and Mr and Mrs Peat and party put to death.

M. Broomhall, Martyred Missionaries of China Inland Mission, China Inland Mission, 1901, pp 299-301

THE PROVINCE OF CHEH-KIANG

Prior to the foundation of the CIM in 1866, Mr Hudson Taylor had in 1857 commenced work in this province. The work then started has been greatly blessed by God. According to the last statistics the China Inland Mission had as many as 3,710 communicants in Cheh-kiang alone.

Recently there has been a time of severe persecution in many of the stations, and not a few native Christians have suffered the loss of all things, and others sealed their testimony by death. The sad outbreak which has occasioned the death of eight members of the Mission and three children, had nothing, as far as we can see, to do with the Boxer movement. It was a local rebellion.

The following are the names of those martyred: stationed at K'u-chau- fu, Mr and Mrs D. B. Thompson, and their two boys, Edwin and Sidney, Miss J. Desmond, Miss Edith Sherwood, and Miss Etta Manchester; stationed at Ch'ang-shan, Mr and Mrs G. F.

Ward and infant, Herbert, and Miss E.A. Thirgood.

On July 21, the day after Mr Thompson wrote, "God, our Father, take care of us, or take us," God took them to himself for ever.

A large and unmanageable crowd gathered at the Mission premises, and commenced to loot and destroy everything, and Mr Thompson was badly bruised on the head. The evangelist Ch'en-Ts'ien-fu escaped through the back door, and sought aid from the Tao-t'ai (intendant of circuit), who practically refused to interfere.

When the evangelist returned to the Mission-house the ladies were sent to the Tao-t'ai's Yamen, but only to find the district (Hsien) magistrate being beheaded in the court of Yamen itself. They at once returned to the already destroyed Mission premises. About noon they again went to the Tao- t'ai's Yamen, and as a report had gained currency that the rebels were attacking the city, all the crowd had gone to the city wall, so they found the Yamen quiet.

In the afternoon the people returned. When they found the foreigners there, they first seized Mr Thompson, took him outside the front door, and put him to death. They then returned and murdered Mrs Thompson, her two children, and Miss Desmond. The native evangelist says they were killed at once and had no prolonged suffering.

The ladies' house where Miss Sherwood and Miss Manchester resided had been rioted at the same time as the Thompsons', but the ladies were hidden by neighbors until the 24th. The natives then refused to afford them any further shelter. Being discovered they were taken to the city temple, where they were speedily put to death.

Mr Thompson had been expecting Mr and Mrs Ward and Miss Thirgood to arrive from Ch'ang-shan, where the danger was greater. The ladies started to travel by boat, and reached the jetty at K'u-chau. Here they were killed on the afternoon of 22nd July. Mr Ward, with his servant Li-yuen, traveled overland, and were also killed on the morning of the same day about five miles from K'u-chau.

M. Broomhall, Martyred Missionaries of China Inland Mission, China Inland Mission, 1901, pp 182-85

Papers of Sarah Alice (Troyer) Young; 1894-1900

Billy Graham Center: Archives
Brief description

Letters, diary and articles about the work in China of Sarah Alice, a worker with China Inland Mission. The materials in the collection document her preparation and her evangelism activities in Shanxi Province, China, where she worked from 1896 until 1900, when she and her husband John were killed during the Boxer Rebellion. Her papers contain many descriptions of missionary work, the lives and testimonies of individual Christians and Chinese society and culture.

Young, Sarah Alice (Troyer); 1871-1900

Papers; 1894-1900
Birth date April 3, 1871 in Clinton Township, Elkhart County, Indiana, United States (Family moved to Milford, Nebraska when Sarah was in her teens.)

Family

Parents: John D. and Cathrine (Egli) Troyer
Siblings: Daniel, Marietta, Anna, Lydia, Joseph, Emanline, David, Ellen, Martha, John
Marital Status: Married Scottish CIM missionary John Young in China April 1, 1899
Children: none

Education

1894?-1895 Gospel Union Bible Institute, Abilene, Kansas
1895 China Inland Mission Training Home in Toronto, Canada

Career

1896-1900 Missionary involved in evangelism and Bible teaching in Lugan Fu and Kih Cheo, Shanxi Province, China (spelled in the documents in the collection "Shansi")

Other significant information

Sarah Alice was raised in the Amish Mennonite Church, although she also attended the Methodist church in her home town of Milford. Young and her husband John were killed by Chinese militants during the Boxer uprising on July 16, 1900, in Shanxi Province

Letters

In writing to her family, she usually signed herself as "Alice" or "Sade." Sarah wrote most of the letters in the collection and usually signed them Alice or Sade. Almost all are to one or more of her sisters, or in some cases to nieces and nephews. There are no letters to Sarah Alice. There is a letter by her husband John (April 19, 1900) to their nieces and nephews, one by sister Marietta or Ett (labeled by the archivist as "probably 1895") to sister Anna, and a fund raising letter by a John C. Beach apparently sent to Sarah Alice's sister Anna (July 22, 1896).

Subjects

Missionary work in China, the China Inland Mission, Chinese life and culture at the turn of the century.

Notes

The bulk of this collection consists of letters written by Sarah to her sisters during her preparations for missionary service and her four years in Shanxi Province with China Inland Mission. She would often write one letter home which was circulated among her many sisters and family members. This collection does not contain all of her letters but only those kept by her sister Anna. Consequently, there are gaps of information. One considerable gap concerns her future husband, John Young, and their courtship. Several letters describe in detail photographs which were apparently enclosed with the letters, but were not with them when the letters were given to the Archives and therefore are not available in this collection.

Along with the letters and diary, the Archives received a full-text transcript, prepared by Sarah Alice's grandniece, Carol Whiting.

Preface

By Carol (Mizer) Whiting, a relative of Sarah Alice Troyer Young and the transcriber of the letters and diary:

Sarah Alice Troyer was born in 1871, one of 11 children of John D. and Catharine (Egly) Troyer. She was my Grandmother's sister. These are letters she wrote to her sisters and brothers before she became a Missionary and while in training and when she was in China as a Missionary. Her siblings were Daniel, Marietta, Anna (my grandmother), Lydia, Joseph, Emanline, David, Ellen, Martha, and John.

1896
September

Praise the Lord for full salvation provided for the Chinese as well as the Americans! In my July diary I spoke of Mrs Chang's unbinding her feet one Sunday morning after Service. Today she has gone to her home to rid it of it's false Gods and all things dishonoring to the God she now serves. She is a widow and her only child is in Mr. Smith's "Boy's School". There is no one in her home but she is not satisfied to leave it occupied by these false gods. Mrs Gates and Mrs. Smith have gone with her to witness the burning. I began to read with my new teacher this morning. His pronunciation is different from that of Mr. Han and it will doubtedly hinder me for a time. Mr Han was numbered among the enquirers for a time and seemed to be coming out bright but for some time past we have seen falseness in him and last week had to dismiss him. He seemed really to know something of the Savior and we hoped for full conversion but

Satan and the wickedness of the human heart have the victory so far as we can tell. The Lord is able to save him still if we only believe.

September 10

Dear Mrs Chang is suffering severe persecution. An angry Brother-in-law prevented the idols being burned yesterday and she remained until this morning hoping for an opportunity to burn them. Mrs Smith and Miss Gates returned with her son. This morning she came back with the most dreadful story. She had been beaten by brother-in-law and nephew (I find I am wrong about the brother-in-law beating her) and the whole village had come out to mock at her unbound feet. They have threatened to sell her for a wife and will not allow her to stay with Mrs Smith (whom she has been serving) any longer. She has stood bravely and alone in all her village. Mrs Smith returned with her to her home. Later,- Mrs Chang has succeeded in burning her idols but as a result was cast off by all her people. She is again with Mrs Smith. When Mr Smith went to her village to try to make peace one old man, at the head of the house, said,"If you take a big knife and cut my throat for it I will not live at peace with that woman while her feet are unbound". However the Lord will not allow His little ones to suffer more than necessary-A written agreement of peace has been signed by the people of the village.

October 4

The women are not coming in to us much now because so busy in their harvest field, but we go to them. Miss Gates with her woman goes out in the morning and in the afternoon for two hours I go out with her (Miss Gates). The people in the street not visited much still seem afraid of us. It is very sad to see how little they care for the Gospel. Now and again the Lord gives encouragement by giving an interested listener. Yesterday for the morning services we had a number of women in who listened well to Elder Liu as he gave them very faithfully the Gospel. Our woman who has been with us only about six weeks is very much interested and seems really to have a great deal of joy in what little she has learned. Yesterday she said as Miss Gates was talking with her "If my Mother had only known this. She was a good woman and tried all her life to find the right way. She knew there is only one God and prayed to Him but she didn't know Jesus – she didn't know that He is the Savior." I take her for half hour or an hour a day in reading and find her very quick indeed. May the Lord do this own work in her heart. The man who heard the Gospel on the street at the time of the great fair and returned the following Sunday to hear more seems to be coming out clear and bright. He has been in several times and I believe stays all at Mrs. Smiths to hear, even sometimes doing with out his food. After having several talks with him Elder Lui spoke to him about his idols, "O said the man, I tore them down the following day after hearing the true doctrine on the street". He says his wife to is becoming interested. There is a little encouragement in the children's work, too. The Mother of some little ones who live just opposite says every night before they go to bed they pray the little prayer they learned here "Kiu chu kiu o" and I notice some of them trying to sing "Jesus Loves Me " the chorus of which they have learned. In many homes we find the children able to repeat the few words of Gospel which are written on the back of the cards I give them on Sunday afternoon. Sometime, there are so many in that I find it difficult to manage them all. Recently I have not been troubled this way but the poor little ones must care for their baby brothers and sisters and as they are to young to put down they are hindered a great deal by the babes.

Oct 7

Today we went to one of our neighbors who has been a good listener ever since we came. She is from Pekin and has big feet. Dear woman she seemed to drink in the message so different from most of these women, but Satan hinders. She does not come in as at first to hear the Gospel every day but perhaps it is because she is so busy. Then we went to our Land Lady's house and found her ready as always to hear. Oh that these people who see the truth might take a stand for it. My teacher gave me a little encouragement this morning. We were reading the crucifixion and resurrection of Jesus. We had a few words of conversation about it and he said his heart is enlightened and he understands it all and it is good. He said sometime ago to our boy that one word of our Bible is worth more than all the books of Confucius. He also brought some paper idols here to burn and tried to do it privately too. Won't you pray with us for his soul?

Oct. 13

I enjoyed Sunday morning in trying to do a little by bringing in the women from the street. I succeeded in bringing in a few in. In the afternoon I had a number of little ones in spite of the rain. I try to teach them a short text with the character. But it is difficult to do much because they do not come regularly. Today we got into a home in a new neighborhood and are invited to stop when ever we go that way and the three women said they would come and sit in our home, and follow us. It seems very much from the conversation that they expect to get money from our God just as we do. We are constantly asked where we get our money and sometime we are told if we will have our God give them money as He does us they will follow this doctrine. Money seems the root of evil in China as much as at home. We also passed through a Mohammedan street. The people are a much better class, apparently, than those we meet as a rule in other streets, and are particularly clean and neat. It seems very sad to leave them without the Gospel though they are few compared with the other class of Chinese. The Mandarins seem very friendly to us. Last week there was some trouble at the R. Catholic premises created by the scholars who were at the examinations, where upon there came a proclamation from the Mandarin to be put up in the Chapel at the North St. saying that the foreigners must be protected and warning any who might wish to harm. Mr and Mrs Smith have gained access to nearly all or all the Yamens in the city and some of the Lsiens. Many shall yet come from the land of Sinim. Praise God! He is "able to do exceeding abundantly above all that ask or think".

Oct 20

Miss Gates visited a Mohammedan Home today. She was invited into the house and had a little company of men and women who listened well. This is a beginning of answer to prayer."He is not willing that any should perish" and it does seem that these people are so left alone, yet what can we do? We cannot enforce them to listen and they care so little to hear. Occasionally we also find a Roman Catholic family. They as a rule listen well thinking we are the same in faith. The women are coming in more again but many are still in their harvest fields or busy on the thrashing floor. Mrs Chang who has suffered so much persecution in unbinding her feet and destroying her Gods is growing very much. The Lord has to punish His children sometimes. It is so good to remember that He lets nothing come to His little ones but what is for their good. His children were even sent into the land of the Chaldeans for their good. Sent into captivity for their own good. (Jer. 24:5) God glorified Jesus through His crucifixion by those who sought to destroy Him (Acts 3:13-15)

Oct. 26

Yesterday three of the Mohammedan women from the house we visited last week came in and listened a long time. One of them was really wanting to hear more and said she came to hear and when there was a pause in the preaching she would say "go on, go on, I like to hear". She said,"I would like to follow this doctrine but I can't come here to live". Of course she was told that isn't necessary. Oh, these people do so misunderstand! There are at present many evil stories rife about us. The Devil seems stirred up very much. But we are to be thankful in all things, and must remember that our God is an Almighty God I went to see a little sick girl yesterday who a month ago was quite a well looking child, but now poor little one! she is so poor and miserable. We found her on a pile of straw in the corner of a dirty, untidy room, a straw mat under her, a brick for a pillow and a few rags over her poor swollen little limbs.— Oh! such a picture of misery I have never before seen.

Oct. 28

Miss Gates and I take turns in going out now she in the morning and I in the afternoon. Yesterday afternoon I had such a good time several little companies of women listened so attentively and some of them asked many questions which showed their interest. What I did not understand or they not understand the woman with me made clear to us and I though I was really beginning work in earnest. But, O, when shall I be able to give them the Gospel fully and freely. The earnest listeners make me long to be able to give fully and freely the Glorious Gospel of the Crucified Lord. But the best of all is that He can make the bread sufficient for the multitude even though it is so little.

Oct 31

The lord is having prayer for these Mohammedans we entered another home and had a crowd of women and children with a few men in the background. One white haired old man replied when told that Jesus is the Savior "you are very much mistaken". Oh, how sad to see men and women tottering on the edge of the grave still rejecting the only name given under Heaven where by we must be saved. Yesterday morning we went to Mrs Li's village.(our women) Many came in and a few listened well to the Gospel. We were glad to find that Mrs. Li herself has not been forgetting what she learned here but has learned to repeat a number of hymns in the week she has been at home. She went home to prepare her husband's clothing that he might go to the North Street to break off opium, and almost the first thing she told us was that he had gone the night before. Her face just beamed with joy as she spoke.

Nov 1

Mr. Smith left today for the coast to take Algie to school at Chefoo. We took dinner there and saw them off afterward.

Nov 2

We had a good time at our teachers home today. The brother's wife who before cared nothing about the Gospel today listened with much interest and the old father came in and Miss gates, I am sure, had a specially good time in giving him the true way, for her voice and words were very earnest and powerful. One of the women has asked to be taught. We do pray that this "house may be saved".

Nov 4

Today there was a fair in the city and we had many women in, some listened well others cared nothing about the Gospel. When shall this people wake? Not until the tribulation comes upon them? So many, many pass away into eternity without a ray of light. That we who are here in this dark land may be kept in a position before Him that He may use us as He would that He may make us rivers in the desert!

Nov 14

Just returned from a visit to In-ching and Wang-fang, the former a mining town up in the hills. The later place we visited the wife of one of the native workers who has for some time shown a desire to come out for the Lord. We found her hesitating because of fear of her relatives. We believe the visit has not been in vain. This morning we left her very sad. At prayers she prayed earnestly that the Lord forgive her for the past and give her strength for the future. Yesterday she took us to a relatives home in In-ching where we had crowds all day. It was such a joy to be able to give the Gospel to these dear people who had, many of them, never heard it before. Though my vocabulary is very limited it is good to think that He is able to "make the bread sufficient" for the multitude though it is so little.

Nov 18

Went out with Miss. Gates this afternoon

instead of going with the woman as usual. We had such a good time at our teachers house. The Lord surely is working here. Won"t you join us in prayer for this house, two brothers with their families and the old father and mother, also a widow woman who lives in the same "uesutsi" is deeply interested and has asked to be taught more.

Nov 19

Today we went to a village twenty li out where there is a little company of Christians. We had real fellowship with the dear women, had a meeting in the school room which was well attended by the women, Christians and those who are interested, then took our dinner with one of the Christians and returned home. It is so good to go out among the people and to live as they live just for a time and to get near them.

Nov 24

Yesterday morning we went to a village about thirty Li away to see Mrs Li, the eldest member of the church. She is a widow living with her daughter-in-law. We found her much in want of Spiritual food as she has no one to teach her and to our joy she consented to come back with us today. Though she is sixty four years of age she apparently stood the cart ride over the rocky, hilly road as well as either of us. We do pray that she may be helped on in the heavenly way. Her daughter-in-law is holding out against unbinding her feet. She told us this morning that is what is keeping her back. Pray that the Lord Himself may work with Li-ta-soo that she may fear no one but Him. The people of this village are particularly hardened against us and the Gospel, so we had very few people in, compared with other places we have visited.

Nov 27

Went to a village a few miles out this afternoon. Had not many people but those to whom we went were very friendly. They live in the courtyard where our woman, Mrs Li has her rooms. She went with us.

S. Alice Troyer
Lugan Tu Shansi Prov.

December 28

Dear Mr Bagnall:
The Lord is working among us these days. Praise His name! we have been crying to Him for His mighty working among His own children in the station and He has begun, only begun to work- only "begun to show His servants His greatness and His mighty hand". We have felt that some of these dear people settle down in a satisfied state short of the "life more abundant" for which Christ came that we might have. He is graciously arousing many of them now and making them long for that higher life through preaching of Ps l1 by Mr. Smith. Some of them are dying hardly but we trust soon the "God of hope will fill them with all joy and peace in believing" in his power who is "alive forevermore" for us and is able to save us to the uttermost.

Dec 9

I took my first Bible class among outsiders. Miss. Gates not being well I went to the village where we have a company of Christians in her stead. The Lord gave me some liberty in speaking on "Sin in the believer". There was only time for one meeting with the women before we had to return.

Dec 11

Went with the school mistress to Mrs king's village. You will remember Mrs King is the woman Miss. Gates and I went to see some time ago and found her very fearful of her relatives and also found the ancestral tablet still in the house. Praise God it has since been destroyed by the husband who was taught by the word that it was wrong to keep it in his home. This time we found her very bold ready to take her place before any one as a disciple of Jesus. Mr King asked us to pray for his daughter who would soon be married to a heathen husband. The engagement was made before he, Mr King, became a Christian and his only hope now is that they both become converted. They, the husband's people, promised not to have burning of incense at the wedding and for this purpose we went up, to see that none of the idol worship should come into the ceremony of the formal engagement which took place

Dec 14

We prayed much that the Lord should undertake for us, and He did. There was none whatever of the idol worship, and even the red cloth in which the bride is always wrapped was not used. Instead of the heathen book which is always presented to the Husband's people Mrs. King chose the new Testament to present to them. It has however since been returned to Mrs King and the wedding which was not to take place until next year took place a day or two ago because the Husband's people were afraid the bride's feet would next be unbound if they do not make haste to get her into their own power. We trust the Lord will yet work in spite of the people. On Saturday Dec 12 we went to visit the school mistress' aunt in a village a few miles away and found her fearful of her friends. Oh, these dear people! If they could only see the danger they are in. On Sunday we had a few women in to our little morning meeting and afterward went to the street where we had a great crowd to whom we preached. The men soon became loud and said things not good to hear, as the Chinese put it but one dear woman clung to my hands bravely defending what I said and asking to hear more. Indeed the women were all attentive and kind. Tuesday Dec 15 we hired a cart and returned home

Dec 17

Miss Gates went away leaving me for a few days to make use of my words. Prayers with the servants twice a day and giving them the necessary orders gave me opportunity enough to use what I had acquired of the language. It was a great help. Not many women and children come in now. It has been so cold that they seem not to leave their homes. However one woman, a near neighbor, spends a greater part of her time sitting by our fire. We have had no reason to hope for a change in her life very soon, however, she seems more interested than at first and last Sunday for the first time she came without her work to the afternoon meeting. Her name is Chang and we call her the hat-woman because she always works on hats. Won't you pray for her? I was away when last post went out so did not write with my examination papers. Miss Gates kindly sent them for me. Yours Faithfully
S. Alice Troyer
Lugan Tu, Shansi Prov.

1897
Jan 23

The past month has been spent by us all rather in sitting at Jesus feet and hearing what He has to say to us than in work among the people. Tho' there has been some encouraging work done and certainly the Lord is working among His own people as ever before. He is purging out the old leaven that He may purify the lump. Though it is done in a way which we would not have thought, Elder Liu has recently been excommunicated for wife beating. One of the women has been found living in sin- and so the Lord brings out the sin which is in the heart, that it may be put away. Though it is very hard for us that these things should be seen among us it is better that the sin should be brought out that it may be put away from us. The man Liu was converted eight years ago and for a year or more was much persecuted, often beaten by his relatives and finally deserted by all. He has been Mr. Smith's stand by in the work and it is very, very hard for him. The Lord is letting us have some encouragement amid the trial. Two of the young men employed by Mr. Smith have recently asked to go to their own homes that they may preach the Gospel to their own people for "The coming of the Lord draw the nigh". One of these is a young fellow of simple faith in the Lord. He has cast out devils in the name of the Lord. When asked how he did it he said. We alternately read the Lord and pray until the person possessed by the evil spirit is better. The other one is also one of the brightest Christians in the church. May the Lord bless their testimony to the conversion of many souls in their own villages. We hope others will soon go to their own homes.

Saturday Jan 16

Two families destroyed their idols in the presence of Mr. Smith. The hat Woman or Mrs Chang of whom I spoke in the last letter has changed some and says now that she believes, when I asked her what she believes she replied "That Jesus is the true Spirit" but she knows she isn't ready to meet the Lord when he comes. Once she said she will repent after New Year. Our woman Mrs Li says she believes for salvation from sin and she does seem to be earnest, often preaching to the women who come in as much as she knows, and especially does she like to tell the women that worshiping their idols is very wrong and that they cannot help or hurt.
Yours Faithfully
S. Alice Troyer
Lugan Tu, Shansi

Jan 27

Today we visited two homes, one that of an opium smoker who once "broke off" her opium at the "North Street" but once again took to it. She is also a witch but in many ways a very dear woman. The other a nice old lady who often asks us in as we go by. She and her daughter who is a very intelligent woman both listened well and asked intelligent questions.

Jan 29

Liu sien sing confessed in the testimony meeting on Saturday evening but judging from his conduct since it was not real confession. On Tuesday Mr. Smith had a talk with him which, after an hour and a half of venting his anger on Mr. Smith, in the end proved satisfactory. The man finally broke down and cried to the Lord for deliverance from his sin which has hindered more than one, doubtless, from being blessed. His temper has led him to sin grievously many times. While waiting upon our God for a few days was working and in just the way in which we were led to pray that this man would of his own accord go away and so the matter is finally concluded. Please pray for Liu sien sing who has been elder in the church and has thus grievously fallen.

Jan 30

A year ago today I for the first time set foot upon the shores of dark China. The most blessed year of my life has been the year in China. He that hath promised is faithful indeed. The message He gave me just before landing was "He will not fail thee nor forsake thee until thou hast finished all the work of the service of the house of the Lord", and as I thought, but this isn't for me it was spoken to Solomon He turned my eyes to Mal 3:6 "I am the Lord, I change not" so the promise was for me too. We were at a dinner today given in honor of a month old baby. There was not much chance of giving the Gospel to any who had not heard it over and over again so we didn't remain long. The mother and J'o Ju have both been employed by the missionaries in the station and know the Gospel well but do not come out for the Lord though they have gone as far as to put away all their idols. It will be harder for these people in the day of judgement than most of the unsaved Chinese for their light is so much greater. Our little testimony meeting of Saturday evening are sometimes very helpful. Tonight our cook , a young Christian, spoke of how the Lord had been speaking to him of his not showing by his face that he is rejoicing in the Lord, that he should be thankful in all things and alway rejoicing.

Feb 9

This P.M. we went to a village about five Li out to the home of our woman, Mrs Li. Had a good many people in her home and afterward were invited to another home. Our man, in the mean time was selling calendars outside.

Feb 10

Spent the day at Chang lu tsuen with the Christians. Also had a very sad affair to see to-that of telling Mrs Li, one who has been very bright for the Lord, that her name no longer stands among the names of God's people in this church. She denied her sin but calling up witnesses we soon proved it beyond doubt though she continued to deny and at last burst out into a raging fit of anger. Poor people!

Feb 13

This P.M. we went to the home of an enquirer eight Li out of the city to see his wife. She has been possessed with the devil but is better now and seems very anxious to learn. She is a very dear woman. May the Lord show forth His own almighty power in bringing her to the light. We hope to go often to the village trusting that the Lord of the Harvest will open many doors for us. Our teachers wife had been very ill. He came one morning looking so frightened and said he had prayed with her three times and each time she was better but is worse again. We sent him home and in the afternoon of the same day he went to ask Mr Smith and Mr. Glover to go to pray with her for she says nothing but prayer does her any good. So many of these dear people know perfectly that our God is the only true God but they fear to come out from their people. May the Lord soon show forth His power in bringing some of them out!

Feb 15

Spent the day in a village eight or ten Li out in the home of the cook at the North Street. His wife has spent sometime there learning the "doctrine" and seemed much interested but today she seemed very indifferent but invited us to come again. Had many people in all day but few who really wanted to hear the Gospel.

Feb 23

Our teacher is burying his wife today she died last week. He said he would have no heathen rites whatever at the burial. He believes his wife was really saved, "for", he said, "she always asked me to pray when she was conscious and she did believe in Jesus". We had noticed that she was very attentive to the Gospel when she was well. We are praying that this may be the means of bringing him out. Won't you pray too?

In His Service

Alice Troyer

Feb 27

We had a very interesting women in today. She is ill and otherwise a sufferer. Her tears flowed freely as she told something of her story and asked if she might send her cart and remain until evening. She seemed very ready to receive the story of the cross and said she would come again, also invited us to her home. We were much interested to see how our woman, Mrs Li, earnestly preached to her. She especially interests herself in telling all whom she has an opportunity of speaking to how worthless their idols are and how wrong it is to worship them. She has herself been an earnest worshiper of them and says they would be wealthy now if they had not spent as much on their idols. You will remember I told you of her when she first came to us.

March 5

Just now we are interested in a photographer who came to the city last autumn and has been hearing much of the Gospel at the street Chapel, and now asks for baptism. His testimony is that, on the twenty first of last month while reading his Bible he was lead to read some of the miracles of Jesus and he said to himself, "If Jesus could raise the dead He can surely save me from my sins." Then he asked the Lord to save him and he would trust Him henceforth and break the opium which he had twice done before with medicine but could not stand. It is now some days since he took this step and he says he has no desire for it. The Hat woman, Mrs Chang, we believe is coming on slowly. She now keeps the Lords day and when she can walk so far goes with the women to the services at the "North Street". She says the people laugh at her and call her "iang Kui tsi" then she just tells them what she thinks of them. "But", said Miss Gates, "Jesus' disciples should be willing to be laughed at and to be persecuted for His sake" and she answered next time they laugh she would only smile at them. Our women, Mrs Li, is very bright and seems to be really acquainted with Jesus from the testimony given by her to those who come in, but she is not ready yet to go all the way. Yesterday we heard her say to some women who were enquiring of her about unbinding feet that she hasn't unbound hers nor is she going to do so. Won't you pray for these mentioned above, that they may come out fully for the Lord.

March 10

Yesterday "the hat woman" opened her heart to us and we saw that there is more of a change than we had hoped for. She wept bitterly as she told of her evil life and of her present trouble she has had two husbands. The first one sold her only son and she, in her rage, told him for this he should die a public death, and so he did, and she said she was the cause because of these words. She said she had not worshiped her idols or ancestral tablet since last year soon after we came here. This was indeed news to us; but today our hearts are still more rejoiced because of her. She has indeed "repented", as she says, but she hasn't Jesus yet- her heart is not at peace. I was surprised to find such a change in the woman as she told me tonight that use to gamble though she has not done so this year. She says in her home she is constantly talking to Jesus asking Him to save her, though the people who live with her "Ma" (curse) her and say all sorts of things to her because she is "following the foreigners". We are very glad that she is not a woman to do such a thing, follow us. We are perfectly satisfied that the Lord is doing the perfect work in her heart which will cause her to follow Him, not us.

March 23

Mrs Chang "the hat woman" Came in yesterday telling us that her neighbors are persecuting her, because she comes her so much. One man was about to strike her but was hindered by the by standing women. But what hurt her most was their words which truly were "puh hao ting" (not good to listen to) especially what they said about us. They threatened to come at us with sharpened knives and spears but she said no matter how many came she will stand up for us, and our God is stronger than fifty men and would protect us. Two of the Christians at Chang lu tsiun who are farmers have sent another of their brethren out on a preaching tour. He has no land and not being busy they thus shared in the Lord's work. There was a misunderstanding about the photographer's breaking off opium suddenly.- He is doing it gradually but the rest of the story seems true. He shows many signs of a new life and his face is quite changed. His boy who at first laughed at his master now comes regularly to the meetings and says he is a disciple of Jesus. They both seem very real. May the Lord do His work. Pray for us.

S. Alice Troyer
Lugan Tu

March 26 '97

Yesterday Mrs Li the member of whom I wrote last month who had her name taken off the Book came and we are rejoiced to see that she still knows the Lord though her name is not in our Book here. She told us how Romans 5 had been blessed to her especially the phrase "rejoicing in hope". We trust she will soon restore to full fellowship in the Lord. Her husband who a year or two ago stole Mr. Smith's horse and had to leave the country came home some time ago and will be a great hindrance to her. He too was once numbered with the Lord's people. Will you not pray for these two?

March 27

Ex-Elder Liu's wife who has for months been most miserable because holding out against God today opened out her feet—at last taken the step at which alone she has hesitated. She looked much more happy and we trust she will be lead on now. Mr. Liu too is praising the Lord with a loud voice. This is the man who some weeks ago struck his wife because she did not repent. His life for sometime has been changed. That outbreak of sin seems to have shown him what he really is. He seems now to know the Lord better than ever before and certainly is more humble. He often prays that his life before his wife may no longer be a hindrance but a help. Three weeks ago after a time of prayer for his wife he told Mr. Smith he has the assurance that his wife will be saved and so we believed our prayers for her salvation had reached the heart of God and was even then, answered. So much prayer has been made for her by both natives and us. We rejoice too that Mrs King has opened her feet, and is willing to stand alone in her village and testify for her Lord. You will remember her as the one of whom I wrote in my Dec. letter to whose house I went with the school mistress at the time of the engagement of her daughter. We have had our first wedding in the chapel the school mistress and Dong sien seng who is teacher of the boy's school in Tuen liu. It was a happy time -not much like the heathen marriages. The wedding was at ten o'clock, the feast at eleven and at twelve the happy bridegroom started with his young wife to their new home forty or fifty li away. We are soon to have the second wedding. This time the parties are Mrs. Smith's nurse and one of the young men servants. Mrs Chang,"the hat woman," seems to have been drawn back into Satan's Power again. Yesterday in her anger against her persecutors she said "Jesus is afraid of men, he counts for nothing or he would avenge her of this wrong." She says it is now that the Lord should show Himself strong in her behalf and punish her persecutors.

March 29

Mrs Chang is more quite today and says she wants the peace which the Lord promises to him who will come to Him. She made a long prayer but was sobbing so that she could not be understood. More good news today, Mrs Liu's mother is making her shoes to unbind her feet. She has been with her daughter the past few days and we were very much surprised that she didn't try to hinder Mrs. Liu in unbinding her feet now we see the Lord has been working with her too. Last night she could not sleep. The Lord was speaking to her. At last when everybody else was asleep she, alone with the Lord, promised Him to follow Him and this is the first outward step. These two women have heard the Gospel for eight or nine years and are now the first women inside the walls of this city to come out for the Lord. The Lord is able to give much more than this. He has been giving us some very precious promises and sometimes the same text to different members of our little company— such as, "Thou hast began to show thy servant thy greatness and thy mighty hand— The breaker has gone up before them- I will do a new thing, behold now it shall spring forth— The Glory of this latter house shall be greater than of the first."

March 30

More good news today. The mother of one of the young men employed by Mr. Smith has today decided for the Lord and says she will open her feet. Her shoes are being made now. When we asked Mrs. Liu's old mother why she unbound her feet she replied without the slightest hesitancy "Because I have believed in the Lord". She seems very bright indeed and understands so well too. May the Lord do His own work in her life that the few remaining days of her life may be spent in real service for the Lord.

April 3

Spent the greater part of the day in a village some ten li out where there is a three or four day's fair being held. I stayed at the home of the woman who is making her shoes so that she may unbind her feet. She seems to want to know and follow the Lord and laments that her "heart is so stupid" that she cannot remember the things her son tells her. There were a number of the Christians there to tell the Gospel and the crowds of people who came to sell and to buy. Yesterday a number of the women went to this village. Among them were Mrs. Liu and her mother Mrs. Liu at first said she would not go because she was ashamed of her big feet but the Lord got the victory and she seemed very happy in going.

April 5

Yesterday Mrs. Chang spent the day at the "North Street" again. Last Lord's day she didn't go because her persecutors threatened to break her leg if she went once more and she feared them but Miss Gates told her how our God is and that He would not let them hurt those who trust in Him and evidently she believed for yesterday she seemed most bright in going. On Saturday night she having done some work for us, was to take her food here when she refused to eat the food which our people had because it was the first of their month- she would eat nothing. Knowing it to be because of some superstitious idea the boy who is a Christian talked to her about it asking her if she didn't believe in Jesus. She replied, yes ,so he told her that nothing would hurt her if she trusted Him. Miss Gates spoke a few words to her as we were passing thro' the courtyard and when we next looked out she was eating her food with the rest. She seems much more peaceful and happy now and never mentions her persecutors. Pray for her please.

April 8th, and 10th

We had a series of meetings at which nearly all the Christians of the district were present. The subject were "Holiness","Unity", and "Tilling of the Spirit". Mr Smith planned to have a subject each day but when the third day was ended the last subject was still not completed so all were asked to remain over the Lord's Day. It was a time of blessing to all. Four of the natives helpers assisted Mr. Smith in the speaking and two of them spoke with much power on all three subjects. One of these is the young man of whom I wrote Jan 23rd who asked to go to his own home to preach and live the Gospel there and the other one is a very earnest little man upon whom the truth that the Bible is God's word has taken a deep hold. Both of these men are very quiet in manner and plain and simple in words but there is a secret power which draws the attention of all. I understood nearly all of the young mans address and felt the power-it was so refreshing and helpful. Mrs Chang, the hat woman, came in yesterday, the first time after a few day's illness and seemed to be under the impression that the illness had been a punishment from the Lord. I said it may have been punishment because you wouldn't listen to His words or it may have (paper torn at the corner) —teach you more about Himself. She added (corner off) I didn't obey, what I heard at the meeting Unity, and Spirits Power, The Lord evident (corner off)

April 22

Had a great many women in today. There was a fair in the city and many of the women from the villages were in and stopped to see the foreigners. Only three or four of them cared to listen to the Word of Life. Oh, that some of these dear people may soon arise from the dead.

April 23

Went with Miss. Gates to the South Huan (South suburb) this afternoon where we had a company to speak to in the street. Miss. Gates gave the Gospel to them and I also talked with a few women who sat off by themselves.

April 26

Spent Sunday in Chang lu tsuen. Arriving at about six o'clock Saturday evening we all had our suppers and then gathered in the little schoolroom for the weekly testimony meeting. There was a goodly company of men, Christians, and others, assembled the women on, one side of the room and the men, on the other. Sunday morning we had, as is their custom, two meetings lead by two of the Christians and in the afternoon I sent the men out to preach and took the women for a long meeting, in the evening again we all assembled and three of the men spoke, all on the line of holy living a part of which was very helpful. This morning I started home early arriving at about nine o'clock. Our boy, whose home is there was with me. I have planned (D.V.) to spend every second Sunday there with the Christians. There are also a number of women who regularly come to the meetings and say they believe.

May 4

Walked to Uang ki fah's home ten li out this afternoon. After a talk of an hour with the mother who decided some time ago to follow the Lord two women who are interested came in and after a short talk with them I had to come away. The work in this village is opening nicely thro' the efforts of Uang ki fa who spends every Lord's day in his home, with some of the other Christians holding a meeting at his own home in the morning and in the evening at the home of another interested family. Mrs. Uang told me today with a bright face that they now have four families, one in each side of the town who believe in Jesus. May the Lord do His own work in their hearts!

May 6

Spent the day with the Christians in Chang lu tsuen. Had a class with the women and a few men who asked if they might come all are Christians and enquirers.

May 11

Our dear Mrs Chang "the hat woman" has suddenly passed away, we believe, to be with the Lord. Sunday, May 9th, she went to both services at "The North Street" which is not a little distance, took dinner there but when time for afternoon meeting came she had gone home because she felt unwell. We saw no more of her that day and Tuesday she did not come in so we thought she must be ill and Miss. Gates went in to see and found her unconscious. They said she had not spoken that day. Just after dinner one of the women in her garden came to ask us to pray with her. We could not ask for her recovery of the Lord but asked that the Lord would let her speak again. It made the people quite indignant that we did not ask our God to raise her up. Tuesday morning our boy went over early to see how she was and he found that no one had been near her all night tho' she had called to them. When she heard our boy's voice she asked what he had come for and when told it was to see her she said "hao" (good) Miss Gates went soon and found her able to converse a little. She repeated some scripture verses which she had learned and repeated every word Miss. Gates prayed then began to pray but Miss. Gates told her to pray in her heart because she was to weak to pray much. At ten o'clock we went over hoping to arrange her bed a little better for the women (there are only women in this garden) were so afraid that they wouldn't even go into the room except when we went. But when we spoke to her she did not move and we saw that her face had changed and her hands were cold though her body was still very warm. We waited to see whether there would be a change, and – yes. There was a change which left no room for doubt, she was soon cold and with sad hearts we went out to talk a few words to the women who had come about the door but feared to touch the body. We longed to see this woman whom we had learned to love so much again and do something for her but remembering what these people say of us foreigners – that we take the heart and eyes of the dead for medicines – we refrained. We miss her very, very much. It seems that one belonging to us has gone. The place by the window in the women's room where she always sat when here is vacant, the stone at her door where she so often sat when we passed is vacant and no one greets us now as we pass. We are very much comforted by the words of the women in her garden. They told us she use to have a very, very bad temper but for a month past she had not"Cursed" anyone until Friday evening our woman's husband who had a room there provoked her very much and she lost her temper. On Sunday as she was relating it she said "I sinned about it " and the tears came freely, tho' she did not tell us what her sin was she repeatedly said she had sinned. We believe it was this and that the Lord washed it all away. It seems the Lord answered her own prayer in taking her so suddenly. About a month ago she remained for the evening prayers and the first time in our presence asked the Lord to wash away her sins and at the end of her prayer asked the Lord when He wants her soul to take it quickly and not let her lie long on the "K'ang". She was then quite well and we thought it strange that she should pray thus. Our Lord doeth all things well and we know this is done well tho' we cannot understand why He did not leave her for a witness in this South Street. But several times the text "He is able to give the much more than this" has been given us and we believe.

May 17

Spent the afternoon in the home of one of the new converts in Kuan ts'uen, ten li out. They seem hungry for more knowledge of the truth both father and son sitting in the room listening attentively while I taught the dear little woman who now and then exclaimed, "O, it is precious" and her face showed that she had experienced it in her heart. They are very poor now tho' they have seen better days. Mrs. Shao said "I used to be so sad from morning to night but now I am happy all the time whether we have anything to eat or not." We are again having some trial in the church. The parents of our cook who is an earnest Christian, have been trying to force him to marry a heathen girl which he refused to do and finally came to us about it Mr. Smith went yesterday to see the parents and it is not to be so— they have promised Mr. Smith. Mrs Wang, Liu sien seng's mother in law rebound her feet. She could not stand the persecution from her own family. Mrs. Liu seems very bright for her.

May 20

Spent the afternoon in Kuant ts'uin at the home of two enquires. The one is a blind woman. At her home we had a good opportunity to give the Gospel. A number of women came in and listened most attentively to the Gospel. The poor blind woman is very bright, at the other home I found Mother and Daughter ready to listen and the mother is ready to unbind her feet. The daughter is engaged to a man who is not a Christian and they are trying to free her from him and marry her to a Christian. Please pray for these dear people that they may go on and not lack in any particular.

Your in the Master's service

S. Alice Troyer

Lugan Tu Shansi Prov. China

Postal address Tientsin, China C/O C.I.M.

Archives of the Billy Graham Center

John and Betty Stam

The martyrdom of John and Betty Stam took place in China while they were missionaries with the China Inland Mission, CIM (now the Overseas Missionary Fellowship, OMF), in 1934.

An army of two thousand Communists, soon increased to six thousand, was now in possession of the district, and the people, already suffering from semi-famine conditions, had to see their meager supplies disappear as before hungry locusts. But that was a minor misery. For when The Reds abandoned Tsingteh the next morning, they left many dead behind them and carried away many captives. Their next destination was Miaosheo, the little town twelve miles across the mountains; and how John and Betty must have dreaded what that would mean for their dear friends there.

Over the familiar road John walked, a prisoner, carrying his precious little one, not yet three months old. Betty was on horseback part of the way, and they both smiled at the few people who saw them as they passed. That little Helen was there at all seems to have been the first miracle in her deliverance, for her life was to have been taken even before they left Tsingteh. Part of the torture of her parents, it is stated, was that their captors discussed before them whether or not they should kill the infant out of hand, to save trouble. But someone said, "Why kill her? She'll die anyway."

So the captors left the child; that remark had saved her life and John and Betty had their treasure with them as they traveled wearily over the mountains to Miaosheo.

Arrived in the town, how they must have longed to go to the home of their friends the Wangs! But, of course, terror reigned supreme. All who could had fled, before the looting of the place began. Betty and John were hurried into the postmaster's shop and left there under guard, thankful to be out of sight of all that was taking place.

"Where are you going?" asked the postmaster, when he recognized the prisoners.

"We do not know where they are going," John answered simply, "but we are going to heaven."

The postmaster offered them fruit to eat. Betty took some – she had the baby to nurse – but John made the most of the opportunity for writing again to Shanghai. This note he entrusted to the postmaster to forward.

> Miaosheo, An.
> December 7, 1934
> China Inland Mission.
> Dear Brethren,
>
> We are in the hands of the Communists here, being taken from Tsingteh when they passed through yesterday. I tried to persuade them to let my wife and baby go back from Tsingteh with a letter to you, but they wouldn't let her, and so we both made the trip to Miaosheo today, my wife traveling part of the way on a horse.
>
> They want $20,000 before they will free us, which we have told them we are sure will not be paid. Famine relief money and our personal money and effects are all in their hands.
>
> God give you wisdom in what you do and give us grace and fortitude. He is able.
>
> Yours in Him,
> John C. Stam.

Not a word of self-pity or of fear. Not a sign of faltering. He who had sent them was with them. They were strong in the quiet strength of Him who said: "For this cause came I unto this hour. Father, glorify thy name."

Afraid? Of What?
To feel the spirit's glad release?
To pass from pain to perfect peace,
The strife and strain of life to cease?
Afraid? Of What?

Afraid? Of What?
Afraid to see the Savior's face,
To hear His welcome, and to trace
The glory gleam from wounds of grace?
Afraid? Of What?

Afraid? Of What?
A flash, a crash, a pierced heart;
Darkness, light, O heaven's art!
Afraid? Of What?

Afraid? Of What?
To do by death what life could not -
Baptize with blood a stony plot,
Till souls shall blossom from the spot?
Afraid? Of What?

"Baptize with blood a stony plot, till souls shall blossom from the spot" – oh, how John and Betty longed, whether by life or by death, to win precious souls to Christ for South Anhwei!

Little remains to be told, for, thank God, their sufferings were not prolonged. When the Communists again turned their attention to them, they were taken to a house belonging to some wealthy man who had fled. There they were put in a room in an inner courtyard, closely guarded by soldiers, and though Betty seems to have been left free to care for the baby, John was tightly bound with ropes to a post of the heavy bed. How long must have seemed the hours of that cold, winter night, when he was not able to move or even change his position!

I'm standing, Lord:
There is a mist that blinds my sight.
Steep jagged rocks, front, left and right,
Lower, dim, gigantic, in the night.
Where is the way?

I'm standing, Lord: -
Since thou hast spoken, Lord, I see
Thou hast beset – these rocks are Thee!
And since thy love encloses me,
I stand and sing.

No one knows what passed between John and Betty, or what fears assailed those young hearts [they were still only 27 and 28 years of age]. Silence veils the hours sacred to him alone who, for love of us, hung long hours in darkness upon a cross. Certain it is that he who is never nearer than when we need him most sustained his children in that hour of trial. Betty was not overwhelmed, but was enabled to plan with all a mother's tenderness for the infant they might have to leave behind, alone and orphaned, amid such perils. Could that little life survive? And if it did, what then? But had they not given her to God in that so recent dedication service? Would not he care for his own?

Never was that little one more precious than when they looked their last on her baby sweetness, as they were roughly summoned the next morning and led out to die. Yet there was no weakening. Those who witnessed the tragedy marveled, as they testify, at the calmness with which John and Betty faced the worst their misguided enemies could do. Theirs was the moral, spiritual triumph, in that hour when the very forces of hell seemed to be let loose. Painfully bound with ropes, their hands behind them, they passed down the street where he was known to many, while the Reds shouted their ridicule and called the people to come and see the execution.

Like their Master, they were led up a little hill outside the town. There, in the clump of pine trees, the Communists harangued the unwilling onlookers, too terror-stricken to utter protest – But no, one man broke the ranks! The doctor of the place and a Christian, he expressed the feelings of many when he fell on his knees and pleaded for the life of his friends. Angrily repulsed by the Reds, he still persisted, until he was dragged away as a prisoner, to suffer death when it appeared that he too was a follower of Christ.

John had turned to the leader of the band, asking mercy for this man, when he was sharply ordered to kneel – and the look of joy on his face, afterwards, told of the unseen Presence with them as his spirit was released. Betty was seen to quiver, but only for a moment. Bound as she was, she fell on her knees beside him. A quick command, the flash of a sword which mercifully she did not see – and they were reunited.

"Absent from the body . . . present with the Lord."

"Thanks be to God, which giveth us the victory through our Lord Jesus Christ."

"They shall walk with me in white; for they are worthy."

[The baby Helen was miraculously rescued by Evangelist Lo, and became known as the "miracle baby".]

Mrs Howard Taylor, The Triumph of John and Betty Stam, China Inland Mission, 1925, pp 103-8

TWENTIETH CENTURY MARTYRS *1994*

In 1994, Lai Man Peng was a 22 year old Chinese Christian evangelist, was taken from a house church meeting by agents of the Public Security Bureau. Later, in front of his own congregation, he was beaten with truncheons and so badly injured that after he was released he collapsed and died on his way home.

Based on a report written by Mona Charen, a former speech writer in the Reagan White House

On 13 May, Fr. Yan Weiping, an administrator of the Diocese of Yixian, Hebei, was arrested on 13 May by China's security while he was conducting a service in church. That same evening, he was found dead in a street in Beijing. Local Christians believe that Yan had been pushed out of a window after he was killed.

Editor

CENTRAL AMERICA
GUATEMALA
ALFONZO LIMA, A CONTEMPORARY ANABAPTIST MARTYR, MURDERED DECEMBER 29, 1996

[This account was first published in the March-April 1997 newsletter of the sponsoring mission, Mennonite Air Missions, which works in Guatemala.]

Martyred For Faith

He was a Brother beloved. Perhaps not the very best friend to any of the other ministers, being so quiet, reserved, and unassuming. But he was highly appreciated for his firm faith in face of threats to his life and adverse circumstances that seemed to assail his entire walk as a Christian.

When Alfonzo Lima first sought to walk with the Lord it required much literal walking. It took him three hours one way to walk to La Sorpresa either in the warm subtropical sunshine or through the rain during the rainy season.

Rafael Segura, the minister in La Sorpresa at that time, walked the same paths to Pital every two weeks to hold services. During that time Brother Rafael's life was threatened. Thus there was opposition to the gospel in Pital from the very beginning.

At first the services were held under a make-shift arbor of crude stakes, holding up split bamboo sticks, covered with banana leaves; a kind of lean-to against Alfonzo's rustic house. The benches were of split bamboo on stakes planted into the ground, or the large stones around the edges of the construction. It was a simple, temporary, but adequate chapel.

It was to this setting that Harold and Darlene Kauffman, and Urie Sharp came for the first baptismal service, when Alfonzo and Auralia were baptized.

Soon others responded, were saved and baptized; and the church began to grow.

Services were moved to an old dilapidated one-room mud house on the adjoining lot, next to Alfonzo's place. In the meantime plans were being made to build a new chapel. Most of the work on the new chapel was done by local workmen.

During this time the opposition intensified. A group of about 15 men drew up accusations against Alfonzo and presented them to the local township, hoping to get Alfonzo put in jail. The township threw it out of court, however, because they knew that the accusations were not true. The accusers did not give up. There were times when they came to Alfonzo's house, shooting threateningly into the air to intimidate and frighten the family. There were numerous times when Alfonzo sensed that men were lying in wait for him as he walked in and out of the area to go to the City or elsewhere. Sometimes others gave him warning. Alfonzo was always delivered out of the hands of those who were against him.

In spite of adverse circumstances, opposition to the witness, death and sickness in Alfonzo's immediate family, unfaithful brethren, and other trials, Alfonzo remained steadfast. On May 25, 1992 Alfonzo was ordained to the ministry, with Brother Harold Kauffman officiating.

The first baptismal class in the new chapel was made up of nine souls. It seemed like the gospel was taking root in this notoriously wicked and lawless part of Guatemala, that was renowned for it killings and acts of vengeance.

On December of 1996, however, those who opposed the work stepped up their efforts. One night 11 men showed up shortly after nightfall. They demanded that Alfonzo come outside. When he didn't, they broke the light bulb, shot through the roof, and tried to break down the door. The neighbors were alerted, due to all the racket, and before they could get their goal accomplished, the 11 men had to flee.

A few days later, in a regional ministers' meeting, Alfonzo poured out his story. He was concerned that these lawless men might be lying in wait for him on his return. Native pastor, IsaYas Muaeoz offered to take him home on his motorcycle. The rest of us held a prayer meeting in our vehicle as we returned to the City.

All of us were relieved to hear that all went well on Alfonzo's return trip, and even more so when we heard that at least eight of the men who had showed up that night, came back to Alfonzo to apologize to him.

A week later when I went with Amilcar Lopez to a midweek prayer meeting, things looked much more hopeful. Alfonzo wanted to know what he should do. If he left, who was going to look after the work that had begun in his home community. Where would he go to earn a living for his growing family? Also, in Alfonzo's mind was the question: Would his adversaries let him alone even if he left the area? I told him that if he felt that he should stay, then he should do what he felt was right.

Sadly, another change was in store. Just how Alfonzo knew that the men were still planning to kill him, we don't know for sure. About two years and nine months earlier, he had told Wesley King that the Lord showed him that he was going to live for three years yet. Then, too, not long before his death, he gathered his family around him and informed them that the Lord had showed him that he was going to be shot in the stomach and the bullet was going to come out of his back (just the way it happened). He also described the beautiful mansion that he was to move into.

Alfonzo sensed that his life was in imminent danger, and made plans to get out on Thursday, the day after New Year's day. It wasn't to be. Seven men showed up on the evening of December 29th. With one shot, his life was taken. It happened more or less on this wise:

Alfonzo was already in bed with his family when the murderers showed up, cursing, swearing, and demanding that he come out. This time they took a knife and worked the screws loose on the hinges of the door and forced themselves into the cooking area. They shot through the door into the bedroom area where Alfonzo and Auralia were together with six of their children. What horror for the children!

Alfonzo had time to get his trousers on, and then the murderers were in the room. They grabbed him by the belt and jerked him around severely, demanding that he give them the 400 quetzales that he had received for selling a pig, not too many days before. Alfonzo told them that he had already used some, but what was left, they could have. He told them they could take the church offering, the communications radio, or anything they wanted. But robbery did not seem to be their main motive.

Auralia was trying to stand by her husband in a desperate attempt to offer some protection, but she was getting shoved roughly back and forth between the men.

Meanwhile, the terrified children were jumping up and down and screaming. The men fired shots at their feet to try to get them to be quiet. The oldest child present suffered one burn on her leg where a bullet grazed the surface. Thankfully, none of the children and Auralia were seriously hurt, physically.

During this time Alfonzo tried to speak to them about their souls' need. He picked up his Bible, but they ripped it out of his hands and threw it to the ground. Nonetheless, Alfonzo never resisted, nor reviled them.

Finally, Auralia broke free and ran with the children to her parents' place nearby. When Alfonzo was left go, he headed toward his parents' home. A short distance from his house, as he came to the barbed wire fence, he turned and with the reality of the situation, he said to the young man who followed him, "You're going to kill me aren't you!" The youth fired one shot into his stomach. As he fell, the accomplices left. Behind them lay a Christian, dying because he loved the Good Shepherd and His sheep more than his own life. He was identifying with the Lord Who laid down His life for the sheep.

Immediately a vehicle was sent for to take Alfonzo out for medical care. In the meantime, Alfonzo's family gathered around him. They heard him pray for his family, and the little flock. They heard him ask God to forgive his murderers. Near the end, he said they could stop praying for him, for he was now in a better place. When the pickup arrived, Alfonzo was dead, or should we say, he was in heaven?

The pickup took Auralia to Oratorio to inform IsaYas Mu±oz of the murder. IsaYas informed the Mission as early as he could the next morning. Immediately, Harold Kauffman and Amilcar Lopez left with materials to make a vault. Leighton Zook and IsaYas went, also. In the meantime, the other MAM personnel were informed.

Later in the day, when Levi Martins came into the City, they, too, left for Pital.

That night in the Pital chapel, Levi preached to a large crowd, including those of the murder gang. He preached about the need of repenting from their evil deeds.

Some of us didn't hear about it in time to be at that first service, or were too far away. Two vehicle loads of mission folks left early the next day in time for the procession to the grave. On the one-kilometer walk, many of Alfonzo's fellow brethren helped bear the casket. But so did at least one who assisted in the murder. He, the murderer, and other participants of the crime, were present once again at the grave side service.

Brother Harold Kauffman and I had brief meditations. Then the grave was closed.

To me, the words of Jesus are the most fitting epithet: "Greater love hath no man than this, that a man lay down his life for his friends" (John 15:13).

We don't know where the work in Pital will go from here. Alfonzo's parents left the area soon after his death. Because of more threats against Auralia, we've moved her out as well. Most of those who were considered faithful have moved out or are going to do so. Right now tensions are high because there are threats of vengeance from non-Christians who sympathized with Alfonzo as well as counter vengeance from the murderous gang.

We ask for your prayers for those who are lost in this downward spiral of violence. What a cold, empty, condemned life for these Christless people.

Pray for Auralia. Pray especially for the children that they will be able to forgive the murderers, and follow in the godly footsteps of their father. Pray for the church leaders who remain, who must make decisions, carry on, and decide how to move ahead from this point.

May the same God who saved Alfonzo Lima from eternal death be glorified for having called him home.

Duane Eby, by kind permission

North America
Canada
Jesuit martyrs

In the 1600's, Jesuits of French origin did considerable missionary work among the Indians of North America, chiefly in what is now Quebec and in upper New York State. Some of them were killed. They are remembered collectively on 19 October.

Antony Daniel was born at Dieppe, France, in 1601. He joined the Jesuits, and was sent to Canada. From 1637 to 1648 he taught in the Georgian Bay area. He was stationed in the Huron village of Teanaustaye, near Hillsdale, Ontario, when it was attacked by the Iroquois, and he chose to stay with his flock. He was shot, and his body burned with his church. He died 4 July 1648.

Charles Garnier was born in Paris in 1606. He joined the Jesuits and was sent to Canada in 1636. In 1649 the Huron village of Saint Jean, Quebec, where he was stationed, was attacked by the Iroquois. He was shot down while assisting his flock to escape. He struggled to his feet and attempted to reach a dying Huron to give him absolution, but an Iroquois struck him dead with a tomahawk. He died 7 December 1649.

Noel Chabanel was born in France in 1613. He joined the Jesuits and was sent to Quebec in 1643 to work with Charles Garnier. He found the Huron language difficult to learn, and the Huron way of life distasteful, and he suffered from depression. As a precaution against temptation, he took a vow not to leave his post. At the time when Garnier was killed, he had just gone to another village to preach, and was never seen again. Later, a Huron who had been baptized but returned to paganism revealed that he had ambushed Chabanel and killed him out of hostility for the Christian religion. He died somewhere around 7 December 1649.

Isaac Jogues was born in Orleans in 1607, became a Jesuit in 1624 and was sent to Canada in 1636, where he worked among the Mowhawks, traveling as far inland as Lake Superior. Assisting him were two laymen, Rene Goupil and John Lalande (the latter like Daniel a native of Dieppe). Goupil, who had studied surgery, had been unable to enrol as a Jesuit because of bad health, so he came to Canada at his own expense and there volunteered to help with the Indian mission. In 1642 Jogues and Goupil were captured by the Iroquois and kept prisoners at Ossernenon, now Auriesville, New York, during which time they were tortured and Jogues lost the use of his hands. On 29 September 1642 Goupil was tomahawked for making the sign of the cross over the head of an Indian child. After a year of captivity, Jogues escaped, with the help of some Dutchmen from Fort Orange, but three years later returned to Ossernenon as a missionary. When there was an outbreak of sickness, and a failure of the crops, Jogues was accused of witchcraft. He and Lalande were seized, beaten and slashed with knives. That evening (18 October 1646), Jogues was tomahawked, and Lalande was tomahawked the next day.

John de Brebeuf was born in Normandy in 1593. He was one of the first three Jesuits assigned to the Canadian mission. He preached among the Hurons, beginning in 1625, at first with no success. In 1633, he made another attempt, which lasted for nearly sixteen years, and was slightly more successful. In 1648 he was joined by Gabriel Lalemant. Lalemant had been born in Paris in 1610, and joined the Jesuits in 1630, but because of bad health was not sent to Canada until 1646. After two years in Quebec, he joined de Brebeuf on the Huron Mission in 1648, the following spring, the two priests were captured in an Iroquois raid and taken to what is now the village of Saint-Ignace in Ontario, where they were horribly tortured. De Brebeuf survived only a few hours, and died 16 March 1649. His frailer companion, Lalemont, lived through the night and died the following day. A contemporary wrote, "There was no part of his body that was not burnt, even his eyes, for the villains had forced burning embers into the sockets."

Two remarks by way of historical background. Many of the Indian tribes were hereditary enemies of one another. An early French expedition, headed by Samuel de Champlain, founder of Quebec City, "Father of New France," was with a group of Huron Indians when they were attacked by an Iroquois war party. Champlain and his men, using their muskets, drove off the Iroquois, killing many, and from that time on the Iroquois were anti-French (and therefore, when the occasion arose, pro-British), while most other tribes of the area became pro-French and anti-British. This was relevant in subsequent struggles between the British and the French, and later between the British crown and the American colonists.

Many of the Indian tribes placed extreme value on courage and hardihood, as demonstrated by the ability to endure pain without flinching; and so the practice of torturing prisoners taken from other tribes was a kind of competition, in which a prisoner upheld his tribal honor by showing no sign of pain, deriding the tortures that he was undergoing, scorning his captors for a lack of imagination, and assuring them that his discomforts were mere fleabites compared with the tortures which his tribe had invented, and stood ready to inflict on his captors once the tables were turned.
James E. Kiefer, by kind permission

Jesuits martyred in Canada

In 1625, the first Jesuits arrived in Quebec. Their initial work was to care for the spiritual needs of the French settlers and traders and to begin evangelizing the nearby Indians. They soon realized that their missionary efforts would have the greatest success if they focused on the Huron tribe some 800 miles west of Quebec. (About 100 miles north of present day Toronto, Canada.)

In Huronia, the missionaries found a tentative welcome as they visited the scattered Indian villages. They shared lodging with several Indian families who occupied a single long house.

Over the years more missionaries arrived and as their efforts were becoming successful, they decided to construct a Christian settlement where Indian converts could witness the beauty of Christian life and the missionaries could retreat for spiritual renewal. In 1639, they began building Sainte Marie. The settlement began with a single bark-covered Huron-style cabin for ten Jesuits and five workmen. Eventually, it would grow to a fortified village with a residence for 27 priests and 39 French laborers. There was a church for the converts, storehouses for food and equipment, a hospital, and living quarters for visiting Indians. The mission was flourishing as hundreds of Hurons were being prepared for baptism and churches were being built in the villages.

However, the shadow of destruction loomed overhead. The dreaded Iroquois nation to the south-east had stationed ambushes along the supply route to Quebec. Father Jogues and Rene Goupil were among those captured in 1642 as their flotilla tried to make a return trip. By 1648 Iroquois warriors were raiding into Huronia itself. A number of villages were destroyed, including Teanostaye where Father Daniel was killed. That winter, more than 6,000 homeless Hurons would find temporary shelter and food at Sainte Marie. In mid March 1649, an Iroquois war party captured Fathers Brebeuf and Lalemant just three miles from Sainte Marie. They were taken to St. Ignace where they were tortured and killed.

By May, the Iroquois had destroyed fifteen Huron villages. The survivors fled to the safety of Sainte Marie or to neighboring tribes. Knowing that Sainte Marie could not withstand an attack, the Jesuits put their settlement to the torch and retreated to Saint Joseph Island with the remaining Christian Indians. There they endured a winter plagued by starvation and disease. Two more priests, Fathers Garnier and Chabanel, were martyred. In the summer of 1650, the priests and about 300 surviving Indians left Huronia. After forty-nine days they found sanctuary in Quebec.

The names of the Martyrs and their respective dates of death are as follows:
St. Rene Goupil – September 29, 1642
St. Isaac Jogues – October 18, 1646
St. John de Laland – October 19, 1646
St. Anthony Daniel – July 4, 1648
St. John Brebeuf – March 16, 1649
St. Gabriel Lalemant – March 17, 1649
St. Charles Garnier – December 7, 1649
St. Noel Chabanel – December 8, 1649

Anthony Daniel

Huron missionary, born at Dieppe, in Normandy, 27 May 1601, slain by the Iroquois at Teanaostae, near Hillsdale, Limcoe County, Ontario, Canada, 4 July, 1648. After two years' study of philosophy and one of law, he entered the Society of Jesus in Rome, 1 October, 1621. Sent to Canada in 1633 he was first stationed at Cape Breton, where his brother Captain Daniel had established a French fort in 1629. For two years he had charge at Quebec of a school for Indian boys, but with this exception he was connected with the Mission at Ihonatiria, in the Huron country, from July, 1634, until his death fourteen years later. In the summer of 1648, the Iroquois made a sudden attack on the mission while most of the Huron braves were absent. Father Daniel did all in his power to aid his people. Before the palisades had been scaled he hurried to the chapel where the women, children, and old men were gathered gave them general absolution and baptized the catechumens. Daniel himself made no attempt to escape, but calmly advanced to meet the enemy. Seized with amazement the savages halted for a moment, then recovering themselves they discharged at him a shower of arrows. "The victim to the heroism of charity", says Bancroft, "died, the name of Jesus on his lips, the wilderness gave him a grave; the Huron nation were his mourners" (vol. II, ch. xxxii). Here Bancroft is in error. The lifeless body was flung into the burning chapel and both were consumed together. Daniel was the second to receive the martyr's crown among the Jesuits sent to New France, and the first of the missionaries to the Hurons. Father Ragueneau, his superior, speaks of him in a letter to the general of the order as "a truly remarkable man, humble, obedient, united with God, of never failing patience and indomitable courage in adversity" (Thwaites, tr. Relations, XXXIII, 253-269).

Edward P. Spillane, The Catholic Encyclopedia, Volume 4

Gabriel Lalemant

Jesuit missionary, b. at Paris, 10 October, 1610, d. in the Huron country, 17 March 1649. He was the nephew of Charles and Jerome Lalemant, and became a Jesuit at Paris, 24 March 1630. He arrived in Canada, 20 September, 1646 and after remaining in Quebec for two years, was sent to the Huron missions as de Brebeuf's assistant. He was scarcely there a month when the Iroquois attacked the settlement of St. Ignatius which they burned, and then descended on the mission of St. Louis where they found de Brebeuf and Lalemant. After setting fire to the village and killing many of the inhabitants, they led the two priests back to St. Ignatius where they were tied to stakes and after horrible torture put to death. Lalemant stood by while his companion was being killed. De Brebeuf expired at three in the afternoon. Lalemant's suffering began at six that evening and lasted until nine o'clock next morning. When the Iroquois withdrew, the bodies of the two priests were carried over to St. Mary's where they were interred. Some of the relies of Lalemant were subsequently carried to Quebec.

T.J. Campbell, The Catholic Encyclopedia, Volume 8

St. Isaac Jogues

French missionary, born at Orléans, France, 10 January, 1607; martyred at Ossernenon, in the present State of New York, 18 October, 1646. He was the first Catholic priest who ever came to Manhattan Island (New York). He entered the Society of Jesus in 1624 and, after having been professor of literature at Rouen, was sent as a missionary to Canada in 1636. He came out with Montmagny, the immediate successor of Champlain. From Quebec he went to the regions around the great lakes where the illustrious Father de Brébeuf and others were laboring. There he spent six years in constant danger. Though a daring missionary, his character was of the most practical nature, his purpose always being to fix his people in permanent habitations. He was with Garnier among the Petuns, and he and Raymbault penetrated as far as Sault Ste Marie, and "were the first missionaries", says Bancroft (VII, 790, London, 1853), "to preach the gospel a thousand miles in the interior, five years before John Eliot addressed the Indians six miles from Boston Harbor". There is little doubt that they were not only the first apostles but also the first white men to reach this outlet of Lake Superior. No documentary proof is adduced by the best-known historians that Nicholet, the discoverer of Lake Michigan, ever visited the Sault. Jogues proposed not only to convert the Indians of Lake Superior, but the Sioux who lived at the head waters of the Mississippi.

His plan was thwarted by his capture near Three Rivers returning from Quebec. He was taken prisoner on 3 August, 1642, and after being cruelly tortured was carried to the Indian village of Ossernenon, now Auriesville, on the Mohawk, about forty miles above the present city of Albany. There he remained for thirteen months in slavery, suffering apparently beyond the power of natural endurance. The Dutch Calvinists at Fort Orange (Albany) made constant efforts to free him, and at last, when he was about to be burnt to death, induced him to take refuge in a sailing vessel which carried him to New Amsterdam (New York). His description of the colony as it was at that time has since been incorporated in the Documentary History of the State. From New York he was sent; in mid-winter, across the ocean on a lugger of only fifty tons burden and after a voyage of two months, landed Christmas morning, 1643, on the coast of Brittany, in a state of absolute destitution. Thence he found his way to the nearest college of the Society. He was received with great honor at the court of the Queen Regent, the mother of Louis XIV, and was allowed by Pope Urban VII the very exceptional privilege of celebrating Mass, which the mutilated condition of his hands had made canonically impossible; several of his fingers having been eaten or burned off. He was called a martyr of Christ by the pontiff. No similar concession, up to that, is known to have been granted.

In early spring of 1644 he returned to Canada, and in 1646 was sent to negotiate peace with the Iroquois. He followed the same route over which he had been carried as a captive. It was on this occasion that he gave the name of Lake of the Blessed Sacrament to the body of water called by the Indians Horicon, now known as Lake George. He reached Ossernenon on 5 June, after a three weeks' journey from the St. Lawrence. He was well received by his former captors and the treaty of peace was made. He started for Quebec on 16 June and arrived there 3 July. He immediately asked to be sent back to the Iroquois as a missionary, but only after much hesitation his superiors acceded to his request. On 27 September he began his third and last journey to the Mohawk. In the interim sickness had broken out in the tribe and a blight had fallen on the crops. This double calamity was ascribed to Jogues whom the Indians always regarded as a sorcerer. They were determined to wreak vengeance on him for the spell he had cast on the place, and warriors were sent out to capture him. The news of this change of sentiment spread rapidly, and though fully aware of the danger Jogues continued on his way to Ossernenon, though all the Hurons and others who were with him fled except Lalande. The Iroquois met him near Lake George, stripped him naked, slashed him with their knives, beat him and then led him to the village. On 18 October, 1646, when entering a cabin he was struck with a tomahawk and afterwards decapitated. The head was fixed on the Palisades and the body thrown into the Mohawk.

In view of his possible canonization a preliminary court was established in Quebec by the ecclesiastical authorities to receive testimony as to his sanctity and the cause of his death.

T.J. Campbell, The Catholic Encyclopedia, Volume 8

Jean de Brébeuf

Jesuit missionary, born at Conde-sur-Vire in Normandy, 25 March, 1593; died in Canada, near Georgian Bay, 16 March, 1649. His desire was to become a lay brother, but he finally entered the Society of Jesus as a scholastic, 8 November, 1617. According to Ragueneau it was 5 October. Though of unusual physical strength, his health gave way completely when he was twenty-eight, which interfered with his studies and permitted only what was strictly necessary, so that he never acquired any extensive theological knowledge. On 19 June, 1625, he arrived in Quebec, with the Recollect, Joseph de la Roche d' Aillon, and in spite of the threat which the Calvinist captain of the ship made to carry him back to France, he remained in the colony. He overcame the dislike of the colonists for Jesuits and secured a site for a residence on the St. Charles, the exact location of a former landing of Jacques Cartier. He immediately took up his abode in the Indian wigwams, and has left us an account of his five months' experience there in the dead of winter. In the spring he set out with the Indians on a journey to Lake Huron in a canoe, during the course of which his life was in constant danger. With him was Father de No3e, and they established their first mission near Georgian Bay, at Ihonatiria, but after a short time his companion was recalled, and he was left alone.

Brebeuf met with no success. He was summoned to Quebec because of the danger of extinction to which the entire colony was then exposed, and arrived there after an absence of two years, 17 July, 1628. On 19 July, 1629, Champlain surrendered to the English, and the missionaries returned to France. Four years afterwards the colony was restored to France, and on 23 March, 1633, Brebeuf again set out for Canada. While in France he had pronounced his solemn vows as spiritual coadjutor. As soon as he arrived, viz., May, 1633, he attempted to return to Lake Huron. The Indians refused to take him, but during the following year he succeeded in reaching his old mission along with Father Daniel. It meant a journey of thirty days and constant danger of death. The next sixteen years of uninterrupted labors among these savages were a continual series of privations and sufferings which he used to say were only roses in comparison with what the end was to be. The details may be found in the "Jesuit Relations".

In 1640 he set out with Father Chaumonot to evangelize the Neutres, a tribe that lived north of Lake Erie, but after a winter of incredible hardship the missionaries returned unsuccessful. In 1642 he was sent down to Quebec, where he was given the care of the Indians in the

Reservation at Sillery. About the time the war was at its height between the Hurons and the Iroquois, Jogues and Bressani had been captured in an effort to reach the Huron country, and Brebeuf was appointed to make a third attempt. He succeeded. With him on this journey were Chabanel and Garreau, both of whom were afterwards murdered. They reached St. Mary's on the Wye, which was the central station of the Huron Mission. By 1647 the Iroquois had made peace with the French, but kept up their war with the Hurons, and in 1648 fresh disasters befell the work of the missionaries – their establishments were burned and the missionaries slaughtered. On 16 March, 1649, the enemy attacked St. Louis and seized Brebeuf and Lallemant, who could have escaped but rejected the offer made to them and remained with their flock. The two priests were dragged to St. Ignace, which the Iroquois had already captured.

On entering the village, they were met with a shower of stones, cruelly beaten with clubs, and then tied to posts to be burned to death. Brebeuf is said to have kissed the stake to which he was bound. The fire was lighted under them, and their bodies slashed with knives. Brebeuf had scalding water poured on his head in mockery of baptism, a collar of red-hot tomahawk-heads placed around his neck, a red-hot iron thrust down his throat, and when he expired his heart was cut out and eaten. Through all the torture he never uttered a groan. The Iroquois withdrew when they had finished their work. The remains of the victims were gathered up subsequently, and the head of Brebeuf is still kept as a relic at the Haetel-Dieu, Quebec.

His memory is cherished in Canada more than that of all the other early missionaries. Although their names appear with his in letters of gold on the grand staircase of the public buildings, there is a vacant niche on the façade, with his name under it, awaiting his statue. His heroic virtues, manifested in such a remarkable degree at every stage of his missionary career, his almost incomprehensible endurance of privations and suffering, and the conviction that the reason of his death was not his association with the Hurons, but hatred of Christianity, has set on foot a movement for his canonization as a saint and martyr. An ecclesiastical court sat in 1904 for an entire year to examine his life and virtues and the cause of his death, and the result of the inquiry was forwarded to Rome.

T.J. Campbell, The Catholic Encyclopedia, Volume 2

Noel Chabanel

A Jesuit missionary among the Huron Indians, born in Southern France, 2 February, 1613; slain by a renegade Huron, 8 December, 1649. Chabanel entered the Jesuit novitiate at Toulouse at the age of seventeen, and was professor of rhetoric in several colleges of the society in the province of Toulouse. He was highly esteemed for virtue and learning. In 1643, he was sent to Canada and, after studying the Algonquin language for a time, was appointed to the mission of the Hurons, among whom he remained till his death. In these apostolic labors he was the companion of the intrepid missionary, Father Charles Garnier. As he felt a strong repugnance to the life and habits of the Indians, and feared it might result in his own withdrawal from the work, he nobly bound himself by vow never to leave mission, and he kept his vow to the end. In the "Relation" of 1649-50, Father Ragueneau describes the martyr deaths of Chabanal and Garnier, with biographical sketches of these two fathers.

Edward P. Spillane, The Catholic Encyclopedia, Volume 3

René Goupil

Jesuit missionary; born 1607, in Anjou; martyred in New York State, 23 September, 1642. Health preventing him from joining the Society regularly, he volunteered to serve it gratis in Canada, as a donné. After working two years as a surgeon in the hospitals of Quebec, he started (1642) for the Huron mission with Father Jogues, whose constant companion and disciple he remained until death. Captured by the Iroquois near lake St. Peter, he resignedly accepted his fate. Like the other captives, he was beaten, his nails torn out, and his finger-joints cut off. On the thirteen days' journey to the Iroquois country, he suffered from heat, hunger, and blows, his wounds festering and swarming with worms. Meeting half way a band of two hundred warriors, he was forced to march between their double ranks and almost beaten to death. Goupil might have escaped, but he stayed with Jogues. At Ossernenon, on the Mohawk, he was greeted with jeers, threats, and blows, and Goupil's face was so scarred that Jogues applied to him the words of Isaias (liii, 2) prophesying the disfigurement of Christ. He survived the fresh tortures inflicted on him at Andagaron, a neighboring village, and, unable to instruct his captors in the faith, he taught the children the sign of the cross. This was the cause of his death. returning one evening to the village with Jogues, he was felled to the ground by a hatchet-blow from an Indian, and he expired invoking the name of Jesus. He was the first of the order in the Canadian missions to suffer martyrdom. He had previously bound himself to the Society by the religious vows pronounced in the presence of Father Jogues, who calls him in his letters "an angel of innocence and a martyr of Jesus Christ."

Lionel Lindsay, The Catholic Encyclopedia, Volume 6

USA

Kund Iverson

On the afternoon of August 9, 1853, a little Norwegian boy, named Kund Iverson, who lived in the city of Chicago, Ill., was going to the pastures for his cow, as light-hearted, I suppose, as boys usually are when going to the pasture on a summer afternoon. He came at length to a stream of water, where there was a gang of idle, ill-looking, big boys, who, when they saw Kund, came up to him, and said they wanted him to go into Mr. Elstonae's garden and steal some apples."

"No," said Kund promptly; "I cannot steal, I am sure."

"Well, but you've got to," they cried!

They threatened to duck him, for these wicked big boys had often frightened little boys into robbing gardens for them. Little boys, they thought, were less likely to get found out.

The threat did not frighten Kund, so, to make their words good, they seized him and dragged him into the river, and, in spite of his cries and struggles, plunged him in. But the heroic boy, even with the water gurgling and choking in his throat, never flinched, for he knew that God had said; "Thou shalt not steal," and God's law he had made his law; and no cursing, or threats, or cruelty of the big boys would make him give up. Provoked by his firmness, I suppose, they determined to see if they could not conquer. So they ducked him again, but still it was, "No, no"; and they kept him under water. Was there no one near to hear his distressing cries, and rescue the poor child from their cruel grip?

Now there was none to rescue him; and gradually the cries of the drowning child grew fainter and fainter, and his struggles less and less, and the boy was drowned. He could die, but would not steal.

A German boy who had stood near, much frightened by what he saw, ran home to tell the news. The agonized parents hastened to the spot, and all night they searched for the lifeless body of their lost darling. It was found the next morning; and who shall describe their feelings as they clasped the little form to their bosoms? Early piety had blossomed in his little life. He loved his Bible and his Savior. His seat was never vacant at Sunday-school, and so intelligent, conscientious and steadfast had he been, that it was expected that he would soon be received into the church of his parents.

Perhaps the little boy used often to think how when he grew up, be would like to be a preacher or a missionary, and do something for his Lord and Master. He did not know what post he might be called to occupy, even as a little child; and, as he left home that afternoon and looked his last look in his mother's face, he thought he was only going after his cow; and other boys, and the neighbors, if they saw him, thought so too. They did not then know that instead of going to the pasture, he was going to preach one of the most powerful sermons of Bible law and Bible principles the country ever heard. They did not know that he was going to give an example of steadfastness of purpose and of unflinching integrity, such as should thrill the heart of this nation with wonder and admiration. He was then only a Norwegian boy, Kund Iverson, only thirteen years old, but his name was soon to be reckoned with martyrs and heroes. And as the story of his moral heroism winged its way from state to state, and city to city, and village to village, how many mothers cried, with full hearts: "May his spirit rest upon my boy!" And strong men have wept over it and exclaimed: "God be praised for the lad!" And rich men put their hands in their pockets, and said: "Let us build him a monument let his name be perpetuated, for his memory is blessed." May there be a generation of Kund Iverson's, strong in their integrity, true to their Bibles, ready to die rather than do wrong.

Touching Incidents and Remarkable Answers to Prayer, edited by S. B. Shaw

Constance and Her Companions, The Martyrs of Memphis

9 September 1878

In 1878 the American city of Memphis on the Mississippi River was struck by an epidemic of yellow fever, which so depopulated the area that the city lost its charter and was not reorganized for fourteen years. Almost everyone who could afford to do so left the city and fled to higher ground away from the river. (It was not yet known that the disease was mosquito-borne, but it was observed that high and dry areas were safe.) There were in the city several communities of nuns, Anglican or Roman Catholic, who had the opportunity of leaving, but chose to stay and nurse the sick. Most of them, thirty-eight in all, were themselves killed by the fever. One of the first to die (on 9 September 1878) was Constance, head of the (Anglican) Community of St. Mary.

James Kiefer, Christian Biographies, By kind permission

Martin Luther King, Jr

Martin Luther King was assassinated in 1968 in Memphis.

The most perfect peace we can attain in this miserable life, consists in meek and patient suffering. He who has learned to suffer will certainly possess the greatest share of peace. He is the conqueror of himself, the lord of the world, the friend of Christ, and the heir of heaven.

The Imitation of Christ, ascribed to Thomas à Kempis

Champion of civil rights for American blacks, Martin Luther King explained his non-violent approach to smashing injustice in these words: "Our aim must be never to defeat or humiliate the white man, but to win his friendship and understanding. We must come to see that the end we seek is a society at peace with itself, a society that can live with its conscience. That will be a day not of the white man, not of the black man. That will be the day of man as man." In December 1964 he received the Nobel Peace Prize Award, presented by King Olav of Norway, in recognition of his tireless campaign against oppression and prejudice.

Negro dustmen had been on strike in Memphis for a week and Martin Luther King went there to orchestrate a massive non-violent protest. Dr King was being put under great pressure from some other Negro leaders like Stokely Carmichael over his avowedly non-violent approach to gaining simple justice for American blacks. Dr King spoke at a pre-march rally on April 3 in which he made clear exactly what he supported in this unequal struggle. He also referred to the numerous threats of violence that he had received, some threatening his life. He said quite openly that he had been warned not to go to Memphis if he wanted to stay alive. Dr King ended his speech, his last recorded public words with these words: "And then I got into Memphis and some began to talk about the threats of what would happen to me from some of our sick white brothers. But I don't know what will happen now. We've got some difficult days ahead. But it really doesn't matter with me now. Because I've been to the mountain-top and I don't mind. Like anybody, I would like to live a long life, longevity has its place, but I'm not concerned about that now. I just want to do God's will, and he's allowed me to go up to the mountain. And I've looked over and I've seen the Promised Land. I may not get there with you, but I want you to know tonight that we as a people will get to the Promised Land. So I'm happy tonight. I'm not fearing any man. Mine eyes have seen the glory of the coming of the Lord."

Dr King was taking a short break the following morning on the balcony of the Lorraine Motel where he was engaged in a conference. As he turned to return to his room the assassin's bullet rang out, making a direct, deadly hit on Dr King's face. In vain the dying, 39-year-old Dr King was rushed by ambulance to St Joseph's hospital where he never regained consciousness.

On hearing the news American President Johnson said to the nation on the television, "I ask every citizen to reject the blind violence that has struck Dr King." On Dr King's tombstone are inscribed the same words that he spoke on the famous march on Washington, in August 1963:

FREE AT LAST,
FREE AT LAST
THANK GOD ALMIGHTY
I'M FREE AT LAST.

Editor

Cassie Bernall

In 1999 America was stunned to learn of a shooting spree at a Colorado High School. It left 15 people dead and many injured. As the details became known one aspect of the story from the last few seconds of life of one of the students at the Columbine High School was made known. With a gun to her head, Cassie Bernall was asked, "Do you believe in God?" "Yes," she said. She was then shot. Cassie's mom, Misty Bernall, wrote a book about her daughter's journey to faith in Jesus Christ, *She Said Yes*

Editor

Hawaii

Damien, Priest, Missionary, and Martyr

15 April 1889

In the 1800's, the Hawaiian Islands suffered a severe leprosy epidemic, which was dealt with largely by isolating lepers on the island of Molokai. They were simply dumped there and left to fend for themselves. The crews of the boats carrying them there were afraid to land, so they simply came in close and forced the lepers to jump overboard and scramble through the surf as best they could. Ashore, they found no law and no organized society, simply desperate persons waiting for death. A Belgian missionary priest, Joseph Van Veuster (Damien of the Fathers of the Sacred Heart), born in 1840, came to Hawaii in 1863, and in 1873 was sent at his own request to Molokai to work among the lepers. He organized burial details and funeral services, so that death might have some dignity. He taught the people how to grow crops and feed themselves better. He organized a choir, and got persons to sing who had not sung in years. He gave them medical attention. (Government doctors had been making regular visits, but they were afraid of contagion, and would not come close to the patients. They inspected their sores from a distance and then left medicines on a table and fled. Damien personally washed and anointed and bandaged their sores.) There was already a small chapel on the island. It proved too small, and with the aid of patients he built a larger one, which soon overflowed every Sunday. Damien contracted leprosy himself in 1885, and continued to work there until his death on 15 April 1889.

James Kiefer, Christian Biographies, By kind permission

The Far East

Melanasia

New Hebrides: Erromanga, "Martyr Isle"

The island of Erromonga, one small island in the New Hebrides chain, became known as "Martyr Isle," because so many missionaries were martyred there. The first

two martyrs date back to 1839 when James Harris and John Williams were speared to death, thus providing a feast for the cannibals. In 1857 Mr and Mrs George Gordon, Presbyterians from Nova Scotia, were also killed. George Gordon's brother, James, with James McNair attempted to carry on the pioneer missionary work, but both were martyred within four years. These killings eventually came to an end in 1880 when a church was built in the place where the first two martyrs fell, Dillon's Bay, and became known as "Martyr Church". A monument was built listing all the martyred missionaries, along with two Bible verses: "They hazarded their lives for the name of our Lord Jesus" (Acts 15:26); "It is a faithful saying, and worthy of all acceptation, that Christ Jesus came into the world to save sinners" (1 Timothy 1:15).
Editor

NEW GUINEA
JAMES CHALMERS

Let us pray
In the Church
With the Church
For the Church.
For there are three things that preserve
The Church and belong to the Church:
Firstly: to teach faithfully.
Secondly: to pray constantly.
Thirdly: to suffer reverently.
Martin Luther

James Chalmers became the first twentieth-century missionary martyr in the Pacific, after spending thirty-four years engaged in missionary work on these islands. When he arrived he was met by cannibals who wore human jawbones on their arms. When these people stopped their "feasts of human flesh" Chalmers knew that the Christian message was taking root. Chalmers was often invited to preach about Christ in heathen temples which had their walls lined by human skulls. Afterwards the cannibals resolved that there would be "no more man-eating". Chalmers was never content to settle down and was always spurred on by a pioneering spirit. Even after his second wife died in New Guinea Chalmers refused to return home. He set off for Goaribari Island with a few Christians from New Guinea on April 4, 1901. Chalmers went ashore and was invited to be a guest at a banquet. But as he entered the building he was clubbed to death with a stone club. Then his head was cut off, and his body was cooked for eating.
Editor

THE MARTYRS OF NEW GUINEA

2 September 1942

New Guinea (also called Irian), one of the world's largest islands, has a difficult terrain that discourages travel between districts. Consequently, it is home to many isolated tribes, with many different cultures and at least 500 languages. Christian missionaries began work there in the 1860's, but proceeded slowly.

When World War II threatened Papua and New Guinea, it was obvious that missionaries of European origin were in danger. There was talk of leaving. Bishop Philip Strong wrote to his clergy:

"We must endeavor to carry on our work. God expects this of us. The church at home, which sent us out, will surely expect it of us. The universal church expects it of us. The people whom we serve expect it of us. We could never hold up our faces again if, for our own safety, we all forsook Him and fled, when the shadows of the Passion began to gather around Him in His spiritual and mystical body, the Church in Papua."

They stayed. Almost immediately there were arrests. Eight clergymen and two laymen were executed "as an example" on September 2, 1942. In the next few years, many Papuan Christians of all Churches risked their own lives to care for the wounded.
James Kiefer, Christian Biographies, By kind permission

EAST ASIA
NORTH KOREA
TWENTIETH CENTURY MARTYRS

In the 1930s the revival of Japanese militarism resulted in Christians being persecuted for not taking part in Shinto shrine ceremonies as demanded by the Japanese. About 3,000 Christians were imprisoned and about 50 were martyred.

Since 1953 about 300,000 Christians have "disappeared." Anyone found with a Bible may be shot. It is estimated that 400 Christians were executed in 1999 alone.

In 2000, Younghee Lee was executed by firing squad in the market place of Moonsan in Hanmkyung North Province. She was accused of being a traitor to the Labor Party. Younghee had received the Lord after escaping to China in 1998. She had returned to N. Korea to preach the Gospel.

December 1999

Two Christian women were shot in HaeSan city on a fabricated charge of illegal smuggling. Two other Christians were also murdered in HamBuk province. One had his teeth broken because he continued to preach the gospel even as he was being carried off to be executed.

October 1999

Two Christians were shot to death in ChungJ in prison. After much torture they had revealed the names of several Christian co-laborers. However, they did not deny the Lord even when martyred. Fortunately an Open Doors worker warned those whose names had been revealed.

May 1999

The government issued an open warning to its citizens that Christian missionaries must be "ferreted out" being the "tools of imperialism." It claimed that certain underground guerillas have been posing as missionaries.

1987-1992

Soon Ok Yi, claims she witnessed monthly execution of Christians while imprisoned during the time listed. During these executions, Christians were asked to deny their faith in Jesus and Heaven. If they refused, they were beaten to death.

Editor

South East Asia

Indonesia

1966

96.12.18

Sukoharjo, Central Java. D. Mendrofa, pastor of GPdI (Pentecostal Church in Indonesia) Grogol, was brutally beaten by Moslems.

96.10.10

Situbondo, East Java. Muslim Rioters Burn 25 Churches, 2 Christian Schools and an Orphanage in Seven Cities. Pastor Ishak Christian and Family Burned to Death.

1997-1999

Between 1997 and 1999 473 churches were burned down and 14 Christians died as martyrs.

Editor

108 Christians Massacred in Moluccas

On June 21, 2000, it was reported from Jakarta that 108 Christians were killed after an hour-long battle in Duma, a village on the mainly Christian island of Halmahera.

Editor

Thailand

Roy Orpin

"Except a corn of wheat fall into the ground and die, it abideth alone: but if it die, it bringeth forth much fruit" (John 12:24)

Many Christians became missionaries through reading the stories of Christians who became Christian martyrs as they served Christ in foreign countries. Roy Orpin, from New Zealand, had been inspired by reading the stories of John and Betty Stam, and of the five missionaries killed by the Auca Indians in Ecuador. After being accepted by the Overseas Missionary Fellowship, Roy was sent to Thailand, where he married his fiancée, a young English girl whom he had met in Auckland while they were both studying at the New Zealand Bible Training Institute.

The newly married couple tried to make their home in a small village in Namkhet in Thailand, among a tribal people known as the Meos. Within a year of being there, violence erupted around them ominously. Three Thai opium dealers had been killed, even though they begged for their lives. Roy left his pregnant wife in their village as he traveled around surrounding villages. One night he came home having stumbled across the bodies of two more murdered Thais.

Roy, and his wife Gillian, had moved to another village, Bitter Bamboo, in order to teach some new Christians there. Then, as the day for their baby's birth came close, Gillian moved into a mission hospital. Roy had decided to follow Gillian. On the day before he was to join Gillian Roy set out to visit one of the surrounding villages. On his return he was attacked by three men who held him up at gunpoint, demanding that Roy should give them all he had. Roy gave him what little he had, but this hardly satisfied them and they proceeded to shoot him. Roy was able to struggle on with his fatal wound and was taken to a government hospital. Gillian was at Roy's side for four days, as his life slowly ebbed away, until the twenty-six-year-old missionary finally died of kidney failure. During these days Roy asked Gillian to recite one of his favorite choruses:

> Jesus! I am resting, resting
> In the joy of what Thou art,
> I am finding out the greatness
> Of Thy loving heart.

Not many days after Roy's funeral Murray Roy was born. Gillian returned to work among the Meo tribes people when they had just begun to sow their grain seeds. Along with two other single women missionaries, Gillian saw a spiritual harvest when twelve families from the Meo people decided to turn to Christ and burn their pagan charms. This happened just as they were harvesting their crops. "Except a corn of wheat fall into the ground and die, it abideth alone: but if it die, it bringeth forth much fruit" (John 12:24).

Editor

VIETNAM
CATECHIST ANDREW

Vietnam has a host of martyrs. In the 19th century it has been estimated that at least 125,000 people died for their Christian faith.

Andrew became officially recognized as a martyr by the Catholic church in 2,000.

Andrew, born in 1625 in Ran Ran (Vietnam), was blessed with a strongly Christian mother. Andrew became a Christian when he was fifteen years old. In 1644 he was arrested, beaten and shut up in a home. The King of Annam (ancient name of Vietnam) had ordered that Christianity should be prevented from spreading in his kingdom and anyone joining this new religion was severely punished. When Mandarin Ong Nghe Bo offered Andrew the opportunity to renounce his Christian faith, Andrew refused. On July 26th 1644, Andrew was condemned to death and was executed the following day by being hanged in public at Ke Cham.

Editor

JAPAN
MARTYRS IN JAPAN

There is not in the whole history of the Church a single people who can offer to the admiration of the Christian world annals as glorious, and a martyrology as lengthy, as those of the people of Japan. In January, 1552, St. Francis Xavier had remarked the proselytizing spirit of the early neophytes. "I saw them", he wrote, "rejoicing in our successes, manifesting an ardent zeal to spread the faith and to win over to baptism the pagans they conquered." He foresaw the obstacles that would block the progress of the faith in certain provinces, the absolutism of this or that daimyo, a class at that time very independent of the Mikado and in revolt against his supreme authority. As a matter of fact, in the province of Hirado, where he made a hundred converts, and where six years after him, 600 pagans were baptized in three days, a Christian woman (the proto-martyr) was beheaded for praying before a cross. In 1561 he diamyo forced the Christians to abjure their faith, "but they preferred to abandon all their possessions and live in the Bungo, poor with Christ, rather than rich without Him", wrote a missionary, 11 October, 1562. When, under the Shogunate of Yoshiaki, Ota Nobunaga, supported by Wada Koresama, a Christian, had subdued the greater part of the provinces and had restored monarchical unity, there came to pass what St. Francis Xavier had hoped for. At Miyako (the modern Kiyoto) the faith was recognized and a church built 15 Aug., 1576. Then the faith continued to spread without notable opposition, as the daimyos followed the lead of the Mikado (Ogimachi, 1558-1586) and Ota Nobunaga. The toleration or favor of the central authority brought about everywhere the extension of the Christian religion, and only a few isolated cases of martyrdom are known (*Le Catholicisme au Japon*, I, 173).

It was not until 1587, when there were 200,000 Christians in Japan, that an edict of persecution, or rather of prescription, was passed to the surprise of everyone, at the instigation of a bigoted bonze, Nichijoshonin, zealous for the religion of his race. Twenty-six residences and 140 churches were destroyed; the missionaries were condemned to exile, but were clever enough to hide or scatter. They never doubted the constancy of their converts; they assisted them in secret and in ten years there were 100,000 other converts in Japan. We read of two martyrdoms, one at Takata, the other at Notsuhara; but very many Christians were dispossessed of their goods and reduced to poverty. The first bloody persecution dates from 1597.

It is attributed to two causes: (1) Four years earlier some Castilian religious had come from the Philippines and, in spite of the decisions of the Holy See, had joined themselves to the 130 Jesuits who, on account of the delicate situation created by the edict were acting with great caution. In spite of every charitable advice given them, these men set to work in a very indiscreet manner, and violated the terms of the edict even in the capital itself; (2) a Castilian vessel cast by the storm on the coast of Japan was confiscated under the laws then in vigor. Some artillery was found on board, and Japanese susceptibilities were further excited by the lying tales of the pilot, so that the idea went abroad that the Castilians were thinking of annexing the country.

A list of all the Christians in Miyado and Osaka was made out, and on 5 Feb., 1597, 26 Christians, among whom were 6 Franciscan missionaries, were crucified at Nagasaki. Among the 20 native Christians there was one, a child of 13, and another of 12 years. "The astonishing fruit of the generous sacrifice of our 26 martyrs" (wrote a Jesuit missionary) "is that the Christians, recent converts and those of maturer faith, have been confirmed in the faith and hope of eternal salvation; they have firmly resolved to lay down their lives for the name of Christ. The very pagans who assisted at the martyrdom were struck at seeing the joy of the blessed ones as they suffered on their crosses and the courage with which they met death".

Ten years before this another missionary had foreseen and predicted that "from the courage of the Japanese, aided by the grace of God, it is to be expected that persecution will inaugurate a race for martyrdom". True it is that the national and religious customs of the people predisposed them to lay down their lives with singular fatalism; certain of their established usages, religious suicide, hara-kiri, had developed a contempt for death; but if grace does not destroy nature it exalts it, and their fervent charity and love for Christ led the Japanese neophytes to scourgings that the missionaries had to restrain. When this love for Christ had grown strong in the midst of suffering freely chosen, it became easier for the faithful to give the Savior that greatest proof of love by laying down their lives in a cruel death for His name's sake. "The fifty crosses, ordered for the holy mountain of Nagasaki, multiplied ten or a hundred fold, would not have sufficed" (wrote one missionary) "for all the faithful who longed for martyrdom". Associations (Kumi) were formed under the patronage of the Blessed Virgin with the object of preparing the members by prayer and scourgings even to blood, to be ready to lay down their lives for the faith. After the persecution of 1597, there were isolated cases of martyrdom until 1614, in all about 70. The reigns of Ieyasu, who is better known in Christian annals by the name of Daifu Sama, and of his successors Hidetada and Iemitziu, were the more disastrous. We are not concerned now with the causes of that persecution, which lasted half a century with some brief intervals of peace. According to Mr. Ernest Satow (quoted by Thurston in "The Month", March, 1905, "Japan and Christianity"): "As the Jesuit missionaries conducted themselves with great tact, it is by no means improbable that they might have continued to make converts year by year until the great part of the nation had been brought over to the Catholic religion, had it not been for the rivalry of the missionaries of other orders." These were the Castilian religious; and hence the fear of seeing Spain spread its conquests from the Philippines to Japan. Furthermore the zeal of certain religious Franciscans and Dominicans was wanting in prudence, and led to the persecution.

Year by year after 1614 the number of martyrdoms was 55, 15, 25, 62, 88, 15, 20. The year 1622 was particularly fruitful in Christian heroes. The Japanese martyrology counts 128 with name, Christian name and place of execution. Before this the four religious orders, Dominicans, Franciscans, Augustinians and Jesuits, had had their martyrs, but on 10 Sept., 1622, 9 Jesuits, 6 Dominicans, 4 Franciscans, and 6 lay Christians were put to death at the stake after witnessing the beheading of about 30 of the faithful. From December until the end of September, 1624, there were 285 martyrs. The English captain, Richard Cocks (Calendar of State Papers: Colonial East Indies, 1617-1621, p. 357) "saw 55 martyred at Miako at one time. . .and among them little children 5 or 6 years old burned in their mother's arms, crying out: "Jesus receive our souls". Many more are in prison who look hourly when they shall die, for very few turn pagans". We cannot go into the details of these horrible slaughters, the skillful tortures of Mount Unaen, the refined cruelty of the trench. After 1627 death grew more and more terrible for the Christians; in 1627, 123 died, during the years that followed, 65, 79, and 198. Persecution went on unceasingly as long as there were missionaries, and the last of whom we learn were 5 Jesuits and 3 seculars, who suffered the torture of the trench from 25 to 31 March, 1643. The list of martyrs we know of (name, Christian name, and place of execution) has 1648 names. If we add to this group the groups we learn of from the missionaries, or later from the Dutch travelers between 1649 and 1660, the total goes to 3125, and this does not include Christians who were banished, whose property was confiscated, or who died in poverty. A Japanese judge, Arai Hakuseki, bore witness about 1710, that at the close of the reign of Iemitzu (1650) "it was ordered that the converts should all lean on their own staff". At that time an immense number, from 200,000 to 300,000 perished. Without counting the members of Third Orders and Congregations, the Jesuits had, according to the martyrology (Delplace, II, 181-195; 263-275), 55 martyrs, the Franciscans 36, the Dominicans 38, the Augustinians 20. Pius IX and Leo XIII declared worthy of public cult 36 Jesuit martyrs, 25 Franciscans, 21 Dominicans, 5 Augustinians and 107 lay victims. After 1632 it ceased to be possible to obtain reliable data or information which would lead to canonical beatification. When in 1854, Commodore Perry forced an entry to Japan, it was learned that the Christian faith, after two centuries of intolerance, was not dead. In 1865, priests of the foreign Missions found 20,000 Christians practicing their religion in secret at Kiushu. Religious liberty was not granted them by Japanese law until 1873. Up to that time in 20 provinces, 3404 had suffered for the faith in exile or in prison; 660 of these had died, and 1981 returned to their homes. In 1858, 112 Christians, among whom were two chief-baptizers, were put to death by torture. One missionary calculates that in all 1200 died for the faith.

Louis Delplace, The Catholic Encyclopedia, Volume 9

Martyrs of 1597

Nearly one million indigenous Japanese Christians who were martyred for their faith in the Kirishtan Holocaust over a 250-year period beginning February 5, 1597.

Francis Xavier arrived in Japan in 1549, baptized great numbers, and whole provinces received the faith. The great kings of Arima, Bungo, and Omura, sent a solemn embassy of obedience to pope Gregory XIII in 1582: and in 1587 there were in Japan over 200,000 Christians, and among these several kings, princes and bonzas, but in 1588, Cambacundono, the haughty emperor, having usurped the honors of a deity, commanded all the Jesuits to leave his dominions within six months: however, many remained there disguised.

In 1592, the persecution was renewed, and several Japanese converts received the crown of martyrdom. The emperor Tagcosama, one of the proudest and most vicious of men, was worked up into a rage and jealously by a suspicion suggested by certain European merchants desirous of the monopoly of this trade, that the view of the missionaries in preaching the Christian faith was to facilitate the conquest of their country by the Portuguese or Spaniards. Three Jesuits and six Franciscans were crucified on a hill near Nangasaqui in 1597. The latter were partly Spaniards and partly Indians, and had at their hand F. Peter Baptist, commissary of his Order, who was born in Avila, in Spain. As to the Jesuits, one was Paul Michi, a noble Japanese and an eminent preacher, at that time thirty-three years old. The other two, John Gotto and James Kisai, were admitted into the Society in prison a little before they suffered.

Several Japanese suffered with them. The martyrs were twenty-six in number, and among them were three boys, two aged fifteen and one aged twelve. Each showed great joy and constancy in their sufferings. Of these martyrs, twenty-four had been brought to Meaco, where only part of their left ears was cut off, by a mitigation of the sentence which had commanded the amputation of their noses and both ears. They were conducted through many towns and public places, their cheeks stained with blood, for a terror to others. When the twenty-six soldiers of Christ arrived at their place of execution near Nangasaqui, they were fastened to crosses by cords and chains, about their arms and legs, and a iron collar about their necks, were raised into the air, the foot of each cross falling into a hole prepared for it in the ground. The crosses were planted in a row, about four feet apart, and each martyr had an executioner near him with a spear ready to pierce his side; for such is the Japanese manner of crucifixion. As soon as all the crosses were planted, the executioners lifted up their lances, and at a signal given, all pierced the martyrs almost in the same instant; upon which they expired and went to receive the reward of the sufferings.

Alban Butler, The Lives of the Saints, Dublin, 1833, volume 1, p 201

Martyrs of 1602-22

In 1599, one hundred Jesuit missionaries converted 40,000 Japanese people, and in 1600 over 30,000 Japanese were converted and fifty churches were built. But bloody persecution resulted in many Japanese converts being beheaded, crucified or burned.

In 1614, new cruelties were exercised to overcome their constancy, as by bruising their feet between certain pieces of wood, cutting off or squeezing their limbs one after another, applying red-hot irons or slow fires, flaying off the skin of the fingers, putting burning coals to their hands, tearing off the flesh with pincers, or thrusting reeds into all parts of their bodies, and turning them about to tear their flesh, till they should say they would forsake their faith: all which, innumerable persons, even children, bore with invincible constancy till death.

In 1616, Xogun succeeding his father Cubosama in the empire, surpassed him in cruelty. The most illustrious of these religious heroes was F. Charles Spinola. He was of a noble Genoese family, and entered the Society of Nola, whilst his uncle cardinal Spinola was bishop of that city. Out of zeal and a desire of martyrdom, he begged to be sent on the Japanese mission. He arrived there in 1602; labored many years in that mission, gained many to Christ, by his mildness, and lived in great austerity, for his usual food was only a little rice and herbs. He suffered four years a most cruel imprisonment, during which, in burning fevers, he was not able to obtain from his keepers one drop of cold water apart from his meals: yet he wrote from his dungeon: "Father, how sweet and delightful is it to suffer for Jesus Christ! I have learned this better by experience than I am able to express, especially since we are in these dungeons where we fast continually. The strength of my body fails me, but my joy increases as I see death draw nearer. O what a happiness for me, if next Easter I shall sing the heavenly Alleluia in the company of the blessed!'

In a long letter to his cousin Maximilian, Charles Spinola wrote:

Letter from Omura, a Japanese prison, 1622
O, if you had tasted the delights with which God fills the souls of those who serve him, and suffer for him, how would you condemn all that the world can promise! I now begin to be a disciple of Jesus Christ, since for his love I am in prison, where I suffer much. But I assure you, that when I am fainting with hunger, God hath fortified me by his sweet consolations, so that I have looked upon myself as well recompensed for his service. And though I were yet to pass many years in prison, the time would appear short, through the extreme desire which I feel of suffering for him, who even here so well repays our labors. Besides other sickness, I have been afflicted with a continual fever a hundred days without any remedies or proper nourishment. All this time my heart was so full of joy, that it seemed to me too narrow to contain it. I have never felt any equal to it, and I thought myself at the gates of paradise.

His joy was excessive at the news that he was condemned to be burnt alive, and he never ceased to thank God for so great a mercy, of which he owned himself unworthy. He was conducted from his last prison at Omura to Nangasaqui, where fifty martyrs suffering together on a hill within sight of that city, nine Jesuits, four Franciscans, and six Dominicans, the rest beheaded. The twenty- five stakes were fixed all in a row, and the martyrs were tied to them. Fire was set to the end of the pile of wood twenty-five feet from the martyrs, and gradually approached them, two hours before it reached them. F. Spinola stood unmoved, with his eyes lifted up towards heaven, till the cords which tied him being burnt, he fell into the flames, and was consumed on September 2, 1622, being fifty-eight years old. Many others, especially Jesuits, suffered variously, being either burnt at slow fires, crucified, beheaded, or thrown into a burning mountain, or hung with their heads downwards in pits, which cruel torment usually put an end to their lives in three or four days.

Alban Butler, The Lives of the Saints, Dublin, 1833, volume 1, pp 201-202

20,000 MASSACRED, 1662

Some Portuguese missionaries were the first to introduce Christianity into Japan. They landed on the island in 1552, and their efforts were more successful than they dared to anticipate. Their labors continued to be successful until 1616, when they were accused of being implicated in a conspiracy to overthrow the government and dethrone the emperor. For a few years they remained unmolested, though the greatest jealousy existed against them at the court; but in 1662 a dreadful persecution broke out against both the foreign and native Christians. It is asserted that between 1662 and 1666 no less than 20,000 Christians were massacred. The churches were shut and any profession of Christianity was punished with death. At length the Christians moved to the town of Siniabara, on the island of Ximio, where they determined to defend themselves to the last. The Japanese army followed them and besieged the town. The Christians, although much inferior in discipline, equipment and resources, defended themselves with the greatest

bravery, and resisted all attacks for three months. Then, as their provisions were so scarce they became weak and had to surrender. Every age and sex were then ruthlessly murdered by the conquerors, and Christianity, after its brief existence, was completely extirpated from the dominions of the Tycoon.
John Foxe, The Book of Martyrs, revised with notes and an appendix by W. Bramley-Moore, London, 1869, pp 170-71

Martyrs of 1660-1673

After the downfall of the insurgents of Shimabara in 1638 the Catholics in Japan were completely isolated from the Mother Church, while the government, both central and feudal, persecuted them severely and persistently. In 1640 the central Shogunate government organized a Commission for Inquisition, and the Chief Commissioner was endowed with the power to control the several feudal states in regard to their measures of inquisition and persecution. In most cases the arrested were first examined by the local authorities, then detained in their local prisons to induce the converts to apostatize – to "turn over" (korobu), as it was termed. Those who withstood were sent to Nagasaki, where further measures were taken to cause them to "turn over'; when they were obstinate enough to defy persuasion or threats or temptations, they were sentenced to death. In many cases the prisoners died in prison within less than a year, but some lasted imprisonment for up to sixteen years.
Editor

Fate of hundreds of people of Matsudaira Yamato-no-kami

The Matsudaira document records the cases of hundreds of people arrested during 1660-73. (see table below)
We classify under four heads:
1 Those who were executed
2 Those who died in prison
3 Those who remained in prison, supposedly, somewhere
4 Those who were released on investigation or on promising to give up their faith
In the province of Bungo, which included the feudal territory of Matsudaira, between 1660-73 at least 472 people were persecuted, 77 being executed and 103 died in prison.
* The oldest among the executed was Ichisuke, 73 years old when arrested and 74 when executed.
* The oldest among those who died in prison was Kichizaemon, 74 when arrested and 75 when he died.
* The youngest executed was Fuji, aged 14 when arrested and 16 when executed.
* The youngest who died in prison were Tsuru, 12 when arrested and 16 when she died, and Shio, 14 when arrested and 20 when she died.
Some previously unrecorded Japanese martyrdoms of the Catholic Church, in the second half of the seventeenth century are

Village community	Executed	Died in prison	Still in prison	Released
Katsuragi	27	24	932	92
Monden	18	12	10	19
Kami-Mitsunaga	2	11	4	
Shimo-Mitsunaga	6	9	84	27
Mera	13	4		
Magaya	3	31	7	
Kobu-gari	0	2	0	2
Senzai	2	22	6	
Otozu	2	3	5	
Yamazu	2	2		
Takajo-mura	3	1	4	
Harumura	1	1		
Takajo-machi	1	1	2	
Tsumori 2	21	5		

set out in a study of newly disclosed documents from the prefectural library of Nagasaki. Masaharu Anesaki writes a chapter about this topic in the book *Scritti di Storia E Paleografia*, Volume III, Roma, Biblioteca Apostolica Vaticana, 1924, pp 343-57
Editor

Manchurian martyrs

Japan took over the southern part of Manchuria in 1905. They discovered that thousands of the people of Manchuria had turned to Christ. The Japanese believed that their emperor was an incarnation of the Sun Goddess and should be worshiped as a god. However, the new Christians in Manchuria refused to honor the emperor in this way. The Japanese soldiers indulged in wholesale massacres of Christians as they burnt the homes of Christian villages. When they arrived in a Christian village they started by setting fire to huge sacks of straw and barley. As the men left their homes they were shot, and any who did not die outright were covered with burning straw or bayoneted. Then the houses were set alight, often with women and children left inside. Up to 150 Christians were killed in one village in this way.
Editor

South America
Bolivia
The Ayore Indians

In the jungle between Brazil and Paraguay Bolivian Indians who have been abused for many decades live. Five missionaries from the New Tribes Mission became the first martyrs to be killed by these Indians. The concept behind the founding of the New Tribes Mission in 1942 by Paul Fleming and Cecil Dye was simple: to take the gospel to new tribes who had never been visited by Christians before. In 1944 Paul Fleming, Cecil Dye, together with three others, Bob Dye, Dave Bacon and George Hosbach arrived in Bolivia to reach the Ayores, who were known to the Bolivians as "the tribe that was impossible to tame." The five men, three of whom were married, left their wives and the Flemings' three children at their base camp in the jungle at Santo Corazon, and went further into the jungle seeking the Ayores. Before they left on November 10, 1944, they told two men colleagues to search for them if they had not returned within a month. After a month nothing had been heard from them, so Clyde Collins, Wally Wright and four Bolivians went in search of the missionaries. They managed to track their trail until they saw a group of Ayores who immediately scattered on seeing them. Soon after this they came across some personal belongings of the missionaries: a sock belonging to Cecil, a machete of George's and a cracked camera lens. They decided to return from their search when Wally was shot and wounded by an arrow.

A bigger search party, consisting only of Bolivians, was then sent out. Although they reached an Ayore plantation and found some more personal belongings of the missionaries, they did not discover their bodies. When the second search party returned an army commander was keen to send in some troops and teach the Ayores a lesson, but the three wives prevented this by stressing that they wanted to reach the Ayores for Christ and not exact revenge. A year later some missionaries, including Jean Dye, moved further into the territory of the Ayores. Three years later, in 1948, a group of naked Ayores came to the mission station in the jungle with no warning. The missionaries tried to show them friendship and gave them gifts before they disappeared back into the jungle. Six weeks later these Indians came back and slept the night with the missionaries. The next day they told the missionaries how a different clan from them had met and killed five white men and thrown their bodies into the river. However, next year, Jean Dye was told by a member of the Ayore tribe, Degui, that his warriors had killed five men and buried them. Further details about the killing of the five missionaries emerged from another Ayore friend of Degui. They were killed with spears and machetes and clubs.

A number of friends of the killers came to Christ and expressed their sorrow to the wives of the three dead missionaries. One of

the ringleaders responsible for the death of the missionaries, Upoide, came to the mission station, and as soon as he realized that the wives of the missionaries had forgiven him, became a Christian himself. Since then a permanent mission station in the jungle for the Ayores has been established and no further killings have taken place.
Editor

Ecuador
The Martyrs of the Ecuador Mission
8 January 1956

In the dense rain-forests of Ecuador, on the Pacific side of the Andes Mountains, lives a tribe of Indians who call themselves the Huaorani ("people" in their language, Huao), but whose neighbors have called them the Aucas ("savages" in Quechua). For many generations they have been completely isolated from the outside world, disposed to kill any stranger on sight, and feared even by their head-hunting neighbors, the Jivaro tribe.

In 1955, four missionaries from the United States who were working with the Quechas, Jivaros, and other Indians of the interior of Ecuador became persuaded that they were being called to preach the Gospel to the Huaorani as well.

Nate Saint was 32 years old (born 1923), and devoted to flying. He had taken flying lessons in high school and served in the Air Force in WWII. After the war, he enrolled in Wheaton College to prepare for foreign mission work but dropped out to join the Missionary Aviation Fellowship. With his wife, Marjorie Farris, he established a base at Shell Mera (an abandoned oil exploration camp in Ecuador) in September 1948, and flew short hops to keep missionaries supplied with medicines, mail, etc. Once his plane crashed, but a few weeks later he returned to work in a cast from his neck to his thighs.

The other three, Ed McCully, Jim Elliot, and Peter Fleming, all Plymouth Brethren, came to Ecuador in 1952 to work for CMML (Christian Missions in Many Lands).

Ed McCully was 28 years old (born 1927). He had been a football and track star at Wheaton College and president of his senior class. After Wheaton, he enrolled at Marquette to study law, but dropped out to go to Ecuador. He and his wife, Marilou Hobolth, worked with the Quechuas at Arajuno, a base near the Huaorani. Half a dozen Quechuas had been killed at the base by Huaorani in the previous year.

Jim Elliot was 28 years old (born 1927) and an honors graduate of Wheaton College, where he had been a debater, public speaker, and champion wrestler. In Ecuador, he married Elisabeth Howard. They did paramedic work, tending broken arms, malaria, snakebite. They taught sanitation, wrote books in Quechua, and taught literacy.

Peter Fleming was 27 years old (born 1928), from the University of Washington, an honor student, and a linguist. With his wife, Olive Ainslie, he ran a literacy program among the Quechuas.

Nate and Ed found a Huaorani settlement from the air in late September 1955. Nate made four more flights on Thursday, 29 September, and found a settlement only fifteen minutes from their station. They told Jim and Pete, and the four planned their strategy.

They would keep the project secret from everyone but their wives, to avoid being joined by adventurers and the press, with the chance that someone not dedicated to the mission would start shooting at the first sign of real or imagined danger, and destroy the project.

They had one language resource, a Huaorani girl, Dayuma, who had fled from her tribe years earlier after her family was killed in a dispute. Dayuma, who spoke both Huao and Quechua, was now living with Nate's sister Rachel. From her the missionaries learned enough of the language to get started.

They would fly over the village every Thursday and drop gifts as a means of making contact and establishing a friendly relationship. Eventually they would try for closer contact. Nate had discovered that, if he lowered a bucket on a line from the plane, and flew in tight circles, the bucket remained almost stationary, and could be used to lower objects to the ground. He had devised a mechanism to release the bucket when it touched down.

On Thursday, 6 October, one week after locating the village, they dropped an aluminum kettle into an apparently deserted village. On the next flight, several Huaorani were waiting, and the missionaries dropped a machete. On the third flight, they dropped another machete to a considerably larger crowd. Beginning with the fourth flight, they used a loudspeaker system to call out friendly messages in Huao.

Soon the Huaorani were responding with gifts of their own tied to the line: a woven headband, carved wooden combs, two live parrots, cooked fish, parcels of peanuts, a piece of smoked monkey tail.... They cleared a space near their village and built platforms to make the exchanges easier.

After three months of air-to-ground contact, during which they made far more progress than they had hoped, the missionaries decided that it was time for ground contact. They feared that they could not keep their activities secret much longer, and that delay risked a hostile encounter between the Huaorani and some third party.

They decided that the expedition needed a fifth man, so they brought in Roger Youderian, a 31-year-old (born 1924) former paratrooper who had fought in the Battle of the Bulge (a major German offensive in Belgium in the last stages of WWII) and had been in General Eisenhower's honor guard. Roger and his wife, Barbara Orton, were working with the Jivaros, and Roger was thoroughly at home in the jungle, accustomed to living like the Jivaros and blessed with acute survival instincts.

They located a beach that would serve as a landing strip, about four miles from the village, and decided to go in on Tuesday, 3 January 1956. After some discussion, they decided to carry guns, having heard that the Huaorani never attacked anyone who was carrying a gun, and having resolved that they would, as a last resort, fire the guns into the air to ward off an attack, but would shoot no one, even to save their own lives.

On Tuesday they flew in and made camp, then flew over the village to invite the Huaorani to visit them. The first visitors showed up on Friday: a man, a woman, and a teen-aged girl. They stayed for several hours in apparent friendliness, then left abruptly. On Saturday, no one showed, and when the plane flew over the village, the Huaorani seemed frightened at first, but lost their fright when presents were dropped. On Sunday afternoon, 8 January 1956, at about 3 PM, all five missionaries were speared to death at their camp. A search party the next day found no signs of a struggle, and the lookout who was to be stationed in a tree-house overlooking the camp at ground level had come down, so it appeared that the meeting had originally seemed friendly, and that the attack had been a surprise. Ed McCully's body was seen and identified, but was swept away by the river and not recovered. The other four, at the request of their wives, were buried at the site of the camp where they had died. Besides their wives, they left behind a total of nine children.

The effort to reach the Huaorani was not abandoned but rather intensified. Within three weeks, Johnny Keenan, another pilot of the Ecuador Mission, was continuing the flights over the Huaorani village. More than twenty fliers from the United States promptly applied to take Nate's place. More than 1000 college students volunteered for foreign missions in direct response to the story of the Five Martyrs. In Ecuador, Indian attendance at mission schools and church services reached record levels, and the number of conversions skyrocketed. A Jivaro undertook to go at once to another Jivaro tribe that had been at war with his own tribe for years, bearing the Christian message, and his visit brought peace between the two tribes. Truly, as Tertullian said 1800 years ago, the blood of the martyrs is the seed of the Church.

In less than three years, Rachel Saint (sister of Nate Saint) and Elisabeth Elliot (widow of Jim Elliot) had not only renewed contact but had established permanent residence in a Huaorani settlement, where they practiced basic medicine and began the process of developing a written form of the language.

Nine years after the murder of the five missionaries, two of those who had killed Nate Saint and his companions baptized two of Nate's children, Kathy and Stephen Saint. In June 1995, at the request of the Huaorani, Nate's son Stephen moved to the settlement with his wife, Ginny, and their four children, to assist the Huaorani in developing greater internal leadership for a church committed to meeting the medical, economic, and social needs of their own people as a means of showing them God's love and his desire to provide for their eternal needs as well.

Why did the Huaorani suddenly turn hostile? Much later, one of the Huaorani who had helped to kill the five martyrs explained that the tribe, who had had almost no contact with outsiders that did not involve killing or attempted killing on one side or another, wondered why the whites wanted to make contact with them; and while they wanted to believe that their visitors were friendly, they feared a trap. After the killings, they realized their mistake. When they were attacked, one of the missionaries fired two shots as warnings, and one shot grazed a Huaorani who was hiding in the brush, unknown to the missionaries. It was therefore clear that the visitors had weapons, were capable of killing, and had chosen not to do so. Thus, the Huaorani realized that the visitors were indeed their friends, willing to die for them if necessary. When in subsequent months they heard the message that the Son of God had come down from heaven to reconcile men with God, and to die in order to bring about that reconciliation, they recognized that the message of the missionaries was the basis of what they had seen enacted in the lives of the missionaries. They believed the Gospel preached because they had seen the Gospel lived.

James Kiefer, Christian Biographies, By kind permission

Jim Elliot

With four Christian friends, Jim Elliot was killed in Ecuador by the Aucas in 1956.

"He is no fool who gives what he cannot keep to gain what he cannot lose." (Jim Elliot, written aged 22)

Soon after Jim Elliot graduated from Wheaton College, Wheaton, Illinois, USA, in 1949, he had premonitions that he would die young in God's service. He became convinced that God was calling him to pioneer missionary work in Ecuador. He spent most of 1952 in Quito, Ecuador, learning Spanish and orientating to a new culture. Jim then went to Shandia, and helped to build up a jungle mission station, where he also had to learn a new language so he could speak with the Quichua Indians.

Since his college days Jim had been fascinated by a remote Stone Age tribe who lived in Ecuador, known as the Aucas. Jim knew that they had a deserved reputation for killing anyone, Indian or white, who dared to intrude into their land. Nevertheless, Jim felt it right to pray especially for these Aucas. While he worked with his recently married wife Elisabeth among the Quichua Indians Jim's thoughts often turned to how he might be able to contact the Aucas.

Then, in September 1955 a pilot with the Mission Aviation Fellowship, Nate Saint, spotted from the air a small Auca settlement, while he was flying with Ed McCully. They quickly reported their discovery to Jim Elliot. The three of them, Ed, Nate and Jim then spent the next three months making weekly flights over the Aucas, dropping gifts of ribbons and cloth on every occasion. Soon the Aucas would leave their oval-shaped, leaf-thatched houses and dugout canoes and wait for the weekly visit from the air. They even started to reciprocate gifts and managed to pop into the rope-suspended bucket a lovely feather crown. Another Auca had made a model of their plane and raised it on a pole outside his house. When the plane circled overhead the men surprised the Aucas at first, by shouting in their own language, "We like you." "We are your friends." "We are your friends."

At the beginning of 1956 the four men,

together with Pete Fleming and Roger Youderian from the Gospel Missionary Union, who had now joined their team, thought it right to try and meet up with the Aucas. Nate had found a suitable flat beach on the Curray River where he could land his Piper Family Cruiser. Then, on January 3, Nate landed Jim, Ed, Roger and Pete in a number of shuttle flights, on the beach. There they built a tree house and looked forward to meeting the Aucas from the neighboring jungle. The plane then flew over the Aucas and they could hardly believe their ears when they were heard the words in their own language: "We are on the Curray." "Come and see us." To the delight of the missionaries three young Aucas, two men and one woman, visited them. The visit seemed to be a total success. They gave them hamburgers and lemonade, and one of the Aucas, named "George" by the missionaries, even went for a ride in the plane. However, three days later, Nate saw ten Aucas leaving their Indian village heading for their airstrip. Nate returned to the other four with this news. Together they all sang:

We rest on Thee, our Shield and our
  Defender,
We go not forth alone against the foe.
Strong in Thy strength, safe in thy keeping
  tender,
We rest on Thee, and in Thy name we go.

Yea, in Thy name, O Captain of Salvation,
In Thy blest name, all other names above,
Jesus our Righteousness, our sure
  Foundation,
Our Prince of Glory, and our King of Love.

We go in faith, our own great weakness
  feeling,
And needing more each day Thy grace to
  know,
Yet from our hearts a song of triumph
  pealing,
We rest on Thee, and in Thy name we go.

We rest on Thee, our Shield and our
  Defender,
Thine is the battle, Thine shall be the praise
When passing through the gates of pearly
  splendor,
Victors, we rest with Thee through endless
  days.

The five missionaries did not use the guns they had, but were speared to death by the primitive wooden spears of these ten Aucas. Their plane was destroyed.
Editor

UPDATE ON THE AUCA INDIANS
Waorani New Testament

When the first translators came to Ecuador and were introduced to the President as people interested in minority groups, they were warned to avoid the notorious Waorani (Auca) Indians. When the President's plane had flown over Waorani territory, they had thrown spears at it. But he was surprised by the bold reply, "When God opens the door, it will be safe to go."

Five young men were killed at the hands of the Waorani when they made their first approach. But after much prayer and persistence their confidence was gained, translation began, and a number of them became Christians.

When the President heard that Waoranis (of all people) had become Christians he arranged to visit some of them. His plane landed in a clearing in the jungle, where a group of Waorani men were standing quietly waiting for him. When they were presented to the President they were wide-eyed with astonishment, because he was completely bald! One of them stepped forward with his arm stretched out in front of him. Not knowing quite what was coming, the President backed away, but the man just wanted to rub the top of the President's head!

The President for his part, amazed at the change in the Waorani people, turned to the translator and said, "Do you really think these people can understand theology?"

"Ask them," came the wise reply.

So the President addressed one of them, "What do you know about Jesus?" Immediately the man's eyes lit up and for a good thirty minutes he preached the gospel to the President of the Republic.

Back in the capital, the President summoned his cabinet to meet the translator. "I was a believer, but I have wandered away from the Truth," he said. Turning to his cabinet ministers, he asked them, one by one, "What about you?" After much embarrassment, the President resumed, "This man will tell you about the power that is transforming the people in our jungle."

Last month, thirteen people were baptized and the Waorani New Testament was presented to the people. Two of the pastors present were involved in the deaths of the missionaries thirty-six years before. One Waorani leader said in his speech, "We no longer want to live like those who killed each other and outsiders. We want to live by what God says. Ever since I was a small boy I have heard that we were going to get this book; now we have it."

Press release, June 1992, from Wycliffe Bible Translators

Columbia
Señor Juan P. Coy

After being in jail for two weeks, Pedro Moreno was released without having signed, as had been demanded by the mayor, a statement that he would not return to that region to preach the Gospel. Early next morning, after his release, Pedro, together with others of the believers in Saboya, received word that Senor Juan P. Coy, who had been in jail with Pedro for one day, had been severely wounded in three places. Pedro and the wounded man's brother-in-law went to the home of Senor Coy and found him in agony. He had been shot in the morning when he went out to attend to the cattle. They were able to ask him a few questions, and then took him to Chiquinquira to the doctor, but while they were entering the town he died.

When Pedro returned to Saboya where he had been threatened in the street by the priest who told the people to stone him. Three policemen refused him protection, but finally two stood by him. In company with a brother of the dead man, we were able to obtain an interview with the Minister of Justice and he sent a special investigator to the scene of the happening. We have been able to write, speak to, and pray with these people, and the words of consolation given to them were from Colossians 1:24, "Who now rejoice in my suffering for you, and fill up that which is behind of the afflictions of Christ in my flesh for his body's sake, which is the Church." These people are not really the imprisoned, the wounded, and the killed of the enemies of the Gospel, but sufferers with Jesus, and they are filling up his sufferings on behalf of the Church in that region, and we expect to see it work mightily for the building up of the Church and the salvation of still more unbelievers.

Pat and Helen Symes, WorldWide, March 1958

More twentieth century martyrs

September 1999

According to Pastor Hector Pardo, at least 25 evangelical pastors have been killed and 300 churches have been closed in the past six months. The majority of the murdered pastors belonged to Assembly of God churches.

June/July, 1999

Five guerrillas wearing masks kidnaped evangelical Hector Chavez, 24, from his home in Galindo on June 22 demanding that $10,000 be paid as ransom. The guerrillas released Chavez three weeks later after an anonymous benefactor gave the guerrillas $2,500.

May 8, 1999

Evangelical Pastor Rincon Galindo, his wife, her sister, and a neighbor were murdered by perpetrators unknown in Cali.

May 19, 1997

Two employees of the Center for Investigation and Popular Education, a Jesuit-run human rights monitoring group, were murdered.

Editor

San Salvador

Archbishop Romero

Romero was shot as he said mass in 1980 in San Salvador.

"If they succeed in killing me, I pardon and bless those who do the deed." Archbishop Romero

"Martyrdom is considered by the church to be an eminent grace and the supreme proof of charity." Vatican II

When Romero became Archbishop of San Salvador in 1977 few expected that he would become an internationally known opponent of the oppressive regime that killed people and priests alike. Romero preferred to champion the status quo and the establishment and viewed some of the more revolutionary theological ideas with deep suspicion. This all changed when a close friend of Romero's, Rutilio Grande, was assassinated. Grande worked with some young Jesuits among 30,000 peasants in the parish of Aguilares. The peasants were ruthlessly exploited, often having no land of their own, and were forced to work for tiny wages during the cane harvest. In the eyes of those in power Grande's "crime" was his suggestion that the peasants should become "delegates of the Word". When they organized themselves into small communities and read the Bible together for the first time they discovered that God hated injustice, was on the side of the poor, and that a laborer is worthy of his hire. Romero learned about the details of Grande's assassination. As Grande walked through a sugar cane field, with a 15-year-old teenager and an old man a rain of bullets fell on them and killed them in the open field.

Romero's change of attitude to those in ecclesiastical and government authority underwent a sea change. Commenting on this some writers have called this his "conversion". Although Archbishop Romero was even-handed in his condemnation of evil government practices, and violent guerrilla attacks, he became identified as the voice of the poor. Six weeks before he was killed, on 2nd February 1980 he told a conference of Latin American bishops about the rampant injustice and inhumane treatment of poor people in his country. He told them that defending the poor now brought about something new in their church – persecution. He went on to enumerate some of the atrocities of the past three years: 6 priests killed as martyrs, 50 priests attacked; many others tortured and expelled. Hundreds and even thousands of peasants, delegates of the Word, catechists, assassinated or tortured. Romero emphasized how the ordinary poor Christian people bore the brunt of these persecutions.

On the night before he was assassinated, Romero pleaded with the army, in a radio broadcast, "Stop the oppression." He did not mince his words, he even ordered them in God's name to stop the killings.

On March 24, 1980, Archbishop Romero was celebrating mass in a hospital in San Salvador. The reading from the gospel during the service had been, "Jesus replied: "The hour has come for the Son of Man to be glorified. I tell you the truth, unless a grain of wheat falls to the ground and dies, it remains only a single seed. But if it dies, it produces many seeds. The man who loves his life will lose it, while the man who hates his life in this world will keep it for eternal life" (John 12:23-25, NIV). Romero took these words as the text of his sermon. He pointed out how his own work was bound to bring risks to his own personal safety, but that anyone who is killed in Christ's service is just like the grain of wheat. It dies. But the reality is that it only appears to die. He continued: "If they kill me I shall rise again in the Salvadorean people. As a pastor, I am obliged by divine decree to give my life for those I love – for all Salvadoreans, even for those who may be about to kill me. From this moment I offer my blood to God for the redemption and resurrection of El Salvador."

Soon after saying these words, Romero was gunned down on the steps of the altar. The bullets had hit him in the stomach. He was rushed into the emergency area of the hospital, but died within minutes.

Editor

AFRICA

ALGERIA

Over one hundred killed

Four hundred people in isolated villages in the Relizane region were killed by Islamic extremists on the first night of Ramadan. Most of the victims had their throats slit or were decapitated. The BBC reported that more than one hundred people were killed in other incidents over that weekend.

Report based on International Christian Concern, Press Release, December 30, 1997

EGYPT

TWO YOUNG CHRISTIAN MEN

August 14, 1998

Two young Christian men were killed in the village of El-Kosheh, Dar Assalam and Governate of Soha, Egypt. The local Coptic Bishop reported that the consensus of the village was that the killers were three Muslim men who were known to police. The police made no effort to apprehend these individuals but rather rounded up nearly 1,200 Christians, including men, women, and children, during the course of the following week. During their detainment, it is reported that these people suffered verbal abuse and physical abuse that included electrical shock, whippings, beatings, and being hung from their feet for extended periods of time. It is believed much of this activity was aimed at obtaining false confessions to the murders. It was been reported that 11 year-old Romani Boctor was suspended from a spinning ceiling fan for several hours in an attempt to get his father to confess to the murders. It is also reported that a fourteen-month-old baby was beaten in front of her mother to get the mother to confess.

Report based on International Christian Concern, Press Release

COPTIC CHRISTIAN FAKHRI AYYAD MUS'AD

July 26, 2000

Coptic Christian Fakhri Ayyad Mus'ad was shot to death when local Muslims discovered he was building a church in a nearby field. Three other men were also injured.

Based on International Christian Concern, Press Release

MOZAMBIQUE

BERNARD MIZEKI, CATECHIST AND MARTYR IN AFRICA

18 June 1896

Bernard Mizeki was born in Portuguese East Africa (Mozambique) in about 1861. When he was twelve or a little older, he left his home and went to Capetown, South Africa, where for the next ten years he worked as a laborer, living in the slums of Capetown, but (perceiving the disastrous effects of drunkenness on many workers in the slums) firmly refusing to drink alcohol, and remaining largely uncorrupted by his surroundings. After his day's work, he attended night classes at an Anglican school. Under the influence of his teachers, from the Society of Saint John the Evangelist (SSJE, an Anglican religious order for men, popularly called the Cowley Fathers), he became a Christian and was baptized on 9 March 1886. Besides the fundamentals of European schooling, he mastered English, French, high Dutch, and at least eight local African languages. In time he would be an invaluable assistant when the Anglican church began translating its sacred texts into African languages.

After graduating from the school, he accompanied Bishop Knight-Bruce to Mashonaland, a tribal area in Southern Rhodesia (now Zimbabwe), to work there as a lay catechist. In 1891 the bishop assigned him to Nhowe, the village of paramount-chief Mangwende, and there he built a mission-complex. He prayed the Anglican hours each day, tended his subsistence garden, studied the local language (which he mastered better than any other foreigner in his day), and cultivated friendships with the villagers. He eventually opened a school, and won the hearts of many of the Mashona through his love for their children.

He moved his mission complex up onto a nearby plateau, next to a grove of trees sacred to the ancestral spirits of the Mashona. Although he had the chief's permission, he angered the local religious leaders when he cut some of the trees down and carved crosses into others. Although he opposed some local traditional religious customs, Bernard was very attentive to the nuances of the Shona Spirit religion. He developed an approach that built on people's already monotheistic faith in one God, Mwari, and on their sensitivity to spirit life, while at the same time he forthrightly proclaimed the Christ. Over the next five years (1891-1896), the mission at Nhowe produced an abundance of converts.

Many black African nationalists regarded all missionaries as working for the European colonial governments. During an uprising in 1896, Bernard was warned to flee. He refused, since he did not regard himself as working for anyone but Christ, and he would not desert his converts or his post. On 18 June 1896, he was fatally speared outside his hut. His wife and a helper went to get food and blankets for him. They later reported that, from a distance, they saw a blinding light on the hillside where he had been lying, and heard a rushing sound, as though of many wings. When they returned to the spot his body had disappeared. The place of his death has become a focus of great devotion for Anglicans and other Christians, and one of the greatest of all Christian festivals in Africa takes place there every year around the feast day that marks the anniversary of his martyrdom, June 18.
James Kiefer, Christian Biographies, By kind permission

RUANDA
500,000 Christian martyrs

Altogether, the 1993-1995 civil unrest in the area (of Ruanda) has been responsible for over 300,000 refugees. This displacement is causing stress on all forms of humanitarian relief and ministry in Burundi, and in the region generally. But worse, many thousands have been killed as what we are defining as Christian martyrs. We calculate that, following our definition of a martyr as "a believer in Christ who loses his or her life, prematurely, in a situation of witness, as a result of human hostility," the above events have resulted in over 500,000 more Christian martyrs, including many pastors, priests, church members, Bible society associates, and lay leaders of all kinds.
Global Monitor, August 1996

UGANDA
CATHOLIC AND PROTESTANT MARTYRS

"Nothing is more acceptable to God, and more beneficial to the soul, than to suffer for the sake of Christ." The Imitation of Christ, ascribed to Thomas à Kempis

Cardinal Lavigerie set about the evangelization of equatorial Africa by sending, in 1878, ten French White Fathers, into the interior of Africa, as far as the great lakes. Five of these missionaries established a base at Rubaga in Buganda [Uganda], where a number of slaves, children and pages from king Mwanga's court turned to the Christian faith.

However, the ambitions of European colonialization arrived in Africa at the same time as these missionaries. Mwanga decided to oppose them both. A local prophecy predicted that an invader from the east would "devour" Buganda. Unfortunately Mwanga identified the traveling Anglican Bishop Hannington as this invader and had him killed [see entry on James Hannington].

The leader of the African Christians in Rubaga, a man called Joseph Mukasa, was also the king's chief page, and acted as the king's counselor. King Mwanga became most upset when Joseph managed to spirit away the catechumens whenever he wanted to indulge in his homosexual activities with them. The king then thought of Joseph as a rival king to him. When the king had a fever Joseph had given him a pill to swallow, but the king's fever grew worse. When the king recovered he accused Joseph of attempting to poison him and ordered the executioner to burn Joseph. The executioner, out of love for Joseph, beheaded him, before burning his body. Joseph's last words to the executioner were, "Tell Mwanga that I forgive him for killing me for no good reason." Thus, Joseph became the first Catholic martyr in Uganda, being martyred on 15th November, 1885.

The number of pages at king Mwanga's court who embraced Christianity greatly upset the king. They were nicknamed "the praying ones" and were accused of being unpatriotic because they refused to take part in some of the ancestral customs and to indulge in any of the king's homosexual practices.

In May, 1886, Mwanga had over forty Christians put to death. On May 27 "the praying ones" were tied up and thrown into little huts, at Namugongo, while Mwanga's men collected wood for their execution. The older Christians encouraged the younger Christians, saying, "Do not be afraid. Our Christian friends are with the Lord. We shall soon join them." Among the Christian prisoners were Abudala, a Muslim, and Aliwali, who did not pray. Two of the Anglicans told their guards about Abudala and Aliwali and they were set free.

Editor

The twenty-six Catholic and Protestant martyrs of Uganda

The sixteen Catholic martyrs were young men or youths:

NAME	AGE
Luke Banabakintu	34
Bruno Serunkuma	30
James Buzabaliawo	29
Charles Lwanga	?
Adolph Mukasa Ludigo	early 20s
Anatole Kiriggwajjo	?
Mukasa Kiriwawanvu	?
Achilles Kiwanuka	18
Ambrose Kibuka	18
Gyavira	17
Mugagga	17
Mbaga Tuzinde	17
Denis Kamyuka	?
Simeon Sebutta	13-15
Charles Werabe	?
Kisito	?

The ten Anglican martyrs were also young men or youths:

NAME	COMMENT
Kiwanuka	
Mukasa	
Lwanga	Young pages
Dani Nnakabanda	
Mubi	
Noah Walukagga	The king's chief smith
Kifamunyanya	
Frederick Kizza	
Alexander Kadoko	Brother of Bruno Serunkuma
Albert Munyagabyanyo	

On the evening of June 2 the sixteen Christians heard the tam tam and death chants and realized what would follow in the morning. The Anglicans and Catholics encouraged each other and their one hundred executioners, with their faces painted red and black, dressed in animal skins and headdresses, were amazed that the Christian martyrs approached death as if it was a festival. The sixteen martyrs, bound hand and foot, were wrapped up in reeds, placed on top of a great mound of wood. Then more wood was placed on top of them and set alight so that the whole spectacle looked like a giant hut on fire.

Editor

James Hannington

"I am about to die for the Baganda and have purchased the road to them with my life." (Bishop Hannington's last words)

The Church Missionary Society decided, in 1884, that the mission churches of Eastern Equatorial Africa should be placed in the hands of a bishop. The one they chose, James Hannington, said at his farewell meeting, that he intended to became "a very troublesome bishop". Hannington arrived in Freetown, the diocesan headquarters, in January 1885, where he discovered that 12 clergy and 11 lay workers looked after all the CMS stations. Hannington consecrated the first African CMS deacons in East Africa as he passionately believed that educated Africans should not be relegated to menial work. When he met violent African chiefs who looked to him for guns Hannington persuaded them to receive a Christian teaching instead.

Hannington longed to travel to Uganda, a journey which had caused him to have a breakdown three years earlier on his previous visit to Africa. As he pondered his plans, he found himself reading words from Psalm 146, "The Lord preserveth the strangers." He took this to be a message from God and gathered together his 200 porters for his 600 mile journey. After Hannington tried to complete the last part of the journey with a party of 50 men, he himself was attacked and captured by twenty men from the Mwanga tribe. That night Hannington recorded in his dairy that he "sang 'Safe in the Arms of Jesus' and then laughed at the very agony of my situation." Hannington was kept in an airless hut for eight days and then taken out to an open space where he was surrounded by his own men. Hannington thought that they were going to be allowed to proceed. But they were attacked and killed by the Mwanga tribe, and only four people escaped with their lives, and they were only spared so that they could explain how Hannington's luggage could be opened. According to one of these four men, Hannington's last words were, "I am about to die for the Baganda and have purchased the road to them with my life.'

Editor

JAMES HANNINGTON AND THE MARTYRS OF UGANDA

29 October 1885

Among the new nations of Africa, Uganda is the most predominantly Christian. Mission work began there in the 1870's with the favor of King Mutesa, who died in 1884. However, his son and successor, King Mwanga, opposed all foreign presence, including the missions.

James Hannington, born 1847, was sent out from England in 1884 by the Anglican Church as missionary Bishop of Eastern Equatorial Africa. As he was traveling toward Uganda, he was apprehended by emissaries of King Mwanga. He and his companions were brutally treated and, a week later, 29 October 1885, most of them were put to death. Hannington's last words were: "Go tell your master that I have purchased the road to Uganda with my blood."

The first native martyr was the Roman Catholic Joseph Mkasa Balikuddembe, who was beheaded after having rebuked the king for his debauchery and for the murder of Bishop Hannington. On 3 June 1886 (see Biography), a group of 32 men and boys, 22 Roman Catholic and 10 Anglican, were burned at the stake. Most of them were young pages in Mwanga's household, from their head-man, Charles Lwanga, to the thirteen-year-old Kizito, who went to his death "laughing and chattering." These and many other Ugandan Christians suffered for their faith then and in the next few years.

In 1977, the Anglican Archbishop Janani Luwum and many other Christians suffered death for their faith under the tyrant Idi Amin.

Thanks largely to their common heritage of suffering for their Master, Christians of various communions in Uganda have always been on excellent terms.

James Kiefer, Christian Biographies, By kind permission

THE MARTYRS OF UGANDA

3 June 1886

On 3 June 1886, thirty-two young men, pages of the court of King Mwanga of Buganda, were burned to death at Namugongo for their refusal to renounce Christianity. In the following months many other Christians throughout the country died by spear or fire for their faith.

These martyrdoms totally changed the dynamic of Christian growth in Uganda. Introduced by a handful of Anglican and Roman missionaries after 1877, the Christian faith had been preached only to the immediate members of the court, by order of King Mutesa. His successor, Mwanga, became increasingly angry as he realized that the first converts put loyalty to Christ above the traditional loyalty to the king. Martyrdoms began in 1885. Mwanga first forbade anyone to go near a Christian mission on pain of death, but finding himself unable to cool the ardor of the converts, resolved to wipe out Christianity.

The Namugongo martyrdoms produced a

result entirely opposite to Mwanga's intentions. The example of these martyrs, who walked to their deaths singing hymns and praying for their enemies, so inspired many of the bystanders that they began to seek instruction from the remaining Christians. Within a few years the original handful of converts had multiplied many times and spread far beyond the court. The martyrs had left the indelible impression that Christianity was truly African, not simply a white man's religion. Most of the missionary work was carried out by Africans rather than by white missionaries, and Christianity spread steadily. Uganda now has the largest percentage of professed Christians of any nation in Africa.

Several years ago I heard an African clergyman, born of pagan parents, tell of his conversion. He said:

One afternoon I was bicycling along a road and met a young man about my own age bicycling in the opposite direction. He promptly turned about and began to ride beside me and to talk. He spoke with great enthusiasm about Jesus, whom I had never heard of before, and how He had destroyed the power of death and evil by dying and rising again, and how He was God become man to reconcile man with God. I heard what my companion had to say, and before we parted I had accepted Jesus Christ as my Lord and Savior. Now, the young man who preached the Good News of Jesus Christ to me that afternoon had himself heard of Jesus for the first time that morning.

Renewed persecution of Christians in the 1970's by the military dictatorship of Idi Amin proved the vitality of the example of the Namugongo martyrs. Among the thousands of new martyrs, both Anglican and Roman, was Janani Luwum, Archbishop of the (Anglican) Church of Uganda.

James Kiefer, Christian Biographies, By kind permission

Martyrdom of Archbishop Luwum (1)

Janani Luwum, Archbishop of Uganda, Martyr

Born: 1922, martyred 16 Feb. 1977, Aged 54 or 55

The Church in Uganda began with the deaths of martyrs. Around 1900, Uganda became a British protectorate, with the chief of the Buganda tribe as nominal ruler, and with several other tribes included in the protectorate. In 1962 Uganda became an independent country within the British Commonwealth, with the Bugandan chief as president and Milton Obote, of the Lango tribe, as Prime Minister. In 1966, Obote took full control of the government. In 1971, he was overthrown by General Idi Amin, Chief of Staff of the Armed Forces. Almost immediately, he began a policy of repression, arresting anyone suspected of not supporting him. Hundreds of soldiers from the Lango and Acholi tribes were shot down in their barracks. Amin ordered the expulsion of the Asian population of Uganda, about 55,000 persons, mostly small shopkeepers from India and Pakistan. Over the next few years, many Christians were killed for various offenses. A preacher who read over the radio a Psalm which mentioned Israel was shot for this in 1972.

Early in 1977, there was a small army rebellion that was put down with only seven men dead. However, Amin determined to stamp out all traces of dissent. His men killed thousands, including the entire population of Milton Obote's home village. On Sunday, 30 January, Bishop Festo Kivengere preached on "The Preciousness of Life" to an audience including many high government officials. He denounced the arbitrary bloodletting, and accused the government of abusing the authority that God had entrusted to it. The government responded on the following Saturday (5 February) by an early (1:30am) raid on the home of the Archbishop, Janani Luwum, ostensibly to search for hidden stores of weapons. The Archbishop called on President Amin to deliver a note of protest at the policies of arbitrary killings and the unexplained disappearances of many persons. Amin accused the Archbishop of treason, produced a document supposedly by former President Obote attesting his guilt, and had the Archbishop and two

Cabinet members (both committed Christians) arrested and held for military trial. The three met briefly with four other prisoners who were awaiting execution, and were permitted to pray with them briefly. Then the three were placed in a Land Rover and not seen alive again by their friends. The government story is that one of the prisoners tried to seize control of the vehicle and that it was wrecked and the passengers killed. The story believed by the Archbishop's supporters is that he refused to sign a confession, was beaten and otherwise abused, and finally shot. His body was placed in a sealed coffin and sent to his native village for burial there. However, the villagers opened the coffin and discovered the bullet holes. In the capital city of Kampala a crowd of about 4,500 gathered for a memorial service beside the grave that had been prepared for him next to that of the martyred bishop Hannington. In Nairobi, the capital of nearby Kenya, about 10,000 gathered for another memorial service. Bishop Kivengere was informed that he was about to be arrested, and he and his family fled to Kenya, as did the widow and orphans of Archbishop Luwum.

The following June, about 25,000 Ugandans came to the capital to celebrate the centennial of the first preaching of the Gospel in their country, among the participants were many who had abandoned Christianity, but who had returned to their Faith as a result of seeing the courage of Archbishop Luwum and his companions in the face of death.

James Kiefer, Christian Biographies, By kind permission

Martyrdom of Archbishop Luwum (2)

Archbishop Janani Luwum was assassinated on the orders of Idi "Papa" Amin, in 1977.

"I am the Archbishop. I must stay." (Archbishop Luwum, replying to the suggestion that he should escape from Amin.)

Archbishop Luwum's assassination was the spur that made the Dean and Chapter of Canterbury Cathedral set aside a special chapel in Canterbury Cathedral to commemorate twentieth-century Christian martyrs.

Idi Amin and his reign of terror in Uganda came to a head in February 1977 when he ordered the massacre of thousands of supporters, both soldiers and civilians, of the former president Milton Obote. However it was Amin's murder of the Archbishop of Uganda, Janani Luwum, along with two other Christians, former cabinet ministers, that hit the headlines around the world and prompted Time magazine to call Amin "The Wild Beast of Africa".

Luwum did not hesitate to publicly point out the evils of Amin's regime. Amin retaliated. Eight of his soldiers burst into the Archbishop's home at 1.30 on Saturday morning, while the Archbishop and his wife were in bed. They ransacked his house, on the pretext of looking for hidden guns. As one soldiers pressed a gun into the archbishop's stomach he told the soldiers that the only armament he had was the Bible. He also told them that he prayed for the President, and prayed that he would learn to rule Uganda without destroying it.

The Anglican bishops sent a very strongly worded letter to Amin stating: "We are deeply disturbed. In the history of our country such an incident in the Church has never before occurred. This is a climax of what has been constantly happening to our Christians. We have buried many who have died as a result of being shot and there are many more whose bodies have not yet been found; yet their disappearance is connected with the activities of some members of the Security Forces." Archbishop Luwum delivered the letter to President Amin personally on February 12. Amin gave the archbishop a cup of tea but accused him of plotting to overthrow him and informed him that a secret supply of arms had been found near his house. On the 16th of February Amin angrily summoned Luwum and six of his bishops. After a two-hour wait in the blazing sun Luwum was subjected to a mock "trial" in front of 3,000 soldiers. With a cache of arms on display in front of him the archbishop was accused of striking a deal with Obote. The vice-President, who was orchestrating the trial, called out: "These men are traitors. What should be done with them?'

The obedient soldiers, baying for blood, shouted back, "Kill them. Kill them." Amin said that the archbishop with the two former cabinet ministers would be taken away and given military trials. When Archbishop Luwum left Bishop Festo Kivengere for the last time he told him something that he had not previously shared with him. Three days before a girl had come to the archbishop and told him about a conversation she had overheard in which she heard that the archbishop was on the security forces' death list. She had advised the archbishop to escape but he told her kindly, "I cannot. I am the Archbishop. I must stay.'

Amin called them in for questioning. Later Bishop Festo Kivengere saw a Mercedes Benz race pass him with the two government ministers, Erinayo Oryema and Oboth Ofumbi, and the archbishop inside. The following morning Radio Uganda announced that the three of them had been killed in a car accident: "The archbishop and two ministers were killed in an automobile accident." Nobody believed the official version of the archbishop's death as it became known on 17th February.

The true story of Luwum's death started in a torture room where the archbishop was taken with the two Christian cabinet ministers. There, they found four other men who were condemned prisoners. Luwum puts his hands on each of the men's heads as he prayed for them. From this room the archbishop and cabinet ministers were forced into a Land Rover and taken to a secret location outside the capital. Amin appeared later and demanded that the archbishop should sign a confession about his involvement in a plot to overthrow him. The archbishop constantly refused and was eventually stripped of his clothes and made to lie on the floor. Amin then ordered two soldiers to whip the archbishop mercilessly. Luwum did not sign the confession, but prayed for his torturers. Amin, in a fit of rage, hit out at the archbishop and forced the soldier to carry out perverted sexual acts with the archbishop before he shot the archbishop through the heart twice with his own revolver.

Editor

Madagascar Persecutions in the 19th Century

Agents of the London Missionary Society reached Madagascar in 1818, and received a most cordial welcome from this enlightened monarch. They reduced its language to writing, arranged its grammar, and translated the Holy Scriptures. In the space of ten years 15,000 natives could read, and a large number write, while multitudes were converted to Christianity. But in 1828 a reaction set in led by the monarch's wife. The schools were closed, the old regime reinstated, and the idol keepers once more held their pernicious sway over the heathen. In 1835 it was enacted that no Malagasy should profess Christianity, and the missionaries are the foreign artisans were ejected from the island. On their departure, many who were suspected of being Christians had to pass through the ordeal of drinking the tanjena, or poison water, and the following year several others were punished by fine, imprisonment, and perpetual slavery.

The first Christian martyr suffered in 1837 and during the last twenty-six years more than a hundred martyrs have been added to the Church triumphant. The missionaries were expelled in 1836, but they left behind them the oracles of God. The history of Christianity in this island is remarkable as the secretly circulated Word of God maintained spiritual life in the island. After the exile of the teachers various persecutions broke out. The converts wandered about in the deserts and caves of the earth, until, in 1842, sixteen of them were arrested while trying to escape from the island, and nine of them were put to death in the capital. But, as of old times, the wrath of man fulfilled the purposes of God, and general attention was thus drawn to the subject of the Christian religion. In 1846 the

Crown Prince renounced heathenism, and was baptized, and proved himself a faithful protector. His conversion greatly angered the queen mother, who regarded him as the victim of witchcraft, and vented her wrath in the violent persecution of 1849, when more than 2,000 people were mulcted in some form or other, and many put to death. We subjoin some details, extracted from the work of the Rev William Ellis, who visited Madagascar in 1853, 1854, and 1856:

"The authorities in Madagascar, who sought, by torture and death, to extinguish the Christian faith, by whatever motives they may have been actuated, only imitated the Diocletians of the early ages, and the Alvas, the Medicis, and the Marys of more recent times, and with corresponding results in the invincible constancy of those who fell, and the subsequent fruits of the imperishable seed which was scattered in the martyrs' blood. The following verbatim statements refer to the severe persecution in 1849:

On 14th March, 1849 the officer before whom the Christians were examined, said, "Do you pray to the sun, or the moon, or the earth?"

R—— answered, "I do not pray to these, for the hand of God made them."

"Do you pray to the twelve mountains that are sacred?"

R—— answered, "I do not pray to them, for they are mountains."

"Do you pray to the idols that render sacred the kings?"

R——: "I do not pray to them, for the hand of man made them."

"Do you pray to the ancestors of the sovereigns?"

R——: "Kings and rulers are given by God that we should serve and obey them, and render them homage. Nevertheless, they are only men like ourselves. When we pray, we pray to God alone."

"You make distinct and observe the Sabbath-day."

R——: "This is the day of the great God; for in six days the Lord made all his works. But God rested on the seventh, and he caused it to be holy; and I rest or keep sacred that day."

And in similar manner answered all the Christians. Before dawn on the following day the people assembled at A——y. Then they took the eighteen brethren that chose God and bound them hand and foot, and tied each of them to a pole, wrapped in mats, and placed them with the other prisoners. When the officers, and troops, and judges arrived, they read over the names of each class of prisoner, and then placed them by themselves, and stationed around them soldiers with muskets and spears; and the sentences were then delivered, consigning some to fine and confiscation, others to slavery, others to prison and chains, some to flogging, and eighteen to death – four to be burnt, and fourteen to be hurled from the rocky precipice, and afterwards burnt to ashes.

And the eighteen appointed to die, as they sat on the ground, surrounded by the soldiers, sang this hymn:

When I shall die, and leave my friends
When they shall weep for me,
When departed has my life,
Then I shall be happy.

After this hymn they sang the hymn that ended, "When I shall behold him rejoicing in the heavens."

And when the sentences were all pronounced, and the officer was about to return to the chief authorities, the four sentenced to be burned requested him to ask that they might be killed first, and then burned; but they were burned alive. When the officer was gone, they took those eighteen away to put them to death. The fourteen they tied by their hands and their feet to long poles, and carried on men's shoulders. And these brethren prayed and spoke to the people as they were being carried along. And some who beheld them said that their faces were like the faces of angels. And when they came to the top of Nampaminarina, they cast them down, and their bodies were afterwards dragged to the other end of the capital, to be burned with the bodies of those who were burned alive.

And as they took the four that were burned alive to the place of execution, these Christians sang the 90th hymn, beginning,

"When our hearts are troubled," each verse ending with "Then remember us." Thus they sang on the road. And when they came to Faravohitra, there they burned them, fixed between split bars. And there was a rainbow in the heavens at the time, close to the place of burning. Then they sang the hymn:

There is a blessed land,
Making most happy;
Never shall the rest depart,
Nor cause of trouble come.

That was the hymn they sang after they were in the fire. Then they prayed, saying, "O Lord, receive our spirits, for thy love to us has caused this to come to us; and lay not this sin to their charge." Thus they prayed as long as they had any life. Then they died; but softly, gently: indeed, gently was the going forth of their life. And astonished were all the people around that beheld the burning of them there.'"'

John Foxe, The Book of Martyrs, revised with notes and an appendix by W. Bramley-Moore, London, 1869, pp 694-698

Swaziland
Swazi Tidings

The latest news from Swaziland is that all stations appear to be in good order, with one exception of Mount Hermon, where Mr and Mrs Wehmeyer have been working. The native Christians have been persecuted, and in some case have had to lay down their lives: some have given way under the very severe test, but the majority remained true to God. . . .

On April 3 the messenger arrived at Ezulwioni (Miss Harris and Miss Thomson's Station).

He found Jan, the evangelist, in good health and the place generally in good condition, but alas, the few Christians had sadly gone back. They were very weak in the faith, and we, in our highly favored circumstances, little know what fearful testing and persecution they might have had to go through by remaining faithful to their Lord.

As an instance of this, we hear that one native Christian living not far from Ezulwini Station was murdered, and Jan, our evangelist, was afraid for his own life at the hands of those bloodthirsty Swazis, sent forth to do such awful work.

We are very sorry to hear from our friend Mr Dawson, of the Alliance Mission, Swaziland, that his house has been broken into, and everything wantonly destroyed. This was the work of the heathen Swazis. A lady worker in the same mission, named Miss Moe, who remained in the country during the war, has wonderfully proved God's faithful care. A letter was received from her recently saying that she had been imprisoned in Pietretief, a small town in the Transvaal, for two months, but was then allowed to return to her station in Swaziland, where God has greatly used her. She gives the sad details of the murder of a Christian native who lived near Ezulwini. The wild, heathen Swazis came upon him to kill him. He besought them to take his cattle, and spare his wife and himself. This they refused to do, and he then prayed to God. As the "Amen" came from his lips, they stabbed him to death.

How sad, and yet what a glorious home-going! "The noble army of martyrs praise thee," and this one has entered the presence of the King, having been "faithful unto death". His wife escaped to the hills.

And so it has gone on – month after month – this terrible "killing off." The orders given to the murderers were that they were to kill off every one, old and young, so that there should be on one left to tell the white people when they returned.

This ends our report, and gives the condition of things up to 12 May. We pray that ere long God will open up the way for our return to work among them again.

George F. Gale, Durban, Natal, 22 August, 1900. Printed in The South African Pioneer, October, 1900, published by Africa Evangelical Fellowship

Liberia
Tom and June Jackson

The report in the Liberian Daily Observer was brief and to the point. "An American national and his British wife have been reported killed during fighting between government troops and rebel forces in Nimba County. The two reported killed have been identified as missionary Thomas K. Jackson and his wife June M. Jackson. Mr and Mrs Jackson were killed in fighting near Bahn City last Saturday, March 24th. The two were members of Liberia Inland Church.'

Tom Jackson left Canada for Liberia on 21 February 1941. On the same boat was another WEC candidate, Billie Price, unknown to him at that time. However, in 1943 they were married and assigned to Bahn where they began a life-long ministry to the Gio people. Tom was a brilliant linguist and translator and their loving and happy home was used in outreach and fellowship.

For a few years Tom took up two pastorates in the States because of deterioration in Billie's health. In 1978 Billie was called home and Tom returned to his other beloved land, Liberia.

There, in 1980, he married British Weccer June Hobley, also a gifted translator. Between them they spoke fluently Bassa, Gio and Mano and completed the translation of the New Testament in each of these languages. At the time of their death they were working on Old Testament books.

The Jacksons were in Monrovia on business when hostilities began with the invasion of Nimba Country on 24 December. In spite of dangers they decided to return to Bahn on 10 January.

"We had sought the Lord and he had give us peace," Tom wrote in his last newsletter dated 14 January. "It was so right for us to come as we have been able to help and reassure our people.'

Tom and June now rejoice together in glory.

Worldwide, July/August, 1990, published by Worldwide Evangelization Crusade

Congo

Winnie Davies, aged 51, 1967

Clutching her Bible, she staggered at the head of the rebel column.

It was their vain attempt to escape the Congolese troops. After the skirmish Winnie Davies (51) was beyond the reach of further suffering. General Ngalo had killed her – and fled. It was May 17th, 1967.

Winnie was born in Coedpoeth, Denbighshire, and educated at Penygelli. She became secretary to a dental surgeon, and later trained as a nurse, gaining her SRN, SRFN, and CMB. From 1941, she was for two years a student of the Emmanuel Bible College, Birkenhead, and on July 25th, 1946 sailed for Congo with Worldwide Evangelization Crusade. Posted early to Nebobongo, she reopened the maternity center closed by the home-call of Mrs Edith Moules. In 1961, after an evacuation of missionaries from Congo, she accepted the invitation of the Church at Opienge to return. The believers were aware of the danger and promised to guard her. On July 17th, 1964 Mr Arthur Scott left Opienge and was the last Crusader to see her alive.

The Simba rebellion took her into captivity a few weeks later. At irregular intervals it was reported that she was alive, and nationwide prayer was focused for her release. It is now known that she was killed on May 27th, 1967.

In addition to Winnie Davies the following four missionaries were killed, in 1964, in this uprising: Jim Rodger, Bill McChesney, Cyril Taylor and Muriel Harman.

Editor

Report on the death of a Protestant missionary by a Dutch Roman Catholic missionary

Thirty-four months of captivity

The last European in the hands of the Congo Rebels was Reverend Father Alphonse Strijbosh, a Dutch Roman Catholic missionary, freed by the Congolese Army on May 27th, 1967.

Alphonse Strijbosh gave the only details we shall ever be likely to know about Winnie's captivity and death. At the airport in Kinshasa, Congo, where he was in transit to Brussels, he reported:

Miss Davies had served as a midwife in the Rebel Camp. The General Gaston Ngalo had ten wives. The other rebels had their wives also with them. For my part, I baptized thirteen infants. Miss Davies was taken captive with me at the commencement of hostilities in 1964. Although she was never maltreated, her health failed. She suffered from having to accompany the rebels when they were "on the run" from 1965-67. This was very hard for her, but she held services for the rebels to the end.

Jungle camp

We lodged at first in the jungle at Batama, some 100 miles north of Opienge, at the camp of the late Minister of Defense of the Congo rebels, Dominique Babu, also of Peking and Moscow. He was a convinced communist.

The morale of Miss Davies was high and General Ngalo himself promised her in the jungle to release her. Twice, on May 15th this year, he was aware by radio of the efforts of the British Ambassador in Kinshasa to bring about a surrender. He did not seem hostile to the idea. But he was not going to let the National Army take Miss Davies by force of arms. In any case, it is to the English that I owe the fact that I am still alive today. As soon as the General knew the Army was in the area, the rebel group fled at his orders. We marched three days without food, save for a little elephant meat at the end of the march.

At dawn on the fourth day, a fresh start was made by the column with Miss Davies at its head. I was at the end with an old rebel porter. It is to him I owe my deliverance. I could not keep up any longer. I had crossed two rivers and was lost in a maze of buffalo and elephant paths. Suddenly I saw Miss Davies.

Resting?

At first I thought she was resting, being exhausted by the long marches through the jungle. Then I saw two knife wounds in her face and throat, and blood coming from her mouth. I realized she was dead. It must have been fifteen minutes since she was killed. They had stolen her watch, but it was about 10 am. I was smitten with consternation. I rearranged my haversack and said to myself, "My turn is to come." Suddenly I saw three soldiers on the path. I thought they were Simbas and again said to myself, "This is the end." But they were regular Congolese Army soldiers, and I was saved.

Miss Davies' body was to be transported to Kisangani and interred in the communal grave of those massacred on the Congo River in 1964.

Winnie's last message to us in the WEC was at the June Month-end conference in 1961, a month prior to her sailing. Her text was Philippians 1:20: "It is my eager expectation and hope that I shall not be at all ashamed, but with full courage, now as always, Christ will be honored in my body, whether by life or by death" (RSV). This triumphant entry into His Presence is surely the fulfilment of the Spirit's word that day.

Len Moules, in Worldwide, July-August, 1967, published by Worldwide Evangelization Crusade

SENEGAL
PIERRE SENGHOR, AGED 19, A YOUNG DIOLA, MARTYRED 1959

Alastair and Helen Kennedy writing from France say that they have had this sad but triumphant latter from Andy and Betty Macindoe, Senegal, with the news of the martyrdom of a young Diola. Pierre found the Lord just before they left Ziguinchor, and gave his fine testimony in the church there just a few days before they came away.

"Our beloved brother, Pierre, was called into the presence of the Lord on Sunday July 19th, at around 10.45 am. On Saturday he was here with us, left his work just after 7 pm, said he'd see us tomorrow and spent part of the evening with Amathe laughing and chatting. On Sunday morning about breakfast time a youngster called up to tell us that Pierre was ill and could not get up. We thought that his rheumatism was worse or that he had fever or something. When we had finished breakfast Andy and I (Betty) went down in the car to his home. I took a few medicines with me thinking to be of some help. But when we got there we were shocked to find Pierre already unconscious, his face swollen, his eyes dilated, saliva coming out of his mouth, his breathing then stertorous and his pulse exceedingly rapid. We were alarmed and called for the chief of his compound, a Moslem and told him we'd have to get medical help at once.

"Then we rushed off to hospital not knowing what we'd find or whom we'd find there to help on a Sunday morning. By the time we arrived in the hospital Pierre's pulse had weakened, and his breathing was almost imperceptible. The Chief (doctor) came and ordered injections which they gave as soon as Pierre had been moved into the ward. But within a few minutes he had passed away to be with the Lord.

"When I talked with the chief of the compound I asked him if Pierre had eaten his supper. He said he had taken a good meal, but in the night he had vomited a lot, had cried a lot and then gone unconscious and that he had not rallied. When they took him off his mattress at the hospital I noticed that his saliva was blood-stained. When I looked at him in the house I had very grave suspicions, and as soon as we were in the car I said to Andy what I thought – poisoning – and he had the same thought. As soon as Amathe heard he voiced the same opinion, and so did Dominique. We have no proof, but what can say? After all, he is with the Lord now, having courageously, faithfully and zealously fought the good fight which for him lasted only seven hot months. A few weeks ago Pierre visited his own village of Kadyinor for the first time since his conversion, and although he was there at the time of a big fetish feast, and although he stayed in the compound of the fetish-chief, he did not hide his light. But he held meetings right there in the village, and had times of witnessing especially to the young men.

"We cannot understand, we do not try to, all the ways of the Lord. If wicked men have devised this young man's death, then may the Lord turn this sad and tragic event to his glory. If he has become our first Christian martyr in the Casamance, then may the "blood of the martyr be the seed of the Church."'

Worldwide*, *September-October, 1959, published by Worldwide Evangelization Crusade

Indian subcontinent
Kashmir
Ron Davies, 1947

"Congratulations, Ron. You lived a Crusader's life and died a Crusader's death. Ron Davies always warmed my heart. He had this abandonment of a Crusader. He lived out the words of the pilgrim song, "I'll fling the world away to go crusading." I can imagine the warmth of the meeting with his Lord on that day of sudden promotion in Kashmir.

"Before the war he loved his work among the Kashmiris in north India. He was fond of wearing native dress, which sometimes got him into difficult situations, but certainly gave him his heart's desire of getting into the hearts of the people. With the war [in India] ended Ron went back to England on leave before demobilisation, and he had only one thought – back to Kashmir with the Gospel in the shortest possible time. We found him just the same lovable Ron, but with this difference, responsibility had made him more capable himself of taking responsibility. so he went back this time as leader of the WEC Northern Kashmir field, a territory which also relieves the work around Haripur in N.W.F. He went with five workers, four women and a man.

"Then came his earthly end, like a bolt from the blue – from the rifle of one of those whom he loved and went to save. He died as we would expect Ron to die – saving others physically and spiritually. He went to rescue the three lady workers in danger from the Pathan invasion. He was seeing them off to safety, but stayed himself behind, we understand, as there was not transport for all. Then the wild tribesmen came – and silence.

"He has gone gloriously from the battle line – all one for Christ and souls. Congratulations, Ron. By God's grace we will fill up the gaps and carry on with the holy war of preaching the Gospel to all Kashmir.'

The above comes from the pen of Norman Grubb concerning this soldier of the Cross, who both lived and died, seeking the evangelization of the people to whom he had been sent.

World Conquest, published by the Worldwide Evangelization Crusade

INDIA
GRAHAM STEWART STAINS, 58, AND HIS TWO SONS, PHILIP, 10, AND TIMOTHY, 8

Baptists killed: Graham Stewart Stains, 58, and his two sons, Philip, 10, and Timothy, 8

This e-mail report came from a fellow-missionary, dated Jan. 24, 1999

Bro. Sam Varughese called late today and said that a Baptist Missionary and his two children were burned to death as they slept in a jeep. They had been preaching to a leper colony.

Their funeral will be today. He was weeping and very upset, though it was not one of his preachers. Today is also a holiday (the day has already begun there) and he and other Christians were meeting for prayer and to raise the Christian flag.

People there are blaming Christians for all their woes and want to make India a Hindu nation. He doesn't know what may happen.

We need the urgent prayers all over the country for all the Christians in India, especially Sam, his family and his church. Please pass this on to as many people as you can. Love in Christ, Sandy Snyder

A mob of rampaging Hindus burned to death an Australian missionary and his two sons as they slept in a jeep in eastern India yesterday, the first deaths in a recent spate of Hindu-Christian violence.

Graham Stewart Stains, a secretary of the Evangelical Missionary Society, and his sons were attacked by activists from the radical Bajrang Dal, a group affiliated with the ruling Hindu nationalist Bharativa Janata Party, police said.

Stains, 58, had been working with leprosy victims in India for 34 years. He and his sons, Philips, 10, and Timothy, 8, died shortly after midnight Friday when about 40 people doused the jeep with kerosene and set it ablaze, said witnesses.

Until now, the violence had mostly consisted of clashes in the western state of Gujarat, damaging at least 12 Christian churches and 24 Hindu temples. The unrest began after radical Hindus accused Christian missionaries of converting people to their faith.

At a memorial service for her husband and sons, Gladys and her daughter led the congregation in singing:

Because he lives, I can face tomorrow.
Because he lives, all fear is gone.
Because I know He holds the future,
And life is worth the living just because He lives.

Based on information in an Article in Ft. Worth-Star Telegram, New Delhi, India

MORE 20TH CENTURY MARTYRDOMS IN INDIA
THE REV ASHISH PRABASH MASIH

June 13, 2000

The Rev Ashish Prabash Masih, a 23-year-old preacher, was found murdered in Punjab state. The Punjab Christian Association believe that the killing was the outcome of a concerted campaign against its community by Hindu nationalists.

Based on a report in The Irish Times

MR. YESU DASU

September 12, 2000

A Christian preacher was beheaded in Karimnagar. Unidentified assailants struck Mr. Yesu Dasu in the neck with an axe several times before he died.

FATHER VICTOR CRASTA

July 25, 2000

Catholic priest Father Victor Crasta, and three missionaries were killed when a militant group opened fire on them in Balucherra, north Tripura district.

Vijay Ekka

June 10, 2000

Vijay Ekka, a tribal Christian from Raigarh District, Madhya Pradesh, died while in police custody. Ekka was an eye witness to the murder of Brother George Kuzhikandum (see June 7, 2000 below) and had been called in for questioning. Two Mathura police have since been arrested and accused of killing Mr. Ekka by beating him and giving him electric shock.

Brother George Kuzhikandum

June 7, 2000

Brother George Kuzhikandum, a Catholic priest, was murdered on the Brother Polus Memorial School Campus near Mathura, Uttar Pradesh. He was hit with iron rods until he died.

Pakistan

Nine Christians butchered

Gruesome terrorist attack claims live of Christian family, one month old baby in Pakistan

On Wednesday the 18th of November 1998, it was reported that a band of terrorists killed nine Christians, eight from the same family, in a city named Noshehra, which is situated in the north-east of the North Western Frontier Province of Pakistan. They were butchered with a sharp knife, and most of them had their throats cut.

It was reported that the murderers later wrote on the wall with the blood of these slain Christians, "No more black magic." The youngest member of the family slain was only one month old.

According to initial reports, the father of the slain family, Sabir John Bhatti, was involved in praying for the sick. Often Muslims as well as Christians would come to him to ask for pray for healing. This offended some of the extremist Muslim groups. Some Christians in the community believe that the reason for killing the whole family was an attempt to threaten other Christians involved in evangelism or other ministry work among Muslims.

Among the slain, apart from Mr. Sabir John Bhatti, was his wife Ruth, his daughter Shaheen, daughter in law Rosina, grandson Mohsin (1 year), grandson Romi (8 years), grand daughter Sobia (10 years), a one month old grandson (name unknown), and a young friend visiting the family, Ifzal (14 years).

Newspaper reports

More 20th century martyrdoms in Pakistan

Christians who are accused of blasphemy are often killed while awaiting trial. Between 1990 and 1998 at least 5 Christians were murdered after being charged with blasphemy. Mukhtar Masih was allegedly tortured to death in police custody. Tahir Iqbal was poisoned while in prison. Bantu Masih, Manzoor Masih, and Namat Ahmer were killed by armed attackers. Five Christians that were acquitted on blasphemy charges left the country, fearing for their safety.

October 1999

Christian pastor Ejaz Masih was shot to death by a Muslim youth when he answered the front door.

Newspaper reports

Russian and Eastern Europe

Albania

Savage campaign against Catholic Church

Since its inception in 1944, the Albanian Communist Party and Government has pursued a vicious campaign aiming to exterminate all vestiges of religion, in particular, every trace of the Catholic Faith.

A chronology of the government's actions to wipe out the Catholic Church.

December 1944

Franciscan Father Leke (Alexander) Luli is murdered by Yugoslav-Albanian Communist guerilla forces. According to a British war commander, his captors cut Luli's throat and dumped him in an unmarked grave is Kosova.

March 1945
Distinguished poet and humanist Father Lazer Shantoja is mercilessly tortured and shot.

Bishop of Lezha, 80 year-old Venerable Luigj Bumci, who headed the Albanian delegation at the Paris Peace Talks in 1918, dies under house arrest after uninterrupted harassment.

December 1945
Father Ndre (Andrew) Zadeja, poet and writer, tortured and shot without trial.

February 1946
Franciscan Father Anton Harapi, towering religious and cultural figure, executed after mock trial.

March 1946
Jesuit Vice Provincial, Gjon Fausti, rector of the Pontifical seminary, Daniel Dajani, Franciscan Father Gjon Shllaku, and seminarian Mark Cuni, are executed after mock trial.

May 1946
Metropolitan Archbishop of Shkodra, and head of the Catholic Church in Albania, Gasper Thaci, dies under house arrest after continued harassment and humiliation for not accepting government pressure to cut ties with the Vatican.

January 1947
Sigurimi (the Albanian security police) plants cache of arms and ammunition in main Franciscan church in Shkodra. When "discovered," many Franciscan priests and brothers are arrested, tortured, and executed. Among them, their provincial, Father Cyprian Nika. All their schools and monasteries are closed, properties confiscated, and the order disbanded.

February 1948
Forty-four-year-old Bishop of Sappa, Gjergj (George) Volaj is executed after horrible torture.

March 1948
Abbot Frano Gjini, substitute Apostolic Delegate in Albania, is executed after torture and mock trial, along with 17 other clerics and lay people.

February 1949
Metropolitan Archbishop of Durres, author and poet Vincent Prendushi, dies in prison after much torture and suffering.

August 1951
Communist daily, Zeri Populli (Voice of the People), falsifies contents of charter and declares the Catholic Church in Albania has broken all ties with the Vatican. The Catholic clergy denounces from pulpits the false-hood and emphasizes strong allegiance to the Pope. A new wave of persecution washes over the Church once more. Between 1951 and 1965, dozens of priests and religious are executed, imprisoned, or sent to forced labor camps in Southern Albania. Among these, Fathers Ded (Dominic) Malaj, Zef Bici, Nikol Mazrreku, Andrew Lufi, Tom Laca, Gjon and Engjel Kovaci, Anton Suma, and Konrad Gjolaj.

February 1972
Father Shtjefen (Stephen) Kurti is executed for baptizing a child.

April 1979
Titular Bishop of Shkodra, Ernest Coba (Cho-ba) dies in labor camp from police beatings for holding an Easter celebration.

Summary
The forty years of the Albanian government's savage campaign against the Catholic Church have resulted in the arrest and death of two archbishops, five bishops, an abbot, sixty-four diocesan priests, thirty-three Franciscans, fourteen Jesuits, ten seminarians and eight nuns.
Editor

Grave violations of religious rights in Albania

The Orthodox Church

The Albanian Orthodox and their Church have not always had an easy time professing their faith and national identity. Declared as Greeks because of their adherence to Orthodoxy by the Greek clergy and politicians, they have struggled vigorously to identify themselves with the Albanian nation. Because of the traditional nationalistic character of the Orthodox Church, the government's plan was to use it in the first place as an instrument for mobilizing the Orthodox population behinds its policies. At the same time, steps were undertaken to eliminate elements within the Church which were considered "unreliable." To succeed in this plan, all churches and monasteries were infiltrated by Communist agents and sympathizers. Soon after this was implemented, the regime brought the entire Church under its control. Their only seminary was closed, while some church buildings and monasteries, such as those of Ardenica, Narta, Vlora and Voskopoja, were confiscated.

The elimination of the leaders of the Orthodox Church was carried out in the same way as it was against the Muslim and Catholic clergy – by murder, execution, imprisonment and torture. Thus, during a period of less than five years, the regime killed or put into prison and labor camps the majority of the hierarchy, which included: Visarion Xhuvani, Archbishop of Elbasan; Bishop Irine of Apollonia (Pojan); Bishop Agathangjel Cance of Berat; Bishop Irine, Deputy Metropolitan of Korca and Gjirokastra; Papas Josif Papmihaili, a promoter of the Byzantine Church; and many other simple priests and deacons. The highly cultured Archbishop Kristofor Kisi, head of the Albanian Orthodox Church, was deposed and sent to prison where he died after much humiliation. He was replaced by the government with Pais Vodica, an archimandrite and Communist agitator.

As in the case of the Muslim religion, the government also used the Orthodox Church for its foreign policy purposes. During the Soviet tutelage of Albania, the Autocephalous Orthodox Church of Albania was forced to closely cooperate with the Moscow Patriarchate and Pais Vodica participated on behalf of the Albanian Orthodox Church in all peace conferences organized by the Soviet Union. However, after Albania broke with Moscow in 1961, the ties between the two churches were abruptly cut.

The Catholic Church

Although the government directed its anti-religious campaign against all three religious groups, Catholics felt the main brunt of the assaults. Despite being a minority, Albanian Catholics and particularly their clergy, were admired and loved by Orthodox and Muslims for their traditionally strong patriotic and cultural dedication. Jealous of the strength of influential Catholic clergy and afraid of the unity among their believers, the government employed all kinds of legal and illegal means to erode and destroy the foundation of the Catholic Church. For centuries, the Catholic clergy had taught and worked with all the people without religious distinction. Many visitors to Albania noted how they cared for and served people selflessly, sharing daily joys and sorrows. It was this religious tradition the new government sought to shatter. By the end of 1946, almost half of the Catholic clergy were imprisoned, all foreign clergy expelled and 20 priests and religious put to death. At the same time, Enver Hoxha, at that time General Secretary of the party and Head of the government, directed all his efforts toward fomenting resentment against the Catholic church leaders. The church, however, stood firm and united in opposition to the government's plan to establish a new church organization, severed from Rome, which would serve the purposes of Communist indoctrination throughout the land.

The actions of the Albanian government and Party to wipe out Catholicism from public and private life can be divided into three main periods: 1944-1948, 1949-1967 and 1967-1984.

1944-1948

Hoxha's plan to establish a Catholic Church severed from Rome began to take shape in May 1945 when he expelled the Apostolic

Delegate to Albania, Archbishop Leone G.B. Nigris. Then, hastily summoning the Metropolitan Archbishop of Shkodra, Primate of the Church, Gasper Thachi, and the Archbishop of Durres, Vincent Prendushi, a nationally famed poet and writer, he demanded that they separate from Rome, establish a new national church and give their allegiance to his new regime. In exchange he offered the government's "conciliatory attitude" and material help in maintaining the Church's institutions. Both prelates bravely refused, and paid for this stand with their lives. Thachi died in 1946 while under house arrest. Prendushi was sentenced to twenty years at hard labor and died in prison in 1949 after enduring horrible tortures.

The government's onslaught now turned against the priests. On June 21, 1945, two Jesuit teachers, Frs. Jak Gardin and Gjergj Vata were arrested and, after a trial filled with illegal proceedings and marked by the withdrawal of their defenders from the court in protest of the proceedings were sentenced to many years in prison. Immediately after the first elections, on December 31, 1945, in which no opposition party was allowed to participate, the police arrested Frs. Gjon Fausti, Vice-Provincial of the Jesuits and Daniel Dajani, Rector of the Pontifical Seminary of Shkodra. A month later the government ordered the immediate expulsion of all non-Albanian members of religious orders. The number expelled exceeded two hundred. During a mock trial on January 30, 1946, Jesuit Fathers Fausti and Dajani, Franciscan Father Gjon Shllaku, and seminarians Mark Cuni and Gjergj Bici were sentenced to death along with 13 laymen. The execution took place on march 4, 1946, outside the Catholic cemetery in Shkodra and their bodies were thrown into a common grave. Their last words were of pardon for their persecutors and of praise to God and Albania as they shouted "Long live Christ. Long live Albania." Exactly one month later all Jesuit institutions were closed and the Order outlawed.

As soon as the shock of the executions had had its effect, Enver Hoxha summoned Bishop Fran Gjini in Tirana to order him, as he had done the year before with Bishops Thachi and Prendushi, to cut his ties to Rome and to sway the clergy and Catholic population over the government's side. Gjini had become the Substitute Apostolic Delegate and the leader prelate after the death of Thachi. Hoxha threatened him with a similar fate to that of his predecessor unless he capitulated; Bishop Gjini refused, saying "I will never separate myself and my flock from the Holy See." Nevertheless, fearing great reprisals against those under his care if a compromise could not be reached, Gjini attempted to bring about a reconciliation between the government and the Catholic Church in Albania. He courageously wrote an open letter to Hoxha, in which Gjini offered the Church's cooperation in "reconstructing the nation, binding the wounds and surmounting the existing difficulties." He expressed "hope for the realization of not only material advantages, but also spiritual benefits for all Albanians." Hoxha ignored the message and ordered the arrest of Gjini on the charge of spreading anti-Communist propaganda. After a year of torture and much humiliation, Bishop Gjini was executed on March 8, 1948, along with a group of eighteen clergy and lay people.

Just a month earlier, another Bishop, Gjergj Volaj, had been executed along with other priests and lay people on the charge of being "enemies of the people." By now the persecution had reached its peak. Besides the Jesuits, the Franciscans had also been disbanded, along with all the orders of religious sisters. Their property, even their personal belongings, were confiscated. The hierarchy had been completely decimated, with only one bishop still alive.

1949-1967

In 1949 external and internal pressures prompted the Albanian government to slow its drive against the Catholic Church and religion in general. The expulsion of Yugoslavia from the Cominform at Stalin's orders, in June, 1948, had created an unexpected danger for the Albanian leaders and its Party. Groups of pro-Tito sympathizers and Albanian escapees to Yugoslavia were being organized by Yugoslavia to overthrow the Hoxha regime. In order to meet the challenge, Hoxha took the offensive against Yugoslavia, publicly blaming Albania's neighbor for all of the misfortunes of Albania since the "liberation." As a tactic designed to forestall Catholics from joining forces against him, Hoxha delegated his Minister of the Interior, Tuk Jakova, to meet with Jakova's former schoolmate, the Franciscan priest Marin Sirdani, in the swamps near Elbasan (central Albania) where Fr. Sirdani was serving a long sentence of forced labor. Jakova blamed and condemned Yugoslavia for the policies of brutality against Catholics and their clergy during past years, and assured Fr. Sirdani of the government's desire for rapprochement with the Church. Stunned by Jakova's statements, Fr. Sirdani nevertheless rejoiced and promptly accepted his invitation to mediate between the government and the Catholic hierarchy, which was now reduced to one elderly Bishop, the Venerable Bernardin Shllaku, Ordinary of the Diocese of Pulti.

Fr. Sirdani informed the Bishop of the government's approach and both the Bishop and the government agreed to begin negotiations. Several organizational charters governing the Catholic Church were prepared between 1949 and 1951. Bishop Shllaku and his aides tried their best to accommodate the government's demands and conditions, while at the same time taking into account the articles of Canon Law. Satisfied with the goodwill of the Church leaders, the government pressed for complete separation of the Church from the Vatican. In order to force compliance, new arrests of intransigent priests were made. Stubbornly, Catholics refused to give in despite the fact that the government charters for the Muslim and Orthodox faiths had already been worked out and approved by the government a few years earlier. Finally, after lengthy and painful discussions, a compromise was reached in which the government allowed the Church to keep its spiritual sovereignty and its links with the Holy See.

However, the official Communist press falsified the original text of the Charter and announced that all ties between the Albanian Catholic Church and the Vatican had been broken. The Catholic clergy were angered and saddened by this betrayal. They denounced the lies and misinterpretations regarding the Charter and emphasized their strong allegiance to the Holy Father.

In signing the Charter the government promised to allow churches and seminaries to reopen and to provide a subsidy for their maintenance. The government had also agreed to allow parents to bring their children into the Church for religious instruction. When these promises were not kept, the Church tried to accommodate itself to the government's wishes in order to perform its religious duties toward Albanian Catholics. The Catholic faithful, who understood the Communists' hatred of them and religion in general, suffered greatly. They witnessed helplessly the destruction of Catholic institutions and the imprisonment and execution of their priests. In the midst of this turmoil, and despite the oppression and pillage directed against the Catholic minority, Catholics filled the churches for regular services. It was an open and eloquent testimony of their dedication to the Church and its clergy.

The leaders of the Church and faithful were certainly aware that the government's attempt to nationalize the churches was only a temporary measure to prevent the growth of discontent. Adamantly, they refused to subordinate themselves to this kind of constitutional pressure and blocked all compromises concerning the fundamental teaching of the Catholic Church. As a consequence, a new wave of persecution washed over the Church. Between 1955 and 1965 more than a dozen priests and religious were shot. Many others were either imprisoned or sent to forced labor camps. Among the executed priests were Fathers Ded Malaj, Zef Bici, and Franciscan Konrad Gjolaj. Diocesan offices and parishes were constantly harassed, and religious services impeded by agents of the government.

Titular Bishops and vicars were forced to clean streets and public bathroom wearing clown outfits with paper signs across their chests reading "I have sinned against the people." The entire Catholic Church was slowly being martyred.

1967-1984

This period is the final intensified attempt of the Albanian Communist Party and the Albanian government to wipe out the Church and all religious activity. Enver Hoxha again set the stage for action with his infamous speech of February 6, 1967, urging the Albanian youth to fight "religious superstitions." A ruthless campaign against all religion followed. Everywhere churches were burned or turned into sports arenas, dance halls, movie theaters, apartments, etc. Priests and Bishops were publicly beaten. The Franciscan church of Arramadhe in Shkodra, together with the Friary, was set afire one evening and four elderly Franciscans were burned to death.

During 1967, according to the journal of Albanian writers, Nendori (November), about 2200 mosques, churches, chapels, monasteries and other religious buildings were vandalized and closed. Of that number 327 were Roman Catholic. On November 22, 1967, the government published Decree No. 4337 ordering the annulment of the religious charters and of all laws pertaining to state-church relationships. All religious rites were prohibited and grave penalties were imposed on violators. The remaining priests were sent to forced-labor camps for "re-education." The Albanian Party and government boasted that it had become the first totally atheistic state in the world. Their actions had broken Article 18 of the country's 1946 Constitutions which states that all citizens are guaranteed freedom of conscience and faith, and that religious communities are free in the exercise of their beliefs and practices. Their decree also violated the Universal Declaration of Human Rights (U.N.) which guarantees religious freedom.

The abolition of religion in Albania passed almost without notice abroad and aroused little protest, with the exception of the Vatican's daily, L'Observatore Romano, which published reports on anti-religious violence. The Free Albania Committee, located in New York, made a strong protest in the name of the silenced Albanian people, to the United Nations General Secretary, and urged that immediate steps be taken "to stop the savage religious persecution" in Albania. The Albanian Catholic Center in New York, under the leadership of Msgr. Joseph J. Oroshi, denounced the abolition of religion by the Albanian government and pleaded to American Catholics for their concern and support. Th American-Albanian Charity Organization of Detroit, in turn, distributed an informational brochure (in three languages) documenting accounts of the ongoing religious persecution there, since 1944. Unfortunately, other than these steps, the plea for support went unheeded by religious and civic leaders until 1972 when Pope Paul VI strongly protested the execution of Father Shtjefen Kurti for baptizing a child in a labor camp. Since that time, the late Cardinal Humberto Medeiros of Boston, the late Bishop Mark Lipa of the Albanian Orthodox diocese of America, Pope John Paul II, the German Catholic Bishops' Conference and the United Churches of Christ-USA have defended the right of Albania's citizens to practice freely their religion.

However, Albanian leaders remain deaf to these international pleas and continued to attack religion. Moreover, they proudly defend the destruction of churches, monasteries and mosques; the killing of hundreds of priests and religious; the inhuman persecution of believers. They even attack with vehemence the Soviet Union, China, Poland, Yugoslavia and other Eastern countries for their "anti-revolutionary" stand toward religion. Needless to say, all these Communist governments which Albania criticizes persecute religion. Nevertheless, they at least formally guarantee religious freedom in their constitutions and allow, with restrictions, some private and public exercise of religion.

To show their disapproval of such

"lenience" toward religion, Albania's government adopted in 1976 a new Constitution whose Articles 37 and 55 boastfully proclaimed that the State recognizes no religion whatsoever, and forbids all religious activities and organizations, while encouraging atheism.

Article 37

The State does not recognize any religion at all and supports and develops atheistic propaganda in order to implant in people the scientific-materialistic world view.

Article 55

The formation of any organization of a fascist, anti-democratic, religious or anti-socialist nature is forbidden. Fascist, religious, warmongerish, anti-socialist activity and propaganda are forbidden, as is the incitement to hatred between peoples and races.

With these articles Albania became the only country in the world where the suppression of religion and the propagation of atheism have become a constitutionally mandated state policy. In June, 1977, a new Albanian penal code was issued, clause 55 of which lays down the penalties to be exacted for religious activity. It states that "religious propaganda, and also the production, distribution or storage of literature of this kind" will be punished with imprisonment for between three years and ten years. In time of war or if the offenses are deemed to be serious, imprisonment is not for less than ten years and the death penalty can be imposed.

Prior to the actual enactment of such official acts, the government manifested the same kind of suppression of religion. Fr. Stephen Kurti was executed in 1972 for baptizing a child in a labor camp at the parents' request. In 1974 the government also sentenced the three remaining Catholic Bishops to detention camps for conducting religious services in private. Following the constitutional outlawing of religion, in 1977 Fran Mark Gjoni of Shkodra was brought to trial for the possession of Bibles. Gjoni admitted, when presented with Bibles taken from his home, that he had found them in parks and at the seashore where they had been left by tourists or floated in by sea. For his "crime" Gjoni was sentenced to 12 years in prison. In spite of a total blackout in regard to the case by the government-controlled news media monopoly, everyone in Albania was aware of the trial and took great interest in it. The trial ironically helped to testify to the continued existence of religious faith in Albania, as well as highlighting the outrageous reactions made by the Albanian government to even the most mild expression of that faith! For religious criminals such as Gjoni, according to reports from recent refugees, the government has at least six prisons, nine concentration camps and 14 areas of internal exile.

An even more terrible example of the continuing anti-religious campaign of the Albanian government is that of Catholic Bishop Ernest Coba (Choba), Apostolic administrator of Shkodra. Bishop Coba, confined since 1974 to the labor camp of Paperr near the city of Elbasan in central Albania, celebrated a secret Easter service in 1979 at the request of his fellow prisoners. Unfortunately, the police were informed and at the beginning of the service prison guards entered the barracks and some began assaulting the Bishop, tearing off his vestments and breaking the cross, while others began beating the prisoners who had gathered for the celebration. The old, nearly blind, venerable prelate was seriously injured in the melee and died the following morning. His body was immediately removed and buried by the police in an undisclosed site.

Another recent victim of the Albanian government's war against religion is Fr. Ndoc Luli, S.J. Father Luli, after much hesitation, in May of 1980, baptized, at the request of his sister-in-law, her newborn twins at the Agricultural Cooperative, Mali Jushit, near Shkodra, where he was confined. The event leaked out somehow, first to the secretary of the Communist cell, then to the police. Father Luli was arrested immediately, along with his sister-in-law, and both were interrogated and treated harshly. At the public trial, which took place in the recreation room of the cooperative, Fr. Luli's sister-in-law was sentenced to eight years in prison at hard labor, while he received the sentence ambiguously termed "life until death." His fate is unknown and many believe that Fr. Luli died at the bottom of some mine, a victim of the dreaded Sigurimi (Albanian Secret Police).

With the death of Bishop Coba, the only remaining Catholic Bishop in Albania is the 70-year old Nikoll (Nicholas) Troshani, titular Bishop of Cisamo and Apostolic Administrator of Lezha and Durres. He is confined in the labor camp of Tepelana near the seaport of Vlora. The third of the surviving Bishops who were detained in 1974, Antonin Fishta, died several years ago while still in confinement. The few priests and religious still alive remain in prison and forced labor camps. Among these is Mark Hasi who, for the second time, is serving a long prison sentence for "conducting religious services." Confined to labor camps are also Fathers Injac Gjoka, Rrok Gjuraj, Ndoc Sahatcia, Zef Nikolla, Ndrec Gega, Jesuit Gjergj Vata, Simon Jubani, and Simon's older brother, Lazer, Fran Illia, Federik Mazi and two Franciscans.

Amnesty International has been interceding in vain for the release of Bishop Troshani and the other priests and lay religious believers who are kept in prison solely for their beliefs. In 1977, Cardinal Humberto Medeiros of Boston, together with Albanian Orthodox Bishop Mark Lipa, issued a "Joint Appeal for Religious Freedom" which condemned the anti-religious laws of Albania. Again on November 28, 1981, Medeiros and Lipa issued a "Declaration for Religious Freedom" on the sixty-ninth anniversary of the establishment of an independent Albanian state. In the declaration the religious leaders called for "respect for human rights, and especially for religious freedom in Albania." They asked the Albanian government that the churches, mosques and religious institutions be allowed to reopen. They also stated their conviction that Church life and faith in God "promotes good social order." On October 5, 1980, Pope John Paul II, referring to the many martyrs or modern day Albania, asked all the faithful to pray for Christians and other believers who are persecuted for their faith. He reminded his listeners that "to be spiritually close to all those in Albania, who are suffering violence because of their faith, is a special duty of all Christians, according to the tradition inherited from the first centuries." In addition, he exhorted all "to pray also for those who persecute them, repeating Christ's invocation on the Cross, addressed to His father: "Forgive them; for they know not what they do.'" The Pope also defended the martyrs from the charges that they were guilty of political crimes by drawing attention to Christ's having been condemned on the political charge of having claimed he was a king.

In 1981, the Bishops of Greece also denounced religious persecution in Albania, particularly stressing the fate of the Orthodox believers. However, their appeal had chauvinistic overtones, claiming that 400,000 Albanian Orthodox were Greek nationals. Unfortunately, their distortion, instead of helping, hurt the Orthodox believers in Albania by giving Hoxha the pretext to continue his drive against religion.

Another positive indication that world opinion is becoming interested in the plight of Albanian believers, came from Eastern Europe. On October 7, 1982, in Bucharest, Romania, an international, inter-faith colloquium was held under the auspices of the Conference of European Churches of the World Council of Churches. The Ecumenical Press Services of the World Council of Churches published a part of the document from this colloquium which deals with the religious situation in Albania. The document reports the radical suppression of any organized religious activity in Albania. While denouncing the present religious oppression, it suggests that Christians outside of Albania utilize this period in order to prepare the way for an eventual future dialogue with the Albanian government regarding the fate of Albanian believers.

In March of 1983, the representative of the Foreign Ministry of Denmark presented the issue of religious oppression in Albania at the 39th meeting of the United Nations Human Rights Commission in Geneva. He urged the Commission to take formal steps to protest the attitude of the Albanian government toward its citizens wishing to practice their faith. Two months later another strong voice on behalf of Albanian believers was heard from the United Churches of Christ-USA. At their annual meeting on May 13, 1983 in San Francisco, they adopted a resolution vigorously condemning religious oppression in Albania.

Religious Activity in Albania Today

Religion continues secretly to influence the life of Albanians of all faiths despite the brutality of anti-religious campaigns. Evidence of this is given by official news media agencies, including the government leaders. At various times the Albanian press has repeatedly stated that "religion has still not been uprooted in our country," "religion is still alive among our working class;" "enemies of the people who believe in God do not sleep, they continue to look with sympathy and hope to the Vatican; these kinds of enemies are inside our Party lines and active in our organizations." These statements verify the reports which have come from Albania that some religious practices are alive there, such as the observance of major feast days, the wearing of "disguised" religious symbols, and even participation in religious pilgrimages.

Several young Albanian refugees reaching the United States within the last two years have given details of how the people have continued to practice their Catholic faith in the secrecy of their homes. It is almost certain that the remaining Catholic priests still alive are in prison. The people now rely on lay leadership for their religious services. The eldest family member is chosen to lead prayer service and to perform the rites of baptism and marriage. Religious medals, crucifixes, pictures and rosaries are kept hidden by families due to the threat of raids by the Albanian security police. Decree 5339 of 1975 has discouraged the giving of religious names to the newborn by threatening parents who do so. In 1980 the government complained that the children were being called by their saint's name at home. Such all-pervasive repressive measures against religion are greatly resented as being foreign to Albania's heritage. Their parents and grandparents who still remain in Albania note that even during the Ottoman rule of Albania, when forced conversions took place, no such attempts to totally eradicate Christianity were made.

"Grave Violations of Religious Rights in Albania" was originally published in Albanian Catholic Bulletin, Palok Plaku, Vol. VI, 1985. Albanian Catholic Information Center, By kind permission

Armenia
The Martyrs of Armenia
24 April 1915

Armenia is located at the east end of modern Turkey, with some of its traditional territory now in Turkey and some across the border in the former Soviet Union. The Armenians were converted to Christianity around 280 or 290, and are accounted the first country to become predominantly Christian. Their country is located at a spot where empires have clashed for centuries, and they have often been caught in the middle. For centuries they have been dominated by their Moslem neighbors, most recently the Turks of the Ottoman Empire.

The Turks were concerned about the possibility of an Armenian revolt. In 1895 and 1896 the Turkish Army killed about 100,000 Armenian civilians. Then in 1915, early in World War I, with Turkey fighting on the side of Germany and Austria-Hungary, and Russia fighting in alliance with the British and French on the other side, the Turkish government accused the Armenians of plotting with the Russians to assist a Russian invasion of Turkey. That spring, around 600,000 Armenians were killed by the Turkish Army, in an attempt to exterminate the Armenians completely. Much of the slaughter took place on 24 April 1915. The survivors were driven eastward and escaped into Russia. On 29

November 1920, most of Armenia was annexed by the Soviet Union.

It is sometimes said that the issues here were national, political, and ethnic rather than religious, and that the victims therefore do no qualify as martyrs. However, many of the Armenians, when about to be killed, were given the option of saving their lives by converting to Islam. Few did.

James Kiefer, Christian Biographies, By kind permission

Russia After the 1917 Revolution

Hungarian Report from 1933

"For whosoever will save his life shall lose it: and whosoever will lose his life for my sake shall find it." (Matthew 16:25)

After the Russian "Revolution" (coup d'état) of 1917, Christianity suffered great persecution in Bolshevik Russia. Unfortunately, very little information is available on this subject.

The article "Protestant World Report" by Hungarian university professor Charles Karner appeared in the Hungarian Protestant Almanac of 1933. The following excerpts present the state of the Protestant Church in Russia. Just a small portion of Russian Christians was Protestant; we can infer that the more extensive Orthodox Church suffered a much greater loss.

In the same context, we shall at least refer to the situation that emerged after the collapse of the czarist Russia, as far as that concerned Protestantism. The nations living on the west border of the empire declared their independence in the midst of the revolutionary turmoil that turned upside down the old Russian Empire starting the spring of 1917. This happened most quietly in Finland where the order was quickly established. This country has an almost exclusively Lutheran population: the church had been independent before and could adapt to the new circumstances without much difficulty. The situation was much more difficult in the case of the so called Baltic Provinces. Their territories had mostly been battle-fields, afterwards they suffered all the brutality of the emerging Bolshevik power. The old nobility of these provinces had mainly been Lutheran but the rest of the population also had a high percentage of Lutherans. The revolutionary turmoil also greatly ravaged these countries: most of the German nobility became victims of the agitated masses, the rest had to flee; there are only a few remaining today. The reign of the Bolsheviks, though temporary, caused a lot of harm to the people. Besides, the few months of Bolshevik power degenerated into the persecution of the Lutheran church in Latvia. Eight Lutheran pastors were martyred in Riga and 23 more in the countryside by the Bolsheviks during 1918-1919. At the same time eight more pastors died due to persecution. These confessors testified with death-defying courage until the last minute of the following words of the apostle: "For to me to live is Christ, and to die is gain." (Phil. 1:21). Their martyrdom clearly stated again the vital force of the Scriptures: let their memory also be blessed by those reading these words. Since the rebels, united with the German volunteer crops, drove out the Bolshevik army from the Baltic States in May, 1919, the situation slowly stabilized and the building work of the Church could start again.

In all these countries, although after perilous times, the regular work of the Church could start again. But in Soviet Russia the state of the whole Christianity, and along with it that of Protestantism is still critical.

Since the Soviet have overcome the inner crisis originating from the so called "wartime communism", it is relentless in its fight for the communist state-ideal. In this ideal Christianity and religion usually have no place.

This is why the persecution of Christians started with increased force in the spring of 1929. Laws and government decrees have already been immobilizing the religious work of the Church; they also completely discontinued religious schooling. The persecution of Church personnel by police regulations, high tax-burden, etc., also played an important role. The decree issued on April 8, 1929 made even the most minimal and restrained charitable work of the Church impossible, as well as forbade all forms of religious "propaganda". This meant that all Church activity was brought to a standstill. The decree was followed by further church confiscations, imprisonment of pastors, and in many cases their exile or martyrdom. The Protestant Church has already suffered a lot during the first years of the revolution, but as a result of these decrees its situation became almost hopeless. Most of the congregations perished or faded away due to their persecution, many pastors were martyred; and there is no new supply. We do not have concrete figures for it is impossible to gather statistical information about the Church, and generally, it is difficult to obtain reliable information on events happening in Russia. However, we can get an idea of the extent of the destruction if we consider that there were 1,200,000 Protestants living in pre-war Russia and their number was 900,000 even before the persecution wave of 1929. But professor Elert from Erlangen stated in 1929 that the number of Russian Lutherans barely reached 600,000 ("Religion in Geschichte und Gegenwart", 2nd ed., III, p.1785) this number could have greatly decreased since then.

Charles Karner

Ukraine
Yakim Bely and Iosyf Tyshkevich

In the early 1870s Christians in the Ukraine were persecuted by the Russian establishment, as well as by the some conservative members of the Orthodox Church. A Mennonite pastor, Johann Wieler, braved the authorities by holding a communion service in Russian in Rohrbach. Some Ukrainian Christians who had only recently been baptized attended this service. After the service the local police arrested Johann Wieler. His place was taken by Mykhaolo Ratushny, but six months after Wieler's arrest eleven more Christians were arrested and imprisoned in Tarashcha. In the spring of 1873 eight of these prisoners were taken to Kiev prison, tortured and put on trial. The first two Ukrainian evangelical martyrs, Yakim Bely and Iosyf Tyshkevich, died during their imprisonment at Kiev.

Editor

Soviet Union

The martyrdom of thousands upon thousands of Christians in Russia in the twentieth century is reminiscent of Nero's persecution of the Christians in Rome. When the communists came to power in 1917 they launched a wholesale attack on the Orthodox churches. Stalin became Party Secretary in 1922, and Premier in 1929.

8,100 martyrs

In 1922, when valuables which belonged to the Orthodox churches were confiscated, over eight thousand clergy were either tortured to death or shot. 2,691 "white" clergy, 1,962 monks and 3,447 lay-sisters and monks suffered in this way. The number of Christians martyred varied greatly from region to region: in Moscow there were 36 martyrs, but in the Barnaul region 441, in Odessa- Kherson 191, in the Stavropol region 139, and in the Poltava there were 124 martyrs.

Editor

General Registers of martyrs, 1917-1922

These extracts record the death of 416 of these martyrs.

The following table sets out a general register, from 1918-1922, of some of the Russian laymen and clergy who were martyred by the Communists.

1917

Archpresbyter John Kochurov from Tsarskoe Selo became the first clergyman to be martyred.

1918-1922

One clergyman from the Kherson region was crucified.

Three priests were crucified in the Kherson region.

Archimandrite Matthew, who was rector of the Perm Ecclesiastical Academy, was cut into pieces by swords.

Rev Koturov, fleeing from Cherdin, was caught by the Communists. In the sub-zero temperatures they forced him to undress and poured cold water over him until he became an icy statue.
During 1918-19, seventy clergymen were martyred from the Kharkov region.
In Kuban province, at Krasnodar, six priests were killed; and in the Stavropol diocese one elder, three psalm-readers, four deacons and fifty-two priests were killed.
Father Michael, aged twenty-eight, had just finished conducting the Divine Liturgy when he was seized by communists in front of his congregation. They wept as the was taken away, but they just heard him say, "Do not weep for me, but weep for yourselves and your children." His dead body was lifted up on the bayonets of soldiers of the Red Army. He left a widow and two children behind.
A priest, a deacon and a psalm-reader. In the village of Bezopasny, Leonid Soloviev, a priest, aged 27, Vladimir Ostrikov, a deacon, aged 45, and a 51- year-old psalm-reader, Alexander Fleginsky were martyred, even though no charges were ever brought against them. The communists forced them to go to an area where diseased cattle had been buried, then made them dig their own grave, before mutilating with swords and burying them while they were still alive.
An old man, more than eighty years old, the Rev Zolotovsky, was taken by some Red soldiers, dressed in women's clothes and ordered to dance in front of them. He refused and so was summarily hanged.
Nikolai Milutkin, a clergyman from Novo-Nikolsky, was brought before the local CHEKA who beat him with the buts of their guns and wounded his head, removing half his scalp, and one of his legs with two strokes of a sword. Then they released him, before arresting him again two hours later, shooting him at point blank range and mutilating his dead body. They then stripped the body and dumped it in the river Don hoping it would float downstream to Novocherkask and serve as an example to the people there, where they intended to go next week.

1918

Archpresbyter John Vostorgov, rector of St Basil's Cathedral, Moscow
Archpresbyter Alexander Veraskin, from Chercassi, was hanged on the outside of the gates of his own home.
Rev Peter Diakonov, from the Nadezhdinsky factory, in the Verhouturie district, was buried alive, up to his head, and then shot.
Archpresbyter Gregory Pospelov from Kronstadt was shot for taking a funeral service for sailors who had fought against the communists. Pospelov was shot clutching the ceremonial cross in his hands which the communists were unable to take away from him.

1919

The communists occupied the city of Voronezh in December 1919, and shot 160 priests from the diocese of Voronezh before the end of 1919.

1920

Rev Nikodim Pedicoultzev, from Kamen, was hacked to death with a kitchen knife while in prison.

1921

Seven priests, Dobrolubov, Friazinov, Nadezhdin, Lorlov, Sokolov, Vishniakov, and Zaozersky, and an Archimandrite, Telegin, were all shot in Moscow.
In the Tobolsk region of West Siberia over ninety priests were shot in 1921.
Serge Shein, Secretary of the Moscow all-Russian Council, was killed in Petrograd.
Rev John Moslovsky from a village called Verhne-Poltavky was shot dead through the window of his own house.
Rev Seraphim Sarichov, from Gondatievka, after taking the Paschal Liturgy was shot.
Rev Joakim Frolov was burnt on a haystack outside his village of Mikhailovsk. A metal cross was the only thing found in the ashes.
Archpresbyter Serapion Chernikh, from Nikolaevsk, was conducting a service on the eve of Palm Sunday, consecrating willow branches, when he was thrown into the river Amur, and drowned, still wearing his vestments.

Martyrs from the monasteries

Between 1917 and 1922, monasteries of the Russian Orthodox church were ransacked and many monks martyred.

The Spasovsky monastery

A sailor, Dibenko, took a seventy-five-year-old Archimandrite Radion from his monastery and scalped him, before cutting his head off.

Alexandro-Svirsky monastery

A novice Ivan, hiding himself in the monastery's loft, lived to recount the following attack on the Alexandro-Svirsky monastery and the martyrdom of five of its brothers and the Superior Eugene.

When the monks refused to hand over the keys to the rooms so that their treasures could be taken they were forced to dig their own graves in the courtyard of the monastery. When this was completed they were told to line up on the edge of the graves so that they could be shot. The monks requested that they should be allowed to sing "Christ is risen," a short Paschal hymn, as it was the third day of the Pascha. They were refused permission but started to sing anyway as the young soldiers fired their rifles.

Solovky monastery

The last igumen of the Solovky monastery, Archimandrite Benjamin, lived as a hermit in a poor peasant's hut on the outskirts of Archangel. The communists sealed its windows and doors and then set fire to the hut with Benjamin inside it.

Mary Magdalene monastery

On June 27, 1918, the Rev Gregory Nikolsky of the Mary Magdalene monastery, was taken out through the gates of his own monastery by the communists. They forced Gregory to open his mouth, shouted, "We will also give you the Sacrament" and then shot him in the mouth.

Spasov Skete monastery

The Rev Athanassy, a priest from Spasov Skete monastery, was taken out to be executed by a Red soldier. Athanassy knelt to pray, crossed himself and then stood up to bless the soldier, who then fired two shots into the pastor's head.

Poltava Krestovozdvizhensky monastery

The Rev Mil from Poltava Krestovozdvizhensky monastery was interrogated many times. The Red soldiers found him so obstinate that they "were forced to spend thirty-seven roubles on him" – the price of a bullet. On July 4th, 1918, with two others, he was shot in the forest. When his body was examined it revealed the extent of the terrible tortures this martyr had endured during his interrogations.

Spaso-Preobrazhensky monastery

The Red soldiers decided to take over Spaso-Preobrazhensky monastery. They rounded up twenty-five monks and Prior Ambrose. They were commanded to bring in fire-wood and told that they would be burnt at the stake. When the Reds realized that the anti-Red Volunteer army was nearby, they took the priests to the local railway station. Commissar Bakai started the massacres of these martyr-monks and shot Prior Ambrose. Seventeen of the monks were killed outright as they were shot, but the eight other monks, who were not fatally injured, pretended that they were dead as they were shot in the dark, and later, were able to escape.

NKVD Martyrs

The NKVD (secret police) became feared, in the 1930s, for their midnight calls. During this time up to 22,000 evangelical Christians were picked up in the early hours of the morning by van and carted off to the Siberian prison camps, from where the majority never returned. One such arrest took place on Christmas Day 1937. Konstantin Korneichuk, pastor of Alma-Ata, asked for Yefrem Mikhailovich. When Mikhailovich heard his friend's voice he thought that he must have been released from prison. His happiness was short-lived, as he realized that something sinister was afoot. Paster Korneichuk had endured

unspeakable torture in prison, but had managed to resist revealing the names of members of his congregation until they put him in the electric chair and turned on the electricity. When Mikhailovich opened his door he was confronted with two men in uniform, members of the militia, who took Mikhailovich away, after he had been allowed to pray with his family. Subsequently he received a ten year prison sentence. That night scores of other Christians were arrested. Among those arrested, along with Mikhailovich, who never saw their families again were five preachers, Rybak, Slepov, Serkyuk, Kvasha, and Levkovich. Korneichuk was rewarded for his betrayal by dying in a concentration camp.
Keston College

Chronicle of martyrs in the Soviet Union, 1974–83

Between 1974 and 1983 Christians were still being frequently martyred in Russia and behind the Iron Curtain, in the Communist Block of countries. The full extent of these killings is hard to appreciate as so many Christians were martyred in circumstances that were hidden from the media in the West, and are only now surfacing. The following table of twenty-two martyrs is in the form of a chronicle. Many of these people died in suspicious circumstances which make it almost impossible to prove that they were murdered. However, whether they were forced to commit suicide, openly murdered, or just died in suspicious circumstances, they are all treated as martyrs in this chronicle.

1. Ivan Ostapenko

Ostapenko, the presbyter of Shevehenko Evangelical-Christian Baptist congregation, had been imprisoned for four years, and then exiled for three years. He was told that he would be able to serve his exile near his home if he gave up his Christian beliefs. Ivan refused to do this. He was discovered hanging in a basement of a house on January 26th 1974.

2. Mikhailo Lutsky

The body of a Uniate minister, Lutsky, was found in a wood near Lvov, in 1975, in the Drogobych district of Ukraine. While the authorities claimed that he had committed suicide there were reports that the secret police had murdered him.

3. Ivan Biblenko

Ivan Biblenko was a Baptist, and had already served a three year prison sentence from 1972-75. He went to Dnepropetrovsk on a church meeting on 13 September, 1975, from which he never returned. Eventually his family tracked him down to a hospital where it was claimed that he had died on 24 September, as a result of a road accident. After his body was examined it became clear to his family that he had died as a result of being tortured.

4. Mindaugas Tamonis

Mindaugas Tamonis, 1941-75, a Roman Catholic, was a poet from Lithuania who played an active role in the Lithuanian Catholic nationalistic movement. At 34 years old he committed suicide by throwing herself under the wheel of a moving train.

She refused to hand back a monument to the Red Army and had written to the Central Committee of the Communist Party seeking a referendum so that Christians could participate in an election where their interests would be catered for. At Vilnius psychiatric hospital Mindaugas was subjected to a 564-point questionnaire about religious beliefs and put on depressant drugs.

5. Raisa Ivanova

Raisa Ivanova, 1929-1977, belonged to the True Orthodox Church. She was interned in the Mordovian camp, where she refused to work. From there she was transferred to Kazan Special Psychiatric Hospital, after being pronounced mentally ill. There she endured great suffering from the "treatment" they gave her, and in December 1977 she hanged herself.

6. Tatyana Krasnova

Tatyana Krasnova, 1903-1979, a member of

the True Orthodox Church, had endured one prison sentence from which she was released in 1955, three years exile and was in the eighth year of a nine year prison sentence when at, 76, she died in prison.

7. Fr Anatoli Gurgula

Anatoli Gurgula, 1906-1980, remained pastor to the Ukrainian Catholics around his village of Tomshivtsy in the region of Kalush. The bodies of the 74-year- old priest and his wife were discovered on 27 February 1980 in their home where they had been burnt to death, where they were believed to have been murdered.

8. Bronius Laurinavicius

Bronius Laurinavicius was a Roman Catholic and pastor at Adutiskis. Over a period of twenty years, since 1960, he had signed petitions against the Soviet authorities interfering in the affairs of the church. He died in a road accident in Vilnius, where a lorry ran over him. Two witnesses say that he was pushed into the oncoming lorry on the orders of KGB officers.

Keston College (Note: Keston College, now in Oxford, England, has been monitoring and recording the persecution and martyrdom of Christians in communist lands. In *Religion in Communist Lands* Volume II, No 1, Spring 1983, Carolyn Burch complied a "Chronicle" of thirty-seven people who had been martyred in communist countries.)

Keston College

Chronicle of Martyrs in Eastern Europe, 1974-1983

A. Czechoslovakia

Cardinal Stepan Trocta

Under Dubcek's liberal government Trocta was made a cardinal in 1969. Trocta, ordained in the Roman Catholic church in 1932, and consecrated bishop of Litomerice in 1948, spent many years in prison. He had spent the war years in prison, was arrested again in 1951 and sentenced to 25 years' hard labor in 1954. In 1974 he was subjected to prolonged and brutal interrogations and he died the next day after a cerebral hemorrhage, and was immediately declared a martyr by the Czech Catholics.

Milan Gono

One of the people Cardinal Trocta ordained in secret was Milan Gono. Gono was arrested on trumped up charges in March 1979. He was given a two-year prison sentence for his unauthorized priestly activities. In July 1979 he died in prison, as a result of falling off scaffolding, according to the authorities. However, the doctor who examined the body declared that Gono had been dead before he fell. Gono's prison warder admitted that he had been interrogated as they tried to make him divulge the names of other people who had been secretly ordained, and that Gono died as a result of these severe tortures.

Father Premysl Coufal

Father Coufal was a Roman Catholic secret priest and was frequently harassed by the secret police for this reason. In January 1981 he was given an ultimatum by the secret police. He had until 23 February to cooperate with them, which would have meant divulging names of other secret priests. On 24 February Coufal's friends found him dead in his flat. The authorities claimed that Coufal committed suicide by gassing himself. Coufal's friends found his head had been very badly wounded.

B. Albania

Bishop Ernesto Coba

Coba, a Roman Catholic, had been the Apostolic Administrator of Shkodra before he was incarcerated in the Elbasan labor camp in 1974. He celebrated mass on Easter Day in 1979, but was caught in the act, and received a severe beating as a result. The elderly clergyman was beaten up so badly that he died from his injuries on the following day. The authorities claimed that he died of natural causes.

C. Romania

Ioan Clipa

Ioan Clipa, a Baptist, was taken into custody by the authorities and savagely interrogated, accused of distributing Bibles in Romania.

By the time the security police had finished with him Clipa was reduced to being a nervous wreck. In 1981 he was arrested for a second time, had a nervous breakdown and committed suicide.

Keston Collge (Keston College, now in Oxford, has been monitoring and recording the persecution and martyrdom of Christians in communist lands. In *Religion in Communist Lands* Volume II, No 1, Spring 1983, Carolyn Burch complied a "Chronicle" of thirty-seven people who had been martyred in communist countries.)

POLAND
JERZY POPIELUSZKO, 1947-84

After being overrun by the Nazi in World War II Poland became a satellite state of Russia after the war. This predominantly Catholic country did not take kindly to being ruled as a Marxist-Leninist state and so made five brave, but unsuccessful, attempts between 1945 and 1989 to throw off the shackles of Russian domination. A man who came to symbolize this struggle was born in 1947 in the village of Okopy, in eastern Poland, Jerzy Popieluszko.

In 1965 Popieluszko entered the Warsaw seminary to train for the priesthood just at a time when the authorities were inflicting another purge on the Catholic Church. Even though people in training for the priesthood were officially exempt from national service Popieluszko had to endure a two-year course of atheistic political indoctrination. During this time a soldier caught Popieluszko with a rosary in his hand. Popieluszko refused to throw it on the ground as he was ordered and so was beaten up and locked in solitary confinement for a month. In 1972 Popieluszko was eventually ordained.

A popular mass movement called Solidarity was born in 1980-81 as a result of illegal strikes in Poland's naval dockyards at Gdansk, with Lech Walesa as one of its early, ardent supporters. During August 1980 strikes spread throughout Poland. 10,000 steel workers at Huta Warszana demanded that a mass should be celebrated in their factory. Jerzy Popieluszko was the popular choice of both the archbishop and the strikers for this symbolic and brave act of faith and defiance. Jerzy Popieluszko became the first priest ever to enter that factory and from then on Popieluszko was known as the pastor of Solidarity. Popieluszko felt at one with the aspirations of the down-trodden workers.

In April 1981 Popieluszko started to hold services in which members of the congregation could take a greater part, singing hymns, clapping and reciting poetry. These services soon became monthly celebrations, held on the last Sunday of every month, as a kind of "mass for the nation". They ensured a focal point after Solidarity became a banned trade union in December 1981. The authorities became more and more angry with Popieluszko as he told the thousands of people who attended his popular masses, in his short sermons, "you must speak of evil as a disease if you are to serve God." Martial law soon followed with many ringleaders of Solidarity being arrested. Popieluszko's masses for Poland now became masses for the victims of martial law. Popieluszko became a folk hero throughout Poland but he also began to receive death threats through the post, in which he was told, "You also will hang on a cross.'

During the first six months of 1984 Popieluszko was arrested and interrogated thirteen times, before being impeached on July 12. On October 19 Popieluszko took part in a Worker's Mass at Bydgoszcz. Three KGB assassins were waiting for him and bundled him unceremoniously into a car at the end of the service. Popieluszko was never seen alive again. He was tortured, beaten, almost suffocated by a gag, before being thrown into a weir, with his body weighed down by two sackfuls of stones.

The 400,000 grateful Polish people who attended his funeral on November 1, 1984, all knew that Popieluszko had given his life for Solidarity. Poland soon became the first country formerly controlled by Russia to successfully reject atheistic communism.

Editor

Western Europe

Germany

Maria Skobtsova, 1891-1945

"Live today as if you were going to die a martyr this evening." Charles de Foucauld

Maria Skobtsova, whose maiden name was Elizabeth (Lisa) Yurievna Pilenco, was brought up in the rarified atmosphere of the Russian Czars. After the Revolution she went to Paris and became a latter-day Dr Barnardo, caring for everyone in need who crossed her path, especially outcasts. In 1932 she made a monastic profession in the Orthodox Church in the Church of the institute of St Sergius in Paris. But she joined no cloistered way of life. As Metropolitan Eulogus said when he gave her name, Maria, it was "in memory of St Mary of Egypt." The Metropolitan told Maria, "Like this Mary lived a life of penitence in the desert to and speak and minister in the desert of human hearts." The world became Maria's monastery. She lived at 77 rue de Lourmel, which became a spiritual center (Nicolas Berdyaev gave one of his lectures there), and a center of compassion for the poor. It became the springboard for the formation of Orthodox Action, founded in 1935. The Orthodox group campaigned for the social welfare of the poor and made Maria Skobtsova their first president.

At the outbreak of World War II Maria made no secret of her hatred of Hitler and all he stood for. It was no surprise, therefore, that the SS broke up her work during a visit to her home on 8 February, 1947. Maria was arrested and ended up in the notorious Ravensbruck concentration camp, after a stint in camps at Romainville and Compiegne. In Ravensbruck Maria still carried on caring for all those suffering around her, in answer to her own prayer which she prayed shortly after her arrest: "Lord, I am your messenger. Throw me like a blazing torch into the night."

Prisoner 19263, from Block 27, gave courage, hope and encouragement to all around her, counseling her fellow prisoners in the most appalling human misery, "Don't let your spirit's flame die." With her swelling feet, ankles and legs, and becoming weaker and weaker, Maria became a mother to many of the women prisoners who went to her for a hug. One young girl had managed somehow to smuggle in a prayer book and Maria read aloud the words of the Gospel and Epistle, adding her own short meditation afterwards.

The final days of Maria's life are shrouded in mystery. One account of her death tells how she became so weak that she was unable to walk and so was callously condemned to death by the Nazis. Himmler had sent orders that all sick people should be killed, in a vain attempt to cover up the inhuman treatment and medical experimentations that had been carried on in these camps. A second version of Maria's last days is very much in keeping with the tenor of her whole life. Maria exchanged places with a woman who was in a queue of condemned prisoners and went voluntarily to her martyrdom in order to help her companion to live. What is certain is that Maria's name is on the list of those people who were gassed to death on 31 March, 1945, Easter Eve. The next day, Easter Day, the Red Cross arrived at Ravensbruck camp, a day too late for Maria.

Editor

Martyrdom of Maximilian Kolbe (1)

Maximilian Kolbe, Friar, Martyr
14 August 1941

Raymond Kolbe (who took the name Maximilian when he became a friar) is known chiefly for the manner of his death, but his life was also noteworthy. He was born in 1894 near Lodz (51:49 N 19:28 E) in a part of Poland then under Russian rule, of parents who worked at home as weavers. In 1910 he became a Franciscan, taking the name Maximilian. His parents then undertook the monastic life, his mother as a Benedictine and his father as a Franciscan. His father left the order (I assume before taking life vows) to run a religious bookstore, and then enlisted with Pilsudski's army to fight the Russians. He was captured and hanged as a traitor in 1914.

Maximilian studied at Rome and was

ordained in 1919. He returned to Poland and taught Church history in a seminary. He left the seminary (1) to found an association named for the Virgin Mary and dedicated to spreading the Roman Catholic faith and assisting those who held it to learn more about it; and (2) to establish a printing press and publish a periodical for the members of his association, consisting largely of Christian apologetics. He built a friary just west of Warsaw (52:15 N 21:00 E), which eventually housed 762 Franciscans and printed eleven periodicals (one with a circulation of over a million), including a daily newspaper. In 1930 he went to Asia, where he founded friaries in Nagasaki (34:25 N 129:52 E) and in India. In 1936 he was recalled to supervise the original friary near Warsaw. When Germany invaded Poland in 1939, he knew that the friary would be seized, and sent most of the friars home. He was imprisoned briefly and then released, and returned to the friary, where he and the other friars sheltered 3000 Poles and 1500 Jews, and continued to publish a newspaper encouraging its readers.

In May 1941 the friary was closed down and Maximilian and four companions were taken to Auschwitz, where they worked with the other prisoners, chiefly at carrying logs. Maximilian carried on his priestly work surreptitiously, hearing confessions in unlikely places and celebrating the Lord's Supper with bread and wine smuggled in for that purpose.

In order to discourage escapes, the camp had a rule that if a man escaped, ten men would be killed in retaliation. In July 1941 a man from Kolbe's bunker escaped. The remaining men of the bunker were led out and ten were selected, including a Sergeant Francis Gajowniczek. When he uttered a cry of dismay, Maximilian stepped forward and said, "I am a Catholic priest. Let me take his place. I am old. He has a wife and children." The officer had more use for a young worker than for an old one, and was happy to make the exchange. The ten men were placed in a large cell and left there to starve. Maximilian encouraged the others with prayers, psalms, and meditations on the Passion of Christ. After two weeks, only four were alive, and only Maximilian was fully conscious. The four were killed with injections of carbolic acid on 14 August 1941.

James Kiefer, Christian Biographies, By kind permission

Martyrdom of Maximilian Kolbe (2)

Maximilian Kolbe, born Raymond Kolbe, was born in Zdunska Wola, in Poland on 8th January, 1894. He became a Franciscan at sixteen. Then he founded the Niepokalanon friars who grew to 763 in number by the outbreak of the Second World War. Maximilian set up a printing press which became the envy of all printers in Poland where the circulation of his Knights magazine eventually rose to a 60,000 monthly circulation. As Hitler began to overrun Poland in 1939, Maximilian Kolbe, who by then was something of a celebrity, was arrested and taken to Amtlitz concentration camp. After being freed once, he was rearrested on 17th February 1941 for helping Jews escape from the Germans. On 28th May 1941, after a journey by cattle truck with 300 other prisoners, Maximilian arrived at the dreaded death camp at Auschwitz.

In Auschwitz Kolbe continued to inspire and encourage other prisoners, and heard confessions, said masses and preached, even though each of these activities was punishable by death. One morning sirens droned their frightening sound, announcing the escape of another prisoner of war. Everyone knew what that meant. Ten prisoners would die as a reprisal, but they were made to die in a terrible way. They were placed in airless concrete bunkers. In that underground position they were then left to slowly die of thirst and hunger.

The day after the escape the camp's Deputy Commandant, Karl Fritsch, had an important visiting guest to take with him along the pathetic lines of prisoners – Gestapo chief Gerhardt Palitsch. Colonel Fritsch said tersely, "The escaped prisoner has not been found. Ten of you will die." They pointed to different men, who were thus selected for this painfully slow form of execution. The ninth man they selected could not bear the thought. "I don't want to die. I'm young. I can work for you. I have a wife. I have young children. I shall never see them again."

At that moment a smaller man, wearing wire rimmed glasses, came forward, without asking anyone's permission. The Franciscan stood to attention in front of the Deputy Commandant. "What do you want, Polish pig?" screamed the Deputy Commandant.

The little man replied, "I would like to die in the place of this man. I am a Catholic priest, whereas he has a wife and family." They allowed prisoner 16670 to be a substitute for Francis Gajowniczek. The ten condemned men went through agonies before they died, although the sound of praying and singing of Christian songs could be heard from under the ground at Block 13. One by one the men died, as they were deprived of water and food. They were so desperate for fluid to drink that they even drank their own urine. By August 14th four prisoners were left alive. Then the moment came for a lethal injection of phenol to be administered in the left arms of the four men, including Kolbe. Kolbe prayed and gave his arm to his executioner.

News of Maximilian's death spread through the camp and was spoken of as if it had been some victory. Szczepanski wrote later, "The lunatic program of the Nazis was not defeated by military might. The definitive answer was given by a death in August 1941 in an underground cell in Block 13, the Block of Death, in Auschwitz concentration camp. It was given by a Polish Franciscan, Father Maximilian Kolbe, who gave an answer which no dialectic could ever provide." On 17 October 1971 Pope Paul VI beatified Maximilian, thus making him the first Nazi victim to be proclaimed blessed by the Roman Catholic Church. John Paul II, in 1982, elevated Maximilian to the official status of martyr in the Roman Catholic Church.

Editor

Franz Jõgerstõtter, Martyr

9 August 1943

Franz Jõgerstõtter was an Austrian Christian executed for his refusal to serve in the armies of the Third Reich. He was born out of wedlock in 1907 in the small town of St. Radegund (47:11 N 15:29 E), about 13 kilometers north of Graz. His natural father was killed in World War I. His mother married Herr Jõgerstõtter, a small farmer, who adopted Franz. After gaining a reputation as a rather wild young man, perhaps fathering an illegitimate child, Franz married and settled down to a typical peasant life.

In addition to his farm and household duties, Jõgerstõtter became sexton of the parish church, and was known for his diligent and devout service, particularly in refusing donations for conducting bereavement services, and for joining the bereaved as a fellow mourner. After taking up this work, he began to receive Holy Communion daily.

He also became known for his opposition to the Nazi regime, casting the only local vote against the Anschluss (the annexation of Austria by Germany in March 1938), eschewing the local taverns and political argument, but typically responding "Pfui Hitler" when greeted by a "Heil." He also engaged in long discussions with his cousin, a Jehovah's Witness, having strong theological disagreements, but gaining great respect for the Jehovah's Witnesses' stand against service to Hitler.

When Jõgerstõtter was called to active duty in the military, he sought counsel from at least three priests and his bishop. Each tried to counter his conscience and assure him that this military service was compatible with his Christianity. His earlier experiences left him with a great horror of lies and double-dealing, and Jõgerstõtter reconciled his church's advice of subservience to the governing authorities with his conscience by reporting to the induction center but refusing to serve. Imprisoned in Linz (48:19 N 14:18 E) and Berlin (53:32 N 13:25 E), he was convicted in a military trial and beheaded on August 9th, 1943. He was survived by his wife and three daughters, the eldest of whom was six. He also left behind a small and moving set of essays and letters from prison.

His sacrifice was uniformly regarded as foolish by his neighbors, and his story almost forgotten, but for a book written by an American, Gordon Zahn, who heard of Jõgerstötter when researching the subject of German Roman Catholics' response to Hitler. This book, In Solitary Witness, influenced Daniel Ellsberg's decision to stand against the Vietnam War by bringing the Pentagon Papers to public attention. It is also the source for this report, and of the following quote, taken from one of Jõgerstötter's last letters.

"Just as the man who thinks only of this world does everything possible to make life here easier and better, so must we, too, who believe in the eternal Kingdom, risk everything in order to receive a great reward there. Just as those who believe in National Socialism tell themselves that their struggle is for survival, so must we, too, convince ourselves that our struggle is for the eternal Kingdom. But with this difference: we need no rifles or pistols for our battle, but instead, spiritual weapons—and the foremost among these is prayer.... Through prayer, we continually implore new grace from God, since without God's help and grace it would be impossible for us to preserve the Faith and be true to His commandments....

"Let us love our enemies, bless those who curse us, pray for those who persecute us. For love will conquer and will endure for all eternity. And happy are they who live and die in God's love."

James Kiefer, (guest biography by Paul Bellan-Boyer), Christian Biographies, By kind permission

Martyrdom of Dietrich Bonhoeffer

Dietrich Bonhoeffer, Pastor and Theologian

10 April 1945

Bonhoeffer was born in 1906, son of a professor of psychiatry and neurology at the University of Berlin. He was an outstanding student, and at the age of 25 became a lecturer in systematic theology at the same University. When Hitler came to power in 1933, Bonhoeffer became a leading spokesman for the Confessing Church, the center of Protestant resistance to the Nazis. He organized and for a time led the underground seminary of the Confessing Church. His book Life Together describes the life of the Christian community in that seminary, and his book The Cost Of Discipleship attacks what he calls "cheap grace," meaning grace used as an excuse for moral laxity. Bonhoeffer had been taught not to "resist the powers that be," but he came to believe that to do so was sometimes the right choice. In 1939 his brother-in-law introduced him to a group planning the overthrow of Hitler, and he made significant contributions to their work. (He was at this time an employee of the Military Intelligence Department.) He was arrested in April 1943 and imprisoned in Berlin. After the failure of the attempt on Hitler's life in April 1944, he was sent first to Buchenwald and then to Schoenberg Prison. His life was spared, because he had a relative who stood high in the government; but then this relative was himself implicated in anti-Nazi plots. On Sunday 8 April 1945, he had just finished conducting a service of worship at Schoenberg, when two soldiers came in, saying, "Prisoner Bonhoeffer, make ready and come with us," the standard summons to a condemned prisoner. As he left, he said to another prisoner, "This is the end – but for me, the beginning – of life." He was hanged the next day, less than a week before the Allies reached the camp.

Some of his later writings insist that many Christians do not take seriously enough the existence and power of evil. Because of this and other statements of his, some theological advocates of "secularist Christianity" in the 1960's attempted to claim him as their own. In my judgement, a study of his writings (even his later writings) as a whole does not support this claim. However, it is true that he never had a chance to edit his prison letters and papers, or put them into context, and accordingly it is not surprising that they contain some statements that baffle the reader.

Church leaders remember Dietrich Bonhoeffer

Fifty years after the execution of Dietrich Bonhoeffer at the age of 39 on April 9, 1945, at the hands of one of Hitler's special commandos in the concentration camp of Flossenbuerg, church leaders have paid tribute to the German Lutheran theologian who joined the political opposition to Hitler. At a recent memorial service in Flossenbuerg, Klaus Engelhardt, the presiding bishop of the Evangelical Church in Germany (EKD), described how Bonhoeffer refused to be placed on the prayer list of the Confessing Church after his imprisonment in 1943. "Bonhoeffer believed that only those who were imprisoned because of their proclamation or actions in the service of the church belonged on the prayer list, but not those imprisoned as political conspirators," he said. Engelhardt asserted that the church today should think again about how it supports those who exercise their resistance to injustice through political means. "Is our Protestant church not in the position and not prepared to support or pray for those who take the path of political resistance to inhumanity or the perversion of law and order?" he asked. "They are among those who hunger and thirst for righteousness and whom Jesus praises in the beatitudes."

James Kiefer, Christian Biographies, By kind permission

Martyrdom of Dietrich Bonhoeffer (2)

Bonhoeffer was hanged by the Nazis at Flossenburg death camp on 9th April, 1945. A memorial stone in the church at Flossenburg says: "Dietrich Bonhoeffer, a witness of Jesus Christ among his brethren."

Bonhoeffer was born on 4th February, 1906, in Breslau, Germany. He grew up in Berlin, where his father was a Professor of Psychiatry and Neurology at Berlin University. He was the sixth of eight children in a prosperous, middle-class family.

In 1923, when he was seventeen, Bonhoeffer went to Tübingen University to study theology. He immersed himself in his studies, proving to be an independent and original thinker. His ambition was to lecture in theology at the university. As a student politics did not interest him. As a good Lutheran he believed it was his duty to support the state, but, step by step, in obedience to Christ, he was led to resist the growing evil of Nazism until he was thrown into prison and killed only three weeks before Hitler himself committed suicide.

When he was twenty-four Bonhoeffer went to America for a year, to study at Union Theological Seminary in New York. He taught Sunday School and gave Bible classes in the black ghetto of Harlem. Among these black Christians he found fellowship in Christ – a true Christian community of faith and love. And for the first time he experienced the horror of racial hatred.

Returning to Germany, he was ordained and became a student pastor and lecturer at the university of Berlin. Increasing numbers of Christians – especially Protestants in the Lutheran churches – supported Hitler's National Socialist movement. Many regarded Hitler as their country's savior, and defender against communism. At the university, where students and lecturers were impassioned Nazis, Bonhoeffer lectured on the evils of war.

On 30th January, 1933, Hitler became Chancellor of Germany. That spring the first anti-Jewish laws were announced. To a congregation of Lutheran pastors Bonhoeffer said that the church must oppose the state when it made wrong judgements. If a car, he said, were driven by a mad driver and went out of control, then it was not enough to bind up the wounds of injured people. A spoke must be put in the wheels. Many of his congregation walked out in disgust at his words.

When the Protestant Church of Germany voted to support Hitler, Bonhoeffer became one of the leaders of the breakaway Lutheran group called "Young Reformers". They vowed to be true to God's word and to oppose the Aryan laws. Asked to prepare a Confession of Faith for Christians opposed to Hitler, he went to stay at Bethel – a community for the physically and mentally disabled. Here he enlisted his father's medical help to oppose the implementation of Hitler's euthanasia law. Malcolm Muggeridge writes: "It was quite clear to him that to suppose the sick and infirm could be disposed of in this barbarous way was a worse sickness than any had to deal with at Bethel. Von Bodtchwingh [the Director of Bethel] . . . when challenged demonstrated conclusively that at Bethel there were no useless lives. The most stricken inmates could still communicate, if not in words, then in God's language of love."

In 1933 German support for Hitler reached fever pitch. Protestants who would not support Hitler joined together to form the Confessing Church. In 1935 Bonhoeffer became head of its theological seminary at Finkenwalde. Bonhoeffer's anti-Nazi views became well-known. He lost his job at Berlin University, and in 1937 the Seminary was closed down. Bonhoeffer wrote articles for a number of periodicals. His condemnation of government policies resulted in his being condemned for meddling in politics.

In 1939, as warfare mounted Bonhoeffer found himself in a dilemma. He was a pacifist. All war was abhorrent to him. It was impossible for him to fight for Germany. But to refuse the call-up would endanger his friends in the Confessing Church. Unable to make a decision, he sailed for America where his friends hoped he would stay till peace returned. But he could not turn his back on Germany. He wrote, "I must live through this difficult period of our national history with the Christian people of Germany. I shall forfeit the right to share in the reconstruction of Christian life in Germany after the war, if I do not share the trials of this time with my own people."

So after a very short time he returned – and he went back determined to do all he could to rid Germany of Hitler. In 1940 he was forbidden to preach or publish. He began to work as a German double agent. He traveled in Europe, ostensibly for the church on ecumenical missions. In reality, while pretending to find out allied military secrets, he was working with a group of conspirators seeking to destroy Hitler. He helped Jewish refugees to escape from Germany. In the winter of 1942-43 two assassination attempts failed. During this time Bonhoeffer tried to enlist the help of the British Government in the plot to assassinate Hitler, and to set up an alternative government.

When Bonhoeffer was eventually arrested in 1943 it was for his involvement in smuggling fourteen Jews out of Germany. He was at first thrown into Tegal prison. This was a military prison not a Gestapo prison. Here, for the first twelve days he was allowed visits from his family, and he was also allowed to read and write letters. He hid his connection with the conspirators, whilst still communicating to them in code. Bonhoeffer spent eighteen months in Tengel prison, and here "the theologian became a mystic, the pastor became a martyr, and the teacher produced in his Letters and Papers from Prison, one of the great contemporary classics of Christian literature."

One year after his arrest, when no evidence had been found implicating him in conspiracy, the charge was dropped. Whilst he was at Tengel he was given the opportunity to escape – with the help of the guards. However, he refused to run away because this would have put his uncle and brother – fellow prisoners – in danger. In July 1944 the assassination plot was discovered and the conspirators were executed. On 23rd August 1949 he wrote: "You must never doubt that I'm traveling with gratitude and cheerfulness along the road where I'm being led. My past life is brim full of God's goodness, and my sins are covered by the forgiving love of Christ crucified."

In October 1944 a secret file was discovered which revealed that Bonhoeffer had been working with the anti-Hitler conspirators for many years. He was moved to the Gestapo prison in Prinz-Albrecht Strasse. Here he was brutally tortured but remained unbroken, calm, cheerful, and trusting. On 7th February, 1945, he was transferred to Buchenwald, where he was kept in the cellar of a house outside the main concentration camp. A British officer, imprisoned at Buchenwald, wrote, "Bonhoeffer was different; just quiet calm and normal, seemingly perfectly at his ease. His soul really shone in the dark desperation of our prison. He was all humility and sweetness. He was one of the very few men I have ever met to whom his God was real and close to him." The war was drawing to a close. The prisoners could hear American guns and expected to be released. Then, after seven weeks, Bonhoeffer was taken to the village of Sclonberg. They stayed in a village school. But just after he had left, diaries were found, clearly implicating Bonhoeffer in the conspiracy. On 8th April, Low Sunday, Bonhoeffer preached a sermon on the text, "Through his wounds we are healed". Just as it was over, the SS arrived. "Prisoner Bonhoeffer, get ready and come with us." Bonhoeffer asked an Englishman, Payne Best, to give a message to Bishop Bell of Chichester, "Tell him that for me this is the end but also the beginning."

Not long after all the conspirators met together at Flossenburg. The prison doctor described what happened:

"Through the half-open door in one room of the huts I saw Pastor Bonhoeffer, before taking off his prison garb, kneeling on the floor praying fervently to his God. I was most deeply moved by the way this lovable man prayed, so devout and so certain that God heard his prayer. At the place of execution, he again said a short prayer and then climbed the steps to the gallows, brave and composed. His death ensued after a few seconds. In almost fifty years that I worked as a doctor, I have hardly ever seen a man die so entirely submissive to the will of God."
Editor

Italy
Agostina; also known as: Livia Pietrantoni; Livia Petrantoni

Livia is referred to as a martyr of charity. She was a nurse at the Holy Spirit Hospital, near the Vatican, in Rome in 1886. The next year she joined the Sisters of Charity, dedicated to service to the sick, taking the name Agostina. She worked with the critically ill and contagious, catching typhus and malaria in the process. After she caught tuberculosis, she worked in the TB ward where a patient, Giuseppe Romanelli, stabbed her to death, on 13 November 1913 during a rape attempt; she died praying for his forgiveness.
Editor

France
Martyrs of the Paris Commune

The secular priests and the religious who were murdered in Paris, in May 1871, on account of their sacred calling. They may be divided into three groups:

first, those who on the 24th of May were executed within the prison of La Roquette;

second, the Dominican Fathers, who, on the following day, were shot down at the Barriaphre d' Italie; and third, the priests and religious who, on the 26th of May were massacred at Belleville.

The revolutionary party which took possession of the city after the siege of Paris by the Prussians began, in the last days of March, to arrest the priests and religious to whom personal character or official position gave a certain prominence. No reason was given for these arbitrary measures, except the hatred with which the leaders of the Commune regarded the Catholic Church and her ministers.

(1) At the head of the first group of martyrs is the Archbishop of Paris, Monseigneur Georges Darboy, to whom the discomforts of his prison life were peculiarly trying on account of his feeble health. His fellow sufferers were: the Abbé Duguerry, curé of the important parish of La Madeleine, an old man, well-advanced in years, but bright and vigorous; the Abbé Allard, a secular priest, who had rendered good service to the wounded during the siege, and two Jesuit-Fathers Ducoudray and Clerc. The first was rector of the Ecole Sainte-Geneviphave, a well known preparatory school for the army: the second had been a distinguished naval officer; both were gifted and holymen. To these five

ecclesiastics was added a magistrate, Senator Bonjean. After several weeks of confinement, first in the prison or Mazas, then at La Roquette, these six prisoners were executed on 24 May. There was no pretense made of judging them, neither was any accusation brought against them. This revolutionary party still held possession of the east of Paris, but the regular army, whose headquarters were at Versailles, was fast approaching, and the leaders of the Commune, made desperate by failure, wished to inflict what evil they could on an enemy they no longer hoped to conquer. The priests had, one and all, endured their captivity with patience and dignity the Jesuits, their letters prove it, had no illusions as to their probable fate, Archbishop Darboy and the Abbé Deguerry were more sanguine. "What have they to gain by killing us? What harm have we done them?" often said the latter. The execution took place in the evening. The archbishop absolved his companions who were calm and recollected. They were told to stand against a wall, within the precincts of the prison, and here they were shot down at close quarters by twenty men, enlisted for the purpose. The archbishop's hand was raised to give a last blessing: "Here take my blessing", said one of the murders and by discharging his gun he give the signal for the execution.

(2) The Dominican Fathers, who perished the following day 25 May, belonged to the College of Arcueil, close to Paris. Their superior was Father Captier, who founded the college and under whose government it had prospered. With him were for religious of his order: Fathers Bourard, Delhorme Cottrault, and Chatagneret, and eight laymen, who belonged to the college, either as professors or as servants. They were arrested on the 19th of May and imprisoned in the outlying fort of Bicütre, where they suffered from hunger and thirst. On the 25th of May they were transferred from Bicütre to a prison within the city, situated on the Avenue d' Italie. The excitement and anarchy that reigned in Paris, and the insults that were leveled at the prisoners as they were led from one prison to another prepared them for the worst; they made their confession and prepared for death. Towards five in the afternoon, they were commanded to go into the street one by one: Father Captier, whose strong faith sustained his companion's courage, turned to them: "Let us go, my friends, for the sake of God". The street was filled with armed men who discharged their guns at the prisoners as they passed. Father Captier was mortally wounded; his companions fell here and there; some were killed on the spot; others lingered on till their assassins put them out of their pain. Their dead bodies remained for twenty-four hours on the ground, exposed to an insult; only the next morning, when the troops from Versailles had conquered the Commune, were they claimed by the victims' friends and conveyed to Arcuil.

(3) The third group of martyrs perished on the 26th of May; the revolutionists were now driven back by the steady advance of the regular troops, and only the heights of Belleville were still in the possession of the Commune. Over fifty prisoners were taken from the prison of La Roquette and conducted on foot to this last stronghold of the revolution. Among them were eleven ecclesiastics: three Jesuits, four members of the Congregation of the Sacred Heart and Mary, three secular priests, and one seminarist. All displayed heroic courage, the best known among them was Father Olivaint, rector of the Jesuit house of the Rue de Saphvres, who thirsted for martyrdom. After a painful journey through the streets, which were filled with an infuriated rabble, the prisoner were into an enclosure, called the cite Vincennes, on the height os Belleville. Here they were hacked to pieces by a crowd of men, women, and even children. There was no attempt to organize a regular execution like the one at La Raquette; the massacre lasted an hour, and most of the bodies were disfigured beyond recognition. Only a few hours later the regular troops forced their way to La Roquette, delivered the prisoners that still remained there, and took possession of Belleville, the stronghold of Commune.

Barbara de Courson, The Catholic Encyclopedia, Volume 4

Middle East

Iran

Twentieth century martyrs

Since the 1979 Muslim takeover of Iran, governmental sponsored persecution, imprisonment, and torture of Christians is the norm. This is especially true of church leaders who are put in prisons for months or years. Even if there is international pressure to release the Christian prisoners, after their release they are killed by governmental sponsored groups.

Hossein Soodmand

Hossein had been pastor of the church in Mashad and was executed by hanging in prison in 1990.

Rev. Sayyah

Rev. Sayyah, a minister in Shiraz had his throat cut.

Bahram Deghani-Tafti

Bahram Deghani-Tafti, the son of the Anglican bishop, was shot.

Rev. Tateos Michaelian

Also in 1994 the sixty-two year old leader of the Presbyterian church, Rev. Tateos Michaelian, was murdered after taking over Bishop Hovsepian's position as Chairman of the Protestant Council of Ministers.

Bishop Haik Hovsepian – Church of Tehran

Bishop Haik disappeared from the streets of Tehran on January 19, 1994. The authorities reported his death to his family on January 30. Haik was a man of God who believed in the God-given right of a person to believe according to his conscience. He loved the people of Iran whether Christian or Muslim. For their religious freedom, he gave his life.

Pastor Haik Hovsepian-Mehr did not believe in succumbing to government pressure and chose instead to "tell the world" about the plight of Iranian Christians. He said: "If we go to jail or die for our faith, we want the whole Christian world to know what is happening to their brothers and sisters."

Rev. Mehdi Dibaj

Rev. Mehdi Dibaj who was born into a Muslim family became a Christian 45 Years ago. On December 21, 1993 an Islamic court in the city of Sari condemned him to die. The conviction was based on the charge of apostasy, i.e. that Rev. Dibaj had abandoned Islam and embraced Christianity. Once the news of Rev. Dibaj's death sentence reached the rest of the world, the reaction was one of disbelief followed by prayer and action.

Written Defense of the Rev. Mehdi Dibaj Delivered to the Sari Court of Justice

Sari, Iran, December 3, 1993

"In the Holy Name of God who is our life and existence"

With all humility I express my gratitude to the Judge of all heaven and earth for this precious opportunity, and with brokenness I wait upon the Lord to deliver me from this court trial according to His promises. I also beg the honored members of the court who are present to listen with patience to my defense and with respect for the Name of the Lord.

I am a Christian. As a sinner I believe Jesus has died for my sins on the cross and by His resurrection and victory over death, has made me righteous in the presence of the Holy God. The true God speaks about this fact in His Holy Word, the Gospel (Injil). Jesus means Savior "because He will save His people from their sins." Jesus paid the penalty of our sins by His own blood and gave us a new life so that we can live for the glory of God by the help of the Holy Spirit and be like a dam against corruption, be a channel of blessing and healing, and be protected by the love of God.

In response to this kindness, He has asked me to deny myself and be His fully surrendered follower, and not to fear people even if they kill my body, but rather rely on the creator of life who has crowned me with the crown of mercy and compassion. He is the great protector of His beloved ones as well as their great reward.

I have been charged with "apostasy!" The invisible God who knows our hearts has given assurance to us, as Christians, that we are not among the apostates who will perish but among the believers who will have eternal life. In Islamic Law (Sharia'), an apostate is one who does not believe in God, the prophets or the resurrection of the dead, We Christians believe in all three!

They say "You were a Muslim and you have become a Christian." This is not so. For many years I had no religion. After searching and studying I accepted God's call and believed in the Lord Jesus Christ in order to receive eternal life. People choose their religion but a Christian is chosen by Christ. He says, "You have not chosen me but I have chosen you." Since when did He choose me? He chose me before the foundation of the world. People say, "You were a Muslim from your birth." God says, "You were a Christian from the beginning." He states that He chose us thousands of years ago, even before the creation of the universe, so that through the sacrifice of Jesus Christ we may be His. A Christian means one who belongs to Jesus Christ.

The eternal God who sees the end from the beginning and who has chosen me to belong to Him, knew from the beginning those whose heart would be drawn to Him and also those who would be willing to sell their faith and eternity for a pot of porridge. I would rather have the whole world against me, but know that the Almighty God is with me. I would rather be called an apostate, but know that I have the approval of the God of glory, because man looks at the outward appearance but God looks at the heart. For Him who is God for all eternity nothing is impossible. All power in heaven and on earth is in His hands.

The Almighty God will raise up anyone He chooses and bring down others, accept some and reject others, send some to heaven and other to hell. Now because God does whatever He desires, who can separate us from the love of God? Or who can destroy the relationship between the creator and the creature or defeat a life that is faithful to his Lord? The faithful will be safe and secure under the shadow of the Almighty! Our refuge is the mercy seat of God who is exalted from the beginning. I know in whom I have believed, and He is able to guard what I have entrusted to Him to the end until I reach the Kingdom of God, the place where the righteous shine like the sun, but where the evil doers will receive their punishment in the fire of hell.

They tell me, "Return!" But to whom can I return from the arms of my God? Is it right to accept what people are saying instead of obeying the Word of God? It is now 45 years that I am walking with the God of miracles, and His kindness upon me is like a shadow and I owe Him much for His fatherly love and concern.

The love of Jesus has filled all my being and I feel the warmth of His love in every part of my body. God, who is my glory and honor and protector, has put his seal of approval upon me through His unsparing blessings and miracles.

This test of faith is a clear example. The good and kind God reproves and punishes all those whom He loves. He tests them in preparation for heaven. The God of Daniel, who protected his friends in the fiery furnace, has protected me for nine years in prison. And all the bad happenings have turned out for our good and gain, so much so that I am filled to overflowing with joy and thankfulness.

The God of Job has tested my faith and commitment in order to increase my patience and faithfulness. During these nine years he has freed me from all my responsibilities so that under the protection of His blessed Name, I would spend my time in prayer and study of His Word, with a searching heart and with brokenness, and grow in the knowledge of my Lord. I praise the lord for this unique opportunity. God gave me space in my confinement, brought healing in my difficult hardships and His kindness revived me. Oh what great blessings God has in store for those who fear Him!

They object to my evangelizing. But if one finds a blind person who is about to fall in a well and keeps silent then one has sinned. It is our religious duty, as long as the door of God's mercy is open, to convince evil doers to turn from their sinful ways and find refuge in Him in order to be saved from the wrath of the

Righteous God and from the coming dreadful punishment.

Jesus Christ says "I am the door. Whoever enters through me will be saved." "I am the way, the truth and the life. No-one comes to the father except through me." "Salvation is found in no-one else, for there is no other name under heaven given to men by which we must be saved." Among the prophets of God, only Jesus Christ rose from the dead, and He is our living intercessor for ever.

He is our Savior and He is the (spiritual) Son of God. To know Him means to know eternal life. I, a useless sinner, have believed in this beloved person and all His words and miracles recorded in the Gospel, and I have committed my life into His hands. Life for me is an opportunity to serve Him, and death is a better opportunity to be with Christ. Therefore I am not only satisfied to be in prison for the honor of His Holy Name, but am ready to give my life for the sake of Jesus, my Lord, and enter His kingdom sooner, the place where the elect of God enter everlasting life. But the wicked enter into eternal damnation.

May the shadow of God's kindness and His hand of blessing and healing be and remain upon you for ever. Amen. With Respect,

Your Christian prisoner, Mehdi Dibaj

"I have always envied those Christians who were martyred for Christ Jesus our Lord. What a privilege to live for our Lord and to die for Him as well. I am filled to overflowing with joy; I am not only satisfied to be in prison. . .but am ready to give my life for the sake of Jesus Christ." Mehdi Dibaj

One of the people who worked very hard to overturn the death sentence handed out to Rev. Dibaj was Bishop Haik Hovsepian-Mehr. Bishop Haik, an Armenian pastor, shared the news of Rev. Dibaj's death sentence as well as other violations of religious freedom of Christians in Iran with the world. Due to the world's reaction, Rev. Dibaj was released on January 16, 1994.

Five months after the release from prison, Rev. Mehdi Dibadj was abducted mysteriously and suffered martyrdom in June, 1994.

Pastor Mohammed Bajher Yusefi

Mohammad Bajher Yusefi was the seventh Christian leader to be killed in Iran since the 1979 revolution. At the beginning of the revolution the Anglican Church, which was mainly made up of converts from Islam was attacked.

Pastor Mohammed Bajher Yusefi, affectionately known by his flock as "Ravanbaksh" (soul giver), was slain on Saturday September 28, 1996. Pastor Yusefi had left his house in Sari at 6 a.m. to spend time in prayer, but he never returned. The Iranian authorities notified the family later that evening that his body had been found hanging from a tree in a nearby forest.

The 35-year-old pastor converted from Islam at the age of 24. After attending Bible school, he entered into full-time ministry and became pastor of the Assembly of God churches in Sari, Gorgan, and Shahr in the province of Mazandaran.

News Reports

South Pacific
Futuna Island
St. Peter-Louis-Marie Chanel

Born at Cuet, Diocese of Belley, France, 1802; died at Futuna, 28 April, 1841. He was ordained priest in 1827, and engaged in the parochial ministry for a few years; but the reading of letters of missionaries in far-away lands inflamed his heart with zeal, and he resolved to devote his life to the Apostolate. In 1831 he joined the Society of Mary, and in 1836 he embarked for Oceania. He was assigned by his bishop to the Island of Futuna, and landed in Nov., 1837. No Christian missionary had ever set foot there, and the difficulties Peter encountered amidst those savage tribes were almost incredible. Nevertheless, he was beginning to see the results of his efforts, when Niuluki, king and also pontiff of the island, already jealous of the progress of the new religion, was exasperated by the conversion of his son and daughter. At his instigation, one of the ministers gathered some of the enemies of Christianity and Peter was cruelly assassinated without uttering a word of complaint. Through his death, the venerable martyr obtained what he had so ardently desired and earnestly worked for, the conversion of Futuna. In 1842, two Marist missionaries resumed his work, and nowhere has the preaching of the Gospel produced more wonderful results. Peter was declared Venerable by [Ven.] Pius IX in 1857, and beatified by Leo XIII on 17 November, 1889.

Joseph Freri, Catholic Encyclopedia, Volume 11

3. Christian writings

A collection of the writings, prayers and the spoken words of the martyrs and about the martyrs and martyrdom and persecution of Christians from the seventeenth to the twenty-first centuries.

A. Quotations

Sister Agostina understood that the love of Jesus requires generous service to one's brothers, in whose faces, especially that of the neediest, is reflected the face of Christ. "God" was the only "compass" which guided all the decisions of her life. The evangelical ideal of charity to the brethren, specially the smallest, the sick, the abandoned, also led Agostina to the heights of sanctity. Ready to face any sacrifice – an heroic witness of charity – she paid with her blood the price of faithfulness to Love.

Pope John Paul II

The sad chapter of the Martyrology of the Church has been opened again in the African region of the Great Lakes.

The Vatican Observer, January 13, 2000

The servant of Christ must never be surprised if he has to drink of the same cup with his Lord.

J.C. Ryle

Persecution for righteousness' sake is what every child of God must expect.

Charles Simeon

Lord, if any have to die this day, let it be me, for I am ready.

Billy Bray

The true Christian is like sandalwood, which imparts its fragrance to the axe which cuts it, without doing any harm in return.

Sundar Singh

Martyrdom does not end something; it is only the beginning.

Indira Gandhi

The tyrant dies and his rule ends, the martyr dies and his rule begins.

Søren Kierkegaard

One of the shocking untold stories of our time, is that more Christians have died this century simply for being Christians than in any century since Christ was born.

A. M. Rosenthal, The New York Times

It is sad that the United States has capitulated to China on fundamental human rights issues as China continues its maltreatment of innocent civilians whose only desire is to gather for prayer and Bible study. If the silence continues, it is only a matter of time until a form of quasi-democracy spreads worldwide where economic wealth is elevated as god and religious conviction is trodden down.

Steven L. Snyder, President of International Christian Concern

Christians have become the targets of opportunity to the thug regimes around the world, and they are many. What's going on now is monumental, and it's affecting millions, tens of millions, of people. We're talking not about discrimination, but persecution of the worst sort: slavery, starvation, murder, looting, burning, torture.

Michael Horowitz

It is the cause, not the death, that makes the martyr.

Napoleon

Love makes the whole difference between an execution and a martyrdom.

Evelyn Underhill

I will not purchase corruptible life at so dear a rate; and indeed, if I had a hundred lives, I would willingly lay down all in defense of my faith.

Christopher Buxton

Jesus promised his disciples three things – that they would be completely fearless, absurdly happy and in constant trouble.
G.K. Chesterton

Great spirits have often encountered violent opposition from weak minds.
Albert Einstein

B. Prayers and a poem

Ravensbruck prayer

O Lord, remember not only the men and women of good will, but also those of ill will. But do not remember all the suffering they have inflicted on us; remember the fruits we have brought, thanks to this suffering – our comradeship, our loyalty, our courage, our generosity, the greatness of heart which has grown out of all this, and when they come to judgment let all the fruits which we have borne be their forgiveness.
Prayer found near the body of a dead child in the Ravensbruck concentration camp

Hassan Dehqani-Tafti's prayer

This prayer was written by Bishop Hassan Dehqani-Tafti of Iran, on the martyrdom of his son.
O God
We remember not only our son but also his murderers;
Not because they killed him in the prime of his youth and made our hearts bleed and our tears flow,
Not because with this savage act they have brought further disgrace on the name of our country among the civilized nations of the world;
But because through their crime we now follow thy footsteps more closely in the way of sacrifice.
The terrible fire of this calamity burns up all selfishness and possessiveness in us;
Its flame reveals the depths of depravity and meanness and suspicion, the dimension of hatred and the measure of sinfulness in human nature;
It makes obvious as never before our need to trust in God's love as shown in the cross of Jesus and his resurrection;
Love which makes us free from hate towards our persecutors;
Love which brings patience, forbearance, courage, loyalty, humility, generosity, greatness of heart;
Love which more than ever deepens our trust in God's final victory and his eternal designs for the Church and for the world;
Love which teaches us how to prepare ourselves to face our own day of death.
O God
Our son's blood has multiplied the fruit of the Spirit in the soil of our souls;
So when his murderers stand before thee on the day of judgement
Remember the fruit of the Spirit by which they have enriched our lives.
And forgive.
Hassan Dehqani-Tafti

Madame Guyon's poem
Joy in Martyrdom

Sweet tenants of this grove!
Who sing without design,
A song of artless love,
In unison with mine:
These echoing shades return
Full many a note of ours,
That wise ones cannot learn,
With all their boasted powers.
O thou! whose sacred charms
These hearts so seldom love,
Although thy beauty warms
And blesses all above;
How slow are human things,
To choose their happiest lot!
All-glorious King of kings,
Say why we love thee not?
This heart, that cannot rest,
Shall thine for ever prove;

Though bleeding and distressed,
Yet joyful in thy love:
'Tis happy though it breaks
Beneath thy chastening hand;
And speechless, yet it speaks,
What thou canst understand.
Madame Guyon, translated by William Cowper

Bibliography

Allen, William Cardinal, *Martyrdom of Father Campion and his Companions,* Burns & Oates, 1908

Bede, *Ecclesiastical History of the English People*, translated Leo Sherley- Price, Penguin, 1955

Birnie, Ian H., *Four Working for Humanity*, Edward Arnold, 1969

Bosanquet, Mary, *The Life and Death of Dietrich Bonhoeffer*, Harper & Row, 1971

Bourdeaux, Michael, *Faith on Trial in Russia*, Hodder and Stoughton, 1971

Bowden, John (trans.), *The Book of Christian Martyrs,* New York, Crossroad, 1990

Bower, H. M., *The Fourteen of Meaux*, Longman, 1894

Bowersock, G.W., *Martyrdom & Rome,* Cambridge, Cambridge University Press, 1995

Bray, Gerald (ed.), *Documents of the English Reformation,* Minneapolis, Fortress, 1994

Broomhall, A. J., *Martyred Missionaries of the China Inland Mission and Perils of Some Who Escaped*, Marshall, Morgan & Scott, 1901

Bruce, F. F., *The Spreading Flame*, Paternoster, 1958

Budge, E. A. Wallis (ed.), *Coptic Martyrdom etc. in the Dialect of Upper Egypt*, British Museum, 1914

Burton. E. H., and Pollen, J. H., *Lives of the English Martyrs,* Vol 1, 1583-1588, Longman, 1914

Butler, Alban, *The Lives of the Saints*, Dublin: Richard Coyne, 1833

Caraman, Philip (ed.), *The Years of Siege: Catholic Life from James I to Cromwell*, Longman, 1966

Catholic Encyclopedia, Robert Appleton Co., 1910

Chadwick, Henry, *Early Christian Thought and the Classical Tradition,* Oxford: Clarendon Press, 1966

Chadwick, Owen, *The Reformation,* Pelican History of the Church, vol. 3, New York: Penguin Books, 1964

Chenu, Bruno (and others), *The Book of Christian Martyrs*, SCM, 1990

Davies, J. G., *Daily Life in the Early Church*, Lutterworth, 1952

Delehaye, H., *Mélanges d'Hagiographie*, Brussels: Société des Bollandistes, 1966

Dodds, E.R., *Pagans and Christians in an Age of Anxiety,* New York, W.W. Norton, 1965

Dods, M., Trans *Justin Martyr and Athenagoras,*Edinburgh: T. & T. Clark, 1867

Douglas, J.D. (ed.), *Shaff-Herzog Encyclopedia of Religious Knowledge*, Grand Rapids, Mich, Baker Book House, 1991

Ehrman, Bart D., *After the New Testament: A Reader in Early Christianity,* New York: Oxford University Press, 1998

Elliot, Elisabeth, *The Shadow of the Almighty*, Hodders, 1959

Elton, G.R. (ed.), *The Reformation, 1520-1559,* (vol. 2 of The New Cambridge Modern History), Cambridge, Cambridge University Press, 1957

Eusebius, *The History of the Church*, translated by G. A. Williamson, Penguin, 1989

Fox, George, *Journal*, London: W & F. G. Cash, 1852

Foxe, John, *The Book of Martyrs,* revised with notes and an appendix by W. Bramley-Moore, London: Callell, Petter, & Galpin, 1869

Frend, W.H.C., *Martyrdom and Persecution in the Early Church: A Study of a Conflict from the Maccabees to Donatus,* New York: Oxford University Press, 1965

Gallonio, *Tortures and Torments of the Christian Martyrs,* from the ìDe SS. Martyrum Cruciatibusî of the Rev Father Gallonio, translated by A. R. Allinson, London and Paris: printed for the subscribers, 1903

Grant, Robert (ed.), *The Apostolic Fathers: a New Translation and Commentary,* six volumes New York, Nelson

Hefley, J., and Hefley, M., *By Their Blood: Christian Martyrs of the 20th century,* Milford: Mott Media, 1979

Hillerbrand, Hans J. (ed.), *The Oxford Encyclopedia of the Reformation*, 4 vol. New York, Oxford University Press, 1996

Hillerbrand, Hans (ed.), *The Reformation: A Narrative History Related by Contemporary*

Observers and Participants, Grand Rapids, MI, Baker Book House, 1978

Hyatt, Irwin T. Jr, *Our Ordered Lives Confess: Three Nineteenth Century American Missionaries in East Chantung,* Cambridge, Mass., 1976

Karslake, C. J., Alternative Saints: the Post-Reformation British People Commemorated by An Account of the Imprisonment and Martyrdom of Father John Ogilvie, Burns and Oates, 1877

King, Coretta Scott, *My Life with Martin Luther King Jr,* Hodder & Stoughton, 1973

Kreider, Robert S. *Mirror of the Martyrs: Stories of Courage, Inspiringly Retold, of 16th Century Anabaptists Who Gave Their Lives for Their Faith,* Good Books, 1901

Lietzmann, Hans, *A History of the Early Church,* Lutterworth, 1961

Lightfoot, J.B. and Harmer, J.B. (ed.), *The Apostolic Fathers: Greek Texts and English Translations of Their Writings,* 2nd edition, revised by Michael W. Holmes (reprint of 1891 edition), Grand Rapids, MI, Baker Book House, 1991

Lightfoot, J. B., *The Apostolic Fathers,* Macmillan, 1898

Linklater, Eric, *Mary Queen of Scots,* Nelson, 1933

Longford, Frank, *Saints,* Hutchinson, 1987

Lyall, L., *A Passion for the Impossible,* Chicago: Moody Press, 1965

Marshall, Paul, *Their Blood Cries Out,* Word, 1997

Martyrs Omitted by Foxe, being records of Religious Persecutions in the sixteenth and seventeenth centuries, compiled by a member of the English Church, London: John Hodges, 1870

Mason, A. J., *The Historic Martyrs of the Primitive Church,* Longman, 1905

Morgan, Robert, *On This Day: 365 Amazing and Inspiring Stories about Martyrs, Heroes, and Little Known Men and Women of Faith,* Thomas Nelson, 1969

Muggeridge, Malcolm, *A Third Testament,* Collins, 1976

Murusillo, H.A. (ed.), *The Acts of the Christian Martyrs,* Oxford, Clarendon Press, 1972

Norman, Edward, *Roman Catholicism in England, from the Elizabethan Settlement to the Second Vatican Council,* Oxford University Press, 1985

Owen, E. C. E. (trans. with notes), *Some Authentic Acts of the Early Martyrs,* Oxford, 1927

Peel, Albert, *The Noble Army of Congregational Martyrs,* Independent Press, 1948

Peers, E. Allison, *The Life of Ramon Lull,* SCM Press, 1946

Pollen, J. H., *Father Edmund Campion and his Companions,* Burns and Oates, 1908

Polsky, Michael, *The New Christian Martyrs,* Montreal: Monastery Press, 1972

Richardson, Cyril C. (ed.), *Early Christian Fathers,* New York, Macmillan, 1970

Robeck, Cecil M., *Prophecy in Carthage: Perpetua, Tertullian, Cyprian,* Cleveland, Pilgrim Press, 1993

Rowe, Michael, *Russian Resurrection,* Marshall Pickering, 1994

Ruoff, E.G. (ed.), *Ewing, Charles, Death Throes of a Dynasty: letters and diaries of Charles and Bessie Ewing, missionaries to China,* Kent, Ohio, 1990

Salisbury, Joyce E., *Perpetua's Passion: The Death and Memory of a Young Roman Woman,* New York, Routledge, 1998

Scritti de Storia E Paleografia, volume III, Biblioteca Apostolica Vaticana, 1924

Shahid, Irfan, *The Martyrs of Najran: New Documents,* Brussels: Société des Bollandistes, 1971

Shea, Nina, *In the Lions' Den: Persecuted Christians And What The Western Church Could Do About It,* Broodman & Holman Pub., 1997

Staniforth, Maxwell (ed.), (revised ed. by Andrew Louth), *Early Christian Writings: The Apostolic Fathers,* London, Penguin Books, 1987

Symonds, Richard, *Church of England,* Macmillan Press, 1988

Taylor, Mrs Howard, *The Triumph of John and Betty Stam,* China Inland Mission, 1935

Thomson, John H. (ed.), *A Cloud of Witnesses,* Edinburgh: Oliphant,

Anderson, & Ferrier, 1781
Wilken, Robert, *The Christians as the Romans Saw Them,* New Haven, Yale University Press, 1984
Wolf, K. B., *Christian Martyrs in Muslim Spain,* Cambridge University Press, 1988

Keston Institute, 4 Park Town, Oxford, OX2 6SH, UK, has extensive records about the persecution and martyrdom of Christians in communist lands in the nineteenth and twentieth centuries.

Index